T0188831

Lecture Notes in Computer Science   10960

Commenced Publication in 1973
Founding and Former Series Editors:
Gerhard Goos, Juris Hartmanis, and Jan van Leeuwen

More information about this series at http://www.springer.com/series/7407

Osvaldo Gervasi · Beniamino Murgante
Sanjay Misra · Elena Stankova
Carmelo M. Torre · Ana Maria A. C. Rocha
David Taniar · Bernady O. Apduhan
Eufemia Tarantino · Yeonseung Ryu (Eds.)

Computational Science and Its Applications – ICCSA 2018

18th International Conference
Melbourne, VIC, Australia, July 2–5, 2018
Proceedings, Part I

Springer

Editors
Osvaldo Gervasi 🔟
University of Perugia
Perugia
Italy

Ana Maria A. C. Rocha 🔟
University of Minho
Braga
Portugal

Beniamino Murgante 🔟
University of Basilicata
Potenza
Italy

David Taniar 🔟
Monash University
Clayton, VIC
Australia

Sanjay Misra 🔟
Covenant University
Ota
Nigeria

Bernady O. Apduhan
Kyushu Sangyo University
Fukuoka shi, Fukuoka
Japan

Elena Stankova 🔟
Saint Petersburg State University
Saint Petersburg
Russia

Eufemia Tarantino 🔟
Politecnico di Bari
Bari
Italy

Carmelo M. Torre 🔟
Polytechnic University of Bari
Bari
Italy

Yeonseung Ryu 🔟
Myongji University
Yongin
Korea (Republic of)

ISSN 0302-9743   ISSN 1611-3349   (electronic)
Lecture Notes in Computer Science
ISBN 978-3-319-95161-4   ISBN 978-3-319-95162-1   (eBook)
https://doi.org/10.1007/978-3-319-95162-1

Library of Congress Control Number: 2018947453

LNCS Sublibrary: SL1 – Theoretical Computer Science and General Issues

This Springer imprint is published by the registered company Springer International Publishing AG
part of Springer Nature
The registered company address is: Gewerbestrasse 11, 6330 Cham, Switzerland

Preface

These multiple volumes (LNCS volumes 10960–10964) consist of the peer-reviewed papers presented at the 2018 International Conference on Computational Science and Its Applications (ICCSA 2018) held in Melbourne, Australia, during July 2–5, 2018.

ICCSA 2018 was a successful event in the International Conferences on Computational Science and Its Applications (ICCSA) conference series, previously held in Trieste, Italy (2017), Beijing, China (2016), Banff, Canada (2015), Guimaraes, Portugal (2014), Ho Chi Minh City, Vietnam (2013), Salvador, Brazil (2012), Santander, Spain (2011), Fukuoka, Japan (2010), Suwon, South Korea (2009), Perugia, Italy (2008), Kuala Lumpur, Malaysia (2007), Glasgow, UK (2006), Singapore (2005), Assisi, Italy (2004), Montreal, Canada (2003), and (as ICCS) Amsterdam, The Netherlands (2002) and San Francisco, USA (2001).

Computational science is a main pillar of most current research and industrial and commercial activities and it plays a unique role in exploiting ICT innovative technologies. The ICCSA conference series has been providing a venue to researchers and industry practitioners to discuss new ideas, to share complex problems and their solutions, and to shape new trends in computational science.

Apart from the general tracks, ICCSA 2018 also included 33 international workshops, in various areas of computational sciences, ranging from computational science technologies, to specific areas of computational sciences, such as computer graphics and virtual reality. The program also featured three keynote speeches.

The success of the ICCSA conference series, in general, and ICCSA 2018, in particular, is due to the support of many people: authors, presenters, participants, keynote speakers, session chairs, Organizing Committee members, student volunteers, Program Committee members, International Advisory Committee members, International Liaison chairs, and people in other various roles. We would like to thank them all.

We would also like to thank Springer for their continuous support in publishing the ICCSA conference proceedings and for sponsoring some of the paper awards.

July 2018

David Taniar
Bernady O. Apduhan
Osvaldo Gervasi
Beniamino Murgante
Ana Maria A. C. Rocha

Welcome to Melbourne

Welcome to "The Most Liveable City"[1], Melbourne, Australia. ICCSA 2018 was held at Monash University, Caulfield Campus, during July 2–5, 2018.

Melbourne is the state capital of Victoria, and is currently the second most populous city in Australia, behind Sydney. There are lots of things to do and experience while in Melbourne. Here is an incomplete list:

- Visit and experience Melbourne's best coffee shops
- Discover Melbourne's hidden laneways and rooftops
- Walk along the Yarra River
- Eat your favourite food (Chinese, Vietnamese, Malaysian, Italian, Greek, anything, … you name it)
- Buy souvenirs at the Queen Victoria Market
- Go up to the Eureka, the tallest building in Melbourne
- Visit Melbourne's museums
- Walk and enjoy Melbourne's gardens and parks
- Visit the heart-shape lake, Albert Park Lake, the home of the F1 Grand Prix
- Simply walk in the city to enjoy Melbourne experience
- Try Melbourne's gelato ice cream

Basically, it is easy to live in and to explore Melbourne, and I do hope that you will have time to explore the city of Melbourne.

The venue of ICCSA 2018 was in Monash University. Monash University is a member of Go8, which is considered the top eight universities in Australia. Monash University has a number of campuses and centers. The two main campuses in Melbourne are Clayton and Caulfield. ICCSA 2018 was held on Caulfield Campus, which is only 12 minutes away from Melbourne CBD by train.

The Faculty of Information Technology is one of the ten faculties at Monash University. The faculty has more than 100 full-time academic staff (equivalent to the rank of Assistant Professor, Associate Professor, and Professor).

I do hope that you will enjoy not only the conference, but also Melbourne.

David Taniar

---

[1] The Global Liveability Report 2017, https://www.cnbc.com/2017/08/17/the-worlds-top-10-most-livable-cities.html

Organization

ICCSA 2018 was organized by Monash University (Australia), University of Perugia (Italy), Kyushu Sangyo University (Japan), University of Basilicata (Italy), and University of Minho, (Portugal).

Honorary General Chairs

Antonio Laganà   University of Perugia, Italy
Norio Shiratori   Tohoku University, Japan
Kenneth C. J. Tan   Sardina Systems, Estonia

General Chairs

David Taniar   Monash University, Australia
Bernady O. Apduhan   Kyushu Sangyo University, Japan

Program Committee Chairs

Osvaldo Gervasi   University of Perugia, Italy
Beniamino Murgante   University of Basilicata, Italy
Ana Maria A. C. Rocha   University of Minho, Portugal

International Advisory Committee

Jemal Abawajy   Deakin University, Australia
Dharma P. Agrawal   University of Cincinnati, USA
Marina L. Gavrilova   University of Calgary, Canada
Claudia Bauzer Medeiros   University of Campinas, Brazil
Manfred M. Fisher   Vienna University of Economics and Business, Austria
Yee Leung   Chinese University of Hong Kong, SAR China

International Liaison Chairs

Ana Carla P. Bitencourt   Universidade Federal do Reconcavo da Bahia, Brazil
Giuseppe Borruso   University of Trieste, Italy
Alfredo Cuzzocrea   University of Trieste, Italy
Maria Irene Falcão   University of Minho, Portugal
Robert C. H. Hsu   Chung Hua University,Taiwan
Tai-Hoon Kim   Hannam University, South Korea
Sanjay Misra   Covenant University, Nigeria
Takashi Naka   Kyushu Sangyo University, Japan

Rafael D. C. Santos   National Institute for Space Research, Brazil
Maribel Yasmina Santos   University of Minho, Portugal

Workshop and Session Organizing Chairs

Beniamino Murgante   University of Basilicata, Italy
Sanjay Misra   Covenant University, Nigeria
Jorge Gustavo Rocha   University of Minho, Portugal

Award Chair

Wenny Rahayu   La Trobe University, Australia

Web Chair

A. S. M. Kayes   La Trobe University, Australia

Publicity Committee Chairs

Elmer Dadios   De La Salle University, Philippines
Hong Quang Nguyen   International University (VNU-HCM), Vietnam
Daisuke Takahashi   Tsukuba University, Japan
Shangwang Wang   Beijing University of Posts and Telecommunications,
        China

Workshop Organizers

Advanced Methods in Fractals and Data Mining for Applications (AMFDMA 2018)

Yeliz Karaca   IEEE
Carlo Cattani   Tuscia University, Italy
Majaz Moonis   University of Massachusettes Medical School, USA

Advances in Information Systems and Technologies for Emergency Management, Risk Assessment and Mitigation Based on Resilience Concepts (ASTER 2018)

Maurizio Pollino   ENEA, Italy
Marco Vona   University of Basilicata, Italy
Beniamino Murgante   University of Basilicata, Italy
Grazia Fattoruso   ENEA, Italy

Advances in Web-Based Learning (AWBL 2018)

Mustafa Murat Inceoglu   Ege University, Turkey
Birol Ciloglugil   Ege University, Turkey

Bio- and Neuro-inspired Computing and Applications (BIONCA 2018)

Nadia Nedjah	State University of Rio de Janeiro, Brazil
Luiza de Macedo Mourell	State University of Rio de Janeiro, Brazil

Computer-Aided Modeling, Simulation, and Analysis (CAMSA 2018)

Jie Shen	University of Michigan, USA
Hao Chen	Shanghai University of Engineering Science, China
Youguo He	Jiangsu University, China

Computational and Applied Statistics (CAS 2018)

Ana Cristina Braga	University of Minho, Portugal

Computational Geometry and Security Applications (CGSA 2018)

Marina L. Gavrilova	University of Calgary, Canada

Computational Movement Analysis (CMA 2018)

Farid Karimipour	University of Tehran, Iran

Computational Mathematics, Statistics and Information Management (CMSIM 2018)

M. Filomena Teodoro	Lisbon University and Portuguese Naval Academy, Portugal

Computational Optimization and Applications (COA 2018)

Ana Maria Rocha	University of Minho, Portugal
Humberto Rocha	University of Coimbra, Portugal

Computational Astrochemistry (CompAstro 2018)

Marzio Rosi	University of Perugia, Italy
Dimitrios Skouteris	Scuola Normale Superiore di Pisa, Italy
Albert Rimola	Universitat Autònoma de Barcelona, Spain

Cities, Technologies, and Planning (CTP 2018)

Giuseppe Borruso	University of Trieste, Italy
Beniamino Murgante	University of Basilicata, Italy

Defense Technology and Security (DTS 2018)

Yeonseung Ryu	Myongji University, South Korea

Econometrics and Multidimensional Evaluation in the Urban Environment (EMEUE 2018)

Carmelo M. Torre	Polytechnic of Bari, Italy
Maria Cerreta	University of Naples Federico II, Italy
Pierluigi Morano	Polytechnic of Bari, Italy
Paola Perchinunno	University of Bari, Italy

Future Computing Systems, Technologies, and Applications (FISTA 2018)

Bernady O. Apduhan	Kyushu Sangyo University, Japan
Rafael Santos	National Institute for Space Research, Brazil
Shangguang Wang	Beijing University of Posts and Telecommunications, China
Kazuaki Tanaka	Kyushu Institute of Technology, Japan

Geographical Analysis, Urban Modeling, Spatial Statistics (GEO-AND-MOD 2018)

Giuseppe Borruso	University of Trieste, Italy
Beniamino Murgante	University of Basilicata, Italy
Hartmut Asche	University of Potsdam, Germany

Geomatics for Resource Monitoring and Control (GRMC 2018)

Eufemia Tarantino	Polytechnic of Bari, Italy
Umberto Fratino	Polytechnic of Bari, Italy
Benedetto Figorito	ARPA Puglia, Italy
Antonio Novelli	Polytechnic of Bari, Italy
Rosa Lasaponara	Italian Research Council, IMAA-CNR, Italy

International Symposium on Software Quality (ISSQ 2018)

Sanjay Misra	Covenant University, Nigeria

Web-Based Collective Evolutionary Systems: Models, Measures, Applications (IWCES 2018)

Alfredo Milani	University of Perugia, Italy
Clement Leung	United International College, Zhouhai, China
Valentina Franzoni	University of Rome La Sapienza, Italy
Valentina Poggioni	University of Perugia, Italy

Large-Scale Computational Physics (LSCP 2018)

Elise de Doncker	Western Michigan University, USA
Fukuko Yuasa	High Energy Accelerator Research Organization, KEK, Japan
Hideo Matsufuru	High Energy Accelerator Research Organization, KEK, Japan

Land Use Monitoring for Soil Consumption Reduction (LUMS 2018)

Carmelo M. Torre	Polytechnic of Bari, Italy
Alessandro Bonifazi	Polytechnic of Bari, Italy
Pasquale Balena	Polytechnic of Bari, Italy
Beniamino Murgante	University of Basilicata , Italy
Eufemia Tarantino	Polytechnic of Bari, Italy

Mobile Communications (MC 2018)

Hyunseung Choo	Sungkyunkwan University, South Korea

Scientific Computing Infrastructure (SCI 2018)

Elena Stankova	Saint-Petersburg State University, Russia
Vladimir Korkhov	Saint-Petersburg State University, Russia

International Symposium on Software Engineering Processes and Applications (SEPA 2018)

Sanjay Misra	Covenant University, Nigeria

Smart Factory Convergence (SFC 2018)

Jongpil Jeong	Sungkyunkwan University, South Korea

Is a Smart City Really Smart? Models, Solutions, Proposals for an Effective Urban and Social Development (Smart_Cities 2018)

Giuseppe Borruso	University of Trieste, Italy
Chiara Garau	University of Cagliari, Italy
Ginevra Balletto	University of Cagliari, Italy
Beniamino Murgante	University of Basilicata, Italy
Paola Zamberlin	University of Florence, Italy

Sustainability Performance Assessment: Models, Approaches and Applications Toward Interdisciplinary and Integrated Solutions (SPA 2018)

Francesco Scorza	University of Basilicata, Italy
Valentin Grecu	Lucia Blaga University on Sibiu, Romania
Jolanta Dvarioniene	Kaunas University, Lithuania
Sabrina Lai	Cagliari University, Italy

Advances in Spatio-Temporal Analytics (ST-Analytics 2018)

Rafael Santos	Brazilian Space Research Agency, Brazil
Karine Reis Ferreira	Brazilian Space Research Agency, Brazil
Joao Moura Pires	New University of Lisbon, Portugal
Maribel Yasmina Santos	University of Minho, Portugal

Theoretical and Computational Chemistry and Its Applications (TCCA 2018)

M. Noelia Faginas Lago   University of Perugia, Italy
Andrea Lombardi   University of Perugia, Italy

Tools and Techniques in Software Development Processes (TTSDP 2018)

Sanjay Misra   Covenant University, Nigeria

Challenges, Trends and Innovations in VGI (VGI 2018)

Beniamino Murgante   University of Basilicata, Italy
Rodrigo Tapia-McClung   Centro de Investigación en Geografia y Geomática Ing
                             Jorge L. Tamay, Mexico
Claudia Ceppi   Polytechnic of Bari, Italy
Jorge Gustavo Rocha   University of Minho, Portugal

Virtual Reality and Applications (VRA 2018)

Osvaldo Gervasi   University of Perugia, Italy
Sergio Tasso   University of Perugia, Italy

International Workshop on Parallel and Distributed Data Mining (WPDM 2018)

Massimo Cafaro   University of Salento, Italy
Italo Epicoco   University of Salento, Italy
Marco Pulimeno   University of Salento, Italy
Giovanni Aloisio   University of Salento, Italy

Program Committee

Kenny Adamson   University of Ulster, UK
Vera Afreixo   University of Aveiro, Portugal
Filipe Alvelos   University of Minho, Portugal
Hartmut Asche   University of Potsdam, Germany
Michela Bertolotto   University College Dublin, Ireland
Sandro Bimonte   CEMAGREF, TSCF, France
Rod Blais   University of Calgary, Canada
Ivan Blečić   University of Sassari, Italy
Giuseppe Borruso   University of Trieste, Italy
Ana Cristina Braga   University of Minho, Portugal
Yves Caniou   Lyon University, France
José A. Cardoso e Cunha   Universidade Nova de Lisboa, Portugal
Rui Cardoso   University of Beira Interior, Portugal
Leocadio G. Casado   University of Almeria, Spain
Carlo Cattani   University of Salerno, Italy
Mete Celik   Erciyes University, Turkey
Alexander Chemeris   National Technical University of Ukraine KPI, Ukraine
Min Young Chung   Sungkyunkwan University, South Korea

Florbela Maria da Cruz Domingues Correia	Polytechnic Institute of Viana do Castelo, Portugal
Gilberto Corso Pereira	Federal University of Bahia, Brazil
Carla Dal Sasso Freitas	Universidade Federal do Rio Grande do Sul, Brazil
Pradesh Debba	The Council for Scientific and Industrial Research (CSIR), South Africa
Hendrik Decker	Instituto Tecnológico de Informática, Spain
Frank Devai	London South Bank University, UK
Rodolphe Devillers	Memorial University of Newfoundland, Canada
Joana Matos Dias	University of Coimbra, Portugal
Paolino Di Felice	University of L'Aquila, Italy
Prabu Dorairaj	NetApp, India/USA
M. Irene Falcao	University of Minho, Portugal
Cherry Liu Fang	U.S. DOE Ames Laboratory, USA
Florbela P. Fernandes	Polytechnic Institute of Bragança, Portugal
Jose-Jesus Fernandez	National Centre for Biotechnology, CSIS, Spain
Paula Odete Fernandes	Polytechnic Institute of Bragança, Portugal
Adelaide de Fátima Baptista Valente Freitas	University of Aveiro, Portugal
Manuel Carlos Figueiredo	University of Minho, Portugal
Maria Antonia Forjaz	University of Minho, Portugal
Maria Celia Furtado Rocha	PRODEB–PósCultura/UFBA, Brazil
Paulino Jose Garcia Nieto	University of Oviedo, Spain
Jerome Gensel	LSR-IMAG, France
Maria Giaoutzi	National Technical University, Athens, Greece
Arminda Manuela Andrade Pereira Gonçalves	University of Minho, Portugal
Andrzej M. Goscinski	Deakin University, Australia
Sevin Gümgm̈	Izmir University of Economics, Turkey
Alex Hagen-Zanker	University of Cambridge, UK
Malgorzata Hanzl	Technical University of Lodz, Poland
Shanmugasundaram Hariharan	B.S. Abdur Rahman University, India
Eligius M. T. Hendrix	University of Malaga/Wageningen University, Spain/The Netherlands
Tutut Herawan	Universitas Teknologi Yogyakarta, Indonesia
Hisamoto Hiyoshi	Gunma University, Japan
Fermin Huarte	University of Barcelona, Spain
Mustafa Inceoglu	EGE University, Turkey
Peter Jimack	University of Leeds, UK
Qun Jin	Waseda University, Japan
A. S. M. Kayes	La Trobe University, Australia
Farid Karimipour	Vienna University of Technology, Austria
Baris Kazar	Oracle Corp., USA
Maulana Adhinugraha Kiki	Telkom University, Indonesia
DongSeong Kim	University of Canterbury, New Zealand

Jon Rokne	University of Calgary, Canada
Octavio Roncero	CSIC, Spain
Maytham Safar	Kuwait University, Kuwait
Chiara Saracino	A.O. Ospedale Niguarda Ca' Granda - Milano, Italy
Haiduke Sarafian	The Pennsylvania State University, USA
Marco Paulo Seabra dos Reis	University of Coimbra, Portugal
Jie Shen	University of Michigan, USA
Qi Shi	Liverpool John Moores University, UK
Dale Shires	U.S. Army Research Laboratory, USA
Inês Soares	University of Coimbra, Portugal
Takuo Suganuma	Tohoku University, Japan
Sergio Tasso	University of Perugia, Italy
Ana Paula Teixeira	University of Trás-os-Montes and Alto Douro, Portugal
Senhorinha Teixeira	University of Minho, Portugal
Parimala Thulasiraman	University of Manitoba, Canada
Carmelo Torre	Polytechnic of Bari, Italy
Javier Martinez Torres	Centro Universitario de la Defensa Zaragoza, Spain
Giuseppe A. Trunfio	University of Sassari, Italy
Toshihiro Uchibayashi	Kyushu Sangyo University, Japan
Pablo Vanegas	University of Cuenca, Ecuador
Marco Vizzari	University of Perugia, Italy
Varun Vohra	Merck Inc., USA
Koichi Wada	University of Tsukuba, Japan
Krzysztof Walkowiak	Wroclaw University of Technology, Poland
Zequn Wang	Intelligent Automation Inc., USA
Robert Weibel	University of Zurich, Switzerland
Frank Westad	Norwegian University of Science and Technology, Norway
Roland Wismüller	Universität Siegen, Germany
Mudasser Wyne	SOET National University, USA
Chung-Huang Yang	National Kaohsiung Normal University, Taiwan
Xin-She Yang	National Physical Laboratory, UK
Salim Zabir	France Telecom Japan Co., Japan
Haifeng Zhao	University of California, Davis, USA
Kewen Zhao	University of Qiongzhou, China
Fabiana Zollo	University of Venice Cà Foscari, Italy
Albert Y. Zomaya	University of Sydney, Australia

Reviewers

Afreixo Vera	University of Aveiro, Portugal
Ahmad Rashid	Microwave and Antenna Lab, School of Engineering, Korea
Aguilar José Alfonso	Universidad Autónoma de Sinaloa, Mexico
Albanese Valentina	Università di Bologna, Italy
Alvelos Filipe	University of Minho, Portugal
Amato Federico	University of Basilicata, Italy
Andrianov Serge	Institute for Informatics of Tatarstan Academy of Sciences, Russia
Antunes Marília	University Nova de Lisboa, Portugal
Apduhan Bernady	Kyushu Sangyo University, Japan
Aquilanti Vincenzo	University of Perugia, Italy
Asche Hartmut	Potsdam University, Germany
Aslan Zafer	Istanbul Aydin University, Turkey
Aytaç Vecdi	Ege University, Turkey
Azevedo Ana	Instituto Superior de Engenharia do Porto, Portugal
Azzari Margherita	Universitá degli Studi di Firenze, Italy
Bae Ihn-Han	Catholic University of Daegu, South Korea
Balci Birim	Celal Bayar Üniversitesi, Turkey
Balena Pasquale	Politecnico di Bari, Italy
Balucani Nadia	University of Perugia, Italy
Barroca Filho Itamir	Instituto Metrópole Digital da UFRN (IMD-UFRN), Brazil
Bayrak §sengül	Haliç University, Turkey
Behera Ranjan Kumar	Indian Institute of Technology Patna, India
Bimonte Sandro	IRSTEA, France
Bogdanov Alexander	Saint-Petersburg State University, Russia
Bonifazi Alessandro	Polytechnic of Bari, Italy
Borruso Giuseppe	University of Trieste, Italy
Braga Ana Cristina	University of Minho, Portugal
Cafaro Massimo	University of Salento, Italy
Canora Filomena	University of Basilicata, Italy
Cao Yuanlong	University of Saskatchewan, Canada
Caradonna Grazia	Polytechnic of Bari, Italy
Cardoso Rui	Institute of Telecommunications, Portugal
Carolina Tripp Barba	Universidad Autónoma de Sinaloa, Mexico
Caroti Gabriella	University of Pisa, Italy
Ceccarello Matteo	University of Padova, Italy
Cefalo Raffaela	University of Trieste, Italy
Cerreta Maria	University Federico II of Naples, Italy
Challa Rajesh	Sungkyunkwan University, Korea
Chamundeswari Arumugam	SSN College of Engineering, India
Chaturvedi Krishna Kumar	Patil Group of Industries, India
Cho Chulhee	Seoul Guarantee Insurance Company Ltd., Korea

Choi Jae-Young	Sungkyunkwan University, Korea
Choi Kwangnam	Korea Institute of Science and Technology Information, Korea
Choi Seonho	Seoul National University, Korea
Chung Min Young	Sungkyunkwan University, Korea
Ciloglugil Birol	Ege University, Turkey
Coletti Cecilia	University of Chieti, Italy
Congiu Tanja	Università degli Studi di Sassari, Italy
Correia Anacleto	Base Naval de Lisboa, Portugal
Correia Elisete	University of Trás-Os-Montes e Alto Douro, Portugal
Correia Florbela Maria da Cruz Domingues	Instituto Politécnico de Viana do Castelo, Portugal
Costa e Silva Eliana	Polytechnic of Porto, Portugal
Cugurullo Federico	Trinity College Dublin, Ireland
Damas Bruno	LARSyS, Instituto Superior Técnico, Univ. Lisboa, Portugal
Dang Thien Binh	Sungkyunkwan University, Korea
Daniele Bartoli	University of Perugia, Italy
de Doncker Elise	Western Michigan University, USA
Degtyarev Alexander	Saint-Petersburg State University, Russia
Demyanov Vasily	Heriot-Watt University, UK
Devai Frank	London South Bank University, UK
Di Fatta Giuseppe	University of Reading, UK
Dias Joana	University of Coimbra, Portugal
Dilo Arta	University of Twente, The Netherlands
El-Zawawy Mohamed A.	Cairo University, Egypt
Epicoco Italo	Università del Salento, Italy
Escalona Maria-Jose	University of Seville, Spain
Falcinelli Stefano	University of Perugia, Italy
Faginas-Lago M. Noelia	University of Perugia, Italy
Falcão M. Irene	University of Minho, Portugal
Famiano Michael	Western Michigan University, USA
Fattoruso Grazia	ENEA, Italy
Fernandes Florbela	Escola Superior de Tecnologia e Gestão de Braganca, Portugal
Fernandes Paula	Escola Superior de Tecnologia e Gestão, Portugal
Ferraro Petrillo Umberto	University of Rome "La Sapienza", Italy
Ferreira Fernanda	Escola Superior de Estudos Industriais e de Gestão, Portugal
Ferrão Maria	Universidade da Beira Interior, Portugal
Figueiredo Manuel Carlos	Universidade do Minho, Portugal
Fiorini Lorena	Università degli Studi dell'Aquila, Italy
Florez Hector	Universidad Distrital Francisco Jose de Caldas, Colombia
Franzoni Valentina	University of Perugia, Italy

Freitau Adelaide de Fátima Baptista Valente	University of Aveiro, Portugal
Gabrani Goldie	Bml Munjal University, India
Garau Chiara	University of Cagliari, Italy
Garcia Ernesto	University of the Basque Country, Spain
Gavrilova Marina	University of Calgary, Canada
Gervasi Osvaldo	University of Perugia, Italy
Gioia Andrea	University of Bari, Italy
Giorgi Giacomo	University of Perugia, Italy
Giuliani Felice	Università degli Studi di Parma, Italy
Goel Rajat	University of Southern California, USA
Gonçalves Arminda Manuela	University of Minho, Portugal
Gorbachev Yuriy	Geolink Technologies, Russia
Gordon-Ross Ann	University of Florida, USA
Goyal Rinkaj	Guru Gobind Singh Indraprastha University, India
Grilli Luca	University of Perugia, Italy
Goyal Rinkaj	GGS Indraprastha University, India
Guerra Eduardo	National Institute for Space Research, Brazil
Gumgum Sevin	İzmir Ekonomi Üniversitesi, Turkey
Gülen Kemal Güven	Istanbul Ticaret University, Turkey
Hacızade Ulviye	Haliç Üniversitesi Uluslararas, Turkey
Han Longzhe	Nanchang Institute of Technology, Korea
Hanzl Malgorzata	University of Lodz, Poland
Hayashi Masaki	University of Calgary, Canada
He Youguo	Jiangsu University, China
Hegedus Peter	University of Szeged, Hungary
Herawan Tutut	Universiti Malaysia Pahang, Malaysia
Ignaccolo Matteo	University of Catania, Italy
Imakura Akira	University of Tsukuba, Japan
Inceoglu Mustafa	Ege University, Turkey
Jagwani Priti	Indian Institute of Technology Delhi, India
Jang Jeongsook	Brown University, Korea
Jeong Jongpil	Sungkyunkwan University, Korea
Jin Hyunwook	Konkuk University, Korea
Jorge Ana Maria, Kapenga John	Western Michigan University, USA
Kawana Kojiro	University of Tokio, Japan
Kayes Abu S. M.	La Trobe University, Australia
Kim JeongAh	George Fox University, USA
Korkhov Vladimir	St. Petersburg State University, Russia
Kulabukhova Nataliia	Saint-Peterburg State University, Russia
Kumar Pawan	Expert Software Consultants Ltd., India
Laccetti Giuliano	Università degli Studi di Napoli, Italy
Laganà Antonio	Master-up srl, Italy
Lai Sabrina	University of Cagliari, Italy

Laricchiuta Annarita	CNR-IMIP, Italy
Lazzari Maurizio	CNR IBAM, Italy
Lee Soojin	Cyber Security Lab, Korea
Leon Marcelo	Universidad Estatal Península de Santa Elena – UPSE, Ecuador
Lim Ilkyun	Sungkyunkwan University, Korea
Lourenço Vanda Marisa	University Nova de Lisboa, Portugal
Mancinelli Luca	University of Dublin, Ireland
Mangiameli Michele	University of Catania, Italy
Markov Krassimiri	Institute for Information Theories and Applications, Bulgaria
Marques Jorge	Universidade de Coimbra, Portugal
Marvuglia Antonino	Public Research Centre Henri Tudor, Luxembourg
Mateos Cristian	Universidad Nacional del Centro, Argentina
Matsufuru Hideo	High Energy Accelerator Research, Japan
Maurizio Crispini	Politecnico di Milano, Italy
Medvet Eric	University of Trieste, Italy
Mengoni Paolo	Università degli Studi di Firenze, Italy
Mesiti Marco	Università degli studi di Milano, Italy
Millham Richard	Durban University of Technology, South Africa
Misra Sanjay	Covenant University, Nigeria
Mishra Anurag	Helmholtz Zentrum München, Germany
Mishra Biswajeeban	University of Szeged, Hungary
Moscato Pablo	University of Newcastle, Australia
Moura Pires Joao	Universidade Nova de Lisboa, Portugal
Moura Ricardo	Universidade Nova de Lisboa, Portugal
Mourao Maria	Universidade do Minho, Portugal
Mukhopadhyay Asish	University of Windsor, Canada
Murgante Beniamino	University of Basilicata, Italy
Nakasato Naohito	University of Aizu, Japan
Nguyen Tien Dzung	Sungkyunkwan University, South Korea
Nicolosi Vittorio	University of Rome Tor Vergata, Italy
Ogihara Mitsunori	University of Miami, USA
Oh Sangyoon	Ajou University, Korea
Oliveira Irene	University of Trás-Os-Montes e Alto Douro, Portugal
Oluranti Jonathan	Covenant University, Nigeria
Ozturk Savas	The Scientific and Technological Research Council of Turkey, Turkey
P. Costa M. Fernanda	University of Minho, Portugal
Paek Yunheung	Seoul National University, Korea
Pancham Jay	Durban University of Technology, South Africa
Pantazis Dimos	Technological Educational Institute of Athens, Greek
Paolucci Michela	Università degli Studi di Firenze, Italy
Pardede Eric	La Trobe University, Australia
Park Hyun Kyoo	Petabi Corp, Korea
Passaro Tommaso	University of Bari, Italy

Pereira Ana	Instituto Politécnico de Bragança, Portugal
Peschechera Giuseppe	University of Bari, Italy
Petri Massimiliano	Università di Pisa, Italy
Pham Quoc Trung	Ho Chi Minh City University of Technology, Vietnam
Piemonte Andrea	Università di Pisa, Italy
Pinna Francesco	Università degli Studi di Cagliari, Italy
Pinto Telmo	University of Minho, Portugal
Pollino Maurizio	ENEA, Italy
Pulimeno Marco	University of Salento, Italy
Rahayu Wenny	La Trobe University, Australia
Rao S. V.	Duke Clinical Research, USA
Raza Syed Muhammad	Sungkyunkwan University, South Korea
Reis Ferreira Gomes Karine	National Institute for Space Research, Brazil
Reis Marco	Universidade de Coimbra, Portugal
Rimola Albert	Autonomous University of Barcelona, Spain
Rocha Ana Maria	University of Minho, Portugal
Rocha Humberto	University of Coimbra, Portugal
Rodriguez Daniel	The University of Queensland, Australia
Ryu Yeonseung	Myongji University, South Korea
Sahni Himantikka	CRISIL Global Research and Analytics, India
Sahoo Kshira Sagar	C. V. Raman College of Engineering, India
Santos Maribel Yasmina	University of Minho, Portugal
Santos Rafael	KU Leuven, Belgium
Saponaro Mirko	Politecnico di Bari, Italy
Scorza Francesco	Università della Basilicata, Italy
Sdao Francesco	Università della Basilicata, Italy
Shen Jie	University of Southampton, UK
Shintani Takahiko	University of Electro-Communications, Japan
Shoaib Muhammad	Sungkyunkwan University, South Korea
Silva-Fortes Carina	ESTeSL-IPL, Portugal
Singh V. B.	University of Delhi, India
Skouteris Dimitrios	SNS, Italy
Soares Inês	INESCC and IPATIMUP, Portugal
Sosnin Petr	Ulyanovsk State Technical University, Russia
Souza Erica	Universidade Nova de Lisboa, Portugal
Stankova Elena	Saint-Petersburg State University, Russia
Sumida Yasuaki	Kyushu Sangyo University, Japan
Tanaka Kazuaki	Kyushu Institute of Technology, Japan
Tapia-McClung Rodrigo	CentroGeo, Mexico
Tarantino Eufemia	Politecnico di Bari, Italy
Tasso Sergio	University of Perugia, Italy
Teixeira Ana Paula	Universidade Católica Portuguesa, Portugal
Tengku Adil	La Trobe University, Australia
Teodoro M. Filomena	Lisbon University, Portugal
Tiwari Sunita	King George's Medical University, India
Torre Carmelo Maria	Polytechnic of Bari, Italy

Torrisi Vincenza	University of Catania, Italy
Totaro Vincenzo	Politecnico di Bari, Italy
Tran Manh Hung	Institute for Research and Executive Education, Vietnam
Tripathi Aprna	GLA University, India
Trunfio Giuseppe A.	University of Sassari, Italy
Tóth Zoltán	Hungarian Academy of Sciences, Hungary
Uchibayashi Toshihiro	Kyushu Sangyo University, Japan
Ugliengo Piero	University of Torino, Italy
Ullman Holly	University of Delaware, USA
Vallverdu Jordi	Autonomous University of Barcelona, Spain
Valuev Ilya	Russian Academy of Sciences, Russia
Vasyunin Dmitry	University of Amsterdam, The Netherlands
Vohra Varun	University of Electro-Communications, Japan
Voit Nikolay	Ulyanovsk State Technical University, Russia
Wale Azeez Nurayhn	University of Lagos, Nigeria
Walkowiak Krzysztof	Wroclaw University of Technology, Poland
Wallace Richard J.	Univeristy of Texas, USA
Waluyo Agustinus Borgy	Monash University, Australia
Westad Frank	CAMO Software AS, USA
Wole Adewumi	Covenant University, Nigeria
Xie Y. H.	Bell Laboratories, USA
Yamauchi Toshihiro	Okayama University, Japan
Yamazaki Takeshi	University of Tokyo, Japan
Yao Fenghui	Tennessee State University, USA
Yoki Karl	Catholic University of Daegu, South Korea
Yoshiura Noriaki	Saitama University, Japan
Yuasa Fukuko	High Energy Accelerator Research Organization, Korea
Zamperlin Paola	University of Florence, Italy
Zollo Fabiana	University of Venice "Cà Foscari", Italy
Zullo Francesco	University of L'Aquila, Italy
Zivkovic Ljiljana	Republic Agency for Spatial Planning, Belgrade

Sponsoring Organizations

ICCSA 2018 would not have been possible without the tremendous support of many organizations and institutions, for which all organizers and participants of ICCSA 2018 express their sincere gratitude:

Springer International Publishing AG, Germany
(http://www.springer.com)

Monash University, Australia
(http://monash.edu)

University of Perugia, Italy
(http://www.unipg.it)

University of Basilicata, Italy
(http://www.unibas.it)

Kyushu Sangyo University, Japan
(www.kyusan-u.ac.jp)

Universidade do Minho, Portugal
(http://www.uminho.pt)

Keynote Speakers

New Frontiers in Cloud Computing for Big Data and Internet-of-Things (IoT) Applications

Rajkumar Buyya[1,2]

[1] Cloud Computing and Distributed Systems (CLOUDS) Lab,
The University of Melbourne, Australia
[2] Manjrasoft Pvt Ltd., Melbourne, Australia

Abstract. Computing is being transformed to a model consisting of services that are commoditised and delivered in a manner similar to utilities such as water, electricity, gas, and telephony. Several computing paradigms have promised to deliver this utility computing vision. Cloud computing has emerged as one of the buzzwords in the IT industry and turned the vision of "computing utilities" into a reality.

Clouds deliver infrastructure, platform, and software (application) as services, which are made available as subscription-based services in a pay-as-you-go model to consumers. Cloud application platforms need to offer

1. APIs and tools for rapid creation of elastic applications and
2. a runtime system for deployment of applications on geographically distributed computing infrastructure in a seamless manner.

The Internet of Things (IoT) paradigm enables seamless integration of cyber-and-physical worlds and opening up opportunities for creating newclass of applications for domains such as smart cities. The emerging Fog computing is extending Cloud computing paradigm to edge resources for latency sensitive IoT applications.

This keynote presentation will cover:

a. 21st century vision of computing and identifies various IT paradigms promising to deliver the vision of computing utilities;
b. opportunities and challenges for utility and market-oriented Cloud computing,
c. innovative architecture for creating market-oriented and elastic Clouds by harnessing virtualisation technologies;
d. Aneka, a Cloud Application Platform, for rapid development of Cloud/Big Data applications and their deployment on private/public Clouds with resource provisioning driven by SLAs;
e. experimental results on deploying Cloud and Big Data/Internet-of-Things (IoT) applications in engineering, and health care, satellite image processing, and smart cities on elastic Clouds;

f. directions for delivering our 21st century vision along with pathways for future research in Cloud and Fog computing.

Short Bio Dr. Rajkumar Buyya is a Redmond Barry Distinguished Professor and Director of the Cloud Computing and Distributed Systems (CLOUDS) Laboratory at the University of Melbourne, Australia. He is also serving as the founding CEO of Manjrasoft, a spin-off company of the University, commercializing its innovations in Cloud Computing. He served as a Future Fellow of the Australian Research Council during 2012-2016. He has authored over 625 publications and seven text books including "Mastering Cloud Computing" published by McGraw Hill, China Machine Press, and Morgan Kaufmann for Indian, Chinese and international markets respectively. He also edited several books including "Cloud Computing: Principles and Paradigms" (Wiley Press, USA, Feb 2011).

He is one of the highly cited authors in computer science and software engineering worldwide (h-index = 117, g-index = 255, 70,500 + citations). Dr. Buyya is recognized as a "Web of Science Highly Cited Researcher" in both 2016 and 2017 by Thomson Reuters, a Fellow of IEEE, and Scopus Researcher of the Year 2017 with Excellence in Innovative Research Award by Elsevier for his outstanding contributions to Cloud computing.

Software technologies for Grid and Cloud computing developed under Dr. Buyya's leadership have gained rapid acceptance and are in use at several academic institutions and commercial enterprises in 40 countries around the world. Dr. Buyya has led the establishment and development of key community activities, including serving as foundation Chair of the IEEE Technical Committee on Scalable Computing and five IEEE/ACM conferences. These contributions and international research leadership of Dr. Buyya are recognized through the award of "2009 IEEE Medal for Excellence in Scalable Computing" from the IEEE Computer Society TCSC.

Manjrasoft's Aneka Cloud technology developed under his leadership has received "2010 Frost & Sullivan New Product Innovation Award". He served as the founding Editor-in-Chief of the IEEE Transactions on Cloud Computing. He is currently serving as Co-Editor-in-Chief of Journal of Software: Practice and Experience, which was established over 45 years ago. For further information on Dr. Buyya, please visit his cyberhome: www.buyya.com.

Approximation Problems for Digital Image Processing and Applications

Gianluca Vinti

Department of Mathematics and Computer Science,
University of Perugia, Italy

Abstract. In this talk, some approximation problems are discussed with applications to reconstruction and to digital image processing. We will also show some applications to concrete problems in the medical and engineering fields. Regarding the first, a procedure will be presented, based on approaches of approximation theory and on algorithms of digital image processing for the diagnosis of aneurysmal diseases; in particular we discuss the extraction of the pervious lumen of the artery starting from CT image without contrast medium. As concerns the engineering field, thermographic images are analyzed for the study of thermal bridges and for the structural and dynamic analysis of buildings, working therefore in the field of energy analysis and seismic vulnerability of buildings, respectively.

Short Bio Gianluca Vinti is Full Professor of Mathematical Analysis at the Department of Mathematics and Computer Science of the University of Perugia. He is Director of the Department since 2014 and member of the Academic Senate of the University. Member of the Board of the Italian Mathematical Union since 2006, member of the "Scientific Council of the GNAMPA-INdAM "(National Group for the Mathematical Analysis, the Probability and their Applications) since 2013, Referent for the Mathematics of the Educational Center of the "Accademia Nazionale dei Lincei" at Perugia since 2013 and Member of the Academic Board of the Ph.D. in Mathematics, Computer Science, Statistics organized in consortium (C.I.A.F.M.) among the University of Perugia (Italy), University of Florence (Italy) and the INdAM (National Institute of High Mathematics).

He is and has been coordinator of several research projects and he coordinates a research team who deals with Real Analysis, Theory of Integral Operators, Approximation Theory and its Applications to Signal Reconstruction and Images Processing.

He has been invited to give more than 50 plenary lectures at conferences at various Universities and Research Centers. Moreover he is author of more than 115 publications on international journals and one scientific monography on "Nonlinear Integral Operators and Applications" edited by W. de Gruyter. Finally he is member of the Editorial Board of the following international scientific journals: Sampling Theory in Signal and Image Processing (STSIP), Journal of Function Spaces and Applications, Open Mathematics, and others and he holds a patent entitled: "Device for obtaining informations on blood vessels and other bodily-cave parts".

Contents – Part I

High Performance Computing and Networks

Geometric Modeling, Graphics and Visualization

Advanced and Emerging Applications

Information Systems and Technologies

Short Papers

Keynote Papers

Software-Defined Multi-cloud Computing: A Vision, Architectural Elements, and Future Directions

Rajkumar Buyya and Jungmin Son[✉]

Cloud Computing and Distributed Systems (CLOUDS) Laboratory,
School of Computer Science and Software Engineering,
The University of Melbourne, Melbourne, Australia
jungmins@student.unimelb.edu.au

Abstract. Cloud computing has been emerged in the last decade to enable utility-based computing resource management without purchasing hardware equipment. Cloud providers run multiple data centers in various locations to manage and provision the Cloud resources to their customers. More recently, the introduction of Software-Defined Networking (SDN) and Network Function Virtualization (NFV) opens more opportunities in Clouds which enables dynamic and autonomic configuration and provisioning of the resources in Cloud data centers.

This paper proposes architectural framework and principles for Programmable Network Clouds hosting SDNs and NFVs for geographically distributed Multi-Cloud computing environments. Cost and SLA-aware resource provisioning and scheduling that minimizes the operating cost without violating the negotiated SLAs are investigated and discussed in regards of techniques for autonomic and timely VNF composition, deployment and management across multiple Clouds. We also discuss open challenges and directions for creating auto-scaling solutions for performance optimization of VNFs using analytics and monitoring techniques, algorithms for SDN controller for scalable traffic and deployment management. The simulation platform and the proof-of-concept prototype are presented with initial evaluation results.

1 Introduction

Cloud computing is the fulfilment of the vision of Internet pioneer, Kleinrock [1], who said in 1969: *"Computer networks are still in their infancy, but as they grow up and become sophisticated, we will probably see the spread of 'computer utilities' which, like present electric and telephone utilities, will service individual homes and offices across the country."*

Cloud computing delivers infrastructure, platform, and software as a service, which are made available to customers on demand as subscription-oriented services based on a pay-as-you-go model. This is supported by dynamic provisioning of computing resources of data centers using Virtual Machine (VM) technologies for consolidation and environment isolation purposes [2]. Many ICT infrastructure service providers including Amazon, Google, Microsoft, IBM, and Telstra are rapidly deploying data

© Springer International Publishing AG, part of Springer Nature 2018
O. Gervasi et al. (Eds.): ICCSA 2018, LNCS 10960, pp. 3–18, 2018.
https://doi.org/10.1007/978-3-319-95162-1_1

centers around the world to support customers worldwide. Furthermore, there is a wide array of services (e.g., standard and spot market priced VM/computing services in case of IaaS) offered by each provider for each model, and each service can be configured with different parameters.

Furthermore, the emerging IoT (Internet-of-Things) paradigm is enabling the creation of intelligent environments supporting applications such as smart cities, smart transportations, and self-driving vehicles. They demand services that are delivered with low latency to meet their QoS (Quality-of-Service) requirements. This triggers the need for distributed Clouds, which are placed near edge-oriented IoT applications.

1.1   The Programmable Network Cloud: Challenges and Requirements

Offering a variety of services creates a challenge for service providers to enforce committed Service Level Agreements (SLAs), which are made up of QoS expectations of users, rewards, and penalties in case it is not achieved. Since SLA establishment is legally required for compliance and has potential impact on revenue, meeting these SLAs is a primary concern of service providers. One elementary approach to guarantee SLA compliance is provisioning of resources for peak requirements of a given service. This approach is not economically viable, i.e., over-provisioning increases the cost of running the service as these provisioned resources are often underutilized.

As data centers are made up of large numbers of servers and switches, they consume significant amounts of energy. According to the Natural Resources Defense Council, **data centers in the U.S. consumed** about 90 billion kilowatt-hours of electricity in 2013, which is roughly **twice of the electricity consumption** in New York City. The energy cost incurred by data centers in 2014 was estimated at **54 billion dollars**. It is reported that energy expense typically accounts for more than **75% of Cloud data center operating expenditure**.

Operators can utilize a new paradigm called "Programmable Network Cloud" [3], which provides scalable services efficiently through a combination of Software-Defined Networking (SDN) [4] and Network Functions Virtualization (NFV) [5] along with integrated use of virtualized computing and storage resources. This enables efficient sharing of resources and helps in meeting SLA requirements while minimizing the operational cost.

SDN allows separation of the control and configuration of the network routes from the forwarding plane (provided by networking devices) [6]. This offers flexibility to the network control plane by enabling the network to be easily adapted to changes via the software called *controller*. OpenFlow [7] is a de facto standard interface for SDN controllers. It allows controllers to communicate with the forwarding plane and makes dynamic changes to the network. This real-time responsiveness to traffic demand is an effective feature to deal with the dynamic nature of the telecom operators' networks, as huge numbers of network resources are constantly joining and leaving the network.

NFV concerns the migration of network functions, such as load balancing, network address translation, and firewalls, to the software layer to enable better interoperability of equipment and advanced network functions. While SDNs focus mostly on separating the control and forwarding planes, NFV focuses on other types of networking functions that are commonly embedded on networking devices or realized in the form of *middleboxes*, i.e., hardware appliances that implement a specific network function such as filtering unwanted or malicious traffic. The deployable elements of NFV are known as *Virtualized Network Functions (VNFs)* that are hosted in containers/virtual machines in Clouds and benefit from its elasticity.

Nevertheless, offering a variety of services in a timely manner while maximizing user experience across the world and at the same time minimizing operational costs (OpEx) creates a number of challenges in the design and realization of the Programmable Network Cloud. New services often need resources and application components that reside in different Clouds or network domains, and in this aspect, it diverges significantly from the behavior of traditional services deployed in traditional siloed data centers. The current centralized data centers impose a number of limitations on the way network and application services are delivered. The utilization of multiple distributed Clouds brings applications closer to the access network/devices, which will enable substantially lower latencies [3]. This is not a trivial task as multiple data centers with different platforms need to be managed simultaneously, with efficient approaches for resources provisioning, service placement, and distribution of the workload.

SDN and NFV can serve as building blocks for achieving traffic consolidation thus saving cost while also supporting QoS at network level in Cloud data centers [3]. However, this requires joint host-network consolidation optimization techniques that not only minimize the energy cost by consolidating network traffic and VMs onto the least number of links and hosts, but also avoid negative impacts on user experience.

In addition, the ability to allocate resources elastically is one of the major advantages of a Programmable Network Cloud that can significantly reduce OpEx. Although by leveraging the Cloud, network operators can scale resources up or down according to changes in demand, the key question is when auto-scaling should be triggered and how much capacity shall be added or removed. With millions of nodes operating in the network, manual management of elasticity is not feasible. Hence, there should be an automated approach in place that utilizes Big Data analytics along with efficient monitoring to detect/predict anomalies in service performance and act accordingly.

Moreover, provisioning of new resources and services taking months or even weeks to be performed is not acceptable in the current competitive markets. Therefore, a Cloud agnostic deployment configuration management (DevOps) solution that automates the deployment of VNFs and applications across multiple data centers running different platforms is of extreme importance.

Without SDNs, dynamic and quick reaction in response to variation in application condition while maintaining service quality cannot be achieved at the network level. It continues to be challenging, as existing SDN controllers are still rudimentary and they need scalable and automated algorithms for achieving integration of such features to enable performance-driven management. SDN and NFV technologies do not, by themselves, solve any of the problems related to QoS nor represent an improvement over traditional networks if the controller is not properly instrumented. Therefore, new algorithms and techniques need to be developed and incorporated in the controller to realize the benefits of the Programmable Network Cloud.

The main objective of this paper is to explore ***the above-mentioned challenges by going beyond traditional Cloud services and proposing solutions*** for auto-scaling, cross-cloud cost and SLA-aware VNF/VM provisioning and consolidation, scalable

SDN-controller traffic management, Cloud agnostic deployment configuration management techniques, use of open source initiatives, and Data Analytics-enabled VNF performance tuning in multi-cloud computing environments.

1.2   Research Methodology

A methodology for solving the problem of cost-efficient and SLA-aware management of geographically distributed Cloud data centers where network functions and applications can be instantly deployed and managed to meet acceptable service levels of customers world-wide is as follows:

- Define an architectural framework and principles for cost-efficient and SLA-aware management of future network resources and applications distributed across multiple Cloud data centers.
- Propose new algorithms for cost-efficient and SLA-aware management of resources by joint host and network optimization.
- Create new data analytics techniques for auto-scaling, performance tuning, and failure recovering of network services.
- Propose techniques for autonomic VNF (Virtualized Network Function) and application deployment and their management across multiple Clouds to accelerate new service deployment processes.
- Propose new algorithms for autonomic VNF composition and management aiming at enabling efficient execution of applications by increasing the efficiency in the utilization of the data center network. This includes techniques for placement and consolidation of VNF compositions.
- Develop new algorithms and optimization techniques for SDN controllers for traffic and deployment management to decrease cost of data centers while honoring Service-Level Agreements.
- Design and develop a proof-of-concept software platform incorporating the above techniques and demonstrate their effectiveness through a series of applications.

The rest of this paper is organized as follows: First, a brief survey on the existing literature in SDN usage in Clouds is presented. Next, we propose a system architecture of Software-Defined Multi-Cloud platform and explain its elements in detail, followed by the simulation framework implementation and some preliminary experiments and results to show the potential effectiveness of the proposed approach. Finally, the paper concludes with discussion on future directions.

2   State-of-the-Art in SDN Usage in Clouds

Although recent research has addressed the application of SDN concepts in Clouds [9, 10, 29, 33], little attention has been given on how to enable network performance allocation to different customers with diverse priorities beyond best effort. Therefore, the user segmentation and bandwidth allocation proposed in this paper make novel contributions for the topic of Cloud networking.

On the topic of energy efficiency, existing works [11–13] focus mainly on improving energy efficiency of servers. Only a few recent works started to look at the problem of energy efficient Cloud networking [8]. As the available works are in early stage, they make too many assumptions that do not hold in real data centers.

Regarding NFV, previous research [14–17] investigated the problem of middlebox virtualization. Some works proposed migration of middleboxes functionalities to the Cloud, whereas others focused on enabling virtual middleboxes by using SDNs. These approaches do not target energy efficiency of the infrastructure, but rather best effort while moving the functionalities from hardware appliances to Cloud virtual machines.

Virtualization technology enables energy-efficiency via workload or computing server consolidation [11, 13]. The next research step in this direction concerns algorithms that jointly manage consolidation of VMs and network traffics to the minimum subset of hosts and network resources.

Furthermore, many energy-efficient resource allocation solutions proposed for various computing systems [18–20] cannot be implemented for Software-Defined Clouds. This is because they do not explicitly consider the impact of their solution on SLA requirements of different classes of users with diverse priorities. Hence, they do not emphasize SLA and energy-aware resource management mechanisms and policies exploiting VM and network resource allocation for Cloud services offered in different QoS.

3 System Architecture

Figure 1 shows the high-level unified architecture that accelerates and simplifies the deployment of network functions along with other applications in distributed Cloud data centers. The architecture leverages the state-of-the-art technologies and paradigms to deliver reliable and scalable network functions while minimizing the operational cost of data centers and meeting QoS requirements of users. In the following sections, we present components of the framework, their related research problems, and potential solutions.

The framework is designed in such a way that it enables network service placement across multiple platforms in distributed Multi-Cloud environments. It allows deployment and migration of VNFs and user applications across Cloud platforms. This is best achieved by the following principles:

- Use of open Cloud standards and execution environments such as OpenDaylight, OpenFlow, OpenStack, Open Virtualization Format (OVF), and Open Container Format (OCF).
- Use of abstractions and virtualization techniques that allow seamless deployment and migration of services across multiple platforms.
- Utilization of Cloud characteristics of elasticity and auto-scaling to adapt the platform to changes in demand.
- Use of automation techniques and tools including DevOps to accelerate new service deployments.

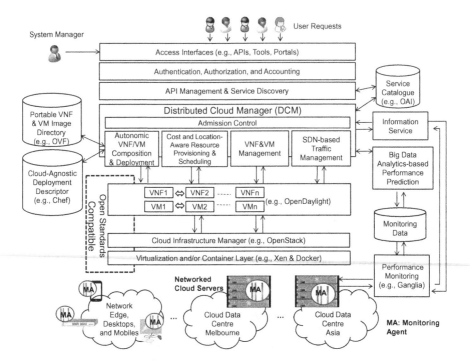

Fig. 1. System architecture for distributed cloud data centers with NFV.

- Use of open APIs formats for service exposures and discovery to enable 3rd party innovations.

As noted in Fig. 1, the input of the system consists of *static* and *dynamic requests*. *Static requests* are issued by the System Manager and consist of instructions for provisioning and configuration of VMs/containers and VNFs. Once VMs/containers that host applications and VNFs that host network operations are placed and the network configuration is completed, the system is ready to receive *dynamic requests* that are issued by end users.

The **Distributed Cloud Manager (DCM)** is the core component of the architecture and consists of a set of subcomponents with specialized functions. The *Cost and Location-aware Resource Provisioning and Scheduling* component uses monitoring data as input and aims at improving efficiency of the data center while minimizing SLA violations via efficient VM/container and traffic placement and consolidation across multiple Clouds. The architecture further minimizes SLA violations and (energy) cost by dynamically finding the shortest path for each network flow via the *SDN-based Traffic Management* component. *Monitoring Data* is collected regarding the servers' utilization and service performance. Such information is obtained by *Monitoring Agents (MA)* stored in a database that is available to DCM components through the *Information Service* component. To ensure the highest level of SLA satisfaction, DCM utilizes the *Autonomic VNF&VM Management* component that is responsible for auto-scaling and failure recovery. Timely scaling and recovery is made possible with the help of the *Performance Prediction* component that consumes historical data (collected using benchmarking of VNFs deployed on various VM types) and predicts performance anomalies. Finally, the *Autonomic Composition, Configuration and Deployment Management* component is responsible to store the deployment information and simplify the deployment of VNFs using preconfigured images.

4 Architectural Elements, Challenges, and Directions

In this section, we discuss various key elements identified in system architecture along with challenges and issues involved in their realization.

4.1 API Management and Service Discovery

A key issue with the way services provided over the Web are consumed is the method of access. No assumption can be made these days about the nature of access devices or services that utilize them. Indeed, one cannot even assume that a service is being consumed by humans as Web services can be made up of many disparate simpler services. Such microservices promote reuse and isolation, resulting in higher tolerance to failures.

The *Service Catalogue* component serves as a directory/registry maintaining information related to the available services and their access methods. It can be accessed by users and other services/brokers to discover them. The *API Management and Service Discovery* component uses information from the Catalogue to determine which particular services are required for each incoming request, and to keep track of the health of the corresponding microservices. New algorithms can be developed to enable composition of the complex services and workflow execution required to perform the activities of other components of the architecture.

4.2 Admission Control

Given that Cloud infrastructure is composed of a finite amount of physical resources, it is unrealistic to assume that there is an infinite amount of computing and network power available for processing an arbitrary number of requests. Thus, if the number of incoming requests exceeds the infrastructure capacity, requests will experience delays and poor QoS, resulting in violation of SLAs. Thus, the key research challenge to prevent QoS degradation is *SLA-Aware Admission Control* algorithms.

Because providers are subject to penalties for SLA violations, it is necessary to evaluate which requests should be accepted and which ones should be rejected. To enable a rational decision and **to increase provider revenue, the decision should be based on user segmentation**. In this case, requests belong to users with different service levels, and requests from higher levels have priority over the lower level ones for admission purposes. Regardless the service level, it is important to avoid starvation, a problem where requests from lower levels are never accepted, as this leads to abandonment of the service by customers.

4.3 Cost and Location-Aware Resource Provisioning and Scheduling

The existing centralized Cloud deployments limit the way certain network services can be delivered. In order to offer satisfactory Quality of Experience (QoE), providers require resources that reside in Cloud data centers distributed across different geographical locations. The load on each individual Cloud can vary with time, sometimes in unexpected ways. This necessitates a solution that manages multiple resource pools with different platforms that can exploit elasticity and auto-scaling properties of Clouds and at the same time is equipped with optimization algorithms that both maximize the QoE of users and minimize the operational cost.

Over-provisioning of resources (e.g., CPU and memory) is one of the major causes of cost escalation although the average utilization of servers is reported to be between 10–30% for large data centers [21]. Hence, to improve the server cost efficiency, VM/container placement, consolidation, and migration techniques play an important role. Likewise, provisioning of network capacity for the peak demand leads to bandwidth wastage. With the emergence of SDN, it is possible to investigate approaches to dynamically manage bandwidth per flow and thus consolidate network traffic. However, poor traffic and VM/container consolidation can have a negative effect on the quality of service (QoS) that clients receive from the system and it can impact the system profitability. Therefore, optimization algorithms are required that can minimize cost via consolidation while still meeting QoS requirements.

The Host-Network resource provisioning problem is a variant of the multi-commodity flow problem and can be solved by linear programming solvers. As they have high computational complexity, online greedy bin-packing algorithms or heuristics can be used to substitute the optimal solution. They not only find the minimum subset of hosts and network resources that can support a given workload, but also dynamically identify resources that satisfy SLA requirements of users such as latency by considering users locations. For efficient overbooking and VM/container and flow consolidation, workload correlation analysis and prediction methods can be utilized [22].

To address the above issues, *cost-efficient joint VM/container and VNF provisioning* needs to be investigated in the context of this framework component. Furthermore, the problem of *resource and workload placement* needs to be addressed in the context of SDN in Clouds, as it has not been explored so far in the literature, resulting in a lack of solutions that can handle the scale of distributed Cloud infrastructure while meeting SLA demands of applications. **Therefore, it is worth to investigate optimization techniques that simultaneously optimize the VM/Container placement and traffic consolidation to jointly maximize SLA satisfaction and minimize the cost (including energy).**

Furthermore, client requests directed to the applications deployed on the platform need to be scheduled in a timely manner so that the expected QoS of the application is achieved. The application may contain several VNFs that are subject to different load levels. Thus, it is important that the request is scheduled to a VNF (or VNF path) that can complete its execution within the agreed service level. Considering the importance of the scheduler component for the success of the framework, it is crucial to consider the following three key elements:

The first element is an *analytical model* for SDN-enabled Cloud data centers that combines *network-aware scheduling* and *load balancing*. It is capable of capturing SDN principles and at the same time sufficiently flexible to handle priorities defined for each flow. The analytical modelling of SDN has not been investigated deeply and it is attempted only in a few research works in the literature [21, 23]. These proposed models generally cannot be extended to more than one switch in the data plane and have not considered the priority of flows. Therefore, it is necessary to build a model based on priority networks [23] that can deal with the aforementioned shortcomings and can efficiently be used for analysis of SDN networks and validation of results from experiments conducted via simulation.

The second element, *network-aware scheduling and load balancing* in distributed Clouds, serves users with different priorities. The main objective is the exploration of SDN capabilities for dynamic bandwidth management on a per flow basis for each class of users. SDN can prioritize traffic of users with higher classes by dynamically configuring queues in switches, which can be utilized by resource allocation policies. Combining this problem with the problem of capacity management including scaling, VM/VNF placement and migration makes this research topic even more challenging. Finally, in order to move towards more realistic scenarios, the original problem invested above should be extended to simultaneously consider the two objectives of **adhering to SLA constraints of different classes of users and minimizing operational cost in the data center**. This can be achieved with the utilization of the network topology and the relative distance between hosts during the formulation of the scheduling problem.

4.4   Autonomic Configuration, Deployment Management, and VNF Composition

A high-level network service is usually composed of many smaller services that are well described and widely used in computer networks. Implementation of traffic policies normally requires the combination of services such as network address translation (NAT), firewalling, load balancing, and LAN and WAN optimization. Each of these services manipulates the input network packets and modifies it to achieve its goals. These operations are usually CPU-intensive and occur for hundreds or thousands of packets per second. In current competitive markets, service rollout that takes months or even weeks is not acceptable. Hence, it is important that the service composition can be performed efficiently and automatically. It can be realized by defining VNF composition and its role for efficient execution of applications. A VNF composition is called a VNF Graph and enables advanced networking services. The automatic composition methods can adopt AI planning techniques. Also, online optimization algorithms are necessary for placement and consolidation of VNF Graphs and for scheduling and load balancing of user requests on VNF Graphs across multiple Cloud data centers. Each virtualized function may be scaled out independently to support the observed demand. **Thus, auto-scaling and elasticity capabilities can be achieved.**

Once the configuration of VNF graphs is finalized, and the decision on mapping of VM/container instances to hosts has been made, the deployment and configuration metadata has to be persisted in such a format that can later be used to accelerate the redeployment of VMs/containers and VNFs in case of a failure in a new platform. Storage of metadata also enhances reusability, as it enables functionalities similar to those provided by automation tools such as Chef [24], which utilizes reusable definitions and data bags to automate deployment. Therefore, **a new approach is necessary to persist specifications of required VNFs and their configuration information**, such as scaling settings, in a format we termed as Deployment Descriptor by leveraging and extending current DevOps technologies. The format has to include instance description (e.g. name, ID, IP, status), image information, etc. This metadata is used by the Configuration Manager and DCM to manage the whole stack of VNFs even if they are deployed across multiple Clouds. One possible solution is to extend existing vendor-agnostic formats such as the Open Virtualization Format (OVF) [25], which is an open specification for the packaging and distribution of virtual machine images composed of one or more VMs. OVF can be further enhanced to facilitate the automated and secure management of not only virtual machines in our system but also the VNF as a functional unit.

4.5   Performance Management of VMs and VNFs

Apart from physical resources management, virtual resources also require monitoring. VMs executing user applications and VNFs providing networking support for applications are CPU-intensive and are subject to performance variation caused by a number of factors, such as overloaded underlying hosts, failure in hardware components, or bugs in their underlying operating systems. Therefore, to keep a certain level of QoS, VMs and VNFs need to be managed such that their status is constantly monitored, and when problems are detected, corrective actions need to be taken automatically to avoid malfunctions. Considering the importance of autonomic management, **auto-scaling mechanisms** can play important role for VNF Graphs. The auto-scaling mechanism consists of two components:

- **Monitoring** component that keeps track of performance of the VNF Graph. Data collected by the monitoring is used to enable performance prediction.
- **Profiling** component that collects information to build correlations regarding the VNF computing requirements and service time. The main challenge in this regard is the lack of benchmarking tools developed specifically for VNFs. New benchmarks can be proposed to measure performance criteria such as VNFs' throughput, time to deploy, and migration impacts on SLAs. The benchmark can help to design auto-scaling policies that maintain a certain level of QoS once any anomaly in the expected performance is detected.

4.6   Big Data Analytics-Based Performance Prediction for Capacity Planning and Auto-scaling

Several functionalities of the proposed architecture rely on data analytics for proper operation. However, the data generated by the infrastructure and consumed by the proposed architecture has characteristics of volume (because there are thousands of components—from infrastructure to application level—that need to be monitored), velocity (data is being continuously generated, and needs to be processed quickly to enable timely action to incidents), and variety (data is generated in various formats). These are the characteristics of **Big Data analytics**, which need to be handled with specialized systems and algorithms.

The collected data can be used for many purposes inside the architecture. Firstly, it can be used in new methods based on Big Data to detect performance anomalies in VMs, VNFs, and in the network as a whole, and to identify the root cause of the anomaly. This can be done after defining the set of required QoS criteria and metrics; and identifying and modelling the dependency between those criteria. This helps in improving the accuracy of the monitoring system by locating the root cause of a failure. The activity also looks into developing recovery plans related to performance issues caused by hosts and link failures. Big Data analytics frameworks such as Spark can be exploited for rapid detection of anomalies and identify root causes that assist in data center's capacity planning and auto-scaling.

4.7 Software-Defined Network (SDN)-Based Traffic Management

SDN is a prominent technology for data center traffic management that provides flexibility to dynamically assign a path (network capacities) to a data flow through APIs. However, knowing that the operators' networks are dynamic, computing and updating the shortest path per flow must be performed in efficient way. One possible solution is the design and optimization of vertex-oriented graph processing techniques to dynamically find the shortest paths. For this purpose, solutions can be implemented in Apache Giraph [26]. The dynamism and changes in the data center network can be evaluated under different topologies, and graph processing can be applied to recalculate the shortest paths in response to changes. A scalable graph partitioning and processing algorithm is also necessary to takes advantage of Cloud's elasticity. It helps in building efficient controllers that properly utilize elasticity of Cloud computing and provide forwarding rules in a timely manner. In detail, the issue can be investigated in twofold:

- **Efficient heuristics for graph partitioning** that support a vertex-oriented execution model [27] and suit data center network routing problems, which enables scalable and efficient computations.
- **Algorithms for detection of similarities** in network conditions and configurations including topology, traffic, and priority settings (the current and previous network setting retrieved from the history) to accelerate the process of making routing decisions for current network settings.

These techniques can be incorporated into OpenFlow/OpenDaylight stacks for efficient management of network traffic.

4.8 Authentication, Authorization, Accounting, and System Security

Achieving security features such as confidentiality (protecting data from one user from others), availability (make the application available to legitimate by blocking malicious users), and protection against **Distributed Denial of Service (DDoS)** attacks is crucial for any solution deployed in the Internet, and they are specialty important when the solution can be distributed along multiple Clouds. Authorization protocols such as OAuth2 [28] can be used to guarantee that VNFs and VMs are seamlessly deployed across multiple Clouds if necessary.

Besides single sign in capabilities, this module also performs DDoS detection and mitigation. This is a critical feature, because in a dynamic resource provisioning scenario, increase in the number of users causes an automatic increase in resources allocated to the application. If a coordinated attack is launched against the Cloud provider, the sudden increase in traffic might be wrongly assumed to be legitimate requests and resources would be scaled up to handle them. This would result in an increase in the cost of running the application (because the provider will be charged for these extra resources) as well as waste in resources.

In this module, **automatic identification of threats** can be implemented by checking the legitimacy of requests. For this, the module needs to perform analytics on data center logs and feedback from intrusion detection systems, which leads to prevent the scaling-up of resources to respond to requests created with the intention of causing a Denial of Service or other forms of cyber-attacks. The module is also able to distinguish between authorized access and attacks, and in case of suspicion of attack, it can either decide to drop the request or avoid excessive provision of resources to it. To achieve this, techniques already in use for detection of DDoS attacks can be adapted to be able to handle the unique characteristics of Cloud systems.

5   Performance Evaluation - Platforms and Sample Results

In this section, we present both the simulation and real software platforms that support a programmable network Cloud for efficient network services via SDN and NFV and show some of our preliminary experiment results.

5.1   Simulation Platform for SDN and NFV in Clouds

In order to simulate NFV and SDN functionalities in Clouds, we have implemented additional modules in CloudSimSDN simulation toolkit [30]. CloudSimSDN has been developed based on CloudSim [31] to support testing SDN functionalities, such as dynamic flow scheduling, bandwidth allocation, and network programmability for Cloud data centers. On top of CloudSimSDN, our extension modules for NFV support creating VNFs in a data center and composition of multiple VNFs to form a chain of network functions. It also supports altering forwarding rules in SDN switches to enforce specific packets to transfer through VNF chains using defined policies.

As the simulation tool is developed upon CloudSimSDN, it is capable of all the features and functions provided by CloudSimSDN and CloudSim. We can measure the response time of each workload compositing of computing and networking jobs and the energy consumption for each host/switch and the entire data center. It also supports to implement different policies and algorithms for VNF placement and migration which decides a physical host to place a VNF.

5.2 System Prototype

We also developed a software platform named SDCon[1] for empirical evaluation of the proposed architecture in a small-scale testbed [32]. The prototype is implemented upon various open-source software such as OpenStack, OpenDaylight, and OpenVSwitch. The software integrates Cloud manageability and network provisioning into a single platform, which can be exploited for joint host-network optimization, network bandwidth allocation, dynamic traffic engineering, and VM and network placement and migration.

The system prototype is implemented on the in-lab testbed consisting of 9 servers and 10 software switches. We utilize Raspberry-Pi low-cost embedded computers for the software switches, by plugging USB-Ethernet adapters and running OpenVSwitch software. The testbed with the deployed SDCon can easily perform the empirical experiments for SDN usage in the Cloud context.

5.3 Evaluating VNF Auto-scaling Policy in Simulation

In previous subsection, we present the simulation framework for VNF and SDN functionalities in Clouds. Upon the implemented simulation, we undertook preliminary experiments to show the validity of the presented vision in this paper. The experiment is designed to see the effectiveness of VNF auto scaling policies in the VM network performance and energy consumption.

We created 34 VMs and 4 VNFs in a data center with 128 hosts connected with 8-pod fat-tree network topology. All data transmissions between VMs are enforced to pass through a chain of 4 VNFs. We synthetically generate workloads for 10 min including compute (CPU) workload in VMs and network transmission to another VM. We measure CPU processing time, network processing time, and overall response time for each workload in two cases. For the first case, we enabled auto-scaling algorithm for VNFs, which simply adds more VNFs in the data center once the current utilization of a VNF reaches the threshold (70%). In the second case, the auto-scaling algorithm is disabled, so that the number of VNFs are never changed.

Table 1 presents the total capacity of all VNFs at the end of the experiment. With the auto-scaling policy enabled, it keeps adding VMs utilized for VNFs throughout the experiment once the utilization of a VNF reaches the threshold. In the end, the auto-scaling policy added 5 more VMs in total for overloaded VNFs, whereas the number of VMs has not changed when we disabled auto-scaling policy.

Table 1. VNF capacity with different auto-scaling policies

	Initial	Auto-scaling enabled	Auto-scaling disabled
Number of VMs used for all VNFs	4	9	4

---

[1] Source code available at: https://github.com/Cloudslab/sdcon.

Table 2 present CPU, network, and overall processing time of 90,000 workloads sent for 10 min. As shown in the table, the auto-scaling policy for VNFs reduced the average network transmission time by 22.4% from 1579 ms to 1226 ms, which leads to the improvement of the overall response time by 22.2%. As the number of VMs for VNFs has been increased by auto-scaling policy, the packets processed faster with higher capacity of VNFs with the auto-scaling enabled. Although this experiment is preliminary to show the effectiveness of the simulation framework, the toolkit can be used for further NFV and SDN studies in Clouds context to evaluate various composition and migration algorithms, traffic management, and joint compute-network optimization within a single data center, or for Multi-Clouds.

Table 2. Average CPU processing, network transmission, and response time of workloads

	VNF auto-scaling enabled	VNF auto-scaling disabled
CPU processing	27 ms	27 ms
Network transmission	1226 ms	1579 ms
Response time	5018 ms	6454 ms

6 Summary and Conclusions

In this paper, we presented a vision, a model architecture, elements, and some preliminary experimental results of Software-Defined Multi-Cloud Computing. Many opportunities and open challenges exist in the context of NFV and SDN in Cloud computing. As we presented in this paper, joint resource provisioning and scheduling in Software-Defined Cloud computing which considers VM, VNF, storage, and network performance and capacity are one of the most challenging topic. The integration of such resources and modules with a holistic view [32] is necessary in the future Software-Defined data center architecture, so that all the resources can be managed in autonomically. Also, traffic engineering with scalable NFV and programmable SDN is worth to investigate in order to optimize the network performance, SLA fulfillment, and the operational cost of a data center including electricity consumption.

The evaluation of the new architecture and its elements along with proposed or new approaches addressing their challenges can be fostered using our simulation (CloudSimSDN) and/or empirical platforms (SDCon). For a large-scale evaluation, our simulation toolkit can speed up the evaluation process with various measurements. For a practical proof-of-concept experiment, the empirical evaluation platform can be exploited to see the effectiveness of the proposed methodology in the real world. More details of the simulation and empirical platforms have been discussed in [32].

Acknowledgements. We acknowledge Dr. Rodrigo Calheiros, Dr. Amir Vahid Dastjerdi, and Dr. Adel Nadjaran Toosi for their contributions towards various ideas presented in this paper. This work is partially supported by an Australian Research Council (ARC) funded Discovery Project.

References

1. Kleinrock, L.: A vision for the Internet. ST J. Res. **2**(1), 4–5 (2005)
2. Barham, P., et al.: Xen and the art of virtualization. In: Proceedings of 19th ACM Symposium on Operating Systems Principles (SOSP 2003), Bolton Landing, USA (2003)
3. The programmable network cloud. Ericsson White paper. Uen 288 23-3211 Rev B, December 2015. http://www.ericsson.com/res/docs/whitepapers/wp-the-programmable-network-cloud.pdf
4. Open Network Foundation. Software-Defined Networking: The New Norm for Networks. White Paper, April 2012
5. Chiosi, M., et al.: Network Functions Virtualisation—Introductory White Paper. White Paper, October 2012 http://portal.etsi.org/NFV/NFV_White_Paper.pdf
6. Barroso, L., Holzle, U.: The datacenter as a computer: an introduction to the design of warehouse-scale machines. Synth. Lect. Comput. Archit. **4**(1), 1–108 (2009)
7. Jarschel, M., et al.: Modeling and performance evaluation of an OpenFlow architecture. In: Proceedings of the 23rd International Teletraffic Congress (2011)
8. Zheng, K., Wang, X., Li, L., Wang, X.: Joint power optimization of data center network and servers with correlation analysis. In: Proceedings of the 33rd IEEE International Conference on Computer Communications (INFOCOM 2014), Toronto, Canada, April 2014
9. Koponen, T., et al.: Onix: a distributed control platform for large-scale production networks. In: Proceedings of the 9th USENIX Conference on Operating Systems Design and Implementation (OSDI), Broomfield, USA, October 2010
10. Monsanto, C., Reich, J., Foster, N., Rexford, J., Walker, D.: Composing software-defined networks. In: Proceedings of the 10th USENIX Conference on Networked Systems Design and Implementation (NSDI), Lombard, USA, April 2013
11. Beloglazov, A., Buyya, R., Lee, Y., Zomaya, A.: A taxonomy and survey of energy-efficient data centers and cloud computing systems. Adv. Comput. **82**, 47–111 (2011)
12. Guenter, B., Jain, N., Williams, C.: Managing cost, performance, and reliability tradeoffs for energy-aware server provisioning. In: Proceedings of the IEEE Conference on Computer Communications (INFOCOM), Shanghai, China (2011)
13. Beloglazov, A., Buyya, R.: Managing overloaded hosts for dynamic consolidation of virtual machines in cloud data centers under quality of service constraints. IEEE Trans. Parallel Distrib. Syst. **24**(7), 1366–1379 (2013)
14. Sherry, J., Hasan, S., Scott, C., Krishnamurthy, A., Ratnasamy, S., Sekar, V.: Making middleboxes someone else's problem: network processing as a cloud service. SIGCOMM Comput. Commun. Rev. **42**(4), 13–24 (2012)
15. Qazi, Z., Tu, C.-C., Chiang, L., Miao, R., Sekar, V., Yu, M.: SIMPLE-fying middlebox policy enforcement using SDN. In: Proceedings of the ACM 2013 Conference on SIGCOMM, Hong Kong, China, August 2013
16. Gember, A., et al.: Stratos: a network-aware orchestration layer for virtual middleboxes in clouds (2014). http://arxiv.org/abs/1305.0209
17. Hwang, J., Ramakrishnan, K., Wood, T.: NetVM: high performance and flexible networking using virtualization on commodity platforms. In: Proceedings of the 11th USENIX Symposium on Networked Systems Design and Implementation, USA, April 2014
18. Aydin, H., Melhem, R.G., Mossé, D., Mejía-Alvarez, P.: Power-aware scheduling for periodic real-time task. IEEE Trans. Comput. **53**(5), 584–600 (2004)
19. Chase, J.S., Anderson, D.C., Thakar, P.N., Vahdat, A.M.: Managing energy and server resources in hosting centres. In: Proceedings of the 18th ACM Symposium on Operating System Principles, Banff, Canada

20. Zeng, H., et al.: ECOSystem: managing energy as a first class operating system resource. In: Proceedings of the 10th International Conference on Architectural Support for Programming Languages and Operating Systems, San Jose, USA
21. Azodolmolk, S., et al.: An analytical model for software defined networking: a network calculus-based approach. In: Proceedings of the Global Communications Conference (2013)
22. Son, J., Dastjerdi, A.V., Calheiros, R.N., Buyya, R.: SLA-aware and energy-efficient dynamic overbooking in SDN-based cloud data centers. IEEE Trans. Sustain. Comput. **2**(2), 76–89 (2017)
23. Bolch, G., et al.: Queueing Networks and Markov Chains: Modeling and Performance Evaluation with Computer Science Applications. Wiley, Hoboken (2006)
24. Marschall, M.: Chef Infrastructure Automation Cookbook. Packt Publishing Ltd., Birmingham (2013)
25. Distributed Management Task Force. Open Virtualization Format. White Paper, June 2009. www.dmtf.org/standards/published_documents/DSP2017_1.0.0.pdf
26. Apache Giraph. http://giraph.apache.org/
27. Chen, R., et al.: Improving large graph processing on partitioned graphs in the Cloud. In: Proceedings of the Third ACM Symposium on Cloud Computing. ACM, New York (2012)
28. Hardt, D.: The OAuth 2.0 Authorization Framework. Internet Engineering Task Force (IETF) RFC 6749 (2012)
29. Jain, R., Paul, S.: Network virtualization and software defined networking for cloud computing: a survey. IEEE Commun. Mag. **51**(11), 24–31 (2013)
30. Son, J., Dastjerdi, A.V., Calheiros, R.N., Ji, X., Yoon, Y., Buyya, R.: CloudSimSDN: modeling and simulation of software-defined cloud data centers. In: Proceedings of the 15th IEEE/ACM International Symposium on Cluster, Cloud and Grid Computing (CCGrid 2015), Shenzhen, China (2015)
31. Calheiros, R.N., Ranjan, R., Beloglazov, A., De Rose, C.A., Buyya, R.: CloudSim: a toolkit for modeling and simulation of cloud computing environments and evaluation of resource provisioning algorithms. Softw. Pract. Exp. **41**, 23–50 (2011)
32. Son, J.: Integrated provisioning of compute and network resources in software-defined cloud data centers. Ph.D. thesis, The University of Melbourne (2018)
33. Son, J., Buyya, R.: A taxonomy of software-defined networking (SDN)-enabled cloud computing. ACM Comput. Surv. **51**(3), 1–36 (2018)

Approximation Problems for Digital Image Processing and Applications

Danilo Costarelli, Marco Seracini, and Gianluca Vinti[✉]

Department of Mathematics and Computer Science, University of Perugia,
1, Via Vanvitelli, 06123 Perugia, Italy
danilo.costarelli@unipg.it, marco.seracini@dmi.unipg.it,
gianluca.vinti@unipg.it

Abstract. In this note, some approximation problems are discussed with applications to reconstruction and to digital image processing. We will also show some applications to concrete problems in the medical and engineering fields. Regarding the first, a procedure will be presented, based on approaches of approximation theory and on algorithms of digital image processing for the diagnosis of aneurysmal diseases; in particular we discuss the extraction of the pervious lumen of the artery starting from CT image without contrast medium. As concerns the engineering field, thermographic images are analyzed for the study of thermal bridges and for the structural and dynamic analysis of buildings, working therefore in the field of energy analysis and seismic vulnerability of buildings, respectively.

1 Introduction

In the diagnosis of vascular pathologies, such as stenosis of main vessels or aneurysms, CT (computer tomography) images play a central role (see e.g., [19]). In particular, in order to diagnose aneurysm of the aorta artery (see e.g., [23]) it is necessary to identify inside the artery, the pervious lumen of the vessel, i.e., the zone in which the blood flows, and to quantify the rate of the possible occlusion. In CT images, is not possible to distinguish the contours of the lumen from the rest of the vessel.

In general, to solve the above problem the vascular surgeons and the radiologists resort to CT image with contrast medium, which makes the blood radiopaque, and therefore recognizable with respect to other anatomical structures. However, for patients with severe kidney's diseases or allergic problems, the introduction of contrast medium is not possible. For this reason, becomes crucial to have techniques for the automatic segmentation of the lumen of the vessels in CT images without contrast medium, since the gold-standard procedure to diagnose aneurysms of the aorta artery is the CT.

We develop a procedure to accomplish the above task (see [12]); starting from CT images without contrast medium, of size $n \times n$, we process the ROI using the sampling Kantorovich (SK) algorithm. The latter algorithm provides

© Springer International Publishing AG, part of Springer Nature 2018
O. Gervasi et al. (Eds.): ICCSA 2018, LNCS 10960, pp. 19–31, 2018.
https://doi.org/10.1007/978-3-319-95162-1_2

a techniques of digital image processing which allows to reconstruct a given image with an increased resolution of $nR \times nR$ pixels, where R is a suitable integer scaling factor. The above algorithm can be deduced from the theory of sampling Kantorovich operators S_w [6,11,13–15,18], and their approximation results in various setting; for other approximation results by means of other kind of operators, see e.g., [1,7,16,17]. Then the above procedure is based on the application of suitable algorithms of digital image processing, such as wavelet decomposition, normalization, equalization, and thresholding.

In the last years, the SK algorithm has been successfully applied in seismic and energetic engineering. For what concerns applications in seismic engineering, some models have been developed for studying the behaviors of buildings under seismic action starting from thermographic images. While, for what concerns energetic engineering, the SK algorithm has been applied in order to derive an automatic procedure for the detection of thermal bridges from thermographic images and to study energy performance of buildings.

2   Multivariate Sampling Kantorovich Operators

The multivariate sampling Kantorovich operators are defined as follows:

$$(S_w^{\chi} f)(\underline{x}) := \sum_{\underline{k} \in \mathbb{Z}^n} \chi(w\underline{x} - t_{\underline{k}}) \cdot \left[w^n \int_{R_{\underline{k}}^w} f(\underline{u}) \, d\underline{u} \right] \qquad (\underline{x} \in \mathbb{R}^n, w > 0),$$

where $f : \mathbb{R}^n \to \mathbb{R}$ is a locally integrable function, such that the above series is convergent for every $\underline{x} \in \mathbb{R}^n$, see [14], and

$$R_{\underline{k}}^w := \left[\frac{k_1}{w}, \frac{k_1 + 1}{w} \right] \times \left[\frac{k_2}{w}, \frac{k_2 + 1}{w} \right] \times \ldots \times \left[\frac{k_n}{w}, \frac{k_n + 1}{w} \right],$$

$\underline{k} := (k_1, \ldots, k_n) \in \mathbb{Z}^n$, are the sets in which we consider the mean values of the signal f. The SK algorithm for image reconstruction and enhancement consists in an optimized implementation of the above sampling operators, with kernels $\chi : \mathbb{R}^n \to \mathbb{R}$ satisfying the following assumptions [13]:

(χ1) χ is summable on $\mathbb{R}^n$, and bounded in a ball containing the origin of $\mathbb{R}^n$;
(χ2) For every $\underline{x} \in \mathbb{R}^n$:

$$\sum_{\underline{k} \in \mathbb{Z}^n} \chi(\underline{x} - \underline{k}) = 1;$$

(χ3) For some $\beta > 0$, we assume that the discrete absolute moment of order β is finite, i.e.,

$$m_\beta(\chi) := \sup_{\underline{u} \in \mathbb{R}} \sum_{\underline{k} \in \mathbb{Z}^n} |\chi(\underline{u} - \underline{k})| \cdot \|\underline{u} - \underline{k}\|^\beta < +\infty.$$

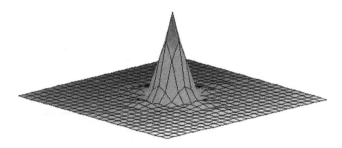

Fig. 1. The bivariate Fejér kernel.

where $\| \cdot \|$ denotes the Euclidean norm.

We immediately provide some typical examples of kernels χ that can be used according to the required assumptions. The most used method to construct multivariate kernels is to consider the product of n kernels of one variable. Indeed, for instance, the definition of the multivariate Fejér kernel can be formulated as follows:

$$\mathcal{F}_n(\underline{x}) = \prod_{i=1}^{n} F(x_i), \qquad \underline{x} = (x_1, \ldots, x_n) \in \mathbb{R}^n, \tag{1}$$

where $F(x)$, $x \in \mathbb{R}$, denotes the univariate Fejér kernel, which is defined by:

$$F(x) := \frac{1}{2} \operatorname{sinc}^2 \left(\frac{x}{2} \right), \qquad x \in \mathbb{R}, \tag{2}$$

where the well-known *sinc*-function is that defined as $\sin(\pi x)/\pi x$, if $x \neq 0$, and 1 if $x = 0$ (see Fig. 1).

By the *sinc*-function it is possible to define another class of kernels, which is widely used, i.e., the Jackson-type kernels. The multivariate expression of the Jackson-type kernels, is the following:

$$\mathcal{J}_k^n(\underline{x}) := \prod_{i=1}^{n} J_k(x_i), \qquad \underline{x} = (x_1, \ldots, x_n) \in \mathbb{R}^n, \tag{3}$$

where $J_k(x)$, $x \in \mathbb{R}$ are defined by:

$$J_k(x) := c_k \operatorname{sinc}^{2k} \left(\frac{x}{2k\pi\alpha} \right), \qquad x \in \mathbb{R}, \tag{4}$$

with $k \in \mathbb{N}$, $\alpha \geq 1$, and c_k is a non-zero normalization coefficient, given by:

$$c_k := \left[\int_{\mathbb{R}} \operatorname{sinc}^{2k} \left(\frac{u}{2k\pi\alpha} \right) du \right]^{-1}.$$

Figure 2 shows an example of the bivariate Jackson type kernel of first order with $\alpha = 1$.

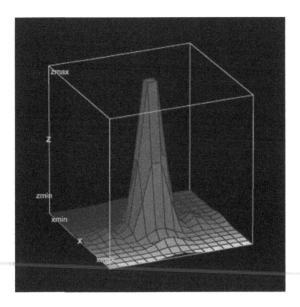

Fig. 2. The bivariate Jackson type kernel of first order with $\alpha = 1$.

Since the *sinc*-function has unbounded support, we usually say that $F(\underline{x})$ and $\mathcal{J}_k^n(\underline{x})$ are not duration limited kernels. To know the duration of a kernel is important in order to implement the numerical evaluation of the operators studied in this section. In fact, operators based upon kernels with unbounded duration, need to be truncated for the evaluation. For the latter reason, we also provide examples of duration limited kernels. For instance, we can consider the well-know central B-spline of order s, defined by:

$$M_s(x) \; := \; \frac{1}{(s-1)!} \sum_{i=0}^{s} (-1)^i \binom{s}{i} \left(\frac{s}{2} + x - i\right)_{+}^{s-1}, \tag{5}$$

where the function $(x)_{+} := \max\{x, 0\}$ denotes the positive part of $x \in \mathbb{R}$. The corresponding multivariate spline kernels are then defined by:

$$\mathcal{M}_s^n(\underline{x}) \; := \; \prod_{i=1}^{n} M_s(x_i), \qquad \underline{x} = (x_1, \ldots, x_n) \in \mathbb{R}^n. \tag{6}$$

Figure 3 shows an example of the bivariate B-spline type kernel of order 3.

For the sampling Kantorovich operators, with kernels e.g., as above, the following approximation results hold.

Theorem 2.1 ([13]). *Let $f : \mathbb{R}^n \to \mathbb{R}$ be a given bounded signal. Then:*

$$\lim_{w \to +\infty} (S_w^\chi f)(\underline{x}) \; = \; f(\underline{x}),$$

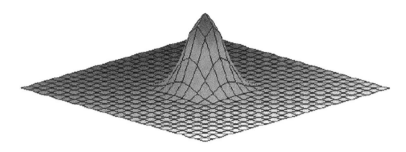

Fig. 3. The bivariate B-spline kernel of order 3.

at any point of continuity of f. Moreover, if f is uniformly continuous on $\mathbb{R}^n$, it turns out that:

$$\lim_{w \to +\infty} \|S_w^\chi f - f\|_\infty = \lim_{w \to +\infty} \sup_{\underline{x} \in \mathbb{R}^n} |(S_w^\chi f)(\underline{x}) - f(\underline{x})| = 0.$$

Finally, if the signal f belongs to $L^p(\mathbb{R}^n)$, $1 \le p < +\infty$, we have:

$$\lim_{w \to +\infty} \|S_w^\chi f - f\|_p = \lim_{w \to +\infty} \left(\int_{\mathbb{R}^n} |(S_w^\chi f)(\underline{x}) - f(\underline{x})|^p \, d\underline{x} \right)^{1/p} = 0.$$

Increasing the sampling rate and choosing an appropriate kernel χ, it is possible to enhance the images/signals f under consideration. For more details concerning the SK algorithm, see e.g., [4,5,13].

3   Digital Image Processing by Sampling Kantorovich Operators

Multivariate sampling Kantorovich operators, with kernels as above, are suitable to be used in order to process digital images, see [4,5,14,20].

A bi-dimensional digital gray scale image A (matrix) can be represented by using a step function I belonging to $L^p(\mathbb{R}^2)$, $1 \le p < +\infty$. I is defined by:

$$I(x,y) := \sum_{i=1}^{m} \sum_{j=1}^{m} a_{ij} \cdot \mathbf{1}_{ij}(x,y) \quad ((x,y) \in \mathbb{R}^2),$$

where $\mathbf{1}_{ij}(x,y)$, $i, j = 1, 2, \ldots, m$, are the characteristics functions of the sets $(i-1, i] \times (j-1, j]$ (i.e., $\mathbf{1}_{ij}(x,y) = 1$, for $(x,y) \in (i-1, i] \times (j-1, j]$ and $\mathbf{1}_{ij}(x,y) = 0$ otherwise). The above function $I(x,y)$ is defined in such a way that, to every pixel (i,j) the corresponding gray level a_{ij} is associated. Now the family of bivariate sampling Kantorovich operators applied to the function I, $(S_w I)_{w>0}$ (for some kernel χ) approximates I pointwise at the continuity points and in L^p-sense, so it is possible to use it for the reconstruction and enhancement of the original image. To achieve a new image (matrix), $S_w I$ (for some $w > 0$)

is sampled with a fixed sampling rate. In particular, the reconstruction of the approximating images (matrices) is available considering different sampling rates; this is possible since we know $S_w I$ analytically in all its domain.

If the sampling rate is chosen higher than the original one, a new image with an increased resolution with respect to the original, is obtained. The above procedure has been implemented by using MATLAB, in order to achieve an algorithm based on the multivariate sampling Kantorovich theory.

For the sake of completeness, the pseudo-code of the above algorithm is reported (see Table 1).

Practical reconstruction and enhancement of some biomedical and engineering images that lead to interesting results from the "diagnostic" point of view are presented in the following section.

4   Applications to Biomedical Images

Thanks to relatively recent developments in the field of medical imaging, a big amount of data is nowday available for the diagnosis of different pathologies.

It is auspicable to apply the SK algorithms, together with other Digital Image Processing (D.I.P.) techniques, to support doctors in the diagnostic process. In this direction, a particular version of the SK algorithm has been specifically developed for the segmentation of the pervious lumen of the aorta artery in CT (computer tomography) images without contrast medium.

For patients with severe kidney's diseases or allergic problems the introduction of contrast medium must be avoided. For this reason, the availability of techniques for the automatic segmentation of the lumen of the vessels in CT images without contrast medium becomes crucial, since the goal standard procedure to diagnose aneurysms of the aorta artery is the CT.

The numerical procedure for the detection of the pervious area of the lumen of the aorta artery has the following crucial steps:

- enhancement of the original CT image without contrast medium;
- application of a wavelet decomposition method in 5 levels and computation of the residual component of the image;
- application of normalization and equalization;
- classification of the pixel's histogram associated to each processed image and computation of the threshold value for the segmentation of the pervious lumen of the aorta artery.

The above procedure, together with some numerical results, have been schematically depicted in Fig. 4.

For the validation of the method, specific indexes of performance can be introduced so that a comparison with a reference set of images is possible. Practically, the reference consists of a corresponding acquisition performed in the same patient after the introduction of the contrast medium. Due to the fact that the acquisitions are performed in different times and that the patient could change position during the exam (think for example to the natural expansion of

Table 1. Pseudo-code of the SK algorithm for image reconstruction and enhancement.

Objective: Reconstructing and improving the resolution of the original bivariate image I by sampling Kantorovich operators based upon the bivariate kernel χ.

Inputs: Original image I ($n \times n$ pixel resolution), the parameter $w > 0$ and the scaling factor R.

- Choice and definition of the kernel function χ;
- Size of the reconstructed image: $(n \cdot R) \times (n \cdot R)$;
- Computation of matrices of the mean values (samples) of I by means of the Kronecker matrix product.
- Definition of the vectors containing the arguments of χ.

Iteration: Summation over $\underline{k}$ of all non zero terms of the form
$$\chi(w\underline{x} - \underline{k}) \cdot \left[w^2 \int_{R_{\underline{k}}^w} I(\underline{u})\, d\underline{u} \right],$$
for a suitable fixed grid of points $\underline{x}$.

Output: The reconstructed image of resolution $(n \cdot R) \times (n \cdot R)$.

---

the chest during normal breathing), it is difficult to individuate a strictly univocal reference. The image registration procedure, i.e., the necessity to superimpose images coming from different CT sets, influences the estimation of the numerical results.

With the aim to take into account of these problems in terms of quantitative evaluation (see e.g., [21]), multiple measurements can be performed using:

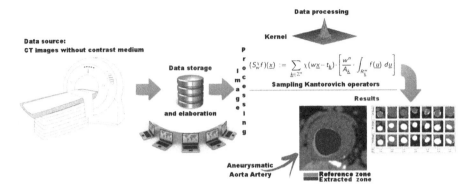

Fig. 4. The schematic plot of the procedure for the segmentation of the pervious lumen of the aorta artery.

- the number of the pixels wrongly classified;
- the number of pixels wrongly classified compared to the number of pixels included in the Region Of Interest (R.O.I.);
- the circularity of the extracted zone (see [22]);
- the ratio of the circularity between the extracted zones;
- the area of the extracted zone compared with the contrast medium reference;
- the Hausdorff distances between the contours of the extracted zone compared with the contrast medium reference;
- the Hausdorff distance between the full sets of the extracted zone compared with the contrast medium reference.

The Hausdorff distance measures the mismatch level between two sets of points, A and B, considering the maximum value of the distance of A from B and viceversa. Let $A = \{a_1, a_2, \ldots, a_n\}$ and $B = \{b_1, b_2, \ldots, b_m\}$ be two non-empty discrete subsets of a metric space (M, d); the Hausdorff distance d_H is defined as:

$$d_H = max\{d(A, B), d(B, A)\}$$

where:

$$d(A, B) = \max_i \min_j |a_i - b_j|$$

$$d(B, A) = \max_j \min_i |a_i - b_j|$$

with $i \in [1, n], j \in [1, m]$.

Figure 5 shows an example of Hausdorff distance between two discrete sets of points.

The main advantages of this approach relies in the potential possibility of performing diagnosis concerning vascular pathologies even for those patients who exhibit severe kidney's diseases or allergic problems, for which CT images with contrast medium cannot be used.

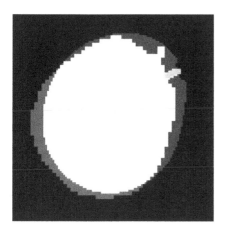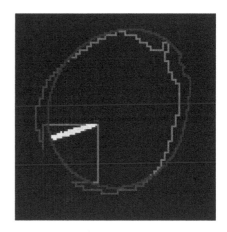

Fig. 5. Hausdorff distance d_H between two discrete sets of points, A and B: on the left, in green, d_H between the full sets. The white zone represents the intersection between the two sets of pixels, the red zone contains the points belonging only to A, the blue zone the ones belonging only to B. The length of the green line is $d_H = 7.616$. On the right d_H between the borders ($d_H = 26.24$). Both images are of size 111×111 pixels. (Color figure online)

5   Applications to Engineering Problems

SK algorithms can be successfully applied in civil engineering, from one hand to improve the thermal bridges quantitative assessment by infrared thermography, from the other hand to support non invasive and non destructive structural analysis.

In the first contest, the intervention on the existing building envelope thermal insulation is the main and effective solution in order to achieve a significant reduction of the building stock energy needs. The infrared technique [8] is the methodology of the energy diagnosis aimed to identify qualitatively the principal causes of energy losses: the presence of thermal bridges. Those weak parts of the building envelope in terms of heat transfer result not easy to treat with an energy efficiency intervention, while they are gaining importance in the buildings total energy dispersion, as the level of insulation of opaque and transparent materials is continuously increasing. It is generally possible to evaluate the energy dispersions through these zones with a deep knowledge of the materials and the geometry using a numerical method. The analysis of surface temperatures of the undisturbed wall and of the zone with thermal bridge, allows to define the Incidence Factor of the thermal Bridge (I_{tb}), see [3]. This parameter is strongly affected by the thermographic image accuracy, therefore, SK algorithm enhances the image resolution and the consequent accuracy of the energy losses assessment. An experimental campaign in a controlled environment (hot box apparatus) has been conducted on three typologies of thermal bridge, firstly performing the thermographic survey and then applying the enhancement SK

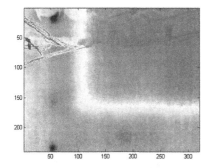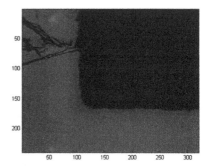

Fig. 6. On the left, a thermographic image depicting a beam-pillar-joint 2D thermal bridge, while on the right we have in red the profile of the thermal bridge extracted by the above method after the application of the SK algorithm. (Color figure online)

algorithm to the infrared images in order to compare the I_{tb} and the linear thermal transmittance ψ values. Results show that the proposed methodology could bring to an accuracy improvement of the total buildings envelope energy losses evaluated by quantitative infrared thermography.

SK algorithm allows the implementation of a further process applicable to the images, in order to extract the physical boundaries of the hidden materials causing the thermal bridge, so revealing itself as a useful tool to identify exactly the suitable points of intervention for the thermal bridge correction. The application of the imaging process on the quantitative infrared thermography is an innovative approach that makes more accurate the evaluation of the actual heat loss of highly insulating buildings and reaching a higher detail on the detection and treating of thermal bridges.

Concerning the application of the SK algorithm to the energetic engineering, in [4,5] a segmentation method has been developed and applied in order to detect the shape of thermal bridges of the building envelope from thermographic images (see Fig. 6). Generally speaking, a thermal bridge is characterized by a significant temperature gradient compared with the average value of the surrounding area (undisturbed zones). The temperature gradient is high when a change of material due to the geometrical contours of thermal bridge structure exists (e.g. contour of a pillar or a beam). Analysing the histogram associated to the infrared thermal bridge image, which can be interpreted as the distribution of probability of temperature occurring on the thermal map, two peaks (P1 and P2) representing the homogeneous temperature areas can be identified: one of the undisturbed area of the wall and the other one of the thermal bridge. Between these two peaks it is possible to find a minimum value which, in view of the above probabilistic interpretation of the data, can be associated to the minimum error due to the wrong classification of pixels located inside the thermal wall but classified as external, and viceversa. The temperature Tm, which corresponds to the value that minimizes the above misclassification error, identifies the suitable threshold value to segment the thermal bridge shape from the background. (see Fig. 7).

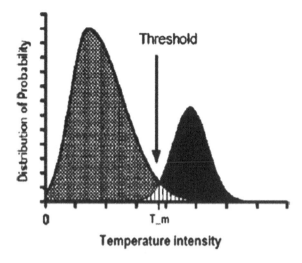

Fig. 7. Generic distribution of probability for the temperature in a thermal bridge.

First of all, we enhance the original thermographic image by the SK algorithm and then we determine the threshold value by means of a sort of probabilistic method (see [4,5] again) based on the analysis of the pixel's histogram of the thermographic data. Moreover, it also allows to determine the heat losses of the buildings, using a suitable *incidence factor of thermal bridge*, introduced in [2,3]. It has been proved that the application of the SK algorithm is crucial in order to have an accurate estimate of the heat losses of the buildings.

Finally, we recall that in [9,10] the SK algorithm has been used in order to enhance the thermographic images of walls, to improve the texture procedure, which allows the automatic separation of mortar and bricks in the masonries (see Fig. 8), to extract the elastic parameters and finally, to study the dynamic behavior of buildings under seismic action. Also here, the application of SK algorithm revealed to be crucial.

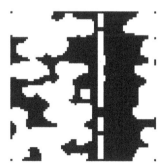 

Fig. 8. On the left, the texture of a wall starting from a thermographic image, while on the right we have the texture after the application of the SK algorithm to the original thermographic image.

Acknowledgments. The authors are members of the Gruppo Nazionale per l'Analisi Matematica, la Probabilitá e le loro Applicazioni (GNAMPA) of the Istituto Nazionale di Alta Matematica (INdAM).

The authors are partially supported by the "Department of Mathematics and Computer Science" of the University of Perugia (Italy). Finally, the first two authors of the paper have been partially supported within the 2017 GNAMPA-INdAM Project "Approssimazione con operatori discreti e problemi di minimo per funzionali del calcolo delle variazioni con applicazioni all'imaging".

The research related to this paper is part of the project: "Metodi di Approssimazione e Applicazioni" funded by the basic research fund, 2015 of the University of Perugia.

References

1. Angeloni, L., Vinti, G.: Approximation with respect to Goffman-Serrin variation by means of non-convolution type integral operators. Numer. Funct. Anal. Optim. **31**, 519–548 (2010)
2. Asdrubali, F., Baldinelli, G.: Thermal transmittance measurements with the hot box method: calibration, experimental procedures, and uncertainty analyses of three different approaches. Energy Build. **43**, 1618–1626 (2011)
3. Asdrubali, F., Baldinelli, G., Bianchi, F.: A quantitative methodology to evaluate thermal bridges in buildings. Appl. Energy **97**, 365–373 (2012)
4. Asdrubali, F., Baldinelli, G., Bianchi, F., Costarelli, D., Evangelisti, L., Rotili, A., Seracini, M., Vinti, G.: A model for the improvement of thermal bridges quantitative assessment by infrared thermography. Appl. Energy **211**, 854–864 (2018)
5. Asdrubali, F., Baldinelli, G., Bianchi, F., Costarelli, D., Rotili, A., Seracini, M., Vinti, G.: Detection of thermal bridges from thermographic images by means of image processing approximation algorithms. Appl. Math. Comput. **317**, 160–171 (2018)
6. Bardaro, C., Butzer, P.L., Stens, R.L., Vinti, G.: Kantorovich-type generalized sampling series in the setting of Orlicz spaces. Sampl. Theory Signal Image Process. **6**(1), 29–52 (2007)
7. Bardaro, C., Karsli, H., Vinti, G.: Nonlinear integral operators with homogeneous kernels: pointwise approximation theorems. Appl. Anal. **90**(3–4), 463–474 (2011)
8. Bianchi, F., Pisello, A., Baldinelli, G., Asdrubali, F.: Infrared thermography assessment of thermal bridges in building envelope: experimental validation in a test room setup. Sustainability **6**(10), 7107–7120 (2014)
9. Cluni, F., Costarelli, D., Minotti, A.M., Vinti, G.: Enhancement of thermographic images as tool for structural analysis in earthquake engineering. NDT E Int. **70**, 60–72 (2015)
10. Cluni, F., Costarelli, D., Minotti, A.M., Vinti, G.: Applications of sampling Kantorovich operators to thermographic images for seismic engineering. J. Comput. Anal. Appl. **19**(4), 602–617 (2015)
11. Costarelli, D., Minotti, A.M., Vinti, G.: Approximation of discontinuous signals by sampling Kantorovich series. J. Math. Anal. Appl. **450**(2), 1083–1103 (2017)
12. Costarelli, D., Seracini, M., Vinti, G.: A segmentation procedure of the aorta artery from CT images without contrast medium (2018, submitted)

13. Costarelli, D., Vinti, G.: Approximation by multivariate generalized sampling Kantorovich operators in the setting of Orlicz spaces. Boll. U.M.I. **9**(IV), 445–468 (2011). Special volume dedicated to Prof. Giovanni Prodi
14. Costarelli, D., Vinti, G.: Approximation by nonlinear multivariate sampling Kantorovich type operators and applications to image processing. Numer. Funct. Anal. Optim. **34**(8), 819–844 (2013)
15. Costarelli, D., Vinti, G.: Degree of approximation for nonlinear multivariate sampling Kantorovich operators on some functions spaces. Numer. Funct. Anal. Optim. **36**(8), 964–990 (2015)
16. Costarelli, D., Vinti, G.: Approximation by max-product neural network operators of Kantorovich type. Results Math. **69**(3), 505–519 (2016)
17. Costarelli, D., Vinti, G.: Max-product neural network and quasi-interpolation operators activated by sigmoidal functions. J. Approx. Theory **209**, 1–22 (2016)
18. D. Costarelli, G. Vinti.: An inverse theorem of approximation by sampling Kantorovich series. In: Proceedings of the Edinburgh Mathematical Society (2018, in Print). arXiv:1801.08695
19. Deserno, T.M.: Biomedical Image Processing. Biological and Medical Physics, Biomedical Engineering. Springer, Heidelberg (2011). https://doi.org/10.1007/978-3-642-15816-2
20. Kaijser, T.: Computing the Kantorovich distance for images. J. Math. Imag. Vis. **9**, 173–191 (1998)
21. Meijering, E.H.W., Niessen, W.J., Viergever, M.A.: Quantitative evaluation of convolution-based methods for medical image interpolation. Med. Image Anal. **5**, 111–126 (2001)
22. Olson, E.: Particle shape factors and their use in image analysis part 1: theory. J. GXP Compliance **15**(3), 85–96 (2011)
23. Takayama, T., Yamanouchi, D.: Aneurysmal disease: the abdominal aorta. Surg. Clin. **93**(4), 877–891 (2013)

Computational Methods, Algorithms and Scientific Applications

An Assessment of Reordering Algorithms to Speed Up the ICCG Method Applied to CFD Problems

Sanderson L. Gonzaga de Oliveira[1]([⊠]), Guilherme Oliveira Chagas[1],
Júnior Assis Barreto Bernardes[1], Diogo T. Robaina[2],
and Mauricio Kischinhevsky[2]

[1] Universidade Federal de Lavras, Lavras, Minas Gerais, Brazil
`sanderson@dcc.ufla.br`, `guilherme.chagas@computacao.ufla.br`,
`jrassis@posgrad.ufla.br`
[2] Universidade Federal Fluminense, Niterói, Rio de Janeiro, Brazil
{`drobaina,kisch`}`@ic.uff.br`

Abstract. Previous publications analyzed a large number of heuristics for bandwidth and profile reductions, and 14 heuristics were selected as promising low-cost heuristics for these problems. Based on extensive numerical experiments, this paper evaluates these heuristics when applied to matrices contained in systems of linear equations arising from computational fluid dynamics problems and the most promising heuristics are identified when reducing the zero-fill incomplete Cholesky-preconditioned conjugate gradient method.

Keywords: Bandwidth reduction · Profile reduction
Sparse matrices · Graph labeling · Conjugate gradient method
Reordering algorithms

1 Introduction

An essential task in several scientific and engineering applications is the solution of systems of linear equations in the form $Ax = b$, where A is an $n \times n$ large-scale sparse matrix, x is the unknown n-vector solution which is sough, and b is a known n-vector. It is generally a part of the simulation that demands a high processing time [1].

Modern hierarchical memory architecture and paging policies favor programs that take locality of reference into consideration [1,2]. Thus, spatial locality (a sequence of recent memory references is clustered locally rather than randomly in the memory address space) is relevant when designing an algorithm in this context.

For the low-cost solution of large and sparse linear systems, an appropriate vertex labeling in a graph is desirable to ensure that the corresponding coefficient matrix A will have narrow bandwidth and small profile. Specifically, heuristics

O. Gervasi et al. (Eds.): ICCSA 2018, LNCS 10960, pp. 35–52, 2018.
https://doi.org/10.1007/978-3-319-95162-1_3

for bandwidth or profile reductions return a sequence of graph vertices with spatial locality. Thus, these heuristics are used to reach low computational costs when solving large sparse systems of linear equations [1,2].

The bandwidth reduction problem consists of labeling the vertices of a graph with positive integer labels aiming at minimizing the maximum absolute difference between labels of adjacent vertices. It is isomorphic to the problem of reordering the rows and columns of a symmetric matrix so that the objective is to locate non-null coefficients as close as possible along the main diagonal [3]. Let $A = [a_{ij}]$ be an $n \times n$ symmetric matrix associated with a connected undirected graph $G = (V, E)$ composed of a set of vertices V and a set of edges E. The bandwidth of row i is $\beta_i(A) = i - \min_{1 \leq j \leq i} [j : a_{ij} \neq 0]$, for $a_{ii} \neq 0$. Bandwidth $\beta(A)$ is the largest distance between the non-null coefficient of the lower triangular matrix and the main diagonal considering all rows of the matrix, that is, $\beta(A) = \max_{1 \leq i \leq n} [\beta_i(A)]$. Equivalently, the bandwidth of G for a vertex labeling $S = \{s(v_1), s(v_2), \cdots, s(v_{|V|})\}$ (i.e., a bijective mapping $s : V \rightarrow \{1, 2, \cdots, |V|\}$) is $\beta(G) = \max_{v \in V} [(\{v, u\} \in E) |s(v) - s(u)|]$, where $s(v)$ and $s(u)$ are labels of vertices v and u, respectively. The profile of A can be defined as $profile(A) = \sum_{i=1}^{n} \beta_i(A)$, or equivalently, $profile(G) = \sum_{v \in V} \max_{\{v,u\} \in E} [|s(v) - s(u)|]$. The bandwidth and profile minimization problems are NP-hard [4,5] and, since the mid-1960s, several heuristics have been proposed to solve the bandwidth and profile reduction problems [2,6–8] due to the existence of extensive connections between these problems and a large number of other scientific and engineering problems [1].

A prominent method for solving large sparse systems of linear equations is the preconditioned conjugate gradient method (CGM) when the matrix contained in them are symmetric and positive definite. The number of iterations of the CG method depends on the structure of the matrix A, its condition number, the accuracy to be achieved, and the preconditioner used [1]. Thus, the most important result of a reordering algorithm in conjunction with the preconditioner is to return a matrix A with a reduced condition number (or equivalently better cluster of eigenvalues). The reordering algorithm should provide spatial locality. Moreover, the application should use a data structure that depends neither on the bandwidth nor the profile of the matrix A, as is the case in the experiments presented in this paper. Consequently, the resulting linear system is much easier to solve than the original linear system, even when the linear system is composed of multiple right-hand side vectors [1].

A specific preconditioner is applied to speed up the conjugate gradient method depending on the problem in context. Among various preconditioners proposed (e.g., see [9]) for the conjugate gradient method, the incomplete Cholesky (IC) factorization is especially useful [1]. The IC(l) preconditioner with $l > 0$ will obtain a better approximation to A than IC(0) at the cost of increased memory requirements and processing times. Thus, we used the IC(0) preconditioner. The zero-fill incomplete Cholesky-preconditioned conjugate gradient method (ICCGM) has been employed promisingly in the solution of various problems (see [1] and references therein).

One can reduce computational costs using the conjugate gradient method by applying an adequate ordering of the vertices of the corresponding graph of A to improve cache hit rates. Such ordering can be reached using a heuristic for bandwidth reduction (see [1] and references therein).

Systematic reviews [2,6–8] identified almost 140 heuristics for bandwidth and profile reductions. This number is increasing each year [1,10,11]. Therefore, an important decision in this context is to choose the best reordering algorithm among several alternatives for the problem at hand. Furthermore, in previous publications [10–13], various heuristics for bandwidth and profile reductions were evaluated with the intention of reducing the execution cost of the Jacobi-preconditioned conjugate gradient method. Additionally, in a recent publication [1], several heuristics for bandwidth and profile reductions were evaluated. This publication [1] also identified the most promising heuristics for several application areas when reducing the computational cost of the ICCG method. Among 55 instances (arising from several application areas) used in this publication [1], it evaluated the heuristics for bandwidth and profile reductions when applied to only three linear systems originating from computational fluid dynamic (CFD) problems. Thus, this present work aims to evaluate the same 14 heuristics for bandwidth and profile reductions to speed up the ICCG method when applied to several instances that arise from this application area. To provide more specific details, systematic reviews [1,2,6–8] reported 14 promising low-cost heuristics for bandwidth (Burgess-Lai [14], FNCHC [15], GGPS [16], VNS-band [17], KP-band [3], CSS-band [18], and RBFS-GL [1]) and profile (Snay [19], Sloan [20], MPG [21], NSloan [22], and Sloan-MGPS [23]) reductions. Additionally, this paper [1] evaluated the reverse Cuthill-McKee method with pseudo-peripheral vertex given by the George-Liu algorithm (RCM-GL) [24] and GPS algorithm [25] in both contexts of bandwidth and profile reductions. Therefore, 14 heuristics were evaluated in this work. Thus, our work provides an extensive computational experiment employing heuristics for bandwidth and profile reductions aiming at reducing the computational time of the ICCG method applied to 23 instances originating from CFD problems. To be more precise, the main contribution of our work is the comparison of results obtained when using 14 heuristics for bandwidth and profile reductions to symmetric matrices contained in linear systems (with sizes nearly 300,000 unknowns) arising from CFD problems solved by the ICCG method.

The remainder of this manuscript is organized as follows. Section 2 describes how this paper conducted the simulations in this computational experiment. Section 3 presents and analyzes the results. Finally, Sect. 4 provides the conclusions.

2 Description of the Tests

This computational experiment uses a 64-bit executable program of the VNS-band heuristic. One of the heuristics' authors kindly provided this program. Additionally, a heuristics' author kindly provided the C programming language source code of the FNCHC heuristic. Then, we converted this source code to the C++ programming language. The 12 other heuristics were also implemented in the C++ programming language to compare the computational costs of the heuristics. Furthermore, we used a data structure based on the Compress Row Storage, Compress Column Storage, and Skyline Storage Scheme data structures to implement the ICCG method. Previous publications described details of our implementations, testing, and calibration of the heuristics [1, 2].

The three datasets (composed of real symmetric instances) that are part of the simulations carried out on each machine are (Intel® Core™): (*i*) systems of linear equations (ranging from 7,332 to 277,118 unknowns) arising from finite-volume discretizations of the Laplace equation [26], originally using a random order, with executions performed on a workstation that contains an i3-2120 CPU 3.30 GHz, 3 MB of cache, 8 GB DDR3 1.333 GHz of main memory, Linux kernel 3.13.0-39-generic; (*ii*) linear systems (ranging from 4,846 to 232,052 unknowns) originating from finite-volume discretizations of the heat conduction equation with meshes generated using Voronoi diagrams (and Delaunay triangulations) [27], with executions performed on a workstation that contains an i3-550 CPU 3.20 GHz, 4 MB cache, 16 GB DDR3 1.333 GHz of main memory, Linux kernel 3.13.0-39-generic; (*iii*) 11 instances (ranging from 1,733 to 81,920 unknowns) contained in the SuiteSparse matrix (SSM) collection [28], with executions performed on a workstation that contains an i7-4790K CPU 4.00 GHz, 8 MB cache, 12 GB DDR3 1.6 GHz of main memory, Linux kernel 3.19.0-31-generic (Intel; Santa Clara, CA, United States). The Ubuntu 14.04 LTS 64-bit operating system was used in the simulations. A dataset used in each machine was chosen arbitrarily.

The convergence criterion used in the ICCG method was a reduction of the computed residual $|Ax = b|$ (i.e., a final backward error) to less than 10^{-16}. Thus, the final attainable accuracy in our numerical experiments is related to this precision. Three sequential runs were performed for each instance with both a reordering algorithm and with the ICCG method. This present work employs the GNU Multiple Precision Floating-point Computations with Correct-Rounding library to make it possible to obtain high precision in the computations.

3 Results and Analysis

This section presents and analyzes the results obtained in simulations using the ICCG method computed after executing heuristics for bandwidth and profile reductions. Sections 3.1 and 3.2 show the results obtained from the solutions of linear systems arising from finite-volume discretizations of the heat conduction (with instances ranging from 4,846 to 232,052 unknowns) and Laplace equations (with instances ranging from 7,322 to 277,188 unknowns), respectively.

Section 3.3 shows the results obtained from the solutions of 11 systems of linear equations (ranging from 1,733 to 81,920 unknowns) contained in the SuiteSparse matrix collection [28].

Tables contained in this section show the number of unknowns (n), the name of the reordering algorithm applied, the bandwidth and profile results, the results of the heuristics in relation to the computational times, in seconds (s), and the memory requirements, in mebibytes (MiB). These tables provide the computational times of the IC(0) preconditioner and the conjugate gradient method separately. It was decided to distinguish these costs because the renumbering produced using the reordering algorithms also affects the computational cost of the IC(0) preconditioner. These tables also present the number of iterations and the total computational times, in seconds, of the ICCG method. Moreover, in spite of the small number of executions for each heuristic in each instance, these tables provide the standard deviation σ and coefficient of variation $C_v = \sigma/\mu$ (where μ is the mean of the results analyzed), referring to the total execution cost of the ICCG method. Additionally, the first line of each instance presented in these tables shows results for systems of linear equations solved using the ICCG method without applying a reordering algorithm. These lines are indicated as "—" in these tables. With this result, one can check the speed-up (or speed-down) of the ICCG method provided by employing a reordering algorithm (i.e., the time of the ICCG method without applying a reordering algorithm divided by the time of the ICCG method executed in conjunction with a reordering algorithm), which is exhibited in the last columns of the tables below. Numbers in boldface are the best results. In addition, several figures in this section are presented as line charts for clarity.

3.1   Instances Arising from Finite-Volume Discretizations of the Heat Conduction Equation

Tables 1, 2 and Fig. 1, developed from an ample collection of heuristics for bandwidth and profile reductions that compose this work, show the average results obtained from the use of the ICCG method applied to instances derived from finite-volume discretizations of the heat conduction equation. These instances arise from the use of meshes generated by employing Voronoi diagrams (and Delaunay triangulations) [27].

Increasing the runtime of the VNS-band heuristic does not reduce the total cost of the whole simulation [10, 11]. Table 2 and Fig. 1b show that several heuristics increased the processing time of the ICCG method or the speed-up is marginal when applied to various instances contained in this dataset (e.g., see the results related to the linear system composed of 50,592 unknowns in Table 2). Moreover, although Sloan's heuristic [20] reached the best results when applied to the smallest instances contained in this dataset (see Table 1), the RCM-GL method [24] yielded similar results to Sloan's [20] heuristic in these instances, and the RCM-GL method [24] obtained, in general, the best results in the largest linear system (see Table 2). Therefore, this method achieved on average the best

Table 1. Results from the solution of systems of linear equations (up to 23,367 unknowns and derived from finite-volume discretizations of the heat conduction equation [27]) using the ICCG method and vertices labeled by heuristics for bandwidth and profile reductions (continued on Table 2).

n	Heuristic	β	Profile	Heuristic t(s)	m.(MiB)	IC(0) t(s)	CGM t(s)	ICCGM iter.	ICCGM t(s)	σ	C_v (%)	Speed-up
4846	—	4769	9116750	—	—	**2**	6	144	8	0.02	0.26	—
	Sloan	882	297009	0.006	0.2	3	3	85	7	0.02	0.29	**1.26**
	Sloan-MGPS	809	299210	0.025	0.0	3	3	86	7	0.02	0.37	1.24
	MPG	1084	305791	0.006	0.2	3	3	91	7	0.02	0.36	1.21
	Snay	1108	360746	0.285	0.1	3	3	**84**	6	0.02	0.35	1.21
	RCM-GL	152	425223	0.005	0.0	3	4	92	7	0.02	0.34	1.20
	GPS	140	406081	0.166	0.3	3	4	94	7	0.01	0.21	1.16
	RBFS-GL	165	448906	**0.002**	0.0	3	4	95	7	0.06	0.80	1.16
	GGPS	136	409134	0.397	0.6	3	4	94	7	0.01	0.07	1.11
	KP-band	152	471590	0.006	0.0	3	4	106	7	0.01	0.19	1.10
	NSloan	554	448633	0.004	0.0	3	4	106	7	0.03	0.35	1.10
	Burgess-Lai	233	417653	0.533	0.0	3	4	100	7	0.07	1.10	1.05
	VNS-band	154	499797	1.054	44.5	3	4	97	7	0.01	0.09	1.02
	CSS-band	4709	8470608	0.588	19.6	3	6	132	8	0.04	0.61	0.94
	FNCHC	**126**	460851	2.297	2.2	3	4	98	7	0.04	0.62	0.87
10728	—	10626	45314579	—	—	**12**	21	206	32	0.27	0.82	—
	Sloan	1415	**1041059**	0.020	0.3	16	11	124	27	0.28	1.03	**1.22**
	Sloan-MGPS	1521	1056012	0.100	0.3	16	11	124	27	0.16	0.60	1.21
	Snay	1418	1087614	0.880	0.3	16	**10**	**121**	**26**	0.12	0.44	1.19
	MPG	2087	1099888	0.020	0.2	16	11	133	27	0.12	0.43	1.18
	RBFS-GL	241	1455453	**0.007**	0.0	16	12	137	28	0.11	0.42	1.17
	RCM-GL	242	1504910	0.014	0.0	17	11	133	28	0.28	1.01	1.16
	KP-band	249	1645616	0.015	0.0	15	13	152	28	0.10	0.34	1.15
	GGPS	230	1540354	1.122	2.6	16	12	135	28	0.26	0.96	1.13
	GPS	**207**	1358676	0.658	1.5	17	11	133	28	0.11	0.38	1.13
	NSloan	1191	1525236	0.010	0.2	17	13	150	30	0.11	0.36	1.10
	VNS-band	552	1746660	1.148	135.6	17	12	145	29	0.51	1.75	1.07
	Burgess-Lai	398	1365197	5.895	0.0	16	12	141	28	0.06	0.22	0.96
	FNCHC	211	1646613	5.968	2.5	16	12	144	28	0.06	0.22	0.95
	CSS-band	10602	42658429	5.030	83.4	**12**	20	192	32	0.44	1.39	0.89
23367	—	23167	216212086	—	—	71	71	302	142	2.21	1.56	—
	Sloan	2973	3578074	0.080	0.6	95	33	177	129	1.60	1.25	**1.10**
	Sloan-MGPS	2713	3565599	0.334	0.3	96	33	178	129	0.90	0.70	1.09
	RCM-GL	367	4913698	0.050	0.0	94	37	192	130	0.45	0.35	1.09
	Snay	1823	**3413219**	2.942	0.7	95	33	**176**	**127**	0.76	0.60	1.09
	RBFS-GL	355	4786316	**0.020**	0.0	93	38	198	132	0.73	0.56	1.08
	MPG	3060	3493791	0.059	0.3	96	36	193	132	0.56	0.43	1.08
	KP-band	376	5521227	0.050	0.0	91	42	219	132	0.29	0.22	1.07
	GPS	**293**	4221479	3.650	3.3	93	37	194	131	0.45	0.35	1.06
	GGPS	317	5194437	5.220	3.5	93	39	202	132	0.11	0.08	1.04
	VNS-band	1564	8889127	1.500	371.1	94	43	223	137	0.58	0.42	1.02
	NSloan	1590	5012507	0.035	0.3	97	41	217	139	0.37	0.27	1.02
	FNCHC	309	5319151	15.320	3.0	93	40	208	133	0.97	0.73	0.96
	Burgess-Lai	465	4296542	11.190	0.0	96	42	213	137	0.69	0.51	0.96
	CSS-band	23127	203145287	38.630	549.1	**70**	67	276	137	2.80	2.05	0.81

Table 2. Results from the solution of systems of linear equations (ranging from 50,592 to 232,052 unknowns and derived from finite-volume discretizations of the heat conduction equation) using the ICCG method and vertices labeled by heuristics for bandwidth and profile reductions (continued from Table 1).

n	Heuristic	β	Profile	Heuristic t(s)	m.(MiB)	IC(0) t(s)	CGM t(s)	ICCGM iter.	ICCGM t(s)	σ	C_v (%)	Speed-up
50592	—	50461	1020411959	—	—	**384**	220	431	604	0.8	0.14	—
	RCM-GL	553	16182346	0.1	0.0	479	116	278	595	4.0	0.67	1.02
	Snay	2928	**10727635**	9.4	1.4	482	**103**	257	**585**	1.0	0.17	1.02
	Sloan	4590	11711775	0.2	1.1	489	104	258	593	1.1	0.18	1.02
	RBFS-GL	541	16420191	0.1	0.0	478	118	283	597	3.0	0.50	1.01
	KP-band	547	18159371	0.1	0.0	471	128	314	600	0.2	0.03	1.01
	Sloan-MGPS	5150	11866029	1.2	1.1	490	105	**255**	594	2.8	0.48	1.01
	MPG	6604	11565237	0.1	1.1	492	111	275	603	2.4	0.39	1.00
	GPS	**466**	14149442	24.2	5.5	480	116	276	596	4.2	0.71	0.97
	VNS-band	7377	47268027	2.9	967.1	490	130	309	621	0.7	0.11	0.97
	NSloan	2568	16461468	0.1	1.1	499	132	316	631	3.2	0.50	0.96
	FNCHC	507	18166254	42.5	5.6	479	122	299	601	2.9	0.49	0.94
	GGPS	497	16985652	48.5	7.7	479	120	289	599	3.0	0.50	0.93
	CSS-band	50349	953617481	391.6	270.1	401	217	398	618	4.4	0.71	0.60
	Burgess-Lai	961	14447154	493.2	0.0	495	125	291	619	2.2	0.35	0.54
108683	—	108216	4725435534	—	—	**1963**	702	627	2665	3.6	0.13	—
	RBFS-GL	907	55649180	**0.1**	0.0	2166	357	408	2524	2.0	0.08	**1.06**
	RCM-GL	911	55350648	0.3	0.0	2185	352	400	2536	7.0	0.27	1.05
	KP-band	885	59355159	0.3	0.0	2177	400	452	2577	3.4	0.13	1.03
	Snay	3887	**33205366**	28.6	2.9	2248	**318**	**369**	2566	10.9	0.42	1.03
	VNS-band	16676	157588720	8.7	2293.7	2203	395	442	2599	4.2	0.16	1.02
	Sloan	8243	36198196	0.7	2.8	2306	321	370	2627	9.7	0.37	1.01
	MPG	14267	36552907	0.3	2.8	2298	344	396	2642	11.2	0.42	1.01
	Sloan-MGPS	7700	36496358	4.0	2.8	2309	328	371	2637	17.2	0.65	1.01
	FNCHC	756	59671449	116.2	11.6	2164	377	430	2541	7.3	0.29	1.00
	GPS	**642**	48744729	139.0	12.6	2167	355	402	2522	4.3	0.17	1.00
	NSloan	8680	52203136	0.2	2.8	2322	408	453	2730	21.8	0.80	0.98
	GGPS	743	54261170	226.5	23.3	2152	363	416	**2515**	2.1	0.08	0.97
	Burgess-Lai	1262	45836037	609.5	0.0	2259	389	428	2647	16.3	0.61	0.82
	CSS-band	108332	110396292	471.5	596.5	2179	700	575	2879	12.8	0.44	0.80
232052	—	231672	21652820640	—	—	**9339**	2167	908	11506	19.1	0.17	—
	RCM-GL	1231	168178362	0.6	0.0	9726	1081	573	**10807**	21.1	0.20	**1.07**
	RBFS-GL	1275	167101014	**0.3**	0.0	9731	1126	595	10857	8.9	0.08	1.06
	KP-band	1228	180118365	0.6	0.0	9811	1240	654	11050	3.7	0.03	1.04
	Snay	5818	**99995456**	92.3	6.3	10023	986	533	11009	36.1	0.33	1.04
	FNCHC	1148	185662203	286.3	22.4	9729	1171	618	10899	19.9	0.18	1.03
	VNS-band	17036	313594920	33.4	5048.3	9942	1221	636	11163	17.8	0.16	1.03
	Sloan	26898	121163861	2.6	5.2	10258	996	534	11254	23.3	0.21	1.02
	MPG	25623	117501685	0.8	5.2	10279	1070	574	11349	10.5	0.09	1.01
	Sloan-MGPS	26456	122023395	14.8	5.1	10424	1014	534	11438	50.5	0.44	1.01
	GPS	**1104**	148697458	584.6	25.4	9757	1108	580	10866	13.7	0.13	1.01
	NSloan	12010	166693574	0.5	5.2	10396	1275	657	11671	61.8	0.53	0.99
	GGPS	1190	172865013	1297.7	43.8	9694	1122	595	10816	11.5	0.11	0.95
	CSS-band	231315	2916471097	4486.6	841.4	11254	2207	830	13471	29.5	0.22	0.64
	Burgess-Lai	2048	153659093	47698.4	0.0	10287	1219	621	11472	6.5	0.06	0.19

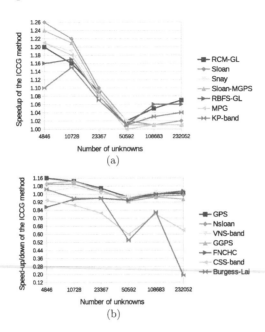

(a)

(b)

Fig. 1. Speed-ups/downs of the ICCG method obtained when using 14 heuristics for bandwidth and profile reductions applied to matrices contained in systems of linear equations derived from finite-volume discretizations of the heat conduction equation (see Tables 1 and 2).

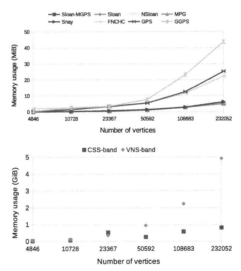

Fig. 2. Memory requirements of 10 heuristics for bandwidth and profile reductions applied to matrices contained in systems of linear equations derived from finite-volume discretizations of the heat conduction equation (see Tables 1 and 2).

results in reducing the computational time of the ICCG method when applied to systems of linear equations contained in this dataset.

Figure 2 shows memory requirements of 10 heuristics for bandwidth and profile reductions. The RCM-GL [24], Burgess-Lai [14], KP-band [3], and RBFS-GL [1] heuristics are in-place algorithms (if one implements the label as an attribute of a vertex).

3.2 Instances Originating from Finite-Volume Discretizations of the Laplace Equation

This section shows simulations using seven linear systems ranging from 7,322 to 277,118 unknowns. In particular, these instances (arising from finite-volume discretizations of the Laplace equation) were ordered randomly because irregular triangulations were employed to generate them [26].

Tables 3, 4 and Fig. 3 show that the RCM-GL method [24] dominated the other heuristics when considering the speedup of the ICCG method applied to these instances. In particular, Fig. 3 does not show the results obtained from the use of the CSS-band and Burgess-Lai heuristics because these two heuristics performed less favorably than the other heuristics applied to the instances contained in this dataset (see Tables 3 and 4). Snay's heuristic [19] was dominated by other heuristics so that we did not apply this algorithm to instances larger than 34,238 unknowns contained in this dataset.

Figure 4 shows memory requirements of eight heuristics for bandwidth and profile reductions applied to matrices contained in linear systems arising from finite-volume discretizations of the Laplace equation. This figure does not show the results from the use of the VNS-band and CSS-band heuristics because these two heuristics showed larger storage costs than the other heuristics when applied to instances contained in this dataset (see Tables 3 and 4).

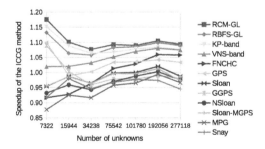

Fig. 3. Speed-ups/downs of the ICCG method obtained when applying 12 heuristics for bandwidth and profile reductions (see Tables 3 and 4) to matrices contained in linear systems with random order originating from finite-volume discretizations of the Laplace equation.

Table 3. Results from the solution of systems of linear equations (up to 34,238 unknowns, derived from finite-volume discretizations of the Laplace equation and composed of matrices with random order) using the ICCG method and vertices labeled by heuristics for bandwidth and profile reductions (continued on Table 4).

n	Heuristic	β	Profile	Heuristic t(s)	mem.	IC(0) t(s)	CGM t(s)	ICCGM iter.	ICCGM t(s)	σ	C_v (%)	Speed-up
7322	—	7248	16083808	—	—	**3**	8	271	11	0.01	0.05	—
	RCM-GL	80	397878	0.005	0.0	4	5	201	**9**	0.01	0.12	**1.18**
	RBFS-GL	80	398377	**0.003**	0.0	4	6	202	10	0.01	0.06	1.13
	KP-band	80	406461	0.006	0.0	4	5	208	10	0.02	0.24	1.15
	Burgess-Lai	152	407458	0.151	0.0	4	6	201	10	0.01	0.11	1.12
	GPS	78	404414	0.362	0.2	4	5	203	10	0.11	1.12	1.10
	GGPS	80	403391	0.323	1.3	4	6	204	10	0.02	0.27	1.09
	VNS-band	1599	966638	1.061	75.9	4	6	214	10	0.07	0.67	1.02
	Sloan-MGPS	296	**374434**	0.031	0.2	5	7	**197**	12	0.08	0.71	0.96
	Sloan	407	377055	0.010	0.2	5	7	199	12	0.02	0.19	0.95
	NSloan	178	425289	0.004	0.2	5	7	204	12	0.01	0.12	0.93
	CSS-band	7185	15979344	0.870	40.9	3	8	271	11	0.10	0.87	0.92
	Snay	1853	448728	0.240	0.3	5	7	199	12	0.28	2.39	0.92
	FNCHC	**71**	423722	2.222	0.5	4	6	205	10	0.02	0.18	0.92
	MPG	846	610304	0.010	0.2	4	8	228	13	0.09	0.75	0.88
15944	—	15902	76482022	—	—	**19**	26	396	45	0.08	0.17	—
	RCM-GL	120	1149124	0.020	0.0	24	17	290	**41**	0.04	0.11	**1.10**
	KP-band	121	1219929	0.020	0.0	24	17	304	41	0.07	0.16	1.09
	RBFS-GL	124	1148009	**0.010**	0.0	25	18	291	42	0.04	0.09	1.06
	Burgess-Lai	212	1144254	1.090	0.0	25	18	291	43	0.14	0.33	1.03
	VNS-band	3916	5108940	1.180	196.7	25	19	319	43	0.28	0.64	1.02
	GGPS	117	1210422	1.790	2.8	25	19	302	43	0.21	0.48	1.00
	GPS	118	1154030	3.610	0.5	25	17	290	42	0.59	1.40	0.99
	Sloan	477	**982724**	0.026	0.3	24	22	286	46	0.24	0.53	0.99
	Sloan-MGPS	473	1003462	0.097	0.3	24	22	284	46	0.11	0.23	0.99
	Snay	5862	1586436	1.027	0.4	23	22	**281**	45	0.24	0.52	0.98
	NSloan	218	1222337	0.014	0.3	24	23	298	47	0.15	0.31	0.96
	MPG	1222	1587797	0.028	0.3	23	25	323	49	0.37	0.76	0.93
	FNCHC	**113**	1315311	5.730	1.3	25	18	301	43	0.13	0.31	0.93
	CSS-band	15724	76687757	8.060	192.7	**19**	26	395	44	0.56	1.26	0.86
34238	—	34609	357518296	—	—	108	82	565	190	0.60	0.32	—
	RCM-GL	192	3413888	0.040	0.0	126	**50**	411	**176**	0.47	0.27	**1.08**
	RBFS-GL	191	3416318	**0.002**	0.0	127	52	412	179	0.75	0.42	1.06
	KP-band	193	3756415	0.040	0.0	125	53	434	178	0.03	0.02	1.06
	VNS-band	2726	6767128	1.670	490.5	127	55	444	182	0.31	0.17	1.03
	Burgess-Lai	334	3282297	4.300	0.0	130	54	419	184	0.01	0.09	1.01
	GPS	191	3545656	9.610	1.6	127	53	418	179	0.80	0.45	1.00
	Sloan	917	**2578022**	0.060	0.8	129	68	395	196	0.94	0.48	0.96
	Sloan-MGPS	845	2672048	0.299	0.9	129	67	**388**	196	1.24	0.63	0.96
	FNCHC	**170**	3910584	15.030	4.0	126	55	436	182	0.76	0.42	0.96
	GGPS	192	3415253	19.630	5.2	126	52	411	178	0.36	0.21	0.96
	Snay	21625	5150148	5.496	1.0	128	67	391	195	1.36	0.70	0.95
	NSloan	366	3608451	**0.033**	0.9	128	73	419	201	0.70	0.35	0.94
	MPG	2111	3965061	0.059	0.9	129	77	448	207	0.42	0.20	0.92
	CSS-band	33953	359290792	68.630	910.7	**107**	81	562	189	2.80	1.48	0.74

Table 4. Results from the solution of systems of linear equations (ranging from 75,542 to 277,118 unknowns, derived from finite-volume discretizations of the Laplace equation and composed of matrices with random order) using the ICCG method and vertices labeled by heuristics for bandwidth and profile reductions (continued from Table 3).

n	Heuristic	β	Profile	Heuristic		IC(0) t(s)	CGM t(s)	ICCGM		σ	C_v (%)	Speed-up
				t(s)	m.(MiB)			iter.	t(s)			
75542	—	75490	1744941733	—	—	591	268	815	859	1.2	0.13	—
	RCM-GL	275	12096902	0.1	0.0	622	164	607	786	0.7	0.08	1.09
	RBFS-GL	275	12128940	0.1	0.0	624	169	616	793	1.4	0.18	1.08
	KP-band	277	13793938	0.1	0.0	625	179	663	804	0.1	0.02	1.07
	VNS-band	21310	42564399	3.7	1198.1	637	176	642	813	2.2	0.26	1.05
	GPS	272	12086603	41.4	3.6	624	166	607	790	0.4	0.05	1.03
	FNCHC	266	13848181	41.5	7.2	630	177	644	806	2.7	0.33	1.01
	Burgess-Lai	460	11175444	42.8	0.0	642	171	612	814	0.8	0.10	1.00
	Sloan	1521	8981209	0.2	1.1	647	214	572	861	5.5	0.63	1.00
	Sloan-MGPS	1236	9245713	1.1	1.1	646	215	568	861	2.0	0.23	1.00
	GGPS	271	12405895	86.2	10.3	625	166	604	792	1.5	0.18	0.98
	NSloan	533	12805775	0.7	1.1	646	250	628	886	2.4	0.27	0.97
	MPG	4020	14107424	0.2	1.1	645	247	653	897	5.4	0.60	0.96
	CSS-band	75031	1747217131	692	3819.2	591	269	819	859	7.6	0.88	0.55
101780	—	101583	3169282786	—	—	1094	405	907	1499	0.1	0.01	—
	RCM-GL	407	21336387	0.1	0.0	1126	249	670	1375	0.6	0.05	1.09
	RBFS-GL	406	21346316	0.1	0.0	1127	254	676	1381	0.7	0.05	1.09
	KP-band	408	23967214	0.1	0.0	1124	265	716	1389	1.8	0.13	1.08
	VNS-band	5207	25033097	5.6	1638.4	1140	256	686	1395	0.7	0.05	1.07
	GPS	405	21399542	73.4	4.9	1125	250	668	1374	3.5	0.25	1.04
	FNCHC	399	25629738	59.9	9.8	1133	265	705	1398	1.0	0.07	1.03
	Sloan	8624	15003839	0.3	2.6	1177	322	640	1498	0.1	0.01	1.00
	Sloan-MGPS	8420	15400014	2.0	2.6	1180	323	635	1503	7.4	0.49	1.00
	NSloan	7730	21163363	0.1	2.6	1165	352	685	1517	8.3	0.54	0.99
	GGPS	402	21624122	152.7	15.5	1128	251	665	1379	2.7	0.19	0.98
	MPG	10570	24189624	0.2	2.6	1185	368	723	1553	0.6	0.04	0.97
	CSS-band	101300	3161769330	227.1	611.4	1093	405	906	1498	9.2	0.61	0.87
	Burgess-Lai	745	19394495	4383.7	0.0	1152	262	683	1414	4.3	0.31	0.26
192056	—	191738	11329772559	—	—	4115	1045	1215	5160	11.0	0.21	—
	RCM-GL	360	42577946	0.2	0.0	4030	642	909	4671	3.9	0.08	1.11
	RBFS-GL	360	42627911	0.1	0.0	4037	659	927	4696	4.2	0.09	1.10
	KP-band	364	48325681	0.3	0.0	4057	704	1000	4761	4.0	0.08	1.08
	VNS-band	11142	99018771	16.6	3195.0	4056	705	992	4761	8.2	0.17	1.08
	FNCHC	344	48743268	115.2	21.0	4056	700	982	4756	7.5	0.16	1.06
	GPS	371	41541059	257.4	10.1	4048	649	911	4696	7.8	0.17	1.04
	Sloan	1963	30916661	0.8	4.6	4219	840	866	5059	18.9	0.37	1.02
	Sloan-MGPS	1733	31860210	4.3	4.6	4249	842	857	5091	33.2	0.65	1.01
	NSloan	753	44591269	0.2	4.6	4223	925	932	5148	8.2	0.16	1.00
	Burgess-Lai	621	40149530	349.5	0.0	4142	682	934	4824	17.2	0.36	1.00
	MPG	5366	47979879	0.5	4.6	4240	953	971	5193	29.0	0.56	0.99
	GGPS	363	42925208	530.0	27.8	4040	645	904	4685	1.5	0.03	0.99
	CSS-band	191322	2731669814	1345.0	1124.9	4101	1047	1211	5148	15.0	0.29	0.80

(continued)

Table 4. (*continued*)

n	Heuristic	β	Profile	Heuristic t(s)	m.(MiB)	IC(0) t(s)	CGM t(s)	ICCGM iter.	t(s)	σ	C_v (%)	Speed-up
277118	—	277019	23512579029	—	—	8563	1766	1430	10329	3.2	0.03	—
	RCM-GL	420	74697812	0.3	0.0	8371	1076	1066	**9447**	7.0	0.07	**1.09**
	RBFS-GL	419	74759303	**0.2**	0.0	8387	1096	1078	9483	2.2	0.02	**1.09**
	KP-band	425	84682829	0.4	0.0	8416	1178	1168	9593	5.4	0.06	1.08
	VNS-band	12132	97666318	32.3	4618.2	8430	1149	1134	9579	11.6	0.12	1.08
	FNCHC	412	85849403	182.4	26.7	8419	1161	1144	9580	8.7	0.09	1.06
	GPS	**399**	72378558	511.5	16.4	8395	1087	1070	9483	23.4	0.25	1.03
	Burgess-Lai	793	66880423	397.9	0.0	8640	1138	1093	9778	2.9	0.03	1.02
	Sloan	2243	**55586225**	1.2	5.6	9070	1392	1012	10463	14.9	0.14	0.99
	GGPS	422	75150257	1051.7	20.7	8412	**1069**	1047	9480	6.1	0.06	0.98
	NSloan	908	77425832	0.3	5.6	9055	1535	1086	10590	66.4	0.63	0.98
	Sloan-MGPS	2094	57033429	7.4	5.6	9206	1399	**1001**	10605	68.3	0.64	0.97
	MPG	6920	89231836	0.8	5.6	9113	1576	1128	10689	44.0	0.41	0.97
	CSS-band	276240	2054061697	3994.8	1679.6	8579	1765	1421	10344	46.6	0.45	0.72

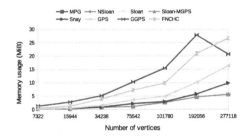

Fig. 4. Memory requirements of eight reordering algorithms applied to matrices contained in systems of linear equations with a random order (see Tables 3 and 4) originating from finite-volume discretizations of the Laplace equation.

3.3 Experiments Using Instances Contained in the SSM Collection

Tables 1, 2, 3, 4 and Figs. 1, 2, 3, 4 show that several heuristics dominated Snay's [19], NSloan [22], and CSS-band [18] heuristics. Moreover, these tables and figures show that the GPS [25], Burgess-Lai [14], FNCHC [15], GGPS [16], and VNS-band [17] algorithms were dominated by the RCM-GL [24], KP-band [3], and RBFS-GL [1] orderings. Hence, we applied six heuristics for bandwidth and profile reductions to a dataset composed of 11 systems of linear equations contained in the SSM collection: the RCM-GL [24], Sloan's [20], MPG [21], Sloan-MGPS [23], KP-band [3], and RBFS-GL [1] heuristics.

Tables 5 and 6 show the instance's name and density (d.). Moreover, these tables and Fig. 5 show the average results obtained by the ICCG method applied to 11 systems of linear equations contained in the SSM collection [28]. Tables 5 and 6 show the 2-norm (a 1-norm) condition number (estimation) $\kappa(A)$ of the instances. Specifically, Tables 5 and 6 show that the ICCG method converges in n iterations, where n is the size of the linear system when applied to ill-conditioned

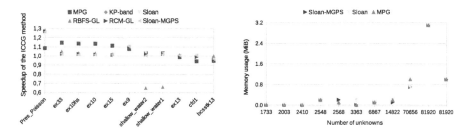

Fig. 5. Speedups of the ICCG method and memory usage obtained when using heuristics for bandwidth and profile reductions (see Tables 5 and 6) applied to 11 systems of linear equations arising from computational fluid dynamics problems contained in the SSM collection [28].

Table 5. Results from the solution of eight systems of linear equations (arising from CFD problems) contained in the SuiteSparse matrix collection [28] employing the zero-fill incomplete Cholesky-preconditioned conjugate gradient method and vertices labeled using reordering algorithms (continued on Table 6).

LS	n	d.	Heuristic	β	Profile	(2-norm) $\kappa(A)$	Heuristic		CGM t(s)	IC(0) t(s)	ICCGM		Speed-up/down
							t(s)	mem.			t(s)	iter.	
ex33	1733	0.74%	—	157	125884	7.0e+12	—	—	18.18	0.4	19	1733	—
			MPG	977	232924	3.1e+11	0.002	0.0	**15.81**	0.4	16	1733	**1.14**
			RBFS-GL	97	71487	3.1e+11	**0.001**	0.0	17.28	0.4	18	1733	1.05
			Sloan-MGPS	569	57790	3.7e+11	0.002	0.0	17.67	0.5	18	1733	1.02
			RCM-GL	97	70259	3.1e+11	0.002	0.0	17.76	0.4	18	1733	1.02
			Sloan	506	**55817**	3.7e+11	**0.001**	0.0	17.70	0.5	18	1733	1.02
			KP-band	**96**	76081	**2.3e+11**	0.001	0.0	17.78	0.4	18	1733	1.02
bcsstk13	2003	2.09%	—	1250	434798	1.1e+10	—	—	64.12	1.8	66	2003	—
			RBFS-GL	521	524853	2.2e+07	**0.001**	0.0	**64.08**	1.5	66	2003	**1.00**
			KP-band	537	644513	**1.8e+07**	0.005	0.0	66.50	1.6	68	2003	0.97
			Sloan-MGPS	1699	522268	1.9e+07	0.022	0.0	66.20	1.9	67	2003	0.97
			Sloan	1790	**512622**	2.5e+08	0.009	0.0	66.72	1.9	69	2003	0.96
			RCM-GL	**502**	519475	1.1e+08	0.006	0.0	67.19	**1.5**	69	2003	0.96
			MPG	1454	729001	1.5e+08	0.012	0.0	67.59	1.9	70	2003	0.95
ex10	2410	0.94%	—	113	170956	9.1e+11	—	—	55.41	**1.3**	57	2410	—
			MPG	1310	437834	2.7e+12	0.004	0.0	**48.62**	1.4	50	2410	**1.13**
			RBFS-GL	112	72752	1.5e+11	**0.001**	0.0	53.82	1.5	55	2410	1.03
			KP-band	**105**	132506	1.2e+11	0.003	0.0	54.24	**1.3**	56	2410	1.02
			RCM-GL	509	247099	2.0e+11	0.002	0.0	54.40	1.4	56	2410	1.02
			Sloan	215	**70891**	1.9e+11	0.004	0.0	54.32	1.5	56	2410	1.02
			Sloan-MGPS	174	71513	**9.5e+10**	0.003	0.0	54.47	1.5	56	2410	1.01
ex10hs	2548	0.88%	—	117	150904	5.5e+11	—	—	61.63	1.5	63	2548	—
			MPG	1236	460152	7.0e+12	0.006	0.2	**54.20**	1.4	56	2548	**1.14**
			RBFS-GL	109	78699	2.1e+11	**0.001**	0.0	59.86	1.5	61	2548	1.03
			KP-band	105	141132	4.5e+11	0.005	0.0	60.21	1.4	62	2548	1.02
			Sloan	199	77868	**1.4e+11**	0.003	0.2	60.33	1.3	62	2548	1.02
			RCM-GL	**105**	**77226**	5.2e+11	0.005	0.0	60.44	1.3	62	2548	1.02
			Sloan-MGPS	176	78605	1.6e+11	0.004	0.2	60.93	1.3	62	2548	1.01

(continued)

Table 5. (*continued*)

LS	n	d.	Heuristic	β	Profile	(2-norm) $\kappa(A)$	Heuristic t(s)	mem.	CGM t(s)	IC(0) t(s)	ICCGM t(s)	iter.	Speed-up/down
ex13	2568	1.15%	—	165	127134	1.2e+15	—	—	77.48	1.9	79	2568	—
			KP-band	167	231828	1.5e+14	0.004	0.0	**76.61**	1.9	79	2568	**1.02**
			RBFS-GL	185	125553	1.5e+14	**0.001**	0.0	76.94	1.9	79	2568	1.01
			Sloan	652	125050	1.5e+14	0.003	0.0	78.11	1.9	79	2568	1.00
			Sloan-MGPS	546	**122369**	1.5e+14	0.003	0.2	77.20	1.9	79	2568	1.00
			RCM-GL	**182**	125123	1.5e+14	0.005	0.0	78.11	1.9	80	2568	0.99
			MPG	1906	1061077	1.5e+14	0.010	0.1	78.60	1.9	80	2568	0.99
ex9	3363	0.88%	—	**85**	**156224**	1.2e+13	—	—	148.30	3.3	152	3363	—
			KP-band	148	288037	2.4e+12	0.005	0.0	**133.51**	3.3	137	3363	**1.11**
			Sloan	604	158613	2.4e+12	0.003	0.2	133.65	3.3	137	3363	1.11
			RBFS-GL	153	159760	2.4e+12	**0.002**	0.0	133.71	4.0	138	3363	1.10
			Sloan-MGPS	406	162327	2.4e+12	0.004	0.0	134.02	3.3	137	3363	1.10
			RCM-GL	147	157476	6.1e+12	0.006	0.0	135.60	3.3	139	3363	1.09
			MPG	2296	1744453	2.4e+12	0.015	0.0	137.55	3.3	141	3363	1.08
ex15	6867	0.21%	—	**67**	450556	8.6e+12	—	—	326.82	7.0	334	6867	—
			MPG	1338	1320684	**1.7e+13**	0.029	0.1	**293.21**	6.6	**300**	6867	**1.11**
			RBFS-GL	83	262534	4.6e+13	**0.001**	0.0	321.70	6.8	328	6867	1.02
			Sloan	139	**250857**	2.0e+13	0.005	0.1	321.55	**6.2**	328	6867	1.02
			Sloan-MGPS	146	251009	6.4e+13	0.008	0.1	323.40	**6.2**	330	6867	1.01
			KP-band	84	267003	2.6e+14	0.006	0.0	323.54	6.8	330	6867	1.01
			RCM-GL	83	261901	3.2e+13	0.005	0.0	324.18	6.8	331	6867	1.01
Pres_Poisson	14822	0.33%	—	12583	9789525	2.0e+06	—	—	77.40	107.8	186	269	—
			KP-band	364	3130744	3.5e+05	0.046	0.0	37.82	107.5	**145**	133	**1.28**
			RBFS-GL	**331**	3024736	1.1e+06	**0.019**	0.0	38.66	106.9	146	137	1.27
			RCM-GL	346	3051085	3.0e+06	0.048	0.0	**37.52**	108.6	146	**132**	1.27
			Sloan-MGPS	640	2832467	2.7e+06	0.114	0.1	39.15	107.6	147	138	1.26
			Sloan	548	**2830658**	**3.2e+05**	0.049	0.2	39.25	107.8	147	138	1.26
			MPG	14168	26556694	7.7e+05	2.399	0.2	64.05	**104.8**	169	220	1.08

instances (i.e., with large condition numbers). Among the information presented in Table 5, in particular, this table shows a small number of iterations for the ICCG method when applied to the *Pres_Poisson* instance, whose condition number is smaller than the other seven linear systems contained in this table. Furthermore, Table 6 shows that the execution times of the ICCG method to solve the *shallow_water1* and *shallow_water2* instances (composed of 81,920 unknowns and with small condition numbers) are approximately four times lower than the execution times to compute the *cfd1* instance (composed of 70,656 unknowns and with a large condition number).

The MPG [21] (KP-band [3]) heuristic obtained the best results when applied to the *ex33*, *ex10*, *ex10hs*, and *ex15* (*ex9* and *Pres_Poisson*) instances. The KP-band [3] (Sloan [20]) heuristic obtained the best results when applied to the *ex13* and *shallow_water1* (*cfd1* and *shallow_water2*) instances, but these gains are marginal.

When setting the same precision in exploratory investigations using standard double-precision floating-point format, the ICCG method converged in a similar

Table 6. Results from the solution of three systems of linear equations (arising from CFD problems) contained in the SSM collection [28] employing the ICCG method and vertices labeled using reordering algorithms (continued from Table 5).

LS	n	d.	Heuristic	β	Profile	(1-norm) $\kappa(A)$ est.	Heuristic t(s)	mem.	CGM t(s)	IC(0) t(s)	ICCGM t(s)	iter.	Speed-up/down
cfd1	70656	0.04%	—	6229	1.0+08	**1.3e+06**	—	—	443	1441	1884	542	—
			Sloan	19834	6.0e+07	1.8e+06	1.0	0.7	**413**	1449	**1862**	499	1.01
			KP-band	3322	1.3e+08	4.1e+06	0.2	0.0	443	1423	1866	539	1.01
			Sloan-MGPS	19186	**5.7e+07**	3.6e+06	4.1	0.7	416	1453	1869	501	1.01
			RBFS-GL	3289	1.2e+08	1.3e+06	**0.1**	0.0	428	1448	1876	524	1.00
			RCM-GL	**3182**	1.1e+08	3.5e+06	0.2	0.0	450	1459	1909	542	0.99
			MPG	56114	4.7e+08	2.8e+06	17.9	1.0	576	**1408**	1984	682	0.94
shallow_water1	81920	0.01%	—	40959	**3.5e+07**	3.6	—	—	20	470	473	7	—
			KP-band	1029	6.8e+07	1.3	0.2	0.0	2	**456**	**458**	6	1.03
			MPG	3619	7.0e+07	1.3	0.8	3.1	2	**456**	**458**	7	1.03
			RCM-GL	**966**	6.6e+07	1.5	0.2	0.0	2	460	462	6	1.02
			Sloan	3070	6.8e+07	1.3	0.7	3.1	2	460	462	6	1.02
			Sloan-MGPS	2578	6.6e+07	1.3	4.0	3.1	2	459	460	6	1.02
			RBFS-GL	322	2.2e+07	2.2	**0.1**	0.0	2	713	715	6	0.66
shallow_water2	81920	0.01%	—	40959	3.5e+07	11.3	—	—	3	464	467	10	—
			Sloan	1225	2.2e+07	1.6	0.2	1.0	3	**447**	**450**	10	**1.04**
			MPG	1226	2.4e+07	1.6	0.3	1.0	3	449	452	10	1.03
			RCM-GL	329	2.2e+07	4.2	**0.1**	0.0	3	458	461	10	1.01
			KP-band	**327**	2.2e+07	1.6	**0.1**	0.0	3	458	461	10	1.01
			Sloan-MGPS	896	2.3e+07	1.6	1.4	1.0	3	462	465	10	1.00
			RBFS-GL	337	3.3e+07	4.2	**0.1**	0.0	3	714	717	9	0.65

number of iterations to using high-precision floating-point arithmetic. Thus, in these experiments, we observed that high-precision floating-point arithmetic does not minimize delay in the convergence of the ICCG method. Figure 5 also shows the memory usage obtained when using three heuristics for bandwidth and profile reductions applied to 11 instances arising from computational fluid dynamics problems contained in the SSM collection [28].

4   Conclusions

Systematic reviews [1, 2, 6–8] reported the most promising low-cost heuristics for bandwidth and profile reductions. Thus, our computational experiment compared the results of the implementations of 14 heuristics for bandwidth and profile reductions when applied to 23 instances arising from CFD problems.

Table 5 shows six promising heuristics for bandwidth and profile reductions to reduce computational times of the ICCG method. In particular, in experiments using instances (with sizes to almost 300,000 unknowns) from three datasets, three out of 14 heuristics for bandwidth and profile reductions evaluated in this computational experiment showed the best overall results in reducing the processing cost of the ICCG method. Specifically, the RCM-GL [24], MPG [21], and

KP-band [3] obtained the most promising results when used to reduce the processing cost of the ICCG method when applied to instances arising from computational fluid dynamics problems. Future studies will reveal whether this may be extended to any preconditioned conjugate gradient method or even to other preconditioned iterative solvers. In particular, the RCM-GL method [24] achieved the best results when applied to instances arising from finite-volume discretizations of the heat conduction and Laplace equations [26,27] (see Tables 2, 3, 4 and Figs. 1a and 3). Thus, the in-place low-cost RCM-GL method [24] remains in the state of the practice in bandwidth reduction when applied to instances originating from CFD problems. On the other hand, the MPG [21] (in four linear systems) and KP-band [3] (in two linear systems) heuristics reached the largest number of best results in simulations with 11 instances contained in the SuiteSparse matrix collection [28].

As a continuation of this work, we intend to implement and evaluate other preconditioners in conjunction with the conjugate gradient method. We also plan to implement parallel approaches of the above algorithms in future investigations.

Acknowledgments. We would like to thank Prof. Dr. Dragan Urosevic, from the Mathematical Institute SANU, for sending us the VNS-band executable program. We would also like to thank Prof. Dr. Fei Xiao for sending us the source code of the FNCHC heuristic.

References

1. Gonzaga de Oliveira, S.L., Bernardes, J.A.B., Chagas, G.O.: An evaluation of reordering algorithms to reduce the computational cost of the incomplete Cholesky-conjugate gradient method. Comput. Appl. Math. (2017). https://doi.org/10.1007/s40314-017-0490-5
2. Gonzaga de Oliveira, S.L., Bernardes, J.A.B., Chagas, G.O.: An evaluation of low-cost heuristics for matrix bandwidth and profile reductions. Comput. Appl. Math. **37**(2), 1412–1471 (2018). https://doi.org/10.1007/s40314-016-0394-9
3. Koohestani, B., Poli, R.: A hyper-heuristic approach to evolving algorithms for bandwidth reduction based on genetic programming. In: Bramer, M., Petridis, M., Nolle, L. (eds.) Research and Development in Intelligent Systems XXVIII, pp. 93–106. Springer, London (2011). https://doi.org/10.1007/978-1-4471-2318-7_7
4. Papadimitriou, C.H.: The NP-completeness of bandwidth minimization problem. Comput. J. **16**, 177–192 (1976)
5. Lin, Y.X., Yuan, J.J.: Profile minimization problem for matrices and graphs. Acta Mathematicae Applicatae Sinica **10**(1), 107–122 (1994)
6. Chagas, G.O., Gonzaga de Oliveira, S.L.: Metaheuristic-based heuristics for symmetric-matrix bandwidth reduction: a systematic review. Proc. Comput. Sci. (Proc. Int. Conf. Comput. Sci. (ICCS)) **51**, 211–220 (2015)
7. Bernardes, J.A.B., Gonzaga de Oliveira, S.L.: A systematic review of heuristics for profile reduction of symmetric matrices. Proc. Comput. Sci. (Proc. Int. Conf. Comput. Sci. (ICCS)) **51**, 221–230 (2015)

8. Gonzaga de Oliveira, S.L., Chagas, G.O.: A systematic review of heuristics for symmetric-matrix bandwidth reduction: methods not based on metaheuristics. In: The XLVII Brazilian Symposium of Operational Research (SBPO), Ipojuca-PE, Brazil, Sobrapo, August 2015

9. Golub, G.H., van Loan, C.F.: Matrix Computations, 3rd edn. The Johns Hopkins University Press, Baltimore (1996)

10. Gonzaga de Oliveira, S.L., de Abreu, A.A.A.M., Robaina, D., Kischinhevsky, M.: A new heuristic for bandwidth and profile reductions of matrices using a self-organizing map. In: Gervasi, O., et al. (eds.) ICCSA 2016. LNCS, vol. 9786, pp. 54–70. Springer, Cham (2016). https://doi.org/10.1007/978-3-319-42085-1_5

11. Gonzaga de Oliveira, S.L., Abreu, A.A.A.M., Robaina, D.T., Kischnhevsky, M.: An evaluation of four reordering algorithms to reduce the computational cost of the Jacobi-preconditioned conjugate gradient method using high-precision arithmetic. Int. J. Bus. Intell. Min. **12**(2), 190–209 (2017)

12. Gonzaga de Oliveira, S.L., Bernardes, J.A.B., Chagas, G.O.: An evaluation of several heuristics for bandwidth and profile reductions to reduce the computational cost of the preconditioned conjugate gradient method. In: Proceedings of the Brazilian Symposium on Operations Research (SBPO 2016), Vitória, Brazil, Sobrapo, September 2016

13. Gonzaga de Oliveira, S.L., Chagas, G.O., Bernardes, J.A.B.: An analysis of reordering algorithms to reduce the computational cost of the Jacobi-preconditioned CG solver using high-precision arithmetic. In: Gervasi, O., et al. (eds.) ICCSA 2017. LNCS, vol. 10404, pp. 3–19. Springer, Cham (2017). https://doi.org/10.1007/978-3-319-62392-4_1

14. Burgess, I.W., Lai, P.K.F.: A new node renumbering algorithm for bandwidth reduction. Int. J. Numer. Meth. Eng. **23**, 1693–1704 (1986)

15. Lim, A., Rodrigues, B., Xiao, F.: A fast algorithm for bandwidth minimization. Int. J. Artif. Intell. Tools **3**, 537–544 (2007)

16. Wang, Q., Guo, Y.C., Shi, X.W.: A generalized GPS algorithm for reducing the bandwidth and profile of a sparse matrix. Prog. Electromagn. Res. J. **90**, 121–136 (2009)

17. Mladenovic, N., Urosevic, D., Pérez-Brito, D., García-González, C.G.: Variable neighbourhood search for bandwidth reduction. Eur. J. Oper. Res. **200**, 14–27 (2010)

18. Kaveh, A., Sharafi, P.: Ordering for bandwidth and profile minimization problems via charged system search algorithm. Iranian J. Sci. Technol.-Trans. Civil Eng. **36**(2), 39–52 (2012)

19. Snay, R.A.: Reducing the profile of sparse symmetric matrices. Bull. Geodésique **50**(4), 341–352 (1976)

20. Sloan, S.W.: A Fortran program for profile and wavefront reduction. Int. J. Numer. Meth. Eng. **28**(11), 2651–2679 (1989)

21. Medeiros, S.R.P., Pimenta, P.M., Goldenberg, P.: Algorithm for profile and wavefront reduction of sparse matrices with a symmetric structure. Eng. Comput. **10**(3), 257–266 (1993)

22. Kumfert, G., Pothen, A.: Two improved algorithms for envelope and wavefront reduction. BIT Numer. Math. **37**(3), 559–590 (1997)

23. Reid, J.K., Scott, J.A.: Ordering symmetric sparse matrices for small profile and wavefront. Int. J. Numer. Meth. Eng. **45**(12), 1737–1755 (1999)

24. George, A., Liu, J.W.: Computer Solution of Large Sparse Positive Definite Systems. Prentice-Hall, Englewood Cliffs (1981)

25. Gibbs, N.E., Poole, W.G., Stockmeyer, P.K.: An algorithm for reducing the band-width and profile of a sparse matrix. SIAM J. Numer. Anal. **13**(2), 236–250 (1976)
26. Gonzaga de Oliveira, S.L., Kischinhevsky, M., Tavares, J.M.R.S.: Novel graph-based adaptive triangular mesh refinement for finite-volume discretizations. Comput. Model. Eng. Sci. **95**(2), 119–141 (2013)
27. Gonzaga de Oliveira, S.L., de Oliveira, F.S., Chagas, G.O.: A novel approach to the weighted Laplacian formulation applied to 2D Delaunay triangulations. In: Gervasi, O., Murgante, B., Misra, S., Gavrilova, M.L., Rocha, A.M.A.C., Torre, C., Taniar, D., Apduhan, B.O. (eds.) ICCSA 2015. LNCS, vol. 9155, pp. 502–515. Springer, Cham (2015). https://doi.org/10.1007/978-3-319-21404-7_37
28. Davis, T.A., Hu, Y.: The University of Florida sparse matrix collection. ACM Trans. Math. Softw. **38**(1), 1:1–1:25 (2011)

A Total Variation Diminishing Hopmoc Scheme for Numerical Time Integration of Evolutionary Differential Equations

Diego N. Brandão[1], Sanderson L. Gonzaga de Oliveira[2(✉)],
Mauricio Kischinhevsky[3], Carla Osthoff[4], and Frederico Cabral[4]

[1] CEFET-RJ, Rio de Janeiro, RJ, Brazil
diego.brandao@eic.cefet-rj.br
[2] Universidade Federal de Lavras, Lavras, MG, Brazil
sanderson@dcc.ufla.br
[3] Universidade Federal Fluminense, Niterói, RJ, Brazil
kisch@ic.uff.br
[4] Laboratório Nacional de Computação Científica (LNCC), Petrópolis, RJ, Brazil
{osthoff,fcabral}@lncc.br

Abstract. This paper concentrates on a total variation diminishing Hopmoc scheme for numerical time integration of evolutionary differential equations. The Hopmoc method for numerical integration of parabolic partial differential equations with convective dominance is based on the concept of spatially decomposed meshes used in the Hopscotch method. In addition, the Hopmoc method uses the concept of integration along characteristic lines in a Semi-Lagrangian scheme based on the Modified Method of Characteristics. This work employs Total Variation Diminishing schemes in order to increase accuracy of the Hopmoc method. Thus, this paper shows that the Hopmoc method in conjunction with a Total Variation Diminishing scheme provides effective improvements over the original Hopmoc method.

Keywords: Higher-order schemes · Total Variation Diminishing
Flux limiters · Hopscotch method · Advection-diffusion equation
Modified Method of Characteristics

1 Introduction

The numerical solution of advection–diffusion transport arises from several relevant scientific and engineering applications, including problems in physics and chemistry. Important examples of its use include the transport of contaminants in air, ground water, rivers, and lagoons, oil reservoir flow, aerodynamics, astrophysics, biomedical applications, in the modeling of semiconductors, geophysical flows, such as meteorology and oceanography [1]. In reactive or environment fluid flow problems, contaminant or chemical species are mainly transported by the fluid in which it is dissolved. Specifically in computational hydraulics and fluid

© Springer International Publishing AG, part of Springer Nature 2018
O. Gervasi et al. (Eds.): ICCSA 2018, LNCS 10960, pp. 53–66, 2018.
https://doi.org/10.1007/978-3-319-95162-1_4

dynamics problems, the advection–diffusion equation can be used to represent quantities such as mass, heat, energy, vorticity, etc. [2]. Thus, the modeling of transport processes is studied in a wide range of fields. Therefore, this is a key topic in numerical mathematics [3].

The Hopmoc method was proposed to solve parabolic problems with convective dominance in parallel architectures [4,5]. This method addresses the entire process of parallelization by devising a spatial decoupling that allows message-passing minimization.

The Hopscotch method [6–10] is a general-purpose approach for the solution of second-order parabolic and elliptic partial differential equations. The Hopmoc method [4,5] is based on Hopscotch concepts in the sense that the set of unknowns is decoupled into two subsets. These subsets are calculated alternately in explicit and implicit semi–steps so that the approach does not involve solving any linear system. The semi–steps are solved along characteristic lines in a Semi-Lagrangian approach following concepts of the Modified Method of Characteristics [11]. The time derivative and the advection term are integrated as a direction derivative, i.e. time steps are calculated in the flow direction along characteristics of the velocity field of the fluid. Specifically, the Hopmoc method uses a strategy based on tracking values along characteristic lines during time stepping. Furthermore, it is an Eulerian-Lagrangian localized adjoint method (ELLAM [12]) since the domain is completely discretized along characteristic lines. In short, an ELLAM-like method provides the accuracy and efficiency of an Eulerian-Lagrangian approach, preserves mass quantity, and systematically handles any sort of boundary condition [13]. In addition, the Hopmoc method is a direct method in the sense that the cost per time step is known *a priori* [1]. Another advantage of the Hopmoc method is that its processing time is linear in the number of unknowns per time step [14].

Discretization of the advective term in transport equations is frequently a difficult task. To avoid abrupt numerical oscillations in the solution, Harten [15] introduced the concepts of Total Variation Diminishing (TVD) techniques and flux limiter. In short, these techniques provide monotonicity-preserving properties of stable higher-order accurate solutions of advection–diffusion problems. Total Variation Diminishing techniques have been successfully employed alongside numerical methods, where recent examples are the publications of Bartels [16] and Fernandes et al. [17].

This paper implements a Total Variation Diminishing technique along with the Hopmoc method. More specifically, this work shows how to combine a total variation diminishing scheme for numerical time integration of parabolic equations with convective dominance when using the Hopmoc method.

The remainder of this paper is divided as follows. Section 2 provides a brief background on the original Hopmoc scheme, which we modify and improve in this paper. Section 3 describes the Total Variation Diminishing scheme employed and the different flux limiters used in this work. Section 4 shows the numerical results. Specifically, this section shows the efficiency of the new scheme over the

original Hopmoc method in terms of numerical errors. Section 5 addresses the
final remarks and a description of future works.

2   The Hopmoc Method

For clarity, we describe below the Hopmoc method in details (see [4,5]). Consider
the one-dimensional advection–diffusion equation in the form

$$u_t + v u_x = d u_{xx}, \tag{1}$$

comprised of appropriate initial and boundary conditions, where v is a constant
positive velocity, d is a positive constant of diffusivity, and $0 \le x \le 1$. Even
though in Eq. (1) u_t refers to the time derivative and not u evaluated at a
discrete time step t, we abuse the notation and now use t to represent a discrete
time step in the range $0 \le t \le T$, for T time steps. Then, $\Delta t = u^{t+1} - u^t$
($\delta t = \frac{\Delta t}{2} = u^{t+\frac{1}{2}} - u^t$) represents a time (semi-) step when considering a typical
finite-difference discretization for Eq. (1). Specifically, this work uses a three-
point finite-difference scheme for the discretization of diffusive terms.

Figure 1 represents the Hopmoc method for a one-dimensional problem. This
figure shows that the characteristic line allows to obtain $\bar{u}\left(\bar{x}_i^{t+\frac{1}{2}}\right)$ and $\bar{\bar{u}}\left(\bar{\bar{x}}_i^t\right)$
in the previous two time semi–steps, for $\bar{x}_i^{t+\frac{1}{2}} = x_i - v \cdot \delta t$ and $\bar{\bar{x}}_i^t = x_i - 2v \cdot \delta t$,
respectively. As described below, an interpolation calculates the variable value
$\bar{\bar{u}}\left(\bar{\bar{x}}_i^t\right)$ [18]. For clarity, a variable in a previous time [semi-] step is represented as
$\bar{\bar{u}}_i^t = u\left(\bar{\bar{x}}_i^t\right)\left[\bar{u}_i^{t+\frac{1}{2}} = u\left(\bar{x}_i^{t+\frac{1}{2}}\right)\right]$ in the foot of the characteristic line originated at
$\bar{\bar{x}}_i^t\left[\bar{x}_i^{t+\frac{1}{2}}\right]$. The Hopmoc method performs this strategy along characteristic lines
in a Semi-Lagrangian scheme based on the Modified Method of Characteristics
[11]. Thus, $\bar{u}_i^t\left[\bar{u}_i^{t+1}\right]$ is a numerical approximation of u in $(x_i, u^t)\left[(x_i, u^{t+1})\right]$. In
addition, a uniform spatial discretization $\Delta x = x_{i+1} - x_i$ is used [18]. Thereby,
the Hopmoc method uses variable values $\bar{u}_i^t\left(\bar{u}_i^{t+\frac{1}{2}}\right)$ to calculate $\bar{u}_i^{t+\frac{1}{2}}\left(u_i^{t+1}\right)$ in
its first (second) time semi–step.

The set of grid points is divided into two subsets during the implementation
of the integration step (see Fig. 1). Then, two distinct updates are alternately
performed, one explicit and one implicit, on each variable in the course of the
iterative process. Each update demands an integration semi step. Similar to the
Hopscotch method, this approach avoids the use of a linear system solver to
calculate the unknowns, as mentioned.

The Hopmoc method employs the finite-difference operator

$$L_h(u_i^t) = d\frac{u_{i-1}^t - 2u_i^t + u_{i+1}^t}{\Delta x^2} \tag{2}$$

so that both consecutive time semi–steps can be written as $\bar{u}_i^{t+\frac{1}{2}} = \bar{u}_i^t +$
$\delta t\left(\theta_i^t L_h \bar{u}_i^t + \theta_i^{t+1} L_h \bar{u}_i^{t+\frac{1}{2}}\right)$ or $u_i^{t+1} = \bar{u}_i^{t+\frac{1}{2}} + \delta t\left(\theta_i^t L_h \bar{u}_i^{t+\frac{1}{2}} + \theta_i^{t+1} L_h u_i^{t+1}\right)$, for

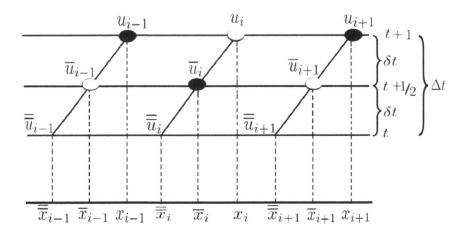

○ Implicit   ● Explicit

Fig. 1. Variable values $\overline{\overline{u}}_i^t$ are used to calculate $\overline{u}_i^{t+\frac{1}{2}}$ in a first time semi–step and subsequently the variable values $\overline{u}_i^{t+\frac{1}{2}}$ are used to calculate u_i^t in the second time semi–step in the Hopmoc method

$\theta_i^t = 1 \ (= 0)$ if $t + i$ is even (odd). In particular, Oliveira et al. [18] presented the convergence analysis of the Hopmoc method for an advection–diffusion equation.

The discretization of the advective term demands to calculate the values of the concentration at midpoints of the sides of each grid interval. Thus, this work employs a flux limiter to obtain these values.

As mentioned, the Hopmoc method employs in each first step a linear interpolation to obtain the initial estimative of the function value in the foot of the characteristic line. Consider a complete Hopmoc step in order to calculate u_i^{t+1} when t is even: $\overline{u}_i^{t+\frac{1}{2}}$ are updated using $\overline{\overline{u}}_i^t$ in the first time semi–step, i.e., $\overline{\overline{u}}_i^t$ are obtained by a linear interpolation using values u_i^t from the previous time step, since these values are already known from the previous time step. When using a linear interpolation, one obtains $\overline{\overline{u}}_i^t = u_{i-q-1}^t + \frac{u_{i-q}^t - u_{i-q-1}^t}{x_{i-q} - x_{i-q-1}} (\overline{\overline{x}}_i - x_{i-q-1})$, where $q = \lfloor \frac{\Delta t}{\Delta x} \rfloor$ is the number of spatial intervals to be jumped to find $\overline{\overline{x}}_i = x_i - v\Delta t$, so that (x_{i-q-1}, x_{i-q}) is the interpolation interval sought. Consequently, $\overline{\overline{x}}_i \in (x_{i-q-1}, x_{i-q})$. Therefore, the linear interpolation is

$$\overline{\overline{u}}_i^t = \frac{\left(x_{i-q} - \overline{\overline{x}}_i\right) u_{i-q-1}^t + \left(\overline{\overline{x}}_i - x_{i-q-1}\right) u_{i-q}^t}{x_{i-q} - x_{i-q-1}}. \tag{3}$$

Substituting $\Delta x = x_{i-q} - x_{i-q-1}$ and $\overline{\overline{x}}_i = x_i - \Delta t$ for $v = 1$ in Eq. (3) yields

$$\overline{\overline{u}}_i^t = \frac{\overbrace{(x_{i-q} - x_i}^{-q\Delta x} + \Delta t)u_{i-q-1}^t + \overbrace{(x_i - x_{i-q-1}}^{(q+1)\Delta x} - \Delta t)u_{i-q}^t}{\Delta x}. \tag{4}$$

Each nodal point in the spatial discretization is given by $x_i = i \cdot \Delta x$, for $i = 0, 1, \cdots, N$ in N spatial intervals. Therefore, substituting $-q\Delta x = x_{i-q} - x_i$ and $(q+1)\Delta x = x_i - x_{i-q-1}$ in Eq. (4) yields

$$\overline{\overline{u}}_i^t = \left(\frac{\Delta t}{\Delta x} - q\right)\left(u_{i-q-1}^t - u_{i-q}^t\right) + u_{i-q}^t. \tag{5}$$

The origin of the error in Eq. (5) occurs as described below [18].

- Error increases if $\Delta t < \Delta x$. In this case, $q = 0$ is obtained and the interpolation step contains a nodal point x_i, i.e., $\overline{\overline{x}}_i \in (x_{i-1}, x_i)$. Rewriting Eq. (5) provides $\overline{\overline{u}}_i^t = \left(\frac{\Delta t}{\Delta x}\right)u_{i-1}^t + \left(1 - \frac{\Delta t}{\Delta x}\right)u_i^t$. When Δt decreases, the foot of the characteristic line approximates x_i. Thus, the factor $1 - \frac{\Delta t}{\Delta x}$ increases. This means that if a higher weight is given to the value u_i^t, the error gradually increases. Nevertheless, u_{i-1}^t represents upstream information. Since $\overline{\overline{x}}_i = x_i - \Delta t$, the foot of the characteristic line approximates x_i when Δt decreases. The expected result is to reduce the maximum error. However, if $\Delta t < \Delta x$, then the error increases when Δt decreases because of the use of a linear interpolation.
- Error oscillates if $\Delta t \geq \Delta x$. The errors of the scheme present oscillations with respect to $\frac{\Delta t}{\Delta x}$. If this quotient is an integer number, the error is smaller; otherwise, it is either increased or reduced, and the analysis is divided into the two cases described below.

1. Δt is multiple of Δx and $\frac{\Delta t}{\Delta x} - q = 0$ in Eq. (5). This means that the foot of the characteristic line $\overline{\overline{x}}_i$ coincides with a nodal point. Thus, each $\overline{\overline{u}}_i^t$ is directly updated from the value u_{i-q}^t, which in turn was updated after a Hopmoc step in the second time semi–step t, i.e. $\overline{\overline{u}}_i^t = u_{i-q}^t$. Therefore, the values $\overline{u}_i^{t+\frac{1}{2}}$ and u_i^{t+1} are updated without any error originated from a linear interpolation. More precisely, a linear interpolation is not carried out if the foot of the characteristic line is a nodal point. For this reason, the error is considerably reduced if compared with simulations where a linear interpolations occurs. This can be observed in Table 1, when considering Eq. (2). In particular, this table shows inherent truncation errors in simulations with the Hopmoc method even without using linear interpolation because the use of large time steps (see rows with $\frac{\Delta t}{\Delta x} \geq 4$ in Table 1).
2. Δt is not multiple of Δx. Considering Eq. (5), the interpolation of the values $\overline{\overline{u}}_i^t$ are calculated as $\overline{\overline{u}}_i^t = \left(\frac{\Delta t}{\Delta x} - q\right)u_{i-q-1}^t + \left[1 - \left(\frac{\Delta t}{\Delta x} - q\right)\right]u_{i-q}^t$.

58   D. N. Brandão et al.

Table 1. Maximum errors when setting $\Delta x = 0.001$ and applying the Hopmoc method with and without (w/o) using linear interpolation (int.)

Δt	$\frac{\Delta t}{\Delta x}$	$d = 0.002$		$d = 0.001$		$d = 0.000\overline{6}$	
		int.	w/o int.	int.	w/o int.	int.	w/o int.
$2.00 \cdot 10^{-4}$	0.2000	1.5138	0.0	3.1551	0.0	4.5060	0.0
$2.50 \cdot 10^{-4}$	0.2500	1.4929	0.0	2.9897	0.0	4.2807	0.0
$31.25 \cdot 10^{-5}$	0.3125	1.3215	0.0	2.7781	0.0	3.9905	0.0
$4.00 \cdot 10^{-4}$	0.4000	1.1678	0.0	2.4721	0.0	3.5678	0.0
$5.00 \cdot 10^{-4}$	0.5000	0.9876	0.0	2.1075	0.0	3.0590	0.0
$6.25 \cdot 10^{-4}$	0.6250	0.7549	0.0	1.6279	0.0	2.3807	0.0
$8.00 \cdot 10^{-4}$	0.8000	0.4141	0.0	0.9066	0.0	1.3410	0.0
$1.00 \cdot 10^{-3}$	1.0000	0.0012	0.0	0.0008	0.0	0.0001	0.0
$1.25 \cdot 10^{-3}$	1.2500	0.3154	0.0	0.6906	0.0	1.0236	0.0
$156.25 \cdot 10^{-5}$	1.5625	0.3375	0.0	0.7272	0.0	1.0742	0.0
$1.00 \cdot 10^{-3}$	4.0000	0.1695	0.0003	0.0803	0.0003	0.0457	0.0002
$1.00 \cdot 10^{-2}$	10.0000	1.0749	0.0021	0.5188	0.0019	0.3011	0.0015

3   A Total Variation Diminishing Scheme

Consider the advection part of Eq. (1), i.e.

$$u_t + v \cdot u_x = 0, \tag{6}$$

for the case when u is constant and positive. In addition, consider u_i^t as a discrete approximation to u in a grid point at time step t. Harten [15] explained that a weak solution of a scalar initial value problem has a monotonicity property as a function of t, i.e. no new local extrema in the solution spatial domain may be created; and the value of a local minimum (maximum) is non-decreasing (non-increasing).

Consider the total variation (TV) at time step t defined as $TV^t = \sum_i |u_{i+1}^t - u_i^t|$. It follows from this monotonicity property that the total variation is non-increasing in t, i.e. a scheme is Total Variation Diminishing if it guarantees that $TV^{t+1} \leq TV^t$.

The Total Variation Diminishing property should be evaluated globally in a solution of an advection scheme. The Total Variation Diminishing property guarantees that the total variation of the solution will not increase as the solution evolves in time. Harten [15] demonstrated that an initially monotonic profile u_i^t remains monotonic after advection by a Total Variation Diminishing scheme. Consider the Eq. (6) rewritten in the form

$$u_i^{t+1} = u_i^t - C_{i-\frac{1}{2}} \left(u_i^t - u_{i-1}^t \right) + D_{i+\frac{1}{2}} \left(u_{i+1}^t - u_i^t \right), \tag{7}$$

where values represented in C and D may depend on unknowns u_i^t as well as on u. Harten [15] showed that the conditions

$$0 \le C_{i+\frac{1}{2}}, \ 0 \le D_{i+\frac{1}{2}}, \ C_{i+\frac{1}{2}} + D_{i+\frac{1}{2}} \le 1, \tag{8}$$

for all i, are sufficient to ensure that the scheme is Total Variation Diminishing. Thus, when building a Total Variation Diminishing scheme, one considers a basic advection scheme, rewrites it in the form of Eq. (7), and then modifies it in a manner that satisfies the conditions in (8). To exemplify this approach, we consider a discretization in the form

$$u_i^{t+1} = u_i^t - c \cdot \left(\hat{u}_{i+\frac{1}{2}} - \hat{u}_{i-\frac{1}{2}} \right), \tag{9}$$

where $c = v\frac{\Delta t}{\Delta x}$ is the Courant number and values represented in $\hat{u}$ are mixing ratios at the grid box edges. To illustrate the definition of $\hat{u}$, we use the Lax–Wendroff scheme $\hat{u}_{i+\frac{1}{2}} = u_i^t + \frac{1-c}{2} \left(u_{i+1}^t - u_i^t \right)$ [19].

The Total Variation Diminishing scheme is built when a factor ϕ is introduced, called *flux limiter*,

$$\hat{u}_{i+\frac{1}{2}} = u_i^t + \phi_i \frac{1-c}{2} \left(u_{i+1}^t - u_i^t \right). \tag{10}$$

In general, ϕ depends on u and then it may change with respect to position and time. Two particular cases are the Lax–Wendroff scheme (when $\phi_i = 1$) and the classical upwind scheme (when $\phi_i = 0$) [20]. Thus, Eqs. (9) and (10) can be combined as $u_{i+1} = u_i^t - c(u_i^t - u_{i-1}^t) \left[1 - \frac{1-c}{2}\phi_{i-1} + \frac{1-c}{2} \cdot \frac{\phi_i}{r} \right]$, where $r = \frac{u_i^t - u_{i-1}^t}{u_{i+1}^t - u_i^t}$. Observing that $c < 1$ and to guarantee that this scheme is Total Variation Diminishing, the conditions $0 \le \phi_i \le \frac{2}{1-c}$ and $0 \le \frac{\phi_i}{r_i} \le \frac{2}{c}$ for all i must be applied. To avoid the CFL condition, those conditions can be rewritten as $0 \le \phi_i \le 2$ and $0 \le \frac{\phi_i}{r_i} \le 2$, for all i. These conditions are satisfied by several flux limiters [3,19,21], and the same approach can be used in conjunction with any high-order basic advection scheme [19].

Flux limiters define the advection scheme based on a ratio of local gradients in the solution field [21,22]. To be used in conjunction with the Hopmoc method, this work compares five flux–limiter formulations based on [23] because the spatial terms are completely separated from the time discretization in their formulations.

- MinMod is a symmetric piecewise-linear scheme proposed by Roe and Baines [23]. It represents the simple expedient of centered gradients from extrema [21]: $\phi(r) = \max[0, min(r, 1)]$.
- Superbee is a symmetric piecewise-linear scheme proposed by Roe [24]: $\phi(r) = \max[0, \min(2r, \max(r, 1), 2)]$. This scheme is a highly compressive transfer function. It was developed to achieve the best possible resolution in discontinuities.

- Van Leer is a symmetric non-linear scheme proposed by Van Leer [25] defined as $\phi(r) = \max[0, \min(\theta r, 1), \min(\theta, r)]$ with $1 \leq \theta \leq 2$, so that $\phi(r) = \frac{r+|r|}{1+|r|}$. It is based on consecutive gradients and is a particular-case TVD scheme that includes extrema both in the upper and lower boundaries.
- Monotonized Central (MC) is a symmetric scheme proposed also by Van Leer [25]. It compares the central difference slope of a centered slope method with twice the one-sided slope to a side: $\phi(r) = max\left[0, min\left(2r, \frac{1+r}{2}, 2\right)\right]$.
- Koren's scheme [26] consists of a non-linear symmetric technique. A version of this scheme applied to variable grid size was presented by Holstad [3]: $\phi(r) = \max\left[0, \min\left(4r, \frac{2}{3}r + \frac{1}{3}, 2\right)\right]$.

The use of a TVD technique does not change the complexity of the 1–D Hopmoc method. This occurs because, similar to the MMOC, the loop that calculates a TVD technique takes $O(n)$ time.

4   Numerical Results and Analysis

Consider the one-dimensional advection–diffusion Eq. (1) with velocity $v = 1.0$ and diffusion coefficient $d = \frac{2}{Re}$. Thus, Eq. (1) is rewritten as

$$u_t + u_x = \frac{2}{Re} u_{xx}. \tag{11}$$

The analytical solution to (11) in a smooth domain is

$$U(x,t) = \frac{exp\left[-\frac{(x-x_o-t)^2}{2\cdot\phi(t)}\right]}{\sqrt{\phi}}, \tag{12}$$

where $\phi(t) = \phi_o\left[1 + \frac{4t}{Re\phi_o}\right]$, x_o is the initial center location of the pulse, $Re = \frac{\rho \cdot L \cdot v}{\mu}$ is the Reynolds number, ρ, L, v, and μ represent density, size of the draining, velocity, and viscosity of the fluid, respectively, and ϕ_0 is the Gaussian pulse amplitude. A Gaussian pulse with amplitude 0.0004, whose initial center location is 0.2, is simulated in our numerical experiments. The initial and boundary conditions simulate the analytical value $U(x,t)$ given by Eq. (12), for $0 \leq x \leq 1$ and $0 \leq t \leq T$.

The workstation used in the execution of the simulations contains an Intel® Core™ i5 with 4 GB of main memory, OS X version 10.10.1 (Intel; Santa Clara, CA, United States). The maximum error was defined as $\max |U(x,t) - u_t^i|$.

As described, Table 1 shows the results of the original Hopmoc method when using interpolation. These results were compared with the results obtained when using a Total Variation Diminishing scheme to determine the foot of the characteristic line in the Hopmoc method. We will refer this approach as TVD–Hopmoc method.

Table 2 shows the maximum errors when establishing $\Delta x = 0.001$ and Reynolds number (Re) as 1000 and, consequently, $d = 0.002$. This table shows the

Table 2. Maximum errors from the TVD-Hopmoc method when setting $\Delta x = 0.001$ and Reynolds number $\mathrm{Re} = 1000$ compared with maximum errors in simulations using the original Hopmoc method. The symbol † indicates that the convergence was not achieved

Δt	$\frac{\Delta t}{\Delta x}$	Hopmoc		TVD–Hopmoc				
		w/o int.	int.	Van Leer	MinMod	Superbee	MC	Koren
$2.00 \cdot 10^{-4}$	0.20	0.0000	1.5138	0.0048	0.0310	0.0306	0.0048	0.0124
$2.50 \cdot 10^{-4}$	0.25	0.0000	1.4929	0.0038	0.0296	0.0284	0.0038	0.0109
$31.25 \cdot 10^{-5}$	0.31	0.0000	1.3215	0.0027	0.0274	0.0255	0.0026	0.0092
$4.00 \cdot 10^{-4}$	0.40	0.0000	1.1678	0.0023	0.0235	0.0215	0.0014	0.0071
$5.00 \cdot 10^{-4}$	0.50	0.0000	0.9876	0.0028	0.0213	0.0163	0.0019	0.0050
$6.25 \cdot 10^{-4}$	0.63	0.0000	0.7549	0.0031	0.0170	0.0104	0.0023	0.0031
$8.00 \cdot 10^{-4}$	0.80	0.0000	0.4141	0.0031	0.0089	0.0028	0.0028	0.0022
$1.00 \cdot 10^{-3}$	1.00	0.0000	0.0012	†				
$1.25 \cdot 10^{-3}$	1.25	0.0000	0.3154					
$156.25 \cdot 10^{-5}$	1.56	0.0000	0.3375					
$4.00 \cdot 10^{-3}$	4.00	0.0003	0.1695					
$1.00 \cdot 10^{-2}$	10.00	0.0021	1.0749					

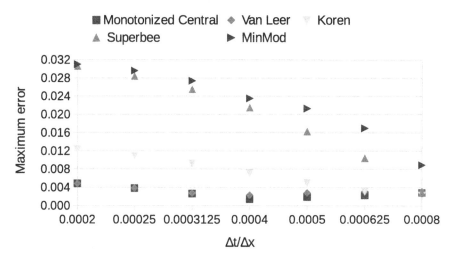

Fig. 2. Maximum errors when setting $\Delta x = 0.001$ and Reynolds number (Re) established as 1000 in simulations employing the TVD–Hopmoc method alongside five flux–limiter formulations

maximum errors of the original Hopmoc method with and without (w/o) using linear interpolation (int.). This table and Fig. 2 show that the Monotonized Central scheme reached the best results when used along with the TVD–Hopmoc method.

Table 3 shows the results when setting the Reynolds number as 2000 ($d = 0.001$) and 3000. Tables 2 and 3 and Figs. 3 and 4 show that the TVD–Hopmoc method in conjunction with the Monotonized Central scheme [25] obtained in general better results than employing the other four flux–limiter schemes. On the other hand, Koren's scheme [26] achieved better results than the other schemes when employed in simulations with $\frac{\Delta t}{\Delta x} = 0.8$. Moreover, Tables 2 and 3 and Fig. 5 show that the TVD-Hopmoc method (along with the Monotonized Central scheme [25]) obtains better accuracy results than the Hopmoc method using an interpolation technique.

Table 3. Maximum errors when setting $\Delta x = 0.001$ and Reynolds number (Re) established as 2000 and 3000 in simulations employing the TVD–Hopmoc along with five flux–limiter formulations and the Hopmoc method with and without (w/o) using a linear interpolation (int.). The symbol † indicates that the convergence was not achieved

Re	Δt	$\frac{\Delta t}{\Delta x}$	Hopmoc		TVD–Hopmoc				
			w/o int.	int.	V. Leer	MinMod	Superbee	MC	Koren
2000	$2.00 \cdot 10^{-4}$	0.20	0.0000	3.1551	0.0142	0.0902	0.0852	0.0139	0.0362
	$2.50 \cdot 10^{-4}$	0.25	0.0000	2.9897	0.0111	0.0845	0.0800	0.0109	0.0318
	$31.25 \cdot 10^{-5}$	0.31	0.0000	2.7781	0.0077	0.0775	0.0733	0.0075	0.0267
	$4.00 \cdot 10^{-4}$	0.40	0.0000	2.4721	0.0058	0.0676	0.0639	0.0035	0.0203
	$5.00 \cdot 10^{-4}$	0.50	0.0000	2.1075	0.0051	0.0566	0.0526	0.0015	0.0140
	$6.25 \cdot 10^{-4}$	0.63	0.0000	1.6279	0.0040	0.0427	0.0389	0.0028	0.0078
	$8.00 \cdot 10^{-4}$	0.80	0.0000	0.9066	0.0036	0.0223	0.0197	0.0037	0.0023
	$1.00 \cdot 10^{-3}$	1.00	0.0000	0.0008	†				
	$1.25 \cdot 10^{-3}$	1.25	0.0000	0.6906					
	$156.25 \cdot 10^{-5}$	1.56	0.0000	0.7272					
	$2.00 \cdot 10^{-3}$	2.00	0.0000	0.0187					
	$2.50 \cdot 10^{-3}$	2.50	0.0001	0.4776					
	$31.25 \cdot 10^{-4}$	3.13	0.0001	0.1717					
	$4.00 \cdot 10^{-3}$	4.00	0.0003	0.0803					
	$6.25 \cdot 10^{-3}$	6.25	0.0007	0.2373					
	$1.00 \cdot 10^{-2}$	10.00	0.0019	1.2599					
3000	$2.00 \cdot 10^{-4}$	0.2	0.0000	4.5060	0.0248	0.1584	0.1441	0.0239	0.0620
	$2.50 \cdot 10^{-4}$	0.25	0.0000	4.2807	0.0195	0.1484	0.1350	0.0187	0.0545
	$31.25 \cdot 10^{-5}$	0.31	0.0000	3.9905	0.0142	0.1360	0.1242	0.0129	0.0457
	$4.00 \cdot 10^{-4}$	0.40	0.0000	3.5678	0.0123	0.1187	0.1086	0.0060	0.0347
	$5.00 \cdot 10^{-4}$	0.50	0.0000	3.0590	0.0103	0.0987	0.0907	0.0030	0.0240
	$6.25 \cdot 10^{-4}$	0.63	0.0000	2.3807	0.0073	0.0738	0.0685	0.0047	0.0133
	$8.00 \cdot 10^{-4}$	0.80	0.0000	1.3410	0.0063	0.0386	0.0365	0.0061	0.0036
	$1.00 \cdot 10^{-3}$	1.00	0.0000	0.0001	†				
	$1.25 \cdot 10^{-3}$	1.25	0.0000	1.0236					
	$156.25 \cdot 10^{-5}$	1.56	0.0000	1.0742					
	$2.00 \cdot 10^{-3}$	2.00	0.0000	0.0097					
	$2.50 \cdot 10^{-3}$	2.50	0.0001	0.7015					
	$31.25 \cdot 10^{-4}$	3.13	0.0001	0.2535					
	$4.00 \cdot 10^{-3}$	4.00	0.0002	0.0457					
	$5.00 \cdot 10^{-3}$	5.00	0.0003	0.0230					
	$6.25 \cdot 10^{-3}$	6.25	0.0005	0.2788					
	$1.00 \cdot 10^{-2}$	10.00	0.0015	0.3011					

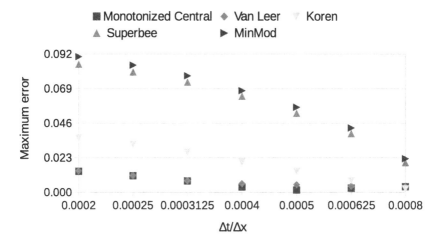

Fig. 3. Maximum errors when setting $\Delta x = 0.001$ and Reynolds number (Re) established as 2000 in simulations employing the TVD–Hopmoc method alongside five flux–limiter formulations

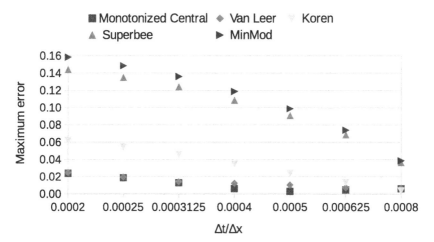

Fig. 4. Maximum errors when setting $\Delta x = 0.001$ and Reynolds number (Re) established as 3000 in simulations employing the TVD–Hopmoc method alongside five flux–limiter formulations

The Hopmoc method is independent of the CFL condition. On the other hand, the TVD–Hopmoc method does not converge for $v \cdot \frac{\Delta t}{\Delta x} \geq 1$ because it is based on the Lax–Wendroff method that was used to obtain the Total Variation Diminishing formulation.

When the foot of the characteristic line is a nodal point (i.e. a very particular case), Tables 2 and 3 show that the results obtained when applying the original Hopmoc method without linear interpolation is better than using Total Variation Diminishing schemes. However, for instance when the velocity field is

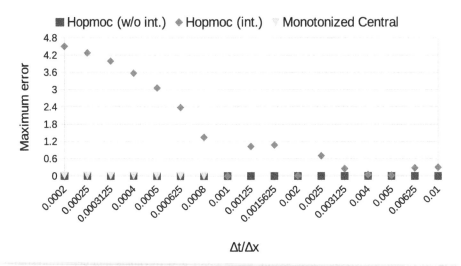

Fig. 5. Maximum errors when setting $\Delta x = 0.001$ and Reynolds number (Re) established as 3000 in simulations employing the Hopmoc and TVD–Hopmoc methods alongside the Monotonized Central scheme [25]

non-uniform, this peculiar circumstance (i.e. the foot of the characteristic line as a nodal point) does not occur.

5   Conclusions and Future Works

This work presented the Hopmoc method along with a Total Variation Diminishing scheme (TVD–Hopmoc for short) for the solution of parabolic equations with convective dominance without solving linear systems. The TVD–Hopmoc method computes previous values by tracking them along characteristic lines and employs a flux–limiter formulation to provide higher precision solutions than the original Hopmoc method. This work compared five flux–limiter formulations along with the Hopmoc method. The Monotonized Central scheme [25] yielded in general better results than the other four schemes in simulations with three Reynolds number regimes. On the other hand, Koren's scheme [26] delivered better results than the other schemes in simulations with $\frac{\Delta t}{\Delta x} = 0.8$ (see Tables 2 and 3). Thus, this paper provided numerical experiments that show the advantages of the new approach compared with the original Hopmoc method. Specifically, the numerical results obtained with the new TVD–Hopmoc strategy provided effective improvements over the original Hopmoc method for simulations with Courant number smaller than 1 since the flux–limiter formulations employed here are based on the Lax–Wendroff method.

Naturally, the Hopmoc method is more accurate when values from previous time steps are obtained from nodal points when tracking them along the characteristic line. However, this situation is a very particular case for a uniform velocity field so that more experiments are necessary to be carried out in the case of non-uniform velocity fields.

Furthermore, the Total Variation Diminishing property does not guarantee that one extrema grows whereas another nearby extrema diminishes [19]. Then, other approaches using positive schemes and universal limiters will be evaluated in future studies. In addition, we intend to evaluate those schemes when applying them to 2–D and 3–D parallel cases so that the scalability of this approach will be also evaluated in future investigations. Additionally, we plan to compare how well the proposed new method performs compared with other approaches, especially one based on an approach of solving systems of linear algebraic equations.

References

1. Cabral, F.L., Osthoff, C., Costa, G., Brandão, D.N., Kischinhevsky, M., Gonzaga de Oliveira, S.L.: Tuning up TVD HOPMOC method on Intel MIC Xeon Phi architectures with Intel Parallel Studio tools. In: 2017 29th International Symposium on Computer Architecture and High Performance Computing Workshops (SBAC-PADW), Campinas, pp. 19–24 (2017). https://ieeexplore.ieee.org/document/8109000/
2. Ding, H., Zhang, Y.: A new difference scheme with high accuracy and absolute stability for solving convectiondiffusion equations. J. Comput. Appl. Math. **230**, 600–606 (2009)
3. Holstad, A.: The Koren upwind scheme for variable gridsize. Appl. Numer. Math. **37**, 459–487 (2001)
4. Kischinhevsky, M.: An operator splitting for optimal message-passing computation of parabolic equation with hyperbolic dominance. In: SIAM Annual Meeting, Kansas City, MO (1996)
5. Kischinhevsky, M.: A spatially decoupled alternating direction procedure for convection-diffusion equations. In: Proceedings of the XXth CILAMCE Iberian Latin American Congress on Numerical Methods in Engineering (1999)
6. Gane, C.R., Gourlay, A.R.: Block hopscotch procedures for second order parabolic differential equations. J. Inst. Math. Appl. **19**, 205–216 (1977)
7. Gordon, P.: Nonsymmetric difference equations. SIAM J. Appl. Math. **13**, 667–673 (1965)
8. Gourlay, A.R.: Hopscotch: a fast second order partial differential equation solver. IMA J. Appl. Math. **6**, 375–390 (1970)
9. Gourlay, A.R., McGuire, G.R.: General Hopscotch algorithm for the numerical solution of partial differential equations. J. Inst. Math. Appl. **7**, 216–227 (1971)
10. Gourlay, A.R., McKee, S.: The construction of Hopscotch methods for parabolic and elliptic equations in two space dimensions with mixed derivative. J. Comput. Appl. Math. **3**, 201–206 (1977)
11. Douglas Jr., J., Russel, T.F.: Numerical methods for convection-dominated diffusion problems based on combining the method of characteristics with finite element or finite difference procedures. SIAM J. Numer. Anal. **19**, 871–885 (1982)
12. Celia, M.A., Russel, T.F., Herrera, I., Ewing, R.E.: An Eulerian-Lagrangian localized adjoint method for the advection-diffusion equation. Adv. Water Resour. **13**, 187–206 (1990)
13. Russel, T.F., Celia, M.A.: An overview of research on Eulerian-Lagrangian localized adjoint methods (ELLAM). Adv. Water Resour. **25**, 1215–1231 (2002)

14. Cabral, F.L., Osthoff, C., Kischinhevsky, M., Brandão, D.: Hybrid MPI/OpenMP/ OpenACC implementations for the solution of convection diffusion equations with Hopmoc method. In: Apduhan, B., Rocha, A.M., Misra, S., Taniar, D., Gervasi, O., Murgante, B. (eds.): 14th International Conference on Computational Science and its Applications (ICCSA) CPS, 196–199. IEEE, July 2014

15. Harten, A.: High resolution schemes for hyperbolic conservation laws. J. Comput. Phys. **49**, 357–393 (1983)

16. Bartels, S., Nochetto, R.H., Salgado, A.J.: A total variation diminishing interpolation operator and applications. Math. Comput. **84**, 2569–2587 (2015)

17. Fernandes, B.R.B., Gonçalves, A.D.R., Filho, E.P.D., Lima, I.C.M., Marcondes, F., Sepehrnoori, K.: A 3D total variation diminishing scheme for compositional reservoir simulation using the element-based finite-volume method. Numer. Heat Transfer, Part A **67**(8), 839–856 (2015)

18. Oliveira, S.R.F., Gonzaga de Oliveira, S.L., Kischinhevsky, M.: Convergence analysis of the Hopmoc method. Int. J. Comput. Math. **86**, 1375–1393 (2009)

19. Thuburn, J.: TVD schemes, positive schemes and universal limiter. Mon. Weather Rev. **125**, 1990–1993 (1997)

20. Courant, R., Isaacson, E., Rees, M.: On the solution of nonlinear hyperbolic differential equations by finite differences. Commun. Pure Appl. Math. **5**(3), 243–255 (1952)

21. Waterson, N.P., Deconinck, H.: Design principles for bounded higher-order convection schemes - a unified approach. J. Comput. Phys. **224**, 182–207 (2007)

22. Sweby, P.K.: High resolution schemes using flux limiters for hyperbolic conservation laws. SIAM J. Numer. Anal. **21**(5), 995–1011 (1984)

23. Roe, P.L., Baines, M.J.: Algorithms for advection and shock problems. In: Viviand, H. (ed.): Proceedings of the Fourth GAMM Conference on Numerical Methods in Fluid Mechanics. Notes on Numerical Fluid Mechanics, vol. 5, pp. 281–290. Vieweg, Paris, France (1982)

24. Roe, P.L.: Some contributions to the modelling of discontinuous flows. In: Engquist, B.E., Osher, S., Somerville, R.C.J. (eds.): Proceedings of the Fifteenth Summer Seminar on Applied Mathematics Large-Scale Computations in Fluid Mechanics. Lectures in Applied Mathematics, vol. 22, pp. 163–193. AMS-SIAM Summer Seminar, American Mathematical Society, La Jolla, CA (1985)

25. van Leer, B.: Towards the ultimate conservative difference schemes. J. Comput. Phys. **14**, 361–370 (1974)

26. Koren, B.: A robust upwind discretization method for advection, diffusion and source terms. In: Vreugdenhil, C.B., Koren, B. (eds.) Numerical Methods for Advection - Diffusion Problems. Notes on Numerical Fluid Mechanics, vol. 45, pp. 117–138. Friedrich Vieweg & Sohn Verlagsgesellschaft, Braunschweig, Germany, October 1993

NLFSR Functions with Optimal Periods

Sultan Almuhammadi$^{(\boxtimes)}$, Ibraheem Al-Hejri, Ghashmi Bin Talib,
and Awadh Gaamel

King Fahd University of Petroleum and Minerals, Dhahran, Saudi Arabia
muhamadi@kfupm.edu.sa, alhejri87@gmail.com,
{g201309530,g201402020}@kfupm.edu.sa

Abstract. Nonlinear feedback shift registers (NLFSRs) are basic components, typically found in stream ciphers and other cryptosystems. The main purpose of these components is to generate pseudorandom sequences of bits. There is no mathematical foundation on how to construct an NLFSR feedback function with optimal period. In this work, we review the existing NLFSR feedback functions, and propose new functions with optimal periods.

Keywords: NLFSR · Pseudorandom · Optimal period

1 Introduction

One of the most prevalent tools used to generate pseudo-random sequences is the feedback shift register (FSR). FSRs have various applications such as data compression [1], cryptography [2], error detection and correction [3] and testing [4]. Research on LFSRs has been developed since early 1960s [5].

Depending on its internal feedback function, the FSR can be either linear (LFSR) or nonlinear (NLFSR). The area of LFSRs is considered well-known and most of the LFSR fundamental problems are solved. A designer only has to use a primitive generator polynomial in order to build a LFSR of size n bits with a maximum period.

Unlike LFSR, the state in NLFSR is a non-linear transformation of the previous state [6]. The importance of NLFSR comes from its ability to produce a very secure pseudorandom sequence which is hard to break. Thus, to determine the structure of an NLFSR, at least $\Theta(2^n)$ sequence bits are needed, where n is the register size [7], while only $2n$ bits are needed to determine the structure of an LFSR. However, NLFSRs still have many fundamental problems, which remain open even with well-known theory. A systematic method to construct an NLFSR with optimal periods is the most significant problem to be solved. This problem remains challenging since there is no mathematical foundation supporting it.

In this paper, we propose new feedback functions with optimal periods for NLFSRs by construction. The rest of the paper is organized as follows. Section 2 presents the concept of feedback shift registers and related definitions. Section 3 reviews the existing NLFSR feedback functions which have optimal periods. Section 4 describes our construction method. Section 5 presents the new feedback functions. Finally, Sect. 6 concludes and outlines future work.

© Springer International Publishing AG, part of Springer Nature 2018
O. Gervasi et al. (Eds.): ICCSA 2018, LNCS 10960, pp. 67–79, 2018.
https://doi.org/10.1007/978-3-319-95162-1_5

2   Preliminaries

An FSR consists of a shift-register to store the state, and a function to compute the feedback bit. The register has n binary storage cells, each cell $i \in \{0, 1, \dots, n-1\}$ holds a single bit x_i in the state register. The feedback function $f : \{0,1\}^n \rightarrow \{0,1\}$ computes a feedback bit used as an input to the register to update the state using a shift operation. Figure 1 illustrates an n-bit FSR general structure.

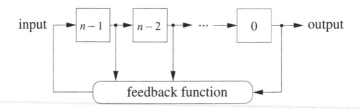

Fig. 1. An n-bit FSR general structure

The state of an FSR is presented by a vector of bits $X = (x_0, x_1, \dots, x_{n-1})$. An FSR generates a pseudorandom sequence of bits obtained by extracting the bits from the shift-register one-by-one. The initial state X_0 is a seed used to generate the output sequence of bits. From the current state, the feedback function computes x_n, which is the input to the FSR and it updates the input cell $(n-1)$, while the value x_0 of the cell 0 determines the output of the FSR.

Due to the limitation of register size, n, there will be a repeated state eventually (when all the 2^n states are exhausted). The *period* of the FSR is defined as the length of the longest unrepeated output sequence. Let us now proceed formally.

Definition 1: Let $\mathbb{F}_2$ be the binary finite field and $\mathbb{F}_2[x]$ represent the ring of polynomials in undefined value of x with coefficients taken from $\mathbb{F}_2$. Assume that, $\mathbb{F}_2^n$ is an n-dimensional vector space over $\mathbb{F}_2$ which consists of n-tuples of $\mathbb{F}_2$ elements. Each function from $\mathbb{F}_2^n$ to $\mathbb{F}_2$ is represented by a Boolean function of n variables. The elements sequence $s = (s_0, s_1, \dots)$ of $\mathbb{F}_2$ is known as a binary sequence. The sequence $s = (s_i)_{i=0}^{\infty}$ is *periodic* when there is a positive integer w such that $s_{i+w} = s_i, \forall i \geq 0$. The least such positive integer is called a *period*.

In a binary n-stage FSR, $\mathbb{F}_2^n$ is mapped into $\mathbb{F}_2^n$ as shown below, where F is the mapping function:

$$F(x_0, x_1, \dots, x_{n-1}) = ((x_1, \dots, x_{n-1}, f(x_0, x_1, \dots, x_{n-1}))$$

The feedback function is the Boolean function f over n-variables. If F is a linear transformation from $\mathbb{F}_2^n$ to itself, it is called a *linear feedback shift register* (LFSR), otherwise it is called a *nonlinear feedback shift register* (NLFSR). Moreover, if the function F is mapped as a bijection, it is called *non-singular* [8].

LFSRs have feedback functions of the following type:

$$f(x_0, x_1, \dots, x_{n-1}) = c_0 \cdot x_0 \oplus c_1 \cdot x_1 \oplus \dots c_{n-1} \cdot x_{n-1}$$

where $c_i \in \{0,1\}$ for $i \in \{0,1,\dots,n-1\}$). All terms in an LFSR are linear, like $(c_i \cdot x_i)$. However, NLFSRs include nonlinear terms. For example, an NLFSR of degree 2 includes at least one term of the form $(x_i \cdot x_j)$, where $i \neq j$.

Definition 2: The sequence of de Bruijn $(a_0, \dots, a_{2^n-1})$ of order n which consists of elements from $\mathbb{F}_2$ has a period of 2^n where each n-tuples appears exactly once.

Sainte-Marie [9] and de Bruijn [10,11] show that the number of sequences which are cyclic equivalent is given by:

$$B_n = 2^{2^{n-1}-n} \tag{1}$$

Definition 3: The modified version of de Bruijn sequence $(a_0, \dots, a_{2^n-2})$ of order n is a sequence which has a period of 2^{n-1}.

In FSR, the all-zeroes state $(X = 0)$ should not be allowed at any given point, or otherwise the FSR will remain locked up at this state. If $X = 0$, then $f(X) = 0$ for all new states. Hence, the sequence s will be all zeros. Therefore, the maximum period of an FSR of size n is at most $2^n - 1$. It is important to include the output bit x_0 in the feedback function to maximize the period. Hence, the FSR can take the following form:

$$f(x_0, x_1, \dots, x_{n-1}) = x_0 + g(x_1, x_2, \dots, x_{n-1}) \tag{2}$$

where g denotes to a Boolean function on $n - 1$ variables.

Mayhew and Golomb [11] investigated sequences satisfying Definition 3. Gammel et al.[12] called these sequences primitive. In LFSRs, these sequences can be produced using primitive polynomials and the theory of such sequences is well-understood [13].

The primitive sequence is a significant factor in the applications of cryptography. The number of primitive sequences jointly (in linear and nonlinear functions) is given by B_n in (1). We have $\phi(2^{n-1})/n$ primitive LFSRs, where ϕ refers to the Euler phi function. Since we have $2^{2^{n-1}}$ Boolean functions on $n-1$ variables, the probability of selecting a primitive NLFSR function of the form in (2) is given by:

$$\frac{(2^{2^{n-1}-n})}{2^{2^{n-1}}} = \frac{1}{2^n} \tag{3}$$

Thus, there are more NLFSRs than LFSRs [8].

Berlekamp-Massey algorithm [14] can be used to generate a given binary sequence of a minimal LFSR. Golomb's postulates [5] have characterized the properties of sequences created by LFSRs statistically.

In LFSR system, there is a unique transformation between the configurations of Galois and Fibonacci. Therefore, we can reverse the order of LFSR's feedback taps and adjust the initial state to get the configuration of Galois from Fibonacci (or vice versa). In contrast, the NLFSR system does not have a unique transformation between Fibonacci and Galois configurations [15–17].

3   Literature Review

Many researchers focused on non-linear feedback shift register functions with
optimal periods. However, much of their work is either restricted to particular
cases [18,19], or limited to a subset of functions for particular values of n (like
$n = 1, 3, 4, 11$–$13, 15$–$17, 19$–$21, 23, 31$–33) [20]. Generally, the NLFSR problem
is very hard due to the lack of the mathematical foundation on how to construct
the feedback functions that give optimal periods.

An NLFSR can be implemented using either Fibonacci or Galois configuration. The Fibonacci configuration applies the feedback only to the input cell ($n-
1$) of the shift register as shown in Fig. 1, while the Galois configuration is able
to potentially apply the feedback to any cell. Figure 2 shows a 4-bit Fibonacci
NLFSR with its feedback function $f(x_0, x_1, x_2, x_3) = x_0 \oplus x_1 \oplus x_2 \oplus x_1 \cdot x_2$.

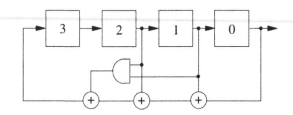

Fig. 2. A 4-bit Fibonacci NLFSR example. [21]

Dubrova [21] presented Fibonacci NLFSR feedback functions of degree 2,
with optimal periods of $2^n - 1$, for $4 \le n \le 25$, in the following three types:

- Type 1: $f(x_0, x_1, \dots, x_{n-1}) = x_0 \oplus x_a \oplus x_b \oplus x_c \cdot x_d$
- Type 2: $f(x_0, x_1, \dots, x_{n-1}) = x_0 \oplus x_a \oplus x_b \cdot x_c \oplus x_d \cdot x_e$
- Type 3: $f(x_0, x_1, \dots, x_{n-1}) = x_0 \oplus x_a \oplus x_b \oplus x_c \oplus x_d \oplus x_e \cdot x_h$

where $a, b, c, d, e, h \in \{1, 2, \dots, n - 1\}$, $x_i \in \{0, 1\}$, and the addition (XOR) and
multiplication (AND) operations are in modulo 2.

Mandal and Gong [22] have defined the relation between an NLFSR and a
regular directed graph on a field extension. They assumed two states k^{th} and $(k+
1)^{st}$ such that $S_k = (a_k, a_{k+1}, \dots, a_{k+n-1})$ and $S_{k+1} = (a_{k+1}, a_{k+2}, \dots, a_{k+n})$,
where $S_{k+1} = f(S_k)$, for $k \ge 0$ and f refers to the feedback function. They used
$G = (V, E)$ to be the directed graph defined as follows:

- Each state S_k is denoted as a vertex $v_k \in V$.
- There is a directed edge $e_k \in E$ between the state S_k to the state S_{k+1}^i.
- $S_{k+1}^i = (a_{k+1}, a_{k+2}, \dots, a_{n+k-1}, a_{n+k}^i)$, where $a_{n+k}^i \ne a_{n+k}^j$, $i \ne j$, for $i =
1, 2, 3, \dots, 2^q$.

The directed graph (G) here is called de Bruijn graph [10, 23], which consists of 2^q regular graphs along with $|V| = 2^{qn}$ and $|E| = 2^{q(n+1)}$. They relied on a uniform probability distribution Ω to define the random feedback functions, as:

$$F = (f, \Omega)$$

where the uniform probability is computed by $p_j = \dfrac{1}{2^q}$, for $j = 1, 2, \ldots, 2^q$. The input state is S_k and the output of F is $S_{k+1}^i, (F(S_k) = S_{k+1}^i)$ for some values of i which is selected depending on f and Ω where S_{k+1}^i is not generated by F. Let S_0 be an initial state, then the random NLFSR sequence, that F can generate, is given by $a = \{a_0, a_1, \ldots, a_k, a_{k+1}, \ldots\}$ and the sequence period is P, for $S_0 = F^P(S_0)$, where $F^P(S) = F^{P-1}(F(S))$.

Mandal and Gong used a random walk definition on the directed graph G. They used it among the vertices v_k and v_{k+1} imposing the distribution of uniform probability defined as follows:

- Assume S_k and S_{k+1} are the states which are corresponding to the vertices v_k and v_{k+1}.
- Next, at v_k, the random walk selects randomly v_{k+1} according to F beneath uniform distribution $Pr(S_{k+1} = F(S_k)) = \dfrac{1}{2^q}$.

Motwan and Raghavan [24] and Banderier and Dobrow [25] considered a basic random walk $R(P)$ on the directed graph G of length P which works as follows:

- Start from any vertex v_0.
- The next vertex v_1 will be selected from v_0 with probability $Pr(S_1 = F(S_0)) = \dfrac{1}{2^q}$, if v_1 has not been visited yet.
- Repeat the second step until it finds v_0.
- If v_0 has been found, stop.

Therefore, the sequence $\{a_i\}$ generated by F and the random walk are equivalent. Obtaining the value of P in $R(P)$ means obtaining the NLFSR sequence period [25].

4   Constructing NLFSR Feedback Functions

In this work, we propose and use an efficient sequential NLFSR function construction method, which sequentially enumerates all feedback functions of a desired type. We then compute the period for each feedback function and verify its optimality. The normal straightforward method to check all values located in a register is very expensive in terms of both time and computational power since the number of functions grows exponentially in terms of n.

4.1   Proposed Construction Method

The proposed construction method consists of two parts:

1. *Sequential Function Generator (SFG)*: which is an enumeration of the feedback functions. Thus, given a specific type of a function f and its size n, the SFG sequentially increments the indices of the variables $(x_a, x_b, x_c, \dots)$ in f such that all nonequivalent functions are enumerated. Since x_0 is a fixed input in all the three types of feedback functions, all other indices are chosen relatively to x_0 such that the constructed functions are nonequivalent. For the linear terms of f, the first index a is initially assigned to 1, while the next index b (in types 1 and 3) is assigned to $a + 1$ and sequentially incremented. When b reaches to the end, the previous index a is incremented and b is reset to $a + 1$ again, and so on. The enumeration of the nonlinear terms of f is done similarly.
2. *Period-Testing Algorithm*: which tests whether the generated function f has an optimal period of $2^n - 1$ or not. This algorithm selects a predefined seed (X_0) and starts searching from this point. We prove in Sect. 4.2 that the seed must appear again in the register since it generates a cycle of periodic states as shown in Fig. 3a. The length of the generated cycle is the period. We argue that the seed cannot be outside the state cycle (Fig. 3b). For a given value of n, if the seed X_0 appears after $2^n - 1$ shift operations, then the maximum period of the given function f is achieved, and f is reported as a feedback function with an optimal period. Otherwise, the function f does not have an optimal period.

4.2   Proof of Correctness

For a seed generating a periodic bit sequence of length p, the seed must also generates p periodic states in the register where each bit in the sequence is the right-most bit in the corresponding state. We examine two scenarios: (A) the seed generates $p - 1$ states then it comes back to itself to make a cycle of length p that includes the seed, and (B) the seed generates a number of states outside the cycle, then it generates p states in a cycle that excludes the seed. Figure 3 illustrates these two scenarios.

In order to properly check for NLFSR periods, our Period-Testing algorithm is based on the following observation: Given a feedback function f of some NLFSR, and its size n, it is sufficient to monitor the state of the register to find the period. This observation follows from the following easy-to-prove theorem, which rules out Scenario B.

Theorem 1. *An NLFSR repeats the same bit sequence if and only if the seed appears again in the register.*

Proof. First, if the seed appears again in the register, then proving that the NLFSR will repeat the sequence $s = (s_0, s_1, \dots)$ is straightforward. Second, to prove the converse, let $y = (y_0, y_1, \dots, y_{n-1})$ and $z = (z_0, z_1, \dots, z_{n-1})$ be two states such that the NLFSR repeats the same sequence $s = (s_0, s_1, \dots)$ if y or z appears in the register (Fig. 3b). Since the first output bit s_0 is the one in the cell 0 of the register, it should be the first bit in y and z, which implies $s_0 = y_0 = z_0$. Similarly, the second output bit $s_1 = y_1 = z_1$ after a shift operation, and hence, the ith output bit $s_{i-1} = y_{i-1} = z_{i-1}$, for $i = 1, 2, \dots, n$. Therefore, the two states y and z generate the same output sequence of bits if and only if $y = z$.   □

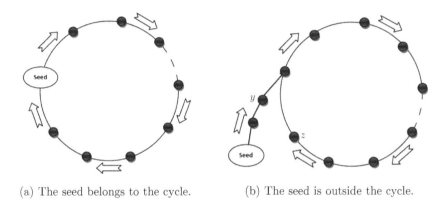

(a) The seed belongs to the cycle.   (b) The seed is outside the cycle.

Fig. 3. Two scenarios for a seed generating periodic states

By construction, the feedback functions generated by the proposed SFG are pairwise nonequivalent. Therefore, they are expected to output nonequivalent pseudorandom bit sequences.

5   New NLFSR Functions with Optimal Periods

In this work, we verify all feedback functions listed by Dubrova [21] for different values of $n \leq 25$ using our Period-Testing algorithm introduced in Sect. 4. We found that all functions give optimal periods. However, the list in [21] is incomplete, and many feedback functions are missing. We extend Dubrova's work by constructing all missing feedback functions with optimal periods for all $n = 4, 5, \dots, 19$. These function are pairwise nonequivalent and different from the existing ones.

Table 1 summarizes the improvement achieved by our construction method in each type of the feedback functions considered by Dubrova [21]. The complete lists of all proposed NLFSR feedback functions with optimal periods are given in Sects. 5.1, 5.2 and 5.3 for the functions of types 1, 2 and 3 respectively. If a constructed function with optimal period is equivalent to an existing function in [21], it will not be listed here.

Table 1. Number of NLFSR feedback functions for $4 \leq n \leq 19$

Type	Proposed	Existing	Total
1	59	61	120
2	209	209	418
3	157	155	312

5.1 Proposed Functions of Type 1

Our construction method found 59 new functions with optimal periods for $n = 4 \dots 16$. However, no new functions were found for $n = 17$, 18 or 19. The new feedback functions of type 1 that have optimal periods are listed below. Each entry below is of the form n $(0, a, b, c, d)$ where n is the size of the feedback function, and a, b, c and d are the indices of the variables in type 1 functions defined in Sect. 3.

4 $(0, 2, 3, 1, 2)$	7 $(0, 3, 6, 4, 6)$	9 $(0, 5, 7, 4, 5)$
4 $(0, 2, 3, 1, 3)$	7 $(0, 5, 6, 1, 5)$	10 $(0, 2, 9, 3, 4)$
4 $(0, 2, 3, 2, 3)$	8 $(0, 2, 7, 1, 7)$	10 $(0, 5, 6, 1, 6)$
5 $(0, 2, 4, 1, 4)$	8 $(0, 2, 7, 2, 3)$	10 $(0, 5, 6, 2, 6)$
5 $(0, 2, 4, 2, 3)$	8 $(0, 2, 7, 3, 4)$	10 $(0, 5, 6, 4, 8)$
5 $(0, 2, 4, 2, 4)$	8 $(0, 2, 7, 4, 6)$	10 $(0, 5, 8, 5, 9)$
5 $(0, 3, 4, 1, 3)$	8 $(0, 2, 7, 6, 7)$	10 $(0, 6, 9, 3, 7)$
6 $(0, 2, 5, 2, 5)$	8 $(0, 3, 6, 1, 5)$	10 $(0, 8, 9, 1, 2)$
6 $(0, 3, 4, 1, 5)$	8 $(0, 3, 6, 3, 4)$	11 $(0, 2, 10, 7, 10)$
6 $(0, 3, 4, 2, 4)$	8 $(0, 3, 6, 4, 6)$	11 $(0, 3, 9, 2, 5)$
6 $(0, 3, 4, 3, 4)$	8 $(0, 3, 7, 3, 7)$	11 $(0, 6, 9, 2, 10)$
6 $(0, 3, 4, 3, 5)$	8 $(0, 4, 5, 1, 2)$	12 $(0, 4, 9, 3, 9)$
6 $(0, 3, 5, 1, 5)$	8 $(0, 4, 5, 1, 4)$	12 $(0, 5, 8, 5, 8)$
6 $(0, 4, 5, 2, 4)$	8 $(0, 4, 5, 1, 6)$	12 $(0, 5, 8, 5, 11)$
6 $(0, 4, 5, 4, 5)$	8 $(0, 4, 5, 2, 4)$	13 $(0, 2, 12, 4, 8)$
7 $(0, 2, 6, 1, 3)$	8 $(0, 4, 5, 4, 5)$	13 $(0, 5, 9, 3, 4)$
7 $(0, 2, 6, 2, 4)$	8 $(0, 4, 5, 4, 6)$	14 $(0, 12, 13, 2, 7)$
7 $(0, 2, 6, 2, 6)$	9 $(0, 3, 8, 1, 5)$	15 $(0, 6, 10, 4, 13)$
7 $(0, 3, 5, 2, 5)$	9 $(0, 3, 8, 3, 5)$	16 $(0, 3, 14, 13, 14)$
7 $(0, 3, 5, 5, 6)$	9 $(0, 5, 6, 2, 6)$	

5.2 Proposed Functions of Type 2

For type 2 functions, we propose 209 new feedback functions with optimal periods for $n = 4 \dots 19$. The proposed feedback functions of type 2 are listed below. The entries are of the form n $(0, a, b, c, d, e)$ where n is the size of the function, and a, b, c, d and e are the indices in type 2 functions.

4 $(0, 2, 1, 3, 2, 3)$	7 $(0, 6, 2, 4, 2, 5)$	10 $(0, 6, 1, 3, 2, 3)$
4 $(0, 3, 1, 2, 2, 3)$	7 $(0, 6, 2, 4, 4, 5)$	10 $(0, 6, 1, 3, 5, 9)$
5 $(0, 3, 1, 2, 3, 4)$	7 $(0, 6, 2, 6, 3, 4)$	10 $(0, 6, 1, 3, 7, 9)$
5 $(0, 3, 1, 3, 1, 4)$	8 $(0, 5, 1, 2, 4, 6)$	10 $(0, 6, 1, 9, 5, 9)$
5 $(0, 3, 1, 3, 2, 4)$	8 $(0, 5, 1, 4, 2, 7)$	10 $(0, 6, 2, 3, 7, 9)$
5 $(0, 3, 1, 4, 2, 3)$	8 $(0, 5, 1, 5, 2, 6)$	10 $(0, 6, 3, 9, 7, 9)$
5 $(0, 4, 1, 2, 3, 4)$	8 $(0, 5, 2, 3, 5, 6)$	10 $(0, 7, 1, 2, 3, 4)$
5 $(0, 4, 1, 3, 2, 4)$	8 $(0, 5, 2, 4, 2, 7)$	10 $(0, 7, 1, 2, 3, 8)$
5 $(0, 4, 1, 4, 2, 3)$	8 $(0, 5, 2, 5, 2, 7)$	10 $(0, 7, 1, 3, 2, 8)$
5 $(0, 4, 2, 3, 2, 4)$	8 $(0, 5, 4, 6, 4, 7)$	10 $(0, 7, 1, 3, 7, 9)$
5 $(0, 4, 2, 3, 3, 4)$	8 $(0, 5, 4, 6, 6, 7)$	10 $(0, 7, 1, 4, 4, 9)$
6 $(0, 3, 2, 3, 2, 5)$	8 $(0, 6, 1, 2, 1, 5)$	10 $(0, 7, 2, 7, 4, 9)$
6 $(0, 3, 2, 4, 2, 5)$	8 $(0, 6, 1, 2, 3, 7)$	10 $(0, 7, 2, 8, 8, 9)$
6 $(0, 3, 2, 5, 3, 4)$	8 $(0, 6, 1, 3, 5, 7)$	10 $(0, 7, 4, 8, 7, 8)$
6 $(0, 4, 1, 2, 1, 5)$	8 $(0, 6, 1, 7, 5, 6)$	10 $(0, 8, 1, 2, 1, 7)$
6 $(0, 4, 1, 3, 2, 3)$	8 $(0, 6, 2, 4, 5, 7)$	10 $(0, 8, 1, 5, 1, 9)$
6 $(0, 4, 1, 3, 3, 4)$	8 $(0, 7, 1, 2, 4, 6)$	10 $(0, 8, 1, 6, 5, 9)$
6 $(0, 4, 1, 3, 3, 5)$	8 $(0, 7, 1, 4, 4, 5)$	10 $(0, 8, 3, 6, 7, 9)$
6 $(0, 4, 1, 5, 2, 4)$	8 $(0, 7, 2, 7, 3, 6)$	10 $(0, 8, 3, 7, 5, 7)$
6 $(0, 4, 2, 3, 3, 5)$	8 $(0, 7, 4, 6, 4, 7)$	10 $(0, 8, 3, 7, 6, 9)$
6 $(0, 4, 2, 4, 3, 5)$	8 $(0, 7, 4, 6, 5, 6)$	10 $(0, 8, 3, 9, 4, 6)$
6 $(0, 5, 1, 2, 4, 5)$	9 $(0, 5, 1, 4, 6, 7)$	10 $(0, 8, 3, 9, 4, 9)$
6 $(0, 5, 1, 3, 3, 5)$	9 $(0, 5, 1, 6, 2, 7)$	10 $(0, 8, 5, 7, 5, 9)$
6 $(0, 5, 1, 4, 3, 4)$	9 $(0, 5, 1, 7, 2, 3)$	10 $(0, 9, 1, 3, 2, 8)$
7 $(0, 4, 1, 4, 3, 6)$	9 $(0, 5, 1, 7, 4, 7)$	10 $(0, 9, 2, 6, 3, 4)$
7 $(0, 4, 1, 6, 3, 4)$	9 $(0, 5, 1, 7, 6, 8)$	10 $(0, 9, 2, 7, 3, 6)$
7 $(0, 4, 1, 6, 4, 6)$	9 $(0, 5, 2, 6, 4, 6)$	10 $(0, 9, 5, 8, 6, 8)$
7 $(0, 4, 2, 3, 4, 5)$	9 $(0, 5, 3, 6, 3, 8)$	10 $(0, 9, 6, 7, 8, 9)$
7 $(0, 4, 2, 4, 2, 5)$	9 $(0, 6, 1, 5, 2, 8)$	11 $(0, 6, 2, 5, 7, 10)$
7 $(0, 4, 2, 4, 2, 6)$	9 $(0, 6, 2, 5, 6, 7)$	11 $(0, 6, 3, 5, 3, 9)$
7 $(0, 4, 4, 5, 5, 6)$	9 $(0, 6, 2, 5, 7, 8)$	11 $(0, 6, 4, 5, 4, 7)$
7 $(0, 5, 1, 2, 1, 4)$	9 $(0, 6, 2, 8, 3, 8)$	11 $(0, 7, 1, 2, 9, 10)$
7 $(0, 5, 1, 2, 1, 6)$	9 $(0, 7, 1, 8, 5, 6)$	11 $(0, 7, 1, 9, 8, 9)$
7 $(0, 5, 1, 3, 1, 5)$	9 $(0, 7, 2, 5, 3, 4)$	11 $(0, 7, 3, 7, 4, 8)$
7 $(0, 5, 1, 3, 2, 5)$	9 $(0, 7, 2, 7, 3, 5)$	11 $(0, 8, 1, 4, 4, 8)$
7 $(0, 5, 1, 3, 5, 6)$	9 $(0, 7, 2, 7, 3, 8)$	11 $(0, 8, 1, 6, 2, 10)$
7 $(0, 5, 1, 4, 1, 6)$	9 $(0, 7, 3, 5, 4, 8)$	11 $(0, 8, 2, 3, 5, 10)$
7 $(0, 5, 1, 5, 2, 6)$	9 $(0, 8, 1, 4, 2, 6)$	11 $(0, 8, 2, 5, 6, 8)$
7 $(0, 5, 1, 6, 3, 5)$	9 $(0, 8, 1, 6, 6, 7)$	11 $(0, 8, 3, 6, 5, 8)$
7 $(0, 5, 2, 4, 3, 5)$	9 $(0, 8, 1, 7, 2, 6)$	11 $(0, 8, 4, 6, 4, 9)$
7 $(0, 5, 3, 4, 3, 6)$	9 $(0, 8, 1, 8, 2, 7)$	11 $(0, 9, 1, 2, 5, 7)$
7 $(0, 6, 1, 2, 5, 6)$	9 $(0, 8, 1, 8, 3, 4)$	11 $(0, 9, 1, 3, 2, 4)$
7 $(0, 6, 1, 6, 2, 3)$	9 $(0, 8, 2, 3, 3, 8)$	11 $(0, 9, 1, 5, 6, 7)$
7 $(0, 6, 2, 3, 2, 5)$	9 $(0, 8, 4, 6, 5, 6)$	11 $(0, 10, 1, 8, 4, 9)$
7 $(0, 6, 2, 3, 3, 4)$	9 $(0, 8, 4, 7, 4, 8)$	11 $(0, 10, 2, 10, 4, 9)$

11 $(0, 10, 3, 4, 4, 8)$	13 $(0, 8, 4, 11, 8, 9)$	15 $(0, 8, 2, 12, 3, 12)$
11 $(0, 10, 3, 8, 4, 8)$	13 $(0, 9, 1, 3, 10, 12)$	15 $(0, 9, 2, 3, 4, 7)$
11 $(0, 10, 3, 9, 4, 10)$	13 $(0, 9, 3, 5, 4, 11)$	15 $(0, 11, 1, 3, 7, 8)$
11 $(0, 10, 6, 7, 8, 9)$	13 $(0, 9, 7, 9, 10, 12)$	15 $(0, 11, 1, 10, 9, 10)$
11 $(0, 10, 6, 9, 7, 8)$	13 $(0, 10, 2, 4, 7, 9)$	15 $(0, 11, 4, 13, 5, 8)$
12 $(0, 9, 1, 7, 2, 6)$	13 $(0, 10, 2, 11, 4, 12)$	15 $(0, 11, 5, 6, 5, 9)$
12 $(0, 9, 2, 5, 4, 11)$	13 $(0, 10, 3, 4, 4, 5)$	15 $(0, 13, 1, 3, 7, 9)$
12 $(0, 10, 1, 4, 1, 7)$	13 $(0, 11, 1, 3, 3, 6)$	16 $(0, 9, 2, 8, 4, 5)$
12 $(0, 10, 1, 5, 3, 5)$	13 $(0, 11, 1, 4, 7, 12)$	16 $(0, 9, 3, 6, 10, 14)$
12 $(0, 10, 1, 9, 3, 9)$	13 $(0, 12, 2, 7, 10, 11)$	16 $(0, 11, 4, 10, 8, 12)$
12 $(0, 10, 1, 11, 2, 11)$	13 $(0, 12, 2, 8, 8, 11)$	16 $(0, 11, 4, 12, 8, 9)$
12 $(0, 10, 3, 5, 9, 10)$	13 $(0, 12, 4, 11, 8, 9)$	16 $(0, 13, 2, 9, 3, 14)$
12 $(0, 10, 3, 7, 3, 9)$	13 $(0, 12, 5, 7, 7, 11)$	16 $(0, 13, 9, 11, 11, 15)$
12 $(0, 10, 4, 10, 5, 11)$	13 $(0, 12, 6, 10, 6, 12)$	17 $(0, 9, 1, 6, 5, 7)$
12 $(0, 10, 6, 9, 9, 11)$	14 $(0, 8, 1, 2, 5, 9)$	17 $(0, 10, 3, 8, 9, 16)$
12 $(0, 11, 1, 4, 2, 3)$	14 $(0, 8, 1, 13, 5, 9)$	17 $(0, 11, 5, 10, 8, 15)$
12 $(0, 11, 2, 4, 4, 5)$	14 $(0, 9, 1, 8, 10, 12)$	17 $(0, 12, 4, 11, 10, 13)$
12 $(0, 11, 2, 6, 4, 10)$	14 $(0, 11, 1, 8, 2, 12)$	17 $(0, 14, 3, 4, 8, 11)$
12 $(0, 11, 2, 9, 7, 10)$	14 $(0, 11, 2, 7, 4, 9)$	17 $(0, 16, 2, 8, 7, 10)$
12 $(0, 11, 8, 9, 9, 10)$	14 $(0, 11, 2, 8, 10, 12)$	18 $(0, 15, 7, 16, 11, 12)$
13 $(0, 7, 1, 11, 8, 12)$	14 $(0, 11, 2, 10, 8, 13)$	18 $(0, 17, 6, 7, 6, 9)$
13 $(0, 8, 1, 10, 2, 4)$	14 $(0, 12, 3, 11, 9, 13)$	19 $(0, 13, 1, 2, 11, 15)$
13 $(0, 8, 1, 12, 2, 6)$	14 $(0, 13, 1, 12, 2, 10)$	19 $(0, 15, 3, 14, 5, 12)$
13 $(0, 8, 4, 9, 7, 10)$	14 $(0, 13, 2, 5, 2, 9)$	19 $(0, 17, 9, 11, 11, 13)$
13 $(0, 8, 4, 9, 8, 12)$	15 $(0, 8, 2, 5, 4, 13)$	

5.3 Proposed Functions of Type 3

We propose 157 new functions of type 3 with optimal periods for $n = 6 \ldots 19$. There are no new functions for $n = 4$ or 5. The new feedback functions are listed below. Each entry is of the form $n \ (0, a, b, c, d, e, h)$ where n is the size of the function, and a, b, c, d, e and h are the indices in type 3 functions.

6 $(0, 1, 2, 3, 4, 1, 5)$	7 $(0, 2, 3, 5, 6, 2, 6)$	8 $(0, 2, 4, 5, 6, 3, 4)$
6 $(0, 1, 2, 3, 4, 3, 5)$	7 $(0, 2, 3, 5, 6, 5, 6)$	8 $(0, 2, 5, 6, 7, 1, 3)$
6 $(0, 1, 2, 3, 5, 1, 4)$	7 $(0, 3, 4, 5, 6, 1, 5)$	8 $(0, 2, 5, 6, 7, 3, 5)$
6 $(0, 1, 2, 3, 5, 2, 3)$	7 $(0, 3, 4, 5, 6, 1, 6)$	8 $(0, 3, 4, 5, 6, 2, 6)$
6 $(0, 1, 3, 4, 5, 2, 5)$	7 $(0, 3, 4, 5, 6, 4, 5)$	8 $(0, 3, 4, 6, 7, 4, 6)$
6 $(0, 1, 3, 4, 5, 3, 4)$	8 $(0, 1, 3, 6, 7, 4, 6)$	8 $(0, 3, 5, 6, 7, 2, 6)$
6 $(0, 2, 3, 4, 5, 1, 3)$	8 $(0, 1, 4, 5, 7, 1, 5)$	9 $(0, 1, 4, 6, 8, 4, 6)$
6 $(0, 2, 3, 4, 5, 1, 5)$	8 $(0, 1, 4, 5, 7, 2, 7)$	9 $(0, 1, 4, 7, 8, 3, 7)$
7 $(0, 1, 4, 5, 6, 1, 5)$	8 $(0, 1, 4, 5, 7, 4, 7)$	9 $(0, 2, 3, 5, 8, 2, 8)$
7 $(0, 1, 4, 5, 6, 2, 6)$	8 $(0, 1, 4, 6, 7, 3, 7)$	9 $(0, 2, 3, 7, 8, 3, 6)$
7 $(0, 1, 4, 5, 6, 4, 6)$	8 $(0, 2, 3, 4, 5, 2, 6)$	9 $(0, 2, 4, 6, 8, 3, 4)$
7 $(0, 2, 3, 5, 6, 1, 5)$	8 $(0, 2, 3, 4, 6, 4, 5)$	9 $(0, 2, 5, 6, 7, 1, 7)$

9 $(0, 2, 5, 7, 8, 3, 8)$

9 $(0, 2, 6, 7, 8, 3, 5)$

9 $(0, 3, 4, 7, 8, 3, 7)$

9 $(0, 3, 4, 7, 8, 3, 8)$

9 $(0, 4, 5, 6, 8, 2, 6)$

9 $(0, 5, 6, 7, 8, 2, 6)$

10 $(0, 1, 5, 6, 9, 1, 5)$

10 $(0, 1, 5, 6, 9, 1, 6)$

10 $(0, 1, 5, 6, 9, 1, 9)$

10 $(0, 2, 5, 6, 8, 6, 8)$

10 $(0, 2, 5, 8, 9, 1, 5)$

10 $(0, 2, 6, 8, 9, 5, 9)$

10 $(0, 2, 6, 8, 9, 6, 8)$

10 $(0, 3, 4, 5, 6, 2, 6)$

10 $(0, 3, 4, 5, 7, 2, 6)$

10 $(0, 3, 4, 5, 7, 4, 6)$

10 $(0, 3, 4, 5, 9, 2, 8)$

10 $(0, 3, 4, 6, 8, 4, 9)$

10 $(0, 3, 4, 7, 9, 4, 9)$

10 $(0, 3, 5, 6, 7, 4, 6)$

10 $(0, 3, 5, 6, 7, 4, 8)$

10 $(0, 3, 6, 7, 9, 4, 7)$

10 $(0, 4, 5, 6, 7, 4, 8)$

10 $(0, 4, 6, 7, 8, 4, 7)$

11 $(0, 1, 4, 7, 10, 2, 10)$

11 $(0, 1, 5, 8, 10, 2, 4)$

11 $(0, 1, 7, 8, 10, 1, 5)$

11 $(0, 1, 7, 9, 10, 2, 8)$

11 $(0, 1, 7, 9, 10, 2, 10)$

11 $(0, 2, 3, 5, 10, 5, 9)$

11 $(0, 2, 4, 6, 10, 3, 9)$

11 $(0, 2, 4, 8, 10, 3, 10)$

11 $(0, 2, 6, 7, 9, 2, 6)$

11 $(0, 3, 4, 8, 9, 1, 4)$

11 $(0, 3, 4, 8, 9, 1, 5)$

11 $(0, 3, 4, 8, 9, 1, 7)$

11 $(0, 3, 4, 9, 10, 1, 2)$

11 $(0, 3, 4, 9, 10, 2, 10)$

11 $(0, 3, 5, 6, 10, 2, 6)$

11 $(0, 3, 5, 8, 10, 3, 5)$

11 $(0, 3, 6, 7, 10, 4, 6)$

11 $(0, 4, 5, 6, 8, 3, 7)$

11 $(0, 4, 5, 7, 8, 8, 9)$

11 $(0, 4, 7, 9, 10, 2, 3)$

11 $(0, 4, 7, 9, 10, 2, 7)$

11 $(0, 4, 7, 9, 10, 8, 9)$

11 $(0, 5, 6, 7, 8, 1, 9)$

11 $(0, 6, 7, 9, 10, 5, 7)$

11 $(0, 6, 8, 9, 10, 5, 7)$

12 $(0, 1, 6, 7, 11, 4, 5)$

12 $(0, 1, 6, 10, 11, 6, 10)$

12 $(0, 2, 3, 7, 11, 5, 6)$

12 $(0, 2, 4, 8, 11, 7, 10)$

12 $(0, 2, 5, 9, 11, 7, 8)$

12 $(0, 2, 6, 7, 10, 2, 10)$

12 $(0, 2, 6, 9, 10, 2, 8)$

12 $(0, 2, 6, 9, 10, 6, 10)$

12 $(0, 2, 8, 9, 10, 4, 9)$

12 $(0, 3, 5, 7, 11, 1, 11)$

12 $(0, 3, 6, 9, 11, 2, 8)$

12 $(0, 3, 6, 9, 11, 3, 11)$

12 $(0, 3, 7, 10, 11, 1, 5)$

12 $(0, 4, 6, 7, 11, 2, 6)$

12 $(0, 4, 6, 7, 11, 6, 8)$

12 $(0, 4, 6, 9, 10, 6, 9)$

12 $(0, 5, 6, 9, 11, 2, 8)$

12 $(0, 7, 9, 10, 11, 3, 7)$

13 $(0, 2, 3, 6, 12, 7, 11)$

13 $(0, 2, 3, 11, 12, 1, 7)$

13 $(0, 2, 5, 10, 11, 3, 12)$

13 $(0, 2, 6, 8, 12, 3, 5)$

13 $(0, 2, 7, 8, 11, 2, 5)$

13 $(0, 3, 6, 7, 11, 1, 5)$

13 $(0, 3, 6, 8, 10, 3, 11)$

13 $(0, 3, 7, 8, 10, 2, 5)$

13 $(0, 3, 8, 9, 12, 5, 9)$

13 $(0, 4, 6, 8, 12, 4, 5)$

13 $(0, 6, 7, 8, 12, 4, 8)$

13 $(0, 7, 9, 10, 12, 3, 7)$

13 $(0, 8, 9, 11, 12, 6, 12)$

14 $(0, 1, 9, 10, 13, 8, 13)$

14 $(0, 2, 4, 8, 13, 5, 7)$

14 $(0, 2, 4, 8, 13, 7, 11)$

14 $(0, 2, 4, 11, 12, 4, 5)$

14 $(0, 2, 5, 7, 13, 1, 11)$

14 $(0, 2, 8, 9, 12, 4, 8)$

14 $(0, 3, 5, 7, 12, 2, 3)$

14 $(0, 3, 7, 10, 13, 3, 13)$

14 $(0, 4, 7, 8, 10, 1, 9)$

14 $(0, 6, 8, 9, 10, 10, 13)$

14 $(0, 6, 9, 10, 13, 6, 12)$

14 $(0, 7, 9, 11, 12, 9, 13)$

14 $(0, 7, 10, 12, 13, 11, 13)$

14 $(0, 9, 11, 12, 13, 11, 13)$

15 $(0, 2, 6, 12, 13, 8, 12)$

15 $(0, 3, 10, 11, 14, 11, 12)$

15 $(0, 5, 8, 10, 11, 1, 14)$

15 $(0, 5, 10, 11, 12, 8, 12)$

15 $(0, 7, 8, 10, 12, 2, 12)$

16 $(0, 2, 3, 11, 15, 1, 2)$

16 $(0, 2, 6, 11, 14, 2, 10)$

16 $(0, 3, 4, 5, 15, 1, 11)$

16 $(0, 3, 8, 9, 14, 1, 13)$

16 $(0, 4, 5, 10, 14, 1, 2)$

16 $(0, 6, 7, 8, 12, 4, 8)$

16 $(0, 6, 8, 9, 14, 10, 13)$

16 $(0, 7, 13, 14, 15, 2, 10)$

17 $(0, 3, 5, 14, 16, 7, 15)$

17 $(0, 5, 8, 13, 15, 1, 11)$

17 $(0, 5, 8, 14, 16, 4, 10)$

17 $(0, 6, 8, 12, 16, 4, 16)$

17 $(0, 7, 10, 11, 14, 2, 8)$

18 $(0, 3, 6, 12, 16, 3, 7)$

18 $(0, 5, 7, 9, 15, 2, 14)$

18 $(0, 6, 7, 13, 17, 9, 17)$

18 $(0, 7, 9, 10, 17, 3, 16)$

18 $(0, 11, 13, 14, 17, 8, 16)$

19 $(0, 2, 11, 15, 18, 6, 18)$

19 $(0, 3, 10, 12, 16, 2, 16)$

19 $(0, 5, 7, 13, 14, 1, 17)$

19 $(0, 11, 14, 15, 18, 4, 14)$

6   Conclusion

In this work, we verified previous study done by Dubrova which provides a list of NLFSR feedback functions in the range $(4 \leq n < 25)$. These functions are of three predefined types, and they all have the optimal period of $2^n - 1$ where n is the size of the register. Since Dubrova's work did not list all feedback functions for many values of n in the specified range, we closed the gap by proposing the missing feedback functions with optimal periods for all $n = 4, 5, \cdots, 19$. The construction method of these functions is briefly explained. As for future work, we suggest extending this work in two ways: (1) construct feedback functions with larger values of n, and (2) explore different types of feedback functions and search for new types with more functions with optimal periods. Since all feedback functions considered in this work are of degree 2, we may also extend the search to include degree 3 functions.

Acknowledgment. The authors would like to thank King Fahd University of Petroleum and Minerals, Dhahran, Saudi Arabia, for supporting this research. Figures and descriptions in this paper were provided by the authors and are used with permission.

References

1. Mrugalski, G., Rajski, J., Tyszer, J.: Ring generators-new devices for embedded test applications. IEEE Trans. Comput. Aided Des. Integr. Circuits Syst. **23**(9), 1306–1320 (2004)
2. Zeng, K., Yang, C.-H., Wei, D.-Y., Rao, T.: Pseudorandom bit generators in stream-cipher cryptography. Computer **24**(2), 8–17 (1991)
3. McCluskey, J.: High speed calculation of cyclic redundancy codes. In: Proceedings of the 1999 ACM/SIGDA Seventh International symposium on Field Programmable Gate Arrays, p. 250. ACM (1999)
4. Ahmad, A.: Achievement of higher testability goals through the modification of shift registers in LFSR-based testing. Int. J. Electron. **82**(3), 249–260 (1997)
5. Golomb, S.: Shift Register Sequences. Aegean, Laguna Hills (1982)
6. Jansen, C.J.A.: Investigations on nonlinear streamcipher systems: construction and evaluation methods (1989)
7. Dubrova, E.: Generation of full cycles by a composition of NLFSRS. Des. Codes Crypt. **73**(2), 469–486 (2014)
8. Rachwalik, T., Szmidt, J., Wicik, R., Zabłocki, J.: Generation of nonlinear feedback shift registers with special-purpose hardware. In: 2012 Military Communications and Information Systems Conference (MCC), pp. 1–4. IEEE (2012)
9. Sainte-Marie, C.F.: Solution to question nr. 48. LâÂŹintermédiaire des Mathématiciens, vol. 1, pp. 107–110 (1894)
10. de Bruijn, F.: A combinatorial problem (1946)
11. Mayhew, G.L., Golomb, S.W.: Linear spans of modified de bruijn sequences. IEEE Trans. Inf. Theor. **36**(5), 1166–1167 (1990)
12. Gammel, B.M., Göttfert, R., Kniffler, O.: The achterbahn stream cipher. Submiss. eSTREAM (2005)

13. Lidl, R., Niederreiter, H.: Introduction to Finite Fields and their Applications. Cambridge University Press, Cambridge (1994)
14. Massey, J.: Shift-register synthesis and BCH decoding. IEEE Trans. Inf. Theor. **15**(1), 122–127 (1969)
15. Dubrova, E.: A transformation from the Fibonacci to the Galois NLFSRS. IEEE Trans. Inf. Theor. **55**(11), 5263–5271 (2009)
16. Chabloz, J.M., Mansouri, S.S., Dubrova, E.: An algorithm for constructing a fastest Galois NLFSR generating a given sequence. In: Carlet, C., Pott, A. (eds.) SETA 2010. LNCS, vol. 6338, pp. 41–54. Springer, Heidelberg (2010). https://doi.org/10. 1007/978-3-642-15874-2_3
17. Dubrova, E.: Finding matching initial states for equivalent NLFSRS in the fibonacci and the galois configurations. IEEE Trans. Inf. Theor. **56**(6), 2961–2966 (2010)
18. Liu, M., Mansouri, S.S. Dubrova, E.: A faster shift register alternative to filter generators. In: Digital System Design (DSD) Euromicro Conference on 2013, pp. 713–718. IEEE (2013)
19. Castro Lechtaler, A., Cipriano, M., García, E., Liporace, J., Maiorano, A., Malvacio, E.: Model design for a reduced variant of a trivium type stream cipher. J. Comput. Sci. Technol. **14**, 55–58 (2014)
20. Fredricksen, H.: A survey of full length nonlinear shift register cycle algorithms. SIAM Rev. **24**(2), 195–221 (1982)
21. Dubrova, E.: A list of maximum-period NLFSRS (2012)
22. Mandal, K., Gong, G.: Probabilistic generation of good span n sequences from nonlinear feedback shift registers. University of Waterloo (2012)
23. Good, I.J.: Normal recurring decimals. J. London Math. Soc. **1**(3), 167–169 (1946)
24. Motwani, R., Raghavan, P.: Randomized algorithms. Cambridge international series on parallel computation (1995)
25. Banderier, C., Dobrow, R.P.: A generalized cover time for random walks on graphs. In: Krob, D., Mikhalev, A.A., Mikhalev, A.V. (eds.) Formal Power Series and Algebraic Combinatorics, pp. 113–124. Springer, Heidelberg (2000). https://doi. org/10.1007/978-3-662-04166-6_10

Towards the Modular Specification and Validation of Cyber-Physical Systems
A Case-Study on Reservoir Modeling with Hybrid Automata

Andre Metelo[1], Christiano Braga[1](✉), and Diego Brandão[2]

[1] Instituto de Computação, Universidade Federal Fluminense,
Niterói, Rio de Janeira, Brazil
{metelo,cbraga}@ic.uff.br
[2] Centro Federal de Educação Tecnológica Celso Suckow da Fonseca CEFET-RJ,
Rio de Janeiro, Rio de Janeiro, Brazil
diego.brandao@eic.cefet-rj.br

Abstract. Cyber-Physical Systems (CPS) are systems controlled by one or more computer-based components tightly integrated with a set of physical components, typically described as sensors and actuators, that can either be directly attached to the computer components, or at a remote location, and accessible through a network connection. The modeling and verification of such systems is a hard task and error prone that require rigorous techniques. Hybrid automata is a formalism that extends finite-state automata with continuous behavior, described by ordinary differential equations. This paper uses a rewriting logic-based technique to model and validate CPS, thus exploring the use of a *formal* technique to develop such systems that combines expressive specification with efficient state-based analysis. Moreover, we aim at the *modular* specification of such systems such that each CPS component is *independently* specified and the final system emerges as the *synchronous product* of its constituent components. We model CPSs using Linear Hybrid Automaton and implement them in Real-Time Maude, a rewriting logic tool for real-time systems. With this method, we develop a specification for the n-reservoir problem, a CPS that controls a hose to fill a number of reservoirs according to the physical properties of the hose and the reservoirs.

1 Introduction

Cyber-Physical Systems (CPS) [2] are ever present in our daily life. They can be intuitively described as systems that are controlled by one or more computer based components tightly integrated with a set physical components, typically described as sensors and actuators that can either be directly attached to the computer components, or at a remote location and accessible through a network connection.

Most CPS have to cope with design requirements that are imposed onto them by their multiple applications in the real world. Typically a CPS has to be

O. Gervasi et al. (Eds.): ICCSA 2018, LNCS 10960, pp. 80–95, 2018.
https://doi.org/10.1007/978-3-319-95162-1_6

specified and tested against environments that require the system to: (i) operate in real-time, (ii) perform reactive computations, (iii) leverage concurrent and distributed processing, (iv) deal with synchronization issues.

In [2], one of the major books on CPS in a *vast* (e.g. [3, 4, 10, 15, 17, 24, 26, 27]) literature on the subject, Alur describes how Linear Hybrid Automata (LHA) can be used for modeling CPS. In this context, the 2-reservoirs problem [17], a text-book problem on dynamic systems where a control system needs to decide to which of two tanks a hose needs to be moved given the reservoirs and hose's physical characteristics, is a CPS and therefore can be modeled as a LHA. In this paper we *generalize* this problem to an *arbitrary* number of reservoirs, each with their *individual* physical characteristics, and by adding *latency* to hose dislocation. We model and analyze both the standard problem description and the generalized version using Rewriting Logic [19], an expressive formalism for the specification and verification of concurrent and distributed systems [22]. Moreover, we specify the 2-reservoir system *modularly* as the *synchronous product* [5] of its constituent components.

This paper contribution is manifold: (i) a precise definition of the synchronous product of real-time rewrite systems, extending [18], (ii) a model of the n-reservoir problem as an LHA, (iii) how to describe a CPS as a LHA in Rewriting Logic by representing its components, sensors, actuators and controllers, as mathematical tuples denoting objects that communicate asynchronously, (iv) a modular specification of the n-reservoir system, based on (i), and (v) its implementation and model checking in Real-Time Maude (RTM) [21], a Rewriting Logic tool designed for the formal specification and analysis of real-time and hybrid systems. This is a first-step in the development of a formal method and its tooling to *modularly* specify and verify Cyber-Physical Systems based on its Rewriting Logic semantics of the associated Linear Hybrid Automata.

The remainder of this paper is organized as follows. Section 2 describes foundational requirements related to LHA and RTM. In Sect. 3, we discuss our prototype implementation of the reservoir problem in RTM. Section 4 presents the synchronous product of rewrite systems and its extension to real-time, together with the modular specification of the 2-reservoir problem. Section 5 describes related work. Section 6 concludes this paper describing the insights and future research based on our findings.

2   Preliminaries

In oder to develop the implementation of the n-reservoirs problem and its model check through the use of Linear Hybrid Automaton and Real-Time Maude an understanding of what they are is required. This section provides a basic introduction of these topics.

2.1   Linear Hybrid Automaton (LHA)

A LHA is a Finite State Machine that is associated with a finite set of variables that are described by ordinary differential equations (ODE). To guarantee that the solutions of the differential equation are well defined, we assume that the ODE are Lipschitz continuous [17]. Moreover, these differential equations are such that any test and attribution within the model of the LHA are affine, that is, a linear equation of the form $a_1x_1 + a_2x_2 + \ldots + a_nx_n \sim 0$ where $\sim$ is a comparison operation that can be one of $<, \leq, =, \geq$ or $>$ and an attribution is in the form $x_i = a_o + a_1x_1 + a_2x_2 + \ldots + a_nx_n$ and $a_0, a_1, \ldots, a_n$ are integer or real constants.

A LHA **HP** consists of: (i) An asynchronous process **P**, where some of its state variables can be of type cont, and appear only in affine tests and affine assignments in the guards and updates of the tasks of **P**; (ii) A continuous-time invariant **CI**, which is a Boolean expression over the state variables **S**, where the variables are continuous (that is, of type cont) and appear only in affine tests; (iii) A rate constraint **RC**, which is a Boolean expression over the discrete state variables and the derivatives of the continuously updated state variables that appear only in affine tests.

Inputs, outputs, states, initial states, internal actions, input actions, and output actions of the LHA **HP** are the same as that of the asynchronous process **P**. Given a state **s** and a real-valued time $\delta > 0$, $s \xrightarrow{\delta} s + \delta r$ is a timed action of **HP**, for a rate vector **r** consisting of a constant r_x for every continuously updated variable x if:

1. The expression **RC** is satisfied for every continuously updated variable x, the derivative $\dot{x}$ is assigned the value r_x and every discrete variable x is assigned the value $s(x)$;
2. The state $s + tr$ satisfies the expression **CI** for all values $0 \leq t \leq \delta$.

As such, a LHA can be represented as an extended state machine as shown in Fig. 1, where the Initial Variables represent the starting values of all constants and discrete variables in the LHA; State(i), $i \in \{1, 2\}$, represents one of the many states in LHA together with tests and assignments that occur while the system is evolving in time while not changing state; the arrow with a test and attribution represents the boolean test that needs to be satisfied for the transition between one state and another to happen, alongside any changes that must be assigned to LHA variables.

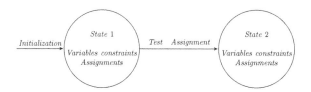

Fig. 1. Simple extended state machine diagram of a LHA

2.2   Real-Time Rewrite Systems and Real-Time Maude

A Rewriting Logic theory is essentially a triple (Σ, E, R) where Σ is a typed (or sorted) signature (many sorted, order-sorted or membership equational, that is, Rewriting Logic is *parameterized* by a choice of equational logic), E is a set of Σ-equations and R is a set of Σ/E-rules where the terms being rewritten are those in the initial Σ-algebra $\mathcal{T}_{\Sigma}$ identified by Σ-equations E.

A real-time rewrite theory is a tuple $R = (\Sigma, E \cup A, R)$ [23], where: (i) $(\Sigma, E \cup A)$ contains an equational subtheory $(\Sigma_{TIME}, E_{TIME}) \subseteq (\Sigma, E \cup A)$, satisfying the *TIME* axioms that specifies sort `Time` as the time domain (which can be discrete or dense) and $\{\_\}$ is a built-in constructor of sort `GlobalSystem`. The rules in R are decomposed into: (i) instantaneous rewrite rules, that do not act on the system as a whole, but only on some system components, and (ii) tick rules that model the elapse of time in a system, having the form $l : \{t\} \xrightarrow{u} \{t'\}$ *if condition*, where t and t' are terms of sort `System`, u is a term of sort `Time` denoting the duration of the rewrite. Given a real-time rewrite theory R, a *computation* is a non-extensible sequence $t_0 \longrightarrow t_1 \longrightarrow \ldots \longrightarrow t_n$ (that is, one for which t_n cannot be further rewritten) or an infinite sequence $t_0 \longrightarrow t_1 \longrightarrow \ldots$ of one-step R-rewrites $t_i \longrightarrow t_{i+1}$, with t_i and $t_i + 1$ ground terms, starting with a given initial term t_0 of sort `System`.

Maude [14] is a system/language that implements concurrent systems through the use of equations and rewrite rules specified in one or more modules. Maude itself has been extended through Full Maude, which is fully written in Maude itself, to add several features to the system/language. These features include, but are not limited to, object-oriented modules, module parameterization, and n-tuple declaration.

Real-Time Maude (RTM) is an extension of Full Maude that includes the requirements and tooling to model and check real-time systems. The time evolution is achieved through tick rules that determine the effects of time in the system. As such, RTM allows for a very granular control over how a system can evolve both in time and instantaneously by means of two classes of rewrite rules that specify either timed or discrete transitions. Although a timed module is parametric on the time domain, Real-Time Maude provides some predefined modules specifying useful time domains. For example, the modules `NAT-TIME-DOMAIN-WITH-INF` and `POSRAT-TIME-DOMAIN-WITH-INF` define the time domain to be, respectively, the natural numbers and the nonnegative rational numbers, and contain the subsort declarations `Nat < Time` and `Pos-Rat < Time`. In Real-Time Maude, tick rules, together with their durations, are specified using the syntax `crl [l] : {t} => {t'}` in time u if condition.

Essentially, an RTM specification representing a hybrid automaton $\mathcal{H} = (S, \rightarrow_t, \rightarrow_d)$, with S the set of states of $\mathcal{H}$, $\rightarrow_t$ the set of timed transitions, and $\rightarrow_d$ the set of discrete transitions, is given by a structure (Σ, E, R_t, R_d) where the equational specification (Σ, E) specifies the set S of states of the hybrid automaton $\mathcal{H}$, R_t is the set of Σ/E-timed rewrite rules representing $\rightarrow_t$ transitions in $\mathcal{H}$, and R_d the set of Σ/E-discrete rewrite rules representing $\rightarrow_d$ transitions in $\mathcal{H}$.

We describe RTM specification language in Sect. 3, by example, while describing the implementation of the 2-reservoir problem.

3   The Reservoir Problem in RTM

The 2-reservoir problem was presented by Lygeros *et al.* in [17]. The problem has been fully defined in that work, alongside its differential equations and its LHA.

Succinctly, the problem has as a pair of reservoirs that are flowing water out of the system at a constant rate. Water is added to the system through a hose that has a constant intake rate. The hose can be moved from one reservoir to the other instantaneously. There is a control system that is designed to make sure that the water level in each reservoir does not fall below a predefined level. This can be seen in Fig. 2.

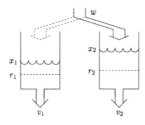

Fig. 2. 2-reservoirs diagram [17]

The LHA of the 2-reservoirs problem is described in Fig. 3, where: x_i is the water level at the reservoir i (that is time dependent), r_i is the flow of water out of the reservoir i, q_i is the state of the system with the hose filling reservoir i, and w is the hose's water flow rate.

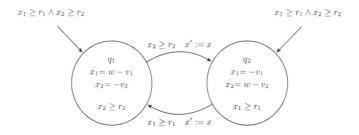

Fig. 3. 2-reservoir LHA diagram

The generalized n-reservoir problem is the extension of the 2-reservoirs problem where the system has a finite non-predetermined number of reservoirs, each with its own individual physical characteristics. In this new structure, the control system has to make the decision to which reservoir it will move the hose to when multiple reservoirs are potentially below the minimum water level threshold.

Although the differential equations of each individual reservoir stay the same, the total number of continuous variables that are tracked by the system scales with the size of the instance (n continuous variables). Additionally, the number of states in the LHA grows with the number of reservoirs as well ($2n$ states). Similarly, the problem will have a considerably larger number of state transitions. These extra states and transitions force the control system to cope with a more complex decision process to choose where to move the hose at any specific point in time ($n(n-1)$ transitions).

We are now ready to inspect how the reservoirs problems can be implemented in RTM with LHA in place and a clear understanding of the differences between the simple (with 2 reservoirs) and the generalized versions of the reservoir problem.

3.1   The 2-reservoir Problem in RTM

The states of the hybrid automaton modeling the 2-reservoir problem is defined in RTM through a triple $\langle \{right, left\}, \mathbb{Q}^+, \mathbb{Q}^+ \rangle$ where $\{right, left\}$ denotes the hose position (either on the right or left reservoir) and $\mathbb{Q}^+$ is the set of positive rational numbers denoting the height of the water column for each reservoir.

The triple and constants can be defined through the code below where keywords *op* and *ops* declare operations for the left and right position of the hose, the system configuration (that is, the triple $\langle \{right, left\}, \mathbb{Q}^+, \mathbb{Q}^+ \rangle$) and constants for the hose flow rate w, each reservoir flow rate v_i, and the water level on each reservoir r_i, with $i \in \{1, 2\}$, and NNegRat is the sort for $\mathbb{Q}^+$, respectively.

```
1  ops left right : −> Hose [ctor].
2  op _‘,_‘,_ : Hose NNegRat NNegRat −> System [ctor].
3  ops w v1 v2 r1 r2 : −> NNegRat.
```

Listing 1.1. Signature for the states of the 2-reservoir hybrid automaton

The movement of the hose can be represented by rules that change the system configuration. Rule *moveright* moves the hose from left to right, while *moveleft* goes the other way around. The rules are triggered when the water level of the proper reservoir reaches the minimum acceptable level.

```
1  vars x1 x2 : NNegRat.
2  crl [moveright] : left,x1,x2 => right,x1,x2 if x2 <= r2.
3  crl [moveleft] : right,x1,x2 => left,x1,x2 if x1 <= r1.
```

The last step is to create the rules specifying how water levels change in time, the so called *tick* rules. The water levels increase in linear time by $w - v_i$ and decreases, also in linear time, by v_i.

```
1  var R : Time.
2  crl [tick−right] :
3    {right, x1, x2} => {right, x1 − (v1 * R), x2 + ((w − v2) * R)} in time R
4  if x1 > r1 [nonexec].
5
6  crl [tick−left] :
7    {left, x1, x2} => {left, x1 + ((w − v1) * R), x2 − (v2 * R)} in time R
8  if x2 > r2 [nonexec].
```

The evolution in time does not happen when the water level of the reservoir with the hose is above the water threshold and the second reservoir is below or at its water threshold. Without this restriction, the system can evolve to undesired configurations where it keeps filing a reservoir that is above minimum threshold while letting the other reservoir dry out.

3.2   The n-Reservoir Problem in RTM

The implementation of the n-reservoir problem requires a dynamic structure to accommodate the run-time defined reservoir count. For that we leverage Maude's sets to create a *System* configuration made of a hose and each individual reservoir as shown below.

```
1  { hose(10, 0) < 0 | thr: (15, 50), hth: 30, rte: 5 > < 1 | thr: (15, 50), hth: 30, rte: 5 > }
```

In this structure we have a hose element that has an in-take rate of 10 units per time unit and it is positioned on top of reservoir 0. The hose is followed by multiple structures in the form < 0 | thr: (15, 50), hth: 30, rte: 5 $>$ that represent a single reservoir with its unique identifier, the upper and lower water thresholds, the current water level and the constant flow of water out of the reservoir.

The hose is defined by:

```
1  sort Hose.
2  op hose : NNegRat Nat −> Hose [format(m! o)].
```

A single reservoir, logically defined as $<$N | List of attributes $>$, can be coded as:

```
1  subsort ReservoirAttribute < ReservoirAttributes.
2  op <_|_> : Nat ReservoirAttributes −> Reservoir [ctor format(b! o b! o b! o)].
3  op _',_ : ReservoirAttributes ReservoirAttributes −> ReservoirAttributes [ctor assoc comm].
```

Then the reservoir attributes are defined.

```
1  *** Upper and Lower Water thresholds
2  op thr: : NNegRat NNegRat −> ReservoirAttribute [ctor format(b! o)].
3  *** Water Level
4  op hth:_ : NNegRat −> ReservoirAttribute [ctor format(b! o b!)].
5  *** Leak Rate
6  op rte:_ : NNegRat −> ReservoirAttribute [ctor format(b! o b!)].
```

The whole system is put together by concatenating a Hose and as many reservoirs as desired.

```
1  subsort Hose Reservoir < System.
2  op __ : System System −> System [ctor assoc comm].
```

Keep in mind that in Maude, computations are identified with rewritings. One of the distinguished features of Maude is to implement rewriting modulo axioms, such as associativity and commutativity. Thus the use of definition of many *assoc* and *comm* in the operators definition.

The next step is to define functions - done through operators in Maude - to fill and drain the reservoirs alongside tests to validate that the evolution in time can occur. First, a function to add water to the reservoir that the hose is currently pointing to:

```
1  *** Vars used across the functions and rules
2  vars N M : Nat.
3  vars L U Ln Un Lm Um Xn Xm Dn Dm W : NNegRat.
4  var T : Time. var S : System.
5  vars RA RAn RAm : ReservoirAttributes.
6
7  op fill : Reservoir NNegRat NNegRat -> Reservoir.
8  eq fill(< N | thr: (L, U), hth: Xn, rte: Dn >, W, T) =
9    < N | thr: (L, U), hth: (Xn + ((W - Dn) * T)), rte: Dn >.
```

Next, a function that drains water from all reservoirs:

```
1  op drain : Reservoir NNegRat -> System.
2  eq drain(< N | thr: (L, U), hth: Xn, rte: Dn >, T) =
3    < N | thr: (L, U), hth: sd(Xn,(Dn * T)), rte: Dn >.
4  eq drain(< N | thr: (L, U), hth: Xn, rte: Dn > S, T) =
5    < N | thr: (L, U), hth: sd(Xn,(Dn * T)), rte: Dn > drain(S, T).
```

and a test to identify if there is a reservoir that needs refill:

```
1  op refill? : System -> Bool.
2  ceq refill?(< N | thr: (L, U), hth: Xn, RAn >) = true if Xn <= L.
3  ceq refill?(< N | thr: (L, U), hth: Xn, RAn > S) = true if Xn <= L.
4  eq refill?(S) = false [owise].
```

Next, the rules to control the movement of the hose and the evolution in time must be defined. A single rule is capable of moving the hose from a reservoir above the lower threshold to one that is below the lower threshold. If there is no reservoir below the lower threshold, or the current reservoir is below the threshold, the hose stays in the same place.

```
1  crl [move-hose] :
2    hose(W, N) < N | thr: (Ln, Un), hth: Xn, RAn >
3    < M | thr: (Lm, Um), hth: Xm, RAm > S =>
4    hose(W, M) < N | thr: (Ln, Un), hth: Xn, RAn >
5    < M | thr: (Lm, Um), hth: Xm, RAm > S
6  if (Xm <= Lm) and (N =/= M) and (Xn >= Ln).
```

In rule *move-hose*, the configuration hose(10, 0) < 0 | thr: (15, 50), hth: 40, rte: 5 > < 1 | thr: (15, 50), hth: 15, rte: 5 > changes to configuration hose(10, 1) < 0 | thr: (15, 50), hth: 40, rte: 5 > < 1 | thr: (15, 50), hth: 15, rte: 5 > as the reservoir 1 *hth* attribute value is less or equal to the lower threshold defined in the *thr* attribute.

Once the system is in a configuration with no reservoir below the lower threshold or if there is at least one reservoir that needs water and the hose is placed on one of them, the system can evolve in time.

```
1  crl [tick] : {hose(W, N) < N | RAn > S} =>
2     {hose(W, N) fill(< N | RAn >, W, T) drain(S, T)} in time T
3  if not refill?(S) [nonexec].
```

In this rule, the system hose(10, 1) < 0 | thr: (15, 50), hth: 40, rte: 5 > < 1 | thr: (15, 50), hth: 15, rte: 5 > can evolve to hose(10, 1) < 0 | thr: (15, 50), hth: 30, rte: 5 > < 1 | thr: (15, 50), hth: 20, rte: 5 > while the system hose(10, 0) < 0 | thr: (15, 50), hth: 40, rte: 5 > < 1 | thr: (15, 50), hth: 15, rte: 5 > is not eligible to evolve in time because there is a reservoir below the lower threshold, and the hose is on a reservoir above the threshold.

Maude offers techniques to search for states that are reachable from the initial states and match a given search pattern. To demonstrate this property, we search the first six steps of the system evolution starting with initial state given by < 0 | hth: 30, rte: 5, thr:(15,50)> < 1 | hth: 30, rte: 5, thr:(15, 50)> < 2 | hth: 30, rte: 5, thr:(15,50)>.

```
1  Timed search in TEST
2     {init2} =>* {S:System}
3  in time < 5 and with mode default time increase 1 :
4
5  Solution 1
6  S:System --> < 0 | hth: 30,rte: 5,thr:(15,50)> < 1 | hth: 30,rte: 5,thr:(15,
7     50)> < 2 | hth: 30,rte: 5,thr:(15,50)> hose(10,0); TIME_ELAPSED:Time --> 0
8
9  Solution 2
10 S:System --> < 0 | hth: 35,rte: 5,thr:(15,50)> < 1 | hth: 25,rte: 5,thr:(15,
11    50)> < 2 | hth: 25,rte: 5,thr:(15,50)> hose(10,0); TIME_ELAPSED:Time --> 1
12
13 Solution 3
14 S:System --> < 0 | hth: 40,rte: 5,thr:(15,50)> < 1 | hth: 20,rte: 5,thr:(15,
15    50)> < 2 | hth: 20,rte: 5,thr:(15,50)> hose(10,0); TIME_ELAPSED:Time --> 2
16
17 Solution 4
18 S:System --> < 0 | hth: 45,rte: 5,thr:(15,50)> < 1 | hth: 15,rte: 5,thr:(15,
19    50)> < 2 | hth: 15,rte: 5,thr:(15,50)> hose(10,0); TIME_ELAPSED:Time --> 3
20
21 Solution 5
22 S:System --> < 0 | hth: 45,rte: 5,thr:(15,50)> < 1 | hth: 15,rte: 5,thr:(15,
23    50)> < 2 | hth: 15,rte: 5,thr:(15,50)> hose(10,1); TIME_ELAPSED:Time --> 3
24
25 Solution 6
26 S:System --> < 0 | hth: 45,rte: 5,thr:(15,50)> < 1 | hth: 15,rte: 5,thr:(15,
27    50)> < 2 | hth: 15,rte: 5,thr:(15,50)> hose(10,2); TIME_ELAPSED:Time --> 3
28
29 No more solutions
```

Next, in order to estimate RTM's efficiency when executing in entry-level computer devices, we executed a search looking for a specific system configuration from the *init2* configuration.

```
1  Timed search in TEST
2     {init2} =>* {< 0 | hth: 45,RA0:ReservoirAttributes > < 1 | hth: 10,
3        RA1:ReservoirAttributes > < 2 | hth: 10,RA2:ReservoirAttributes >}
4  in time < 100 and with mode default time increase 1 :
5
6  No solution
```

In order to make sure we looked through the full state space, a state that the system will not reach was selected, and as Table 1 demonstrates the whole process took 10 ms of processing and executed over 7,000 rewritings to accomplish the task.

Table 1. Evaluation of search technique in Maude

Test	Time (in ms)	Rewrites	Rewrites/second
1	10	7978	730786
2	10	7029	692580

3.3 Model Checking

An RTM specification induces a timed automaton. Standard Maude model checking techniques may be applied to validate timed Linear Temporal Logic formula over a given timed automaton. This is achieved in RTM through a module extension that includes the *TIMED-MODEL-CHECK* module into the reservoir problems implemented.

With the *TIMED-MODEL-CHECK* in a new RTM module, it is possible to verify if the system evolves to a point where it has reservoirs that are below the lower water threshold, and need the hose to be moved to - as a temporal logic: $\models t \,\square\, \neg\lozenge$ *one-down*, where *one-down* represents the event of at least one reservoir below the lower water threshold. The second test executed verified if, at any point in time, all reservoirs need are below the lower treshold - as a temporal logic proposition: $\models t\neg\square \,\lozenge\, macondo$, where *macondo* represents the event of all reservoirs reaching the lower threshold at any point in time.

If the system is well-formed - where $\sum_{i=1}^{n} rte_i = w$ - the checker should not find a state where all reservoirs reach their low threshold or their upper threshold. During the execution of such system up to $n-1$ reservoirs could cross below the low threshold. This behavior is achieved after the model check execution. It can not find a solution where all reservoirs fall below the lower threshold; and it produces a counter example when asked if we can identify a state where the water of a least one reservoir drops to or below the lower threshold.

```
1   Model check{init2} |=t ~[]<> macondo in TEST in time <
2     5 with mode default time increase 1
3   Result Bool :
4     true
5
6   Model check{init2} |=t[]~ <> one-down in TEST in time < 5
7     with mode default time increase 1
8   Result ModelCheckResult :
9     counterexample(
10    {{ < 0 | hth: 30,rte: 5,thr:(15,50)> < 1 | hth: 30,rte: 5,thr:(15,50)>
11       < 2 | hth: 30,rte: 5,thr:(15,50)> hose(10,0)} in time 0,'tick}
12    {{ < 0 | hth: 35,rte: 5,thr:(15,50)> < 1 | hth: 25,rte: 5,thr:(15,50)>
13       < 2 | hth: 25,rte: 5,thr:(15,50)> hose(10,0)} intime 1,'tick}
14    {{ < 0 | hth: 40,rte: 5,thr:(15,50)> < 1 | hth: 20,rte: 5,thr:(15,50)>
15       < 2 | hth: 20,rte: 5,thr:(15,50)> hose(10,0)} in time 2,'tick}
16    {{ < 0 | hth: 45,rte: 5,thr:(15,50)> < 1 | hth: 15,rte: 5,thr:(15,50)>
17       < 2 | hth: 15,rte: 5,thr:(15,50)> hose(10,0)} in time 3,'move-hose}
18    ,{{ < 0 | hth: 45,rte: 5,thr:(15,50)> < 1 | hth: 15,rte: 5,thr:(15,50)>
```

```
19          < 2 | hth: 15,rte: 5,thr:(15,50)> hose(10,1)} in time 3,'move−hose}
20      {{ < 0 | hth: 45,rte: 5,thr:(15,50)> < 1 | hth: 15,rte: 5,thr:(15,50)>
21          < 2 | hth: 15,rte: 5,thr:(15,50)> hose(10,2)} in time 3,'move−hose})
```

Table 2 demonstrates the amount of time required to complete the model checking of the safety and liveness requirements for the system using the *init2* configuration, with both proofs computed under 100 ms in an entry level x86 system, this indicates how efficient the rewriting system in RTM is at running these LTL based model-checks.

Table 2. Model checking evaluation

Test	Time (in ms)	Rewrites	Rewrites/second
1	12	7074	570529
2	21	9580	443046

The RTM code for both the 2-reservoir and the *n*-reservoir modules and the model checking can be retrieved from https://github.com/andremetelo/CPSSources/tree/master/Reservoir.

3.4 Preliminary Analysis of LHA and RTM for CPS Design

A criteria to review a CPS design process has to turn the CPS characteristics into key metrics in its evaluation. The control logic should be embedded in the specification itself. The same should apply for sensors and actuators. Considering that reactive computing and synchronization are intrinsic characteristics of a CPS, the computing model process must naturally support and handle them. Moreover, the time dependency of the differential equations are a constant that has to be managed by the formalization process in order to generate a precise model that represents the physical processes managed by the CPS.

The RTM code used in both variations of the reservoir problem is elegant. It follows a very logical and straight forward principle that satisfies the statements above. Implementing the LHA from Fig. 3 does not pose a challenge in RTM. The model check tools provided by RTM proved to be straight forward once the tests have been formalized in temporal logic.

However, the choice of using LHA as the formalization tool imposes a limitation. A LHA is limited to problems that falls into ordinary differential equations in respect to time. Additionally, it must only use affine tests and attributions. Although many problems that translate into a CPS can fit this model, there are problems that do not fit these requirements.

4 The Synchronous Product of Rewrite Systems and Real-Time Rewrite Systems

The synchronous product of two systems is a procedure to compose such systems such that they evolve simultaneously if they *synchronize* in a given step. A key concept in the synchronous product is the compatibility relation, denoted by $\approx$. Two states, s_1 and s_2, synchronize on a given *action* if they are *compatible*, that is, iff for each property (or atomic proposition) p shared by both states p holds in s_1 iff p holds in s_2.

In [18], the authors specify that given two rewrite systems $\mathcal{R}_i = (\Sigma_i, E_i \cup A_i, R_i)$, for $i = 1, 2$, their synchronous product, denoted $\mathcal{R}_1 \parallel \mathcal{R}_2$, is a new rewrite system $\mathcal{R} = (\Sigma, E \cup A, R)$ as follows, (i) $\Sigma = \Sigma_1 \uplus \Sigma_2 \uplus \Sigma'$, where $\uplus$ denotes the disjoint union of two sets, Σ' contains, among other declarations, (a) a declaration for the operator R.$|=$: R.State $\times$ R.Prop $\rightarrow$ R.Bool, where notation R.*Sort*, or R.*op*, denotes sort *Sort*, or operation *op*, from rewrite system R; (b) a declaration for the predicate R.$\approx$: R_1.State $\times$ R_2.State $\rightarrow$ R.Bool. (ii) $E = E_1 \uplus E_2 \uplus E'$, where E' contains, among other declarations: (a) equations to reduce $s_1 \approx s_2$ to **true**; (iii) $A = A_1 \uplus A_2$; (iv) R is composed of the following set of rules: (a) for each rule label l that exists in both systems, say $[l]s_i \rightarrow s_i' \in R_i$, we have in R the conditional rule $[l]\langle s1, s2 \rangle \rightarrow \langle s_1', s_2' \rangle$ if $s_1' \approx s_2'$, with constructor $\langle \_, \_ \rangle$ denoting the product state; (b) for each rule label l that exists in R_1 but not in R_2, say $[l]s_1 \rightarrow s_1' \in R_1$, we have in R the conditional rule $[l]\langle s_1, x_2 \rangle \rightarrow \langle s_1', x_2 \rangle$ if $s_1' \approx x_2$ (with x_2 a variable of sort R_2.State); (c) correspondingly for rule labels in R_2 but not in R_1.

Now in this paper we propose that given two real-time rewrite systems $\mathcal{R}_i = (\Sigma_i, E_i \cup A_i, R_i \cup R_{t_i})$ with R_i instantaneous rewrite rules and tick rules R_{t_i}, with the same subequational theory for *TIME*, the synchronized real-time system $\mathcal{R} = (\Sigma, E \cup A, R \cup R_t)$ has each individual component composed as above but each tick rule in R_t requires its left-hand side and right-hand side to be *R-compatible*, that is, each r in R_t relate product states that are compatible using the rules in R. Therefore, a (possibly infinite, Zeno) computation $t_0 \longrightarrow t_1 \longrightarrow \ldots$ in the synchronized real-time system $\mathcal{R}$ has a step $\langle s_{1_i}, s_{2_l} \rangle \xrightarrow{u} \langle s_{1_j}, s_{2_k} \rangle$ such that the product state $\langle s_{1_j}, s_{2_k} \rangle$ is reached from $\langle s_{1_i}, s_{2_l} \rangle$ after a computation composed by R-compatible untimed transitions, that is, transitions resulting from the application of rules in R where each state in the computation is compatible with its predecessor.

In what follows, we specify (a simplified version) of a *modular* 2-reservoir problem using the synchronous product extension of Full-Maude available in http://maude.sip.uc.es/syncprod. (An extension of Real-Time Maude with real-time synchronous product as described above is under development.) In Listing 1.2 we specify the behavior of a reservoir as a component whose state is either **below** (its fluid threshold) or **ok**. Whenever the clock ticks, modeled by rule labeled **tick**, the reservoir (actually, *all* of them as they will synchronize with this action) may change its state from **ok** to **below**. And by (re)filling it, it may change from **below** to **ok**. State predicate **refill1?** is true when the state of the reservoir is **below**.

```
1  (mod RESERVOIR1 is
2      including SATISFACTION. --- declares State, Prop, and |=.
3      ops below ok : -> State [ctor].
4      rl [tick] : ok => below.
5      rl [fill1] : below => ok.
6      op refill1? : -> Prop.
```

```
7    eq below |= refill1? = true.
8    eq ok |= refill1? = false.
9  endm)
```

Listing 1.2. Modular specification of a reservoir

Now, the 2-reservoir system is given by the synchronous product of reservoirs 1 and 2, as declared in Listing 1.3 by the statement pr RESERVOIR1 || RESERVOIR2.. Module 2-RESERVOIR-SYSTEM also declares a state proposition specifying that the 2-reservoir system is safe if reservoirs 1 and 2 are not in state below at the same time.

```
1  (mod 2−RESERVOIR−SYSTEM is
2    pr RESERVOIR1 || RESERVOIR2.
3    op safe : −> Prop [ctor].
4    eq S:State |= safe = not (S:State |= refill1? and S:State |= refill2?).
5  endm)
```

Listing 1.3. The 2-reservoir system as the product of reservoirs

We may now model check this specification and prove that it is not the case that the system is always safe starting from state <ok, ok> where both reservoirs are above their thresholds. A counter-example is produced showing the infinite loop <ok, ok> $\xrightarrow{\text{tick}}$ <below, below> $\xrightarrow{\text{fill2}}$ <below, ok> $\xrightarrow{\text{fill1}}$ <ok, ok>.....

```
1  (mod MODEL−CHECK−2−RESERVOIR−SYSTEM is
2    pr 2−RESERVOIR−SYSTEM.
3    inc MODEL−CHECKER * (sort State to Conf).
4    inc LTL−SIMPLIFIER.
5    subsort Conf < State.
6    op init : −> State.
7    eq init = < ok, ok >.
8  endm)
9
10 (red modelCheck(init, [] safe).)
11 reduce in MODEL−CHECK−2−RESERVOIR−SYSTEM :
12   modelCheck(init,[]safe)
13 result [ModelCheckResult] :
14   counterexample({< ok,ok >,'tick},{< below,below >,'fill2}{< below,ok >,
15     'fill1}{< ok,ok >,'tick})
```

Listing 1.4. Model checking the 2-reservoir as a synchronous product

5   Related Work

Even though CPS are not a new concept, to this day an optimal set of formalisms, languages and tools are not properly defined. Broman *et al.* [9] describe an extensive list of formal methods, languages and tools that can be combined to let an entity specify, design, develop and test a CPS.

Some problems were approached through the eyes of the Model checking methodology to verify the safety properties. Akella and McMillin [1] modeled a CPS as a Security Process Algebra. They used model checker, CoPs, to check the confidentially properties. Bu *et al.* [10] analyzed CPS aspects using a statistical model checker. Highlight that in this approach the state space explosion also occurs like in classical model checking problems.

Zhang *et al.* [27] present a model to verify the safety properties in mobile CPS based on a SAT-based model checking algorithm. The system was modeled as a Petri net and presented a lower memory consumption.

A combined model checking and a new version of PALS (physically asynchronous, logically synchronous) were applied to verified an airplane turning control system in [6,7]. Bae *et al.* [7] also present other applications as a networked thermostat controllers and networked water tank controllers with gravity component.

This paper takes advantage of one possible set of such techniques to model (in LHA), develop (in *Maude*) and model check (also in *Maude*) the leaking reservoir problem specified in [17]. Additional formalisms that are capable of modeling the reservoir problem are presented in [9]. Some examples are: *Differential Equations, additional State Machines model beyond LHA, Dataflow, Discrete Events.* Each of these methods can be used alongside a plethora of tools and languages to develop and model check phases of a CPS.

Each technique is going to favor a set of tools and languages when development moves to the next phase. The LHA approach used in this paper favors a model check approach such as *Maude.* Of course other checkers such as *SAL* [20], *Spin* [16], *NuSMV* [13] and *UPPAAL* [8] are viable options for the design process of a LHA based CPS. For an approach based on Discrete Event techniques, the language and tools would most likely been based on Hard Description Languages based on *VHDL* like *Verilog* [25] or *AMS with added extensions* [12]. Meanwhile, a DataFlow based approach is more likely to leverage a language like *Lustre* [11]. Each bringing their own set advantages and limitations, making it even harder to create consensus on a standardized end-to-to process to specify, validate and develop a CPS.

This situation highlights the toughest aspect of CPS design and implementation. Depending on the context of the project sponsors, their perspective can influence the formalism path adopted and push the project toward one of another set of languages and tools. This is an area of CPS design that can be improved through increased availability of references that provide a study case of such methods applied to the same problem, and provide a qualitative and quantitative comparison of the results of each individual implementation. Such works seem to be at a preliminary stage at this point in time.

6   Conclusion

This work presents a first step in creating a formal model to modularly specify and model check CPS by precisely describing the concept of modular CPS modeling and illustrating it with a case study on how to model a CPS as a LHA and effectively implement it in RTM. It creates succinct code to simulate and model check the problem in this study scope.

We are currently developing a tool to support the notion of synchronous product of real-time systems as described in this paper. Our results are encouraging, as illustrated in this paper.

There are also open questions, which require further studies in terms of creating more precise models for the leaking reservoir models and other types of automata that can be used as starting point for CPS modeling alongside their respective implementation in RTM.

Acknowledgment. This work was developed with the support of CAPES - Coordenação de Aperfeiçoamento de Pessoal de Nível Superior (Coordination for Enhancement of Higher Education Personnel, in Brazil) and FAPERJ - Fundação de Amparo a Pesquisa do Rio de Janeiro.

References

1. Akella, R., McMillin, B.: Model-cheking BNDC properties in cyber-physical systems. In: Proceedings of the 33rd Annual IEEE International Computer Software and Applications Conference COMPSAC 2009, pp. 660–663. IEEE (2009)
2. Alur, R.: Principles of Cyber-Physical Systems. The MIT Press, Cambridge (2015)
3. Alur, R., Courcoubetis, C., Henzinger, T.A., Ho, P.-H.: Hybrid automata: an algorithmic approach to the specification and verification of hybrid systems. In: Grossman, R.L., Nerode, A., Ravn, A.P., Rischel, H. (eds.) HS 1991-1992. LNCS, vol. 736, pp. 209–229. Springer, Heidelberg (1993). https://doi.org/10.1007/3-540-57318-6_30
4. Alur, R., Dill, D.L.: A theory of timed automata. Theor. Comput. Sci. **126**(2), 183–235 (1994). https://doi.org/10.1016/0304-3975(94)90010-8
5. Arnold, A.: Finite Transition Systems: Semantics of Communicating Systems. Prentice Hall International (UK) Ltd., Hertfordshire (1994)
6. Bae, K., Krisiloff, J., Meseguer, J., Ölveczky, P.: Designing and verifying distributed cyber-physical systems using multirate pals: an airplane turning control system case study. Sci. Comput. Program. (2015). http://www.sciencedirect.com/science/article/pii/S0167642314004109
7. Bae, K., Ölveczky, P., Kong, S., Gao, S., Clarke, E.M.: SMT-based analysis of virtually synchronous distributed hybrid systems. In: Proceedings of the 19th International Conference on Hybrid Systems: Computation and Control, HSCC 2016, pp. 145–154. ACM, New York (2016). https://doi.org/10.1145/2883817.2883849
8. Bengtsson, J., Larsen, K., Larsson, F., Pettersson, P., Yi, W.: UPPAAL—a tool suite for automatic verification of real-time systems. In: Alur, R., Henzinger, T.A., Sontag, E.D. (eds.) HS 1995. LNCS, vol. 1066, pp. 232–243. Springer, Heidelberg (1996). https://doi.org/10.1007/BFb0020949
9. Broman, D., Lee, E., Tripakis, S., Torngren, M.: Viewpoints, formalisms, languages, and tools for cyber-physical systems. In: Proceedings of the 6th International Workshop on Multi-Paradigm Modeling, pp. 49–54 (2012)
10. Bu, L., Wang, Q., Chen, X.: Toward online hybrid systems model checking of cyber-physical systems time-bounded short-run behavior. ACM SIGBED Rev. **8**, 7–10 (2011)
11. Caspi, P., Pilaud, D., Halbwachs, N., Plaice, J.A.: LUSTRE: a declarative language for real-time programming. In: Proceedings of the 14th ACM SIGACT-SIGPLAN Symposium on Principles of Programming Languages, POPL 1987, pp. 178–188. ACM, New York (1987). https://doi.org/10.1145/41625.41641

12. Christen, E., Bakalar, K.: VHDL-AMS-a hardware description language for analog and mixed-signal applications. IEEE Trans. Circ. Syst. II: Analog Digit. Sig. Process. **46**(10), 1263–1272 (1999). See also: IEEE Trans. Circ. Syst. II: Express Briefs

13. Cimatti, A., Clarke, E., Giunchiglia, E., Giunchiglia, F., Pistore, M., Roveri, M., Sebastiani, R., Tacchella, A.: NuSMV 2: an opensource tool for symbolic model checking. In: Brinksma, E., Larsen, K.G. (eds.) CAV 2002. LNCS, vol. 2404, pp. 359–364. Springer, Heidelberg (2002). https://doi.org/10.1007/3-540-45657-0_29

14. Clavel, M., Durán, F., Eker, S., Escobar, S., Lincoln, P., Martí-Oliet, N., Meseguer, J., Talcott, C.: Maude Manual (Version 2.7.1). SRI International (2016)

15. Henzinger, T.A.: The theory of hybrid automata. In: Inan, M.K., Kurshan, R.P. (eds.) Verification of Digital and Hybrid Systems. NATO ASI Series, vol. 170, pp. 265–292. Springer, Heidelberg (2000). https://doi.org/10.1007/978-3-642-59615-5_13

16. Holzmann, G.: Spin Model Checker, the: Primer and Reference Manual. Addison-Wesley Professional, Boston (2003)

17. Lygeros, J., Tomlin, C., Sastry, S.: Hybrid Systems: Modeling, Analysis and Control. University of California (2008)

18. Martín, Ó., Verdejo, A., Martí-Oliet, N.: Synchronous products of rewrite systems. In: Artho, C., Legay, A., Peled, D. (eds.) ATVA 2016. LNCS, vol. 9938, pp. 141–156. Springer, Cham (2016). https://doi.org/10.1007/978-3-319-46520-3_10

19. Meseguer, J.: Conditional rewriting logic as a unified model of concurrency. Theor. Comput. Sci. **96**(1), 73–155 (1992). https://doi.org/10.1016/0304-3975(92)90182-F

20. Moura, L., Owre, S., Shankar, N.: The SAL language manual. SRI International (2003)

21. Ölveczky, P.: Real-Time Maude 2.3 Manual. University of Oslo (2007). http://heim.ifi.uio.no/peterol/RealTimeMaude/

22. Ölveczky, P.: Designing Reliable Distributed Systems: A Formal Methods Approach Based on Executable Modeling in Maude. Undergraduate Topics in Computer Science. Springer, London (2018). https://doi.org/10.1007/978-1-4471-6687-0

23. Ölveczky, P.C., Meseguer, J.: Specification of real-time and hybrid systems in rewriting logic. Theor. Comput. Sci. **285**(2), 359–405 (2002). https://doi.org/10.1016/S0304-3975(01)00363-2

24. Shafi, Q.: Cyber physical systems security: a brief survey. In: 12th International Conference on Computational Science and Its Applications (ICCSA), Salvador, Brazil, pp. 146–150. IEEE (2012)

25. Smith, D.: VHDL and Verilog compared and contrasted-plus modeled example written in VHDL, Verilog and C. In: Proceedings of the 33rd Annual Design Automation Conference (1996)

26. Thomas, W.: Automata on infinite objects. In: Handbook of Theoretical Computer Science, vol. B, pp. 133–191. MIT Press, Cambridge (1990). http://dl.acm.org/citation.cfm?id=114891.114895

27. Zhang, L., Hu, W., Qu, W., Guo, Y., Li, S.: A formal approach to verify parameterized protocols in mobile cyber-physical systems. Mob. Inf. Syst. (2017). https://doi.org/10.1155/2017/5731678

Influence Maximization in Network by Genetic Algorithm on Linear Threshold Model

Arthur Rodrigues da Silva[1,2], Rodrigo Ferreira Rodrigues[1,2],
Vinícius da Fonseca Vieira[1,2], and Carolina Ribeiro Xavier[1,2(✉)]

[1] Department of Computer Science, Universidade Federal de São
João Del Rei - UFSJ, São João Del Rei, Brazil
carolinaxavier@ufsj.edu.br
[2] Graduate Program in Computer Science, Universidade Federal de São
João Del Rei - UFSJ, São João Del Rei, Brazil

Abstract. The problem of maximum influence on the network consists in the search for a subset of k vertices called seeds which when activated are able to influence as much elements as possible, considering a model to simulate the propagation of influence in a network. This paper proposes a Genetic Algorithm to optimize the selection of seeds for the Linear Threshold Model (LTM), a widely adopted simulation model for influence propagation, by investigating different strategies for initial population configurations based on high centrality nodes. The results obtained by the application of the proposed methodology to the Linear Threshold Model considering real world networks show significant improvements on the convergence of the algorithm.

Keywords: Maximum influence · Genetic algorithm
Linear Threshold Model · Centrality

1 Introduction

According to [5], the maximum influence problem is the optimization problem that consists in finding a group of vertices with size k on a network such that, when the vertices are activated and a propagation model is applied, the global influence is maximized. The most common application of propagation models is in viral marketing on on-line social networks, where the goal is to find a small subset of influent people which is able to attract the attention of the other individuals to posts and publications about new products, services and ideas.

A common approach to study the influence maximization problem is through the modeling of the subject of study as an graph, considering each person as a vertex and their personal relationships as edges of this vertex. Propagation models, like Linear Threshold Model, allow us to study the propagation of the influence in controlled environment. Thus, considering a propagation model, an

O. Gervasi et al. (Eds.): ICCSA 2018, LNCS 10960, pp. 96–109, 2018.
https://doi.org/10.1007/978-3-319-95162-1_7

analyst is able to investigate the level in which a set of vertices is able to influence or activate the others vertices of the network.

According to [9] the definition of the optimal subset of k individuals for the influence optimization problem on a graph is NP-hard. Thus, many heuristics to search for a good set of vertices have been proposed and considered in the literature. Over these strategies, this work highlights the effectiveness and proposed a genetic algorithm for the influence maximization problem.

In order to maximize the influence using a genetic algorithm as a method of seed selection, this work proposes the perturbation of the initial population through a single individual containing the k vertices of greater centrality within the network, rather than considering random initial populations. Thus, the analysis of how much these vertices, considering different strategies, can impact the final solution of GA and the investigation of structural properties of the vertices that correspond to the solution are an important step of the methodology of this work.

Kempe et al. [8] propose a greedy algorithm in order to overcome heuristics based on seed selection by the centrality in their strategy they obtains a solution that is provably within 63% of optimal for several classes of models. However this algorithm depends on the calculation of the propagation of influence.

Chen et al. demonstrate that calculating the influence in directed acyclic graphs (DAGs) can be performed in time linear to the size of the graphs. Based on this, they proposed a scalable algorithm (LDAG) for the Linear Threshold Model an applied it to networks with millions of edges and vertices that is faster than other algorithms in the literature.

Bucur and Iacca, [4] demonstrate in their work that the use of genetic algorithms on the problem of maximizing influence can offer solutions of high level of influence comparable to the heuristics found by other heuristics and viable at runtime. They use the independent cascade model as a fitness function. Also without the need for any assumptions about the network.

The remainder of the work is organized in the following way. First, the centrality measures used in this work (Sect. 2) are presented, and the LTM influence model (Sect. 3) is detailed, then GA fundamentals (Sect. 4). Section 5 describes the proposed methodology for the selection of optimal seeds and the propagation model considered in this work. Finally in Sects. 6 and 7 the results, discussions and conclusions from the work are presented.

2   Background

According to Barabási [1] a network is a catalog of a system's components often called nodes or vertices and the direct interactions between them, called edges. Newman [12] explains that a network (also called graphs in mathematical literature) abound in the world. Examples include the Internet, the World Wide Web, social networks of acquaintance or other connections between individuals, organizational networks and networks of business relations between companies, neural networks, metabolic networks, food webs, distribution networks such as blood vessels and others.

A network contains two basics characteristics:

- Nodes: each node represents an entity of what the network represents and the total number of nodes defines the size of the network.
- Links: represent the connections between the nodes.

Links on a network can be direct or undirected. In cases of networks that model the Internet, considering that each vertex is a website and each edge is a link between these sites, a site A may contain a link to a site B but B does not necessarily have a link to A, and it becomes more appropriate to represent a directed network. Other systems have undirected links, like transmission lines on the power grid, on which the electric current can flow in both directions [1].

2.1 Communities

The nodes of a network can be organized into communities. Communities can be defined as a group of nodes that are more likely to connect to one another than to nodes in other communities. In other words, groups of nodes that have more connections to each other than to nodes that do not belong to this group. Some examples are Work places, circles of friends, or a group of individuals who pursue the same hobby together, or individuals living in the same neighborhood [1].

Among the many algorithms proposed in the literature for community detection, the Multilevel algorithm [3] stands out, due to its capability of finding good community structures in reasonable time, being executed quickly in large networks (millions of vertices). Its operation is divided into two phases repeated iteratively. First, each vertex of the network is considered separately as a member of a community, in this way there are as many communities as there are vertices. Then, for each vertex the algorithm investigates if its insertion in the community of one of its neighbor vertices increases a measure called modularity, frequently used for the assessment of quality of community structures. The vertex is then transferred to the neighbor community that maximizes the modularity or stays in its current community. The process continues until modularity stops improving. According to [3] the order in which the vertices are analyzed has no significant impact on the obtained modularity.

2.2 Centrality

The centrality can reflects the importance of the node on the web, some important metrics used for this study are:

- Degree: When a node has a large number of edges connected to it, it is said that it has a high degree. This degree can be measured in different ways depending on the network. If the network is undirected, the degree of a node is given by the number of edges connected to it.
  If the network is directed, the degree is measured separately. Each vertex has a degree of output (outdegree), given by the number of edges starting from

this vertex, and degree of input (indegree), given by the amount of edges that reach it, or even the total degree, which takes into account the input and output edges. In this work the degree of output will be used.

– Closeness: It is the average distance between a vertex and all the others on the graph using the shorter path. The vertex became more central how much closer it is from the others [2].
– Betweenness: This centrality measure how many times a vertex makes up the shorter path between two vertices on the graph. So, if this vertex has a hight probability of make up a random short path chosen between two others vertices chosen randomly, It contains a high valor of betweenness [6].
– PageRank: In this measure each vertex has a value, calculated according to the amount of input edges that it has, the larger the value the more important it is. When a vertex has an output edge to another vertex, it adds value to this other vertex in proportion to the value that it has divided by its number of output edges. Thus, vertices that have many input edges tend to have greater importance values as well as vertices that receive edges of other important vertices [13].

3   Linear Threshold Model (LTM)

According to [15], the Linear Threshold Model is an influence model that each edges $e \in E$ has a non negative weight, and for each vertex $v \in V$ the sum of the input edges must be less than or equal to one. Therefore, considering $w(e)$ the edge's weight of any incident to v and the amount of edges that connect with the vertex v we have:

$$\sum_{e \in v} w(e) \leq 1. \tag{1}$$

There is also a threshold θ associated to each vertex v which must be defined. This threshold is fixed in a uniformly random way, with a value between zero and one for each vertex. Giving a graph with this characteristics and a initial set of actives vertices, for each iteration t a new one vertex (previously inactive), can be activated at iteration $t + 1$ if the sum of values of their incoming edges starting from an already active vertex is greater than or equal to the threshold of the vertex.

In this way the set of activated vertices, or influenced, by initial set is defined when, after a undefined number of iterations, the total active vertices does not increase. The Fig. 1 illustrated this process for three iterations.

By analyzing Fig. 1 in $t = 0$ the initial set of actives vertex (on gray), and in $t = 1$ the vertices connected to the initial set become actives if the influence created by the set of actives vertex are sufficient. Finally, in $t = 2$ shows the activation of the vertices influenced by the resulting vertices activated set of $t = 1$.

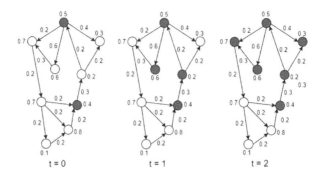

Fig. 1. Representation of the operation of the LTM in three instants of time represented by t.

4   Genetic Algorithm

According to [7] Evolutionary Algorithms are computer programs that solve complex problems imitating the process described by Darwin. In this way the population of individuals competes against each others. Thus, it is expected that individuals evolve and find a better solution than those found previously until the goal or some stop criterion is reached.

In this way, each individual of the population represents a candidate solution for solving the problem, and each individual must be evaluated by a fitness function, that will define the quality of solution that individual represents.

According to [11] a Genetic Algorithm (GA) it is a kind of Evolutionary Algorithm, and even if are several variations of a GA four characteristics are common to all of them: Chromosome populations, fitness selection, crossover and mutation.

4.1   Chromosome Populations

A chromosome populations is the name given to the set of candidate solutions. Each candidate solution (chromosome) has a numerical sequence (genes) [11].

4.2   Fitness Selection

Fitness is the name given to the value of the evaluation function, also used as an operation to selection population members to reproduction. This function allows to check how much a candidate solution fit to the solution. Through it is possible to define the best members of each population [11].

4.3   Crossover

A crossover is an operation in which given two individuals selected as parents, a criterion is established for the characteristics of these two individuals are present in the individuals generated by the operation [11].

For a crossing of the individuals represented by numerical, or binary chains can be used the crossing of n points. In this type of crossing one or more random points are chosen from this chain for the generation of subsequences. This subsequences are linked, containing parts of the individuals selected, forming two new individuals called sons. Figure 2 illustrates the crossover at one point.

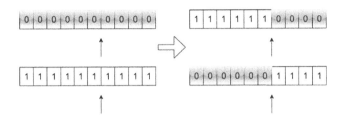

Fig. 2. Crossover of one point, where the parents (on left side) generating two sons (right side) containing parts of their genes

Crossing is responsible for the search intensification, because it explores solutions close to existing solutions.

4.4 Mutation

A mutation occurs when a individual has one of their genes changed. This gene must be randomly chosen and the change probability must be small. The mutation is responsible for diversify the population, because it is change the individual randomly without analyze the informations about previous generations. This strategy is used to escape from local optimums [11].

5 Methodology

For the implementation of the evaluation function an adaptation of the previously presented LTM was performed. Each edge of the network has a relative value for each vertex, so that the sum of the edge values of each vertex is always one. So if a given vertex has x input edges, then the value of each edge for this vertex will be $1/x$. This decision was taken so that each vertex exported an influence proportional to the amount of neighbors of the vertex influenced. In this way it was also possible to use the evaluation function for non-directed networks. The influence is divided evenly between all the edges of each vertex in this networks.

Before to run the GA an influence test with the most central nodes of the network were performed. The 50 best ranked nodes in each centrality measure was chosen as seeds for the influence model simulation later this results will be compare with the GA results.

For the genetic algorithm a population of 50 individuals was defined, each containing 50 genes, and each gene representing one vertex. The parents selection for the next generation was done by tournament, implementing crossing at only one point and using the mutation rate of 10%. In tournament selection four individuals are selected randomly, two at a time, and the two best ones are chosen as parents. Each generation replaces the previous individuals, except for the individual with the best fitness value of the previous generation, which is inserted in the next generation. That is, assuming a n generation, at each iteration the $n + 1$ generation, generated from n, will replace n and will be replaced by the $n + 2$ generation, and so on.

In order to check the impact on the quality of the solution, some disturbances of the initial population were performed. It was added a single individual containing the fifty vertices of greater centrality of the network. This centrality is defined by one of the four previously presented: degree, closeness, betweenness and PageRank. Thus, for each network to be analyzed, the four measures of centrality are applied and each one has one individual inserted in the initial population at a time.

Defining the operation of the algorithm (LTM) and the genetic algorithm, the operation of the proposed method follows the following steps:

1. Calculate the vertex centrality.
2. Generate an individual with the fifty most central vertices of the chosen measure and insert it into the initial population that will be formed.
3. Create the first population
4. Evaluate this population.
5. Crossover.
6. Mutation.
7. Evaluate this population.
8. Elitism (saved the best o previously generation).
9. Return to the 5 step.

The algorithm finishes executing after a predefined number of iterations, for this study we considered 100 generations or when the best fitness value stops growing for 10 consecutive generations.

5.1   Data

In order to test the proposed methodology, three networks were selected and the influence results were compared by applying the seeds selected by the centrality measures directly on the LTM and, inserting them with the rest of the initial AG population.

CA-GrQc. CA-GrQc [10] is a network that represents the collaboration of authors in a same work in the context of General Relativity and Quantum Cosmology. This network is undirected containing 5242 nodes and 14496 edges, such that a node represents a researcher and an edge represents the collaboration of two authors in a publication.

CA-HepPh Network. CA-HepPh [10] is a collaboration network in High Energy Physics - Phenomenology. It is also undirected and contains 12008 vertices and 118521 edges, such that a node represents a researcher and an edge represents the collaboration of two authors in a publication.

Epinions Network. Epinions [14] is an on-line social networks based on the trust of individuals in services reviews. It contains 75879 vertices and 508837 edges, such that a node represents an individual and an edge represents the trusty between two individuals.

6   Results and Discussions

In this section will be present the main results of this work.

For each network, first will be present the graphic with the reach of influence per number of seeds (1 up to 50) for different centrality method to select seeds. So, a graphic with the results of GA by generation, with and without the initial population disturbance will show the different effects of centralities in the GA results. Finally, a table with an analysis of the best fit individuals and its rank for each centrality measure will be discussed.

Figures 3(a), 4(a), and 5(a) represent the diffusion of influence of these networks. Axis y shows the percentage of vertices influenced and axis x shows the quantity of seeds used, without considering the GA.

When GA is used, axis x represents the number of generations passed. It is important mentioning that Figs. 3(b), 4(b) and 5(b) represent the performance of GA with and without the proposes disturbance.

Tables 1, 2 and 3 represent the percentage of the GA results on the last generation to the worst, the average, and the best result of the same tests shown in the charts (Fig. 3-b, 4-b, and 5-b).

In Fig. 3 it can seen that the GA improve the results around 50% when compared with the best set of seeds in case without GA and it is possible to see different behavior for different centralities measure. It show that the simplest GA can give great results in influence maximization problem.

As in previously network, in Fig. 4 the results show an great improve of the GA when compare with the results using only the centrality measures.

Tables 1, 2, and 3 show that the variation around the average value stands below 3% in most cases. This occurs because the GA discards all the worse results then the one already discovered. However, this result also demonstrates how difficult it is to improve a far above average result. This indicates that even if a good result is found, it will not be surpassed very easily.

On Fig. 3 it is noticed that the seeds selected by the calculation of the centrality by betweenness reached greater influence, followed by the seeds selected by Degree. Also, when this same group of seeds was used in the GA not only there was an improvement in the influence but also a great approximation between the results achieved by the measures. The same behavior can be observed in the

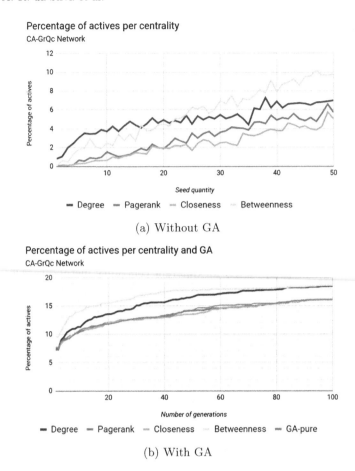

(a) Without GA

(b) With GA

Fig. 3. Difference of -CA-GrQc network influence with and without GA

network Fig. 4 but in this, when GA was used the seeds selected by betweenness generated a significantly better result.

Analyzing Fig. 5 it is possible to observe a similar behavior in the other networks so that the seeds defined by degree and betweenness had better results, however in this network there is a great difference between the best and the worst results when the GA is used. To understand this difference we analyzed the results of the 10 executions for each measure.

For this analysis we made the intersection of the 10 response sets of each mode so that when a vertex appeared in 8 or more groups it was used in the analysis. For each selected vertex it was verified if it was in the ranking of 50 first vertices of each one of the four measures of centrality shown. The objective of comparing the membership of these vertices to the group of the first 50 is justified by the fact that the initial populations received the 50 highest ranked vertices in the graph, in some measure of centrality. In addition, it was checked whether

Table 1. CA-GrQc group

Measure	Worse	Average	Best
Degree	14.7081	18.4872	20.8890
Pagerank	14.3838	16.1599	18.0465
Closeness	14.6509	16.1560	19.1721
Betweenness	15.4140	18.6227	20.2213
GA-pure	14.1740	16.0588	17.8558

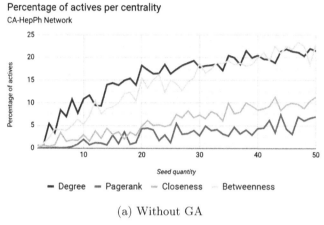

(a) Without GA

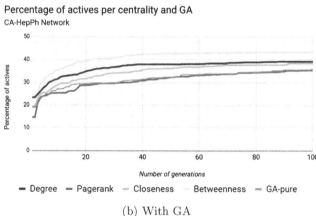

(b) With GA

Fig. 4. Difference of CA-HepPh network influence with and without GA

these vertices made up a community calculated by the multilevel algorithm. The
Tables 4, 5, 6, and 7, show the results of the analysis regarding the position of
the vertices in each measure for each response group:

Table 2. CA-HepPh group

Measure	Worse	Average	Best
Degree	37.6553	39.2080	40.6806
Pagerank	33.4467	35.3464	37.5685
Closeness	36.1048	38.3628	40.4193
Betweenness	41.0287	43.3561	45.1084
GA-pure	34.0023	35.8228	37.8997

Percentage of actives per centrality
soc-Epinions Network

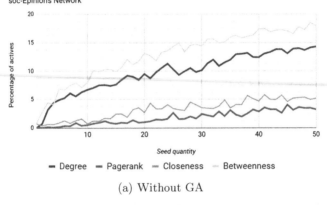

(a) Without GA

Percentage of actives per centrality and GA
soc-Epinions Network

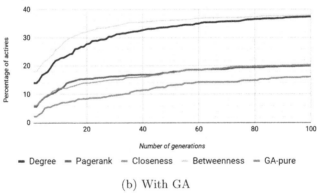

(b) With GA

Fig. 5. Difference of Epinions network influence with and without GA

It is possible to note on Tables 4, 5, 6, and 7 that not all the analyzed vertices are on the group of the top 50 measures like in Tables 6 and 7. Moreover, it is possible to note that almost all the elements of the Table 5 are contained in Table 4. Surprisingly also the closeness and PageRank groups contained the same

Table 3. Epinions group

Measure	Worse	Average	Best
Degree	35.3734	37.4674	38.7327
PageRank	17.0640	20.0053	22.4225
Closeness	19.6721	20.5236	21.6806
Betweenness	37.2382	38.0835	39.6460
GA-pure	10.0225	16.2087	28.9922

Table 4. Betweenness group

Vertex	Betweenness	Degree	Closeness	PageRank
363	4	1	2	307
697	3	32	164	76
1677	1	3	27	375
1867	2	2	7	257
2776	10	11	9	1335
8499	11	21	125	1322

Table 5. Degree group

Vertex	Betweenness	Degree	Closeness	PageRank
363	4	1	2	307
1677	1	3	27	375
1867	2	2	7	257
4971	22	18	29	1857

Table 6. Closeness group

Vertex	Betweenness	Degree	Closeness	PageRank
1138	529	481	613	942
2868	114	218	82	1701
8491	23	65	155	1136

Table 7. PageRank group

Vertex	Betweenness	Degree	Closeness	PageRank
1138	529	481	613	942
2868	114	218	82	1701
8491	23	65	155	1136

vertices. Observing Tables (4, 5, 6, and 7) it is possible to verify that PageRank is not a good measure to choose the seeds. Another verified characteristic is that no vertex shown in the tables occupy the same community together.

7   Conclusion

This work proposed a genetic algorithm for the influence maximization problem. The results shown that the use of GA, with the basic operations can improve significantly the influence results. Moreover, a very simple disturbance in the initial population was propose and the tests showed that the insertion of one individual with vertices with high centrality can improve even more this results.

It is possible to notice in this work the insertion of a special individual in the initial population of GA produced better results than without its insertion. Another visible feature is that the use of Betweenness and Degree measurements obtained better results than other measures. Thus, considering the results obtained, it is reasonable that for the maximization of influence in a network on LTM, it makes sense to consider high-centrality seeds that are not in the same community. It is also possible to realize that good seeds do not necessarily have high centrality. Another relevant factor is that due to the computational cost of calculating the values of centrality by betweenness for each vertex of the network it is possible to obtain very close results using the degree of the vertex (which is computationally cheaper to be calculated). This work comes to demonstrate the quality of results for the maximizing influence using a genetic algorithm and measures of centrality.

References

1. Barabási, A.-L.: Network Science. Cambridge University Press, Cambridge (2016)
2. Bavelas, A.: Communication patterns in task-oriented groups. J. Acoust. Soc. Am. **22**(6), 725–730 (1950)
3. Blondel, V.D., Guillaume, J.L., Lambiotte, R., Lefebvre, E.: Fast unfolding of community hierarchies in large network. J. Stat. Mech. 1008 (2008)
4. Bucur, D., Iacca, G.: Influence maximization in social networks with genetic algorithms. In: Squillero, G., Burelli, P. (eds.) EvoApplications 2016. LNCS, vol. 9597, pp. 379–392. Springer, Cham (2016). https://doi.org/10.1007/978-3-319-31204-0_25
5. Chen, W., Yuan, Y., Zhang, L.: Scalable influence maximization in social networks under the linear threshold model. In: 2010 IEEE 10th International Conference on Data Mining (ICDM), pp. 88–97. IEEE (2010)
6. Freeman, L.C.: A set of measures of centrality based on betweenness. Sociometry **40**, 35–41 (1977)
7. Jones, G.: Genetic and evolutionary algorithms. Encycl. Comput. Chem. **2**, 1127–1136 (1998)
8. Kempe, D., Kleinberg, J., Tardos, É.: Maximizing the spread of influence through a social network. In: Proceedings of the Ninth ACM SIGKDD International Conference on Knowledge Discovery and Data Mining, pp. 137–146. ACM (2003)

9. Kempe, D., Kleinberg, J., Tardos, É.: Influential nodes in a diffusion model for social networks. In: Caires, L., Italiano, G.F., Monteiro, L., Palamidessi, C., Yung, M. (eds.) ICALP 2005. LNCS, vol. 3580, pp. 1127–1138. Springer, Heidelberg (2005). https://doi.org/10.1007/11523468_91

10. Leskovec, J., Kleinberg, J., Faloutsos, C.: Graph evolution: densification and shrinking diameters. ACM Trans. Knowl. Discov. Data (TKDD) **1**(1), 2 (2007)

11. Mitchell, M.: An Introduction to Genetic Algorithms. MIT Press, Cambridge (1998)

12. Newman, M.E.J.: The structure and function of complex networks. SIAM Rev. **45**(2), 167–256 (2003)

13. Page, L., Brin, S., Motwani, R., Winograd, T.: The pagerank citation ranking: bringing order to the web. Technical report. Stanford InfoLab (1999)

14. Richardson, M., Agrawal, R., Domingos, P.: Trust management for the semantic web. In: Fensel, D., Sycara, K., Mylopoulos, J. (eds.) ISWC 2003. LNCS, vol. 2870, pp. 351–368. Springer, Heidelberg (2003). https://doi.org/10.1007/978-3-540-39718-2_23

15. Shakarian, P., Bhatnagar, A., Aleali, A., Shaabani, E., Guo, R.: Diffusion in Social Networks. Springer, Heidelberg (2015). https://doi.org/10.1007/978-3-319-23105-1

Computing the Linear Complexity
in a Class of Cryptographic Sequences

Amparo Fúster-Sabater[1] and Sara D. Cardell[2($\boxtimes$)]

[1] Instituto de Tecnologías Físicas y de la Información, CSIC,
144, Serrano, 28006 Madrid, Spain
amparo@iec.csic.es
[2] Instituto de Matemática, Estatística e Computação Científica, UNICAMP,
Campinas, Brazil
sdcardell@ime.unicamp.br

Abstract. In this work, we present a method of computing the linear complexity of the sequences produced by the cryptographic sequence generator known as generalized self-shrinking generator. This approach is based on the comparison of different shifted versions of a single PN-sequence. Just the analysis of binary digits in these shifted sequences allows one to determine the linear complexity of those generalized sequences. The method is simple, direct and efficient. Furthermore, the concept of linear recurrence relationship and the rows of the Sierpinski's triangle are the basic tools in this computation.

Keywords: Generalized self-shrinking generator · Linear complexity
Linear recurrence relationship · Sierpinski's triangle

1 Introduction

Confidentiality of sensitive information makes use of an encryption function called *cipher* that converts the original message or *plaintext* into the ciphered message or *ciphertext*. In symmetric cryptography (or secret key cryptography) there is a single piece of secret information called *key*. Such a secret key is shared by both legitimate communicating parties. Secret key cryptography is currently divided into two large classes: stream ciphers and block-ciphers depending on whether the encryption function is applied either to each individual bit or to a block of bits, respectively.

Stream ciphers are the fastest and simplest among all the encryption procedures so they are in widespread use and can be found in many technological applications e.g. the encryption system E0 in Bluetooth network specifications [8], the algorithm RC4 in Microsoft Word processor and Microsoft Excel spreadsheet [21] or the SNOW 3G Generator [15] in wireless communication of high-speed data with 4G/LTE (Long-Term Evolution) technology.

The basic problem in stream cipher design is to generate from a short and truly random key a long and pseudorandom sequence called *keystream* sequence.

For encryption, the sender performs the bitwise XOR (exclusive-OR) operation among the bits of the plaintext and the keystream sequence. The result is the ciphertext to be sent to the receiver. For decryption, the receiver generates the same keystream sequence, performs the same bitwise XOR operation between the received ciphertext and the keystream sequence and recovers the original message. Notice that both encryption and decryption procedures use the same XOR logic operation, an extremely simple and balanced operation.

Most keystream generators are based on maximal-length Linear Feedback Shift Registers (LFSRs) [13] whose output sequences, the PN-sequences, are combined in a non linear way to produce pseudorandom sequences of cryptographic application. Combinational generators, non-linear filters, clock-controlled generators or irregularly decimated generators are some of the most popular keystream generators. See [11, 12, 19] for a comprehensive introduction to this topic.

Inside the family of irregularly decimated generators, we can enumerate: (a) the *shrinking generator* [6] that involves two LFSRs, (b) the *self-shrinking generator* [18] involving only one LFSR and (c) the most representative element of this family, the *generalized self-shrinking generator* or family of generators [14], that includes the self-shrinking generator as one of its members. Irregularly decimated generators produce sequences with long periods, good correlation, excellent run distribution, balancedness [9], simplicity of implementation, etc. The underlying idea of this type of generators is the irregular decimation of a PN-sequence according to the bits of another. The decimation result is a sequence that will be used as keystream sequence in the cryptographic procedure. This work focuses on the generalized self-shrinking generators and their output sequences the so-called *generalized self-shrunken sequences*.

Linear complexity, LC, is a much used metric of the security of a keystream sequence [20]. Roughly speaking, LC measures the amount of sequence bits needed to reconstruct the rest of the sequence. In cryptographic terms, linear complexity must be as large as possible; the recommended value is approximately half the sequence period, $LC \simeq T/2$. Traditionally the linear complexity of a sequence is computed by the Berlekamp-Massey algorithm [17] after having processed at least $2 \cdot LC$ bits of such a sequence. For sequences in a cryptographic range ($T = 10^{38}$), the generation and application of such an algorithm can be an extremely hard task. In spite of its importance, the linear complexity of the generalized self-shrunken sequences is a topic never considered nor analysed. In this work, we introduce a simple method of computing the linear complexity of the generalized self-shrunken sequences. No generation of such sequences is needed as we just use different shifted versions of a single PN-sequence.

The work is organized as follows. Fundamental and basic concepts used throughout the work are introduced in Sect. 2. Next in Sect. 3, the main result, a method of computing the linear complexity of generalized self-shrunken sequences, is developed; formulation, discussion and an illustrative example of such a method are also provided. Finally, conclusions in Sect. 4 end the paper.

2   Fundamentals and Basic Concepts

First of all, we introduce the concept of decimation of a binary sequence, which will be used repeatedly throughout this work. Let $\{a_i\}$ $(i = 0, 1, 2, \dots)$ be a sequence defined over the binary field of two elements, $a_i \in \mathbb{F}_2$. The decimation of the sequence $\{a_i\}$ by distance d is a new sequence $\{b_i\}$ $(i = 0, 1, 2, \dots)$ obtained by taking every d-th term of $\{a_i\}$, that is $\{b_i\} = \{a_{d \cdot i}\}$ [7].

Let L be a positive integer, and let $c_0, c_1, \dots, c_{L-1}$ be given elements of the binary field $\mathbb{F}_2$. A sequence $\{a_i\}$ satisfying the relation

$$a_{i+L} = c_1 a_{i+L-1} + c_2 a_{i+L-2} + \dots + c_{L-1} a_{i+1} + c_L a_i, \qquad i \geq 0 \qquad (1)$$

is called an L-th order linear recurring sequence in $\mathbb{F}_2$. A relation of the form given in (1) is called an L-th order homogeneous linear recurrence relationship (l.r.r.). The polynomial of degree L

$$P(x) = x^L + c_1 x^{L-1} + c_2 x^{L-2} + \dots + c_{L-1} x + c_L \in \mathbb{F}_2[x],$$

is called the characteristic polynomial of the linear recurrence relationship.

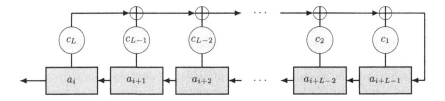

Fig. 1. An LFSR of length L

The generation of linear recurring sequences can be implemented on Linear Feedback Shift Registers (LFSRs). These devices handle information in form of bits and they are based on shifts and linear feedback. An LFSR consists of L interconnected stages (LFSR length) of binary content, the characteristic polynomial $P(x)$ of its linear recurrence relationship and the non-zero initial state (stage contents at the initial instant), see Fig. 2. If $P(x)$ is a primitive polynomial, then the register is said to be a maximal-length LFSR and its output sequence $\{a_i\}$ is called a PN-sequence of period $T = 2^L - 1$ with 2^{L-1} 1's and $(2^{L-1} - 1)$ 0's, see [13]. If α is a root of $P(x)$, then α is a primitive element in $\mathbb{F}_{2^L}$, the extension field of $\mathbb{F}_2$, that consists of 0 and appropriate powers of α [16]. Via the characteristic polynomial, there is a one-to-one correspondence

$$a_i \rightarrow \alpha^i \qquad (i = 0, 1, 2, \dots, 2^L - 2) \qquad (2)$$

between the i-th element, a_i, of the PN-sequence and the i-th power of α, notated α^i. The linear complexity is the length of the shortest LFSR that generates such a sequence or, equivalently, the lowest order linear recurrence relationship that generates such a sequence.

The more representative element in the class of irregularly decimated generators is the generalized self-shrinking generator [14] described as follows:

Definition 1. *Let* $\{a_i\}$ *(*$i = 0, 1, 2, \dots$*) be a PN-sequence generated by a maximal-length LFSR with an L-degree characteristic polynomial. Let* p *be an integer and* $\{v_i\}$ *(*$i = 0, 1, 2, \dots$*) be an p-position shifted version of* $\{a_i\}$ *with* $(p = 0, 1, 2, \dots, 2^L - 2)$*. The decimation rule is very simple:*

1. *If* $a_i = 1$*, then* v_i *is output, that is* $s_j = v_i$*.*
2. *If* $a_i = 0$*, then* v_i *is discarded and there is no output bit.*

In this way, for a fixed p *a balanced output sequence* $s_0 s_1 s_2 \dots$ *denoted by* $\{s(p)_j\}$ *or simply* $\{s_j\}$ *is generated. Such a sequence is called the generalized self-shrunken sequence (GSS) associated with the shift* p*.* ∎

Recall that $\{a_i\}$ remains fixed while $\{v_i\}$ is the sliding sequence or left-shifted version of $\{a_i\}$. When p ranges in the interval $p \in [0, 1, 2, \dots, 2^L - 2]$, then the class of $2^L - 1$ generalized self-shrunken sequences (or simply generalized sequences) is obtained. Let us see a simple example.

Example 1. For an LFSR of length $L = 4$, characteristic polynomial $P(x) = x^4 + x^3 + 1$ and initial state $(1, 1, 1, 1)$, its corresponding PN-sequence is $\{a_i\} = \{111101011001000\}$. Applying the previous decimation rule, we get $2^L - 1 = 15$ generalized sequences $\{s_j\}$ based on $\{a_i\}$ and depicted in Table 1.

The $2^L - 1 = 15$ choices of p result in the 15 distinct shifts of $\{v_i\}$. For each sequence $\{v_i\}$, a new generalized self-shrunken sequence is generated. ∎

Table 1. GSS sequences for Example 1

p	$\{s(p)_j\}$	p	$\{s(p)_j\}$
0	1111 1111	8	1001 0110
1	1110 0100	9	0010 0111
2	1101 1000	10	0100 1110
3	1010 1010	11	1000 1101
4	0101 0101	12	0001 1011
5	1011 0001	13	0011 1100
6	0110 1001	14	0111 0010
7	1100 0011		

The period of the generalized sequences is a divisor of 2^{L-1}. This class of sequences always includes [10] the sequence $\{111111, \dots\}$ for $p = 0$ and the sequences $\{101010, \dots\}$ and $\{010101, \dots\}$ for $p = n, n + 1$, where n is an integer corresponding to the power $\alpha^n \in \mathbb{F}_{2^L}$ satisfying $\alpha^{n+1} = \alpha^n + 1$.

Finally, let $\{u_i\}$ $(i = 0, 1, \ldots, 2^{L-1} - 1)$ be a sequence of period $T = 2^{L-1}$ whose terms u_i are elements of $\mathbb{F}_{2^L}$. Keeping in mind the one-to-one correspondence defined in (2), the terms of $\{u_i\}$ are the powers of α associated with the $1's$ of $\{a_i\}$. Let us see the sequence $\{u_i\}$ for the Example 1.

Table 2. Sequence $\{u_i\}$ for Example 1

$\mathbb{F}_{2^L}:$	1	α	α^2	α^3	α^4	α^5	α^6	α^7	α^8	α^9	α^{10}	α^{11}	α^{12}	α^{13}	α^{14}
$\{a_i\}:$	1	1	1	1	0	1	0	1	1	0	0	1	0	0	0
$\{u_i\}:$	1	α	α^2	α^3		α^5		α^7	α^8			α^{11}			

Thus, the sequence $\{u_i\} = \{1, \alpha, \alpha^2, \alpha^3, \alpha^5, \alpha^7, \alpha^8, \alpha^{11}\}$. It is proved [1] that the sequence $\{u_i\}$ defined as before has a linear complexity upper bounded by:

$$LC(\{u_i\}) \leq 2^{L-1} - (L - 2). \tag{3}$$

3   Linear Complexity of the Generalized Sequences

As the generalized sequences have period power of 2, then the characteristic polynomial of each generalized sequence is of the form $(x + 1)^M$ where $M = LC$. Thus, $(x + 1)^{M+1}, (x + 1)^{M+2}, (x + 1)^{M+3}, \ldots$ are characteristic polynomials of higher degree defining linear recurrence relationships that the generalized sequence has to satisfy. Contrarily, $(x + 1)^{M-1}, (x + 1)^{M-2}, (x + 1)^{M-3}, \ldots$ are not characteristic polynomials meaning that the generalized sequence does not satisfy their corresponding linear recurrence relationships. This is the key idea to compute the LC in the class of generalized self-shrunken sequences.

The coefficients of a polynomial $(x + 1)^M$ are the binomial numbers $\binom{M}{i}$ $(i = 0, 1, \ldots, M)$ of the M-th row of the Pascal's triangle [3,5]. When such a triangle is reduced mod 2, then we get the Sierpinski's triangle, see Fig. 2. Linear Cellular Automata (CA) with rules 102 and 60 [2,4,22] also define the coefficients of this type of polynomial. See the CA-images with these rules in Fig. 3, where black squares represent $1's$ and white squares (inside the figure) represent $0's$.

Next we study the linear recurrence relationships of the sequence $\{u_i\}$ for successive and decreasing values of M.

1. For $M = 2^{L-1} - (L - 2)$:

According to Eq. (3), the sequence $\{u_i\}$ satisfies the l.r.r.

$$\sum_{i=0}^{M} c_i\, u_{i+p} = 0 \qquad (p = 0, 1, 2, \ldots, 2^L - 2), \tag{4}$$

where the c_i are the binary coefficients of the $M - th$ row in the the Sierpinski's triangle or in the CA-images, see Figs. 2 and 3.

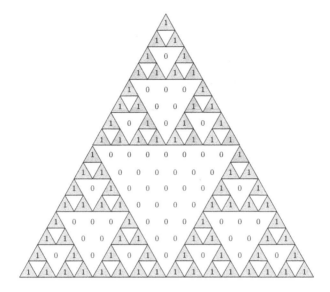

Fig. 2. Binary Sierpinski's triangle

If we denote $u_i = \alpha^{\tau(i)}$, then we can rewrite the correspondence (2) as follows

$$u_i = \alpha^{\tau(i)} \qquad \rightarrow \qquad a_{\tau(i)} \qquad (i = 0, 1, 2, \ldots, 2^L - 2).$$

Therefore,

$$\sum_{i=0}^{M} c_i\, u_{i+p} = \sum_{i=0}^{M} c_i\, \alpha^{\tau(i)+p} = 0 \quad \rightarrow \quad \sum_{i=0}^{M} c_i\, a_{\tau(i)+p} = 0, \tag{5}$$

where $\{a_{\tau(i)+p}\}$ $(i = 0, 1, 2, \ldots)$ denotes the generalized sequence $\{s(p)_j\}$ associated with the shift p. Thus, according to Eq. (5), all the generalized sequences $\{s(p)_j\}$ satisfy $\sum_{i=0}^{M} c_i\, a_{\tau(i)+p} = 0$ and their linear complexities are upper bounded by

$$LC(\{s(p)_j\}) \leq 2^{L-1} - (L - 2) \qquad (p = 0, 1, 2, \ldots, 2^L - 2).$$

So we have already determined an upper bound on the LC of all the generalized sequences.

2. For $M = 2^{L-1} - (L - 2) - 1$:

We check if the sequence $\{u_i\}$ satisfies the l.r.r. with the new value of M and the new row of coefficients c_i in the Sierpinski's triangle or in the CA-images.

$$\sum_{i=0}^{M} c_i\, u_{i+p} = \alpha^m \neq 0 \qquad (p = 0, 1, 2, \ldots, 2^L - 2),$$

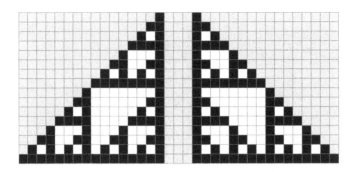

Fig. 3. CA-images: rule 102 (left) and rule 60 (right)

Therefore,

$$\sum_{i=0}^{M} c_i\, \alpha^{\tau(i)+p} = \alpha^m \quad \rightarrow \quad \sum_{i=0}^{M} c_i\, a_{\tau(i)+p} = a_{m+p}.$$

1. If $a_{m+p} = 0$ for some p, then the l.r.r. holds for the corresponding sequences $\{s(p)_j\}$ and their $LC(\{s(p)_j\}) \leq 2^{L-1} - (L-2) - 1$.
2. If $a_{m+p} = 1$ for some p, then the l.r.r. does not hold for the corresponding sequences $\{s(p)_j\}$ and their $LC(\{s(p)_j\}) = 2^{L-1} - (L-2)$.

As a_{m+p} $(p = 0, 1, 2, \ldots, 2^L - 2)$ is the PN-sequence $\{a_i\}$ starting at the term a_m, then we will have $(2^{L-1} - 1)$ terms $a_{m+p} = 0$, that is $(2^{L-1} - 1)$ generalized sequences for which the l.r.r. holds, as well as 2^{L-1} terms $a_{m+p} = 1$, that is 2^{L-1} generalized sequences for which the l.r.r. does not holds.

3. For $M = 2^{L-1} - (L-2) - 2$:

We check if the sequence $\{u_i\}$ satisfies the l.r.r. with the new value of M and the new row of coefficients c_i in the Sierpinski's triangle or in the CA-images.

In fact, for the successive values of p we have two alternative values of this l.r.r.

$$\sum_{i=0}^{M} c_i\, u_{i+p} = \alpha^{m_1} \neq 0 \qquad \sum_{i=0}^{M} c_i\, u_{i+p} = \alpha^{m_2} \neq 0.$$

This yields to:

$$\sum_{i=0}^{M} c_i\, a_{\tau(i)+p} = a_{m_1+p} \qquad \sum_{i=0}^{M} c_i\, a_{\tau(i)+p} = a_{m_2+p}.$$

Therefore, we get two shifted versions of the PN-sequence $\{a_i\}$, one of them starting at the term a_{m_1} and the other at a_{m_2}.

1. If $a_{m_1+p} = a_{m_2+p} = 0$ for some p, then the l.r.r. holds for the corresponding sequences $\{s(p)_j\}$ and $LC(\{s(p)_j\}) \leq 2^{L-1} - (L-2) - 2$.

2. If $a_{m_1+p} = a_{m_2+p} = 1$ for some p, then the l.r.r. does not hold for the corresponding sequences $\{s(p)_j\}$ and $LC(\{s(p)_j\}) = 2^{L-1} - (L-2) - 1$.

Thus, we will have $(2^{L-2} - 1)$ terms $a_{m_1+p} = a_{m_2+p} = 0$, that is there will be $(2^{L-2} - 1)$ generalized sequences with $LC(\{s(p)_j\}) \leq 2^{L-1} - (L-2) - 2$. In the same way, we will have 2^{L-2} terms $a_{m_1+p} = a_{m_2+p} = 1$, that is there will be 2^{L-2} generalized sequences with $LC(\{s(p)_j\}) = 2^{L-1} - (L-2) - 1$. For successive and decreasing values of M, that is $M = (2^{L-1} - (L-2) - 3), (2^{L-1} - (L-2) - 4), (2^{L-1} - (L-2) - 5), \ldots$, we get 4, 8, 16, ... shifted versions of the PN-sequence $\{a_i\}$. The number of generalized sequences that satisfy (do not satisfy) the linear recurrence relationship in one step is half the number of sequences obtained in the previous step. Now a numerical example is provided to clarify the method.

3.1 An Illustrative Example

Let us consider a maximal-length LFSR of length $L = 5$, characteristic polynomial $P(x) = x^5 + x^2 + 1$ and initial state $(1,1,1,1,1)$, its corresponding PN-sequence is $\{a_i\} = \{1111100011011101010000100101100\}$ with period $T = 31$. The sequence $\{u_i\} = \{1, \alpha, \alpha^2, \alpha^3, \alpha^4, \alpha^8, \alpha^9, \alpha^{11}, \alpha^{12}, \alpha^{13}, \alpha^{15}, \alpha^{17}, \alpha^{22}, \alpha^{25}, \alpha^{27}, \alpha^{28}\}$ and $\alpha^{14} = \alpha^{13} + 1$. We compute the linear recurrence relationship for different values of M.

1. For $M = 2^{L-1} - (L-2) = 13$:

The sequence $\{u_i\}$ satisfies the linear recurrence relationship given by Eq. (4), where the coefficients c_i are $(1,1,0,0,1,1,0,0,1,1,0,0,1,1)$, see the **13-th** row in Figs. 2 and 3. As $\sum_{i=0}^{13} c_i a_{\tau(i)+p} = 0$ $(p = 0,1,2,\ldots,30)$, we know that the linear complexity of all the generalized sequences is $LC(\{s(p)_j\}) \leq 13$.

2. For $M = 2^{L-1} - (L-2) - 1 = 12$:

We check if the sequence $\{u_i\}$ satisfies the linear recurrence relationship given by Eq. (4) for $M = 12$ and for the new coefficients c_i $(1,0,0,0,1,0,0,0,1,0, 0,0,1)$, see the **12-th** row in Figs. 2 and 3. In fact, $\sum_{i=0}^{12} c_i a_{\tau(i)+p} = \alpha^6 \neq 0$, then $\{a_{6+p}\}$ $(p = 0,1,2,\ldots,30)$ is the PN-sequence $\{a_i\}$ starting at the term a_6. Thus, according to Table 3, the 15 generalized sequences corresponding to $p = 0, 1, 4, 8, 10, 12, 13, 14, 15, 17, 18, 20, 23, 24, 30$ (the 0's of $\{a_{6+p}\}$ in bold) will satisfy $LC(\{s(p)_j\}) \leq 12$; while the 16 generalized sequences corresponding to the remainder values of p (the 1's of $\{a_{6+p}\}$) will have $LC(\{s(p)_j\}) = 13$. Therefore, we have computed the LC of some generalized sequences just by analysing the binary digits of the PN-sequence $\{a_{6+p}\}$.

Table 3. Linear complexity of GSS sequences

p =	0				4				8				12				16				20				24				28		30
$\{a_{6+p}\}$	0	0	1	1	0	1	1	1	0	1	0	1	0	0	0	0	1	0	0	1	0	1	1	0	0	1	1	1	1	1	0

3. For $M = 2^{L-1} - (L - 2) - 2 = 11$:

We check if the sequence $\{u_i\}$ satisfies the linear recurrence relationship given by Eq. (4) for $M = 11$ and for the new coefficients c_i (1, 1, 1, 1, 0, 0, 0, 0, 1, 1, 1, 1), see the **11-th** row in Figs. 2 and 3. Now , $\sum_{i=0}^{11} c_i \alpha_{\tau(i)+p} = \alpha^{10}, \alpha^{16} \neq 0$, alternatively for the successive values of p. Thus, according to Table 4, the 7 generalized sequences corresponding to $p = 0, 4, 8, 10, 13, 14, 20$ will satisfy $LC(\{s(p)_j\}) \leq 11$. Recall that the previous values of p correspond to the 0's coinciding in the 3 shifted PN-sequences $\{a_{6+p}\} = \{a_{10+p}\} = \{a_{16+p}\} = 0$, see the columns in bold in Table 4.

On the other hand, the 8 generalized sequences corresponding to $p = 1, 12, 15, 17, 18, 23, 24, 30$ will have $LC(\{s(p)_j\}) = 12$. Recall that the previous values of p correspond to the 1's coinciding in the 2 shifted PN-sequences $\{a_{10+p}\} = \{a_{16+p}\} = 1$ (on grey rectangles) but with $\{a_{6+p}\} = 0$, see the columns in Table 4. Therefore, the comparison of binary digits in three shifted version of a single PN-sequence allows us to compute the LC of other generalized sequences.

Table 4. Linear complexity of GSS sequences

p =	0				4				8				12				16				20				24				28		30
$\{a_{6+p}\}$	0	0	1	1	0	1	1	1	0	1	0	1	0	0	0	0	1	0	0	1	0	1	1	0	0	1	1	1	1	1	0
$\{a_{10+p}\}$	0	1	1	1	0	1	0	1	0	0	0	0	1	0	0	1	0	1	1	0	0	1	1	1	1	1	0	0	0	1	1
$\{a_{16+p}\}$	0	1	0	0	0	0	1	0	0	1	0	1	1	0	0	1	1	1	1	1	0	0	0	1	1	0	1	1	1	0	1

4. For $M = 2^{L-1} - (L - 2) - 2 = 10$:

We check if the sequence $\{u_i\}$ satisfies the linear recurrence relationship given by Eq. (4) for $M = 10$ and for the new coefficients c_i (1, 0, 1, 0, 0, 0, 0, 0, 1, 0, 1), see the **10-th** row in Figs. 2 and 3. Now , $\sum_{i=0}^{10} c_i \alpha_{\tau(i)+p} = \alpha^7, \alpha^5, \alpha^{24}, \alpha^{23} \neq 0$, alternatively for the successive values of p. Thus, according to Table 5, the 3 generalized sequences corresponding to $p = 0, 13, 14$ will satisfy $LC(\{s(p)_j\}) \leq 10$. Recall that the previous values of p correspond to the 0's coinciding in the 7 shifted PN-sequences $\{a_{6+p}\} = \{a_{10+p}\} = \{a_{16+p}\} = \{a_{7+p}\} = \{a_{5+p}\} = \{a_{24+p}\} = \{a_{23+p}\} = 0$, see the columns in bold in Table 5.

On the other hand, the 4 generalized sequences corresponding to $p = 4, 8, 10, 20$ will have $LC(\{s(p)_j\}) = 11$. Recall that the previous values of p correspond to the 1's coinciding in the 4 shifted PN-sequences $\{a_{7+p}\} = \{a_{5+p}\} = \{a_{24+p}\} = \{a_{23+p}\} = 1$ (on grey rectangles) but with $\{a_{6+p}\} = \{a_{10+p}\} = \{a_{16+p}\} = 0$, see the columns in Table 5. Now, the comparison of binary digits in seven shifted version of a single PN-sequence allows us to compute the LC of more generalized sequences.

Table 5. Linear complexity of GSS sequences

p =	0				4				8				12				16				20				24				28		30
$\{a_{6+p}\}$	0	0	1	1	0	1	1	1	0	1	0	1	0	0	0	0	1	0	0	1	0	1	1	0	0	1	1	1	1	1	0
$\{a_{10+p}\}$	0	1	1	1	0	1	0	1	0	0	0	0	1	0	0	1	0	1	1	0	0	1	1	1	1	1	0	0	0	1	1
$\{a_{16+p}\}$	0	1	0	0	0	0	1	0	0	1	0	1	1	0	0	1	1	1	1	1	0	0	0	1	1	0	1	1	0	1	1
$\{a_{7+p}\}$	0	1	1	0	1	1	1	0	1	0	1	0	0	0	0	1	0	0	1	0	1	1	0	0	1	1	1	1	1	0	0
$\{a_{5+p}\}$	0	0	0	1	1	0	1	1	1	0	1	0	1	0	0	0	0	1	0	0	1	0	1	1	0	0	1	1	1	1	1
$\{a_{24+p}\}$	0	1	0	1	1	0	0	1	1	1	1	1	0	0	0	1	1	0	1	1	1	0	1	0	1	0	0	0	0	1	0
$\{a_{23+p}\}$	0	0	1	0	1	1	0	0	1	1	1	1	1	0	0	0	1	1	0	1	1	1	0	1	0	1	0	1	0	0	0	1

5. For $M = 9, 8, 7, 6, \ldots, 2$:

We follow with the same procedure but no new values of $\sum_{i=0}^{M} c_i \alpha_{\tau(i)+p}$ are computed.

6. For $M = 1$:

We check if the sequence $\{u_i\}$ satisfies the linear recurrence relationship given by Eq. (4) for $M = 1$ and for the new coefficients c_i $(1,1)$, see the **1**-th row in Figs. 2 and 3. Now , $\sum_{i=0}^{1} c_i \alpha_{\tau(i)+p} = \alpha^{18}, \alpha^{19}, \alpha^{20}, \alpha^{21}, \alpha^{14}, \alpha^{26}, \alpha^{29}, \alpha^{30} \neq 0$, alternatively for the successive values of p. Thus, according to Table 6, the single generalized sequence corresponding to $p = 0$ will satisfy $LC(\{s(0)_j\}) = 1$. It is the identically 1 sequence. Recall that the value $p = 0$ corresponds to the 0's coinciding in the 15 shifted PN-sequences $\{a_{6+p}\} = \{a_{10+p}\} = \{a_{16+p}\} = \{a_{7+p}\} = \{a_{5+p}\} = \{a_{24+p}\} = \{a_{23+p}\} = \{a_{18+p}\} = \{a_{19+p}\} = \{a_{20+p}\} = \{a_{21+p}\} = \{a_{14+p}\} = \{a_{26+p}\} = \{a_{29+p}\} = \{a_{30+p}\} = 0$, see the column in bold in Table 6.

On the other hand, the 2 generalized sequences corresponding to $p = 13, 14$ will satisfy $LC(\{s(p)_j\}) = 2$. They correspond to the generalized sequences $\{1010 \ldots\}$ and $\{0101 \ldots\}$. Recall that the previous values of p correspond to the 1's coinciding in the 8 shifted PN-sequences $\{a_{18+p}\} = \{a_{19+p}\} = \{a_{20+p}\} = \{a_{21+p}\} = \{a_{14+p}\} = \{a_{26+p}\} = \{a_{29+p}\} = \{a_{30+p}\} = 1$ (on grey rectangles) but with $\{a_{6+p}\} = \{a_{10+p}\} = \{a_{16+p}\} = \{a_{7+p}\} = \{a_{5+p}\} = \{a_{24+p}\} = \{a_{23+p}\} = 0$, see the columns in Table 6. In this way, we have computed the LC of the whole family of generalized sequences for this example.

In a general case, there will be 2^{L-1} generalized sequences with $LC = 2^{L-1} - (L-2)$, 2^{L-2} sequences with $LC_1 < 2^{L-1} - (L-2)$, 2^{L-3} sequences with $LC_2 < LC_1$ and so on, until we get the last three generalized sequences $\{101010, \ldots\}$ and $\{010101, \ldots\}$ with $LC = 2$ and the identically 1 sequence $\{111111, \ldots\}$ with $LC = 1$. The intermediate values LC_i are in the interval $2^{L-2} < LC_i \le 2^{L-1} - (L-2)$ although they are not necessarily consecutive values.

3.2 Discussion of the Method

Notice that the method of computing the LC of the generalized self-shrunken sequences involves very simple operations. Indeed, the method is based on the comparison of a single PN-sequence with some of its shifted versions. Only one

Table 6. Linear complexity of GSS sequences

p =	0				4				8				12				16				20				24				28		30
$\{a_{6+p}\}$	0	0	1	1	0	1	1	1	0	1	0	1	0	0	0	0	1	0	0	1	0	1	1	0	0	1	1	1	1	1	0
$\{a_{10+p}\}$	0	1	1	1	0	1	0	1	0	0	0	0	1	0	0	1	0	1	1	0	0	1	1	1	1	1	0	0	0	1	1
$\{a_{16+p}\}$	0	1	0	0	0	0	1	0	0	1	0	1	1	0	0	1	1	1	1	1	0	0	0	1	1	0	1	1	1	0	1
$\{a_{7+p}\}$	0	1	1	0	1	1	1	0	1	0	1	0	0	0	0	1	0	0	1	0	1	1	0	0	1	1	1	1	1	0	0
$\{a_{5+p}\}$	0	0	0	1	1	0	1	1	1	0	1	0	1	0	0	0	0	1	0	0	1	0	1	1	0	0	1	1	1	1	1
$\{a_{24+p}\}$	0	1	0	1	1	0	0	1	1	1	1	1	0	0	0	1	1	0	1	1	1	0	1	0	1	0	0	0	0	1	0
$\{a_{23+p}\}$	0	0	1	0	1	1	0	0	1	1	1	1	1	0	0	0	1	1	0	1	1	1	0	1	0	1	0	0	0	0	1
$\{a_{18+p}\}$	0	0	0	0	1	0	0	1	0	1	1	0	0	1	1	1	1	1	0	0	0	1	1	0	1	1	1	0	1	0	1
$\{a_{19+p}\}$	0	0	0	1	0	0	1	0	1	1	0	0	1	1	1	1	1	0	0	0	1	1	0	1	1	1	0	1	0	1	0
$\{a_{20+p}\}$	0	0	1	0	0	1	0	1	1	0	0	1	1	1	1	1	0	0	0	1	1	0	1	1	1	0	1	0	1	0	0
$\{a_{21+p}\}$	0	1	0	0	1	0	1	1	0	0	1	1	1	1	1	0	0	0	1	1	0	1	1	1	0	1	0	1	0	0	0
$\{a_{14+p}\}$	0	1	0	1	0	0	0	0	1	0	0	1	0	1	1	0	0	1	1	1	1	1	0	0	0	1	1	0	1	1	1
$\{a_{26+p}\}$	0	1	1	0	0	1	1	1	1	1	0	0	0	1	1	0	1	1	1	0	1	0	1	0	0	0	0	1	0	0	1
$\{a_{29+p}\}$	0	0	1	1	1	1	1	0	0	0	1	1	0	1	1	1	0	1	0	1	0	0	0	0	1	0	0	1	0	1	1
$\{a_{30+p}\}$	0	1	1	1	1	1	0	0	0	1	1	0	1	1	1	0	1	0	1	0	0	0	0	1	0	0	1	0	1	1	0

sequence in each group of shifted PN-sequences is needed to determine the positions of $1's$ and $0's$. Thus, for an $M < 2^{L-1}-(L-2)$ given, just a linear recurrence relationship $\sum_{i=0}^{M} c_i \, \alpha_{\tau(i)+p}$ must be checked. It means that in total we will have to analyse $L - 2$ groups. For L in a cryptographic range $(L \simeq 128)$ the efficient of the computational method is quite evident.

From the point of view of the keystream generator design, the procedure here introduced allows the cryptographer to design a generalized self-shrinking generator with a guaranteed maximum linear complexity. In fact, for $M = 2^{L-1}-(L-2) - 1$ and the computation of $\sum_{i=0}^{M} c_i \, \alpha_{\tau(i)+p} = \alpha^m$, the $1's$ of the PN-sequence $\{a_{m+p}\}$ determine the possible shifts p of the generalized self-shrunken sequences $\{s(p)_j\}$ with a maximum complexity of value $LC = 2^{L-1} - (L - 2)$. In brief, we guarantee an easy design of cryptographic sequences at the price of minimum number of computational operations.

On the other hand, we know that the self-shrinking generator is an element in the class of generalized self-shrinking generators. Moreover, the self-shrunken sequence is the generalized self-shrunken sequence corresponding to the shift $p = 2^{L-1}$. Thus, the application of the previous method allows us to determine easily the linear complexity of such a sequence. In fact, $LC = M_0$, where M_0 is the first value of the parameter M for which its corresponding shifted sequence $\{a_{s+p}\}$ satisfies $a_{s+2^{L-1}} = 1$.

4   Conclusions

The class of generalized self-shrunken sequences exhibits good cryptographic properties: balancedness, long period, excellent run distribution, good correlation, speed generation, etc. Nevertheless, a fundamental metric of their security, as the linear complexity, has never been considered for this family of sequences. In this work, we present a method of computing the linear complexity of generalized self-shrunken sequences. The procedure is simple and it is based on the comparison of different shifted versions of a single PN-sequence. In fact, the concepts of linear recurrence relationship, Sierpinski's triangle and linear cellular automata make easy to compute the starting point of the shifted PN-sequences. Later the comparison of their binary digits determines the exact value of the linear complexity for the generalized sequences.

The method here developed guarantees an easy choice of generalized sequences with maximum linear complexity.

As a consequence of this work, we can say that the computation of the exact value of the self-shrunken sequence linear complexity is just the natural application of this method.

Acknowledgements. This research has been partially supported by Ministerio de Economía, Industria y Competitividad (MINECO), Agencia Estatal de Investigación (AEI), and Fondo Europeo de Desarrollo Regional (FEDER, UE) under project COPCIS, reference TIN2017-84844-C2-1-R, and by Comunidad de Madrid (Spain) under project reference S2013/ICE-3095-CIBERDINE-CM, also co-funded by European Union FEDER funds. The second author was supported by FAPESP with number of process 2015/07246-0 and CAPES.

References

1. Blackburn, S.R.: The linear complexity of the self-shrinking generator. IEEE Trans. Inf. Theory **45**(6), 2073–2077 (1999)
2. Cardell, S.D., Fúster-Sabater, A.: Linear models for the self-shrinking generator based on CA. J. Cell. Autom. **11**(2–3), 195–211 (2016)
3. Cardell, S.D., Fúster-Sabater, A.: Recovering the MSS-sequence via CA. Proc. Comput. Sci. **80**, 599–606 (2016)
4. Cardell, S.D., Fúster-Sabater, A.: Modelling the shrinking generator in terms of linear CA. Adv. Math. Commun. **10**(4), 797–809 (2016)
5. Cardell, S.D., Fúster-Sabater, A.: Linear models for high-complexity sequences. In: Gervasi, O., Murgante, B., Misra, S., Borruso, G., Torre, C.M., Rocha, A.M.A.C., Taniar, D., Apduhan, B.O., Stankova, E., Cuzzocrea, A. (eds.) ICCSA 2017. LNCS, vol. 10404, pp. 314–324. Springer, Cham (2017). https://doi.org/10.1007/978-3-319-62392-4_23
6. Coppersmith, D., Krawczyk, H., Mansour, Y.: The shrinking generator. In: Stinson, D.R. (ed.) CRYPTO 1993. LNCS, vol. 773, pp. 22–39. Springer, Heidelberg (1994). https://doi.org/10.1007/3-540-48329-2_3
7. Duvall, P.F., Mortick, J.C.: Decimation of periodic sequences. SIAM J. Appl. Math. **21**(3), 367–372 (1971)
8. Fluhrer, S., Lucks, S.: Analysis of the E0 encryption system. In: Vaudenay, S., Youssef, A.M. (eds.) SAC 2001. LNCS, vol. 2259, pp. 38–48. Springer, Heidelberg (2001). https://doi.org/10.1007/3-540-45537-X_3
9. Fúster-Sabater, A., García-Mochales, P.: A simple computational model for acceptance/rejection of binary sequence generators. Appl. Math. Model. **31**(8), 1548–1558 (2007)
10. Fúster-Sabater, A., Caballero-Gil, P.: Chaotic modelling of the generalized self-shrinking generator. Appl. Soft Comput. **11**(2), 1876–1880 (2011)
11. Fúster-Sabater, A.: Aspects of linearity in cryptographic sequence generators. In: Murgante, B., Misra, S., Carlini, M., Torre, C.M., Nguyen, H.-Q., Taniar, D., Apduhan, B.O., Gervasi, O. (eds.) ICCSA 2013. LNCS, vol. 7975, pp. 33–47. Springer, Heidelberg (2013). https://doi.org/10.1007/978-3-642-39640-3_3

12. Fúster-Sabater, A.: Generation of cryptographic sequences by means of difference equations. Appl. Math. Inf. Sci. **8**(2), 1–10 (2014)
13. Golomb, S.W.: Shift Register-Sequences. Aegean Park Press, Laguna Hill (1982)
14. Hu, Y., Xiao, G.: Generalized self-shrinking generator. IEEE Trans. Inf. Theory **50**(4), 714–719 (2004)
15. Jenkins, C., Schulte, M., Glossner, J.: Instructions and hardware designs for accelerating SNOW 3G on a software-defined radio platform. Analog Integr. Circ. Sig. Process. **69**(2–3), 207–218 (2011)
16. Lidl, R., Niederreiter, H.: Introduction to Finite Fields and Their Applications. Cambridge University Press, Cambridge (1986)
17. Massey, J.L.: Shift-register synthesis and BCH decoding. IEEE Trans. Inf. Theory **15**(1), 122–127 (1969)
18. Meier, W., Staffelbach, O.: The self-shrinking generator. In: De Santis, A. (ed.) EUROCRYPT 1994. LNCS, vol. 950, pp. 205–214. Springer, Heidelberg (1995). https://doi.org/10.1007/BFb0053436
19. Menezes, A.J., et al.: Handbook of Applied Cryptography. CRC Press, New York (1997)
20. Paar, C., Pelzl, J.: Understanding Cryptography. Springer, Berlin (2010)
21. Paul, G., Maitra, S.: RC4 Stream Cipher and its Variants. CRC Press, Taylor and Francis Group, Boca Raton (2012)
22. Wolfram, S.: Cellular automata as simple self-organizing system. Caltrech preprint CALT 68-938 (1982)

Finding a Starting Vertex for the Reverse Cuthill-McKee Method for Bandwidth Reduction: A Comparative Analysis Using Asymmetric Matrices

Sanderson L. Gonzaga de Oliveira[1]($\boxtimes$), Alexandre A. A. M. de Abreu[2], Diogo T. Robaina[3], and Mauricio Kischinhevsky[3]

[1] Universidade Federal de Lavras, Lavras, MG, Brazil
sanderson@dcc.ufla.br
[2] Inst. Federal de Educação,
Ciência e Tec. de Santa Catarina, Canoinhas, SC, Brazil
alexandre.abreu@ifsc.edu.br
[3] Universidade Federal Fluminense, Niterói, RJ, Brazil
{drobaina,kisch}@ic.uff.br

Abstract. The need to find pseudo-peripheral vertices arises from many methods for ordering sparse matrix equations. Several algorithms have been proposed to find proper starting vertices to be used in conjunction with heuristics for bandwidth reductions since the 1970s. This paper reviews the main algorithms for the identification of pseudo-peripheral vertices and selects seven out of these algorithms as potentially being the most promising low-cost methods for solving the problem of finding a proper pseudo-peripheral vertex in a graph. This work evaluates these seven low-cost methods. Extensive experiments among these algorithms in conjunction with the reverse Cuthill-McKee method applied to a large set of standard benchmark instances suggest that Pachl's algorithm is a suitable alternative for reducing the bandwidth of matrices with asymmetric sparsity patterns.

Keywords: Bandwidth reduction · Graph labeling
Reordering algorithms · Reverse Cuthill-McKee method · Sparse matrix

1 Introduction

Many applications in modern engineering require the analysis and solution of large-scale and complex problems defined by a set of linear equations in the form $Ax = b$, where $A = [a_{ij}]$ is an $n \times n$ large-scale sparse matrix, x is the unknown n-vector solution which is sough, and b is a known n-vector. Hence, methods for solving these linear systems are among the most fundamental computational kernels in many numerical simulations, such as in finite-element analysis. The kinds of problems that originate matrices in published matrix benchmark collections [1] give a notion of the number of applications relying on large-scale

© Springer International Publishing AG, part of Springer Nature 2018
O. Gervasi et al. (Eds.): ICCSA 2018, LNCS 10960, pp. 123–137, 2018.
https://doi.org/10.1007/978-3-319-95162-1_9

sparse linear systems. Thus, efforts to develop fast approaches (and experiments to evaluate the state-of-the-art algorithms in this context) with the objective of solving linear systems are quite important since these systems play a major role in a wide range of real-world and applied applications in computational science. In particular, an efficient solution using a direct method requires ordering the variables of the problem. Additionally, another method for solving these types of linear equations, which have found ample use in a finite-element analysis, is a frontal solution scheme. These methods should process the equations in a proper order to compute the solution efficiently. Thereby, it is necessary to order the equations for the algorithm to present a low computational cost. Specifically in finite-element analysis, performing a vertex reordering is equivalent to reorder the equations in the case of one degree of freedom per node. Similarly, performing a vertex reordering is also equivalent to reorder the equations in partial differential equations finite-volume discretizations. Applying a heuristic for matrix bandwidth reductions can reduce the computational cost of iterative solvers for the solution of a sparse linear system of equations (see [2] and references therein). To provide more specific detail, the transfer of information to and from memory is related to the number of non-null coefficients in the rows of the matrix system A. An application obtains a lower rate of cache misses if the non-null coefficients in each row lie in the same level of the memory hierarchy. Thus, this links cache misses to the bandwidth of A. Therefore, an adequate order of vertices of a graph is crucial to maximize locality in iterative linear system solvers and improve performance in graph algorithms.

Systematic reviews [2–6] reported the reverse Cuthill-McKee method (RCM) [7] with starting vertex given by the George-Liu (GL) algorithm [8] as one of the most promising low-cost methods for bandwidth reductions. Specifically, the RCM-GL method [9] is one of the best-known and widely used heuristics for bandwidth reductions [2–6,9–11] because it is capable of obtaining high-quality solutions at low cost. Previous publications [2,6] reported that the RCM-GL method provides better results than metaheuristic-based heuristics for bandwidth reduction if the most relevant subject in this context, i.e., computing time, is taken into account.

The reverse Cuthill-McKee method [7] is an example of heuristics known as level set reorderings, where the vertices in a graph are labeled considering that the algorithm firstly partitions the vertices into level sets. This means that the vertices are partitioned taking into account the distance from a given starting vertex. Thus, the choice of the starting vertex strongly affects the quality of the resulting ordering given by this method. In general, the reverse Cuthill-McKee method obtains better results when the width of a level structure rooted at the starting vertex is small, and its eccentricity is very close to the diameter of the graph. Moreover, the execution cost of an algorithm for finding an appropriate starting vertex for the reverse Cuthill-McKee method can be even higher than the execution cost of the proper reverse Cuthill-McKee method [12]. Thus, the bandwidth results of the reverse Cuthill-McKee method executed after an algorithm for finding a starting vertex must be significantly superior to the results of the reverse Cuthill-McKee method achieved without using an algorithm for the identification of a starting vertex.

A peripheral vertex is a proper starting vertex for heuristics for bandwidth reductions. However, finding peripheral vertices in graphs is computationally expensive, that is, for a graph $G = (V, E)$, one can find a peripheral vertex by executing $|V|$ breadth-first search procedures; however, it takes $O(|V|(|V|+|E|))$ time in these operations. As a result, many heuristics for bandwidth reductions use pseudo-peripheral vertices instead of using peripheral vertices. There exist alternative algorithms for finding peripheral vertices, including Arany's algorithm [13], but these algorithms are still computationally expensive when compared with an algorithm for finding a pseudo-peripheral vertex. Thus, several heuristics for bandwidth reductions require as a first step the determination of a pseudo-peripheral vertex.

As mentioned, users have employed the reverse Cuthill-McKee method [7] with starting vertices given by the the George-Liu algorithm [8] since the 1980s (see [2,4–6,9–11] and references therein). With the objective of providing a proper starting vertex to this method, this paper evaluates the results of the George-Liu algorithm [8] against six promising low-cost algorithms for finding pseudo-peripheral vertices.

This paper is organized as follows. Section 2 reviews background information. Section 3 reviews algorithms for finding pseudo-peripheral vertices and selects seven promising low-cost algorithms for the determination of proper pseudo-peripheral vertices in a graph, i.e., these low-cost algorithms show small hidden constants in the functions that represent the order of growth of their running times. Section 4 describes how the simulations were conducted. Section 5 shows the results. Finally, Sect. 6 provides the conclusions.

2   Definitions and Notation

This section gives definitions related to the characteristics of the graph representation of ordering. Bandwidth $\beta(A)$ is the largest distance between the non-null coefficient of the lower triangular matrix and the main diagonal considering all rows of the matrix. The bandwidth minimization problem is NP-hard [14].

The reverse Cuthill-McKee method [7] is based on graph-theoretical concepts. It labels the vertices of a graph $G(V, E)$ in increasing-distance order from a given pseudo-peripheral vertex v. Specifically, it labels vertices with the same distance from the vertex v in increasing-degree order. Finally, the ordering is reversed. Therefore, the final label of vertex v is $|V|$. Thus, ordering the vertices in such a manner partitions them into *level sets* according to the distance from the pseudo-peripheral vertex v.

The reverse Cuthill-McKee [7] for bandwidth reductions is based on a data structure known as *rooted level structure* (RLS). Given a vertex $v \in V$, the level structure $\mathscr{L}(v)$ rooted at vertex v, with depth $\ell(v)$, is the partitioning $\mathscr{L}(v) = \{L_0(v), L_1(v), \ldots, L_{\ell(v)}(v)\}$, where $L_0(v) = \{v\}$ and $L_i(v) = Adj(L_{i-1}(v)) - \bigcup_{j=0}^{i-1} L_j(v)$, for $i = 1, 2, 3, \ldots, \ell(v)$, $Adj(U) = \{w \in V : (u \in U \subseteq V)\ \{u, w\} \in$

$E\}$, $\ell(v) = \max\limits_{u \in V}[d(v, u)]$ denotes the *eccentricity* of the vertex v, and the *distance* $d(v, u)$ is the length of a shortest path connecting vertices v and u. In particular, the diameter of a graph $G = (V, E)$ is the maximum eccentricity of any vertex in the graph and is defined as $\Phi(G) = \max\limits_{v \in V}(\ell(v))$ and, if $\ell(v) = \Phi(G)$, then v is a peripheral vertex. The *width* of an RLS $\mathscr{L}(u)$ is defined as $b(\mathscr{L}(u)) = \max\limits_{0 \leq i \leq \ell(u)} [\|L_i(u)\|]$.

Since Cuthill and McKee [15] showed that $\beta(A) \leq 2b(\mathscr{L}(v)) - 1$, a method for bandwidth reduction based on an RLS $\mathscr{L}(v)$ with narrow width $b(\mathscr{L}(v))$ is sought. Thus, results of many graph theoretic-based heuristics for bandwidth reductions depend upon the choice of a starting vertex.

3 A Review of Algorithms for Finding Pseudo-Peripheral Vertices and Algorithms Evaluated

In 1973, Cheng [16] used a vertex of minimum degree satisfying some conditions as the starting vertex for the method for bandwidth reduction that the author proposed. In 1976, Gibbs et al. [17] proposed an algorithm to find two pseudo-peripheral vertices for their method.

The George-Liu algorithm [8] (from 1979) is an improvement over the algorithm for the identification of pseudo-peripheral vertices proposed by Gibbs et al. [17]. This algorithm shows low computational costs in practical tests [2,6]. In particular, Smyth [18] verified that the algorithm for finding pseudo-peripheral vertices proposed by Gibbs et al. [17] requires substantially more computer time than the George-Liu algorithm [8]. Thus, the George-Liu algorithm [8] was implemented and evaluated in this computational experiment. In exploratory experiments, we evaluated a modified George-Liu algorithm [8] starting with a random vertex r. It shrinks $L_{\ell(r)}(r)$ also by determining a random vertex. The results of this variation were not competitive with the results of the George-Liu algorithm [8].

In 1983, Arany [19] proposed an algorithm for the identification of pseudo-peripheral vertices that is similar to the George-Liu algorithm [8]. To provide more specific detail, from an arbitrary vertex v, Arany's algorithm [19] shrinks $L_{\ell(v)}(v)$ to the vertex of largest eccentricity u instead of using the vertex of minimum degree in $L_{\ell(v)}(v)$ as it is applied in the George-Liu algorithm [8]. If $\ell(u) = \ell(v)$, then the algorithm stops; otherwise u is attributed to v and the process is repeated. The author provided no comparisons and this algorithm is more expensive than the George-Liu algorithm [8].

Pachl [20] proposed an algorithm for the identification of pseudo-peripheral vertices in 1984. This algorithm grows in $O\left(|E|\sqrt{|V|}\right)$ time [20] and is also implemented and evaluated in our experiments since no publication was found that presented simulations and comparisons in a way that could indicate that this algorithm might be considered to be surpassed by any other algorithm for the identification of pseudo-peripheral vertices. We evaluated in exploratory experiments a modified Pachl's algorithm [20] starting with a vertex with minimum degree v and obtaining also a vertex with minimum degree from $\mathscr{L}(v)$. The results of this variation were not competitive enough with the results obtained by the use of Pachl's algorithm [20].

In 1985, Smyth [18] considered nine algorithms for finding pseudo-peripheral vertices. Two of these algorithms were proposed by Arany, the algorithm of Gibbs et al. [17], the George-Liu algorithm [8], and five algorithms were proposed by the author himself. Arany's and Smyth's [18] algorithms are based on the width of an RLS. Smyth [18] compared four algorithms (the George-Liu algorithm [8], two variants of Arany's algorithm, and Smyth's Maximum Swing algorithm) since the five other algorithms required substantially more computer time than the others. The George-Liu algorithm [8] superseded the other three algorithms that were compared by Smyth [18] since the George-Liu algorithm [8] provided similar results at lower computational times.

In 1986, Sloan [21] proposed an algorithm based on the $\ell(v)$, $b(\mathscr{L}(v))$, and in a shrinking strategy recommended by George and Liu [8] that reduces the number of vertices to be verified, following also the idea of the same authors [8] of sorting vertices by their degree. In 1989, Duff et al. [22] proposed a strategy of rejecting any vertex in $L_{\ell(v)}(v)$ that had a neighbor which has already been tested, but this strategy is more expensive than Sloan's shrinking strategy. Duff et al. [22] also limited the search to one vertex of each degree, which they found to be significantly less expensive while having little effect on the quality of the final ordering. This strategy was also used by Sloan [23], in 1989, so that Sloan's algorithm [23] for the identification of pseudo-peripheral vertices was included in our experiments. Specifically, Sloan's algorithm [23] returns two pseudo-peripheral vertices: a starting vertex v and a target-end vertex u. The pseudo-peripheral vertex u is evaluated to have a narrow width $b(\mathscr{L}(u))$ and this algorithm forces the starting pseudo-peripheral vertex v to present large $\ell(v)$. We also implemented and evaluated a modified Sloan's algorithm [23] starting with an arbitrary vertex instead of starting with a vertex with minimum degree. The results of this modified Sloan's algorithm were not better than the results of Sloan's algorithm [23].

In 2000, Kaveh and Bondarabady [24] (KB2) proposed an algorithm for finding pseudo-peripheral vertices based on Sloan's algorithm [23]. The Kaveh-Bondarabady algorithm was also implemented and evaluated in our computational experiment and we will refer this algorithm as KB2. Another algorithm implemented and evaluated in a previous publication [12] was a slightly modification in the Kaveh-Bondarabady algorithm [24] by starting with an arbitrary vertex instead of starting with a vertex with minimum degree, termed MKB2 algorithm. Its results provided an improvement in the results of the Kaveh-Bondarabady algorithm [24] when considering the bandwidth reduction of asymmetric matrices performed in conjunction with the reverse Cuthill-McKee method [7]. Nevertheless, a previous publication [12] showed that the RCM-GL method [9] dominated both the RCM-KB2 and RCM-MKB2 algorithms.

In 1986, Kaveh [25] proposed six algorithms for finding pseudo-peripheral vertices: we will refer these algorithms as KA, KB,..., KF algorithms. In the same year, Kaveh [26] described also the KF algorithm. In 1991, Kaveh [27] described also the KC and KF algorithms and proposed an algorithm named K91B in our computational experiment. The KA and KD algorithms [25] grow in $O(|V|(|V| + |E|))$ time and the KE algorithm is impractical according to the results presented by Kaveh [25]. The KB, KC, KF [25], and K91B [27] algorithms are faster than the KA and KD algorithms. Additionally, the hidden constant in the function that represent the order of growth of the running times of the K91B algorithm [27] is undoubtedly larger than those presented in the KB and KC algorithms [25]. Moreover, the KF algorithm [25] presents an even larger hidden constant than the K91B algorithm [27]. Kaveh [27] described an algorithm for the identification of pseudo-peripheral vertices named D algorithm by the author. This algorithm is more time consuming than the KB and KC algorithms [25]. In particular, Kaveh [27] showed no example and no comparison among the algorithms described so that the K91B algorithm was also implemented and evaluated in our experiments. In general, Kaveh's algorithms for the identification of pseudo-peripheral vertices follow the recommendation named *short circuiting* by George and Liu [8], i.e., Kaveh's algorithms terminate to construct any RLS whose width exceeds the narrowest RLS so far found.

Kaveh [25] compared the results of the KA, KB,..., KF algorithms. These six algorithms were applied to 13 instances. Then, the author showed the computational costs and bandwidth reductions considering the 4-steps algorithm for bandwidth reduction [25]. The KB and KC algorithms [25] showed the lowest computational costs and the results of the KB algorithm were better than the results of the KC algorithm. Thus, the KB algorithm [25] was implemented and evaluated here.

Kaveh [27,28] proposed algorithms for finding pseudo-peripheral vertices based on the algebraic graph theory in 1990 and 1991. The computational costs of these algorithms are certainly higher than the computational costs of the KB and KC algorithms [25]. In particular, Kaveh [29] provided details about these algorithms and, in 2002, Kaveh and Bondarabady [30] applied algorithms for finding pseudo-peripheral vertices described by Kaveh [29] in a hybrid method for finite-element ordering.

In 1990, Grimes et al. [31] proposed two algorithms for finding pseudo-peripheral vertices based on the eigenvector of the adjacency matrix corresponding to the largest eigenvalue. In 1993, Souza and Murray [32] proposed an alternative algorithm for the identification of pseudo-peripheral vertices that seems to reach higher computational costs than the algorithm for finding pseudo-peripheral vertices proposed by Gibbs et al. [17]. Moreover, the algorithms proposed by Grimes et al. [31] and the Souza-Murray algorithm yielded no promising results in relation to the other algorithms that the authors compared (and have been already reviewed here).

In 1992, Luo [33] proposed an algorithm for the identification of pseudo-peripheral vertices based on the algorithm for finding pseudo-peripheral vertices proposed by Gibbs et al. [17]. Luo's algorithm [33] may be fast. Nevertheless,

Luo's algorithm [33] showed no promising results in relation to the algorithm for finding pseudo-peripheral vertices proposed by Gibbs et al. [17].

In 1994, Paulino et al. [34] proposed an algorithm for the identification of pseudo-peripheral vertices using the first and last vertices of the spectral permutation, without constructing level structures, i.e., the authors employed spectral techniques applied to graphs. The eigensolution scheme proposed made the algorithm very time-consuming when compared to the George-Liu algorithm [8] and the algorithm for finding pseudo-peripheral vertices proposed by Gibbs et al. [17], as examples.

In 1999, Reid and Scott [35] proposed a method based on the George-Liu algorithm [8]. In spite of the Reid-Scott algorithm [35] being more expensive than the George-Liu algorithm [8], it was included in our experiments.

In 2012, Wang et al. [36] (and references therein) proposed an algorithm that combines the widths of RLSs and eccentricities of vertices to define pseudo-peripheral vertices. This algorithm is doubtless more expensive than the George-Liu [8], Luo's [20], and Kaveh's B [25] algorithms.

4 Description of the Tests

Seven algorithms for finding pseudo-peripheral vertices were implemented and evaluated in this computational experiment (George-Liu [8], Pachl's [20], Kaveh's B [25], Sloan's [23], K91B [27], Reid-Scott [35], and KB2 [24]) in conjunction with the reverse Cuthill-McKee method [7] for bandwidth reductions. Additionally, the bandwidth reductions provided by the reverse Cuthill-McKee method are evaluated without using an algorithm for the identification of pseudo-peripheral vertices, i.e., there is no search for a pseudo-peripheral vertex. To provide more specific detail for this method, the first vertex established in the entry file of the instance is used as the starting vertex of the reverse Cuthill-McKee ordering.

To evaluate the bandwidth reductions provided by the selected algorithms, 63 small asymmetric instances [1] were used in this computational experiment. The 63 asymmetric instances were divided into two subsets: (i) 18 instances, ranging from 30 to 199 vertices; and (ii) 45 instances, ranging from 207 to 1104 vertices. This subdivision of the 63 asymmetric instances into two sets of instances is common in the field [6]. Additionally, we used 10 asymmetric instances (with sizes ranging from 659,033 to 1,505,785 vertices and composed of up to 27,130,349 non-null coefficients ($|E|$)) contained in the SuiteSparse matrix collection [1].

The algorithms were implemented in the C++ programming language. Specifically, the g++ version 4.8.2 compiler was used.

The workstation used in the executions of the simulations contained an Intel® Core™ i7-4770 (CPU 3.40 GHz, 8 MB Cache, 8 GB of main memory DDR3 1.333 GHz) (Intel; Santa Clara, CA, United States). The Ubuntu 14.04.4 LTS 64-bit operating system with Linux kernel-version 4.2.0-36-generic was used on this machine.

In this field, a common metric to evaluate the results of heuristics for bandwidth results is to compare the bandwidth results of the heuristics by counting the number of times that the heuristic obtained the smallest bandwidth on the instances used. This metric is also employed in this work. On the other hand, an algorithm can be recognized as the best one in a dataset when it obtains on average the best bandwidth results among all of the algorithms evaluated, without necessarily reaching the largest number of best results. Thereby, to analyze the quality of the bandwidth results attained using the algorithms evaluated, for each algorithm H in each dataset, we use a metric recently proposed [6]. We calculate $\rho = \sum_{i=1}^{N} \frac{\beta_H(i) - \beta_{min}(i)}{\beta_{min}(i)}$ for each instance i, where $\beta_H(i)$ is the bandwidth obtained when using an algorithm H applied to the instance i, $\beta_{min}(i)$ is the smallest bandwidth obtained in the instance i (using the algorithms evaluated or the original bandwidth), and N is the number of instances. In particular, this metric is not bounded, i.e., if an algorithm performs poorly on a given instance i, $\frac{\beta_H(i) - \beta_{min}(i)}{\beta_{min}(i)}$ and ρ can be arbitrarily large. This was exactly the objective when this metric was designed. According to this metric, a more regular algorithm performs better than an algorithm that obtains the best results when applied to many instances but yields poor results in a few instances. Thus, similar to any other metric in this context, the ρ metric strongly depends both on the dataset chosen and the algorithms evaluated.

In addition to the ρ metric, we use here another metric. For each algorithm H in each dataset, we calculate $\upsilon = \sum_{i=1}^{N} \frac{\beta_H(i) - \beta_{min}(i)}{\beta_{max}(i)}$ for each instance i, where $\beta_{max}(i)$ is the largest bandwidth obtained in the instance i (using the algorithms evaluated). This is a bounded metric, i.e., it ensures $0 \leq \upsilon \leq 1$. To the best of our knowledge, this paper is the first (published) instance of this metric being used in the field.

5   Results and Analysis

Tables in this section show the instance's name and size (n), the value of the initial bandwidth (β_0) of the instance, and the average values of bandwidth and runtime obtained by each algorithm in 10 runs performed on each small instance contained in the SuiteSparse matrix collection [1]. Three runs were performed on each large-scale instance used here. Sections 5.1 and 5.2 show the results delivered by the algorithms evaluated in reducing bandwidth when applied to small and large-scale instances contained in the SuiteSparse matrix collections [1], respectively.

5.1   Experiments Using Small Instances

This section presents the bandwidth results of the reverse Cuthill-McKee method executed after seven algorithms for finding pseudo-peripheral vertices. These algorithms are applied to 63 small asymmetric instances.

Table 1 and Fig. 1(a) contain the results of eight algorithms applied to reduce the bandwidth of 18 small asymmetric instances. Table 1 shows that the ρ metric gives a better indication of the performance achieved by these algorithms than the v metric. However, even the ρ metric does not show differences in the performance obtained by the algorithms evaluated.

Table 1. Results of the reverse Cuthill-McKee method [7] along with seven algorithms for finding pseudo-peripheral vertices applied to reduce the bandwidth of 18 small asymmetric instances. The symbol "—" indicates that the reverse Cuthill-McKee method was applied without the use of an algorithm for finding pseudo-peripheral vertices.

Instance	n	β_0	GL	Pachl	KB	Sloan	K91B	RS	KB2	—	Min. found
arc130	130	125	123	126	124	127	125	123	127	123	123
curtis54	54	44	36	28	29	36	31	36	30	36	28
fs_183_1	183	181	164	175	176	180	175	164	172	162	162
gent113	113	101	108	110	105	99	106	108	104	102	99
gre__115	115	101	110	110	110	52	97	107	110	70	52
gre__185	185	60	57	40	45	59	57	57	54	39	39
ibm32	32	26	30	22	30	27	29	30	27	29	22
impcol_b	59	43	48	50	58	48	58	48	56	48	43
impcol_c	137	91	96	96	111	111	96	96	106	100	91
lns__131	131	111	95	94	91	104	103	112	115	118	91
mcca	180	65	106	168	106	106	169	64	88	59	59
pores_1	30	11	14	14	11	14	11	14	14	14	11
steam3	80	43	7	7	7	7	7	7	7	7	7
west0132	132	94	99	105	106	107	106	109	109	105	94
west0156	156	147	149	150	141	149	129	150	147	149	129
west0167	167	158	154	165	165	166	156	154	154	154	154
will199	199	169	181	189	187	184	185	181	196	181	169
will57	57	44	16	16	16	19	16	16	13	21	13
Number of best results		5	3	3	3	3	3	3	3	6	—
	ρ	10	4	4	4	4	5	4	4	3	
	v	3	2	2	2	2	3	2	2	2	

Table 2 and Fig. 1(b) contain the results of eight algorithms applied to reduce the bandwidth of 45 small asymmetric instances. The ρ metric in Table 2 shows that the Reid-Scott [35] and Pachl's [20] algorithms (along with the RCM method [7]) reached the second and third best results (13.1 and 13.2) in this dataset, respectively. This table shows that these two algorithms obtained very close results to the reverse Cuthill-McKee method without using an algorithm for finding pseudo-peripheral vertices (11.3). To recognize that these values are close, a reference value is the value of the metric when applied to the original bandwidth of the instances (32.3). On the other hand, the v metric in Table 2 shows that Pachl's [20] and Reid-Scott [35] algorithms (along with the RCM method) achieved the second and third best results (3.2 and 3.7) in this dataset, respectively. Pachl's algorithm [20] (alongside the RCM method) returned large band-

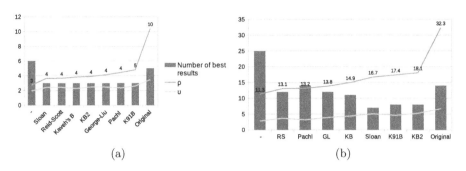

(a)   (b)

Fig. 1. Number of best bandwidth results and the ρ and υ metrics obtained by seven algorithms for finding pseudo-peripheral vertices in conjunction with the reverse Cuthill-McKee method [7] when applied to (a) 18 and (b) 45 small asymmetric instances. The symbol "-" indicates that the reverse Cuthill-McKee method was applied without using an algorithm for finding pseudo-peripheral vertices.

width values when applied to instances such as jpwh_991, mcfe, west0479, and west0989. The Reid-Scott algorithm [35] (in conjunction with the RCM method), however, yielded reasonable results when applied to these instances. Since the υ metric is bounded, the large bandwidth results delivered by Pachl's algorithm [20] in these instances are limited when using this metric.

5.2 Experiments Using Large-Scale Instances

Table 2 shows that both ρ and υ metrics indicate that the reverse Cuthill-McKee method [7] (without the use of an algorithm for finding pseudoperipheral vertices) shows better results than the other algorithms evaluated. Concerning the algorithms for finding pseudoperipheral vertices, both ρ and υ metrics in Table 2 show that Pachl's [20], Reid-Scott [35], and George-Liu [8] algorithms reached the best results in the dataset composed of 45 small asymmetric instances. Thus, these four algorithms were applied to 10 large-scale asymmetric instances contained in the SuiteSparse matrix collection [1].

Table 3 and Fig. 2(a) show bandwidth results of three algorithms for finding pseudo-peripheral vertices in conjunction with the reverse Cuthill-McKee method [7] applied to 10 asymmetric instances contained in the SuiteSparse matrix collection [1]. This table and figure show that both ρ and υ metrics indicate that Pachl's algorithm [20] delivered the best bandwidth results when applied in conjunction with the reverse Cuthill-McKee method [7].

Table 4 and Fig. 2(b) show execution times in simulations using four methods when applied to 10 asymmetric matrices contained in the SuiteSparse matrix collection [1]. For clarity, Fig. 2(b) does not show the execution times of the algorithms when applied to the webbase-1M instance. As expected, the reverse Cuthill-McKee method [7] was the lowest time-consuming algorithm evaluated. In particular, Table 4 shows that an algorithm for finding pseudoperipheral vertices is much slower than the reverse Cuthill-McKee method.

Table 2. Results of the reverse Cuthill-McKee method [7] along with seven algorithms for finding pseudo-peripheral vertices applied to reduce the bandwidth of 45 small asymmetric instances. The symbol "—" indicates that the reverse Cuthill-McKee method was applied without the use of an algorithm for finding pseudo-peripheral vertices.

Instance	Vertices	β_0	GL	Pachl	KB	Sloan	K91B	RS	KB2	—	Min. found
bp_1000	822	820	820	820	820	821	820	820	820	799	799
bp_1200	822	820	815	821	820	821	820	820	821	807	807
bp_1400	822	820	820	821	820	821	821	820	821	806	806
bp_1600	822	820	820	820	820	821	821	821	821	809	809
bp__200	822	820	820	820	820	818	820	820	821	813	813
bp__400	822	820	820	820	820	818	821	820	813	807	807
bp__600	822	820	820	821	821	818	820	820	821	802	802
bp__800	822	820	819	820	820	821	819	820	821	799	799
bp___0	822	820	819	819	821	817	821	818	820	768	768
fs_541_1	541	540	539	539	539	540	540	539	540	539	539
fs_680_1	680	600	670	665	632	624	649	664	624	636	600
fs_760_1	760	740	759	730	724	750	759	759	748	718	718
gre_216a	216	36	36	36	36	36	36	36	36	36	36
gre_343	343	49	49	49	49	49	49	49	49	49	49
gre_512	512	64	64	64	64	64	64	64	64	64	64
hor_131	434	421	101	92	84	101	86	101	96	101	84
impcol_a	207	167	192	181	192	190	200	192	191	193	167
impcol_d	425	406	418	284	419	416	413	414	337	413	284
impcol_e	225	92	177	102	193	193	122	197	196	102	92
jpwh_991	991	197	657	657	657	900	965	510	929	432	197
lnsp_511	511	57	438	436	435	413	488	438	435	494	57
mbeacxc	487	490	486	485	485	486	486	486	486	485	485
mbeaflw	487	490	486	485	485	486	486	486	486	485	485
mbeause	492	490	490	490	490	490	489	490	490	490	489
mcfe	765	187	424	709	424	424	712	424	436	214	187
nnc261	261	64	36	36	36	37	36	36	37	37	36
nnc666	666	262	207	220	220	207	207	207	220	208	207
orsirr_2	886	554	160	138	134	157	160	160	157	161	134
pores_3	532	77	26	17	30	30	26	26	53	17	17
saylr1	238	14	14	14	15	14	15	14	14	14	14
saylr3	1000	100	57	57	57	88	62	57	93	57	57
sherman4	1104	368	27	27	52	60	27	27	52	41	27
shl__200	663	661	661	661	660	658	660	659	662	642	642
shl__400	663	662	662	662	661	659	661	662	662	619	619
shl___0	663	661	659	660	661	659	658	659	662	643	643
steam1	240	146	50	53	50	50	50	50	50	50	50
steam2	600	331	63	63	79	63	79	63	63	63	63
str__200	363	359	349	354	361	360	353	349	356	349	349
str__600	363	359	351	335	349	357	344	351	359	351	335
str___0	363	359	356	361	361	356	360	356	342	361	342
west0381	381	363	376	373	375	375	380	378	380	376	363
west0479	479	388	460	456	454	453	417	402	436	452	388
west0497	497	416	393	393	394	394	414	393	384	419	384
west0655	655	564	650	639	632	650	638	639	635	630	564
west0989	989	855	899	898	875	875	902	865	867	892	855
Number of best results		14	12	14	11	7	8	12	8	25	—
ρ		32.3	**13.8**	**13.2**	14.9	16.7	17.4	**13.1**	18.1	**11.3**	
υ		6.7	**3.9**	**3.2**	4.4	5.1	4.6	**3.7**	5.2	**2.8**	

Table 3. Bandwidth results of three algorithms for finding pseudo-peripheral vertices applied in conjunction with the reverse Cuthill-McKee method [7] to reduce the bandwidth of 10 asymmetric instances contained in the SuiteSparse matrix collection [1]. The symbol "—" indicates that the reverse Cuthill-McKee method was applied without the use of an algorithm for finding pseudo-peripheral vertices.

Instance	Vertices	$|E|$	β_0	Pachl	—	GL	RS
pre2	659033	5834044	117686	97846	106715	106715	106715
ASIC_680k	682862	2638997	682779	682389	682385	682389	682389
ASIC_680ks	682712	1693767	681277	112761	112761	156392	156392
tmt_unsym	917825	4584801	2161	942	1081	946	946
webbase-1M	1000005	3105536	987649	999273	981870	999795	999818
atmosmodd	1270432	881488	21904	7773	7773	7773	7773
atmosmodj	1270432	881488	21904	7773	7773	7773	7773
Hamrle3	1447360	5514242	1442878	1446283	1442845	1442845	1442845
atmosmodl	1489752	1031976	39204	7183	7183	7183	7183
cage14	1505785	27130349	676026	200188	200311	200311	200311
Number of best results			0	8	6	5	4
ρ			17.02	0.02	0.24	0.50	0.50
υ			4.38	0.02	0.21	0.38	0.38

Table 4. Execution times, in seconds, of three algorithms for finding pseudo-peripheral vertices applied in conjunction with the reverse Cuthill-McKee method [7] to reduce the bandwidth of 10 asymmetric instances contained in the SuiteSparse matrix collection [1]. The symbol "—" indicates that the reverse Cuthill-McKee method was applied without the use of an algorithm for finding pseudo-peripheral vertices

Instance	Vertices	$|E|$	—	Pachl	GL	RS
pre2	659033	5834044	0.8	1.9	1.9	3.8
ASIC_680k	682862	2638997	1.0	1.5	2.4	6.0
ASIC_680ks	682712	1693767	1.0	54.2	77.5	101.4
tmt_unsym	917825	4584801	0.4	1.3	1.9	5.4
webbase-1M	1000005	3105536	3450.8	150655.1	282628.8	643198.7
atmosmodd	1270432	881488	0.8	2.0	2.5	6.5
atmosmodj	1270432	881488	0.8	2.0	2.5	6.4
Hamrle3	1447360	5514242	0.7	2.8	2.0	5.00
atmosmodl	1489752	1031976	1.0	2.5	3.0	8.1
cage14	1505785	27130349	3.4	7.5	9.5	25.1

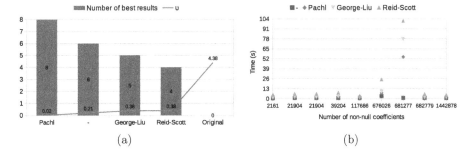

Fig. 2. Number of best bandwidth results, the v metric, and times, in seconds, obtained by three algorithms for finding pseudo-peripheral vertices in conjunction with the reverse Cuthill-McKee method [7] when applied to 10 large-scale asymmetric instances contained in the SuiteSparse matrix collection [1]. The symbol "-" indicates that the reverse Cuthill-McKee method was applied without using an algorithm for finding pseudo-peripheral vertices.

6   Conclusions

The George-Liu algorithm [8] has been used alongside the reverse Cuthill-McKee method [7] for bandwidth reductions since the 1980s. Among several algorithms identified in the literature that were applied to find pseudo-peripheral vertices, seven algorithms were selected as promising low-cost algorithms for the identification of pseudo-peripheral vertices to be used as starting vertices of the reverse Cuthill-McKee method. These algorithms were implemented in this computational experiment. Thereby, eight algorithms (including the reverse Cuthill-McKee method without applying an algorithm for selecting pseudo-peripheral vertices) were evaluated when applied to 63 small and 10 large-scale asymmetric instances contained in the SuiteSparse matrix collection [1]. The reverse Cuthill-McKee method along with Pachl's algorithm [20] provided the best bandwidth results when applied to these asymmetric instances.

We plan to apply the algorithms evaluated in this computational experiment to perform reordering of vertices with the objective of reducing the computational times of direct and iterative methods for solving linear systems composed of asymmetric matrices to verify the best algorithms(s) in this context. Additionally, we intend to evaluate these algorithms for finding pseudo-peripheral vertices in conjunction with other methods for bandwidth reductions, including the GPS [17] algorithm (by determining the target end vertex as a vertex in $\mathscr{L}(v)$ with the minimum degree, where v is the pseudo-peripheral vertex found), Kaveh's algorithms [24,25,27,28,30], and GGPS algorithm [36]. We also intend to study these algorithms when applied to symmetric instances and we plan to investigate parallel approaches of them in future studies.

References

1. Davis, T.A., Hu, Y.: The University of Florida sparse matrix collection. ACM Trans. Math. Softw. **38**(1), 1–25 (2011)
2. Gonzaga de Oliveira, S.L., Bernardes, J.A.B., Chagas, G.O.: An evaluation of reordering algorithms to reduce the computational cost of the incomplete Cholesky-conjugate gradient method. Comput. Appl. Math. (2017). https://doi.org/10.1007/s40314-017-0490-5
3. Chagas, G.O., Gonzaga de Oliveira, S.L.: Metaheuristic-based heuristics for symmetric-matrix bandwidth reduction: a systematic review. Proc. Comput. Sci. **51**, 211–220 (2015). Proceedings of the ICCS - International Conference on Computational Science, Reykjavík, Iceland
4. Bernardes, J.A.B., Gonzaga de Oliveira, S.L.: A systematic review of heuristics for profile reduction of symmetric matrices. Proc. Comput. Sci. **51**, 221–230 (2015). Proceedings of the ICCS - International Conference on Computational Science, Reykjavík, Iceland
5. Gonzaga de Oliveira, S.L., Chagas, G.O.: A systematic review of heuristics for symmetric-matrix bandwidth reduction: methods not based on metaheuristics. In: The XLVII Brazilian Symposium of Operational Research, SBPO, Ipojuca-PE, Brazil, Sobrapo, August 2015
6. Gonzaga de Oliveira, S.L., Bernardes, J.A.B., Chagas, G.O.: An evaluation of low-cost heuristics for matrix bandwidth and profile reductions. Comput. Appl. Math. **37**(2), 1412–1471 (2018). https://doi.org/10.1007/s40314-016-0394-9
7. George, A.: Computer implementation of the finite element method. Ph.D. thesis. Stanford University, Stanford, USA (1971)
8. George, A., Liu, J.W.H.: An implementation of a pseudoperipheral node finder. ACM Trans. Math. Softw. **5**(3), 284–295 (1979)
9. George, A., Liu, J.W.: Computer Solution of Large Sparse Positive Definite Systems. Prentice-Hall, Englewood Cliffs (1981)
10. Benzi, M., Szyld, D.B., Van Duin, A.: Orderings for incomplete factorization preconditioning of nonsymmetric problems. SIAM J. Sci. Comput. **20**(5), 1652–1670 (1999)
11. Camata, J.J., Rossa, A.L., Valli, A.M.P., Catabriga, L., Carey, G.F., Coutinho, A.L.G.A.: Reordering and incomplete preconditioning in serial and parallel adaptive mesh refinement and coarsening flow solutions. Int. J. Numer. Meth. Fluids **69**, 802–823 (2012). https://onlinelibrary.wiley.com/doi/abs/10.1002/fld.2614
12. Gonzaga de Oliveira, S.L., Abreu, A.A.A.M.: The use of the reverse Cuthill-Mckee method with an alternative pseudo-peripheral vertice finder for profile optimization. In: XXXVII National Conference on Computational and Applied Mathematics, CNMAC, São José dos Campos, vol. 6. Sociedade Brasileira de Matemática Aplicada e Computacional (SBMAC), São Carlos (2018)
13. Arany, I.: An efficient algorithm for finding peripheral nodes. In: Lovász, L., Szemerédi, E. (eds.) Colloquia Mathematica Societatis János Bolyai (Hungarian Edition), Theory of Algorithms Pécs, vol. 44, pp. 27–35. North-Holland, Budapest (1984)
14. Papadimitriou, C.H.: The NP-completeness of bandwidth minimization problem. Computing **16**, 177–192 (1976)
15. Cuthill, E., McKee, J.: Reducing the bandwidth of sparse symmetric matrices. In: ACM Proceedings of the 1969 24th International Conference, pp. 157–172. ACM, New York (1969)

16. Cheng, K.: Minimizing the bandwidth of sparse symmetric matrices. Computing **11**, 103–110 (1973)
17. Gibbs, N.E., Poole, W.G., Stockmeyer, P.K.: An algorithm for reducing the bandwidth and profile of a sparse matrix. SIAM J. Numer. Anal. **2**(13), 236–250 (1976)
18. Smyth, W.F.: Algorithms for the reduction of matrix bandwidth and profile. J. Comput. Appl. Math. **12**(13), 551–561 (1985)
19. Arany, I.: Another method for finding pseudo-peripheral nodes. In: Annales, ed. Eotvos Lorand University, Sectio Computatorica, Tomus IV, Universitatis Scientiarum Budapestinensis De Rolando Eotvos Nominatae, vol. 4, pp. 39–49 (1983)
20. Pachl, J.K.: Finding pseudoperipheral nodes in graphs. J. Comput. Syst. Sci. **29**(1), 48–53 (1984)
21. Sloan, S.W.: An algorithm for profile and wavefront reduction of sparse matrices. Int. J. Numer. Methods Eng. **23**, 1693–1704 (1986)
22. Duff, I.S., Reid, J.K., Scott, J.A.: The use of profile reduction algorithms with a frontal code. Int. J. Numer. Methods Eng. **28**, 2555–2568 (1989)
23. Sloan, S.W.: A FORTRAN program for profile and wavefront reduction. Int. J. Numer. Methods Eng. **28**, 2651–2679 (1989)
24. Kaveh, A., Bondarabady, H.A.R.: Ordering for wavefront optimization. Comput. Struct. **78**, 227–235 (2000)
25. Kaveh, A.: Ordering for bandwidth reduction. Comput. Struct. **24**, 413–420 (1986)
26. Kaveh, A.: Multiple use of a shortest route tree for ordering. Commun. Appl. Numer. Methods **2**, 213–215 (1986)
27. Kaveh, A.: A connectivity coordinate system for node and element ordering. Comput. Struct. **41**(6), 1217–1223 (1991)
28. Kaveh, A.: Algebraic graph theory. Comput. Struct. **37**(1), 51–54 (1990)
29. Kaveh, A.: Structural Mechanics: Graph and Matrix Methods. Research Studies Press Ltd., Baldock (2004)
30. Kaveh, A., Bondarabady, H.A.R.: A hybrid method for finite element ordering. Comput. Struct. **80**, 219–225 (2002)
31. Grimes, R.G., Pierce, D.J., Simon, H.D.: A new algorithm for finding a pseudoperipheral node in a graph. SIAM J. Matrix Anal. Appl. **11**, 323–334 (1990)
32. Souza, L.T., Murray, D.W.: An alternative pseudoperipheral node finder for resequencing schemes. Int. J. Numer. Methods Eng. **36**(19), 3351–3379 (1993)
33. Luo, J.C.: Algorithms for reducing the bandwidth and profile of a sparse matrix. Comput. Struct. **44**, 535–548 (1992)
34. Paulino, G.H., Menezes, I.F.M., Gattass, M., Mukherjee, S.: A new algorithm for finding a pseudoperipheral vertex or the endpoints of a pseudodiameter in a graph. Commun. Appl. Numer. Methods **10**, 913–926 (1994)
35. Reid, J.K., Scott, J.A.: Ordering symmetric sparse matrices for small profile and wavefront. Int. J. Numer. Methods Eng. **45**(12), 1737–1755 (1999)
36. Wang, Q., Shi, X., Guo, C., Guo, Y.: An improved GPS method with a new pseudoperipheral nodes finder in finite element analysis. Finite Elem. Anal. Des. **48**(1), 1409–1415 (2012)

Computational Efficiency Improvement for Analyzing Bending and Tensile Behavior of Woven Fabric Using Strain Smoothing Method

Q. T. Nguyen[1(✉)], A. J. P. Gomes[2], and F. N. Ferreira[1]

[1] School of Engineering, Centre for Textile Science and Technology, University of Minho, Campus de Azurém, 4800-058 Guimarães, Portugal
quyenum@gmail.com
[2] Faculty of Engineering, Institute of Telecommunications, University of Beira Interior, R. Marquês de Ávila e Bolama, 6201-001 Covilhã, Portugal

Abstract. The tensile and bending behavior of woven fabrics are among the most important characteristics in complex deformation analysis and modelling of textile fabrics and they govern many aesthetics and performance aspects such as wrinkle/buckle, hand and drape. In this paper, a numerical method for analyzing of the tensile and bending behavior of plain-woven fabric structure was developed. The formulated model is based on the first-order shear deformation theory (FSDT) for a four-node quadrilateral element (Q4) and a strain smoothing method in finite elements, referred as a cell-based smoothed finite element method (CS-FEM). The physical and low-stress mechanical parameters of the fabric were obtained through the fabric objective measurement technology (FOM) using the Kawabata evaluation system for fabrics (KES-FB). The results show that the applied numerical method provides higher efficiency in computation in terms of central processing unit (CPU) time than the conventional finite element method (FEM) because the evaluation of compatible strain fields of Q4 element in CS-FEM model is constants, and it was also appropriated for numerical modelling and simulation of mechanical deformation behavior such as tensile and bending of woven fabric.

Keywords: Plain woven fabric structure · Fabric objective measurement
First-order shear deformation theory
Cell-based smoothed finite element method

1 Introduction

In engineering sectors of textile and apparel industry, numerical modelling and simulation have been widely developed and applied in solving complex problems in the product design and engineering process to predict how an apparel product reacts to real-world forces, moisture absorption, heat transfer and other physical effects and so forth [1–4]. Tensile properties are considered as the most important factor that govern the performance characteristics of textile fabrics. The investigation of tensile properties

© Springer International Publishing AG, part of Springer Nature 2018
O. Gervasi et al. (Eds.): ICCSA 2018, LNCS 10960, pp. 138–148, 2018.
https://doi.org/10.1007/978-3-319-95162-1_10

encounters many difficulties due to the complexity of fabric structure leading to variation strain during deformation [5]. In general, each fabric sheet consists of a large amount of constituent fibers and yarns which will response subsequently to a series of complex movements under any deformation state. This makes the mechanical properties of textile fabrics more complicated due to both fibers and yarns behaving in a non-Hookean law during deformation and presenting hysteresis effect [5, 6]. In addition, mechanical bending properties of textile fabrics govern many aspects of fabric appearance and performance, such as wrinkle/buckle, hand and drape. These are one of the most important characteristics in complex deformation analysis and modelling of textile fabrics.

Numerical modelling of large-deflection elastic structural mechanics from numerical models have been widely applied to examine specific textile fabric engineering and apparel industry problems [6]. The applicability of mechanical modelling of tensile and bending behavior of textile fabrics is very limited because it requires a large number of mechanical parameters and is, therefore, difficult to express in a closed form [3]. The most detailed analysis of the bending behavior of plain-woven fabrics can be found in [7] The tensile and bending properties of woven fabrics have, therefore, received considerable attention in both literature and model experiments.

A strain smoothing operation [8] was proposed recently as a CS-FEM A cell-based strain smoothing method in finite elements (CS-FEM), was improved the accuracy and convergence rate of the existing conventional finite element finite element method (FEM) of elastic solid mechanics problems [9–12]. It was also applied to improve formulation of a locking-free four-node quadrilateral flat shell element (Q4) with five degrees of freedom per node, and able to reduce the mesh distortion sensitivity and enhance the coarse mesh accuracy.

Therefore, this paper presents a numerical solution that offer a better efficiency of computation but effective performance in modelling and simulation of tensile and bending behavior of woven fabric structures. The numerical model is based on the integration scheme of CS-FEM model into the Mindlin-Reissner plate element and the plane-stress element using a four-node quadrilateral element [13–15]. The plain-woven fabric is assumed as an elastic with orthotropic anisotropy for which the constitutive laws formulated are using low-stress mechanical properties obtained from KES-FB [6]. The numerical result is subjected to evaluate and investigate the applicability of CS-FEM models using one smoothing cell to improve the computational efficiency in analyzing the bending and tensile behavior of woven fabric.

2   Formulations of the Shell Structure

Consider a reference plane that occupies a domain $\Omega \in R^3$ bounded by Γ at the middle surface of shell is. Let u, v and w be the translational displacements and transverse displacement, θ_x and θ_y be the rotations in the xz and yz planes in the Cartesian coordinate system as shown in Fig. 1.

The problem domain Ω is discretized into a set of four-node quadrilateral flat shell elements Ω^e with boundary Γ^e. The generalized displacement vector $\boldsymbol{u}^h$ can be then approximated as

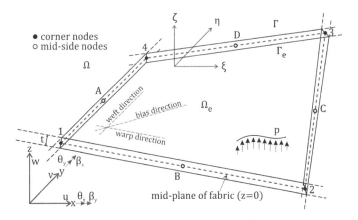

Fig. 1. A four-node quadrilateral flat shell element

$$
\boldsymbol{u}^h = \sum_{I=1}^{4}
\begin{bmatrix}
N_I & 0 & 0 & 0 & 0 \\
0 & N_I & 0 & 0 & 0 \\
0 & 0 & N_I & 0 & 0 \\
0 & 0 & 0 & 0 & N_I \\
0 & 0 & 0 & N_I & 0
\end{bmatrix} \boldsymbol{q}_I,
\tag{1}
$$

in which N_I is shape function and $\boldsymbol{q}_I^T = \{ u_I \quad v_I \quad w_I \quad \theta_{xI} \quad \theta_{yI} \}$ is vector of nodal degrees of freedom associated with each of nodes I.

Based on the FSDT, the generalized strains comprises of three parts, namely ε^m, ε^b and ε^s. The membrane strain ε^m, curvature strain ε^b and transverse shear strain ε^s are defined, respectively, as

$$
\varepsilon^m = \left\{
\begin{array}{c}
\frac{\partial u}{\partial x} \\
\frac{\partial v}{\partial y} \\
\frac{\partial u}{\partial y} + \frac{\partial v}{\partial y}
\end{array}
\right\} = \sum_{I=1}^{4}
\begin{bmatrix}
N_{I,x} & 0 & 0 & 0 & 0 \\
0 & N_{I,y} & 0 & 0 & 0 \\
N_{I,y} & N_{I,x} & 0 & 0 & 0
\end{bmatrix} \boldsymbol{q}_I = \boldsymbol{B}^m \boldsymbol{q},
\tag{2}
$$

$$
\varepsilon^b = \left\{
\begin{array}{c}
\frac{\partial \theta_x}{\partial x} \\
\frac{\partial \theta_y}{\partial y} \\
\frac{\partial \theta_y}{\partial y} - \frac{\partial \theta_x}{\partial y}
\end{array}
\right\} = \sum_{I=1}^{4}
\begin{bmatrix}
0 & 0 & 0 & N_{I,x} & 0 \\
0 & 0 & -N_{I,y} & 0 & 0 \\
0 & 0 & -N_{I,x} & N_{I,y} & 0
\end{bmatrix} \boldsymbol{q}_I = \boldsymbol{B}^b \boldsymbol{q},
\tag{3}
$$

$$
\varepsilon^s = \left\{
\begin{array}{c}
\frac{\partial \mathrm{w}}{\partial x} + \theta_y \\
\frac{\partial \mathrm{w}}{\partial y} - \theta_x
\end{array}
\right\} = \sum_{I=1}^{4}
\begin{bmatrix}
0 & 0 & N_{I,x} & 0 & N_I \\
0 & 0 & N_{I,y} & -N_I & 0
\end{bmatrix} \boldsymbol{q}_I = \boldsymbol{B}^s \boldsymbol{q},
\tag{4}
$$

where superscripts m, b and s stand for the membrane, bending (curvature) and transverse shear elements, respectively, and $\boldsymbol{B}$ is the strain matrices.

The constitutive relations between the stress and train fields of elements are defined as

$$\sigma^m = \left\{ \sigma_x \quad \sigma_y \quad \tau_{xy} \right\}^T = D^m \varepsilon^m, \tag{5}$$

$$\sigma^b = \left\{ \sigma_x \quad \sigma_y \quad \tau_{xz} \right\}^T = D^b \varepsilon^b, \tag{6}$$

$$\sigma^s = \left\{ \tau_{xz} \quad \tau_{yz} \right\}^T = D^s \varepsilon^s, \tag{7}$$

in which the stress components σ_x and σ_y, shear components γ_{xy}, τ_{xy}, τ_{xz} and τ_{yz} lead to the force and moment resultants per unit length. Let subscripts 1 and 2 be associated with directions of the warp and weft yarns, and h, E, v, B, H and G are respectively the thickness of shell, Young's modulus, Poisson's ratios, flexural moduli, torsional rigidity and shear modulus. Then the material matrices related to the plane-stress D^m, bending D^b and transverse shear deformation D^s are defined, respectively, as

$$D^m = \int_{\frac{h}{2}}^{\frac{h}{2}} \begin{bmatrix} \frac{E_1}{1-v_1 v_2} & \frac{v_2 E_1}{1-v_2 v_1} & 0 \\ \frac{v_1 E_2}{1-v_1 v_2} & \frac{E_2}{1-v_2 v_1} & 0 \\ 0 & 0 & G \end{bmatrix} dz,$$

$$D^b = \int_{\frac{h}{2}}^{\frac{h}{2}} z^2 \begin{bmatrix} B_1 & 0 & 0 \\ 0 & B_2 & 0 \\ 0 & 0 & H \end{bmatrix} dz, \quad D^s = \int_{\frac{h}{2}}^{\frac{h}{2}} \frac{5}{6} G \begin{bmatrix} 1 & 0 \\ 0 & 1 \end{bmatrix} dz, \tag{8}$$

The discretized system equations in term of a weak form solution of generalized displacement field u^h that satisfies the Galerkin weak form for the tensile and bending problems can be written as

$$Kq = f, \tag{9}$$

in which f indicates the force vector and $K = K^m + K^b + K^s$ is the global stiffness matrix [16].

3   Cell-Base Strain Smoothing Operation

The cell-based strain smoothing operation [17, 18] performs over the kth smoothing domain Ω_k^s with Γ_k^s of the element Ω^e is addressed as

$$\bar{\nabla} u(x_k) = \int_{\Omega_i^s} \varepsilon(x) \Phi(x - x_k) d\Omega, \tag{10}$$

where Φ is a smoothing or weight function associated with point x_i in Ω_k^s, and $\nabla u(x) \cong \varepsilon(x)$. This smoothing function must satisfy the basic conditions of $\Phi \geq 0$ and $\int_{\Omega_i^s} \Phi d\Omega = 1$. For simplicity, a piecewise constant function is applied here, as given by:

$$\Phi(x - x_k) = \begin{cases} 1/A_k^s, & x \in \Omega_k^s \\ 0, & x \notin \Omega_k^s \end{cases}, \tag{11}$$

where $A_k^s = \int_{\Omega_k^s} d\Omega$ the area of the kth smoothing domain $\Omega_k^s \subset \Omega^e$.

In an CS-FEM model, the strain in smoothing domain Ω_k^s can be further assumed to be a constant and equals $\bar{\varepsilon}(x_k)$. By substituting smoothing function Φ into Eq. (10), the averaged/smoothed gradient of displacement is defined as

$$\bar{\varepsilon}_k = \bar{\varepsilon}(x_k) = \frac{1}{A_k^s} \int_{\Omega_k^s} \varepsilon(x) d\Omega = \frac{1}{A_k^s} \int_{\Gamma_k^s} n(x) \cdot u(x) d\Gamma. \tag{12}$$

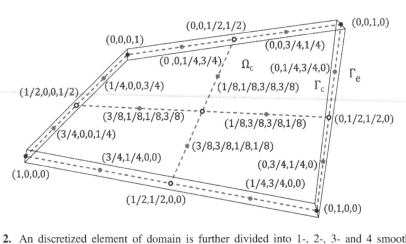

Fig. 2. An discretized element of domain is further divided into 1-, 2-, 3- and 4 smoothing domains (SDs) including the orthogonal nodal shape functions N_I.

The averaged/smoothing strain operation for membrane strains and curvature strains in Eqs. (2) and (3), as shown in Fig. 2, can be reformed as

$$\varepsilon^m(x_k) = \frac{1}{A_k^s} \int_{\Omega_k^s} \varepsilon^m(x_k) d\Omega = \frac{1}{A_k^s} \int_{\Gamma_k^s} n \cdot u(x_k) d\Gamma = \sum_{I=1}^{4} B_{kI}^m(x_k) \cdot q_I^m, \tag{13}$$

$$\varepsilon^b(x_k) = \frac{1}{A_k^s} \int_{\Omega_k^s} \varepsilon^b(x_k) d\Omega = \frac{1}{A_k^s} \int_{\Gamma_k^s} n \cdot u(x_k) d\Gamma = \sum_{I=1}^{4} B_{kI}^b(x_k) \cdot q_I^p, \tag{14}$$

in which n is the outward normal matrix containing the components of the outward unit normal vector to the boundary Γ_k^s and B_{kI} stand for the smoothed gradient matrices defined as

$$B_{kI}^m(x_k) = \begin{bmatrix} \bar{b}_{kIx} & 0 & 0 & 0 & 0 \\ 0 & \bar{b}_{kIy} & 0 & 0 & 0 \\ \bar{b}_{kIy} & \bar{b}_{kIx} & 0 & 0 & 0 \end{bmatrix}, B_{kI}^b(x_k) = \begin{bmatrix} 0 & 0 & 0 & \bar{b}_{kIx} & 0 \\ 0 & 0 & -\bar{b}_{kIy} & 0 & 0 \\ 0 & 0 & -\bar{b}_{kIx} & \bar{b}_{kIy} & 0 \end{bmatrix}, \tag{15}$$

where

$$\bar{b}_{kIx} = \frac{1}{A_k^s} \int_{\Gamma_k^s} n_x N_I d\Gamma = \frac{1}{A_k^s} \sum_{b=1}^{n_b^s} n_{xb} N_I \left(x_b^G\right) l_b,$$

$$\bar{b}_{kIy} = \frac{1}{A_k^s} \int_{\Gamma_{k,c}^e} n_y N_I d\Gamma = \frac{1}{A_k^s} \sum_{b=1}^{n_b^s} n_{yb} N_I \left(x_b^G\right) l_b. \tag{16}$$

In Eq. (16), n_{xb} and n_{yb} indicate the components of the outward unit normal to the bth boundary segment and x_b^G is the cooinate value of Gauss point of the bth boundary segment. Using Eq. (15), the membrane and bending terms of the stiffness matrix K^m and K^b in Eq. (9) can be evaluated using 1 to 4 smoothing cells.

4 Mixed Interpolation of Tensorial Components

Mindlin-Reissner (or FSDT) plate elements exhibit a shear locking phenomenon due to incorrect transverse forces under bending, or in the case of the thickness of the plate tends to zero. To overcome the shear locking phenomena, the approximation of the shear strain fields γ is formulated with the mixed interpolation of tensorial components approaches [13] as

$$\varepsilon^s = \left\{ \begin{array}{c} \gamma_{xz} \\ \gamma_{yz} \end{array} \right\} = J^{-1} \frac{1}{2} \left\{ \begin{array}{c} (1-\eta)\gamma_\xi^B + (1+\eta)\gamma_\xi^D \\ (1-\xi)\gamma_\eta^A + (1+\xi)\gamma_\eta^C \end{array} \right\}, \tag{17}$$

in which

$$\left\{ \begin{array}{c} \gamma_\xi \\ \gamma_\eta \end{array} \right\} = \frac{1}{2} \left\{ \begin{array}{c} (1-\eta)\gamma_\xi^B + (1-\eta)\gamma_\xi^D \\ (1-\xi)\gamma_\eta^A + (1-\xi)\gamma_\eta^C \end{array} \right\}, \tag{18}$$

and J is Jacobian transformation matrix and superscripts A, B, C and D are the mid-side node, as shown in Fig. 1. Expressing $\gamma_\eta^A, \gamma_\eta^C$ and $\gamma_\xi^B, \gamma_\xi^D$ in terms of the discretized fields q_I, the shear part of the stiffness matrix is then rewritten as

$$B_I^s = J^{-1} \begin{bmatrix} 0 & 0 & \frac{\partial N_I}{\partial \xi} & \xi_i \frac{\partial x^M}{\partial \xi} \frac{\partial N_I}{\partial \xi} & \xi_i \frac{\partial y^M}{\partial \xi} \frac{\partial N_I}{\partial \xi} \\ 0 & 0 & \frac{\partial N_I}{\partial \eta} & \eta_i \frac{\partial x^L}{\partial \eta} \frac{\partial N_I}{\partial \eta} & \eta_i \frac{\partial y^L}{\partial \eta} \frac{\partial N_I}{\partial \eta} \end{bmatrix}. \tag{19}$$

The coordinates of the unit square are $\xi_i \in \{-1, 1, 1, -1\}$ and $\eta_i \in \{-1, -1, 1, 1\}$ and the allocation of the mid-side nodes to the corner nodes of element are given as $(i; M; L) \in \{(1; B; A); (2; B; C); (3; D; C); (4; D; A)\}$. Using Eq. (19), the shear term of the stiffness matrix K^s in Eq. (9) can be evaluated using full integration of 2×2 Gauss Quadrature.

5   Numerical Implementation and Results

The numerical results of a four-node quadrilateral flat shell element (Q4) for bending and tensile analysis of a square woven fabric sheet having boundaries include clamped edges (C), simply supported edges (S) and free edges (F) under uniform pressure was implemented for both FEM and CS-FEM models, see Figs. 3 and 4.

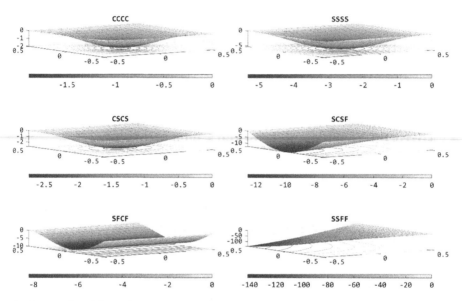

Fig. 3. Bending deformation of a plain-woven fabric sheet, using 20 × 20 Q4 elements and one smoothing cell per element with different boundaries.

Mechanical and physical parameters of a plain-woven fabric sample were computed with KES-FB comprising of the thickness [mm] of $h = 0.0848$, elastic modulus [gf/cm], $E_1 = 3823.7993$, $E_2 = 14092.4464$ and $E_{12} = 6896.5517$, Poisson's ratio $v_1 = 0.0211$ and $v_2 = 0.0778$, bending rigidity $[gf.cm^2/cm]$ of $B_1 = 0.1237$, $B_2 = 0.1333$ and $B_{12} = 0.0880$, transverse shear modulus $[gf.cm^2]$ of $G = 217.3100$.

The computational results for tensile behavior, as illustrated in Figs. 5 and 6, produced an accurate numerical results implemented by one smoothing cell per a four-node quadrilateral shell element and it was compared with the conventional FEM's results, which is clearly well-balanced feature of the CS-FEM.

The numerical results also indicated that the membrane elements implemented by CS-FEM are well refined, not distorted and not coarse even. Thus, the strain smoothing operation for four-node flat shell element are in good agreement with the conventional FEM solution.

In order to compare the accuracy of strain fields evaluated by CS-FEM and FEM, train fields of membrane and curvature of the formulated shell element was implemented using Eqs. (2) and (3) for FEM and Eq. (15) for CS-FEM. Figure 7 indicates

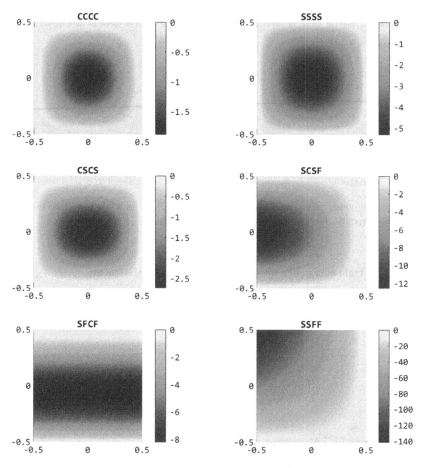

Fig. 4. The stress distribution (magnitude and direction) of fabric sheet yielded by the bending deformed under uniform pressure using 20 × 20 Q4 and one smoothing cell per element.

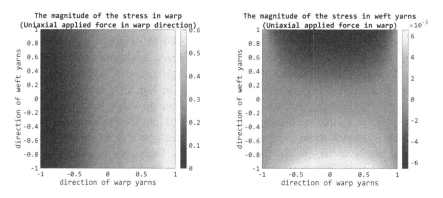

Fig. 5. The magnitude of the stress, under uniaxial applied force in warp direction, using 70 × 70 Q4 elements and one smoothing domains per element.

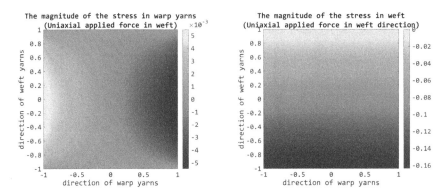

Fig. 6. The magnitude of the stress, under uniaxial applied force in weft direction, using 70 × 70 Q4 elements and one smoothing domains per element.

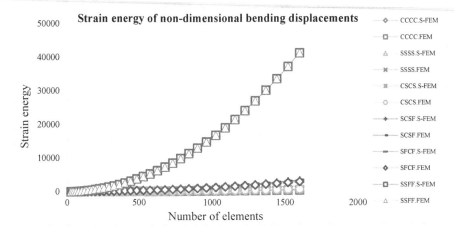

Fig. 7. Strain energy evaluated with FEM and CS-FEM for non-dimensional transverse displacements with different mesh density and boundary conditions subjected uniform load.

that the graphs of strain energy computed by CS-FEM model is approximate and coincided with that one of FEM on the same boundary conditions and mesh density under uniform pressure. However, the linear shape functions of CS-FEM using a point interpolation method (PIM) are constant as shown in Fig. 2. Vice versa, the shape functions of a Q4 element are those of bilinear Lagrange shape functions in natural coordinates (ξ, η, ζ) that are needed to be transformed into Cartesian coordinates (x, y, z) when one evaluates strain gradient matrix. This requires a Jacobian transformation matrix and needs to be evaluated by one or more Gauss points. Thus, the strain smoothing technique reduces the computation time in terms of the central processing unit time.

6 Conclusions

The CS-FEM gives a higher computational efficiency in term of GPU time but effective performance in analyzing the bending and tensile behavior of woven fabric compared with standard FEM. Thus, the application of FOM and CS-FEM to displacement-based low-order finite element formulations, that based on quadrilateral plate/shell finite element models, are well refined and appropriate for numerical modelling and simulation of the mechanical deformation behavior of tensile and bending for woven fabric in terms of elastic material with both isotropy and orthotropic anisotropy.

Acknowledgments. The author (UMINHO/BPD/9/2017) and co-authors acknowledge the FCT funding from FCT – Foundation for Science and Technology within the scope of the project "PEST UID/CTM/00264; POCI-01-0145-FEDER-007136".

References

1. Koustoumpardis, P.N., Aspragathos, N.A.: Intelligent hierarchical robot control for sewing fabrics. Robot. Comput.-Integr. Manuf. **30**(1), 34–46 (2014)
2. Sengupta, S., Debnath, S., Sengupta, A.: Fabric bending behaviour testing instrument for technical textiles. Measurement **87**, 205–215 (2016)
3. Veit, D.: Simulation in Textile Technology: Theory and Applications. Woodhead Publishing Series in Textiles, 1st edn. Woodhead Publishing, Cambridge (2012)
4. Zhang, Y.T., Fu, Y.B.: A micro-mechanical model of woven fabric and its application to the analysis of buckling under uniaxial tension. Part 2: buckling analysis. Int. J. Eng. Sci. **39**(1), 1–13 (2001)
5. Fan, J., Yu, W., Hunter, L.: Clothing Appearance and Fit: Science and Technology. Woodhead Publishing Series in Textiles. Woodhead Publishing, Cambridge (2004)
6. Hu, J.: Fabric Testing. Woodhead Publishing Series in Textiles. Woodhead Publishing, Cambridge (2008)
7. Hu, J.: Structure and Mechanics of Woven Fabrics. Woodhead Publishing Series in Textiles. Woodhead Publishing, Cambridge (2004)
8. Chen, J.-S., et al.: A stabilized conforming nodal integration for Galerkin mesh-free methods. Int. J. Numer. Methods Eng. **50**(2), 435–466 (2001)
9. Liu, G.R., Zeng, W., Nguyen-Xuan, H.: Generalized stochastic cell-based smoothed finite element method (GS_CS-FEM) for solid mechanics. Finite Elem. Anal. Des. **63**, 51–61 (2013)
10. Yue, J., et al.: A cell-based smoothed finite element method for multi-body contact analysis using linear complementarity formulation. Int. J. Solids Struct. **141–142**, 110–126 (2018)
11. Feng, S.Z., Li, A.M.: Analysis of thermal and mechanical response in functionally graded cylinder using cell-based smoothed radial point interpolation method. Aerosp. Sci. Technol. **65**, 46–53 (2017)
12. Tootoonchi, A., et al.: A cell-based smoothed point interpolation method for flow-deformation analysis of saturated porous media. Comput. Geotech. **75**, 159–173 (2016)
13. Bathe, K.-J., Dvorkin, E.N.: A four-node plate bending element based on Mindlin/Reissner plate theory and a mixed interpolation. Int. J. Numer. Methods Eng. **21**(2), 367–383 (1985)
14. Duan, H., Ma, J.: Continuous finite element methods for Reissner-Mindlin plate problem. Acta Mathematica Scientia **38**(2), 450–470 (2018)

15. Wu, F., et al.: A generalized probabilistic edge-based smoothed finite element method for elastostatic analysis of Reissner-Mindlin plates. Appl. Math. Model. **53**, 333–352 (2018)
16. Thai-Hoang, C., et al.: A cell—based smoothed finite element method for free vibration and buckling analysis of shells. KSCE J. Civ. Eng. **15**(2), 347–361 (2011)
17. Liu, G.R., Dai, K.Y., Nguyen, T.T.: A smoothed finite element method for mechanics problems. Comput. Mech. **39**(6), 859–877 (2007)
18. Nguyen-Xuan, H., et al.: A node-based smoothed finite element method with stabilized discrete shear gap technique for analysis of Reissner-Mindlin plates. Comput. Mech. **46**(5), 679–701 (2010)

High Performance Computing and Networks

Inferring Gene Regulatory Networks Using Hybrid Parallel Computing

Jean C. W. K. Ma[1], Marco A. Stefanes[1], Carlos H. A. Higa[1(✉)],
and Luiz C. S. Rozante[2]

[1] Federal University of Mato Grosso do Sul, Campo Grande, MS 79070-900, Brazil
{marco,higa}@facom.ufms.br
[2] Federal University of ABC, Santo Andre, SP 09210-580, Brazil
https://www.facom.ufms.br

Abstract. Gene regulatory networks (GRN) inference is an important bioinformatics problem, with many applications in system biology, in which the gene interactions need to be deduced from gene expression data, such as microarray data or RNA-Seq. Depending on the algorithm, the inference process may take a large amount of time due to the size of the networks and the complexity of the algorithm. The inference algorithm described in this work is based on the seed growing paradigm and has two steps: the seed growing and the inference step. We developed two parallel versions of the inference algorithm with the following approaches: Cluster of CPUs and a hybrid Multi CPU/GPUs. In tests performed in three databases of genes with different samples, these versions present good speedups, scalability, and robustness when compared with the sequential algorithm. Namely, for the seed growing step we achieved speedup of 12.7 with 16 nodes on Cluster of CPUs and speedup of 12.3 on hybrid Multi CPU/GPUs approach using 8 CPU/GPUs. For the inference step, we achieved speedups up to 10 on Cluster of CPUs.

Keywords: Gene regulatory network · Hybrid parallel computing
GPU

1 Introduction

Advancement in technologies to measure gene expression has provided us means to analyze the expression of thousands of genes simultaneously. For instance, the RNA-Seq [16] technology. One consequence of this advancement is the increase of biological data available and, therefore, the need of computational methodologies to process these data. In this context, the inference of gene regulatory networks (GRN) is an important problem in Bioinformatics, whose study help us understand the interactions among genes and their roles in cellular functions.

In the past years, mathematical models of GRN have been proposed, including Boolean networks [12], Bayesian networks [5] and models based on ordinary

Supported by CNPq and UFMS.

differential equations [7], to cite a few of them. Besides these models, several GRN inference algorithms have been proposed. For instance, seed growing approaches can be reviewed in [8,9]. Algorithms based on Boolean networks are very popular: [1,17]. For a complete review of sequential methods, see [11]. Given that each model and algorithm has its own characteristics, we cannot say that there is an algorithm that outperforms the others in every situation. It is worth mentioning that the inference of GRN is an ill-posed inverse problem, *i.e.*, given a set of gene expression data, there could be several solutions (networks) that explain the input data, which makes the problem very difficult.

Another challenge related to GRN inference is the computational cost independently of the method used. As in practice it is desired to infer GRNs with thousands of genes, the use of solutions based on high-performance computing becomes an interesting alternative. In 2011 Shi *et al.* [19] describe a method based on mutual information (used as criterion to measure the relationship between two genes) using CUDA-enabled GPU. In 2013 Borelli *et al.* [2] present an implementation using an exhaustive search approach on Multi-GPUs environment. In 2014, Lee and Hwang [14] design an evolutionary algorithm on the cloud environment. In 2015 Carastan-Santos *et al.* [3] apply hitting set problem for infer GRNs on Multi-GPUs and Xiao *et al.* [22] develop an asynchronous parallel algorithm using mutual information and ODEs on cluster of CPUs. All these methods do not take into account the network dynamics.

In this work we parallelize and evaluate a solution for inferring GRNs in two different computing systems, namely Cluster of CPUs and Multi CPU/GPUs environment using CUDA, based on a sequential algorithm that makes use of the seed growing paradigm proposed in [9]. This algorithm, unlike most of inference algorithms, analyzes the dynamics of a set of networks to rank them according to their stability (entropy). This analysis increases the time consuming, however, it leads to better solutions in terms of stability of networks. Besides that, the algorithm outputs a set of stable networks instead of a single network. This is interesting given that this is an ill-posed inverse problem. It is believed that a small set of genes is responsible for maintaining a specific cellular function [22]. Thus, these gene networks can be inferred concurrently after a clustering process.

In experimental tests performed in two gene databases from HeLa cells [21] and a from the contest DREAM4 [4], these parallel versions presented good speedups, scalability, and robustness when compared with the sequential algorithm. Namely, for the seed growing step we achieved speedup of 12.7 with 16 nodes with the Cluster of CPUs and speedup of 12.3 with the hybrid Multi CPU/GPUs approach using 8 CPU/GPUs. For the inference step, we achieved speedups around 10 using a cluster of CPUs with 16 nodes.

2   Sequential Algorithm

The inference algorithm [9] considered in this work models a GRN as a *thresholded Boolean network* (TBN) in which we have a gene set $X = \{x_1, x_2, \ldots, x_n\}$, $x_i \in \{0, 1\}$, $i = 1, 2, \ldots, n$. The interactions among the genes in X are represented by a *regulatory matrix* $A_{n \times n}$, where $a_{i,j} = 1$ for a positive regulation (activation) from x_j to x_i; $a_{ij} = -1$ for a negative regulation from x_j to x_i; and $a_{ij} = 0$ if there is no regulation among them. The value of each gene at time $t + 1$ is computed through Boolean functions that take into account the regulatory matrix and the values of genes at time t, as described in [9]. A *state* at time t is a binary vector $\mathbf{x}(t) = (x_1(t), x_2(t), \ldots, x_n(t))$. Therefore, the number of states is 2^n: $\mathbf{x}_0, \mathbf{x}_1, \ldots, \mathbf{x}_{2^n-1}$. Applying the Boolean functions to each gene simultaneously, the system transits from a state $\mathbf{x}_i(t)$ to $\mathbf{x}_j(t+1)$. A *state transition diagram* is a graph where a vertex represents a state and there is an edge $\mathbf{x}_i \rightarrow \mathbf{x}_j$ if there is a transition from $\mathbf{x}_i(t)$ to $\mathbf{x}_j(t+1)$. As this system is deterministic and the number of states is finite, there will be cycles in this diagram. A cycle is called an *attractor* and the states that leads to an attractor is part of its *basin of attraction*.

The algorithm is composed by two steps: the *seed growing step* and the *inference step*. In the first step, the seed $S \subset X$ is given as input and the goal is to add genes to an initially empty set Z. A time-series of gene expression $\mathbf{T} = \{\mathbf{s}_1, \mathbf{s}_2, \ldots, \mathbf{s}_m\}$, $\mathbf{s}_i \in \{0, 1\}^n$, is also given. We can view this sequence of samples, $\mathbf{s}_1 \rightarrow \cdots \rightarrow \mathbf{s}_m$, as a sequence of states in a state transition diagram of some TBN which we are trying to infer. The candidate genes to be added are chosen among the genes in $C = X \setminus S \cup Z$ and the growing step is finished once $d > 0$ genes are added, where d is a user parameter. This step is addressed as a feature selection problem and an algorithm known as IFFS (*Improved Forward Floating Selection*) [18] is used. In this feature selection setting, a candidate gene $x^* \in X - (S \cup Z)$ is selected such that

$$x^* = \arg \max_{x_c \in C} J(x_c, S \cup Z), \tag{1}$$

where $J(x_c, S \cup Z)$ is the value of the criterion function relative to the candidate gene x_c. We use the notation $J(x_c, S \cup Z)$ instead of $J(x_c)$ because, as we will see in Sect. 4, the score also depends on sets S and Z when considering its insertion/deletion to/from Z. As defined in [9], to compute the score we take into account the number of consistent networks (regulatory matrices) and the overall entropy of these networks. A consistent network is one possessing a state transition diagram in which the sequence $\mathbf{s}_1 \rightarrow \cdots \rightarrow \mathbf{s}_m$ appears as part of its diagram, when simulated according to the Boolean functions of the TBN. We generate all the consistent networks to compute the proportion $\mathcal{P}(x_c)$ of consistent networks regarding the total number of possible networks. This is done by solving *constraint satisfaction problems* (CSP) as described in [10], which is time consuming. The idea of the entropy is to measure the uncertainty regarding the consistent networks. Recall that a network is a regulatory matrix A where $a_{i,j} \in \{-1, 0, 1\}$. During this part of the algorithm, the size of A is $\ell \times \ell$, where $\ell = |S \cup Z| + 1$. Observing all the consistent networks we can estimate the probabilities $\hat{P}(a_{i,j} = \lambda)$, $\lambda \in \{-1, 0, 1\}$. The entropy of the variable $a_{i,j}$ is then computed by

$$H(a_{i,j}) = -\sum_\lambda \hat{P}(a_{i,j} = \lambda) \lg(\hat{P}(a_{i,j} = \lambda)). \tag{2}$$

In this case, $H(a_{i,j}) \leq -\lg(1/3)$, and the maximum value is achieved when $\hat{P}(a_{i,j} = -1) = \hat{P}(a_{i,j} = 0) = \hat{P}(a_{i,j} = 1)$. As we want to maximize the score for the gene which minimizes the uncertainty, we take the average of $-\lg(1/3) - H(a_{i,j})$:

$$\mathcal{H}(x_c) = \frac{1}{\ell^2} \sum_i \sum_j -[\lg(1/3) + H(a_{i,j})]. \tag{3}$$

The criterion function is a balance between $\mathcal{P}(x_c)$ and $\mathcal{H}(x_c)$:

$$J(x_c, S \cup Z) = (\mathcal{P}(x_c) + \mathcal{H}(x_c))/2. \tag{4}$$

The inference step takes as input the genes in $S \cup Z$ (the output of the seed growing step) and generates several consistent networks representing interactions among the genes in $S \cup Z$. In this step, a sample process is performed where a network A is randomly selected among the consistent networks and its entropy $H(A)$ is computed by analyzing its state transition diagram. Roughly, a network is stable (low $H(A)$) if its transition diagram has few attractors, with large basins of attraction. Therefore we are interested in networks possessing low values of $H(A)$ (details of how to compute $H(A)$ can be found in [9]). Even for small networks, computing $H(A)$ is time consuming.

3   Parallel Algorithms

The seed growing process, which is based on the IFFS method, attempts to find a gene in the candidate set $C = X \setminus S \cup Z$ to add to Z, remove from Z or replace a gene from Z with one from the set C. To find the best candidate gene $x \in C$ to be added to Z we use the SFS (*Sequential Forward Selection*) method. Using the SBS (*Sequential Backward Selection*) method, we find the least significant gene x in Z and we check whether removing this gene improves the score of the set $S \cup Z - \{x\}$. Finally, the IFFS executes the replacement method. This technique replaces each gene in Z with another gene in the candidate gene set C, attempting to increase the overall score. See Fig. 1 for details.

In the next two sections, we describe two parallel implementations of the seed growing algorithm. The first implementation uses cluster of CPUs approach (or Beowulf architecture) [20] and the second implementation uses a hybrid environment where each node consists of a CPU and a GPU [13].

The CPU cluster approach uses the library Gecode [6] in each CPU. This library cannot be used by GPU due to a number of features of Gecode's functions. Hence, we rewrote the functions to be compatible to GPU. The input is given as a set of genes $X = \{x_1, x_2, \ldots, x_n\}$, a subset of genes $S \subset X$ called seed, a time series $\mathbf{T} = \{\mathbf{s}_1, \mathbf{s}_2, \ldots, \mathbf{s}_m\}$, $\mathbf{s}_i \in \{0,1\}^n$, and the user parameter $d > 0$.

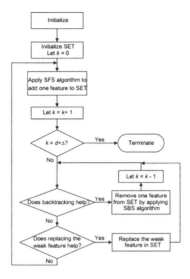

Fig. 1. The IFFS flowchart according to [18].

4   Cluster of CPUs Approach

4.1   Seed Growing

Suppose we have p processing units (nodes) denoted by $P_0, P_1, \ldots, P_{p-1}$. The general idea of this algorithm is to partitionate the set of candidate genes among the p nodes and locally identify the gene with the highest local score, as follows:

1. partition the set C into p subsets $C_0, C_1, \ldots, C_{p-1}$;
2. broadcasts the sets S and Z (initially empty) to the nodes $P_i, 0 \le i \le p-1$;
3. each node P_i determines its highest local score gene. This task is performed by the execution of the IFFS algorithm, which is composed by three algorithms SFS, SBS and Replace, described below;
4. lastly, the algorithm joins all locally obtained score in a master node, which will calculate the highest overall score and the process is repeated to add another gene in several rounds, until we have d genes in Z.

Sequential Forward Selection - SFS

The method SFS (detailed in Algorithm 1) identifies a candidate gene that has a good interaction with the genes in $S \cup Z$. The input of the Algorithm 1 is a set of genes S (the seed), a set of genes Z, which is initially empty, a set C (candidate genes) and a time-series **T**. Each node P_i finds the higher score candidate gene x_c among all genes in the subset C_i (lines 4–7). The score $J(x_c, S \cup Z)$ is computed and compared to the higher score computed so far (line 5) and an update is performed, if necessary. After computing the higher score of the genes of each subset C_i, the master node puts them all together (line 8) and determines the general higher score of the gene among all x_c received from all node (line 9). That score corresponds to the higher score gene in the entire set C. After that, the gene x_c is removed from C and added to Z.

Algorithm 1. SFS_CPUs$(S, Z, C, \mathbf{T})$

---

1 Broadcast the whole set Z among all nodes;
2 Distribute C evenly among the p nodes, such that the subset C_i is attributed to node P_i;
3 *local_score* $\leftarrow -1.0$;
4 **foreach** $x_c \in C_i$ **do**
5 $\quad$ **if** $J(x_c, S \cup Z) > $ *local_score* **then**
6 $\quad\quad$ *local_gene$_i$* $\leftarrow x_c$;
7 $\quad\quad$ *local_score* $\leftarrow J(x_c, S \cup Z)$;
8 $G \leftarrow \bigcup_i \{local\_gene_i\}$;
9 $x_c \leftarrow \max_{x_c \in G}\{J(x_c, S \cup Z)\}$;
10 $C \leftarrow C \setminus \{x_c\}$;
11 $Z \leftarrow Z \cup \{x_c\}$;

Sequential Backward Selection - SBS

The SBS method verifies whether the score of the gene set can be improved when we remove a gene from it. In other words, we verify if there exists a gene x such that the score of $S \cup Z - x$ is higher than the score of the set $S \cup Z$. The algorithm for this method is similar to SFS_CPUs, which can be obtained from it with minor changes. Due to lack of space the pseudo-code is omitted.

Replacement Method

The last step of the seed growing is the replacement method. This method consists of finding the best score of the set Z without increasing its size by replacing each gene in Z with another gene in C. Again, this algorithm can be obtained from Algorithm SFS_CPU with minor changes and the pseudo-code is omitted.

4.2 Inference Step

Now we detail the Inference Step. The input consists of the set $S \cup Z$ generated by the seed growing step, a parameter $\mathcal{M}$ corresponding to the sampling size and s a percent of $\mathcal{M}$. In this step each node of the cluster is responsible to assemble $\mathcal{M}/p$ networks. First, all the consistent rows are generated and stored in the master node's memory and distributed to all nodes. Then each node create a max-heap where it will be inserted the generated networks according to entropy. This heap stores only $s \cdot \mathcal{M}$ of the networks based on the value of the network's entropy $H(A)$. Next, a matrix A is randomly assembled by selecting one consistent row for each gene and inserted into the heap. Notice that, because we want to infer connected GRNs, we consider only connected networks A before computing the transition diagram. After each node generated $s \cdot \mathcal{M}$ networks, it applies a local sorting in increasing order of entropy values $H(A)$. Finally, the master node receives the sorted networks and selects $s \cdot \mathcal{M}$ networks from those received, generating $s\%$ of the networks possessing the lowest entropy values.

5   Hybrid Parallel Algorithm

Parallel seed growing using cluster of CPUs can enhance response time by splitting the set of candidate genes among the nodes, however each node still has a lot of work to perform. In order to obtain a better performance of the parallel solution, we used a hybrid approach where the use of CPUs and GPUs is locally alternated in each node to compute the criterion function. We introduce a parameter ϕ to indicate whether the computation will be run on CPU or GPU, according to the size of $S \cup Z$. Before we describe the hybrid algorithm, we detail how to compute in GPU the criterion function used in the seed growing step.

5.1   Criterion Function on the GPU

The kernel to calculate the criterion function J works as follows. Each block performs the processing of a candidate gene $x_c \in C_i$ and each gene $x_i \in S \cup Z$ is attributed to a thread. The function CSP_GPU (line 3) solves CSPs as described in [10] on the GPU, *i.e.*, it finds the consistent rows for a gene x_i. Using dynamic parallelism, a new kernel is invoked in line 4 to calculate the amount m_{x_i} and the proportion $\mathcal{P}_{x_i}$ of consistent rows. Then, the entropy of x_i is computed in line 6 using Eq. (2). If there is no consistent rows for some gene, the score is set to zero, otherwise two atomic operations are performed: an operation sums up the proportions of consistent rows and another sums up the gene entropies. Next, line 15 computes the score using Eq. (4).

5.2   Seed Growing

The parameter ϕ defines where to compute the criterion function. When computing is done on GPU, the time-series given as input is stored in the GPU's texture memory, since several operations of access are performed on these data. Moreover, this time-series is shrunk to store only genes in $S \cup Z$. After the shrinking if identical transition states appear between consecutive rows, we remove these extra rows. This task is called *producing* of the time-series $\mathbf{T}_A$ for some set A.

Sequential Forward Selection - SFS

The SFS method using hybrid approach is detailed in Algorithm 3. We broadcast the set Z and we evenly split the set C among the nodes such that the set C_i is attributed to node P_i (lines 1–2).

Algorithm 2. f_criterion(dev_score)

---

1 $x_c \leftarrow blockIdx.x$;
2 $x_i \leftarrow threadIdx.x$;
3 $R_{x_i} \leftarrow \text{CSP\_GPU}(x_i, T_{S \cup Z \cup \{x_c\}})$;
4 $c\_lines \mathord{<}\mathord{<}\mathord{<}blocks, threads\mathord{>}\mathord{>}\mathord{>}(R_{x_i}, m_{x_i}, \mathcal{P}_{x_i})$;
5 $cudaDeviceSynchronize()$;
6 $entropy_{x_i} \leftarrow H(x_i)$;
7 **if** $m_{x_i} = 0$ **then**
8 | $atomicAdd(\&shr\_inconsistent, 1)$;
9 $\_syncthreads()$;
10 **if** $shr\_inconsistent=0$ **then**
11 | $atomicAdd(\&shr\_\mathcal{P}, \mathcal{P}_{x_i})$;
12 | $atomicAdd(\&shr\_\mathcal{H}, entropy_{x_i})$;
13 | $\_syncthreads()$;
14 | **if** $x_i = 0$ **then**
15 | | $dev\_score[x_c] \leftarrow (shr\_\mathcal{P} + shr\_\mathcal{H})/2$;

Algorithm 3. Hybrid_SFS($S, Z, C, \mathbf{T}, \phi$)

---

1 Broadcast whole set Z and its score to every node;
2 Distribute C evenly among the p nodes, such that the subset C_i is attributed to node p_i;
3 **if** $|S \cup Z| + 1 < \phi$ **then**
4 | Produce the time-series $\mathbf{T}_{S \cup Z \cup \{x_c\}}$ for all $x_c \in C_i$;
5 | Copy all $T_{S \cup Z \cup \{x_c\}}$ to GPU memory;
6 | $threads \leftarrow |S \cup Z| + 1$;
7 | $blocks \leftarrow |C_i|$;
8 | cudaMalloc($dev\_score, blocks$);
9 | $f\_criterion \mathord{<}\mathord{<}\mathord{<} blocks, threads \mathord{>}\mathord{>}\mathord{>}(dev\_score)$;
10 | $cudaDeviceSynchronize()$;
11 | Copy dev_score from GPU to $score$ in host;
12 | $x'_c \leftarrow \max_{x_c \in C_i}\{score(S \cup Z \cup \{x'_c\})\}$;
13 | $C_i \leftarrow C_i \setminus \{x'_c\}$;
14 | $Z \leftarrow Z \cup \{x'_c\}$;
15 **else**
16 | $x'_c \leftarrow SFS\_CPUs(S, Z, C_i)$;
17 Find the best candidate x_c among all C_i;
18 $C \leftarrow C \setminus \{x_c\}$;
19 $Z \leftarrow Z \cup \{x_c\}$;

If $|S \cup Z| + 1 < \phi$, we compute criterion function of C_i on GPU (lines 4–14). In this case, all possible time-series relative to $S \cup Z \cup \{x_c\}$ for all $x_c \in C_i$ are produced in line 4 and these time-series are transfered to GPU in line 5. Next, line 9 calls the $f\_criterion$ (Algorithm 2) with $|C_i|$ blocks where each *thread* has size $|S \cup Z| + 1$ to calculate the score of $S \cup Z \cup \{x_c\}$. After computing the criterion function on GPU, the scores are transfered to the CPU where the higher score gene x_c is computed (line 12) among all candidate genes received from the GPU. Finally, the best score gene x_c is deleted from C_i and inserted in Z.

If $|S \cup Z| + 1 \geq \phi$ we call *SFS_CPUs* taking as input S, Z and C_i and returns the best gene x'_c in C_i. Next, the master node determines the best gene x_c among all genes in C. At the end, the gene x_c is deleted from C and added to Z.

Sequential Backward Selection - SBS

The SBS method computes the best score of $S \cup Z - \{x\}$ for all $x \in Z$ and verifies whether this score is better than the score of $S \cup Z$. The Algorithm 4 broadcasts the set Z and, additionally, splits the set Z evenly among the nodes such that the set Z_i is attributed to node p_i (lines 1–2).

If $|S \cup Z| - 1 < \phi$, the criterion function of $Z_i - \{x\}$ is computed on GPU in lines 4–12. In this case, the algorithm produces the time-series of $S \cup Z - \{x\}$ for each gene $x \in Z_i$ and transfer it to GPU's memory. Next, kernel *f_criterion* computes the score of $S \cup Z - \{x\}$ using $|Z|$ blocks with $|S \cup Z| - 1$ threads each. In addition, the score of each $S \cup Z - \{x_i\}$ is transfered to the CPU. The weakest gene x is chosen by taking the highest score of $S \cup Z - \{x\}$ for all $x \in Z$. If the score of $S \cup Z - \{x\}$ is greater than the score of $S \cup Z$, the gene x is removed.

If $|S \cup Z| - 1 \geq \phi$, we call *SBS_CPUs* which uses as input S, Z_i and C and returns the best candidate gene x'_c in C_i. Moreover, the master node finds the weakest gene x among all in the entire set Z in line 15, and if the score of $S \cup Z - \{x\}$ is greater than the score of $S \cup Z$, the gene x is removed from Z.

Algorithm 4. Hybrid_SBS$(S, Z, C, \mathbf{T}, \phi)$

---

1 Broadcast whole set Z and its score to every node;
2 Distribute Z evenly among the p nodes, such that the subset Z_i is attributed to node p_i;
3 **if** $|S \cup Z| - 1 < \phi$ **then**
4   Produce the time-series $\mathbf{T}_{S \cup Z - \{x_i\}}$ for all $x_i \in Z_i$;
5   Copy all $\mathbf{T}_{S \cup Z - \{x_i\}}$ to GPU memory;
6      $threads \leftarrow |S \cup Z_i| - 1$;
7      $blocks \leftarrow |Z_i|$;
8   cudaMalloc($dev\_score, blocks$);
9   *f_criterion* $<<<$ *blocks, threads* $>>>$(dev_score);
10   *cudaDeviceSynchronize()*;
11   Copy dev_score from GPU to $score$ in host;
12     $x'_z \leftarrow \max_{x_z \in Z_i} \{score(S \cup Z - \{x_z\})\}$;
13 **else**
14     $x'_z \leftarrow SBS\_CPUs(S, Z_i, C, \mathbf{T})$;
15 Find the weakest x among all Z_i;
16 **if** $J(S \cup Z - \{x\}) > J(S \cup Z)$ **then**
17     $Z \leftarrow Z \setminus \{x\}$;
18     $C \leftarrow C \cup \{x\}$;

Replacement Method

Algorithm 5 details the Replacement Method using hybrid parallel approach. Initially the algorithm broadcasts the whole set Z and its score and splits the set C evenly, $i.e.$ the subset C_i is attributed to the node P_i (lines 1–2).

If $|S \cup Z| < \phi$, the algorithm computes the replacement method on GPU. Each block calculates the score of a different set $S \cup Z$ using its time-series. All these time-series for all different $S \cup Z$ are produced in line 4 and in line 5, which are transfered to GPU. Next, the algorithm calls the *kernel f_criterion* in line 9 to determine the score of each set $S \cup Z$. After that, the weakest gene x_z of Z and the strongest gene x_c of C are identified. If the score of $S \cup Z \cup \{x_c\} - \{x\}$ is greater than the score of $S \cup Z$, the gene x_z is replaced by x_c into the set Z.

If $|S \cup Z| \geq \phi$, the algorithm calculates the criterion function on CPU, by replacing each gene in Z with each gene in C_i (line 14) to increase the score. Each variable x_z and x_c store the weakest gene of Z_i and the best candidate gene of C_i, respectively. After finding the best candidate gene of all subsets C_i, master node calculates in line 15 the best gene $x_c \in C$ that can be replaced by the weakest gene $x_z \in Z$ such that improve the overall score. Finally, if the score can be improved, the algorithm replaces x_z by x_c and x_z comes back to set C.

Algorithm 5. Hybrid_Replace($S, Z, \mathbf{T}, C, \phi$)

---

1 Broadcast whole set Z and its score to every node;
2 Distribute C evenly among the p nodes, such that the subset C_i is attributed to node p_i;
3 **if** $|S \cup Z| < \phi$ **then**
4   Produce the time-series $\mathbf{T}_{S \cup Z}$, by replace each $x_i \in Z$ with each $x_c \in C_i$ in $S \cup Z$;
5   Copy $T_{S \cup Z}$ to GPU memory;
6   threads $\leftarrow |S \cup Z|$;
7   blocks $\leftarrow |Z| * |C_i|$;
8   cudaMalloc(*dev_score, blocks*);
9   *f_criterion* <<< *blocks, threads*>>>(*dev_score*);
10   *cudaDeviceSynchronize()*;
11   Copy *dev_score* from GPU to *score* in host;
12      $(x_z, x_c) \leftarrow \max_{x_z \in Z}^{x_c \in C_i} \{score(S \cup Z \cup \{x_c\} - \{x_z\})\}$;
13 **else**
14   *Replace_CPUs*(S, Z, C_i, x_z, x_c);
15 $(x_z, x_c) \leftarrow \max_{x_z \in Z}^{x_c \in C} \{J(S \cup Z \cup \{x_c\} - \{x_z\})\}$;
16 **if** $J(S \cup Z \cup \{x_c\} - \{x_z\}) > J(S \cup Z))$ **then**
17   Replace x_z by x_c into Z;
18   Replace x_c by x_z into C;

6   Experimental Tests

6.1   Test Environment

The gene databases used in our experiments were those from *HeLa* cells [21] and from the contest DREAM4 [4]. The first database contains two networks: The first network with 20 genes and 12 samples, and the second network with 20 genes and 14 samples. The second database analyzed has 100 genes and 21 samples. The gene expression data were discretized using the algorithm BiKmeans [15]. We set the initial seed with 3 genes and we add up to 8 genes using the IFFS method. During the tests in the hybrid environment the parameter ϕ, which establish the size of set $S \cup Z$, was set to 7, due to small size of memory.

The cluster of CPU implementation was run in a cluster with 16 nodes with processors Xeon CPU X3440 of 4 cores, 4 GB of RAM per node. The experiments with cluster of CPU/GPUs, were performed in a public cloud with processor Xeon E5-2686 v4 (32 vCPUs), 488 GB of RAM and 8 GPUs Nvidia K80.

6.2   Performance Measure

The performance of the seed growing and inference steps were measured separately. In this section, we compare the sequential performance with the performance of the cluster of CPUs and hybrid approaches.

Seed Growing of HeLa 1

First of all, we run the experiments with the network 1 of the *HeLa* cells, using the sequential Gecode with 10 samples of different seeds. These experiments correspond to those experiments performed by [9] with the ten best seeds. Table 1 shows the performance, in seconds, of both cluster of CPUs' implementation for up to 16 nodes and hybrid parallel implementation for up to 8 nodes. For the cluster of CPUs we achieved *speedups* around 2 for two nodes, and the speedup was growing up to 16 nodes (see Fig. 2(a)).

For the hybrid algorithm, we notice that the speedup was around 2 when we used only one CPU/GPU. Increasing this number to 2, the running time dropped by half for many seeds (see Table 1). Figure 2(b) shows the speedups achieved for 1, 2, 4 and 8 CPU/GPUs. The best speedup achieved was 12.3 (ex. seed $\{3, 4, 8\}$), when running with 8 CPU/GPU.

Seed Growing of HeLa 2

We tested our algorithms for network 2 of *HeLa* cells. Table 2 shows the runtime of both implementations. On Cluster of CPUs we obtained speedups around 2 (see Fig. 3) with 2 nodes. Doubling the number of nodes, the speedups range from 2.4 to 3.5. With 8 nodes, we obtained speedups values from 2.8 to 5.8 and with 16 nodes, the best speedup obtained was 11.5 (ex. seed $\{1, 7, 17\}$). For the hybrid algorithm we note that when the run time is low the sequential algorithm is faster than the hybrid algorithm with only one CPU/GPU. However the speedup increases when augmenting the number of CPU/GPUs (see Fig. 3(b)).

Table 1. Performance, in seconds, of seed growing in cluster of CPUs and hybrid approach for network 1 of *HeLa* cells.

*HeLa*1 seed	CPUs					CPUs/GPUs			
	1	2	4	8	16	1	2	4	8
0 2 8	70	48	34	22	13	52	31	22	15
1 7 8	25	16	8	5	3	17	10	6	4
1 7 11	38	25	13	9	6	25	15	9	6
1 8 11	34	21	12	7	5	23	13	8	5
3 4 8	49	26	16	8	5	32	16	10	4
3 4 11	46	27	13	8	6	28	15	8	5
8 9 10	21	11	8	5	4	14	7	5	4
3 10 11	20	12	6	4	3	14	8	5	4
8 13 14	53	29	18	11	7	37	19	12	8
8 16 19	28	16	10	5	4	18	10	7	5

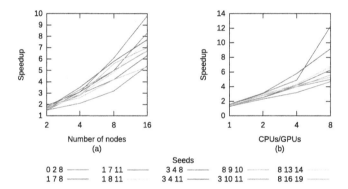

Fig. 2. Speedups of the cluster of CPU and hybrid algorithm of network Hela 1.

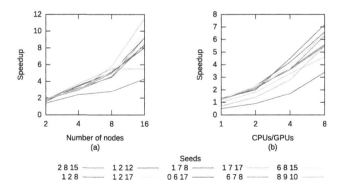

Fig. 3. *Speedups* of the cluster of CPU and hybrid algorithm of network HeLa 2.

Table 2. Performance, in seconds, of seed growing of cluster of CPUs and hybrid for network 2 of *HeLa* cells.

HeLa2 seed	CPUs					CPUs/GPUs			
	1	2	4	8	16	1	2	4	8
2 8 15	50	27	16	10	6	41	23	14	8
1 2 8	67	37	21	15	8	56	32	18	12
1 2 12	46	26	13	9	5	35	20	11	7
1 2 17	39	22	13	8	4	29	17	10	6
1 7 8	17	12	7	6	4	35	18	10	5
0 6 17	72	46	21	14	9	57	36	16	10
1 7 17	23	12	8	4	2	24	13	7	5
6 7 8	83	45	28	18	9	69	38	23	15
6 8 15	52	28	17	10	6	43	23	14	8
8 9 10	11	6	3	2	2	16	8	4	2

Seed Growing of In Silico Data

The last experiment used the *in silico* data. Table 3 shows the runtime of the both implementations. Figure 4(a) shows the obtained speedups for the cluster of CPUs. For two nodes, the speedup was around 2 for most of the seeds. With 4 nodes the speedups were in the range 2.7 to 3.4. With 8 nodes, the speedups were around twice better in relation to 4 nodes and for 16 nodes, the best speedup obtained was 12.7 (ex. seed $\{26, 43, 79\}$).

Table 3. Performance, in seconds, of seed growing in cluster of CPUs and hybrid approach for *in silico* data.

In Silico seed	CPUs					CPUs/GPUs			
	1	2	4	8	16	1	2	4	8
1 2 71	287	171	94	50	31	476	229	110	55
26 62 71	136	86	50	25	16	159	84	47	23
37 52 83	60	33	20	12	7	135	65	31	16
25 37 71	54	32	16	12	6	136	62	28	14
26 43 79	140	82	41	22	11	195	97	46	23
6 37 71	55	30	16	12	6	131	62	29	14
21 71 86	47	28	16	10	8	167	73	31	16
2 71 86	107	63	37	19	14	251	133	59	24
12 25 83	54	35	19	14	9	82	40	20	12
19 20 86	132	78	41	24	15	307	144	66	33

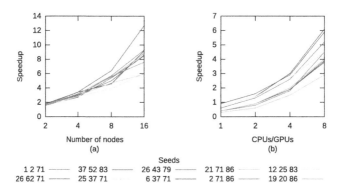

Fig. 4. Speedups in cluster of CPUs and hybrid in the *in silico* data.

We notice that using one CPU/GPU (see Table 3), the time did not reach the sequential time. We also notice that, as from two CPU/GPUs, the hybrid algorithm is faster than the sequential. This behavior demonstrates that the algorithm is scalable with the number of CPU/GPU (see Fig. 4(b)).

When we analyze the experiments we note that in Gecode, if a gene $x_i \in S \cup Z$ does not have consistent rows, the computing of criterion function $J(S \cup Z)$ stops and the function J is no longer computed for x_j, $j > i$. This feature is not present in the GPU algorithm, since the all threads must run the same instruction.

6.3   Inference Step in Cluster of CPUs

The inference step is a sample process where $\mathcal{M}$ consistent networks are generated and only 10% (we set $s = 10$) of these networks with the lowest entropies are considered of interest from the biological point of view.

Figure 5(a) shows the runtime of the algorithm. As expected, the algorithm is scalable and robust independently of the number of generated networks, and in Fig. 5(b) we see the speedup ranging from 1.4 up to 10.1. We note that in Table 4 the time is proportional to the number of networks. This behavior is repeated when we use 2, 4, 8 and 16 CPUs, with different number of networks.

Table 4. Time, in seconds, of the inference step on cluster of CPUs.

# Networks generated	Number of nodes				
	1	2	4	8	16
1000	11,1	8,6	4,4	2,2	1,1
2000	22,2	17,1	8,7	4,6	2,2
3000	33,3	25,7	12,9	6,6	3,3
4000	44,3	34,4	17,2	8,8	4,3
5000	55,5	43,2	21,6	10,9	5,4

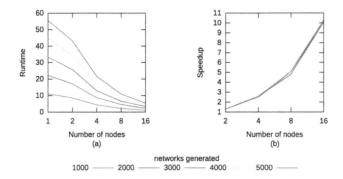

Fig. 5. Runtime (a), in sec., and speedup (b) of the sequential and parallel inference step on cluster of CPUs over five different values of $\mathcal{M}$.

Note that the speedups are very similar for different number of networks. The number of operations of the parallel algorithm is higher when compared to Gecode, since it has to keep its local networks in increasing order of score. Figure 5(b) shows that we achieved speedups of up to 10.1 with 16 nodes. Notice also that the algorithm is scalable when varying the number of CPUs.

7   Conclusion

We presented two parallel implementations for the inference of GRNs in two different parallel computer systems. Despite the high quality of the Gecode solver, we obtained good speedups, and in general our solutions were always scalable.

When we observe the speedups of the cluster of CPU algorithm in the three datasets, we notice that the algorithm is scalable. It is important to observe that the inference step depends on the parameter $\mathcal{M}$. When $\mathcal{M}$ is large enough both algorithms, sequential and parallel, tends to output the same set of networks. In the seed growing step, both provide the same output, once there is no randomness in this step. The validation of the inferred networks is performed in [9].

In general, with the improvement of the CSP solvers on GPU to address constrains, we can expect that the speedups obtained in this work can be improved. We notice that adding more devices to the computer system the algorithm can speedup the process, even when it is slower for a small amount of nodes.

The source code is free software under the GPL license and available at http://git.facom.ufms.br/jean.carlo/seedgrowing.

References

1. Akutsu, T., Miyano, S., Kuhara, S.: Identification of genetic networks from a small number of gene expression patterns under the Boolean network model. In: Pacific Symposium on Biocomputing, pp. 17–28 (1999)
2. Borelli, F., de Camargo, R., Martins, D., Rozante, L.: Gene regulatory networks inference using a multi-GPU exhaustive search algorithm. BMC Bioinform. **14**(Suppl. 18), S5 (2013). https://doi.org/10.1186/1471-2105-14-S18-S5

3. Carastan-Santos, D., de Camargo, R.Y., Martins Jr., D.C.: A multi-GPU hitting set algorithm for GRNs inference. In: IEEE/ACM International Symposium on Cluster, Cloud and Grid Computing, pp. 313–322 (2015)
4. DREAM: DREAM: Dialogue for Reverse Engineering Assessments and Methods (2009). Project website: http://wiki.c2b2.columbia.edu/dream/
5. Friedman, N., Linial, M., Nachman, I., Pe'er, D.: Using Bayesian networks to analyze expression data. J. Comput. Biol. **7**(6), 601–620 (2000)
6. Gecode Team: Gecode: Generic constraint development environment (2006). www.gecode.org
7. Goodwin, B.C.: Temporal Organization in Cells; A Dynamic Theory of Cellular Control Process. Academic Press, Cambridge (1963)
8. Hashimoto, R.F., Kim, S., Shmulevich, I., Zhang, W., Bittner, M.L., Dougherty, E.R.: Growing genetic regulatory networks from seed genes. Bioinformatics **20**(8), 1241–1247 (2004)
9. Higa, C.H.A., Andrade, T.P., Hashimoto, R.F.: Growing seed genes from time series data and thresholded Boolean networks with perturbation. IEEE Trans. Comput. Biol. Bioinform. **10**(1), 37–49 (2013)
10. Higa, C.H.A., Louzada, V.H.P., Andrade, T.P., Hashimoto, R.F.: Constraint-based analysis of gene interactions using restricted Boolean networks and time-series data. BMC Proc. **5**(Suppl. 2), S5 (2011)
11. Karlebach, G., Shamir, R.: Modelling and analysis of gene regulatory networks. Nature **9**, 770–780 (2008)
12. Kauffman, S.A.: Metabolic stability and epigenesis in randomly constructed genetic nets. J. Theor. Biol. **22**(3), 437–467 (1969)
13. Kim, G., Lee, M., Jeong, J., Kim, J.: Multi-GPU system design with memory networks. In: IEEE International Symposium on Microarchitecture (2014)
14. Lee, W.P., Hsiao, Y.T., Hwang, W.C.: Designing a parallel evolutionary algorithm for inferring gene networks on the cloud computing environment. BMC Syst. Biol. **5**(8), 5+ (2014)
15. Li, Y., Liu, L., Bai, X., Cai, H., Ji, W., Guo, D., Zhu, Y.: Comparative study of discretization methods of microarray data for inferring transcriptional regulatory networks. BMC Bioinform. **11**(1), 520+ (2010)
16. Martin, J.A., Wang, Z.: Next-generation transcriptome assembly. Nat. Rev. Genet. **12**(10), 671–682 (2011)
17. Martin, S., Zhang, Z., Martino, A., Faulon, J.L.: Boolean dynamics of genetic regulatory networks inferred from microarray time series data. Bioinformatics **23**, 866–874 (2007)
18. Nakariyakul, S., Casasent, D.P.: An improvement on floating search algorithms for feature subset selection. Pattern Recogn. **42**(9), 1932–1940 (2009)
19. Shi, H., Schmidt, B., Liu, W., Müller-Wittig, W.: Parallel mutual information estimation for inferring gene regulatory networks on GPUs. BMC Res. Notes **4**, 1–10 (2011)
20. Sterling, T., Becker, D.J., Savarese, D., Dorband, J.E., Ranawake, U.A., Packer, C.V.: BEOWULF: a parallel workstation for scientific computation. In: International Conference on Parallel Processing, vol. 95 (1995)
21. Whitfield, M.L., Sherlock, G., Saldanha, A.J., Murray, J.I., Ball, C.A., Alexander, K.E., Matese, J.C., Perou, C.M., Hurt, M.M., Brown, P.O., Botstein, D.: Identification of genes periodically expressed in the human cell cycle and their expression in tumors. Mol. Biol. cell **13**(6), 1977–2000 (2002)
22. Xiao, X., Zhang, W., Zou, X.: A new asynchronous parallel algorithm for inferring large-scale gene regulatory networks. PLoS ONE **3**(10), e0119294 (2015)

Geometric Modeling, Graphics and Visualization

Highest Order Voronoi Processing
on Apache Spark

Putu Eka Budi Pradnyana[1($\boxtimes$)], Kiki Maulana Adhinugraha[1($\boxtimes$)],
and Sultan Alamri[2($\boxtimes$)]

[1] School of Computing, Telkom University, Bandung, Indonesia
budipradnyana@students.telkomuniversity.ac.id,
kikimaulana@telkomuniversity.ac.id
[2] College of Computing and Informatics, Saudi Electronic University,
Riyadh, Saudi Arabia
salamri@seu.edu.sa

Abstract. Voronoi diagram is a method that divides the plane into smaller area based on the nearest distance to an object. There is a new variant of Voronoi diagram where each Voronoi cell has ordered generator points distances called Highest Order Voronoi Diagram (HSVD). The HSVD construction complexity is on $O(m^4)$, where m is the number of generator points. From related works, there are method called Fast Labelling and Interchange Position (FLIP) and Left with Least-Angle Movement (LAM) used to construct highest order voronoi diagram. But, both of this methods implemented on conventional computing/sequential processing and have limitation on number of points that can be processed. Because on sequential processing the process executed sequentially, then there is a process awaits for another process to finish. Beside that, computing resources are only utilized sequentially. To overcome this issues, we can use distributed computing framework that focuses on the optimization of computing resources called Apache Spark. In this paper we adapt FLIP and LAM construction method in Apache Spark framework. Our observation shows that the processing time is 60% faster than previous implementation and also 17% increase on the number of point that can be processed.

Keywords: Voronoi diagram · Highest order · Spark · Spatial · Flip
Lam

1 Introduction

Voronoi diagram is a method that divides the map into smaller area/region based on the nearest distance to an object [1]. Voronoi diagrams are very useful in computational geometry, particularly for representation or quantization problems, and are used in the field of robotics for creating a protocol for avoiding detected obstacles [2]. This work [3] revealed that the complexity of Voronoi diagram is at most quadratic.

© Springer International Publishing AG, part of Springer Nature 2018
O. Gervasi et al. (Eds.): ICCSA 2018, LNCS 10960, pp. 169–182, 2018.
https://doi.org/10.1007/978-3-319-95162-1_12

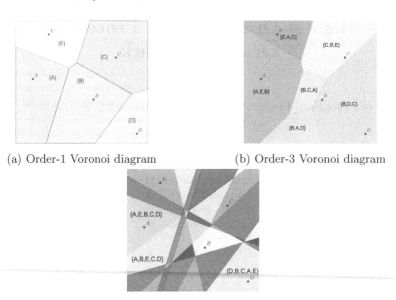

(a) Order-1 Voronoi diagram   (b) Order-3 Voronoi diagram

(c) Highest order Voronoi diagram

Fig. 1. An example of voronoi diagram based on the order.

There are first order Voronoi diagram in Fig. 1(a) that show a Voronoi cell only contain a single information of the nearest generator points, higher order Voronoi diagram order-3 in Fig. 1(b), shows a Voronoi cell contains 3 nearest generator points and highest order Voronoi diagram where we can get all the sequence of the nearest generator pointsin as shown in Fig. 1(c). The complexity of Highest order Voronoi diagram (HSVD) construction is on $O(m^4)$, where m is the number of generator points [1].

There are 2 methods used to construct highest order voronoi diagram called Fast Labelling and Interchange Position (FLIP) and Left with Least-Angle Movement (LAM) [1]. Both of this methods implemented on conventional computing/sequential processing and have limitation on number of points that can be processed. Because on sequential processing the process executed sequentially, then there is a process awaits for another process to finish. Beside that, computing resources are only utilized sequentially.

To overcome this issues, we offer an alternative processing using distributed computing framework that focuses on the optimization of computing resources called Apache Spark. Apache Spark work well on iterative process that reuse a set of data because of the ability to do in-memory processing and distribute the task to all available cores [4]. The aim of this paper is to show that by combining FLIP and LAM construction method in Apache Spark framework, we can achieved 60% faster processing time than previous implementation and also 17% increase on the number of point that can be processed.

This paper is organized as follows. Section 2 discusses about related works, the proposed system methodology are on Sects. 3 and 4 explain about the evaluation of the system's performance, and the conclusion about the paper is on Sect. 5.

2   Related Works

2.1   First Order Voronoi Diagram

First-order Voronoi diagrams is a partition of space into regions of points that are closer to one site than to any other site. In this case the regions are convex polygons (sometimes called cells). An example of a first-order Voronoi diagram in the Euclidean plane can be seen in Fig. 2 below.

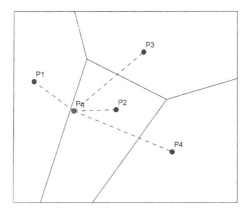

Fig. 2. First-order voronoi diagram

Note that in Fig. 2, the point p4 is closer to p2 than any other generated sites. The Voronoi diagram is composed of three elements: generators, edges, and vertices. Every point on the plane that is not a vertex or part of an edge is a generator point in a distinct voronoi region. A vertex is located at any point that is equidistant from the three (or more) nearest generator points on the plane. The number of edges that meet at a vertex is called the degree of the vertex [2]. A Voronoi diagram can be constructed by merging Voronoi polygons which are generated by the discrete points [5]. This paper [6] shows that Voronoi diagram of n sites in the plane can be computed in O(n) time. This paper [7] shows that Voronoi diagram construction can be facing instability in geometric computation that comes from numerical precision errors, which cause misjudgements of geometric structure, and algorithm failed to process the data.

2.2   Higher Order Voronoi Diagram

In higher order Voronoi diagram, the set of generators points are determined by the order itself. Higher order voronoi diagram also called n-order Voronoi

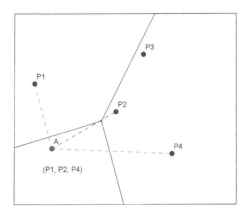

Fig. 3. Order-3 voronoi diagram (Color figure online)

diagram [8]. Here the 'order' means the number of points constituting a generator and 'higher' means more than one point.

In this order, we deal with only R^2, but conceptually the extension from R^2 to R^m is straightforward [8]. Suppose, as is illustrated in Fig. 3, that a set of generator points (the blue circles) is placed in the Euclidean plane. Consider there is a query point A (indicated by the red circle in the Figure), if the distance from A to all points in the point set is sorted, can be seen from the dashed lines, the three nearest points from the location are P1, P2 and P4. Note that we are not concerned with which point is the first nearest point in (P1, P2, P4).

2.3   Highest Order Voronoi Diagram

Highest order voronoi diagram is a new variant of the Voronoi diagram which is derived from Higher order voronoi diagram. HSVD consists of Voronoi cells with distance information to all generator points. In HSVD, no cells have the same m ordered generator points, and no generator points have the same order where m is the number of facility points [1].

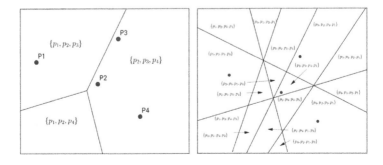

Fig. 4. Order-3 VD (left) and HSVD (right)

As shows in Fig. 4, both of Order-3 VD and HSVD have 4 generators point. Order-3 voronoi diagram each region are labeled with 3 nearest generates points. Unlike HOVD, in HSVD each region are labeled with all sorted generator points from the nearest to the farthest. Label (p1, p2, p3, p4) on region r mean that any query point x in region r will have the information of all ordered generator points from nearest to farthest. In other words, query point x will consider p1 as the nearest generator points, p2 as the second nearest, p3 as the third nearest, and p4 as the farthest generators points.

2.4   Apache Spark

Apache Spark is a distributed computing framework designed for iterative process. The main abstraction in Spark is the resilient distributed dataset (RDD). RDD is a collection of read-only objects that stored in distributed system [9].

Spark uses a master/slave architecture. As we can see in the Fig. 5, it has one central master called Driver Program that communicates with many distributed workers (executors). The driver is s where the conversion process of user program into tasks occur and after that it schedules the tasks to the executors. Executors are worker nodes that running individual tasks in a given Spark job. Once they have run the task they send the results to the driver [10].

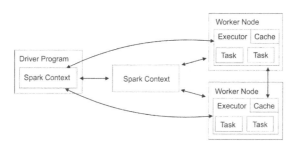

Fig. 5. Apache Spark master/slave architecture

Resilient Distributed Dataset (RDD). An RDD is simply a distributed collection of elements. RDDs are fault-tolerant, parallel data structures that let users explicitly persist intermediate results in memory, control their partitioning to optimize data placement, and manipulate them using a rich set of operators [11] In Spark all work is expressed as either creating new RDDs, transforming existing RDDs, or calling operations on RDDs to compute a result. Under the hood, Spark automatically distributes the data contained in RDDs across cluster and parallelizes the operations we perform on them [12].

Dataframe. DataFrame is a distributed data table organized in rows and columns and having names for each column. Dataframe is developed based on this research paper [13]. DataFrame holds structured data, and it is distributed.

It allows selection, filtering, and aggregation of data, very similar to RDD. The key difference between RDD and DataFrame is that DataFrame stores much more information about the structure of the data, such as the data types and names of the columns, than RDD. This allows the DataFrame to optimize the processing much more effectively than Spark transformations and Spark actions doing processing on RDD [14]. DataFrames not only used for basic data transformations, but also can be used as the input and output format to Spark's libraries (e.g., the machine learning library) [15].

3   System Methodology and Design

3.1   Overview

In this section, we will present the system methodology and design which include the data structure, process overview, and evaluation.

3.2   Data Structure

A Voronoi cell is convex polygon. It consist of segments and a segment consist of vertex. The data structure that will be used in order to construct highest order Voronoi diagram on Apache Spark are shown in Table 1.

3.3   Highest Order Voronoi Diagram Construction

In order to construct a highest order Voronoi diagram, will be combined FLIP method and LAM method [1]. There are several step that must be applied to construct highest order Voronoi diagram. Those steps are explained as follows:

1. The generators points are generated using random uniform distributed method.
2. At the first step, will be created all possible perpendicular bisectors that can be constructed from one point to all other generator points. The bound of workspace area also considered as bisector.
3. The next step is to find all intersection points (vertex) by intersecting one perpendicular bisector to the others bisector.
4. Identify all available segments. A segment is considered as 2 directed vector. The segment constructed by ordering the vertex in X or Y axis for all available bisectors.
5. In order to construct regions, we have to loop through all segments. In Fig. 6, we show how a region is constructed from list of segment. The process to construct a region are explained as follows:
   (a) The first is we select a segment called current segment. The segment we select is the bisector segment, not the boundary segment.
   (b) Then, we have to get all the next segment candidate. Don't select the next segment that are in the same bisector. We can see this step on Fig. 6(a).

Table 1. Highest order Voronoi diagram data structure

Structure name	Attributes	Description
Point	name	Point name
	x	Coordinate on x-axis
	y	Coordinate on y-axis
Bisector	perp_name	Bisector name
	mval	m coefisien of bisector line
	bval	b coefisien of bisector line
	tipe	Type of bisector
	point1	The first bisector point
	point2	The second bisector point
Vertex	vertex_name	Vertex name
	coordinate_X	The coordinate on X axis
	coordinate_Y	The coordinate on Y axis
	bisector1	Tirst bisector to intersect
	bisector2	Second bisector to intersect
Segment	seg_name	Segment name
	X_begin	Starting point of segment on X axis
	Y_begin	Starting point of segment on Y axis
	X_end	Ending point of segment on X axis
	Y_end	Ending point of segment on Y axis
	tipe	Type of segment
	bisector	Bisector origin of the segment
Region	region_name	Region name
	X_begin	Starting point of segment on X axis
	Y_begin	Starting point of segment on Y axis
	X_end	Ending point of segment on X axis
	Y_end	Ending point of segment on Y axis
	tipe	Type of region's segment
Label	region_name	Region name
	label	List of ordered generator points

(c) After we get all the next segment candidates, we do calculation on the inner-angle between current segment to all next segment candidates. This process shown in Fig. 6(b).

(d) We choose the next segment candidates with the smallest inner-angle as the next segment. Then the segment we select from previous process become the current segment as shown in Fig. 7(c).

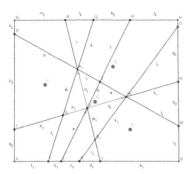 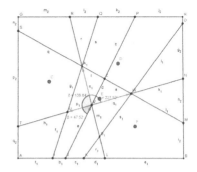

(a) select a segment and get the next seg- (b) Calculate the inner angle
ment candidates

Fig. 6. Region construction process part 1.

(e) The process number (2), (3), (4) then repeated until the next segment is the equal to initial segment. After this process stops then a region is already formed as in Fig. 7(d).

6. After all regions have been identified, the next step is identify the sequence for each voronoi cell. We use centroid method to identify all the sequence for each voronoi cell. In Fig. 8(a), the first step is we have to calculate the centroid of voronoi cell. A centroid must be inside of a voronoi cell. This paper [16] describe one of many method to calculate the centroid of Voronoi cell called the arithmetic mean centroid. Then, we calculate the distance from the centroid to all generator points. After we get the distance information from centroid to all generator points, we have to sort it in ascending order. The result from sorting is the sequence for the voronoi cell. This process repeated to each Voronoi cells as in Fig. 8(b).

3.4 Apache Spark Partitioning

One of the important way to increase parallelism on Apache Spark processing is increase the number of executors on the machine. In Apache Spark we can achieve this using partitioning. Since Apache Spark split data into partitions and executes the data on the partitions in parallel, then the number of partition also affect the performance. But, there are no fixed way to calculate the number of partition. Having too few partition will affect the performance because we aren't utilize all of the available cores. In the other side, if we have too many partition, there will be excessive overhead in executing small tasks.

From Fig. 9, we can see that after spark transforming the data using query that we apply, then the query result return as a set of data. Those data then partition into the number of partition that we specify. The partitioned data then distributed to all executors to do the calculation. At last, the result is combining and collect the result.

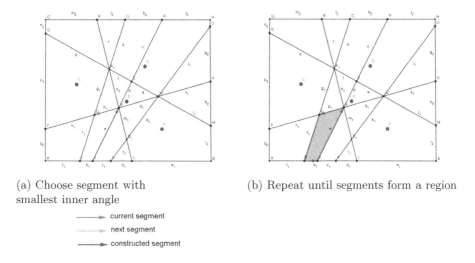

(a) Choose segment with smallest inner angle

(b) Repeat until segments form a region

```
———————▶  current segment
··········▶  next segment
———————▶  constructed segment
```

Fig. 7. Region construction process part 2.

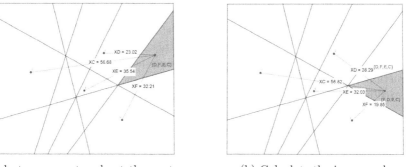

(a) select a segment and get the next segment candidates

(b) Calculate the inner angle

Fig. 8. Labelling process

3.5   Summary

Highest order Voronoi diagram construction use random distributed dataset. The number of points on highest order Voronoi diagram construction will affect the data size that generated. The construction generated large amount of data, so that constructing the highest order voronoi diagram will take more time as the number of points grows up. By using Apache Spark framework, we can query a large dataset then partition the query result to our specified number of partition. Then the partitioned query result distributed evenly to the executors.

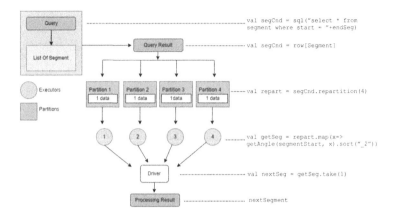

Fig. 9. Partitioning in Apache Spark

4 Evaluation

4.1 Overview

In this section, we will explain about the system performance evaluation. There are 4 aspects that will be the concern in this phase, they are: the number of partition, execution time comparison, labelling method comparison, region construction and region labelling comparison. Three method are compared in term of execution time and number of point that can be processed.

4.2 Number of Partition

Based on Apache Spark documentation that says "In general, we recommend 2–3 tasks per CPU core in your cluster" then we conduct an experiment to determine the number of partitions that could give the fastest execution time. Since our available CPU core is 8, then we had 24, 32 and 40 partitions run separately on our program. We used 15 point, 16 point, 17 point, 18 point and 19 point as the dataset because it will be more obvious if the data is quite large. From Fig. 10, we can see that, few partition doesn't mean faster execution time while many partition doesn't mean faster execution time either. That is why we have to work with an experiment to decide the number of partition that will be used. All of the dataset used in this experiment shows that the number of partition equal to 32 give the fastest execution time among other number of partition.

4.3 Execution Time Comparison

In this execution times evaluation, we do a comparison between this implementation, we called FLIP* and previous implementation [1]. As shown in Fig. 11, FLIP* on Spark run about 60% in average faster than LAM method on conventional computing because we can avoid costly disk accesses by keeping the

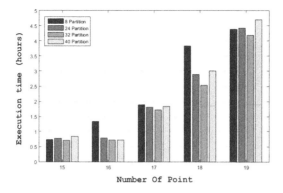

Fig. 10. Number of partition comparison for FLIP* on Apache Spark

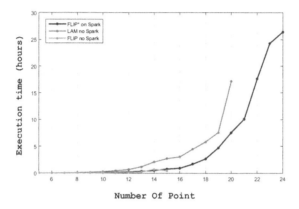

Fig. 11. Method's execution time comparison.

processed data in memory. While on comparison between FLIP* on Spark and previous FLIP implementation [1], FLIP* on Spark is in average 46% slower because on region construction process there are repeatedly changes on input data in memory. It means that we repeatedly retrieves and re-saves data to memory. Previous implementation [1] can only process at maximum of 20 generator points due to point precision problem while FLIP* on Spark manage to process 24 generator points. At first sight we might think that the graph of FLIP* on Spark is exponential, but since the complexity of highest order Voronoi diagram construction is at $O(n^4)$, it stands between cubic and exponential complexity.

4.4 Labelling Method Comparison

In Fig. 12 show that labelling using centroid method perform faster than FLIP method. This is because we utilize the Apache Spark computation advantage on processing immutable data. During FLIP labelling process, we must do some changes on the region data to indicate which region segment has been

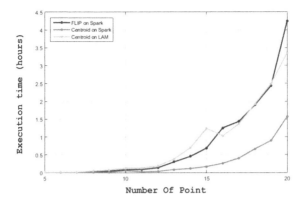

Fig. 12. Labelling method execution time comparison

processed. This process that made us unable to utilize the immutable data processing on Apache Spark. While using centroid labelling, we are able to utilize the immutable data processing on Apache Spark. Since we didn't do any changes on region data, the data can be stored as immutable component and processed in average about 60% faster.

4.5 Region Construction and Labelling Process Comparison on Apache Spark

From Fig. 13, we can see the comparison of region construction and region labelling in term of execution time. Region labelling executed faster than region construction because in region construction we can't efficiently utilize the immutable component and in-memory processing of Apache Spark. We try to reduce the size of the segment data input that used to construct region by removing each segment that already in used. This process resulting in the repeated

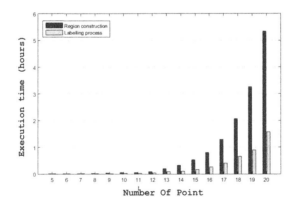

Fig. 13. Region construction and labelling process comparison on Apache Spark

segment data changes in memory and needs to be refreshed into memory. While on labelling using centroid method, we can store the region data input in memory because this method only need to read the region data without do any changes. With this kind of processing, we achieve region labelling run 65% faster than region construction on Apache Spark.

5   Conclusion

We conduct this experiment to increase the generator points that can be processed while reducing the execution time compared to previous implementation. By combining the data structures and method between FLIP and LAM then choosing the best for reducing execution time, we manage to speed up the processing time 62% in average faster than previous implementation and also 17% increase on the number of point that can be processed. This work still have a disadvantage in memory usage as we stored a segment twice.

The future work of this work is use real spatial object dataset such as airport latitude and longitude as generator points input to make the highest order Voronoi diagram more suitable for real world cases.

References

1. Christianto, D.S., Adhinugraha, K.M., Herdiani, A., Alamri, S.: Highest order Voronoi diagram optimization. In: 2017 5th International Conference on Information and Communication Technology (ICoIC7), pp. 1–7, May 2017
2. Dobrin, A.: A review of properties and variations of Voronoi diagrams. Whitman College (2005)
3. De Berg, M., Van Kreveld, M., Overmars, M., Schwarzkopf, O.C.: Computational geometry. In: De Berg, M., Van Kreveld, M., Overmars, M., Schwarzkopf, O.C. (eds.) Computational Geometry, pp. 1–17. Springer, Heidelberg (2000). https://doi.org/10.1007/978-3-662-04245-8_1
4. Zaharia, M., Chowdhury, M., Franklin, M.J., Shenker, S., Stoica, I.: Spark: cluster computing with working sets. HotCloud **10**(10–10), 95 (2010)
5. Zhang, X., Bae, H.Y., Xia, Y.,Wu, X.: Parallel voronoi diagram construction method with mapreduce. In: IJISET, **4** (2016)
6. Aggarwal, A., Guibas, L.J., Saxe, J., Shor, P.W.: A linear-time algorithm for computing the voronoi diagram of a convex polygon. Discrete Comput. Geom. **4**(6), 591–604 (1989)
7. Sugihara, K.: Degeneracy and instability in geometric computation. In: Kimura, F. (ed.) Geometric Modelling. ITIFIP, vol. 75, pp. 3–16. Springer, Boston, MA (2001). https://doi.org/10.1007/978-0-387-35490-3_1
8. Okabe, A., Boots, B., Sugihara, K., Chiu, S.N.: Spatial Tessellations: Concepts and Applications of Voronoi Diagrams, vol. 501. Wiley, Hoboken (2009)
9. Zhang, Y., Cao, T., Li, S., Tian, X., Yuan, L., Jia, H., Vasilakos, A.V.: Parallel processing systems for big data: a survey. Proc. IEEE **104**(11), 2114–2136 (2016)
10. Jangid, H.: Parallel SPARQL query execution using apache spark. Ph.D. dissertation, University of Missouri-Kansas City (2016)

11. Zaharia, M., Chowdhury, M., Das, T., Dave, A., Ma, J., McCauley, M., Franklin, M.J., Shenker, S., Stoica, I.: Resilient distributed datasets: a fault-tolerant abstraction for in-memory cluster computing. In: Proceedings of the 9th USENIX Conference on Networked Systems Design and Implementation, p. 2. USENIX Association (2012)
12. Karau, H., Konwinski, A., Wendell, P., Zaharia, M.: Learning Spark: Lightning-fast Big Data Analysis. O'Reilly Media, Inc., Newton (2015)
13. Armbrust, M., Xin, R.S., Lian, C., Huai, Y., Liu, D., Bradley, J.K., Meng, X., Kaftan, T., Franklin, M.J., Ghodsi, A., et al.: Spark SQL: in relational data processing in spark. In: Proceedings of the 2015 ACM SIGMOD International Conference on Management of Data, pp. 1383–1394. ACM (2015)
14. Thottuvaikkatumana, R.: Apache Spark 2 For Beginners. Packt Publishing, Birmingham (2016)
15. Armbrust, M., Das, T., Davidson, A., Ghodsi, A., Or, A., Rosen, J., Stoica, I., Wendell, P., Xin, R., Zaharia, M.: Scaling spark in the real world: performance and usability. Proc. VLDB Endow. **8**(12), 1840–1843 (2015)
16. Deakin, R., Bird, S., Grenfell, R.: The centroid? Where would you like it to be be? Cartography **31**(2), 153–167 (2002)

Adaptation of k-Nearest Neighbor Queries for Inter-building Environment

Diska Andini[1(✉)], Dawam Dwi Jatmiko Suwawi[1(✉)],
Kiki Maulana Adhinugraha[1(✉)], and Sultan Alamri[2(✉)]

[1] School of Computing, Telkom University, Bandung, Indonesia
diskaandini@student.telkomuniversity.ac.id,
{dawamdjs,kikimaulana}@telkomuniversity.ac.id
[2] College of Computing and Informatics, Saudi Electronic University,
Riyadh, Saudi Arabia
salamri@seu.edu.sa

Abstract. Nearest neighbor (kNN) is a spatial query where its main aim is to find k nearest object around a query point. This query has been widely used in outdoor environment to obtain point of interests in various GIS system, such as navigation and routing. The floor layout of a building can be represented with simple graph network. Unlike outdoor road network that usually only has single layer, an indoor network might have multiple layers which represents floors. In a multi-building area, buildings can be connected with the other buildings and create more complex network, which is called inter-building environment. In this paper, Dijkstra and Floyd Warshall algorithms as kNN algorithm are adapted and implemented in inter-building environment. Our experiments show that these algorithms are be able to adapt three dimensional graph for inter-building environment.

Keywords: Nearest neighbor · Inter-building
Three dimensional network

1 Introduction

Nearest neighbor (kNN) is a spatial query where its main aim is to find k nearest object around a query point. This query has been widely used in outdoor environment to obtain point of interests in various GIS system, such as navigation and routing [10]. In navigational system, kNN is commonly used to identify nearby objects either in static or dynamic objects [3,6], especially in mobile devices to support road navigations [1,9,15].

From Fig. 1 nearest neighbor query can be used to find the objects of interests (such as restaurants) from the query location. Nearest neighbor query in indoor space can be used as in outdoor space to finding the objects of interest type in inter-building environment. But differences in some aspects of indoor and outdoor spaces, nearest neighbor in indoor space should consider the elements

O. Gervasi et al. (Eds.): ICCSA 2018, LNCS 10960, pp. 183–194, 2018.
https://doi.org/10.1007/978-3-319-95162-1_13

Fig. 1. Geo-Positioning system implementation in outdoor

contained in indoor space to be implemented for inter-building environment. In indoor, buildings may have a number of rooms and corridors. Every rooms allows for a variety of doors that connect with another spaces. Moreover, the building can be multi level building or on three dimensional spaces that has stairs, lifts or elevators to move from one level to another level. The entire space must have identified labels as well as connection between the spaces [2, 7].

Although indoor and outdoor have differences in some aspects, but there is similarity in representing data model. The floor layout of a building is similar with road network in outdoor, where this layout can be represented as a graph network. While it's not common in a road network to have multiple layer, in indoor environment, a building can have multiple floors [11]. Therefore, the network structure in indoor space is more complex than the road network. Moreover in a multi-building area, some buildings can be connected with each other and create an inter-building environment. In this paper, adaptation and implementation several kNN algorithm for inter-building environment is proposed. Our experiments show that the algorithms can be well implemented in inter-building environment.

This paper is organized as follows: Sect. 2 discusses the related work and previous studies that used in this case, Sect. 3 will explain the system adaptation analysis. After that will discuss evaluation of this system such as testing, analysis in Sect. 4 and last of section is the conclusion of this study.

2   Related Works

Nearest Neighbor Algorithm

Nearest neighbor is an algorithm to finding the given object of interest that is closest to the query location. From the space perspective, this query can be divided into three categories, which are: (i) Euclidean space, (ii)spatial road network space and (iii) combination of Euclidean and spatial road network space [12]. In Euclidean space, the distance is measured by a straight and direct distance between two spatial objects. The work for NN query in Euclidean distance has been extended to calculate the obstacled during the process [13,14]. The idea is if the Euclidean distance between two spatial objects are obstructed with obstacles, the path from Euclidean distance needs to be bend to avoid the obstacles. Therefore, the distance will be longer (Figs. 2 and 3).

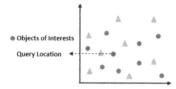

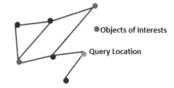

Fig. 2. NN based on Euclidean   **Fig. 3.** NN based on road network

Neighbor query in road networks uses a two dimensional representation of road network as a data structure to support nearest neighbor query, they proposed positioning units to report the query location and location of points of interests. From the representation of road network, measure the distance used the shortest distance between points algorithm. By the positioning system shows the points of interests location, the measure used road network graph representation to finding the nearest object [8]. However, the existing literature does not explain about based nearest neighbor for building in inter-building environment that may have multi-level-floor building.

Indoor Environment

The indoor positioning literature is vast and diverse as it takes advantage of several technologies, including: RFID, Wireless LANs, Infrared, Bluetooth, Ultra-Wide-Band, etc, beside their combinations into hybrid systems. These technologies deliver a promising level of accuracy, comparable to GNSS (Global Navigation Satellite System) that is not efficient in indoors. With the present availability of sensor-rich mobiles which have increased the interest for a variety of indoor buildings location-based services, such as, querying, in-building guidance and navigation [11]. This is important since most of people spend their time in indoor environments such as houses, offices, shopping malls and others [3].

Moreover, most of buildings are multi-floor environments, where many queries can be raised. This clear in Inter-building environment where some queries such as KNN, which shows the importance of adopting this type of query in this environment. For example, a user wants to retrieve the nearest prayer room to its location in Inter-building environment. Note that these inter-building may have buildings with multi-floor environments which gives a higher importance for determining the best path for the user (Figs. 4 and 5).

In [5], they proposed a floor layout information that specified the coordinates of each room and also obtained the coordinates of three base stations. However, this study does not explain the floor layout information that have different floors in a building. [7] proposes a representation in indoor space identify an object

 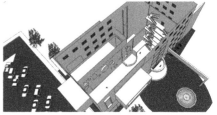

Fig. 4. Inter-building   **Fig. 5.** Indoor space

accurately by storing geographic data that are represented to undirected graph form which has three dimensional attributes x, y, and z, where x and y are the coordinates of a point, and z represents the height level of the points. There are various kinds of elements in indoor spaces such as rooms, doors, corridors, floors, stairs, elevators and the road connection between buildings. Indoor spaces are represented by undirected graph with nodes and edges. The various kinds of elements in indoor can be represented with modeling concept, such as: A cell represent room, edge represent door and one or more cells with one or more edges represent corridor and stair [2,4,7].

From this related work, this paper will define the nearest neighbor adaptation based on road network with the combination by considering indoor environment elements such as the connection between floor. Nearest neighbor for inter-building environment will represent inter-building by graph. The graph used to measure the distance between query location and points of interest.

3   Adaptation Analysis

The general process of this implementation can be modeled with the flowchart below (Fig. 6).

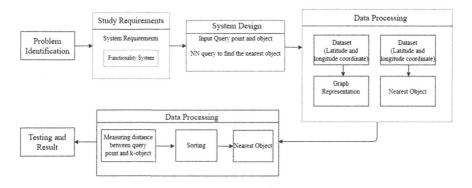

Fig. 6. General system process of proposed system

The first step of adaptation is collecting the dataset. The dataset used in this study is the School of Computing, Telkom University's spatial data in Fig. 7.

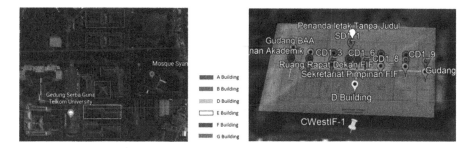

Fig. 7. Dataset location of School of Computing, Telkom University

The dataset is geographic data of latitude and longitude of buildings, rooms, label spaces, coordinates and connectivity between spaces. There are three coordinates, first longitude as x, latitude as y and z represent level of a buildings, stairs an corridors. Figure 7 an example of how to get the coordinate. Every rooms, stairs, label spaces and connectivity between spaces are marked to get the latitude and longitude.

By the dataset, graph data structure will be built by implementing indoor space representation. At this stage it will be built is undirected graph data structure by using a representation of three-dimensional space. Unlike the indoor routing data representation already described, this will represent a phase-storey building in three dimensions based on the location of the coordinates x, y, and z. The value of x is the longitude coordinate, y is the latitude coordinate, and z is the height level of the building.

After building the graph representation, finding the nearest object will be performed on undirected graph through measuring distances between query location and objects of interests. The distances calculate by implement road network for indoor space and use the routing algorithm. The search is performed in general and with the filtration technique implements a closed space. Performance will be measured on the performance of the system is associated with speed of execution time.

3.1   Three Dimensional Representation

The three dimensional representation captures data by x, y and z coordinates. Unlike two dimensional, three dimensional representation difficult to implement two dimensional Euclidean distances cause there are walls, path, stairs and others. Three dimensional represents every rooms, corridors, stairs of a building. Rooms, corridors and stairs representation by nodes. For each rooms (node) will be represented according the door of a room. And for each stairs, a node will be represented as the start of the stair begins and each corner of the stair stop. To represent three dimensional representation, latitude and longitude every rooms, corridors and stair can used as x and y coordinates. For z coordinates will be represent by floor.

Fig. 8. Coordinate point of room, corridor and stair on A building

Figure 8 shows the points that represent rooms, corridor and stairs on first floor A building. For the second and the third and floors will do the same thing. Latitude, longitude coordinate and floor of each point will be used to build graph representation.

3.2   Graph Representation

Graph representation in Table 1 have some nodes with different colors that symbolized different objects. Table 1 is three dimensional representation of buildings that was built represent to graph representation.

Table 1. Graph symbol

1	Black node	Represents the first floor corridors
2	Red node	Represents the third floor corridors
3	Green node	Represents the second floor corridors
4	Grey node	Represents all rooms
5	Blue node	Represents the stairs
6	Line	All segments

The define of graph representation and objects have to related to three dimensional representation. From the three dimensional representation, there are nodes and segment that can used on graph representation to build a graph. Every node is marked by roomid, stairid or corridorid as shown in Fig. 9. It illustrates a graph representation that was built from three dimensional representation.

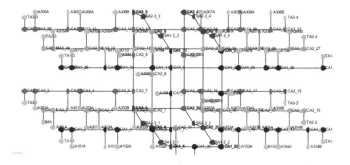

Fig. 9. Graph representation of A and B building (Color figure online)

3.3   NN in Inter-building Environment

This section will describe the adaptation and implementation of Dijkstra and Floyd Marshall algorithm for NN in inter-building environment. There are three steps which are: (i) to find nearest neighbor candidates (objects of interest), (ii) to compute the distance between query location and each objects of interests, (iii) to sort the distances. In this adaptation, the NN query that will be performed is monochromatic query.

At this stage, shortest path algorithms will be implemented. In this case there are Dijkstra's and Floyd Warshall algorithms that adapted to give the shortest path and also to calculate the measure between query location and objects of interests. Those algorithms used to compare the shortest path algorithm that find the shortest path between single node and all pairs of nodes. After all the measure between objects of interests is calculated, by default, the systems shows the nearest object and the path to the nearest object (Table 2).

Table 2. Path symbol

1	Yellow nodes	Represent objects of interests
2	Brown nodes	Represent nodes using Floyd Warshall
3	Purple nodes	Represent nodes using Dijkstra
4	Orange line	Represent segments using Floyd Warshall
5	Pink line	Represent segments using by Dijkstra

In Fig. 10 objects of interest with yellow nodes and the nearest practicum laboratory from IF2.02.02 is IF02.03.05 and there are similar paths between Dijkstra and Floyd Warshall. Figure 10 shows there is no pink line or purple node that represent Dijkstra Algorithm, because the nodes and segments of Dijkstra Algorithm covered by Floyd Warshall.

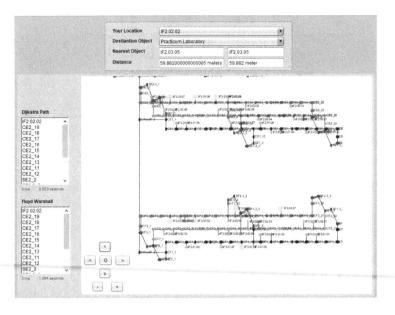

Fig. 10. Nearest practicum laboratory from IF2.02.02 (Color figure online)

4   Evaluation

4.1   Discussion

Based on first section there are two objectives of testing process: Correctness testing to test the correctness of adaptation nearest neighbor query in indoor space and performance testing to analyze the performance of nearest neighbor query.

We proposed some testing scenarios in this study, related to system's accuracy and performance in execution time. The aim of the test of system's accuracy is to compare between the desired objects with different objects. Another testing scenario is to test of system's performance in execution time, the aim is to compare running time between Dijkstra Algorithm and Floyd Warshall Algorithm. Both of algorithms tested five times with same data and scenario to get the execution time and also tested with different data and scenario.

4.2   Experiment and Analysis

There are two parts in this experiment. First, experiment for result of the system's accuracy. "IF3.02.06" were chosen as a query location and "Practicum Laboratory" as desired object. Table 3 shows the distance between query location and each objects that have type "Practicum Laboratory".

Table 3. Distance from IF3.02.06 to Practicum Laboratory

Source	Destination	Length
IF3.02.02	IF2.03.05	285.299 m
IF3.02.02	IF2.03.06	275.899 m
IF3.02.02	IF2.03.07	262.399 m
IF3.02.02	IF3.01.06	60.442 m
IF3.02.02	IF3.03.01	83.332 m
IF3.02.02	IF3.03.03	69.842 m
IF3.02.02	IF3.03.05	60.442 m
IF3.02.02	IF3.03.07	50.058 m
IF3.02.02	B203B	433.650 m

Table 3 shows that between all of the distances from source is IF3.02.02 to destination object: practicum laboratory, IF3.03.07 is the nearest practicum laboratory from IF3.02.02 by the distance is 50.058 m.

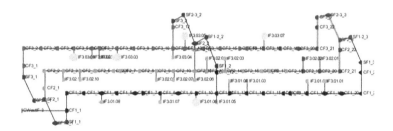

Fig. 11. Nearest practicum laboratory from IF3.02.02 (Color figure online)

Figure 11 shows the visualization of distance from query location and the objects of interests. It shows that there are five practicum laboratories in the same building that represent by yellow nodes. From all of objects of interests, it show that IF3.03.07 is the nearest practicum laboratory from IF3.02.02 and have the same result with Table 3.

Part two, experiments were performed to performance testing of the algorithm. The nearest Assistant Room from A307A were chosen as a sample. This testing do the searching process five times and it take the average value of the execution times as the result. Figure 12 the comparison clearly according to the console output of running execution time the system.

Consider the chart in Fig. 12 it shows the comparison in both shortest path algorithm, Floyd Warshall always give the best result. This is evidenced from the results of execution time that Floyd Warshall Algorithm shows the lower execution for each running program than Dijkstra Algorithm.

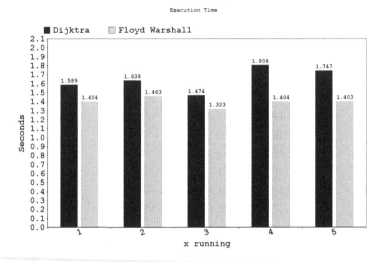

Fig. 12. Execution time comparison

The second test choose different query locations and objects with the different scenarios. Second test is divided into four scenarios: the query location and the object have same floor and same building, query location and the object have different floor and same building, query location and the object have same floor and different building, query location and the object have different floor and different building. The result of Tables 4 and 5 shown in Figs. 13, 14, 15 and 16.

Table 4. Testing result

No	Scenario	Query location	Destination	Result	Distance	Time execution	
						Dijskra	Floyd Warshall
1	Same floor, same building	A101A	Service room	A112	71.367 m	2.362 s	1.342 s
2	Different floor, same building	TA1-2	Musholla	MA	99.79 m	0.86 s	1.338 s
3	Same floor, different building	B109	Service room	A203A	149.07 m	1.502 s	1.332 s
4	Different floor, different building	A101A	Laboratory	B203	189.739 m	8.935 s	1.43 s

From the experiment result, nearest neighbor query can adapt in indoor space and the shortest path algorithm used on this study have different execution times. From Fig. 12 show that Floyd Warshall execution time is more consistent,

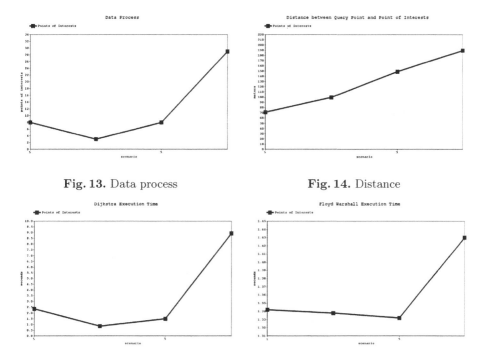

Fig. 13. Data process   **Fig. 14.** Distance

Fig. 15. Dijkstra execution time   **Fig. 16.** Floyd execution time

then Dijkstra algorithm that depends on how much data is executed that shown Figs. 13 and 15 that have same graphic. The more data executed the more time required by Dijkstra algorithm, but not with Floyd Warshall algorithm. Floyd Warshall has consistent execution time because the execution time does not rise or fall much different and does not depend on the amount of data. Based on Figs. 14, 15 and 16 execution time both of Algorithm does not depend on the distance between the query location and objects.

5   Conclusion

While nearest neighbor queries are commonly used in outdoor, the implementation in indoor is very limited. However, since the network structure of indoor environment and outdoor environment are very similar, the adaptation and implementation of well known kNN algorithms are highly possible. In this paper, we have demonstrated that both Dijkstra and Floyd Warshall algorithms are able to cope with inter-building environment.

We are now working with implementation and adaptation with NN types, which is reverse nearest neighbour queries to be implemented in inter-building environment.

References

1. Alamri, S.: An efficient shortest path routing algorithm for directed indoor environments. ISPRS Int. J. Geo-Inf. **7**(4) (2018)
2. Alamri, S., Taniar, D., Safar, M.: Indexing moving objects in indoor cellular space. In: NBiS, pp. 38–44 (2012)
3. Alamri, S., Taniar, D., Safar, M.: A taxonomy for moving object queries in spatial databases. Future Gener. Comput. Syst. **37**, 232–242 (2014)
4. Alamri, S., Taniar, D., Safar, M., Al-Khalidi, H.: Spatiotemporal indexing for moving objects in an indoor cellular space. Neurocomputing **122**, 70–78 (2013)
5. Bahl, P., Padmanabhan, V.N.: RADAR: an in-building RF-based user location and tracking system. In: Proceedings IEEE INFOCOM 2000, Conference on Computer Communications, Nineteenth Annual Joint Conference of the IEEE Computer and Communications Societies, Cat. No. 00CH37064, vol. 2, pp. 775–784 (2000)
6. Cheema, M.A., Lin, X., Zhang, Y., Wang, W., Zhang, W.: Lazy updates: an efficient technique to continuously monitoring reverse knn. Proc. VLDB Endow. **2**(1), 1138–1149 (2009)
7. Dionti, T.A., Adhinugraha, K.M., Alamri, S.M.: Inter-building routing approach for indoor environment. In: Gervasi, O., et al. (eds.) ICCSA 2017. LNCS, vol. 10404, pp. 247–260. Springer, Cham (2017). https://doi.org/10.1007/978-3-319-62392-4_18
8. Jensen, C.S., Kolářvr, J., Pedersen, T.B., Timko, I.: Nearest neighbor queries in road networks. In: Proceedings of the 11th ACM International Symposium on Advances in Geographic Information Systems, pp. 1–8. ACM (2003)
9. Nghiem, T., Green, D., Taniar, D.: Peer-to-peer group k-nearest neighbours in mobile ad-hoc networks. In: 2013 International Conference on Parallel and Distributed Systems, ICPADS, pp. 166–173, December 2013
10. Safar, M.: K nearest neighbor search in navigation systems. Mob. Inf. Syst. **1**(3), 207–224 (2005)
11. Alamri, D.T.S., Nguyen, K.: Vertical indexing for moving objects in multifloor environments. Mob. Inf. Syst. 15 (2018)
12. Taniar, D., Rahayu, W.: A taxonomy for nearest neighbour queries in spatial databases. J. Comput. Syst. Sci. **79**(7), 1017–1039 (2013)
13. Xia, C., Hsu, D., Tung, A.K.H.: A fast filter for obstructed nearest neighbor queries. In: Williams, H., MacKinnon, L. (eds.) BNCOD 2004. LNCS, vol. 3112, pp. 203–215. Springer, Heidelberg (2004). https://doi.org/10.1007/978-3-540-27811-5_19
14. Zhang, J., Papadias, D., Mouratidis, K., Zhu, M.: Spatial queries in the presence of obstacles. In: Bertino, E., Christodoulakis, S., Plexousakis, D., Christophides, V., Koubarakis, M., Böhm, K., Ferrari, E. (eds.) EDBT 2004. LNCS, vol. 2992, pp. 366–384. Springer, Heidelberg (2004). https://doi.org/10.1007/978-3-540-24741-8_22
15. Zhao, G., Xuan, K., Taniar, D.: Path knn query processing in mobile systems. IEEE Trans. Ind. Electron. **60**(3), 1099–1107 (2013)

Advanced and Emerging Applications

A Cognitive Architecture for Agent-Based Artificial Life Simulation

Ronaldo Vieira(✉)⬤, Bruno Dembogurski⬤, Leandro Alvim,
and Filipe Braida

Department of Computer Science, Universidade Federal Rural do Rio de Janeiro,
Nova Iguaçu, Brazil
ronaldo.vieira@ufrrj.br, brunodembogurski@gmail.com, alvim.lgm@gmail.com,
filipebraida@gmail.com

Abstract. The ability to simulate living beings that behave in a credible way is a fundamental aspect in digital games. This is due to its interdisciplinary characteristic, that brings together different fields of knowledge to better understand biological life and its processes. In this context, the design of an intelligent agent is a hard task as it involves a complex system, which has several interconnected components. In this work a virtual mind architecture for intelligent agents is proposed, where it simulates the cognitive processes of an actual brain, in this case attention and memory, in order to reproduce behaviors similar to those of actual living beings. A prototype is then proposed, where the architecture is applied on agents that represent virtual animals in a semantic-modeled ecosystem, and conduct a proof-of-concept experiment with it to demonstrate its effectiveness. In this experiment, the behavior of the virtual animals were consistent with reality, thus, validating the architecture's ability to simulate living beings.

Keywords: Artificial intelligence · Intelligent agents
Cognitive architecture

1 Introduction

The simulation of realistic virtual living beings has many applications, ranging from use in non-player characters (NPCs) in games to crowd and traffic simulation. In games, realism is often a crucial factor to the entertainment of the players, whereas in scientific simulations, realism is needed in order for them to be considered a valid simulation of real life.

Ultima Online [18], one of the earliest massively multiplayer online games released, simulated an ecosystem with various species of virtual animals, where they interacted with each other and with the players. *The Elder Scrolls V: Skyrim* [5], in turn, presented NPCs with daily routines that react to unexpected scenarios, such as the sudden presence of a dragon nearby. The simulation of evacuation of people on accident scenarios also needs that the virtual people behave similar to their real counterparts.

© Springer International Publishing AG, part of Springer Nature 2018
O. Gervasi et al. (Eds.): ICCSA 2018, LNCS 10960, pp. 197–213, 2018.
https://doi.org/10.1007/978-3-319-95162-1_14

The efforts made on this purpose often employ the concept of intelligent agents, from artificial intelligence. In these, the agents carry a virtual mind model that resemble the functioning of an actual brain, providing them with realistic behavior. In this work, the problem of simulating virtual living beings that behave in a credible way is addressed with the proposal of a virtual mind architecture for intelligent agents.

The proposed architecture has the goal to be generic enough to be usable in a variety of applications and flexible enough to allow problem-specific extensions. It also should be sufficiently complex in order to generate complex behavior while sufficiently simple in order for its use to be viable on digital games or other real time applications, where it is often needed to simulate the behavior of hundred or thousands of characters many times per second.

The main contribution of this paper is to introduce a virtual mind architecture that fulfills the aforementioned requirements while using a simple high-level abstraction of the reasoning workflow of a brain that is both computationally cheap and easy to understand and predict. Also in this paper, the proposed architecture is applied in the context of simulating a small ecosystem, where its operation is exemplified.

In Sect. 2, the concept of intelligent agents is presented. Next, in Sect. 3, concepts about the cognitive processes of the brain that are essential to the understanding of the proposed architecture are explained. After that, the proposed architecture, its components and their interaction are described in Sect. 4. A proof-of-concept prototype that uses the architecture is then depicted on Sect. 5, and the experiment is made in Sect. 6. Conclusions and future works are discussed on Sect. 7.

2   Intelligent Agents

In a generic way, an agent can be defined as an autonomous entity that perceives its environment through sensors and act on it through actuators [23]. With this definition, many things can be considered agents: a human being perceives its environment through its sight, hearing, smell, taste and other sensors, while act on it with its hands, feet and voice; a smartphone perceives its environment with the aid of its proximity, luminosity and touch sensors and act through its speakers and screens. However, the concept of agents is explored in depth on the Artificial Intelligence field, and is often used as means to develop complex systems, simulations and games.

Besides sensors and actuators, this definition of agents also have a program, that determines how the agent select its actions based on the inputs captured by its senses. An agent is said to be intelligent when its program can maximize its performance on the tasks it was developed for through its perception of the environment. To demonstrate how the definition of an agent can vary, a reading of the work by Franklin and Graesser [10] is suggested, where a taxonomy for autonomous agents is presented and, also, the many agent definitions used in the literature.

The term autonomous agent has been an intense discussion topic since the early 90's [16], due to its ability to act in complex and changing multiagent environments. The main core of an autonomous agent is its architecture, which comprehends the description of its features (modules and parts) and how they interact with each other. Thus, since its first appearance, numerous architectures have been proposed in order to create better and smarter agents, each presenting different features or expanding the previous ones. For a thorough explanation of the research field and its main threads refer to [16].

Several works make use of intelligent agents to simulate the behavior of human beings or other living beings. [1,9] use them in the context of simulating characters in a narrative, while [3] apply them to build realistic bots for the game *Unreal Tournament 2004*, and [17] applies them in the medical context, as virtual patients and clinical advisors. [4] creates a agent system in order to explain the cognitive processes of a human brain. As can be noted, intelligent agents can be applied to solve a variety of different problems.

The next section explain some of the cognitive processes of human brains on which the proposed mind architecture is based.

3   Cognitive Processes

Cognition can be defined as "the mental action or process of acquiring knowledge and understanding through thought, experience, and the senses" [20]. It encompasses processes such as knowledge, attention, memory, reasoning and problem solving. In this section, concepts of the human memory and attention that are relevant to the proposed architecture are discussed.

3.1   Working Memory

On neuroscientific literature, three types of memory are often accepted to exist: long-term memory, short-term memory and working memory [7]. When new memories are created, they are short-term ones. If any of them is deemed important by the brain (by either conscious or subconscious decision), it gets stored as a long-term memory.

The working memory can be considered a temporary memory where information is kept for immediate use by the brain's cognitive processes. Its existence allows the brain to manipulate information: when comparing two objects, for instance, it is necessary that a representation of both of them be stored in the working memory so that the comparison can be made.

Some cognitive architectures [1,4] make use of both long-term and short-term storing. They are out of the scope of this work. Their future addition, however, is noted in Sect. 7.2.

3.2   Attention

Though the human field of vision seem to be wide, our eyes can only perceive with precision, in fact, within a few centimeters radius from the point where we are focusing. The human hearing often has gaps that are filled with what our brain sees fit [24]. However, even with those and other known limitations of our sensory systems, the brain is constantly bombarded with information from our surroundings. It was necessary during evolution the development of a mechanism to decide which information was relevant and which was not. That mechanism is called attentional filter [12].

The attentional filter's job is to allow only the most relevant information to enter consciousness (and, consequently, the working memory). After driving for a while, for example, the attentional filter will eventually prevent the engine noise from entering consciousness. However, if the engine starts producing an unfamiliar noise – possibly due to some mechanism needing attention –, this information is promptly brought to consciousness. That is the first principle used by the attentional filter: change. The other principle, importance, can be exemplified by when someone in a full bus starts paying attention to a specific conversation once something important, such as their own name, was cited.

4   Proposed Architecture

This section explains in details the proposed architecture, each of its components and the interaction between them.

There are several mind architectures in the literature, AuRA (Autonomous Robot Architecture) [2], The Soar Cognitive Architecture [11], IRMA [6], BDI (Belief-Desire-Intention) architecture model [22], FAtiMA [8] and ORIENT [13], just to name a few. The latter is built on top of FAtiMA (which uses the OCC - cognitive theory of emotions [19]) plus motivational and learning components from the PSI theory [21]. In this paper, however, the agents behaviors are derived from a much simpler workflow, where a motivation system is abstracted as their needs and, combined with their perception of the environment, results in dynamic realistic agents whose behavior can still be directed/predicted.

The virtual mind model proposed here simulates in a high level of abstraction both the architecture and cognitive flow of an actual brain, in order to allow intelligent agents carrying this artificial mind, once disposed in an semantic-modeled environment, to display behaviors that are similar to those of actual living beings.

Despite all the technology and scientific knowledge available nowadays, it is still impossible to perfectly simulate a working brain. Thus, this work's objective is not to try such feat, but to find a complexity level for the architecture that is both high enough for it to be able to generate credible behavior and low enough to make its use on real time applications – such as games – viable.

An abstraction of the senses, needs and goals of a living being, along with some cognitive processes (perception, memory, attention and reasoning) and a semantic-modeled environment or world are the components of the proposed virtual mind architecture.

4.1   Semantic Representation

For the virtual mind be able to reason, it needs information about the surroundings of the agent. Thus, the architecture requires a semantic-modeled world, that is, an environment where each perceivable entity has semantic attributes that represent its meaning. For instance, an object can have attributes for its size, color, what it is made of, whether it is alive, *etc.* The agents are not an exception – as any other entity in the world, they also must have these semantic information.

The semantic information of an entity can be represented with any data structure able to hold key-value entries. However, a frame system [15] is recommended, since it allows for complex semantic modeling with inheritance and commonsense reasoning [25].

4.2   The Agent

Different from the static objects in the world, the agents can move and interact with near objects and agents. That is possible because they have senses which perceive their surroundings, needs that guide their goals and actions, and a mind where the actual reasoning happens. In the following sections, each of these components will be described in terms of its role in the architecture and its properties (Fig. 1).

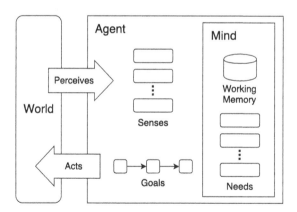

Fig. 1. Architecture of an agent.

4.3   Senses and Perceptions

The role of the human senses, such as sight and hearing, is to obtain information from its environment and make them available to the brain so that it has sufficient inputs to decide which actions to take. Analogously, in this architecture, in order for an agent to interact with the world, it should have one or more senses.

Here, a sense's job is to capture semantic information from the entities in the world that are within its range.

In a Sight sense, for instance, a field-of-view algorithm may be used as its range in order to simulate the sight of a living being. It may be able to perceive attributes like size, color and distance. These captured semantic information are made available to the agent's mind in the form of perceptions.

A perception is, basically, a subset of semantic information of an object or agent extracted by a sense, and can be represented with the same data structure. At the moment of its creation, some non-static attributes can also be filled by the sense, such as the distance attribute, which can only be determined at perception creation time.

4.4   Goals

In the other end of the agent's interaction with the world are the goals. While the senses are responsible for reading the current world state, the goals' role is to alter them. The agent is at all times executing a goal, and the choice of the most suitable goal to execute is byproduct of the reasoning cycle of the agent's mind. The goals of an agent in this work are directly mapped to actions in the environment, unlike [1,9], where goals and actions are hierarchically structured.

Fig. 2. A goal chain. The arrows denote prerequisite relationships.

A goal should have the following properties:

- A set of **completion conditions**. A goal is considered as completed if and only if each of its completion conditions are satisfied. A Go-to goal, for instance, may have the unique completion condition of the distance between the agent and its target being less than a specified threshold.
- Optionally, a **previous goal** (or prerequisite goal). The previous goal should be necessarily completed in order for the current goal to be executed. If during the execution of an goal its prerequisite ceases to be completed, the agent will execute its prerequisite instead until it is completed again.
- Optionally, a **next goal**. The next goal is the next goal in the goal chain, that is, the goal that will be executed after the completion of the current one.
- Optionally, a **target**. It is represented by a perception that represents the target of the goal. An Attack goal, for instance, may require a target which will be attacked. Not all goals will require a target, though. It may be the case for a Sleep goal, for example. The goal's target is inherited from previous goals to next goals in a goal chain or manually defined at its creation. In Fig. 2, the Find-food goal may not require a target beforehand, but may set its target

as any potential food source once it has found one so that the next goal – Go-to – will then inherit it as its target.
– A **execution cycle**. The execution cycle of a goal is an algorithm that is executed on each reasoning cycle of the agent. That algorithm will, often, perform actions on the goal's target, in the agent itself or alter the world's state. The execution cycle of a Eat goal, for instance, may have instructions to decrease the intensity of the agent's Hunger need and also reduce the weight attribute of the target entity.

The structure formed by goals and their next and previous goals is named goal chain. In the subsequent sections, the term goal will be used to refer to both single goals and goal chains. The management of a goal chain, that is, the choice of the next goal once the current is completed and the choice of the previous goal once it ceases to be completed is one of the steps of the agent's reasoning cycle.

4.5   Needs

According to Maslow [14], the human being has various needs to be fulfilled simultaneously, such as breathing, temperature, feeding, safety, health, shelter, being part of a group or community and happiness. Some of them have greater priorities than others, forming a hierarchy of needs. A human being will not give much thought to its need to be respected if, say, their need to breathe is not being at least reasonably satisfied.

The needs of an agent are the central aspect in their decision-making process. Each need is bound to a goal that will satisfy it. The current goal of an agent in a given moment will always be the goal bound to the need with the most priority among its needs at that moment. The calculation of the priority of a need will be explained in detail on Sect. 4.7.

The need to feed or sleep, for example, are derived from a number of biological processes of an animal's body. However, their intensity increase over time can be represented in a simpler way without a significant loss of realism through a increase rate. That way, the needs should have, besides their bound goal and a intensity value, a increase rate. This rate define how quickly the intensity value of a need will increase over time.

Some needs, such as safety and shelter, may not possess the behavior of increasing their intensity over time. In that case, they can be assigned with a zero increase rate, causing their intensity value to be fixed. Furthermore, it is convenient to set their initial intensity value to a reasonable value.

At last, a need should be able to evaluate how relevant is a given perception. The relevancy evaluation of perceptions can be implemented as either a set of logic rules such as "if the perception source is a bigger animal, then return 1", a set of fuzzy rules such as "if the size attribute from the perception ranges between 1 and 2, then return the interpolated value between 0 and 1" or any other algorithm or equation.

The aforementioned needs hierarchy proposed by Maslow [14] raises a diverse list of needs of human beings that are usable in this architecture. However, it is important to note that any simulation aspect that fits in the description of a need can be represented as one.

In summary, needs should have the following properties:

- An **intensity value**. A value in the range $[0, 1]$ that represents how intense is the need in a given moment. A hungry agent, for instance, would have a value near 1 as the intensity of their Hunger need.
- An **increase rate**. A rate that defines how quickly the intensity of the need will increase. A need with an increase rate of 0.2 per minute would take exactly five minutes to go from fully satisfied (intensity 0) to critically neglected (intensity 1).
- A **bound goal**. A goal or goal chain that will be executed by the agent whenever the need is chosen as the one with the most priority by the reasoning cycle.
- A **relevancy evaluator**. An algorithm that, given a perception, returns its relevancy score to the need in the $[-1, 1]$ interval. Positive scores amplify the need's intensity, while negative scores inhibit it.

4.6 The Mind

The mind of an agent translate perceptions obtained by its senses in goals, in order to satisfy its needs. It consists of a working memory and the reasoning cycle algorithm.

The working memory stores a limited set of perceptions and serves as a temporary memory, representing the current thoughts of the agent. It has a capacity limit that defines how many perceptions it is able to store simultaneously. In [1], the short-term memory is in charge of this aspect. [3] also has a working memory module, where a number of different sensory inputs compete for attention. In this architecture, however, the perceptions in the working memory already represent the agent's attention.

The agent's attentional filter, in the reasoning cycle, guarantees that only the most relevant perceptions will enter the working memory. The reasoning cycle is the core of the architecture. It represents the agent's process of thought and decision-making through its limited perception of the world.

4.7 Reasoning Cycle

The first step in an agent's reasoning cycle is to obtain a new set of perceptions of the world through the agent's senses. Each sense is queried for its current set of perceptions, then all perceptions that share the same source are merged. The agent's working memory can already be filled with perceptions from earlier reasoning cycles, so those are also considered for the merging. At this point, each entity in the world is represented in the agent's mind by at most one perception.

Then, each need n of the agent will assign a relevancy score $r(p, n) \in [-1, 1]$ to each perception p using its relevancy evaluator. That way, each perception will be assigned a number of different relevancy scores, one for each of the agent's needs.

The working memory is then updated to carry only the k most overall relevant perceptions, where k is its capacity limit. The overall relevancy of a perception ($r(p)$) is just the sum of the absolute values of all the relevancy scores assigned to it, as shown by Eq. 1. A perception that got 0.8 and -0.5 as relevancy scores by the two needs of the agent, for instance, will have a overall relevancy score of 1.3. This step works as an attentional filter to the agent's mind, ensuring that only the most relevant entities perceived by its senses will be considered.

$$r(p) = \sum_n |r(p,n)| \tag{1}$$

With the working memory updated, the agent is ready to decide which of its needs demands more attention at the moment. That decision is made using Eq. 2, by choosing the need n that presents the highest priority value $p(n)$, given as a function of its intensity $i(n)$ and relevancy $r(n)$ values.

$$p(n) = i(n) * (1 + r(n)) \tag{2}$$

The relevancy of a need n, as shown in Eq. 3, is given as a function of each of the relevancy scores $r(p,n)$ assigned by it to the perceptions currently in the agent's working memory W. In this case, however, each relevancy score is penalized by a factor of the distance of the perception to the agent.

$$r(n) = \sum_{p \in W} \frac{r(p,n)}{1 + \ln(1 + d(p))} \tag{3}$$

It can be noted on Eq. 2 that when an agent does not have any perception stored in its working memory, $r(n)$ will be null, and the priority of the needs will be based solely on its intensity. On the other hand, when two needs have the same intensity value, their priority values will vary based only on the current perceptions of the agent. A virtual human being whose Hunger and Thirst needs have the same intensity at a given moment, for example, would easily choose to satisfy their hunger should an apple be near them. Besides, it is guaranteed that any need with a non-null increase rate, if neglected long enough, will eventually have a high enough intensity value, causing it to be chosen by the agent.

In Eq. 3, in turn, can be noted that the primary factor to determine the relevancy of a need is how relevant to this need are the current perceptions in the agent's working memory. For a virtual animal, for example, a perception that represents a threatening animal would hold a positive relevancy score to its Safety need and, thereafter, would have a positive impact on the relevance of that need. Still, if many members of its own specie were near, generating negative relevancy scores and impacting negatively the Safety's relevance, the threatening animal would then not look so threatening.

The relevance of the perceptions are penalized proportionally to the natural logarithm of the distance of those perceptions to the agent. That way, a virtual human being with a Hunger need would prefer a near apple than an apple that is 50 m away. The natural logarithm is used in order to reduce the penalizing impact of the distance – an apple that is 50 m away is still reasonably more relevant to a Hunger need than no apple at all.

Once the need with the most priority is identified, if its bound goal is already being executed by the agent, then nothing is done. Otherwise, the agent's current goal is replaced with that need's bound goal.

The last step on the reasoning cycle consists in executing the execution cycle of the current goal. The goal management also happens: if the current goal is completed or if the previous one is not, the appropriate arrangements are made.

4.8   Extensions

Although the proposed architecture is based on high-level abstractions of cognitive processes of human beings and its design is focused to use on digital games, it can be adapted to other contexts, such as (i) transit simulations, with agents as vehicles in a road or city; (ii) crowd simulations, with agents as people; (iii) narratives, as in [1], with agents as characters in a story; (iv) simulation of ecosystems, as described in Sect. 5; and even (v) population-based metaheuristics, to solve combinatorial optimization problems.

5   Prototype

This section has the objective to present one of the possible applications of the architecture, provide a concrete example and allow for experiments to demonstrate its operation.

The chosen context for this prototype is the simulation of a small ecosystem, with the animals as agents and other static entities. For this ecosystem, two species of animals were chosen to represent respectively the prey and predator roles: rabbit and fox. Also, a grass entity was created to represent the prey's food and a rock entity to represent a object that is not important to any of the agents. The objective of this prototype is to use the proposed virtual mind architecture in intelligent agents simulating virtual animals. For that, their senses, needs and goals were chosen accordingly to those of real animals in a ecosystem.

In the following subsections, the semantic model used, as well as the chosen senses, needs and goals are described.

5.1   Semantic Model

A implementation of Minsky's frames [15] was used as the data structure to represent the semantic information of the prototype's world.

Each entity in the world (fox, rabbit, grass and rock) possess a instance frame containing its semantic attributes. That instance frame, in turn, inherits attributes from a generic frame in the semantic hierarchy. This way it is possible to infer that, for example, a rabbit has four legs, since it is a mammal, and the mammal generic frame it inherits from possess a "legs" attribute set to four.

5.2   Senses, Needs and Goals

The Sight and Hearing senses were created to represent – unsurprisingly – the sight and hearing of the virtual animals, respectively. Their perception ranges are depicted graphically by Fig. 3. The parameters and initial values of these senses as well as those of the needs and goals were chosen empirically, with values that provided a satisfactory level of realism while working in a similar way to the senses of the corresponding animals in nature.

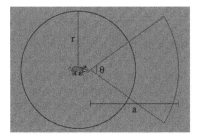

Fig. 3. Graphic representation of the range of the agent's sight (red) and hearing (blue). (Color figure online)

Two needs were created for the agents: Hunger and Safety. They represent two of main aspects of the survival in a ecosystem: feeding and avoiding potential threats. Their bound goals were defined as the goal chains depicted by Fig. 4, respectively. The detailed description of each need and goal is omitted, but can be assumed to act abstractly as they would in real life.

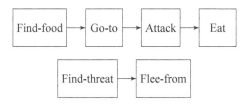

Fig. 4. Goal chains bound to the Hunger (on top) and Safety (on bottom) needs.

6   Experiment

The proposed experiment involves placing four entities reasonably close to each other in a world: a fox, a rabbit, a grass and a rock. It is expected, as the virtual mind architecture described on Sect. 4 is used with the accordingly developed components described on Sect. 5, that the agents display behaviors similar to reality. As the agent's reasoning cycle is executed dozens of times per second in the simulation, a single moment was chosen to present and explain the operation of the architecture and justify some of the behaviors shown by the agents (Fig. 5).

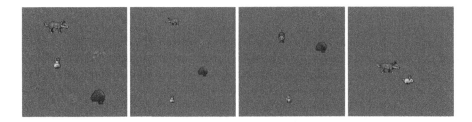

Fig. 5. Initial setting and some key moments of the experiment.

The chosen moment happens right at the start of the simulation, when the rabbit will decide to flee from the fox. The following paragraphs will demonstrate their reasoning cycles in that moment of the simulation.

Initially, all entities are close to each other. As the first execution of the agent's reasoning cycle, their working memories will be first filled with perceptions from the world and their first goals will be defined.

The fox's reasoning cycle starts with the retrieval of its current perceptions from its senses. In Fig. 6 the perceptions retrieved from the Sight and Hearing senses are described. Though the agent does not know, it can be noted that these perceptions come, respectively, from the rabbit, grass and rock.

The rabbit's perception was assigned with a 1.0 relevancy score from the fox's Hunger need, since it fits its criteria for potential food sources. The fox, rabbit, grass and rock's perceptions will be referred to as, respectively, p_f, p_r, p_g e p_o.

Perception 1	**Perception 2**	**Perception 3**
(other attributes)	(other attributes)	(other attributes)
distance: 4.896	distance: 6.326	distance: 10.191
r(Hunger): 1.0	r(Hunger): 0.0	r(Hunger): 0.0
r(Safety): 0.0	r(Safety): 0.0	r(Safety): 0.0

Fig. 6. Perceptions retrieved by the fox's senses. Each box represents a perception, where their semantic attributes and relevancy scores are listed.

The working memory of the agents was defined to hold up to four perceptions simultaneously. This way, all the three obtained perceptions will be included in the fox's working memory. Should its capacity limit be reduced to one perception, only the rabbit's perception would be stored as its overall relevance value equals 1.0, while all the others have 0.0.

In this moment, the intensities of the Hunger and Safety needs are, respectively, 0.15 and 0.3. Their relevance is calculated using the perceptions currently stored in the working memory.

$$r(\text{Hunger}) = \frac{r(p_r, \text{Hunger})}{1 + \ln(d(p_r))} + \frac{r(p_g, \text{Hunger})}{1 + \ln(d(p_g))} + \frac{r(p_o, \text{Hunger})}{1 + \ln(d(p_o))}$$

$$= \frac{1}{1 + \ln(5.896)} + \frac{0}{1 + \ln(7.326)} + \frac{0}{1 + \ln(11.191)} \qquad (4a)$$

$$= 0.36$$

$$r(\text{Safety}) = \frac{r(p_r, \text{Safety})}{1 + \ln(d(p_r))} + \frac{r(p_g, \text{Safety})}{1 + \ln(d(p_g))} + \frac{r(p_o, \text{Safety})}{1 + \ln(d(p_o))}$$

$$= \frac{0}{1 + \ln(5.896)} + \frac{0}{1 + \ln(7.326)} + \frac{0}{1 + \ln(11.191)} \qquad (4b)$$

$$= 0$$

As shown by Eqs. 4a and 4b, the relevancy scores respective to the Hunger and Safety needs are 0.36 and 0. With these values, is then possible to calculate the priority score of them. The Eqs. 5a and 5b depict the necessary calculations.

$$p(\text{Hunger}) = i(\text{Hunger}) * (1 + r(\text{Hunger}))$$
$$= 0.15 * (1 + 0.36) \qquad (5a)$$
$$= 0.204$$

$$p(\text{Safety}) = i(\text{Safety}) * (1 + r(\text{Safety}))$$
$$= 0.3 * (1 + 0) \qquad (5b)$$
$$= 0.3$$

This way, it can be noted that the Safety's priority score (0.3) is higher than Hunger's (0.204), thus, Safety is the chosen need. Once having chosen a need, the agent's current goal will become the first goal of the goal chain bound to that need. In this case, the bound goal chain is composed by the Find-threat and Flee-from goals, and the former will become the fox's current goal.

The goal management is the last step of the fox's reasoning cycle. The mind will check that the current goal's completion conditions are not satisfied and no previous goal is present, and will thus execute it. As part of the goal's execution cycle, it will check the perceptions currently on the agent's working memory for any potential threats. However, no such perception will be found. The fox will then keep searching for threats in the next reasoning cycles, until its Hunger (which intensity value increases with time) become the need with the highest priority score. And so ends the fox's reasoning cycle.

The rabbit's reasoning cycle starts retrieving its current perceptions from its Sight and Hearing senses. Figure 7 describes the perceptions obtained by them that refers to, respectively, the fox, grass and rock. It can be noted that the perception relative to the grass and fox received 1.0 as relevancy score from the Hunger and Safety needs, respectively.

The rabbit's attentional filter also permits all three perceptions to enter its working memory. It is then calculated which of its needs will be satisfied, following the same process as made by the fox.

Perception 1	Perception 2	Perception 3
(other attributes)	(other attributes)	(other attributes)
distance: 4.896	distance: 5.046	distance: 6.352
r(Hunger): 0.0	r(Hunger): 1.0	r(Hunger): 0.0
r(Safety): 1.0	r(Safety): 0.0	r(Safety): 0.0

Fig. 7. Perceptions retrieved by the rabbit's senses. Each box represents a perception, where their semantic attributes and relevancy scores are listed.

$$
\begin{aligned}
r(\text{Hunger}) &= \frac{r(p_f, \text{Hunger})}{1 + \ln\left(d(p_f)\right)} + \frac{r(p_g, \text{Hunger})}{1 + \ln\left(d(p_g)\right)} + \frac{r(p_o, \text{Hunger})}{1 + \ln\left(d(p_o)\right)} \\
&= \frac{0}{1 + \ln\left(5.896\right)} + \frac{1}{1 + \ln\left(6.046\right)} + \frac{0}{1 + \ln\left(7.352\right)} \qquad (6a) \\
&= 0.357
\end{aligned}
$$

$$
\begin{aligned}
r(\text{Safety}) &= \frac{r(p_f, \text{Safety})}{1 + \ln\left(d(p_f)\right)} + \frac{r(p_g, \text{Safety})}{1 + \ln\left(d(p_g)\right)} + \frac{r(p_o, \text{Safety})}{1 + \ln\left(d(p_o)\right)} \\
&= \frac{1}{1 + \ln\left(5.896\right)} + \frac{0}{1 + \ln\left(6.046\right)} + \frac{0}{1 + \ln\left(7.352\right)} \qquad (6b) \\
&= 0.36
\end{aligned}
$$

As shown in the Eqs. 6a and 6b, the relevancy scores respective to the Hunger and Safety needs are 0.357 e 0.36. Is then possible to calculate their priority scores, which is made by Eqs. 7a and 7b using the intensity values (0.15 for Hunger and 0.3 for Safety) and the obtained relevancy scores.

$$
\begin{aligned}
p(\text{Hunger}) &= i(\text{Hunger}) * (1 + r(\text{Hunger})) \\
&= 0.15 * (1 + 0.357) \qquad (7a) \\
&= 0.204
\end{aligned}
$$

$$
\begin{aligned}
p(\text{Safety}) &= i(\text{Safety}) * (1 + r(\text{Safety})) \\
&= 0.3 * (1 + 0.36) \qquad (7b) \\
&= 0.408
\end{aligned}
$$

With the obtained results, the rabbit will choose its Safety need (0.408) to be satisfied rather than its Hunger (0.204). For that reason, the goal chain formed by the Find-threat and Flee-from goals will be chosen as its current goal.

The rabbit's goal management step proceeds similarly to that of the fox. However, in the execution cycle of the Find-threat goal, a potential threat perception is found. That perception – that refers to the fox – is set as the target of the current goal so that, in the next reasoning cycle, the mind will check that the goal's completion conditions were satisfied and will move on to the next goal in the chain: Flee-from.

In the subsequent reasoning cycles, the Flee-from goal will move the rabbit away from the fox. Even though it possesses a wide field of view, by moving in the opposite direction, the rabbit will not be able to detect the fox with its Sight sense. However, it will still be able to know its location by the Hearing sense, and will keep running away until it reaches a sufficient distance.

After the chosen moment, the rabbit will run in the opposite direction of the fox until it feels safe enough: the distance from the fox will trigger the completion of its Flee-from goal. Eventually, the fox's Hunger need will become sufficiently intense, causing it to be chosen by the reasoning cycle. The fox, then, will chase the rabbit until it is close enough to attack. After feeding itself, the fox will have satiated its hunger and will be back to exploring the world.

As depicted in the chosen moment and in the rest of the simulation, the architecture was able to choose dynamically an appropriate behavior for the virtual animals in all situations through their reasoning cycles. The rabbit, having a threat and a food source at sight, decided to take care of its safety and flee. The fox, on the other hand, ignored the presence of the rabbit until it was hungry enough, and then chased it.

7 Conclusion

Simulating virtual living beings that behave in a realistic way is not a trivial problem. In order to perfectly represent a living being, it would be necessary to simulate the low level interaction between the chemical elements in its body, which is impossible by the currently available technology and scientific knowledge. That being said, the current approaches to this problem in the literature often make use of models with higher levels of abstraction where virtual minds emulate, in a simplified way, the functioning of real brains.

7.1 Proposal

In this work a cognitive architecture for intelligent agents was proposed, that is, an architecture that simulates the functioning of a brain and it cognitive processes, whose objective is to reproduce on agents behaviors similar to those of living beings, once they are disposed in a semantic-modeled virtual world.

The proposed architecture translates the concept of sensors of intelligent agents as living beings' senses. The job of a sense is to capture information about the surroundings of the agent in order to foment its reasoning. These information are passed to the agent's mind in the form of perceptions. Once inside the mind, its attentional filter ensures that only the most relevant perceptions enters the agent's working memory, and thus, be considered in its reasoning process. The mind then decides which of the agent's needs demands most attention taking into account its current intensity and the content of the working memory. The goal chain associated to that need is then executed by the agent. The goals encompass the concept of actuators of intelligent agents. This way, the agent perform actions that are consistent with its internal state and its perception of the external world.

A prototype that simulates virtual animals in a small ecosystem was developed in order to validate the architecture. In the experiment made, the two agents acted accordingly to what would be expected of actual animals pursuing their survival and, therefore, demonstrated the proposed architecture's ability to simulate living beings.

7.2 Research Directions

As future improvements to the architecture, would be interesting to have (i) grouping of similar perceptions into one collective perception; (ii) occasional errors on the senses' detection; (iii) goals uncoupled from the needs; (iv) satisfaction of multiple needs simultaneously; and (v) a short-term and a long-term memory.

As for the developed prototype, some interesting features are (i) non-binary relevancy scores; (ii) implement reproduction as a need; (iii) learning by experience; and (iv) allow evolution and natural selection.

References

1. Araujo, S., Chaimowicz, L.: Atores Virtuais Autônomos para Sistemas Narrativos Interativos. Master's thesis, Universidade Federal de Minas Gerais (2009)
2. Arkin, R.C.: Integrating behavioral, perceptual, and world knowledge in reactive navigation. Rob. Auton. Syst. **6**(1), 105–122 (1990). http://www.sciencedirect.com/science/article/pii/S0921889005800314, designing Autonomous Agents
3. Arrabales, R., Ledezma, A., Sanchis, A.: Towards conscious-like behavior in computer game characters. In: IEEE Symposium on Computational Intelligence and Games, CIG 2009, pp. 217–224. IEEE (2009)
4. Bach, J.: Principles of Synthetic Intelligence PSI: An Architecture of Motivated Cognition, vol. 4. Oxford University Press, Oxford (2009)
5. Bethesda Game Studios: The Elder Scrolls V: Skyrim. [PC CD-ROM] (2015)
6. Bratman, M.E., Israel, D.J., Pollack, M.E.: Plans and resource-bounded practical reasoning. Technical report 425, AI Center, SRI International, 333 Ravenswood Ave., Menlo Park, CA 94025, September 1988
7. Cowan, N.: What are the differences between long-term, short-term, and working memory? Prog. Brain Res. **169**, 323–338 (2008)
8. Dias, J., Mascarenhas, S., Paiva, A.: FAtiMA modular: towards an agent architecture with a generic appraisal framework. In: Bosse, T., Broekens, J., Dias, J., van der Zwaan, J. (eds.) Emotion Modeling. LNCS (LNAI), vol. 8750, pp. 44–56. Springer, Cham (2014). https://doi.org/10.1007/978-3-319-12973-0_3
9. Franco, A.O., Maia, J.G., Neto, J.A., Gomes, F.A.: An interactive storytelling model for non-player characters on electronic RPGs. In: 2015 14th Brazilian Symposium on Computer Games and Digital Entertainment (SBGames), pp. 52–60. IEEE (2015)
10. Franklin, S., Graesser, A.: Is it an agent, or just a program?: a taxonomy for autonomous agents. In: Müller, J.P., Wooldridge, M.J., Jennings, N.R. (eds.) ATAL 1996. LNCS, vol. 1193, pp. 21–35. Springer, Heidelberg (1997). https://doi.org/10.1007/BFb0013570. http://dl.acm.org/citation.cfm?id=648203.749270

11. Laird, J.E.: The Soar Cognitive Architecture. The MIT Press, Cambridge (2012)
12. Levitin, D.J.: The Organized Mind: Thinking Straight in the Age of Information Overload. Penguin, London (2014)
13. Lim, M.Y., Dias, J., Aylett, R., Paiva, A.: Creating adaptive affective autonomous NPCs. Auton. Agent. Multi-Agent Syst. **24**(2), 287–311 (2012). https://doi.org/10.1007/s10458-010-9161-2
14. Maslow, A.H.: A theory of human motivation. Psychol. Rev. **50**(4), 370 (1943)
15. Minsky, M.: A framework for representing knowledge. Psychol. Comput. Vis. **73**, 211–277 (1975)
16. Müller, J.P.: Architectures and applications of intelligent agents: a survey. Knowl. Eng. Rev. **13**(4), 353–380 (1999)
17. Nirenburg, S., McShane, M., Beale, S., Catizone, R.: A cognitive architecture for simulating bodies and minds. In: AMIA Annual Symposium Proceedings, vol. 2011, p. 905. American Medical Informatics Association (2011)
18. Origin Systems: Ultima online. [CD-ROM] (1997)
19. Ortony, A., Clore, G.L., Collins, A.: The Cognitive Structure of Emotions. Cambridge University Press, Cambridge (1990)
20. Oxford Dictionaries: Cognition - Definition of Cognition in English—Oxford Dictionaries (2010). https://en.oxforddictionaries.com/definition/cognition. Accessed 07 July 2017
21. Prisnyakov, V.F., Prisnyakova, L.M.: Mathematical modeling of emotions. Cybern. Syst. Anal. **30**(1), 142–149 (1994). https://doi.org/10.1007/BF02366374
22. Rao, A.S., Georgeff, M.P.: Modeling Rational Agents within a BDI-Architecture (1991)
23. Russell, S.J., Norvig, P.: Artificial Intelligence: A Modern Approach, 2nd edn. Pearson Education, New York (2003)
24. Warren, R.M., et al.: Perceptual restoration of missing speech sounds. Science **167**(3917), 392–393 (1970)
25. Winston, P.H.: Frames and commonsense. In: Artificial intelligence, 3rd edn. (repr. with corrections 1993), Chap. 10, pp. 209–230. Addison-Wesley (1993)

A Multimodal Approach for Cultural Heritage Information Retrieval

Erasmo Purificato[1] and Antonio M. Rinaldi[1,2(✉)]

[1] Department of Electrical Engineering and Information Technologies,
University of Naples, Federico II Napoli, Via Claudio, 21, 80125 Naples, Italy
erasmopurif@gmail.com, antoniomaria.rinaldi@unina.it
[2] IKNOS-LAB Intelligent and Knowledge Systems - LUPT, University of Naples,
Federico II Napoli, Via Toledo, 402, 80134 Naples, Italy

Abstract. The daily use of mobile devices and the expansion of the
world-wide-web lead multimedia information to an uncontrolled growth.
In this context, the use of smart interfaces and the combination of different features in the information retrieval process are crucial aspects.
In particular, for a cultural heritage application it is important to consider that a digitized artwork is only a representation of a real object,
represented under specific conditions (camera position, brightness, etc.).
These issues could be causes of alterations during the features extraction task. In this paper we propose a multimodal approach for cultural
heritage information retrieval combining geographic and visual data. Our
approach has been implemented in a mobile system based on open source
technologies. It is composed of three main parts related to image matching functionalities, Geographic Information Retrieval task, and a combination strategy for multimedia and geographic data integration. An
Android application has been developed to give a user friendly interface
and a case study together with some experimental results are presented
to show the effectiveness of our approach for the user satisfaction.

1 Introduction

Art and culture have always represented an important part in human lives. Over
the years, public and private organizations have preserved and used our cultural
heritage as fundamental sources of education and learning. Due to these reasons,
in recent times, there is a great interest on the archiving of ancient historical
and cultural materials in digital forms for future generations [1]. Digitalization is
a very important task, because computers and mobile devices have become the
principal medium for learning and visiting digital art galleries from any corner
of the world; furthermore, artworks tend to be preserved from deterioration and
natural or human damages [2]. Such increasing digitization has lead to uncontrolled growth of data with several issues very closely the Big Data challenges
[3] in every phase of the data life cycle, from storage to analytic and visualization [4–6].

© Springer International Publishing AG, part of Springer Nature 2018
O. Gervasi et al. (Eds.): ICCSA 2018, LNCS 10960, pp. 214–230, 2018.
https://doi.org/10.1007/978-3-319-95162-1_15

In such a scenario, a significant role is played by a set of technologies generally referred to as *Content-Based Image Retrieval* (CBIR). Also known as Query By Image Content (QBIC) or Content-Based Visual Information Retrieval (CBVIR), CBIR is the application of computer vision to image retrieval. Its goal is to limit the use of textual descriptions and to develop techniques for retrieving images on the basis of automatically-extracted multimedia features, such as colour, edge, texture and shape, from a user query image or user-specified image features [7]. The image content refers to measurable visual properties. As an example, for a computer scientist the content of a painting like *Mona Lisa* is a combination of textures, edges, shapes and colours, while for a tourist at the Louvre museum the content normally refers to represented the person, the author Leonardo Da Vinci, painting techniques, historical models.

In the context of CBIR, a large number of methods have been proposed and investigated but, as stated in [8], they still not provide general solutions.

On the other hand, spatial information has becoming an important feature in the information retrieval process. The concepts of *Geographic Information Retrieval* and *Spatial Query* are explained starting from the interpretation of Larson in [9]. He defines GIR as a specialization of the terms *Information Retrieval* (IR) and *Geographic Information System* (GIS) which provide access to georeferenced information sources. IR means finding information resources of an unstructured nature relevant to an information need (user query) from a document collection (e.g. web) [10]. Moreover, Geographic Information System is defined as the development and use of theories, methods, technologies and data for understanding geographic processes, relationships and patterns [11]. Eventually, Geographic Information Retrieval could be described ad as the set of technologies and processes to index, query, retrieve and browse georeferenced information. GIR is supposed to be able to better understanding the geographic knowledge in documents and user queries, and provides a more accurate answer to user needs. From this point of view, *spatial queries* could be recognized as queries about the spatial relationship of entities geometrically defined and located in the space. This kind of query requires that the space will be well-defined using a coordinate systems of the "real world". The use of different features related to objects and user behaviour could improve the quality in the whole retrieval process [12].

In this paper, an approach to integrate Image Content matching techniques, *Geographic Information Retrieval* (GIR) and spatial queries is proposed. Our approach has been implemented in a system based on a mobile interface.

The remainder of the paper is structured as follows: in Sect. 2 some of the principal recent works produced in last decades about Content-Based Image Retrieval and Geographic Information Retrieval are discussed; the architecture of the proposed system and the Android application developed as case study are described, respectively, in Sects. 3 and 4; some experimental results are presented and discussed in Sect. 5; eventually, conclusions and future works are presented in Sect. 6.

2   Related Works

Content-Based Image Retrieval is a fervent research topic where theories and technology to organize digital image archives represented by their visual contents are studied and developed. This community is composed by people from different fields, such as computer vision, data mining, human-computer interaction, information retrieval, statistics, information theory and also psychology. Smeulders published a paper presenting a review of two hundred references in CBIR [13]. According to his work, CBIR applications can be divided into three board categories: Search by association, Search at specific image and Category search. *Search by association* is a class of methods and systems aimed at search in large sets of images from unspecified sources. It implies iterative search refinement with similarity measure or examples with which the search was started. This kind of systems are typically highly interactive. The search results can be manipulated interactively by relevance feedback [14]. *Search at specific image* aims to obtain an accurate example of the same object represented in a user image. These systems are suitable for searching for stamps, artworks, industrial component, and catalogues. *Category search* goal is in the retrieval of a random image representative of a specific class of objects. Categories can be derived from labels or inferred from databases [15]. CBIR systems represents images by numeric values, called *features* or *descriptors*, that are used to describe the properties of images and allow the retrieval of visual information. There are two approaches called discrete and continuous respectively. The *discrete approach* is inspired by textual information retrieval and uses techniques like text retrieval metrics and inverted files indexing. In this approaches all features have to be mapped to binary features and an image feature is considered as a word in a text document. The main advantage of the discrete approach is that techniques from textual information retrieval can easily be transferred (e.g., storage handling and user interaction). The *continuous approach* is very similar to nearest neighbour classification. In fact, all the images are represented by a feature vector and these vectors are compared using distance-based evaluation measures. As the retrieval process result, the images ranked highest are those with lowest distances.

In the last few years, CBIR systems have been consider has an exciting application domains for several research fields in computer science. In [16] a Content-Based Image Retrieval technique based on genetic algorithms with support vector machines and user feedbacks for image retrieval is proposed using a web 3.0 architecture. Karamti *et al.* [17] present an image retrieval framework which includes a vectorization technique combined with a pseudo relevance model. *Geographic Information Retrieval* and its applications spread on different areas as urban planning, urban architecture, environmental protection, transport and logistic, engineering networks, real estate and military planning and so on. Google and Microsoft introduced commercial GIR system in 2005, respectively *Google Maps*[1] and *Live Search Maps* (since 2010 and presently *Bing Maps*[2])

---

[1] https://www.google.com/maps. Last seen May 7, 2018.

[2] https://www.bing.com/maps. Last seen May 7, 2018.

and these are currently the most used on-line GIR services. In 2007 a group of researchers of the University of California, Irvine, proposed a framework for GIR systems focusing on indexing strategies that can process spatial-keywords queries efficiently [18]. The paper shows through experiments that the indexing strategies lead to significant improvement in efficiency of answering spatial-keywords queries as regards to other techniques already present. A search engine called *TexSpaSearch* was presented at the University of New Brunswick, Fredericton, Canada [19]. It is a geo-textual index and search methodology that simultaneously supports text only, text with search radius, and point location with radius queries. In addition to other similar systems, TexSpaSearch supports simultaneous indexing of text having geometric figures describing their location. In [20] an automatic approach for discovering location names in WWW data selected from different domains is proposed. The described approach is based on *Apache Tika*, *Apache OpenNLP*, and *Apache Lucene* frameworks. A very interesting general-purpose geographic search engine was presented in [21]. This Geographic Information Retrieval system, called *Frankenplace*, is an interactive thematic map search engine that uses geographic context as a way to discover, organize, and interactively visualize documents related to a search query. Frankenplace is also an ad-hoc search site designed to help users in finding relevant documents that match a query[3], and visualizing the interaction between the thematic and geographic content of documents. The current version of Frankenplace (May 2015) indexes over five million articles from the English version of Wikipedia and online travel blog entries.

The increasing of computational power of microprocessors improves the research in CBIR field in terms of different directions, such as applications to art and cultural imaging. For centuries, our memory institutions (i.e. libraries, archives, museums) have spent their efforts on collecting and describing artefacts and social phenomena to preserve and give access to our cultural heritage. In this context, several questions related to digital libraries management and information storage and retrieval represent hard issues and exciting challenges.

Mobile applications represent a fast and smart solution to achieve information about cultural heritage. Smartify[4] and GetCOO Travel[5] are interesting examples. Smartify is a free app that allows to scan and identify artworks, access rich interpretation and build a personal art collections in some of best museums and galleries around the world. GetCOO Travel is a smartphone application developed for tourists. They can take pictures of monuments to receive information about it.

In this context, we propose a novel multimodal information retrieval approach used to improve the user satisfaction during his/her roaming for cultural heritage information. Our approach has been completely developed in a mobile system based on open source technologies. One of the improving of the proposed system is in the use of on board sensors as GPS device, in fact, if it is activated

---
[3] http://frankenplace.com/. Last seen May 7, 2018.
[4] https://smartify.org. Last seen May 7, 2018.
[5] https://www.travel.getcoo.com. Last seen May 7, 2018.

by the user during an artwork recognition, it allows to effectively exploit the combination between location of the considered artwork and the multimedia data provided from the image matching task. The location of an artwork, based on the geographic position of the user is used to filter the results obtained from a multimedia search, considering only the artworks sited in the place resulting from the geographic search. In the author opinion the use of spatial information is a basic feature to implement smart systems in different application contexts and to analyse complex scenarios [22,23].

In according to the use of mobile technologies for digital cultural heritage access, we implement an Android application and test our framework and system in a real use case scenario about museums in the Italian city of Napoli.

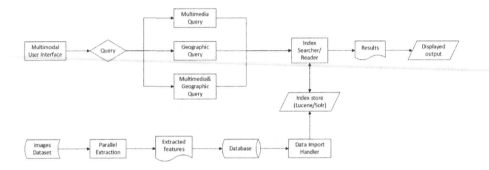

Fig. 1. System architecture

3   The Proposed Approach

The aim of our approach is to integrate Content-Based Image Retrieval and Geographic Information Retrieval to improve the accuracy of results in the retrieval process and give an easy user interface for multimodal query. The final goal is to have an enhancement of user satisfaction. Our approach has been implemented in a system and its architecture is shown in Fig. 1. In our discussion we introduce the used Content-Based Image Retrieval features starting from the description of the multimedia search implementation. In the second part the integration between multimedia and geographic data has been explained, focusing on the spatial data processing and the combination between the results obtained from CBIR and GIR. In the last part we'll present a *points of interest* (POI) *search*.

The system has been implemented using *Apache Solr* queries performed on a dataset composed of artworks located in Naples's museums. In the following sections, the three system main functionalities will be described.

3.1   Multimodal Query

The main aim of Content-Based Image Retrieval is to develop techniques for retrieving images on the basis of automatically-extracted features. For this reason the tasks of the *Multimedia Query* functionality provides to extract multimedia/visual features from an image previously loaded, and perform a search using the features vector obtained as result of the extraction. The *Geographic Query* functionality consists in points of interest search and, in our context they are represented by a museum, a church, an art gallery. In particular, for this functionality, the museums that are near to the user location are considered as points of interest. To perform this type of search, a radius has to be set to define the circle in which the museums can be retrieved. The idea of combining geographic data with multimedia data comes from observation of multimedia queries results. Most of the artworks submitted to the system was not retrieved in useful position and often the item in the top results are far from the user position. Therefore the use of a functionality based on the geolocation of the user could be useful to filter the results of a standard multimedia query. Obviously, filtering is possible only if the user geographic position is available at real-time by mobile devices.

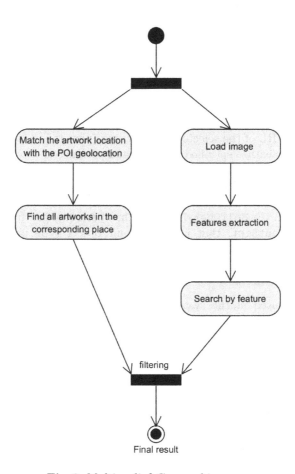

Fig. 2. Multimedia&Geographic query

The first step in the *Multimedia&Geographic Query* functionality is similar to the Multimedia Query and have the same purpose in features extraction from the loaded image and the searching by this feature vector. Afterward, a Geographic Query is performed to match the artwork location, based on the user geographic position, with the corresponding POI geolocation, to discover the place in which the user, and thus the artwork, is sited. The result of this query is used to find all the artworks in that place. Finally, the list of artworks is used in order to filter the multimedia results and obtain a more accurate result.

The Activity Diagram of this functionality is shown in Fig. 2. The artworks and their information are stored in a *Neo4J* instance. This database is used in the implementation and it is composed of the nodes drawn in Fig. 3: *Cultural Object*, *Author*, *Multimedia Representation* and *Place*.

It is important to point out that *location* is an exclusive attribute of *Place* node. Between this node and the *Cultural Object* one, there is relationship representing the current position of the artwork. This relationship is used to retrieve the POI in which the artwork is located, in the Multimedia&Geographic Query functionality, and has to be dynamically modified when an artwork changes location.

3.2 Multimodal Query Implementation

The *Multimedia Query* class is developed using the *SolrJ* library and it is composed of two queries provided by LIRe plug-in for Solr:

1. *Extract*: the URL of the selected (or captured) picture is passed to the query to extract the feature specified in the `field` parameter;
2. *Search by feature*: this query receives the results of the previous one as the `hashes` and `feature`. To manage easily the results of this query, the `doSearch` method of Lux's `LireRequestHandler` class has been modified: the type of the return value in the `SolrQueryResponse` has been changed from `LinkedList` to `SolrDocumentList`, that is, the default object type provided in SolrJ library for the queries response. In this way, the analysis of the results list from the response became immediate, being able to use the standard methods provided by the library.

The dataset used in the system includes Solr documents with the information of six Naples's museums: Museo nazionale di Capodimonte, Gallerie di palazzo Zevallos Stigliano, Museo nazionale di San Martino, Cappella Sansevero, Museo archeologico nazionale di Napoli, Museo civico di Castel Nuovo. Within these information, there is also the `location` field, expressed as a "latitude-longitude" string and configured in the `managed-schema` file as values of the `LatLonPointSpatialField` type. The *Geographic Query* method consists in a *points of interest* (POI) *search* to retrieve all the museums at a radial distance of one kilometer from the user. The Solr Spatial Query is performed using the `location` field of the Solr documents and the `geofilt` filter. As shown above, the *Multimedia&Geographic Query* functionality consists of the four steps listed below with the methods used in the implementation:

1. The first steps are equals to Multimedia Query and have the same purpose:
   (a) *Extract* query to get the feature vector from the captured image;
   (b) *Search by feature* query.
2. A Geographic Query is performed to match the artwork location, based on user's device GPS location, with the corresponding POI geolocation, to discover the place in which the user, and thus the artwork, is sited. For this query, the `geofilt` filter is used and a radial distance of 200 meters is set (`d = 0.2`).
3. The result of the previous query is sent as a parameter of the join query that is performed to find all the artworks in that place.
4. The resulting list is used as the filter for the results of the *Search by feature* query performed at point 1(b).

The final result of these steps is the most similar artwork to the captured image that is located in the POI where the user is.

3.3   The Used Technologies

The technologies used to implement the functionalities previously described are now presented. These description is useful to understand the whole framework and put in evidence the complete open source vision of our work.

Apache Lucene is an open source Java-based search library providing Application Programming Interfaces (APIs) for performing common search and search related tasks like indexing, querying, highlighting, language analysis, and many others [24]. The main capabilities of Lucene are centered on the creation, maintenance and accessibility of the *Lucene inverted index*. In particular, it has implemented a modified vector space model that supports incremental index modifications. As regards querying, Lucene supports a variety of query types, including: fielded term with boost, wildcards, fuzzy (using Levensthein Distance), boolean operators (AND, NOT, OR) and proximity searches. Furthermore, the version 3.6.0 has added support for regular expressions, complex phrases, spatial distances and arbitrary scoring functions based on values in a field.

Apache Solr is an open source, enterprise-ready, and highly scalable search platform, from the Apache Lucene Project [25]. It is written in Java, runs as a stand-alone server and also provides a web based graphical administrator interface for simple monitoring. Solr is *config-based* and the main configuration files are `solrconfig.xml` and `managed-schema`. The second one of these two files primarily defines the fields of the schema and their behaviour, that is how the text must be tokenized while indexing and querying. There is also a possibility to use Solr schemaless and let to Solr itself create fields while indexing the data. Solr provides libraries in various languages for server connection, documents indexing and queries handling. The library used in the proposed system is *SolrJ*, written in Java. Furthermore, Solr supports geographic data for use in spatial/geospatial searches. The main characteristics of this kind of query are: indexing points or other shapes; filtering search results by a bounding box, circle, or other shapes; sorting or boost scoring by distance between points, or relative area between

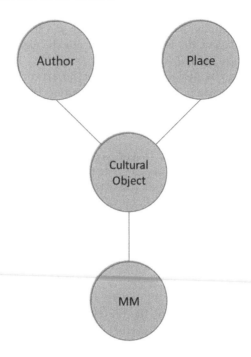

Fig. 3. Neo4J nodes

rectangles; generating a 2D grid of facet count numbers for heatmaps generation or point plotting.

LatLonPointSpatialField is the field type for most common use-cases for "latitude-longitude" point data, and for this reason it is the type used in our system. It replaced LatLonType which still exists for backwards compatibility. Two *Spatial Query Parsers* are provided for geospatial search: geofilt and bbox. The geofilt filter allows the user to retrieve results based on the geospatial distance, also know as "great circle distance", from a given point. This circular shape filter returns all results within a circle of the considered radius around the center point.

The bbox filter is very similar to the previous one. It takes the same parameters as geofilt, but it uses the bounding box of the calculated circle. The rectangular shape is faster to compute and for this it is often used when it is acceptable to have points outside the circle.

LIRe is a Java library for Content-Based Image Retrieval [26] used to extract image features from the dataset images and store them in a Lucene index for later retrieval. It has a very simple approach, in fact only a few lines of code are needed to integrate this library in any CBIR application. The integration of additional image features is made to further extend the functionality of LIRe.

LIRe Request Handler is a Solr plug-in that provides a Content-Based Image Retrieval server, allowing the combination of a Apache Solr search server with the LIRe CBIR Java-based library [27]. The LIRe Solr plug-in includes a

RequestHandler which supports the different types of queries used in the system. *Extracting features* query extracts the histogram (Base64 encoded string) and the hashes from an image, selecting the feature with `field` parameter and the number of query terms should be in the queries with `accuracy` parameter. The return values are ordered by ascending document frequency values and distance from the image to the respective reference point. *Search by feature vector* query returns an image that looks like the one the given features were extracted. This method is used if the client extracts the features from the image. Mandatory parameters to set are: `field`-the feature to search for; `hashes`-string of white space separated numbers representing the hashes of the image feature; `feature`-the Base64 encoded feature histogram. This query is used to match the feature just extracted with the ones extracted from images stored in Solr indexes and retrieve the correct artwork and the information linked to it. Furthermore, to extract features from a group of images (i.e., the whole dataset) and to index it, a Java runnable class called `ParallelSolrIndexer` can be used. It creates XML documents to be sent to Solr server and indexed in Lucene, taking in input a text file containing the paths of each image. Unfortunately, this class provides the extraction of global features only. To bridge the gap, a new Java runnable class for the local feature parallel extraction has been implemented. Due to the large amount of possible data, we use a NoSQL database. For our purpose we choice to use Neo4J, an open source graph database management system developed in Java. It is based on the *property graph model*, in which a node is described with properties and labels. Neo4J is accessible from software written in other languages using the *Cypher Query Language* through a transactional HTTP endpoint. The database instance has been indexed directly into Solr with the help of Neo4J `JDBC Driver` and the Solr `Data Import Handler` (DIH) feature. The Data Import Handler provides a mechanism for importing content from a data store and indexing it. In addition to relational databases, DIH can also index content from NoSQL DB, HTTP based data sources such as RSS feeds, e-mail repositories, and structured XML with an XPath processor is used to generate fields[6]. The DIH has to be registered in `solrconfig.xml`, and the only required parameter is the `config`, which specifies the location of the handler configuration file that contains specifications for the data source, the way to fetch data, type of fetched data, and how to combine nodes and relations in the Neo4J database to create entities related to the desired structure and generate the Solr documents to be posted to the indexer.

4   A Case Study on Cultural Heritage Domain

The described system has been designed using a client-server paradigm and implemented in an Android application. We describe the whole process presenting both user interaction tasks and implementation details to better understand our application.

---

[6] https://cwiki.apache.org/confluence/display/solr/Uploading+Structured+Data+St ore+Data+with+the+Data+Import+Handler. Last seen May 7, 2018.

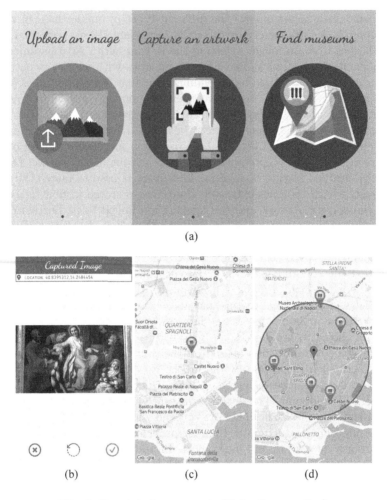

Fig. 4. User interface example (Color figure online)

The client-side application allows users to: *upload* an image from device gallery to retrieve information about artwork represented in the given image; *take a picture* of an artwork in a POI to retrieve information about it. The user can enable his/her position given by GPS sensor to improve the accuracy of image retrieval; *discover* the location of the museums closest to him/her. The server-side system is able to: *receive* and *manage* data sent by client application to call the right method, based on data types received in the request; *establish* the connection with the `SolrClient`; *perform* the necessary `SolrQuery`; *get* results as `SolrDocument`; *send* the response to client. The connection between client and server is obtained via the HTTP protocol, and in particular by the POST request method realized by an `HttpURLConnection` Java object. JSON (JavaScript Object Notation) structures are used as *content type* of the POST requests and response; it represents the standard type of format for data interchange between a client and a server. The *media type* for JSON is `application/json`. To handle the JSON object received both on server (HTTP request) and on client (HTTP response), methods provided by *Google-Gson* library[7] are applied.

On server, the `fromJson()` method is used to convert the request into an object, having as attributes the three possible data types sent by client: `base64String`, the Base64-encoded string of the image uploaded or captured by user (`null` in case of Geographic Query); `type`-the string representing the type of uploaded image file or captured by user (`null` in case of Geographic Query); `userPosition`-the string representing the user's geographic location, in "latitude, longitude" format (`null` in case of Multimedia Query).

On client, instead, the `fromJson()` method is used to get the results from the response and store them in a Java class to be managed and displayed by the device. The results structure contains: `title`, `author`, `place` (the name of the POI in which the retrieved artwork is sited), `location` (the geographic location of the POI in which the retrieved artwork is sited, in "latitude, longitude" format), `placeUrl` (the *Wikipedia* page web address of the POI in which the retrieved artwork is sited), `base64image` (Base64 encoded string of the image of the retrieved artwork), and `imageUrl` (the *Wikipedia* page web address of the retrieved artwork, if available).

In Fig. 5 a Use Case Diagram representing a static and formal description of the application functionalities is shown.

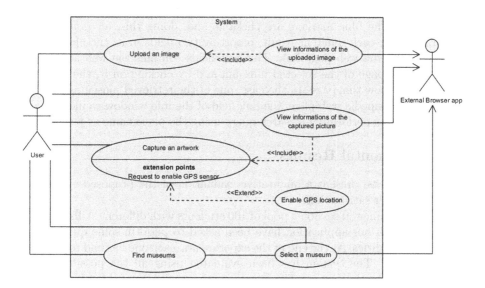

Fig. 5. Use case diagram

---

[7] https://github.com/google/gson. Last seen May 7, 2018.

On startup, the application checks if the internet connection is available, because this is a needful requirement for the work of the entire system. In the case that no connection is enabled, an *alert dialog* is shown warning the user to provide to turn it on. Enabled the internet connection, the user visualizes the home screen of each functionality, that allows him to click on the circular button placed at the center of the screen, Fig. 4(a). A picture representing an artwork can be submitted to the system both loading it from the device storage or taking it by device camera. In this second option, once the photo is taken, the application displays an *alert dialog* to the user asking him/her the possibility of using position, given by GPS sensor, to improve the image retrieval, allowing the filtering based on location. The image in Fig. 4(b) shows the case in which the user chooses to improve the image retrieval with position, and under the screen title a *location* field displays the geographic data, represented as "latitude, longitude". After the server side computation, a map with a marker is displayed to show the result as depicted in Fig. 4(c). The marker indicates the location of the retrieved artwork and, by clicking on it, an *info window* appears with the information about title, author, place and a web link regarding the artwork. The *link* field can contain a Wikipedia address, if the artwork has a dedicated web page, or a Google address that leads to a search query in which title and author of the artwork are used as keywords.

In Fig. 4(d) results of a points of interest search are shown. After the server computation, a map is displayed. On it a red marker indicates the user position and a red circle shows the area in which the POI search is performed. Within this circle one or more customized markers can be displayed if the retrieval produces some results. The blue markers are clickable and, doing this, an *info window* appears, one for each different result, reporting two fields in it: the place name and the Wikipedia web page link. This last fields contains the web address of the Wikipedia page of the selected museum and by clicking on it, the Browser app opens to show this page. In the case, one of the retrieved museums has not a dedicated Wikipedia web page, the link field of the info window would contain a Google address performing a search query using the place name as parameter.

5   Experimental Results

In this section, we present a qualitative evaluation of the proposed system to measure the user satisfaction.

In the experimental session a pool of 100 students with different skills without experiences with our application have been asked to perform some queries and use all functionalities. At the end of the experiments, each one has had to compile a questionnaire. The system has been evaluated using all the possible query types proposed by the system. The query and the used data set have been based on some cultural places and objects in the city of Naples. The questionnaire is structured following a methodology presented in [28] to evaluate system usability and user satisfaction. For each of the five questions selected, the user gives a score from *strongly disagree* (1) to *strongly agree* (7) (Y-axis), for the corresponding statement. The questions contain the following statements (X-axis):

1. Overall, I am satisfied with how easy it is to use this system;
2. It was simple to use this system;
3. I was able to complete the tasks quickly using this system;
4. It was easy to learn to use this system;
5. It was easy to find the information I needed.

The number of scale values (7) has been defined through a trade-off between reliability and easiness for the tester. Data from any questionnaire have been gathered and analyzed. Figure 6 show the mean of obtained results for each types of query (MQ = Multimedia Query, GQ = Geographic Query, M&GQ = Multimedia&Geographic Query).

The geographic query has slightly better values with questions 1, 2 and 4 which refer to simpleness and ease to learning. This could probably caused by the fact that the geographic query is quite similar to other widely information systems. However the strong difference is in questions 3 and 5, which are about completing the task and finding information where the combined query show an improvement. Thus, we can deduce that with a very small effort into adapting to the new way of querying, the users achieve better results.

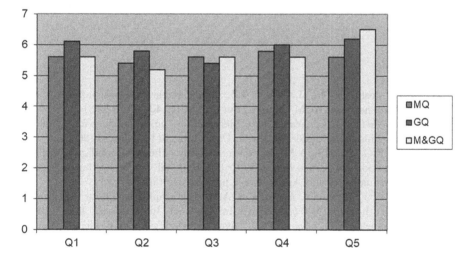

Fig. 6. Qualitative evaluation results

6   Conclusion and Future Work

In this paper a system providing a multimodal user interface for cultural heritage information retrieval has been presented. We present a complete design an implementation of our proposed approach using an Android application. It presents three functionalities: a method for the image matching based on visual descriptors, called *Multimedia Query*; a points of interest search called the

Geographic Query, and the *Multimedia&Geographic Query*, which provide the combination between geographic and multimedia data to improve the accuracy of image retrieval process. In particular, this functionality is based on the geolocation of the artwork, derived from the user geographic position who perform the query, which filter the results of a standard multimedia/visual query. The satisfaction of users has been measured using a formal methodology and our results suggest several directions for future investigations and researches. An in-depth study of the principal visual descriptors actually used in image retrieval should be analyzed in order to measure their performances and recognize the best features to use in the system implementation. Focusing on the multimodal user interface, instead, it could be expanded with other functionalities that provide, for example, the possibility to the posing query process, a vocal query could be implemented using techniques and methods for speech recognition. Furthermore, semantic web oriented techniques can be investigated and eventually exploited in order to enhance the query construction also adopting matchmaking strategies [29,30] using cultural heritage resources collected from heterogeneous databases. In addition, some improvements could be done on the extension of the image dataset to include other artworks and different cultural features. Eventually, a more specific quantitative experiments using precision and recall measures should be carried out to compare our strategy with other presented in literature.

References

1. Datta, R., Joshi, D., Li, J., Wang, J.Z.: Image retrieval: ideas, influences, and trends of the new age. ACM Comput. Surv. (CSUR) **40**(2), 5 (2008)
2. Chen, C., Wactlar, H.D., Wang, J.Z., Kiernan, K.: Digital imagery for significant cultural and historical materials. Int. J. Digit. Libr. **5**(4), 275–286 (2005)
3. Caldarola, E.G., Rinaldi, A.M.: Big data: a survey - the new paradigms, methodologies and tools. In: Proceedings of 4th International Conference on Data Management Technologies and Applications, pp. 362–370 (2015)
4. Caldarola, E.G., Picariello, A., Rinaldi, A.M.: Big graph-based data visualization experiences: the WordNet case study. In: 2015 7th International Joint Conference on Knowledge Discovery, Knowledge Engineering and Knowledge Management (IC3K), vol. 1, pp. 104–115. IEEE (2015)
5. Caldarola, E.G., Rinaldi, A.M.: Improving the visualization of WordNet large lexical database through semantic tag clouds. In: 2016 IEEE International Congress on Big Data (BigData Congress), pp. 34–41. IEEE (2016)
6. Caldarola, E.G., Picariello, A., Rinaldi, A.M.: Experiences in WordNet visualization with labeled graph databases. In: Fred, A., Dietz, J.L.G., Aveiro, D., Liu, K., Filipe, J. (eds.) IC3K 2015. CCIS, vol. 631, pp. 80–99. Springer, Cham (2016). https://doi.org/10.1007/978-3-319-52758-1_6
7. Shete, D.S., Chavan, M., Kolhapur, K.: Content based image retrieval. Int. J. Emerg. Technol. Adv. Eng. **2**(9), 85–90 (2012)
8. Deselaers, T., Keysers, D., Ney, H.: Features for image retrieval: an experimental comparison. Inf. Retr. **11**(2), 77–107 (2008)

9. Larson, R.R.: Geographic information retrieval and spatial browsing. Geographic information systems and libraries: patrons, maps, and spatial information. Papers Presented at the 1995 Clinic on Library Applications of Data Processing, 10–12 April 1995 (1996)

10. Manning, C.D., Raghavan, P., Schütze, H., et al.: Introduction to Information Retrieval. Cambridge University Press, Cambridge (2008)

11. Mark, D.M.: Geographic information science: defining the field. Found. Geograph. Inf. Sci. **1**, 3–18 (2003)

12. Moscato, V., Picariello, A., Rinaldi, A.M.: A recommendation strategy based on user behavior in digital ecosystems. In: Proceedings of the International Conference on Management of Emergent Digital EcoSystems, pp. 25–32. ACM (2010)

13. Smeulders, A.W., Worring, M., Santini, S., Gupta, A., Jain, R.: Content-based image retrieval at the end of the early years. IEEE Trans. Pattern Anal. Mach. Intell. **22**(12), 1349–1380 (2000)

14. Frederix, G., Caenen, G., Pauwels, E.J.: Panoramic, adaptive and reconfigurable interface for similarity search. In: Proceedings of the 2000 International Conference on Image Processing, vol. 3, pp. 222–225. IEEE (2000)

15. Giuca, A.M., Seitz, K.A., Furst, J., Raicu, D.: Expanding diagnostically labeled datasets using content-based image retrieval. In: 2012 19th IEEE International Conference on Image Processing (ICIP), pp. 2397–2400. IEEE (2012)

16. Irtaza, A., Jaffar, M.A., Muhammad, M.S.: Content based image retrieval in a web 3.0 environment. Multimed. Tools Appl. **74**(14), 5055–5072 (2015)

17. Karamti, H., Tmar, M., Visani, M., Urruty, T., Gargouri, F.: Vector space model adaptation and pseudo relevance feedback for content-based image retrieval. Multimed. Tools Appl. **77**, 1–27 (2017)

18. Hariharan, R., Hore, B., Li, C., Mehrotra, S.: Processing spatial-keyword (SK) queries in geographic information retrieval (GIR) systems. In: 19th International Conference on Scientific and Statistical Database Management, SSBDM 2007, p. 16. IEEE (2007)

19. Han, A., Nickerson, B.G.: Efficient combined text and spatial search. In: Gervasi, O., Murgante, B., Misra, S., Gavrilova, M.L., Rocha, A.M.A.C., Torre, C., Taniar, D., Apduhan, B.O. (eds.) ICCSA 2015. LNCS, vol. 9157, pp. 713–728. Springer, Cham (2015). https://doi.org/10.1007/978-3-319-21470-2_52

20. Mattmann, C.A., Sharan, M.: An automatic approach for discovering and geocoding locations in domain-specific web data (application paper). In: 2016 IEEE 17th International Conference on Information Reuse and Integration (IRI), pp. 87–93. IEEE (2016)

21. Adams, B., McKenzie, G., Gahegan, M.: Frankenplace: interactive thematic mapping for ad hoc exploratory search. In: Proceedings of the 24th International Conference on World Wide Web, pp. 12–22. ACM (2015)

22. Di Pinto, V., Rinaldi, A.: A configurational approach based on geographic information systems to support decision-making process in real estate domain. Soft Comput. 1–10 (2018). https://link.springer.com/article/10.1007/s00500-018-3142-9#citeas

23. Rinaldi, A.: A GIS-based system for electromagnetic risk management in urban areas. J. Locat. Based Serv. **3**(1), 3–23 (2009)

24. Białecki, A., Muir, R., Ingersoll, G., Imagination, L.: Apache lucene 4. In: SIGIR 2012 Workshop on Open Source Information Retrieval, p. 17 (2012)

25. Shahi, D.: Apache Solr: an introduction. In: Shahi, D. (ed.) Apache Solr, pp. 1–9. Springer, Heidelberg (2015). https://doi.org/10.1007/978-1-4842-1070-3_1

26. Lux, M., Chatzichristofis, S.A.: LIRE: lucene image retrieval: an extensible Java CBIR library. In: Proceedings of the 16th ACM International Conference on Multimedia, pp. 1085–1088. ACM (2008)
27. Lux, M., Macstravic, G.: The LIRE request handler: a solr plug-in for large scale content based image retrieval. In: Gurrin, C., Hopfgartner, F., Hurst, W., Johansen, H., Lee, H., O'Connor, N. (eds.) MMM 2014. LNCS, vol. 8326, pp. 374–377. Springer, Cham (2014). https://doi.org/10.1007/978-3-319-04117-9_39
28. Lewis, J.R.: IBM computer usability satisfaction questionnaires: psychometric evaluation and instructions for use. Int. J. Hum.-Comput. Interact. **7**(1), 57–78 (1995)
29. Caldarola, E.G., Rinaldi, A.M.: An approach to ontology integration for ontology reuse. In: 2016 IEEE 17th International Conference on Information Reuse and Integration (IRI), pp. 384–393. IEEE (2016)
30. Caldarola, E.G., Rinaldi, A.M.: A multi-strategy approach for ontology reuse through matching and integration techniques. In: Rubin, S.H., Bouabana-Tebibel, T. (eds.) FMI/IRI 2016 -2016. AISC, vol. 561, pp. 63–90. Springer, Cham (2018). https://doi.org/10.1007/978-3-319-56157-8_4

A Platform for Exploring Social Media Analytics of Fast Food Restaurants in Australia

Chang Liu$^{(\boxtimes)}$ (iD) and Richard O. Sinnott$^{(\boxtimes)}$ (iD)

University of Melbourne, Melbourne, VIC 3010, Australia
a609640147@gmail.com, rsinnott@unimelb.edu.au

Abstract. Social media is one of the primary communication tools for Internet users. Twitter, one of the most popular social medias, has more than one hundred million daily active users. These tweeters tweet a large number of tweets every day containing a rich and diverse collection of information. At the same time, the problem of obesity is becoming a serious issue all over the world. In this paper, we consider the impact of the geographical location of fast food restaurant on the body mass index (BMI) and levels of obesity of individuals in Melbourne through data analytics around social media.

Keywords: Social media · Twitter · Content analysis · Fast food restaurant

1 Introduction

In 2000, the world health organization (WHO) gave a warning that obesity had become one of the most serious health problems of the 21st century. In 2016, the WHO identified that there are about 1.9 billion overweight adults of whom at least 650 million are medically obese [1]. Obesity can lead to many secondary disorders, such as cardiovascular issues, diabetes and cancer. However, as with many health issues, levels of BMI and obesity is a personal issue, and access to such personal BMI information is limited because of individual level privacy [2]. To tackle such issues, one approach is to aggregate data to spatial areas, e.g. postcode averages.

Human activities are rarely completely isolated and independent, and hence the interconnection of otherwise independent data resources has many advantages especially in health settings. In the Internet-era, people are now dependent on using and exchanging information. From email to blogs to Social Network Services such as Twitter, human activities are increasingly captured, and people are now paying more attention to the subsequent use of data from these services.

As one example, Twitter is an online micro-blogging service and social networking tool. It has more than one hundred million daily active users. In Australia, there are 2.9 million tweeters in the total population of 24.13 million people [3]. These tweeters tweet a large number of tweets every day. On average, there are around 6,000 tweets are sent every second with over 350,000 tweets sent per minute, 500 million tweets sent per day, and over 200 billion tweets sent per year. Twitter offers a low cost, real-time and extensive resource to understand a wide range of phenomenon, e.g. if a person

© Springer International Publishing AG, part of Springer Nature 2018
O. Gervasi et al. (Eds.): ICCSA 2018, LNCS 10960, pp. 231–244, 2018.
https://doi.org/10.1007/978-3-319-95162-1_16

tweets 'I need to lose weight' there is a high probability that this person is overweight. Identifying population-wide patterns in such tweets can reveal societal patterns [4].

This paper focuses on such capabilities. It involves large-scale data collection and data pre-processing with keyword-based methods derived from Natural Language Processing approaches with supervised classification and long-short term memory models from machine learning. Lydecker and Cotter used 'fat' as the keyword [9] and Anwar and Yuan used 11 hashtags as keywords [10] to gather tweets. These keywords are widely used and easily understood by a majority of people, but they may not enough to cover most tweet which describe 'fat' and 'fast food'. Besides, the obesity-related conversations are not very socially and personally rooted [10]. In this paper, we used existing keywords to get some tweets. Then Word Frequency was used to get more proper keywords basing on these tweets.

The specific research question explored here is to establish the relationship between the number of overweight people and the number of fast food restaurants in a particular area. Specifically, we focus on collecting data on fast food restaurants in Melbourne, via the Google Maps API and from Twitter. We combine these data sets with other official data sets on health and wellbeing from the Australian Urban Research Infrastructure Network (AURIN – www.aurin.org.au) resource to explore the correlation between people's health and the distribution of fast food restaurant. Such analysis can be used to influence policy on establishment of restaurants for example.

The remainder of this paper is organized as follows. Section 2 focuses on the background and provides a literature review. Sections 3 presents the methods used and the implementation details. Section 4 focuses on the analysis and presentation of results. Finally, Sect. 5 concludes this paper and discusses areas of future work.

2   Background

2.1   Spatial Aggregation Levels

There are many ways to classify the use of land: postcodes, states, countries. In Australia, Statistical Area such as Statistical Area Level 2 (SA2) are one way to partition the use of land in Australia. They typically represent a community such as a named suburb that aggregates data across a range of social and economic aspects relevant to that SA2. In 2016, there were 2310 SA2 regions in Australia. It is noted that there are many other spatial aggregation levels that exist: local government areas (LGAs), functional economic regions, census districts, and statistical areas (SA4-SA1) amongst numerous others. It is also noted that these spatial levels evolve over time, e.g. as cities grow and change their population profiles.

2.2   Twitter

Twitter is an online micro-blogging service and social networking tool that allows users to post and interact with other users by using short message 'tweets'. Tweets are 140-character long messages including space and punctuation. Many tweets contain pictures, links to content and emojis. By using Twitter, users can connect with a community of people who share the same interests.

The majority of tweets are broadcast publicly and everyone that uses Twitter can access and read them. Tweets track details of the time when these tweets were posted. The timeline is one primary way people engage with the Twitter. Tweets from other accounts that the user follows will appear in the timeline chronologically, and the timeline will update in real time. '@' which is a symbol known as mentions are used to reply to tweets. The '@' mentions are added at the start of tweets, followed by the user who is replying. Twitter uses this feature to track the association between the tweets as a form of 'conversation.' The last important feature that Twitter provides is hashtags. In Twitter, the hashtags turn words into clickable links that relate to another tweet sharing the same hashtag. This provides a search mechanism for contents included in a set of tweets [5].

The users of Twitter generate a large amount of information every day, and many tweets contain the location information of the users. Such major (global) volumes of data allow for a rich range of subsequent uses for Twitter analytics.

2.3 Deep Learning

Deep learning is a field stemming from origins in artificial neural networks and machine learning and specifically multi-layer artificial neural networks. A layer of the neural network will typically use a large number of matrix numbers as input, then use the non-linear activation method to achieve the associated weight, before generating another data set as the output [8].

There are two main models driving forward rapid evolution in the area of deep learning: Convolution Neural Networks (CNNs) and Recurrent Neural Networks (RNN). In this paper we focus on RNNs.

An RNN is a form of artificial neural network which can be used to identify serial data from resources as diverse as text, genome, handwriting and voice. When reading an article, a human will use the understanding of the preceding text to understand the current text, rather than simply reading the current text and discarding any understanding of the older/previous text. Human memory is persistent. However traditional neural networks cannot infer the next text classification based on the previously classified text. The RNN solves this problem by including loops which can keep the previous information [8].

Long-Short Term Memory (LSTM) is a special form of RNN model that can be used to solve problems with gradient disappearance. LSTM preserves errors for reverse delivery over time and layers. It keeps errors at a more constant level, allowing the recursive network to perform many time steps thereby opening opportunities for establishing long distance causal links. LSTM stores the information in a gated unit outside the normal recursive network traffic. These units can store, write or read information. The unit determines which information is stored through a switch that allows to read, write, or clear the information. Unlike the digital memory in a computer, these gates are analog and contain element-by-factor multiplication of the sigmoid function with all the output ranges between 0 and 1. Compared to digital storage, the advantages of analog values can be differentiated, hence they are suitable for reverse propagation.

The gates are switched depending on the received signal as similar to the nodes of a neural network. They use their own weight sets to filter the information and decide whether or not to allow information to be passed according to its strength and content. These weights, like the weights of the modulation input and the hidden state, are adjusted by the recursive network learning process. That is, the memory unit will, by estimation, support error back propagation, with a gradient descent that adjusts the weight of the iterative process to learn when to allow data to enter, leave or be deleted from the network.

3   Method and Data Processing

3.1   Google Maps API

To obtain the detailed address information of fast food restaurants in Melbourne, a radar search method is used [7]. As the name implies, this method searches the target based on keywords associated with a given centroid.

Melbourne has many fast food restaurants. The area from [−37.5, 144.5] to [−38.5, 145.5] is broken into several 5 km circular areas, as shown in Fig. 1. To ensure no omission of fast food restaurants, these circles have overlaps covering all of the areas from [−37.5, 144.5] to [−38.5, 145.5].

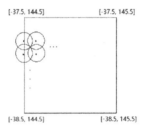

Fig. 1. Partition method of the Google Maps radar search

This approach means that fast food restaurants located in overlapping areas may be recorded more than once. To remove duplicate fast food restaurants' their geo-information is used directly. In this work, a known set of fast food chains was explored and their associated keywords used to collect the branch location information. Specifically the fast food chains and keywords included 'KFC,' 'McDonalds,' 'Maccas', 'Subway,' 'Domino,' 'Pizza Hut,' 'Nandos' and 'fastfood.' The collected results are shown in Table 1 below.

After removing the duplicate information and the restaurant out of range, 762 fast food restaurants' and their geo-information was obtained from Twitter.

Table 1. Different Melbourne fast food restaurants identified via Twitter

Keyword	Number	Keyword	Number
KFC	154	Pizza Hut	77
McDonalds (maccas)	208	Nandos	97
Subway	108	Fastfood	526
Domino	245		

3.2 Data Pre-processing

In order to perform natural language processing (NLP) tweets need to be pre-processed. The first step of NLP is tokenization, e.g. identifying terms and removing stop words. Tweet text is different from normal prose since it may have hashtags, mentions, emojis and URLs. In order to tokenize a tweet, a tokenizer is built using regular expressions. In this work, eight regular expressions were used to tokenize the tweet text. The second step is tweet normalization. Initially, all of the characters in the token should translate to lowercase letters. Then, lemmatization is used to solve word tense problems. The third step is removing the meaningless token from the Tweet text token list, e.g. removing stopwords. The punctuation, stopwords, retweets (prefixed with RT) and via (used to mention the original author of a tweet or a retweet) were removed.

3.3 Word Count

The word count is the easiest analysis used to find fast food restaurant-related words. Through this method, the word which most commonly used in the data set can be found. A bag-of-words is used to get the word counts. A bag-of-words model can represent a sentence or a document as a feature vector. The basic idea is to treat text as a collection of words. By searching for tweets which contain at least one of the aforementioned eight keywords, 6229 tweets were identified that contained at least one of the nine words. By identifying bigrams and combining the tf-idf value of all words and phrases with the high-frequency words and phrases, 38 normal words and 9 search words were chosen as the basis for fast food restaurant related words:

```
['#maccas', '#McDonald', '#kfc', '#dominos', '#subway', '#nandos', '#pizza hut'
'fastfood', 'fast food', 'carry-out', 'eat in', 'drive thru', 'franchise', 'menu', 'combo',
'nutrition', 'beverage', 'soft drink', 'fountain drink', 'slushie', 'smoothie', 'coffee', 'sub',
'bun', 'muffin', 'scone', 'biscuit', 'sides', 'condiments', 'dressing', 'fries', 'fried chicken',
'hash browns', 'onion rings', 'burger', 'chicken', 'sausage', 'hotdog', 'bacon', 'beef']
```

By using the keywords 'fat', 'overweight' and 'obese' to find all tweets related to being overweight in the data set, 2574 tweets, which contained at least one of the three words were found. Combining the tf-idf value of all words and phrases with the high-frequency words and phrases, 68 normal words and phrases were chosen as the overweight related words:

[' fat ', 'overweight', 'obese', 'obesity', 'lose weight', 'low fat', 'slim', 'reduce', 'keep fit', 'fatty', 'adipose', 'fatty tissue', 'chubby', 'plump', 'podgy', 'tubby', 'blubber', 'sebaceous', 'corpulent', 'pudgy', 'greasy', 'avoirdupois', 'portly', 'rotund', 'zaftig', 'fatten', 'blubbery', 'fleshy', 'oily', 'potbellied', 'dumpy', 'juicy', 'paunchy', 'porcine', 'buxom', 'buttery', 'thick', 'jowly', 'thickset', 'rich', 'embonpoint', 'oleaginous', 'stocky', 'gross', 'profitable', 'weighty', 'fatten up', 'heavyset', 'stout', 'fill out', 'heavy', 'fertile', 'compact', 'productive', 'rounded', 'fruitful', 'abdominous', 'double-chinned', 'endomorphic', 'fatten out', 'fattish', 'flesh out', 'loose-jowled', 'plump out', 'pyknic', 'suety', 'superfatted', 'zoftig']

There were only 83 tweets which contained at least one of the fast food restaurant keywords and at least one overweight keyword. Since this was insufficient for training, the, 47 fast food restaurant-related words and phrases were also used as keywords.

3.4 Long-Short Term Memory Network (LSTM)

A unique feature of NLP data is that every word in a sentence depends on the previous words and impacts on the subsequent word. Because of this dependency, an RNN is used to analyze this kind of series data. The LSTM is a special RNN, it preserves long-term dependency information in text. To get the training set, the tweets data set needs to be pre-processed. In this work, only three features were used: 'created_at', 'text' and 'user_id'. By using the 47 fast food restaurant related words and 68 fat related words identified above to search these tweets the specific obesity related tweets were obtained. After data pre-processing and searching, 13,420 tweets were identified which contained obesity related words, and 922 tweets found which contained both fast food restaurant related words and obesity-related words.

The input of the LSTM should be a word vector. Before building the LSTM model, the training data should be changed from text to word vectors. Key to this is ensuring that the size of the vocabulary of the model includes sufficient different words. This is because this vocabulary is used to build the one-to-one correspondence between the word and value. Building the vocabulary is an important step to change a sentence into a word vector [6]. A low frequency word which may just appear one time in the text may not need to be added into the vocabulary. Words which are not in the vocabulary are replaced by the pseudo word 'UNK'. After processing all the text in the data set, 24,490 different words existed in this data set with 6,748 words appearing more than twice. As a result, the size of the vocabulary was set to 6,750 with the first 6758 words sorted by the word frequency from large to small in the training set with one pseudo word UNK.

The length of sentence should also be fixed, since in the RNN model the word vectors are analyzed in a matrix. The longest sentence contains 32 words. Since a tweet text can contain at most 140 characters, the length of the sentence is set as 30. If a sentence is less than 30 terms, the filling word 0 should be added to the short sentence until it reaches a length of 30.

A lookup table is used to convert the words and their appearances based on the vocabulary. All of the text in the data set is converted into word vectorx by using the lookup table. After the conversion, if the word vector is longer than 30 terms, the part which is out of range is cut off. If the word vector is shorter than 30, the filling word 0 is added until the length reaches 30. After these processes, the text has been changed into a fixed length word vector matrix.

Following this, the word vector data set is split with 80% of the data used as the training set and the rest used as the test set. These data sets are used to train the LSTM. The LSTM model from Keras is used with the loss function based on '*binary_crossentropy*' and optimization method using 'adam'. Using the model on the test set, the results are as follows (Fig. 2):

```
predict label   label       text
      0           0     pho noodle bowls ready for our rich bone broth # warming # UNK # UNK
      0           0     it only takes grams of UNK per day to reduce oral bacteria aka
      1           1     why am laying in bed at am craving juicy burger
      1           1     did someone say breakfast pick up bag of our mouth-watering thick cut UNK bacon express
      0           0     17 bottles of chocolate cherry stout # craftbeer # homebrew # UNK
      0           0     download the # UNK app and listen to the latest mix by the # legend # UNK # UNK
```

Fig. 2. Part of the test result

After training, the LSTM model had an accuracy of 96.1%. Using the trained LSTM model on the 2.7 million tweets data set (from all over the Australia), there were 37,889 predicted tweets. We then used this model on the 153,984 tweets data set obtained from Melbourne to obtain 18,775 predicted tweets.

4   Data Analysis

There were three main analysis undertaken. The first one used the SA2 as the partition criterion to analyze tweets data. The second analysis focused specifically on the Melbourne CBD (SA2). The last one focused on the McDonald's fast food restaurants using both the tweet data sets and the SA2 partition criteria.

4.1   Visualization

Visualization of all data gives a general impression of the work as a whole. The visualization of all the collected fast food restaurants is shown in Fig. 3.

As seen, fast food restaurants are distributed across Melbourne evenly with the exception of the Melbourne CBD. There are 53 fast food restaurants located in the Melbourne LGA, and 32 fast food restaurants located in the Melbourne CBD (SA2). The fast food restaurants are obviously more concentrated in the Melbourne CBD. The visualization of all tweets predicted by the LSTM model are shown in Fig. 4.

Fig. 3. Visualization of the collected fast food restaurants

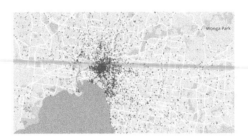

Fig. 4. Visualization of all tweets

4.2   SA2

SA2 areas are relatively small, so all SA2 areas located in the area [−37.5, 144.5] to [−38.5, 145.5] can be considered as a single area. There are 213 SA2 areas in this region. After processing the 762 fast food restaurants, the 37,889 and 18,775 predicted tweets, there were 160 areas that contained both the collect tweets and the collected fast food restaurants. The obesity related data from AURIN also uses the SA2 partition criteria as follows (Table 2):

Table 2. Data separated into SA2 areas

Sa2_name	Overweight	Obesity	Fastfood	Tweet_old	Tweet_new
Melbourne	4217.22	1478.83	32	893	10027
Epping	6070.65	4651.30	11	20	4
Narre Warren	5499.92	4484.96	11	7	21
Dandenong	5802.12	5034.52	10	27	20
Preston	6959.97	5138.12	10	22	52
......					
Ivanhoe	2660.90	1318.37	1	5	4
Newport	3885.22	2476.24	1	9	16

Here tweet_old is based on a large collection of historic tweets from the Melbourne eResearch Group and tweet_new, the tweets collected between April–July 2017. Here the Melbourne (SA2) can be regarded as a singularity due to the amount of data and activity more generally. Removing the data from the Melbourne CBD, the scatter plot matrix for the SA2s are shown in Fig. 5.

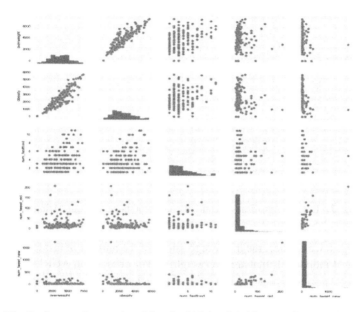

Fig. 5. Scatter plot matrix of data in SA2 level (without Melbourne (SA2))

After processing, the linear regression of the parameters is shown in Fig. 6:

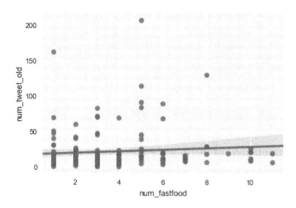

Fig. 6. Linear regression of fastfood and tweet_old (without Melbourne)

From the figure above, we can see that the linear regression for the number of fast food restaurant and the number of historic tweets (2011–2014) is positive.

From Fig. 7 we can see the linear regression of the number of fast food restaurants and number of fast food related tweets (2017.4–2017.7) is positive.

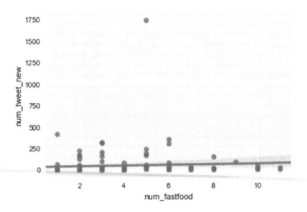

Fig. 7. Linear regression of fastfood and tweet_new (without Melbourne)

From Fig. 8 we can see, the linear regressions of the number of fast food restaurants and number of individuals that are overweight and/or obese from AURIN are also both positive. We use the Pearson Correlation Coefficient to calculate the similarity as shown below (Table 3).

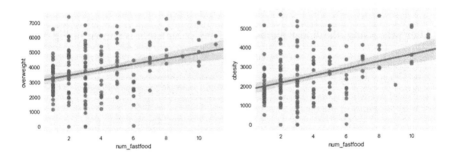

Fig. 8. Linear regression of fastfood and overweight (without Melbourne)

As seen, the correlations of the four parameter-pairs are all positive. It is noted that the data of the Melbourne (SA2) has a huge influence on the result and it is not appropriate to simply remove this data. The following section considers the Melbourne CBD area explicitly.

Table 3. Pearson Correlation Coefficient in SA2 level

Parameter pair	All data	All data (without Melbourne)
num_ff and num_tweet_old	0.65388565626	0.092830718422
num_ff and num_tweet_new	0.67563521684	0.061814196975
num_ff and overweight	0.22830948095	0.28745296698
num_ff and obesity	0.21536339828	0.34973838419

4.3   SA2

There are 32 fast food restaurants and 3,813 tweets (2011–2014) identified in the Melbourne CBD. This area was divided into four segments as shown in Fig. 9.

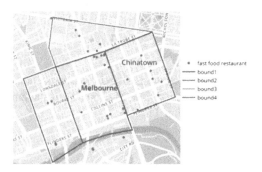

Fig. 9. Partitioning the Melbourne SA2

Since AURIN does not have overweight data based on partition, only the number of historic tweets (2011–2014) were taken into consideration. After processing, the data was as follows (Table 4):

Table 4. Melbourne CBD data separated into four parts

num_ff	num_tweet
16	387
7	327
5	98
4	72

We consider a linear regression on these data:

From Fig. 10 we can see that the linear regression of the number of fast food restaurants and number of tweets (2011–2014) is positive. The Pearson Correlation Coefficient is 0.83554998008. This represents a strong positive correlation between the number of fast food restaurant and the number of tweets.

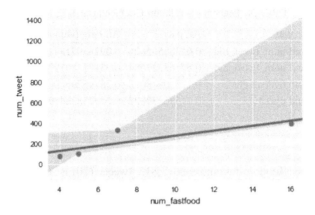

Fig. 10. Linear regression of restaurants and tweets in four partitions of Melbourne SA2

4.4 McDonalds/Maccas Analysis

In this part, only the McDonald's restaurants and the tweets containing the keyword of 'maccas' or 'mcdonalds' are analyzed. The McDonald's restaurants and the tweets for all of Melbourne are shown in (Fig. 11).

Fig. 11. Visualization of the collected McDonald's restaurants and tweets

The visualization of the McDonald's restaurants and the tweets in the Melbourne SA2 are shown in Fig. 12.

From the image above, we can see that about 80% tweets about McDonald's are sent near a McDonald's restaurants, and 20% tweets are sent some distance from a McDonald's restaurants. From the tweet points around the McDonald's restaurant, we can see that people are likely to post tweet about fast food when waiting for meals and/or having meals.

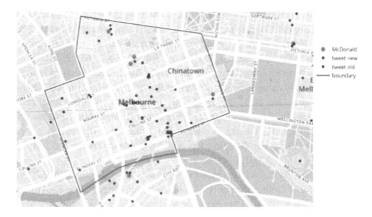

Fig. 12. Visualization of the collected McDonald's and tweets in the Melbourne SA2

5 Conclusions and Future Work

The research question explored in this paper is to establish the relationship between overweight people and the number of fast food restaurants in a particular area. The work focused on collecting data of fast food restaurant via the Google Maps API and the Twitter API. By combining these data with other official data on health and wellbeing from the AURIN project, a strong correlation was observed, i.e. overweight people are more likely to live in an area with increased number of fast food restaurants. This seemingly obvious result is important nonetheless since social media data is ubiquitous and can be used to provide broader information that is more real time in nature that can/should inform policy on establishment of fast food outlets and/or improved understanding of population health issues.

There are several parts of this work that could be improved in the future. The performance of the LSTM model can be improved. The parameters of the LSTM can be optimized and a method that improves the keywords-based method, might also be used to label the input training data. Other machine learning models may also be used to analyze the data with support for cross-validation root mean square error approaches to find the best model. Furthermore, this work assumes (naively) that the geographic information of the tweet is where the potentially overweight/obese person may live however they may simply be tourists/visitors and hence no inference should be made. Future work could factor in logic to determine whether a tweet is actually a resident or non-resident based on the number of tweets sent over a given time period.

References

1. Hacker, J., Wickramasinghe, N., Durst, C.: Can health 2.0 address critical healthcare challenges? Insights from the case of how online social networks can assist in combatting the obesity epidemic. Australas. J. Inf. Syst. **21**, 1–17 (2017)
2. Jensen, P., Jensen, L., Brunak, S.: Mining electronic health records: towards better research applications and clinical care. Nat. Rev. Genet. **13**(6), 395–405 (2012)

3. Sinnott, R.O., Cui, S.: Benchmarking sentiment analysis approaches on the cloud. In: 2016 IEEE 22nd International Conference on Parallel and Distributed Systems (ICPADS) (2016)
4. Hamed, A., Wu, X., Erickson, R., Fandy, T.: Twitter K-H networks in action: advancing biomedical literature for drug search. J. Biomed. Inf. **56**, 157–168 (2015)
5. Chae, B.: Insights from hashtag #supplychain and Twitter analytics: considering Twitter and Twitter data for supply chain practice and research. Int. J. Prod. Econ. **165**, 247–259 (2015)
6. Corso, A.J., Alsudais, K.: GIS, Big Data, and a tweet corpus operationalized via natural language processing. In: 21st Americas Conference on Information Systems (2015)
7. Kobayashi, S., Fujioka, T., Tanaka, Y., Inoue, M., Niho, Y., Miyoshi, A.: A geographical information system using the Google Map API for guidance to referral hospitals. J. Med. Syst. **34**(6), 1157–1160 (2009)
8. Putra, Y.A., Khodra, M.L.: A deep learning approach towards cross-lingual tweet tagging. In: 2016 International Conference on Data and Software Engineering (2016)
9. Lydecker, J.A., Cotter, E.W., Palmberg, A.A., Simpson, C., Kwitowski, M., White, K., Mazzeo, S.E.: Does this Tweet make me look fat? A content analysis of weight stigma on Twitter. Eat. Weight Disord. **21**(2), 229–235 (2016)
10. Anwar, M., Yuan, Z.: Linking obesity and tweets. In: Zheng, X., Zeng, D.D., Chen, H., Leischow, S.J. (eds.) ICSH 2015. LNCS, vol. 9545, pp. 254–266. Springer, Cham (2016). https://doi.org/10.1007/978-3-319-29175-8_24

Midsaggital Plane Detection in Magnetic Resonance Images Using Phase Congruency, Hessian Matrix and Symmetry Information: A Comparative Study

Paulo Guilherme de Lima Freire$^{(\boxtimes)}$ (iD), Bruno César Gregório da Silva(iD),
Carlos Henrique Villa Pinto(iD), Camilo Aparecido Ferri Moreira(iD),
and Ricardo José Ferrari(iD)

Department of Computing, Federal University of São Carlos,
Rod. Washington Luís, Km 235, Mailbox 676, São Carlos, SP 13565-905, Brazil
{paulo.freire,rferrari}@ufscar.br
http://bipgroup.dc.ufscar.br

Abstract. The human brain has two hemispheres that are separated by a midsaggital plane (MSP) in the medial longitudinal fissure. By using the MSP, it is possible to assess clinically relevant information such as brain atrophy and asymmetry. In this paper, we evaluate the performance of three techniques (phase congruency, Hessian-based and symmetry-based approaches) for MSP detection using the normal angle difference and average Z-distance metrics to assess accuracy. The datasets were comprised of simulated and clinical magnetic resonance (MR) images with different weights, levels of noise and intensity inhomogeneities. Our results indicate the phase congruency approach is the most accurate of the three techniques, with an average normal angle difference of 0.446° and 0.395 average Z-distance for the simulated database and 0.705° and 0.753 for the clinical database. The Hessian-based approach has the best trade-off between accuracy and execution time; on average, the Hessian-based algorithm takes roughly 9 seconds to detect the MSP, 10-fold faster than the other two techniques. The symmetry-based approach presented the worst results regarding accuracy and execution time. Given these findings, it is possible to conclude that the phase congruency MSP detection approach is the appropriate choice in scenarios where precision is of paramount importance. However, in situations where accuracy is essential, but not crucial, and there are hundreds of images to be processed, the Hessian-based technique is indicated to promptly detect the plane.

Keywords: Midsaggital plane · Phase congruency · Hessian matrix
Symmetry information · Magnetic resonance imaging

© Springer International Publishing AG, part of Springer Nature 2018
O. Gervasi et al. (Eds.): ICCSA 2018, LNCS 10960, pp. 245–260, 2018.
https://doi.org/10.1007/978-3-319-95162-1_17

1   Introduction

The human brain has two hemispheres that can be separated by a midsaggital plane (MSP). Both hemispheres usually present a fair match of similar regions and counterparts, and, therefore, analysis of these parts provides clinically relevant information in studies of neurodegenerative diseases, such as level of brain atrophy and asymmetry. The brain's longitudinal fissure (LF) is commonly used as a reference to guide manual delineation of the MSP, and although the separation surface is not exactly a plane surface, a planar approximation is enough for many applications [1].

Many techniques to automatically detect the MSP in magnetic resonance images (MRI) have been proposed in the literature over the years [2–4]. There are mainly two different classes of algorithms used to detect MSPs. The first one searches for the plane that maximizes a specific symmetry measure derived from information of the left and right brain hemispheres; the second one focus on estimating a plane from points that lie on the LF region.

To this day, there is no consensus regarding which algorithm works best for all scenarios. In this work, we used three different approaches for MSP detection. The first method [5] makes use of phase congruency (PC) information [6] to find a suiting plane, whereas the second approach is based on Hessian matrix and gradient features [7]. These two techniques fall under the category of algorithms that use the LF to estimate the MSP. For the sake of comparison, we used a publicly available symmetry-based MSP detection algorithm from Rupert *et al.* [1] to serve as a reference.

We applied all three algorithms to two databases, one with simulated [8] and the other with clinical images [9]. The purpose of using a simulated database was to generate different levels of noise and intensity inhomogeneity to assess how well the techniques would perform in adverse scenarios. Similarly, the clinical database was comprised of images from subjects with multiple sclerosis (MS). Since MS lesions have no well-defined shape, size or location, these images presented a certain degree of asymmetry, thus allowing us to verify if that would pose a challenge to MSP detection.

To quantitatively assess the algorithms, we used two well-known metrics for MSP detection: angle difference and average Z-distance. The first is used to calculate the difference in angle between a ground truth and an automatically detected MSP. Though widely used, this metric has the disadvantage of not taking into account specific situations such as when both planes are parallel but translated apart from each other. To circumvent this issue, we used the average Z-distance proposed in [1], which calculates the MSP estimation error as a function of the distances between corresponding voxels of each plane. These two metrics combined provide an excellent way to analyze any given MSP detection and compare one algorithm to another.

Our results show the PC and Hessian-based approaches outperformed the reference algorithm on angle difference and average Z-distance on both databases. The PC technique was the most accurate of all three algorithms, while the Hessian algorithm was the fastest. We also observed the symmetry-based approach fail on some images of the simulated database.

This paper is divided as follows: in Sect. 2 we describe our methodology, including the PC-, Hessian- and symmetry-based approaches as well as the databases and metrics used in this work. We present and discuss our results in Sect. 3 and also provide images used to visually assess the algorithms' outputs. Our final considerations are made in Sect. 4.

2   Materials and Methods

In this section we elaborate on the PC, Hessian matrix and symmetry techniques and how they were used for the purpose of MSP detection. We also describe the databases and metrics used in this paper.

2.1   Phase Congruency

The PC technique is an intensity and contrast invariant approach used to highlight relevant visual features in an image [6,10]. The main idea of the PC technique is to search for image patterns having a similar order in the phase components of the Fourier transform. However, instead of working directly on the Fourier components, the PC technique, which can be proved to be proportional to the local energy of a signal, is implemented via convolution of the original image with a bank of complex band-pass filters in quadrature. For its implementation, Kovesi [6,11,12] proposed the use of log-Gabor filters, since they have zero mean components for arbitrarily large bandwidth that can be tuned to generate filters with minimal spatial extent. For efficiency, in this work the convolution of an input image with each complex filter in the bank was implemented in the frequency domain.

In this paper, we used the MSP-PC algorithm proposed by Ferrari *et al.* [5], where the MSP was estimated using the PC-technique proposed in [13] and a weighted least-squares algorithm [14] (Chap. 5) on voxels enhanced by a sheet-ness measure. The PC of an image is calculated, and then a sheetness measure is used on the PC output to enhance voxels that are likely to be located in the LF region. This measure is calculated based on the eigenvalues of a second-order moments local matrix of the 3D PC responses centered around a given spatial location x, given by

$$M_{PC}(x) = \begin{bmatrix} M_{200}(x) & M_{110}(x) & M_{101}(x) \\ M_{110}(x) & M_{020}(x) & M_{011}(x) \\ M_{101}(x) & M_{011}(x) & M_{002}(x) \end{bmatrix}, \tag{1}$$

where $M_{pqr}(x)$ is the local moment of order $p + q + r$ calculated from the PC map.

Ratios can be devised to relate to certain geometric structures, assuming the eigenvalues of $M_{PC}(x)$ are sorted as $|\lambda_1| \leq |\lambda_2| \leq |\lambda_3|$. These relations are shown in Table 1. Since a MSP is represented by a sheet-like structure, R_{sheet} is the ratio of interest in this case.

Table 1. Eigenvalue ratios and their relations with local geometric structures

Eigenvalue ratios	Sheet	Tube	Blob	Noise
$R_{sheet}(\boldsymbol{x}) = \lambda_2/\lambda_3$	0	1	1	-
$R_{blob}(\boldsymbol{x}) = (2\lambda_3 - \lambda_2 - \lambda_1)/\lambda_3$	2	1	0	-
$R_{noise}(\boldsymbol{x}) = \sqrt{\lambda_1^2 + \lambda_2^2 + \lambda_3^2}$	λ_3	$\lambda_3\sqrt{2}$	$\lambda_3\sqrt{3}$	0
$R_{tube}(\boldsymbol{x}) = (\lambda_3 - \lambda_2 + \lambda_1)/\lambda_3$	1	0	1	-

Two parameters related to the sheetness measure were set to different values from those proposed in [5]. Using the same notation as the authors, $\alpha = \delta = 0.10$ instead of $\alpha = \delta = 0.15$. This subtle change proved to yield better results for the databases analyzed in this paper. Every other parameter related to the sheetness measure, PC and bank of filters remained the same. We recommend referring to [5] for an in-depth explanation of this technique.

2.2 Hessian Matrix

A local Hessian matrix can be seen as a local shape descriptor which its eigenvalues carry important information about a structured object. Given a particular point $\boldsymbol{x}$ of an image I with dimension k, the local Hessian matrix is defined as

$$
H_\sigma(I; \boldsymbol{x}) = \begin{bmatrix} I_{\sigma x_1^2} & I_{\sigma x_1 x_2} & \cdots & I_{\sigma x_1 x_k} \\ I_{\sigma x_2 x_1} & I_{\sigma x_2^2} & \cdots & I_{\sigma x_2 x_k} \\ \vdots & \vdots & \ddots & \vdots \\ I_{\sigma x_k x_1} & I_{\sigma x_k x_2} & \cdots & I_{\sigma x_k^2} \end{bmatrix}, \tag{2}
$$

where σ in H_σ indicates a multiscale framework that is calculated by convolving the original image with Gaussian kernels $G(\boldsymbol{x}, \sigma)$. In this case, the second order derivatives in Eq. 2 correspond to

$$
I_{\sigma x_i^2} = I_0(\boldsymbol{x}) * \left(\sigma^{2\gamma} \frac{\partial^2}{\partial x_i^2} G(\boldsymbol{x}; \sigma) \right), \tag{3}
$$

$$
I_{\sigma x_i x_j} = I_{\sigma x_j x_i} = I_0(\boldsymbol{x}) * \left(\sigma^{2\gamma} \frac{\partial^2}{\partial x_i x_j} G(\boldsymbol{x}; \sigma) \right). \tag{4}
$$

These equations are also called γ-parameterized normalized derivatives since the term γ is introduced to overcome the problem of increasingly smoothed responses [15]. A value of $\gamma = 1.25$ was used in this work, as suggested by Majer [16]. The factor 2 in 2γ follows the order of the derivative.

By examining the second-order variations in image intensities, a Hessian eigenvalue decomposition can be done to better understand local shape information. In this work, we followed the idea presented by Descoteaux *et al.* [7], inspired by the works of [17–19]. By doing so, we were able to differentiate 3D tube-like, sheet-like and blob-like structures. In this sense, assuming our eigen-values follow the ordering $|\lambda_1| \leq |\lambda_2| \leq |\lambda_3|$, the same three ratios presented in Table 1 can be devised.

For sheet-like structures, the eigenvalues must be $\lambda_1 \approx \lambda_2 \approx 0$ and $|\lambda_3| \gg 0$, so measure R_{sheet} can easily differentiate sheet-like structures from others, while R_{blob} reinforces sheetness features. Finally, the Frobenius norm, R_{noise}, helps to suppress random noise effects in the background.

In order to enhance the desired shaped structures, Descoteaux et $al..$ defined a sheetness measure, S, in which its maximum response over all scales σ corresponds to the acceptance level that a sheet-like structure is present in a particular image position and is given by

$$S(\boldsymbol{\lambda}) = \max_{\sigma \in \Sigma} S_\sigma(\boldsymbol{\lambda}), \tag{5}$$

where

$$S_\sigma(\boldsymbol{\lambda}) = \begin{cases} 0, & \text{if } \lambda_3 < 0, \\ \exp\left(-\frac{R_{sheet}^2}{2\alpha^2}\right) \times \\ \left(1 - \exp\left(-\frac{R_{blob}^2}{2\beta^2}\right)\right) \times \\ \left(1 - \exp\left(-\frac{R_{noise}^2}{2c^2}\right)\right), & \text{otherwise.} \end{cases} \tag{6}$$

In Eq. 6, $\Sigma = \{2.0, 4.0\}$ is a finite set of scales and α, β and c can be adjusted to control the sensitivity of the filter components. We performed a grid search over all possible combinations in range $[0, 1]$ with steps of 0.05 to set $\alpha = 0.75$ and $\beta = 0.10$. Parameter c was calculated following the suggestion of Dzyubak and Ritman [20] as one-tenth of the maximum Laplacian image value.

An important observation must be made about the sign of λ_3 in Eq. 6, since it dictates the intensity feature of the structure we are interested in. In T1-weighted images, the LF is dark, so we use the equation as is. For T2- and PD-weighted images, however, the LF is bright, so in these cases, $S_\sigma(\lambda) = 0$ if $\lambda_3 > 0$.

As a result of the Hessian-based approach, voxel values closer to 1 indicate a higher probability of having sheet-like structures in a real-valued image. Similar to [5], plane estimation was performed by a weighted least-squares algorithm [14] in a coarse-to-fine manner applied to voxels enhance by the sheetness measure.

2.3   Symmetry Analysis

In Ruppert et $al.$ [1], a bilateral symmetry algorithm based on the maximization of symmetry measure was used to find the best plane that divides the brain into its hemispheres. The authors applied a 3D Sobel operator and thresholding to generate a binary-edge feature image, which was then used as input to the symmetry measure algorithm. Since evaluating all possible planes was unfeasible, the authors proposed a 3-stage coarse-to-fine multi-scale approach to reduce the search space. The plane with the highest symmetry score on a coarser scale was used as input to a finer scale, and then the region around the plane was analyzed to refine the MSP estimation.

Formally, let I^o be the binary image resulting from applying a threshold to the Sobel output and I^f its flipped copy with respect to a candidate plane. Then the symmetry measure S is defined as

$$S = \frac{\sum_i^w \sum_j^h \sum_k^d I_{ijk}^o I_{ijk}^f}{\sqrt{\left(\sum_i^w \sum_j^h \sum_k^d I_{ijk}^o I_{ijk}^o\right)\left(\sum_i^w \sum_j^h \sum_k^d I_{ijk}^f I_{ijk}^f\right)}}, \tag{7}$$

where w, h, d are width, height and depth of the 3D image and I_{ijk}^f, similar to I_{ijk}^o, is the value in $\{0,1\}$ of a voxel at a given coordinate (i, j, k).

They assessed their algorithm on MRI and computation tomography (CT) images using angle difference and average Z-distance and compared their results to other three approaches. Considering accuracy and execution time, the authors concluded their technique outperformed the other three algorithms.

2.4   Databases

The MSP algorithms investigated in this work were assessed using two different sets of MR images, described in details in this section.

BrainWeb. We used 45 synthetic MR (T1-, T2- and PD-weighted) images from the publicly available McGill University BrainWeb MRI simulator [8]. We used images with five different noise levels (0%, 1%, 3%, 5% and 7%) and three intensity inhomogeneity percentages (0%, 20% and 40%), thus generating fifteen images for each MR weight. Every image had a voxel resolution of $1\,mm^3$ and dimensions $181 \times 217 \times 181$.

MS. The MS database used in this paper came from the training data of the 2015 Longitudinal MS Lesion Segmentation Challenge [9]. This database was comprised of five MS subjects with a total number of 21 time-points and lesion volumes ranging from 2 ml to 32 ml. Each time-point had T1-, T2-, PD-weighted and FLAIR images acquired on a 3T MR scanner. For this research, we used only T1-weighted images because of the high contrast and anatomical information such weight provides. Every T1-weighted image had a voxel resolution of $1\,mm^3$ and dimensions $181 \times 217 \times 181$.

2.5   Metrics

We used the angle difference (in degrees) and average Z-distance (in voxels) to assess how accurately the algorithms detected the MSP. These metrics are described in the following sections.

Angle Difference. The angle difference measures the angle between normal vectors of two given planes as

$$\alpha = \arccos \left(\frac{<\mathbf{u}, \mathbf{v}>}{\|\mathbf{u}\|.\|\mathbf{v}\|} \right) \times \frac{180}{\pi}, \tag{8}$$

where α is the angular difference in degrees, $\mathbf{u}$ and $\mathbf{v}$ are two given normal vectors, $<, >$ is the canonical inner product and $\|\|$ is the vector norm function. The closer α is to zero, the smaller is the angle between planes.

Average Z-distance. The average Z-distance was proposed in [1] to measure the distance in voxels between two planes. This metric improves the quantitative analysis of the MSP detection, since the angle difference alone may be misleading in situations where both planes are parallel but translated from one another, for example.

To find this distance, the z coordinate of each plane is calculated using the plane equations and their x and y coordinates. The absolute differences between the z coordinates from the ground truth, and the estimated plane are summed up and divided by $dim(x) \times dim(y)$, where dim is the image dimension of a given axis, thus providing the average Z-distance in voxels between both planes. Formally,

$$Z\text{-distance} = \frac{\sum_{(x,y)} \left(|z_{coord}(GT) - z_{coord}(Aut)| \right)}{dim(x) \times dim(y)}, \tag{9}$$

where GT and Aut are the ground truth and automatically estimated MSPs, respectively.

3   Results and Discussion

In this section we present the MSP detection results for both BrainWeb and MS databases and discuss the advantages and drawbacks of each technique.

3.1   BrainWeb Database

The results for the PC, Hessian and symmetry approaches on the BrainWeb database are shown in Tables 2, 3 and 4.

Of the three techniques assessed in this paper, the symmetry approach was not able to correctly detect the MSP for some images in the BrainWeb database (indicated by *). These cases were not taken into account when calculating the average angle difference and Z-distance of the three techniques since they would artificially increase the average and standard deviation results of the symmetry approach.

The symmetry results shown in Tables 2, 3 and 4 indicate that this technique had a rather poor behaviour in situations where images were noisy and presented a high-intensity inhomogeneity level. Examples of MSPs detected on T2 image weights with 7% noise and 40% intensity inhomogeneity levels are shown in

Table 2. MSP detection results for PC-, Hessian- and symmetry-based algorithms on the BrainWeb database with intensity inhomogeneity = 0%. Rows in bold were not taken into account to calulate mean and standard deviation values.

Image	Phase congruency		Hessian		Symmetry	
	Angle diff. (°)	Z-dist. (voxels)	Angle diff. (°)	Z-dist. (voxels)	Angle diff.(°)	Z-dist. (voxels)
PD 0%	0.196	0.156	0.719	1.013	0.318	1
PD 1%	0.185	0.147	0.719	1.012	0.318	1
PD 3%	0.290	0.238	0.016	0.013	0.318	1
PD 5%	0.703	0.558	0.016	0.013	0.318	1
PD 7%*	**1.194**	**1.134**	**0.017**	**0.014**	**90**	**0**
T1 0%	0.144	0.114	1.639	1.347	0.318	1
T1 1%	0.142	0.113	1.674	1.380	0.318	1
T1 3%	0.147	0.117	1.819	1.506	0.318	1
T1 5%	0.146	0.116	1.700	1.396	0.265	1
T1 7%	0.132	0.105	1.608	1.320	0.265	1
T2 0%	0.759	0.666	0.388	0.422	0.318	1
T2 1%	0.750	0.657	0.386	0.418	1.591	2.052
T2 3%	0.802	0.711	0.384	0.415	0.318	1
T2 5%*	**0.835**	**0.747**	**0.385**	**0.416**	**0**	**51.5**
T2 7%	0.867	0.784	0.383	0.413	0	0.5
Mean (std)	0.404 (0.310)	0.344 (0.278)	0.881 (0.696)	0.821 (0.553)	0.383 (0.373)	1.042 (0.333)

Fig. 1. These results can be explained by the fact that this technique uses a bilateral symmetry measure and searches for a plane that maximizes it. Part of the algorithm consists of smoothing and applying a Sobel operator to the input image to detect edges. The output of the Sobel operator is then used to calculate the symmetry measure and find the best plane. Since we had some images with a high level of intensity inhomogeneity, we believe the level of smoothing used by this technique was not enough, leading the Sobel algorithm to detect noise as edges, which in turn caused the MSP detection to become rather erratic.

The PC approach had the smallest average Z-distance in both scenarios of intensity inhomogeneity and a very low angle difference on average. We can state that, on average, the PC-based algorithm was less than 0.5° and 0.5 voxels off compared to the ground truth. It is also possible to note that this technique was somewhat invariant to noise and intensity inhomogeneity given any image weight, which is strongly related to the frequency-domain aspect of PC [6]. But high accuracy and invariance come with a cost, since it took roughly 91 seconds to detect the MSP of each image in this database using phase congruency.

Table 3. MSP detection results for PC-, Hessian- and symmetry-based algorithms on the BrainWeb database with intensity inhomogeneity = 20%. Rows in bold were not taken into account to calulate mean and standard deviation values.

Image	Phase congruency		Hessian		Symmetry	
	Angle diff. (°)	Z-dist. (voxels)	Angle diff. (°)	Z-dist. (voxels)	Angle diff.(°)	Z-dist. (voxels)
PD 0%	0.183	0.145	0.016	0.013	0.636	1.5
PD 1%	0.158	0.125	0.016	0.013	0	1.5
PD 3%	0.181	0.144	0.017	0.013	0	1.5
PD 5%	0.275	0.223	0.017	0.014	0	1.5
PD 7%*	**1.266**	**1.197**	**1.142**	**1.016**	**90**	**0**
T1 0%	0.144	0.114	2.542	2.254	0.318	1
T1 1%	0.145	0.115	2.871	2.544	0.318	1
T1 3%	0.149	0.118	2.559	2.261	0.636	1.5
T1 5%	0.156	0.124	2.463	2.162	0.265	1
T1 7%	0157	0.125	0.981	0.782	0	0.5
T2 0%	0.711	0.615	0.456	0.475	0.318	1
T2 1%*	**0.685**	**0.586**	**0.456**	**0.474**	**0**	**51.5**
T2 3%*	**0.749**	**0.658**	**0.454**	**0.471**	**0**	**52.5**
T2 5%*	**0.813**	**0.727**	**0.452**	**0.469**	**89.681**	**10536.776**
T2 7%	0.849	0.759	0.473	0.484	1.273	1.067
Mean (std)	0.282 (0.250)	0.237 (0.226)	1.128 (1.212)	1.001 (1.066)	0.342 (0.389)	1.187 (0.334)

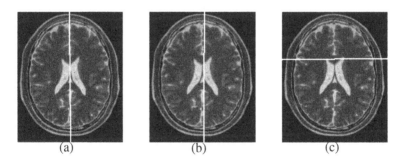

(a)   (b)   (c)

Fig. 1. BrainWeb MSP comparison (axial view) of the three approaches assessed in this paper on T2-weighted images with 7% noise and 40% intensity inhomogeneity. (a) PC-based MSP detection, (b) Hessian-based MSP detection and (c) Symmetry-based MSP detection.

The Hessian-based algorithm was the least accurate approach on this database considering angle difference. However, it outperformed the symmetry technique on average Z-distance in all three intensity inhomogeneity scenarios. Since the Hessian algorithm is heavily based on image gradients, it is not as

Table 4. MSP detection results for PC-, Hessian- and symmetry-based algorithms on the BrainWeb database with intensity inhomogeneity = 40%. Rows in bold were not taken into account to calulate mean and standard deviation values.

Image	Phase congruency		Hessian		Symmetry	
	Angle diff. (°)	Z-dist. (voxels)	Angle diff. (°)	Z-dist. (voxels)	Angle diff.(°)	Z-dist. (voxels)
PD 0%	0.168	0.133	0.017	0.014	0.636	1.5
PD 1%	0.188	0.149	0.017	0.014	0	1.5
PD 3%	0.168	0.134	1.064	0.907	0	1.5
PD 5%	0.391	0.313	1.070	0.913	0	1.5
PD 7%*	**1.074**	**1.017**	**0.017**	**0.014**	**90**	**0**
T1 0%	0.144	0.114	0.952	0.756	0.318	1
T1 1%	0.145	0.115	0.949	0.753	0.318	1
T1 3%	0.148	0.118	0.932	0.740	0.265	1
T1 5%	0.16	0.127	0.952	0.756	0.265	1
T1 7%	0.134	0.107	0.292	0.307	0	0.5
T2 0%	0.593	0.499	0.646	0.609	0.318	1
T2 1%*	**0.619**	**0.523**	**0.646**	**0.610**	**0**	**44.5**
T2 3%*	**0.673**	**0.576**	**0.654**	**0.615**	**89.364**	**7504.408**
T2 5%*	**0.779**	**0.685**	**0.676**	**0.627**	**90**	**0**
T2 7%*	**0.797**	**1.067**	**0.668**	**0.599**	**89.363**	**5255.808**
Mean (std)	0.223 (0.149)	0.180 (0.127)	0.689 (0.423)	0.577 (0.341)	0.212 (0.210)	1.150 (0.337)

robust as phase congruency and is susceptible to highlight high-gradient areas that are not related to the LF. These areas interfere with the MSP detection and can cause the plane to be slightly dislocated compared to the ground truth. This drawback can be seen in T1-w results since this weight presents a high-contrast between tissues. On the other hand, the Hessian technique was faster than the other two algorithms by a 10-fold, since the MSP detection took approximately 9 seconds using this approach. Qualitative analysis indicates the automatically detected MSPs correctly divided the brain hemispheres into two, though the planes did not precisely halve the LF. Examples of MSP detections on T1-w images using the Hessian algorithm are shown in Fig. 2.

It is worth pointing out that both PC and Hessian approaches detected the MSPs regardless of noise and intensity inhomogeneity. However, we cannot state this for the symmetry approach, since the number of failures increased as the intensity inhomogeneity level increased. We understand that certain levels of noise and inhomogeneity - for instance, 7% and 40%, respectively - are no longer encountered in research or clinical work, but we used them to check the algorithms' robustness in extreme situations.

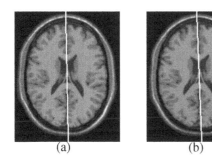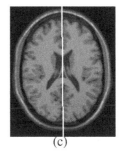

(a)   (b)   (c)

Fig. 2. BrainWeb MSP comparison (axial view) of MSPs detected by the Hessian approach on T1 images with 0% noise and (a) 0% and (b) 20% intensity inhomogeneity levels. Note that the hemispheres are correctly split, but the planes do not precisely halve the LF.

3.2   MS Database

The results for the PC, Hessian and symmetry approaches on the MS database are shown in Tables 5, 6 and 7.

We can see that the PC approach had the best results (both for angle differences and Z-distance), followed by Hessian matrix and symmetry information. It is worth remembering that though this database had T1-, T2-, PD-weighted and FLAIR images, we used only T1 images to detect the MSP. Compared to PC, the Hessian matrix and symmetry techniques had approximately 36% and 42% difference in the angle measurement and 28% and 36% difference on the Z-distance metric, respectively. But all three techniques, on average, were less than $1.3°$ and 1.2 voxels off compared to the ground truth. Based on the results shown in Tables 5, 6 and 7 indicate, all three techniques had a significant average performance regardless of lesion volume. Qualitatively, it was not possible to distinguish one method from another for any given detected MSP in this database. The average execution time for the PC, Hessian-based and symmetry-based algorithms on this database were 92 seconds, 9 seconds and 293 seconds, respectively, on an Intel Core i7 3.2 GHz with 16GB of RAM. Note that these times were very similar to those mentioned in Sect. 3.1. Examples of planes detected by the three techniques compared to the manually delineated planes in an MS image with high lesion load is shown in Fig. 3.

It is important to note that visual assessment of the planes detected by all three approaches in the MS database indicated the brain hemispheres were correctly separated. However, some points need to be highlighted. For instance, compared to the Hessian-based algorithm, PC requires a bank of filters to work, and while it is true that this bank is created only once and then used on every image, the convolution of the image with all filters in the bank, performed in the frequency domain, is time-consuming. Besides, there is also an overhead for generating the bank of filters. In this work, we designed it to work best with image dimensions $181 \times 217 \times 181$, which were the image dimensions for both BrainWeb and MS databases. Another significant highlight is that we observed

Table 5. PC-based MSP detection results for the MS database.

Subject number	Time points	Avg. lesion load (ml)	Avg. angle diff. (°)	Avg. Z-distance (voxels)
1	4	17.877	0.734	0.648
2	4	31.167	0.512	0.712
3	5	6.616	1.041	0.831
4	4	2.711	0.233	0.809
5	4	4.257	0.923	0.794
			Mean (std)	Mean (std)
			0.705 (0.339)	0.753 (0.125)

Table 6. Hessian-based MSP detection results for the MS database.

Subject number	Time points	Avg. lesion load (ml)	Avg. angle diff. (°)	Avg. Z-distance (voxels)
1	4	17.877	1.341	1.190
2	4	31.167	1.192	1.076
3	5	6.616	1.105	0.897
4	4	2.711	0.187	1.025
5	4	4.257	1.643	1.328
			Mean (std)	Mean (std)
			1.094 (0.579)	1.044 (0.321)

the Hessian-based approach runs 10-fold faster than PC. The same goes for the symmetry approach; similar to the Hessian matrix, the symmetry technique does not require a bank of filters, but it is approximately 32 times slower than the Hessian-based MSP detection. This result is an enormous advantage when working with hundreds of images in real-life scenarios such as clinical trials.

Finally, to visually assess the robustness of the three techniques even further, we applied them to MR FLAIR images either with glioma or post-brain tumor resection to analyze how well they would perform in a strong asymmetric scenario. The results are shown in Figs. 4 and 5.

In Fig. 4, the MR image came from a subject with glioma. In Fig. 5, the subject had undergone a medical removal procedure which left asymmetric holes in the brain.

As it can be seen in Figs. 4 and 5, the PC technique outperformed the other two approaches; however, the same observation made earlier regarding execution time also holds true for these strong asymmetric cases. So in a scenario where accuracy is of paramount importance, the PC algorithm would be the best choice. On the other hand, if time is of the essence and accuracy is essential, but not crucial, then the Hessian-based MSP detection would be a good alternative.

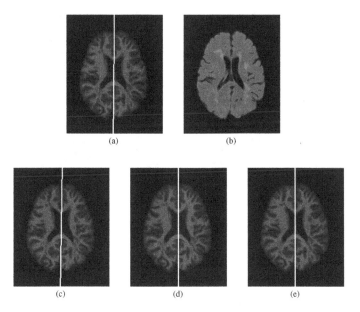

Fig. 3. Comparison between MSP detection techniques on an image with an average lesion load of 31.167 ml. (a) Ground truth, (b) FLAIR image where lesions are more easily identified, (c) PC-based MSP detection, (d) Hessian-based MSP detection, (e) Symmetry-based MSP detection.

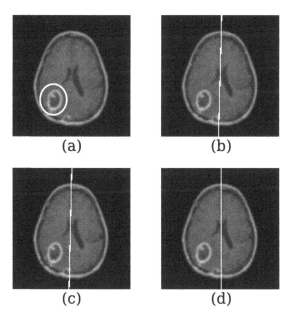

Fig. 4. Comparison between MSP detection techniques on an image with glioma. (a) Pathology indication, (b) PC-based MSP detection, (c) Hessian-based MSP detection, (d) Symmetry-based MSP detection.

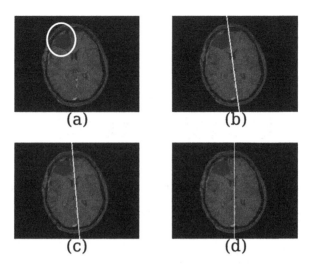

Fig. 5. Comparison between MSP detection techniques on a post-operation image with asymmetric holes. (a) Asymmetry indication, (b) PC-based MSP detection, (c) Hessian-based MSP detection, (d) Symmetry-based MSP detection.

Table 7. Symmetry-based MSP detection results for the MS database.

Subject number	Time points	Avg. lesion load (ml)	Avg. angle diff. (°)	Avg. Z-distance (voxels)
1	4	17.877	2.339	2.078
2	4	31.167	0.662	0.626
3	5	6.616	0.791	0.792
4	4	2.711	0.270	1.035
5	4	4.257	2.115	1.679
			Mean (std)	Mean (std)
			1.214 (0.903)	1.172 (0.644)

4   Conclusions

This paper presented and compared three automatic MSP detection techniques applied to simulated and clinical databases. One of the techniques was a publicly available MSP detection algorithm based on symmetry analysis, while the other two were based on phase congruency and Hessian matrix, respectively, to find the brain's LF and estimate a plane from it. We assessed the algorithms' performance using the angle difference and average Z-distance metrics.

Our results show the PC approach was the most accurate technique on both databases, followed by the Hessian- and symmetry-based algorithms.

The accuracy of PC was strongly related to its frequency-domain aspect, which makes it contrast-invariant and more robust to noise and intensity variations.

The Hessian approach, though not as accurate as PC, proved to be the fastest of all techniques by a 10-fold. This fast execution time feature brings enormous advantage in scenarios where hundreds of images need to be processed such as in clinical trials. Visual assessment of MSPs detected by the Hessian algorithm indicated the brain hemispheres were correctly split into two, but the LFs were not necessarily halved.

We observed the symmetry-based algorithm was affected by high levels of noise and intensity inhomogeneity, which led to incorrect plane estimations. On the other hand, this approach was able to correctly estimate MSPs for the clinical database and images with glioma and tumor resection. However, it had the worst execution time compared to the other two approaches.

As mentioned in Sect. 1, there is no consensus regarding which MSP detection approach in MRI works best for all scenarios. Given the three techniques analyzed in this paper, we can conclude that if accuracy is of paramount importance, then the PC approach provides an excellent MSP estimation. But a trade-off between accuracy and execution time points to the Hessian-based algorithm as a better alternative to divide the brain hemispheres into two.

References

1. Ruppert, G., Teverovskiy, L., Yu, C., Falcão, A., Liu, Y.: A new symmetry-based method for mid-sagittal plane extraction in neuroimages. In: IEEE International Symposium on Biomedical Imaging: From Nano to Macro, Chicago, IL, USA, pp. 285–288 (2011)
2. Jayasuriya, S., Liew, A., Law, N.: Symmetry plane detection in brain image analysis: a survey. Curr. Med. Imaging Rev. $9(3)$, 230–247 (2013)
3. Liu, Y., Collins, R., Rothfus, W.: Robust midsaggital plane extraction from normal and pathological 3-D neuroradiology images. IEEE Trans. Med. Imaging $20(3)$, 175–192 (2001)
4. Prima, S., Ourselin, S., Ayache, N.: Computation of the mid-saggital plane in 3-D brain images. IEEE Trans. Med. Imaging $21(2)$, 122–138 (2002)
5. Ferrari, R., Pinto, C., Moreira, C.: Detection of the midsagittal plane in MR images using a sheetness measure from eigenanalysis of local 3D phase congruency responses. In: IEEE International Conference on Image Processing, Phoenix, AZ, USA, pp. 2335–2339, September 2016
6. Kovesi, P.: Phase congruency: a low-level image invariant. Psychol. Res. $64(2)$, 136–148 (2000)
7. Descoteaux, M., Audette, M., Chinzei, K., Siddiqi, K.: Bone enhancement filtering: application to sinus bone segmentation and simulation of pituitary surgery. Comput. Aided Surg. $11(5)$, 247–255 (2006)
8. Aubert-Broche, B., Griffin, M., Pike, G., Evans, A., Collins, D.: Twenty new digital brain phantoms for creation of validation image data bases. IEEE Trans. Med. Imaging $25(11)$, 1410–1416 (2006)

9. Carass, A., Roy, S., Jog, A., Cuzzocreo, J., Magrath, E., Gherman, A., Button, J., Nguyen, J., Prados, F., Sudre, C., Jorge Cardoso, M., Cawley, N., Ciccarelli, O., Wheeler-Kingshott, C., Ourselin, S., Catanese, L., Deshpande, H., Maurel, P., Commowick, O., Barillot, C., Tomas-Fernandez, X., Warfield, S., Vaidya, S., Chunduru, A., Muthuganapathy, R., Krishnamurthi, G., Jesson, A., Arbel, T., Maier, O., Handels, H., Iheme, L., Unay, D., Jain, S., Sima, D., Smeets, D., Ghafoorian, M., Platel, B., Birenbaum, A., Greenspan, H., Bazin, P., Calabresi, P., Crainiceanu, C., Ellingsen, L., Reich, D., Prince, J., Pham, D.: Longitudinal multiple sclerosis lesion segmentation: resource and challenge. Neuroimage **148**(1), 77–102 (2017)
10. Morrone, M., Burr, D.: Feature detection in human vision: a phase-dependent energy model. Proc. R. Soc. Lond. B **235**, 221–245 (1988)
11. Kovesi, P.: Image features from phase congruency. Videre: J. Comput. Vis. Res. **1**(3), 2–26 (1999)
12. Kovesi, P.: Phase congruency detects corners and edges. In: VIIth DICTA Conference on The Australian Pattern Recognition Society, Sydney, Australia, pp. 309–318 (2003)
13. Ferrari, R., Allaire, S., Hope, A., Kim, J., Jaffray, D., Pekar, V.: Detection of point landmarks in 3D medical images via phase congruency model. J. Braz. Comput. Soc. **17**(2), 117–132 (2011)
14. Montgomery, D., Peck, E., Vining, G.: Introduction to Linear Regression Analysis. Series in Probability and Statistics, 5th edn. Wiley, Hoboken (2012)
15. Lindeberg, T.: Feature detection with automatic scale selection. Int. J. Comput. Vis. **30**(2), 79–116 (1998)
16. Majer, P.: The influence of the Gamma-parameter on feature detection with automatic scale selection. In: Kerckhove, M. (ed.) Scale-Space 2001. LNCS, vol. 2106, pp. 245–254. Springer, Heidelberg (2001). https://doi.org/10.1007/3-540-47778-0_21
17. Frangi, A.F., Niessen, W.J., Vincken, K.L., Viergever, M.A.: Multiscale vessel enhancement filtering. In: Wells, W.M., Colchester, A., Delp, S. (eds.) MICCAI 1998. LNCS, vol. 1496, pp. 130–137. Springer, Heidelberg (1998). https://doi.org/10.1007/BFb0056195
18. Lorenz, C., Carlsen, I.-C., Buzug, T.M., Fassnacht, C., Weese, J.: Multi-scale line segmentation with automatic estimation of width, contrast and tangential direction in 2D and 3D medical images. In: Troccaz, J., Grimson, E., Mösges, R. (eds.) CVRMed/MRCAS -1997. LNCS, vol. 1205, pp. 233–242. Springer, Heidelberg (1997). https://doi.org/10.1007/BFb0029242
19. Sato, Y., Nakajima, S., Shiraga, N., Atsumi, H., Yoshida, S., Koller, T., Gerig, G., Kikinis, R.: Three-dimensional multi-scale line filter for segmentation and visualization of curvilinear structures in medical images. Med. Image Anal. **2**(2), 143–168 (1998)
20. Dzyubak, O., Ritman, E.: Automation of hessian-based tubularity measure response function in 3D biomedical images. Int. J. Biomed. Imaging **2011**(920401), 1–16 (2011)

Automatic Segmentation and Quantification of Thigh Tissues in CT Images

Jonas de Carvalho Felinto[1]([✉]) [iD], Katia Maria Poloni[1] [iD],
Paulo Guilherme de Lima Freire[1] [iD], Jessica Bianca Aily[2] [iD],
Aline Castilho de Almeida[2] [iD], Maria Gabriela Pedroso[2] [iD],
Stela Márcia Mattiello[2] [iD], and Ricardo José Ferrari[1] [iD]

[1] Department of Computing, Federal University of São Carlos,
Rod. Washington Luís, Km 235, Mailbox 676, São Carlos, SP 13565-905, Brazil
{jonas.felinto,rferrari}@ufscar.br
[2] Department of Physical Theraphy, Federal University of São Carlos,
São Carlos, SP 13565-905, Brazil
stela@ufscar.br
http://bipgroup.dc.ufscar.br

Abstract. Quantification and distribution of the thigh adipose tissues in CT images have clinical implication in prognostic chronic disease including type 2 diabetes and osteoarthritis. Although there are studies in the literature addressing the quantification of thigh tissues, only a handful of them aims to segment and quantify thigh adipose tissues in CT images automatically. In this study, we propose an automated technique for the segmentation and quantification of muscle, inter- and intra-muscular adipose tissue and subcutaneous adipose tissue in thigh CT images. Our technique combines morphological operations, thresholding, a Gaussian mixture model and the use of an accumulator matrix to map the number of adipose tissue pixels about muscle pixels and thus, to allow an automatic differentiation between SAT and Inter-MAT. Our method was quantitatively assessed using 144 thigh images extracted from 72 leg (left and right) CT scans. All images were manually segmented and the tissues quantified by a specialist with the help of a computer software and used for further comparative analysis. Our technique obtained precision of 0.998 and 0.982, respectively, for the fascia and thigh regions with corresponding recall values of 0.978 and 0.975. Also, the Dice similarity coefficient for both areas was close to 0.98.

Keywords: Thigh tissue segmentation · Automatic segmentation
Computer-assisted image analysis · Subcutaneous adipose tissue
Inter-muscular adipose tissue · Computed tomography

1 Introduction

The adipose tissue is not just a reservoir of calories, but due to its property to expand throughout life, it is the most significant endocrine organ of the human body [1]. The increase in adipose mass is directly related to the immoderate consumption of saturated fatty acids, which are responsible for the systemic condition of low-grade inflammation and insulin resistance [2].

The excessive accumulation of adipose tissue (known as obesity) is currently the top health problem in the world. Such issue is already reaching epidemic characteristics, according to the World Health Organization[1], besides being the most prominent risk factor for diseases such as hypertension, osteoporosis, type 2 diabetes, and osteoarthritis [3].

Although adipose tissue has been deposited in different regions of the human body, the fat deposit located between muscle cells (intra-muscular adipose tissue - Intra-MAT), and beneath the muscle fascia (Inter-muscular adipose tissue - Inter-MAT) is a significant predictor of both muscle function and mobility function in older adults [4]. Hight levels of Inter-MAT are associated with insulin resistance and represent the driving factor leading to type 2 diabetes in humans, loss of strength and decrease in mobility [5,6].

Thus, the quantification of Inter-MAT is of paramount importance for the diagnosis and prevention of chronic diseases. The most common imaging techniques used for the quantification of this type of tissue are computed tomography (CT) and magnetic resonance imaging (MRI).

Although MRI provides higher soft-tissue contrast and better differentiation between normal and abnormal tissue without using ionizing radiation, CT produces images with higher resolutions in a shorter period and is less expensive [7–9]. For this reason, CT is the typical choice in clinical trials, since they involve a large number of images that require individual tissues labeling.

In a CT scan, the attenuation coefficient is an arbitrary measure created by Hounsfield [10] to quantify the attenuation of the X-ray beam after passing through the body. The representation of each tissue in the Hounsfield unit (HU) scale varies according to how much of X-ray photons it absorbs, allowing a quantitative and standardized evaluation. Water, in this case, corresponds to the zero value in the scale.

Semi-automatic segmentation of anatomical structures in CT images, with the aid of an image editing software, is currently the most used approach to measure body fat percentage [11]. This method usually applies a set of predefined intensity windows on the Hounsfield scale to segment fat tissues in the CT images.

In addition to being a time-consuming and an expensive task, semi-automatic segmentation is susceptible to inter- and intra-observer variations [10,12] and has low reproducibility [13]. Although automated methods for the segmentation of different adipose tissues in CT images are very desirable for the clinical use, the process for generating the region of interest (ROI) automatically to quantify the tissues is quite complicated [14].

---

[1] http://www.who.int/mediacentre/factsheets/fs311/en/.

2   Related Works

There are some proposed studies in the literature addressing the problem of automatic segmentation of adipose tissues [11,15–21]. However, most of them are developed to work on MR images. Only a handful number of them works on the segmentation and quantification of thigh tissues in CT images [18,22].

Senseney and Hemler [22], for instance, proposed an automated computer system for automatic segmentation of thigh, bone, and marrow in CT images. Their method uses region growing, morphological operations, and thresholding technique applied to the HU scale. Although their system has shown to segment the thigh region on CT images successfully, there is no indication regarding the estimation of the Inter-MAT.

Tan *et al.* [18] proposed a variational Bayesian Gaussian mixture model to cluster regions of interest in thigh CT and MR images into adipose tissues (fat and marrow), muscle, bone, and background. Their method uses information of the detected marrow tissue as a reference to segment the other classes. Furthermore, a combination of parametric and geodesic active contour models is used to distinguish different adipose tissues in the images. They applied their method to five volumetric mid-thigh axial datasets of MR and CT images from clinical trials and compared the results with manual annotations from a specialist. Results for MR images have shown dice similarity coefficients of 0.94, 0.87 and 0.86, respectively, for muscle, Inter-MAT, and Intra-MAT. For CT images, the corresponding numbers were 0.98, 0.92 and 0.89. Despite the excellent results, their method needs a more thorough evaluation using a large image dataset.

Kullberg *et al.* [23] recently proposed a new technique for thigh and abdominal tissues quantification on CT images. They created a technique called inside lean tissue (ILT) filter to separate SAT from Inter-MAT in thighs. For each pixel in the image, lean tissues are traced in different directions, and their occurrence is used to compute a probability map to represent the amount of lean tissue surrounds the analyzed pixel. The authors have used 1089 images, and their method achieved high Dice coefficients (0.97 and 0.88) for SAT and Inter-MAT, respectively, in thigh quantifications. However, regarding the assessment of the Inter-MAT, the authors have chosen only 57 images where the fascia was visible (approximately 5% of the dataset).

Despite the importance of quantifying Inter-MAT to study different diseases, such as diabetes and osteoarthritis [4], to the best of our knowledge, to date, there is no tool available to the medical community for automatic segmentation of thigh tissues in CT images. Therefore, our study contributes in providing an automated computer technique for the segmentation and measurement of adipose tissues of the thigh region in CT images. Our results were compared with the ones obtained from manual annotations of a specialist and show that our approach is a viable alternative to segment thigh tissues and quantify Inter-MAT consistently.

This study is organized as follows: Sect. 3 describes the used methodology, followed by results in Sect. 4, discussions in Sect. 5, and conclusions in Sect. 6.

3   Materials and Methods

In this section, we describe the dataset and methodology used in this study.

3.1   Image Dataset

A total of 72 patients from the University Hospital of São Carlos, SP - Brazil underwent CT imaging scans. Subjects (36 men; 65.5 years $\pm$ 14.9, weight 73.6 $\pm$ 11.6 Kg, and 36 women; 54.2 years $\pm$ 14.9, weight 69.6 $\pm$ 11.0 Kg) were imaged using a Multislice CT scanner (Brilliance CT 16-slice, Phillips) that produces DICOM images of the mid-thigh region with a spatial resolution of $0.793 \times 0.793 \times 1\,\mathrm{mm}^3$ and a matrix of size $512 \times 512 \times 10$ voxels.

All patients participating in this study were informed about using their CT scans and other medical information for this research. Ethical approval for this study was ob- tained from the local Human Research Ethics Committee of the Federal University of São Carlos (number CAAE: 64171617.9.0000.5504). The methods applied were carried out in accordance with the relevant guidelines and regulations. Written informed consent was obtained from all subjects.

The proposed automatic segmentation method is applied slice-by-slice to the whole image volume. However, for comparative analysis, the left and right thigh regions from the middle slice of all 72 volumetric CT images were manually segmented by a specialist with the help of a computer software (ITK-Snap [24]). As a result, a total of 144 thigh 2D image regions were obtained and used for the assessment of adipose tissue measurements. A subset of images (19 images) was selected (among all 72 images) and manually segmented by three specialists using the same procedure as indicated above. These images were used for assessment of the variability between the specialists.

3.2   CT Image and Thigh Tissue Attenuations

A CT imaging system produces cross-sectional images or "slices" of an anatomy. The gray levels in each slice correspond to X-ray attenuation, which reflects the proportion of X-rays absorbed or scattered as they pass through the human body [25] (Chap. 15). The X-ray attenuation is primarily a function of the X-ray energy and the density and composition of the imaged material. In CT, the matrix of reconstructed linear attenuation coefficients ($\mu_{material}$) is transformed into a corresponding matrix of Hounsfield units ($\mathrm{HU}_{material}$), where the HU scale is expressed according to the linear attenuation coefficient of water (0 HU, for this case) at room temperature [25]. Using water as a reference, the maximum brightness of a pixel (called CT number) is -1000 HU and appears as white in a CT image. The opposite end of the HU scale is maximum darkness, which is $+1000$ HU and is represented by black. Between these extremes are various shades of gray. Giving as an example: bone structures have high-intensity levels in CT images, and because of that they can be separated from soft tissue using threshold methods [26].

In the mid-thigh CT image in Fig. 1, the subcutaneous adipose thigh tissue (SAT) corresponds to the adipose tissue that lies between the skin (red contour) and the fascia[2] (yellow contour). Inter-MAT is the adipose tissue underneath the fascia and between muscle groups, and intramuscular adipose tissue (Intra-MAT) is fat that infiltrates the muscle [4]. Table 1 provides the range of CT numbers (HU) for each thigh tissue type [16,27].

3.3   Manual Annotation of Thigh Tissues

For this study, three specialists have manually annotated three specific regions on the CT images using the contours indicated in Fig. 1(b): red for the entire thigh region, yellow for the fascia and green for the bone-marrow area. Each outlined part is composed of different tissues, which can be SAT, Inter-MAT and Intra-MAT, muscle, and bone marrow. With the help of a computer software (ITK-Snap [24]) and using a window of intensity determined by the range of HU values, each specialist counted the number of pixels for each type of tissue within the regions defined by the contours. The results were saved in a computer disk for further analysis.

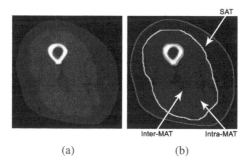

(a)   (b)

Fig. 1. (a) Original mid-thigh CT image; (b) manual contours delineated by a specialist for thigh tissue quantification

Table 1. CT numbers (Hounsfield units) corresponding to the thigh tissue types

Thigh tissue types	CT numbers (HU)
SAT and Inter-MAT	−190 to −30
Intra-MAT	0 to 29
Muscle	30 to 100
Bone marrow	over 200

---

[2] Fascia is a sheet of connective tissue beneath the skin that attaches, stabilizes, encloses, and separates muscles and other internal organs.

3.4   Automatic Segmentation of Thigh Tissues

By examining the CT numbers in Table 1, we can argue the most challenging problem is to develop an algorithm that can differentiate between Inter-MAT and SAT. Because SAT and Inter-MAT have similar HU, applying a thresholding on the HU values is not sufficient to separate these two classes of tissue. As previously discussed, manual annotation of Inter-MAT is performed using the fascia (yellow contour in Fig. 1(b)) as a guideline. Therefore, if a computer algorithm, similar to a human expert, could segment the fascia region (the interior area delimited by the fascia), then a thresholding technique could be applied separately to segment the tissues inside and outside this region.

However, since the fascia is not always visible in CT images, our method uses an accumulator matrix to help determine adipose tissue pixel positions near muscle pixels. This procedure aims to predict the approximate location of the fascia and to create a closed contour (yellow contour in Fig. 1) encompassing the Inter-MAT, Intra-MAT and muscle tissues. This rationale provides a better differentiation between SAT and Inter-MAT.

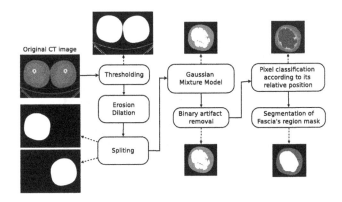

Fig. 2. Block diagram of the proposed method showing intermediate results

The proposed method is composed of two main steps: first, it works to generate the right and left thigh binary masks and second, it generates the fascia region binary mask. Figure 2 illustrates the complete diagram of our method.

3.5   Generation of the Left and Right Thigh Binary Masks

The main reason for creating the left and right thigh binary masks is to limit the region used for tissue quantification. This task can be successfully accomplished by thresholding the original CT image with a fixed threshold value of -190 HU, since all tissues inside the thigh region have a grey level intensity equal or higher than -190, as indicated in Table 1. Therefore, image pixels with intensity values higher than this threshold will be labeled as foreground (white), while the rest will be part of the background (black).

To eliminate the edges of the CT scanner table, which often appear in the resulting binary image, we apply an erosion operation with a disk-shaped structuring element of radius equal to 7. Although this procedure removes the undesirable scanner table edges, it also reduces the area of the binary image. Therefore, a dilation operation using the same structuring element of the erosion is applied to the eroded image to recover its original area.

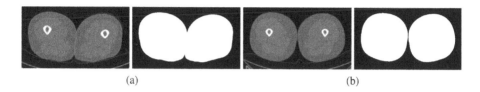

(a)   (b)

Fig. 3. Example on CT image with (a) thighs touched and (b) separated

Because there are cases in which the thighs touch each other, creating one single binary object (as indicated in Fig. 3(a)), we developed a strategy to separate them and thus allow for a proper segmentation. In this case, if we detect only one object in the binary image, it will be considered the joint of both thighs and, therefore, we use the procedure described as follows to split it into the corresponding left and right thighs.

To separate the left and right thighs, we first look for the two pairs of points, $(T1, T2)$ and $(B1, B2)$, illustrated in Fig. 4(a). Point T1 is the first foreground (white) pixel found by scanning the left half of the image, starting from left-right and top-down. Similarly, the same procedure is used on the right half of the image to find point T2. Next, points $(B1, B2)$ are determined identically as $(T1, T2)$, with the exception that a bottom-up searching was used instead of top-down one. After that, we define P1 as the object boundary point, between T1 and T2 shortest path, with the highest y-axis component and point P2 as the object boundary point, between B1 and B2 shortest path, with the lowest y-axis component. Finally, the two thigh regions are split by using a straight line formed by the points P1 and P2, as shown in Fig. 4(b).

(a)   (b)

Fig. 4. Steps to separate the thighs (a) points used for thigh separation and; (b) separated thigh using points (P1, P2)

3.6   Generation of the Fascia Region Binary Mask

After obtaining the left and right thigh binary images, the next step is to create a binary mask of the region delineated by the fascia, which will be further used to quantify the amount of Inter-MAT, Intra-MAT, and muscle tissues. As discussed previously, this is an essential and challenging task, since, in most cases, the fascia is either not visible or very difficult to identify in a CT image. The proposed method works by predicting the location of fascia region relatively to each adipose pixel.

First, to get an initial estimate of each region of interest, we apply a Gaussian Mixture Model (GMM) clustering technique adapted from [28] to each thigh mask. The main difference from the clustering algorithm proposed in [28] is that we used Gaussian probability density functions (pdf) instead of Student's t pdf due to the simplicity of the former. Since there are three tissues of interest, we segment each thigh into three clusters (adipose tissue, non-adipose tissue, and background). The result of this step is shown in Fig. 5(a).

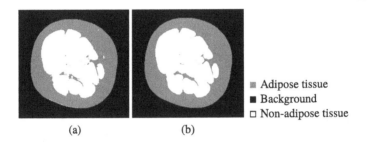

    (a)   (b)

■ Adipose tissue
■ Background
□ Non-adipose tissue

Fig. 5. Initial steps for generation of fascia region (a) image after applying the Gaussian Mixture Model (GMM), and (b) image after spurious artifacts removal

Second, small spurious artifacts of non-adipose tissue, created by the image segmentation (especially along the thigh edges) that may affect the next step, are removed. For that, we apply morphological operations (erosion followed by dilation) only to the non-adipose pixels. A disk-shaped structuring element of radius 5 pixels is used in this case. The result of this step is shown in Fig. 5(b).

Third, an accumulator matrix, $A(x, y)$, of the same size of the original image is created to store and count the occurrences of two specific cases that occur when assessing the pixel labels located in different orientations and positions, relative to the location (x, y), in the image using digital lines.

The procedure used in such analysis is as follows. For each adipose pixel at $I(x, y)$, all pixels on each of the sixteen digital straight line orientations (equally spaceAll patients participating in this study were informed about using their CT scans and other medical information for this research. Ethical approval for this study was obtained from the local Human Research Ethics Committee of the Federal University of São Carlos (number CAAE: 64171617.9.0000.5504). The methods applied were carried out in accordance with the relevant guidelines and

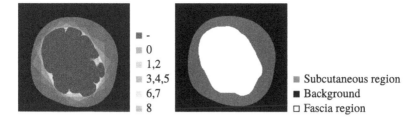

Fig. 6. (a) Example of the accumulator matrix mapped in color for easy inspection, (b) binary mask for the fascia region obtained after thresholding (a).

regulations. Written informed consent was obtained from all subjects apart by 22.5 degrees) are scanned and analyzed. In this case, if a pixel of background value is found, then, we increment the accumulator matrix at $A(x, y)$ position and halt the procedure for the corresponding line. On the other hand, if a pixel of non-adipose value is found, we interrupt that line scanning without changing the accumulator. After applying the above procedure for all digital lines, the number of counts on each accumulator cell is used to predict the location of the adipose pixels related to the fascia region. An example of the accumulator matrix resulting from this procedure is shown in Fig. 6(a).

The procedure described above is similar to the "shooting rays" idea used by the inside lean tissue (ILT) filter [23]. However, instead of accumulating lean tissue counts by ray directions, our method stores the number of digital line directions that reaches the background before entering a different tissue.

As it can be seen in Fig. 6(a), pixels closer to thigh edges (outer regions) have a higher score (dark red) while pixels in the inner areas have lower scores (light blue). Finally, a threshold is applied to the accumulator matrix $A(x, y)$ to define the region enclosed by the fascia lata. A threshold value equal to half the maximum accumulator value was found to provide the best trade-off between false-positives and false-negatives pixels in the final segmented image. The result from the threshold is shown in Fig. 6(b).

3.7 Evaluation Metrics

For validation of the proposed method, the mean value of the Dice similarity coefficient (DSC) and the relative error (RE) were used for comparison of the automated and manual results. These metrics are computed as

$$\text{DSC} = \frac{2\text{TP}}{2\text{TP} + \text{FP} + \text{FN}}, \tag{1}$$

$$\text{RE} = \frac{\text{FP} + \text{FN}}{\text{TP} + \text{FN}}, \tag{2}$$

where TP, TN, FP and FN are, respectively, the number of pixels correctly identified (true-positive), correctly rejected (true-negative), incorrectly identified (false-positive) and incorrectly reject (false-negative) as tissue labels. In addition, the mean Precision, Recall and F_1-score metrics [29], computed as

$$\text{Precision} = \frac{\text{TP}}{\text{TP} + \text{FP}}, \tag{3}$$

$$\text{Recall} = \frac{\text{TP}}{\text{TP} + \text{FN}}, \tag{4}$$

$$F_1\text{-score} = 2\left(\frac{\text{Precision} \cdot \text{Recall}}{\text{Precision} + \text{Recall}}\right), \tag{5}$$

were also used to evaluate the overall performance of our method.

4   Results

The proposed method for segmentation and quantification of adipose tissues in thigh CT images was quantitatively evaluated using 144 images. We compared the results of our technique with the ones of a manual procedure for the segmentation of both the binary masks and individual tissues. Also, we selected a group of 38 images to assess the specialist's variability.

In the first assessment, we evaluate the results of our method to generate the thigh and fascia binary masks with relation to the manual annotations. Such analysis is essential because obtaining precise binary masks has a high impact on the quantification success of all thigh tissues. Results of this evaluation are presented in Table 2.

Table 2. Comparative analysis of the binary masks automatically obtained and manually generated. Results are presented as mean ± standard deviation within all images of the dataset

Metrics	Tissue types	
	Thigh	Fascia
Precision	0.998 ± 0.002	0.982 ± 0.010
Recall	0.978 ± 0.008	0.975 ± 0.016
F_1-score	0.988 ± 0.003	0.978 ± 0.008
DSC	0.988 ± 0.003	0.978 ± 0.008
RE	0.022 ± 0.007	0.041 ± 0.016

The second assessment was to compare the quantification of each thigh tissue resulting from the automatic method with the ones obtained by the specialists. The results are given in Table 3. Figure 7 shows the scatter plots of pixel counts of SAT, muscle, Inter-MAT, and Intra-MAT resulting from manual and automatic segmentation, with the corresponding regression lines and R-values.

Table 3. Quantitative results for the quantification of all thigh tissues in CT images

Tissue types	Metrics				
	Precision	Recall	F_1-score	DSC	RE
SAT	0.995 ± 0.006	0.972 ± 0.014	0.983 ± 0.008	0.983 ± 0.008	0.031 ± 0.016
Intra-MAT	0.994 ± 0.006	0.997 ± 0.007	0.996 ± 0.005	0.996 ± 0.005	0.007 ± 0.009
Inter-MAT	0.814 ± 0.094	0.742 ± 0.110	0.767 ± 0.063	0.767 ± 0.063	0.446 ± 0.117
Muscle	0.999 ± 0.000	0.999 ± 0.001	0.999 ± 0.000	0.999 ± 0.000	0.0006 ± 0.001

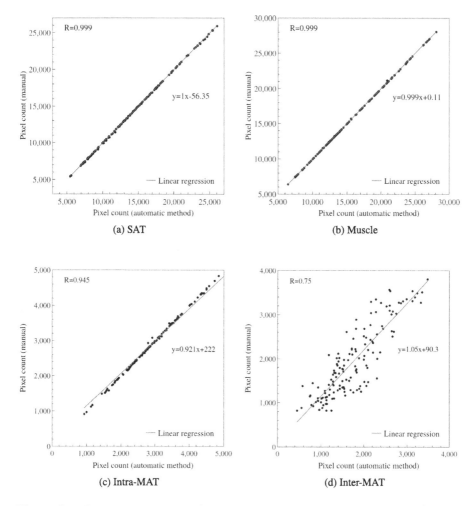

(a) SAT   (b) Muscle

(c) Intra-MAT   (d) Inter-MAT

Fig. 7. Correlation analysis of thigh tissues calculated for the manual and automatic segmentation results

A third analysis was performed with 38 thigh images to compare the performance of our method against specialists for the quantification of IMAT. For this analysis, we could only get two annotations per specialist (JBA, ACA, and MGP) per image. Therefore, we decide to average and compute the standard deviation of all six annotations per image. The results of this analysis is illustrated in Fig. 8. Black dots are used to indicate the mean values of manual annotations with their respective standard deviations, and the red dots show the results of the automatic segmentation method.

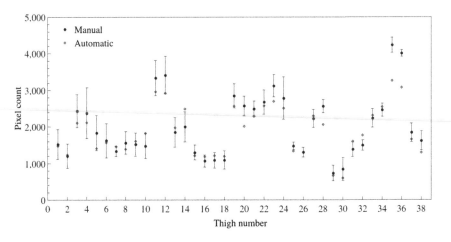

Fig. 8. Average results from six annotations (two annotations per specialist) compared to our proposed method (red dot) for the Inter-MAT quantification

5   Discussions

Results in Table 2 show an excellent agreement between the manual and automatic segmentation of both thigh and fascia regions, with corresponding values of precision, recall, DSC and F1-score of 0.998, 0.978, 0.988 and 0.988 for the thigh and 0.982, 0.975, 0.978 and 0.978 for the fascia regions. Although all metrics have shown very high values (over 0.9 for all metrics), the numbers for the fascia regions are slightly lower than the thighs. This result can be explained by the inherent difficulty to precisely draw contours in the internal thigh parts due to the lacking of contrast.

Regarding the segmentation results for the individual thigh tissues, the values obtained for the precision, recall, F_1-score and DSC indicate in Table 3 were very high for all thigh tissues. Because the muscle tissue has a very different HU range compared to adipose tissues, as we explain in Subsect. 3.2, it was the one with the highest average score numbers for the precision (0.999), recall (0.999), F_1-score (0.999) and DSC (0.999), and the smallest relative error, RE = 0.001. On the other hand, the Inter-MAT, which is the tissue with less quantity in the thigh and that interfaces with and has same HU range as SAT, presented the lowest average score numbers for precision (0.814), recall (0.742), F_1-score (0.767) and DSC (0.767) and the highest relative error, RE = 0.446. Figure 9 illustrates an example of disagreement between the automatic and manual annotated fascia contour, which directly contributes to the low score numbers for this tissue, as pointed in Table 3.

Correlation analysis, calculated from manual and automatic segmentation results in Fig. 7, show almost perfect correlation for SAT (R = 0.999) and muscle (R = 0.999), and an excellent agreement for Intra-MAT (R = 0.945). On the other hand, the correlation result for the Inter-MAT (R = 0.75) is much lower compared to the other tissues. These results can be explained by the fact that SAT and muscle are much more abundant than Inter-MAT and that Intra-MAT has a distinctive HU range compared to others adipose tissues. Therefore, similar errors in absolute terms result in different errors in percentage, leading to a lower correlation for Inter-MAT.

By inspection of the results in Fig. 8, we can notice a high variability between the specialist annotations, particularly for the thigh numbers 4, 11, 12 and 24. We can also verify that, except for nine thighs, the results from the proposed method are within the standard deviation. In the nine cases in which our approach deviated from the specialists, we have identified the same type of problem as indicated in Fig. 9. This fact is due mainly to the difficulty in determining the fascia location on the CT images. Although the results of Inter-MAT quantification were lower than the other tissues, we may minimize the problem if we consider the high variability between specialists in this case.

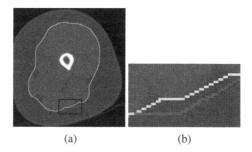

(a)   (b)

Fig. 9. CT image with (a) the fascia's boundary detected by the automatic proposed method (yellow) and the manually annotated by the specialist (red) for the purpose of thigh tissue quantification; (b) image zoom to illustrating a disagreement between the automatic and manual annotated contour

6   Conclusions

In this work, we presented a fully automatic method for the segmentation and quantification of adipose tissue in thigh CT images. Adipose tissue accumulated in the muscles and the abdominal cavity is associated with chronic inflammation, increased cholesterol, decreased strength, and mobility in adults. Thus, the localization and quantification of adipose tissue by using CT images have a clinical importance in the prognosis of chronic diseases. Despite the simplicity of the proposed method, the obtained results proved its efficacy and showed that the automatic quantification of adipose thigh tissues in CT images is feasible.

The main contribution of this work relies on a new proposed algorithm for the prediction of the fascia lata region in CT images since this connective tissue is difficult to detect by mere visual observation. Also, our algorithm allows quantifying the amount of all tissues in the thigh in a straightforward manner.

By assessing the results, it can be noticed that the automatic quantification of the Inter-MAT is lesser accurate than expected. The reason is probably related to the inherent difficulty in delineating the fascia region; a task that is even hard for the specialists to accomplish. Therefore, differences between contours manually drawn, and the ones obtained automatically for the fascia region will lower down the quantification precision for the Inter-MAT tissue. Moreover, in general, the amount of Inter-MAT is much smaller than SAT, which in turn is spatially connected to the Inter-MAT in thigh CT images and the Inter-MAT and SAT have the same HU ranges. So a small disagreement between the specialist and the automated method on the absolute quantification of the Inter-MAT tissue will result in a significant percentage error in quantitative outcomes.

Finally, this study was done with the intention and motivation to assist medical specialists to automate and streamline the manual process of annotating and quantifying thigh tissues. Because the quantification of Inter-MAT is very sensitive, the goal is to provide the community with software capable of producing the region markings automatically, allowing specialists to intervene and modify the automatic annotations in cases where they do not accept the results.

Conflict of interest
The authors declare that they have no conflict of interest.

Acknowledgments. The authors would like to thank the São Paulo Research Foundation (FAPESP) (grant number 2016/15661-0) and the Coordination for the Improvement of Higher Education Personnel (CAPES) for the finantial support of this research.

References

1. Stehno-Bittel, L.: Intermuscular fat: a review of the consequences and causes. Phys. Ther. **88**(11), 1265–1278 (2008)
2. Sartori-Cintra, A.R., Aikawa, P., Cintra, D.E.C.: Obesity versus osteoarthritis: beyond the mechanical overload. Einstein (São Paulo) **12**(3), 374–379 (2014)
3. Goodpaster, B.H., Krishnaswami, S., Resnick, H., Kelley, D.E., Haggerty, C., Harris, T.B., Schwartz, A.V., Kritchevsky, S., Newman, A.B.: Association between regional adipose tissue distribution and both type 2 diabetes and impaired glucose tolerance in elderly men and women. Diabetes Care **26**(2), 372–379 (2003)

4. Addison, O., Marcus, R.L., LaStayo, P.C., Ryan, A.S.: Intermuscular fat: a review of the consequences and causes. Int. J. Endocrinol. **2014**(309570), 1–11 (2014)
5. Visser, M., Goodpaster, B.H., Kritchevsky, S.B., Newman, A.B., Nevitt, M., Rubin, S.M., Simonsick, E.M., Harris, T.B.: Muscle mass, muscle strength, and muscle fat infiltration as predictors of incident mobility limitations in well-functioning older persons. J. Gerontol. Ser. A: Biol. Sci. Med. Sci. **60**(3), 324–333 (2005)
6. Visser, M., Kritchevsky, S.B., Goodpaster, B.H., Newman, A.B., Nevitt, M., Stamm, E., Harris, T.B.: Leg muscle mass and composition in relation to lower extremity performance in men and women aged 70 to 79: the health, aging and body composition study. J. Am. Geriatr. Soc. **50**(5), 897–904 (2002)
7. Karampinos, D.C., Baum, T., Nardo, L., Alizai, H., Yu, H., Carballido-Gamio, J., Yap, S.P., Shimakawa, A., Link, T.M., Majumdar, S.: Characterization of the regional distribution of skeletal muscle adipose tissue in type 2 diabetes using chemical shift-based water/fat separation. J. Magn. Reson. Imaging **35**(4), 899–907 (2012)
8. Martínez-Martínez, F., Kybic, J., Lambert, L., Mecková, Z.: Fully automated classification of bone marrow infiltration in low-dose CT of patients with multiple myeloma based on probabilistic density model and supervised learning. Computers in Biology and Medicine 71(Supplement C), 57–66 (2016)
9. Wattjes, M.P., Kley, R.A., Fischer, D.: Neuromuscular imaging in inherited muscle diseases. Eur. Radiol. **20**(10), 2447–2460 (2010)
10. Yoshizumi, T., Tadashi-Nakamura, R.T., Yamane, M., Waliul-Islam, A.H.M., Menju, M., Yamasaki, K., Arai, T., Kotani, K., Funahashi, T., Yamashita, S., Matsuzawa, Y.: Abdominal fat: standardized technique for measurement at CT. Radiology **211**, 283–286 (1999)
11. Kim, Y.J., Park, J.W., Kim, J.W., Park, C.S., Gonzalez, J.P.S., Lee, S.H., Kim, K.G., Oh, J.H.: Computerized automated quantification of subcutaneous and visceral adipose tissue from computed tomography scans: development and validation study. JMIR Med. Inform. **4**(1), e2 (2016)
12. Rodrigues, É., Rodrigues, L., Oliveira, L., Conci, A., Liatsis, P.: Automated recognition of the pericardium contour on processed CT images using genetic algorithms. Computers in Biology and Medicine 87(Supplement C), 38–45 (2017)
13. Yu, P., Poh, C.L.: Region-based snake with edge constraint for segmentation of lymph nodes on CT images. Computers in Biology and Medicine 60(Supplement C), 86–91 (2015)
14. Athertya, J.S., Kumar, G.S.: Automatic segmentation of vertebral contours from CT images using fuzzy corners. Computers in Biology and Medicine 72(Supplement C) (2016) 75–89
15. Tan, C., Li, K., Yan, Z., Yang, D., Zhang, S., Yu, H.J., Engelke, K., Miller, C., Metaxas, D.: A detection-driven and sparsity-constrained deformable model for fascia lata labeling and thigh inter-muscular adipose quantification. Comput. Vis. Image Underst. **151**, 80–89 (2016)
16. Nemoto, M., Yeernuer, T., Masutani, Y., Nomura, Y., Hanaoka, S., Miki, S., Yoshikawa, T., Hayashi, N., Ohtomo, K.: Development of automatic visceral fat volume calculation software for CT volume data. J. Obes. **2014**, 495084 (2014)
17. Ciecholewski, M.: Automatic liver segmentation from 2D CT images using an approximate contour model. J. Sig. Process. Syst. **74**(2), 151–174 (2014)
18. Tan, C., Yan, Z., Zhang, S.: An automated and robust framework for quantification of muscle and fat in the thigh. In: 22nd International Conference on Pattern Recognition. ICPR 2014, Stockholm, Sweden, pp. 24–28. IEEE, August 2014

19. Positano, V., Christiansen, T., Santarelli, M.F., Ringgaard, S., Landini, L., Gastaldelli, A.: Accurate segmentation of subcutaneous and intermuscular adipose tissue from MR images of the thigh. J. Magn. Reson. Imaging 29(3), 677–684 (2009)

20. Peng, Q., McColl, R.W., Ding, Y., Wang, J., Chia, J.M., Weatherall, P.T.: Automated method for accurate abdominal fat quantification on water-saturated magnetic resonance images. J. Magn. Reson. Imaging 26(3), 738–746 (2007)

21. Positano, V., Gastaldelli, A., Santarelli, M.F., Lombardi, M., Landini, L.: An accurate and robust method for unsupervised assessment of abdominal fat by MRI. J. Magn. Reson. Imaging 20(4), 684–689 (2004)

22. Senseney, J., Hemler, P.: Automated segmentation of computed tomography images. In: IEEE Symposium on Computer-Based Medical Systems, CBMS-2009, pp. 1–7. IEEE, New Mexico, August 2009

23. Kullberg, J., Hedström, A., Brandberg, J., Strand, R., Johansson, L., Bergström, G., Ahlström, H.: Automated analysis of liver fat, muscle and adipose tissue distribution from CT suitable for large-scale studies. Sci. Rep. 7(1), 1–11 (2017)

24. Yushkevich, P.A., Piven, J., Hazlett, H.C., Smith, R.G., Ho, S., Gee, J.C., Gerig, G.: User-guided 3D active contour segmentation of anatomical structures: significantly improved efficiency and reliability. Neuroimage 31(3), 1116–1128 (2006)

25. Hendee, W.R., Ritenour, E.R.: Medical Imaging Physics, 4th edn. Wiley, New York (2002)

26. Zhang, J., Yan, C.H., Chui, C.K., Ong, S.H.: Fast segmentation of bone in CT images using 3D adaptive thresholding. Comput. Biol. Med. 40(2), 231–236 (2010)

27. Goodpaster, B.H., Thaete, F.L., Kelley, D.E.: Composition of skeletal muscle evaluated with computed tomography. Ann. New York Acad. Sci. 904(1), 18–24 (2000)

28. Freire, P.G.L., Ferrari, R.J.: Automatic iterative segmentation of multiple sclerosis lesions using Student's t mixture model and probabilistic anatomical atlases in FLAIR images. Computers in Biology and Medicine 73(Supplement C) (2016) 10–23

29. Goutte, C., Gaussier, E.: A probabilistic interpretation of precision, recall and F-score, with implication for evaluation. In: Losada, D.E., Fernández-Luna, J.M. (eds.) ECIR 2005. LNCS, vol. 3408, pp. 345–359. Springer, Heidelberg (2005). https://doi.org/10.1007/978-3-540-31865-1_25

Multi-objective Based Road-Link Grading for Health-Care Access During Flood Hazard Management

Omprakash Chakraborty$^{(\boxtimes)}$ iD, V. Yeshwanth, Pabitra Mitra,
and Soumya K. Ghosh

Indian Institute of Technology (IIT) Kharagpur, Kharagpur, West Bengal, India
omchakrabarty@gmail.com, yeshwanthv5@gmail.com,
pabitra@cse.iitkgp.ernet.in, skg@cse.iitkgp.ac.in

Abstract. Health-care centers form a critical part in citizen services during disaster management. Road networks play an important role in facilitating access to such services from settlements. The importance of a road depends on its utility in this respect along with its geospatial characteristics. In this article, road importance measures are proposed that consider spatial properties as well as path utlizations. These metrics are then utilized to identify optimal links of the network in terms of safety and sustainability towards relief-facility access even in severe hazard conditions. A case study is presented for a flood scenario in the Bankura district of West Bengal, India. The proposed approach provides a more realistic assessment of the road importance as compared to conventional link analysis. The identification of optimal road links help in several mitigation and rescue strategies for disaster management.

1 Introduction

Amongst all natural hazards, floods pose one of the highest threats [1] to the populace and their properties in the Indian sub-continent. The entire coastal areas of the sub-continent are the most resource rich areas leading to high population density and drawing continuous stream of migrant population [1]. The increasing population density and the changing pattern of the monsoons pose a higher risk in these areas. A study on floods and their societal impacts has been carried out in Bangladesh [2]. Incidentally, Bangladesh lies in the Indian sub-continent and shares similar experience with flood related vulnerability. West Bengal has in past, experienced several large floods, most of these can be attributed to tropical cyclones or monsoonal rains [3]. The socio-economic characteristics of the flood prone areas are such that most of these floods have left behind irreparable losses. These losses can be characterized into *direct losses* - losses incurred due to mortality and morbidity of population, loss to physical property, damaging of standing crops, loss to livestock, and *indirect losses* - outbreak of epidemics, forced migration [3].

© Springer International Publishing AG, part of Springer Nature 2018
O. Gervasi et al. (Eds.): ICCSA 2018, LNCS 10960, pp. 277–293, 2018.
https://doi.org/10.1007/978-3-319-95162-1_19

The disaster mitigation strategies for affected communities can be subdivided into two parts, first is a pre-disaster strategy of moving population to flood reliefs and second being the provision of emergency response services [3]. The flood reliefs have a catchment area and the population residing within that catchment moves in before the disaster strikes. It also has provisions for safeguarding livestock during the disaster. However, post disaster response activities, as considered in our case, involve emergency medical-care, medical support, threat of epidemic and other public health issues, mortuary services apart from other relief operations like fooding provisions, drinking water, etc. It is evident that both the pre- and post-disaster operations is dependent on road connectivity. The pre-disaster connectivity is mostly limited to community level, fair weather conditions whereas, post disaster connectivity needs to be addressed at the regional level.

Spatial analysis or statistics is a wide and interdisciplinary scientific topic including a variety of techniques, many still in their early development, using different analytic approaches and applied in diverse fields. Spatial analysis is applied to structures at the human scale, most notably in the analysis of geographic data. In case of disaster management also, Geographic Information Systems (GIS) techniques have vast implementations which are still being explored with alternative perspectives and extensive approaches.

Urban and Regional Studies deal with large tables of spatial data obtained from several heterogeneous sources. It is necessary to channelize the huge amount of detailed information through a fixed work-flow in order to extract the main trends. As GIS based service oriented approach is needed to integrate social and environmental data as a map for carrying out the analysis. This study aims to implement a framework to retrieve diverse spatial data and incorporate it to analyze road networks and compute key measures such as node importance and edge importance of the network.

In our study, we aim to analyze the road network of a region to facilitate the mitigation strategies during disasters. We utilize spatial properties of the region to assess the vulnerability of the road links followed by its diverse utilization by the affected populace in reaching different healthcare facilities. Road importance measures have been proposed for the same. We also provide a relevant case study to depict the results of our approach.

2   Related Works

The analysis of roads from various perspectives and different disaster circumstances have been carried out over a decade. [4] gives an overview of the road reliability, various approaches towards vulnerability and effective risk analysis aimed to optimize the service provisions. The discussions can be related to most of the present day road network with variable traffic flow and usages. [5] promotes the approach of network robustness index of the edge links for improvement over the congested critical links. The index is derived based on the change in the time caused due to the re-routing of traffic within the system owing to the instability of that road edge. The transport network resilience has been studied by [6], in terms of the *critical capacity* of the network. The approach involves a genetic algorithm based approach to analyze the resilience in the view of a maxmin optimization problem. [7] gives an approach to derive the safety criteria for the vehicles in roads subjected to urban flood risks.

[8] evaluates the impact and risk of pluvial flash flood in the city center of Shanghai, China. It depicts a method to measure the impact of pluvial flash flooding and its risk on intra-urban road networks. The results indicate the local origination of road floods and synchronization with the timing of rainfall is generally proportionate to the magnitude of precipitation. Our previous work, [9], also aimed at the risk mapping for critical flood affected regions utilizing varied heterogeneous sources. It proposed a service oriented framework for the depiction of risk zones in a disaster prone region. Some interesting results revealed larger water-bodies possessing a great effect towards water level risk in terms of flood assessment. The final result depicted the division of final risk zones with variation in regional elevation within the study region.

3   Road Importance Grading Framework

The overall framework is shown in Fig. 1. The system takes different spatial data (road network, elevation map, facility locations etc.) as inputs, and grades the links to identify the least vulnerable paths. The approach modules are illustrated in the respective sections later.

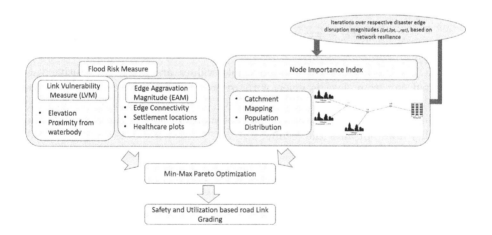

Fig. 1. Overview of the road importance grading framework

4   Flood Risk Measure

In case of a road network, the identification of risk at the edge level can be determined by the spatial vulnerability of the individual links as well as the effects of the link disruption on the overall connectivity of the road system. These critical factors are addressed using *two* proposed measures namely: (i) *Link Vulnerability Measure (LVM)* and (ii) *Edge Aggravation Magnitude (EAM)*.

The road network is modeled as a weighted undirected multi-graph $G = (V, E)$, where the set of vertices V denote the population settlements (villages or towns) and E, the set of edges represent the connecting roads between them.

4.1   Link Vulnerability Measure (LVM)

LVM is proposed to predict the likeliness of the road-links for getting disrupted. That would be the measure of how vulnerable that particular link is in the case of floods. The flood based vulnerability is computed based on the elevation of the link and proximity of the edge to a water-body, that if an area is at higher elevation and far from a water-body, it is less likely to get submerged. Therefore the link would stay intact and so has a lower risk. Thus we can say that the probability of a link getting disrupted (vulnerability) is inversely proportional to the elevation of that link and its proximity from a water-body,

$$Pr(e_i) \propto \frac{1}{Elevation(e_i) \times Proximity(e_i)},$$

where $Proximity(e_i)$ is the shortest distance of the link from the closest water-body.

So, the vulnerability relative to the sample points can be computed using Eq. 1.

$$Pr(e_i) = \frac{\frac{1}{1+\sqrt{Elevation(e_i) \times Proximity(e_i)}}}{\sum_{e \in E} \frac{1}{1+\sqrt{Elevation(e_i) \times Proximity(e_i)}}} \tag{1}$$

Note that both elevation and proximity values are taken as positive values. Usual elevation data is given with respect to sea level. So it is possible to encounter negative values. These negative values were normalized. Since we are finding out relative probability, the choice of function used to calculate the probability does not alter the results.

5   Edge Aggravation Magnitude (EAM)/Edge Criticality Index

Applying the proposed EAM concept to the road networks, we calculate the criticality of an edge in terms of the overall connectivity for optimal functioning of the road network. This may seem to be straightforward that the probability of the link getting disrupted (LVM) is the direct measure of edge criticality index as a link is more susceptible to disruption it is more critical. However, it is not the case as shown using a sample a road network connecting six villages shown in Fig. 2.

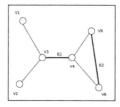

Fig. 2. Toy example to show that vulnerability doesn't necessarily imply criticality

Say, the edge E_2 has highest probability of getting disrupted. We can't plainly say that edge E_2 has the highest EAM index among all the edges. Because E_2 is connecting vertices V_5 and V_6 which are also connected by $V_5 - V_4 - V_6$ path. So even if E_2 gets disrupted we can reach $V6$ from $V5$. Now suppose the edge E_1 that is connecting V_3 and V_4 gets disrupted, this would mean that the network is disconnected. Suppose there is a district hospital in V_4, if E_1 gets disrupted there is no way that people from V_1, V_2 and V_3 can access that hospital in V_4. Thus, we need to consider the population and resource flow while calculating the EAM index of an edge. Putting the above discrepancy in theoretical terms, the magnitude of aggravation associated with the link disruption in addition to the vulnerability of the link should also be considered in order to complete the formulation of criticality. To calculate the EAM mertic, the utilization of the links are getting analyzed. If a link that is very frequently used to access a hospital, then that particular link staying functional is very important and there is an inconvenience to huge population caused with its disruption hence it can be termed as critical.

For the study purpose, a facility is defined as a place equipped with providing a particular service. For example - Hospitals, Banks, Education Institutes. Now, to capture the data of population flow and resource flow, we initially consider the catchment of particular facility. Catchment area of a facility refers to the region that is being served by that particular facility. The whole network is divided into different catchments with respect to a particular facility based on the shortest path distances from the facilities. The concept of catchment mapping is illustrated in the toy example in Fig. 3.

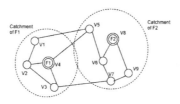

Fig. 3. Toy example to illustrate the concept of catchment

To define the concept of catchment mapping mathematically, the road network is considered as weighted undirected multi-graph $G = (V, E)$. Let the vertex set $V = v_1, v_2, \ldots, v_n$ be the set of all population settlements and edge set E be the connecting roads between them weighted based on the travel cost along the road. Let $F^i = f_1^i, f_2^i, \ldots, f_n^i$ be the set of facilities of type i such as hospitals. It is reasonable to assume that for a given node v_k, the nearest facility in terms of travel distance is the one which serves it. We define a distance function $dist(v_k, f^i)$ as the cost of traveling from settlement v_k to facility f_j^i along the shortest path in the road network represented by the multi-graph $G = (V, E)$. Then the Catchment CM of facility f_j^i is the union of nodes that are served by f_j^i and is represented as,

$$CM^F(f_i) = \{\bigcup s_k | s_k \in V \ \& \\ dist(s_k, f_i) = min(dist(s_k, f_1), dist(s_k, f_2), \ldots, dist(s_k, f_m))\} \quad (2)$$

where $1 \leq i \leq m$ and $1 \leq k \leq n$

However, there is one fundamental assumption in the above approach that we say that a particular settlement v_k is served only by the facility f_j^i. But this is not necessarily true in all cases. So instead of dividing the graph into catchments, we compute the probability with which a settlement v_k is served by the facility f_j^i say Probabilistic Catchment (pCM). To calculate this probability we again consider the distance function that was defined before and argue that higher the $dist(v_k, f^i)$ lower the probability that people from the settlement v_k are going to choose f_j^i as their primary facility. So inverse of the distance is considered for calculating the probability. To handle the zero distance cases we add a bias term 1 while calculating the probability. Now we define pCM as,

$$pCM(v_k, f^i) = \frac{\frac{1}{1+dist(v_k, f^i)}}{\sum_{i=1}^m \frac{1}{1+dist(v_k, f^i)}},$$

where $1 \leq i \leq m$ and $1 \leq k \leq n$

pCM gives the probability of a particular settlement choosing a particular facility. Next step would be reaching the facility starting from the settlement. It can be intuitively said that the people from a given settlement will choose the shortest available path from the settlement to the facility. But it is not necessary that the people choose the shortest path to reach the facilities always. There can be many other parameters such as safety, public transport service. So giving importance only for the edges that come in the shortest path is not a good way of looking at the problem. The alternate paths should be considered as well. People will usually go for first few alternatives and the rest can be discarded. Therefore, as a trade off, we consider the first K shortest paths to calculate the edge aggravation magnitude. Now of course we can't assume that all the K shortest paths have equal effect in calculating edge aggravation. So based on the length of the paths we assign weights to each of the paths and then add up to the aggravation for each edge appearing in the paths.

Based on these analysis, the magnitude of aggravation associated with each edge getting disrupted can be computed based on the following Algorithms 1–3.

Algorithm 1. EAM(u,v)

Input   : G, F, pCM(v,f), k.

Output: Magnitude of aggravation associated with each edge getting disrupted with respect to the accessibility of the facilities available in set F

1 Initialize the Edge Aggravation Magnitude $EAM(u,v) = 0 \forall (u,v) \in E$

2 **for** s in V **do**

3 | **for** $f_i in F$ **do**

4 | | $P = GET\_K\_SHORTEST\_PATHS(s, f_i, k) UPDATE\_EAM(EAM, P)$

5 Return EAM

Algorithm 2. $GET\_K\_SHORTEST\_PATHS(s, f_i, k)$

---

1 Initialize a set $P = \phi$

2 Initialize $Count[u] = 0 \forall u \in V$

3 Insert $P_s = s$ into Q with $Cost[P_s] = 0$

4 **while** $Q \neq \phi$ and $Count[f_i] < k$ **do**

5 | Let P_u be the root of the heap with $Cost[P_s] = c$

6 | Pop the root from the heap. $Q = Q - P_u$

7 | Increment the count of node u by 1. $Count[u] = Count[u] + 1$

8 | If we have reached the destination i.e. $u = f_i$: Update the set P. $P = P \cup P_u$

9 | **if** $Count[u] < k$ **then**

10 | | **for** $each vertex v adjacent to u$ **do**

11 | | | **if** $v \notin P_u$ **then**

12 | | | | Let P_v be a new path with cost $c + weight(u,v)$ formed by concatenating the (u,v) to path P_u

13 | | | | $Q = Q \cup P_v$

14 Return P

The algorithm calculates the Edge Aggravation Magnitude(or Edge Criticality) of each edge in the network with respect to one particular type of facility. In addition to EAM we have Link Vulnerability Measure(LVM). By combining these two parameters we calculate the risk associated with each edge.

$$Risk(e_i) = LVM(e_i) \times EAM(e_i) \qquad (3)$$

where $LVM(e_i)$ is the Link Vulnerability Measure that is given by the probability calculations of the relative probability of link, e_i getting disrupted. $EAM(e_i)$ is the Edge Aggravation Magnitude i.e. the measure of impact associated with the loss of that edge. The mapping of the link-risks along the road network is followed by the grading of the links based on the population flow along the roads for accessing the relief-facilities. This is computed using the *Node Importance Index*.

Algorithm 3. $UPDATE\_EAM(EAM, P)$

---

1 Initialize $weight(P_i) = 0 \forall P_i \in P$

2 Initialize $sumcost = 0$ for $P_i \in P$ do

3 $\quad | \quad sumcost = sumcost + \frac{1}{(1+P.cost)}$

4 for $P_i \in P$ do

5 $\quad | \quad$ Calculate the weight of the path

6 $\quad | \quad weight(P) = \frac{\frac{1}{(1+P.cost)}}{sumcost}$ Initialize current index

7 $\quad | \quad curr = 0$ Initialize $vulenrable\_pop = 0$ Initialize $destination(dest)$ to the last vertex in the path P_i while $curr < length(P_i)$ do

8 $\quad | \quad | \quad$ Update the vulnerable population by adding the population of the current settlement weighted by the probability that the people from the current settlement choosing the facility destination vertex.

9 $\quad | \quad | \quad vulnerable\_pop = vulnerable\_pop + population[P_i[curr]] \times pCM(P_i[curr], dest)$

10 $\quad | \quad | \quad$ Update the edge aggravation magnitude of the edge joining the current vertex and the next vertex

11 $\quad | \quad | \quad EAM(P_i[curr], P_i[curr + 1]) = $
   $\quad | \quad | \quad EAM(P_i[curr], P_i[curr + 1]) + vulenrable\_pop \times weight(P_i)$

12 $\quad | \quad | \quad$ Move to the next node by incrementing the current index

13 $\quad | \quad | \quad curr = curr + 1$

---

6 Node Importance Index (NII)

The *Node Importance Index (NII)* is a modification of the Edge Importance Index (EII) [10], in which the importance is analyzed not for the intermediate edges of the network, but for the end-nodes of the road links along the path sets between the village centroids and the facilities. It not only withholds the path importance indices from the villages to catchment facilities but the complete node set of the entire road network. Once the road features are converted to a di-graph revealing the corresponding edge and node sets, the individual nodes of the path are treated with the village population as weights. The analysis is proceeded based on the node's significance towards its utilization by the people of different villages. More the number of people from different villages use the links of the path, and passes through the nodes, the greater importance it gets. Thus for calculations, the nodes are assigned weights, the values of which are incremented with the population of the particular villages that use it.

Let $SP_{O \to D}$ denote shortest path from origin, O and destination, D

$$SP_{O \to D} = arg\ min\{dist(P^*_{O \to D})\}, \tag{4}$$

where, $dist(P^*_{O \to D})$ represents the distance function for length of the paths in P^*.
The resultant node importance for a given node n can be depicted as in Eq. 6.

$$NII(n) = C_c(n)\frac{\sum \mathbb{P}_{OD}}{\mathbb{P}_O}, if\ n \in SP_{O \to D} \tag{5}$$

where, $\mathbb{P}_{OD}$ is the population of O accessing facility, D. $C_c(n)$, is the *closeness centralities* of nodes n.

The closeness centrality of a node is the measure of its shortest path lengths to other nodes of the corresponding layer. It is denoted as,

$$C_c(u) = \left[\sum_{v=1}^{n} dist(u, v) \right]^{-1}$$

The centrality measure helps in better access to the road networks for faster dispersion and citizen check-outs.

As the road-link utilizations change with the increase in hazard-scale, the NII values for the individual links also get altered to address the dynamics of the population flow for relief-access. Let $D = \{\rho_1, \rho_2, \ldots, \rho_n\}$, be the considered disaster scales. These scales are represented by the observed percentage of road-link disruption which implicitly reflect the level of water. The NII correspond-ing to the respective scales can be represented as Let $NII^{\rho_1}, NII^{\rho_2}, \ldots, NII^{\rho_n}$ respectively. For identifying the overall node importances, the net NII is taken as an average over all the corresponding values as,

$$NII = \frac{1}{D} \sum_{\rho=\rho_1}^{\rho=\rho_n} NII^{\rho_n} \tag{6}$$

7   Optimization Towards Multiobjective Edge-Grading

The safety of the path traversals to access the respective relief-facilities are based on the risk and utilization parameters of the links and nodes forming the paths. To identify paths with highest overall importance, the grading should satisfy the criteria of being safe even at adverse disaster scenarios while having most utility in reaching the different relief facilities. This scoring can be formalized as a max-min multi-objective optimization (MOO) approach on a ranking function, say ϕ, to minimize *Risk* and maximize NII parameters as in Eq. 7.

$$max\ \phi = \begin{cases} min\ Risk(e_i) \\ max\ NII(n) \end{cases} = \begin{cases} LVM(e_i) \times EAM(e_i) \\ \frac{1}{D} \sum_{\rho=\rho_1}^{\rho=\rho_n} C_c(n) \frac{\sum \mathbb{P}_{OD}}{\mathbb{P}_O} \end{cases} \tag{7}$$

We implement the concept of Pareto optimality to grade the edges in the MOO model. The optimal edges at a given iteration are identified through the computation of the Pareto frontier. These edges, intuitively, represent the solu-tions in which one of the attributes cannot be further maximized without wors-ening the other. The edges are ranked based on their location on the respective Pareto frontier grades, which are iteratively computed during the MOO opti-mization process.

8   Case Study

Bankura (Fig. 4) is one of the inland districts (area of 6882 km^2) located on the western side of the state of West Bengal. It has been recognized as a major flood prone area in the state of West Bengal [11]. Bankura has a unique physiography where four rivers run across the district from west to east direction (Damodar on the northern periphery, Dwarekeshwar river below it, followed by Silai and river Kasai at the southern end of the district), which incidentally is prevalent gradient of the land. There are zones of plateau between the undulating hilly western side (covered by reserved forests) and gradually sloped eastern part of the district.

The hierarchy of roads reveals that the district is connected to its adjoining districts by a system of state highways (SH). The SH-9 runs from south to the north connecting Bankura to Paschim Medinipur (in south) to Bardhhaman (in the north). Similarly, SH-2 runs from west to east connecting Puruliya to Hugli via Bankura. The SH-5 joins the eastern part of the state to the northern part, whereas the SH-4 primarily serves the south-western part of the district. There are other arterial/sub-arterial road system in the district, which connect to this network of SH. The network of the district (up to the collector street level system) was taken up for this study (Fig. 5). The objective of this study is to understand the network connectivity at extreme weather conditions. However, the base case for a further scenario generation and simulation is assumed from fair weather connectivity.

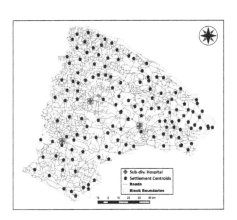

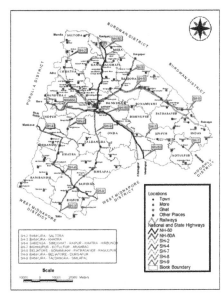

Fig. 4. Case study region: Bankura, West Bengal, India; area: 6,882

Fig. 5. National and state highways of Bankura. [Source: National Informatics Center, Bankura]

8.1   Results

The results of Link Vulnerability Measure calculated with elevation and proximity to water body data are shown in Fig. 7. To compute LVM values of the road links, we need to identify the distribution of river-basins of the region, the portion of land being drained by a particular river, which encompasses the road network and the spatial aspect of the links. The entire district of Bankura lies within the basins of the rivers Damodar and Rupnarayan respectively [12], where the latter more prominently infamous for causing flash floods, monsoonal floods in the region [13]. Simultaneously, its upper catchments consist of $12°$–$21°$ slopes where as the slope in the middle portion is $7°$–$12°$. That is the reason the water in the middle part does not get back to its upper catchments. The upper catchment's water level getting higher and higher than its lower potion give backward onrush of water. The middle portion of the river gets flooded. That is the reason of monsoonal flood in its middle portion. Although, the rivers significantly dry out during the summer months, they overflow each year during the monsoons. Bankura receives flooding conditions due to discharge from upper basin areas through these four rivers, large volume of surface runoff, build-up of water due to heavy rainfall, and the unique elevation profile of the region (as in Fig. 6).

Fig. 6. Road network links graded based on the regional elevation profile

The Edge Aggravation Magnitude (EAM) of the road links to access the relief-facility, healthcare in this case are, as discussed in Algorithm 1, based on the connectivity of the vulnerable population flow paths along the probable catchment maps. The EAM values for the individual facilities is depicted in Fig. 8.

The road segment node importances, NII analyses the population traversal based importance index of the all the 3839 intermediate node sets of the road network for the respective facilities across the considered hazard scales. We have considered the percentage of edge-disruption owing to flood-level rise as the

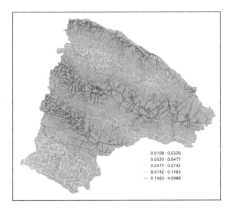

Fig. 7. The LVM grading of the road links

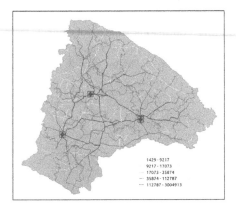

Fig. 8. Healthcare access routes graded by EAM levels

hazard scales initiating from fair weather conditions iteratively upto 16% edge disruptions, post which the road network fails to provide access to any health-care centers. The results reflecting significant importance changes are reflected in Figs. 9, 10 and 11. The figures portray a significant shift the node importances with the rise in flood adversity. Table 1 depicts the overall NII results for some of the nodes.

Finally, these results are utilized for grading the road links for sustainable relief-facility access during disaster times as discussed in Sect. 7. The Pareto based grading can be conceptualized using Fig. 12. The plots contain all the road link-nodes of the region that participate in forming paths for health-care access. The roads having same grade values are marked using a common and unique color band. The color-coded edges in the graph denote the min-max Pareto frontiers for the respective grades. Figure 13 portrays the road network of the study region consisting of top four graded links which form the safest path for health-care access from the respective settlements.

Table 1. NII Analysis of all intermediate path nodes of the road network

SL_No	Longitude	Latitude	NII
1	86.85690308	22.86751938	14616
2	87.03074646	23.15146446	0
3	86.76268768	23.12214851	12687
...	...	...	...
68	87.25009918	23.20824242	0
69	87.11117554	23.10203362	21016
...	...	...	...
134	87.05408478	22.99751091	18699
136	87.17552948	23.11337852	0
...	...	...	...
1000	87.23303223	23.31071472	0
1500	86.84412384	23.11271477	0
...	...	...	...
2000	87.17552948	23.45362663	142800
2500	87.00985718	23.53209496	0
...	...	...	...
3000	87.44976807	23.14036751	0
3839	86.93696594	23.16602707	0

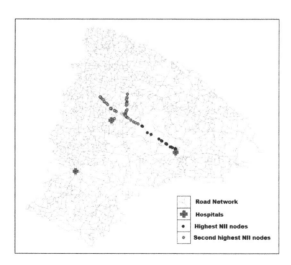

Fig. 9. Highest NII valued nodes for healthcare access in normal conditions

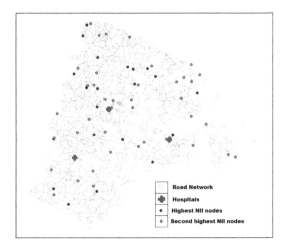

Fig. 10. Highest NII valued nodes for healthcare access at 7% edge disruption

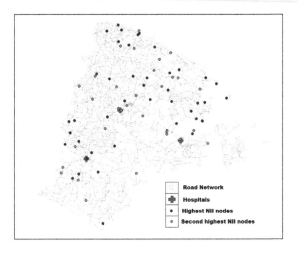

Fig. 11. Highest NII valued nodes for healthcare access at 16% edge disruption

8.2 Discussion

Besides the primary results of the work, the approach also reveals some interesting inferences. The LVM values (Fig. 7) reflect the high overall proximity of the roads in the region that lead to their higher natural propensity to disrupt. The road network dissected almost at equal intervals by the main rivers of the region. Furthermore, majority of the region lies in low elevation area (refer Fig. 6), except the north-western part causing higher flood adversities. Within the road layout, the central part plays a critical part in holding sustainable connectivity (Fig. 8) and this may be one of the reasons for centralized location of the health-care centers. Based on the available locations, it is found that the

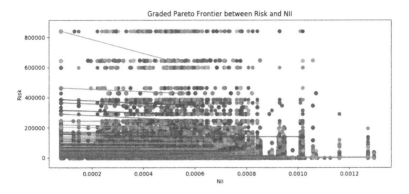

Fig. 12. Road link grading based on min-max Pareto optimality (Color figure online)

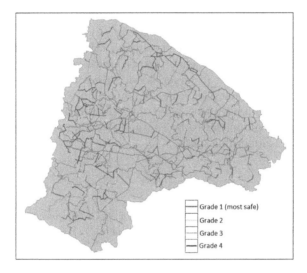

Fig. 13. Top *four* ranges of highest graded road-links within the region. The grade 1 (green path) links serve as the optimal links that provide the highest utilizations for health-care access and also have low risk from flood adversities. (Color figure online)

utilization of the roads by the populace to access the health-cares are mostly concentrated in the northern region (as in Figs. 9 and 11) which indeed hold the safer paths to the facilities. Also, an extensive migration of the highest node importances is observed from the central (Fig. 9) to the northern region post 7% edge disruptions within the network. The Pareto optimal plots reveal the moderate utilization as well as risk of most of the common road links. However, the min-max frontiers highlight the importance of few yet low utilized roads (left-most frontier nodes of Fig. 12) that may facilitate safer health-care access routes. Finally, the optimal links (refer Fig. 13) emphasize the utilization of the major roads in the central region. The results significantly coincide with some of the major state and national highways of the region (as in Fig. 5). This also acts as a validation as usually these roads are of the superior quality and preferred during disaster management.

9   Conclusion

The identification of vital roads links for relief accesses by the populace along with alternate travel strategies, is a crucial factor for disaster management schemes. It also promotes the safeguarding of the links for better service usabilities in disaster cases. In our study, we carry out an analysis of the road segments in terms of its spatial layouts, contribution towards reliable paths for facility access and alternate routes. We illustrate the road network based on three importance factors of link vulnerability, edge criticality and resilience of the auxilary paths. The approach considers most of the aspects influencing the capability of roads to provide the emergency services during disasters. However, the work can be extended to encompass other vulnerability influencing parameters to enhance the efficiency further more. in the future, we also aim to implement the framework in larger flood regions and also explore the spatial attributes to a more detailed scale. The multi-objective based optimization of the road-network enhances the analytical capabilities by identifying only the facility-relevant link properties to be considered within the different input sets of importance measure evaluations.

References

1. Mukherjee, A., Saha, D., Harvey, C.F., Taylor, R.G., Ahmed, K.M., Bhanja, S.N.: Groundwater systems of the Indian sub-continent. J. Hydrol.: Reg. Stud. **4**, 1–14 (2015)
2. Masuya, A., Dewan, A., Corner, R.J.: Population evacuation: evaluating spatial distribution of flood shelters and vulnerable residential units in Dhaka with geographic information systems. Nat. Hazards **78**(3), 1859–1882 (2015)
3. Nath, S.K., Roy, D., Thingbaijam, K.K.S.: Disaster mitigation and management for West Bengal, India - an appraisal. Curr. Scie.-Bangalore **94**(7), 858 (2008)
4. Berdica, K.: An introduction to road vulnerability: what has been done, is done and should be done. Transp. Policy **9**(2), 117–127 (2002)
5. Scott, D.M., Novak, D.C., Aultman-Hall, L., Guo, F.: Network robustness index: a new method for identifying critical links and evaluating the performance of transportation networks. J. Transp. Geogr. **14**(3), 215–227 (2006)
6. Bhavathrathan, B., Patil, G.R.: Capacity uncertainty on urban road networks: a critical state and its applicability in resilience quantification. Comput. Environ. Urban Syst. **54**, 108–118 (2015)
7. Kramer, M., Terheiden, K., Wieprecht, S.: Safety criteria for the trafficability of inundated roads in urban floodings. Int. J. Disaster Risk Reduct. **17**, 77–84 (2016)
8. Yin, J., Yu, D., Yin, Z., Liu, M., He, Q.: Evaluating the impact and risk of pluvial flash flood on intra-urban road network: a case study in the city center of Shanghai, China. J. Hydrol. **537**, 138–145 (2016)

9. Chakraborty, O., Das, J., Dasgupta, A., Mitra, P., Ghosh, S.K.: A geospatial service oriented framework for disaster risk zone identification. In: Gervasi, O., et al. (eds.) ICCSA 2016. LNCS, vol. 9788, pp. 44–56. Springer, Cham (2016). https://doi.org/10.1007/978-3-319-42111-7_5

10. Chakraborty, O., Das, A., Dasgupta, A., Mitra, P., Ghosh, S.K., Mazumder, T.: A multi-objective framework for analysis of road network vulnerability for relief facility location during flood hazards: a case study of relief location analysis in Bankura district, India. Trans. GIS (2017). https://doi.org/10.1111/tgis.12314

11. Roy, P., Samal, N., Roy, M., Mazumdar, A.: Integrated assessment of impact of water resources of important river basins in Eastern India under projected climate conditions. Glob. Nest J. **17**(3), 594–606 (2015)

12. Bandyopadhyay, S., Kar, N., Das, S., Sen, J.: River systems and water resources of West Bengal: a review. In: Rejuvenation of surface water resources of India: potential, problems and prospects. GeolSoc India, Bengaluru, Special Publication, vol. 3, pp. 63–84 (2014)

13. Vass, K.K., Das, M.K., Tyagi, R., Katiha, P.K., Samanta, S., Srivastava, N., Bhattacharjya, B., Suresh, V., Pathak, V., Chandra, G., et al.: Strategies for sustainable fisheries in the Indian part of the Ganga-Brahmaputra river basins. Int. J. Ecol. Environ. Sci. **37**(4) (2011)

Zen Cat: A Meditation-Based Brain-Computer Interface Game

Gabriel Alves Mendes Vasiljevic$^{(\boxtimes)}$ (iD),
Leonardo Cunha de Miranda (iD), and Bruna Camila de Menezes (iD)

Department of Informatics and Applied Mathematics, Federal University of Rio
Grande Do Norte (UFRN), Natal, RN 59078-970, Brazil
gabrielvasiljevic@outlook.com,
leonardo@dimap.ufrn.br, brunacamilamenezes@gmail.com

Abstract. Brain-Computer Interfaces (BCIs) are specialized systems that allow any person, including patients suffering from physical paralysis, to control applications using only their brain waves. Recently, BCI started to find applications outside of the medical field, as the development of consumer-grade BCI technology allowed the implementation of entertainment systems, which are more accessible for the general public, although there are still many challenges regarding the design and development of this kind of game. This work presents the development process and the evaluation of the Zen Cat software, a computer game application based on BCI interaction which incentives players to relax using neurofeedback. The game was developed using an iterative process, and evaluated for two weeks by sixteen volunteer subjects. The results of the evaluation may be of guidance for the development of future BCI-based games.

Keywords: BCI · EEG · NeuroSky MindWave · HCI · Evaluation
Games

1 Introduction

The advancement of novel interface technologies led to the development of new ways to interact with the computer [3], such as with speech [13] and gestures [19, 26], that provide a greater immersion of the user with the virtual platform. Emerging applications are starting to employ physiological data from the user as an input modality to alter or control the virtual environment, such as his/her breath [4], muscle movements [25] and heart rate [27]. In the past few decades, researchers also started to investigate the employment of brain waves as a control mechanism for computer applications.

Brain-Computer Interfaces (BCIs) are computer systems that allow users to control such specialized applications using their brain waves [20]. BCI systems started to gain attention as they can be potentially used by any person, including physically impaired ones [12], as the signal commands are sent directly to the computer from the brain [9]. This direct channel of communication can be employed in many different applications, such as medical treatments, psychological evaluation tools and training programs [23], opening various research possibilities for the field of Human-Computer Interaction (HCI).

© Springer International Publishing AG, part of Springer Nature 2018
O. Gervasi et al. (Eds.): ICCSA 2018, LNCS 10960, pp. 294–309, 2018.
https://doi.org/10.1007/978-3-319-95162-1_20

The recent advancements in BCI technology allowed the development of systems not only for medical purposes, but for entertainment and domestic applications as well [5, 10, 11]. The advent of consumer-grade BCI devices based on electroencephalography (EEG), such as the NeuroSky MindWave and the Emotiv Epoc, made the development of applications for the general public easier, as several layers of signal processing and brain wave classification are abstracted and the devices are easier to use [14, 15]. In addition, the relative low cost and easiness of use in comparison to medical-grade devices make the employment of these consumer-grade devices attractive for games and scientific experiments [22, 24].

However, there are still numerous challenges to be overcome in relation to the design and development of BCI-based computer games: brain waves, as physiological signals, may have a high degree of variation and its control may be difficult for most users [1]. In addition to the current limitations of BCI technology, the game designer must take this biological instability in consideration to create a game with reliable controls that still feels natural to the player in comparison to other traditional controls, like mouse and keyboard [13].

In this context, this work presents the Zen Cat game application. The game is based on BCI interaction and allows for players to control the game using only neurofeedback interaction. Details about its interface and development process are highlighted, and the results of the iterative testing and an evaluation involving sixteen subjects over two weeks are presented and discussed. These results may help game designers in the process of developing future BCI-based computer games.

This paper is organized as follow: Sect. 2 presents the related work in the area; Sect. 3 introduces the Zen Cat game, its concept, development details and interfaces; Sect. 4 explains the performed evaluation and its results; Sect. 5 discusses the obtained results; and Sect. 6 concludes the paper.

2 Related Work

There are a number of developed games that employed a BCI-based control scheme. Although there is a large diversification of control signals on which they are based upon and the device that is employed to capture the player's signal, this section will focus at games that specifically employed the meditation control signal.

Antle et al. [2] describe two meditation-based games. In the first one, the goal is to help a paraglide to descend from a hill to the ground. The paraglide only starts to descend when the player's meditation has reached a base level, which must be maintained until the match is completed. In the second one, the player must also maintain his/her meditation above a base level to gain score. A virtual pinwheel is present to symbolize that the player must blow to help to relax and increase the meditation level; it also starts to move when the base level is reached and the player start scoring.

Laar et al. [17] presents an adapted version of an online RPG game, in which the player can control the shape of his/her character by maintaining a high or a low meditation value. With a high meditation value, the character can perform long-ranged combat with magic spells; when the player is stressed with a low meditation value, the character shifts its form into a bear with close-range combat skills. Choo and May [7] describe a game that aims at helping players to meditate. After each session of the game, the player is awarded with points that can be exchanged with new content, such as lessons and scenarios. A racing game is described in the work of Jiang and Johnstone [16] and the goal of the game is to win the race using the meditation levels, which in turn control the speed of the character: the more relaxed the player is, the faster s/he gets. In the work of Liarokapis et al. [18], the authors present a BCI-adapted Tetris game. In this version of the game, the player can control the speed of the falling blocks using his/her meditation: the more the player is relaxed, the slower the blocks fall.

Some games also employ other control signals, such as the player's level of attention, in combination with the meditation control. The game described in the work of Cho and Lee [6], for example, employs the attention and meditation to control environmental traits. When the attention of the player is high, the environment becomes lighter, while the fog becomes denser the less relaxed the player is (i.e., with lower meditation levels). Coulton et al. [8], on the other hand, describes a mobile game in which the player must use his/her smartphone's accelerometer to move and conduct a ball in a labyrinth. The player must reach a specific location on the map to win, and may use his/her attention and meditation scores to open shortcuts and new paths.

Table 1 summarizes the data from the related games. The table shows which control scheme was employed (BCI only or hybrid control); the EEG device; the paradigm, i.e. whether the control was employed to actively or passively control any aspect of the game; and whether the game was adapted from an existing one.

Table 1. Related work

Work	Control	Device	Paradigm	Adapted
[2]	BCI only	NeuroSky MindWave	Active	No
	BCI only	NeuroSky MindWave	Active	No
[17]	Hybrid	Emotiv Epoc	Passive	Yes
[7]	BCI only	Emotiv Epoc	Active	No
[16]	BCI only	NeuroSky MindWave	Active	No
[18]	Hybrid	NeuroSky MindSet	Passive	Yes
[6]	Hybrid	NeuroSky MindSet	Passive	No
[8]	Hybrid	NeuroSky MindSet	Passive	No

One can notice, based on the described games, that the meditation control signal can be applied in a number of different contexts depending on the game. While some works employed the BCI signal to actively control the game, others have employed it to passively change the game itself. In our work, the game was entirely designed to fully employ the BCI signal as a direct, active control scheme. The evaluation was performed as a mean to verify the feasibility, the design implications, impacts on the entertainment aspects and gameplay changes of applying this specific control mode.

3 Zen Cat

The Zen Cat software is an open-source BCI-based game, which was developed to be played using only the player's brain waves. The player controls a cat that must meditate in order to levitate and reach the highest height as possible. To achieve that goal, the player must also meditate, i.e., must maintain his/her average meditation, which is calculated using his/her brain waves, above a certain threshold. If his/her average meditation falls below the threshold, which is defined by the cat's current height, the cat starts to wake from his meditative state and stops levitating.

The game software was developed by the Zen Cat Development Team (Dev Team), composed of two researchers and a designer, in the C++ programming language, using the Simple and Fast Multimedia Library (SFML). The SFML was employed to manage the game's graphics and sounds. To capture the players' level of meditation, the NeuroSky MindWave headset was employed, which is a consumer-grade BCI device that is able to measure the levels of concentration and meditation of a person using a single electrode, positioned at the forehead (position Fp1 in the International 10–20 System [21]). The game can be played in three different difficulty settings: easy, medium, and hard, each with unique scenarios, animations, sound effects and challenges. The players are ranked according to their performance on each difficulty, and are able to unlock achievements related to specific tasks in the game.

The game application is composed of several interfaces in addition to the game match itself. The main menu, which appears right after opening the application, is composed of an animated background, representing a night sky with moving clouds of various speeds and forms. In the bottom left of the screen there is the exit button, which closes the application; in the bottom right, the configuration button and the about button, which provides, respectively, various options to change in the game, such as language and sound volume; and information about the Zen Cat Dev Team. The logo of the game appears at the top, with two buttons bellow it: on the center, a big play button, followed by a golden button that leads to the achievements interface. The main interface of the application is shown on Fig. 1.

Fig. 1. Main interface.

Fig. 2. Difficulty selection interface, with the (a) easy, (b) medium, and (c) hard difficulties selected.

The difficulty selection interface (Fig. 2), which appears after clicking the play button, is composed of four main elements: in the top, the headset status, which indicates the connection and the signal strength of the BCI device (and remains in the screen when the game starts), and the title of the screen; in the bottom, a button that leads to the previous screen, the play button and the ranking button, which opens the ranking of the top 10 players for the selected difficulty; and in the center, the selected difficulty, which is represented by a cat-themed board with the name of the difficulty on the top and an image in the center that previews the corresponding difficulty scenario. The medium and hard difficulties start locked, with a lock icon above the image of the scenario, and stays so until the player beats the game at the previous difficulty. To beat the game, the player must reach a certain height of the scenario.

The game match interface is composed of four main elements: (i) the headset status bar (Fig. 3a), which indicates the current status of the headset (i.e. whether it is connected, the battery charge, and the signal strength); (ii) the height indicator (Fig. 3b), which represents the current height of the cat in relation to the total scenario's height; (iii) a clock (Fig. 3c), which indicates the remaining time to the end of the match (each game match has a fixed duration of two minutes); and (iv) a meditation bar (Fig. 3d), which shows the current meditation threshold, the player's average meditation from the last 20 s and his/her current meditation.

Fig. 3. Game match interface. (a) Headset status; (b) height indicator; (c) game clock; (d) meditation bar.

The game has three possible background scenarios, each corresponding to a difficulty setting (i.e., easy, medium and hard). The main idea is that the player starts in an urban area and moves to more peaceful locations, while his/her meditation skills increases. From the middle to the top, every scenario starts to have the same identity, as the cat is levitating into the outer space. However, each scenario has its own unique characteristics. The easy scenario (Fig. 4a) is a backyard, with grass on the floor and a fence on the background. The concept is that the cat is on an urban environment, and encounters birds and airplanes while ascending. The medium scenario (Fig. 4b), on the other hand, is closer to the nature, as the cat is near a waterfall. In this scenario, the airplanes are replaced by balloons, and different birds and insects appear. The concept of the hard scenario (Fig. 4c) is a temple, located deep in the nature and symbolizing the player's higher level of meditation skills. In contrast with the other two scenarios, which are represented in daytime, the hard scenario takes turn in night time, and have insects like dragonflies and fireflies passing by around the player.

Fig. 4. Zen Cat interface in the (a) easy, (b) medium, and (c) hard difficulty level.

All scenarios from the mid to the top starts to look alike, as the cat is leaving the atmosphere and entering in the outer space. The animations, in this case, starts with falling stars, rockets and spaceships, and become comets and alien spaceships while the player reaches higher heights. The planets are represented by balls of wool, given the cat-like theme of the game. The top of the scenario has a special theme, which contains no animations and represents the cat entering a high state of mind (Fig. 5). The game is designed so that the player only reaches this special region with an exceptionally good performance.

Each floor in the scenario also represents a difficulty progression. Each floor, for each difficulty, has a specific threshold value for the minimum average meditation that the player must maintain in order to continue ascending. The Eq. (1) that defines this threshold for each floor is:

$$T_v = B_v + F_v + F_c \tag{1}$$

In Eq. (1), T_v is the threshold value, B_v is a constant base value (defined as 40), and F_c is the floor constant (i.e., 0 for the first floor, 5 for the second, 14 for the third, 24 for the fourth, and 35 for the fifth), and F_v is the floor value and is defined in Eq. (2):

Fig. 5. Last floor of the game.

$$F_v = (5 + \text{Floor}) * \text{Diff} \tag{2}$$

In Eq. (2), Diff is a numeric value for the selected difficulty (i.e., 0 for easy, 1 for medium, and 2 for hard), and Floor is the numeric value for the current floor (i.e., 0 for the first floor, 1 for the second floor, and so on). The constant values were defined empirically.

The achievements interface is composed of a board with nine slots, representing the nine achievements that are unlocked throughout the game. When the player unlocks a new achievement by completing a special task, the empty slot corresponding to that achievement is replaced by a medal with an image engraved in its center. By clicking in the medal or in the empty slot, a pop-up screen appears with the title of the corresponding achievement and its description, with details of how to obtain it. This screen is presented in Fig. 6.

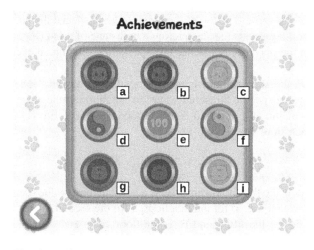

Fig. 6. Achievements interface, with all achievements (a)–(i).

The first three achievements (from left to right, top to bottom) are related to the win condition of the game, which is to reach the fourth floor (roughly 60% of the total height of the scenario), and are represented visually by the face of the cat. This also unlocks the next difficulty, if it has not been unlocked yet. The following three achievements are related to specific challenges regarding the control of the meditation value. Two of them are represented each by a half of the yin-yang symbol, and are obtained by maintaining a very high or very low average meditation. The "ThouZENd" achievement is obtained by reaching the highest possible value of meditation (i.e., 100) ten times in a single match.

Finally, the next three achievements are related to reaching the top of the scenario on each of the three difficulties of the game, which is only possible by always maintaining the average meditation above the minimum threshold (there is a small tolerance in the easy difficulty). They are also represented by the cat, but with its eyes closed and a third-eye open on its forehead. Table 2 shows each achievement individually, with its title and the description of how to obtain it.

Table 2. Game achievements

Icon	Title	Description
Figure 6a	Zen town	Win a game on the easy difficulty
Figure 6b	Zen mountain	Win a game on the medium difficulty
Figure 6c	Zen temple	Win a game on the hard difficulty
Figure 6d	Zen disaster	Keep your average meditation below 15 for 10 s
Figure 6e	ThouZENd	Reach 100 meditation ten times
Figure 6f	Zen master	Keep your average meditation above 85 for 10 s
Figure 6g	Revelation	Reach the Beyond on the easy difficulty
Figure 6h	Ascension	Reach the Beyond on the medium difficulty
Figure 6i	Nirvana	Reach the Beyond on the hard difficulty

The ranking interface, which is accessed through the difficulty selection interface, shows the top 10 players with highest scores of each difficulty. The score of a player is defined by three factors: the highest height that the player reached; the average meditation value throughout the entire match; and the performance score. Players are first ranked by the performance score. If the performance scores are equal, the tie is break using the highest height. If they are also equal, the highest average meditation will decide the tie.

The performance score is represented by a scale that ranges from one to five stars, and is calculated by the maximum height that the player reached (each floor counts for one star) and the current height in which s/he ended the game (minus one star for each floor below the highest floor). The titles of the scores are "Awful...", "Bad", "Good", "Great", and "Perfect!", each having a corresponding icon of the face of the cat, that goes from a sad to an excited expression, and a corresponding number of stars. Figure 7 shows these corresponding icons.

Fig. 7. Performance score representations.

Finally, the post-game interface, which is shown after the time limit ends and the game is over, presents the result of the match, with three main elements: the maximum height that the player reached; his/her average meditation; and the performance score, with its corresponding icon and a title. This interface also has two buttons: one for returning to the difficulty selection screen, and one for playing again. Figure 8 shows an example of this interface.

Fig. 8. Post-game result interface.

4   Evaluation

In order to evaluate the user interaction and the game design, an evaluation study was conducted with volunteer participants, as part of a larger controlled experiment. The subjects played the game in its current version after several months of development and iterative testing, and qualitative data regarding their interaction with the system was collected. The evaluation was performed in a timespan of two weeks and helped gathering important data and insights regarding the development of meditation-based neurofeedback games.

4.1 Subjects and Procedure

In total, 16 volunteer subjects participated in the evaluation, being 14 male and two female. Their age ranged from 22 to 35 years. They were all graduate or undergraduate students, and the majority had never used a BCI system before. Figure 9 shows all participants, placed at a random order, playing the game in one of the sessions of the evaluation, while Table 3 provides demographic data about the participants.

Fig. 9. All 16 participants of the evaluation.

Table 3. Demographic data of the subjects

ID	Age	Gender	Scholarship	BCI knowledge
S01	25	Male	Graduate	Know and not used
S02	24	Male	Graduate	Don't know
S03	24	Male	Graduate	Don't know
S04	24	Male	Graduate	Know and used
S05	25	Male	Graduate	Don't know
S06	24	Male	Graduate	Know and used
S07	25	Female	Graduate	Don't know
S08	32	Male	Graduate	Don't know
S09	25	Male	Graduate	Don't know
S10	20	Male	Undergraduate	Know and used
S11	23	Male	Undergraduate	Don't know
S12	23	Male	Graduate	Know and not used
S13	35	Male	PhD	Don't know
S14	22	Male	Graduate	Know and not used
S15	25	Male	Graduate	Know and used
S16	24	Female	Graduate	Don't know

Each subject participated in three individual evaluation sessions and played four consecutive matches of the game, being the first one for calibration only and excluded from the evaluation. At the end of the session, the participant filled out a questionnaire and answered a short semi-structured interview regarding the game experience. In the first session, participants filled a demographic form and watched a short gameplay video while a researcher explained how the game works and how to play it with the BCI device. All matches were set to the easy mode as default.

All sessions were conducted in a closed, silent and climatized room, where only the subject and a researcher were present. Also, every subject used the same computer and the same BCI equipment for all game matches. All sessions were also recorded, with the written consent of the subjects, by two cameras positioned at the front and the lateral of the subjects. The desktop screen was also recorded. The videos were analyzed after the evaluation in order to acquire more details about the interaction. An example of a recorded video from the evaluation is shown in Fig. 10.

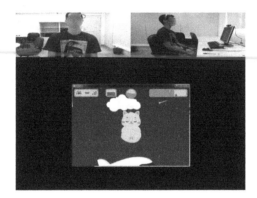

Fig. 10. Recorded video frame from the evaluation.

4.2   Results

The results were analyzed based on the observations from the researchers, the video analysis of the experimental sessions, the data from the applied questionnaires, and the answers provided by the subjects in the semi-structured interview conducted at the end of each session.

Regarding the employed strategies by the subjects, some were employed more frequently across them. The most common strategy was to close the eyes and to try to mentally concentrate in a thought or a physiological phenomenon, such as the breath or the heart beat frequency. In general, subjects tried to alternate between the employed strategies even when the current one has shown good results, in order to test the result in the game. Other strategies included trying to sleep, thinking about calm places, music or memories, and paying attention to the sounds of the game. Performance-wise, most players realized relatively soon that closing their eyes was the most efficient strategy, as they noticed that, as soon as their eyes were opened, their meditation would decrease almost instantly. Secondarily, focusing on the breath appears to have the higher meditation outcome. Surprisingly, trying to think about nothing in particular was the strategy with the lowest performance among the employed ones.

In relation to the difficulty of the game, the majority of players, in the first sessions of the evaluation, thought that the game was hard, even on the easy mode. Although this opinion persisted for some subjects in the later sessions as they were still trying to find a good strategy, most of them thought that the game became easier with each session, as they were able to reach higher scores and maintain the average meditation higher for longer periods of time. When looking at each session individually, however, subjects usually had a slightly higher performance in the first match, while it decreased over time and usually had its lower scores in the last two matches, probably due to fatigue effects. This difference is shown in Fig. 11a. However, the performance per subject shows that, despite the difficulty of the game, players in general achieved an average meditation above or close to 60 across all three sessions, which may be considered slightly elevated. The boxplots in Fig. 11b present these values.

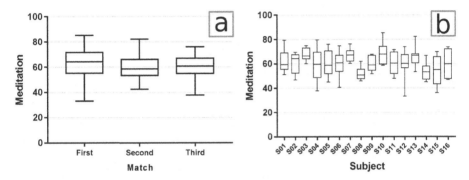

Fig. 11. (a) Boxplots of the average performance per match of the 16 subjects; (b) Boxplots of the subjects' average performance in the three matches of all three sessions.

Still regarding the difficulty of the game, some subjects reported that a few specific sounds were relaxing, while others could have disrupted the meditation control. Examples of these sounds were the birds and the waterfall sounds, which the subjects deemed as tranquilizing and relaxing, and the airplane sound, which many subjects considered annoying and disruptive. These sounds may have played a major role on the subjects' performance and the result of the game matches, as many of them played the game with their eyes closed, focusing only on the sound effects.

In relation to the game's graphics and visual design, all subjects rated it as satisfying and stated that the game's theme was in accordance with the meditation control, i.e., meditate in order to help the cat to levitate. In general, most players did not report feeling any discomfort regarding the use of the headset device. However, there had been cases in which subjects commented that the device made them feel uncomfortable, as it kept a pressure on the right lobe and limited the movement of the head, as some movements, such as inclining the head forward, might cause a displacement of the device on the head and, as a result, increase the noise on the collected and processed signal.

5 Discussion

The evaluation allowed drawing many insights about the development of BCI-based games, especially those based on the meditation control signal. By analyzing how the subjects played the game using their state of mental relaxation, several adjustments and updates could be made to complement the game in its current state.

As stated in Sect. 4, some participants reported that the game seemed too hard, especially in the first sessions of the evaluation. There is an intrinsic challenge on balancing the difficulty of a BCI-based game, as each person may have biological differences between their cognitive states. In the case of the Zen Cat, the challenge is a bit harder as there are five difficulty progressions within each difficulty itself: the minimum threshold that the player must keep his average meditation above increases each time the avatar levitates one fifth of the scenario's total height. This complexity was made in order to force the player to increase and maintain his average meditation throughout the entire match, and make it a challenge to reach the top even in the easy difficulty. The chosen strategy was to implement a linear function (Eq. (1)) based both on the selected difficulty and the current height of the player. The increase is more evident in harder difficulties, as the base value of the current floor is added to a constant, then added to another constant multiplied by a number that represents the difficulty (zero for easy, one for medium and two for hard). The resulting values for the easy, medium and hard difficulties are, respectively, 40, 45 and 50, for the 1st floor; 45, 51 and 57, for the 2nd floor; 54, 61 and 68, for the 3rd floor; 64, 72 and 80, for the 4th floor; and 75, 84 and 93, for the 5th floor. Although it seemed hard for the majority of players in the early development tests, the idea is that the player progresses through time and increases his/her potential in order to unlock the achievements related to reaching the top of the scenario.

Regarding the strategies employed by the subjects to play the game, it is interesting to notice that the majority tried to play at least once with their eyes closed, before realizing that their performance was increased when closing them. This is particularly important in the context of meditation-based games, as it suggests that auditory cues and sound effects may play a major role in those games in contrast to the visual design. Many subjects suggested that it would be interesting to have more sounds in the game, especially to indicate whether the cat was moving up or down. They stated that, after playing a few matches, they could get clues of whether their strategies were working by the sound of the animated elements, as the sound of the birds, for example, appear only on the first floor, while the airplane only appears at the second one. The sounds of the game could be applied both to try to disrupts one's meditation, thus increasing the difficulty of the game, or to create a more relaxing atmosphere and help the player to better meditate.

The subjects' comments on the gameplay using the meditation signal were also interesting. A few participants suggested that the meditation could be employed as a secondary or passive control, to change some characteristic of the game without directly controlling it. These suggestions were based, according to the interviews, on the difficulty that these participants had on controlling the meditation signal. As stated in Sect. 4, the strategy with the lowest resulting performance was trying to think of nothing, clearing the mind or simply trying to focus on relaxing. This may seem a contradictory idea for the subjects, as the idea of the game is to mentally meditate, but intentionally trying to focus in doing so may be more mentally demanding than to just try to remember a calm song or a relaxing scenario. Some sort of background music, in this case, could have helped the subjects, as they could, even unintentionally, focus on the relaxing music in order to better meditate.

The employment of the BCI control signal as a secondary form of control, as suggested by some participants, is in accordance with others works in the literature, such as the game developed by Cho and Lee [6], described in Sect. 2. Given the technology limitations, the constant biological oscillation in the signals and the learning curve of the players to control the brain waves, it makes sense that specific brain signals could possibly be employed as a complementary control rather than a direct control interface. Also, with more advanced BCI devices, multimodal BCI games could employ two or more control signals. Both of these controls could be used to actively control the game, or one could be used as the active control while the other would be a complementary one. Furthermore, BCI control could also be employed to enhance the typical gaming experience provided by traditional controllers, such as mouse, keyboard and joystick.

Given that the game is open-source and its logging feature, it could be easily adapted not only to other BCI devices, but also to employ other control signals, such as attention or motor imagery, and used as a tool for scientific research in the field. The game could also be adapted to other platforms or compiled to other operating systems – given that the target platform has the necessary support for the respective BCI device – thus increasing the number of applications and research areas to which the game could be employed.

5.1 Limitations

The limitations are related to the evaluation and the game itself. Regarding the evaluation, the opinion of the players on the design and gameplay of the game could have been influenced by the novelty of the control scheme. In relation to the limitations of game itself, it is available for the computer platform alone, and adapted for only one BCI device, i.e., the NeuroSky MindWave.

6 Conclusion

In this work, the development process and the evaluation of the Zen Cat game was presented. The game uses the players' brain waves to measure their level of meditation and employs it as its main control scheme. The evaluation and its results are discussed, as well as the implications and the design challenges of developing a BCI-based computer game. The results of the evaluation shows that the game can indeed be entertaining, despite being solely controlled by the player's brain waves. This work may help game designers and developers in the implementation of future BCI-based games, especially the ones based on meditation. Also, the application could be employed to conduct scientific research on the field of BCI.

In future works, the game could be adapted to employ other control signals, in contrast with the level of meditation. Also, the game could be adapted for other BCI devices, such as the Emotiv Epoc, and other platforms, such as mobile devices.

Acknowledgments. This work was supported by the Physical Artifacts of Interaction Research Group (PAIRG) at the Federal University of Rio Grande do Norte (UFRN), and partially funded by the Brazilian National Council of Scientific and Technological Development (CNPq), under grants 130158/2015-1 and 146931/2017-3. We also would like to thank by resources of the PAIRG's Laboratory of Physical and Physiological Computing (PAIRG L2PC) at UFRN, and the subjects who volunteered to participate in the evaluation of the Zen Cat.

References

1. Allison, B.: The I of BCIs: next generation interfaces for brain–computer interface systems that adapt to individual users. In: Jacko, Julie A. (ed.) HCI 2009. LNCS, vol. 5611, pp. 558–568. Springer, Heidelberg (2009). https://doi.org/10.1007/978-3-642-02577-8_61
2. Antle, A.N., Chesick, L., Levisohn, A., Sridharan, S.K., Tan, P.: Using Neurofeedback to teach self-regulation to children living in Poverty. In: IDC 2015, pp. 119–128. ACM (2015)
3. Bento, A.A., Miranda, L.C.: Steering all: infinite racing game controlled by haar cascade through OpenCV. In: SVR 2015, pp. 245–254. IEEE (2015)
4. Bingham, P.M., Bates, J.H.T., Thompson-Figueroa, J., Lahiri, T.: A breath biofeedback computer game for children with cystic fibrosis. Clin. Pediatr. **49**(4), 337–342 (2010)
5. Bos, D.P.O., Reuderink, B., Laar, B., Gürkök, H., Mühl, C., Poe, M., Nijholt, A., Heylen, D.: Brain-computer interfacing and games. In: Tan, D., Nijholt, A. (eds.) Brain-Computer Interfaces: Applying Our Minds to Human-Computer Interaction, pp. 149–178. Springer, Heidelberg (2010). https://doi.org/10.1007/978-1-84996-272-8_10
6. Cho, O.H., Lee, W.H.: BCI sensor based environment changing system for immersion of 3D game. Int. J. Distri. Sens. Netw. **10**(5), 1–8 (2014)
7. Choo, A., May, A.: Virtual mindfulness meditation: virtual reality and electroencephalography for health gamification. In: GEM 2014, pp. 1–3. IEEE (2014)
8. Coulton, P., Wylie, C.G., Bamford, W.: Brain interaction for mobile games. In: MindTrek 2011, pp. 37–44. ACM (2011)
9. Fatourechi, M., Bashashati, A., Ward, R.K., Birch, G.E.: EMG and EOG artifacts in brain computer interface systems: a survey. Clin. Neurophysiol. **118**, 480–494 (2007)
10. Ferreira, A.L.S., Marciano, J.N., Miranda, L.C., Miranda, E.E.C.: Understanding and proposing a design rationale of digital games based on brain-computer interface: results of the AdmiralMind battleship study. SBC J. Interact. Syst. **5**(1), 3–15 (2014)
11. Ferreira, A.L.S., Miranda, L.C., Miranda, E.E.C., Sakamoto, S.G.: A survey of interactive systems based on brain-computer interfaces. SBC J. 3D Interact. Syst. **4**(1), 3–13 (2013)
12. Gervasi, O., Magni, R., Macellari, S.: A brain computer interface for enhancing the communication of people with severe impairment. In: Murgante, B., et al. (eds.) ICCSA 2014. LNCS, vol. 8584, pp. 709–721. Springer, Cham (2014). https://doi.org/10.1007/978-3-319-09153-2_53
13. Gürkök, H., Hakvoort, G., Poel, M., Nijholt, A.: User expectations and experiences of a speech and thought controlled computer game. In: ACE 2011, pp. 1–6. ACM (2011)
14. Hendricks, J.C., Semwal, S.K.: EEG: the missing gap between controllers and gestures. WCECS **2014**, 1–6 (2014)

15. Jadav, G.M., Vrankic, M., Vlahinic, S.: Monitoring cerebral processing of gustatory stimulation and perception using emotiv epoc. In: MIPRO 2015, pp. 643–645. IEEE (2015)
16. Jiang, H., Johnstone, S.J.: A preliminary multiple case report of neurocognitive training for children with AD/HD in China. SAGE Open 5(2), 1–13 (2015)
17. Laar, B., Gürkök, H., Bos, D.P.O., Poel, M., Nijholt, A.: Experiencing BCI control in a popular computer game. IEEE Trans. Comput. Intell. AI Games 5(2), 176–184 (2013)
18. Liarokapis, F., Vourvopoulos, A., Ene, A.: Examining user experiences through a multimodal BCI Puzzle game. In: iV 2015, pp. 488–493. IEEE (2015)
19. Miranda, L.C., Hornung, H.H., Baranauskas, M.C.C.: Adjustable interactive rings for iDTV. IEEE Trans. Consum. Electron. 56(3), 1988–1996 (2010)
20. Nicolas-Alonso, L.F., Gomez-Gil, J.: Brain computer interfaces. Rev. Sens. 12(2), 1211–1279 (2012)
21. Niedermeyer, E., Silva, F.L.: Electroencephalography: Basic Principles, Clinical Applications, and Related Fields. Lippincott Williams & Wilkins, Philadelphia (2004)
22. Ratti, E., Waninger, S., Berka, C., Ruffini, G., Verma, A.: Comparison of medical and consumer wireless EEG systems for use in clinical trials. Front. Hum. Neurosci. 11, 398 (2017)
23. Reuderink, B.: Games and brain-computer interfaces: the state of the art. Technical report TR-CTIT-08-81, University of Twente (2008)
24. Rogers, J.M., Johnstone, S.J., Aminov, A., Donnelly, J., Wilson, P.H.: Test-retest reliability of a single-channel, wireless EEG system. Int. J. Psychophysiol. 106, 87–96 (2016)
25. Uriarte, I.L.O., Garcia-Zapirain, B., Garcia-Chimeno, Y.: Game design to measure reflexes and attention based on biofeedback multi-sensor interaction. Sensors 15(3), 6520–6548 (2015)
26. Vasiljevic, G.A.M., Miranda, L.C., Miranda, E.E.C.: A case study of MasterMind chess: comparing mouse/keyboard interaction with kinect-based gestural interface. Adv. Hum.-Comput. Interact. 2016, 1–10 (2016)
27. Wollmann, T., Abtahi, F., Eghdam, A., Seoane, F., Lindecrantz, K., Haag, M., Koch, S.: User-centred design and usability evaluation of a heart rate variability biofeedback game. IEEE Access 4, 5531–5539 (2016)

Construction and Application of a Probabilistic Atlas of 3D Landmark Points for Initialization of Hippocampus Mesh Models in Brain MR Images

Katia Maria Poloni$^{(\boxtimes)}$ ⓘ, Carlos Henrique Villa Pinto ⓘ, Breno da Silveira Souza ⓘ, and Ricardo José Ferrari ⓘ

Department of Computing, Federal University of São Carlos,
Rod. Washington Luís, Km 235, Mailbox 676, São Carlos, SP 13565-905, Brazil
{katia.poloni,rferrari}@ufscar.br
http://bipgroup.dc.ufscar.br

Abstract. The magnetic resonance (MR) imaging has become an indispensable tool for diagnosis and study of various brain diseases. To perform an accurate diagnosis of a brain disease and monitor its evolution and treatment outcomes, a neuroradiologist often needs to measure the volume and assess the changes of shapes in specific brain structures along a series of MR images. In general, brain structures are manually delineated by a radiologist and, therefore, they highly dependend on the professional's skills. In this study, we proposed the construction of a probabilistic atlas consisting of 3D landmark points automatically detected in a set of MR images. Also, we aimed at investigate its applicability to guide the initial positioning of mesh models based on the deformation of the hippocampus in brain MR images. The normalized Dice Similarity Coefficient (DSC) and the Hausdorff Average Distance (HAD) were used for the quantitative performance evaluation of the proposed method. The results showed that the average values obtained by our atlas-based landmark approach were significantly better (DSC = 0.74/0.70, HAD = 0.70/0.73, for left and right hippocampus, respectively) than our previous initial approaches, such as the template-based landmark (DSC = 0.65/0.61, HAD = 0.88/0.91) and the affine transformation (DSC = 0.58/0.53, HAD = 1.10/1.22).

Keywords: Atlas of 3D landmarks · Deformable mesh models
Alzheimer's disease · MRI

1 Introduction

Magnetic resonance imaging (MRI) has become an important imaging modality to help radiologists in the diagnosis and study of various neurological diseases, such as the Alzheimer's disease (AD) and multiple sclerosis. This is mainly due

© Springer International Publishing AG, part of Springer Nature 2018
O. Gervasi et al. (Eds.): ICCSA 2018, LNCS 10960, pp. 310–322, 2018.
https://doi.org/10.1007/978-3-319-95162-1_21

to the high sensitivity of MRI, which provides images with superior contrast and exquisite anatomical details [1].

For accurate diagnosis of a neurological disease, a medical specialist (radiologist) often needs to measure the volume and evaluate changes in the shape of specific brain structures over a series of magnetic resonance (MR) images. As an example, we can mention the assessment of volumetric reduction and shape alterations that occur in the hippocampus and corpus callosum of patients with AD [2].

In the last decades, deformable mesh models have demonstrated significant success in several applications of medical image processing [3]. The primary advantage of this approach is the ability to incorporate the mean structural shape that is going to be segmented in the image into the mesh model, making it less susceptible to noise and to situations in which the local image contrast is low [4]. More sophisticated techniques, a priori, use the knowledge about the neighboring regions of the analyzed structure and include, for example, adaptive spatial constraints on the deformable model [5] or use atlases built from specific populations [6] to improve model adaptation.

The success of deformable mesh models in image segmentation highly depends on the initial positioning of the mesh [3]. The mesh must be placed near the target structure in the image to be successful in the segmentation task. In general, this is a semi-automatic procedure which demands manual landmarks written in the image by a radiologist. However, for tasks such as clinical trials, this method can be prohibitive considering the large number of MR images to be processed. Also, a proper mesh positioning can be problematic for images containing a large number of structures close to one another.

Within this context, some studies in the literature have been using landmark points[1] as anchors for the positioning of the models [7–9]. In these studies, the landmark points (landmarks) and their respective descriptors are computed for both template and clinical images and then matched against each other. However, in this type of approach, herein named template-based landmark positioning, the landmarks detected in the template or clinical image may not represent stable points (or hold anatomical distinctions) across a population and, therefore, the mesh positioning may fail to yield a proper placement.

In this study, we proposed the construction of a probabilistic atlas which automatically detects 3D landmark points in MR images. In addition, we suggested that it can be used for the initial positioning of deformable mesh models of the hippocampi of the brain. The probabilistic atlas is intended to provide quantitative information about the stability of landmarks on intersubject variations. Therefore, by weighting the landmarks considering their spatial occurrence (stable points) across an image dataset of healthy subjects and using them to match points detected in a clinical image, we expect to obtain a more efficient

---

[1] The term "landmark point" or "salient point" refers to an image point that stands locally due to its specific characteristic (e.g., high degree of curvature) and is usually visible to the naked eye. It does not necessarily represent an anatomical reference point that would be marked by an expert, although this is usually the case.

and less noisy transformation for the positioning of the hippocampus meshes. To the best of our knowledge, this is the first time that a probabilistic atlas of 3D landmark points is proposed and used for the positioning of mesh models in MR images.

The study is organized as follows: Sect. 2 shows the image datasets and the methodology, followed by results and discussions in Sect. 3 and conclusions in Sect. 4.

2   Materials and Methods

2.1   Image Datasets

The image datasets used in this study consist of 3D clinical MR images and triangle meshes representing the hippocampus, described as follows.

NAC Brain Atlas. This dataset was developed by the Neuroimage Analysis Center[2] (NAC). It consisted of a set of 149 3D triangle meshes, each one representing a distinctive brain structure, including the left (LH) and right hippocampus (RH). The meshes were spatially aligned to a T1-weighted (T1-w) MRI image (reference or fixed image), with an isotropic resolution of 1 mm and size of $256 \times 256 \times 256$ voxels.

IXI Dataset. The "Information eXtraction from Images[3] (IXI)" dataset consists of clinical brain MR images (T1-w, T2-w, PD-w, Magnetic Resonance Angiography – MRA, and Diffusion Tensor Imaging – DTI), acquired from three different hospitals in London – Hammersmith Hospital (HH), Guy's Hospital (GH) and Institute of Psychiatry (IoP). A total of 185 images from the HH and 322 from the GH hospitals had the size of $256 \times 256 \times 150$ and resolution of $0.94 \times 0.94 \times 1.2$, while the ones from the IoP hospital (74 images) had the same characteristics as the images from the HH and GH hospitals, except for the size of $256 \times 256 \times 146$. Images from this dataset were used to construct the probabilistic atlas of 3D landmark points.

EADC-ADNI. The image dataset of the European Alzheimer's Disease Consortium – Alzheimer's Disease Neuroimaging Initiative Harmonized Protocol (EADC-ADNI HarP)[4] resulted from a project started in 2010, aiming to create a harmonized protocol for segmentation of hippocampal subfields. For this study, we used 129 T1-w RM images with the LH and RH segmented by five specialists using the HarP protocol. In addition to the segmented images, the EADC-ADNI also provides instructions to download the ADNI images and the studies describing the harmonization protocol developed [10].

---

[2] http://nac.spl.harvard.edu.
[3] http://www.brain-development.org.
[4] http://www.hippocampal-protocol.net.

2.2   Image Preprocessing

Previous to the atlas construction, all MR images were preprocessed through the following steps: (a) image denoising using the Non-Local Means (NLM) technique [11], (b) biasfield correction using the N4-ITK technique [12], (c) MR image intensity standardization [13], (d) registration of the affine transformation of all images to the NAC reference image [14] and (e) brain extraction [15].

2.3   Detector of 3D Landmark Points

The detector of 3D landmark point used in this study [16] was based on the phase congruency (PC) model proposed by Morrone et al. [17]. In this model, image landmarks are detected at points where the Fourier components are in maximum moment of phase congruency, instead of searching for them at points of maximum intensity gradient changes. In [16], the PC measure was computed via convolution of the original image with a bank of log-Gabor filters and further used to implement the detector of 3D landmark point.

2.3.1   PC-Based Landmark Detector

The PC-based landmark detector used the relationship of the eigenvalues computed from local 3×3 matrices of second-order PC moments to detect 3D landmark points in MR images. It had the advantage over methods using gradient-based optimization, which are less sensitive to image contrast and intensity variations. If there is a prominent image characteristic at position x, the direction of the principal axis of dispersion of the local matrix of second-order PC moments will indicate its dominant orientation, and the dispersions in the perpendicular axes will evidence the significance of this characteristic in 3D. If all three values are high, this means that the salient feature in x has a strong 3D component associated with it and therefore x is a potential landmark point to be considered. This situation usually occurs in corners and high curvature points of the 3D image.

2.3.2   Landmark Descriptor

The landmark descriptor used in this study [16] was a 3D adaptation of the shape contexts technique [18] initially proposed to quantify similarities in shapes and to find corresponding points between 2D objects. In our case, the shape contexts technique relied on the 3D PC maps to represent the shape information of the object. Also, it used a log-spherical histogram to split the image space around each landmark regarding η_r relative radial distances, η_a relative azimuth angles and η_e relative elevation angles. The accumulated values in the log-spherical histogram bins expressed the feature significance of the edges placed inside them.

2.3.3   Matching of Landmark Descriptors

The $\chi 2$ distance was used as a dissimilarity function [16] to measure the similarity between pairs of descriptor vectors. This metric was particularly appropriate because it considers the differences between histogram bin sizes. Therefore, small differences between values from larger bins (which typically accumulate larger values) result in a smaller distance, different from the small difference between values of smaller bins (which accumulate small values) [18]. After computing the $\chi2$ distance of descriptor vectors of a pair of landmark points, we decided to verify whether there was a correspondence between the points by using the "forward-backward" nearest neighbor. In this case, a match between the two descriptor vectors h_1 and h_2 would exist only if h_1 was the nearest neighbor of h_2 and h_2 was the nearest neighbor of h_1.

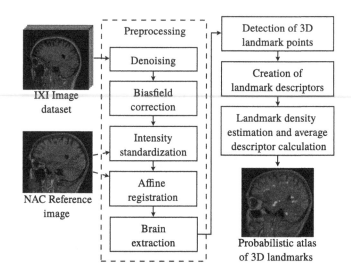

Fig. 1. Steps for construction of the probabilistic atlas of 3D landmark points

2.4 Construction of the Probabilistic Atlas of 3D Landmark Points of the Hippocampal Regions

The probabilistic atlas of 3D landmark points, illustrated in Fig. 1, was built using every image from the IXI dataset (referred here as training images) after the pre-processing stage and detection of 3D landmarks (Sects. 2.2 and 2.3, respectively). The atlas construction started by estimating the probability density function (pdf), $p(x) : X \subset \mathbb{N}^3 \longrightarrow [0, 1]$, representing the spatial density of all detected landmarks in the training images. The pdf estimation was performed using the non-parametric Manifold Parzen Windows (MPW) estimator [19], which represented a $p(x)$ of a set of l d-dimensional samples by a finite mixture of diagonal Gaussian kernels as

$$p(x) = \frac{1}{l} \sum_{i=1}^{l} \frac{1}{\sqrt{(2\pi)^d |\Sigma_i|}} \exp\left(-\frac{1}{2}\Delta(x)\right), \tag{1}$$

where $\Sigma_i = \Sigma_{\mathcal{K}_i} + \sigma^2 I_3$ is the covariance matrix of the ith kernel component and $\Delta(\boldsymbol{x})^2 = (\boldsymbol{x} - \boldsymbol{x}_i)^t \, \Sigma_i^{-1} \, (\boldsymbol{x} - \boldsymbol{x}_i)$ is the Mahalanobis distance. The first component, $\Sigma_{\mathcal{K}_i}$, of the covariance matrix Σ_i is computed as

$$\Sigma_{\mathcal{K}_i} = \frac{\sum_{j=1...l, j\neq i} \mathcal{K}\,(\boldsymbol{x}_j, \boldsymbol{x}_i)\,(\boldsymbol{x}_j - \boldsymbol{x}_i)^t\,(\boldsymbol{x}_j - \boldsymbol{x}_i)}{\sum_{j=1...l, j\neq i} \mathcal{K}\,(\boldsymbol{x}_j, \boldsymbol{x}_i)}, \qquad (2)$$

where $\mathcal{K}\,(\boldsymbol{x}, \boldsymbol{x}_i) = G_{\mu=\boldsymbol{x}_i, \Sigma=\sigma I_3}(\boldsymbol{x}_i)$ is a Gaussian function which associates an influence weight to each sample $\boldsymbol{x}$ in the neighborhood of $\boldsymbol{x}_i$. This neighborhood can be limited to k_{cov} samples. The second component, $\sigma^2 I_3$, of Σ_i is a 3×3 isotropic Gaussian added to $\Sigma_{\mathcal{K}_i}$ to avoid ill-conditioned inverse problems.

The density calculation, at each point in space, could be simplified if the combination of Gaussian functions was restricted to only k_{eval} components, corresponding to the closest k_{eval} neighbor points. In this study, we used the MPW estimator from the Insight Segmentation and Registration Toolkit (ITK) library [20]. Samples consisted up of the locations of outgoing points $\{\boldsymbol{x}\}$ and the default values of the MPW parameters remained unchanged, which, in this case, are: $\sigma^2 = 1$, $k_{cov} = 50$, and $k_{eval} = 5$.

The aforementioned process resulted in a volumetric image in which each voxel intensity was proportional to the greater or lesser presence of landmark points projected at that location along the training images, as illustrated in Fig. 2. After the pdf estimation, a mean descriptor $\overline{h}$ was calculated for each maximal position of $p(\boldsymbol{x})$. Mean descriptors were used to represent the stable 3D landmark points of the atlas.

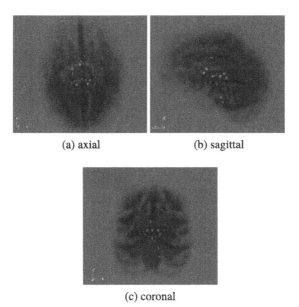

(a) axial   (b) sagittal

(c) coronal

Fig. 2. Two dimensional projections of the resulting probabilistic atlas of 3D landmark points (red dot clouds) (Color figure online)

2.5   Proposed Method for Initialization of the Mesh Models of Hippocampus

The complete schematic of the proposed mesh model initialization for automatic segmentation of the hippocampus in MR images is illustrated in Fig. 3. Our method started with the image registration of affine transformation of a clinical T1-w image (moving image) to the template T1-w image (fixed image from the NAC dataset), which was already aligned to the proposed probabilistic atlas and the hippocampus meshes. Then, landmark points were detected and their descriptors were computed from the clinical image, as described in Sects. 2.3.1 and 2.3.2. Subsequently, the matching algorithm described in Sect. 2.3.3 was used to find as many correct matches as possible between the clinical image landmarks and the ones from the probabilistic atlas, while avoiding both wrong and missed matches. Finally, from the set of pairs of 3D landmark points, $\{(x_{1,m}, x_{2,m})\}$, representing the matching point locations, a deformable B-spline transformation [21] was estimated. The transformation, which can be represented by a deformation vector field, mapped the spatial locations of the points $\{x_{1,m}\}$ to $\{x_{2,m}\}$ with minimal error, interpolating values to the rest of the vertices of the reference model. In this study, the probability density of each point in the atlas was used as a weighting factor by the B-spline transformation. Therefore, high-density points will contribute more to the mesh positioning than others with lower density. The estimated transformation was applied to the hippocampus mesh vertices to move them to a position and configurate them in a shape that was as close as possible to the structure of interest in the target image.

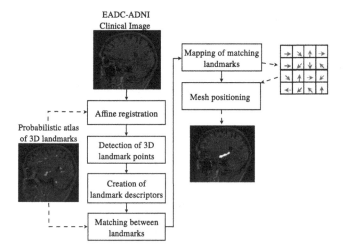

Fig. 3. Schematic of the proposed method for initialization of mesh models for automatic segmentation of the hippocampus in MR images

2.6 Assessment Results

The effectiveness of our method was quantitatively assessed by measuring the overlapping between the binary images of the ground-truth mesh and the mesh after positioning using the Dice Similarity Coefficient (DSC) and the Hausdorff average distance (HAD) between them. The HAD is defined as the average of all minimum distances with any negative distance set to zero since they indicate overlapping regions.

This study aimed to place the hippocampus meshes correctly for further adaptation and not achieve the final segmentation. Therefore because the ground-truth meshes differed in volume, the DSC was always less than the unit, even for the best possible case in which the meshes overlapped entirely with each other. For this reason, we normalized each DSC value by dividing it by the maximum possible DSC value it could assume for the two corresponding meshes.

For a thorough analysis, the results of all 129 processed images from the EADC-ADNI dataset were stratified into four groups: Normal Cognitive (NC), Mild Cognitive Impairment (MCI), Late Mild Cognitive Impairment (LMCI) and AD. Also, DSC and HAD metrics were computed separately for both LH and RH structures. The template-based technique proposed in [16] was used for comparison with our new approach.

3 Results and Discussions

In a previous study [16], we developed a technique for the initialization of deformable models with the same 3D PC-based landmark point detector used in this study. The method, which was tested only on synthetic and artificially deformed MR images, used the corresponding landmarks detected in the template and an MR (or synthetic) image to estimate a non-rigid B-spline transformation, which was further used to place the hippocampus and corpus callosum meshes into the image. Different from [16], this had an atlas of 3D landmark points to help to identifying the most stable points in clinical MR images. Therefore, to achieve the positioning of the hippocampus meshes in a clinical image, we first matched the landmark points of the atlas to landmarks extracted from the clinical image and then, considering the matched points and their corresponding density values in the atlas as weight factors, we estimated a deformable B-spline transformation for the positioning of the hippocampus meshes. In addition, we tested our new approach using clinical MR images of healthy, MCI, LMCI and AD patients and compared the results with affine and our previous template-based landmark methods.

3.1 Probabilistic Atlas of 3D Landmark Points of Brain Images

The proposed probabilistic atlas of 3D landmark points in Fig. 2, constructed from brain MR images of healthy patients, demonstrated to be effective in providing the location of stable landmarks across the images. By examining the atlas, many critical landmarks can be found in the ventricular system of the brain. Moreover, shown in the axial and coronal views, Figs. 2(a) and (c), the landmark points are symmetrically displaced around about the midsagittal plane, i.e., they have a high degree of hemispheric symmetry. As discussed in [22], the symmetry and consistency of landmarks are useful attributes that should be considered when assessing the robustness of a feature detector. In our case, the fact that our atlas has a symmetrical landmark distribution may benefit the positioning of the hippocampus meshes.

3.2   Positioning of 3D Triangular Hippocampus Meshes

The experimental results for positioning the 3D triangles hippocampus meshes are summarized in Tables 1 and 2. As can be noticed, the atlas-based landmark approach provided the best results (the highest average DSC and the lowest average HAD values) for all cases (with and without population stratification) and both hippocampi. Although, on average, DSC and HAD metrics had negative correlation with each other, some cases may not consider that these two meshes (template and ground-truth) have different volumes. Therefore, in cases whose meshes are entirely overlapped (i.e. with the same maximum DSC values), we may still have two different HAD values.

Table 1. Normalized DSC results for the positioning of the left (LH) and right (RH) hippocampus using affine transformation and template- and atlas-based landmark mapping

Patients (n)	Normalized DSC (Avg ± SD)					
	Affine transformation		Template-based		Atlas-based	
	LH	RH	LH	RH	LH	RH
All (129)	0.55 ± 0.18	0.50 ± 0.18	0.59 ± 0.14	0.56 ± 0.14	0.72 ± 0.12	0.67 ± 0.12
CN (42)	0.58 ± 0.15	0.53 ± 0.16	0.60 ± 0.13	0.58 ± 0.13	0.72 ± 0.09	0.68 ± 0.10
LMCI (17)	0.57 ± 0.14	0.51 ± 0.12	0.65 ± 0.11	0.61 ± 0.12	**0.74 ± 0.12**	**0.70 ± 0.10**
MCI (26)	0.57 ± 0.21	0.48 ± 0.22	0.61 ± 0.13	0.55 ± 0.14	0.74 ± 0.11	0.67 ± 0.13
AD (44)	0.49 ± 0.20	0.47 ± 0.18	0.56 ± 0.16	0.53 ± 0.15	0.70 ± 0.15	0.64 ± 0.14

Table 2. HAD results for the positioning of the left (LH) and right (RH) hippocampus using affine transformation and template- and atlas-based landmark mapping

Patients (n)	HAD (Avg ± SD)					
	Affine transformation		Template-based		Atlas-based	
	LH	RH	LH	RH	LH	RH
All (129)	1.37 ± 0.85	1.45 ± 0.88	1.08 ± 0.48	1.12 ± 0.53	0.82 ± 0.41	0.86 ± 0.42
CN (42)	1.10 ± 0.56	1.22 ± 0.73	0.98 ± 0.41	0.99 ± 0.51	**0.70 ± 0.30**	**0.73 ± 0.37**
LMCI (17)	1.16 ± 0.46	1.27 ± 0.49	0.88 ± 0.30	0.91 ± 0.38	0.72 ± 0.30	0.74 ± 0.26
MCI (26)	1.37 ± 0.85	1.63 ± 1.11	1.06 ± 0.42	1.18 ± 0.57	0.79 ± 0.29	0.92 ± 0.42
AD (44)	1.72 ± 1.07	1.64 ± 0.92	1.28 ± 0.58	1.29 ± 0.54	0.98 ± 0.54	1.00 ± 0.47

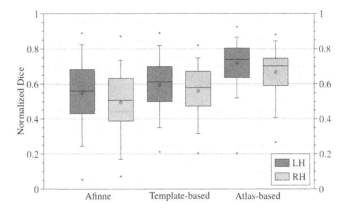

Fig. 4. Boxplot results for the normalized DSC obtained for the left and right hippocampus positioning using all 129 MR images

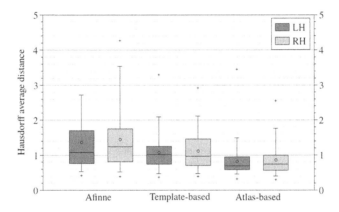

Fig. 5. Boxplot results for the HAD obtained for the left and right hippocampus positioning for all 129 MR images.

Box plots in Fig. 4 shows the DSC and HAD values obtained for the left and right hippocampus using all 129 MR images. As can be seen, the mesh positioning approach using affine transformation was the one with the lowest DSC and highest HAD averages and with the highest dispersions for both metrics. The intermediate and best average results were obtained, respectively, for the template- and atlas-based landmark approaches. The atlas-based approach also provided the minimum dispersion. For the approach of affine transformation, the interquartile range (IQR) for the DSC was 0.25 for both LH and RH. Considering the template- and atlas-based approaches, the IQRs for both LH and RH were 0.20 and 0.16. As can be noticed, the IQR for the DSC of the proposed atlas-based landmark was less spread than the other methods.

By using the Mann-Whitney U test (with significance level $\alpha = 0.01$), we proved that, for all stratified groups, there were statistically significant

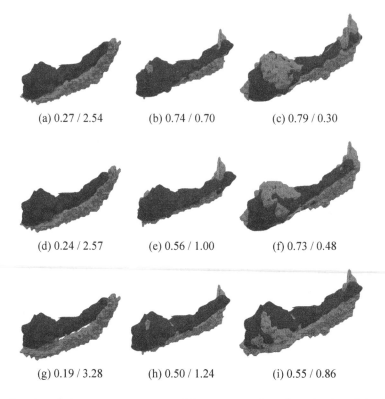

(a) 0.27 / 2.54   (b) 0.74 / 0.70   (c) 0.79 / 0.30

(d) 0.24 / 2.57   (e) 0.56 / 1.00   (f) 0.73 / 0.48

(g) 0.19 / 3.28   (h) 0.50 / 1.24   (i) 0.55 / 0.86

Fig. 6. Results of the worst, average, and best cases using the atlas-based landmark method (first row), template-based landmark (second row) and affine (third row) approaches on the same cases. Violet meshes are the ground-truths while blue meshes are the ones automatically positioned. DSC and HAD values are indicated in the image subcaptions (Color figure online)

differences between both LH and RH average values for the proposed atlas-based and the two other, template-based (p-value < 0.00001) and affine transformation (p-value < 0.00001) mappings. Although the Mann-Whitney U test also showed statistically significant differences for the LH and RH results when using the same method, this is likely because the volume of the left template mesh is larger than the right mesh, which makes the normalized DSC values higher for the left side. This effect is unnoticeable for the HAD in Fig. 5 since it requires no normalization. The HAD values in Fig. 5 also indicated the advantage of the atlas-based landmark method, since the average HAD values were significantly smaller (p-values < 0.00001) and had less spread than both the affine transformation and the template-based approaches.

Figure 6 shows the worst, the average and the best results (in relation to the HAD metric on the RH) of mesh positioning using the atlas-based landmark approach (first row). For direct comparison, results of the same cases obtained by the template-based landmark (second row) and affine transformation (third row) mappings are also illustrated. The violet mesh is the ground-truth mesh while the blue is the one automatically positioned by the respective registration techniques. As observed and numerically assessed by the DSC and HAD values in the sub-captions, the results for the mesh positioning using the proposed method are better than the other two approaches.

4   Conclusions

In this study, we constructed a probabilistic atlas of 3D landmark points automatically detected in MR images and applied it for the initialization of mesh models of hippocampus. We tested our method using 129 clinical MR images and compared its results with affine transformation and landmark-based mesh initialization approaches. The results have demonstrated that our method outperformed the other two mentioned approaches. Besides, quantitative results have shown that our new method was more stable (lower IQR ranges) than the other two methods used for comparison. Although our new proposed method has shown a satisfactory performance, we believe that using multiple atlases of 3D landmark points, computed from an age-stratified population, may improve our results significantly. We consider this because hippocampal atrophy and ventricular enlargement may vary considerably with age, which can cause a substantial reduction in the correct matching between the landmark points.

Acknowledgments. The authors would like to thank the São Paulo Research Foundation (FAPESP) (grants no. 2014/11988 0 and 2015/02232 1) and the Coordination for the Improvement of Higher Education Personnel (CAPES) for the financial support of this research.

References

1. Johnson, K.A., Fox, N.C., Sperling, R.A., Klunk, W.E.: Brain imaging in Alzheimer disease. Cold Spring Harb. Perspect. Med. **2**(4), 1–23 (2012)
2. Shen, K.K., Fripp, J., Mériaudeau, F., Chételat, G., Salvado, O., Bourgeat, P.: Detecting global and local hippocampal shape changes in Alzheimer's disease using statistical shape models. NeuroImage **59**(3), 2155–2166 (2012)
3. Farag, A.: Deformable Models: Biomedical and Clinical Applications. Springer, Heidelberg (2007). https://doi.org/10.1007/978-0-387-68413-0
4. Pekar, V., McNutt, T.R., Kaus, M.R.: Automated model-based organ delineation for radiotherapy planning in prostatic region. Int. J. Radiat. Oncol. Biol. Phys. **60**(3), 973–980 (2004)
5. Liu, C.Y., Iglesias, J.E., Tu, Z.: Deformable templates guided discriminative models for robust 3D brain MRI segmentation. NeuroInformatics **11**(4), 447–468 (2013)
6. Ghose, S., Mitra, J., Oliver, A., Marti, R., Llado, X., Freixenet, J., Vilanova, J.C., Sidibe, D., Meriaudeau, F.: A coupled schema of probabilistic atlas and statistical shape and appearance model for 3D prostate segmentation in MR images. In: 19th IEEE International Conference on Image Processing (ICIP), Orlando, FL, pp. 541–544. IEEE (2012)

7. Ferrari, R.J., Allaire, S., Hope, A., Kim, J., Jaffray, D., Pekar, V.: Detection of point landmarks in 3D medical images via phase congruency model. J. Braz. Comput. Soc. **17**(2), 117–132 (2011)
8. Qazi, A.A., Pekar, V., Kim, J., Xie, J., Breen, S.L., Jaffray, D.A.: Auto-segmentation of normal and target structures in head and neck CT images: A feature-driven model-based approach. Med. Phys. **38**(11), 6160–6170 (2011)
9. Zhang, J., Chen, L., Wang, X., Teng, Z., Brown, A.J., Gillard, J.H., Guan, Q., Chen, S.: Compounding local invariant features and global deformable geometry for medical image registration. PLoS ONE **9**(8), e105815 (2014)
10. Apostolova, L.G., Zarow, C., Biado, K., Hurtz, S., Boccardi, M., Somme, J., Honarpisheh, H., Blanken, A.E., Brook, J., Tung, S., et al.: Relationship between hippocampal atrophy and neuropathology markers: a 7T MRI validation study of the EADC-ADNI harmonized hippocampal segmentation protocol. Alzheimer's Dement. **11**(2), 139–150 (2015)
11. Buades, A., Coll, B., Morel, J.M.: A non-local algorithm for image denoising. In: Proceedings of the 2005 IEEE Computer Society Conference on Computer Vision and Pattern Recognition (CVPR), Washington, DC, USA, vol. 2, pp. 60–65. IEEE Computer Society (2005)
12. Tustison, N.J., Avants, B.B., Cook, P.A., Zheng, Y., Egan, A., Yushkevich, P.A., Gee, J.C.: N4ITK: improved N3 bias correction. IEEE Trans. Med. Imaging **29**(6), 1310–1320 (2010)
13. Nyul, L.G., Udupa, J.K., Zhang, X.: New variants of a method of MRI scale standardization. IEEE Trans. Med. Imaging **19**(2), 143–150 (2000)
14. Ourselin, S., Stefanescu, R., Pennec, X.: Robust registration of multi-modal images: towards real-time clinical applications. In: Dohi, T., Kikinis, R. (eds.) MICCAI 2002. LNCS, vol. 2489, pp. 140–147. Springer, Heidelberg (2002). https://doi.org/10.1007/3-540-45787-9_18
15. Iglesias, J.E., Liu, C.Y., Thompson, P., Tu, Z.: Robust brain extraction across datasets and comparison with publicly available methods. IEEE Trans. Med. Imaging **30**(9), 1617–1634 (2011)
16. Villa-Pinto, C.H., Ferrari, R.J.: Initialization of deformable models in 3D magnetic resonance images guided by automatically detected phase congruency point landmarks. Pattern Recogn. Lett. **79**, 1–7 (2016)
17. Morrone, M.C., Ross, J., Burr, D.C., Owens, R.: Mach bands are phase dependent. Nature **324**(6094), 250–253 (1986)
18. Belongie, S., Malik, J., Puzicha, J.: Shape matching and object recognition using shape contexts. Pattern Anal. Mach. **24**(4), 509–522 (2002)
19. Vincent, P., Bengio, Y.: Manifold parzen windows. In: Becker, S., Thrun, S., Obermayer, K. (eds.): Advances in Neural Information Processing Systems 15, pp. 849–856. MIT Press (2003)
20. Lee, S., Wolberg, G., Shin, S.Y.: The ITK Software Guide, 4th edn. Kitware, Inc., Clifton Park (2017)
21. Lee, S., Wolberg, G., Shin, S.Y.: Scattered data interpolation with multilevel B-splines. IEEE Trans. Vis. Comput. Graph. **3**(3), 228–244 (1997)
22. Henderson, C., Izquierdo, E.: Symmetric stability of low level feature detectors. Pattern Recogn. Lett. **78**, 36–40 (2016)

Reverse Engineering of Gene Regulatory Networks Combining Dynamic Bayesian Networks and Prior Biological Knowledge

Mariana C. de Souza⬤ and Carlos H. A. Higa$^{(\boxtimes)}$⬤

Federal University of Mato Grosso do Sul, Campo Grande, MS 79070-900, Brazil
mariana.caravanti@aluno.ufms.br, higa@facom.ufms.br
https://www.facom.ufms.br

Abstract. An important problem in the Systems Biology field is the reverse engineering of gene regulatory networks from gene expression data. In this work, we addressed this problem using a probabilistic graphical model known as Dynamic Bayesian Network to model the regulatory relations among the genes. We also used a Boolean formalism, assuming that each gene can take on two possible values: 0 (not expressed) and 1 (expressed). To learn the Dynamic Bayesian Network from time-series gene expression data we search for the network structure that best matches the data using the Bayesian Information Criterion score and the BDe score and compared them. Besides that, we used a source of prior biological knowledge from a database named STRING, unlike most of the reverse engineering algorithms that does not take into account any source of additional information. The results show that this approach can improve the quality of the inferred networks, and we also showed that the Dynamic Bayesian Network performs better than its standard version, Bayesian Network.

Keywords: Gene regulatory network · Dynamic Bayesian Network
Reverse engineering

1 Introduction

The reverse engineering of Gene Regulatory Networks (GRN) is an important problem studied in the Systems Biology and Bioinformatics field. The importance of dealing with this problem is that it can help us to understand the regulatory mechanisms of a biological phenomenon under study. For instance, researchers have studied GRN in the context of cell cycle [15], circadian cycle of plants [18], and more important, diseases such as cancer [9,19]. Given the importance of this problem, several models of GRN along with algorithms for the inference of GRN have been proposed over the years. Generally, these algorithms receive a dataset of gene expression as input and outputs a regulatory

---

Supported by CNPq and UFMS.

O. Gervasi et al. (Eds.): ICCSA 2018, LNCS 10960, pp. 323–336, 2018.
https://doi.org/10.1007/978-3-319-95162-1_22

network represented by a specific model. The input data are those provided by technologies such as DNA microarrays [22] and, more recently, RNA-Seq [27].

Among the proposed mathematical models of GRN are the Boolean networks [12], Bayesian networks [4], models based on ordinary differential equations [6], to name a few of them. To review a set of models of GRN we suggest the papers [7,11,17]. Algorithms for the reverse engineering of GRN are based on mathematical models and each one has its own characteristics besides advantages/advantages. We can not say that there is an algorithm that outperforms the others in every situation. For instance, some algorithms are specific to work with time-series data while some others work with steady-state data. It is worth mentioning that the reverse engineering of GRN is an ill-posed problem, *i.e.*, given a set of gene expression data, there could be several consistent solutions (networks) with these data. This fact makes the problem a very difficult one.

In this work, we modeled the gene expression in a Boolean fashion where a gene can take on two possible values: 0 (not expressed) and 1 (expressed). We also used a probabilistic graphical model known as Dynamic Bayesian Network, which is commonly used to represent complex stochastic processes. It differs from the standard Bayesian Network in the sense that it models the stochastic evolution of a set of variables over time. Both models are defined by a graphical structure and a set of parameters, which together specify a joint distribution over the random variables. Algorithms for learning the parameters and the structure of such networks have been developed [14,21]. In this paper, to learn the structure of Dynamic Bayesian Networks from time-series gene expression data we search for the network structure that best matches the data using the Bayesian Information Criterion score [23] and the BDe score [8].

Most of the reverse engineering algorithms of gene regulatory networks do not take into account any sources of prior biological knowledge. The approach of using additional biological information in this problem has shown interesting results, as can be seen in [5,26,29]. The source of prior knowledge used in this work is a database called STRING [20,25], which covers more than 2000 organisms in its latest version (10.0). In [13] a similar approach was performed using the Boolean network model and a feature selection algorithm. Here, we use a different model and approach do infer the model, but using the same source of prior biological knowledge. Because we are facing an ill-posed problem, this approach aims to improve the inference of gene interactions, once we take into account some interactions already supported by the literature.

To validate the methodology we used data from the DREAM challenge [2]. We also applied the methodology in a dataset of yeast (*Saccharomyces cerevisiae*) cell-cycle gene expression [24] and compared the results against the literature through the KEGG (Kyoto Encyclopedia of Genes and Genomes) database [10].

In the next section, we present the methodology, beginning with the introduction of the Dynamic Bayesian Networks, followed by the definitions of the score functions used in the learning process. We also explain how the prior biological knowledge database was used in the process. In Sect. 3 we discuss the results, followed by our conclusions, in Sect. 4.

2   Methodology

In this section we present the mathematical model of GRN used in our methodology along with the methodology to learn the model from the data. We also present the source of prior biological knowledge used and how it is used in the process of reverse engineering a GRN. In the final part of the section we discuss how the methodology is validated.

2.1   Dynamic Bayesian Networks

A *Dynamic Bayesian Network* (DBN) is a probabilistic graphical model defined by a network structure and a set of parameters to specify the joint probability of random variables. Let $\mathcal{X} = \{X_1, X_2, \ldots, X_n\}$ be a set of random variables where each variable X_i can assume values in the finite set $\text{Val}(X_i)$. In DBN, unlike standard Bayesian networks, the time is taken into account such that $X_i[t]$ is the value of X_i at time t. Thus, $\mathcal{X}[t]$ is the set of all random variables at time t.

To represent the beliefs about the process, a probability distribution over the variables $\mathcal{X}[0] \cup \mathcal{X}[1] \cup \mathcal{X}[2] \cup \cdots$ is necessary. We assume that the process is Markovian in the sense that $\text{P}(\mathcal{X}[t+1] \mid \mathcal{X}[0], \ldots, \mathcal{X}[t]) = \text{P}(\mathcal{X}[t+1] \mid \mathcal{X}[t])$. The probability $\text{P}(\mathcal{X}[t+1] \mid \mathcal{X}[t])$ is time independent.

A DBN representing the joint distribution over all possible trajectories of a process is composed of: (i) a prior network B_0 specifying a distribution over $\mathcal{X}[0]$; (ii) a transition network $B_\rightarrow$ over $\mathcal{X}[0] \cup \mathcal{X}[1]$ that is taken to specify $\text{P}(\mathcal{X}[t+1] \mid \mathcal{X}[t])$ for all t. In Fig. 1(a) and (b) we can see a simple example. The transition probability of this network is given by

$$\text{P}_{B_\rightarrow}(\mathcal{X}[1] \mid \mathcal{X}[0]) = \prod_{i=1}^{n} \text{P}_{B_\rightarrow}(X_i[1] \mid \mathbf{Pa}(X_i[1])), \tag{1}$$

where $\mathbf{Pa}(X_i)$ is the parents of X_i. Thus, the structure of a DBN is defined by a pair $(B_0, B_\rightarrow)$ corresponding to a network over the variables $\mathcal{X}[0], \ldots, \mathcal{X}[\infty]$. In practice, we reason only about the finite interval $0, \ldots, T$. To this end, we "unroll" the DBN structure into a Bayesian Network over $\mathcal{X}[0], \ldots, \mathcal{X}[T]$. In slice 0, the parents of $X_i[0]$ are specified in B_0. In slice $t+1$, the parents of $X_i[t+1]$ are nodes in slices t and $t+1$ corresponding to the parents of $X_i[1]$ in $B_\rightarrow$. In Fig. 1(c) we can see the result of unrolling the network for 3 time slices. Given a DBN, the joint distribution over $\mathcal{X}[0], \ldots, \mathcal{X}[T]$ is

$$\text{P}(\mathcal{X}[0], \ldots, \mathcal{X}[T]) = \text{P}_{B_0}(\mathcal{X}[0]) \prod_{t=0}^{T-1} \text{P}_{B_\rightarrow}(\mathcal{X}[t+1] \mid \mathcal{X}[t]). \tag{2}$$

2.2   Learning DBN from Complete Data

In this work, the reverse engineering of gene networks is treated as a problem of learning a DBN from complete data. The data in question is a time-series gene expression dataset $\mathcal{D}$ consisting of K complete observation sequences

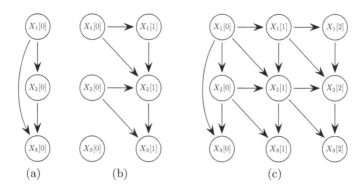

Fig. 1. (a) A prior network B_0 and (b) a transition network $B_\rightarrow$ for three variables. In (c) is the corresponding "unrolled" network. Figure adapted from [4].

$D_1, D_2, \ldots, D_K$. Each sequence D_ℓ has length N_ℓ and specifies values for the variables $\mathbf{x}^\ell[0], \mathbf{x}^\ell[1], \ldots, \mathbf{x}^\ell[N_\ell]$. Thus, we have K initial instances of initial slices to learn B_0 and $N = \sum_\ell N_\ell$ instances of transitions to learn $B_\rightarrow$.

Formally, the reverse engineering problem is stated as follows. Given a dataset $\mathcal{D}$ of instances of $\mathcal{X}$, find a DBN $\mathcal{B}$ with structure $\mathcal{G} = (B_0, B_\rightarrow)$ and its parameters Θ that best matches $\mathcal{D}$. We use a scoring function to measure how a DBN matches the data. The score combines the *likelihood* of the data according to the network, $L(\mathcal{B} : \mathcal{D}) = \log \mathrm{P}(\mathcal{D} \mid \mathcal{B})$, with some penalty according to the complexity of the network.

BIC Score. We define the *Bayesian Information Criterion score* and the *BDe score* according to [3]. First, let us define

$$\theta^{(0)}_{i,j'_i,k'_i} = P(X_i[0] = k'_i \mid \mathbf{Pa}(X_i[0]) = j'_i) \tag{3}$$

and similarly

$$\theta^{\rightarrow}_{i,j_i,k_i} = P(X_i[0] = k_i \mid \mathbf{Pa}(X_i[0]) = j_i) \tag{4}$$

for $t = 1, \ldots, T$. The notation for the sufficient statistics is given by

$$N^{(0)}_{i,j'_i,k'_i} = \sum_\ell I(X_i[0] = k'_i, \mathbf{Pa}(X_i[0]) = j'_i; \mathbf{x}^\ell) \tag{5}$$

and

$$N^{\rightarrow}_{i,j_i,k_i} = \sum_\ell \sum_t I(X_i[0] = k_i, \mathbf{Pa}(X_i[t]) = j_i; \mathbf{x}^\ell) \tag{6}$$

where $I(\cdot; \mathbf{x}^\ell)$ is an indicator function which takes on value 1 if the event $\cdot$ occurs in $\mathbf{x}^\ell$, and 0 otherwise.

Using Eq. 2 and rearranging the terms, the likelihood function is decomposed according to the DBN structure:

$$P(\mathcal{D}\,|\,\mathcal{G},\boldsymbol{\Theta}_{\mathcal{G}}) = \prod_i \prod_{j_i'} \prod_{k_i'} (\theta_{i,j_i',k_i'}^{(0)})^{N_{i,j_i',k_i'}^{(0)}} \times \prod_i \prod_{j_i} \prod_{k_i} (\theta_{i,j_i,k_i}^{\rightarrow})^{N_{i,j_i,k_i}^{\rightarrow}} \qquad (7)$$

and the log-likelihood is given by

$$L(\mathcal{B}:\mathcal{D}) = \sum_i \sum_{j_i'} \sum_{k_i'} N_{i,j_i',k_i'}^{(0)} \log \theta_{i,j_i',k_i'}^{(0)} + \sum_i \sum_{j_i} \sum_{k_i} N_{i,j_i,k_i}^{\rightarrow} \log \theta_{i,j_i,k_i}^{\rightarrow}. \qquad (8)$$

This decomposition facilitates the computation of the BIC and BDe scores.

Using the standard maximum likelihood estimate for multinomial distributions, we get the following expression for $\hat{\boldsymbol{\Theta}}_{\mathcal{G}}$:

$$\hat{\theta}_{i,j_i',k_i'}^{(0)} = \frac{N_{i,j_i',k_i'}^{(0)}}{\sum_{k_i'} N_{i,j_i',k_i'}^{(0)}}, \qquad (9)$$

and similarly for the transition case. Thus, the BIC score is given by

$$\mathrm{BIC}(\mathcal{G}:\mathcal{D}) = \mathrm{BIC}_0 + \mathrm{BIC}_{\rightarrow}, \qquad (10)$$

where

$$\mathrm{BIC}_0 = \sum_i \sum_{j_i'} \sum_{k_i'} N_{i,j_i',k_i'}^{(0)} \log \hat{\theta}_{i,j_i',k_i'}^{(0)} - \frac{\log K}{2} \#G_0 \qquad (11)$$

and

$$\mathrm{BIC}_{\rightarrow} = \sum_i \sum_{j_i} \sum_{k_i} N_{i,j_i,k_i}^{\rightarrow} \log \hat{\theta}_{i,j_i,k_i}^{\rightarrow} - \frac{\log N}{2} \#G_{\rightarrow}, \qquad (12)$$

where $\#G_0$ and $\#G_{\rightarrow}$ are the number of parameters in B_0 and $B_{\rightarrow}$, respectively.

BDe Score. The BDe score is computed by evaluating the following integral:

$$P(\mathcal{D}\,|\,\mathcal{G}) = \int P(\mathcal{D}\,|\,\mathcal{G},\boldsymbol{\Theta}_{\mathcal{G}}) P(\boldsymbol{\Theta}_{\mathcal{G}}\,|\,\mathcal{G})\, d\boldsymbol{\Theta}_{\mathcal{G}}. \qquad (13)$$

Using Eq. 7 and assuming *Dirichlet* priors we can obtain a closed form. A Dirichlet prior for a variable X is specified by a set o *hyperparameters* $\{N_x' : x \in \mathrm{Val}(X)\}$:

$$P(\boldsymbol{\Theta}_X) = \mathrm{Dirichlet}(N_x' : x \in \mathrm{Val}(X)) \propto \prod_x \theta_x^{N_x'-1}. \qquad (14)$$

The hyperparameters can be interpreted as pseudo counts. Assuming that for each structure $\mathcal{G}$ we have hyperparameters $N_{i,j'_i,k'_i}^{'(0)}$ and $N_{i,j_i,k_i}^{'\rightarrow}$ we can rewrite $P(\mathcal{D} \mid \mathcal{G})$ as a product of two terms

$$
\prod_i \prod_{j'_i} \frac{\Gamma(\sum_{k'_i} N_{i,j'_i,k'_i}^{'(0)})}{\Gamma(\sum_{k'_i} N_{i,j'_i,k'_i}^{'0} + N_{i,j_i,k_i}^{'\rightarrow})} \times \prod_{k'_i} \frac{\Gamma(N_{i,j'_i,k'_i}^{'(0)} + N_{i,j'_i,k'_i}^{(0)})}{\Gamma(N_{i,j'_i,k'_i}^{'(0)})}, \tag{15}
$$

and similar for the transition case where $\Gamma(x) = \int_0^\infty t^{x-1}e^{-t}dt$ is the *Gamma* function satisfying $\Gamma(1) = 1$ and $\Gamma(x+1) = x\Gamma(x)$. Following [8], we assign the Dirichlet hyperparameters as

$$
N_{i,j'_i,k'_i}^{'(0)} = \hat{N}^{(0)} \times P_{B'_0}(X_i[0] = k'_i | \mathbf{Pa}(X_i[0]) = j'_i) \quad \text{and} \tag{16}
$$

$$
N_{i,j_i,k_i}^{'\rightarrow} = \hat{N}^{\rightarrow} \times P_{B'_{\rightarrow}}(X_i[1] = k_i | \mathbf{Pa}(X_i[1]) = j_i), \tag{17}
$$

given two *equivalent sample sizes* $\hat{N}^{(0)}$ and $\hat{N}^{\rightarrow}$.

2.3   Prior Biological Knowledge

The source of prior biological knowledge used is the STRING database (Search Tool for the Retrieval of Interacting Genes/Proteins) [25]. This database aims to provide a critical assessment and integration of protein-protein interactions, including direct (physical) as well as indirect (functional) associations. The current version of STRING is v10 and it covers more than 2000 organisms. Besides that, an API interface for the R computing environment is available, allowing us to easily retrieve the information about gene interactions.

The interactions are derived from multiple sources: (i) known experimental interactions are imported from primary databases, (ii) pathway knowledge is parsed from manually curated databases, (iii) automated text-mining is applied to uncover statistical and/or semantic links between proteins, based on Medline abstracts and a large collection of full-text articles, (iv) interactions are predicted *de novo* by a number of algorithms using genomic information as well as by co-expression analysis and (v) interactions that are observed in one organism are systematically transferred to other organisms, via pre-computed orthology relations [25].

For each pair of genes of a given organism, the STRING database provides a set of scores based on association evidence type: conserved neighborhood, gene fusions, phylogenetic co-occurrence, co-expression, database imports, large-scale experiments and literature co-occurrence. There is also a *combined score* expressing confidence when an association is supported by several types of evidence. For details see reference [20].

Let $s(X_i, X_j)$ be the combined score for a pair of genes obtained from STRING. First, we normalize the scores so that $0 \leq s(X_i, X_j) \leq 1$. Given that, the *biological score* is defined as the mean

$$\beta(X_i, \mathbf{Pa}(X_i)) = \frac{1}{|\mathbf{Pa}(X_i)|} \sum_{X_j \in \mathbf{Pa}(X_i)} s(X_i, X_j). \tag{18}$$

The decomposition in Eq. 8 facilitates the computation of the BIC and BDe scores. Notice that the likelihood is expressed as a sum of terms, where each term depends only on the conditional probability of a variable X_i given its parents $\mathbf{Pa}(X_i)$. Thus, when computing the BIC or BDe score, we add the term $\omega \cdot \beta(X_i, \mathbf{Pa}(X_i))$, where $\omega \in \mathbb{R}$ is the weight given to the prior biological knowledge. Obviously, $\omega = 0$ means that we are not taking into account the biological knowledge.

2.4 Validation

To validate and analyze the methodology, assume that $\mathcal{G}^*$ is the gold standard network and $\mathcal{G}$ is the output network. Then, it is possible to fill the entries of a *confusion matrix* [28] according to Table 1. According to this table, if an edge/connection is present in the gold standard and it is correctly inferred, then it counts as a true positive (TP).

Table 1. Confusion matrix. TP = true positive; FP = false positive; FN = false negative; TN = true negative.

Edge	Inferred in $\mathcal{G}$	Not inferred in $\mathcal{G}$
Present in $\mathcal{G}^*$	TP	FN
Absent in $\mathcal{G}^*$	FP	TN

To quantify the quality of the output network, we used a similarity [1] measure defined as

$$\text{Similarity}(\mathcal{G}^*, \mathcal{G}) = \sqrt{\text{PPV} \times \text{Specificity}}, \tag{19}$$

where

$$\text{PPV} = \frac{\text{TP}}{\text{TP} + \text{FP}} \quad \text{and Specificity} = \frac{\text{TN}}{\text{TN} + \text{FP}}. \tag{20}$$

2.5 Implementation

The methodology was implemented by extending an open source package named Pgmpy (http://pgmpy.org), which is a Python library for working with probabilistic graphical models. This is an ongoing project and for DBN only the parameters inference was implemented. We extended the library by implementing the learning of DBN structure given a gene expression dataset and a source of prior biological knowledge provided by the STRING database.

3 Results and Discussion

In order to apply the proposed methodology, we performed experiments using data from the DREAM4 Challenge (Dialogue for Reverse Engineering Assessments and Methods) [2] and a yeast (*Saccharomyces cerevisiae*) cell cycle study [24]. All datasets used were discretized using an algorithm called Bikmeans [16].

3.1 DREAM4 Data Results

The DREAM4 *in silico* challenge data consists of a time series generated from networks of 10 and 100 genes. There are 5 networks of size 10 and for each of them there are 5 datasets of 21 time points. For the network of size 100 the number of networks is also 5, but there are 10 datasets of 21 time points each. This experiment validates the methodology without the use of prior biological knowledge, once it consists of synthetic data.

In Fig. 2 we compare the standard Bayesian Network (BN), the Bayesian Network considering the time factor (BN with time), and Dynamic Bayesian Network (DBN) by using the BIC score. The BN with time simply means that, when estimating the conditional probabilities for a gene $X_i[t]$, the values of its parents in the samples are taken at time $t+1$. Networks from 1 to 5 are composed by 10 genes and from 6 to 10 by 100 genes. We can observe that DBN performs better in most cases.   In Fig. 3 we performed the same comparison, but using

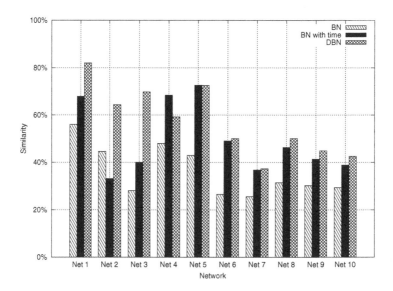

Fig. 2. Comparison between the standard Bayesian Network and the Dynamic Bayesian Network, using the BIC score.

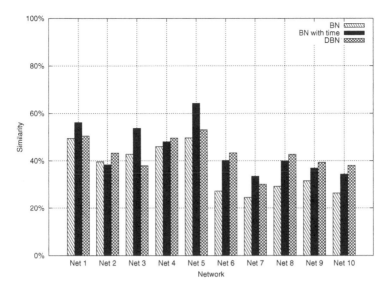

Fig. 3. Comparison between the standard Bayesian Network and the Dynamic Bayesian Network, using the BDe score.

the BDe score. In some cases DBN presented better results, but in others the BN with time was better.

We also compared the true positive rate between BIC and BDe scores. In Fig. 4 we can observe that the BDe score performs slightly better in most experiments. From 1 to 10 we used BN with time, where from 1 to 5 are the networks of size 10 genes and, from 6 to 10 are networks of size 100. From 11 to 20 we used DBN, where from 11 to 15 are networks of size 10 and, from 16 to 20 of size 100.

3.2   Yeast Cell Cycle Data Results

We tested the methodology using a dataset of yeast cell cycle gene expression provided by [24]. This dataset was obtained from six experiments, named cln3 (2 time points), clb2 (2), alpha (18), cdc15 (24), cdc28 (17) and elutriation (14). In this experiment, we selected 11 genes considered to be key regulators of the cell cycle process according to [15]. The gold standard network was obtained from the KEGG database.

In Fig. 5 we show the similarities values when using the BIC score and the prior biological knowledge for $\omega = 1, 2, 4$. The completeData bars was generated using all six experiments together. Because the experiments cln3 and clb2 are composed by only 2 samples each we did not use them individually. We can observe that the biological knowledge improves the quality of the output network specially in the cdc28 and alpha experiments.

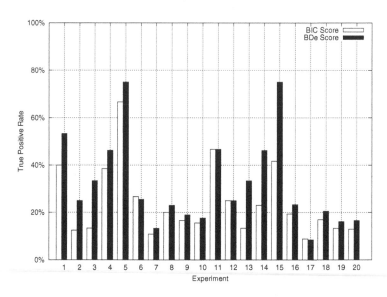

Fig. 4. Comparing the true positive rates obtained when using BIC and BDe score for the DREAM4 data.

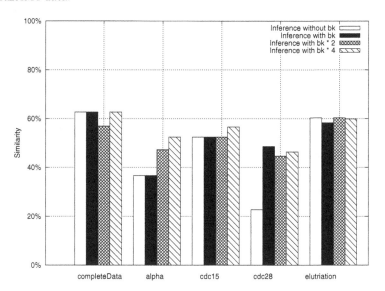

Fig. 5. Similarity of the yeast cell cycle network using BIC score and considering biological knowledge with $\omega = 1, 2, 4$.

In Fig. 6 the show the results when using the same data, but with the BDe score. We can observe that the similarity values are slightly worst when compared to the BIC score experiment. It is also possible to notice a soft improvement of the quality when considering the biological knowledge.

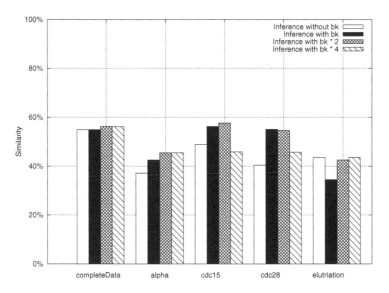

Fig. 6. Similarity of the yeast cell cycle network using BDe score and considering biological knowledge with $\omega = 1, 2, 4$.

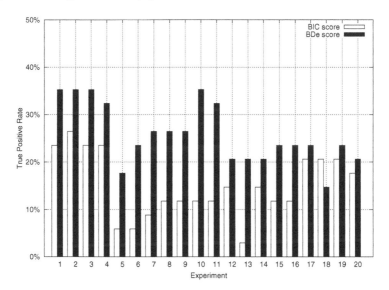

Fig. 7. Comparing the true positive rates obtained when using BIC and BDe score for the yeast cell cycle data.

Comparing the true positive rates between BIC and BDe scores shows that BDe performs better in most of our experiments, as we can observe in Fig. 7. In experiments 1 to 4 we used the completeData with biological knowledge plus $\omega = 0, 1, 2, 4$, respectively. In experiments 5 to 8 the alpha dataset was used, following the same pattern of ω. Experiments 9 to 12 correspond to the cdc15 dataset, 13 to 16 correspond to the cdc28 dataset, and from 17 to 20 to the elutriation dataset.

4   Conclusion

In this work, we proposed a methodology for the reverse engineering of gene regulatory networks from time series gene expression using dynamic bayesian networks as well. We also proposed the use of a source of prior biological knowledge, known as STRING, to improve the quality of the inferred networks. The methodology was tested on two datasets: artificial dataset provided by the DREAM4 *in silico* challenge and a biological dataset from a yeast cell cycle study.

To learn the structure of the DBN we search for the network that best matches the data, based on a score function. We used two types of functions, BIC and BDe scores, and compared them. The results show that BDe score performs better in most of the experiments.

We also compared the standard Bayesian Network model against the Dynamic Bayesian Network, showing that the DBN provides better results than its standard version. One important point to highlight is that our methodology considers a source of prior biological knowledge, when available, unlike most of the reverse engineering algorithms. We showed through our experiments that this approach can improve the quality of the inferred networks. As a future work, we can explore how to use various sources of biological knowledge instead of only one.

Acknowledgement. This research was supported by CNPq (Conselho Nacional de Desenvolvimento Científico e Tecnológico) and UFMS (Universidade Federal de Mato Grosso do Sul).

References

1. Dougherty, E.R.: Validation of inference procedures for gene regulatory networks. Curr. Genomics **8**(6), 351–359 (2007)
2. DREAM: DREAM: Dialogue for Reverse Engineering Assessments and Methods (2009). http://wiki.c2b2.columbia.edu/dream/
3. Friedman, N., Murphy, K., Russell, S.: Learning the structure of dynamic probabilistic networks. In: 15th Annual Conference on Uncertainty in Artificial Intelligence, pp. 139–147. Morgan Kaufmann (1999)
4. Friedman, N., et al.: Using Bayesian networks to analyze expression data. J. Comput. Biol. **7**(6), 601–620 (2000)
5. Gao, S., Wang, X.: Quantitative utilization of prior biological knowledge in the Bayesian network modeling of gene expression data. BMC Bioinf. **12**(1), 359+ (2011)
6. Goodwin, B.C.: Temporal Organization in Cells; A Dynamic Theory of Cellular Control Process. Academic Press, Cambridge (1963)
7. Hecker, M., et al.: Gene regulatory network inference: data integration in dynamic models - a review. BioSystems **96**, 86–103 (2009)

8. Heckerman, D., Geiger, D., Chickering, D.: Learning Bayesian networks: the combination of knowledge and statistical data. Mach. Learn. **2**(3), 197–243 (1995)
9. Huang, S., Ernberg, I., Kauffman, S.: Cancer attractors: a systems view of tumors from a gene network dynamics and developmental perspective. Semin. Cell Dev. Biol. **20**(7), 869–876 (2009)
10. Kanehisa, M., Goto, S., Kawashima, S., Nakaya, A.: The KEGG databases at GenomeNet. Nucleic Acids Res. **30**, 42–46 (2002)
11. Karlebach, G., Shamir, R.: Modelling and analysis of gene regulatory networks. Nature **9**, 770–780 (2008)
12. Kauffman, S.A.: Metabolic stability and epigenesis in randomly constructed genetic nets. J. Theor. Biol. **22**(3), 437–467 (1969)
13. Koike, C.Y., Higa, C.H.A.: Inference of gene regulatory networks using coefficient of determination, Tsallis entropy and biological prior knowledge. In: Proceedings of the IEEE 16th International Conference on Bioinformatics and Bioengineering (2016)
14. Koller, D., Friedman, N.: Probabilistic Graphical Models: Principles and Techniques, 1st edn. MIT Press, Cambridge (2012)
15. Li, F., Long, T., Lu, Y., Ouyang, Q., Thang, C.: The yeast cell-cycle network is robustly designed. PNAS USA **101**(14), 4781–4786 (2004)
16. Li, Y., Liu, L., Bai, X., Cai, H., Ji, W., Guo, D., Zhu, Y.: Comparative study of discretization methods of microarray data for inferring transcriptional regulatory networks. BMC Bioinf. **11**(1), 520+ (2010)
17. Linde, J., Schulze, S., Henkel, S.G., Guthke, R.: Data and knowledge-based modeling of gene regulatory networks: an update. EXCLI J. **14**, 346–378 (2015)
18. Locke, J.C.W., Millar, A.J., Turner, M.S.: Modelling genetic networks with noisy and varied experimental data: the circadian clock in Arabidopsis thaliana. J. Theor. Biol. **234**(3), 383–393 (2005)
19. Madhamshettiwar, P.B., Maetschke, S.R., Davis, M.J., Reverter, A., Ragan, M.A.: Gene regulatory network inference: evaluation and application to ovarian cancer allows the prioritization of drug targets. Genome Med. **4**(5), 1–16 (2012)
20. von Mering, C., Jensen, L.J., Snel, B., Hooper, S.D., Krupp, M., Foglierini, M., Jouffre, N., Huynen, M.A., Bork, P.: STRING: known and predicted protein-protein associations, integrated and transferred across organisms. Nucleic Acids Res. **33**(Database issue), D433–D437 (2005)
21. Russell, S.J., Binder, J., Koller, D., Kanazawa, K.: Local learning in probabilistic networks with hidden variables. In: IJCAI, pp. 1146–1152 (1995)
22. Schena, M., Shalon, D., Davis, R.W., Brown, P.O.: Quantitative monitoring of gene expression patterns with a complementary DNA microarray. Science **270**(5235), 467–470 (1995)
23. Schwarz, G.: Estimating the dimension of a model. Ann. Stat. **6**(2), 461–464 (1978)
24. Spellman, P.T., Sherlock, G., Zhang, M.Q., Iyer, V.R., Anders, K., Eisen, M.B., Brown, P.O., Botstein, D., Futcher, B.: Comprehensive identification of cell cycle-regulated genes of the yeast Saccharomyces cerevisiae by microarray hybridization. Mol. Biol. Cell **9**, 3273–3297 (1998)
25. Szklarczyk, D., Franceschini, A., Wyder, S., Forslund, K., Heller, D., Huerta-Cepas, J., Simonovic, M., Roth, A., Santos, A., Tsafou, K.P., Kuhn, M., Bork, P., Jensen, L.J., von Mering, C.: STRING v10: protein-protein interaction networks, integrated over the tree of life. Nucleic Acids Res. **43**(Database issue), D447–D452 (2015)
26. Wang, Z., Xu, W., Lucas, F., Liu, Y.: Incorporating prior knowledge into gene network study. Bioinformatics **29**(20), 2633–2640 (2013)

27. Wang, Z., Gerstein, M., Snyder, M.: RNA-Seq: a revolutionary tool for transcriptomics. Nat. Rev. Genet. **10**(1), 57–63 (2009)
28. Webb, A.R.: Statistical Pattern Recognition, 2nd edn. Wiley, Hoboken (2002)
29. Werhli, A.V., Husmeier, D.: Reconstructing gene regulatory networks with Bayesian networks by combining expression data with multiple sources of prior knowledge. Stat. Appl. Genet. Mol. Biol. **6**(1), 15 (2007)

An Investigative Analysis of Quality of Service Metrics on OpenStack

Edna Dias Canedo$^{(\boxtimes)}$, Ítalo Paiva Batista, Emilie Trindade de Morais, and Aleteia Patricia Favacho de Araujo

University of Brasília - UnB, P.O. Box 4466, Brasília, DF 70910-900, Brazil
{ednacanedo,aleteia}@unb.br, italo.paiva.b@gmail.com, emilie.morais.t@gmail.com

Abstract. Cloud computing is a paradigm that is becoming widespread because of its benefits. The cloud services are structured in three modules: Software as a Service (SaaS), Platform as a Service (PaaS) and Infrastructure as a Service (IaaS). This last one use the hardware resources to provide services on virtual machines. A lot of tools have been created to support this type of service. OpenStack is an open-source tool created to provide cloud services on IaaS models through several inter-related projects. An important point of attention in cloud services is the Quality of Service (QoS) and cloud computing tools should provide metrics to monitor and ensure the QoS. The purpose of this work was to gather the QoS metrics provided the OpenStack and compare them to the QoS metrics for cloud computing services found in the literature. The metrics show that OpenStack provides approximately 24.25% of the metrics found in the literature.

Keywords: Metrics · Quality of service · Infrastructure as a service
Cloud computing · OpenStack

1 Introduction

The cloud computing frameworks and environments are able to address different issues in current distributed and ubiquitous computing systems. The availability of infrastructure as a service and platform as a service environments provided a fundamental base for building cloud computing based applications.

Cloud Computing is an on-demand resource delivering paradigm, providing infrastructure, platforms and software. This paradigm has widely due to its benefits, like resource scalability, software flexibility, pay-per-use, consolidated management and maintenance system, reliability and reduction of carbon emissions [19]. With the spread of the use of cloud computing services, some studies [2,12,16,18,22,23] have been developed in order to help choose the more appropriate service by analyzing intrinsic aspects of cloud computing services and Quality of Service (QoS). [24] states that the quality of service in cloud computing is critical, but is hard to analyze.

© Springer International Publishing AG, part of Springer Nature 2018
O. Gervasi et al. (Eds.): ICCSA 2018, LNCS 10960, pp. 337–352, 2018.
https://doi.org/10.1007/978-3-319-95162-1_23

According to [14], measurements support management, processes and product improvement. It is a key discipline in quality assessment and, according to [17], cloud computing services measurement is one of the essential characteristics.

The work presented by [5] states that measurements allow transparency to both provider and client, and that measuring cloud services helps to accomplish the agreed service level agreements.

OpenStack [11] is an open source, cloud computing platform that allows the management and development of cloud computing infrastructure in a datacenter. It is currently maintained by the OpenStack Foundation and is used by several companies [4,10]. In this context of cloud service selection and the increasing use of OpenStack, the research question of this study is:

1. **Which QoS metrics for cloud computing services proposed in the literature are provided by OpenStack?**

The goal of this paper was to identify QoS metrics, proposed in the literature, available natively in OpenStack.

The article is organized as follows. Section 2, Cloud Computing Services presents some cloud computing concepts and its quality are presented and a general view of the OpenStack tool is presented. In the Materials and Methods, Sect. 3 are presented the stages involved in this work accomplishment, as well as the used methods. In Sect. 4, the work's execution steps are presented. Finally, the conclusions are presented in Sect. 5.

2   Cloud Computing Services

According to [1] cloud computing refers to applications that deliver services using the Internet. These services are provided using the hardware and software of data centers. [20] conceptualize cloud computing as services that offers mechanisms to provide virtual access to unlimited resources based on Pay-per-use model.

Cloud computing is structured in three modules: Software as a Service (SaaS), Platform as a Service (PaaS) and Infrastructure as a Service (IaaS), ordered by abstraction level, from high to low, respectively. SaaS provides all the functions of a traditional application, but provides access to specific applications through Internet. The SaaS mod-el reduces concerns with application servers, operating systems, storage, application development, etc. Hence, developers may focus on innovation, and not on infrastructure, leading to faster software systems development. SaaS systems re-duce costs since no software licenses are required to access the applications. In-stead, users access services on demand. Since the software is mostly Web based, SaaS allows better integration among the business units of a given organization or even among different software services. PaaS is the middle component of the service layer in the cloud. It offers users software and services that do not require downloads or installations. PaaS provides an infrastructure with a high level of integration in order to implement and test cloud applications. The user does not manage the infra-structure (including network, servers, operating systems and storage), but he controls deployed applications and, possibly, their configurations. PaaS provides an operating system, programming languages and application programming environments [17].

IaaS is the portion of the architecture responsible for providing the infrastructure necessary for PaaS and SaaS. Its main objective is to make resources such as servers, network and storage more readily accessible by including applications and operating systems. Thus, it offers basic infrastructure on-demand services. IaaS has a unique interface for infrastructure management, an Application Programming Interface (API) for interactions with hosts, switches, and routers, and the capability of adding new equipment in a simple and transparent manner. In general the, user does not manage the underlying hardware in the cloud infra-structure, but he controls the operating systems, storage and deployed applications. Eventually he can also select network components such as firewalls. The term IaaS refers to a computing infrastructure, based on virtualization techniques that can scale dynamically, increasing or reducing resources according to the needs of applications. The main benefit provided by IaaS is the pay-per-use business model [17].

According to [5,17], cloud services has the following characteristics: self-service on demand, large network access, resource grouping, fast elasticity and service measurement. The work presented by [20] characterizes the IaaS as a hardware resource provided on virtual machines. The client maintains the applications, databases and servers while the server maintains the cloud virtualization, hardware, storage and networks.

To [3] the IaaS model is the service of delivering hardware (server, storage and network) and associated software (files system and systems virtualization). The authors established the following services as IaaS: virtual infrastructure (server, storage and network); deployment of web-based applications with easy on-demand availability; load balancing; establishing service-level agreements the clients; CPU, data and network security; and management and account provisioning.

2.1   Quality of Service

Quality of Service (QoS) denotes the levels of performance, reliability, and availability offered by an application and by the platform or infrastructure. QoS is fundamental for cloud users, who expect providers to deliver the advertised quality characteristics, and for cloud providers, who need to find the right trade-offs between QoS levels and operational costs.

The QoS in cloud computing can be considered as the performance of the provided service in a general mode [10]. The work presented by [5] characterizes the QoS in two approaches: **network and application**. The network approach deals with the requirements to ensure the QoS. The application approach deals with the attributes that on the fulfill of the service level agreement. The QoS can be divided into two points of view: the client's and the provider's [3,10]. The scope of this work is focused only on the metrics for the provider's point of view which, is more concerned with the cloud is overall performance.

2.2 OpenStack

OpenStack is a tool that provides cloud services an IaaS model. It consists of a group of interrelated sub-projects that control a set of processing resources (*Nova* subproject), storage (*Cinder* and *Swift* sub-projects), and network (*Neutron* subproject). Each subproject is a module of OpenStack and forms a computing cloud infrastructure [4,10].

OpenStack also provides some shared services between the different modules, such as the authentication and authorization service (*Keystone* subproject), the image service (*Glance* subproject) and the telemetry service (*Ceilometer* subproject). These are just the main services provided by OpenStack, the complete description of all its services can be seen in the tool's documentation [10].

OpenStack is fairly robust. It is capable of a large number of computational resources in a datacenter. This characteristic requires good hardware infrastructure for full operation. The cloud infrastructure management and control can be performed using a web application (*Horizon* subproject), via the command line and/or RESTful APIs [4,10].

The internal module integration is performed by RESTful APIs and Remote Procedure Call (RPC) via RabbitMQ (a tool that implements the inter-process communication following the Advanced Message Queue Protocol) [4]. More details about the module integration can be seen in the study made by [4]. Figure 1 shows the conceptual architecture of OpenStack, presenting the relationship between the modules.

3 Materials and Methods

The methodology used in this study was organized into five steps as shown in Fig. 2.

– **Collection of existing metrics:** This step consisted of researching the QoS metrics for cloud services in the literature and documenting them, using a literature review;
– **Metrics filtering:** From the metrics identified in the literature review, this step involved in filtering the results according to the previously defined criteria;
– **Metrics comparison:** To verify which metrics proposed in the literature were implemented natively in OpenStack, this step verified the existence of the filtered metrics in OpenStack, based on the documentation and the execution of the tool. The way that the tool presents the metrics was also identified. In addition, the metrics provided by OpenStack that were not found in the literature, but were related to the metrics found, were identified and documented;
– **Metrics exemplification:** This step consisted of verifying if the compared metrics were in the tool and how they were provided. The verification was performed through the simple collection of the identified metrics present in OpenStack with the execution of the tool in a test scenario; This step also involved the following activities:

- *Characterize scenario/context:* In this activity the context of the execution and the test scenario were described. The scenario was described considering items as the environment for the execution, tool version, topology and available tools and resources.
- *Collect data:* In this activity the identified metrics in the previous step were collected and documented.
- **Analysis and results report:** In this step the results obtained in the previous step were interpreted and then documented.

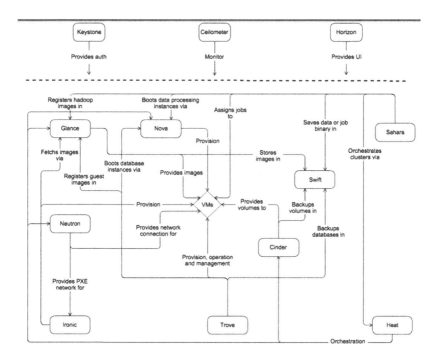

Fig. 1. Conceptual architecture of the OpenStack [10]

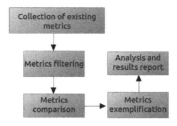

Fig. 2. Proposed methodology.

4 Execution

A literature review was performed in order to find existing QoS metrics proposed in other studies. Six papers that explicitly presented QoS metrics for cloud services were found. These papers were analyzed and **68 metrics** identified, as can be seen in the Table 1. The papers found are:

- **Paper 1:** *QoS Metrics for Cloud Computing Services Evaluation* [2];
- **Paper 2:** *On a Catalogue of Metrics for Evaluating Commercial Cloud Services* [16];
- **Paper 3:** *IaaS Cloud Service Selection using Case-Based Reasoning* [22];
- **Paper 4:** *SMICloud: A Framework for Comparing and Ranking Cloud Services* [12];
- **Paper 5:** *Cloud Services Measures for Global Use* [21];
- **Paper 6:** *An End-To-End QoS Mapping Approach for Cloud Service Selection* [15].

Four criteria were defined to filter the metrics based on the context and scope of the work. The evaluation of the collected metrics can be seen in Table 2. The criteria explanation follows:

- **Criterion 1 - Is the meaning known?**
  - This criterion was used to assess if the meaning of the metric and its calculation method were known.
- **Criterion 2 - Does it apply to the IaaS service model?**
  - This criterion was used to select metrics most applicable to the IaaS model, due to its singular characteristics.
- **Criterion 3 - Can it be collected objectively?**
  - This criterion was used to select the metrics that can be collected objectively, because this kind of metric can be collected using automated tools.
- **Criterion 4 - Is it from the provider's perspective?**
  - This criterion was used to select which metrics were related to the cloud computing service provider is point of view (Table 3).

4.1 Metrics Comparison

After the filtering step, 34 metrics remained to be compared against OpenStack. In order to accomplish this, the metrics were divided into static and dynamic metrics. Static metrics do not require tool execution to be collected, while dynamic metrics do. Furthermore, the metrics were categorized based on the study performed by [2].

The categories used were: Reliability, Economy, Memory, Performance, Security and General. It is worth mentioning that two equivalent metrics were identified: Transfer Speed bit/byte TCP/UDP/IP and Bandwidth (download, upload). Considering this, only bandwidth was used in the comparison.

Table 1. Metrics found in the literature

Metric	Category	Paper
Cryptography algorithms	Security	Paper 6
Service learnability	Usability	
Access control	Security	
Data control	Data control	
Defects per million (DPM)	-	
Ease of use	Usability	
IaaS instalability	Usability	
Data privacy	Security	
Mean time between failures (MTBF)	Reliability	
Access control policies	Security/privacy	Paper 5
VM Cost	Cost	Paper 5 Paper 4
Storage (HD)	-	Paper 3
NoSQL databases support	-	
Application layers	-	
CPU frequency	-	
I/O performance	-	
Bandwidth (download, upload)	-	
Application maximum latency	-	
Number of load balancers	-	
Number of instances	-	
Number of CPU cores	-	
Concurrent users maximum number	-	
Region	-	
Application servers	-	
Operational System (Type, Platform, Version)	-	
Relational database support	-	
Application type	-	
Security (general metric)	-	Paper 3 Paper 6
Memory (RAM required for the instance)	Reliability/sustainability	Paper 3 Paper 4
Application response time	Performance	
Availability	-	Paper 3 Paper 4 Paper 6

(*continued*)

Table 1. (*continued*)

Metric	Category	Paper
Transfer latency TCP/UDP/IP	Performance/communication	Paper 2
Transfer speed bit/byte TCP/UDP/IP	Performance/communication	
Confidentiality	Security/authentication	Paper 1
Effectiveness	Security/authentication	
Auditability	Security/data security	
Modularity	-	
Sensitivity	Security/authentication	
Boot time	Economy/elasticity	
Computation time	Performance	
Resources utilization	Efficiency	
Memory speed	Performance/memory	
CPU load	Performance/computation	Paper 1 Paper 2
Component resources cost	Economy/cost	
FLOP cost	Economy/cost	
Fixed time cost	Economy/cost	
Total cost	Economy/cost	
Instance efficiency	Performance/computation	
Packet loss frequency	Performance/communication	
Latency over SLL	Security/data security	
Price/performance ratio	Economy/cost	
Is SSL applicable?	Security/data security	
RAM update rate	Performance/memory	
Connection errors rate	Performance/communication	
FLOPs (Float Point Operations Per Second) rate	Performance/computation	
Communication time	Performance	
Deletion time	Economy/elasticity	
Deploy time	Economy/elasticity	
Suspension time	Economy/elasticity	
Acquisition total time	Economy/elasticity	
Supported users on a fixed budget	Economy/cost	
Interoperability	-	
Memory reponse time	Performance/memory	
Accuracy	-	Paper 4
Adequacy	-	
Reliability (errors numbers)	-	
Elasticity	-	
Transparency	-	

Table 2. Metrics evaluation according to defined criteria (approved metrics).

Metric	Criterion 1	Criterion 2	Criterion 3	Criterion 4
Transfer latency TCP/UDP/IP	Yes	Yes	Yes	Yes
Bandwidth (download, upload)	Yes	Yes	Yes	Yes
CPU load	Yes	Yes	Yes	Yes
Reliability (errors numbers)	Yes	Yes	Yes	Yes
Access control	Yes	Yes	Yes	Yes
CPU frequency	Yes	Yes	Yes	Yes
Total cost	Yes	Yes	Yes	Yes
Instance efficiency	Yes	Yes	Yes	Yes
Elasticity	Yes	Yes	Yes	Yes
Packet loss frequency	Yes	Yes	Yes	Yes
Auditability	Yes	Yes	Yes	Yes
Latency over SLL	Yes	Yes	Yes	Yes
Application maximum latency	Yes	Yes	Yes	Yes
Concurrent users maximum number	Yes	Yes	Yes	Yes
Memory (RAM required for the instance)	Yes	Yes	Yes	Yes
NoSQL databases support	Yes	Yes	Yes	Yes
Number of CPU cores	Yes	Yes	Yes	Yes
Number of instances	Yes	Yes	Yes	Yes
Number of load balancers	Yes	Yes	Yes	Yes
Operational System (Type, Platform, Version)	Yes	Yes	Yes	Yes
Relational database support	Yes	Yes	Yes	Yes
Memory response time	Yes	Yes	Yes	Yes
Is SSL applicable?	Yes	Yes	Yes	Yes
Storage (HD)	Yes	Yes	Yes	Yes
Boot time	Yes	Yes	Yes	Yes
Communication time	Yes	Yes	Yes	Yes
Deletion time	Yes	Yes	Yes	Yes
Deploy time	Yes	Yes	Yes	Yes
Application response time	Yes	Yes	Yes	Yes
Suspension time	Yes	Yes	Yes	Yes
Mean time between failures (MTBF)	Yes	Yes	Yes	Yes
Acquisition total time	Yes	Yes	Yes	Yes
Transfer speed bit/byte TCP/UDP/IP	Yes	Yes	Yes	Yes
I/O performance	Yes	Yes	Yes	Yes

Table 3. Metrics evaluation according to defined criteria (rejected metrics).

Metric	Criterion 1	Criterion 2	Criterion 3	Criterion 4
Accuracy	Yes	Yes	Yes	No
Availability	Yes	Yes	Yes	No
Adequacy	Yes	No	-	-
Service learnability	Yes	Yes	No	-
Data Control	Yes	Yes	No	-
Fixed time cost	Yes	Yes	No	-
Defects per million	Yes	No	-	-
Ease of use	Yes	Yes	No	-
IaaS instalability	Yes	Yes	No	-
Interoperability	Yes	Yes	No	-
Access Control Policies	Yes	Yes	No	-
Transparency	Yes	Yes	No	-
VM Cost	Yes	Yes	No	-
Cryptography algorithms	No	-	-	-
Application servers	No	-	-	-
Application layers	No	-	-	-
Application type	No	-	-	-
Confidentiality	No	-	-	-
Component resources cost	No	-	-	-
FLOP cost	No	-	-	-
Effectiveness	No	-	-	-
Modularity	No	-	-	-
Data privacy	No	-	-	-
Price/Performance ratio	No	-	-	-
Region	No	-	-	-
Security (general metric)	No	-	-	-
Sensitivity	No	-	-	-
RAM update rate	No	-	-	-
FLOPs (Float Point Operations Per Second) rate	No	-	-	-
Computation time	No	-	-	-
Supported Users on a Fixed Budget	No	-	-	-
Resources utilization	No	-	-	-
Memory speed	No	-	-	-
Connection errors rate	No	-	-	-

The categorization and the metrics comparison is presented in Tables 4 and 5 that represents the static metrics and dynamic metrics, respectively.

The existing metrics in OpenStack can be summarized in the follow items. Besides the identical metrics, some related metrics were also identified. All metrics provided by the tool can be consulted in the documentation [10]. The metrics presented with the dot notation ('some.metric.presented'), this is the name as presented in OpenStack by its telemetry module.

Table 4. Evaluation of the static metrics in OpenStack.

Statics		
Category	Metrics	Is it in OpenStack?
Economy	Total cost	-
General	NoSQL databases support	Yes
	Operational System (Type, Platform, Version)	Yes
	Relational database support	Yes
	Access control policies	Yes
Security	Is SSL applicable?	Yes
	Auditability	Yes

- **Memory (RAM required for the instance)**
  - Volume of RAM allocated to the instance (memory);
  - Volume of RAM used by the instance from the amount of its allocated memory (memory.usage);
  - Volume of RAM used per project.
- **Storage (HD)**;
  - Size of root disk (disk.root.size);
  - Permanent memory used per project.
- **Application maximum latency**
  - Average disk latency (disk.latency);
  - Average disk latency per device (disk.device.latency).
- **Number of CPU cores**
  - Number of virtual CPUs allocated to the instance (vcpus);
  - Number of virtual CPUs per project;
  - Average CPU utilization (cpu_util).
- **Number of instances**
  - Number of active instances.
- **Number of load balancers**
  - Existence of a LB pool (network.services.lb.pool);
  - Existence of a LB VIP (network.services.lb.vip);
  - Existence of a LB member (network.services.lb.member);
  - Existence of a LB health probe (network.services.lb.health_monitor);
  - Total connections on a LB (network.services.lb.total.connections);
  - Active connections on a LB (network.services.lb.active.connections).
- **Bandwidth (download, upload)**
  - Bytes through this l3 metering label (Network layer routers) (bandwidth).
- **CPU load**
  - CPU load in the past 1 min (hardware.cpu.load.1 min);
  - CPU load in the past 5 min (hardware.cpu.load.5 min);
  - CPU load in the past 10 min (hardware.cpu.load.10 min).
- **CPU frequency**
  - CPU frequency (compute.node.cpu.frequency).

Table 5. Evaluation of the dynamic metrics in OpenStack.

Dynamics		
Category	Metrics	Is it in OpenStack?
Reliability	Reliability (errors numbers)	No
	Mean time between failures (MTBF)	No
Economy	Elasticity	No
	Boot time	No
	Deletion time	No
	Deploy time	No
	Suspension Time	No
	Acquisition total time	No
Memory	Memory (RAM required for the instance)	Yes
	Storage (HD)	Yes
Performance	Application maximum latency	No
	Concurrent users maximum number	No
	Number of CPU cores	No
	Number of instances	Yes
	Number of load balancers	No
	Application response time	No
	Bandwidth (download, upload)	Yes
	CPU load	Yes
	CPU frequency	Yes
	Instance efficiency	Yes
	Packet loss frequency	No
Security	Transfer latency TCP/UDP/IP	No
	I/O Performance	Yes
	Memory response time	No
	Communication time	No
	Latency over SLL	No

- **Instance efficiency**
    - CPU utilization (compute.node.cpu.percent).
- **Packet loss frequency**
    - Number of incoming packets (network.incoming.packets);
    - Average rate of incoming packets (network.incoming.packets.rate);
    - Number of outgoing packets (network.outgoing.packets);
    - Average rate of outgoing packets (network.outgoing.packets.rate).
- **I/O Performance**
    - Number of read requests (disk.read.requests);
    - Average rate of read requests (disk.read.requests.rate);

- Number of write requests (disk.write.requests);
- Average rate of write requests (disk.write.requests.rate);
- Volume of reads (disk.read.bytes);
- Average rate of reads (disk.read.bytes.rate);
- Volume of writes (disk.write.bytes);
- Average rate of writes (disk.write.bytes.rate).

4.2   Metrics Exemplification

In order to verify how the presented metrics were presented in OpenStack, a tool usage test scenario was performed to collect the metrics shown in Sect. 4.1. Subsect. 4.2 describes scenario used and Subsect. 4.2 discusses the obtained results.

Test Scenario. The data collection was performed in the following scenario/-context:

- Laboratory with machines that had simple hardware features;
    - Maximum of 4 GB of RAM.
- OpenStack Kilo version;
- Cent OS 7 operational system;
- Use of the topology of an OpenStack installation (Fig. 3);
    - Two interconnected computers were used to distribute the processing load between them so that a computer had the Controller node and the other computer had the Processing (Compute) and the Network nodes as shown in Fig. 3;
    - The topology used was based on the topology proposed by Ahmad Imanudin in [13];
- Creation of two instances.

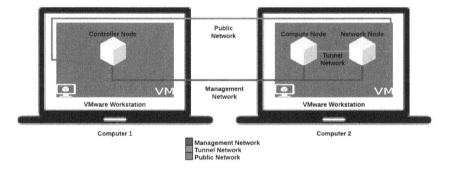

Fig. 3. Topology used in OpenStack installation. Source: Authors.

Two instances (using 512 MB of RAM and operational system CirrOS) were created in OpenStack as a test scenario to collect data. The topology used as test scenario can be seen in Fig. 4.

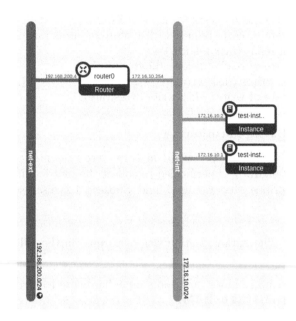

Fig. 4. Topology used as test scenario. *Image taken from OpenStack.*

Table 6. Collected metrics in test scenario.

OpenStack metric	Max	Min	Average	Unit
cpu_util	16.11	0	7.9	%
memory	512	512	512	MB
memory.usage	-	-	-	MB
disk.root.size	1	1	1	GB
vcpus	1	1	1	n vCPUs
network.incoming .packets	19	8	11.75	packets
network.incoming .packets.rate	0.0016	0.00011	0.00011	packets/s
network.outgoing .packets	9	9	9	packets
network.outgoing .packets.rate	0	0	0	packets/s
disk.read.requests	1122	877	1032.77	requests
disk.read .requests.rate	0.23	0	0.015	requests/s
disk.write.requests	134	55	111.9	requests
disk.write .requests.rate	0.091	0	0.001	requests/s
disk.read.bytes	20436992	18510848	20245043.2	bytes
disk.read.bytes.rate	3700.63	0	206.49	bytes/s
disk.write.bytes	397312	206848	348262.4	bytes
disk.write.bytes.rate	268.85	0	22.14	bytes/s

The Kilo [8] version of OpenStack was used because it is a stable and lighter version, necessary to the limited resources available. It is worth mentioning that although the support for the Kilo version has been terminated by the OpenStack maintainers, its architecture is not far from its successor, OpenStack Liberty, which does not significantly impact or invalidate this work [9].

Results Obtained. The metrics were collected through the OpenStack data collection service (Ceilometer module) and web application (Horizon module). With the test scenario fulfilled, the collected metrics can be seen in Table 6.

It is possible to see that OpenStack is a very powerful tool that provides a good measurement service (Ceilometer module). In the simple scenario (creation of two instances in the tool) several metrics are generated and can be monitored to guarantee QoS.

5   Conclusions

With a literature review it was possible to collect 68 metrics of QoS into cloud services. In OpenStack, 34 of these metrics were evaluated. In the evaluation it was found that OpenStack provides approximately 24.25% of the metrics, as well as, providing additional related metrics.

The number of metrics can be related to the fact that OpenStack has a specific module to collect metrics. The results obtained in this study can be used in other related studies and for tools that provide a cloud services selection, supporting the collection of possible metrics that can be found in OpenStack.

Beyond the telemetry module, OpenStack offers some mechanisms of quality of service assurance, such as: establishing limits for files size, RAM memory, instances and virtual CPUs; creating security rules to limit specific traffic on instances; and the creation of QoS rules to limit bandwidth on instances and to assure a minimum bandwidth [6,7].

An identified limitation of this study is that the metrics were identified using a simple literature review. In this way, it was not possible to obtain the visibility of a higher number of studies. The use of an old version of the tool was identified as another limitation.

Future work could involve a systematic review to find more metrics and then to apply them to a most current version of OpenStack.

References

1. Armbrust, M., Fox, A., Griffith, R., Joseph, A.D., Katz, R., Konwinski, A., Lee, G., Patterson, D., Rabkin, A., Stoica, I., et al.: A view of cloud computing. Commun. ACM **53**(4), 50–58 (2010)
2. Bardsiri, A.K., Hashemi, S.M.: QoS metrics for cloud computing services evaluation. Int. J. Intell. Syst. Appl. **6**(12), 27 (2014)
3. Bhardwaj, S., Jain, L., Jain, S.: Cloud computing: a study of infrastructure as a service (IaaS). Int. J. Eng. Inf. Technol. **2**(1), 60–63 (2010)

4. Bui, T.A.: Cloud network performance analysis: an OpenStack case study. Master's thesis, Université Catholique de Louvain (2016)
5. Filho, L., Machado, D.: A influência das informações de hardware e software nos serviços de IaaS: uma abordagem sobre desempenho de máquinas virtuais em nuvem. Ph.D. thesis, Universidade de São Paulo (2016)
6. O. Foundation. Neutron QoS API Models and Extension
7. O. Foundation. OpenStack neutron QoS
8. O. Foundation. OpenStack kilo (2015)
9. O. Foundation. OpenStack Liberty Release Notes (2015)
10. O. Foundation. OpenStack Kilo Installation Guide, May 2016
11. O. Foundation. OpenStack Website (2016)
12. Garg, S.K., Versteeg, S., Buyya, R.: SMICloud: a framework for comparing and ranking cloud services. In: 2011 Fourth IEEE International Conference on Utility and Cloud Computing (UCC), pp. 210–218. IEEE (2011)
13. Imanudin, A.: How to Install OpenStack Kilo Multi-node (2015)
14. Systems and software engineering - Measurement process. Standard, International Organization for Standardization, Switzerland, October 2007
15. Karim, R., Ding, C., Miri, A.: An end-to-end QoS mapping approach for cloud service selection. In: 2013 IEEE Ninth World Congress on Services, pp. 341–348. IEEE (2013)
16. Li, Z., O'Brien, L., Zhang, H., Cai, R.: On a catalogue of metrics for evaluating commercial cloud services. In: Proceedings of the 2012 ACM/IEEE 13th International Conference on Grid Computing, pp. 164–173. IEEE Computer Society (2012)
17. Mell, P., Grance, T.: The NIST Definition of Cloud Computing (2011)
18. Quarati, A., Clematis, A., D'Agostino, D.: Delivering cloud services with QoS requirements: business opportunities, architectural solutions and energy-saving aspects. Future Gener. Comput. Syst. 55, 403–427 (2016)
19. Rehman, M.S., Sakr, M.F.: Teaching the cloud-experiences in designing and teaching an undergraduate-level course in cloud computing at the Carnegie Mellon University in Qatar. In: 2011 IEEE Global Engineering Education Conference (EDUCON), pp. 875–879. IEEE (2011)
20. Sefraoui, O., Aissaoui, M., Eleuldj, M.: OpenStack: toward an open-source solution for cloud computing. Int. J. Comput. Appl. 55(3), 260–276 (2012)
21. Siegel, J., Perdue, J.: Cloud services measures for global use: the service measurement index (SMI). In: 2012 Annual SRII Global Conference, pp. 411–415. IEEE (2012)
22. Soltani, S.: IaaS Cloud Service Selection Using Case-Based Reasoning (2016)
23. Sun, L., Dong, H., Hussain, F.K., Hussain, O.K., Chang, E.: Cloud service selection: state-of-the-art and future research directions. J. Netw. Comput. Appl. 45, 134–150 (2014)
24. Xia, Y., Zhou, M., Luo, X., Zhu, Q.: A comprehensive QoS determination model for infrastructure-as-a-service clouds. In: 2013 IEEE International Conference on Automation Science and Engineering (CASE), pp. 122–127. IEEE (2013)

Dynamic Composable Analytics on Consumer Behaviour

Jin-Quan Goh and Fang-Fang Chua$^{(\boxtimes)}$

Faculty of Computing and Informatics, Multimedia University,
63000 Cyberjaya, Selangor, Malaysia
jqgoh@hotmail.com, ffchua@mmu.edu.my

Abstract. Large enterprises and companies often use different tools and systems that distributed across their company branches to operate daily business operations. The collected data and logs have significant potential of providing useful information and insights for the company; however, staffs may spend massive time and effort to process the raw data into useful information as raw data is scattered and distributed across different platforms. This study proposes a framework called *Dynamic Composable Analytic Framework (DCAF)*, which is able to accept and compose raw data from different systems or tools, and performs analytics on the composed data to identify or predict the consumer behavior. The proposed framework is able to perform data receiver, data composition, data massaging and data analytic job with minor human interaction. *DCAF* provides contribution as an end-to-end solution for converting raw data to predicted customer behavior information and thus improving the customer analytics efficiency.

Keywords: Data composition · Consumer analytic · Dynamic data integration
Consumer behavior prediction · Big data

1 Introduction

Nowadays, we use systems or tools to aid our daily routine and tasks. These tools might contain activity logs or produce data in different formats, and we could get a lot of helpful information and insights from these data. The emergence of data analytic is able to provide valuable information to improve tools, decision-making and productivity. Besides, organizations that embrace analytic driven management yield a better business performance. MIT Sloan Management Review collaborates with IBM Institute of Business Value by conducting a research which includes global survey as well as in-depth interview. The outcome of the survey indicates that top performing companies are using data analytic five times more than low performance company [1] and affirms that the implementation of data analytic is correlated with the good performance of the organization. Through Ren's team [2] and Mariya's research [3], data analytic is performed to allow user to gain business value from system or stakeholder information to improve business performance. Ren's team applies machine learning and big data analytic on data from energy utility companies and it allows them to gain insight on millions of customer within a short time. Apart from that, big data analytic can improve new product success rate. In Xu and his team research, big data analytic is better in dealing with drastic change in technology and market requirement as big data analytic has better understanding in stakeholder information compared with traditional marketing [4]. However, these benefits can only be utilized if the data analytic process is completed successfully and useful information is extracted from the data. One of the essential factors for data analytic is that the data has to be clean and well structured. Besides, the steps to perform data integration and data composition on heterogeneous data from different data sources are also playing a crucial part to increase effectiveness of data analytic [5]. Meanwhile, there are not many relevant tools in market, which can give a hand to perform data analytic on heterogeneous data.

A framework called *Dynamic Composable Analytic Framework (DCAF)* is proposed to overcome the problem addressed earlier. There are three main objectives of *DCAF*. The available tools in the market are able to perform e jobs for each objective separately but there is no tool in the market that is able to meet the all objectives at the same time. The first objective of our proposed work is to provide feature that accept data coming from different data sources and in different forms such as different structure or format but containing same semantic meaning; and then convert the data which is in heterogeneous forms into an expected file type. This is to ease data composition or data analytic job. The second objective is to discover and compose information in real time scenario and enabling *DCAF* to accept data input from different sources in real time automatically. Besides, *DCAF* allows newly discovered data source to communicate with it or receive data from new data source. The third objective is to provide consumer analytic feature for the user on composed dataset. *DCAF* is a framework that composes of different technology like.NET, Window Workflow Foundation (WF), Window Communication Foundation (WCF) and R.NET. There are three core elements in *DCAF*: (1) dynamic environment element which improves the flexibility of the framework and enable the framework to handle real time data, (2) composable element which improve the interoperability of the framework and allows the framework to compose the information from different data sources, and (3) consumer analytic element that provide consumer analytic feature. The remainder of this paper is organized as follows: Sect. 2 presents background study and related works, Sect. 3 discusses structure and three core elements proposed in *DCAF*, Sect. 4 presents the testing and results and Sect. 5 concludes with discussion and future work.

2   Related Works

DCAF chooses orchestration service which focuses on recursively compose of services [6]. Based on orchestration service, there will be one master module that acts as central service or controller that coordinating all modules among the whole environment. In *DCAF*, central service will be the point of contact for the child service to pass the dataset, and central service is also the service that responsible to compose and analyze the data. Apart from that, *DCAF* uses workflow to handle the dynamic environment. There is a Workflow Management System (WFMS) in *DCAF* which manages the flow of data from data acceptations stage to data analytic stage. To ensure that WFMS meets its objective, WFMS is configured to collaborate with Knowledge Library (KL) which is a rule-based library to provide guidance to convert the dataset to correct file type and data composition. Besides, *DCAF* contains analytic modules that provide consumer analytic feature. *DCAF*'s analytic module adopts RFM (recency, frequency, monetary) analytic model, introduced by Hughes [7] to identify the Customer Lifetime Value (CLV) which can be used to forecast future profit of a customer, and rank the potential important customers. During literature reviews, we find methods or tools which carry out composition job, handle dynamic data and perform consumer analytic. However, there is no identical framework that offers functionality like *DCAF*. The current method, framework and tools that can be found from the market do not provide the end-to-end solution as offered by DCAF, hence the literature review for this study is done based on the comparison of the core elements in *DCAF*. The summary of the related works is shown in Table 1.

Table 1. Summary of related works

References	Related work's methods	Related feature in *DCAF*
Coetzee [8]	Uses rule-based class to provide pre and post condition to handle dynamic environment	Dynamic environment handling
Siriweera [9]	Uses a layer architecture that contain intelligent layer to manage dynamic data	Dynamic environment handling
Hughes [7]	Uses RFM analytic model to identify the Customer Lifetime Value	Consumer analytic
Benatallah and Sheng [10]	Uses layered architecture to dynamically composes web service and allows the web service to have P2P communication	Composition method
Chen [11]	Allows the web services to select correct web service to communicate	Composition method
Kluskas [12]	Integrated visualisation analysis on phenotyping plant data	Composition method
Fielder and Dasey [13]	The proposed tool allows user to add the wanted data source and then compose and analyze the data	Data composition and dynamic environment handling

A dynamic analysis allows data from the analysis process change constantly and support real time analysis. This means that the analytic model should be able to feed in new data in real time mode and perform immediate analysis on the data. There are many events in the world which requires real time analysis, for example natural disaster prevention [14] and medical research activities [15]. Special written or design of library, module or architecture would require the tools or systems to handle dynamic environment like the proposed framework by Coetzee [8] and Siriweera [9]. In terms of handling dynamic environment part, *DCAF* will rely on rule-based class to handle dynamic variable like how Coetzee did, but the rule-based class in *DCAF* which called KL will work with WFMS. On consumer analytic part, the RFM analytic model that proposed by Hughes [7] is able to identify the value of customer. Hence, *DCAF* will use RFM analytic model to group the customer based on the customer value, so that the prediction can be done on important customer group. On composition method part, there are different composition methods from the literature like web service composition method from Benatallah and Sheng [10] and Chen [11], and data composition method from Kluskas [12]. The composition method from Kluskas is more suitable for *DCAF*, because *DCAF* need data composition for analytic purpose to merge the data and standardizing sematic meaning of the data. However, the proposed method from Kluskas is focusing on image data while *DCAF* is focusing on text-based data. Thus, *DCAF* will have its own composition method, which relies on Service-Oriented Architecture (SOA) to obtain the data from child service and then use WFMS to collaborate with Knowledge Library (KL) to compose the data. There is an existing tool called Composable Analytics which is able to compose data from different sources and then provide the summary of the data to user in current market [13]. *DCAF* offers better flexibility than Composable Analytics as *DCAF* allows any registered child service to call the central service to pass input dataset in *DCAF* when child service provides the metadata. Besides, *DCAF* offers more precise analytic feature compared to Composable Analytics, because *DCAF* provides consumer analytic feature while Composable Analytics only provides basic analytic features with charts.

3 Dynamic Composable Analytic Framework (DCAF)

Dynamic Composable Analytic Framework (DCAF) provides data composition and consumer analytic feature on real time data with minor human interaction. Dynamic environment element uses Workflow Management Systems (WFMS) to handle the input of real time data and SOA to improve the flexibility in data exchange between the tools; composable element uses Knowledge Library (KL) which is a rule- base library to guide the *DCAF* on data composition and data cleaning; consumer analytic element uses RFM analysis model to group the customer. Further details will be discussed in the sub section of this section. Figure 1 illustrates the process within *DCAF*. Firstly, the data sources will call the main service function and pass the received data into WFMS which in charge of the logical controls and workflow. Next, data will be compiled into correct file format at file storage, and analytic module will then perform analytic by retrieving the file from the file storage. Analysis result will be displayed at UI application. In this framework, knowledge library provides support for data cleaning, conversion of file type and column data type.

3.1 Services in DCAF

The services in *DCAF* are developed using Windows Communication Foundation (WCF) from .Net framework [16]. There are two type of services in *DCAF*: child service and central service. Child service is the data source that provides the input data to central service, while central service is the place that carries out data composition and data analytic process. The list of functions from central service is listed in Table 2.

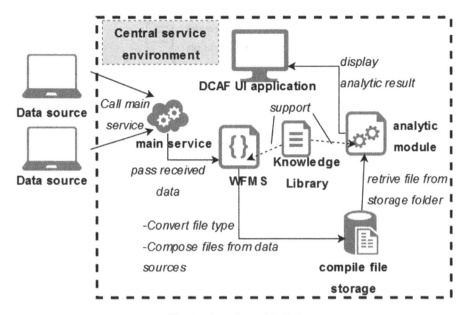

Fig. 1. Overview of *DCAF*

Table 2. List of functions from central service

Function name	Descriptions
CS_GetData	Child services call this method to pass the dataset to central service
CS_GetMetaData	Child services call this method to pass the metadata for dataset from the particular child service to central service
CS_SendMetaDataTemplate	Child service call this method to get the metadata template from central service

3.2 Workflow Management System in DCAF

DCAF is adopting concepts from Business Process Management (BPM) to handle and compose input data from multiple data sources. BPM is an approach using Workflow Management System (WFMS) to automate business process that involves different resources like human, organisation, application and source of information in business [17]. The Workflow Management System will be developed by using Windows Workflow Foundation (WF) on .Net framework 4.5 [18]. WF allows the user to declare workflow or business logic to control the logic and flow of the activities in applications or services using Visual Basic or C# language. WFMS will be the logical and operation controller in *DCAF*. It is ensuring the input data passing thru file type conversion process and data compilation process correctly, and the data analytic job is triggered continuously. Figure 2 illustrates the overview process flow for WFMS.

When child service triggers the web service function from central service, central service will execute the "WorkFlow_FileConverter" workflow to convert input data file

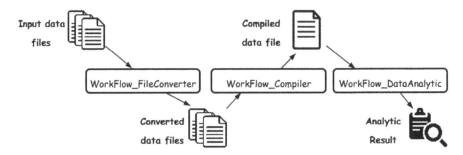

Fig. 2. Overview of WFMS process flow

into expected file type. Next, the "WorkFlow_Compiler" will notice the existing of new data file and consolidate the input data file into single compiled data file. After that, "WorkFlow_DataAnalytic" will retrieve the data from file into analytic module to perform analytic accordingly. The analytic result will be displayed in *DCAF* application UI after the data analytic job is completed.

3.3 Knowledge Library in *DCAF*

Knowledge Library (KL) is a rule-based class that provides information for the workflow to perform data composition. KL can be divided into three parts as shown in Fig. 3. KL is a class that written in C# programming language, and uses .Net Framework Class Library to support file type conversation and use R.net library to support data type conversation activities. The difference between convert file type feature and convert column data type feature is that convert file type feature will focus on converting the data file type, while convert column data type will focus on converting the column variable type like string or integer to correct column variable type.

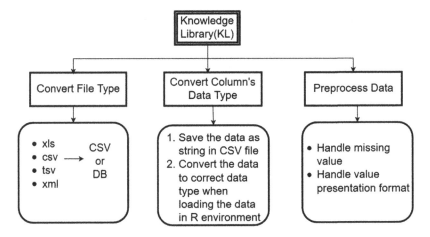

Fig. 3. Knowledge library overview

3.4   Consumer Analytic in *DCAF*

DCAF has an analytic module that will analyze the customer transaction history to predict the consumer behavior and convert the result in chart or list of suggestion via displayed text on *DCAF* user interface. The analytic module starts when analysis function is triggered from data analytic workflow. First, composed data will be then retrieved, and secondly data cleaning is performed. Next, data summary will be displayed and then dataset will be discretized for RFM analysis. The customer segmentation is then reformed based on RFM result and a chart is plotted. Lastly, one of the customer from the "best customer" (the way to identifier "best customer" will be explained in this section) segment is selected and the top five potential interest products are being identified and displayed.

RFM Analysis

The analytic module uses RFM analytic model to identify Customer Lifetime Value (CLV) from customer transaction dataset. In marketing field, CLV is applying on customer acquisition, customer selection, customer retention, marketing strategic decision and resource allocation [19]. While in *DCAF*, the CLV from RFM analysis has been used on customer selection to identify the "best customer" group, who has the most interest to the shop product and sales. The "best customer" will score the highest mark in three attributes of RFM analysis namely recency, frequency and monetary. Marketer and shop manager are unlikely to focus on every customer's needs and interests as the customer pool can be huge and variant. Matching with Pareto principle (also known as 80/20 rule), they may apply the concept by just focusing 20% of the shop customer to gain the 80% income of the shop [20]. *DCAF* analytic module is using the same concept from Pareto principle. It will only target on prominent customer group like "best customer" segment which is mostly the big spender and loyal customer.

Algorithm 1. RFM Analysis

---

1. **Set** a target date that represent recent date
2. Select the transaction that match with the target customer id
   and not more than 1 year different with target date
3. **With** the selected transaction perform step 4 to step 7
4. **Set** Recency = target date - latest transaction date
5. **Set** Frequency = **Sum**(invoice count)
6. **Set** Monetary = **Sum**(total spend of every transaction)
7. Add new row to RFM_Analysis data table with
   customer id, Recency, Frequency, Monetary as new row of record
8. Repeat from step 2 until acquire RFM value for all the customers
9. Discretize the Recency into 5 equal equal size group by labeling
   first 20% of data = 5 , next 20% of data = 4 and so on ...
10. Discretize the Frequency into 5 equal equal size group by labeling
    first 20% of data = 1 , next 20% of data = 2 and so on ...
11. Discretize the Monetary into 5 equal equal size group by labeling
    first 20% of data = 1 , next 20% of data = 2 and so on ...
12. Perform segmentation according to preset rule

Algorithm 1 shows the pseudocode for RFM analysis and it is also the steps for *DCAF* to obtain the RFM score. The RFM analysis will start from setting the target date. The target date will be the recent date or today's date, which will be used to find the Recency dimension value. After setting the target date, analytic module will find the transaction that is not more than one year's difference with the target date and match with the target customer id. After that, *DCAF* will find the Recency, Frequency and Monetary dimension value from the subset of transaction. Recency value can be obtained from the difference between the target date and the most recent transaction date in the subset. Summing up the total invoice count that represents the number transactions then we can get the frequency value while the Monetary value is calculated from the total spend of the customer in every transaction. After having RFM value for all customers, *DCAF* discretizes each dimension into five equal groups. For Recency dimension, the first 20% of the value will be labeled as 5 and the next 20% of the value will be label as 4 and so on. This means that the customer with the more recent transaction will have higher score in Recency dimension. For Frequency and Monetary dimension, the first 20% of the value will be labelled as 1 and the next 20% of the score will be labelled as 2 and so on. This means that the customer with higher frequency of visit and purchase at the shop and higher total spent in the shop will get higher score in Frequency and Monetary dimension respectively. After *DCAF* obtains RFM score of each customer, it will then perform customer segmentation according to pre-set rule that is shown in Table 3.

Table 3. RFM customer segments

Segment	RFM score			Description
	R	F	M	
Best customer	5	5	5	Customers who visit and often spend a lot in the shop, and this group customer visit the shop recently
Lost cheap customer	1	–	1	Customers who have not visit the shop for long time and do not spending much money in this shop
Lost big spend customer	1	–	5	Customer who have not visited the shop for long time and spend a lot of money in this shop
Almost lost big spender	2	–	5	Customer who spend a lot in this shop but have not visit the shop for sometime
Almost lost	2	–	–	Customer who have not visited the shop for sometime
Loyal	–	5	–	Customer visit the shop for many time
Big spender	–	–	5	Customer spend a lot in this shop

Predicting product that customer might be interested in

After *DCAF* identifies the "best customer" from the input transaction, it will then predict the best prospect product based on the transaction history of the customer from "best customer" group. The best prospect product is being identified based on sales profit from the product being purchased and the probability of the item that will be purchased from the history. *DCAF* will list out the top five highest amount of purchase products along with the probability of the product being purchased in the *DCAF* user interface. The product sales amount presents customer's demand to the product, while the probability of the product being purchased presents how often the customer needs the product. Hence, the combination of both of the statistics will able to improve the accuracy on predicting the potential interest product.

4   Testing and Results

A framework testing has been performed to evaluate *DCAF*. The testing process is divided into three parts: (1) Workflow Management testing, (2) Knowledge Library testing and (3) Consumer Analytic module testing. Workflow Management testing aims to verify whether the WFMS working correctly as expected in dynamic environment; Knowledge Library testing is to verify whether KL is giving the correct instruction to *DCAF* for data composition purpose; Consumer Analytic module testing is to check whether proposed method in analytic module is performing analysis correctly if the framework accepts the data dynamically. Checklist questions which are used in the framework testing are shown in Table 4. *DCAF* is required to pass all the questions in checklist questions in order to pass the framework testing.

Table 4. Testing checklist question

Type of testings	Checklist questions
Workflow Management testing	Is WFMS getting the data from child services and pass to the central services?
Workflow Management testing	Is WFMS handling constant input from real time data source?
Workflow Management testing	After child service stop providing the data, will WFMS becomes not responding?
Knowledge Library testing	Is KL in *DCAF* converting the data type of the column correctly?
Knowledge Library testing	Is KL in *DCAF* composing the columns that have same semantic meaning correctly?
Consumer Analytic module testing	Will the consumer analytic module able to accept new data input dynamically and then perform the analysis without error?

The testing will start with creating a scenario which assuming there are two child services registered in *DCAF*. The scenario will assume that one of the registered child services is from Singapore, while the other child service is from China. The Singapore service will provide dataset in excel format (.xlsx file), while the China service will provide the dataset in tab separated value format (.tsv file). Both of the child services dataset will contain the required columns for the consumer behaviour prediction purpose, but both datasets will contain extra unwanted columns. Hence, *DCAF* will need to convert the child datasets into CSV format and find the wanted columns in both child data sets for consolidation purpose. To find the wanted column, *DCAF* will need to match the columns name between different datasets. *DCAF* will use the column name from the parent dataset as the searching criteria to check the availability of wanted column in child dataset. The *DCAF* should able to adapt to the dynamic environment because it is assumed that both child services will have inconstant time to send the child data set to central service. Besides, it is assumed that both child service and central service are having corrected and error free metadata file.

Dataset for testing
DCAF is being evaluated by using an online retail dataset from http://archive.ics.uci. edu/ml/datasets/online+retail. Chen from School of Engineering, London South Bank University generates this dataset [21]. The dataset is collected from an UK-based company which having its non-store retail business over Europe and UK. The online retail dataset is having the sales transaction from 01/02/2010 to 09/12/2011. There are more than 4000 customers contribute to this dataset, and it has more than 500,000 of row record with 8 attributes in each row to record the customer purchase history. Apart from the retail dataset from Chen, self-created datasets will also be included in the evaluation process. The self-created datasets will be having file type like comma separated file, tab separated file and excel file to evaluate the data composition ability of *DCAF*. Although this self-created dataset is being randomly generated, it is still able to match with the main retail dataset, because the stock code and unit price for the self-created dataset is from the main retail dataset. In the framework testing, the central services will have the downloaded online retail dataset, while the both child services will send the self-created dataset to the central service.

4.1   Test Results

Workflow Management Testing Result. When the testing started, the child service will send in the self-created datasets without a consistent time to create dynamic environment. These self-created datasets will be handled by WFMS and converted to CSV file type and stored at temporary file location and pending consolidator workflow to compose. Thus, to verify the correctness of WFMS, checking is required on temporary folder. If WFMS working correctly, CSV file will be generated in temporary folder as WFMS will trigger the workflow that is able to convert the child dataset to CSV file and then store the converted CSV file at temporary folder. The testing result shows that WFMS is working correctly as before the execution, the temporary file location is empty, but after the testing is started, it contains two CSV files. These two CSV files are the dataset from China and SEA child services. After performing five round of testing and monitoring the files changes of temporary folder, we found that WFMS done its job correctly as it is able to handle the inconstant dataset input. From this, we can verify *DCAF* pass the first testing stage.

Knowledge Library Testing Result. The child service dataset will be composed correctly if KL is working correctly without error. To verify whether the child service dataset been composed into expected file structure, user can check the composed file at "Compose" folder. The "Compose" folder will have the compose dataset which being generated or updated after composing the CSV file from temporary location. After verified the column structure and content of the consolidate CSV file is correct, then we said that KL provides the correct rules and instruction to "WorkFlow_Compiler" workflow as "WorkFlow_Compiler" workflow done it job correctly without error. To verify the composed file having correct column structure, we did manually checking on the composed file to ensure that it has the required columns by comparing the columns from all the CSV files in temporary folder. On the other side, to verify the content of consolidate file, we checked whether the all the required row of data exist in the consolidate file. Apart from that, to verify that the KL works well, we also check whether summary and chart from the *DCAF* analytic result tab reflect the changes correctly. *DCAF* analytic result tab displays the result in text or chart form correctly without application crash or error message during the testing. Hence from the checking and verification, the KL is verified and passed both checklist questions.

Consumer Analytic Module Testing. To verify the analytic module is working correctly, we need to ensure the analysis result is correctly displayed at DCAF data analytic tab. The analytic module shall display the dataset summary like number of customer, oldest transaction date and latest transaction date of the dataset at the analytic result tab's "summary" section correctly, customer value segmentation bar chart in result tab's "plot" section correctly, and the predicted important customer interested item in result tab's "result" section correctly (as shown in Fig. 4). The tester had use native tools to run the analysis on the same dataset separately, so that the tester can

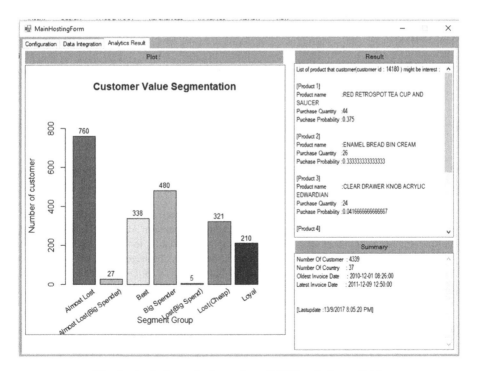

Fig. 4. Analytic result shown from *DCAF* analytic result tab

verify that the displayed result is correct. After complete the comparison between the result from DCAF and the result of testing tool, the analytic module can be verified as working correctly as the result from both tools is the same.

5   Conclusion

DCAF is a framework that is able to compose the data dynamically and then perform consumer analytic on the compose dataset automatically with minimum human interaction. Besides, *DCAF* has high interoperability characteristic. It is able to communicate with tools or other service easily by just providing the main service URL for other tools and service to call it. *DCAF* is been verified and tested and it is able to provide its functions correctly. The drawback of *DCAF* is it needs to rely on dataset's metadata to match the columns between different dataset and perform data composition accordingly. This drawback will reduce the efficiency of data composition because there is possibility that the column is named differently but having the same semantic meaning and it prompts to human error as it requires user to key in the metadata manually. Thus, in future work, Nature language Processing (NLP) will be applied in *DCAF*, so that we would able to understand the semantic meaning of the columns' name and thus improve the accuracy and flexibility of data composition. Besides, the analytic module will be further developed so that the prediction accuracy and performance for *DCAF* can be improved.

References

1. LaValle, S., Lesser, E., Shockley, R., Hopkins, M.S., Kruschwitz, N.: Big data, analytics and the path from insights to value. MIT Sloan Manag. Rev. **52**(2), 21 (2011)
2. Ji-fan Ren, S., Fosso Wamba, S., Akter, S., Dubey, R., Childe, S.J.: Modelling quality dynamics, business value and firm performance in a big data analytics environment. Int. J. Prod. Res. **55**(17), 5011–5026 (2017)
3. Sodenkamp, M., Kozlovskiy, I., Staake, T.: Gaining is business value through big data analytics: a case study of the energy sector (2015)
4. Xu, Z., Frankwick, G.L., Ramirez, E.: Effects of big data analytics and traditional marketing analytics on new product success: a knowledge fusion perspective. J. Bus. Res. **69**(5), 1562–1566 (2015)
5. Jagadish, H.V., Gehrke, J., Labrinidis, A., Papakonstantinou, Y., Patel, J.M., Ramakrishnan, R., Shahabi, C.: Big data and its technical challenges. Commun. ACM **57**(7), 86–94 (2014)
6. Ross-Talbot, S.: Orchestration and choreography: Standards, tools and technologies for distributed workflows. In: NETTAB Workshop-Workflows Management: New Abilities for the Biological Information Overflow, Naples, Italy, vol. 1, p. 8, October 2005
7. Hughes, A.M.: Strategic database marketing. McGraw-Hill Pub, New York (2005)
8. Coetzee, P., Jarvis, S.A.: Goal-based composition of scalable hybrid analytics for heterogeneous architectures. J. Parallel Distrib. Comput. (2016)
9. Siriweera, T.H.A.S., Paik, I., Kumara, B.T., Koswatta, K.R.C.: Intelligent big data analysis architecture based on automatic service composition. In: 2015 IEEE International Congress on Big Data (BigData Congress), pp. 276–280. IEEE, June 2015

10. Benatallah, B., Sheng, Q.Z., Dumas, M.: The self-serv environment for web services composition. IEEE Internet Comput. **7**(1), 40–48 (2003)
11. Chen, P.Y., Hwang, S.Y., Lee, C.H.: A dynamic service composition architecture in supporting reliable web service selection. In: 2013 Fifth International Conference on Service Science and Innovation (ICSSI). IEEE (2013)
12. Klukas, C., Chen, D., Pape, J.M.: Integrated analysis platform: an open-source information system for high-throughput plant phenotyping. Plant Physiol. **165**(2), 506–518 (2014)
13. Fielder, L.H., Dasey, T.J.: Systems and Methods for Composable Analytics (No. MIT/LL-CA-1). Massachusetts Inst of Tech Lexington Lincoln Lab (2014)
14. Sakaki, T., Okazaki, M., Matsuo, Y.: Earthquake shakes Twitter users: real-time event detection by social sensors. In: Proceedings of the 19th International Conference on World Wide Web, pp. 851–860. ACM, April 2010
15. Derveaux, S., Vandesompele, J., Hellemans, J.: How to do successful gene expression analysis using real-time PCR. Methods **50**(4), 227–230 (2010)
16. What Is Windows Communication Foundation. (n.d.). https://msdn.microsoft.com/en-us/library/ms731082(v=vs.110).aspx. Accessed 14 May 2017
17. Weske, M.: Business process management architectures. Business Process Management, pp. 333–371. Springer, Heidelberg (2012). https://doi.org/10.1007/978-3-642-28616-2_7
18. Milner, M.: A Developer's Introduction to Windows Workflow Foundation (WF) in .NET 4, April 2010. https://msdn.microsoft.com/en-us/library/ee342461.aspx. Accessed 13 May 2017
19. Gupta, S., Lehmann, D.R.: Customers as assets. J. Interact. Mark. **17**(1), 9–24 (2003)
20. Dunford, R., Su, Q., Tamang, E.: The Pareto principle. Plymouth Stud. Sci. **7**(1), 140–148 (2014)
21. Chen, D., Sain, S.L., Guo, K.: Data mining for the online retail industry: a case study of RFM model-based customer segmentation using data mining. J. Database Mark. Cust. Strategy Manag. **19**(3), 197–208 (2012)

Citation Count Prediction Using Non-technical Terms in Abstracts

Takahiro Baba[1] and Kensuke Baba[2]

[1] Kyushu University, Fukuoka 819-0395, Japan
[2] Fujitsu Laboratories, Kawasaki 211-8588, Japan
baba.kensuke@jp.fujitsu.com

Abstract. Researchers are required to find previous literature which is related to their research and has a scientific impact efficiently from a large number of publications. The target problem of this paper is predicting the citation count of each scholarly paper, that is, the number of citations from other scholarly papers, as the scientific impact. The authors tried to detect the high and low of the citation count of scholarly papers using only their abstracts, especially, non-technical terms used in them. They conducted a classification of abstracts of scholarly papers with high and low citation counts, and applied the classification also to the abstracts modified by deleting technical terms from them. The results of their experiments indicate that the scientific impact of a scholarly paper can be detected from information which is written in its abstract and is not related to the trend of research topics. The classification accuracy for detecting scholarly papers with the top or bottom 1% citation counts was 0.93, and that using the abstracts without technical terms was 0.90.

Keywords: Citation count prediction · Document classification
Text analysis · Machine learning

1 Introduction

Researchers are required to find previous literature which is related to their research and has a scientific impact efficiently from a large number of publications. The number of scholarly papers, especially, those available on-line is rapidly increasing. Ideally, researchers should make a survey over all the possible publications for their research, but it seems to be difficult to read their main texts carefully. Therefore, efficient methods are necessary for picking out scholarly papers which are relevant to the research concerned and have scientific impacts from huge data.

The target problem of this paper is predicting scientific impacts of scholarly papers, where the measure of impact is the *citation count* of a paper, that is, the number of citations from other papers to the paper. Predicting citation count enables us to screen scholarly papers to find those which potentially have high impacts. Citation count is a reasonable feature of scholarly papers for formalizing

© Springer International Publishing AG, part of Springer Nature 2018
O. Gervasi et al. (Eds.): ICCSA 2018, LNCS 10960, pp. 366–375, 2018.
https://doi.org/10.1007/978-3-319-95162-1_25

a kind of scientific impact. The impact factor [6], which is often referred as a "quality" measure of journal titles, is defined for a journal using the citation counts of the articles published in the journal. The h-index [7], which is a measure of a contribution of a researcher to the society concerned, is also based on the citation counts of scholarly papers written by the researcher. As we can see from the definition, citation count will increase with the lapse of time, and hence is not appropriate for measuring the impacts of brand-new papers. We need to use other features which can be extracted from papers to predict their future impacts.

The novelty of our study is that we tried to predict the citation count of scholarly papers using only their abstracts, especially, non-technical terms used in them. The problem of citation count prediction [9] has been widely studied, and a variety of features can be used for the prediction [5]. We addressed the text data obtained from scholarly papers themselves as the target of our analysis. The text data, especially, the abstracts which are usually available as the metadata of papers, are directly related to the contents of papers, while the other metadata including the authors, authors' institutions, and journal (conference) titles need extra processes to map the evaluations defined for the attributes to that for the contents. However, analyzing abstracts for citation count prediction can sink into trivial findings of the trend of research topics. Therefore, we also conducted the classification with the abstracts modified by deleting technical terms from them.

We conducted a classification of abstracts of scholarly papers with high and low citation counts using the distribution of word occurrences. Additionally, we applied the classification also to the abstracts modified by deleting technical terms from them. We aimed to find a lead to the citation count prediction in surface level information obtained from the text data, rather than realizing a prediction of high accuracy by using many kinds of features. Although most of previous literature related to citation count prediction conduct regression analyses, we conducted the binary classification and gave a deeper examination into the statistics of word occurrences.

The results of our experiments indicate that the scientific impact of a scholarly paper can be detected from information which is written in its abstract and is not related to the trend of research topics. Scholarly papers with high and low citation count could be classified using their abstracts with an accuracy. Additionally, deleting technical terms from the abstracts caused only a slight decrease of the accuracy. We can use the resulting classifier with other methods for predicting citation counts to find potentially high-impact publications more efficiently.

The rest of this paper is organized as follows. Section 2 formalizes the target problem as a classification of documents, and describes the experimental methods. Section 3 reports the experimental results. Section 4 gives considerations on the results and future directions of our study.

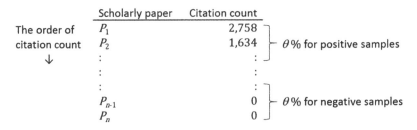

Fig. 1. Main idea of generating samples for the classification of scholarly papers with high and low citation count using a threshold θ.

2   Methods

This section formalizes predicting the future impacts of scholarly papers as the problem of a classification of documents, and describes the experimental methods.

2.1   Citation Count Prediction

Our objective is to determine whether the future impact of a scholarly paper can be detected from its abstract, especially, using non-technical terms. We formalized this task as follows. As the measure of impact of a scholarly paper, we used the citation count of the paper. Then, we tried to classify papers with large citation counts and papers with small citation counts instead of regression. Figure 1 shows the idea of generating positive and negative samples. As the features for the classification, we used the distribution of word n-grams [8] in abstracts. The classifier was the support vector machine (SVM) with a linear kernel. We also applied this binary classifier to the abstracts modified by deleting technical terms, to clarify the effects of factors unrelated to the trend of research topics on classification accuracy.

2.2   Data

We used abstracts and citation counts of papers published in Proceedings of the National Academy of Sciences (PNAS) [4] for our experiments. We obtained the metadata from Europe PubMed Central (Europe PMC) [1].

We conducted a prior experiment, and selected the data of papers published in PNAS from 1981 to 2003 (and available from Europe PMC) according to the result. Figure 2 shows the annual numbers of papers published from 1915 to 2017 and the annual average of citation counts, where the citation counts were the values as of the time we obtained the data in June, 2017. As shown in the figure, the average citation count is decreasing from 2004, which indicates that the citation counts of papers published after 2004 can be potentially larger in the future. Therefore, we used the data of papers published before 2004. Additionally, there are two peaks in the graph of average citation count at 1970's, which can

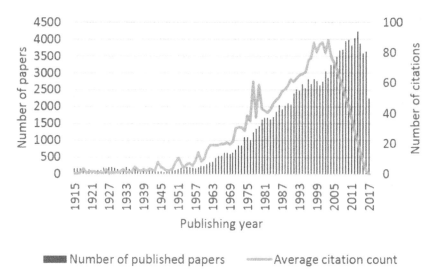

Fig. 2. Annual number and average of citation counts of papers published in PNAS and available from Europe PMC.

be caused by some exceptional factors. Therefore, we used the data of papers published after 1980.

As the corpus for defining technical terms, we used Medical Subject Headings (MeSH) [3], the medical thesaurus controlled by the National Library of Medicine. We used all the "Descriptors" defined in the latest version as of February 2018 of MeSH as the stop words for our experiment. We identified the singular and plural forms of each word for matching using a library [2] for string transformation.

2.3 Experiments

We used the data of papers published from 1981 to 2000 as training data and those from 2001 to 2003 as test data. In the selected data, the total number of the papers that have their abstracts was 52,425. The numbers of the two data sets were 44,218 and 8,207, respectively.

We selected the top and bottom $\theta\%$ papers as positive and negative samples, respectively, after normalizing the citation count of each paper by dividing the number by the average citation count of its publishing year. The threshold θ was set to be 2^i for $0 \leq i \leq 5$. Therefore, the size of experimental data was $\theta\%$ of the total data for each classification.

We applied the linear SVM classifier to the multisets of the 1-, 2-, and 3-grams of abstracts (the *normal* data) and those processed using the stop words (the data *without technical terms*). An *n-gram* of a given sequence is a contiguous n elements appear in the sequence. For example, the (word-level) 1- and 2-grams of "that is impossible" is "that", "is", "impossible", "that is", and "is impossible".

Table 1. Confusion matrix of the classification with the normal data (and the data without technical terms) for $\theta = 1$ and 2.

Predicted class\Actual class	High citation count	Low citation count	Precision
$\theta = 1$			
High citation count	144 (140)	6 (7)	0.96 (0.95)
Low citation count	20 (24)	158 (157)	0.89 (0.87)
Recall	0.88 (0.85)	0.96 (0.96)	
$\theta = 2$			
High citation count	144 (140)	6 (7)	0.96 (0.95)
Low citation count	20 (24)	158 (157)	0.89 (0.87)
Recall	0.88 (0.85)	0.96 (0.96)	

Then, we predicted "positive" or "negative" using vectors obtained from the multisets whose dimensionality is the vocabulary size. We didn't use the phrases that appeared in more than 50% of the training data for the classification. The vocabulary size was 22,063,049.

The *accuracy* is defined to be the ratio of the number of the correct predictions to the number of the total predictions examined in a test. The *precision* and the *recall* are defined, for each class, to be the ratio of the number of the correct predictions to a class to the number of the predictions to the class, and the ratio of the number of the correct predictions to a class to the actual number of samples of the class, respectively.

3   Results

Figure 3 shows the classification accuracy against the threshold θ for generating positive and negative samples. Table 1 shows the confusion matrices of the classifications with the normal data and the data without technical terms for $\theta = 1$ and 2. The accuracy generated by the normal data was 0.93 for $\theta = 1$ and 0.92 for $\theta = 2$. The accuracy generated by the data without technical terms was 0.90 for $\theta = 1$ and 0.91 for $\theta = 2$. Since the positive and negative sets of the test data had the same number of samples, the accuracy even for a large θ was better than that of a random prediction. The decrease of accuracy by deleting technical terms was small.

Tables 2 and 3 show the top and bottom 20 phrases in the order of coefficients of the support vector used in the classifier, for the normal data and the data without technical terms. The phrases with large (or small) coefficients are expected to be distinctive of papers with high (resp. low) citation counts. The bold phrases in Table 2 are those included in the stop words and deleted in the classification for the data without technical terms. The phrases "lt" and "gt" mean "<" and ">", respectively.

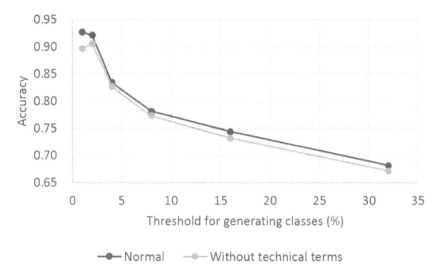

Fig. 3. Classification accuracy of scholarly papers with high and low citation counts.

4   Discussion

This section makes examinations of the experimental results.

4.1   Main Conclusion

We can conclude that the future impact of a scholarly paper can be detected using non-technical terms appear in its abstract. We found that papers with high and low citation counts could be classified using only their abstracts with an accuracy. Even though technical terms were deleted form the abstracts, the decrease of accuracy was small. We used a simple classifier and straight-forward features of abstracts, hence there is yet room for improvement in the classification.

4.2   Key Findings

We examine some phrases that are distinctive of each of the two classes in the classification.

The high and low of citation counts of papers could be detected with high accuracy using technical terms used in their abstracts. As shown in Table 2, some technical terms including "DNA" and "cell(s)" were put large weights. These phrases are supposed to be distinctive of frequently cited papers. This result can be finding active research subjects in addition to high impact papers.

A number of non-technical terms which were distinctive of the low citation count class were related to the types of research rather than the subjects. In Table 3, the technical terms with large weights were deleted. Some phrases that

Table 2. Phrases with large and small coefficients in the classification of papers with high and low citation counts for the normal data for $\theta = 1$, where the bold phrases are included in the stop words.

Large coef. (distinctive of high CC)	Small coef. (distinctive of low CC)
dna	theory
cells	**paper**
protein	**electron**
human	space
gene	**solutions**
cell	problem
sequence	if
brain	lt
proteins	equations
receptor	finite
beta	this paper
expression	chains
or	given
sequences	considered
mice	law
disease	equation
genes	**galaxies**
blood	dimensional
data	gt
amino	**light**

represent a type of research including "theory" and "equation(s)" were put low weights. These results are supposed to indicate that papers whose abstracts mention of theoretical issues are tend not to be cited frequently.

Long phrases are expected to express the tendency of writing style. Table 4 shows the distinctive phrases of length two or three words in the result of Table 3, that is, top and bottom 20 phrases made by more than one word in the order of coefficients of the support vector used in the classification for the data without technical terms for $\theta = 1$. As shown in the table, the phrase "it is shown that" seems to be distinctive of abstracts of papers with low citation counts. Some ungrammatical phrases with large coefficients are supposed to be the results of deleting technical terms. This result also suggests that technical terms are effective for the classification.

Table 3. Phrases with large and small coefficients in the classification of papers with high and low citation counts for the data without technical terms for $\theta = 1$.

Large coef. (distinctive of high CC)	Small coef. (distinctive of low CC)
protein	theory
sequence	space
expression	equations
or	if
beta	problem
receptor	finite
sequences	lt
were	equation
was	chains
these	given
amino	considered
data	dimensional
specific	gt
coli	atoms
antibody	states
endothelial	is shown
within	fusicoccin
cox	quantum
from	glc
induced	bond

4.3 Future Directions

Improving the classifier is one of our future work. We used the simple classifier based on SVM and the straightforward features based on word occurrences in documents. We can simply apply other machine learning methods to the classification and examine the effects on the accuracy. However, we need a way of explaining the mechanism of a classification when we use a complex method.

The results of the experiments can be used for an automatic proofreading of scholarly papers. When we have multiple expressions possible for writing an issue in scholarly papers, the classifier used in our experiments can suggest a better phrase expected to lead a high citation count. An approach using our result with language models [8] is expected to be effective for this application.

Table 4. Phrases made by more than one word with large and small coefficients in the classification of papers with high and low citation counts for the data without technical terms for $\theta = 1$.

Large coef. (distinctive of high CC)	Small coef. (distinctive of low CC)
in and	is shown
in vitro	values of
expression of	it is shown
we have	that the
amino acid	is shown that
in vivo	on the
nitric oxide	shown that
has been	number of
by using	it is
the to	to the
in addition	is given
variety of	for the
of these	heavy chains
appears to	is considered
sequence of	values of the
associated with	the system
response to	of finite
and in	theory of
involved in	in this
of from	the existence

5   Conclusion

The future impact of a scholarly paper can be detected from its abstract with an accuracy. Additionally, it can be detected using only non-technical terms with a slight decrease of the accuracy. We classified abstracts of papers with high and low citation counts, and the classification accuracy was 0.93 for detecting the top and bottom 1%. The accuracy for abstracts without technical terms was 0.90, which indicates that the future citation count of a scholarly paper might be related to the type of research and the style of writing of the paper in addition to the trend of research topics.

Acknowledgement. This work was supported by JSPS KAKENHI Grant Number 15K00310.

References

1. Europe PMC: Europe PubMed Central. https://europepmc.org/. Accessed 5 Feb 2018
2. Inflection. https://pypi.org/project/inflection/. Accessed 11 May 2018
3. MeSH: Medical Subject Headings. https://www.nlm.nih.gov/mesh/. Accessed 5 Feb 2018
4. PNAS: Proceedings of the National Academy of Sciences. http://www.pnas.org/. Accessed 5 Feb 2018
5. Dong, Y., Johnson, R.A., Chawla, N.V.: Can scientific impact be predicted? IEEE Trans. Big Data **2**(1), 18–30 (2016)
6. Garfield, E.: The history and meaning of the journal impact factor. JAMA **295**(1), 90–93 (2006)
7. Hirsch, J.E.: An index to quantify an individual's scientific research output. PNAS **102**(46), 16569–16572 (2005)
8. Manning, C.D., Raghavan, P., Schütze, H.: Introduction to Information Retrieval. Cambridge University Press, Cambridge (2008)
9. Yan, R., Tang, J., Liu, X., Shan, D. Li, X.: Citation count prediction: learning to estimate future citations for literature. In: Proceedings of the 20th ACM International Conference on Information and Knowledge Management, CIKM 2011, pp. 1247–1252. ACM, New York (2011)

Improving Online Argumentation Through Deep Learning

Ke Kang and Richard O. Sinnott[✉]

School of Computing and Information Systems, University of Melbourne,
Melbourne, Australia
rsinnott@unimelb.edu.au

Abstract. Critical thinking and reasoning are essential for making informed judgments. This can be especially important for the intelligence community and associated government agencies. In this paper, we explore methods to evaluate critical thinking and reasoning. We focus on a public opinion/argument-based website - Yourview. We introduce the Yourview platform and present the annotated Yourview dataset that was created following a pilot period that focused on collecting public opinion on a range of topics. We then propose a method to classify arguments and their components related to the comments in the Yourview dataset. We assess the influence of components of argumentation as the basis for critical thinking and subsequently score and visualize these relations. Building on this, we predict critical thinking scores for what makes a good argument using a multilayer perceptron (MLP). The results of these models help enhance reasoning and establishment of knowledge from persuasive texts.

Keywords: Critical thinking · Argument component classification
Text analysis

1 Introduction

Critical thinking and reasoning are vital for society. Critical thinking and reasoning can be described as the ability to interpret, analyze, evaluate and ultimately establish insightful and reasoned judgments. Such reasoning influences what to believe and ultimately what to do encompassing diverse ideas and opinions that reflect beliefs and values, and where possible avoid bias. It would be highly desirable to automate the process of evaluating critical thinking and reasoning ability of individuals and crowds more generally. This is the goal of the US Intelligence Advanced Research Projects Activity (IARPA – www.iarpa.gov) Crowdsourcing Evidence, Argumentation, Thinking and Evaluation (CREATE) program. The aim of CREATE is to improve intelligence analysis by supporting improved, collective wisdom.

The CREATE program includes four teams from all over the world. The Smartly-assembled Wiki-style Argument Marshalling (SWARM – www.swarmproject.info) is one such team based at the University of Melbourne. The SWARM project has three innovations. First, it introduces a method called *argument marshaling* to combine structured analytical methods with crowdsourcing. The second innovation is to deploy

© Springer International Publishing AG, part of Springer Nature 2018
O. Gervasi et al. (Eds.): ICCSA 2018, LNCS 10960, pp. 376–391, 2018.
https://doi.org/10.1007/978-3-319-95162-1_26

this technique onto a collaborative platform similar to Google docs with wiki-based capabilities. The third innovation is to improve collective reasoning by aggregating individual's contributions. Figure 1 provides a snapshot of the SWARM front-end. This includes: a question with background information and evidence (left pane); the proposed answers/responses to the question together with how they are ranked by the crowd (middle pane) and a chat/discussion room related to the question (right pane). A range of analytics is currently being developed to support rating of the quality of a given answer. The highest quality answers (reasoning) will ultimately be ranked accordingly and appear at the top of the multiple answers that a given crowd might generate.

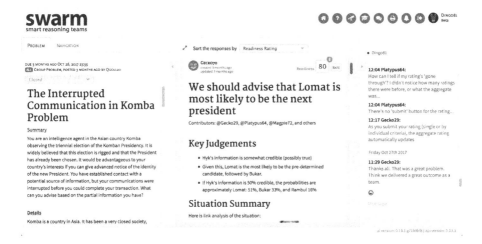

Fig. 1. SWARM platform

The SWARM project runs for up to 4 years over 3 phases. At present the work is nearing the end of Phase 1. The SWARM project builds upon the use of a crowd to establish the best possible reasoning and analysis, however the focus of this paper is to consider the extent that machine learning and especially deep learning can be used to automate the quality of reasoning. This builds upon a range of techniques and pre-existing platforms with extensive data that has already been collected.

One example of such a crowdsourcing platform was Yourview (https:// timvangelder.com/category/yourview/). The Yourview platform developed a website that allowed people to discuss and debate on a range of topics of relevance to Australians, e.g. arguments for or against gay marriage. Users on this website could vote for issues they wanted to talk about, post comments, and vote and reply on other people's comments. The reputation system used credibility scores for each user as the critical thinking competency. Users could improve this score by posting high quality comments and get up-votes from other users. The Yourview platform had in total 2,563 comments with a critical thinking score that ranged from 0 to 7.

In this paper, we focus on building models to classify argument components and analyze the argument structure of comment using the Yourview dataset. We then predict the critical thinking score using features extracted from the comments. The ultimate goal is to explore the extent that deep learning approaches can recognize the quality of a given argument.

The rest of this paper is organized as follows. Section 2 introduces the background to critical thinking and argument mining. In Sect. 3, we describe the detailed format, size and features of the Yourview data set. We illustrate the models for argument component classification in Sect. 4. In Sect. 5, the critical thinking score prediction models are described. Finally, in Sect. 6 we present the results of our research.

2   Background

Critical thinking and reasoning are vital for society and indeed humanity. One obvious example is in the voting process where critical thinking and reasoning should be used to elect sensible leaders with sound policies. With the development of technology, automation and assessment of critical thinking has recently become more possible. Argument mining is one important approach for assessing critical thinking.

2.1   Argument Mining

Argument Mining is used for mining the structure and relations of arguments that can subsequently be used to assess and measure the quality of arguments. Stab and Gurevych [3] classified arguments into three components: *major claims*, *claims* and *premises*. The relations between these components were used to analyze argument structures. A *major claim* is the author's stance on the given topic whilst a *claim* is typically part of a major claim or an attempted major claim that does not get community-wide support. A *premise* is used to support claims and persuade readers. The boundary between a major claim and a claim is not obvious in many works.

Numerous methods have been applied for classifying argument components. Moens et al. [10] utilized features such as unigram, keywords, punctuations and Parts of Speech (POS) to predict argument components. These features have been commonly used in many argument-mining approaches.

Rooney et al. [11] presented a Kernel method to recognize arguments. This method used a convolution kernel method to compare the similarities between sequences. In this work, POS tags were considered. However, this method was complex and there has been no evidence that shows it could significantly improve the accuracy.

Persing and Ng [6] proposed an end-to-end argument mining method. This method was implemented in a pipeline based on Integer Linear Programming. They showed that the objective function (F-score) could be directly optimized. Specifically, the method achieved an 18.5% reduction of the F-score in identifying argument components.

Arguments in the legal domain often have clearer structure. [12] proposed a model with context-free grammar to identify the argument structure in ten annotated legal documents based on the European Court of Human Rights (ECHR). However, this method needed to identify the grammars used for the relations in arguments manually.

The grammar in different documents can change significantly. As a result, context-free grammar methods could not easily be applied either in other contexts or with new documents.

Identifying the relations between units in text such as sentences and clauses is a challenging task. The Penn Discourse Treebank (PDTB) provides an annotated dataset that labels the relations between textual units, such as clauses, sentences, and paragraphs. In order to classify implicit relations, Lin et al. [13] built a classifier using the PDTB dataset. The features they used included the relation context, dependency parse trees and word pairs. Although the accuracy in classifying implicit relations was only 40.2%, this was a significant improvement compared to other approaches.

Louis et al. [14] added features including grammar information, syntactic forms and coherence information. They claimed that results built on these features were better than random baseline models, however such accuracy requirements came at the cost of manually establishing implicit relation classifications.

In the research of Peldszus and Stede [15], the task of predicting the structure was separated into subtasks, e.g. central claim identification, relation identification and role classification. Subtasks were combined for different structure prediction tasks. It was claimed that this method improved the accuracy of central claim identification and function classification.

One major subtask in argument mining is evaluating argument quality. The quality of arguments can be evaluated from a higher level using information including argument components and their relations. One key application area is (student) essay scoring. Due to the heavy burden in scoring essays and providing feedback for every student, the ability to automatically score student essays is often essential. It has been demonstrated that automated scoring can have a higher efficiency and consistency than manual scoring. As one example, E-rator is one of the most popular automated essay scoring systems. Attali and Burstein [4] built a new feature set containing: grammar errors, essays organization, lexical complexity and prompt-specific vocabulary usage. They showed improvements automated marking of 500 labeled student essays. Due to the different systems and various feature sets, [16] investigated and summarized existing methods and developed a task-independent feature set. This feature set was based on different essay grading tasks.

In addition to automated essay scoring, Feng et al. [5] presented a method to measure coherence with discourse relations, where coherence reflects the quality of being consistent and logical in persuasive texts. They used Rhetorical Structure Theory (RST) to label discourse relations in persuasive texts. By comparing shallow RST-style discourse relations with a complete set of RST-style discourse relations, they found that deep discourse structure was important in measuring coherence.

Persing and Ng [17] annotated a corpus of student essays and assigned a coherence score on a 4-point scale. They predicted the coherence score with N-grams and Keywords. The result showed that the model could improve the results by 16.6%.

Stab and Gurevych [18] showed an empirical study based on the theory that high quality claims need enough evidence to persuade readers. By evaluating an annotated corpus, they achieved an accuracy of 84% in identifying insufficient arguments. The results showed that sufficient evidence from premises was essential for well-reasoned arguments.

Convincingness is another measure of argument quality. Habernal and Gurevych [7] proposed a Long Short Term Memory (LSTM) model to evaluate the convincingness of web arguments. They trained 16k argument pairs and achieved a 0.76-0.78 accuracy in predicting which argument was convincing. However, they only compared the convincingness of argument pairs, and not convincingness of arbitrary arguments. In further work, they assessed other properties of convincingness [19]. For this purpose, they annotated 9k argument pairs into 17 convincingness classes. They then used Support Vector Machines (SVM) and LSTM models to predict the argument convincingness.

Wachsmuth et al. [20] surveyed existing argument quality assessment approaches and categorized them into several classes: Logic, Rhetoric and Dialectic. They then derived a systematic taxonomy for argument quality assessment.

2.2 Critical Thinking and Reasoning

Critical thinking and reasoning involve the ability to interpret, analyze, evaluate and make inferences resulting in a range of typically verbal or textually formulated judgments. People with high competence in critical thinking and reasoning can understand the relationship and logic between different events, as well as detect the relevance between different ideas that reflect their beliefs and values. A key aspect of critical thinking is avoiding bias.

In many works, individual competency in thinking and reasoning can be measured through psychometric tests. Abrami et al. [8] summarized available empirical evidence to measure critical thinking skills. Although these individualized methods have been demonstrated to be effective, they are costly and cumbersome. Such psychometric tests are hard to apply across a multitude of people with diverse reasoning abilities, e.g. some people are more mathematically inclined, others visually inclined etc.

Other works have evaluated people's digital traces on the Internet to explore their reasoning. Youyou et al. [1] tried to predict personalities using the digital footprints of individuals on the Internet. They analyzed digital traces such as purchasing records for music and books. With this kind of data, they were able to analyze user personalities. Their results showed that they were more accurate in identifying personalities and reasoning competency than judgments made by family and friends [1].

Many reputation systems have been built for reasoning using online forums. One widely adopted example is StackOverflow. This web forum offers a question and answer website related to software programming although numerous other versions have now appeared in different application domains. The reputation system is built by leveraging users' contribution to the website in responding to questions [2]. A high reputation score means the user gives high-quality answers based on assessment by the crowd (in this case, other software developers). A high reputation score thus reflects the ability of an individual for providing sound reasoning with software solutions to targeted questions.

Underpinning the analysis of arguments and argument quality is data.

3   Data

In this research, we focus on exploring enhanced reasoning through deep learning. To support this, we use three datasets: data from the Yourview platform; student essay datasets with labeled argument components [3], and a labeled subset of the Youview data with the same annotation method used for the essay dataset. We describe the details of the format and content of these datasets below.

3.1   Yourview Dataset

The Yourview dataset contained 2,563 comments from 805 users on a range of topics. The structure of the Yourview dataset is shown in Table 1 below.

Table 1. Details of features in the Yourview dataset

Feature	Definition
Id	Unique id for every comment
Issue title	The title for the debate issue
Total votes	Total number of votes received
Commenter credibility	Credibility score of the commenter
Type	Whether the comment supports or is opposed to the premise of the issue or is a reply
Comment text	The text for every comment
Mean evaluation	The average critical thinking score based on assessment by three evaluators

The system assigned a credibility score for each commenter. This score was assigned by the reputation system of the Yourview system and was based on the user's activities on the platform. For example, the number of comments and replies posted on the platform by the user; the number of votes for other users, especially for users with opposing ideas and the number of votes they received from other users.

Every comment was assigned a critical thinking (CT) score by three independent evaluators (PhD students with backgrounds in logic and philosophy). The critical thinking score reflected a direct measure of a user's critical thinking ability. The evaluators assigned a CT score manually using an annotation guide. The average of the three scores was used as the "mean evaluation" in the Yourview dataset.

High CT score comments typically involved an in-depth analysis of the problem and clear conveyance of understanding. For a given issue, a higher CT score reflected a clear and insightful position and used clear persuasive examples or reasoning. This meant that the structure was well organized and clearly expressed their ideas. On the other hand, a low CT score for a comment meant that the comment was unclear and without enough evidence to support their position. The comment was also likely to be poorly organized and contain serious grammar errors, or even be off topic.

Figure 2 shows the distribution of the number of comments for each critical thinking score. As seen there was a spread of scores. A score of 5 was the most prevalent score with almost 4 times the number of scores of 0 and score 7. Here a score of 7 means that it is the strongest argument, i.e. it is well-structured, with strong reasoning and enough evidence to support the argument. A score of 0 is likely to be off-topic and/or have bad structure and poor reasoning.

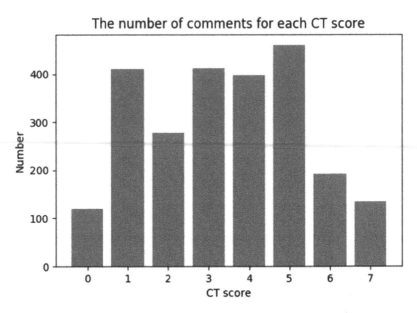

Fig. 2. The CT score distribution for comments from Yourview

3.2 Argument Annotated Essays Dataset

The argument annotated essays dataset [3] originated at the Ubiquitous Knowledge Processing (UKP) Lab in Germany. This dataset has mainly been used in research focused on identifying argument components and their relations in persuasive student essays. As the data size in the Yourview was small, it was necessary to pre-train the model used for classifying argument components in this dataset.

The argument annotated essays dataset was built based on 402 student essays. It comprised 7116 sentences including 1506 claims, 3832 premises and 751 major claims amongst other components.

In order to evaluate the argument component classifying efficiency of our model using the Yourview dataset, we manually labeled a subset of the dataset of 100 sentences using the annotation guide of the argument annotated essays dataset.

4 Argument Component Classification

In this section, we focus on argument component classification using the Yourview comments. To support this, a classifier was required at the sentence level. Four types of argument components were classified: major claims, claims, premises and other types. Because the size of Yourview dataset was relatively small, the model first had to be trained on the argument annotated essays dataset, where the argument components of sentences were labeled. Two classifiers were built using approaches based on Support Vector Machines (SVM) and Convolutional Neural Networks (CNN). We describe the details of these models below.

4.1 Support Vector Machines

Support Vector Machines (SVM) are a widely adopted classifier used in supervised machine learning. The main idea behind an SVM is to find the hyper plane in training data, i.e. to find the optimal hyper plane separating data belonging to different classes. An SVM model is a form of binary classifier. In this work we applied *one-vs-rest* approach for the argument component classification. Before applying the model, we first tokenized the comments, removing low frequency words and transforming every sentence into a term-frequency vector. We then applied the SVM against the vector to predict the argument components.

4.2 Convolutional Neural Networks

Besides image processing, Convolution Neural Networks (CNN) have been applied in many other application domains including natural language processing. In image processing, the convolution usually operates on a block of the image. In text processing, the input of a CNN is a matrix of word vectors. As a result, when using a CNN to process texts, the kernel can cover words over several rows. Through this method, the model can capture features such as multiple consecutive words.

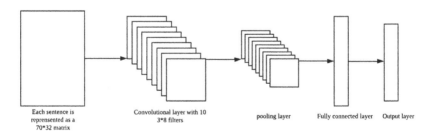

Fig. 3. The architecture of the Convolutional Neural Network used for sentence classification

In this work, we adopt the CNN architecture of Kim [28] as seen in Fig. 3. We fixed the sentence length to a limit of 70. We padded sentences lower than 70 with zeros and truncated sentences longer than 70. Each word was itself represented as a

32-length vector. As a result, every sentence was transformed into a 70 * 32 matrix used as input to the CNN. In the network, the first layer used was the convolution layer. We utilised 10 filters of size 3 * 8. The second layer was a max-pooling layer. The outputs of this layer were used as inputs to a fully connected layer and ultimately an output layer. We apply a *Dropout* method to prevent over-fitting problems.

5 Comment Score Prediction

The critical thinking score of comments in the Yourview dataset was based on the evaluation of an individual's critical thinking competency. As noted, there were 2,563 comments in the Yourview dataset. From this, 80% were used to train the models, while the rest were used to test and evaluate critical thinking scores. For the CT score prediction, we used and extracted various kinds of features including: *length features, occurrence features, error features* and *argument component features*.

Length Features are based on the length of comments, i.e. the number of words in a comment. This is a very simple feature. Intuitively high CT users are likely to invest more time and energy into their inputs, e.g. a good argument will use more evidence and reasoning. To extract the comment length, we first tokenized the comments and then counted the number of tokens.

Occurrence Features are based on the number of specific linguistic phenomena in the comments. In this research we considered five features: *links count, punctuation count, sentence numbers, paragraph numbers* and *average number of sentences per paragraph*. For the links count, the writer will typically provide more evidence to support their arguments, e.g. links to referenced articles and posts. *Punctuation* is another simple but valuable feature to consider. Based on the work of Mahana et al. [29], the amount of punctuation including quotations, commas and exclamation marks can be valuable information in predicting the quality of student essays. For example, complex sentences usually have more semi-colons and commas. Sentence numbers and paragraph numbers are also useful indicators of the quality and completeness of writing. For example, different claims will typically be in different paragraphs.

Error Features including grammar and spelling errors are two most obvious features for evaluating the quality of comments. Skilled reasoners will take care in minimising such errors. To detect spelling errors, a corpus containing all words in the English language was required. A word that has spelling error is one that cannot be found in this list. A standard Python package to check for grammar errors was used. The package returns the number and location of errors.

Argument Component Features are indicators of the argument structure contained in comments. They can help to analyze the reasoning quality and critical thinking abilities of users. As noted, we focus on various types of information contained in arguments: *Major Claims, Claims, Premises* and other types of information. Using several types of argument components can suggest a better overall argument. We consider the number of sentences belonging to each kind of argument component. We also consider the ratio of each argument component type and sentence numbers against the total number of sentences. This provides a degree of normalization for the data. This feature can also be used to infer further structure of the inputs. Finally, we consider the word count for each kind of argument component and the ratio of each type of word count to the total word count.

Following feature extraction, the comments are transformed into 29-length vectors corresponding to the features above. These features are input into the models and algorithms used to predict the critical thinking score. Specifically, we consider models using linear regression, a multilayer perceptron (MLP), and MLP together with Principal Component Analysis (PCA).

6   Results and Discussion

In this section, we present the classification outcomes of our models and discuss and visualize the result. As noted, to support this work we designed and applied two models for identifying argument components: SVM and CNN. The results of these models are shown in Table 2.

Table 2. Accuracy of argument component classification for models based on the annotated argument essays dataset and the Yourview dataset.

Model	Essay dataset	Yourview dataset
SVM	0.61	0.50
CNN	0.82	0.69

As noted, due to the limited size of the Yourview dataset, the models were pre-trained on the annotated argument dataset. From the results, we identify that the four models had different effectiveness levels in classifying argument components. CNN achieved an accuracy of 0.69 on the Yourview dataset, whilst SVM only achieved an accuracy of 0.50. Furthermore, a model that works well on the essays dataset may give poor results on the Yourview dataset, e.g. due to over-fitting problems. In the training process, models capturing too many details specific to the training set do not generalize well.

As shown in Table 2, the result of the CNN model was significantly higher than that of SVM. This illustrates that deep learning models are more effective in argument component classification. It is noted that feature representation is important. The input to the SVM is transformed with a bag-of-words, while the CNN uses the *word2vec*.

In order to analyze the influence of argument components on critical thinking score, we analyzed the relations between the data contained in argument components and critical thinking scores from several aspects. Firstly, we analyze the relation between the component type numbers and the critical thinking score. As there are many types of argument, we want to check if comments with higher scores have more argument component types. This is shown in Fig. 4.

As seen, the number of argument component increases with the critical thinking score, i.e. writers with higher scores for their comments will use more argument component types. Lower score writers, produce comments using only one to two kinds of types. We also consider the number of sentences for each argument component, i.e.

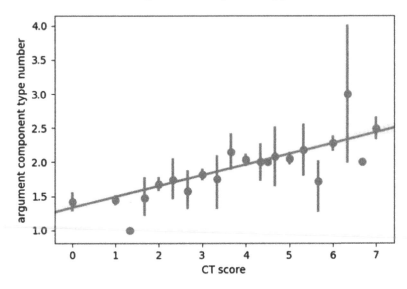

Fig. 4. Relation between the number of argument component types and critical thinking score

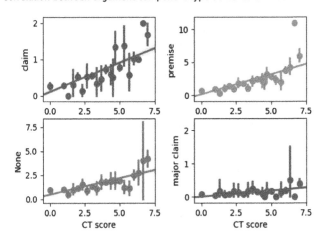

Fig. 5. Correlation between argument component count and the critical thinking score

how many sentences are claims and how many sentences are premises. The result is shown in Fig. 5.

From Fig. 5, we observe that each kind of component will increase with the critical thinking with the exception of *major claims*. As mentioned above, a high score writer tends to write more content to support their arguments. However as seen, the sentence number for major claims is not significantly increased. This may be due to several reasons. Firstly, each comment often has only one major claim. As a result, the number does not increase with the critical thinking. Secondly, the argument component labels are first introduced in student essays and these are far longer than inputs and comments on the Yourview system. As a result, the boundary between claims and major claims is often unclear.

We considered the ratio of each argument component sentence against the total sentence count in each comment. For each comment, we compute the ratio of every argument component with each comment at the sentence level. The result is shown in Fig. 6, where as seen, the ratio of premises increases with the critical thinking score, while the ratio of non-arguments drops. As the ratio of claims and major claims do not have obvious changes, the number of claims within a comment is limited. However, a good argument typically needs to be supported by several premises. As a result, the premise ratio increases with the overall critical thinking score.

Correlation between argument component sentence ratio and CT score

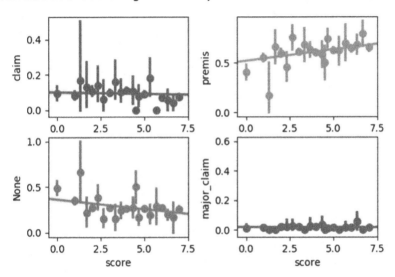

Fig. 6. Correlation between the ratio of each argument component sentence count and the critical thinking score.

As noted, the inputs and comments on the Yourview data were labeled with a critical thinking score by three independent evaluators. In order to predict the score for comments, several models were built with the labeled Yourview data. Specifically, a linear regression model, a multilayer perceptron (MLP) model and an MLP with Principal Component Analysis (PCA) was explored. The linear regression was used as the baseline model. Due to high dimensions of the input vectors, the PCA method was applied before training using the MLP. The results considered the mean absolute error (MAE) and the mean squared error (MSE).

Table 3. Results for predicting critical thinking scores of comments in the Yourview dataset

Models	MSE	MAE
Linear regression	2.50	1.29
MLP	6.38	1.74
MLP + PCA	2.25	1.19

From Table 3, we observe that whilst the linear regression model is one of the simplest regression models, it also shows good performance for prediction of the critical thinking score. The results are far better than just using the MLP model. The reason is most likely due to an over-fitting problem. The MLP model is too complex and in the training, it is over-fitted on the training dataset and hence does not generalize well. As a result, it exhibits a bad performance with the testing data. Since the input vector has too many features and many features are correlated, the PCA method is applied to extract the most important information from the input data. After applying the PCA model, the result is improving considerably.

In order to improve the model further, we analyzed the comments where the predicted value was significantly different from the labeled score. Representative examples are given in Table 4.

Table 4. Examples of comments and corresponding scores in the Yourview dataset

Comment	Scores
"Its time to bring the law into line with current practice"	6.0
"Plenty room for it"	2.0
"Why donate if not expecting a return? Altruism?"	3.0

In these examples, each comment is short however as seen, the score can be quite different. It is hard to predict these scores with the features mentioned in this work. Comments containing negative information and sensitive information are also scored very low. The information is hard to detect just using the features mentioned above. Furthermore, some comments need further background knowledge, e.g. news and related information needs to be considered as well as the reliability (trust) of external resources that are used to augment arguments. This is especially pertinent in the era of fake news.

7   Conclusions

In this paper, we focused on enhancing reasoning through deep learning approaches. The models were developed against a web-based platform (Yourview) designed to extract opinions from the Australian population. This dataset was manually labeled with a critical thinking score by domain experts. In order to evaluate the potential for automating critical thinking assessment, we built a range of models to classify argument components used in these comments. With these deep learning models, we achieved a classification result with accuracy of 80.21%. The influence of argument components for critical thinking scores was evaluated and the extent that they captured an individual's critical thinking ability. The result of the models demonstrated a result with mean squared error 2.25 and mean absolute error 1.19. The results show that our models are effective in predicting the critical thinking score of comments from individuals.

For the future, we will consider analysis of the semantic information included in other datasets. As described in the results, just using the features of length, occurrence and error is insufficient for truly evaluating critical thinking ability. The argument relations, background knowledge, contextual information, sensitive information amongst other aspects need to be considered in the evaluation also. Furthermore, we intend to also apply other deep learning approaches to conduct further in-depth analysis using reasoning mechanisms against persuasive texts.

The work will also utilize the results form the SWARM platform. It is noted that the SWARM platform will have a much larger crowd (expected to be over 840 users in 30–40 teams) and many questions (expected to be 40) that will garner far more data over an extended time period. The success of the SWARM project will ultimately depend on the improvements of the platform for quality of reasoning compared to control groups using other technologies, e.g. crowds using solutions such as Googledocs. Automating the ability to assess the quality of reasoning and argumentation will be hugely important for the future for SWARM project logistics as well as for the intelligence community more generally.

Acknowledgements. The authors would like to thank the SWARM team and especially Tim van Gelder for providing access to the Yourview data set. This research is based upon work supported in part by the Office of the Director of National Intelligence (ODNI), Intelligence Advanced Research projects Activity (IARPA), under Contract [2017-16122000002]. The views and conclusions contained herein are those of the authors and should not be interpreted as necessarily representing the official policies, either expressed or implied, of ODNI, IARPA, or the U.S. Government. The U.S. Government is authorized to reproduce and distribute reprints for governmental purposes notwithstanding any copyright annotation therein.

References

1. Youyou, W., Kosinski, M., Stillwell, D.: Computer-based personality judgments are more accurate than those made by humans. Proc. Natl. Acad. Sci. **112**(4), 1036–1040 (2015)
2. Movshovitz-Attias, D., Movshovitz-Attias, Y., Steenkiste, P., Faloutsos, C.: Analysis of the reputation system and user contributions on a question answering website: stackoverflow. In: Proceedings of the 2013 IEEE/ACM International Conference on Advances in Social Networks Analysis and Mining, pp. 886–893. ACM (2013)
3. Stab, C., Gurevych, I.: Annotating argument components and relations in persuasive essays, pp. 1501–1510 (2014)
4. Attali, Y., Burstein, J.: Automated Essay Scoring with E-rater® v. 2.0. ETS Research Report Series, vol. 2004, no. 2 (2004)
5. Feng, V.W., Lin, Z., Hirst, G., Holdings, S.P.: The impact of deep hierarchical discourse structures in the evaluation of text coherence. In: COLING, pp. 940–949 (2014)

6. Persing, I., Ng, V.L.: End-to-end argumentation mining in student essays. In: Proceedings of Human Language Technologies: The 2016 Annual Conference of the North American Chapter of the Association for Computational Linguistics, pp. 1384–1394 (2016)
7. Habernal, I., Gurevych, I.: Which argument is more convincing? Analyzing and predicting convincingness of web arguments using bidirectional LSTM. In: ACL, no. 1 (2016)
8. Abrami, P.C., Bernard, R.M., Borokhovski, E., Waddington, D.I., Wade, C.A., Persson, T.: Strategies for teaching students to think critically: a meta-analysis. Rev. Educ. Res. 85(2), 275–314 (2015)
9. van Gelder, T.: Cultivating deliberation for democracy. J. Public Delib. 8(1) (2012)
10. Moens, M.-F., Boiy, E., Palau, R.M., Reed, C.: Automatic detection of arguments in legal texts. In: Proceedings of the 11th International Conference on Artificial Intelligence and Law, pp. 225–230. ACM (2007)
11. Rooney, N., Wang, H., Browne, F.: Applying kernel methods to argumentation mining. In: FLAIRS Conference (2012)
12. Mochales, R., Moens, M.-F.: Study on the structure of argumentation in case law. In: Proceedings of the 2008 Conference on Legal Knowledge and Information Systems, pp. 11–20 (2008)
13. Lin, Z., Kan, M.-Y., Ng, H.T.: Recognizing implicit discourse relations in the Penn Discourse Treebank. In: Proceedings of the 2009 Conference on Empirical Methods in Natural Language Processing: Volume 1, pp. 343–351. Association for Computational Linguistics (2009)
14. Louis, A., Joshi, A., Prasad, R., Nenkova, A.: Using entity features to classify implicit discourse relations. In: Proceedings of the 11th Annual Meeting of the Special Interest Group on Discourse and Dialogue, Association for Computational Linguistics, pp. 59–62 (2010)
15. Peldszus, A., Stede, M.: Joint prediction in MST-style discourse parsing for argumentation mining. In: EMNLP, vol. 2015, pp. 938–948 (2015)
16. Zesch, T., Wojatzki, M., Scholten-Akoun, D.: Task-independent features for automated essay grading. In: BEA@ NAACL-HLT, pp. 224–232 (2015)
17. Persing, I., Ng, V.: Modeling prompt adherence in student essays. In: Proceedings of the 52nd Annual Meeting of the Association for Computational Linguistics: Volume 1: Long Papers, pp. 1534–1543 (2014)
18. Stab, C., Gurevych, I.: Recognizing insufficiently supported arguments in argumentative essays. In: Proceedings of the 15th Conference of the European Chapter of the Association for Computational Linguistics: Volume 1, Long Papers, vol. 1, pp. 980–990 (2017)
19. Habernal, I., Gurevych, I.: What makes a convincing argument? Empirical analysis and detecting attributes of convincingness in web argumentation. In: EMNLP, pp. 1214–1223 (2016)
20. Wachsmuth, H., Naderi, N., Hou, Y., Bilu, Y., Prabhakaran, V., Thijm, T.A., Hirst, G., Stein, B.: Computational argumentation quality assessment in natural language. In: Proceedings of the 15th Conference of the European Chapter of the Association for Computational Linguistics, vol. 1, pp. 176–187 (2017)
21. Mikolov, T., Chen, K., Corrado, G., Dean, J.: Efficient estimation of word representations in vector space. arXiv preprint arXiv:1301.3781 (2013)
22. Duchi, J., Hazan, E., Singer, Y.: Adaptive subgradient methods for online learning and stochastic optimization. J. Mach. Learn. Res. 12(Jul), 2121–2159 (2011)
23. Zeiler, M.D.: Adadelta: an adaptive learning rate method. arXiv preprint arXiv:1212.5701 (2012)
24. Kingma, D., Ba, J.: Adam: a method for stochastic optimization. arXiv preprint arXiv:1412.6980 (2014)

25. LeCun, Y., Bottou, L., Bengio, Y., Haffner, P.: Gradient-based learning applied to document recognition. Proc. IEEE **86**(11), 2278–2324 (1998)
26. Hochreiter, S., Schmidhuber, J.: Long short-term memory. Neural Comput. **9**(8), 1735–1780 (1997)
27. Srivastava, N., Hinton, G.E., Krizhevsky, A., Sutskever, I., Salakhutdinov, R.: Dropout: a simple way to prevent neural networks from overfitting. J. Mach. Learn. Res. **15**(1), 1929–1958 (2014)
28. Kim, Y.: Convolutional neural networks for sentence classification. arXiv preprint arXiv: 1408.5882 (2014)
29. Mahana, M., Johns, M., Apte, A.: Automated essay grading using machine learning. Machine Learning Session, Stanford University (2012)

Location Analytics for Optimal Business Retail Site Selection

Ahmad Murad Bin Mohamed Rohani and Fang-Fang Chua[(⊠)]

Faculty of Computing and Informatics, Multimedia University, 63000 Cyberjaya,
Selangor, Malaysia
muradmy@gmail.com, ffchua@mmu.edu.my

Abstract. The issue on location placement for next business establishment is always a challenging topic. It presents businesses with many opportunities to uncover the most sophisticated approach on selecting the next location of physical stores to establish its presence. The traditional approach of manual survey of land, competition landscape and also related to demographic factor analysis comes with high cost and longer time to complete. Our proposed work leveraging Google Maps to survey the surrounding and records the existing characteristics such as whether the shop is a corner shop lot, can be viewed from main road or having a sizable parking space. Based on the findings, the characteristics listing mainly relates to the business type. The approach of this paper can be used as one of the alternative input to decision making for physical placement of store. With the proposed work, optimal store location placement is determined based on a set of characteristics of an existing location. This research may help new business to gain optimal in flux of customers based on the location identified.

Keywords: Location analytics · Association rule mining · Retails placement

1 Introduction

Much effort need to be considered from inception till materialized for investing in a new place for a brick and mortar kind of establishment. Factors affecting the locational decision making includes external & internal environment, locational management activities and their portfolios [1]. For instance: Where will your next shop be located? Is it near the main road or a corner shop lot? What are the important aspects in the surrounding area that need to be observed in order to assure that you have the best return from the investment for the new place? These are part of the questions that need to be considered when choosing the location for new shops. Due to its fixed in nature, location cannot be modified in a short period of time and this is conflicting with elements such as price, customer service, or advertising [2] which can be adjusted accordingly following the needs and demand using forecasting and other related tools.

This research will leverage the availability of data over the internet via web medium by examining location characteristics and the corresponding business types that exist within the nearby area. Then, data mining techniques are performed to determine the top ranking characteristics that exist based on a pool of recorded

© Springer International Publishing AG, part of Springer Nature 2018
O. Gervasi et al. (Eds.): ICCSA 2018, LNCS 10960, pp. 392–405, 2018.
https://doi.org/10.1007/978-3-319-95162-1_27

information from various location establishments. The result later can be aggregated with other traditional methods for the decision on the next retail business establishment investment and in turn help to increase the turnover of the business. With the correct information and approaches, they can make an intelligent choice for a good place and perhaps will yield the most visitors.

This paper aims to achieve the objectives based on the data mining techniques and analysis: (a) to propose the attributes of location characteristics that influence the placement of retails shop. (b) to analyse the characteristics of location placement and propose the method for selection. (c) to evaluate the proposed method by using the data mining techniques. Relationship between the characteristics of a location with a particular business is extracted. Examples of businesses type include mini market, food and beverages, laundry, etc. Using Google Maps, this study surveys the area of interest and records the attributes. These attributes can be in terms of characteristics of location and type of stores within the surveyed area. Beginning with selecting the location as the starting points of search, this research will drill down to the particular site and start recording the attributes of the surrounding within predefined radius. Each occurrence will be recorded as binary of zero (0) for non-existence and one (1) if it exists. Based on the collected information, mining will be performed to find the association among the attributes and types of stores that typically exist. From the result, suggestions related to the store and location characteristic will be proposed.

Section 2 provides an overview of related works. In Sect. 3, we describe the research methodology that uses Google Maps for data collection and how it is used in this proposed work. Subsequently this paper will elaborate the analysis of findings in Sect. 4. Section 5 presents the results and discussion with some research contribution and finally, Sect. 6 presents the conclusion.

2   Related Works

The previous work on selecting location factors are mainly using the traditional qualitative approach of interviewing, observation and survey [3]. The newer approaches of location analytics are using rich social media data such as Facebook [4] and Foursquare [5]. Another online resource is using the search query data from Baidu Maps [6]. We are focusing on location attributes concerning the physical characteristics using association rule [7–9] which produce ranks by using lift as a result for related location characteristics given a business type.

2.1   Location Characteristics Attributes

Selection of location is always being prioritized in order to start a business. The location characteristics refer to the feature or quality belonging to a place that can be observed. This is important because the retailers can create differentiation through locational preferences based around the projection of image and identity [10]. The characteristics of the surrounding location encourage the gathering behavior and contribute to place attachment in selected coffee shops. The store must also be relatively close to major roads, the ability to walk from surrounding neighborhoods. An

access to nearby shops, parking availability, along with other exterior or site considerations also needs to be considered for shop placement [3].

Other research on location selection is based on the largest number of check-ins
using data taken from Foursquare check-ins that published in twitter [5]. This check-in
data is used to frame the problem of optimal retail store placement in the context of
location-based social networks. The study focusing on three factors, which are the
density, heterogeneity and also competitiveness of a place. Method being used is by
producing ranking based on data mining technique. This includes the Normalized
Discounted Cumulative Gain (NDGC) and also supervised learning such as Support
Vector Regression and Linear Regression. The ranking of the location is using the
RankNet which is based on Neural Network algorithm. Information on location
selection also using a different approach through the search query requested to the
pages via Baidu Maps [6]. Pair it with the location features, the supply side is already
showing the potential customer for the targeted location.

Research on location analytics using Facebook page data of user check-in and
identify the key feature that correspond to the suitable matric for business popularity
[4] is another methodology of using online data. The research employs gradient
boosting machine as the predictive model to gain insight on feature importance metrics
for location selection. A set of relevant characteristics extracted and a predictive model
is developed to estimate the popularity of a business location. The research reveals that
the popularity of neighboring business is the key features to perform accurate prediction. The more popular the shops around the area, with more check-in, the more
suitable it is for new business to be established around that area. Another research on
location strategies indicates that one of the primary motivation by the retailers in
placing their outfit is based on the close proximity to capital city residents, due to their
high discretionary incomes which likely to become the customers [11].

2.2   Types of Store

The shop characteristics is an important aspect when choosing the location. For
example on stores carrying the fashion based merchandize, they require more selective
location when placing their establishment [12]. The researches focus on the expansion
direction of fashion designer retailers within central area city of London and New York
and investigate the main factor driving the chosen location selection. The new retail
places, spaces and sites includes the department store and the mall where it confines to
certain location such as the primary business street of towns or cities, especially in the
United Kingdom [10]. As for the street, it reveals that the retailers choose certain
location in order to create differentiated spaces of consumption through locational
preferences, which contributed to the exclusive image and identity. This is important
because through differentiation it will create the brand exclusivity and attract more
people who are rich or of a high social class [13]. Other example of store includes the
shoe stores aggregate at the town shopping center, while furniture stores are partially
dispersed on secondary poles and drugstores are strongly dispersed across the whole
town [14]. The criteria for each location are different because it attracts certain type of
customers with particular needs.

2.3   Location Intelligence and the Use of Spatial Data

Businesses use data to improve their company performance. More location-based data can be collected using applications like Google Maps and Microsoft's Bing Maps. These applications provide free or low-cost and comes with easily accessible mapping capabilities. According to [15], it allows people using the simple Application Programming Interface, to put data on maps and integrate the analytical and geospatial capabilities. Location Intelligence is the ability to process complex data using Business Intelligence and geographic analysis [16]. It positions business and geographically referenced data to uncover the relationship of location to people, transactions, facilities, events and assets. Other research introduced Smart Data Localization to promote the design and implementation of a Decision Support Systems [17]. The step involves include data extraction and modelling, integration of business data with spatial data, data analysis and also data visualization.

The research on co-location pattern proposes a notion of user-specified neighborhoods in place of transactions to specify groups of items. This define the spatial co-location rule as well as interest measures, and propose an algorithm to find co-location rules. It determines that the problem for patterns discovery for the subset of feature located together is different from the association rule problem [18]. Retailers make use of the spatial technology to acquire new client, retain the existing/current customers and stay competitive with changing user requirements [19]. Research by [8] on discovery of spatial association rules in geographic information databases proposed an efficient method for mining strong spatial association rules in geographic information databases. However, for the spatial association, the rule indicating certain association relationship among a set of spatial and possibly some non-spatial attributes are not straightforward and can lead to misinterpretation.

3   Research Methodology

This research followed a classic data mining process and depicted as diagram below (Fig. 1).

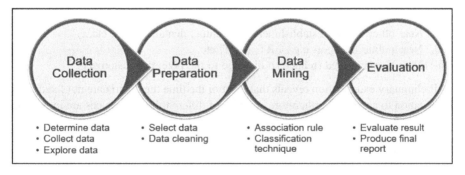

Fig. 1. Research methodology

3.1 Data Collection

The study begins with the selection of location as a base target for the data captured. We targeted Klang Valley area in Malaysia where most of the businesses establish their presence. A favorable location has the ability to meet users' demands, having less competition and also can attract a significant number of customers. In the proposed work, we aim to first figure out what are the characteristics that exist within the vicinity of the retails shops and then produce some ranking based on the statistical analysis. The location selected is using a retail shop as a base target for data capture. We have chosen the one of the successful Malaysian home grown mini market, 99 Speedmart as the starting location. This store was chosen for two reasons:

i. This establishment has grown to be the largest mini markets in Malaysia with sales up to RM 2.1 billion in 2014 [20], surpassing more shops such as 7-eleven.
ii. The list of all locations where 99 Speedmart located can be easily accessed through their own website (http://www.99speedmart.com.my/) under store locator. We can choose the desired location where in our case is the Klang Valley region, which includes Kuala Lumpur and Selangor area.

Data gathered through observation using Google Maps based on the listed location. All the observation will be recorded as "1" for having the characteristics and "0" otherwise. From the observation, all the characteristics of the surrounding within the radius of 100 to 200 m from the shop are recorded. This radius is considered as the size of retails trade area. This area is normally determined by the types of goods offered at the retail outlets. For example, in our case, the mini market is selling products which are easily substituted and affordable by majority of customers. This creates a smaller retail zone compared to exclusive store such as Cars outlet [19]. The radius is also considered an optimal location because it defines as the distance that a customer is willing to travel in order to buy the grocery [14] and also how newly open store in the area that will potentially attract the largest number of visits. The characteristics identified in this research include:

i. Facing road view (visibility from main road)
ii. Ample parking space
iii. Corner shop lot
iv. Near other building e.g., school, hospital, etc....
v. Near other type of shops e.g., laundry, restaurant, etc....
vi. Near other type of establishment e.g., clinic, dental, offices, etc....
vii. Near public transport e.g., LRT, MRT, etc....
viii. Near Housing area (related to distance to the potential customer)

Preliminary examination reveals that most of the time the criteria are not fixed from one location to another. Furthermore, number of different business types are increasing as new location is added and this also increases the number of variables.

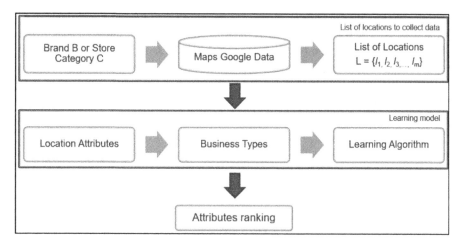

Fig. 2. Overall framework

3.2 Data Preparation

Our data values are using quantitative variables belonging to a set of items. In our case, the raw data are originated from the original source, which is using Google Maps and is difficult to be analyzed in its original format. These data need to be pre-processed and converted to a processed data before any analysis can be performed. Consistent data is data that is fit for statistical and predictive model building [21]. Missing values, special values, (obvious) errors and outliers are either removed, corrected or imputed.

3.3 Data Mining

We adopt the association rule using Apriori algorithm and also classification techniques with Decision Tree to help in extracting meaningful information from the collected data.

3.4 Proposed Framework

The framework used is adopted from research by [6] on ranking the best location for new business. The difference is on the target output where the original framework focuses in ranking the location whereas in our research, we are ranking the attributes.

Referring to Fig. 2, in one region, there can be many locations to choose for opening a store. Our first step is to determine several places $L_d = \{l1, l2, l3,..., lm\}$ as candidate locations for a store Category C or a specific brand of chain stores B. Google Maps data is used to find the specific place where the attributes and the type of businesses within the particular locations will be recorded for further analysis. Then these attributes will then be transformed into a ranking problem. Our goal is to produce the ranking list of attributes based on the business selected. We achieve this by using association rule based on lift.

Association Rule Mining – Apriori
Apriori algorithm is used for spatial association rule. A spatial association rule of the form $X \rightarrow Y$ where X and Y are sets of predicates and some of which are spatial ones

[8], this rule describes the effect of one or a set of features by another set of features in spatial data set. The reference feature is referring to a selected business area and we are using the spatial association rule with the desired business type to identify the related corresponding characteristics. The characteristics ranking is based on the outcome of the association rule mining using Apriori based on their Lift's score. In general, association rule mining can be viewed as a two-step process [22]:

a. "Find all frequent itemsets: By definition, each of these itemsets will occur at least as frequently as a predetermined by minimum support count."
b. "Generate strong association rules from the frequent item sets: By definition, these rules must satisfy minimum support and minimum confidence."

Classification Technique
Classification is used to predict group membership for data instance [23]. The aim is to examine what Business Type that is likely to appear when we set the characteristics of the location. Decision tree is used to predict the type of businesses that will likely to occur based on the chosen characteristics. This is important in order for us to build the prototype to predict the Business type based on location characteristic chosen. We train a supervised ML with the attributes of a particular location. The features are mined from an area L_d. The location centered at L_d with radius r = 200 m as this yields the best experimental results [5].

4   Analysis of Findings

4.1   Data Overview – Descriptive

From the pre-processed data, we proceed with the processing and generate an initial overview of the data based on the data summary.

Table 1. Descriptive data for three attributes

District	Business Type	Business Name
Petaling Jaya : 221	EateryPlace : 125	99 Speedmart : 45
Puchong : 118	Mini Market : 45	7 Eleven : 12
Shah Alam : 93	Saloon: 39	Hong Leong Bank : 4
Subang Jaya : 78	Clinic : 37	KK Supermart : 3
Seri Kembangan : 57	Learning : 35	POS Malaysia : 3
(Other) : 165	(Other) : 451	(Other) : 665
Total = 20 level	Total = 58 level	Total = 662 level
(a)	(b)	(c)

We separate the table based on the attributes with multiple levels from Table 1. In Table 1(a), the District Petaling Jaya has the highest number of location count. The specific location is in various places. This district is considered as one of the most critical business area with high density of population. Table 1(b) showing the highest count for Business Type in our data set. The Eatery Place is dominating the count of 127 outlets. Corresponding outlet under this category includes restaurant, café and other related food establishment found in the area of observation. We have chosen location characteristics as listed in Table 2.

Table 2. Location characteristics with details description

Location characteristics	Description
Ample parking	The surrounding has a sufficient parking place. For example, availability of parking on each side of the road in front of the stores or near to parking area
Corner shop lot	The shops are located at the end corner shop lot
Housing	Near to housing area such as an Apartment or a common accommodation are such as Taman or Kampung
Facing road view	The stores are visible from the outer road or main road
Road entry	Entry to the stores is located near to road entrance
Hospital	Near to Hospital such as government Hospital
LRT	Near to LRT or public transport
School	Near to School such as Primary or Secondary government schools

#No of location characteristics = 8

4.2 Data Integration – Correlation Analysis Using Fisher's Test

Correlation analysis is to remove data redundancy in a dataset. This analysis measures the strength of association between two variables and the direction of the relationship. Our data consists of multi variables and we would like to measure how the Dependent Variable = Business. Type is significant with each variable. Beginning with the null hypothesis (Ho) where each variable is independent from each other with the p-value is >0.05. However, if the p-value < 0.05, the Ho will be rejected and the alternative hypothesis (H$_1$) will be accepted, where the variable is significant with the dependent variable. To proceed further, we run the Fisher Test on each attributes. Tables 3 and 4 shows the result separated between p-value < 0.05 (statistically significant) and p-value > 0.05 (statistically insignificant):

Table 3. Attributes with p-value < 0.05

#	Attributes	p-value	#	Attributes	p-value
1	CornerShopLot	0.0004998	15	Hardware	0.006497
2	FacingRoadView	0.04948	16	Hotel	0.04648
3	RoadEntry	0.005997	17	KitchenCabinet	0.002499
4	24HrsConvenience	0.0009995	18	Laundry	0.0009995
5	BakeryShop	0.007996	19	Learning	0.0004998
6	Bank	0.0004998	20	MedicalShop	0.01249
7	CarAccessories	0.01399	21	MotorcyleShop	0.0004998
8	CarWorkshop	0.0004998	22	Office	0.002499
9	Clinic	0.0009995	23	Pets	0.01699
10	EateryPlaceMamak	0.004498	24	Telecommunication	0.001999
11	EateryPlace	0.002499	25	Travel	0.0004998
12	Saloon	0.0004998	26	WellnessCentre	0.006997
13	FashionAndClothing	0.0004998	27	WorkAgency	0.003498
14	FitnessCentre	0.01299			

Table 4. Attributes with p-value > 0.05

#	Attributes	p-value
1	AmpleParking	0.30330
2	Housing	0.38980
3	Hospital*	Error
4	LRT	0.49430
5	School	0.25840
6	Bookshop	0.56870
7	OtherMiniMarket	0.74060
8	FastFood	0.20390
9	FruitsShop	0.40580
10	Music	0.11190
11	Optical	0.07296
12	Pajak	0.08946
13	Printing	0.1384

*x having only 1 value

4.3   Mining Process

Association Rule

We are interested in the top Businesses that appear in our listing in Table 1(b). We set the right-hand-side of the Apriori function following the chosen business type of interest. The support and confidence percentage will be changed accordingly following the number of rules outcome that is suitable to be used. This is based on the right-hand-side parameter following the Business Type. The ranking of the attributes is summarized in Table 5:

Table 5. Ranking of attributes based on the Business Type

Business Type	Attributes Ranking
Eatery Place	1. CornerShopLot=yes, 2. RoadEntry=no, 3. Clinic=yes, 4. Office=yes, 5. Pets=no 6. Saloon=yes, 7. CarWorkshop=yes, 8. WellnessCentre=yes 9. EateryPlaceMamak=no 10. Laundry=yes, 11. MedicalShop=no

(a)

Business Type	Attributes Ranking
Mini market	1. CornerShopLot=yes, 2. RoadEntry=yes, 3. Clinic=yes, 4. Hardware=no 5. 24HrsConvenience=no 6. FashionAndClothing=no, 7. Hotel=no 8. Bank=no, 9. FitnessCentre=no, 10. Pets=no 11. CarAccessories=no, 12. CarWorkshop=no

(b)

Business Type	Attributes Ranking
Saloon	1. CornerShopLot=no, 2. FacingRoadView=yes, 3. CarWorkshop=no, 4. Hardware=yes, 5. Laundry=no, 6. Pets=no 7. RoadEntry=no, 8. CarAccessories=yes, 9. EateryPlaceMamak=no, 10. Learning=no 11. WellnessCentre=no

(c)

Classification – Decision Tree

We proceed further with the supervised learning using classification method. This is to predict the Business Type based on the location attributes. The rationale of using decision tree is to get the insight from the data based on the known set of data. The insight is related to the Business Type that likely to appear based on the surrounding location characteristics. From the information on the ranks of attributes, we can make this as the predictor to determine the possible Business Type that might be suitable to be operated. Based on the outcome from the association, we will run the Decision Tree classification to predict the Business Type based on the characteristics. As can be observed from the decision tree, we summarize the outcome in Table 6:

Table 6. Summary of decision tree outcome/result based on selected location characteristics

Attributes	Business type
All attributes	EateryPlaceMamak EateryPlace Bank MiniMarket
CornerShopLot + RoadEntry + Clinic + Office + Pets + Saloon + CarWorkshop + WellnessCentre + EateryPlaceMamak + Laundry + MedicalShop	EateryPlaceMamak EateryPlace MiniMarket
CornerShopLot + RoadEntry + Clinic + Hardware + 24HrsConvenience + FashionAndClothing + Hotel + Bank + FitnessCentre + Pets + CarAccessories + CarWorkshop	EateryPlace Bank MiniMarket
CornerShopLot + FacingRoadView + CarWorkshop + Hardware + Laundry + Pets + RoadEntry + CarAccessories + EateryPlaceMamak + Learning + WellnessCentre	EateryPlace MiniMarket

Based on the summarized information, the Business Type output is in conformance with the earlier association ranking of characteristics, where the top business such as Eatery Place and Mini Market appear in all classification output. Other businesses such as Bank also appear due to these stores are having the same characteristics as our top business type stores. As a comparison, when we use the same characteristics from the output of Association as an input for the Classification, we can see that the output result occurred is similar with the Business Type which in our case the Eatery Place and Mini Market (which serve as the input for the Association). The intention of using both method is different. We used Association to get the Location Characteristics whereas the intention of using Classification is to get the Business Type.

5   Discussion

5.1   Mapping of Results to Research Questions

Below are some of the discussions based on the research findings.

a. What are the types of businesses that can be found at certain location?
   We want to gauge the overall data and what information can be extracted. Our data is taken from around twenty different Districts in Klang Valley region. From the data gathered, we found that there exist around 58 Business Type. Table 7 shows the top ten businesses (based on count) that occur.

Table 7. Top ten businesses from the data set

#	Business type	Frequency
1	Eateryplace	125
2	Mini market	45
3	Saloon	39
4	Clinic	37
5	Learning	35
6	Carworkshop	34
7	Office	34
8	Other mini market	32
9	Eatery place mamak	29
10	Wellness centre	25

Based on the outcome, these are the type of stores exist in our data set. The coverage of district as mentioned can be considered as a high population area with many business activities that take place. Based on the outcome of this research, we know that each location is having different characteristics that attract certain businesses. However, looking at the data gathered, given an area with similar characteristics, we can foresee and have an idea of the suitable type of businesses that can be opened in that particular area.

b. What are the top location characteristics that can be reported from the data?

We selected top three Businesses Type with the most number of outlets in order to list down the top characteristics as shown in Table 8.

Table 8. Summarized characteristics based on three top business type

Business type	Attributes ranking
Eatery place Mini market Saloon	1. CornerShopLot = yes, 2. RoadEntry = no, 3. Clinic = yes, 4. RoadEntry = yes, 5. Hardware = no 6. 24HrsConvenience = no 7. CornerShopLot = no, 8. FacingRoadView = yes, 9. CarWorkshop = no, 10. Pets = no

All three businesses type will generally have these characteristics existed in their surroundings with the related type of shops as part of the attributes. Interestingly in the combination above, it is observed that attribute CornerShopLot showing a "yes" and "no" value. We need to highlight that these two opposite characteristics are coming from two different businesses, which is Mini Market and Saloon.

c. Given a set of characteristics of a location, what are the most suitable businesses that can be opened at the particular area?

We can use Decision Tree classification in order to predict the suitable business to be opened given the attributes of the location. For example, in our case for a combination of characteristics with corner shop lot and a road entry plus a laundry and a motorcycle workshop, the suggested business to be opened is related to:

    i. a restaurant (eatery place),
    ii. grocery shop (mini market) and
    iii. a polyclinic establishment (clinic).

We can run other similar scenario by giving a different input of the characteristics and will yield another set of suitable business type.

6 Conclusion

This paper presented the methodology of producing the result beginning with the data collection, data preparation and the mining technique to determine the optimal business location selection. We contribute on the data collection presented using Google Maps. As far as the usage of data online, it is a novel approach whereby data being presented in such a way where manual records is done in order to capture the physical characteristics of a location. Although it's a manual process of opening and browsing the maps, it presented the opportunity over traditional method in many ways. This paper also suggested the usage of data mining techniques in order to do some prediction on the type of businesses that suitable to be opened, given some characteristics. We presented the proposed solution on each of the processes and presented the related R codes in order to produce the result using the data mining technique. It gives indication to the interested party on the characteristics that may have more value to the business. For example, we can target the business owner in order to decide where to open their businesses. For future work, this research can be extended using more data from other input such as: (1) Financial performance of the stores - to compare whether the physical characteristics having any significance relation with the stores turnover or sales revenue (2) Number of customer of the premises – to study on the traffic of patron to the shop in relation to the top location characteristics chosen in this research (3) The social media data for number of check-ins or likes – to study on the possibility of higher check-ins or likes for the location with high ranks of characteristics.

References

1. Hernandez, T., Bennison, D.: The art and science of retail location decisions. Int. J. Retail Distrib. Manag. **28**(8), 357–367 (2000)
2. Zentes, J., Morschett, D., Schramm-Klein, H.: Store location – trading area analysis and site selection. In: Strategic Retail Management, pp. 203–225 (2011)
3. Waxman, L.: The coffee shop: social and physical factors influencing place attachment. J. Inter. Des. **31**(3), 35–53 (2006)
4. Lin, J., Oentaryo, R., Lim, E.P., Vu, C., Vu, A., Kwee, A.: Where is the goldmine? Finding promising business locations through Facebook data analytics. In: Proceedings of the 27th ACM Conference on Hypertext and Social Media, pp. 93–102. ACM, New York (2016)

5. Karamshuk, D., Noulas, A., Scellato, S., Nicosia, V., Mascolo, C.: Geo-spotting: mining online location-based services for optimal retail store placement. In: Proceedings of the 19th ACM SIGKDD International Conference on Knowledge Discovery and Data Mining, pp. 793–801. ACM, New York (2013)
6. Xu, M., Wang, T., Wu, Z., Zhou, J., Li, J., Wu, H.: Store location selection via mining search query logs of Baidu maps (2016). arXiv:1606.03662
7. Agrawal, R., Srikant, R.: Fast algorithms for mining association rules in large databases. In: Proceedings of the 20th International Conference on Very Large Data Bases, pp. 487–499. Morgan Kaufmann Publishers, San Francisco (1994)
8. Koperski, K., Han, J.: Discovery of spatial association rules in geographic information databases. In: Egenhofer, Max J., Herring, John R. (eds.) SSD 1995. LNCS, vol. 951, pp. 47–66. Springer, Heidelberg (1995). https://doi.org/10.1007/3-540-60159-7_4
9. Kouris, I.N., Makris, C., Theodoridis, E., Tsakalidis, A.: Association Rules Mining for Retail Organizations. Encyclopedia of Information Science and Technology, 2nd edn., pp. 262–267. IGI Global, Hershey (2009)
10. Crewe, L.: Geographies of retailing and consumption. Prog. Hum. Geogr. 24(2), 275–290 (2000). https://doi.org/10.1191/030913200670386318
11. Hollander, S.C.: Multinational Retailing. Institute for International Business and Economic Development Studies, Michigan State University (1970)
12. Fernie, J., Moore, C.M., Lawrie, A.: A tale of two cities: an examination of fashion designer retailing within London and New York. J. Prod. Brand Manag. 7(5), 366–378 (1998)
13. Radon, A.: Luxury brand exclusivity strategies – an illustration of a cultural collaboration. J. Bus. Adm. Res. 1(1), 106 (2012)
14. Jensen, P.: Network-based predictions of retail store commercial categories and optimal locations. Phys. Rev. E 74(3), 035101 (2006)
15. Garber, L.: Analytics goes on location with new approaches. Computer 46(4), 14–17 (2013). https://doi.org/10.1109/MC.2013.123
16. ESRI: Using Location Intelligence to Maximize the Value of BI, 16 November 2011. http://www.cio.in/whitepaper/using-location-intelligence-maximize-value-bi-moved. Accessed 5 Aug 2017
17. Angelaccio, M., Buttarazzi, B., Basili, A., Liguori, W.: Using geo-business intelligence to improve quality of life. In: 2012 IEEE First AESS European Conference on Satellite Telecommunications (ESTEL), pp. 1–6. IEEE (2012)
18. Shekhar, S., Huang, Y.: Discovering spatial co-location patterns: a summary of results. In: Jensen, Christian S., Schneider, M., Seeger, B., Tsotras, Vassilis J. (eds.) SSTD 2001. LNCS, vol. 2121, pp. 236–256. Springer, Heidelberg (2001). https://doi.org/10.1007/3-540-47724-1_13
19. Niti, D.: Retail location analysis: a case study of Burger King & McDonald's in Portage & Summit Counties, Ohio. Kent State University (2007)
20. The edge [News], 9 June 2014. http://www.equatoassist1.com/CMS_99SMart2/Admin/uploads/news/839bfa4c-049d-4fa9-9dff-a0b5f9cf1d9a/Pages%20from%2020140609_TEM_1018.pdf. Accessed 30 Aug 2017
21. Fayyad, U., Piatetsky-Shapiro, G., Smyth, P.: From data mining to knowledge discovery in databases. AI Mag. 17(3), 37 (1996). https://doi.org/10.1609/aimag.v17i3.1230
22. Han, J., Kamber, M., Pei, J.: Mining frequent patterns, associations, and correlations: basic concepts and methods. In: Han, J., Kamber, M., Pei, J. (eds.) Data Mining, 3rd edn. Morgan Kaufmann, Boston (2012)
23. Gupta, M., Agarwal, N.: Classification techniques analysis. In: Proceedings of National Conference on Computational Instrumentation, pp. 120–128 (2010)

Detection and Classification of Hippocampal Structural Changes in MR Images as a Biomarker for Alzheimer's Disease

Katia Maria Poloni🄳 and Ricardo José Ferrari$^{(\boxtimes)}$🄳

Department of Computing, Federal University of São Carlos, Rod. Washington Luís, Km 235, Mailbox 676, São Carlos, SP 13565-905, Brazil
{katia.poloni,rferrari}@ufscar.br
http://bipgroup.dc.ufscar.br

Abstract. Alzheimer's disease (AD) is the most common form of dementia, comprising around 60% of all dementia cases and affecting 20% of the population over 80 years of age. AD may affect people in different ways. The most common symptom pattern begins with a gradually worsening ability to remember new information, difficulty to solve problems and perform familiar tasks at home, confusion about time or place, and trouble understanding visual images. Currently, the volume reduction of the two hippocampi is the most used structural magnetic resonance imaging (MRI) biomarker of AD. However, despite its clinical use, hippocampal volume reduction is involved not only in AD but also in other dementias and even in healthy aging. In this study, we propose a new computational framework for the detection and classification of hippocampal structural changes in MR images as a biomarker for AD. First, we built a probabilistic atlas of 3D salient points using a dataset of healthy brain images. Then, we detected 3D salient points in a training dataset with cognitively normal (CN) and mild-AD brain images and used them to label each point on the atlas. Next, the 3D salient points detected in each image from the training dataset were matched against the labeled points in the atlas, and their descriptor vectors were used to train a support vector machine with radial basis function (SVM-RBF). Last, we detected 3D salient points, extracted their descriptor vectors, matched them against the atlas and classified them using the SVM-RBF classifier, for each image from the testing dataset. Finally, we attribute a class label (CN/mild-AD) according to the majority of points classified in the corresponding class. We tested our proposed framework using a stratified age group image dataset (551 MR images in total) and assessed the results using a 10-fold cross-validation and ROC methodology. The highest accuracy value achieved by our method was 85% (up to 82.59% sensitivity and 88.50% specificity) for the age group 70–89, and the highest area under the curve was 0.9227.

Keywords: Atlas of 3D landmarks
Alzheimer's disease classification · Feature extraction · MRI · SVM

O. Gervasi et al. (Eds.): ICCSA 2018, LNCS 10960, pp. 406–422, 2018.
https://doi.org/10.1007/978-3-319-95162-1_28

1   Introduction

Alzheimer's disease (AD) is an irreversible, progressive brain disorder that slowly destroys cognitive functions, and eventually the ability to perform the simplest tasks. AD is the most frequent cause of dementia, responsible for almost 60% of cases, currently it is one of the most significant health problems in the world due to the population aging. In 2010, the World Health Organization estimated that 35.6 million people worldwide had dementia and that the number of cases would double by 2030 (65.7 million) and again by 2050 (115.4 million) [1]. AD still has no cure, and its late diagnosis can lead to death.

Aging involves multiple structural changes in the brain that can affect cognition [2,3], however, these changes are usually more frequent and severe in neurodegenerative diseases. AD exists along a spectrum, from forgetfulness and memory changes to functional dependence and death. The initial damage seems to occur in the hippocampal regions, the part of the brain essential in forming memories. Additional parts of the brain are affected and start to shrink as more neurons die. By the final stage of AD, the damage is widespread, and brain tissue has shrunk significantly [1,4].

Despite decades of research, there is still no definitive test to diagnose AD. A careful evaluation of Magnetic Resonance (MR) images and a clinical interview with the person and someone close to them who can corroborate the person's memory loss are the primary steps to establish if physical and cognitive changes are part of a healthy aging process or indicative of Mild Cognitive Impairment (MCI) or AD. Eliminating other possible causes of memory loss is also an essential part of diagnosing this disease.

Clinical practice routinely uses anatomical magnetic resonance (MR) images to diagnosis patients with cognitive disturbances [5], due to its excellent contrast on soft tissues. Therefore, the development of a quantitative MR image biomarker that could be used to differentiate brain structural changes caused by healthy aging and mild-AD would be of great benefit and have a minimal cost impact.

Hippocampal and whole-brain atrophy rates have been recognized as two essential markers in measuring AD progression [6] with hippocampal rates being considered a more specific marker of AD. Reductions in hippocampal volume, for instance, appear to correspond to the onset of memory decline.

Hippocampal volume reduction (HVR) over time is still widely used to diagnose AD, however, HVR can also be related to other dementias, such as vascular dementia [7], or even be a part of healthy aging [2,4,8]. Therefore, volumetric measurements of the hippocampus may not be the most efficient form of predicting AD progression.

Devanand et al. [9] suggest that the nature of hippocampal degeneration and surrounding structures, such as the entorhinal cortex and the parahippocampal gyrus, is different in AD than in other dementias and healthy aging. Their results are further corroborated by the study of Eskildsen et al. [10], they have also investigated structural brain changes in the hippocampal region of three population groups: cognitively normal (CN), mild cognitive impairment (MCI) and AD.

A critical task in AD research is to observe and understand the progression of this disease over an extended period and find trends in its development before the clinical manifestations. Given this context, this study proposes a new technique for the detection and classification of brain structural changes in MR images to be used as a biomarker for the diagnosis of AD.

The contributions of our study can be summarized as follows. First, we proposed a probabilistic atlas of 3D salient points automatically detected in MR brain images, which can be used for different tasks in neuroimaging, such as to the positioning of deformable meshes, landmark-based image registration and, as in this study, to capture structural changes. Second, we proposed a methodology to label the salient points of the proposed atlas and use them to capture structural changes in the hippocampal regions caused by Alzheimer's disease, which is different from healthy aging. Third, we proposed the use of support vector machine (SVM) classifiers to classify salient points detected in an MR image, and use their class-labels to decide if the image is a case of mild-AD or CN.

2   Materials and Methods

In this section, we describe the dataset and methodology used in this study.

2.1   Image Datasets

In this study, we used images from three different datasets: the Neuroimage Analysis Center (NAC) [11], the Alzheimer's Disease Neuroimaging Initiative (ADNI) [12] and the Information eXtraction from Images (IXI[1]) datasets.

The NAC dataset consists of 149 3D triangular meshes, each representing a distinct brain structure. The meshes are spatially aligned to both T1-weighted (T1-w) and T2-weighted (T2-w) MRI sequences (reference images) of the same patient. Both images have an isotropic resolution of 1 mm and size of $256 \times 256 \times 256$ voxels. In addition to the meshes, this dataset provides the reference images and the labeling of brain structures made by a specialist.

The ADNI dataset is part of a project initiated in 2003 by a group of research institutions, private pharmaceutical companies, and nongovernmental organizations to study the progression of AD. The dataset includes pre-processed and post-processed T1-w images, as well as hippocampal labels for some images. The images were acquired using a wide variety of 1.5 T and 3T scanners and protocols from the three leading manufacturers (Philips, General Electric, and Siemens), so the specifications of the images (size, resolution, etc.) are diverse and will be omitted here. The acquisition sites are also variated[2]. For this study, we selected only images with T1-MPRAGE protocol and without preprocessing

---

[1] http://www.brain-development.org.

[2] http://adni.loni.usc.edu/about/centers-cores/study-sites/.

for CN and mild-AD subjects. CN patients showed no signs of depression, mild cognitive impairment or dementia. Mild-AD patients were evaluated and met an established criteria for a probable AD, as summarized in Table 1. Since structural changes in the brain caused by Alzheimer's disease have significant similarities to the changes caused by healthy aging [13], we stratified the database by age groups of 10, 20 and 40 years.

The IXI dataset consists of clinical brain MR images of normal healthy patients obtained from three different London hospitals, namely: Hammersmith Hospital (HH), Guy's Hospital (GH) and Institute of Psychiatry (IoP). The HH and GH have 185 and 322 images, respectively, both of size $256 \times 256 \times 150$ voxels and resolution $0.94 \times 0.94 \times 1.2$ mm^3, the IoP hospital has 74 images of same resolution as the ones from the HH and GH hospitals and size of $256 \times 256 \times 146$ voxels. This dataset is composed of 581 images in total. The age range of patients considered in this study varied between 20 and 86 years.

Table 1. Age group stratification of the ADNI images used for the training and testing stages of our proposed method

Age group	Training images			Testing images		
	CN	Mild-AD	Total	CN	Mild-AD	Total
60–69	34	30	64	4	3	7
70–79	151	98	249	17	11	28
80–89	91	76	167	10	8	18
60–79	185	128	313	21	14	35
70–89	242	174	416	27	19	46
55–89	282	214	496	31	24	55

2.2 Overview of the Proposed Framework

The primary idea of the proposed framework is to build a probabilistic atlas of salient points using MR images of a healthy population and then compare the most frequently detected points (high-density salient points) to both CN and mild-AD classes (training dataset) to determine which categories present the highest discriminative classification. In this case, the descriptor vectors associate to each salient point in the atlas, summarizing local anatomical brain character-istics. This, in turn, account for the distinctive nature of structural changes in the hippocampal regions.

Figure 1 illustrates a schematic diagram of our proposed framework for CN/mild-AD classification. Each step of the block diagram is explained in detail as follows.

Preprocessing. All MR images used in this study were pre-processed using the following ordered steps: (a) noise removal using the Non-Local Means (NLM)

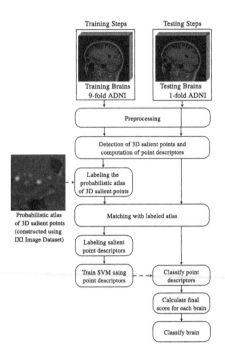

Fig. 1. Block diagram of the proposed method

technique [14], (b) bias field correction using the N4-ITK technique [15], (c) image intensity standardization [16] and (d) image registration using the Nifty-Reg tool [17]. Steps (c) and (d) were performed using the T1-w reference image from the NAC dataset.

To ensure that all structural changes in the MR brain images were considered during the training and testing of the classifier designed to distinguish between CN and mild-AD cases, the dataset images were registered to the reference using only affine registration. However, images from the IXI dataset, that were used to build the probabilistic atlas of 3D salient points, were registered for reference using a composition of affine and free-form B-Spline transformations.

Since the region of interest (ROI) in this study is the two hippocampal regions, the left and right hippocampi meshes from the NAC dataset were converted to binary masks and expanded with a morphological dilation operation. This procedure guarantees the incorporation of surrounding structures (*e.g.*, the amygdala and parahippocampal gyrus) around the two hippocampi. The dilation operation used a 3D sphere of 12 voxels radius as a structuring element. Figure 2 illustrates both the 3D volume rendering and the final binary masks representing the left and right hippocampal regions.

3D Salient Point Detector. The term "salient point" used in this study refers to an image point that stands out locally due to showing some specific feature

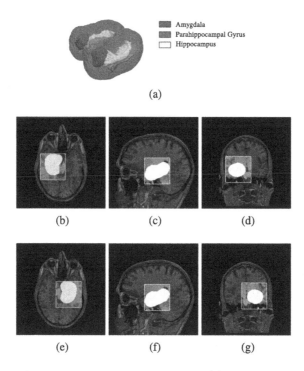

Fig. 2. Regions of interest analyzed in this study. (a) 3D rendering indicating the anatomical regions included in the ROIs. (b-e) axial view, (c-f) sagittal view and (d-g) coronal view

(*e.g.*, a high degree of curvature), and it is usually visible to the naked eye. This point does not necessarily represent an anatomical reference point that would be marked by a specialist, although this is usually the case.

Phase Congruency-Based Detector: We used the detector proposed by Villa-Pinto and Ferrari [18] to detect the 3D salient points in the MR images, the detected points helped to guide the initialization of 3D mesh models of brain structures. This method is based on the phase congruency (PC) model [19], which assumes the position of image features at locations where Fourier components are maximally in phase rather than intensity changes (gradient). However, instead of using a Fourier series to compute the PC measure, Venkatesh and Owens [20] showed that the PC measure is proportional to the local energy of the signal and that it can be calculated via convolution of the original image with a bank of spatial filters in quadrature. Villa-Pinto and Ferrari [18] computed the PC response maps via convolution of the original image with a bank of log-Gabor filters. The measure of saliency for a given point was defined as the highest eigenvalue of a 3×3 matrix of second order moments of inertia of the directional PC response maps.

Salient Point Descriptor: The method used for the description and matching of salient points is an extension of the shape contexts technique [21,22], initially proposed to quantify shape similarities and corresponding points on brain structures whose contours are represented by sets of 2D points.

The shape contexts technique for 3D images requires using an image edge map to represent the shape information of the object and a log-spherical histogram to divide the image space around each salient point in η_r relative radial distances, η_a relative azimuth angles and η_e relative elevation angles. The accumulated values in the bins of the log-spherical histogram express the feature significance of the edge points placed inside them. The values used were $\eta_r = 5$, $\eta_a = 12$ and $\eta_e = 6$ [18]. Therefore, each salient point descriptor has 360 attributes in total.

In this study, descriptor vectors associated to each salient point in the atlas summarize local anatomical brain characteristics, which, in turn, account for the distinctive nature of structural changes in the hippocampal regions.

Point Matching: To measure the similarity between two pairs of descriptor vectors (say, h_1 and h_2) of two salient points (p_1 and p_2), the χ^2 distance was used as a dissimilarity function. The χ^2 distance is computed as

$$\chi^2\left(h_1, h_2\right) = \frac{1}{2} \sum_{i=0}^{\eta_r \eta_a \eta_e - 1} \frac{[h_1(i) - h_2(i)]^2}{h_1(i) + h_2(i)}, \tag{1}$$

where $h_1(i)$ and $h_2(i)$ are the ith bin of the descriptor vectors h_1 and h_2, respectively. This metric is particularly appropriate due to considering the differences between the sizes of the histogram bins, which means that small differences between values obtained from larger bins result in a smaller distance than a small difference between values of the smaller bins [21].

After computing the χ^2 distance of descriptor vectors of a pair of salient points, we determined if these two points matched by using the "forward-backward" nearest neighbor. Therefore, a match between the descriptor vectors h_1 and h_2 only exists if h_1 is the nearest neighbor of h_2 and h_2 is the nearest neighbor of h_1. Please refer to [18] for an in-depth explanation of the detector of 3D salient points (including the salient point descriptor) used in this study.

Probabilistic Atlas of 3D Salient Points in the Hippocampal Region.

A probabilistic atlas in medical image analysis provides essential information regarding the shape or grayscale value variability of a specific training population [23]. Probabilistic atlases are widely used in image segmentation and registration tasks [24]. In this study we proposed a probabilistic atlas of 3D salient points automatically detected in T1-w MR images and used it to aid in CN/mild-AD classification. Our technique was different from the conventional atlases in the studies mentioned in the literature review, since it only considers the information of the salient points instead of the brain tissues.

The rationale behind this idea, which is inspired in the feature-based morphometry technique [25], is two-fold. First, the probabilistic atlas of 3D salient points can be used directly to represent invariant anatomical local brain regions in MR images across a healthy population. Second, points with high-density values in the atlas can be labeled according to their occurrence in the CN and mild-AD classes and, by using their descriptors, further applied to capture the distinct nature of structural changes in the brain.

The construction of the probabilistic atlas of 3D salient points is made after applying the preprocessing (please refer to Sect. 2.2) and detecting the 3D salient points (using the detector described in Sect. 2.2) in all training images, *i.e.*, MR images of healthy patients from the IXI dataset. Figure 3 illustrates the entire sequence of steps of this process, which does not require any human interaction.

Two steps are used to build the atlas. First, a probability density function (pdf), $p_x : X \subset \mathbb{N}^3 \longrightarrow [0, 1]$, which expresses the location distribution of the detected points in the training images, is estimated. Second, the mean descriptors $\overline{h}$ are calculated for all maximal positions of p_x.

The Manifold Parzen Windows [26] estimator is used to estimate the density of salient points. For such, a finite mixture of diagonal Gaussian-kernels is used to represent the probability density function, $p(x)$, of a set of l samples, as

$$p\left(x\right) = \frac{1}{l} \sum_{i=1}^{l} \frac{1}{\sqrt{(2\pi)^d |\Sigma_i|}} \exp\left(-\frac{1}{2}\Delta(x)\right), \tag{2}$$

where d is the sample dimensionality, $\Sigma_i = \Sigma_{\mathcal{K}_i} + \sigma^2 I_3$ is the covariance matrix of the ith kernel component, $\sigma^2 I_3$ is a 3×3 isotropic Gaussian with $\sigma^2 = 1$ added to $\Sigma_{\mathcal{K}_i}$ to avoid ill-conditioned inverse problems and $\Delta(x) = (x - x_i)^t \Sigma_i^{-1} (x - x_i)$ is the squared Mahalanobis distance. The first component, $\Sigma_{\mathcal{K}_i}$, of the covariance matrix Σ_i is computed as

$$\Sigma_{\mathcal{K}_i} = \frac{\sum_{j=1...l, j \neq i} \mathcal{K}\left(x_j, x_i\right)\left(x_j - x_i\right)^t\left(x_j - x_i\right)}{\sum_{j=1...l, j \neq i} \mathcal{K}\left(x_j, x_i\right)}, \tag{3}$$

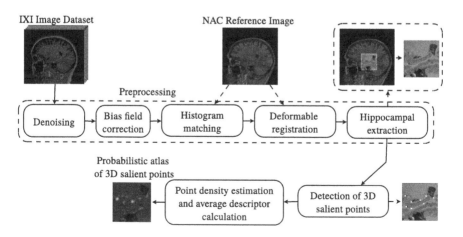

Fig. 3. Processing steps to build the probabilistic atlas of 3D salient points

where $\mathcal{K}(\boldsymbol{x}_j, \boldsymbol{x}_i) = G_{\mu=\boldsymbol{x}_i, \Sigma=\sigma I_3}(\boldsymbol{x}_j)$ is a Gaussian function which associates each sample $\boldsymbol{x}_j$ of the neighbor of $\boldsymbol{x}_i$ with a weighting factor.

Figure 4 illustrates the density map (overlaid to the original template T1-w MR image) created as a result of the process described above. In this case, the intensity of each voxel is proportional to the greater or lesser presence of points projected at that location along the training images.

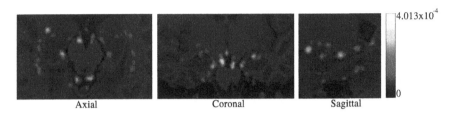

Fig. 4. Probabilistic atlas of 3D salient points of the hippocampal region overlaid to the original MR image (axial, coronal, and sagittal views)

After estimating the density for each voxel corresponding to a maximal point of $p(\boldsymbol{x})$, a mean descriptor $\overline{\boldsymbol{h}}$ is calculated as the average of all descriptors detected in any training image within a neighboring region around the corresponding maximal peak. For simplicity, from now on, we will refer to the maximal points of $p(\boldsymbol{x})$ as "salient points of the atlas."

Labeling the Probabilistic Atlas of 3D Salient Points. First, the number of matchings (m_i) between each salient point (p_i) of the atlas and the points detected in all images from the training dataset is calculated within each class (CN and mild-AD). In this study, we use a constraint on the χ^2 distance, Eq. (1), to avoid matchings between points farther apart than 0.35. Next, we normalize the number of matchings per point $(\hat{m}_i)$ in the interval of $[0, 1]$ by dividing all m_i by the largest m_i value $(max(m_i))$ found in each class (CN and mild-AD). This normalization is required since the number of images per class is different, which prevents a direct comparison between the number of matchings in both classes. After that, all salient points p_i of the atlas are labeled as (○) concomitant and (★) structural changes indicator by using the following rule:

$$p_i = \begin{cases} \star & , if \left| \hat{m}_i^{\mathrm{CN}} - \hat{m}_i^{\mathrm{mild\text{-}AD}} \right| > T_s \\ \circ & , \text{otherwise} \end{cases}, \tag{4}$$

where T_s controls the matching similarity.

In summary, Eq. (4) defines that concomitant points are the ones showing similar values of matching in both classes while the others points are considered as indicators of structural changes.

Extracting Morphometric Image Features for Classification. After labeling all salient points of the atlas as "concomitant" and "structural change indicators," salient points are extracted from each image in the training dataset and matched against the ones of the atlas using the nearest neighbor search (see Sect. 2.2). The class labels (CN and mild-AD) of the training images are known, for this reason the descriptor vectors of all points of a given training image are used as sample features for their respective class, being matched against points that are indicators of structural changes. Also, points in a training image matching to concomitant points in the atlas will have their descriptors considered as sample features for a third class, named "concomitant class."

Classifier Design. To classify an MR clinical image in one of the two classes (CN or mild-AD), we designed a SVM classifier [27,28], with an RBF kernel for each age group using the python sklearn library[3]. For such, we use morphometric image features extracted from the training dataset, as described in Sect. 2.2.

For the SVM-RBF, two kernel parameters needed to be tuned, C and gamma (γ). Parameter C controls the trade-off between training error and the generalization of the solution. The higher C is, the lesser the final training error will be. However, if C is increased too much, there is a risk of losing the generalization properties of the classifier, because it will try to fit all training sample as best as possible (including possible errors or noise, present in your dataset). In addition, a high C value usually increases the time needed for training. The gamma parameter acts as the inverse of the radius of influence of samples selected by the model as support vectors. If γ is too high, the radius of the area of influence of the support vectors only includes the support vector itself, and no amount of regularization with C will be able to prevent overfitting. When gamma is very low, the model is too constrained and unable to capture the complexity of the data [28].

In this study, we used a grid-search to select the best (regarding accuracy) set of parameters for the SVM in each age group, according to the methodology proposed in [29]. The parameters were first varied using a coarse grid with C ranging from $[2^{-5}; 2^{15}]$, and γ from $[2^{-15}; 2^{3}]$, with steps of 2^{2} and 5-fold cross validation. After finding the best grid range, the best SVM kernel parameters were assessed again using a finer grid with C ranging from $2^{(\log_2 \tilde{C})-1}; 2^{(\log_2 \tilde{C})+1}]$ and γ from $[2^{(\log_2 \tilde{\gamma})-1}; 2^{(\log_2 \tilde{\gamma})+1}]$, with steps of $2^{0.5}$ and 5-fold cross validation. Table 2 summarizes the results of these experiments. Given the nature of our feature set, in this stage we have an unbalanced dataset, *i.e.*, the number points labeled as concomitant is higher than CN and mild-AD. Therefore, to correct for this uneven class representation, we adjust the weights as inversely proportional to class frequencies.

Image Classification. Our developed computational framework classifies a given MR brain image as CN or mild-AD through the following steps. First,

---

[3] http://scikit-learn.org/stable/modules/generated/sklearn.svm.SVC.html.

Table 2. Best set of parameters for the SVM-RBF classifier

Age group (n)	SVM-RBF					
	C	Gamma (γ)	f1-score (%)	Precision (%)	Recall (%)	Accuracy (%)
60–69 (64)	$2^{0.5}$	$2^{-7.8}$	57.00	57.00	57.00	59.00
70–79 (249)	$2^{2.5}$	$2^{-7.8}$	63.00	63.00	64.00	69.00
80–89 (167)	$2^{1.0}$	$2^{-8.8}$	64.00	65.00	63.00	66.00
60–79 (313)	$2^{2.0}$	$2^{-7.8}$	70.00	79.00	70.00	71.00
70–89 (416)	$2^{1.0}$	$2^{-7.8}$	65.00	65.00	65.00	66.00
55–89 (496)	$2^{4.5}$	$2^{-8.3}$	80.00	79.00	80.00	81.00

salient points are detected in the image. Second, they are matched with the atlas and the designed SVM-RBF classifies the salient points into three classes: concomitant, CN, and mild-AD. Third, the ratio between the number of AD and CN points is calculated. Finally, the image is classified as mild-AD if the ratio is higher than a defined threshold T_r; otherwise, it is classified as CN.

2.3 Performance Evaluation

The performance of our proposed computational framework was assessed using 10-fold cross-validation. The classification results were calculated using accuracy (ACC), sensitivity (SEN), specificity (SPE), standard error (SE), the receiver operating characteristic (ROC) curve and the area under curve (AUC) [30].

3 Experimental Results and Discussions

Fig. 4 illustrates the axial, coronal and sagittal views of a specific cut-plane of the probabilistic atlas of 3D salient points built for the hippocampal regions. We have overlaid the salient point densities to the T1-w MR image (reference image) to better illustrate their anatomical positions. The high-density of points were found in image locations with high 3D curvature information. Furthermore, some of the salient points seen in the sagittal view correspond to actual anatomical landmarks, such as the hippocampus tail and the posterior apex of the hippocampal uncus, which is usually used by neuroradiologists during semi-manual delineation of the hippocampus.

The atlas labeling procedure in Sect. 2.2 considers the similarity between the number of matchings of a given point in the atlas within both classes (CN and mild-AD), which is controlled by the threshold T_s. In this study, for each age group, the difference $\hat{m}_i^{CN} - \hat{m}_i^{mild\text{-}AD}$ was plotted and the values for all groups were between 0 and 0.25. However, values greater than 0.12 represented only 13% of all points in the atlas (less than 10 points). Therefore, T_s varied from 0.02 to 0.12, with steps of 0.02, as illustrated in Fig. 5. We performed the proposed framework on each fixed value of T_s using the testing images, calculating a ROC curve and its respective AUC, as shown in Fig. 6a. The ROC curve was drawn

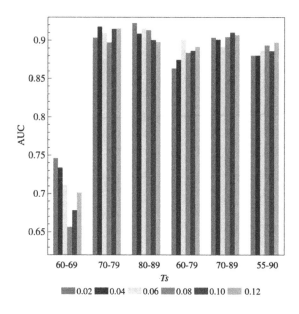

Fig. 5. Assessment of the atlas labeling parameter (T_s)

by varying the threshold T_r from 0 to 5 with 0.01 steps. T_r is applied to the ratio between the number of AD and CN salient points classified by the SVM-RBF.

Table 3. Average classification results of the 10-fold cross-validation using all images from the testing dataset for different age groups

Age group (n)	AUC	Specificity $\overline{SPE}$ (%) $\pm$ SE	Sensitivity $\overline{SEN}$ (%) $\pm$ SE	Accuracy $\overline{ACC}$ (%) $\pm$ SE
60–69 (64)	0.7459	77.50 ± 10.03	57.50 ± 5.53	67.50 ± 5.36
70–79 (249)	0.9178	85.29 ± 2.89	84.55 ± 1.91	84.99 ± 1.66
80–89 (167)	0.9227	**83.27 ± 3.05**	**86.39 ± 4.53**	**84.73 ± 2.63**
60–79 (313)	0.9010	86.19 ± 2.07	82.86 ± 3.26	84.86 ± 2.06
70–89 (416)	**0.9101**	82.59 ± 1.59	**88.50 ± 1.74**	**85.12 ± 0.99**
55–90 (496)	0.8970	89.38 ± 1.97	77.50 ± 1.10	84.28 ± 1.18

By assessing the plots in Fig. 5, we can notice that the highest variation of the T_s parameter occurs in the 60–69 group, with a difference up to 10% between the lowest and highest values. For the other groups, the differences are lower than 5%. Another point to be considered is that regardless of T_s variation, the AUC values for the 60–69 age group are much smaller than the others. The highest AUC value (0.92) was obtained for the 80–89 group with a T_s value equal to 0.02.

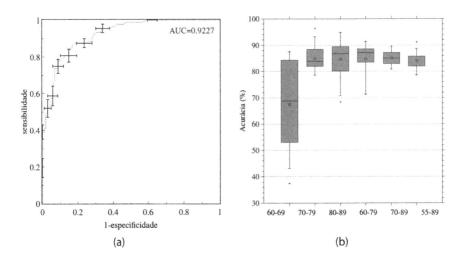

Fig. 6. (a) ROC curve and its corresponding AUC value for the age group 80–89 years. (b) Boxplots for 10-fold cross-validation accuracy values for all age-groups

Stratifying the population by age is crucial to avoid misjudgment regarding brain structural changes caused by Alzheimer's disease or by healthy aging, which would introduce bias into our analysis.

Thus, we started to evaluate our method by stratifying our database (Table 1) with intervals of 10 years. For this case, as previously discussed, the 60–69 age range presented much lower AUC values when compared to other ranges. Our initial hypothesis was that the relatively small number of images (64 training images) when compared to the 70–79 and 80–89 age groups (over 167 training images) was the cause for such a difference. To confirm, we stratified our database at intervals of 20 to increase the number of images in the new age groups. We also assessed our method using all images from the ADNI database. As a result, the AUC values increased significantly for the group with the fewer images, going from 0.7459 (60–69 age group) to 0.9010 (60–79 age group), which confirmed our hypothesis.

Figure 6b shows the boxplots for 10-fold cross-validation accuracy for all age groups. We can notice that the interquartile range (IQR) is about 30% for the 60–69 age group, which is the group with the least training images. Furthermore, we observe a trend for the IQR values in which the IQR decreases as the number of training images increases. Finally, by assessing the boxplots, we noticed that the average accuracy values are similar for all age groups but the 60–69.

Table 3 presents the average classification results of the 10-fold cross-validation using all images from the testing dataset. For the analysis, we use the T_s parameter values that provide the best AUC values for the age groups, Fig. 5. All results were obtained by choosing the operating point in the ROC curve that is the closest point to the (0, 1) position and gives an excellent trade-off between sensitivity and specificity values. The best accuracy result is highlighted in boldface.

Because in this study we used a larger dataset compared to the other methods published in the literature, a direct comparison is not possible. However, in a recent work, Sørensen *et al.* [31] has used a dataset similar to one of our age group (70–79 years) which allow us to compare the results. In their work, [31] combined hippocampus volume, texture and CSF for classification of CN vs AD. For the optimization of their method, the authors also used the AUC metric. The results obtained for the 70–79 age group have shown comparable AUC and accuracy values; $AUC = 0.9101$ and $accuracy = 84.99\%$ for our method versus 0.932 and 85.6% for the Sørensen *et al.* [31].

4   Conclusions

In this study, we proposed a novel computational framework for the detection and classification of hippocampal structural changes in MR images as a biomarker Alzheimer's disease. Our method uses a labeled probabilistic atlas of labeled 3D salient points to extract morphometric features from a given image, we used them to design a SVM-RBF classifier to distinguish structural changes caused by mild-AD from healthy aging. We demonstrated that our method can distinguish images from the CN and mild-AD classes with a high accuracy in different age groups. The highest value (85%) achieved was for the middle age group. Despite the good results, we believe that our method can provide even better results (accuracy classification rates) if we consider brain regions other than the hippocampal region. Our experiments also demonstrated that a smaller number of brain images decreases the accuracy and AUC metrics, significantly. Therefore, by adding a more significant number of images per age group, the accuracy may increase. Despite applying our proposed framework only on hippocampal regions, the experimental results suggest that our method can distinguishing between CN and mild-AD patients, having great potential for practical use in clinical settings. Considering these results, we plan to apply our method on other brain regions with the objective of finding more predictive regions, and to add the MCI class to our analyses.

Acknowledgments. Data collection and sharing for this project was funded by the Alzheimer's Disease Neuroimaging Initiative (ADNI) (National Institutes of Health Grant U01 AG024904) and DOD ADNI (Department of Defense award number W81XWH-12-2-0012). ADNI is funded by the National Institute on Aging, the National Institute of Biomedical Imaging and Bioengineering, and through generous contributions from the following: AbbVie, Alzheimer's Association; Alzheimer's Drug Discovery Foundation; Araclon Biotech; BioClinica, Inc.; Biogen; Bristol-Myers Squibb Company; CereSpir, Inc.; Cogstate; Eisai Inc.; Elan Pharmaceuticals, Inc.; Eli Lilly and Company; EuroImmun; F. Hoffmann-La Roche Ltd and its affiliated company Genentech, Inc.; Fujirebio; GE Healthcare; IXICO Ltd.; Janssen Alzheimer Immunotherapy Research & Development, LLC.; Johnson & Johnson Pharmaceutical Research & Development LLC.; Lumosity; Lundbeck; Merck & Co., Inc.; Meso Scale Diagnostics, LLC.; NeuroRx

Research; Neurotrack Technologies; Novartis Pharmaceuticals Corporation; Pfizer Inc.; Piramal Imaging; Servier; Takeda Pharmaceutical Company; and Transition Therapeutics. The Canadian Institutes of Health Research is providing funds to support ADNI clinical sites in Canada. Private sector contributions are facilitated by the Foundation for the National Institutes of Health (www.fnih.org). The grantee organization is the Northern California Institute for Research and Education, and the study is coordinated by the Alzheimer's Therapeutic Research Institute at the University of Southern California. ADNI data are disseminated by the Laboratory for Neuro Imaging at the University of Southern California.

Funding Statement. The authors would like to thank the São Paulo Research Foundation (FAPESP) (grant numbers 2015/02232-1 and 2014/11988-0) and the Coordination for the Improvement of Higher Education Personnel (CAPES) for the finantial support of this research.

References

1. Chan, M.: Dementia: a public health priority. World Health Organization and Alzheimer's Disease International (2017)
2. Fjell, A.M., McEvoy, L., Holland, D., Dale, A.M., Walhovd, K.B.: What is normal in normal aging? Effects of aging, amyloid and Alzheimer's disease on the cerebral cortex and the hippocampus. Prog. Neurobiol. **117**, 20–40 (2014)
3. Guo, H., Song, X., Vandorpe, R., Zhang, Y., Chen, W., Zhang, N., Schmidt, M.H., Rockwood, K.: Evaluation of common structural brain changes in aging and Alzheimer disease with the use of an MRI-based brain atrophy and lesion index: a comparison between T1WI and T2WI at 1.5T and 3T. Brain **35**(3), 504–512 (2014)
4. Abbott, A.: Dementia: a problem for our age. Nature **475**(7355), S2–S4 (2011)
5. Narayanan, L., Murray, A.D.: What can imaging tell us about cognitive impairment and dementia? World J. Radiol. **8**(3), 240–254 (2016)
6. Frisoni, G.B., Fox, N.C., Jack-Jr, C.R., Scheltens, P., Thompson, P.M.: The clinical use of structural MRI in Alzheimer disease. Nat. Rev. Neurol. **6**(2), 67–77 (2010)
7. Dolek, N., Saylisoy, S., Ozbabalik, D., Adapinar, B.: Comparison of hippocampal volume measured using magnetic resonance imaging in Alzheimer's disease, vascular dementia, mild cognitive impairment and pseudodementia. J. Int. Med. Res. **20**(2), 717–725 (2012)
8. De Leon, M., George, A., Stylopoulos, L., Smith, G., Miller, D.: Early marker for Alzheimer's disease: the atrophic hippocampus. Lancet **334**(8664), 672–673 (1989)
9. Devanand, D.P., Bansal, R., Liu, J., Hao, X., Pradhaban, G., Peterson, B.S.: MRI hippocampal and entorhinal cortex mapping in predicting conversion to Alzheimer's disease. Neuroimage **60**(3), 1622–1629 (2012)
10. Eskildsen, S.F., Coupé, P., Fonov, V.S., Pruessner, J.C., Collins, D.L.: Structural imaging biomarkers of Alzheimer's disease: predicting disease progression. Neurobiol. Aging **36**(1), S23–S31 (2015)
11. Halle, M., Talos, I.F., Jakab, M., Makris, N., Meier, D., Wald, L., Fischl, B., Kikinis, R.: Multi-modality MRI-based atlas of the brain. Brigham and Women's Hospital, Harvard Medical School, Boston, MA, USA, Technical report, Surgical Planning Laboratory, Department of Radiology (2017)

12. Jack, C.R.J., Bernstein, M.A., Fox, N.C., Thompson, P., Alexander, G., Harvey, D., Borowski, B., Britson, P.J., Whitwell, J.L., Ward, C., Dale, A.M., Felmlee, J.P., Gunter, J.L., Hill, D.L., Killiany, R., Schuff, N., Fox-Bosetti, S., Lin, C., Studholme, C., DeCarli, C.S., Krueger, G., Ward, H.A., Metzger, G.J., Scott, K.T., Mallozzi, R., Blezek, D., Levy, J., Debbins, J.P., Fleisher, A.S., Albert, M., Green, R., Bartzokis, G., Glover, G., Mugler, J., Weiner, M.W.: The Alzheimer's disease neuroimaging initiative (ADNI): MRI methods. J. Magn. Reson. Imaging 27(4), 685–691 (2017)
13. Teverovskiy, L.A., Becker, J.T., Lopez, O.L., Liu, Y.: Quantified brain asymmetry for age estimation of normal and AD/MCI subjects. In: 5th IEEE International Symposium on Biomedical Imaging: From Nano to Macro, Paris, France, pp. 1509–1512. IEEE (2008)
14. Buades, A., Coll, B., Morel, J.M.: A review of image denoising algorithms, with a new one. Multiscale Model. Simul. 4(2), 490–530 (2005)
15. Tustison, N.J., Avants, B.B., Cook, P.A., Zheng, Y., Egan, A., Yushkevich, P.A., Gee, J.C.: N4ITK: improved N3 bias correction. IEEE Trans. Med. Imaging 29(6), 1310–1320 (2010)
16. Nyúl, L.G., Udupa, J.K., Zhang, X.: New variants of a method of MRI scale standardization. IEEE Trans. Med. Imaging 19(2), 143–150 (2000)
17. Ourselin, S., Stefanescu, R., Pennec, X.: Robust registration of multi-modal images: towards real-time clinical applications. In: Dohi, T., Kikinis, R. (eds.) MICCAI 2002. LNCS, vol. 2489, pp. 140–147. Springer, Heidelberg (2002). https://doi.org/10.1007/3-540-45787-9_18
18. Villa-Pinto, C.H., Ferrari, R.J.: Initialization of deformable models in 3D magnetic resonance images guided by automatically detected phase congruency point landmarks. Pattern Recogn. Lett. 79, 1–7 (2016)
19. Morrone, M.C., Ross, J., Burr, D.C., Owens, R.: Mach bands are phase dependent. Nature 324(6094), 250–253 (1986)
20. Venkatesh, S., Owens, R.: On the classification of image features. Pattern Recogn. Lett. 11(5), 339–349 (1990)
21. Belongie, S., Malik, J., Puzicha, J.: Shape matching and object recognition using shape contexts. Pattern Anal. Mach. 24(4), 509–522 (2002)
22. Mortensen, E.N., Deng, H., Shapiro, L.: A SIFT descriptor with global context. In: 2005 IEEE Computer Society Conference on Computer Vision and Pattern Recognition, San Diego, CA, USA, pp. 184–190 (2005)
23. Carmichael, O.T., Aizenstein, H.A., Davis, S.W., Becker, J.T., Thompson, P.M., Meltzer, C.C., Liu, Y.: Atlas-based hippocampus segmentation in Alzheimer's disease and mild cognitive impairment. Neuroimage 27(4), 979–990 (2005)
24. Kalinic, H.: Atlas-based image segmentation: a survey. Technical report, Universiy of Zagreb, Zagreb, Croatia (2008)
25. Toews, M., Wells-III, W., Collins, D.L., Arbel, T.: Feature-based morphometry: discovering group-related anatomical patterns. Neuroimage 49(3), 2318–2327 (2010)
26. Vincent, P., Bengio, Y.: Manifold Parzen windows. In: Advances in Neural Information Processing Systems, vol. 15. MIT Press, Cambridge (2003)
27. Chang, C.C., Lin, C.J.: LIBSVM: a library for support vector machines. ACM Trans. Intell. Syst. Technol. 2(3), 1–27 (2011)
28. Nell, C., Shawe-Taylor, J.: An Introduction to Support Vector Machines and Other Kernel-based Learning Methods. Cambridge University Press, Cambridge (2000)

29. Hsu, C.W., Chang, C.C., Lin, C.J.: A practical guide to support vector classification. Technical report, Department of Computer Science, National Taiwan University, Taiwan, May 2016

30. Fawcett, T.: An introduction of ROC analysis. Pattern Recogn. Lett. **27**(8), 861–874 (2006)

31. Sørensen, L., Igel, C., Liv Hansen, N., Osler, M., Lauritzen, M., Rostrup, E., Nielsen, M., Alzheimer's Disease Neuroimaging Initiative and the Australian Imaging Biomarkers and Lifestyle Flagship Study of Ageing: Early detection of alzheimer's disease using MRI hippocampal texture. Hum. Brain Mapp. **37**(3), 1148–1161 (2016)

A Discrete Bacterial Chemotaxis Approach to the Design of Cellular Manufacturing Layouts

Camilo Mejía-Moncayo[1]([✉]) [ID], Alix E. Rojas[1] [ID], and Ivan Mura[2] [ID]

[1] Universidad EAN, Bogotá, Colombia
{cmejiam,aerojash}@universidadean.edu.co
[2] Universidad de los Andes, Bogotá, Colombia
i.mura@uniandes.edu.co

Abstract. The design of cellular manufacturing layouts is a very important process, because an adequate placement of machines can reduce costs and waiting times, and ultimately improve the yield of the system. The design process includes two main optimization sub-problems. The first one is a clustering problem, the so-called cell formation, consisting in the definition of groups (the cells) of machines that produce sets of related product parts. The second step is a location-allocation problem, which has to be solved to define the relative position of the cells and of the machines inside each cell. Both problems offer significant challenges from a computational point of view. This paper presents a novel approach for the design of cellular manufacturing layouts through an optimization algorithm based on bacterial chemotaxis. The proposed approach solves simultaneously the two optimization sub-problems mentioned above by minimizing transport cost and maximizing clustering of cells, taking into account the sequencing of production steps, the volume of production and the batch sizes. The performance of the proposed algorithm was tested through benchmark problems, and the results were compared with a genetic algorithm and analytical solutions modeled in GAMS. In all cases our proposal achieves better performance than Genetic Algorithm in quality and time, and comparable results with exact analytical solutions.

1 Introduction

Facility layout is a crucial element of every manufacturing system. According to the estimates presented by several authors in the literature, the layout of a plant determines a significant share of the operational costs, close to 25%, see for instance [1]. The continuous changes in technology and market trends pose significant challenges to manufacturing systems. In particular, they have led manufacturing enterprises to introduce flexible structures in their layouts, with the purpose to damp the demand variability through the high efficiency continuous production of small product batches.

© Springer International Publishing AG, part of Springer Nature 2018
O. Gervasi et al. (Eds.): ICCSA 2018, LNCS 10960, pp. 423–437, 2018.
https://doi.org/10.1007/978-3-319-95162-1_29

Cellular manufacturing provide an example of this flexible facility layout arrangement [2, 3]. A cellular manufacturing layout is an application of the group technology philosophy [4], which mixes the job-shop and flow-shop layouts to deploy small mini-plants or *cells* that produce groups of pieces called *family parts*. These configurations are appropriate for manufacturing systems with diversity of products and variable productions volumes, because manufacturing cells can adapt to changes with less effort and reduced time than pure job-shop or flow-shop layouts can do.

Designing good cellular manufacturing layouts is a complex optimization problem, which requires to form cells and define their inter and intra cells layouts. Typically, the complexity linked with these processes is handled by a step decomposition approach, which sequentially solves each separate sub-problem. However, while such a decomposition grants a relevant simplification of the design, it cannot guarantee the optimality of the proposed solution. Consequently, the performance of the designed manufacturing system may be suboptimal.

This work presents a novel approach to the design of cellular manufacturing layouts, through the application of a Discrete Bacterial Chemotaxis Optimization Algorithm (DBCOA), which solve a model where the Cellular Manufacturing layout problem is formulated as a single optimization problem, combining cell formation and inter and intra cell layout design definition. We tested the performance of our proposal on five benchmark problems and we compared our results with those provided by a Genetic Algorithm (GA) and by an analytical solution modeled in GAMS. The outcomes of the evaluation indicate a better performance of DBCOA in quality and time than GA and of the analytical solution for three out of five considered benchmark problems. For the other two, the results are similar for the three methods.

The rest of this paper is structured as follows. First, we present in Sect. 2 a description of the cellular manufacturing layout problem, followed in the Sect. 3 by the mathematical formulation of the problem as an integer non-linear optimization problem. In Sect. 4 we describe the logic of the BFOA meta-heuristic algorithm, which was originally proposed by Passino in [5]. In Sect. 5 we present our adaptation of the BFOA to the cell layout problem, introducing the DBCOA algorithm. In Sect. 6 we describe the methodology we used for evaluating the merits and the performance of our proposed approach, while the results of this evaluation are presented in Sect. 7. Finally, Sect. 8 wraps up the paper by providing conclusions and suggesting directions for future research work.

2   Cellular Manufacturing Layout

A cellular manufacturing layout is designed to optimize a manufacturing system, with the objectives of moving product parts as fast as possible, reducing work in process and material handling, simplifying the flow of similar products to be assembled, and limiting as much as possible waste. Cells are sets of machines that produce similar product parts in batch, with the parts flowing through the cell like in an assembly line. The modular design of cellular manufacturing layouts have clear advantages in terms of efficiency and flexibility compared to job shop and flow shop arrangements [6] .

The definition of manufacturing cell layout includes two processes [7]:

- cell formation, which has the objective of clustering the machines into cells and product parts into families;
- definition of the intra and inter cell layout, whose objective is to establish the relative position of machines into cells and the relative positions of its between them.

Cell formation can be performed sequentially or simultaneously to obtain manufacturing cells and parts families. In [8], a classification of the approaches used for cell formation is provided, which includes descriptive, cluster analysis, graph partitioning, mathematical programming and artificial intelligence methods. Later on, [9] added to this classification heuristic algorithms and metaheuristics methods, in addition, [10] provide a clear description of the cell formation methods based on similarity coefficients. Many meta-heuristic techniques have been applied to cell formation, including simulated annealing [11], tabu search [12], genetic algorithms [13]), ant colony optimization [14], particle swarm optimization [15] and BFOA [16,17]. In [18], the authors proposed a mathematical formulation of the problem of formation of manufacturing cells and compared the performance of genetic algorithms, ant colony optimization and simulated annealing approaches for its solution. The results of their comparative evaluation indicate that genetic algorithm approaches are the most effective ones when solving the cell formation problem.

The intra and inter cell layout definition problem has been formulated as the problem of minimizing transportation and handling material costs. For instance, in the intra-cell layout design approach described by [19], the cell layout depends on the transport and material handling systems, because they define the flows of materials into the cells and between them. In addition, the inter cell layout problem can be formulated considering the relationships between the cells (which can be quantitatively or qualitatively characterized), as suggested in [20]. Another way to formulate it is by considering the flow of materials between the cells as an assignment problem, as for instance presented in [21].

However, design manufacturing cells with a sequential process that first solves cell formation and then decides for the inter and intra cells layout cannot ensure that an optimal solution will be obtained, given that the decisions taken at each step are indeed affecting the other one. Therefore, in this work we focus our attention of the simultaneous solution of the cell formation and inter and intra cells layout, as described in the following sections.

3 Mathematical Formulation of the Optimization Problem

In this section we present a formalization of the cellular manufacturing layout optimization problem as a non-linear integer (binary) optimization problem, with the objective of defining a reference model and a non-ambiguous notation for the parameters and the decision variables to be set. The model structure also allows to understand the elements that add to the complexity of this optimization problem.

The model considers simultaneously the formation of manufacturing cells and the definition of layout intra and inter cells. The first aspect is modeled by mean of the metric called *grouping efficacy* (Γ), which was originally proposed in [22]. This metric has a simple structure, which allows guiding the search process to the optimum solution. For modeling the second aspect, we use the cost of transportation and handling materials (TC) to define a layout with multi-rows, where the machines are arranged in a straight line within each cell, and the cells are arranged in parallel.

In our work, the cost of transportation and material handling considers operations sequences, production volumes (PV_j) batches sizes (B_j) for each movement and movements types. For the sake of modeling, these factors are integrated in the variable distance ($d_{pp'}$) and the values of the cost of each movement ($C_{pp'}$).

Finally, the proposed model groups together into a single objective function the cost of transport and handling of materials (TC) and the grouping efficacy (Γ). Since the optimal solution will minimize the first and maximize the latter, in the mathematical formulation we set as objective the minimization of the ration $TC/(\Gamma+1)$, where the unitary shift in the denominator is added to avoid division by zero.

The model formulation is as follows:

$$\text{Minimize} \quad \frac{TC}{\Gamma+1} \tag{1}$$

Subject to:

$$\sum_{k=1}^{mc}\sum_{p=1}^{mp} X_{ikp} = 1, \quad \forall \ i, \ i = 1,\ldots,m \tag{2}$$

$$\sum_{k=1}^{mc} Y_{jk} = 1, \quad \forall \ j, \ j = 1,\ldots,n \tag{3}$$

$$\sum_{i=1}^{m} X_{ikp} \leq 1, \quad \forall \ k,p, \ k = 1,\ldots,mc \ \land \ p = 1,\ldots,mp \tag{4}$$

$$\sum_{j=1}^{n}\sum_{i=1}^{m} a_{ij}Y_{jk}\sum_{p=1}^{mp} X_{ikp} \geq 1, \quad \forall \ k, \ k = 1,\ldots,mc \tag{5}$$

$$X_{ikp}, Y_{ik} \in \{0,1\} \tag{6}$$

Where the terms of the objective function are as follows:

$$TC = \sum_{j=1}^{n}\sum_{i=1}^{m}\sum_{i'=1}^{m}\sum_{k=1}^{mc}\sum_{p=1}^{mp}\sum_{k'=1}^{mc}\sum_{p'=1}^{mp} W_{ii'j}X_{ikp}X_{i'kp'}C_{kpk'p'}d_{kpk'p'}\frac{PV_j}{B_j} \tag{7}$$

$$\Gamma = \frac{e}{e_1 + e_2 - e} \tag{8}$$

$$e = \sum_{k=1}^{mc} \sum_{j=1}^{n} \sum_{i=1}^{m} a_{ij} Y_{jk} \sum_{p=1}^{mp} X_{ikp} \tag{9}$$

$$e_1 = \sum_{j=1}^{n} \sum_{i=1}^{m} a_{ij} \tag{10}$$

$$e_2 = \sum_{k=1}^{mc} \left[\left(\sum_{j=1}^{n} Y_{jk} \right) \left(\sum_{i=1}^{m} \sum_{p=1}^{mp} X_{ikp} \right) \right] \tag{11}$$

Parameters and indices used in the model are as follows:

m : number of machines
n : number of parts
mc : maximum number of cells
mp : maximum number of positions
i : machine index; $i = 1, \ldots, m$
j : part index; $j = 1, \ldots, n$
k : cell index; $k = 1, \ldots, mc$
p : position index; $p = 1, \ldots, mp$
$a_{ij} = 1$ if machine i processes part j, $a_{ij} = 0$ otherwise (a_{ij} is the incidence matrix)
$W_{ii'j} = 1$ if part j needs to be moved from machine i to machine i' for processing
$d_{pp'}$: distance from position p to position p'
$C_{pp'}$: cost of moving from position p to position p'
PV_j : production volume of part j
B_j : size of batch for each movement of part j

The decision variables are as follows:

$X_{ikp} = 1$ if machine i belongs to cell k and is assigned position p, $X_{ikp} = 0$ otherwise;
$Y_{jk} = 1$ if part j belongs to cell k, $Y_{jk} = 0$ otherwise.

The model described above minimizes the cost of transportation and material handling (Eq. 6), while maximizing the clustering of manufacturing cells through the grouping efficacy (Eq. 8). Additionally, it includes uniqueness constraints to ensure that each machine and part can only be assigned to a single cell (Eq. 2) or family (Eq. 3), that each layout position is assigned only to one machine (Eq. 4) that each cell will belong to one family (Eq. 5) and finally that values assigned to decision variables are binary (Eq. 6).

4 Bacterial Foraging Optimization Algorithm

The Bacterial Foraging Optimization Algorithm (BFOA), originally proposed in [5], belongs to the field of Bacteria Optimization Algorithms and Swarm Optimization, which groups Ant Colony Algorithms, Particle Swarm Optimization and Bees Algorithms, among others. These meta-heuristic optimization algorithms have in common the capacity to avoid local optima through exploration and communication processes among individuals of the swarm.

BFOA models the food-seeking and reproductive behavior of common bacteria such as *E. coli*, in order to solve optimization problems in continuous search spaces. In the nature bacteria moves in their environment by mean of flagella movements, which allows them swimming and tumbling to follow food trace, or avoid noxious substances that can kill them. Furthermore, bacteria reproduce by duplication and create new individuals that can disperse to increase the probability of survival of the species. All of these behaviors were captured by Passino in the optimization process of the BFOA, whose pseudo-code is the following one:

Algorithm 1. BFOA

Generation of initial bacteria θ
Evaluation of objective function $J(\theta^i)$ $\forall i$, $i = 1, \ldots, S$
for $t = 1$ **to** Ned **do**
  for $u = 1$ **to** Nre **do**
    for $v = 1$ **to** Nc **do**
      for $l = 1$ **to** S **do**
        $Chemotaxis(\theta^l)$
      end for
    end for
    $Reproduction(\theta, J)$
  end for
  $EliminationDispersion(\theta^i)$ $\forall i$, $i = 1, \ldots, S$, $\wedge$ $p_{ed}^l < P_{ed}$
end for

---

where:

l, v, u, a, t are indexes of population, chemotaxis cycle, reproduction cycle and elimination and dispersion cycle.

N_c : is the maximum number of chemotaxis cycles.

N_{re} : is the maximum number of reproduction cycles.

N_{ed} : is the maximum number of elimination and dispersion cycles.

θ : is the bacteria population.

S : is the number of individuals of θ or the size of bacteria population.

$J(\theta^i)$: is the value of objective function for the individual θ^i.

p_{ed}^l : is a random number to realize the elimination and dispersion of θ^i.

P_{ed} : is the probability of elimination and dispersion.

The BFOA searches for optimum through the movement in the space of solutions by mimicking bacterial chemotaxis and swarming processes that bacteria use to locate and exploit sources of food. It avoids premature convergence to local optima by creating in the elimination-dispersion process new individuals that randomly disperse across the space of possible solutions, and finally uses a reproduction scheme that selects the fittest individuals of the population.

Although BFOA has been applied to the solution of many continuous optimization problems in different fields, as described in [23], only a few examples of applications of bacterial algorithms to manufacturing problems are available from the literature [17,24,25]. This clearly indicates the existence of an opportunity to expand bacterial algorithms for more directly addressing problems of discrete nature in manufacturing systems. In the next section we introduce a modified version of BFOA that can effectively deal with the optimization problem of the cell manufacturing layout we formalized in Sect. 3.

5   Discrete Bacterial Chemotaxis Optimization Algorithm

Discrete Bacterial Chemotaxis Optimization Algorithm - DBCOA, is an optimization algorithm for the solution of discrete or combinatorial optimization problems, like the design of cellular manufacturing layout. It emulates bacterial chemotaxis in a discrete search space by mean of a set of hierarchical steps where bacteria are randomly modified. The DBCOA exploits the exploration skills of BFOA in discrete optimization problems. Since the BFOA was developed for continuous optimization problems, it is necessary to modify the original exploration structure of BFOA to achieve an efficient chemotactic process. The structure of DBCOA is explained next, together with the details of the solution encoding, chemotaxis and the others processes implemented to optimize the design of cellular manufacturing layout.

5.1   Structure of DBCOA

The DBCOA shares with BFOA the same structure that is the one shown in the pseudo-code of Algorithm 1. First, it generates a random initial population of bacteria, and the objective function or nutrient level of each bacterium is evaluated. Then, chemotactic cycles, reproduction cycles and elimination and dispersion cycles take place. The chemotactic process is the core of algorithm and it is repeated for each artificial bacterium. When chemotactic cycles end, the reproduction processes duplicate the fittest bacteria. Finally, the elimination and dispersion processes randomly (according to a threshold probability P_{ed}) eliminate individuals and create new ones in the search space. These processes will repeat until a termination criterion based on the convergence of the objective function value has not been met. Each ones of the processes described before is explained below.

5.2   Coding and Initial Population

The codification is the way by which variables that represent individual and populations are encoded into data structures suitable to be manipulated computationally by the software implementing the DBCOA processes. We selected a coding based on the approach presented in [26], where, each solution or bacterium θ^l is encoded by five vectors $\theta^l = (\theta^l_{mp}, \theta^l_{pp}, \theta^l_{cn}, \theta^l_{cl}, \theta^l_{fl})$. The first and second vectors are respectively machines permutation θ^l_{mp} and parts permutation θ^l_{pp}, the third vector represents the cells number θ^l_{cn} , the fourth and fifth vectors are the cells limits θ^l_{cl} and families limits θ^l_{fl}. For example, if we consider a cellular manufacturing system with five machines and seven parts, one possible solution for the cell manufacturing layout design problem, i.e. a bacterium θ^l would be encoded as shown below:

$$\theta^l = (\theta^l_{mp}, \theta^l_{pp}, \theta^l_{cn}, \theta^l_{cl}, \theta^l_{fl})$$

$$\theta^l = [(5, 3, 1, 2, 4), (6, 3, 7, 2, 4, 1, 5), (2), (3, 5, 0, 0, 0), (4, 7, 0, 0, 0)]$$

This bacterium is defining the following cells and families: $Cell_1 = [5, 3, 1]$, $Cell_2 = [2, 4]$, $Family_1 = [6, 3, 7, 2]$ and $Family_2 = [4, 1, 5]$. To get this information out of θ^l it is necessary to check the number of cells or families θ^l_{cn}, which for this example is 2. Next, we look at the first element the vector θ^l_{cl} of the limits of cells, in this case (3). This number defines the number of elements belonging the first cell, starting from the first element of vector θ^l_{mp}, which gives as result $Cell_1 = [5, 3, 1]$. As for $Cell_2$, we use the second element of θ^l_{cl}, which is (5). This number establishes the position in the vector θ^l_{mp}, of the last element to be assigned to $Cell_2$. The first element of $Cell_2$ is the element adjacent to the last element assigned to $Cell_1$, in this example the fourth element of θ^l_{mp}. This gives the definition of the machines $Cell_2 = [2, 4]$. In a similar way we proceed with the parts permutation and limits of families vectors to fully define $Family_1$ and $Family_2$.

5.3   Chemotaxis

The Chemotaxis implemented in DBCOA has a hierarchical structure that imitates the movements carried out by bacteria in their natural environment through swimming and tumbling via flagella. This process has the objective of exploring the search space to find optimal solutions and avoid local optimal. Given the nature of the cell manufacturing layout, the movements of swim and tumble performed by the bacteria in a continuous search space have to be discretized. We chose to implement hierarchical changes into the encoded solutions, by changing the vector-based representation through swap, insertions and changes of the number of cells and of their limits. The modified individuals are then compared with the original ones (in terms of their objective function value) and retained if a fitness improvement occurs. This process, summarized in Algorithm 2, is repeated until no more changes are possible. In Algorithm 2, the following shorthand notation is used:

- $SPM()$ is a function that swaps two elements of θ^l_{mp} to produce θ^l_{spm}.
- $SPP()$ is a function that swaps two elements of θ^l_{pp} to produce θ^l_{spp}.
- $IPM()$ is a function that inserts one element in θ^l_{mp} to produce θ^l_{ipm}.
- $IPP()$ is a function that inserts one element in θ^l_{pp} to produce θ^l_{ipp}.
- $NLM()$ is a function that modifies the limits of θ^l_{lm} to produce θ^l_{nlm}.
- $NLP()$ is a function that modifies the limits of θ^l_{lp} to produce θ^l_{nlp}.

Algorithm 2. DBCOA chemotaxis

$\theta^l_{spm} \leftarrow SPM(\theta^l)$
if $J\left(\theta^l_{spm}\right) < J\left(\theta^l\right)$ then
    $\theta^l \leftarrow \theta^l spm$
else
    $\theta^l_{spp} \leftarrow SPP(\theta^l)$
    if $J\left(\theta^l_{spp}\right) < J\left(\theta^l\right)$ then
        $\theta^l \leftarrow \theta^l spp$
    else
        $\theta^l_{ipm} \leftarrow IPM(\theta^l)$
        if $J\left(\theta^l_{ipm}\right) < J\left(\theta^l\right)$ then
            $\theta^{il} \leftarrow \theta^l ipm$
        else
            $\theta^l_{ipp} \leftarrow IPP(\theta^l)$
            if $J\left(\theta^l_{ipp}\right) < J\left(\theta^l\right)$ then
                $\theta^l \leftarrow \theta^l ipp$
            else
                $\theta^l_{nlm} \leftarrow NLM(\theta^l)$
                if $J\left(\theta^l_{nlm}\right) < J\left(\theta^l\right)$ then
                    $\theta^l \leftarrow \theta^i nlm$
                else
                    $\theta^l_{nlp} \leftarrow NLP(\theta^l)$
                    if $J\left(\theta^l_{nlp}\right) < J\left(\theta^l\right)$ then
                        $\theta^l \leftarrow \theta^i nlp$
                    end if
                end if
            end if
        end if
    end if
end if

5.4 Reproduction

The reproduction is the process by which the fittest bacteria are duplicated and replace the least healthy bacteria, which eventually disappear from the population. Reproduction by duplication produces exact copies of fittest bacteria, i.e. individuals located in the same point of the solution space as their mothers bacteria, just like an asexually reproduction of bacteria in the nature. New bacteria replace bacteria who dies to keep constant the size of the swarm.

5.5 Elimination and Dispersion

Elimination and dispersion are random processes. Bacteria are selected for elimination based on a random sampling: if bacterium θ^l obtains a random number p_{ed}^l that less than the threshold probability of elimination P_{ed}, then θ^l is eliminated from the population, and a new bacterium is created according to the generation process that provides of first bacterial population when the DBCOA initializes.

6 Performance Evaluation Approach

To evaluate the performance of the DBCOA algorithm presented in this work for the solution of cellular manufacturing layout optimization problems, we considered two distinct phases. First, we explored the tuning of the algorithms parameters, whose correct setting is a non trivial problem. Second, we conducted a comparative evaluation of our proposed method performance against a Genetic Algorithm (GA) and the analytical solution obtained from GAMS (using LINDO solver), for the following five benchmark problems based on the well known cell formation problems from the literature[1].

1. Vitanov et al. (5 machines and 7 parts) [27]
2. Seifoddini and Djassemi (7 machines and 11 parts) [28]
3. King (14 machines and 24 parts) [29]
4. Burbidge (35 machines and 20 parts) [30]
5. Chandrasekharan and Rajagopalan (24 machines and 40 parts) [31]

A summary of the parameters that characterize the benchmark problems is provided in Table 1. The algorithms were coded using the programming language Fortran, and executed on a standard machine with an Intel Core i7-6500U, processor of 2.5 GHz and 8 GB RAM of memory. The response variables considered were the minimum value of objective function and the time needed to obtain it. The stopping criteria was set to one million calls to the objective function, a number of 10 replicas were executed for each combination of tuning parameters and 100 replicas were run for the sake of the comparison with the GA and with the exact solution approach. Finally, we included penalizations in GA and DBCOA to the number of cells and number of positions, with the purpose of guarantee the maximum values of table 1 and in this way to run these algorithms in the same conditions of the exact solution approach.

---

[1] In the following link, are available the five benchmark problems in GAMS format: https://sites.google.com/view/dbcoa-cml/problems.

Table 1. Parameters of problems

Problem No.	Machines (m)	Parts (n)	Max-cells (mc)	Max-positions (mp)
1	5	7	3	3
2	7	11	3	4
3	14	24	4	4
4	35	20	4	10
5	24	40	7	5

7   Results and Discussion

In this section, we first explain the parameters tuning process, and then we present the results of the comparative performance evaluation.

The process realized for parameters tuning aims at guaranteeing a performance evaluation under the best possible conditions. To find the best parameter setting for the meta-heuristic approaches we resorted to an experimental design approach, where each one of the parameters of GA and DBCOA were evaluated in three different levels, for each one of the five problems described above. The response variable considered in this case was the value of objective function. The best results obtained with this process are summarized in the Tables 2 and 3.

Table 2. Parameters of GA

Parameter	Value
(Pop) Population size	100
(Pe) Percentage of elite	20%
(Pc) Probability of crossover	0.9
(Pm) Probability of mutation	0.05

Table 3. Parameters of DBCOA

Parameter	Value
(S) number of Bacteria	100
(Nc) Number of chemotaxis cycles	100
(Nre) Number of reproduction cycles	50
(Ned) Number of elimination and dispersion cycles	10
(Ped) Probability of elimination and dispersion	0.05

The values of parameters listed in Tables 2 and 3 are those used to instantiate the meta-heuristics for the final performance evaluation. The results of the performance evaluation are shown in Table 4, and in Figs. 1 and 2, which report the comparison among GA and DBCOA provided results with the analytical solutions modeled in GAMS and solved with the LINDO solver (provided by NEOS-SERVER[2] [32]).

Table 4 provides the comparison among the solutions obtained by analytical method modeled in GAMS, GA and DBCOA. For the meta-heuristic approaches, the value of the best found solution and the average of objective function (across the 100 replicas), as well as the average replica computation time, is reported. By analyzing the best values, which are highlighted in bold for each problem, we notice that for the first two problems, GA and DBCOA achieve equal results, and coincide with the optimal, exact analytical solution. For the third problem, only DBCOA was able to find the optimal solution. For the others two problems, which have a larger size, DBCOA achieves the best result, clearly outperforming both GA and analytical solution. In summary, DBCOA gets the best solution for the five problems in lower time than GA. We show in Figs. 1 and 2 a better characterization of the quality of the results achieved by GA and DBCOA for the five considered benchmark problems.

Table 4. Results of performance evaluation

Problem		GAMS	GA			DBCOA		
No.	Machines × parts		Min	Average	Average time (sec)	Min	Average	Average time (sec)
1	5 × 7	**3087**	**3087**	3092	0.36	**3087**	3091	0.02
2	7 × 11	**642**	**642**	697.1	1.37	**642**	667.6	0.17
3	14 × 24	**5840**	6106	10012	4.42	**5840**	6349	3.80
4	35 × 20	41989	84943	203605	27.97	**26982**	46117	22.39
5	24 × 40	208166	203853	277508	45.58	**169821**	193238	40.21

Fig. 1 shows the boxplots of the best values found, while Fig. 2 shows the boxplots of computation time. Is it possible to observe that DBCOA has a lower

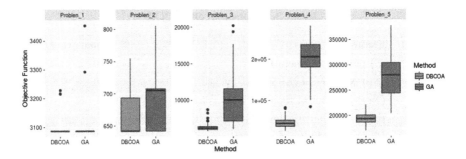

Fig. 1. Comparison between GA and DBCOA best found solutions for the five benchmark problems

[2] https://neos-server.org/neos/.

dispersion of both the best values found and of the computation time, when compared with GA. This behavior of DBCOA allows achieving a consistent quality of solutions for the cellular manufacturing layout problem.

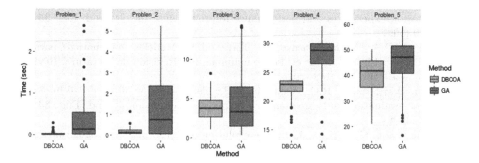

Fig. 2. Comparison between GA and DBCOA computation times in the solutions of five benchmark problems

8   Conclusions and Future Work

In this work a novel approach for the design of cellular manufacturing layouts was proposed, called DBCOA. This proposal achieved the best results in the solution of five benchmark problems found in the literature, and requires a lesser computational effort than the others methods evaluated in this work. The DBCOA considers the problem as an integer non linear constrained model, blending into one single objective function the cell formation and the inter and intra cells layout problems.

The version of DBCOA presented in this work demonstrated a good performance in the solution of the five benchmark problems, showing its potential to solve different optimization problems and in particular those related with manufacturing systems. Our results are promising and provide leeways for the application of bacterial algorithms to other complex discrete optimization problems. Finally, from the vision of authors, the next step in this research will be to include into our discrete meta-heuristic approach mechanisms to emulate swarming processes, as well as to explore multi-objective models to provide multiple design alternatives for a more realistic design.

References

1. Tompkins, J.A.: Facilities Planning. Wiley, Hoboken (2010)
2. Pattanaik, L.N., Sharma, B.P.: Implementing lean manufacturing with cellular layout: a case study. Int. J. Adv. Manufact. Technol. **42**(7–8), 772–779 (2008)
3. Mejía-Moncayo, C., Lara-Sepúlveda, D.F., Córdoba-Nieto, E.: Technological kinship circles. Ingeniería e Investigación **30**(1), 163–167 (2010)

4. Halevi, G.: Expectations and Disappointments of Industrial Innovations. LNMIE, pp. 15–33. Springer, Cham (2017). https://doi.org/10.1007/978-3-319-50702-6
5. Passino, K.M.: Biomimicry of bacterial foraging for distributed optimization and control. IEEE Control Syst. **22**(3), 52–67 (2002)
6. Wemmerlov, U., Johnson, D.J.: Cellular manufacturing at 46 user plants: implementation experiences and performance improvements. Int. J. Prod. Res. **35**(1), 29–49 (1997)
7. Romero, G.A., Mejía-Moncayo, C., Torres, J.A.: Modelos matemáticos para la definición del layout de las celdas de manufactura. Revisión de literatura. Revista Tecnura **19**(46), 135–148 (2015)
8. Selim, H.M., Askin, R.G., Vakharia, A.J.: Cell formation in group technology: review, evaluation and directions for future research. Comput. Ind. Eng. **34**(1), 3–20 (1998)
9. Papaioannou, G., Wilson, J.M.: The evolution of cell formation problem methodologies based on recent studies (1997–2008): review and directions for future research. Eur. J. Oper. Res. **206**(3), 509–521 (2010)
10. Yin, Y., Yasuda, K.: Similarity coefficient methods applied to the cell formation problem: a taxonomy and review. Int. J. Prod. Econ. **101**(2), 329–352 (2006)
11. Xambre, A.R., Vilarinho, P.M.: A simulated annealing approach for manufacturing cell formation with multiple identical machines. Eur. J. Oper. Res. **151**(2), 434–446 (2003)
12. Lei, D., Wu, Z.: Tabu search approach based on a similarity coefficient for cell formation in generalized group technology. Int. J. Prod. Res. **43**(19), 4035–4047 (2005)
13. Onwubolu, G., Mutingi, M.: A genetic algorithm approach to cellular manufacturing systems. Comput. Ind. Eng. **39**(1–2), 125–144 (2001)
14. Li, X., Baki, M.F., Aneja, Y.P.: An ant colony optimization metaheuristic for machinepart cell formation problems. Comput. Oper. Res. **37**(12), 2071–2081 (2010)
15. Durán, O., Rodriguez, N., Consalter, L.A.: Collaborative particle swarm optimization with a data mining technique for manufacturing cell design. Expert Syst. Appl. **37**(2), 1563–1567 (2010)
16. Nouri, H., Tang, S.H., Hang Tuah, B.T., Anuar, M.K.: BASE: a bacteria foraging algorithm for cell formation with sequence data. J. Manufact. Syst. **29**(2–3), 102–110 (2010)
17. Mejia-Moncayo, C., Rojas, A.E., Dorado, R.: Manufacturing cell formation with a novel Discrete Bacterial Chemotaxis Optimization Algorithm. In: Figueroa-García, J.C., López-Santana, E.R., Villa-Ramírez, J.L., Ferro-Escobar, R. (eds.) WEA 2017. CCIS, vol. 742, pp. 579–588. Springer, Cham (2017). https://doi.org/10.1007/978-3-319-66963-2_51
18. Saeedi, S.: Heuristic approaches for cell formation in cellular manufacturing. J. Softw. Eng. Appl. **03**(07), 674–682 (2010)
19. Hamann, T., Vernadat, F.: The intra-cell layout problem in automated manufacturing systems. Technical report (1992)
20. Elwany, M., Khairy, A.B., Abou-Ali, M., Harraz, N.: A combined multicriteria approach for cellular manufacturing layout. CIRP Ann.- Manuf. Technol. **46**(1), 369–371 (1997)
21. Solimanpur, M., Vrat, P., Shankar, R.: An ant algorithm for the single row layout problem in flexible manufacturing systems. Comput. Oper. Res. **32**(3), 583–598 (2005)

22. Suresh Kumar, C., Chandrasekharan, M.P.: Grouping efficacy: a quantitative criterion for goodness of block diagonal forms of binary matrices in group technology. Int. J. Prod. Res. **28**(2), 233–243 (1990)

23. Niu, B., Fan, Y., Tan, L., Rao, J., Li, L.: A review of bacterial foraging optimization part II : applications and challenges. In: Huang, D.-S., McGinnity, M., Heutte, L., Zhang, X.-P. (eds.) ICIC 2010. CCIS, vol. 93, pp. 544–550. Springer, Heidelberg (2010). https://doi.org/10.1007/978-3-642-14831-6_71

24. Nouri, H.: Development of a comprehensive model and BFO algorithm for a dynamic cellular manufacturing system. Appl. Math. Model. **40**(2), 1514–1531 (2016)

25. Atasagun, Y., Kara, Y.: Bacterial foraging optimization algorithm for assembly line balancing. J. Neural Comput. Appl. **25**(1), 237–250 (2015)

26. Gen, M., Lin, L., Zhang, H.: Evolutionary techniques for optimization problems in integrated manufacturing system: State-of-the-art-survey. Comput. Ind. Eng. **56**(3), 779–808 (2009)

27. Vitanov, V., Tjahjono, B., Marghalany, I.: Heuristic rules-based logic cell formation algorithm. Int. J. Prod. Res. **46**(2), 321–344 (2008)

28. Seifoddini, H., Djassemi, M.: A new grouping measure for evaluation of machine-component matrices. Int. J. Prod. Res. **34**(5), 1179–1193 (1996)

29. King, J.R.: Machine-component group formation in group technology. Omega **8**(2), 193–199 (1980). https://doi.org/10.1016/0305-0483(80)90023-7

30. Burbidge, J.L.: The Introduction of Group Technology. Wiley, Hoboken (1975)

31. Chandrasekharan, M.P., Rajagopalan, R.: MODROC: an extension of rank order clustering for group technology. Int. J. Prod. Res. **24**(5), 1221–1233 (1986)

32. Czyzyk, J., Mesnier, M., More, J.: The NEOS server. IEEE Comput. Sci. Eng. **5**(3), 68–75 (1998)

A Firefly Algorithm Based Wrapper-Penalty Feature Selection Method for Cancer Diagnosis

Ramit Sawhney[✉], Puneet Mathur, and Ravi Shankar

Department of Computer Engineering,
Netaji Subhas Institute of Technology, New Delhi, India
{ramits.co,puneetm.co,ravis.co}@nsit.net.in

Abstract. Advances in cancer diagnosis methods have led to the development of highly accurate, detailed and voluminous data. Unfortunately, high dimensional data often leads to poor accuracy and high processing time. Swarm intelligence based feature selection methods have been highly efficient in the biomedical domain, which motivates the exploration of more adaptive and newer wrapper based methods such as the Firefly algorithm. This paper explores the inclusion of a penalty function to the existing fitness function promoting the Binary Firefly Algorithm to drastically reduce the feature set to an optimal subset, and shows an increase in both classification accuracy as well as feature reduction using a Random Forest classifier for the diagnosis of Breast, Cervical and Hepatocellular Carcinoma - Liver Cancer by the proposed method in comparison to other contemporary methods such as those based on Deep Learning, Information Gain and others.

Keywords: Binary Firefly Algorithm · Feature selection
Random forest classifier · Fitness function · Cancer diagnosis

1 Introduction

Evolution of modern computation techniques has enabled the application of machine learning algorithms in the biomedical domain so as to unravel unexplored potential in the areas of pattern recognition and signal processing. But despite this, the presence of high-dimensional voluminous data has obscured the relative leverage of advances in computational feasibility. The existence of misleading, irrelevant and redundant features in the data degrade the learning capabilities of a classifier leading to a loss in generality of the underlying automated processes. Thus, feature selection [1] methods and related optimizations are required to employ the most representative subset of features from a dataset and improve the processing, storage and predictive powers of the classification algorithms. This paper describes the use of the Firefly Algorithm (FFA) [2,3] to empirically determine the most optimal subset of features by maximizing the fitness function used in the wrapper method over a Random Forest classifier.

© Springer International Publishing AG, part of Springer Nature 2018
O. Gervasi et al. (Eds.): ICCSA 2018, LNCS 10960, pp. 438–449, 2018.
https://doi.org/10.1007/978-3-319-95162-1_30

A dataset consisting of n features will have at most 2^n subsets of feature combinations. Even for the most moderately sized datasets, exploration of exponential possibilities of optimal feature sub-groups is an impractical task. The decision to adopt a particular feature in the final subset of optimal features is in itself exhaustive and needs to be treated as a binary optimization problem in a search space comprising of selecting or not selecting a particular feature.

Fireflies are biologically capable of producing short and rhythmic flashes of light so as to attract mating partners and warn enemies from a considerable distance. The movement of each fly is assumed to be random with its brightness being dependent on an objective function. The proposed Binary Firefly Algorithm (BFA) has been formed by considering such naturally inspired restricted occurrences and acts as the cornerstone for the subsequent experimentation stage.

Cancer remains a significant cause of mortality due to the subjective nature of clinical diagnosis and treatment. Cytology-based screening programs including early prediction of cervical and breast cancer are usually beyond the capacity of many primary health services. Early and accurate diagnosis of acute risk factors and prediction of tumor category in patients can potentially improve the standard of living for millions affected by the disease [4]. The progress in the existing research methodologies to classify the breast cancer type as benign or malignant can lead to a revision in accuracy and abatement in computational resources requirement which ultimately justifies the high economic and social value of the proposed modifications to the state of the art. Hepatocellular Carcinoma (HCC) [5] a typical hepatic malignancy caused due to increment in non-alcoholic fatty liver diseases. Another contributor to this phenomenon is the high prevalence of untreated Hepatitis B due to the negligence of patients and medical professionals alike. Cervical cancer is another mortal disease in the category of tumors that is majorly attributed to various causes such as reproductive factors [6], smoking [7], exposure to Human Papillomavirus (HPV) and early sexual history [8] amongst many others. Soft computing techniques complimented by machine-guided learning allows us to model the HCC survival expectation problem in terms of a mathematical framework in order to give a credible predictive analysis on the issue. In an effort to achieve this long-standing goal, the paper encourages the application of BFA to outperform state of the art research endeavors and identify major risk factors in case of affected patients.

In summary, this paper's contributions can be highlighted as:

- Development of a Firefly-based wrapper feature selection method using Random Forest Classifiers for Cancer Diagnosis.
- Modification of existing fitness functions with the inclusion of a penalty factor to promote feature reduction.
- Comparative study of existing Swarm intelligence based feature selection methods in terms of Accuracy and Feature reduction.

The rest of the paper is organized as follows: Sect. 2 presents a literature review of the current state-of-the art in the domain of both Firefly algorithms as well as Feature selection. The methodology is outlined in Sect. 3 with emphasis on the Firefly algorithm and the penalty based fitness function. Section 4 describes the experiment settings and evaluation metrics. A detailed analysis of the results obtained is presented in Sect. 5. Finally, Sect. 6 encompasses a brief conclusion and the scope for future work.

2   Related Work

Machine learning techniques rest on a double-edged sword of data, which can enhance as well as degrade the classification performance of target models. While lack of data inhibits the training of neural weights, the abundance of no-correlated information becomes detrimental to such algorithms. Feature selection algorithms come handy in such cases where a subset of suitably correlated data features boost the performance metrics of classification as portrayed by Chandrashekar and Sahin [9] and Vafaie and Jong [10].

The use of feature selection principles for medical datasets has started attracting the special interest of the bio-informatics community [11]. It is evident from past literature by Cruz and Wishart [12] that artificial neural networks, in general, can be used to substantially improve the accuracy of predicting cancer susceptibility, recurrence, and mortality. Chen et al. [13] proposed an architecture of rough-set based feature selection to remove the redundant features from data and further improve the diagnostic accuracy using SVM based classifier. Ant colony optimizations incorporated with the artificial neural network have also been demonstrated as an effective feature selection strategy (Kabir et al. [14]). In the direction of reducing the dimensionality of complex data, various binary heuristic search algorithms were proposed like Binary Cuckoo Search (BCS) by Rodrigues et al. [15] and Binary Bat Algorithm (BBA) by Nakamura et al. [16].

Firefly algorithm has been extensively studied as an optimization instrument that can even outperform traditional meta-heuristic algorithms such as Particle Swarm Optimization (PSO) [2]. The technique has been previously extended for continuous constrained optimization tasks [17]. Recent advances in the application of FFA for mathematical applications like thinning of concentric two-ring circular array antenna encourages the application of FFA to improve the accuracy of well known medical datasets [18]. The first dataset used in this paper is Breast Cancer Wisconsin (Original) Dataset [19,20]. The subsequent dataset which was tested with the proposed algorithm is Cervical cancer (Risk Factors) Dataset [21]. The last dataset used is HCC Survival Dataset [22] which contains several demographic, risk factors, laboratory and overall survival features of 165 real patients diagnosed with Hepato-Cellular Carcinoma (HCC).

3   Methodology

This paper presents a novel feature selection approach for a classification model consisting of Firefly Algorithm (FFA) along with Random Forest Classifier (RF). The challenge of the continuous constrained optimization problem in feature selection has been tackled by the involvement of a penalty function with the Random Forest classifier in the fitness function of the model.

3.1 The Firefly Algorithm (FFA)

The Firefly Algorithm [23], inspired by the biochemical and social aspects of a real firefly (Lampyridae), makes use of the following mathematical model for synergic local search.

A search space S is initialized having m dimensions corresponding to the features in the dataset under observation. In this binary feature space, each feature can be present (1) or absent (0), which makes the total possible subsets of the features exponential in the count. Space is randomized with n fireflies, whose position is denoted by x_i, and having intensity I_i respectively. The luminous intensity of each firefly is associated with an objective function $f(x)$ such that: BFA focuses on the definition of two parameters for modeling the behavior of fireflies: the variation of light intensity and the formulation of attractiveness. The light intensity I of a firefly representing the optimal feature subset s is proportional to the value of the fitness function as $I(s) \propto f(s)$, whilst the light intensity $I(r)$ varies according to the following equation:

$$I(r) = I_0 e^{-\gamma r^2} \tag{1}$$

where I_0 denotes the light intensity of the source, and the light absorption is approximated using the fixed light absorption coefficient γ. The singularity at $r = 0$ in the expression I/r^2 is avoided by combining the effects of the inverse square law and an approximation of absorption in Gaussian form. The attractiveness β of fireflies is proportional to their light intensities $I(r)$. Therefore, a similar equation to Eq. (1) can be defined, in order to describe the attractiveness β:

$$\beta = \beta_0 e^{-\gamma r^2} \tag{2}$$

where β_0 is the attractiveness at $r = 0$.

The distance between any two fireflies s_i and s_j is expressed as Euclidean distance as:

$$r_{ij} = ||s_i - s_j|| = \sqrt{\sum_{k=1}^{k=n} (s_{ik} - s_{jk})^2} \tag{3}$$

where n denotes the dimensionality of the problem. The movement of the i-th firefly is attracted to another more attractive firefly j. In this manner, the following equation is applied:

$$s_i = s_i + \beta_0 e^{-\gamma r_{ij}^2} (s_j - s_i) + \alpha \epsilon_i \tag{4}$$

where ϵ_i is a random number drawn from the Gaussian distribution. The movements of fireflies consist of three terms: the current position of i-the firefly, attraction to another more attractive firefly, and a random walk that consists of a randomization parameter α and the randomly generated number from the interval $[0, 1]$. When $\beta_0 = 0$ the movement depends on the random walk only. On the other hand, the parameter γ has a crucial impact on the convergence speed.

As feature selection constitutes of finding an optimal solution in a binary search space, we use the following equations to encapsulate map the problem to a discrete space.

$$s_i^k(t+1) = \begin{cases} (s_i^k(t))^{-1} & \text{if } rand < T(s_i^k(t)) \\ s_i^k(t) & \text{if } rand \geq T(s_i^k(t)) \end{cases} \tag{5}$$

$T(s_t^k)$ is calculated using:

$$T(x) = |erf(\frac{\sqrt{\pi}}{2}x)| = |\frac{\sqrt{2}}{\pi} \int_0^{\frac{\sqrt{\pi}}{2}x} e^{-t^2} dt| \tag{6}$$

where $s_i^k(t)$ represents the position of firefly i at time t in the k-th dimension. We use the error function as shown in Eq. 6 due to it's proven ability for mapping continuous values into a discrete binary space effectively [24].

3.2 Fitness Function

The feature subset selection aims at binary optimization of the fitness function through the exclusion of redundant and inclusion of meaningful features. The objective of maximizing the fitness function is two-fold:

- Feature Reduction
- Improve Classification accuracy

The fitness function mentioned above is described as:

$$\rho(b, d) = A(b, d) - \phi(b) \tag{7}$$

where ρ is the fitness function, b represents the feature vector, d represents the dataset, A is the classification accuracy, ϕ is the penalty function over a feature subset b defined as:

$$\phi(b) = \frac{\lambda|x|}{|N|} \tag{8}$$

$|x|$ is the total number of features in the dataset, $|N|$ is the total number of features in the selected subset and λ is a parameter corresponding to the weight given to the penalty function. Algorithm 1 summarizes the steps of the modified FFA algorithm.

Algorithm 1. BINARY FIREFLY ALGORITHM

Input: Dataset, D consisting of N features.
Output: Optimal subset of features of d, $b \subset N$; Best value of fitness function (Accuracy)

1. Initialize random firefly population $X_i(i = 1, 2, .., n)$.
2. Light intensity I_i at x_i is known by $f(x_i)$
3. Define light absorption parameter γ
4. If $(I_j > I_i)$
   Then move firefly i towards j in m-dimensional space.
5. Vary attractiveness with distance r as $e^{-\gamma r^2}$.
6. Evaluate new solutions and update light intensity.
7. Rank the fireflies and find the current best.
8. Repeat steps 4 to 7 till $time <$ Maximum Generation $\forall i, j$.

4 Experiment Settings

4.1 Dataset and Tools

The three datasets used in the experiment have been sourced from UCI ML repository under the tags of:

- Original Wisconsin Breast Cancer Database
- Cervical cancer (Risk Factors) Data Set
- HCC Survival Data Set

Table 1 spells out the specifications of the multivariate datasets A, B and C.

Table 1. Dataset specifications

Dataset name	Instances	Number of attributes	Missing values
Breast cancer wisconsin (Original)	699	10	Yes
Cervical cancer (Risk Factors)	858	36	Yes
HCC survival	165	49	Yes

4.2 Experiment Setting

The Random Forest (RF) classifier is empirically setup with a 10-trees and runs with a 70-30 train-test split to derive the best results. The algorithm is run 20 times with maximum epochs set to 200 with a population size of 20.

The λ parameter in the penalty equation is varied from 0.05 to 0.5 and its value is fixed to 0.12 for optimal accuracy. The value of γ, the light absorption coefficient is set as 1. Additionally, $\beta_0 = 0.2$ and $\alpha = 0.25$.

The computational infrastructure used herein comprises of Intel Core 2 Duo processor, 3.06 GHz CPU and 4 GB of RAM. The stochastic nature of the algorithm compels the adoption of the average of the accuracy and selected features over the numerous iterations of the experiment obtained by randomly seeding the initial model weights.

4.3   Evaluation Metrics

We evaluate and compare our RF-FFA algorithm combined with the *penalty* function with:

1. Random Forest Classifier (RF) with no feature selection.
2. Random Forest Classifier with Firefly Algorithm (BFA).
3. Random Forest Classifier with Firefly Algorithm and Penalty function.
4. Random Forest Classifier with Binary Genetic Algorithm (BGA).
5. Random Forest Classifier with Binary Particle Swarm Optimization (BPSO).
6. Random Forest Classifier with Sequential Forward Search.

The chosen comparison metric of accuracy is defined as:

$$A = \frac{T_p + T_n}{T_p + T_n + F_p + F_n} \tag{9}$$

where,

T_p is the number of True Positives,
T_n is the number of True Negatives,
F_p is the number of False Positives,
F_n is the number of False Negatives.

Another metric for comparison of the performance of these approaches is the number of reduced features given by $|x|$.

5   Results and Discussion

Experimental simulation results for the various feature selection methods are shown in Tables 2, 3 and 4. In general, Swarm Intelligence [25] wrapper based methods lead to a drastic improvement in terms of both classification accuracy as well as the number of reduced features that accounts for dimensionality reduction. While Sequential Forward Search is also successful at feature reduction, the selection of features is less fitting, leading to a slight decrease in accuracy for Breast Cancer and Cervical Cancer datasets and a decent improvement for the HCC Survival dataset. Swarm Intelligence methods perform better than general methods such as Sequential Feature selection due to their ability to fine tune

Table 2. Comparison of various approaches for breast cancer dataset

Algorithm	Accuracy (%)	Number of reduced features
RF	95.62	9
BFA + RF	**97.69**	6
BFA + Penalty + RF	96.18	**2**
BGA + RF	97.14	6.8
BPSO + RF	97.02	5.6
Sequential Forward Search + RF	95.27	4.6

Table 3. Comparison of various approaches for Cervical cancer dataset

Algorithm	Accuracy (%)	Number of reduced features
RF	94.92	34
BFA + RF	97.26	4.875
BFA + Penalty + RF	**97.36**	**4.6**
BGA + RF	96.64	22
BPSO + RF	97.33	15.22
Sequential Forward Search + RF	92.5	18.3

over various iterations as well as model the final feature vector in terms of a stronger correlation between the features in cancer diagnosis datasets.

An interesting observation is the scalability of swarm intelligence [26] methods particularly the proposed BFA + Penalty + RF-based approach that performs drastically better as compared to other methods employing feature selection than those just using simple classifiers such as RF, as the total number of features increases. This improvement can be attributed to the ability of the proposed method to overcome the Curse of Dimensionality [27].

Table 4. Comparison of various approaches for HCC survival dataset

Algorithm	Accuracy (%)	Number of reduced features
RF	65.25	48
BFA + RF	**83.5**	10.5
BFA + Penalty + RF	83	**8**
BGA + RF	79.50	21.25
BPSO + RF	82.25	24.25
Sequential Forward Search + RF	80.00	27.26

The proposed method BFA + Penalty + RF is the most successful in reducing the number of features across all datasets, while not compromising on the

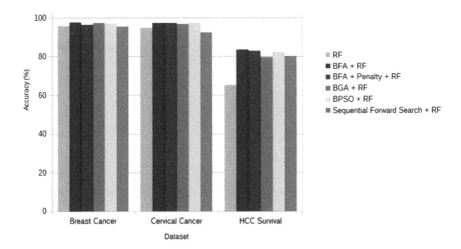

Fig. 1. Performance comparison in terms of classification accuracy

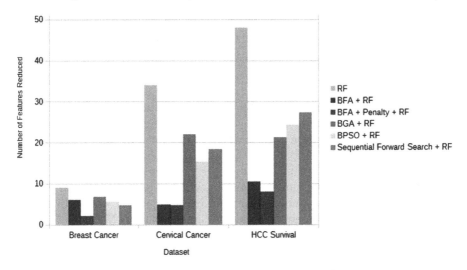

Fig. 2. Performance comparison in terms of feature reduction

classification accuracy. The inclusion of the penalty function greatly reduces the dimensionality which reduces processing time and overheads successfully. In the case of the Cervical Cancer dataset, the proposed method outperforms the other models in terms of both feature reduction and accuracy.

Finally, the Firefly algorithm outperforms other contemporary feature selection methods such as BGSA, BPSO and BGA in terms of both accuracy and feature reduction.

In all cases, the new fitness function produces a final feature subset with lesser number of features without much degradation in classification accuracy.

A comparative analysis on the basis of number of reduced features as well as classification accuracy across the techniques and datasets is shown in Figs. 1 and 2.

6 Conclusion and Future Work

The increase in efficient cancer diagnosis methods on high dimensional detailed data warrants for an efficient optimal feature selection as an important pre-processing step for classification of disease outcomes. Feature selection methods need to be carefully designed in order to reduce the computational cost along with improving classification accuracy.

In this work, we compare the performance of a relatively new evolutionary computation algorithm, the firefly algorithm, with and without a penalty function, with existing methods for feature selection. The new penalty function appears to be highly effective in reducing the number of features which in turn saves computational overhead and combats the Curse of Dimensionality while not compromising drastically on classification accuracy. This paper modifies the existing wrapper feature selection using the firefly algorithm and random forest classifiers, which outperforms standard methods for the same in the domain of cancer diagnosis.

In the near future, we aim to broaden our study by experimenting with other penalty functions as well as with larger datasets for cancer diagnosis extracted using the latest cutting-edge oncology based techniques. Furthermore, this approach can be extended using various other classifiers as well as evolutionary computation techniques along with comparing them to other feature selection methods such as Principal component analysis [28], Harmony Search [29], Two particle swarm optimization [30], Moth flame optimization [31] etc.

References

1. Guyon, I., Elisseeff, A.: An introduction to variable and feature selection. J. Mach. Learn. Res. **3**(Mar), 1157–1182 (2003)
2. Yang, X.-S.: Firefly algorithms for multimodal optimization. In: Watanabe, O., Zeugmann, T. (eds.) SAGA 2009. LNCS, vol. 5792, pp. 169–178. Springer, Heidelberg (2009). https://doi.org/10.1007/978-3-642-04944-6_14
3. Soto, C., Valdez, F., Castillo, O.: A review of dynamic parameter adaptation methods for the firefly algorithm. In: Melin, P., Castillo, O., Kacprzyk, J. (eds.) Nature-Inspired Design of Hybrid Intelligent Systems. SCI, vol. 667, pp. 285–295. Springer, Cham (2017). https://doi.org/10.1007/978-3-319-47054-2_19
4. Danaei, G., Vander Hoorn, S., Lopez, A.D., Murray, C.J., Ezzati, M., Comparative Risk Assessment collaborating group (Cancers), et al.: Causes of cancer in the world: comparative risk assessment of nine behavioural and environmental risk factors. Lancet **366**(9499), 1784–1793 (2005)
5. Bruix, J., Sherman, M.: Management of hepatocellular carcinoma: an update. Hepatology **53**(3), 1020–1022 (2011)

6. Brinton, L.A., Hamman, R.F., Huggins, G.R., Lehman, H.F., Levine, R.S., Mailin, K., Fraumeni Jr., J.F.: Sexual and reproductive risk factors for invasive squamous cell cervical cancer. J. Natl Cancer Inst. **79**(1), 23–30 (1987)
7. Slattery, M.L., Robison, L.M., Schuman, K.L., French, T.K., Abbott, T.M., Overall, J.C., Gardner, J.W.: Cigarette smoking and exposure to passive smoke are risk factors for cervical cancer. Jama **261**(11), 1593–1598 (1989)
8. Bosch, F., Munoz, N., De Sanjosé, S., Izarzugaza, I., Gili, M., Viladiu, P., Tormo, M., Moreo, P., Ascunce, N., Gonzalez, L., et al.: Risk factors for cervical cancer in Colombia and Spain. Int. J. Cancer **52**(5), 750–758 (1992)
9. Chandrashekar, G., Sahin, F.: A survey on feature selection methods. Comput. Electr. Eng. **40**(1), 16–28 (2014)
10. Vafaie, H., De Jong, K.: Genetic algorithms as a tool for feature selection in machine learning. In: Proceedings of the Fourth International Conference on Tools with Artificial Intelligence, TAI 1992, pp. 200–203. IEEE (1992)
11. Saeys, Y., Inza, I., Larrañaga, P.: A review of feature selection techniques in bioinformatics. Bioinformatics **23**(19), 2507–2517 (2007)
12. Cruz, J.A., Wishart, D.S.: Applications of machine learning in cancer prediction and prognosis. Cancer Inform. **2**, 117693510600200030 (2006). https://doi.org/10.1177/117693510600200030
13. Chen, H.L., Yang, B., Liu, J., Liu, D.Y.: A support vector machine classifier with rough set-based feature selection for breast cancer diagnosis. Expert Syst. Appl. **38**(7), 9014–9022 (2011)
14. Kabir, M.M., Shahjahan, M., Murase, K.: A new hybrid ant colony optimization algorithm for feature selection. Expert Syst. Appl. **39**(3), 3747–3763 (2012)
15. Rodrigues, D., Pereira, L.A., Almeida, T., Papa, J.P., Souza, A., Ramos, C.C., Yang, X.S.: BCS: a binary cuckoo search algorithm for feature selection. In: 2013 IEEE International Symposium on Circuits and Systems (ISCAS), pp. 465–468. IEEE (2013)
16. Nakamura, R.Y., Pereira, L.A., Costa, K., Rodrigues, D., Papa, J.P., Yang, X.S.: BBA: a binary bat algorithm for feature selection. In: 2012 25th SIBGRAPI Conference on Graphics, Patterns and Images (SIBGRAPI), pp. 291–297. IEEE (2012)
17. Łukasik, S., Żak, S.: Firefly algorithm for continuous constrained optimization tasks. In: Nguyen, N.T., Kowalczyk, R., Chen, S.-M. (eds.) ICCCI 2009. LNCS (LNAI), vol. 5796, pp. 97–106. Springer, Heidelberg (2009). https://doi.org/10.1007/978-3-642-04441-0_8
18. Basu, B., Mahanti, G.: Thinning of concentric two-ring circular array antenna using fire fly algorithm. Scientia Iranica **19**(6), 1802–1809 (2012)
19. Wolberg, W.H., Mangasarian, O.L.: Multisurface method of pattern separation for medical diagnosis applied to breast cytology. Proc. Nat. Acad. Sci. **87**(23), 9193–9196 (1990)
20. Zhang, J.: Selecting typical instances in instance-based learning. In: Machine Learning Proceedings 1992, pp. 470–479. Elsevier (1992)
21. Fernandes, K., Cardoso, J.S., Fernandes, J.: Transfer learning with partial observability applied to cervical cancer screening. In: Alexandre, L.A., Salvador Sánchez, J., Rodrigues, J.M.F. (eds.) IbPRIA 2017. LNCS, vol. 10255, pp. 243–250. Springer, Cham (2017). https://doi.org/10.1007/978-3-319-58838-4_27
22. Santos, M.S., Abreu, P.H., García-Laencina, P.J., Simão, A., Carvalho, A.: A new cluster-based oversampling method for improving survival prediction of hepatocellular carcinoma patients. J. Biomed. Inform. **58**, 49–59 (2015)
23. Fister, I., Fister Jr., I., Yang, X., Brest, J.: A comprehensive review of firefly algorithms. CoRR abs/1312.6609 (2013). http://arxiv.org/abs/1312.6609

24. Mirjalili, S., Lewis, A.: S-shaped versus v-shaped transfer functions for binary particle swarm optimization **9**, 1–14 (2013)
25. Wang, X., Yang, J., Teng, X., Xia, W., Jensen, R.: Feature selection based on rough sets and particle swarm optimization. Pattern Recogn. Lett. **28**(4), 459–471 (2007)
26. Bonyadi, M.R., Michalewicz, Z.: Particle swarm optimization for single objective continuous space problems: a review (2017)
27. Donoho, D.L., et al.: High-dimensional data analysis: the curses and blessings of dimensionality. AMS Math Chall. Lect. **1**, 32 (2000)
28. Li, W., Shi, T., Liao, G., Yang, S.: Feature extraction and classification of gear faults using principal component analysis. J. Qual. Maint. Eng. **9**(2), 132–143 (2003)
29. Manjarres, D., Landa-Torres, I., Gil-Lopez, S., Del Ser, J., Bilbao, M.N., Salcedo-Sanz, S., Geem, Z.W.: A survey on applications of the harmony search algorithm. Eng. Appl. Artif. Intell. **26**(8), 1818–1831 (2013)
30. Xue, B., Zhang, M., Browne, W.N.: Particle swarm optimization for feature selection in classification: a multi-objective approach. IEEE Trans. Cybern. **43**(6), 1656–1671 (2013)
31. Mirjalili, S.: Moth-flame optimization algorithm: a novel nature-inspired heuristic paradigm. Knowl.-Based Syst. **89**, 228–249 (2015)

Mental War: An Attention-Based Single/Multiplayer Brain-Computer Interface Game

Gabriel Alves Mendes Vasiljevic$^{(\boxtimes)}$ (iD),
Leonardo Cunha de Miranda (iD), and Bruna Camila de Menezes (iD)

Department of Informatics and Applied Mathematics,
Federal University of Rio Grande do Norte (UFRN),
Natal, RN 59078-970, Brazil
gabrielvasiljevic@outlook.com,
leonardo@dimap.ufrn.br, brunacamilamenezes@gmail.com

Abstract. Brain-Computer Interfaces (BCIs) are a novel kind of user interface that allows the recognition of specific user intentions by reading the user's brain activity, translating it into commands and transmitting them to the computer. With increasing advances in the technology behind these interfaces, gaming applications using cerebral input are becoming more common, although the employment of this kind of control for games is still relatively low in comparison to other traditional input modalities. This paper presents Mental War, a brain-controlled multiplayer computer game, in which two or more players are able to compete against each other, or work together in a collaborative mode to achieve a common goal, both using only their mental state alone. Their level of concentration is measured using a single-sensor BCI headset and translated into force to pull a rope in a tug-of-war game. The design and implementation process of the game are detailed and discussed. An evaluation process was performed with a total of 24 participants to acquire qualitative data regarding the interaction with the BCI platform, validating the design and providing insights for developers in future BCI-based research.

Keywords: BCI · EEG · NeuroSky MindWave · HCI · Evaluation
Games

1 Introduction

The field of computer games is rapidly growing in the past few years [6], with increasing interest not only for entertainment, but for scientific researches as well. A number of past works in this field explored novel control schemes for games, aiming at improving the game experience, evaluating their application in a real-world scenario, and providing a greater level of immersion for players. Examples of those works include a multimodal slingshot game with haptic feedback [6], a gestural-based chess game [19], adjustable interactive rings for games [16, 17], a breath-controlled coordination game [2], and even an infinite racing game controlled with a banana through computational vision [1]. Recently, researchers started to adapt and develop advanced

O. Gervasi et al. (Eds.): ICCSA 2018, LNCS 10960, pp. 450–465, 2018.
https://doi.org/10.1007/978-3-319-95162-1_31

games that could be modified or controlled using the player's brain waves, using their own mental state as an input modality. These emerging applications could provide an even greater level of immersion for the player, as his/her emotions and intentions could be directly employed in the game.

Brain-Computer Interface (BCI) is a field of neuroscience and Human-Computer Interaction (HCI) that allow users to interact with the computer serving as a bridge, sending the commands directly from the brain to be transmitted to the standard input of the computer [8, 13]. The great advantage of BCIs over other user interfaces is their capacity to be utilized by any person, even those who has their body completely paralyzed, as only the brain activity is required to its operation [9, 15]. The first BCI-based systems appeared in the decade of 1970 and required brain implants to be used [11]. Thanks to electroencephalography (EEG), cheaper and more practical equipment were developed, allowing the development of both more accessible medical applications and general-purpose systems, especially with the advent of commercial headsets such as the NeuroSky devices (e.g., MindSet and MindWave) and the Emotiv devices (e.g., Emotiv Epoc and Emotiv Insight).

A kind of BCI application that is arising due to the development of new technologies and techniques are brain-controlled games, in which the user utilizes a specific kind of brainwave to directly control actions in the game, or uses it as a complementary type of control, while maintaining the standard inputs. However, it is still a challenge to adapt those biological signals as an input to control a game. In addition to the natural variation and fluctuation that occurs in the brain signals, each person can have its own brain wave patterns [5], so that a method for controlling one's waves may not work for another person. In this sense, the design and implementation of such games can be a difficult task [7], especially when involving multiple users at the same time.

In this sense, this work presents the development of a multiplayer brain-controlled computer game. The game's design and architecture are discussed, along with the design challenges and technical issues regarding its implementation. The focus of this game is the multiplayer interaction, in which few BCI games are designed upon. The developed game is designed to allow multiple users to work in either competitive and collaborative manners, or playing solo against the computer, using their attention level to control it. We seek to evaluate the proposed BCI platform and validate the game with external subjects in a controlled evaluation. Both single and multiplayer game modes were evaluated with qualitative data acquired from the participants.

This paper is organized as follow: Sect. 2 presents the related work in the field; Sect. 3 presents the concept, design and implementation of the developed BCI-based game; Sect. 4 describes the evaluation of the game; Sect. 5 discusses the results of this work; and Sect. 6 concludes the paper.

2   Related Work

Although there are numerous games that were developed or adapted to be played using a BCI, only a few of them allows for multiplayer interaction. The relatively low cost and easiness of employment of consumer-grade EEG devices has made possible the emergence of many multiplayer BCI games in the past few years. These games are particularly difficult to conceive, as the challenges of designing an entertaining game with multiplayer interaction and employing a BCI control must both be considered.

The work of Schwarz et al. [18] presents an adaptation of the classic Pong game, called BrainPong, in which two players compete by moving their respective paddles up and down using the motor imagery control signal, in order to bounce the ball back to the opponent. The game is controlled using an Emotiv Epoc device and was developed for education purposes. Crawford et al. [4] describe a simulation game in which the player, playing individually or together with another one, must control a robot and reach a certain destination in the virtual map. In the cooperative mode, each player controls one specific action, being either moving the robot or rotating it. The controls are performed using imagined movement captured by an Emotiv Epoc device, with the push movement signalizing a move action, while the right hand movement translates as a clockwise rotation.

The work of Laar et al. [12] presents alpha-WoW, which is an adapted version of the role-playing game World of Warcraft (WoW). The game uses the player's alpha waves to measure his/her level of meditation, and uses this level to control the transformation of the character, which can alternate between long-range (low stress) and close-range (high stress) combat. In the work of Hazrati and Hofmann [10], the authors also present an adapted version of an existing game. In the "game", called Second Life, the player can walk and interact with the virtual ambient or with other players, using the motor imagery control signal to walk (imagined foot movement) and to move left or right (imagined hands movements). Both works also use an Emotiv Epoc device to acquire the brain signals.

Bonnet et al. [3] describe a simple BCI football game, in which the two players must use the imagined movement to push the ball in the respective goal. The game can be played both collaboratively and competitively, in which the players can compete against the computer or against each other, respectively. Maby et al. [14] developed and evaluated an adaptation of the game "Connect Four", in which two players compete against each other using the P300 control signal. The game was evaluated with two participants, whose brain signals were captured using electrode caps with nine sensors each, achieving over 82% of precision from the signals. Both works employed an electrode cap to capture the players' brain waves.

One can notice, based on these related works, that the majority of past works employed either an Emotiv Epoc device or a clinical electrode cap. The advantages of those equipment are that, by having a higher number of sensors, they have also a higher spatial resolution in relation to other lower-cost consumer-grade devices. However, they also require specific technical knowledge to capture and handle the data, which can increase the difficulty of the development process of the game; moreover, these devices also require a setup time before being used, which includes the application of saline solutions to increase the quality of the captured signals. Our approach, in this sense, is to develop an entertainment game based on a simple one-sensor device that could potentially be played by any person, without necessarily requiring technical knowledge of the equipment.

3 Mental War

The Mental War game is an open-source computer software that enables users to play a game using their brainwaves against the computer or other players. The game software was developed by the Mental War Development Team (Mental War Dev Team) composed by two researchers and a designer. The game was designed as a virtual version of a tug-of-war game, in which the player has to pull the opponent to the center of the screen while avoiding being pulled. The players are connected through a rope, and are pulled while the force made in the other side is greater in intensity than the force that the player himself is making.

The game is mainly controlled using the NeuroSky MindWave input, which represents the player's level of attention. The MindWave is a headset device that uses a single electrode, positioned at the forehead, which is able to measure the levels of concentration and meditation of a person using a set of algorithms called eSense, and to detect whether the user is blinking an eye.

There are three possible game modes that the game is intended to offer to the player, i.e., solo (single player), collaborative and competitive (both multiplayer). This division was based on the work of Bonnet et al. [3]. In the single player mode, the player is set to play against the computer itself in three difficult levels, i.e., easy, medium and hard. In the competitive mode, players compete against each other. In this case, the average level of attention of each player is subtracted and the result is the resultant force. Thus, the player with higher attention score will pull the other player with more force to its side.

In the collaborative mode, the players work together to defeat the enemy team. In this mode, the level of attention of each player is added to the ones of their team and the mean of the sum is used as the total level of attention of the group. As each player has the same degree of contribution in the total attention of the group, if one player is performing badly, the rest of the group must perform much better to compensate.

These game modes can be mixed, i.e., players can play collaboratively in teams against the other team. In this case, the same rules apply as in the collaborative and competitive modes. For each team, the total attention is the mean value of each player's average attention in that group, and the resultant force is the difference between the total attentions of both teams. Alternatively, two or more players can form a team to compete against a single player.

The game user interface was designed to be simple, intuitive and yet maintaining all the necessary information to the player. Upon opening the game, the player is presented with the main interface, where s/he can choose to play a single or a multiplayer match. Upon selecting the desired mode, the player is moved to either the difficulty selection interface, in the case of the single player mode, or the team selection interface, in the case of the multiplayer mode.

In the single player difficulty selection interface, there are three buttons, each representing a difficulty level and its correspondent color. Each difficulty option also has an icon representing the computer opponent in the correspondent mode. In the multiplayer team selection interface (or multiplayer lobby), each player is represented by his name and a picture of his character, and is placed in one of the two teams. The player has the option to check if s/he is ready to begin the match and to add or remove computer players of any difficulty in both teams.

The game's main interface (Fig. 1a) is composed of four elements: the two group of players (area 4 in Fig. 1a); the blink charges (area 2 in Fig. 1a); a force meter (area 3 in Fig. 1a); and a focus meter (area 1 in Fig. 1a) for each side. The focus meter serves as an indicator to the MindWave device's input, which is a number ranging from 0 to 100. The force meter indicates to which side the force is tending, and is roughly the difference between the forces on both sides. The players move according to the resultant force, and the game is over when one of them reaches the center of the screen.

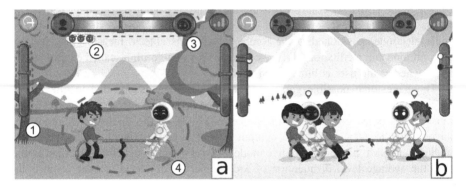

Fig. 1. (a) Game match elements; and (b) multiplayer game interface. (Color figure online)

In addition to the level of attention, the game also uses the blink detection feature of the MindWave headset. At the beginning of each match, the player has three blink charges, represented by three open-eye icons. When the player voluntarily blinks his eyes, s/he spends a blink charge and temporarily gains a small force boost. When a blink charge is spent, one of the open-eye icons disappears from the screen, representing that the player can no longer use this charge in this match.

The game can be played in four scenarios, each representing a difficulty level in a single player match, i.e., easy (Fig. 2a), medium (Fig. 2b) and hard (Fig. 2c), or a multiplayer match (Fig. 1b). Some of the interface elements changes in the multiplayer mode, such as the arrows that indicate the level of attention of each player individually and the background scenario.

Fig. 2. Single player game interfaces in the (a) easy, (b) medium, and (c) hard difficulty level. (Color figure online)

The game software was implemented in the C++ programming language using the Simple and Fast Multimedia Library (SFML) and compiled for the Windows operating system. The SFML was used to manage the game's graphics, sounds and network. To receive the input from the NeuroSky headset, a software module was created to serve as an interface to the NeuroSky C header and the game implementation itself. This module is responsible for establishing a connection with the headset, updating the brain waves' values as soon as a new packet arrives from the device, and updating the headset status, such as the connection status and the signal quality. The architecture of the game client is presented in Fig. 3.

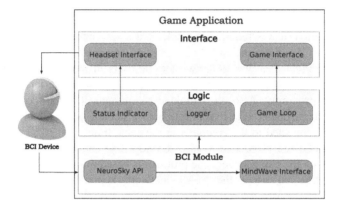

Fig. 3. Game client architecture.

The module tries to establish a connection with the headset as soon as the game software is open. If no connection was found, the module tries again every two seconds. Once a connection is established, the module opens a thread that keeps listening to the headset connection to receive any incoming packet as soon as it arrives (usually one packet every second). The module then updates the headset's status, such as the values for each brainwave (i.e., delta, theta, alpha, beta and gamma), the eSense (i.e., attention and meditation), and signal quality. When an eSense value is acquired, the next requisition will only return a valid number if a packet has arrived with the most updated value. This prevents the headset from returning repeated values due to poor signal quality or interference.

The game itself mainly uses the attention value received from the headset. Once the game begins, the main loop will continuously try to read a value from the headset, and if the value is valid, it is inserted into an array. As the number read from the MindWave is a biological signal, its value may change abruptly over a short period of time. Initial gameplay tests showed that this variation caused a strange effect both in visual and game flow, as there was no constancy in the movement of the characters and the input from the headset appeared to be randomized from the player's perspective. Being so, it was chosen to use the average of the player's attention over the duration of the match, as it would represent the player's overall attention during the game. Thus, every two seconds, the game calculates the average of the values in the array and compares it to the average of the enemy team, then moves the players accordingly. This interval of time was used to slow the game's pace, so the match could have a minimum duration. Also, at the start of the game match, there is a three seconds countdown to prevent it to start instantaneously and give the player time to prepare.

The difficulties of the single player game mode were implemented to start at a base value of 50 attention and increase by 10 for each difficulty. Every second, the computer adds a random number between 0 and 10 to its base attention and inserts the sum into its own array. Thus, the average attention of the computer is approximately 55, 65 and 75 for the easy, medium and hard difficulties, respectively. For the player to win the game, s/he must maintain his/her average attention higher than the computer's for most of the time.

The multiplayer game modes have a similar logic, but were implemented in a different way. First, it was required to implement a server for connecting the players, also written in C++ using the SFML library, and compiled for the Linux operating system. The original idea was to allow multiple users in the same computer to play multiplayer matches, but the MindWave headset suffers from interference from other devices in the proximity. Also, the ThinkGear communication protocol, used by the NeuroSky devices, opens a TCP connection in a default port (13854), so only one device can be connected to the computer at the same time.

A custom network protocol was also developed to control the connection of the game clients with the game server. The protocol is based on packets sent through TCP sockets, implemented using the SFML network support. Architecture-wise, the received packets are parsed by a connection handler, which in turn passes the packet with its identifier and origin to the network facade. Then, the contents of the packet, which depends on its type, are passed to the server control module or the game control module, depending on the state of the server ('waiting for players' or 'in game'). Depending on the packet, the server can send a response to the origin client, or broadcast a message to all connected clients. This scheme is represented in Fig. 4.

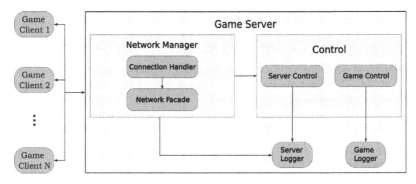

Fig. 4. Game server architecture.

Upon connecting to the server, the player enters in one of the two available teams. The player then can check if s/he is ready to begin the match. The game can only start when all players in the two teams are ready. There is a maximum of three players in each team, and the two teams can have different numbers of players. The server is responsible for receiving the attention value for each player, log it and send it to all players, including the one who send it to the server, so that all players update the attention values at approximately the same time.

The averaged values of each team allows for a more collaborative gameplay, as both members should maintain their average attention high enough so the mean attention is higher than the other team. Also, it allows for one single player to be able to compete with two or three other players without penalties, and to create "custom" difficulties by combining two or more machine players of different difficulty levels. Some key features are also different from the single player mode. In the single player mode, the player force is calculated by averaging all attention values during the match, and the difference between this averaged value and the computer's average is taken as the resultant force (Eq. 1).

$$F = \frac{\sum_{i=1}^{N} A_i}{N} - \frac{\sum_{i=1}^{M} B_i}{M} \tag{1}$$

In Eq. (1), F is the resultant force, N is the number of read attention values for the player, M is the number of attention values generated for the computer player (roughly, the same number of seconds passed since the beginning of the match), A_i is the i-th attention value of the human player and B_i the i-th attention value of the computer player. This value is calculated every two seconds: if F > 0, the human player pulls the computer player; if F < 0, the computer player pulls the human player; and if F = 0, both players will remain at the same position until the next resultant force value is calculated. The speed and distance that both players will move in the next two seconds following this calculation is directly proportional to F.

In the multiplayer mode, in order to avoid long match durations due to stagnation of the averaged value, only the last 20 attention values are considered in the average calculation (Eq. 2). This creates a more variable force values during the match, allowing for the player to recover from a period of low attention, and forcing him/her to try maintaining the attention high during all match.

$$F = \frac{\sum_{k=1}^{L} \frac{\sum_{i=N-19}^{N} A_{ki}}{20}}{L} - \frac{\sum_{k=1}^{R} \frac{\sum_{i=M-19}^{M} B_{ki}}{20}}{R} \tag{2}$$

In Eq. (2), F is the resultant force, L is the number of players in the left team ($1 \leq L \leq 3$), R is the number of players in the right team ($1 \leq R \leq 3$), N is the number of read attention values of the k-th player of the left team, M is the number of read attention values of the k-th player of the right team, A_{ki} is the i-th attention value of the k-th player of the left team, and B_{ki} is the i-th attention value of the k-th player of the right team. The same rules of the single player mode for the values of F apply for the multiplayer mode.

The blinking of the eye is calculated by the MindWave device as a number ranging from 0 to 255, where the higher the value, the stronger the player blinked his/her eyes. As there was no parameter to differentiate the value of an involuntary blink to a voluntary one, empirical tests were made to find the best value for the player to intentionally blink his/her eyes and be recorded as such. The value of 128 was chosen as the default threshold. It was noticed that unintentional blinks had values ranging from 40 to 90, approximately. Unlike the attention value, which is updated every second, the blink value is updated as soon as the player blinks his/her eyes, so the game checks and updates this value every iteration of the main application.

The game also has an embedded log feature, which records data related to the game and the player. The development of the log feature had the objective of allowing easiness in conducting scientific research with the game. At the end of the match, the logger creates two files: one with details about the game in general, such as the players' nickname, the duration of the match, and the total average attention value; and the other containing all the raw read values during the entire course of the match. The game server also has a logging feature, which logs all events that occurred both in relation to the game (i.e., the game logger) and the server itself (the server logger).

4 Evaluation

In order to aid in the process of the user interaction design of the game and validate this design, two evaluations with users were conducted, one being of the single player mode, and one of the multiplayer mode. Each evaluation was performed as part of a series of controlled experiments that aimed at investigating specific aspects of the users' interaction with the BCI platform, and consists of the qualitative data gathered in this process. Every session was recorded using a set of cameras, with the written consent of the participants.

4.1 Procedure and Subjects

The evaluation process was divided into two main steps: the single player evaluation and the multiplayer evaluation. Before each evaluation, pilot tests were also conducted in order to assess key aspects of the implementation, such as bugs, gameplay characteristics, general interface issues, as well as qualitative aspects of the interaction.

The first pilot study and evaluation were conducted after the initial release of the game, in which only the single player mode was available. All evaluation process was performed in a closed, climatized and noise-free room, and the matches were all played in the same computer. This first evaluation was focused on investigating primary aspects of the players' interaction with the BCI platform, such as the functionality of the basic gameplay elements and the overall satisfaction and motivation of the players towards the game.

Single Player Pilot and Evaluation. The main objective of the single player pilot study was to test the game with an unbiased player for the first time, as all other tests were made by the Mental War Dev Team itself. The participant was a 28 years old, male volunteer subject with no previous knowledge of BCI systems. The subject played five consecutive matches of the game in the easy difficulty setting, and was interviewed for observations and opinions on his recent experience with the platform. This first experience allowed identifying a number of changes and corrections that needed to be done before the evaluation, such as adjustments on the interface elements that represent the current status of the headset device and minor balance changes in the pace of the game.

After the changes and corrections from the pilot study, the single player evaluation was performed with eight volunteer subjects, being seven male and one female, with age ranging from 19 to 26 years. Each subject participated in six individual sessions, and played five consecutive matches in each session. After each match, a short semi-structured interview was conducted in order to assess subjective data about the game experience. Moreover, demographic data and other details about the experience were also collected through forms and questionnaires. These questionnaires were composed of general questions about the matches, such as which strategies were employed, whether the user felt tired, and whether there were any discomforts while playing. Figure 5a shows a subject playing during one session of the evaluation.

Following the development of the multiplayer game mode, the second evaluation was performed. This second study aimed at investigating the multiplayer mode, its design and gameplay, and the subjective experience of the players towards this multiplayer interaction, while considering the interaction with the BCI platform itself. We also sought to compare the differences between the collaborative and the competitive gameplay and how would each mode impact in the game experience of the subjects.

Multiplayer Pilot and Evaluation. The pilot session was conducted with two volunteer subjects, which played five competitive matches. Both participants were male. After the matches, they filled out a questionnaire about the game experience and answered a semi-structured interview. As with the pilot study from the first evaluation, the main goal of this study was to validate the multiplayer mode of the game with unbiased players in a real case scenario. The interview was performed with both participants simultaneously, while the questionnaire was individual.

The second evaluation itself followed the same procedure of the pilot study. Sixteen volunteer subjects, with age ranging from 20 to 32 years, were divided in pairs, and each pair participated in a single evaluation session. Each of those sessions was conducted with the pair of subjects playing either competitively or collaboratively, equally distributed. Figure 5b shows a pair of subjects playing during the evaluation.

Fig. 5. (a) Single player match; (b) competitive match during multiplayer evaluation.

4.2   Results

Based on the results of the single player mode evaluation, a new development stage began aiming to improve the game experience and incorporate new features, especially those related to the multiplayer mode. A major change was the representation of the machine player: in the first versions of the game, the computer avatar was represented by a default combination of hair, shirt and pants. This combination confused some of the players, as the machine character resembled the human avatar that the player controls. The design decision was to have a unique avatar that only the machine player could use; given the nature of this player, it was represented by a robot character.

To distinguish the difficulty modes, in addition to the background scenario, three models were created, one for each difficulty: a green, a yellow, and a red robot, with changes on the details and the face expressions (Fig. 2). This distinguish was necessary for the multiplayer mode, as all players would be in the same scenario regardless of difficulty. Some design changes were also made throughout the development of the multiplayer mode as a result of gameplay tests, such as the colors of the interface elements and a representing icon for every face and number of players in each team.

The first pilot study has also contributed to the refinement of the game. It was noticed that the cursor would still remain in the screen after the game starts, and the user had to move it away to avoid being distracted by it in the match, especially as the game requires the user to focus. After the pilot study, the game was modified to hide the cursor after the game starts in both modes. Another fact that led to adapt the game design was the occasional poor signal received from the headset. If a poor signal is detected, no attention value is received and the game does not update the player's status. This is particularly hard to notice if the player is not visually focusing on the attention bar at the moment. To avoid this kind of problem, after the first pilot study the two status icons were added and were showed even before the game starts. Also, before the second evaluation, the game was adapted to automatically pause if the received signals are of poor quality.

After the single player evaluation, the only feature that was not implemented in the multiplayer mode was the blinking attention booster. Although the implementation of the blink detection worked fine for the first pilot study, it was noticed during the single player evaluation that this detection hardly worked for different players. As afore-mentioned, the blink signal received from the headset is a number that ranges from 0 to 255, and there is no default threshold for distinguishing between a voluntary and an involuntary blink. Several threshold values were empirically tested during the development of the game, such as 90, 100, 128 and 150, with 128 wielding the best results. However, the detection presented several problems during the evaluation, such as the charges being rapidly consumed unintentionally, or the subject losing a lot of attention trying to use the charges and failing to do so, even after several attempts. This led to the majority of subjects giving up on using the feature at all. For this reason, the blink detection was not included for the evaluation of the multiplayer mode, as the same problems would probably appear in the evaluation process.

The qualitative data from the evaluations also provided important insights about the design and development of BCI-based computer games, especially those based on neurofeedback. One of the suggestions that were frequent among subjects was that the game could have more sound effects, as there are just the sounds that indicate whether the match has begun or ended. One of the reasons we were cautious about adding more in-game sound effects was the possibility of those sounds impacting in the performance of the players, as the game is based solely on the attention control signal. It is not known to which extension background music, for example, could hinder or help the participants to concentrate, or whether there would be no effect at all.

The data from the first evaluation also motivated the changes in Eq. (1) that originated Eq. (2) for the multiplayer mode. By using all attention data collected throughout the match in the calculation of the resultant force, the duration of the matches tend to increase the more the player maintains his/her attention close to the computer player's average. This also tends to increase the player's fatigue over time and, consequently, lower his/her performance and increase his/her level of stress. This can be observed by comparing the average duration of matches from the single player evaluation and the ones from the multiplayer evaluation: while the single player matches had an average duration of 90.99 s ($SD = 113.2$), the multiplayer matches had an average duration of 56.22 s ($SD = 38.5$); not taking into consideration that the dynamics of playing against the computer may be different from playing with or against another person. This difference can be visualized in Fig. 6(a). After validating Eq. (2) in the multiplayer evaluation (as no subject complained or commented about the duration or the flow of the match), the single player mode was adapted to also employ this equation for the resultant force.

The boxplots in Fig. 6(b) shows the average attention from both game modes. There was no significant difference between the performance of the single and multi-player matches, with the participants in the single player evaluation obtaining an average of 53.49 attention ($SD = 14.48$), while the participants in the multiplayer evaluation obtained an average of 52.42 attention ($SD = 13.0$).

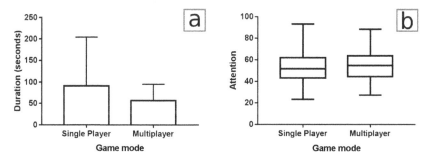

Fig. 6. (a) Column bars of match durations from both game modes; and (b) boxplot of average attention from both game modes.

The data gathered from the multiplayer evaluation served as guideline to the next development iteration, which resulted in the game in its current version. There are improvements that are yet to be discussed based on the opinion of the players, especially regarding the difficulty of the machine players. Initially, the machine players always maintained the same average attention on the course of the match. It was soon realized that this approach provided little immersion, as the player was competing against a static, fixed value. The static value was soon modified to a variable one, and balance changes on the values of each difficulty were made accordingly.

With the adaptation of the computer avatar from the default character to a robot one, the animation of the moving status bar was also made to appear more robotic: while the player's status bar slowly moves towards the new captured value, the machine's bar moves much faster and then stops at its final location, causing a more artificial impression to match the character. Players' had a divergent opinion regarding the difficulty of the machines: while some stated that the game was actually easy even in the hardest difficulty, others had trouble defeating the first difficulty of the game. These opposed opinions may be caused by the natural differences in the learning curve of each individual player, which any game is susceptible to.

5   Discussion

This section discusses the main results from both the design and implementation of the game, and the results gathered during the evaluation of the platform.

Regarding the problems that occurred with the blink detection feature, one possible reason for the difference between the detection precision between players may be the anatomical differences between their skulls. It is known, for example, that the calibration of the device took much longer for some subjects, and had to be adjusted a few times before being able to capture good quality signals. As it is also known that the MindWave device uses artefacts and noise generated by the movement of the blink to detect it, it may be easier or harder to detect this signal for certain players, depending on their anatomy. With increased precision, this feature could be implemented in the multiplayer version of the game. The initial idea was that, in the multiplayer mode, each player had his/her own three charges, each providing a little individual boost each time used. However, in the case of two or three players, this boost could become insignificant when the player's individual attention would be averaged with the others' attention. The second idea was to provide one blink charge for each player, with all charges displayed in the team's side for both teams. Using each individual charge would produce no bonus; however, when all players of the same team had used his/her individual charge, the whole team would gain the attention boost. This could create a more collaborative use of the feature.

After the development of the final version of the game and player tests, one question that arose based on the users' interaction was the employment of a full BCI-based game control. Although the game was intended to use only BCI control, the gameplay tests showed that players usually try to perform other actions other than fixing the gaze at the screen, in order to passively increase their attention. In this case, in which the attention of the player is employed to directly control the game, it would be interesting to also have a complementary control to increase the immersion of the player with the game. This hybrid control scheme could use the cognitive state of the player as a passive control: a higher cognitive status could unlock new features, heal the player or change the weather, for example, as shown in some of the related games in the literature. This way, the use of the hybrid system could increase the player's immersion without jeopardizing the gameplay.

The developer must also take into consideration the total duration of the game match while developing a neurofeedback game. Player tests showed that, after playing multiple matches or a match with long duration, the performance of the players quickly drops and takes a couple of minutes to recover. This mental fatigue effect can be avoided by giving either a limited duration to the match (i.e., a time limit) or forcing a minimum interval between consecutive matches. The size of the sliding window that calculates the average cognitive value must also be taken into consideration in this case, as a match without time limit, using the whole duration of the match to calculate the average (given that a value is given every second) could easily last for a long time. If the game win/lose condition is to reach a certain threshold or maintain the average above or below a certain value for a given amount of time, the choice of the window size will greatly impact both the results and the duration of the matches.

The size of this sliding window, in the case of the Mental War, was defined as twenty, after a series of empirical tests. It was noticed that the average value could easily become stagnated when using the values from the full time of the match to calculate the result. Although this sliding window size has shown good results for stabilizing the average while allowing for it to change relatively quickly, the developer must try to find an adequate size according to the intended application. The full range of values may be adequate for a considerably short game or task duration, but the general tendency is that the value stabilizes at some point in time.

Regarding the difficulty of the game, based on the evaluation of the single player mode and the opinion of the subjects, it appears that a possible more adequate (yet more complex) solution would be to adapt the game difficulty according to the performance of the player. The game could maintain an individual player profile with data about past games, and adapt the difficulty of the machine players accordingly. Another adaptation, as suggested by the subjects, would be to increase the variation of the attention values generated by the machine: in the current version, the machine always generates values in the same interval. The proposed idea is to start at a base, lower value and slowly increase the generated attention value until the arriving at the current interval. Of course, for the multiplayer machine players, the game could still use the fixed interval for the generated valued, as combining the data from multiple players to create a fair challenge could be unfeasible.

As for the validation of the platform itself, it appears that the game was indeed entertaining and fun, based on the subjects' opinions. All subjects stated that they would play the game again for training their attention. Although this opinion may be biased with a possible novelty effect caused by the BCI platform, we are positive that the game could be largely used for both entertainment and training purposes. Also, as the game is made available both for download and modification with its open-source code, we are confident that it could also be employed for future BCI experiments, as the log feature allows for easily collecting data from the subjects, and the game can be adapted to employ other control signals, even with another BCI device, according to the objectives of the research.

6 Conclusion

In this paper, the Mental War software was presented and discussed. Mental War allows users to play the game using their level of attention, captured and processed by a NeuroSky MindWave headset, pulling other players in a game of tug-of-war. The game is available in three modes, allowing the user to play a solo match against the machine, against other players in a competitive mode or together with other players in the collaborative mode. Two evaluations were performed in order to access qualitative data from the subjects regarding their interaction with the game, both in single player and multiplayer modes. The data obtained from the evaluations allowed to further develop the game and, mainly, validate its design and implementation in a controlled environment with external players. These results may help developers with the development of future BCI-based games, while the platform itself can be employed to conduct future scientific research in the field.

Acknowledgments. This work was supported by the Physical Artifacts of Interaction Research Group (PAIRG) at the Federal University of Rio Grande do Norte (UFRN), and partially funded by the Brazilian National Council of Scientific and Technological Development (CNPq), under grants 130158/2015-1 and 146931/2017-3. We also would like to thank by resources of the PAIRG's Laboratory of Physical and Physiological Computing (PAIRG L2PC) at UFRN, and the subjects who volunteered to participate in the evaluation of the Mental War.

References

1. Bento, A.A., de Miranda, L.C.: Steering all: infinite racing game controlled by haar cascade through OpenCV. In: SVR 2015, pp. 245–254. IEEE (2015)
2. Bingham, P.M., Bates, J.H.T., Thompson-Figueroa, J., Lahiri, T.: A breath biofeedback computer game for children with cystic fibrosis. Clin. Pediatr. **49**(4), 337–342 (2010)
3. Bonnet, L., Lotte, F., Lécuyer, A.: Two brains, one game: design and evaluation of a multiuser BCI video game based on motor imagery. IEEE Trans. Comput. Intell. AI Games **5**(2), 185–198 (2013)
4. Crawford, C.S., Andujar, M., Jackson, F., Remy, S., Gilbert, J.E.: User experience evaluation towards cooperative brain-robot interaction. In: Kurosu, M. (ed.) HCI 2015. LNCS, vol. 9169, pp. 184–193. Springer, Cham (2015). https://doi.org/10.1007/978-3-319-20901-2_17
5. DelPozo-Banos, M., Travieso, C.M., Weidemann, C.T., Alonso, J.B.: EEG biometric identification: a thorough exploration of the time-frequency domain. J. Neural Eng. **12**(5), 056019 (2015)
6. Eid, M., Issawi, A.E., Saddik, A.E.: Slingshot 3D: a synchronous haptic-audio-video game. Multimedia Tools Appl. **71**(3), 1635–1649 (2014)
7. Ferreira, A.L.S., Marciano, J.N., de Miranda, L.C., Miranda, E.E.C.: Understanding and pro-posing a design rationale of digital games based on brain-computer interface: results of the AdmiralMind battleship study. SBC J. Interact. Syst. **5**(1), 3–15 (2014)
8. Ferreira, A.L.S., de Miranda, L.C., Miranda, E.E.C., Sakamoto, S.G.: A survey of interactive systems based on brain-computer interfaces. SBC J. 3D Interact. Syst. **4**(1), 3–13 (2013)

9. Gervasi, O., Magni, R., Macellari, S.: A brain computer interface for enhancing the communication of people with severe impairment. In: Murgante, B., et al. (eds.) ICCSA 2014. LNCS, vol. 8584, pp. 709–721. Springer, Cham (2014). https://doi.org/10.1007/978-3-319-09153-2_53

10. Hazrati, M.K., Hofmann, U.G.: Avatar navigation in second life using brain signals. In: WISP 2013, pp. 1–7. IEEE (2013)

11. Kos'myna, N., Tarpin-Bernard, F.: Evaluation and comparison of a multimodal combination of BCI paradigms and eye tracking with affordable consumer-grade hardware in a gaming context. IEEE Trans. Comput. Intell. AI Games 5(2), 150–154 (2013)

12. Laar, B., Gürkök, H., Bos, D.P.O., Poel, M., Nijholt, A.: Experiencing BCI control in a popular computer game. IEEE Trans. Comput. Intell. AI Games 5(2), 176–184 (2013)

13. Liarokapis, F., Vourvopoulos, A., Ene, A.: Examining user experiences through a multimodal BCI puzzle game. In: iV 2015, pp. 488–493. IEEE (2015)

14. Maby, E., Perrin, M., Bertrand, O., Sanchez, G., Mattout, J.: BCI could make old two-player games even more fun: a proof of concept with "connect four". In: Advances in Human-Computer Interaction 2012, pp. 1–8 (2012)

15. Marshall, D., Coyle, D., Wilson, S., Callaghan, M.: Games, gameplay, and BCI: the state of the art. IEEE Trans. Comput. Intell. AI Games 5(2), 82–99 (2013)

16. de Miranda, L.C., Hornung, H.H., Baranauskas, M.C.C.: Adjustable interactive rings for iDTV. IEEE Trans. Consum. Electron. 56(3), 1988–1996 (2010)

17. de Miranda, L.C., Hornung, H., Pereira, R., Baranauskas, M.C.C.: Exploring adjustable interactive rings in game playing: preliminary results. In: Marcus, A. (ed.) DUXU 2013. LNCS, vol. 8013, pp. 518–527. Springer, Heidelberg (2013). https://doi.org/10.1007/978-3-642-39241-2_57

18. Schwarz, D., Subramanian, V., Zhuang, K., Adamczyk, C.: Educational neurogaming: EEG-controlled videogames as interactive teaching tools for introductory neuroscience. In: AIIDE 2014, pp. 49–52. AIII (2014)

19. Vasiljevic, G.A.M., de Miranda, L.C., Miranda, E.E.C.: A case study of MasterMind chess: comparing mouse/keyboard interaction with kinect-based gestural interface. In: Advances in Human-Computer Interaction 2016, 10 p. (2016)

Information Systems and Technologies

An Implementation of the OAuth 2.0 for an Enterprise Service Bus

Alysson de Sousa Ribeiro$^{(\boxtimes)}$, Edna Dias Canedo,
and Sérgio Antônio de Andrade Freitas

Computer Science Department - Professional Masters in Applied Computing,
University of Brasília - UnB, Brasília, DF 70910-900, Brazil
{alyssonribeiro,ednacanedo,sergiofreitas}@unb.br
http://cic.unb.br/

Abstract. The utilization of Service-Oriented Architecture (SOA) offers certain benefits, such as low coupling and interoperability. Considering its benefits, SOA is being used for integration of systems and applications within organizations. In order to evaluate and to provide evolution of legacy systems, SOA is an option for the modernization of the legacy systems. Regarding authorization with SOA, the OAuth 2.0 protocol was implemented as part of the solution of the Enterprise Service Bus (ESB) that is be used as important step for modernization of legacy systems. This research presents a case of study of a systematic mapping regarding the authentication and authorization mechanisms in SOA applied to legacy systems maintained and that are in use by students and professionals at University of Brasília (UnB). Performance tests were carried out in the solution allowing to check the increase in the latency introduced by the Protocol and the average flow supported. Simulations were carried out with the objective to verify the behavior of the Protocol implemented when exposed to a replay attack.

Keywords: Security · OAuth 2.0 · Authorization · SOA · ESB

1 Introduction

The modernization of legacy systems - software that remains active but implemented with outdated technology and old criterias - is a topic seen increasing discussion in companies and institutions. The modernization process is expected to reduce the maintenance cost for legacy systems and increase the integration of business fluxes between the system [1]. However, it has some challenges, such as the integration between the systems that are being modernized and systems with update technologies.

The need to modernize legacy systems started discussions in order to adopt solutions based on Service Oriented Architecture (SOA). In SOA an organization is able to create services and share them in order to interact in real time with other services within the institution or even other organizations, considering for

O. Gervasi et al. (Eds.): ICCSA 2018, LNCS 10960, pp. 469–484, 2018.
https://doi.org/10.1007/978-3-319-95162-1_32

instance a federation approach [27]. Also SOA has been used by organizations to support the modernization of legacy systems, offering integration between new and old systems [14].

Agilar et al. [1] proposed Erlangms as an Enterprise Service Bus (ESB) solution to modernize legacy systems regarding authorization and authentication. The proposed solution uses Representational State Transfer (REST) [12,26] and it was developed in Erlang functional language [18]. Considering a security perspective, this approach has security concerns such as the possibility to access information by unauthorized agents. Also, given the importance of the legacy systems and the shared information provided by distributed authentication, security measures have to be addressed when implementing authentication solutions with SOA.

This paper presents an implementation of the Open Authorization (Oauth) Protocol version 2.0 as a service of ErlangMS ESB [1] to protect the authorization and authentication processes to allow users to safely access legacy systems.

The main contribution of this work is the implementation of an authorization solution (named ErlangMS) to support the modernization of legacy systems. Results of this research were applied in legacy systems maintained and in use by students and professionals at University of Brasilia (UnB). The Oauth 2.0 protocol was chosen after an analysis of the solution found through the systematic mapping shown in [8] and the necessary requirements for the ErlangMS architecture defined.

The article is organized as follows. Sections 2 and 3 presents the main concepts used in this work. The proposed authorization solution, as well as the requirements for its implementation, is presented in Sect. 4. In Sect. 5, the performance tests are presented. The security tests are presented in Sect. 6. Section 7 presents related studies. In Sect. 8, there are the conclusions, the impressions obtained throughout the study, and the objectives to be mapped in future studies.

2   Modernization of Legacy Systems

Legacy modernization, or software modernization, refers to the conversion, rewriting or porting of a legacy system to a modern computer programming language, software libraries, protocols, or hardware platform. Legacy transformation aims to retain and extend the value of the legacy investment through migration to new platforms.

Modernization involves more extensive changes than maintenance, but conserves a significant functionalities of the existing system. These changes often include system restructuring, important functional enhancements, or new software attributes. Modernization is used when a legacy system requires more pervasive changes than those possible during maintenance, but it still has business value that must be preserved. System modernization can be distinguished by the level of system understanding required to support the modernization effort. Modernization that requires knowledge of the internals of a legacy system is called white-box modernization, and modernization that just requires knowledge of the external interfaces of a legacy system is called black-box modernization.

The study conducted by Aguilar in [1] proposes the usage of SOA adopting a Representation State Transfer (REST) in the modernization of legacy systems at University of Brasília. The solution named ErlangMS is an enterprise service bus (ESB) being developed in the Erlang language [2], using the JSON format to exchange messages with the client.

The service bus is based on the concept of a service catalog, allowing the reutilization of software components, since it can be accessed by other applications once it has been published in the service bus. The study [1] presented the systematic mapping and the proposed architecture implementation.

The bus communication scheme occurs through two routes. In the first route, there's the client communication via REST (regardless of programming language or platform) to consume a given service in the bus. In the second route, there's communication between the bus and the service, which is implemented in a programming language. This communication takes place through a messaging system available in Erlang [1], allowing for asynchronous communication with a myriad of programming languages in a fast manner, due to its binary data transportation and low network latency. Therefore, the function of the implemented bus is to route the REST requisitions for another service to process and return the result to the client.

3   The OAuth 2.0 Authorization Framework

The 2.0 version of the OAuth 2.0 Authorization Framework offers a brand new protocol when compared to version 1.0, which was published in 2007, and is not backward compatible [9]. The protocol makes use of the REST architecture and JSON messages. OAuth 2.0 defined four types of authorization grants [11]: *Through Authorization Code; Implicit; Resource Owner Password Credentials*; Client Credentials.

3.1   OAuth 2.0 Vulnerabilities

Replay Attack with the Authorization Code. Critical communication occurs during the request for the access code, as the data is exposed to the user's agent (such as a browser). The authorization code in conjunction with the client's secret can be used to obtain the token. If a malicious agent captures the authorization code in the communication between the user's agent and the client, it can resend the code to do client and begin a session with the account associated to the one who began the authorization process [29].

Impersonation Attack with the Authorization Code. The attack may also behave like a middleman between the user's agent and the client. In this case, the attacker can capture the authorization code and interrupt the true request of the user's agent to keep the code functional (since it can only be used once, as indicated in the specification [11]).

Capture of the Access Token. OAuth 2.0 uses tokens by default, which give access to the protected resource independently from another type of verification (bearer token). This way, if the attacker obtains the access code, they will be able to request the protected resource at any moment throughout the validity of the token.

Cross-Site Request Forgery. When a user logs into a site, a cookie is usually generated to identify the session. All the subsequent requests from the browser to the site include is identification, and thus the website associated the request to the user's session. The CSRF (Cross-site Request Forgery) occurs when the site bases itself only on the cookie to authorize operations related to security. A malicious site can fool the user's agent and send a cross site request to the vulnerable site (using JavaScript, HTTP redirect, or through a link). The browser will then automatically forward the user's sessions cookie with the forged request. This way, the vulnerable site will authorize the malicious request without the users knowledge [3]. In OAuth 2.0, the invader makes the user's agent follow a malicious URI to a trustworthy server, allowing for a malicious client to inject the authorization code or access token, which can result in the client using the token associated to the malicious agent and not the victim. In this case, the attacker can obtain personal information from the victim, for instance [16,23].

4   Authorization Solution

The authorization solution requirements proposed in this study are:

Requirement 1–(Req1): Authorization. The protocol shall grant authorization only to the resources the authenticated client has rights to. The authorizations will be valid for a finite period of time.

Requirement 2–(Req2): Administrator. The administrator of the resource must be capable of revoking granted authorizations at any given time.

Requirement 3–(Req3): Integrity. It must be possible to identify illicit alterations in the messages during the authentication and authorization process.

Requirement 4–(Req4): Privacy. Restricted data exchanged during the authorization process must be kept hidden from unauthorized people and services.

Requirement 5–(Req5): Compatibility with the ErlangMS bus. The protocol must use the REST [21] architecture and the JSON format for message exchange [20]. This is necessary as the proposed solution will work as a service in the bus proposed in [1].

Requirement 6–(Req6): Low Coupling. The protocol must not couple with UnB's business rules, thus maintaining the low coupling characteristic of ErlangMS.

Table 1 presents a comparison between the solutions encountered in the systematic mapping according to the established requirements.

Table 1. Comparison between solutions.

Solutions	Req1	Req2	Req3	Req4	Req5	Req6
Oauth 2.0	X	X	X	X	X	X
SAML			X	X		X
OpenID connect			X	X	X	X
XACML	X	X	X	X		X

OpenID Connect and SAML are authentication-oriented solutions. Normally, they're used for identity federation, process in which different domains agree that a designated cluster of users can be authenticated through a determined set of criteria [30]. Therefore, these solutions don't adhere to requirement 1 nor requirement 2, as they deal in authentication and not in SOA authorization. As for requirements 3 and 4, all solutions have mechanisms to ensure the integrity and privacy of the data used in the authentication or authorization processes. However, the specification of Oauth 2 is restricted to the TLS (Transport Layer Security) protocol.

Oauth 2.0 and OpenID Connect use the same architectural style (REST) and the same pattern for message exchange (JSON) as the bus, being compatible with requirement 5. The SAML and XACML patterns utilize the SOAP pattern and the XML language for message exchange, so that neither are compatible with ErlangMS, failing at requirement 5. The OAuth 2.0 protocol is compatible with all the requirements defined and will be implemented and tested in this study. The XACML solution adheres to the security requirements, but is not compatible with ErlangMS (requirement 5). This pattern can be implemented in conjunction to SAML, creating a more complete authentication and authorization solution.

4.1 Oauth 2.0 and ErlangMS

The solutions encountered in the Systematic Mapping [8] and the definition of the requirements for the security solution that will be used in the ErlangMS bus acted as support for the choice of authorization protocol. In this way, Oauth 2.0 was implemented in the authorization protocol as a bus service [1]. OAuth 2.0 implementation was facilitated by the use of the libraries available on the bus and the Erlang language to handle HTTP/REST requests. ErlangMS already supports the use of TLS, in this way, OAuth 2.0 has been implemented respecting the requirements of integrity and privacy.

Service Catalogue. An important element inside the ErlangMS bus is the service catalogue. In this catalogue there is the description, in JSON, of the APIs of services through the definition of service contracts. For such, the services must be specified with metadata, like the URL, the type of REST requirement (GET, POST, PUT, DELETE), the parameters, the owner of the service, the type of authorization, and others. The publishing of a service in the catalogue allows for the Dispatcher module of the bus to route the REST requirements to the services requested by the user [1]. The service catalogue of OAuth 2.0 describes the requests supported by the solution according to the RFC 6729 specification [11] for instance, specifies an authorization request of the HTTP GET kind, which must be sent using the/authorize URL for the OAuth 2.0 service to begin.

4.2   Security Considerations

In this section, we present the solutions adopted in the implementation in order to deal with the vulnerabilities presented by protocol.

Replay Attack with the Authorization Code. To diminish the risk of this vulnerability, the authorization code - representing the user's authorization to access the protected resources, in the concession flux–must be discarded after the request for the access token [11]. In this case, the vulnerability could only be explored if the attacker managed to capture the authorization code and perform the request for the access token to the authorization server before the legitimate client does.

Attack of Representation with the Authorization Code. To lower the probability of this attack, it's recommended to use the TLS protocol to protect the confidentiality of the communication and intercept the messages exchanged in the authorization process. For this, the bus must use a digital certificate emitted by a certification authority (CA) which is subordinate to the ICPEdu hierarchy.

Capture of the Access Token. The token used by default in OAuth 2.0 (Bearer Token) is not linked to any other security parameter, allowing it to be used by anyone who obtains it. For the solution adopted in ErlangMS, MAC token support was added. This kind of token is used in the 1.0a version of protocol OAuth. Next, the processes used to access a resource using a bearer token and a MAC token will be shown. The access code is sent together with the client's credentials (in the "Authorization" field of the HTTP header) and the redirection URI. After checking the parameters, the OAuth 2.0 server grants the bearer token as shown in Fig. 1. The answer also contains the duration of the token ("expires_in") and the refresh token ("refresh_token"), which is a credential used to obtain a new access token after the current one expires.

To access the protected resource, you simply send the access token characters to the protected resource's requisition. The request for an access token in OAuth 1.0a is more complex than in the 2.0 version, as shown in Fig. 2.

```
HTTP/1.1  200  OK
Content-Type:  application/json;charset=UTF-8
{
  "access_token":"2YotnFZFEjr1zCsicMWpAA",
  "token_type":"bearer",
  "expires_in":3600,
  "refresh_token":"tGzv3JOkF0XG5Qx2TlKWIA",
}
```

Fig. 1. OAuth 2.0 access token.

```
POST /request_token HTTP/1.1
Host:  server.example.com
Authorization:  OAuth
  oauth_consumer_key="jd83jd92dhsh93js",
  oauth_token="hdk48Djdsa",
  oauth_signature_method="HMAC-SHA1"
  oauth_verifier="473f82d3",
  oauth_nonce="asadaggfr",
  oauth_timestamp="134657964",
  oauth_signature="ja893SD9%26xyz4992k83j47x0b"
```

Fig. 2. Access token request in OAuth 1.0a.

In version 1.0, there exists a pair of temporary token credentials to request the access token. The temporary token ("oauth_token") is sent as a request parameter, the secret of the temporary token ("oauth_token_secret") is used as key, together with the client's secret, to generate the signature ("oauth_signature"). The signature, a MAC code to verify the message, is generated according to the following formula:

$$| \; oauth\_signature = HMAC - SHA1(chave, string)$$

Where the key is formed by the secret of the temporary token and by the secret of the client, separated by the & character; the string is the concatenation of the request elements in a single sequence of characters [10]. The nonce and time-stamp parameters are used to avoid the execution of a replay attack in the request. The "oauth_nonce" is a random sequence of characters, generated by the client to allow the server to verify if a request had never been made before. The value of nonce must be exclusive in all requests with the same time-stamp, and client and token credentials [10].

Together with the MAC token, the secret used to generate the message authentication code (MAC) is issued. It is used to sign certain components of HTTP/HTTPS requests. This signature is sent together with the token in the request to access the protected resource. This process is the same as the one used in the request for the access token. Figure 3 shows a request to access protected content using a MAC token.

MAC Token in ErlangMS OAuth 2.0. In the MAC token request in OAuth 2.0, the access code is sent alone, different from what occurs with the bearer token. This is due to the fact that the client's secret must be the key to generate

```
GET /recurso HTTP/1.1
Host: unb.br
Authorization:
 oauth_consumer_key="dpf43f3p2l4k3l03",
 oauth_token="nnch734d00sl2jdk",
 oauth_signature_method="HMAC-SHA1",
 oauth_timestamp="137131202",
 oauth_nonce="chapoH",
 oauth_signature="MdpQcU8iPSUWoN%2FUDMsK2sui9I%3D"
```

Fig. 3. Request using a MAC token.

the resource's request signature, so it shouldn't be sent during the authentication process. The response of the access token request is identical to the one used in OAuth 1.0. The token's secrets are added to the answer, as they will be used to generate the signature. The request to access a protected resource using a MAC token is similar to the one in OAuth 1.0a, differing only in the naming of parameters to respect the RFC 6749 [11].

Cross-Site Request Forgery. To avoid this attack, the specification of OAuth 2.0 recommends that the client generate a value linked to the session of the resource's owner, and which is hard to be guessed (a cookie hash, for instance) and acts like the state variable in the authorization code or access token request. The authorization server simply returns this parameter in its answer, so the client can verify if the returned token or code is destined to the current session [11]. With the definition of the solution that will be implemented at UnB, it is necessary to evaluate the impact of the protocol in the Computer Centers environment. This chapter presents the performance evaluation of the OAuth 2.0 protocol implemented in ErlangMS.

5   Performance Test

The objective of carrying out performance tests is to determine if the performance of the system is adequate to its requirements [5,15]. For the performance test, we used the GQM approach, proposed by van Solingen in [4,28]. This approach suggests that the definition of metrics must be top-down, based in the objectives and questions. The first step is to define the objective that will specify the metric's purpose. In the second step, questions that characterize the measuring object in relation to a quality problem are drafted. In the third step, we define the metrics necessary to answer the drafted questions. One metric can be used to answer different questions with the same objective.

The following objectives were defined for the performance test:

Objective 1: Verify the increase in response time added by the implemented authorization protocol (Latency).
Objective 2: Verify the behavior of the protocol for the demand of requests expected for UnB (Throughput).

With this, we will carry out two types of performance tests: a load test and a stress test. Load tests evaluate the performance of the system using a realistic load of simultaneous users, and stress tests evaluate the performance using the maximum number of simultaneous users that the system can support [17]. These types of tests are important for the systems developed for UnB, given the huge quantity of active users in the University.

5.1 Test Environment

With the objective of evaluating the impact of the protocol, a bus service that returns network information from ErlangMS was implemented. The service was implemented in three test scenarios according to the access mode:

Scenario 1: In the first scenario, the service returns the information publicly (no need for authorization) and without the TLS protocol;

Scenario 2: In the second scenario, the information is obtained after presenting an OAuth 1.0 token. The token is given after the protocol's authorization process, and all messages exchanged between client and authorization server are signed and verified using MAC codes.

Scenario 3: In the third scenario, the information is returned after presenting an OAuth 2.0 token, given through an authorization code process. In this case, the authorization and resource servers were in the same machine.

Scenario 4: In the fourth scenario, the information is returned after presenting an OAuth 2.0 MAC token given through an authorization code process. The messages exchanged during the process are the same as the ones in Scenario 3. The only difference is in the service access request, which now goes through an integrity check through the MAC code.

To carry out the test, two network servers were used, with the same hardware configuration, in which the client and authorization/resource servers were installed. The services were developed in the Erlang language. All the machines are connected to the same switch and are in the same logic network, as shown in Fig. 4. All the machines used the Ubuntu Server 16.04.2 LTS operation system. The requests were done from the desktop. In Table 2, the computational infrastructure used in the tests is specified. Different quantities of requisitions were generated to verify the average latency and throughput in the three authorization scenarios, through the Apache JMeter tool [13].

5.2 Results

To answer Question 1, the latency values on the four previously defined scenarios (direct access to data, access via OAuth 1.0a, access via OAuth 2.0, and access via OAuth 2.0 with MAC tokens) were analyzed. The scenarios were submitted to different numbers of requests, as shown in Table 3.

The result evidences the increase in latency due to the use of authorization protocols, as shown in Table 3, which was already expected given the increase in

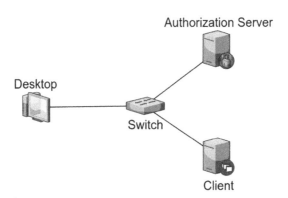

Fig. 4. Test environment.

Table 2. Hardware infrastructure used in the tests.

	Type	Characteristics
Client	Server	Processor Intel Xeon E31220 3.10 GHz, 4 GB RAM
Authorization and resource server	Server	Processor Intel Xeon E31220 3.10 GHz, 4 GB RAM
Desktop	Desktop	Processor Intel Core i5-2500 3.30 GHz, 4 GB RAM

the number of messages introduced by OAuth 1.0 and by the kind of authorization in OAuth 2.0. Scenarios 2, 3 and 4 use five different requests, aside from using a third entity for authorization. Besides that, the use of the TLS protocol and the authentication of messages using HMAC contribute to the increase in latency. It's possible to observe the increase in latency caused by the authentication of messages of OAuth 1.0 (Scenario 2) and OAuth 2.0 using MAC (Scenario 4) tokens. To answer question 2, a throughput metric was used. The average number of accesses to the main systems of UnB was defined. The accesses were generated and the system behavior, verified. Table 4 presents the variation of flow according to the number of requests.

Table 3. Latency in the 4 scenarios.

Request	Scenario 1		Scenario 2		Scenario 3		Scenario 4	
	Average	Median	Average	Median	Average	Median	Average	Median
100	3	2	106	100	105	103	101	99
1000	3	2	413	160	128	109	230	116
5000	11	6	608	372	471	194	510	258
10000	28	2	1231	922	634	350	996	892

Table 4. Flow (requests/s).

Requests	Scenario 1	Scenario 2	Scenario 3	Scenario 4
100	49.6	45.5	45.9	45.9
1000	447.8	231.6	231.2	252.3
5000	2032.5	285.9	269.1	226.6
10000	3940.1	252.7	302.5	247.0

The flow value was considered acceptable for the current situation at UnB. We can observe that the flow didn't vary much with the increase in requests for the scenarios that used the OAuth protocol (Table 4). Comparing the scenarios, it's possible to observe a higher flow in public access (Scenario 1). OAuth 2.0 had a slightly higher flow than OAuth 1.0.

6 Security Test

With the objective of testing the security of the protocol implemented in this study, two attack simulations were done (replay attack with the authorization code and with the access token). The computational structure used was the same as in the performance test, detailed in Fig. 4 and in Table 2.

6.1 Replay Attack with the Authorization Code

The objective of this simulation is to verify the efficiency of the OAuth 2.0 protocol in the ErlangMS bus faced with a replay attack in the access token request. The information is accessed after presenting an OAuth 2.0 MAC token, given through an authorization code process. However, during the test, the token request is repeated, simulating a replay attack.

The authorization code must be single-use, so it is expected from the protocol to deny the requests containing an expired authorization code. It's possible to observe that as the requests increased, the repeated requests were more successful. This can be due to the increase in latency of the protocol when the number of requests is high, thus increasing the chance that a forged request sent after the original one be processed by the bus first. Its also possible for network errors to have occurred, causing the original requests to be lost. Table 5 shows the results.

6.2 Replay Attack with the *MAC Token*

The objective of this simulation is to verify the efficiency of the OAuth 2.0 protocol in the ErlangMS bus during a replay attack in the request to access a protected resource. The information is accessed after presenting an OAuth 2.0 MAC token, given through an authorization code process. However, during the test, the request for the protected resource is repeated, simulating a replay attack.

Table 5. Replay attack using the authorization code.

Requests	Repetitions	Successful repetitions
100	100	0
1000	1000	0
5000	5000	3
10000	10000	12

The MAC tokens contain random numbers (nonce parameter) that identify the request to access the protected resource. In this way, the protocol doesn't accept two requests with the same value in the nonce parameter, considerably reducing the chance of success of a replay attack using a MAC token. Table 6 shows the results of the simulation. It's possible to see that as the number of requests increased, the repeated requests had more success, much like in the previous section.

Table 6. Replay attack using the MAC Token.

Requests	Repetitions	Successful repetitions
100	100	0
1000	1000	0
5000	5000	4
10000	10000	10

6.3   Discussion of Results

With the performance test, it was possible to verify the impact of using OAuth 2.0 in UnB's environment. When compared to the access without ah authorization protocol, there is a significant increase in latency.

This increase was already expected, given the number of messages exchanged, since OAuth 2.0 uses the TLS protocol. Another factor that increases the latency is the usage of hash function for message signature, which can be observed in the difference in results between Oauth 1.0a and 2.0.

OAuth 2.0 using MAC tokens had a better performance than OAuth 1.0. This is because version 1.0a authenticates all messages exchanged between client and authorization server, whereas version 2.0 does it only in the request to access the protected resource.

The results of the flow are considered satisfactory for all scenarios with an authorization protocol. For 10000 requests, all protocols registered above 247 requests per second. The service that most closely answers to requests at the University of Brasília is the DNS, averaging 235000 requests every 15 min (data taken from the firewall equipment of the Computer Center), giving it an average flow of 261.11 requests per second. The number is close to the one reached by the OAuth 2.0 protocol in ErlangMS. However, ErlangMS was tested in an environment with no customizations and limited hardware, when compared to the DNS server.

In the security tests, two replay attack situations were simulated. In both cases, the attacks were efficient in a small percentage of the attempts (0.12% at the most). The simulations, however, only tested the security mechanisms of the OAuth 2.0 protocol implemented in ErlangMS. In a real scenario, the occurrence of these attacks would be made even harder thanks to the TLS protocol (in the test scenario, the attacks came from a trustworthy entity). As such, the performance of OAuth 2.0 in the security tests was considered satisfactory.

7   Related Work

This Section presents the related works that deal with the theme modernization of legacy systems and authentication and authorization in SOA.

Study [7] presents an evaluation on the techniques, tools, and procedures used to ensure safety in SOA. To this end, a systematic mapping took place, using the string: SOA and Security in the IEEE Xplorer, ACM, and DBLP libraries [8]. After all the stages of the mapping, a total of 25 papers was selected. In one of the raised research questions, authenticity was identified as the most addressed security attribute.

The study [7] proposes a safe authentication and authorization protocol. The protocol is adherent to the style (REST), strives to allow for the adoption of a service-oriented architecture as a single integration alternative, and incorporates security mechanisms such as cryptography, digital signature, and the use of digital certificates. The protocol is analyzed according to the BAN logic [25].

The study [22] proposes a unified access control model named UACM, based in the SAML (Security Assertion Markup Language) security access control technology. This model is used to provide access control for the sharing of educational resources based on the SOA architecture. The UACM (Unified Access Control Model for Inter-platform Educational Resources) is divided in two parts to ensure safety in SOA. The SOAP security agent (SMSA) utilizes asymmetrical keys to secure the authenticity of users. Another openSAML-based module is responsible for validating the identity and authorizing access to the services.

UACM was tested in a man-in-the-middle attack, which did not achieve success, thus demonstrating the efficacy of the cryptography of the messages. Another test was related to the access of resources by authorized or unauthorized users. The test also concluded in a success.

In [24], an authorization model (AAuth) is proposed, for the access of cloud-based files using the OAuth protocol and tokens with cryptography based in attribute (ABE Attribute-based encryption). The confidentiality and integrity of the data are guaranteed by the cryptography scheme used and by the utilization of certificates registered by the participating entities. The performance test showed an increase in latency, considered small in relation to the use of

OAuth. The study [19] proposes a model to integrate services using REST and the OAuth 2.0 protocol to carry out the authorization of accesses.

The work [29] presents some experiments with the objective of studying the vulnerabilities in protocol OAuth 2.0. The tests were executed both client-side and on the authorization servers. The following tests were done: replay test on top of the authorization code (the codes must be used only once according to the specification [11]), pushing attacks (where a malicious client steals the users data) and impersonation attack (where a malicious agent steals the access code). Finally, the study discovered some vulnerabilities in current implementations of OAuth 2.0.

In [6], proposed the user authentication method using E-mail for the user and 3rd Party application authentication as the measure solving the security problem that can be happened in OAuth protocol. And when the user authentication being completed and issuing the Access Token and storing, although the Access Token was dispersed and it stored and the attacker won the some of user information, it would not allow to use for the user authentication.

Works [22,24] add new cryptography functionalities to provide security in unsafe channels. Our proposal uses MAC tokens to guarantee the integrity of this type of channel.

Mechanisms were tested and implemented in order to protect the architecture from certain vulnerabilities (Replay attack, Impersonation Attack, and CSRF) in OAuth, as reported in works [6,29].

8   Conclusions

The SOA architecture possesses characteristics that support the modernization process of the legacy systems. The study [1] allowed for the SOA to start being used in the modernization of the legacy systems at CPD/UnB. This approach, however, lacks a few security concerns, such as the authorization to services published in the bus.

With the systematic mapping that was done in [8], it was possible to identify the main solutions presented for authentication and authorization in SOA and in REST. From this mapping, it was possible to conclude that the Oauth 2.0 protocol is the solution which most adheres to the bus proposed for the modernization of legacy systems at UnB, meeting our security needs.

The implementation of Oauth 2.0 seeks to grant access to resources and services published in the bus only in applications (clients) with the privilege for such. This requirement is essential for ErlangMS, contributing for the safe utilization of the SOA architecture in the modernization process of the legacy systems at UnB. ErlangMS is available for the academic community at https://github.com/erlangMS.

After a security analysis, we saw the need to add support to access tokens with message authentication via HMAC (MAC tokens). The main advantage that the MAC tokens offer is an integrity check of the messages through the use of MAC codes.

A performance test was carried out with the proposed solution, making it possible to observe the increase in latency caused by a higher number of messages exchanged in the authorization process. The solution was compared with OAuth 1.0a (a different protocol, incompatible with version 2.0). It was possible to observe that version 2.0 had a lower increase in latency and higher flow than version 1.0a. This is due to the fact that version 1.0a authenticates all of the messages exchanged between client and authorization server via MAC code. The protocol supported high amounts of requests, showing a satisfactory result, taking in account the high number of users of UnB.

References

1. Agilar, E., Almeida, R., Canedo, E.: A systematic mapping study on legacy system modernization. In: The 28th International Conference on Software Engineering and Knowledge Engineering, San Francisco Bay, California, USA - SEKE, pp. 345–350 (2016)
2. Armstrong, J.: Programming Erlang: Software for a Concurrent World. Pragmatic Bookshelf, Armstrong (2007)
3. Bansal, C., Bhargavan, K., Maffeis, S.: Discovering concrete attacks on website authorization by formal analysis. In: 2012 IEEE 25th Computer Security Foundations Symposium, pp. 247–262, June 2012
4. Basili, V., Trendowicz, A., Kowalczyk, M., Heidrich, J., Seaman, C., Münch, J., Rombach, D.: Phase 2: define goals, strategies, and measurement. Aligning Organizations Through Measurement. TFISSSE, pp. 29–67. Springer, Cham (2014). https://doi.org/10.1007/978-3-319-05047-8_5
5. Bhatia, R., Ganpati, A.: In depth analysis of web performance testing tools. IRACST Eng. Sci. Technol. Int. J. (ESTIJ) 6(5), 15–19 (2016). ISSN 2250–3498. In Depth
6. Chae, C.-J., Kim, K.-B., Cho, H.-J.: A study on secure user authentication and authorization in OAuth protocol. Cluster Comput. 20, 1–9 (2017)
7. da Conceição, R.A.: Um Protocolo de Autenticação e Autorização Seguro para Arquiteturas Orientadas a Serviços. Ph.D. thesis, Universidade de Brasília (2014)
8. de Sousa Ribeiro, A., Canedo, E.D.: Solutions analysis of authentication and authorization for service oriented architectures. In: 2016 11th Iberian Conference on Information Systems and Technologies (CISTI), June Gran Canaria, Spain, pp. 1–6 (2016)
9. Hammer-Lahav, E.: Introducing OAuth 2.0. Hueniverse, May 2010
10. Hammer-Lahav, E.: The OAuth 1.0 protocol. Internet engineering task force (IETF). Request for comments: 5849, April 2010
11. Hardt,D.: The OAuth 2.0 authorization framework (2012)
12. Honko, H., Andalibi, V., Aaltonen, T., Parak, J., Saaranen, M., Viik, J., Korhonen, I.: W2E–wellness warehouse engine for semantic interoperability of consumer health data. IEEE J. Biomed. Health Inf. 20(6), 1632–1639 (2016)
13. Jha, N., Popli, R.: Comparative analysis of web applications using JMeter. Int. J. 8(3), 774–777 (2017)
14. Juric, M.B.: SOA Approach to Integration: XML, Web Services, ESB, and BPEL in Real-world SOA Projects. Packt Publishing Ltd., Birmingham (2007)

15. Kao, C.H., Lin, C.C., Lu, H.T.: Toward automatic performance testing for rest-based web applications. In: The Eleventh International Conference on Software Engineering Advances - ICSEA 2016 - Rome, Italy, pp. 81–87 (2016)

16. Kaur, G., Aggarwal, D.: A survey paper on social sign-on protocol OAuth 2.0. J. Eng. Comput. Appl. Sci. **2**(6), 93–96 (2013)

17. Kotzé, R., Ricci, S., Birkhofer, B., Wiklund, J.: Performance tests of a new non-invasive sensor unit and ultrasound electronics. Flow Measur. Instrum. **48**, 104–111 (2016). https://doi.org/10.1016/j.flowmeasinst.2015.08.013

18. Laurent, S.S.: Introducing Erlang: Getting Started in Functional Programming. O'Reilly Media, Inc., Newton (2017)

19. Memeti, A., Selimi, B., Besimi, A., Çiço, B.: A framework for flexible rest services: decoupling authorization for reduced service dependency. In: 2015 4th Mediterranean Conference on Embedded Computing (MECO), pp. 51–55, June 2015

20. Munro, M.C.: Text functions (JSON). In: Munro, M.C. (ed.) Learn FileMaker Pro 16, pp. 313–320. Apress, Berkeley (2017). https://doi.org/10.1007/978-1-4842-2863-0_14

21. Nguyen, H.V., Tolsdorf, J., Lo Iacono, L.: On the security expressiveness of REST-based API definition languages. In: Lopez, J., Fischer-Hübner, S., Lambrinoudakis, C. (eds.) TrustBus 2017. LNCS, vol. 10442, pp. 215–231. Springer, Cham (2017). https://doi.org/10.1007/978-3-319-64483-7_14

22. Shang, C., Yang, Z., Liu, Q., Zhao, C.: SAML based unified access control model for inter-platform educational resources. In: 2008 International Conference on Computer Science and Software Engineering, vol. 5, pp. 909–912, December 2008

23. Shernan, E., Carter, H., Tian, D., Traynor, P., Butler, K.: More guidelines than rules: CSRF vulnerabilities from noncompliant OAuth 2.0 implementations. In: Almgren, M., Gulisano, V., Maggi, F. (eds.) DIMVA 2015. LNCS, vol. 9148, pp. 239–260. Springer, Cham (2015). https://doi.org/10.1007/978-3-319-20550-2_13

24. Tassanaviboon, A., Gong, G.: OAuth and abe based authorization in semi-trusted cloud computing: Aauth. In: Proceedings of the Second International Workshop on Data Intensive Computing in the Clouds, DataCloud-SC 2011, pp. 41–50. ACM, New York (2011)

25. Wen, J., Zhang, M., Li, X.: The study on the application of ban logic in formal analysis of authentication protocols. In: Proceedings of the 7th International Conference on Electronic Commerce, pp. 744–747. ACM (2005)

26. Williams, J.L., Cramer, D.: System and method for validating documentation of representational state transfer (rest) services. US Patent 9,621,440, 11 April 2017

27. Xu, J., Zhang, D., Liu, L., Li, X.: Dynamic authentication for cross-realm SOA-based business processes. IEEE Trans. Serv. Comput. **5**(1), 20–32 (2012)

28. Yahya, F., Walters, R.J., Wills, G.B.: Using goal-question-metric (GQM) approach to assess security in cloud storage. In: Chang, V., Ramachandran, M., Walters, R.J., Wills, G. (eds.) Enterprise Security. LNCS, vol. 10131, pp. 223–240. Springer, Cham (2017). https://doi.org/10.1007/978-3-319-54380-2_10

29. Yang, F., Manoharan, S.: A security analysis of the oauth protocol. In: 2013 IEEE Pacific Rim Conference on Communications, Computers and Signal Processing (PACRIM), pp. 271–276, August 2013

30. Yuan, Y., Li, B., Kreger, H.: SOA reference architecture: standards and analysis. In: Qiu, M. (ed.) SmartCom 2016. LNCS, vol. 10135, pp. 469–476. Springer, Cham (2017). https://doi.org/10.1007/978-3-319-52015-5_48

Intelligent Context-Based Pattern Matching Approaches to Enhance Decision Making

Gaik-Yee Chan[(⊠)], Kim-Loong Ong, Tong-Sheng Wong,
and Lork-Yee Yvonne Chow

Faculty of Computing and Informatics,
Multimedia University, Cyberjaya, Malaysia
gychan@mmu.edu.my

Abstract. In this Internet and Cloud Computing era, every second, there is huge volume of data, whether structured or unstructured, is being stored or retrieved by various applications for use in different ways to support decision making. These business applications certainly require effective and accurate means to store and retrieve information on contextual basis to support decision making. Merely using pattern matching methods without considering the context may not help to retrieve the most suitable and accurate information for decision making. This paper therefore introduces three web applications that apply intelligent pattern matching approaches to retrieve accurate information to enhance decision making on contextual basis. In the first study, stemming and Boyer-Moore methods are incorporated with company policies to auto search, and recommend the right candidate to attend the most appropriate training course. The second study, through several iterations of pattern matching using a lookup table, locates the best three real estate properties that match potential buyer's preferences. In the third study, a color matching scheme is used to find users' preferred images or photos stored in a Cloud storage. Testing and performance evaluation of these methods using the web applications show results that could effectively enhance decision making.

Keywords: Context-based · Decision making · Pattern matching
Stemming

1 Introduction

In this current Internet and Cloud Computing technology era, every second, there is huge volume of data, whether structured or unstructured, is being stored or retrieved by various applications for use in different ways to support decision making. To have a feel of how tremendous the volume, how fast the speed and how varied the content is, take for example, Google which on average, processes over 40,000 search queries every second and this could translate to over 3.5 billion searches per day and 1.2 trillion searches per year worldwide [1]. At another instance as of March 2015, You Tube has created 10,000 videos leading to generation of one billion over views and 70 million plus hours of watch time [2]. Not to forget social media, for example, Facebook, could generate up to 2.7 billion "like" actions and 300 million of photos per day [3]. In view

© Springer International Publishing AG, part of Springer Nature 2018
O. Gervasi et al. (Eds.): ICCSA 2018, LNCS 10960, pp. 485–497, 2018.
https://doi.org/10.1007/978-3-319-95162-1_33

of this wave of big data, effective decision-making has to be data-driven and coupled with intelligent analytic tools [4].

In view of such wave, many organizations as mentioned in [3], be it in health care, telecommunication, finance industries, government agencies, the academia and other businesses are recognizing the fact that data analytics could help their business entities in locating the right data and interpret them according to their business requirements, hence more customer-centric. These businesses or their businesses applications therefore require effective and accurate means to store and retrieve information on contextual basis through data analytics to enhance decision making. Moreover, merely locating or searching data without considering the context may not help to retrieve the most suitable and accurate information for decision-making. Consequently, research in [5] has developed a framework that incorporates data analytic tools and techniques into the decision making process. This framework integrated with intelligent techniques aims to enhance the quality of the decision making process while dealing with big data.

For our paper, we introduce three web applications that apply intelligent pattern-matching approaches to retrieve accurate information to enhance decision making on contextual basis. In the first study, stemming and Boyer-Moore methods are incorporated with company policies to auto search, and recommend the right candidate to attend the most appropriate training course. In the second study, through several iterations of pattern matching in a brute-force manner to locate the best three real estate properties that match potential buyer's preferences. In the third study, a color matching scheme is used to find images or photos stored in a Cloud storage.

This paper is organized as follows, Sect. 2 provides background study, Sect. 3 discusses methodologies used, Sect. 4 presents the three case studies with performance evaluation and analysis of results and Sect. 5 concludes with indication for future work.

2 Background Study

Generally, a keyword search engine should be sufficient in providing retrieval of information. However, most often, these general purpose search engines will retrieve a list of most likely matched results for the users. The users still have to go through each item in the list to find the most suitable one. Hence, much unproductive time is wasted in this search manner. Some web applications although provide information retrieval, but are not incorporated with intelligent search algorithms or data analytic techniques and hence not able to provide accurate and timely support for decision making.

For example, some existing employees training management systems [6–8] do provide functionality for managing their employees' training, but allow only the department manager to select and register the training course for the employees. The selection and registration for the training course is not based on employees training needs or preference. This could create the problem that the employees are not receiving the most suitable training according to their needs.

For some web-based real estate or properties search engine such as [9–11] they do provide search function to allow users to obtain information of properties on sales or rent. However, these applications merely list out the information of the properties and do not do much analytics. For example, they do not have the intelligent search, match and recommend function to offer users some property choices according to their preferences hence assisting users in decision making.

Other web applications such as photo album organizers [12–14] do provide keyword search function for users to search and list out their photos stored in the Cloud storage. However, many of them do not allow image matching whereby photos with similar color schemes could be displayed thus providing users another convenient way to store and retrieve the color photos based on their choices.

Consequently, this leads to our studies being focus on contextual data analytics and intelligent pattern matching methods to auto search and recommend the most suitable choices according to users' preferences.

3 Pattern Matching Methods

This section describes some information retrieval methods such as Stemming algorithm, Boyer-Moore algorithm and color matching schemes. A point to note is that information retrieval or pattern matching methods are not limited to these few mentioned above. They are mentioned here due to our research work makes use of these methods or variations in the development of our intelligent context-based pattern matching applications to auto search, select and recommend the best choices depending on users' preferences. Additionally, the aim of this study is not on the improvement of these pattern matching methods but rather to investigate the feasibility and effectiveness of such methods as used in our applications to provide timely and real-time data analytics for better and more accurate decision making.

3.1 Stemming Algorithm

Research has been on going to find the best method for effective information retrieval. Many of these researches focus on the Stemming algorithm [15, 16] whereby the algorithm shall recognize the different variants of the word and then stemmed to a root word. For example, the words programming, programed, and programs could all be stemmed to the root word 'program'. To achieve stemming, the words need to be conflated to its various variants [17]. There are many automatic approaches towards stemming, such as Affix Removal, Table Lookup, Successor Variety and n-gram [18]. Although there are many variations of the stemming algorithms developed for many different languages, but the Porter's stemming algorithm, originally developed for the stemming of the English-language texts, had become the standard stemming model for processing of other languages [19].

The following sections describe only the stemming approaches used in our case studies such as Affix Removal and Table Lookup.

Affix Removal method involves five steps where each step has defined set of morphological rules to remove the affixes of words sequentially [15]. For example, the first step is to deal with plurals, past or present participles and transforming the last character 'y' to an 'i'. Take for example the word "specializations" shall be transformed to "specialization", "disagreed" to "disagree" and "lucky" to "lucki". The second step then handles double suffixes, for example, the word "generalization" is converted to "generalize". In the third step, suffixes not handled in the second step is further removed, for example, "generalize" is changed to "general". The forth step removes remaining suffixes, example, "general" becomes "gener". The last step deals with words ending with 'e' or double consonant, for example, "contribute" becomes "contribut" and "oscill" becomes "oscil".

The Table Lookup method [18] uses a table to store the stemmed words and their morphological variants. During queries or indexes search, the lookup table will be scanned for the corresponding root word. Storage overhead may be a concern for lookup table and usually, B-tree or hash table is used for more efficient searching.

3.2 Boyer-Moore Algorithm

There are many string searching algorithms and one of it is pioneered by researchers in year 1977 [20] namely the Boyer-Moore string searching algorithm. Since then, more and more research in improving this algorithm is being conducted such as in [21–25]. For our paper, the aim is not to improve on this Boyer-Moore algorithm, but to apply it to our application for fast contextual information searching. Therefore, only the basic concept of this algorithm is discussed in this section.

Generally, Boyer-Moore algorithm starts comparing the pattern from the leftmost part of text and moves it to the right. Thus, there are two observations of pattern that are important in this algorithm, namely, the good-suffix or matching shift and bad-character or the occurrence shift. When there is a mismatch or complete match of the whole pattern, it uses the good-suffix and bad-character to shift the window to the right. A point to note is that Boyer-Moore algorithm has to optimize its use between the good-suffix shift and bad-character shift in order to avoid negative bad-character shifts. Further details regarding Boyer-Moore algorithm could be referred to [20].

4 Pattern Matching - Case Study

This section presents three case studies in which each case study has developed a web application that makes use of pattern matching approaches to intelligently perform data analytics based on users' preferences and auto search, select and recommend suitable choices for them. Based on these choices, the users can still subjectively decide which is the best solution for them. In the first study, stemming and Boyer-Moore methods are incorporated with company policies to auto search, and recommend the right candidate to attend the most appropriate training course. The second study, through several iterations of pattern matching using a lookup table, locates the best three real estate properties that match potential buyer's preferences. In the third study, a color matching scheme is used to find users' preferred images or photos stored in a Cloud storage.

4.1 Pattern Matching Using Stemming and Boyer-Moore Algorithms

A web-based employee training profile management system is developed with the aim to provide companies with a systematic and efficient way, in particular, to auto select and recommend the most appropriate training courses for the employees according to their interests or preferences, qualification or expertise levels, and work requirements. The matching algorithms involved are the Stemming algorithm and Boyer-Moore algorithm.

Basically, there are 5 main stages of searching, matching and recommending the appropriate training course to the suitable employees. Refer to Fig. 1 for step by step process of the auto search, match and recommend stages.

The 5 main stages of matching appropriate training course to suitable employee

Stage 1) *Matching training interest with training type*
For example, the newly added training course has Training type belonging to Information Technology. So the system will search through all the employees' training interest in the database and match those related records. An example of training interest: "I like to learn more about Information Technology, especially obtaining programming skills".
First, the Stemming algorithm will make all the words in training interest to its stem form to make matching easier. These similar terms in stem form (already predefined and stored in database) are for example, Information Technology would be IT, programming would be program and skills would become skill. Then, Boyer-Moore algorithm will take place to match those words having similar terms such as Information Technology, IT, or program. If any of the similar term is matched, the score will be added by 1 from zero.

Stage 2) *Matching training preference with training type*
Next, the system will then check whether the training preference of the employee matches   with the training type. For example, Training preference is Information Technology and Training type is Information Technology, this indicates the training preference matched with the training type, so the match score from Stage (1) will be incremented by 1 to become a cumulative score of 2. Otherwise, the cumulative score is not incremented.

Stage 3) *Matching employee qualification with training name*
The system will then check through the qualification of the employee with the training name. For instance, the employee has already obtained skill in C# and the training course to be matched is also C#. By referring to the training qualification of the employee which is predefined in the database, the system finds a match between training qualification of the employee with training name, which is C#. This increases the cumulative score from Stage (2) to 3. This means the employee already has knowledge of C#, so the next thing to check is in what level of qualification the employee has, is it beginner, intermediate or expert level.

Stage 4) *Matching employee qualification level with training level*
The system will then check through the qualification level of the employee with the training level. For instance, the employee has already achieved C# at Intermediate level, he is still eligible for C# training at the Expert level. Thus the cumulative score is further increased by 1 to become 4. However, if the training level for the training course is Beginner level, the system is smart enough to detect that the employee already obtained Intermediate level and so the cumulative score will not be incremented by 1. In the case that Stage (3) does not match, then no matter what the qualification of the employee, the cumulative score will not be incremented by 1 as well.

Stage 5) *Matching employee department with training type*
At Stage 5, the accuracy of matching will be enhanced by matching the employee department with the training type. For example, if both the employee department (Information Technology) and training type (Information Technology) matched, the cumulative score from Stage (4) is increased by 1 to become a final score of 5. Finally, a recommendation will be made to the specific employee through email notification. At any stage if there is no match found, then the cumulative score at that stage will not be incremented by 1. Therefore, the range of score shall be from 0-5 and the corresponding recommendation would be 'not recommend', 'slightly recommend', 'recommend', 'strongly recommend', 'highly recommend' and 'truly recommend'.

Fig. 1. The 5 stages of searching, matching and recommending training course

This provides the company the flexibility to tailor their policies to cater for employee training, for example, the company may set the cut-off point at 2, meaning a score of 2 or greater, than only the employee is qualified to attend the recommended training.

Refer to Fig. 2 for detail explanation of the stemming and Boyer-Moore algorithms as applied in this application.

Applying Stemming and Boyer-Moore Algorithms

The Stemming and Boyer-Moore algorithms are applied in the auto search, match and recommend function using an example of training interest from an employee:
"I would like to obtain programing skills. Programing skills can enhance the effectiveness of my work. Although I am from Finance department, I want to learn to code useful programs and build web application."

Stemming algorithm is then applied to change all the words in this training interest sentence to the respective stem words.

Partial pseudo codes for the Stemming algorithm:

```
if (substr($word, -1) == 's') { self::replace($word, 'sses', 'ss')
                OR self::replace($word, 'ies', 'i')
                OR self::replace($word, 'ss', 'ss')
                OR self::replace($word, 's', ''); }
```
e.g. **skills -> skill**
e.g. **programs -> program**

```
if ( preg_match("#$v+#", substr($word, 0, -3)) &&
    self::replace($word, 'ing', '')
    OR preg_match("#$v+#", substr($word, 0, -2)) &&
    self::replace($word, 'ed', ''))
```
e.g. **programming -> program**

```
case 's':
                self::replace($word, 'iveness', 'ive', 0)
                OR self::replace($word, 'fulness', 'ful', 0)
                OR self::replace($word, 'ousness', 'ous', 0)
                OR self::replace($word, 'alism', 'al', 0);
                break;
```
e.g. **effectiveness -> effect**

```
case 'o':
                self::replace($word, 'ization', 'ize', 0)
                OR self::replace($word, 'ation', 'ate', 0)
                OR self::replace($word, 'ator', 'ate', 0);
                break;
```
e.g. **application -> applicate**

```
case 'u':
                self::replace($word, 'ful', '', 0);
                break;
```
e.g. **useful -> use**

The expected output after Stemming algorithm being applied:
"I would like to obtain **program skill**. **Program skill** can enhance the **effect** of my work. Although I am from Finance department, I want to learn to code **use program** and build web **applicate**."

Suppose now there is a training course named "Build web program with Java". Boyer-Moore algorithm is applied to this training name by moving through each character in the name from right to left until the pattern that matches is found with respect to good-suffix and bad-character shifts.

Partial pseudo codes for Boyer-Moore algorithm

```
function badCharHeuristic($str, $size, &$badchar)
                {
                for ($i = 0; $i < 256; $i++)
                    $badchar[$i] = -1;
                for ($i = 0; $i < $size; $i++)
                    $badchar[ord($str[$i])] = $i;
                }
```
Hence, the first matched stemmed word is 'program', and other matched words such as 'web' and 'build' are already in their root forms.

Fig. 2. Applying stemming and Boyer-Moore Algorithms

This web application is tested with different scenarios of employee interest, qualification level, departments and so on. The algorithms work satisfactorily to stem and match, hence the scores are computed correctly and the corresponding recommendation is accurate. Refer to Fig. 3 for the accurate recommendation generated.

Scenario 1

Human Resource Employee, Jane logins to system and added the new training course: Web Application Development in PhP, Expert Level, Training room 01, 2017-03-03, Information Technology

Scenario 2
A normal employee with the following information received "not recommended" notification after the new training course from Scenario 1 is entered into the system.
Tan Chin Sing
Training interest: I always like to equip myself with the latest Administration knowledge that can help in my work
Training Preference: Administration
Training qualification: C++
Qualification level: Expert
Employee department: Information Technology
After going through the auto search, match and recommend function according to the user's inputs, the results are displayed as shown in the screenshot below.

ID	: 204
Name	: Web Application Development in
Training Interest	: Not matched
Training Preference	: Not matched
Training Qualification	: Not matched
Training Qualification Level	: Not matched
Employee Department	: Not matched
Status	: Not Recommended

✖ Remove

Scenario 3

A normal employee with the following information received "truly recommended" notification after the new training course from Scenario 1 is entered into the system.
Chan Wan Kim
Training interest: I always like to equip myself with the latest Information Technology knowledge that can help in my work
Training Preference: Information Technology
Training qualification: Web Application Development in PHP
Qualification level: Intermediate
Employee department: Information Technology
After going through the auto search, match and recommend function according to the user's

ID	: 194
Name	: Web Application Development in
Training Interest	: Matched
Training Preference	: Matched
Training Qualification	: Matched
Training Qualification Level	: Matched
Employee Department	: Matched
Status	: Truly Recommended

✖ Remove

Fig. 3. Recommendations generated to match most suitable training course

4.2   Pattern Matching Using Lookup Table

A web application, the real estate property recommender, aims to provide an easy, convenient and accurate way for users to obtain properties information based on their own preferences. It is implemented with a search, match and recommend function. This function goes through three iterations to search for the right properties in the order of the first, second and third users' preferences. For each iteration, the preferences shall be matched to a pre-defined lookup table and those matched records shall be saved in a temporary table. After the third match, three best matched properties are found to be recommended. This web application saves the potential buyers time and solve the problem or difficulty of users looking through newspaper, property magazine, and even contact the property agent in order to gather information about the property they intend to purchase. Additionally, information gathered through this web application shall ensure timeliness, completeness and accuracy since the property database shall be constantly updated with new and most current information, hence assisting the potential property buyers to make the most appropriate decision regarding the purchase.

Refer to Fig. 4 for step by step process of the auto search, match and recommend function for top-3 best matched properties.

The real estate property auto search, match and recommend function

1.   Users input of preferences
      1.1 Users choose the State and Area. An example of State is 'S' and Area is 'P' with pre-defined numeric values stored in a lookup table as 1 and 2 respectively.
      1.2 Users select 3 out of 5 main categories of criteria as the first, second and third preferences.
      An example of selection:
      First preference, number of bedrooms is two has corresponding numeric values of 3 and 2 respectively. Second preference, property build-up area of less than 3,000 sq.ft. has corresponding numeric values of 2 and 2 respectively from the lookup table.
      Third preference, property type is condominium has corresponding numeric values of 1 and 2 respectively from the lookup table.
2.   The search, match and recommend algorithm will search in the property database to sort out the property matching the State and Area that users have entered. The matching records are stored in a table, "SearchedProperty".
3.   The table "SearchedProperty" is saved in the database as "Propertydata".
4.   Retrieve from Propertydata all records that do not match the user's first preference and delete these
5.   records.
6.   Update the "Propertydata" database.
7.   Retrieve from "Propertydata" all records that do not match the user's second preference and delete these records.
7.   Update the "Propertydata" database.
8.   Retrieve from "Propertydata" all records that do not match the user's third preference and delete these
9.   records.
10.   Update the "Propertydata database which now contains all records that match the first, second and third preferences of the user.11
11.   Display the sorted top 3 best matched properties.

Fig. 4. Auto search, match and recommend function for top-3 best matched properties

This web application is tested with different scenarios of users' preferences and the results show the auto search, match and recommend function is working as expected to produce the three best matching properties according to user's first, second and third preferences. Refer to Fig. 5 for the results of four different scenarios.

Scenario 1	Scenario 2
User's inputs	*User's inputs*
State is S, Area is P.	State is T, Area is Q.
1st preference – Property Price, <$600,000.	1st preference – Property Type, Bungalow.
2nd preference - Property Type, Apartment.	2nd preference - Property Price, >$1,000,000.00.
3rd preference – Number of bedrooms, 3.	3rd preference – Number of bedrooms, 5.

Displayed results (3 best choices)

Displayed results (3 best choices)

Analysis of results

All 3 recommended properties satisfy the user's preferences.

The highest priced apartment is PRIMA with build-up area of 1098 Sq.ft., followed by SRI PIE with build-up area of 853 Sq. ft. and lastly KIA APARTMENT with build-up area of 790 Sq. ft. Based on these results, user can still make the decision whether to sacrifice build-up area with the price. The more the build-up area, the higher is the price but still within the user's criteria of less than RM600,000.

Analysis of results

All 3 recommended properties satisfy the user's preferences.

The highest is ALPA with build-up area of 4031 Sq.ft., followed by RECIDENT with build-up area of 3678 Sq. ft. and lastly the VILLA, with build-up area of 4,300 Sq. ft. Although the highest priced bungalow does not have the largest built-up area, but it has 1 extra bathroom as compared to the other two. Based on these results, user can select the best choice according to his/her affordable budget.

Scenario 3	Scenario 4
User's inputs	*User's inputs*
State is U, Area is R.	State is V, Area is S.
1st preference – Property Build-up Area, <3000 Sq ft.	1st preference – Property Type, Semi-Detached House
2nd preference - Property Type, Terrace House.	2nd preference - Property Area, <4500 Sq.ft.
3rd preference –Property Price, <$800,000.	3rd preference –Property Price, <$600,000.

Displayed results (3 best choices)

Displayed results (3 best choices)

Analysis of results

All 3 recommended properties satisfy the user's preferences.

The highest priced is SONATA with the least build-up area of 2300 Sq.ft., followed by SIEERA with greatest build-up area of 2573 Sq. ft. and lastly NUSA, with build-up area of 2,500 Sq. ft.

Although both the highest and the lowest priced terrace house have 4 bedrooms, the difference in price is more than $200,000. This may be due to it is located in a new housing area or the internal furnishing is in good conditions and so on. The user can contact the sales agent to request for an on-site visit to the mentioned properties before making the final decision.

Analysis of results

All 3 recommended properties satisfy the user's preferences.

The highest priced is TIARA with 5 bedrooms and build-up area of 3,200 Sq.ft. The second highest priced is PERDANA which also has 5 bedrooms but a built-up area of 2,600 Sq.ft only. The lowest priced is RESTU which has 4 bedrooms but the largest built-up area of 3,600 Sq. ft.

To sacrifice one bedroom but gaining 400 Sq. ft. by choosing RESTU instead of TIARA the user can gain a saving of greater than $120,000.

Fig. 5. Results of three different scenarios for best matched properties

4.3   Image Matching Using Color Scheme

The personal photo album organizer, is a web application developed with the aim to enhance the users experience in storing and retrieving photos and videos in the Cloud storage. It has functionality that allows users to upload and download photos or videos through a web page easily using Internet access. It allows the users to search for their photos and videos by matching keywords, date and time, and images. This web application saves the users time and solve the problem or difficulty of users looking up a photo or video one by one in order to locate the specific photo or video. Particularly, there is an image matching function whereby images are matched using a color scheme algorithm. This thus provides the users with another convenient way to store and retrieve photos besides using just the keyword, date and time searching and matching.

Refer to Fig. 6 for step by step process of the color scheme image matching function.

The color scheme image matching function

1. This function accepts photos or images in JPG and PNG format only.
2. Resize the image and form into 8x8 square.
3. Store the 8x8 square image into a temporary folder.
4. Function "ColorMeanValue"
   - two nested FOR loops will each run through 8 times to sum up each pixel's color value.
   - results returned is the mean of all pixel's color values and a list of all pixel's color values.
5. Function "Bits"
   -a FOR loop to go through 64 times to compare each pixel's color value with the mean color value computed in step 4.
   -if a pixel's color value is bigger than the mean color value, return 1, else return 0.
6. Call the main function "Compare"
   // images stored in the database will be compared one by one with the one stored in the temporary folder.
   -each image in the database to be compared have to be resized into 8x8 square before comparison.
   -filter both images' grayscale.
   -Call function "ColorMeanValue" and function "Bits".
   -a FOR loop will run 64 times (8x8=64) to calculate the out-of-range distance for a pair of corresponding bit values.
   -each time a pair of corresponding bit values are not equaled and out-of-range distance will be incremented by 1.
   -the bigger the out-of-range distance, the most likely they are not the same images.
   - the smaller the out-of-range distance means the images are more similar in the color ranges.
   -a perfect match of the two photos will be that each pair of corresponding bit values are equal and zero out-of-range distance is returned.

Fig. 6. The color scheme image matching function

This web application is tested with different color images and the results show the search and match color scheme algorithm is working as expected to display the correct images. Refer to Fig. 7 for the results of four different scenarios.

Scenario 1
To find Google logo in the database.

Displayed results

The color scheme function displays those images containing the google logo colors (red, orange, green, blue, white). However, the one with perfect match (out-of-range distance is zero) will be displayed as the first image.

Results analysis
Those images with black and white colors are also displayed is because the image is compared as 8 x 8 square with the four corners surrounding the image always in white color. These images with their out-of-range distance as compared to the google logo are (left to right, top to bottom) are 0, 15, 16, 23, 16, 20, 21. Thus, the greater the out-of-range distance between the two images the greater the chance that they are entirely different.

Scenario 3
To find an exact matched image.

Displayed results
The perfect matched image is displayed.

Results analysis
The search function displays the exact matched image with out-of-range distance of zero. No other image in the database has the closest match in color range with it.

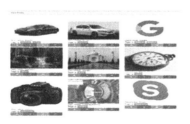

Scenario 2
To find an image with mainly black and white colors.

Displayed results
The matched image is displayed as the first image with out-of-range distance of zero.

Results analysis
The searched image is found together with another image with mainly black and white colors (white color contains in the four corners of the 8 x 8 square).
However, the out-of-range distance for these two images is 24 indicating that indeed they are two entirely different images.

Scenario 4
No matched image found. Image used is two toy cars.

Displayed results
No image is found.

Results analysis

After the search by image using the color scheme function, the display shows no matched image found.

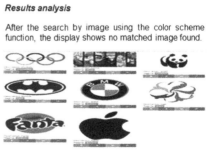

The displayed result is correct because actually the image is not stored in the database.

Fig. 7. Results of four different scenarios for correct matched color images (Color figure online)

5 Conclusion and Future Work

As can be seen from the three web applications that pattern matching techniques incorporated with intelligent contextual data analytics are able to retrieve timely and accurate information based on users' inputs, thus assisting in decision making. Future work shall include evaluation of these applications over the Cloud environment using real-time transactions for efficiency measure such as time and load performances.

References

1. Google Search Statistics. www.internetlivestats.com/google-search-statistics/. Accessed 14 Dec 2017
2. YouTube Press Statistics. https://www.youtube.com/yt/bout/press/. Accessed 14 Dec 2017
3. Mukherjee, S., Shaw, R.: Big data-concepts, applications, challenges and future scope. Int. J. Adv. Res. Comput. Commun. Eng. 2, 66–74 (2016)
4. Batarseh, F.A., Latif, E.A.: Assessing the quality of service using big data analytics with application to healthcare. Big Data Res. 4, 13–24 (2016)
5. Elgendy, N., Elragal, A.: Big data analytics in support of the decision making process. Proc. Comput. Sci. 100, 1071–1084 (2016)
6. Etq. http://www.etq.com/employee-training-software/. Accessed 1 July 2016
7. Halogen software. http://www.halogensoftware.com/ae/products/learning-management. Accessed 1 July 2016
8. Intelex. http://www.intelex.com/products/applications/training-management. Accessed 1 July 2016
9. iProperty.com. https://www.iproperty.com.my/. Accessed 1 Aug 2016
10. Propertyguru.com. https://www.propertyguru.com.my/. Accessed 1 Aug 2016
11. Propwall.my. https://propwall.my/. Accessed 1 Aug 2016
12. Dropbox (2015). https://www.dropbox.com/home. Accessed 22 Nov 2016
13. TinyPic (2011). http://tinypic.com/. Accessed 22 Nov 2016
14. Google Photos (2015). https://photos.google.com/. Accessed 3 Sept 2016
15. Karaa, W.B.A.: A new stemmer to improve information retrieval. Int. J. Netw. Secur. Appl. 5(4), 143–154 (2013)
16. Paik, J.H., Mitra, M., Parui, S.K., Järvelin, K.: GRAS: an effective and efficient stemming algorithm for information retrieval. ACM Trans. Inf. Syst. 29(4), 1–24 (2011). Article 19
17. Shama, D.: Stemming algorithms: a comparative study and their analysis. Int. J. Appl. Inf. Syst. 4(3), 7–12 (2012)
18. Kumar, R., Mansotra, V.: Applications of stemming algorithms in information retrieval-a review. Int. J. Adv. Res. Comput. Sci. Softw. Eng. 6(2), 418–423 (2016)
19. Wilett, P.: The porter stemming algorithm: then and now. Program 40(3), 219–223 (2006)
20. Boyer, R.S., Moore, J.S.: A fast string searching algorithm. Commun. ACM Mag. 20(10), 702–772 (1977)
21. Lecrog, T.: A variation on the Boyer-Moore algorithm. Theor. Comput. Sci. 92, 119–144 (1992)
22. Watson, B.W., Watson, R.E.: A Boyer-Moore-style algorithm for regular expression pattern matching. Sci. Comput. Program. 48(2–3), 99–117 (2003)

23. Danvy, O., Rohde, H.K.: On obtaining the Boyer-Moore string-matching algorithm by partial evaluation. Inf. Process. Lett. **99**, 158–162 (2006)
24. Xiong, Z.: A composite Boyer-Moore Algorithm for the string matching problem. In: The 11th International Conference on Parallel and Distributed Computing, Applications and Technologies, pp. 492–496 (2010)
25. Yuan, L.: An improved algorithm for Boyer-Moore string matching in Chinese information processing. In: The 11th International Conference on Computer Science and Service System, pp. 182–184 (2011)

A Machine Learning Model for Detection and Prediction of Cloud Quality of Service Violation

Tong-Sheng Wong, Gaik-Yee Chan[(✉)], and Fang-Fang Chua

Faculty of Computing and Informatics, Multimedia University,
63000 Cyberjaya, Malaysia
gychan@mmu.edu.my

Abstract. Cloud services connect user with cloud computing platform where services range from Infrastructure as a Service, Software as a Service and Platform as a Service. It is important for Cloud Service Provider to provide reliable cloud services which are fast in performance and to predict possible service violation before any issue emerges so then remedial action can be taken. In this paper, we therefore experiment with five different machine learning algorithms namely Support Vector Machine, Random Forest, Naïve Bayes, Neural Network, and k-Nearest Neighbors for the detection and prediction of cloud quality of service violations in terms of response time and throughput. Experimental results show that the model created using SVM incorporated with 16 derived cloud quality of service violation rules has consistent accuracy of greater than 99%. With this machine learning model coupled with 16 decision rules, the Cloud Service Provider shall be able to know before hand, whether violation of services based on response time and throughput is occurring. When transactions tend to go beyond the threshold limits, system administrator shall be alerted to take necessary preventive measures to bring the system back to normal conditions. This shall reduce the chance for violation to occur, hence mitigating lose or costly penalty.

Keywords: Cloud services · Machine learning · Quality of service violations

1 Introduction

Cloud computing could shape how the internet and hardware services look in the future. Although there have been many formal definitions by both the industry and academia, the one provided by NIST [1] is being used widely in the Cloud Computing community. As defined in [1], Cloud Computing provides convenient uses of resources that could be shared and configurable through the demand of network accesses. These resources are networks, servers, storage, applications, and services which could be provisioned and released with least interaction from the service provider and management effort. Generally, Cloud services are offered through services models such as Infrastructure as a Service (IaaS), Software as a Service (SaaS) or Platform as a Service (PaaS). Currently, Cloud Service Provider (CSP) such as Amazon EC2, Google Cloud Platform, Microsoft Azure do provide these Cloud services to businesses or individuals

© Springer International Publishing AG, part of Springer Nature 2018
O. Gervasi et al. (Eds.): ICCSA 2018, LNCS 10960, pp. 498–513, 2018.
https://doi.org/10.1007/978-3-319-95162-1_34

on a pay-on-use basis. These two parties, the Cloud users and CSP are therefore bounded by the Service Level Agreement (SLA). This SLA has to be formally defined before services are deployed or provided so as to ensure CSPs are constantly providing trustworthy and smooth services to the Cloud users. Additionally, to prevent quality of service violations, this SLA serves as a monitoring tool to guide the performance, availability and quality of service of the CSPs [2]. Any SLA or cloud service violation could incur heavy cost for both the CSP and Cloud user.

The SLA contains important contents which might lead to how the cloud services could be improved in the future. One key element between a Cloud user and CSP in the SLA is the Service Level Objectives (SLO). This SLO composes of one or more Quality-of-Service (QoS) metrics agreed by both the CSP and Cloud user for measuring the performance of the services provided. Example of SLOs' measurable cloud metrics are throughput, availability, reliability, and response time [3]. In order for these metrics to be made known in a transparent way for both parties to enable detection and prediction of QoS violation, there is an urgent need to find an intelligent model for such purpose. Consequently, in this paper, we carry out research with the aim to identify the most efficient and effective machine learning algorithm for detection and prediction of cloud service violations on throughput and response time over a certain time period. We carry out experiments with five different machine learning algorithms such as Support Vector Machine (SVM), Random Forest (RF), Naïve Bayes (NB), Neural Network (NN), and *k*-Nearest Neighbors (*k*-NN) over five datasets from WS-DREAM [4]. Each of these five datasets is split into two partitions, 70% for training and 30% for testing. Classification accuracy is computed using R version 3.4.3 [5], an open source programming language for statistical computing, on each algorithm and their performances are summarized and tabulated for analysis to determine the optimum model.

The remainder of this paper is organized as follows: Sect. 2 presents background study and related works, Sect. 3 discusses the five machine learning algorithms used for predicting cloud service violation, Sect. 4 presents our proposed approach in determining an optimum model for cloud service violations, Sect. 5 analyses the performances of the models and Sect. 6 concludes with discussion on future works.

2 Background Study and Related Works

As technology keeps innovating and becoming more complex throughout the decades, cloud services provided by IaaS, SaaS and PaaS have increased in number with the price for cloud storages decreasing. For example, a CSP may offer as low as 0.06 US Dollar per GB of storage. Due to this price lowering competition but yet maintaining the quality of service, there is a need for CSPs to overcome SLA violations in order to avoid further penalty. Vigorous research in detecting and predicting cloud service violations is, therefore, on-going in recent years. For example, research in [6] has proposed a Cloud Application SLA Violation Detection (CASViD) architecture for detection of SLA violation at application layer. The architecture has tools for allocating, scheduling and deploying cloud resources as well. However, this architecture has no SLA violation prediction feature. Similarly, another research in [7], proposes a SLA–based violation detection mechanism based on the number of allocated processors in the cloud platform. The mechanism checks on the number of processors allocated by broker to client with the number of processes requested by the client's jobs to detect any violation for the SLA.

For SLA prediction using machine learning approach, the research in [8] proposes a prediction model to predict SLA violation during runtime. In this research, inputs to the model could be the service composition or quality of used services. A machine learning regression technique is then used for training data captured from historical process instances. Research in [9] proposes a model using time series analysis based SVM for regression to predict SLA violation. The dataset with values of response time and throughput are collected by WEKA data mining tool on a cloud service server. For experimental purpose, the first 90 days' data was used for training and the 30 days' in advance data was used for testing. This prediction model is able to produce greater than 80% prediction accuracy. However, this prediction model has limitation that it is not able to scale to real world data which is much voluminous and volatile in nature.

The research in [10] proposes a SLA violation prediction model with Naïve Bayesian Classifier and the training datasets are obtained from WS-DREAM Dataset with only response time as the input value. The model is able to make a decent score in mean square error (MSE) with response time value as the only feature. Another Bayesian model is proposed by researchers in [11] for predicting host load using Google's one- month trace data collected through thousands of machines running up to 16 h. This prediction model uses CPU and memory as input metrics. Researchers in [12] conduct an experiment to overcome challenges of predicting SLA violations. According to these researchers, SLA violation is a rare event in the real world with only 20% probability of occurrence. Hence, classification or detection task shall be difficult. Subsequently, they use Google Cloud Cluster trace as the dataset to experiment with various machine learning techniques and find that Random Forest classifier with SMOTE-ENN resampling method provides the best performance with accuracy of 99%.

Motivated by these researches and as there is still room for improvement using the various machine learning algorithms, we therefore carry out research with five machine learning algorithms namely, SVM, RF, NB, NN and k-NN. This research thus aims to determine an optimum machine learning model for the detection and prediction of cloud QoS violation.

3   Machine Learning Algorithms

Machine learning refers to the ability of computers on learning while detecting meaningful patterns of data [13]. Computer learning can be supervised learning and unsupervised learning. For supervised learning, input and output variables are fed to the machine learning algorithms to learn patterns. This supervised machine learning approach is used in our research to work on multiclass classification problem. Multiclass classification problem is the logical extension of binary classification where data are classified into range of different classes instead of only two classes [13]. The following sub sections discuss five machine learning algorithms used in determining an optimum model for the detection and prediction of cloud QoS violations.

3.1 Support Vector Machine (SVM)

Support Vector Machine (SVM) is a machine learning method for regression and classification that could be used to solve problems such as optimization, theoretical convergence, multiclass classification, probability estimates, and parameter selection [14]. Research in [15] has found that for SVM multiclass classification, "one-against-one" or "pairwise coupling" seems to be a more competitive approach. Under this "pairwise coupling", the sum of $k\,(k-1)/2$ will determine the total number of classifiers and k is the number of classes. For two-class classification problem, each classifier would train data based on two classes, from i^{th} to j^{th} classes, for example. This classification problem with two classes could be solved by Eqs. 1–3.

$$min_{wij;bij;\xi ij} \frac{1}{2}\left(w^{ij}\right)^{T} w^{ij} + C \sum_{t} \xi_{t}^{ij} \tag{1}$$

$$subject\ to \quad \left(w^{ij}\right)^{T}\varphi\left(x_{t}\right)+b^{ij} \geq 1 - \xi_{t}^{ij}, \quad if\ x_{t}\ in\ the\ ith\ class \tag{2}$$

$$subject\ to \quad \left(w^{ij}\right)^{T}\varphi\left(x_{t}\right)+b^{ij} \leq -1 + \xi_{t}^{ij}, \quad if\ x_{t}\ in\ the\ jth\ class$$
$$where\ \xi_{t}^{ij} \geq 0. \tag{3}$$

Note that $C > 0$ represents penalty parameter while $\varphi(x_{t})$ maps x_{t} into a higher dimensional space. Therefore, this dual problem in (1) could be solved when vector variable, w exhibits high dimensionality, where the number of variables and data are the same in the two classes.

Generally, the classification of any unknown pattern goes according to the maximum voting, where each SVM votes for one class. For example, the "Max Win" voting strategy that says if x belongs to i^{th} class, then increase i^{th} class vote by one else add that vote to j^{th} class. This shall finally lead to predicting x to belong to the class having the greatest count of votes. When two classes have the same number of votes, the smaller indexed class shall be selected.

A point to note is that SVM requires user-defined parameters with appropriate values combining with the right kernel in order to provide optimum performance. According to [14], the Radial Basis Function (RBF) or Gaussian kernel is the first choice for multiclass classification. While linear kernel is limited by its ability to handle cases where the relation between class-label and the attributes is non-linear, the RBF kernel has the ability to map non-linear samples into a higher dimensional space. RBF kernel is defined in Eq. (4).

$$K_{RBF}(x,x') = \exp\left[\gamma\|x - x'\|^{2}\right] \tag{4}$$

RBF kernel consists of a penalty parameter C with exact performance as linear kernel. Additionally, γ sets the width of the bell shape curve, which represents the "spread" of the kernel. In other words, the greater the value of γ, the narrower the bell shape curve. Contrary, the lower the value of γ will result in a wide bell shape curve where the vector points distance against one and another are further apart.

3.2 Naïve Bayes

Naïve Bayes classifier is a powerful algorithm that performs classification and prediction based on Maximum A Posteriori (MAP). According to [16], this algorithm
determines the class with the highest probability to be the most likely wanted class
using Eq. (5).

$$P(C_k|x) = \frac{P(x|c_k)P(C_k)}{P(x)} \tag{5}$$

When given a dataset with k number of classes as $(C_1, \ldots, C_k)$, and n unique feature
$x = \{x_1, \ldots, x_n\}$, $P(x|c_k)$ and $P(c_k)$ are the likelihood and class prior probability
respectively. $P(C_k|x)$, the posterior probability, gives updated calculation on prior
probability based on observed data and $P(x)$ is the predictor prior probability, a constant which is identical for all classes. Using Naïve Bayes classifier on multiclass
classification could result in complicated computation. This is because the classifier
makes the assumption that in a given class, each unique feature such as $x_1, x_2, \ldots, x_n$ are
independent of each other.

3.3 Neural Network

Neural network mimics the action of the human brain and nerve system and consists of
a pool of processing elements that send signals to each other over a number of weighted
connections [17]. Neural networks are adaptive to changing environment by learning
on their own initiative. For multiclass classification, multilayer perceptron is the most
frequently used neural network [17]. In a multilayer perceptron neural network with
feed-forward structure, the signals are transmitted from input layer to output layer in
only one direction with no looping [18]. For a multilayer perceptron classifier, sets of
data with features are fed as input and the weights of each neural net in the network are
adjusted in the hidden layer to output the target classes. Using backpropagation
algorithm for training, the network would turn into a better model as weights of each
neural nets in the network is adjusted based on propagation error in the real outputs
compared with the network target outputs.

3.4 k-Nearest Neighbor (k-NN)

The k-NN is an effective and simple non-parametric classification algorithm used to
classify unknown item and predict the target class by finding the nearest neighboring
class [19]. Refer to Fig. 1 for a graphical illustration of k-NN classification model. As
shown in Fig. 1, the unknown item is represented as the shape of a triangle, while
Class A and Class B are represented as the shape of rectangle and circle respectively.
To classify the unknown item, there is a need to measure distances from the unknown
to every training data by distance measures, such as the Euclidean distance. To find the
nearest neighbor is by ranking the distances between the unknown with the other

classes. As seen from Fig. 1, the inner most circle representing k = 3 nearest neighbors contain one item from Class B and two items from Class A. By considering this example and use voting to determine the target class, *k*-NN, therefore predicts that the triangular item belongs to Class A having two votes instead of Class B having only one vote. On the other hand, if k = 5, the prediction would be the item belongs to Class B with three votes instead of Class A with two votes. Hence, the value of k needs to be determined using cross validation when using *k*-NN.

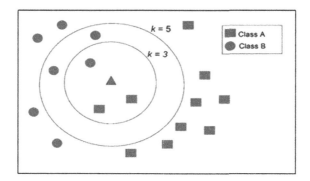

Fig. 1. Graphical illustration example of *k*-Nearest Neighbor (*k*-NN)

3.5   Random Forest

Random Forest is an ensemble machine learning algorithm based on combination of "n" numbers of randomly created trees. The higher the number of decision trees created, the more robust is the algorithm to lead to greater prediction accuracy [20]. The decision tree is the main building block for random forest. The root of the decision tree is split into internal nodes based on defined rules. Splitting is repeated for each internal node until the leaf nodes of all branches of the tree are formed. Random Forest classifies items by constructing "n" number of decision trees by means of bagging. For predicting the output class, random forest uses the concept of majority voting to select the class that has the highest vote from "n" number of trees constructed.

4   Proposed Approach

This section discusses our proposed approach in determining an optimum model for cloud QoS violations among five different machine learning algorithms. An over view of the approach is shown in Fig. 2 (read from left to right, top to bottom following steps 1–8 in sequence).

Referring to Fig. 2 step 1, we make use of WS-DREAM [4] data set in our experiments to determine an optimum multiclass classification model for detection and prediction of cloud QoS violation. WS-DREAM [4] data set as generated by research in [21] contains traces of real-world QoS evaluation results from 142 users on 4,532 Web

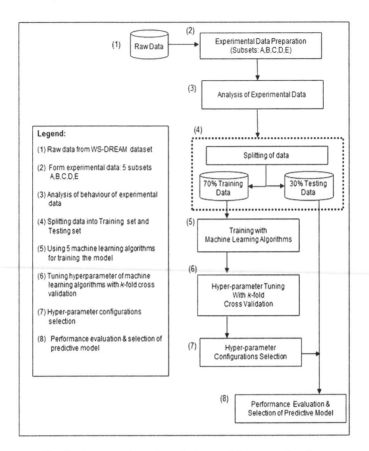

Fig. 2. An over view of predictive model construction flow

Services over 64 different time slots. WS-DREAM data set reflects Web Service in service computing and cloud computing. Every instance of WS-DREAM consists of three features such as the SLO metrics of response time in seconds, throughput in kilobytes per second (kbps), and Time Slot ID representing the 64 different time slots in which each time slot serves a time zone with 15-min time interval. Response time measures the time interval between when a request is made by user and when the response is received by the client, while throughput calculates the amount of workload per unit of time over the measurement period [22].

For our experiments (Fig. 2, step 2), we selected from WS-DREAM [4] data set, 50 users on 5 different servers on 64 different time slots and form into five sub datasets, namely data set A, B, C, D and E. Each of these sub datasets contains a total of 3200 measurable values of response time with corresponding throughput values. Since we are implementing supervised learning technique, all data shall be labeled with joint decision rules which will be discussed at subsequent paragraphs of the paper. These five sub data sets are again divided into two portions, one with 70% of the data as training dataset and another with 30% of the data as testing data set. The splitting of datasets into two portions (Fig. 2, step 4) is to cater for model training and hyper parameter tuning using 5-fold cross validation based on 70% training data while the remaining 30% of data is used as testing for model classification and prediction accuracy.

Before identification of any cloud service violation, there is a need to determine the normal ranges of values of QoS based on SLOs metrics through SLA. However, due to the lack of access on any SLA documents, hence, for our research and experiments, we first have to perform data analysis on our five data sets in order to determine the normal ranges of both response time and throughput as non-violation condition or threshold values for cloud services. We apply normal distribution for determining range of values for throughputs, while cumulative frequency distribution (CDF) technique is used for determining the range of values for response time. Refer to Fig. 2, step 3, the analysis of the dataset features for the five data sets A, B, C, D, and E are tabulated as shown in Table 1.

Table 1. Analysis of dataset features in datasets A–E

Features	Dataset	Min	Mean	Max	Standard deviation
Response time (second)	A	0.376	1.400	20.000	2.307
	B	0.538	1.558	20.000	2.468
	C	0.275	0.898	20.000	1.721
	D	0.313	1.297	20.000	2.246
	E	0.433	1.676	20.000	2.443
Throughput (kbps)	A	0.010	0.577	0.992	0.273
	B	0.001	0.648	0.980	0.276
	C	0.003	0.652	1.134	0.312
	D	0.001	0.629	1.087	0.252
	E	0.001	1.463	2.764	0.722
Time slot ID (0–63) (a slot has 15-min interval)	A–E	0.00	31.50	63	18.476

By just looking at the values of response time and throughput over 64-time slots of Table 1 may not be able to make any conclusive relationships between response time and throughput. Subsequently, scatterplots of the five datasets based on response time and throughput are drawn and all these scatterplots behave similarly as shown in Fig. 3 which is showing one of the sample scatterplot for data set A.

As can be seen from Fig. 3, the longer the response time, the lower would be the throughput values. Vice versa, the higher the throughput, the shorter would be the response time values. Hence response time and throughput are inversely proportional to each other [22]. Consequently, long response time or low throughput values which are over the threshold limits shall cause cloud QoS violations.

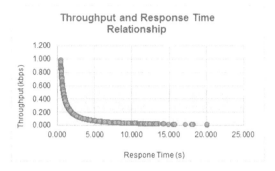

Fig. 3. Scatterplot of data set A based on response time and throughput

In order to find more meaningful relationships between throughput and response time over their ranges of values, response time and throughput are tagged with linguistic terms according to the ranges of values as shown in Table 2 based on sample data set A.

Table 2. Category and range of values for data set A

Response time linguistic category	Response time (range of values)	Response time (# of transactions)	Response time (# of transactions in %)
Short	0 – 0.439	585	18.28%
Normal	0.440 – 2.553	2230	69.69%
Long	2.554 – 6.014	266	8.31%
Very Long	6.015 – 20.00	119	3.72%

a

Throughput linguistic category	Throughput (range of values)	Throughput (# of transactions)	Throughput (# of transactions in %
High	0.850 – 0.992	585	18.28%
Normal	0.304 – 0.849	1956	61.13%
Low	0.032 – 0.303	623	19.47%
Very Low	0.000 – 0.031	36	1.13%

b

As can be seen from Table 2 (Table 2a for response time: Column 4 Row 3 and Table 2b for throughput: Column 4 Row 3) that majority (more than 60%) of the transactions are in the normal range while the lowest ends contribute towards to less than 4% (Table 2a, Column 4 Row 5 and Table 2b, Column 4 Row 5) which are those out of threshold limits transactions or transactions in violation. This is considered to be normal behavior for both response time and throughput values. In order to link response time and throughput to get joint decision on QoS violation, the outcomes of decision or joint decision rules are categorized into four types, namely, certainly no violation, normal, probably violation and certainly violation as shown in Table 3. This categorization goes according to the inverse relationship of response time and throughput.

According to Table 3, all together there are 16 decision outcomes or joint decision rules depending on the combined category of response time and throughput. The following section explains how these rules could be interpreted.

When response time is short while throughput is high (Table 3, Rule 1), certainly there is no QoS violation under this condition. For rules 2-4 when either response time or throughput is in normal range and none is in the very long or very low zone, then decision outcome is that they transacted in a normal condition. Refer to Table 3, Rules 5–9 indicate that either response time is in the long zone or throughput is in the low zone. This means these transactions have the tendency to go beyond the threshold limits, so decision is tagged to probably violation to create necessary alerts. The condition for certainly violation (Table 3, Rules 10–16) is that response time is either in the very long category or throughput is in the very low category which is out of the threshold limits.

Table 3. Joint decision outcome for response time and throughput

Rule #	Response time category	Throughput category	Joint decision rules
1	Short	High	Certainly no violation
2	Short	Normal	Normal
3	Normal	High	Normal
4	Normal	Normal	Normal
5	Short	Low	Probably violation
6	Normal	Low	Probably violation
7	Long	High	Probably violation
8	Long	Normal	Probably violation
9	Long	Low	Probably violation
10	Short	**Very low**	**Certainly violation**
11	Normal	**Very low**	**Certainly violation**
12	Long	**Very low**	**Certainly violation**
13	**Very long**	High	**Certainly violation**
14	**Very long**	Normal	**Certainly violation**
15	**Very long**	Low	**Certainly violation**
16	**Very long**	**Very low**	**Certainly violation**

To analyze further these datasets after being labelled with joint decision rules, statistical data displaying distribution of each category in percentage is shown in Table 4.

Table 4. Analysis of target classes for each dataset

Class	Dataset				
	A	B	C	D	E
Certainly no violation	585	375	446	546	544
	18.28%	11.72%	13.96%	17.06%	17.00%
Normal	1956	2213	2267	2046	1963
	61.13%	**69.16%**	**70.84%**	**63.94%**	**61.34%**
Probably violation	540	322	279	475	571
	16.88%	10.06%	8.72%	14.85%	17.84%
Certainly violation	119	290	208	133	122
	3.72%	**9.06%**	**6.50%**	**4.16%**	**3.81%**

As can be seen from Table 4 that the number of transaction belonging to the normal decision outcome is still in the majority of over 60% (Table 4, Row 6: 61.13%–70.84%) while the out of threshold limit transactions or transactions in QoS violation are still in minority of less than 10% (Table 4, Row 10: 3.72%–9.06%). The reason for quite a wide gap between these percentages might be due to that these data from WS-DREAM were gathered from different servers with different configurations in terms of processing speed and memory. Nevertheless, they show consistency across all the 64-time slots thus indicating fitness for use in our further experiments.

Refer to Fig. 2 (steps 4–7), the five datasets of A, B, C, D and E are split into two portions with 70% of the data as one portion as training dataset while the rest of 30% of data serve as the testing dataset. Five different machine learning algorithms such as Support Vector Machine (SVM), Random Forest (RF), Naïve Bayes (NB), Neural Network (NN), and k-Nearest Neighbors (k-NN) are used in our experiments in determining the optimum model. All our experiments are carried out using the tool, R version 3.4.3 [5], under the environment with hardware specification of Intel Core i5-4460 3.20 GHz with 8 GB of RAM on a 64-bit based operating system. This tool comes with many different library functions or packages that could be used mainly for training and prediction based on machine learning algorithms such as RF, NN, SVM with RBF Kernel, NB, and k-NN. Likewise, we make use of the library functions contained in [5] to perform training on our five datasets for our proposed machine learning model.

First, the training dataset has to be validated or undergo hyper-parameter tuning using k-fold cross validation. This step is important for determining the most suitable parameters for our proposed model. The training and validation data will be partitioned into k equal sized subset where each subset will go through a process of validation to evaluate the accuracy of the model, while the remaining $(k - 1)$ equal sized subset is used to train the model. The process stops when the last subset has been used exactly once for validation.

Our experiments use 5-fold cross validation for tuning of each model. Due to the wide range of possible values for hyper-parameters, selection of which hyper-parameters to be used for each algorithm are evaluated based on Area Under the Curve (AUC) values generated using 5-fold cross validation process. Hyper-parameter configurations that resulted with the best mean AUC value (refer to Table 5) will get chosen for building the final model. This thus resulted in Table 6 showing the best hyper-parameter configurations used for each datasets of each machine learning algorithms based on the 5-fold cross validation.

Table 5. Best mean AUC values

Dataset	Average AUC value				
	SVM with RBF kernel	Naïve Bayes	Neural network	k-Nearest Neighbor (k-NN)	Random forest
A	0.9998	0.9999	0.9999	0.9697	1.0000
B	0.9982	0.9968	0.9982	0.9324	1.0000
C	0.9984	0.9998	0.9997	0.9485	1.0000
D	0.9958	0.9997	0.9999	0.9722	1.0000
E	0.9976	0.9999	0.9999	0.9856	1.0000

After the best set of hyper-parameters for each algorithm on each dataset is confirmed as shown in Table 6, the next step (refer to Fig. 2, step 8) is to evaluate the performance of each algorithm based on these hyper-parameters for each testing datasets of A, B, C, D, and E. Details of this step is explained in the next section, Sect. 5.

Table 6. Best hyper-parameter configurations

Dataset	Machine learning algorithms					Description for hyperparameters
	SVM with RBF kernel	Naïve Bayes	Neural network	k-NN	Random forest	
A	Cost = 2^{10}, gamma = 2^{-1}	L = 0	S = 5, decay = 0	k = 5	Ntree = 500	**Cost:** Cost of misclassification
B	Cost = 2^{10}, gamma = 2^{-4}	L = 0	S = 5, decay = 1e−04	k = 5	Ntree = 500	**Gamma:** Inverse of the standard deviation **Laplace:** Values to
C	Cost = 2^{10}, gamma = 2	L = 0	S = 3, decay = 0	k = 5	Ntree = 500	control Laplace smoothing **Size S:** Number of neurons
D	Cost = 2^{10}, gamma = 2^{-7}	L = 0	S = 5, decay = 1e−04	k = 5	Ntree = 500	on hidden layer **Decay:** Weight decay **Size k:** Number of
E	Cost = 2^{10}, gamma = 2^{-7}	L = 0	S = 5, decay = 1e−04	k = 5	Ntree = 500	neighbours **Ntree:** Number of random trees generated

5   Performance Evaluation and Analysis of Results

To measure the classification and prediction accuracy of the predictive models, we make use of three metrics, namely, Confusion Matrix for Multi-class, Receiver Operating Characteristics (ROC) and Cohen's kappa value.

According to [23], a multiclass classification model can be evaluated and assessed based on confusion matrix in terms of accuracy, the fraction of correct predictions over total number of instances evaluated; precision, the fraction of true positive over the sum of true positive and false positive; recall, the fraction of true positive over the sum of true positive and false negative; and the F1-score, a measurement that conveys the mean or balance between recall and precision.

Another metric that could be used for performance evaluation of the model is by means of a receiver operating characteristics (ROC) graph. This is a technique that applies visualization, organization and selection of classifiers based on performances [24]. The area under the ROC graph or AUC, represents the probability that a randomly selected positive instance is scored higher than a randomly selected negative instance. The value of AUC ranges between 0–1.0, hence, the higher value closer to 1.0 represents almost perfect prediction while values lower than 0.5 represent unsatisfactory or almost failed classification.

Cohen's kappa value can also be used as a measure of accuracy for multiclass classification model. Cohen's kappa is a robust statistic useful for either inter rater or inter rater reliability testing [25]. The kappa value can range from −1 to +1, with 0 representing the amount of agreement that can be obtained from random chance. Hence, positive values closer to 1 indicate perfect agreement between the feature and target classes of the multiclass classification model, while values below 0 indicate no agreement between the features and target classes.

For our experiment, the per-class metrics such as precision, recall, F1-score and AUC are averaged over total number of classes resulting in an averaged metrics giving equal weight to the classification of each class.

The five machine learning algorithms except for RF, based on the hyper-parameters as suggested in Table 6, are evaluated through hyper-parameter tuning with 5-fold cross validation using testing datasets of A, B, C, D, and E. Our research goal is to find an optimum model and not a perfect one with 100% accuracy. Therefore, RF algorithm is excluded as it is able to achieve a mean AUC value of 1.0 for all the five datasets. This might be due to it is too sensitive to the many repetitive data instances leading to over fitting issue. Nevertheless, the results of accuracy performances of four other algorithms are summarized and tabulated as shown in Table 7.

Refer to Table 7, it can be seen that the average accuracy measure for SVM with RBF Kernel ranges from 0.9897–0.9963 (Table 7, Row 7); for NB from 0.9664–0.9876 (Table 7, Row 13); for NN from 0.9477–0.9913 (Table 7, Row 19) and for k-NN from 0.7775–0.9094 (Table 7, Row 25). Therefore, the highest accuracy value achieved by SVM with RBF Kernel is 0.9963 which out performs NB, NN and k-NN. Hence, SVM with RBF Kernel together with the 16 derived joint decision rules for cloud QoS violation on response time and throughput becomes our proposed machine learning model.

Table 7. Performance evaluation of the 5 machine learning models

Machine learning algorithms	Dataset	Accuracy	Precision	Recall	F1-score	AUC	Kappa
SVM with RBF kernel	A	0.9959	0.9884	0.9873	0.9878	0.9931	0.9909
	B	0.9959	0.9918	0.9918	0.9918	0.9950	0.9915
	C	0.9938	0.9846	0.9866	0.9864	0.9924	0.9864
	D	0.9990	0.9983	0.9926	0.9954	0.9962	0.9980
	E	0.9969	0.9965	0.9904	0.9934	0.9944	0.9942
	Average	**0.9963**	**0.9919**	**0.9897**	**0.9908**	**0.9942**	**0.9922**
Naïve Bayes	A	0.9835	0.9618	0.9868	0.9741	0.9911	0.9644
	B	0.9876	0.9754	0.9779	0.9766	0.9864	0.9745
	C	0.9835	0.9618	0.9868	0.9741	0.9911	0.9644
	D	0.9772	0.9674	0.9635	0.9654	0.9783	0.9573
	E	0.9845	0.9778	0.9865	0.9821	0.9909	0.9716
	Average	**0.9833**	**0.9688**	**0.9803**	**0.9745**	**0.9876**	**0.9664**
Neural network	A	1.0000	1.0000	1.0000	1.0000	1.0000	1.0000
	B	0.9928	0.9849	0.9907	0.9878	0.9940	0.9852
	C	1.0000	1.0000	1.0000	1.0000	1.0000	1.0000
	D	0.9659	0.9528	0.7573	0.8439	0.8737	0.9344
	E	0.9979	0.9906	0.9906	0.9906	0.9950	0.9962
	Average	**0.9913**	**0.9857**	**0.9477**	**0.9645**	**0.9725**	**0.9832**
k-Nearest Neighbor (k-NN)	A	0.8831	0.8943	0.7191	0.7972	0.8134	0.7079
	B	0.8697	0.8517	0.7342	0.7886	0.7886	0.7019
	C	0.8831	0.8965	0.7176	0.7971	0.8124	0.7070
	D	0.9255	0.9449	0.8496	0.8947	0.9022	0.8515
	E	0.9566	0.9597	0.9279	0.9435	0.9531	0.9190
	Average	**0.9036**	**0.9094**	**0.7897**	**0.8442**	**0.8603**	**0.7775**

6   Conclusion and Future Work

We carried out experiments with five different machine learning algorithms namely SVM, RF, NB, NN and k-NN to identify the most efficient and effective algorithm for detection and prediction of cloud service violations on throughput and response time over a certain time period. It is observed from our experimental results that SVM with RBF Kernel together with the 16 derived joint decision rules for cloud QoS violation on response time and throughput is the optimum model. This proposed machine learning model coupled with 16 decision rules thus contributed towards allowing the Cloud Service Provider to predict the occurrence of the violation of services based on response time and throughput. When there is a tendency for the transactions to go beyond the threshold limits (joint decision outcome is probably violation), system administrator shall take necessary preventive measures to bring the system back to normal conditions. This shall reduce the chance for violation to occur, hence mitigating lose or costly penalty. Nevertheless, in the event that violations do occur, remedial action has to be in place to prevent future occurrence. Future work therefore will incur further research to determine mechanisms for preventive measure and remedial action in the cloud QoS domain based on voluminous real-time data.

Acknowledgement. This work is supported by the funding of Fundamental Research Grant Scheme (FRGS) from the Ministry of Higher Education of Malaysia with grant number FRGS/1/2016/ICT01/MMU/02/1.

References

1. Mell, P., Grance, T.: The NIST definition of cloud computing. national institute of standards and technology. U.S. Department of Commerce, Special Publication 800-145 (2011)
2. Mirobi, G.J., Arockiam, L.: Service level agreement in cloud computing: an overview. In: International Conference on Control, Instrumentation, Communication and Computational Technologies, ICCICCT, pp. 753–758. IEEE, Kumaracoil (2015). https://doi.org/10.1109/iccicct.2015.7475380
3. OSG Cloud Working Group: Report on Cloud Computing to the OSG Steering Committee. https://www.spec.org/osgcloud/docs/osgcloudwgreport20120410.pdf. Accessed 20 July 2017
4. WSDREAM Data Set. https://github.com/wsdream/wsdream-dataset/tree/master/dataset2. Accessed 20 July 2017
5. R version 3.4.3: A language and environment for statistical computing. https://wbc.upm.edu.my/cran/. Accessed 20 July 2017
6. Emeakaroha, V.C., Ferreto, T.C., Netto, M.A.S., Brandic, I., De Rose, C.A.F.: CASViD: application level monitoring for SLA violation detection in clouds. In: IEEE 36th Annual Computer Software and Applications Conference. IEEE, Izmir (2012). https://doi.org/10.1109/compsac.2012.68
7. Musa, S.M., Yousif, A., Bashi, M.B.: SLA violation detection mechanism for cloud computing. Int. J. Comput. Appl. **133**, 8–11 (2016)
8. Leitner, P., Wetzstein, B., Rosenberg, F., Michlmayr, A., Dustdar, S., Leymann, F.: Runtime prediction of service level agreement violations for composite services. In: Dan, A., Gittler, F., Toumani, F. (eds.) ICSOC/ServiceWave -2009. LNCS, vol. 6275, pp. 176–186. Springer, Heidelberg (2010). https://doi.org/10.1007/978-3-642-16132-2_17
9. Hani, A.F.M., Paputungan, I.V., Hassan, M.F.: Support vector regression for service level agreement violation prediction. In: International Conference on Computer, Control, Informatics and its Applications, IC3INA. IEEE, Jakarta (2013)
10. Tang, B., Tang, M.: Bayesian model-based prediction of service level agreement violations for cloud services. In: Theoretical Aspects of Software Engineering Conference, TASE. IEEE, Changsha (2014)
11. Sheng, D., Kondo, D., Cirne, W.: Host load prediction in a Google compute cloud with a Bayesian model. In: Proceedings of the International Conference on High Performance Computing, Networking, Storage and Analysis, SC 2012. IEEE, Salt Lake City (2012)
12. Hemmat, R.A., Abdelhakim, H.: SLA violation prediction in cloud computing: a machine learning perspective. eprint arXiv:1611.10338 (2016)
13. Smola, A., Vishwanathan, S.V.N.: Introduction to Machine Learning, 1st edn. Cambridge University Press, Cambridge (2008)

14. Chang, C.C., Lin, C.J.: LIBSVM: a library of support vector machine. ACM Trans. Intell. Syst. Technol. **2**, 1–27 (2011)
15. Hsu, C.W., Lin, C.J.: A comparison of methods for multiclass support vector machines. IEEE Trans. Neural Netw. **13**, 415–425 (2002)
16. Rish, I.: An empirical study of the naive Bayes classifier. In: IJCAI 2001 Workshop on Empirical Methods in Artificial Intelligence, vol. 3, pp. 41–46 (2011)
17. Popescu, M.C., Balas, V.E., Perescu-Popescu, L., Mastorakis, N.: Multilayer perceptron and neural networks. WSEAS Trans. Circ. Syst. **8**, 579–588 (2009)
18. Bishop, C.M.: Neural Networks for Pattern Recognition. Clarendon Press, Oxford (1995)
19. Guo, G., Wang, H., Bell, D., Bi, Y., Greer, K.: KNN model-based approach in classification. In: Meersman, R., Tari, Z., Schmidt, D.C. (eds.) OTM 2003. LNCS, vol. 2888, pp. 986–996. Springer, Heidelberg (2003). https://doi.org/10.1007/978-3-540-39964-3_62
20. Breiman, L.: Random forests. Mach. Learn. **45**, 5–32 (2001)
21. Zheng, Z., Zhang, Y., Lyu, M.R.: Investigating QoS of real-world web services. IEEE Trans. Serv. Comput. **7**, 29–32 (2014)
22. IBM Informix Documentation Team: IBM Informix Performance Guide. Version 12.10. IBM, USA (2016)
23. Hossin, M., Sulaiman, M.N.: A review on evaluation metrics for data classification evaluations. Int. J. Data Min. Knowl. Manag. Process (IJDKP) **5**(2), 1–11 (2015). https://doi.org/10.5121/ijdkp.2015.5201
24. Fawcett, T.: An introduction to ROC analysis. Pattern Recognit. Lett. **27**, 861–874 (2006)
25. McHugh, M.L.: Interrater reliability: the kappa statistic. Biochem. Med. **22**(3), 276–282 (2012)

A Citation-Based Recommender System for Scholarly Paper Recommendation

Khalid Haruna[1,2(✉)], Maizatul Akmar Ismail[1],
Abdullahi Baffa Bichi[2], Victor Chang[3], Sutrisna Wibawa[4],
and Tutut Herawan[4,5,6]

[1] Department of Information Systems,
Faculty of Computer Science and Information Technology,
University of Malaya, Kuala Lumpur, Malaysia
[2] Department of Computer Science,
Faculty of Computer Science and Information Technology,
Bayero University, Kano, Nigeria
kharuna.cs@buk.edu.ng
[3] IBSS Xi'an Jiaotong Liverpool University, Suzhou, China
[4] Universitas Negeri Yogyakarta, Yogyakarta, Indonesia
[5] Universitas Teknologi Yogyakarta, Yogyakarta, Indonesia
[6] Politeknik Negeri Malang, Malang, Indonesia

Abstract. Several approaches have been proposed to help researchers in acquiring relevant and useful scholarly papers from the enormous amount of information (information overload) that is available over the internet. The significant challenge for those approaches is their assumption of the availability of the whole contents of each of the candidate recommending papers to be freely accessible, which is not always the case considering the copyright restrictions. Also, they immensely depend on priori user profiles, which required a significant number of registered users for the systems to work effectively, and a stumbling block for the creation of a new recommendation system. This paper proposes a citation-based recommender system based on the latent relations connecting research papers for the scholarly paper recommendation. The novelty of the proposed approach is that unlike the existing works, the latent associations that exist between a scholarly paper and its various citations are utilised. The proposed approach aimed to personalise scholarly recommendations regardless of the user expertise and research fields based on paper-citation relations. Experimental results have shown significant improvement over other baseline methods.

Keywords: Contextual information · Paper-citation relations
Publicly available metadata · Recommender system

1 Introduction

Results of various academic findings are disseminated in the forms of journal articles, conference proceedings, seminars, symposia, theses and etcetera [1], to serve as guidelines for the use of future generations. However, the voluminous amount of this information makes information seeking process very much wearisome [2, 3].

© Springer International Publishing AG, part of Springer Nature 2018
O. Gervasi et al. (Eds.): ICCSA 2018, LNCS 10960, pp. 514–525, 2018.
https://doi.org/10.1007/978-3-319-95162-1_35

The use of the generic search engines when searching for related information over the internet has become the most common and convenient method among researchers [4]. A reasonable level of expertise needs to be achieved to locate relevant and promising information efficiently [5]. Additionally, researchers follow the list of references to the papers they have already possessed for more explorations [6]. However, the coverage of this approach is insufficient and cannot trace the papers that are published after the possessed documents [4].

On the other hand, digital libraries such as IEEE, ScienceDirect, and SpringerLink, can provide proactive systems capable of recommending scholarly papers that match researcher's interests in a timely fashion [7]. Fortunately, they require considerable attention from the users to explicitly state their interests, which is tedious and take up much of researcher's valuable time.

To solve the above problems, research paper recommender systems have been proposed [6–15], to recommend scholarly papers to individual researchers proactively. The challenge is to provide relevant papers to the right researchers in the right way [4]. However, the vital concern to these approaches is that they presumed the whole contents of each of the candidate recommending papers to be freely accessible, which is not always the case considering the copyright restrictions. Furthermore, the approaches largely depend on priori user profiles, which required some registered users for the systems to work effectively, and a stumbling block for the creation of new research paper recommender system.

While there are lots of approaches based on citation-relations for scholarly paper recommendations [16–20], they do not leverage the latent relations across research papers, instead employed direct relations such as the co-citation relations presented in [20]. Identifying and incorporating the latent relations across research papers could play a significant role and improve the recommendation performance.

An initial approach to solving the above problems has been proposed in [6]. The authors mined the hidden relation between a target paper and its references to present utile recommendations. Differently, the hidden association between a target paper and its citation relations is leveraged in this paper. The novelty of the proposed approach are twofold;

a. Firstly, an independent research paper framework that utilises public contextual metadata to personalise scholarly papers regardless of the user expertise and research field is proposed.
b. Secondly, the proposed approach does not require a priori user profile.

The remaining sections of this paper are as follows. Section 2 presents some related work on recommending research papers. Section 3 presents the proposed citation-based recommender system for the scholarly paper recommendation. Section 4 describes the experimental setup and discusses the experimental results. Section 5 concludes the paper.

2 Related Works

The pattern of information seeking behaviour among different researchers has been reviewed in [21, 22]. Their findings reveal that expert researchers are more proficient in using search engines as compared to novice researchers. While [23] discussed the processes of identifying researchers' information need and in [24], a positive step in associating researcher's information seeking behaviour with the design of an ideal system has been reported.

Research paper recommender systems have also been utilised [7–14, 16] to ease the tasks of information seeking process, by suggesting relevant scholarly papers based on some information that is more elaborate than a few keywords. Different researchers have proposed different use of user-provided information. To be specific, [16] explored the use of collaborative filtering approach to recommend scholarly papers to a researcher from the set of citations to one of his/her papers. The aim was to test the ability of the collaborative filtering approach in recommending some set of citations that would be much significant as additional references to a target paper. The experimental results across six different algorithms reveal that the choosing algorithm affects the recommendation results. Also, some algorithms provide either very novel recommendations or very much relevant recommendations, but no single algorithm achieved both.

A citation-network has been explored in [16], to enhance the recommendation performance. However, the approach generates sparsity problem in the paper-citation network and thereby making the recommendation process very much tricky. In alleviating the sparsity problem, [12] applied the concept of the collaborative filtering approach to identify potential citation papers from the list of papers authored by a researcher. The experimental results show that recommendations after discovering the potential citation papers are more effective than collaborative filtering with binary or similarity values. Still, the approach generates poor prediction results for multidisciplinary scholars that work on several research topics. The research was later extended in [25] to cater the problem of multidisciplinary problems by proposing an adaptive neighbour selection. Also, the authors investigate the different sections of scholarly papers to find a better and adequate representation. The best result was achieved by considering the full paper text and conclusion and thus, can serve as a better representation of scholarly papers.

In the above systems, those initial information provided by the users are used to represent their interests in user profiles, and the system searches for similar items to make recommendations. The main weakness of those methods is that they presumed the whole contents of each of the candidate recommending papers to be freely accessible, which is not always the case considering the copyright restrictions.

Different from the above researches, [11] proposed a framework that generates potential queries using terms from only publicly available metadata, title and abstract of a target paper. The approach then applies the content-based approach to rank recommending papers that are more related to the target paper. The authors in [6] have also utilised the only publicly available contextual metadata using the concept of a collaborative approach to mine the hidden relations between a target paper and its references to present essential recommendations. While [6] utilised paper-reference relations, in this paper, the latent associations that exist between paper-citations relations are leveraged to personalise recommendations regardless of the user expertise and research field.

Based on a depth study of existing related works above, the problem is defined as follows:

Given a target paper p_i as a query, extract all the set of citations Cf_j of the target paper p_i. For each of the citations Cf_j, retrieve all other papers p_{ri} that reference. Measure the extent of similarity $W^{p_i \cdots p_{ri}}$ between p_{ri} and p_i, recommend the top- N most similar papers.

Algorithm: A Citation-Based Recommender System
Input: Target Paper
Output: Top-N Recommendation

Given a target paper p_i as a query,

(1) Extract the set of its citations Cf_j.

(2) For each citations Cf_j, retrieve all other papers p_{ri} that Cf_j referenced.

(3) Measure the extent of similarity $W^{P_i \to P_{ri}}$ between p_{ri} and p_i.

(4) Recommend the top-N papers.

Algorithm 1: A Citation-Based Recommender System

3   Proposed Citation-Based Recommender System for Scholarly Paper Recommendation

The proposed approach starts by transforming the corpus into a paper-citation matrix. Rows of the matrix represent the candidate papers, and columns denote the citations (see Table 1). A target paper (Pi) is defined as the paper to which a researcher has possessed and wants to receive other recommendations similar to it. Upon receiving the user's query, the proposed approach identifies the target-paper from the paper-citation matrix and Algorithm 1 is then applied. The algorithm extracts the target paper's citations, and for each citation, it retrieves from the web other papers that referenced any of the target papers citations. Equation 1 is then used to measure the extent of similarity between the target paper and each of the retrieved papers. Finally, it recommends the top-N papers to the researcher.

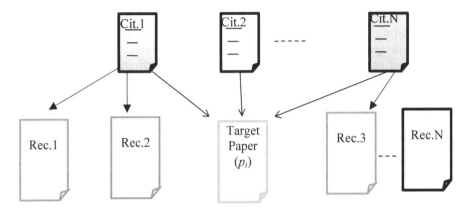

Fig. 1. Proposed citation-based recommendation scenario

To understand the proposed approach clearly, Fig. 1 portrays a target-paper (p_i) with citations *(Cit.1* to *Cit.N)*, in which each of the citations has referenced some set of other papers *(Rec.1* to *Rec.N)*. The goal is to measure the extent of similarity $(W^{P_i \to Rec_j})$ between the target-paper (Pi) and each of the co-referenced papers $(R_{ec.j})$. To do this, the contextual relations between the target paper and its neighbouring papers are mined to transform the paper-citation matrix into a relational matrix to represent the target paper (Pi) concerning each of its neighbouring papers $(R_{ec.j})$. The top-N recommendation list from the results of these associations is then presented to the user.

Table 1. Paper-citation relation matrix

Paper/citation	c_1	c_2	c_3
p_i	1	1	1
p_1	1	1	–
p_2	–	–	1
p_3	–	1	1
p_4	–	–	1
p_5	1	–	–

For illustration, assume that a target paper (Pi) is identified from the user's query and arrived at the paper-citation relations matrix depicted by Table 1 after extracting all other references $(R_{ec.j})$ to the target paper's citations. To get the relationship between the target paper (Pi) and each of the neighbouring papers $(R_{ec.j})$, a single-role relational matrix is obtained from the double-role relational matrix as depicted in Table 2. For simplicity, two papers are considered significantly co-occurring if both have at least a common cited-paper. Additionally, a binary value of one (1) or zero (0) is used to state the co-occurrence or otherwise between two citing papers. Equation (1) is then applied to measure the extent of similarity $(W^{P_i \to Rec_j})$ between (Pi) and $(R_{ec.j})$.

Table 2. Pair-wise paper similarity matrix

	p_i	p_1	p_2	p_3	p_4	p_5
p_i	1	1	1	1	1	1
p_1	1	1	0	1	0	1
p_2	1	0	1	1	1	0
p_3	1	1	1	1	1	0
p_4	1	0	1	1	1	0
p_5	1	1	0	0	0	1

3.1 Similarity Measure

In identifying similar research papers to the target paper (Pi), it becomes imperative to not only consider how similar the candidate recommending papers are to the target paper (Pi) but also how they deviate. It is therefore felt as in [26], that Jaccard similarity coefficient J given by Eq. (1) is more suitable for measuring the similarity and diversity between (Pi) and $(R_{ec.j})$.

$$J = W^{P_i \rightarrow \mathrm{Re}\,c.j} = \frac{Z_{11}}{Z_{01} + Z_{10} + Z_{11}} \tag{1}$$

Where Z_{11} is the total attributes where both X and Y are having a value of 1. Z_{01} is the total attributes where X is 0 and Y is 1 and Z_{10} is the total attributes where X is 1 and Y is 0.

4 Experimental Setup

4.1 Dataset

Similar to the works presented in [4, 25], the publicly available dataset presented in [12] has also been utilised in this paper. Some statistics of the utilised dataset is presented in Table 3.

Table 3. Statistics of the utilized dataset

Total number of researchers	50
Average number of researchers' publications	10
Average number of citations of each researchers' publications	14.8 (max. 169)
Average number of references to each researchers' publications	15.0 (max. 58)
Total number of recommending papers	100,351
Average number of citations of the recommending papers	17.9 (max. 175)
Average number of references to the recommending papers	15.5 (max. 53)

4.2 Experimental Evaluation

To measure the quality and effectiveness of the proposed approach, 5-fold cross-validation is performed to each of the target paper's citations by selecting 20% as a test set. Mean average precision (MAP) and mean reciprocal rank (MRR) given by Eqs. 2 and 3 respectively are used to measure the system's ability in recommending essential papers at the top the recommendation list. This is important because users usually browse only top-ranked recommendations [27]. Precision, recall, and F1 measures given by Eqs. 4, 5 and 6 respectively, are also used to assess the general performance of the proposed approach. These formulas are related and have been used in similar work [4, 6]. The recommendation results obtained are then compared with two (2) other baseline methods presented in [6] and [16].

$$MAP = \frac{1}{I}\sum_{i\in I}\frac{1}{ni}\sum_{k=1}^{N}P(R_{ik}) \tag{2}$$

$$MRR = \frac{1}{N_p}\sum_{i\in I}\frac{1}{rank(i)} \tag{3}$$

$$precision = \frac{\sum(relevant\_papers)\cap\sum(retrieved\_papers)}{\sum(retrieved\_papers)} \tag{4}$$

$$recall = \frac{\sum(relevant\_papers)\cap\sum(retrieved\_papers)}{\sum(relevant\_papers)} \tag{5}$$

$$F1 = \frac{2\times precision\times recall}{precision+recall} \tag{6}$$

5 Results and Discussions

The aggregate results obtained by the proposed approach from the publication lists across the 50 researchers using the said dataset is presented in this section. Figures 2 and 3 demonstrate the results comparisons based on (MAP) and (MRR) respectively.

As can easily be seen from Fig. 2 that the proposed approach has tremendously and unanimously outperformed the baseline methods for all N recommendations values based on mean average precision (MAP). Co-Citation performs the worst of the three results, while as expected, the performance of the proposed approach decreases as the number of N increases. This is because as the number of N increases, the tendency of retrieving irrelevant results also increases and thereby affecting the cumulative MAP results. However, the highest results based on (MAP) is obtained when N = 10 (N@10).

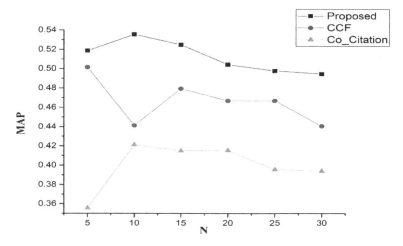

Fig. 2. Mean average precision (MAP)

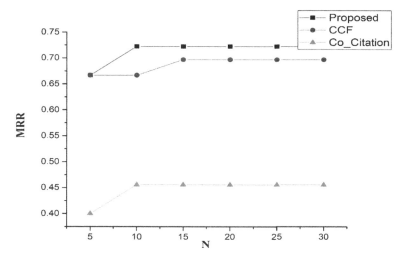

Fig. 3. Mean reciprocal rank (MRR)

On the other hand, the results comparison based on (MRR) is depicted in Fig. 3. The results difference between the proposed method and the CCF is not much significant. However, both the two approaches have significantly outperformed the Co-Citation method. This is because, the two approaches can leverage the latent associations that exist between a scholarly paper and its various citations, and different from the Co-Citation method that only uses the common citations relations.

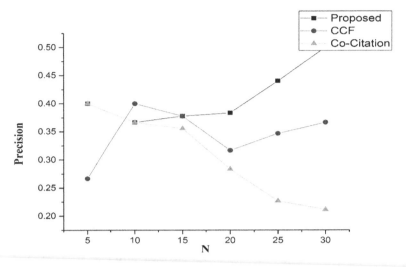

Fig. 4. Precision performance on the dataset

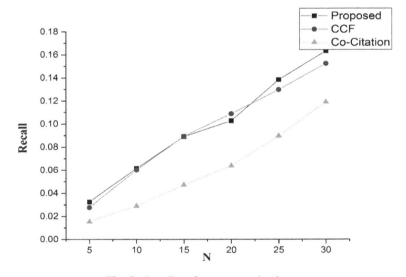

Fig. 5. Recall performance on the dataset

Figures 4 and 5 respectively represent the results comparisons based on Precision and Recall. From Fig. 4, the Precision result of the proposed approach is significant over the baseline methods for all N recommendations values. However, the CCF approach outperformed the proposed approach when N = 10 (N@10). The improvement of the proposed approach over the other baseline methods becomes outstandingly significant when the number of recommendations (N) is higher than 15. The Co-Citation results start with encouraging results specifically when N = 5 (N@5), but becomes less significant as the number of recommendations (N) increases.

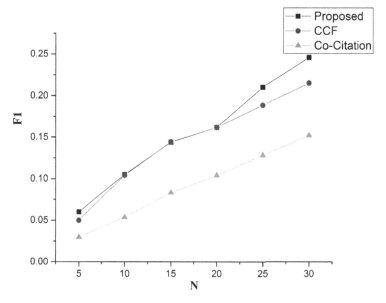

Fig. 6. F1 performance on the dataset

The results comparisons based on recall is depicted in Fig. 5. The CCF method performs better than the proposed approach when $N = 20$ (N@20). Averagely, the performance difference between the proposed and CCF approaches is not much significant. However, both approaches have statistically outperformed the Co-Citation method based on recall.

Figure 6 provides the results comparison based on the F1 measure. Similar to the results of recall depicted in Fig. 5, the performance difference between the CCF and the proposed approach based on the F1 measure is not much significant. However, results of the proposed approach start to be significant as the number of N increases, especially when N is above 20. Also, both the proposed and CCF approaches have shown significant improvement over the Co-Citation method based on the F1 measure.

In conclusion, as can easily be deduced from the presented results (Figs. 2, 3, 4, 5 and 6) that identifying and incorporating the latent relations across research papers plays a significant role in scholarly paper recommendations, and could result to improved recommendation performance. Furthermore, while the results difference between the proposed approach and CCF is not much significant, both the two results have unanimously outperformed the Co-Citation method for all N recommendations values. This is attributed to the direct relations employed by the Co-Citation method.

Additionally, while the proposed approach does not show much significant improvement over CCF method based on the simulated experiments using the static dataset, it is asserted that the proposed approach would sufficiently and statistically outperform the CCF method when a live user study with the real participant is conducted.

6   Conclusion and Future Work

Considering the challenge researchers faced, in acquiring relevant and useful scholarly papers from the enormous amount of information (information overload) that is available over the internet, this paper has successfully proposed a citation-based recommender system for the scholarly paper recommendation. The proposed approach has utilised the latent associations that exist between a scholarly paper and its various citations to personalise recommendations based on paper-citation relations.

Using a publicly available dataset, the proposed approach has improved the baseline methods in recommending useful and utile recommendation based on (MAP) and (MRR). The proposed approach has also shown significant improvement over the other baseline methods in assessing the general recommendation performance based on precision, recall and F1 measures.

One advantage of the proposed approach is its ability to leverage the latent associations that exist between a scholarly paper and its various citations. The next target is to add more strict rules in measuring the relativity between a target paper and the recommending papers to improve the recommendation utility.

Acknowledgement. This research is supported by collaborative research fund from Universitas Negeri Yogyakarta, Indonesia.

References

1. Robson, C., McCartan, K.: Real World Research. Wiley, Hoboken (2016)
2. Haruna, K., Ismail, M.A.: Scholarly paper recommendation using publicly available contextual metadata: conceptual paper. In: Seminar on Information Retrieval and Knowledge Management (SIRKM 2017), 19 July 2017. Faculty of Computer Science and Information Technology, Universiti Putra Malaysia (2017)
3. Haruna, K., Ismail, M.A., Suhendroyono, S., Damiasih, D., Pierewan, A.C., Chiroma, H., et al.: Context-aware recommender system: a review of recent developmental process and future research direction. Appl. Sci. **7**, 1211 (2017)
4. Haruna, K., Ismail, M.A., Damiasih, D., Sutopo, J., Herawan, T.: A collaborative approach for research paper recommender system. PLoS One **12**, e0184516 (2017)
5. Kai-Wah Chu, S., Law, N.: The development of information search expertise of research students. J. Librariansh. Inf. Sci. **40**, 165–177 (2008)
6. Liu, H., Kong, X., Bai, X., Wang, W., Bekele, T.M., Xia, F.: Context-based collaborative filtering for citation recommendation. IEEE Access **3**, 1695–1703 (2015)
7. Sugiyama, K., Kan, M.-Y.: Scholarly paper recommendation via user's recent research interests. In: Proceedings of the 10th Annual Joint Conference on Digital Libraries, pp. 29–38 (2010)
8. Agarwal, N., Haque, E., Liu, H., Parsons, L.: Research paper recommender systems: a subspace clustering approach. In: International Conference on Web-Age Information Management, pp. 475–491 (2005)
9. Gori, M., Pucci, A.: Research paper recommender systems: a random-walk based approach. In: IEEE/WIC/ACM International Conference on Web Intelligence 2006, WI 2006, pp. 778–781 (2006)

10. Gipp, B., Beel, J., Hentschel, C.: Scienstein: a research paper recommender system. In: Proceedings of the International Conference on Emerging Trends in Computing (ICETC 2009), pp. 309–315 (2009)
11. Nascimento, C., Laender, A.H., da Silva, A.S., Gonçalves, M.A.: A source independent framework for research paper recommendation. In: Proceedings of the 11th Annual International ACM/IEEE Joint Conference on Digital Libraries, pp. 297–306 (2011)
12. Sugiyama, K., Kan, M.-Y.: Exploiting potential citation papers in scholarly paper recommendation. In: Proceedings of the 13th ACM/IEEE-CS Joint Conference on Digital Libraries, pp. 153–162 (2013)
13. Beel, J., Langer, S., Genzmehr, M., Nürnberger, A.: Introducing Docear's research paper recommender system. In: Proceedings of the 13th ACM/IEEE-CS Joint Conference on Digital Libraries, pp. 459–460 (2013)
14. Haruna, K., Ismail, M.A.: An ontological framework for research paper recommendation. Int. J. Soft Comput. 11, 96–99 (2016)
15. Haruna, K., Ismail, M.A.: Evaluation techniques for context-aware recommender systems: a systematic mapping. J. Inf. Retrieval Knowl. Manage. 3, 23–35 (2017)
16. McNee, S.M., Albert, I., Cosley, D., Gopalkrishnan, P., Lam, S.K., Rashid, A.M., et al.: On the recommending of citations for research papers. In: Proceedings of the 2002 ACM Conference on Computer Supported Cooperative Work, pp. 116–125 (2002)
17. An, Y., Janssen, J., Milios, E.E.: Characterizing and mining the citation graph of the computer science literature. Knowl. Inf. Syst. 6, 664–678 (2004)
18. Price, D.J.D.S.: Networks of scientific papers. Science 149, 510–515 (1965)
19. Newman, M.E.: The structure of scientific collaboration networks. Proc. Nat. Acad. Sci. 98, 404–409 (2001)
20. Small, H.: Co-citation in the scientific literature: a new measure of the relationship between two documents. J. Assoc. Inf. Sci. Technol. 24, 265–269 (1973)
21. Catalano, A.: Patterns of graduate students' information seeking behavior: a meta-synthesis of the literature. J. Doc. 69, 243–274 (2013)
22. Lazonder, A.W.: Exploring novice users' training needs in searching information on the WWW. J. Comput. Assist. Learn. 16, 326–335 (2000)
23. Ismail, M.A.: Identifying how novice researchers search, locate, choose and use web resources at the early stage of research. Malays. J. Libr. Inf. Sci. 3, 67–85 (2011)
24. Ismail, M.A.: Support system for novice researchers (SSNR): usability evaluation of the first use. Int. Arab J. Inf. Technol. 9, 361–367 (2012)
25. Sugiyama, K., Kan, M.-Y.: A comprehensive evaluation of scholarly paper recommendation using potential citation papers. Int. J. Digit. Libr. 16, 91–109 (2015)
26. Leydesdorff, L.: On the normalization and visualization of author co-citation data: Salton's Cosine versus the Jaccard index. J. Assoc. Inf. Sci. Technol. 59, 77–85 (2008)
27. Hildreth, C.R.: Accounting for users' inflated assessments of on-line catalogue search performance and usefulness: an experimental study. Inf. Res. 6(2) (2001)

A Social Media Platform for Infectious Disease Analytics

Yang Hong$^{(\boxtimes)}$ ⓘ and Richard O. Sinnott$^{(\boxtimes)}$

School of Computing and Information Systems, University of Melbourne,
Melbourne, Australia
hongyang47198@gmail.com, rsinnott@unimelb.edu.au

Abstract. The effect of seasonal epidemics and potentially pandemics represents a significant issue for public health. In this context, early warnings and real time tracking of the spread of disease is highly desirable. In this paper, we address the problem of detecting disease outbreaks through an automated, scalable Cloud-based system for collecting, tracking and analyzing social media data. Specifically, the focus here is targeted to three prevalent diseases (flu, chickenpox and measles) across three Australian cities using data from the Twitter micro-blogging platform. The epidemics related tweets are extracted using an ensemble learning classifier consisting of a combination of Support Vector Machines, Naïve Bayes and Logistic Regression and comparing the results with the Google Trend data to assess the effectiveness of the overall approach.

Keywords: Twitter · Big data · Machine learning · Infectious disease

1 Introduction

Short dynamic micro-blogging messages from services such as Twitter are now in widespread use. Millions of users utilize a real-time communication platform for posting and sharing a variety of dynamic topics from the environment, medicine, sports and politics. The total number of monthly active Twitter users is over 328 million[1] and the total number of Tweets sent per day has now surpassed 500 million[2] in 2017.

Twitter is an ideal data resource for detecting the trends related to many diverse events: population-wide sentiment analysis [1], prediction of elections [2], disaster detection [3] and public health applications amongst many others [4]. One major advantage of Twitter is its real time nature. This offers many benefits for analysis and prediction of infectious disease outbreaks such as flu, measles and chicken pox. The goal of this study is to verify if Twitter data can be used for tracking the trend and spread of infectious diseases.

In this context, one key problem is how to filter the noise coming from tweets with similar terms but irrelevant content [5]. Many noise filters have been developed and presented in previous works. Song and Lee provided a graph based filtering strategy.

---

[1] http://twitter.com.
[2] https://www.omnicoreagency.com/twitter-statistics/.

© Springer International Publishing AG, part of Springer Nature 2018
O. Gervasi et al. (Eds.): ICCSA 2018, LNCS 10960, pp. 526–540, 2018.
https://doi.org/10.1007/978-3-319-95162-1_36

They focused on ensuring that noise features should not be connected with desired features or connected through weak relationships [6]. de Oliveira presented another lightweight stream filter [7].

They proposed a grammar-rule independent method called filter stream named entity recognition (FS-NER) to identify meaningful tweets by analyzing the characteristic and context of words in the tweet.

Another approach that is often used is to find the sentiment polarity of tweets based on machine learning approaches. The approach typically involves tweet-based text analysis comprising two significant methods: extracting sensitive information about infectious diseases according to a list of key words related to diseases such as fever, headache, rash and cough, and subsequently employing Twitter sentiment analysis using machine learning and natural language processing (NLP) algorithms.

Machine learning and NLP can be applied for classifier generation through the features present in the 140 characters (text) of tweets. When a new tweet is obtained, the classifier is able to determine the sentiment polarity (positive or negative mood). The success of the combination of both aspects achieves higher accuracy by removing (filtering) irrelevant tweets. Google Trends provides another source of data that is often used as the basis for social media verification. The processed tweets and Google Trend data are compared to identify their similarity as the evidence for the verification [9].

In this paper we investigate the relationship between social media data and Google Trend data with specific focus on infectious diseases. We present an efficient and scalable system design leveraging a Cloud-based system architecture based on the Australian National eResearch Collaborative Tools and Resources (NeCTAR – www. nectar.org.au) Research Cloud.

The rest of paper is organized as follows. Section 2 covers related background work. Section 3 describes related tools and presents an overview of the system architecture. Section 4 focuses on the data collection modules. Section 5 discusses data processing with specific focus on the classifier used for automated tweet analytics. Section 6 presents the analysis and discussion of the result. Finally, Sect. 7 provides conclusions and areas of future work.

2   Related Work

The global population increasingly uses the web. Individuals now commonly use Google to search for health related issues. Google Trends represent a simple way to identify patterns of web usage and health issues that might arise in particular locations, e.g. people searching for "flu remedies". Similarly, the rise of social media during the last years has greatly increased the amount of content generated by the public. Of particular relevance here is public-generated data using location-based services associated with many mobile devices that allows identification of the precise location of data that is generated.

Social media analytics in the health domain is not new. Zaldumbide et al. focused on an architecture and realisation for real time health events [9]. The work was limited due to the global nature of Twitter and the challenges of high velocity data set issues when dealing with globally significant resources such as Twitter. Chew et al. [10]

analysed H1N1 related data from Twitter over a 6-month period in 2009 and the interaction/overlap with official emergency events. They selected H1N1 because it was the first major (global) event in the Web 2.0 era. They compared their data with official information from the Centre for Disease Control (CDC) and Public Health Agency of Canada. Despite the fact that the behaviour obtained in their research was very close to the official information, they concluded: "These numbers may give us a sense of population demographics; however, those who tweet about H1N1 may not necessarily be representative of the Twitter population, and the Twitter population is not representative of the general population [10]." Finally, they suggested that an improved approach could be performed using geo-location [11].

Aramaki et al. [12] used a different approach to obtain a better accuracy in their results. They recognised the fact that a tweet containing "influenza" or "flu", may not mean that the twitter user has got flu; they may be just talking about the topic. To tackle this, they classify tweets into negative (suspicious, questions or news) and positive (the most accurate tweets). They compared several classifier methods such as Logistic Regression, Naive Bayes, Nearest Neighbour and Support Vector Machine (SVM). They based their studies comparing data from the Infection Disease Surveillance Center in Japan. They found that 42% of their analysed tweets were negative. This high value directly impacted the final results. For their analysis, they used an SVM-based classifier. They noted that their method outperformed the Google Trend-based methods applied to the same area of Japan.

St Louis et al. [13] focused on using Twitter to predict disease outbreaks? Almost all public health agencies rely on classic sources of information to monitor outbreaks such as doctors and hospital reports. One issue with these reports is that despite the fact they can be very accurate, they have a significant lag behind the actual events – diseases can spread in real-time and lags of knowledge capture can be critical, especially in pandemic situations. On the other hand, efforts of projects such as http://www.healthmap.org/ often have a large amount of information, but their results cannot be formally verified with other sources.

Ji et al. [14] analysed tweets from a different point of view. They focused on how concerned people are about disease outbreaks. They used sentiment classification on tweets based on a two-step approach including classifying Tweets as personal or negative. First they divided Tweets into personal and non-personal and then classified Tweets into negative and neutral and applied machine learning-based classifiers for tweet classification. When comparing data with official information sources however they did not achieve high degrees of similarity.

Khan et al. [15] focused on early detection of outbreaks before they transform into full-blown pandemics. They identified three kinds of tweet generators: media and news that posts, tweets related to publicity or advertisement of medicines and tweets created by users that contain key words. The scope of their study was to analyse the last group of tweets to identify true reports of symptoms in the person tweeting. They applied NLP by training a subset of data and applying pre-processing techniques. They used unigram and bigram models to compare their proposed model to obtained a precision of 88.7% compared to other models.

Lampos et al. [16] focused on reducing the impact of an epidemic disease such as the flu. They analysed tweets from the United Kingdom for a period of 24 weeks. They compared this data with official data from the Health Protection Agency. In this work, they used textual analysis and not just a count of occurrences of words, e.g. flu. They obtained a high correlation but noted that the results could be more accurate if they applied methods to remove media hype and discussions around health events.

Achrekar et al. [17] tried to go further by attempting to predict flu trends. In their work, they regarded Twitter users as sensors. They removed retweets and tweets from the same user, and labelled tweets with data related to influenza-like illness (ILI). In order to collect data from Twitter, they use the search API using keywords such as flu, swine flu and H1N1. They compared their results with data from the Center for Disease Control and Prevention and obtained a strong correlation with a Pearson's correlation coefficient of 0.9846.

Signorini et al. [18] explored the analysis and tracking of H1N1 activity including symptoms and medications. Using the timestamp and geo-location information stored in tweets, they used Google Maps to show tweet distributions and their temporal dependencies.

Doan et al. [19] used tweets collected over 36 weeks. The number of tweets collected in that period of time was over 587 million from approximately 24.5 m users. They used this data to compare data from CDC's U.S. Outpatient Influenza-like Illness Surveillance Network (ILINet)3. This institution compiles more than 25 million patient registers per year. They used two methods to filter the information. The first method was based on four keywords: flu, cough, headache and sore throat. With this method, they got a Pearson's correlation coefficient of 0.95. They compared various methods but one key conclusion they reached was that the keywords list was directly related to the official information, i.e. an increase or decrease in keywords correlates directly with the accuracy of official information.

Hirose et al. [20] proposed a method to forecast influenza outbreaks through Twitter, again using ILINet[3] as the official data source used for comparison. They filtered tweets into two groups: positives and negatives. Negatives are tweets contained symptom words but not really expressing influenza reports, e.g. "Football fever this weekend!!!". On the other hand, they identified that positive tweets are more likely connected to real symptoms. They identified that performing multiple linear regressions could improve the accuracy of the prediction.

Jin et al. [21] revealed in their study that rumours can spread across Twitter, e.g. how rumours such as "Health officials might inject Ebola patients with lethal substances". These tweets spread quickly in countries like Ghana, Nigeria and Kenya. They analysed three cases: one case from Dallas, another from New York and the case of Dr Spencer case who volunteered in Guinea and became infected with the Ebola virus. They calculated the time of response for retweets on a specific topic and created a ratio table. They identified a shorter time for Reponses on News Stories than for Twitter rumours.

---

[3] Influenza-Like Illness Surveillance Network (http://www.cdc.gov/flu/weekly/).

3   System Architecture

The platform for infectious disease analytics utilized the Australia-wide NeCTAR Research Cloud. NeCTAR offers access to over 30,000 physical servers across multiple availability zones. All Australian academics and students can request and acquire servers and storage for their own research needs. The overall architecture of the platform utilized in this paper is shown in Fig. 1.

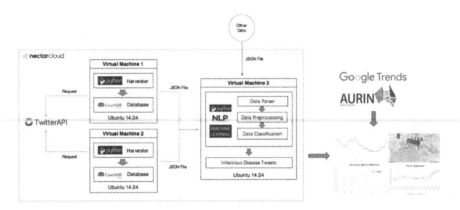

Fig. 1. System architecture.

The system includes three modules: a data collection module, a data processing module and a data analysis module. The first two modules were implemented directly on the NeCTAR Research Cloud. Two virtual machines were used to run Twitter harvesting scripts. Each harvester sends requests to the Twitter server using an API provided, and saves the resultant (JSON) data in a noSQL database (CouchDB). The collected data was integrated and processed by the text analysis components in the third virtual machine. Finally, the processed results were sent to the third module for data analysis.

In the architecture, the virtual machines were based on Ubuntu 14.04 operating system with 8 GB RAM, 2 vCPU and 60 GB memory storage. One virtual machine was required to do more computational tasks so was allocated 16 GB RAM, 4 vCPU and 120 GB memory. It is noted that further virtual machines can be allocated on the fly, e.g. when further data needs to be collected.

4   Data Collection Module

Data was collected from three resources for different purposes. To establish the relationship between tweets and infectious disease in Australia, it was essential to obtain tweets with geo-location (lat/long), i.e. based on uses tweeting with the location-based service (GPS) on their phone activated. It is the case that the majority of Twitter data does not include a geo-location (typically around 15% of tweets), hence it was required to obtain many more tweets and filter those without a geo-location. To aid this work, the University of Melbourne has established a Twitter resource comprising over 100 m tweets – many of which are geo-located. Furthermore, when obtaining tweets, it is possible to restrict the areas of interest through the setting of a bounding box. The bounding boxes for three major cities of Australia were chosen in this work (Melbourne, Sydney and Adelaide). The platform can readily be repurposed by setting new bounding boxes, e.g. for new cities or indeed new countries.

A further data resource was also utilized[4]. This data provides researchers with huge amounts of annotated tweets suitable for sentiment analysis. This included a training dataset and testing dataset. Since the number of positive tweets and negative tweets is the same in the training data, one of the advantages of this dataset is that it was not necessary to solve dataset imbalance issues. In order to generate a suitable classifier, we applied machine learning algorithms to the training data and compared the performance with different model parameters.

The total amount of data used in this work comprised 6,764,090 tweets (18.63 GB) with 3,160,086 tweets from Melbourne, 1,795,170 tweets from Sydney, 208,834 from Adelaide and 1,600,000 from the rest of the world (Tables 1, 2 and 3).

Table 1. Tweets collected from harvester.

City	Size (GB)	Tweets	Time period
Melbourne	8.07	1,945,588	Mar 5th 2017 – Sep 24th 2017

Table 2. Tweets collected from UniMelb Twitter resource.

City	Size (GB)	Tweets	Time period
Melbourne	3.99	1,214,498	July 28th 2014 – June 13th 2016
Sydney	5.66	1,795,170	July 28th 2014 – June 13th 2016
Adelaide	0.67	208,834	July 28th 2014 – June 13th 2016
Total	10.32	3,218,502	

Table 3. Tweets collected from Sentiment140.

Data type	Size (KB)	Polarity	Tweets
Training data	238,800	Positive	800,000
		Negative	800,000
Test data	74	–	14,076

[4] http://help.sentiment140.com/home.

5 Data Processing Module

A raw tweet contains considerable amounts of information – a 140-character tweet typically contains 9 kb of associated metadata. Hence, it is typically necessary to parse the data and reduce the data size. In this work, only a few fields were required for infectious disease analysis. These included:

- *text* field, which forms the main body of the tweet. It contains a 140-character long set of terms.
- *created_at* field indicates the Coordinated Universal Time when the user posted the tweet.
- *coordinates* field provides the GPS location of the tweet [8]. Many tweets omit this information if the location-based network on the device is turned off. Nevertheless, tweets can often be approximately geo-located based on the metadata associated with the tweet, e.g. if the profile mentions Melbourne then it can be associated (retrieved) from a harvester requesting tweets from Melbourne.

Once tweets are harvested and parsed, they are stored in a Cloud-based database. It is also noted that a unique identifier is associated with each tweet. This identifier assists in data operations and ensures that no duplicate tweets are stored.

In order to generate the appropriate data for subsequent classification, a sequence of text processing procedures is applied to process the text field. This includes tokenization, conversion to lower case, stop word removal and word normalization. The preprocessed data also removes non-English language word, punctuation and emoji.

Using the resultant processed data, the next phase involved extracting illness-related tweets related to infectious diseases. The approach taken combined two aspects: keyword and sentiment analytics. The key words list adopted were taken from the public data of Centers for Disease Control and Prevention (CDC). The text fields of tweets were checked if they contained relevant key words (flu, measles, chicken pox) to

Table 4. Infectious disease key words.

Disease type	Key words
Flu	Flu, cough, runny…
Measles	Measles, rash, chill…
Chicken pox	Pox, blister, bump…

Table 5. Infectious disease key words

Tweets	Polarity	Key words	Target tweets
Have a nice day	Positive	No	No
I don't like this food	Negative	No	No
I had a cold. Feel terrible	Negative	Yes	Yes
Crazy sushi fever!	Positive	Yes	No

decide if they were related to the corresponding infectious disease. Table 4 provides part of key word in the work. In addition, sentiment analysis was used to establish the tweet polarity: positive or negative sentiment. Positive tweets were discarded since it can be assumed that tweets related to infectious disease should express negative sentiment. In order to build an effective sentiment classifier, various experiments were carried out. Potential infectious disease tweets contain key words that have negative sentiment. Table 5 provides examples used for tweet selection.

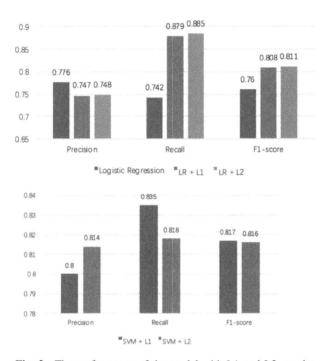

Fig. 2. The performance of the model with L1 and L2 penalty

A set of tweets was used to generate the classifier used for sentiment analysis. A Bag of Word approach was used to extract the features from processed training data. The text model after fitting had a feature space with 777,666 features. The feature vector then was applied to all of the data, whereby the data sharing the same vector had the same dimension. We evaluated the data with test dataset.

In undertaking this we compared three algorithms: Logistic Regression (LR), Support Vector Machine (SVM) and Naïve Bayes (NB). We considered the effect of L1 penalty and L2 penalty with regards to the performance of LR and SVM.

The evaluation of L1 and L2 penalty for LR is described in Fig. 2. Non-regularization LR is used as the baseline. The recall increased from 18.4% with L1 to 19.2% with L2. This indicates that both L1 and L2 reduce false negative errors and greatly improve positive tweet classification. However, their precision drops slightly, which means that the penalty parameter is more sensitive to a positive polarity rather than negative polarity.

The enhancement of the F1-score proves that the penalty parameter is able to improve the model performance. L1 is generally considered more powerful for handling data with sparse features. Comparing L1 and L2, the F1-score of L2 is 1.8% higher than L1 in our experiment, which indicates that L2 actually outperforms L1 with our dataset. Therefore, we chose L2 as the penalty for LR model when building the ensemble classifier. However, unlike LR, the experiment in SVM exhibits different results. The L1 and L2 penalty are evaluated when the penalty term parameter is 0. Although L2 shows a more balanced evaluation, the F1-score of L1 was slightly higher than L2. This indicates that L1 has better performance than L2. Therefore, we choose L2 as the penalty type for the SVM model.

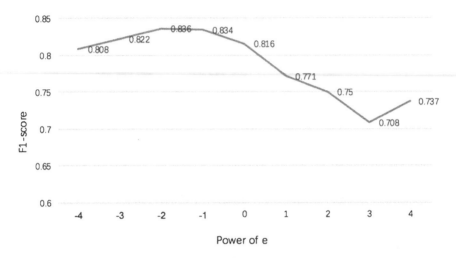

Fig. 3. Penalty term parameter on performance of SVM

The investigation of the penalty term parameter of SVM is displayed in Fig. 3. This parameter plays a significant role in the performance of the model, since the parameter can determine how much the penalty will affect the weight choice in the SVM model. A very large parameter value can make the penalty close to zero, which means it nearly has minimal influence on weight. A small value of parameter has the opposite effect. In Fig. 3, the x-axis represents the power of e, whilst the y-axis represents the F1-score of the model. As seen, the model has the best performance when the power of e is −2. This indicates that the parameter has a small value between 0 and 1. Moreover, we find that the correlation of performance and the parameter is non-monotonic. Hence, the figure shows that the performance of power 4 is higher than power 3.

Figure 4 shows the evaluation of the different machine learning classifiers. Even after adding the L2 penalty parameter, LR still has the worst performance (0.811). The SVM classifier has the best performance (0.836) when considering a single classifier where the F1-score is slightly greater than NB (0.819). The ability of NB and SVM for predicting positive tweets and negative tweets is more balanced than LR. The percentage of positive tweets and negative tweets is unknown in advance. To address

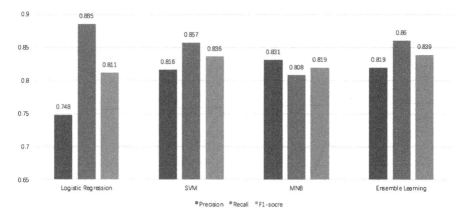

Fig. 4. Comparison of machine learning classifiers

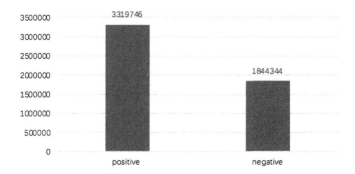

Fig. 5. Overall amount of positive and negative tweets in the dataset

this, we build an ensemble classifier to reduce the impact of an unbalanced dataset. This method considers the characteristics of the three classifiers. It is noted that ensemble learning with hard voting suffers from lower precision than MNB, with F1-score (0.839) higher than SVM (0.836). This indicates that the combination of classifiers is more powerful than any single classifier. It is also noted that the ensemble classifier has balanced tendency to positive or negative sentiment hence the classifier for both polarities is reliable. Figure 5 shows the percentage of positive and negative tweets in the dataset. The figure illustrates that our dataset includes 64.3% positive tweets and 35.7% negative tweets.

6   Results and Analysis

In this section, we analyze and compare our data against a more official data source. Our analysis focuses on three specific infectious diseases: flu, chicken pox and measles. In order to compare this data with Google Trend data, our starting method is grouping our data into time ranges. Specifically, data is categorized into every half-month data

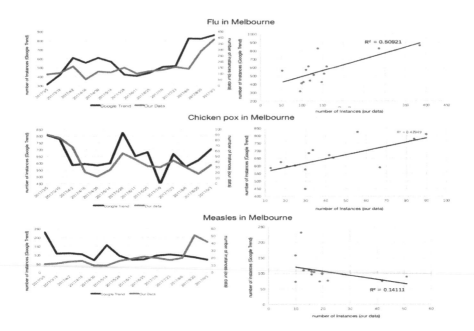

Fig. 6. Infectious disease events in Melbourne

for Melbourne and Sydney. Since we only have a (relatively) minimal data from Adelaide, this is categorized into 28-day periods.

The analysis of results of each disease needs to be rescaled before comparing against Google Trend data. We present a scatter plot and calculate the Pearson Coefficient to indicate the degree of correlation. Moreover, we try to find the interval with 50 units along x-axis that can cover the majority points in scatter plot. From this we calculate the average value of points in the interval, which can subsequently be used as a possible alarm value for an infectious disease outbreak in a given city (Fig. 6).

As seen, for flu in Melbourne, the two lines in the graph both increase from June 11th and keep rising to a peak on September 3rd. It is noted that this period reflects the season change to winter. The scatter plot shows the majority of points are distributed around 139 instances. If there are more flu tweets found over this value at certain time point, it is possible that a flu outbreak is to occur. For chicken pox in Melbourne, two instances both exhibit a downtrend between March 5th to April 2nd. After this decline, the peak of Google Trend is shown on May 28th, which is same as the peak of our data. Points in the scatter plot of chicken pox are random distributed so that we cannot decide a given threshold value. The measles instances do not show any similarity with Google Trend data, i.e. the scatter plot shows a negative correlation between two social media data and Google Trend.

For flu in Sydney, the two graphs show the same downtrend from August 1st to September 12th due to the effect of the season change. The majority of points are distributed in the range of 80 to 130. This interval contains 10 points and their average values are 110, which can be used as a threshold value to indicate a potential outbreak

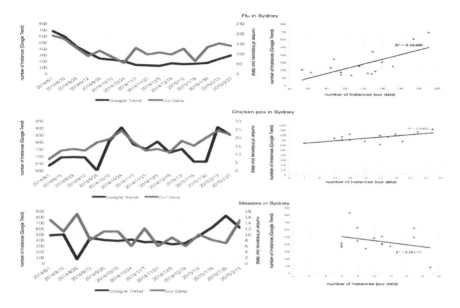

Fig. 7. Infectious disease events in Sydney

of flu in Sydney. For chicken pox, both our data and Google Trend had a peak on October 24th and February 13th. We found 24 tweets with 905 instances respectively on the first peak and 24 tweets with 908 instances on the second peak. However as with as Melbourne, the measles data in Sydney does not show any similarity between the two instances (Fig. 7).

For flu in Adelaide, the two instances show the same trend from August 1st to October 24th. However, the peak of our data occurred on November 21st, which is not indicated in Google Trends. Another similarity is that both charts begin to increase from December 19th. Moreover, points are randomly distributed in the scatter plot. For chicken pox in Adelaide, two instances show a degree of similarity in the two intervals. Although we found that the majority of points are centered at around 24 instances, this value cannot be regarded as a possible alarm value. The main reason is that the size of observed Chicken pox events in Adelaide was too small. For measles in Adelaide, the two instances have a degree of similarity from August 1st to August 29th and from December 19th to January 16th (Fig. 8).

As shown in Table 6, flu has a relatively high degree of correlation in Melbourne, Sydney and Adelaide, which demonstrates that our data is consistent with the Google Trend data for flu. Therefore, we may reasonably assert that tweets can be used as an indicator of flu outbreaks. Similarly, we see that infectious disease data fluctuates along with the changing of the season, i.e. both our data and Google Trend data peak in winter.

Chicken pox also shows a reasonable correlation with a moderate correlation in Sydney and a higher degree of correlation in Melbourne and Adelaide. However,

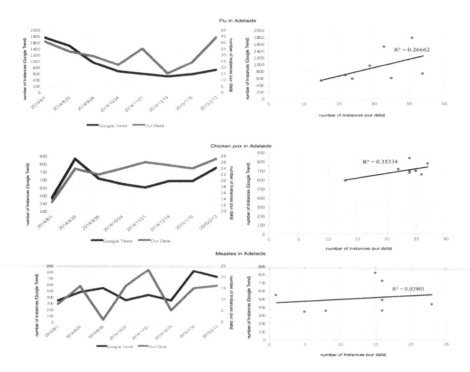

Fig. 8. Infectious diseases data in Adelaide

Table 6. Summary of correlation degree

City	Disease type	R^2	Pearson coefficient	Correlation degree
Melbourne	Flu	0.50	0.71	High
	Chicken pox	0.43	0.66	High
	Measles	0.14	−0.38	Moderate
Sydney	Flu	0.46	0.68	High
	Chicken pox	0.44	0.50	Moderate
	Measles	0.08	−0.44	Moderate
Adelaide	Flu	0.27	0.65	High
	Chicken pox	0.35	0.55	High
	Measles	0.03	0.17	Low

unlike flu, there is no strong evidence that indicates that the peak of chicken pox has a direct relationship with the season.

Measles does not show any correlation between our data and Google Trend data. Indeed, for Melbourne and Sydney, the correlation is negative, which is opposite to expectations. Furthermore, measles shows no change with the changing of the season.

7 Conclusions and Future Work

This project mainly has explored whether social media is capable of tracking and analyzing the trend of the infectious diseases. Unlike other approaches, we combine both sentiment analytics and event detection. This offers enhancements that have not been explored in other works.

We compared our data against Google Trend data. The performance of flu and chicken pox displayed a high correlation with tweet data, which suggests that Twitter data can be used to track flu and chicken pox outbreaks. However, there was no similarity observed for measles. Flu is a seasonal disease. Since there is a difference in geo-location and weather between the three cities, the time period for outbreaks of flu was exhibited during the winter but the specific time was slightly different. Unlike flu, outbreaks of chicken pox and measles are more irregular.

In the future, other aspects will be taken into account to increase the performance of the model. First, we will use more data to train our classifier. Learning more diverse types of data is the most efficient and straight way for model improvement. Second, we will more carefully tune the parameters in each of machine learning model. Third, we will come up with improved methods for sentiment classification, e.g. employ word vectors to extract the features in the text and build neural networks to train the model.

References

1. Liu, B.: Sentiment analysis and opinion mining. Synth. Lect. Hum. Lang. Technol. **5**(1), 1–167 (2012)
2. Tumasjan, A., et al.: Predicting elections with twitter: what 140 characters reveal about political sentiment. In: ICWSM 2010, vol. 1, pp. 178–185 (2010)
3. Sakaki, T., Makoto, O., Yutaka, M.: Earthquake shakes Twitter users: real-time event detection by social sensors. In: Proceedings of the 19th International Conference on World Wide Web. ACM (2010)
4. Callison-Burch, C., Dredze M.: Creating speech and language data with Amazon's mechanical turk. In: Proceedings of the NAACL HLT 2010 Workshop on Creating Speech and Language Data with Amazon's Mechanical Turk. Association for Computational Linguistics (2010)
5. Szomszor, M., Kostkova, P., de Quincey, E.: #Swineflu: Twitter predicts swine flu outbreak in 2009. In: Szomszor, M., Kostkova, P. (eds.) eHealth 2010. LNICST, vol. 69, pp. 18–26. Springer, Heidelberg (2011). https://doi.org/10.1007/978-3-642-23635-8_3
6. Song, J., Lee, S., Kim, J.: Spam filtering in twitter using sender-receiver relationship. In: Sommer, R., Balzarotti, D., Maier, G. (eds.) RAID 2011. LNCS, vol. 6961, pp. 301–317. Springer, Heidelberg (2011). https://doi.org/10.1007/978-3-642-23644-0_16
7. de Oliveira, D.M., Laender, A.H., Veloso, A., da Silva, A.S.: FS-NER: a lightweight filter-stream approach to named entity recognition on twitter data. In: Proceedings of the 22nd International Conference on World Wide Web, pp. 597–604. ACM, May 2013
8. Burton, S.H., et al.: "Right time, right place" health communication on Twitter: value and accuracy of location information. J. Med. Internet Res. **14**(6), e156 (2012)

 9. Zaldumbide, J.P., Sinnott, R.O.: Identification and verification of real-time health events through social media. In: IEEE International Conference on Data Science and Data Intensive Systems, Sydney, Australia, December 2015

10. Chew, C., et al.: Pandemics in the age of Twitter: content analysis of tweets during the 2009 H1N1 outbreak. PLoS One 5(11), e14118 (2010)

11. Byun, C., et al.: Automated Twitter data collecting tool for data mining in social network. In: Proceedings of the 2012 ACM Research in Applied Computation Symposium. ACM (2012)

12. Aramaki, E., et al.: Twitter catches the flu: detecting influenza epidemics using Twitter. In: Proceedings of the Conference on Empirical Methods in Natural Language Processing. Association for Computational Linguistics (2011)

13. St Louis, C., et al.: Can Twitter predict disease outbreaks? BMJ, 344 (2012)

14. Ji, X., et al.: Monitoring public health concerns using Twitter sentiment classifications. In: 2013 IEEE International Conference on Healthcare Informatics (ICHI). IEEE (2013)

15. Khan, M.A.H., et al.: A robust and scalable framework for detecting self-reported illness from Twitter. In: 2012 IEEE 14th International Conference on e-Health Networking, Applications and Services (Healthcom). IEEE (2012)

16. Lampos, V., et al.: Tracking the flu pandemic by monitoring the social web. In: 2010 2nd International Workshop on Cognitive Information Processing (CIP). IEEE (2010)

17. Achrekar, H., et al.: Predicting flu trends using Twitter data. In: 2011 IEEE Conference on Computer Communications Workshops (INFOCOM WKSHPS). IEEE (2011)

18. Signorini, A., et al.: The use of Twitter to track levels of disease activity and public concern in the US during the influenza A H1N1 pandemic. PLoS One 6(5), e19467 (2011)

19. Doan, S., et al.: Enhancing Twitter data analysis with simple semantic filtering: example in tracking influenza-like illnesses. In: 2012 IEEE Second International Conference on Healthcare Informatics, Imaging and Systems Biology (HISB). IEEE (2012)

20. Hirose, H., et al.: Prediction of infectious disease spread using Twitter: a case of influenza. In: 2012 Fifth International Symposium on Parallel Architectures, Algorithms and Programming (PAAP). IEEE (2012)

21. Jin, F., et al.: Misinformation propagation in the age of Twitter. Computer 47(12), 90–94 (2014)

Improvement on a Biometric-Based Key Agreement and Authentication Scheme for the Multi-server Environments

Jongho Moon[1] (ID), Youngsook Lee[2], Hyungkyu Yang[3], Hakjun Lee[1], Sewan Ha[1], and Dongho Won[1(✉)]

[1] Department of Electrical and Computer Engineering, Sungkyunkwan University, 2066 Seobu-ro, Jangan-gu, Suwon-si, Gyeonggi-do 16419, Korea
{jhmoon,hjlee,hsewan,dhwon}@security.re.kr
[2] Department of Cyber Security, Howon University, 64 Howondae 3-gil, Impi-myeon, Gunsan-si, Jeonrabuk-do 54058, Korea
ysooklee@howon.ac.kr
[3] Department of Computer and Media Information, Kangnam University, 40 Gangnam-ro, Giheung-gu, Yongin-si, Gyeonggi-do 16979, Korea
hkyang@kangnam.ac.kr

Abstract. With the rapid spiraling network users expansion and the enlargement of communication technologies, the multi-server environment has been the most common environment for widely deployed applications. Wang et al. recently have shown that Mishra et al.'s biohasing-based authentication scheme for multi-server was insecure, and then presented a fuzzy-extractor-based authentication protocol for key-agreement and multi-server. They continued to assert that their protocol was more secure and efficient. After a prudent analysis, however, their enhanced scheme still remains vulnerabilities against well-known attacks. In this paper, the weaknesses of Wang et al.'s protocol such as the outsider and user impersonation attacks are demonstrated, followed by the proposal of a new fuzzy-extractor and smart card-based protocol, also for key agreement and multi-server environment. Lastly, the authors shows that the new key-agreement protocol is more secure using random oracle method and Automated Validation of Internet Security Protocols and Applications (AVISPA) tool, and that it serves to gratify all of the required security properties.

Keywords: Multi-server · Authentication · Fuzzy-extractor
Biometrics

1 Introduction

Transmission environments of the information become more open and dynamic, research on the trustworthiness of large-scale network has become progressively more crucial [1]. The typical previous user authentication schemes verify the

© Springer International Publishing AG, part of Springer Nature 2018
O. Gervasi et al. (Eds.): ICCSA 2018, LNCS 10960, pp. 541–557, 2018.
https://doi.org/10.1007/978-3-319-95162-1_37

entered credentials with the stored databases. Since the first authentication scheme that is based on password was presented by Lamport [2] in 1981, a variety of authentication schemes [3–5] which are based on password have been presented. Regarding password authentication scheme, however, a server needs to store a list which is stored the password for the identification of the credentials of a remote user; the server thus must make arrangements for additional storage or memory for the storage of the password table. Furthermore, several researcher studies have shown that the password-based authentication protocols are vulnerable against some attacks such as the off-line password guessing or stolen smart card [6,7]. For these reasons, many researchers have suggested a new user authentication protocol for key-agreement using biometrics. The biometrics has a major characteristic which is the uniqueness. Numerous remote user authentication schemes [8–11] have used biological characteristics. In multi-server environments (MSE), each user can approach any type of application server, regardless of their physical location, by using a single registration; for this reason, a secure remote user authentication protocol is required in the MSE. Figure 1 delineates this structure, which incorporates a one-time registration, a single smart card, and the same credentials. For this reason, the MSE requires a secure and forceful remote user authentication protocol.

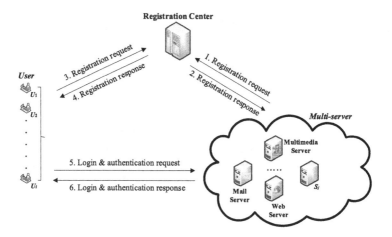

Fig. 1. The basic architecture of multi-server

During the past decade, many researchers have presented user authentication protocols for the MSE. In 2008, Tsai [12] proposed user authentication scheme without verification record using hash function; after that, Liao and Wang [13] presented an user authentication protocol using a dynamic identity. Hsiang and Shih [14], however, have shown that Liao and Wang's protocol was vulnerable against the replay, server spoofing, and stolen-verifier attacks, and aimed to provide mutual authentication, forward secrecy, and user anonymity.

In 2012, Li et al. [15] presented an user authentication protocol using a dynamic identity and smart card; however, Xue et al. [16] showed that Li et al.'s protocol was insecure against some attacks which are replay, eavesdropping, insider, impersonation, and denial of service (DoS), and then presented a new authentication protocol for key agreement using dynamic identity. Nevertheless, Lu et al. [17] have shown that Xue et al.'s protocol was vulnerable against some type of attacks which are masquerade, off-line password guessing and insider. To overcome these vulnerabilities, Lu et al. then presented a meliorated identity-based key-agreement protocol. Chuang and Chen [18] presented a trust computing-based authentication protocol that uses biometrics and smart cards, and they asserted that improved protocol can achieve a variety of security features; unfortunately, Mishra et al. [19] have shown that their protocol was not secure to user impersonation, server spoofing and stolen smart card attacks, and presented a new authentication protocol for key agreement using biometrics; however, Lu et al. [20] have shown that Mishra et al.'s protocol was insecure to the replay attack, and also does not provide an effective password change phase; furthermore, Wang et al. [21] have shown that Mishra et al.'s protocol was vulnerable against masquerade, replay and DoS attacks, and it cannot satisfy perfect forward secrecy. To overcome these problems, Wang et al. suggested a meliorated, authentication protocol for key agreement using biometrics; unfortunately, their proposed protocol is still insecure against some type of attacks which are outsider and user impersonation.

In this paper, we review the authentication protocol of Wang et al. [21] and show how the adversary can impersonate a legal user. Wang et al. [21] have improved the vulnerabilities of previous authentication schemes, and shown the efficient computational cost. Their scheme consists only a hash function and fuzzy-extraction technique. After demonstrating these problems, an improved fuzzy extractor-based authentication protocol is presented for MSE. Our contribution is to prove and overcome the weaknesses of Wang et al.'s protocol [21]. Lastly, the improved protocol is analyzed according to the security properties and the computational cost.

The remainder of the paper is constituted as follows: Some definitions such as threat assumptions and fuzzy extractor that are adopted for the proposed scheme are briefly introduced in Sect. 2; in Sects. 3 and 4, Wang et al.'s protocol is reviewed and analyzed, respectively; in Sect. 5, an improved fuzzy extractor-based authentication scheme is presented; in Sect. 6, a formal and informal analysis and simulation result of the improved protocol is demonstrated; Sect. 7 shows the comparison of security and performance of the improved protocol with the previous protocols; lastly, in Sect. 8, the conclusion is demonstrated.

2 Preliminaries

Some definitions of the threat assumptions and the fuzzy extractor which are useful to understand this paper are demonstrated in this section.

2.1 Threat Assumptions

The Dolev-Yao threat model [22] is introduced here, and the risk of side-channel attacks [23] is considered for the construction of the threat assumptions [8] that are demonstrated as follows:

(TA1) A remote user can be either an adversary AD or a legal user. In other words, a legitimate user can perform as any adversary AD.
(TA2) The AD can intercept, modification such as insert or delete, or reroute any transmitted communication message over public channel.
(TA3) Using the examining the power consumption, the AD can pull out the stored information from the any issued smart card.

2.2 Fuzzy Extractor

The fuzzy extractor can convert from the biometrics to a random string, is described here. Based on the Refs. [24,25], the fuzzy extractor is made of the two procedures (Gen, Rep).

- $Gen(Biometrics) \rightarrow \langle \alpha, \beta \rangle$
- $Rep(Biometrics^*, \beta) = \alpha$ if $Biometrics^*$ is reasonably close to Biometrics.

The probabilistic generation procedure Gen can extract some binary string $\alpha \in \{0,1\}^k$ and string $\beta \in \{0,1\}^*$ from the biometrics, where α is nearly random string and β is an auxiliary binary, and the deterministic reproduction procedure Rep can recover a nearly random binary string α from the auxiliary string β and any biometrics $Biometrics^*$ when the $Biometrics^*$ is pretty similar the $Biometrics$. Additional information can be found in the research [26].

3   Review of Wang et al.'s Protocol

Wang et al.'s fuzzy extractor-based authentication protocol for key agreement is reviewed here. Their protocol consists of three entities, as follows: user, server, and registration authority. Six phases relate to their protocol, and they are the server registration, user registration, login, authentication, password changing, and revocation or re-registration phases. For convenience, Table 1 describes some of the expressions that are used in this paper.

3.1 Server Registration

(SR1) S_j sends the message to the registration authority RA for server registration request.
(SR2) RA sends PK which is the pre-shared key to S_j through Internet Key Exchange Protocol version 2 (IKEv2) [27] by using a secure communication route.

Table 1. Expressions

Notation	Description
U_i, S_j, SC_i	User i, server j and smart card of U_i
$\mathcal{AD}$	Adversary
RA	Registration authority
ID_i, PW_i, BIO_i, DID_i	Identity, password, biometrics and dynamic identity of U_i
SID_j	Identity of S_j
TR_i	Registration time of U_i
R_i	Positive random integer unique to U_i
x	Master secret key selected by RA
α_i, β_i	U_i's nearly random and auxiliary binary strings
PK	Secure key pre-shared by RA and S_j
$\oplus$, $\|$	XOR and concatenation operation
$h(\cdot)$	Collision-resistance one-way hash function

3.2 User Registration

(UR1) U_i gives one's biometrics BIO_i at the biometrics scan sensor. The sensor then scans the BIO_i, pulls out the two random strings (α_i, β_i) from the computation $Gen(BIO_i) \rightarrow (\alpha_i, \beta_i)$, and keeps the β_i in the temporary storage. U_i hence chooses ID_i and PW_i, and calculates $DPW_i = h(PW_i \| \alpha_i)$. Lastly, U_i sends the message $\langle ID_i, DPW_i \rangle$ to RA for user registration by using a secure communication network.

(UR2) RA registers a new user record $\langle ID_i, UR_i = 1 \rangle$ into the database, where UR_i is the registration frequency of U_i. RA then calculates $V_i = h(ID_i \| x \| TR_i)$, $W_i = DPW_i \oplus h(V_i)$, $X_i = W_i \oplus h(PK)$, $Y_i = PK \oplus V_i \oplus h(PK)$ and $Z_i = h(ID_i \| DPW_i)$, where TR_i is the registration time of U_i.

(UR3) RA replies a new SC_i to U_i, which is composed of $\langle W_i, X_i, Y_i, Z_i, h(\cdot) \rangle$ by using a secure communication network.

(UR4) After receiving the smart card, U_i stores β_i into SC_i.

3.3 Login

(L1) U_i inserts own SC_i into a card recognizing device, enters ID_i and PW_i, and gives BIO_i^* at the biometrics scan sensor. The sensor hence scans the BIO_i^*, and recovers α_i from the $Rep(BIO_i^*, \beta_i) \rightarrow \alpha_i$.

(L2) SC_i then computes $DPW_i = h(PW_i \| \alpha_i)$, and checks whether $h(ID_i \| DPW_i)$ is same to the stored Z_i. If this holds, SC_i further calculates $h(PK) = W_i \oplus X_i$.

(L3) Next, SC_i chooses some random digits RN_1, and calculates $DID_i = ID_i \oplus h(RN_1)$, $M_1 = DPW_i \oplus RN_1 \oplus h(PK)$ and $M_2 = h(DID_i \parallel RN_1 \parallel DPW_i \parallel SID_j \parallel TS_i)$, where TS_i is the timestamp.

(L4) Lastly, SC_i sends the message $\langle DID_i, M_1, M_2, W_i, Y_i, TS_i \rangle$ to S_j for login request by using a public communication network.

3.4 Authentication

(A1) S_j verifies whether $TS_j - TS_i \leq \triangle TS$ is reasonable, where $\triangle TS$ is the minimum acceptable time interval and TS_j is the actual arrival time of the message. If this holds, S_j proceeds on the next stage; otherwise, S_j rejects the request.

(A2) S_j computes $V_i = PK \oplus Y_i \oplus h(PK)$, $DPW_i = W_i \oplus h(V_i)$, $RN_1 = DPW_i \oplus M_1 \oplus h(PK)$, and checks whether $h(DID_i \parallel RN_1 \parallel DPW_i \parallel SID_j \parallel TS_i)$ is same to the received M_2.

(A3) If this holds, S_j chooses some random digits RN_2, and calculates the common session secret key $SK_{ji} = h(DID_i \parallel SID_j \parallel RN_1 \parallel RN_2)$.

(A4) S_j computes $M_3 = RN_2 \oplus h(DID_i \parallel RN_1) \oplus h(PK)$ and $M_4 = h(SID_j \parallel RN_2 \parallel DID_i)$, and replies the response message $\langle SID_j, M_3, M_4 \rangle$ to U_i by using a public communication network.

(A5) SC_i computes $RN_2 = M_3 \oplus h(DID_i \parallel RN_1) \oplus h(PK)$, $SK_{ij} = h(DID_i \parallel SID_j \parallel RN_1 \parallel RN_2)$, and then checks whether $h(SID_j \parallel RN_2 \parallel DID_i)$ is same to the received M_4. If this holds, SC_i calculates $M_5 = h(SK_{ij} \parallel RN_1 \parallel RN_2)$, and sends $\langle M_5 \rangle$ to S_j by using a public communication network.

(A6) S_j checks whether $h(SK_{ji} \parallel RN_1 \parallel RN_2)$ is equal to the received M_5. If this holds, S_j can accept the session key SK_{ji} in this session; otherwise, S_j rejects any request message.

3.5 Password Change

(P1) U_i first inserts own SC_i into a card recognizing device, enters ID_i and PW_i, and gives BIO_i^* at the biometrics scan sensor. The sensor then scans BIO_i^*, and recovers α_i from the computation $Rep(BIO_i^*, \beta_i) \to \alpha_i$.

(P2) SC_i then computes $DPW_i = h(PW_i \parallel \alpha_i)$, and checks whether $h(ID_i \parallel DPW_i)$ is same to the stored Z_i. If this holds, SC_i trying to ask the user about the new password; otherwise, SC_i immediately terminates the password change phase.

(P3) After inputting the new PW_i^{new}, SC_i computes $DPW_i^{new} = h(PW_i^{new} \parallel \alpha_i)$, $W_i^{new} = W_i \oplus DPW_i \oplus DPW_i^{new}$, $X_i^{new} = X_i \oplus W_i \oplus W_i^{new}$ and $Z_i^{new} = h(ID_i \parallel DPW_i^{new})$.

(P4) Lastly, SC_i replaces W_i, X_i and Z_i with W_i^{new}, X_i^{new} and Z_i^{new}.

3.6 Revocation or Re-registration

If any user U_i wants to revoke his/her right, it is necessary that the U_i sends the message $\langle DPW_i \rangle$ to RA for revocation and verification by using a secure communication network. RA checks whether U_i is legitimate. If this holds, RA then updates the user's record by setting $\langle ID_i, UR_i = 0 \rangle$. Similarly, after receiving the message for re-registration request by using a public communication network, RA performs the same steps explained in Sect. 3.2, and it changes the user record from $\langle ID_i, UR_i \rangle$ to $\langle ID_i, UR_i = UR_i + 1 \rangle$.

4 Cryptanalysis of Wang et al.'s Protocol

Security weaknesses of Wang et al.'s protocol is shown here, and the authors shows that Wang et al.'s protocol is vulnerable to outsider, user impersonation and privileged insider attacks.

4.1 Outsider Attack

Outsider attack means that a legitimate user who issued a smart card uses his/her card to extract a meaningful value for attack. Let AD, who is the legitimate user but malicious, he/she then can extract the stored information $\{W_{AD}, X_{AD}, Y_{AD}, Z_{AD}, \beta_{AD}, h(\cdot)\}$ from the one's smart card; then, the AD can easily calculate $h(PK) = W_{AD} \oplus X_{AD}$, which is the same for any legitimate user and the pre-shared server key's hash result.

4.2 User Impersonation Attack

Suppose an adversary AD eavesdrops any user U_i's request message $\langle DID_i, M_1, M_2, W_i, Y_i, TS_i \rangle$ for login. AD can then perform the user impersonate attack by using message modification.

(UA1) Outsider adversary AD obtains $h(PK) = W_{AD} \oplus X_{AD}$ from his/her smart card.

(UA2) AD randomly generates some nonce RN_{AD}.

(UA3) AD then computes $W_i^* = W_i \oplus h(PK)$, $Y_i^* = h(PK)$, $M_1^* = W_i \oplus RN_{AD} \oplus h(PK)$ and $M_2^* = h(DID_i \parallel RN_{AD} \parallel W_i \parallel SID_j \parallel TS_{AD})$, where the TS_{AD} is the current timestamp.

(UA4) AD sends the message $\langle DID_i, M_1^*, M_2^*, W_i^*, Y_i^*, TS_{AD} \rangle$ to the server S_j for login by using a public communication network.

(UA5) S_j checks whether $TS_j - TS_{AD} \leq \triangle TS$ is valid. This holds, because the TS_{AD} has a fresh value.

(UA6) S_j retrieves $V_i = PK \oplus Y_i^* \oplus h(PK) = PK \oplus h(PK) \oplus h(PK) = PK$, $DPW_i = W_i^* \oplus h(V_i) = W_i \oplus h(PK) \oplus h(PK) = W_i$ and $RN_{AD} = DPW_i \oplus M_1^* \oplus h(PK) = W_i \oplus W_i \oplus RN_{AD} \oplus h(PK) \oplus h(PK)$, and verifies whether $h(DID_i \parallel RN_{AD} \parallel W_i \parallel SID_j \parallel TS_{AD})$ is equal to the received M_2^*.

(UA7) This holds, S_j then proceeds on the protocol without being detected. Lastly, $\mathcal{AD}$ and S_j "successfully" conclude the session; unfortunately, the S_j faultily decides that he/she is communicating with U_i.

5   The Improved Authentication Protocol

In this section, a new fuzzy extractor-based authentication protocol is proposed. Six phases relate to the proposed protocol, and they are the server registration, user registration, login, authentication, password changing, and revocation or re-registration phases.

5.1   Server Registration

(SR1) S_j sends the message to RA for registration request.
(SR2) RA replies PK which is pre-shared key and second master key x to S_j using the Internet Key Exchange Protocol version 2 (IKEv2) [27] by using secure communication network.

5.2   User Registration

(UR1) U_i imprints own biometrics BIO_i at the biometrics scan sensor. The sensor then scans the BIO_i, pulls out the two random strings (α_i, β_i) from the computation $Gen(BIO_i) \to (\alpha_i, \beta_i)$, and keeps the β_i in the temporary storage. U_i hence chooses ID_i and PW_i, and calculates $T_i = h(ID_i \parallel \alpha_i)$ and $DPW_i = h(PW_i \parallel \alpha_i)$. Lastly, the U_i sends the request message $\langle ID_i, DPW_i \rangle$ to RA for user registration by using a secure communication network, and stores T_i in the memory.
(UR2) RA registers a new user record $\langle ID_i, UR_i = 1 \rangle$ to the database, where UR_i is the registration frequency of U_i. RA then calculates $V_i = h(ID_i \parallel x \parallel R_i)$, $W_i = DPW_i \oplus h(V_i)$, $X_i = h(R_i \parallel PK)$, $Y_i = PK \oplus R_i \oplus h(PK)$ and $Z_i = h(ID_i \parallel DPW_i)$, where R_i is a positive random integer unique to the user.
(UR3) RA replies the new SC_i to U_i, which is composed of $\{W_i, X_i, Y_i, Z_i, h(\cdot)\}$ by using a secure communication network.
(UR4) U_i computes $X_i^* = X_i \oplus T_i$, replaces X_i with X_i^*, stores β_i into SC_i, removes β_i and T_i from the memory, and initialize the authentication environments.

5.3   Login

(L1) U_i first inserts own SC_i into a card recognizing device, enters ID_i and PW_i, and gives BIO_i^* at the biometrics scan sensor. The sensor then scans the BIO_i^*, and recovers α_i from the computation $Rep(BIO_i^*, \beta_i) \to \alpha_i$.
(L2) SC_i then computes $DPW_i = h(PW_i \parallel \alpha_i)$, and checks whether $h(ID_i \parallel DPW_i)$ is same to the stored Z_i. If this holds, SC_i further calculates $h(R_i \parallel PK) = X_i \oplus h(ID_i \parallel \alpha_i)$.

(L3) Next, SC_i chooses some random digits RN_1, and calculates $DID_i = ID_i \oplus h(RN_1)$, $M_1 = RN_1 \oplus h(R_i \parallel PK)$ and $M_2 = h(DID_i \parallel RN_1 \parallel DPW_i \parallel SID_j \parallel TS_i)$, where TS_i is the current timestamp.

(L4) Lastly, SC_i sends the message $\langle DID_i, M_1, M_2, W_i, Y_i, TS_i \rangle$ to S_j for login request by using a public communication network.

5.4 Authentication

(A1) S_j verifies whether $TS_j - TS_i \leq \triangle TS$ is reasonable, where $\triangle TS$ is the minimum acceptable time interval and TS_j is the actual arrival time of the message. If this holds, S_j proceeds on the next stage; otherwise, S_j rejects the login request.

(A2) S_j retrieves $R_i = PK \oplus Y_i \oplus h(PK)$, $RN_1 = M_1 \oplus h(R_i \parallel PK)$ and $ID_i = DID_i \oplus h(RN_1)$, and computes $V_i^* = h(ID_i \parallel x \parallel R_i)$ and $DPW_i = W_i \oplus h(V_i^*)$, and checks whether $h(DID_i \parallel RN_1 \parallel DPW_i \parallel SID_j \parallel TS_i)$ is same to the received M_2.

(A3) If this holds, S_j chooses some random digits RN_2, and calculates the common session secret key $SK_{ji} = h(DID_i \parallel SID_j \parallel h(V_i) \parallel RN_1 \parallel RN_2)$.

(A4) S_j computes $M_3 = RN_2 \oplus RN_1$ and $M_4 = h(SID_j \parallel SK_{ji} \parallel RN_1 \parallel RN_2 \parallel DID_i)$, and replies the authentication response message $\langle M_3, M_4 \rangle$ to U_i by using a public communication network.

(A5) SC_i computes $RN_2 = M_3 \oplus RN_1$, $SK_{ij} = h(DID_i \parallel SID_j \parallel W_i \oplus DPW_i \parallel RN_1 \parallel RN_2)$, and then checks whether $h(SID_j \parallel SK_{ij} \parallel RN_1 \parallel RN_2 \parallel DID_i)$ is same to the received M_4. If this holds, SC_i can accept the session key SK_{ij} in this session; otherwise, U_i terminates this session.

5.5 Password Change

(P1) U_i first inserts own SC_i into a card recognizing device, enters ID_i and PW_i, and gives BIO_i^* at the biometrics scan sensor. The sensor then scans the BIO_i^*, and recovers α_i from the computation $Rep(BIO_i^*, \beta_i) \rightarrow \alpha_i$.

(P2) SC_i then computes $DPW_i = h(PW_i \parallel \alpha_i)$, and checks whether $h(ID_i \parallel DPW_i)$ is same to the stored Z_i. If this holds, SC_i trying to ask the user about the new password; otherwise, SC_i immediately terminates the password change phase.

(P3) After inputting the new PW_i^{new}, SC_i computes $DPW_i^{new} = h(PW_i^{new} \parallel \alpha_i)$, $W_i^{new} = W_i \oplus DPW_i \oplus DPW_i^{new}$ and $Z_i^{new} = h(ID_i \parallel DPW_i^{new})$.

(P4) Lastly, SC_i replaces W_i and Z_i with W_i^{new} and Z_i^{new} into the smart card.

5.6 Revocation or Re-registration Phase

User revocation phase is same as the user revocation phase in Wang et al.'s protocol. If user U_i want to re-registration, the registration authority RA reissues the smart card to the user. The RA checks the UR_i value at the time of the user's login request, and if the UR_i is greater than 1, RA uses the value UR_i to calculate V_i^*.

(RR1) After receiving the request from U_i for re-registration, RA updates a user record $\langle ID_i, UR_i = UR_i + 1 \rangle$ to the database. RA then calculates $V_i = h(ID_i \parallel x \parallel UR_i \parallel R_i)$, $W_i = DPW_i \oplus h(V_i)$, $X_i = h(R_i \parallel PK)$, $Y_i = PK \oplus R_i \oplus h(PK)$ and $Z_i = h(ID_i \parallel DPW_i)$, where R_i is a positive random integer unique to the user.

(RR2) RA replies the new SC_i to U_i, which is composed of $\{W_i, X_i, Y_i, Z_i, h(\cdot)\}$ by using a secure communication network.

(RR3) U_i computes $X_i^* = X_i \oplus T_i$, replaces X_i with X_i^*, stores β_i into SC_i, removes β_i and T_i from the memory, and initialize the authentication environments.

6   Cryptanalysis of the Proposed Protocol

The improved protocol, which maintains the merits of Wang et al.'s protocol, is demonstrated, and it can resist some type of possible attacks and supports all of the security features. The cryptanalysis of the improved protocol was organized with threat assumptions.

6.1   Informal Security Analysis

We explain the improved protocol can resist various kinds of known attacks.

Outsider Attack. Outsider attack means that a legitimate user who issued a smart card uses his/her card to extract a meaningful value for attack. Assume that an adversary AD who issued a smart card extracts $\{W_{AD}, X_{AD}, Y_{AD}, Z_{AD}, \beta_{AD}, h(\cdot)\}$ from the one's smart card. AD can retrieve $h(R_{AD} \parallel PK) = X_{AD} \oplus h(ID_{AD} \parallel \alpha_{AD})$; however, R_{AD} is a positive random integer that has the different value, and PK is the pre-shared key between RA and S_j. AD cannot obtain and use this value to the other attack, and the proposed protocol can therefore avoid the outsider attack.

Modification Attack. Assume that AD intercepts the transmitted informations $\{DID_i, M_1, M_2, W_i, Y_i, TS_i, M_3, M_4\}$; however, the AD cannot retrieve RN_1, RN_2, R_i and PK from these messages. Even if AD uses his/her $h(R_{AD} \parallel PK)$, A cannot generate M_1 without the DPW_i. To compute DPW_i, the second master key x is needed. The proposed protocol can therefore avoid the modification attack.

Off-Line Password Guessing Attack. Assume that U_i's SC_i is lost or AD steals SC_i of U_i, AD can then obtain $\{W_i, X_i, Y_i, Z_i, \beta_i, h(\cdot)\}$; however, he/she cannot guess the password of U_i. To guess the password from $h(PW_i \parallel \alpha_i)$, α_i is needed; however, α_i is in possession of the high entropy; moreover, the same biometrics are not present between any two people. The proposed protocol can therefore avoid the off-line password guessing attack.

User Impersonation Attack. Assume that $\mathcal{AD}$ intercepts the transmitted informations $\{DID_i, M_1, M_2, W_i, Y_i, TS_i, M_3, M_4\}$; however, $\mathcal{AD}$ cannot make the reasonable message $\{DID_i, M_1, M_2, W_i, Y_i, TS_i\}$ for login request. This is because R_i is a positive random integer that is different from the other user's thing, and RN_1 is some random digits that is selected by U_i. To make M_2, the second master key x is needed. The proposed protocol can therefore avoid the user impersonation attack.

Stolen Smart Card Attack. Suppose that $\mathcal{AD}$ steals U_i's SC_i, he/she then extracts $\{W_i, X_i, Y_i, Z_i, \beta_i\ h(\cdot)\}$.; however, $\mathcal{AD}$ cannot obtain any sensitive information of U_i. Although $\mathcal{AD}$ obtains the $h(R_{\mathcal{AD}} \parallel PK)$ from one's smart card, $R_{\mathcal{AD}}$ and R_i are the different values. The proposed protocol can therefore avoid the stolen smart card attack.

Table 2. Algorithm $EXP_{HASH,A}^{BASMK}$

1. Eavesdrop the login request message $\langle DID_i, M_1, M_2, W_i, Y_i, TS_i \rangle$
2. Call the oracle. Let $(RN'_1, DPW'_i) \leftarrow Reveal(M_2)$
3. Eavesdrop the authentication response message $\langle M_3, M_4 \rangle$
4. Use the oracle. Let $(SK'_{ji}, RN''_1, RN'_2) \leftarrow Reveal(M_4)$
5. **if** $(RN'_1 = RN''_1)$ **then**
6.   Compute $ID'_i = DID_i \oplus h(RN'_1)$ and $H_1 = M_1 \oplus RN'_1 = h(R_i \parallel PK)$
7.   Use the oracle. Let $(R'_i, PK') \leftarrow Reveal(H_1)$
8.   Compute $H_2 = Y_i \oplus R'_i \oplus PK' = h(PK)$
9.   Use the oracle. Let $(PK'') \leftarrow Reveal(H_2)$
10.   **if** $(PK' = PK'')$ **then**
11.   Compute $RN''_2 = M_3 \oplus RN'_1$
12.   **if** $(RN'_2 = RN''_2)$ **then**
13.   Call the oracle. Let $(PW'_i, \alpha'_i) \leftarrow Reveal(DPW'_i)$
14.   Compute $h(V_i) = W_i \oplus DPW'_i$
15.   Compute $SK'_{ij} = h(DID_i \parallel SID_j \parallel h(V_i) \parallel RN'_1 \parallel RN''_2)$
16.   **if** $(SK'_{ji} == SK'_{ij})$ **then**
17.   Accept $ID'_i, PW'_i, \alpha'_i, R'_i$ as the correct $ID_i, PW_i, \alpha_i, R_i,$ PK', SK_{ij} as the correct PK and SK_{ij}, respectively.
18.   **return** 1 (Success)
19.   **else**
20.   **return** 0 (Failure)
21.   **else**
22.   **return** 0 (Failure)
23.   **end if**
24.   **else**
25.   **return** 0 (Failure)
26.   **end if**
27. **else**
28.   **return** 0 (Failure)
29. **end if**

6.2   Formal Security Analysis

The formal analysis using random oracle method is demonstrated here, and its security is shown. First, the following hash function is defined Refs. [8,28]:

Definition 1. *The secure and collision-resistance hash function $\mathcal{H}(\cdot) : \{0, 1\}^* \rightarrow \{0, 1\}^k$ picks up any input as a binary string $a \in \{0, 1\}^*$ which has a randomly length, extracts a binary string $\mathcal{H}(a) \in \{0, 1\}^k$, and satisfies the following conditions:*

(i) *Given the $b \in B$, it's mathematically impossible to find out a $a \in A$ such that $b = \mathcal{H}(a)$.*
(ii) *Given the $a \in A$, it's mathematically impossible to find out the another $a' \neq a \in A$, such that $\mathcal{H}(a') = \mathcal{H}(a)$.*
(iii) *It's mathematically impossible to find out a pair $(a', a) \in A' \times A$, with $a' \neq a$, such that $\mathcal{H}(a') = \mathcal{H}(a)$*

Theorem 1. *According to the assumptions that if the hash function $\mathcal{H}(\cdot)$ closely performs like an oracle, then the protocol is certainly secure to the adversary AD for the protection of the meaningful information including the identity ID_i, the password PW_i, the nearly random binary string α_i, the positive random integer R_i, the pre-shared key PK and the common session key SK_{ij}.*

Proof. Formal proof of the proposed protocol is analogous to those in Refs. [8, 20, 28, 29], and it uses the following random oracle model to construct the AD, who will have the ability to recover the ID_i, PW_i, α_i, R_i, PK and SK_{ij}.

Reveal. The random oracle can obtain the input a from the hash result $b = \mathcal{H}(a)$ without failure. AD now performs the experimental algorithm as shown in Table 2, $EXP_{HASH, A}^{BASMK}$ for the proposed protocol as BASMK. Let's define the probability of success for $EXP_{HASH,A}^{BASMK}$ as $Success_{HASH, A}^{BASMK} = |Pr[EXP_{HASH, A}^{BASMK} = 1] - 1|$, where $Pr(\cdot)$ means the probability of $EXP_{HASH,A}^{BASMK}$. The advantage function for this algorithm then becomes $Adv_{HASH, A}^{BASMK}(t, q_R) = max_{Success}$, where t and q_R are the execution cost and number of queries. Consider the algorithm as shown in Table 2. If the AD has the capability to crack the problem of hash function given in Definition 1, AD can then immediately obtain the ID_i, PW_i, α_i, R_i, PK and SK_{ij}. In that case, AD will detect the complete connections between the U_i and S_j; however, the inversion of the input from the given hash result is impossible computationally, i.e., $Adv_{HASH, A}^{BASMK}(t) \leq \epsilon$, for all $\epsilon > 0$. Therefore, $Adv_{HASH, A}^{BASMK}(t, q_R) \leq \epsilon$, since $Adv_{HASH, A}^{BASMK}(t, q_R)$ depends on $Adv_{HASH, A}^{BASMK}(t)$. In conclusion, it is no method for AD to detect the complete connections between the U_i and S_j, the proposed protocol thus is certainly secure to AD for retrieving $(ID_i, PW_i, \alpha_i, R_i, PK, SK_{ij})$.

Table 3. The result of the analysis using OFMC backend

```
% OFMC
% Version of 2006/02/13
SUMMARY
  SAFE
DETAILS
  BOUNDED_NUMBER_OF_SESSIONS
PROTOCOL
  /home/span/span/testsuite/results/testrv4.if
GOAL
  as_specified
BACKEND
  OFMC
COMMENTS
STATISTICS
 parseTime: 0.00s
 searchTime: 71.86
 visiteNodes: 11440 nodes
 depth: 9 piles
```

6.3 Simulation Using AVISPA

We perform to simulate the improved protocol for formal analysis using the widely accepted AVISPA. The main contribution of this simulation is to verify whether the proposed protocol is invulnerable to two attacks which are replay and man-in-the middle. AVISPA is composed of four back-ends: (1) On-the-fly Model-Checker; (2) Constraint-Logic-based Attack Searcher; (3) SAT-based Model Checker; and (4) Tree Automata based on Automatic Approximations for the Analysis of Security Protocols. The protocol is implemented in High Level Protocol Specification Language (HLPSL) [28] in AVISPA. The fundamental classes available in the HLPSL are [30]. The simulation result of the proposed protocol using OMFC is shown in Table 3. The result shows that two attacks which are man-in-the middle and replay have no effect on the proposed protocol.

7 Functionality and Performance Analysis

The comparisons of the functionality and computational cost of the proposed protocol with the other previous protocols [15,16,18–21] are demonstrated here.

7.1 Functionality Analysis

Table 4 itemizes the avoidance comparisons of various biometric-based key agreement protocols for MSE. The result shows that the proposed protocol is distinctly secure and achieves all of the security requirements.

Table 4. The comparison of the attack resistance

	Li et al. [15]	Xue et al. [16]	Chuang et al. [18]	Mishra et al. [19]	Lu et al. [20]	Wang et al. [21]	Ours
P1	×	×	×	×	×	×	√
P2	×	×	√	×	√	√	√
P3	√	√	√	√	√	×	√
P4	×	×	√	√	√	√	√
P5	×	×	√	√	√	√	√
P6	√	×	√	√	√	×	√
P7	×	√	×	√	×	×	√
P8	√	√	×	√	×	×	√
P9	√	√	×	×	√	√	√
P10	√	×	√	√	√	√	√

√: Resist to the attack; ×: Vulnerable to the attack; P1: outsider attack; P2: replay attack; P3: modification attack; P4: stolen verifier attack; P5: off-line guessing attack; P6: insider attack; P7: stolen smart card attack; P8: user impersonation attack; P9: DoS attack; P10: server spoofing attack.

Table 5. The comparison of computational cost

	Registration	Login	Authentication	Total	Time(ms)
Li et al. [15]	$6T_H$	$6T_H$	$13T_H$	$25T_H$	5.0
Xue et al. [16]	$7T_H$	$6T_H$	$19T_H$	$31T_H$	6.4
Chuang et al. [18]	$3T_H$	$4T_H$	$13T_H$	$20T_H$	4.0
Mishra et al. [19]	$7T_H$	$6T_H$	$11T_H$	$24T_H$	4.8
Lu et al. [20]	$5T_H$	$5T_H$	$12T_H$	$22T_H$	4.4
Wang et al. [21]	$5T_H$	$4T_H$	$11T_H$	$20T_H$	4.0
Our proposed	$7T_H$	$5T_H$	$9T_H$	$21T_H$	4.2

7.2   Performance Anaylsis

The computational costs are compared. Table 5 itemizes a comparison of the computational spending of the protocol with the related previous protocols, where the definition of T_H is hash function's computational times. According to the results obtained in [31], T_H is less than 0.2 ms on average, in MSE (Core: 3.2 GHz, Memory: 3.0 G). Compared with Wang et al.'s protocol, the proposed protocol requires a slightly higher computational overhead, as the proposed scheme computes the one extra hash operations; however, the proposed scheme possesses all of the properties in terms of the security.

8   Conclusion

Recently, Wang et al. demonstrated the security weaknesses of Mishra et al., and presented a fuzzy extractor-based authentication protocol. They also asserted that their protocol is more secure and guarantees user anonymity; however, Wang et al.'s protocol was insecure to outsider and user impersonation attacks. To overcome these security weaknesses, the authors propose an improved fuzzy extractor-based authentication protocol for the multi-server environment that continues to have the merits of Wang et al.'s scheme. Furthermore, the proposed protocol comprises inclusive security properties. The formal and informal analysis of this paper make clear or explain why the proposed protocol is more secure.

Acknowledgments. This research was supported by Basic Science Research Program through the National Research Foundation of Korea (NRF) funded by the Ministry of Education (NRF-2010-0020210).

References

1. Zhang, X., Li, W., Zheng, Z.M., Guo, B.H.: Optimized statistical analysis of software trustworthiness attributes. Sci. China Inf. Sci. **55**(11), 2508–2520 (2012)
2. Lamport, L.: Password authentication with insecure communication. Commun. ACM **24**(11), 770–772 (1981)
3. Jeon, W., Kim, J., Nam, J., Lee, Y., Won, D.: An enhanced secure authentication scheme with anonymity for wireless environments. IEICE Trans. Commun. **95**(7), 2505–2508 (2012)
4. Kim, J., Lee, D., Jeon, W., Lee, Y., Won, D.: Security analysis and improvements of two-factor mutual authentication with key agreement in wireless sensor networks. Sensors **14**(4), 6443–6462 (2014)
5. Sun, D.Z., Huai, J.P., Sun, J.Z., Li, J.X., Zhang, J.W., Feng, Z.Y.: Improvements of Juang's password authenticated key agreement scheme using smart cards. IEEE Trans. Ind. Electron. **56**(6), 2284–2291 (2009)
6. Khan, M.K., Zhang, J.: Improving the security of 'a flexible biometrics remote user authentication scheme'. Comput. Stand. Interfaces **29**(1), 82–85 (2007)
7. He, D., Kumar, N., Khan, M.K., Lee, J.H.: Anonymous two-factor authentication for consumer roaming service in global mobility networks. IEEE Trans. Consum. Electron. **59**(4), 811–817 (2013)
8. Moon, J., Choi, Y., Jung, J., Won, D.: An Improvement of robust biometrics-based authentication and key agreement scheme for multi-server environments using smart cards. PLoS ONE **10**(12), 1–15 (2015)
9. Moon, J., Choi, Y., Kim, J., Won, D.: An improvement of robust and efficient biometrics based password authentication scheme for telecare medicine information systems using extended chaotic maps. J. Med. Syst. **40**(3), 1–11 (2016)
10. Lu, Y., Li, L., Peng, H., Yang, Y.: An enhanced biometric-based authentication scheme for telecare medicine information systems using elliptic curve cryptosystem. J. Med. Syst. **39**(3), 1–8 (2015)
11. Choi, Y., Nam, J., Lee, D., Kim, J., Jung, J., Won, D.: Security enhanced anonymous multi-server authenticated key agreement scheme using smart cards and biometrics. Sci. World J. Article ID 281305, 1–15 (2014)

12. Tsai, J.L.: Efficient multi-server authentication scheme based on one-way hash function without verification table. Comput. Secur. **27**(3–4), 115–121 (2008)
13. Liao, Y.P., Wang, S.S.: A secure dynamic ID based remote user authentication scheme for multi-server environment. Comput. Stand. Interfaces **31**(1), 24–29 (2009)
14. Hsiang, H.C., Shih, W.K.: Improvement of the secure dynamic ID based remote user authentication scheme for multi-server environment. Comput. Stand. Interfaces **31**(6), 1118–1123 (2009)
15. Li, X., Ma, J., Wang, W., Xiong, Y., Zhang, J.: A novel smart card and dynamic ID based remote user authentication scheme for multi-server environments. Math. Comput. Model. **58**(1–2), 85–95 (2013)
16. Xue, K.P., Hong, P.L., Ma, C.S.: A lightweight dynamic pseudonym identity based authentication and key agreement protocol without verification tables for multi-server arahitecture. J. Comput. Syst. Sci. **80**(1), 195–206 (2013)
17. Lu, Y., Li, L., Peng, H., Yang, X., Yang, Y.: A lightweight ID based authentication and key agreement protocol for multi-server architecture. Int. J. Distrib. Sens. Netw. **11**(3), 1–9 (2015). 635890
18. Chuang, M.C., Chen, M.C.: An anonymous multi-server authenticated key agreement scheme based on trust computing using smart cards and biometrics. Expert Syst. Appl. **41**(4), 1411–1418 (2014)
19. Mishra, D., Das, A.K., Mukhopadhyay, S.: A secure user anonymity-preserving biometric-based multiserver authenticated key agreement scheme using smart cards. Expert Syst. Appl. **41**(18), 8129–8143 (2014)
20. Lu, Y., Li, L., Yang, X., Yang, Y.: Robust biometrics based authentication and key agreement scheme for multi-server environments using smart cards. PLoS ONE **10**(5), 1–13 (2015)
21. Wang, C., Zhang, X., Zheng, Z.: Cryptanalysis and improvement of a biometric-based multi-server authentication and key agreement scheme. PLoS ONE **11**(2), 1–25 (2016)
22. Dolev, D., Yao, A.C.: On the security of public key protocols. IEEE Trans. Inf. Theory **29**(2), 198–208 (1983)
23. Kocher, P., Jaffe, J., Jun, B., Rohatgi, P.: Introduction to differential power analysis. J. Cryptogr. Eng. **1**(1), 5–27 (2011)
24. Das, A.K.: A secure and effective biometric-based user authentication scheme for wireless sensor networks using smart card and fuzzy extractor. Int. J. Commun. Syst. **30**(1), 1–25 (2015)
25. Dodis, Y., Kanukurthi, B., Katz, J., Reyzin, L., Smith, A.: Robust fuzzy extractors and authenticated key agreement from close secrets. IEEE Trans. Inf. Theory **58**(9), 6207–6222 (2012)
26. Dodis, Y., Reyzin, L., Smith, A.: Fuzzy extractors: how to generate strong keys from biometrics and other noisy data. In: Cachin, C., Camenisch, J.L. (eds.) EUROCRYPT 2004. LNCS, vol. 3027, pp. 523–540. Springer, Heidelberg (2004). https://doi.org/10.1007/978-3-540-24676-3_31
27. RFC 4306: Internet key exchange (IKEv2) protocol (2005)
28. Das, A.K.: A secure and effective user authentication and privacy preserving protocol with smart cards for wireless communications. Netw. Sci. **2**(1–2), 12–27 (2013)
29. Das, A.K., Paul, N.R., Tripathy, L.: Cryptanalysis and improvement of an access control in user hieraRAhy based on elliptic curve cryptosystem. Inf. Sci. **209**, 80–92 (2012)

30. von Oheimb, D.: The high-level protocol specification language HLPSL developed in the EU project AVISPA. In: Proceedings of the Applied Semantics 2005 Workshop, Frauenchiemsee, Germany, pp. 1–17 (2005)
31. Xue, K., Hong, P.: Security improvement on an anonymous key agreement protocol based on chaotic maps. Commun. Nonlinear Sci. Numer. Simul. **17**(7), 2969–2977 (2012)

Mining on Line General Opinions About Sustainability of Hotels: A Systematic Literature Mapping

Thiago de Oliveira Lima[✉], Methanias Colaco Junior[✉], and Maria Augusta S. N. Nunes[✉]

Federal University of Sergipe (UFS), São Cristóvão, Sergipe, Brazil
thiagodeolima@gmail.com, mjrse@hotmail.com, gutanunes@gmail.com

Abstract. Context: Nowadays, people do not only navigate, but also contribute content to the Internet. Thoughts and opinions are written on rating sites, forums, social networks, blogs and other media. Such opinions constitute a valuable source of information for companies, governs and consumers, but it would be humanly impossible to analyze and locate the opinions in those assessments, due to the large volume and different origins of the data. For this, approaches and techniques of opinion mining in texts are used. **Objective:** To identify and characterize the techniques used for mining data in public opinion repositories regarding hotels, since the opinion mining area has offered necessary subsidies for decision-making related to hotel management. Besides, to identify, specifically, studies that investigated the opinions about the sustainability of hotels. **Method:** A systematic mapping was performed to characterize the research area. **Results:** It was identified that, among the main approaches, 31% of the works found use only data mining, while 55% exclusively use machine learning techniques, and 14% both. **Conclusion:** The most relevant studies in such research lines adopt machine learning algorithms such as Naive Bayes, SVM, LDA, decision tree, besides aspect-based techniques and SentiWordNet lexicon dictionaries. There are still opportunities to explore opinion mining solutions in online hotel reviews, mainly by taking into consideration aspects related to sustainable practices and sustainability levels practiced by each hotel.

Keywords: Data mining · Big data · Machine learning · NLP Sustainability

1 Introduction

The specialized websites and the social networks have become the most popular platforms for sharing traveling information, with varied commentaries of diverse virtual origins, published every day. The automatically generated hotel reviews could help travelers when selecting hotels [1]. A convenient approach to divulging

© Springer International Publishing AG, part of Springer Nature 2018
O. Gervasi et al. (Eds.): ICCSA 2018, LNCS 10960, pp. 558–574, 2018.
https://doi.org/10.1007/978-3-319-95162-1_38

and promoting the tourism industry is through website, fact that has been improving nowadays. The researchers noted that the reviews and commentaries gathered by websites are useful information for clients and hotel managers [2].

However, the analysis of the huge set of review texts is a hard task not only for clients, but also for the parties interested in hotel management. On the other hand, the analysis of information based on few items may generate biased situations [3]. In the last years, some researchers have proposed opinion extraction systems, domain-independent mainly, to automatically extract structured representations of opinion contained in such texts [1,4–7]. As an example, consumers have been verifying the opinion of other consumers before buying a product with the intention to make a good purchase [8].

This systematic mapping aims to identify the techniques used for data mining in public written reviews on the Web. The purpose is to evaluate the state of the art of data mining in textual repositories aiming to extract the opinion of the consumers on hotels, in the context of tourists and managers in the hospitality field. A secondary goal was to verify the existence of works that mined the opinion of guests on the practice of sustainable initiatives by the hotels by analyzing the popularity of the opinions and possibly gauge the level of sustainability practiced by each hotel. Sustainability is certainly an ample term, but the present research has as secondary goal to verify if the sustainable practices implemented by the hotels such as: selective garbage collection, rain water captation, use of organic foods, use of low-consumption light bulbs, motion sensors to automatically turn light bulbs on and off in the environments, regular treatment of swimming pool water, may or may not influence the opinion polarity of the guests reviews. With such purpose, articles from important databases for computer science were mapped.

In such context, it is intended to answer the following research questions: **Q1**: What are the most used text mining techniques to detect the opinion of consumers in online reviews? **Q2**: Are the online text mining techniques used for detecting the consumers' satisfaction regarding the sustainable practices by the hotels and gauging the sustainability levels practiced by each hotel? **Q3**: What are the countries that have more researchers publishing on the theme? **Q4**: What years had more publications in the area? **Q5**: What are the main periodicals and conferences on the theme?

It was identified, when answering these questions, that Data Mining, with 31%, and Machine Learning, with 55%, were the most used approaches. Among the main approaches, we found opinion analysis based on lexicon dictionaries [4,6,7,9–12], emoticon [4], interjection [4] and acronym dictionaries [4], besides statistical methods such as Cohen's Kappa [5], maximum entropy [4,5,9] and Chi-Square [2]. In other studies, we also identified aspect-based methods [8,13–16], grammatical classes of words, supposedly named POS-Tagging [9,17] and Machine Learning algorithms, such as k-medoids [1], J48 [6,18], SVM [4,6,12,18–22], logistic regression [23], Naive Bayes [3,4,6,11,12,18,20], LDA [7,20,24–27], AdaBoost [19,20], decision tree [3,6,12,20], LSA (Latent Semantic Analysis) [28], linear regression [28] and TSC (Topic Sentiment Criteria) [29]. In relation to the aspects and sustainability levels practiced by hotels, we identified only one study which relates the influence of sustainable issues on the opinion of the clients [24].

On the technical resources for opinion mining, the Naive Bayes algorithms [3,4,6,11,12,18,20] and SVM [4,6,12,18–22] were the ones which highlighted more in the Machine Learning sphere, while the lexicon dictionary related to the identification of texts in English named SentiWordNet had the greatest highlight in the Data Mining area [4,6,7,9,12]. In relation to countries all over the world, the USA was the country with more publications in the area.

This article is organized in the following way: in Sect. 2, the method adopted in this mapping is presented; in Sect. 3, the analysis results are described; in Sect. 4, the threats to validity are presented; finally, in Sect. 5, the conclusion is presented.

2   Method

The Systematic Mapping consists of a systematic protocol for search and selection of relevant studies aiming to extract information and map the results for a specific research issue [30,31]. Such protocol was proposed by Kitchenham et al. for systematic review in 2004 and Petersen et al. for systematic mapping in 2008. The objective of this work is limited to developing a Systematic Mapping with the intention to identify, analyze and evaluate case studies, primary works or surveys, to characterize the use of algorithms, methods and techniques for opinion mining in public reviews of hotels that take or do not take sustainability aspects into consideration. Initially, for the definition of research questions, the approaches that used opinion mining in texts related to the public reviews of hotels were detailed.

Thus, aiming to follow the systematic mapping method, how the process of search and selection of primary studies was developed is described in the following section. To that end, it was necessary to define the research questions, search and selection strategy and selection criteria. Thus, the detailed description of the process of search and selection of primary studies follows below.

2.1   Research Questions

To achieve the objective proposed by this mapping, the following research questions were elaborated:

- **Q1:** What are the most used text mining techniques to detect the opinion of consumers in online reviews?
- **Q2:** Are the online text mining techniques used for detecting the consumers' satisfaction regarding the sustainable practices by the hotels and gauging the sustainability levels practiced by each hotel?
- **Q3:** What are the countries that have more researchers publishing on the theme?

- **Q4:** What years had more publications in the area?
- **Q5:** What are the main periodicals and conferences on the theme?

For the characterization of the used computing approaches, we initially believed that the studies would be contained in the three computing areas that deal with pattern recognition: Data Mining, Artificial Intelligence and Machine Learning. As Data Mining is the application of specific algorithms for the extraction of patterns from a database [32], such area commonly presents an overlapping with the areas of Artificial Intelligence, Statistics and Database. The studies were classified as Data Mining when they explicitly referred to the term. If they did not, even if the study had used Artificial Intelligence, we consider Data Mining when the use of algorithm was made from a Database Managing System (DMS) with data aspects.

The separate classification of the Machine Learning area in an area originated from Artificial Intelligence, actually happened due to the fact that such area has periodicals and exclusive conferences, such as: Machine Learning, ISSN: 0885-6125; Machine Learning (DORDRECHT. ONLINE), ISSN: 1573-0565; ICML - International Conference on Machine Learning and ICMLA - IEEE International Conference on Machine Learning and Applications. Besides, it is an area classified on the same level as Artificial Intelligence, by the ACM classification system and in conferences indexed by IEEE.

2.2   Research Scope

For the execution of the Systematic Mapping, the Scopus database was used. For unrestricted downloads in the database the access to the Capes periodical portal [33] was used.

The choice of the Scopus database happened due to the fact that its collection incorporates articles from many other databases, such as: IEEE, ACM, Springer and Elsevier. Those databases are responsible for publishing the main periodicals in the computer science area.

The sources were select according to the availability of consultation over the Internet, which were indexed in the databases cited above, being able to be found through keyword search. In relation to the language, only works in English and Portuguese were selected. In relation to the area, only works referring to Computer Science were selected. In relation to the type of publication, only articles published in conferences, periodicals or book chapters were selected.

In the Scopus database, after using the search function by title, summary or keyword, the advanced search option to select only results belonging to the Computer Science area only in the English or Portuguese languages was used, and results that referred to recapitulations of conferences and notes were also excluded.

2.3   Publication Search Method

The sources were accessed over the Internet. The Search String that was later used in the selected database generated through the combination of keywords is:

Search String 01. ((TITLE-ABS-KEY (("review" OR "evaluation" OR "rating OR "appraisal" OR "valuation" OR "appreciation" OR "rate" OR "estimate" OR "reckoning" OR "appraisement" OR "account" OR "putting" OR "opinion" OR "avaliação" OR "opinião" OR "comentário") AND ("hotel" OR "hospitality" OR "hostel" OR "house for season" OR "hospitabilidade" OR "pousada" OR "casa para temporada") AND ("data mining" OR "data analytics" OR "big data" OR "business intelligence" OR "data science" OR "artificial intelligence" OR "NLP" OR "natural language" OR "opinion mining" OR "sentiment classification" OR "sentiment analysis" OR "mineração de dados" OR "análise de dados" OR "ciência de dados" OR "inteligência artificia" OR "PLN" OR "linguagem natural" OR "mineração de opinião" OR "machine learning" OR "aprendizado de máquina")))) AND (LIMIT-TO (SUBAREA, "COMP")) AND (EXCLUDE (DOCTYPE, "cr") OR EXCLUDE (DOCTYPE, "no")).

Search String 02. ((TITLE-ABS-KEY (("review" OR "evaluation" OR "rating" OR "appraisal" OR "valuation" OR "appreciation" OR "rate" OR "estimate" OR "reckoning" OR "appraisement" OR "account" OR "putting" OR "opinion" OR "avaliação" OR "opinião" OR "comentário") AND ("hotel" OR "hospitality" OR "hostel" OR "house for season" OR "hospitabilidade" OR "pousada" OR "casa para temporada") AND ("data mining" OR "data analytics" OR "big data" OR "business intelligence" OR "data science" OR "artificial intelligence" OR "NLP" OR "natural language" OR "opinion mining" OR "sentiment classification" OR "sentiment analysis" OR "mineração de dados" OR "análise de dados" OR "ciência de dados" OR "inteligência artificial" OR "PLN" OR "linguagem natural" OR "mineração de opinião" OR "machine learning" OR "aprendizado de máquina")))) AND ("sustainability" OR "sustainable" OR "tenable" OR "sustentável" OR "sustentabilidade") AND (LIMIT-TO (SUBAREA, "COMP")) AND (EXCLUDE (DOCTYPE, "cr") OR EXCLUDE (DOCTYPE, "no")).

The search was performed during October 2017, the search string returned 250 results. After the search stage, the article selection stage, which will be detailed below, was initiated.

2.4   Criteria Selection Procedures

The performed searches used the string search from Sect. 2.3 and the collected results were calculated taking into consideration only the selected studies for evaluation. The results that obeyed the inclusion criteria were selected for summary reading and titles. The selected articles were read, analyzed and sent to the result extraction stage.

The inclusion criteria were:

1. The result must contain the theme of this study in the title, summary or keywords;
2. The result must be available for online search;
3. The result must explore an algorithm, technique, mechanism or approach of opinion mining in online hotel reviews;
4. The articles must have indicatives of how the opinion of the consumers is influenced by sustainable practices of the hotels that used them (exclusive for the research question Q2).

The exclusion criteria were:

1. Articles that do not have relation with the computer science field;
2. Secondary studies, because they deal with approaches from third parties;
3. Unavailable articles;
4. Preliminary studies.

Among the 250 works found, after the inclusion and exclusion criteria, 29 were selected for complete reading and analysis. Figure 1 shows the amount of articles by scientific repository after the application of the selection criteria and primary studies analyses.

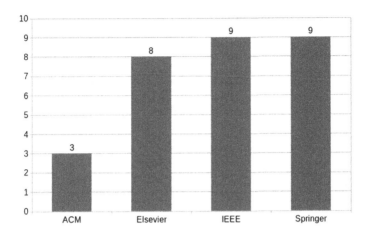

Fig. 1. Selection of articles by base

In Table 1, we can identify a general summary of the research result and application of the selection criteria, resulting in 29 studies.

Table 1. Results of the research in the databases and results of the application of the selection criteria.

Data repository	Research result	Application of selection criteria
ACM	24	4
Elsevier	19	9
IEEE	65	8
Springer	70	8
Others	72	0
Total	**250**	**29**

3   Discussion and Results

In this section, the analysis results of the primary study answering the previously defined research questions are presented. In Table 2, the 29 articles selected for this work, as well as the reference to each author are listed.

Table 2. Referred papers.

Paper title	Reference number
Sentiment analysis method for tracking touristics reviews in social media network	[4]
Word2Vec approach for sentiment classification relating to hotel reviews	[5]
Sentiment Classification of Consumer-Generated Online Reviews Using Topic Modeling	[24]
Aspect based recommendations: Recommending items with the most valuable aspects based on user reviews	[23]
Word of mouth quality classification based on contextual sentiment lexicons	[6]
The analysis and prediction of customer review rating using opinion mining	[3]
Opinion mining from online hotel reviews - A text summarization approach	[1]
Aspect identification and ratings inference for hotel reviews	[13]
Proposal of LDA-Based Sentiment Visualization of Hotel Reviews	[7]
Sentiment Polarity Classification Using Structural Features	[9]
An Investigation of Effectiveness Using Topic Information Order to Classify Tourists Reviews	[20]
Sentiment analysis of hotel reviews in greek: A comparison of unigram features	[21]
Learning sentiment based ranked-lexicons for opinion retrieval	[10]
A novel deterministic approach for aspect-based opinion mining in tourism products reviews	[14]
Are influential writers more objective? An analysis of emotionality in review comments	[11]
Opinion mining and summarization of hotel reviews	[12]
Incorporating appraisal expression patterns into topic modeling for aspect and sentiment word identification	[25]
Hierarchical multi-label conditional random fields for aspect-oriented opinion mining	[15]
The ensemble of Naive Bayes classifiers for hotel searching	[2]
OpinionZoom, a modular tool to explore tourism opinions on the Web	[17]
A boosted SVM based sentiment analysis approach for online opinionated text	[19]
A distant supervision method for product aspect extraction from customer reviews	[26]
Long autonomy or long delay?' the importance of domain in opinion mining	[16]
Identifying customer preferences about tourism products using an aspect-based opinion mining approach	[8]
Analyzing user reviews in tourism with topic models	[29]
Machine learning approach to recognize subject based sentiment values of reviews	[18]
A Study on Text-Score Disagreement in Online Reviews	[22]
Aspect based Sentiment Oriented Summarization of Hotel Reviews	[27]
Business intelligence in online customer textual reviews: Understanding consumer perceptions and influential factors	[28]

In the chart in Fig. 2 the characterization of the main approaches found for opinion mining is presented. As an answer to research question **Q1**, the most used approaches were the SVM machine learning techniques (27.5%) [4,6,12,18–22], *Naive Bayes* (24%) [3,4,6,11,12,20] and the LDA machine learning algorithm [7,20,24–26], followed by aspect-based data mining techniques [8,13–16,18] and the SentiWordNet lexicon dictionary [4,6,7,9,12], both with 17.24%. In 13.79% of the works analyzed, the machine learning algorithm based on decision tree was adopted, [3,6,12,20]. Machine learning statistical methods based on maximum entropy were used in 10.34% of the studies [4,5,9]. With 6.9% of the primary studies, the application of the AdaBoost machine learning algorithm

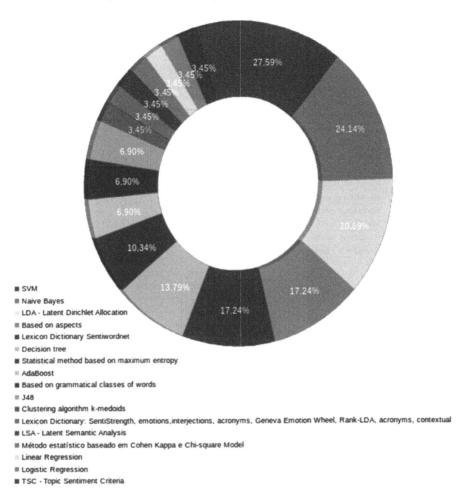

SVM
Naïve Bayes
LDA - Latent Dirichlet Allocation
Based on aspects
Lexicon Dictionary Sentiwordnet
Decision tree
Statistical method based on maximum entropy
AdaBoost
Based on grammatical classes of words
J48
Clustering algorithm k-medoids
Lexicon Dictionary: SentiStrength, emotions,interjections, acronyms, Geneva Emotion Wheel, Rank-LDA, acronyms, contextual
LSA - Latent Semantic Analysis
Método estatístico baseado em Cohen Kappa e Chi-square Model
Linear Regression
Logistic Regression
TSC - Topic Sentiment Criteria

Fig. 2. Characterization of approaches, techniques and mechanisms

[19,20] and data mining based on word classes (Pos-Tagging) [9,17] and J48 [6] were identified. Finally, with 3.45%, we found data mining techniques based on the SentiStrength Lexicon dictionary [4,6,7,9,12], emoticon dictionary [4], interjection dictionary [4], acronym dictionary [4], Geneva Emotion Wheel [11], Rank-LDA [10], contextual dictionary [6] and machine learning algorithms such as logistic regression [23], k-medoids clustering [1] and Cohen's Kappa statistical methods [5], Chi-square Model [2], linear regression [28], LSA - Latent Semantic Analysis [27] and TSC - Topic Sentiment Criteria [29].

Table 3 brings a detailed mapping of the identified approaches, techniques and mechanisms. By performing a deeper analysis of the synthesized data, it was verified that the works [4,6,7,9–12] combine machine learning and data mining techniques.

Table 3. Results of the research in the databases and results of the application of the selection criteria.

Num.	Approach, technique and mechanism	Reference number
01	SentiWordnet Lexicon Dictionary	[4,6,7,9,12]
02	SentiStrength Lexicon Dictionary	[7]
03	Emoticons Dictionary	[4]
04	Interjections Dictionary	[4]
05	Acronyms Dictionary	[4]
06	GALC lexicon dictionary based on Geneva Emotion Wheel	[11]
07	Lexicon Dictionary based on Rank-LDA	[10]
08	Contextual Lexicon Dictionary	[6]
09	Based on aspects	[8,13–16]
10	Based on grammatical classes of words	[9,17]
11	Statistical method based on Cohen Kappa	[5]
12	Statistical method based on maximum entropy	[4,5,9]
13	Statistical method based on Chi-square Model	[2]
14	K-medoids clustering algorithm	[1]
15	J48	[6] [18]
16	SVM	[4,6,12,18–22]
17	Logistic regression	[23]
18	Naive Bayes	[3,4,6,11,12,20,27]
19	LDA - Latent Dirichlet Allocation	[7,20,24–26]
20	LSA - Latent Semantic Analysis	[28]
21	TSC - Topic Sentiment Criteria	[29]
22	AdaBoost	[19,20]
23	Decision tree	[3,6,12,20]

In Fig. 3, the uses of approaches, techniques and mechanisms in primary studies are presented. The Naive Bayes machine learning techniques [3,4,6,11, 12,18,20] and SVM [4,6,12,18–22] have the highest number of works (7), followed by aspect-based techniques [8,13–16], LDA [7,20,24–27] and the SentiWordNet lexicon dictionary (6) [4,6,7,9,12].

As the answer to research question **Q2**, only one work gauged questions related to sustainability [24]. According to Calheiros et al., from the 401 reviews used as corpus of the work, 13% were from the TripAdvisor website, 68% from the Suggestion book, 10% from follow-up emails, 1% from the website review, 6% from direct emails and 1% from other means. However, there were only 95 reviews indicating that the sustainable practices performed by hotels positively influenced the clients opinion.

To answer the research question **Q3**, according to Fig. 4, we verified that the USA had the highest number of publications (9), while Thailand, Japan, India, Portugal, England, Australia and Canada (2) and only with one publication Holland, Greece, Scotland, South Korea, Austria, Australia and Germany.

Research question **Q4** can be answered through the analysis of Fig. 5. It has been verified a considerable increase of interest in researches on the opinion mining area applied to opinion mining in the last two years. Five studies in 2013, six studies in 2014, only two studies in 2015, five studies in 2016 were

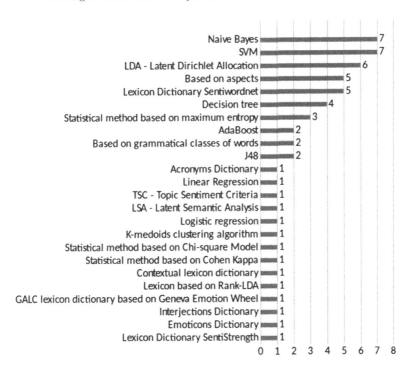

Fig. 3. Use of approaches, techniques and mechanisms

selected, while eight studies in 2017 that are adequate for our research line were considered.

Figure 6 presents a refinement of the graphic present in Fig. 5, in which we can observe the distribution of publications per year, divided by their respective means of publication. The conferences were responsible for the highest number of publications in all years.

Lastly, the answer to **Q5** is found in Table 4, where it can be observed that the primary studies were published in different periods or conferences, in which we can observe that the most popular means of publication of articles on the theme is the conferences. Such pattern does not surprise us, because the conferences are famously the most accessible means for scientific publications. The Scopus database, for example, indexes more than 100 thousand events of conference worldwide, while the number of indexed journals is almost 22 thousand [34]. What surprises us is the absolute low number of publications in journals, because such fact can denote that the works published in conferences did not stand out to deserve any extension in a journal, it means, they may not have been well-executed. Besides, they may not have gotten enough riveting results for their continuity and deepening. We can conclude that conferences The International Conference on Data Mining Workshop (ICDMW) and International Conference on Advances in Computing & Communications had, together, the largest number of publications (4).

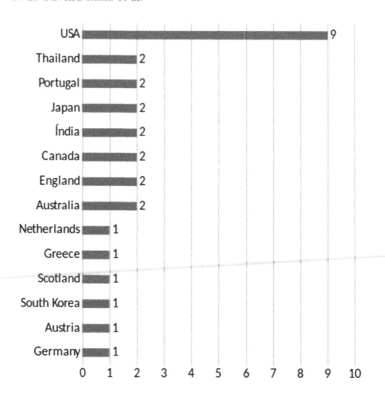

Fig. 4. Articles by country

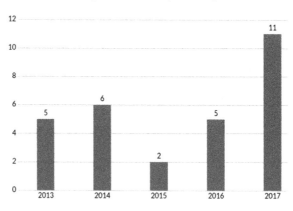

Fig. 5. Publications by year

We must highlight that the journals were published and conferences occurred in more than 12 distinct countries, characterizing homogeneity of publications and interests in different countries. In Fig. 7 we can observe the highest number of publications in conferences (17) and journals (12).

Table 4. Papers vs vehicles

Vehicles	Publications	Journal	Proceedings
Smart Innovation, Systems and Technologies	1		X
2014 International Computer Science and Engineering Conference, ICSEC 2014	2		X
Advances in Intelligent Systems and Computing	1		X
Expert Systems with Applications	2	X	
Information Processing and Management	2	X	
Journal of Hospitality Marketing and Management	1	X	
Knowledge-Based Systems	1	X	
Lecture Notes in Computer Science (including subseries Lecture Notes in Artificial Intelligence and Lecture Notes in Bioinformatics)	1		X
Procedia Computer Science	1		X
Proceedings - 15th IEEE International Conference on Data Mining Workshop, ICDMW 2015	2		X
Proceedings - 2013 IEEE 7th International Conference on Semantic Computing, ICSC 2013	1		X
Proceedings - 2013 IEEE/WIC/ACM International Joint Conference on Web Intelligence and Intelligent Agent Technology - Workshops, WI-IATW 2013	1		X
Proceedings - 2014 6th International Conference on Computational Intelligence and Communication Networks, CICN 2014	1		X
Proceedings - 2015 International Conference on Computer Application Technologies, CCATS 2015	1		X
Proceedings - 2017 15th IEEE/ACIS International Conference on Software Engineering Research, Management and Applications, SERA 2017	1		X
Proceedings of the 2013 Research in Adaptive and Convergent Systems, RACS 2013	1		X
Proceedings of the ACM SIGKDD International Conference on Knowledge Discovery and Data Mining	1		X
Springer Proceedings in Mathematics	1		X
World Wide Web	1	X	
Information Technology and Tourism	1	X	
2nd International Moratuwa Engineering Research Conference, MERCon 2016	1	X	
Cognitive Computation	1	X	
7th International Conference on Advances in Computing & Communications	2		X
WWW 2014 Companion - Proceedings of the 23rd International Conference on World Wide Web	1		X

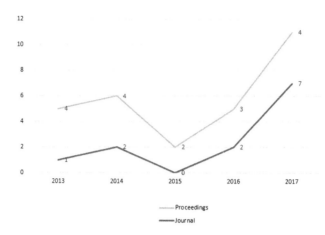

Fig. 6. Publications type vs year

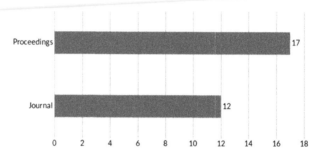

Fig. 7. Distribution of publications and journals

4   Threats to Validity

The threats to the validity of this study were:

– **Construction Validity:** The search String and the research questions used may not cover the opinion mining area in online reviews of hotels. To mitigate such threat, we tried to build a string that was as comprehensive as possible, regarding the terms that could be used in the area, using a control article and the opinion of 3 researchers.
– **Internal Validity:** (Data extraction): As three researchers were responsible for classifying and extracting the main algorithms from each publication, biases or problems in the data extraction may threaten the validity of data characterization; (Selection bias): In the beginning of the study, the articles were included or excluded from the mapping according to the judgment of the researchers themselves. It means that some studies may have been categorized incorrectly. To mitigate such threats, the selection and extraction reviews were performed by all the involved researchers, with a final voting due to disagreements.

– **External Validity:** Besides the fact that the Scopus database is the largest scientific literature database with more than 21,500 journals and 60 million registers [34], it is not possible to affirm that the results of this mapping comprehended the whole computer science area. However, this work presented evidence of the main techniques used, identifying gaps to be explored and serving as a guideline for future studies in this research line.

5   Conclusion

In this work, we performed a systematic mapping that aimed to identify and analyze approaches, techniques and mechanisms used in computer science for promoting data mining in online reviews of hotels.

The systematic mapping process was conducted by using a search protocol and study selection that specified the method used in this work. The data from 29 articles that meet the chosen research line were extracted and analyzed from the specified method.

Some strategies and approaches were used for data mining in online reviews of hotels. However, the most relevant ones were identified through Bayesian classifiers [3,4,6,11,12,20], SVM [4,6,12,19–21], LDA [7,20,24–26], aspect based [8,13–16], through the SentiWordNet lexicon dictionary [4,6,7,9,12] and based on maximum entropy [3,6,9,12,20] **(Q1)**.

Based on the results, we verified that there is a huge potential to be explored referring to the guests' opinions on the sustainable initiative practices by part of the hotels. As it was mentioned before, only the study [24] gauges the positive influences of sustainable practices **(Q2)**. In this regard, another potentiality is to identify, in the guests' commentaries, sustainability levels in their opinions, independent of the polarities of the reviews. It means, to elaborate data mining strategies to list the most sustainable hotels in relation to pre-established sustainability levels. We can also deepen in the aspect-based mining techniques to verify if it is viable to identify the sustainability levels of the hotels.

Among the primary studies selected for this mapping, we identify that Canada, India, Japan, Portugal, Thailand and the USA are responsible for about 60% of the countries with researches in our research line **(Q3)**.

Through the analysis, we can gauge that the last two years (2016 and 2017) were responsible for about 55% of the study databases that contribute towards the data collection proposed in this mapping **(Q4)**. Finally, we found 24 distinct conferences with publications in the research line, being 58% of the studies published in conferences and 42% in journals **(Q5)**.

Besides the apparent need to deepen the researches in the area under discussion, the results found in this work map the state of the art of opinion mining in online reviews of hotels, making it clear that it is an area of interest for researchers from various countries and it has great growth potential.

As a future work, we will investigate the gaps identified in this systematic mapping. We believe that this research presents relevant results for the academic field, providing support on how the mining opinion in hotels and sustainable aspects were discussed in the Computer Science field, becoming a relevant consulting source for this research line.

This mapping can be extended by modifying the research search strings, the research questions or inclusion and exclusion criteria. A systematic review may be performed in this research line.

References

1. Hu, Y.H., Chen, Y.L., Chou, H.L.: Opinion mining from online hotel reviews - a text summarization approach. Inf. Process. Manag. **53**(2), 436–449 (2017). https://doi.org/10.1016/j.ipm.2016.12.002
2. Srisuan, J., Hanskunatai, A.: The ensemble of Naïve Bayes classifiers for hotel searching. In: 2014 International Computer Science and Engineering Conference, ICSEC 2014, no. 1, pp. 168–173 (2014)
3. Songpan, W.: The analysis and prediction of customer review rating using opinion mining. In: Proceedings - 2017 15th IEEE/ACIS International Conference on Software Engineering Research, Management and Applications, SERA 2017, pp. 71–77 (2017)
4. Chaabani, Y., Toujani, R., Akaichi, J.: Sentiment analysis method for tracking touristics reviews in social media network. In: De Pietro, G., Gallo, L., Howlett, R.J., Jain, L.C. (eds.) KES-IIMSS 2017. SIST, vol. 76, pp. 299–310. Springer, Cham (2018). https://doi.org/10.1007/978-3-319-59480-4_30
5. Polpinij, J., Srikanjanapert, N., Sopon, P.: Word2Vec approach for sentiment classification relating to hotel reviews. In: Meesad, P., Sodsee, S., Unger, H. (eds.) IC2IT 2017. AISC, vol. 566, pp. 308–316. Springer, Cham (2018). https://doi.org/10.1007/978-3-319-60663-7_29
6. Hung, C.: Word of mouth quality classification based on contextual sentiment lexicons. Inf. Process. Manag. **53**(4), 751–763 (2017)
7. Chen, Y.S., Chen, L.H., Takama, Y.: Proposal of LDA-based sentiment visualization of hotel reviews. In: Proceedings - 15th IEEE International Conference on Data Mining Workshop, ICDMW 2015, pp. 687–693 (2016)
8. Marrese-Taylor, E., Velásquez, J.D., Bravo-Marquez, F., Matsuo, Y.: Identifying customer preferences about tourism products using an aspect-based opinion mining approach. Procedia Comput. Sci. **22**, 182–191 (2013)
9. Ansari, D.: Sentiment polarity classification using structural features. In: 2015 IEEE International Conference on Data Mining Workshop (ICDMW), pp. 1270–1273 (2015). http://ieeexplore.ieee.org/document/7395814/
10. Peleja, F., Magalhães, J.: Learning sentiment based ranked-lexicons for opinion retrieval. In: Hanbury, A., Kazai, G., Rauber, A., Fuhr, N. (eds.) ECIR 2015. LNCS, vol. 9022, pp. 435–440. Springer, Cham (2015). https://doi.org/10.1007/978-3-319-16354-3_47
11. Martin, L.: Are influential writers more objective? An analysis of emotionality in review comments categories and subject descriptors. In: WWW, pp. 799–804 (2014). https://doi.org/10.1145/2567948.2579242
12. Raut, V.B., Londhe, D.D.: Opinion mining and summarization of hotel reviews. In: Proceedings - 2014 6th International Conference on Computational Intelligence and Communication Networks, CICN 2014, pp. 556–559 (2014)
13. Xue, W., Li, T., Rishe, N.: Aspect identification and ratings inference for hotel reviews. World Wide Web **20**(1), 23–37 (2017). https://doi.org/10.1007/s11280-016-0398-9

14. Marrese-Taylor, E., Velásquez, J.D., Bravo-Marquez, F.: A novel deterministic approach for aspect-based opinion mining in tourism products reviews. Expert Syst. Appl. **41**(17), 7764–7775 (2014). https://doi.org/10.1016/j.eswa.2014.05.045

15. Marcheggiani, D., Täckström, O., Esuli, A., Sebastiani, F.: Hierarchical multi-label conditional random fields for aspect-oriented opinion mining. In: de Rijke, M., Kenter, T., de Vries, A.P., Zhai, C.X., de Jong, F., Radinsky, K., Hofmann, K. (eds.) ECIR 2014. LNCS, vol. 8416, pp. 273–285. Springer, Cham (2014). https://doi.org/10.1007/978-3-319-06028-6_23

16. Cruz, F.L., Troyano, J.A., Enríquez, F., Ortega, F.J., Vallejo, C.G.: 'Long autonomy or long delay?' The importance of domain in opinion mining. Expert Syst. Appl. **40**(8), 3174–3184 (2013)

17. Marrese-Taylor, E., Velasquez, J.D., Bravo-Marquez, F.: OpinionZoom, a modular tool to explore tourism opinions on the Web. In: Proceedings - 2013 IEEE/WIC/ACM International Joint Conference on Web Intelligence and Intelligent Agent Technology - Workshops, WI-IATW 2013, vol. 3, pp. 261–264 (2013)

18. De Mel, N.M., Hettiarachchi, H.H., Madusanka, W.P., Malaka, G.L., Perera, A.S., Kohomban, U.: Machine learning approach to recognize subject based sentiment values of reviews. In: 2nd International Moratuwa Engineering Research Conference, MERCon 2016, pp. 6–11 (2016)

19. Sharma, A., Dey, S.: A boosted SVM based sentiment analysis approach for online opinionated text. In: Proceedings of the 2013 Research in Adaptive and Convergent Systems on - RACS 2013, pp. 28–34 (2013). http://dl.acm.org/citation.cfm?doid=2513228.2513311

20. Nakamura, S., Okada, M., Hashimoto, K.: An investigation of effectiveness using topic information order to classify tourists reviews. In: Proceedings - 2015 International Conference on Computer Application Technologies, CCATS 2015, pp. 94–97 (2016)

21. Markopoulos, G., Mikros, G., Iliadi, A., Liontos, M.: Sentiment analysis of hotel reviews in greek: a comparison of unigram features. In: Katsoni, V. (ed.) Cultural Tourism in a Digital Era. SPBE, pp. 373–383. Springer, Cham (2015). https://doi.org/10.1007/978-3-319-15859-4_31

22. Fazzolari, M., Cozza, V., Petrocchi, M., Spognardi, A.: A study on text-score disagreement in online reviews. Cogn. Comput. 1–13 (2017). https://www.scopus.com/inward/record.uri?eid=2-s2.0-85026501769&doi=10.1007%2Fs12559-017-9496-y&partnerID=40&md5=e59e090854e197e0cf9d52d61659282a

23. Bauman, K., Liu, B., Tuzhilin, A.: Aspect based recommendations. In: Proceedings of the 23rd ACM SIGKDD International Conference on Knowledge Discovery and Data Mining - KDD 2017, pp. 717–725 (2017). http://dl.acm.org/citation.cfm?doid=3097983.3098170

24. Calheiros, A.C., Moro, S., Rita, P.: Sentiment classification of consumer-generated online reviews using topic modeling. J. Hosp. Mark. Manag. **8623**(March), 1–19 (2017)

25. Zheng, X., Lin, Z., Wang, X., Lin, K.J., Song, M.: Incorporating appraisal expression patterns into topic modeling for aspect and sentiment word identification. Knowl.-Based Syst. **61**, 29–47 (2014). https://doi.org/10.1016/j.knosys.2014.02.003

26. Bross, J.: A distant supervision method for product aspect extraction from customer reviews. In: Proceedings - 2013 IEEE 7th International Conference on Semantic Computing, ICSC 2013, pp. 339–346 (2013)

27. Akhtar, N., Zubair, N., Kumar, A., Ahmad, T.: Aspect based sentiment oriented summarization of hotel reviews. Procedia Comput. Sci. **115**, 563–571 (2017). https://doi.org/10.1016/j.procs.2017.09.115
28. Xu, X., Wang, X., Li, Y., Haghighi, M.: Business intelligence in online customer textual reviews: understanding consumer perceptions and influential factors. Int. J. Inf. Manag. **37**(6), 673–683 (2017). https://doi.org/10.1016/j.ijinfomgt.2017.06.004
29. Rossetti, M., Stella, F., Zanker, M.: Analyzing user reviews in tourism with topic models. Inf. Technol. Tourism **16**(1), 5–21 (2016)
30. Kitchenham, B.: Procedures for performing systematic reviews, vol. 33, no. 2004, pp. 1–26. Keele University, Keele, UK (2004)
31. Petersen, K., Feldt, R., Mujtaba, S., Mattsson, M.: Systematic mapping studies in software engineering. In: EASE, vol. 8, pp. 68–77 (2008)
32. Fayyad, U., Piatetsky-Shapiro, G., Smyth, P.: From data mining to knowledge discovery in databases. AI Mag. **17**(3), 37 (1996)
33. Periódicos CAPES (2017). https://www.periodicos.capes.gov.br/
34. Scopus: Scopus - Elsevier Database (2017). http://www.scopus.com/

Event Detection over Continuous Data Stream for the Sustainable Growth in Agriculture Context

Janagan Sivagnanasundaram[1]([⊠]), Athula Ginige[1],
and Jeevani Goonetillake[2]

[1] Western Sydney University, Sydney, Australia
{j.sivagnanasundaram, A.Ginige}@westernsydney.edu.au
[2] University of Colombo, Colombo, Sri Lanka
jsg@ucsc.cmb.ac.lk

Abstract. The coordination failure is a concept that explains the failure of people to coordinate and act on a real-world problem properly. The failure of coordination among human communities can lead to social problems in many domains including in transportation, health care, disaster management, agriculture etc. and ultimately affects the sustainable growth of a country as a whole. The recent advancements in Information and Communication Technologies (ICT) have introduced a new trend called Collaborative Consumption - *the peer-to-peer based coordination and sharing of information through online by human communities* has been expected to solve these social problems identified in the above domains. The tremendous adaptation of people towards ICTs ultimately resulted in huge, fast-moving and heterogeneous data contributed by people in a collaborative manner. In here, most of these data describe real-time events associated with the people based on their context. The way of coordinating user communities to contribute data, detecting events from it and effective delivery of required information to needful parties would be a possible solution to overcome the coordination problem. In this paper, the result of a systematic literature review is performed to understand the current state of the event detection methods used in information systems. Furthermore, we have proposed a user centered mobile based information system that assists the detection of pest outbreak events in agriculture domain for an effective and timely delivery of actionable information to farmers.

Keywords: Event detection · Coordination failure · Agriculture sustainability
Pest management

1 Introduction

Information sharing is a prerequisite for a country's development. Without the exchange of information, no innovation would be able to spread and will results in information gaps. The unavailability of access for human communities to the needful information based on a problem will lead to many problems and need to be overcome as soon as possible. According to Maslow's hierarchy of needs theory as shown in

© Springer International Publishing AG, part of Springer Nature 2018
O. Gervasi et al. (Eds.): ICCSA 2018, LNCS 10960, pp. 575–588, 2018.
https://doi.org/10.1007/978-3-319-95162-1_39

Fig. 1, a human's basic needs for own growth can be divided into following levels; physiological, safety, belonging, self-esteem, and self-actualization [1]. Of these, the lowest level "physiological" is the only one that can be fulfilled by as an individual. But for the levels above it, the individuals need to work as a community to achieve theses. Once the communities are formed, there is coordination and exchange of information tends to happen among the individuals in the community. The unavailability of coordination among human communities and delivery of actionable information at the right time to needful parties will lead to many problems such as difficulties in delivering required information to people when they need it most, guiding people to take precautionary actions in the right time, making effective decisions etc. [2]. Thus, a proper coordination among human communities is a necessity for effective fulfillment of human needs.

Fig. 1. Maslow's hierarchy of needs [1]

Recent advancement in ICTs, Internet of Things (IoT) and the internet has had an enormous effect on many facets of our day to day life. The portable devices such as smartphones have become an increasingly important part of our lives and capable of supplementing our daily activities. In addition, the application of smartphones has provided a new way of making tentative decisions much easily than before, which leads to the improved social attachment and social relationships with other people of human communities. According to a report by Statista [3], for 2019 the total number mobile phone users are expected to pass 5 billion worldwide. Due to these tremendous adaptation and contribution of human communities towards ICTs ultimately resulted in a new trend called Collaborative Consumption - *the peer-to-peer based coordination and sharing of information through online by human communities* and created massive, fast-moving, and heterogeneous data. The tremendous availability of these data is generated from various sources including continuous usage of disparate sensors, social media applications, satellite, IoT etc. The smartphone devices have enabled the distribution and sharing of information to be performed nearly at our fingertips. According to Kaplan and Haenlein [4], many people adapted towards using smartphones because of the increasing ubiquity, widespread application and the user empowerment provided by social media applications. Thus, the smartphone has the potential to become a tool to solve many societal problems.

The study in [4] further states that, social media allows it users to create and exchange contents and such information could be used for various operations such as to explore what's happening around us, to take precautionary actions, to communicate with others etc. A new event update triggered by an individual is also considered as a first alert about something going on. In this case, social media applications could be used as an emergency notification tool. This widespread collaboration among human communities enabled the creation of a new paradigm called "crowd sensing": a collaboration network which targets mobile users to form a network and allow them to share local knowledge acquired by their mind and sensor-enhanced devices. In here, a user is considered as a *sensor* and each tweet generated by the user is considered as *sensory information*. Hence, these sensors are called together as *social sensors*.

The large set of these data contributed by human communities contains information about various events happening around the world. In here an event can be defined as a situation initiated by an individual, followed by others of a human community within a specific time interval. The detection of such events from human contributed data and sharing it among needful parties will help the human communities to act on a problem precisely. The topic called event detection has been an active research topic for a variety of domains and serves as fundamental for many real-world applications related to predictions, monitoring, diagnosis etc. In addition, event detection can be explained as a problem of detecting a target event has occurred or not, from a given data stream and can be considered as multi-stream event detection when there are multiple data streams [5]. It is known that more than 80% of the user-contributed data associated with events are primarily complex, streamed, unstructured and without contextual information [6]. For an efficient implementation of this, the system should be less complex, simple in design and must adapt to the changing conditions of the surrounding environment to capture contextual information [7].

The agriculture is the fundamental source of food for all the countries in the world. Due to the heavy pressure of population growth, the demand for food is continuously increasing at a faster rate. The mixed effect of green revolution and human population has made the need for food production to double over the past years. If agriculture fails to satisfy the rising requirement for food products, it is found to affect a country's economic growth. The productivity and availability of crops grown for human consumption can be affected due to many reasons and one of the important reasons is due to the pest attacks leads to the reduction of crop performance and low yield production [8]. A thorough study in [9] revealed that due to the unavailability of targeted delivery methods, farmers and other parties including agro-chemical companies, agriculture authorities and policy makers of the agriculture domain is not published with the required information such as pests or disease outbreaks and possible remedies, when they need it most. The study further states that the lack of proper framework, for managing crop losses and pesticide use had ultimately contributed to difficulties in producing enough food for future dietary needs.

Therefore, in this paper, a thorough review is presented on the state of the event detection techniques used in other applications and a multi-stream event detection model is proposed in an attempt to detect real-time pest/disease related events to solve the identified crop losses problem in the agriculture context. The multi-stream event detection model is suitable here because the information we are considering is sourced from diverse data sources such as user-contributed data (crowd sensing), weather data, images and spatial-temporal information. The rest of the paper is structured as follows; Sect. 2 of the paper presents the motivation behind this work with possible challenges. Section 3 presents the related works on event detection techniques and similar applications. The proposed solution for the identified problem is discussed in Sect. 4. The results and, the conclusion work are presented in Sects. 5 and 6 respectively.

2 Motivation and Challenges

The motivation behind this research was based on a case study from Sri Lanka. A research team consists of researchers from different universities initiated a project called "Digital Knowledge Ecosystem for Sustainable Agriculture Production" to explore a possible solution to address a problem related to crop cultivation in Sri Lanka [10]. The problem identified in Sri Lanka was, the farmers growing the same crops as others without knowing what others are growing and resulted in overproduction and underproduction of vegetables [11, 12]. The research team has explored a mobile solution to address this issue where farmers get published static information about vegetables, sowing and harvesting methods, and real-time dynamic information including current production levels of crops and prices. With this real time information, farmers, agriculture departments, agriculture agencies and agro-chemical companies can take optimal decisions to effectively plan their tasks.

In worldwide, approximately 35% of crop production is lost due to the pests and disease attacks. In the meantime, as stated previously, the agriculture has to satisfy the global level requirement for food, and other bio-based commodities as well. According to FAO [13], food security is the initial step towards building a greater economy of a country and it exists when all the human communities have the physical and economical access to foods at all the times to satisfy their dietary needs for a healthy life. In order to satisfy the increasing food demands, these crops must be protected from pest or disease attacks [14]. Thus, helping farmers to safeguard their crops will be a vital factor in promoting food security. The recent advancement in ICTs has alleviated many societal problems and undoubtedly holds many of the keys to ensure food security globally. The best combination of these available technologies has to be used to make agriculture more productive and profitable to satisfy the standards of human health. A thorough analysis of information systems developed for agriculture domain revealed that [15], most of the applications were widely used as farm activity journals, farm management tools and communication platforms. None of them were specifically designed and developed for managing crop losses.

In this research work, pest management is used as an exemplar scenario for managing it through a multi-stream event detection technique with the use of an information system, as crop losses are something which has got a significant negative impact on the food security. The development of a mobile-based information system would be a viable solution for this problem because of the wide-spread applicability of smartphones among human communities and even farmers in rural areas, without worrying about their low-level education, literacy, and language, used to carry their mobile phone to the farm, and use it in their daily activities.

The advancement in ICTs effectively exploded diverse types of data and the amount of available data. These diverse types of data include text, images, audio, video, sensory information, spatial-temporal information etc. Thus, the heterogeneous way of monitoring real-world events is one of the challenges to capture diverse properties at a spatial-temporal point. In here, to detect disease or pest outbreak events we are considered using crowd sourced data including images contributed by farmers, atmosphere weather information from weather stations, and spatial-temporal information via the access to farmers location using context aware computing. Another challenge associated with the proposed system for pest or disease event detection is Design. Due to the lack of knowledge and literacy rate among rural farming communities, the proposed system has to be simple in design with necessary features that are desirable and effective without a need for extra efforts.

3   Background

3.1   Definitions

The unavailability of the proper definition for event detection initiates several problems since this topic is complex and many of the aspects of this technique are not clear. Over the years there have been number efforts by scholars to give a concrete definition for this concept but, most of the definitions are lack of satisfying the properties of an event such as context, an action which triggered it etc. In here, we will present such definitions proposed by other scholars in the literature for event detection and propose a new definition that unifies the common traits observed in the literature. According to a work in [16], an event is defined as "something that happens at specific place within a time slot with some consequences". The consequences in this regard are people get motivated about a particular event and action made by them via sharing and messaging to others promptly with the use of wide range of social media applications.

Weng and Lee [17] state that, an event is "a stream of user contents having similar topic and words posted within a time interval". McMin et al. [18] propose an event as "a significant occurrence that happens within a specific time and place". Aggarwal and Subbian [19] state an event as "something that happens at a specific place and time and interest to the mass media". In here, an event takes place at a particular location and time will automatically stimulate people around that place to post contents about it. As a conclusion, all of these definitions have some properties in common and defined based on micro-blog data generated in social media applications.

Proposed Definition

Based on the observations of common traits in the above definitions and a focus on user-contributed data we define *event detection* as: **Given a stream of actions A_n by users U_m of the collaboration network N, detection of real-world event e of a context C along with the spatial information L_e and temporal information T_e.**

Let consider each of the words used in the above definition:

a. **action (a):** In a crowdsourcing network N, an action a is a post of a new content by a user u.

b. **collaboration network (N):** A network of users U_m formed together to perform a series of actions A_n *to* contribute some needful knowledge.
c. **user (u):** An individual who can perform an action a in a crowdsourcing network N.
d. **event (e):** Describing a situation initiated by a user u as an action a, followed by others in a human community within a specified time interval T_e *(t_{start}* to *t_{end})* and location L_e.
e. **context (C):** The description of an environment where the event e happened.
f. **spatial-temporal information ($\mathbf{L_e}$ & $\mathbf{T_e}$):** Having spatial-temporal qualities or space-time properties of an event e.

3.2 Event Detection Techniques – State of the Art

In recent years, many researchers tried to detect events such as trending news stories, life threating situations, traffic reports, epidemic disease outbreaks etc. by exploring the data contributed by human communities. According to [20], the most of the detected events can be categorized into three distinct groups as stated in Table 1.

Table 1. Event categories

Event group	Event type	Examples
A	Emerging events	Live & Trending news etc.
B	An event due to natural or human intervention	Earthquake, Flood, Fire etc.
C	Public feedback events	Electoral polls, Traffic control, Disease management etc.

The main challenge associated with event detection is to select appropriate tools and techniques. A survey of event detection methodologies used in the above identified groups is discussed in Table 2.

3.3 Problems Identified

According to the table above, the majority of the research works have been conducted related to event detection, organization, and prediction in other domains such as transportation, disaster management etc. and none of them were specifically designed for the agricultural domain. In addition, all the identified information systems were based on social media applications and micro-blogs as the source of information. The social media applications like Twitter, Facebook etc. generally have low signal to noise ratio [28, 29]. The people all over the world generate tweets more than several million times per day, resulting in the noisy and informal presentation of 140-characters. The information in a tweet is generally subjective and confined to text format. To make a decision precisely and effectively, human communities must understand the data they get hold is a fact or an opinion. The appropriate way to differentiate facts and opinions is a problem in micro-blogs based application such as Facebook, Twitter etc. Basically,

Table 2. Taxonomy of event detection applications

Event identified	Detection technique	Type of data stream	Features used	Application category	References
Breaking news	Naïve Based Classifier & Online Clustering	Microblogs	Terms in the text, Hashtags	A	[21]
Trending news	Discrete Wavelet Analysis & Graph Partitioning	Microblogs	Individual words	A	[17]
Earthquake	SVM	Microblogs	No of words, No of keywords	B	[22]
Disaster	Named Entity Recognition, Filtering	Microblogs	No of similar words	B	[23]
Traffic	Keyword analysis, Abbreviation analysis	Microblogs	Keyword existence	C	[24]
Flu trend	Keyword analysis, Group average clustering	Microblogs	Keyword existence	C	[25]
Epidemic outbreak	Eventshop, Classification and segmentation of Images	Microblogs	Average of tweets/day Image pixel (intensity value)	C	[26]
Flood	Eventshop, Classification and segmentation of Images	Microblogs	Image pixel (intensity value)	C	[26]
Asthma risk	Eventshop, segmentation of Images, interpolation of fixed sensor values	Microblogs, sensor values, photos	Image pixel (intensity value)	C	[27]

the accuracy of detected events relies upon the quality of data. Thus, micro-blogs created in social media applications can't be used as sources to detect the events, as it has some negative concerns about the quality of data.

Over the years, multimedia data is the largest data sources contributed by human communities. Every second, thousands of images and videos are uploaded by people via computers, smartphones etc. Some of these multimedia data have geo-tagged information. One of the important features of this geo-tagged information is its spatial-temporal information. When an interesting event happens, people capture those events as images, which allow the discovery of events promptly, by visualizing the photo. In [30], Flickr data with geo-tagged information has been used to understand the users' interest. Organizing these multimedia data for further analysis is a difficult task due to its varied levels of meanings about its concepts. Over the years, there is a huge effort made to carry out an analysis using automatic semantic classification on multi-media to classify it into a set of predefined concepts [31]. Even though, having mul-timedia data over text data is beneficial, utilizing concepts for situation detection based on it will be a challenging task.

The previous works establish a basis for improving the quality of data generated by human communities and ultimately contributes to detection of events. Incorporation of multimedia data instead of textual data can improve the quality of the data stream up to some certain level but, the accuracy wise there is a negative impact due to the varied level of understandings. According to [32], most of the agricultural projects fail because when systems were designed for farmers, characteristics such as context, culture and socio-economic were not considered which leads to not being able to develop and recommend appropriate technologies that are compatible with the target group. With the advancements in context aware computing, crowd sensing, and weather models, it is possible to allow farmers to share the observations on their field with the descriptors along with spatial-temporal, weather information. The use of such diverse streams of data and matching it with the knowledge base of diseases/pests, personalized information or alerts could be provided to farmers and other stakeholders. This will help all the related parties of the agriculture domain to act on a problem precisely without further thinking.

4   Proposed Solution

In here, the solution has been given for the problem of managing pests or diseases through a multi-stream event detection technique with the use of a mobile-based information system. Nowadays, the smartphones are equipped with diverse types of built-in sensors such as positioning sensors, motion sensors, cameras and microphones which make the smartphone a promising tool for assisting farmers. Our solution for protecting crops from pests and diseases achieves early and real-time detection of pest and disease outbreaks through capturing farm-field observations as events through data contributed by farmers via mobile phones. Then, by verifying observed events through aggregating similar events generated by other farmers and correlating with weather data, prompt communication back to the farming community is achieved to confirm an outbreak, including disease type and remedies. The major reason for the spread of pests or disease is extreme weather changes. Thus, it is important to incorporate the weather data stream to validate the data contributed by farmers.

The proposed model lends itself to learn from initial observations and over time to change the model to predict the most probable types of pest and disease outbreak events to a predictive model. By collecting data verifying pests and disease outbreaks on a farm, and weather data leading to those outbreaks, it is possible to establish a better correlation between different types of disease/pest outbreaks and weather data patterns leading up to such outbreaks. With such insights, we will be able to predict the onset of outbreaks based on weather data rather than waiting for it to happen and verify it using aggregated farmer collected data. Being able to proactively predict rather than reactively verify will give farmers more time to take necessary precautionary actions to further minimize crop losses due to pest and disease outbreaks.

Converting the above-proposed solution to a practical system has many challenges that we plan to address in this research. We have formulated the following set of research questions to be investigated; (a) what is the optimal mobile user interface for farmers to report an observed pest or disease event with as much information as possible, taking into account their level of mobile literacy, native language and constraints due to farm environment; (b) what is the best model to predict the probability of an outbreak event based on weather data; (c) how best to identify the nature (pest or disease or pathogen) and specific details of the outbreak to work out possible remedies; (d) what is an effective way of providing information about identified outbreak events and remedies to the farming community for them to take action to mitigate the crop losses.

In our solution, the farmers can register their farm and take a photo of their affected crops with the descriptors from a menu as shown in Figs. 2 and 3. We have structured the field observations as menu into 3 levels; type of attack, type of organism and severity. Then these geo-tagged and time-stamped farmer observations can be aggregated based on location and time to find the intensity of observations at a given location within a specified time window. If the intensity in a specific geographical area reaches a threshold value we can conclude that the area has a pest or disease outbreak. There is scientific knowledge relating to onset of different diseases and pest outbreaks during different weather conditions. We can thus get weather data from existing weather stations and dynamically adjust the threshold values of aggregated farmer observations to decide whether there is a valid outbreak in that geographical area.

Fig. 2. Registering farm

Fig. 3. Event reporting screen with 3 levels of menu

Fig. 4. Knowledgebase of disease information [11]

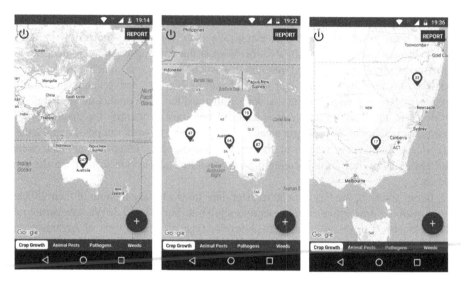

Fig. 5. Events belongs to country

Fig. 6. Events belongs to states

Fig. 7. Events belongs to suburbs

During the process of event reporting, the diverse data streams such as crowd sourced data stream, image data stream, and weather data stream will be captured. In here, the crowd sourced data stream will contain information such as the type of crop grown, soil information, type of attack (pests/pathogens), severity of attack (using color codes) and spatial-temporal information; image data stream will contain the image of the affected crops, weather data stream will contain information related to temperature, humidity, soil moisture, soil temperature, soil temperature at 10 cm depth, rainfall etc. The validation of the reported incident will be performed through aggregating similar incidents reported from the same geographical area and through weather patterns. Once validated, the reported event information is used to search the knowledge base of crop disease information and communicated back to farmers via the same mobile application and deliver an alert notification to others to take precautionary actions. For this work, we will be using the same knowledge base of crop disease information developed for the DKES project [10] as depicted in Fig. 4. Finally, the detected events will be pointed in a map scaled from country wise to suburb wise as shown in Figs. 5, 6 and 7 to give as a summary of detected events.

To capture the weather information of the reported event, we have used the APIs provided by openweathermap.org [33]. These APIs provided the access to the atmosphere weather information and soil information at global scale. In order to verify the accuracy of the generated weather data from weather station, we deployed weather sensors to monitor weather changes remotely as shown in Fig. 8. Following parameters such as temperature, rainfall, pressure, wind speed and direction, humidity, soil temperature and soil humidity were observed in real time. After some period of continuous observation, we have compared the data collected from weather station and remote weather sensors. Based on the comparison, we considered using the weather station data to capture weather patterns instead of deploying remote weather sensors. From our results, the weather station data shows high correlation with the result of remote weather sensors, is available at global scale, and cost effective. The result of the comparisons is discussed in Sect. 5.

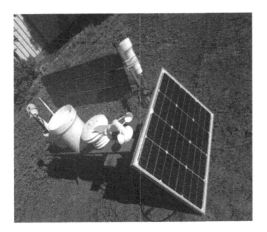

Fig. 8. Deployed weather sensors

5   Results

The comparison performed to verify the accuracy of weather station data (from openweathermap.org) and data from weather sensors reveals that there is a high correlation between these two. The comparison of various weather parameters between weather station data (red) and remote weather sensor data (blue) are shown in Figs. 9 and 10.

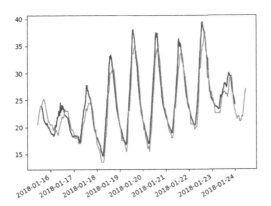

Fig. 9. Atmosphere temperature (Color figure online)

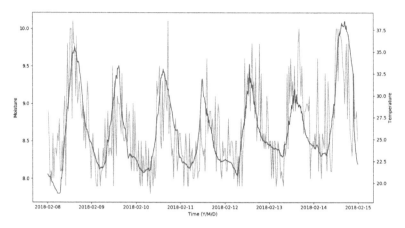

Fig. 10. Soil moisture (sensors) vs atmosphere temperature (weather station) (Color figure online)

Based on the results, we have decided to incorporate the weather station data with the proposed mobile based application. So, when a farmer reports an event, all the information related to weather and soil of the corresponding farm will be extracted via the access to farmer's location.

6   Conclusion

The coordination failure is a concept that explains the failure of people to coordinate and act on a real-world problem properly. The failure of coordination among human communities can lead to social problems in many domains including in transportation, health care, disaster management, agriculture etc. and ultimately affects the sustainable growth of a country as a whole. Without the exchange or sharing of information, no innovation would be able to spread and will result in information gaps. The information gaps are direct barriers to a country's development and must be overcome as soon as possible to limit further problems. The rapid uptake of mobile phones has enabled the sharing of information to be performed quickly and effectively. Such large digitally connected communities create a new way to investigate and perceive varied aspects of human behavior, starting from personal events to high risk environments. A combination of such events can be detected from user-contributed data translated into signifi- cant information and modeled to explore the world around us to control adverse situation promptly.

A thorough analysis of information systems developed for agriculture domain revealed that most of it were widely used as farm management tools. The analysis further emphasize that none of the applications were specifically developed for reporting and managing crop losses. In this paper, pest management is used as an exemplar scenario for managing crop losses through a multi-stream event detection technique with the use of a mobile based information system. Early management of crop losses is important as it something which has got significant negative impact on the food security. The following diverse data streams such as farmer observation data (crowd sourced data), weather data, images and spatial-temporal information were used to detect pest or disease outbreak events. With the use of different streams of data and matching it with the knowledge base of diseases/pests, personalized information or alerts will be generated to farmers with possible remedies. This will empower the farmers to take precautionary actions promptly to safeguard their crops before any losses.

References

1. Maslow's hierarchy of needs. https://en.wikipedia.org/wiki/Maslow%27s_hierarchy_of_ needs
2. Hamari, J., Sjöklint, M., Ukkonen, A.: The sharing economy: why people participate in collaborative consumption. J. Assoc. Inf. Sci. Technol. **67**, 2047–2059 (2015)
3. Number of mobile phone users worldwide 2013–2019—Statista. https://www.statista.com/ statistics/274774/forecast-of-mobile-phone-users-worldwide/
4. Kaplan, A., Haenlein, M.: Social media: back to the roots and back to the future. J. Syst. Inf. Technol. **14**, 101–104 (2012)
5. Cherichi, S., Faiz, R.: Upgrading event and pattern detection to big data. In: Nguyen, N.-T., Manolopoulos, Y., Iliadis, L., Trawiński, B. (eds.) ICCCI 2016. LNCS, vol. 9876, pp. 377–386. Springer, Cham (2016). https://doi.org/10.1007/978-3-319-45246-3_36
6. Chbeir, R., Oria, V.: Editorial preface: special issue on multimedia data annotation and retrieval using web 2.0. Multimed. Tools Appl. **64**, 1–5 (2012)
7. Cohen, J., Dolan, B., Dunlap, M., Hellerstein, J., Welton, C.: MAD skills. Proc. VLDB Endow. **2**, 1481–1492 (2009)
8. Oerke, E.: Crop losses to pests. J. Agric. Sci. **144**, 31 (2005)
9. Selvarajah, A., Thiruchelvam, S.: Factors affecting pesticide use by farmers in Vavuniya district. Trop. Agric. Res. **19**, 380–388 (2007)
10. Ginige, A., Walisadeera, A., Ginige, T., De Silva, L., Di Giovanni, P., Mathai, M., Goonetillake, J., Wikramanayake, G., Vitiello, G., Sebillo, M., Tortora, G., Richards, D., Jain, R.: Digital knowledge ecosystem for achieving sustainable agriculture production: a case study from Sri Lanka. In: 2016 IEEE International Conference on Data Science and Advanced Analytics, DSAA (2016)
11. Hettiarachchi, S.: N'Eliya carrot farmers in the dumps: bumper harvest, but prices low (2018)
12. Hettiarachchi, S.: Leeks cultivators desperate as price drops to record low (2011)
13. How to Feed the World in 2050. http://www.fao.org/wsfs/forum2050/wsfs-forum/en/
14. Popp, J.: Cost-benefit analysis of crop protection measures. Journal für Verbraucherschutz und Lebensmittelsicherheit **6**, 105–112 (2011)
15. Pongnumkul, S., Chaovalit, P., Surasvadi, N.: Applications of smartphone-based sensors in agriculture: a systematic review of research. J. Sens. **2015**, 1–18 (2015)
16. Allan, J.: Introduction to topic detection and tracking. In: Allan, J. (ed.) Topic Detection and Tracking. INRE, vol. 12, pp. 1–16. Springer, Boston (2002). https://doi.org/10.1007/978-1-4615-0933-2_1
17. Weng, J., Lee, B.: Event detection in Twitter. In: Fifth International Conference on Weblogs and Social Media (2011)

18. McMinn, A., Moshfeghi, Y., Jose, J.: Building a large-scale corpus for evaluating event detection on Twitter. In: Proceedings of the 22nd ACM International Conference on Information & Knowledge Management, CIKM 2013 (2013)

19. Aggarwal, C., Subbian, K.: Event detection in social streams. In: Proceedings of the 2012 SIAM International Conference on Data Mining, pp. 624–635 (2012)

20. Hasan, M., Orgun, M., Schwitter, R.: A survey on real-time event detection from the Twitter data stream. J. Inf. Sci. (2017). https://doi.org/10.1177/0165551517698564

21. Sankaranarayanan, J., Samet, H., Teitler, B., Lieberman, M., Sperling, J.: TwitterStand. In: Proceedings of the 17th ACM SIGSPATIAL International Conference on Advances in Geographic Information Systems, GIS 2009 (2009)

22. Sakaki, T., Okazaki, M., Matsuo, Y.: Earthquake shakes Twitter users. In: Proceedings of the 19th International Conference on World Wide Web, WWW 2010 (2010)

23. Abel, F., Hauff, C., Houben, G., Stronkman, R., Tao, K.: Twitcident. In: Proceedings of the 21st International Conference Companion on World Wide Web, WWW 2012 Companion (2012)

24. Zeng, K., Liu, W., Wang, X., Chen, S.: Traffic congestion and social media in China. IEEE Intell. Syst. **28**, 72–77 (2013)

25. Achrekar, H., Gandhe, A., Lazarus, R., Ssu-Hsin, Yu., Liu, B.: Predicting flu trends using Twitter data. In: 2011 IEEE Conference on Computer Communications Workshops, INFOCOM WKSHPS (2011)

26. Singh, V., Jain, R.: Situation Recognition Using EventShop. Springer, Heidelberg (2016). https://doi.org/10.1007/978-3-319-30537-0

27. Tang, M.: Geospatial multimedia data for situation recognition. In: Proceedings of the 2016 ACM on Multimedia Conference, MM 2016 (2016)

28. Barbosa, L., Feng, J.: Robust sentiment detection on Twitter from biased and noisy data. In: Proceedings of the 23rd International Conference on Computational Linguistics: Posters, vol. 36 (2010)

29. Derczynski, L., Ritter, A., Clark, S.: Twitter part-of-speech tagging for all: overcoming sparse and noisy data. In: Proceedings of Recent Advances in Natural Language Processing, RANLP, pp. 198–206. Association for Computational Linguistics (2013)

30. Kisilevich, S., Krstajic, M., Keim, D., Andrienko, N., Andrienko, G.: Event-based analysis of people's activities and behavior using Flickr and Panoramio geotagged photo collections. In: 2010 14th International Conference Information Visualisation (2010)

31. Chang, S., Ellis, D., Jiang, W., Lee, K., Yanagawa, A., Loui, A., Luo, J.: Large-scale multimodal semantic concept detection for consumer video. In: Proceedings of the International Workshop on Multimedia Information Retrieval, MIR 2007 (2007)

32. Iqbal, M.: Concept and implementation of participation and empowerment: reflection from the coffee IPM-SECP. Makara Hum. Behav. Stud. Asia **11**, 58 (2007)

33. Current weather and forecast – OpenWeatherMap. https://openweathermap.org/

A Technique for Assessing the Quality of Volunteered Geographic Information for Disaster Decision Making

Arindam Dasgupta$^{(\boxtimes)}$, Soumya K. Ghosh, and Pabitra Mitra

Indian Institute of Technology Kharagpur, Kharagpur, West Bengal, India
adgkgp@gmail.com, skg@iitkgp.ac.in,
pabitra@cse.iitkgp.ernet.in

Abstract. The volunteered geographic information has been considered as a valuable source of information for disaster management. It may provide rapid essential information from the disaster area. However, this information has been generated by general people without any knowledge in spatial data concept. It is found that the quality of volunteered data have not considered for any emergency decision making. In the work, a statistical framework has been developed to validate the citizen generated spatial data for emergency decision making.

Keywords: Volunteered geographic information · Disaster risk management
Quality assessment · Statistical analysis

1 Introduction

In disaster situation, the local people may provide the most authentic situational information to the emergency response agencies. The social media users may also participate in the disaster response and management [1]. The people may share the situational information of their area into the Volunteered Geographic Information (VGI) platform to enhance the efficiency of disaster response. The traditional methods of creating flood risk map such as satellite imagery, hydrological analysis and flood plain simulation may be time consuming and expensive. Further, the risk map generation takes longer time and may not be useful for the management of disaster. Again, it is a challenging task to capture large scale data for generating flood risk map for comparatively small rural area (say, 500 km^2 or less) by using such traditional methods. If the flood risk map can be generated in real-time by accessing the data from VGI platform, then it is useful to create the contingency plan for disaster management.

Recently, social network plays an important role in emergency response management. It acts as a special form of VGI platform and reveals the opportunity to get free and real-time data. This platform can be used as a complement data source along with the authoritative data sources. However, the quality evaluation of this type of data is an essential factor before using in disaster management. In this work, a conceptual model has been developed to assess the usability of VGI data obtained of the different media for the purpose of real-time emergency response.

© Springer International Publishing AG, part of Springer Nature 2018
O. Gervasi et al. (Eds.): ICCSA 2018, LNCS 10960, pp. 589–597, 2018.
https://doi.org/10.1007/978-3-319-95162-1_40

In Sect. 2, the related work regarding the quality issues of VGI data have been discussed. In Sect. 3, the quality assessment methodology has been explained. The experimental results have been shown in Sect. 4. Finally, conclusion of the work has been discussed.

2 Related Work

There are various research work related to quality evaluation of VGI data have been reported. The potential benefits of integrating social network for crisis mapping have discussed by Linna and Goodchild [2]. After the Haiti earthquake, a community of volunteers has been involved immediately for the development of crisis map by using Open Street Map (OSM) for the support of rescuer [3]. The available VGI platforms such as Ushahidi and OSM have been utilized by various humanitarian aid organizations and emergency response teams to improve the situational awareness and coordinate their disaster response measures [4].

In most of the research work, the VGI data have been evaluated by comparing with the authoritative sources. The quality of OSM data for the disaster management has been studied and evaluated by Girres and Touya [5]. In the work of Ballatore and Zipf [6], a framework has been proposed to extract the meaning of VGI data shared by the different people. This is an important concept for the semantic decoding of VGI data along with finding the fitness for the purpose of the dataset. With the help of OSM data, Barron et al. [7], developed a framework for intrinsic analyses of VGI data without comparing with the authoritative datasets. In this work, various methods and indicators have been presented to evaluate the quality of the OSM data. According to the work of Poser and Dransch [8], the credibility of VGI data should be considered in disaster mitigation phase and the accuracy of the VGI data should be considered in disaster response phase. Schade et al. [9] proposed a validation technique for evaluating Twitter data. In this work, the data obtained from the multiple media have been aggregated and processed for determining relevance in a given context.

3 Integration of Authoritative Data Sources with VGI

The authoritative spatial data sources have been available from multiple private and public organizations. These data can be accessed through different web services technologies. A data sharing platform has been needed to construct the Enterprise GIS (EGIS) platform for the purpose of accessing data in uniform format. Again, the data obtained from various sources such as social media and mobile messages related to a specific disaster area can be considered as the sources of volunteered data. After retrieving the volunteered data these data sources, a data cleaning procedure has been needed for structuring and validating data syntactically. The validated data should be enriched with the information of the disaster situation, location of disaster area, and source of the information. The main aim this work is to assess credibility and relevance of the volunteered data for the disaster events. Before dissemination of the validated data to the decision makers, the EGIS platform has been utilized to integrate with the cleaned volunteered data. In Fig. 1, the overview of the framework has been described. The following components of the framework have been used for assessing quality of volunteered data. Each component has been explained in the subsequent subsections.

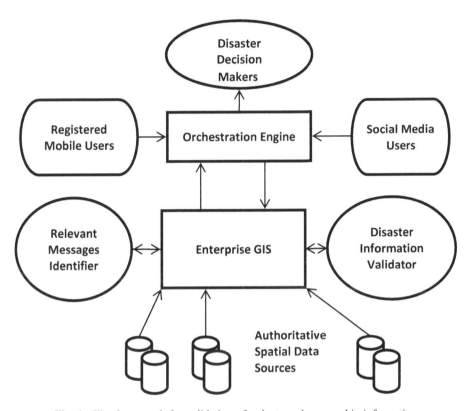

Fig. 1. The framework for validation of volunteered geographic information

3.1 Enterprise GIS

In order to generate information from the heterogeneous datasets provided by different organizations, an Enterprise GIS platform has been developed through the use of web services technology. The architecture of enterprises GIS typically describes the way of integrating relevant data services and provides a platform for the orchestration engine to generate essential information. In emergency situation, the orchestration engine executes a set of data processing operations for producing information based on uniform data services from this platform. In order to develop an interoperable geospatial data services from the heterogeneous resources, Weiser and Zipf [10] developed a standard interface for providing geospatial data services by considering the specifications of Open Geospatial Consortium (OGC). It is a widely adopted standard utilized in most of the GIS applications to access spatial data from different data sources over the network. This platform provides the opportunity to collect the volunteered data from different sources and store into the VGI database. Therefore, the orchestration engine is able to access the volunteered data along with the authoritative data for producing essential information for disaster management.

3.2 Orchestration Engine

The purpose of orchestration engine is to access the multiple geospatial web services according to predefined sequence of data accessing and processing logic for producing useful information. It also parses the messages delivered by the volunteers and stores into the VGI database. It constructs a chain of web services by linking the output of one web service as an input of another web service based on predefined rules. It executes various quality assessment processes to validate the volunteered data.

3.3 Identification of Relevant Messages

The keywords related to the particular type of disaster category have been parsed initially. However, this approach is simple and may have several limitations. Again, the vital information regarding a disaster location cannot be obtained. There is a huge number of research works available to resolve semantic aspects of messages. In this work, the semantic information retrieval and text mining technique methodology have been utilized to identify the relevant messages. In case of mobile messages, the registered volunteers use a mobile application to transfer the messages to this framework. This application provides a data capturing form along with the relevant attributes needed for disaster management. According to the attributes, the volunteers generate the messages of the situational information of their area.

3.4 Validation of Extracted Information

The extraction of the location information related to a message, it is needed to execute various processes for spatial and temporal analyses. Smart et al. [11] developed an approach which enables extract the location of the message without coordinate information. If different messages have been obtained from same location then the minimum distance between the volunteer location and the disaster location has been considered. After cross-referencing with the other information provided by the authoritative organizations, the validation processes of the have been. After that volunteered data have been utilized for disaster responses.

4   Quality Assessment Methodology

The data quality of disaster information provided by the local people is a vital factor for any decision making. In the work of Degrossi et al. [12], a statistical approach has been proposed for flood risk management. It is a process of an experimental evaluation to verify the volunteered data obtained through a crowdsourcing platform. According to Longueville [13], the credibility of VGI can be understood as a subjective concept which describes whether a piece of information can be trusted for disaster management by considering any possible intentional or unintentional omission or exaggeration error. In this work, a web services interface has been developed to collect volunteer information from different sources with respect of a disaster area. In order to become a volunteer, the local people should be registered through a mobile application along with their details. Initially, the messages provided by registered volunteers have been considered as authentic information for the disaster response. Again, the volunteers who are not registered may also provide messages related to the disaster situation. Their messages have been considered for disaster response if sufficient messages have not obtained from the disaster area to generate relevant information.

In this work, a context of flood scenario has been considered for the assessment of quality VGI data. These data can be analyzed by comparing with the data from different authoritative sources. In order to store volunteered information in real-time, a relational schema, called 'FloodVGI' has been created with the following attributes.

FloodVGI (VolunteerID, Date and Time, Point Geometry, Water Height, Rain Intensity, Apparent Visibility, Road Appearance, Runoff Type).

For example, the current *Water Height* around the location a volunteer has been considered by the discrete values such as 'Ankle height', 'Knee height', 'Waist height' and 'No Water'. Similarly for other flood related information, discrete values will be requested from the volunteers.

In order to evaluate the quality of the volunteered data, the statistical hypothesis testing has been conducted. There are two statements have been considered for hypothetical testing.

Statement 1: *Whether the volunteered geographic information is 50% useful in disaster management.*

Statement 2: *Whether the average value of information observed by the volunteers is same as average value of information obtained from the authoritative data sources.*

Initially, each question has been considered as a null hypothesis. An alternative hypothesis has been needed to prove each statement. For statement 1 the two hypotheses were defined as

Null Hypothesis (H_0): *The effectiveness of volunteered geographic information is 50% or less than the information from authorized sources in disaster management*

$$\mu(50\% \text{ of volunteered data}) \leq \mu(\text{Authoritative data})$$

Alternative Hypothesis (H_1): *The effectiveness of volunteered geographic information is more than 50% the information from authorized sources in disaster management*

$$\mu(50\% \text{ of volunteered data}) > \mu(\text{Authoritative data})$$

For statement 2 the two hypotheses were defined as

Null Hypothesis (H_0): *the average of volunteered information is equal to the average of authoritative data*

$$\mu(\text{Average of observed data}) = \mu(\text{Average of authoritative data})$$

Alternative Hypothesis (H_1): *the average of volunteered information is different from the average of authoritative data*

$$\mu(\text{Average of observed data}) \neq \mu(\text{Average of authoritative data})$$

In order to assess the result, the statistical hypothesis tests such as Shapiro-Wilk Test, Levene Test, T Test and Mann-Whitney Test have been carried out. The Shapiro-Wilk Test [14] has been used to check that the samples of the VGI data are within the normal distribution. If samples are within the normal distribution, then the Levene's Test [15] has been executed to verify if the samples have equal variance. After that the T Test [16] was performed to compare the sample's average statistically and thus reject or accept the null hypothesis. If samples did not have a normal distribution, the Mann-Whitney U Test was performed.

5   Case Study

In this case study, a flood prone area, named Ghatal Block is considered as study area which lies between 22.5847E to 22.7936E and 87.6061N to 87.8189. This area is situated under the Paschim Medinipur District, West Bengal, India with population 2,00,000 and the flood has been occurred almost every year. In this case study, a web based platform has been developed to communicate VGI data with the volunteers in this area. There are 2000 volunteers registered with the web based platform. A mobile application has been provided to the volunteers. In Fig. 2, the interface of the mobile application for flood disaster management has been shown. The application contains a predefined form with disaster parameters. The Twitter data also has been considered along with the data provided by the local volunteer for quality assessment. The authoritative data have been collected from the state spatial data infrastructure and irrigation department.

Initially, 2000 data of register volunteers and 500 Twitter data have been considered for the sampling purposes. There are 10 samples have been created for the hypothesis test. In order check the effectiveness volunteered geographic information, the categories of VGI data given in Table 1 have been considered.

The VGI data have been collected after the flood disaster within the EGIS. The Twetter data have cleaned by identifying location context along with message relevance. After cleaning, these data have become structured and included in the EGIS. In order to test the average values of the observed data, each attributed data provided by all volunteers have been considered separately. The average observed data have been divided into 10 samples. The disaster area is divided into multiple zones. The samples are selected based on these zones. In Table 2, the sample of collected VGI data have been given.

Initially, it is necessary to analyze whether the samples have equal variance. The statistical significance of each sample has been tested by the Shapiro-Wilk Test and T Test. The result shows that the data provided by the volunteers have not been within the

Table 1. Categories of VGI data effectiveness

Category	Effectiveness in disaster
Insufficient	Less than 25%
Satisfactory	Between 26% to 50%
Suitable	Between 51% to 75%
Acceptable	More than 75%

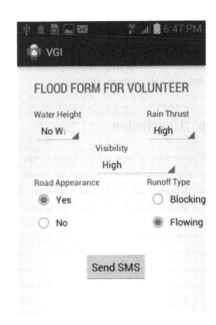

Fig. 2. The mobile application interfaces

Table 2. Sample of the collected VGI data

Geom	Water height	Rain thrust	Visibility	Road appearance	Runoff type
87.615,22.521	Knee	NA	Clear	No	Flowing
87.8045,22.6621	Waist	High	Hazy	No	Flowing
87.716,22.721	Waist	NA	Hazy	Yes	Blocking
86.804,22.675	Ankle	NA	Hazy	Yes	Flowing
87.689,22.857	Waist	High	Dark	No	Flowing
87.749,22.762	Knee	NA	Hazy	Yes	Blocking
87.654,22.857	Ankle	High	Dark	No	Flowing
87.692,22.67	Waist	Low	Clear	No	Blocking
87.72,22.685	Knee	Low	Clear	No	Flowing

range of normal distribution. After that Levene Test has been performed and the experiment shows that the samples do not have equal variance because the value of p-value is smaller than the significance level. The T Test was carried out in order to reject the null hypothesis.

The result shows that the null hypothesis cannot be refuted because the p-value is higher than the significance level. The T test can conclude that there is not statistically significant difference between the 50% of volunteered data and the authoritative data. The average result is equal to the confidence level of 80%. The results indicate that volunteered information is useful for flood risk management context, even with the lack of experience of participants. This can be explained by the fact that participants went through training before the execution. Thus, we can assert that the training was sufficient for enabling participants to produce useful volunteered information for the disaster risk management.

6 Conclusion

The result of statistical hypothesis testing signifies that the use of volunteered geographic information obtained from volunteered data sources provide valuable information for disaster management. The EGIS platform has been integrated with the volunteered data sources to enable rapid validation of volunteered data. The data obtained for the local registered volunteers of a disaster area is more reliable than the data from social media. It is found that the average result of observed data is equivalent to 80% of authoritative data. Since web service technique has been used, so it is possible to execute the statistical testing of VGI data in real-time. As a result, rapid decision making volunteered data can be possible.

In this work, a disaster area related to flood has been considered. It is needed execute this methodology for different disaster data in different area in future work. There is a need of technique for extracting essential information from users from social media. Therefore, it is necessary to develop more flexible VGI platform for any type of disaster management.

References

1. Goodchild, M.F.: Citizens as sensors: the world of volunteered geography. GeoJournal **69**(4), 211–221 (2007)
2. Linna, L., Goodchild, M.F.: The role of social networks in emergency management: a research agenda. Int. J. Inf. Syst. Crisis Response Manag. (IJISCRAM) **2**(4), 48–58 (2012)
3. Zook, M., Graham, M., Shelton, T., Gorman, S.: Volunteered geographic information and crowdsourcing disaster relief: a case study of the Haitian earthquake. World Med. Health Policy **2**, 7–33 (2010)
4. Meier, P.: Crisis mapping in action: how open source software and global volunteer networks are changing the world, one map at a time. J. Map Geogr. Libr. **8**(2), 89–100 (2012)
5. Girres, J., Touya, G.: Quality assessment of the French OpenStreetMap dataset. Trans. GIS **14**(4), 435–459 (2010)

6. Ballatore, A., Zipf, A.: A conceptual quality framework for volunteered geographic information. In: Fabrikant, S.I., Raubal, M., Bertolotto, M., Davies, C., Freundschuh, S., Bell, S. (eds.) COSIT 2015. LNCS, vol. 9368, pp. 89–107. Springer, Cham (2015). https://doi.org/10.1007/978-3-319-23374-1_5
7. Barron, C., Neis, P., Zipf, A.: A comprehensive framework for intrinsic OpenStreetMap quality analysis. Trans. GIS 18(6), 877–895 (2014)
8. Poser, K., Dransch, D.: Volunteered geographic information for disaster management with application to rapid flood damage estimation. Geomatica 64, 89–98 (2010)
9. Schade, S., Díaz, L., Ostermann, F., Spinsanti, L., Luraschi, G., Cox, S., Nunez, M., De Longueville, B.: Citizen-based sensing of crisis events: sensor web enablement for volunteered geographic information. Appl. Geomatics 5, 3–18 (2013)
10. Weiser, A., Zipf, A.: Web service orchestration of OGC web services for disaster management. In: Li, J., Zlatanova, S., Fabbri, A.G. (eds.) Geomatics Solutions for Disaster Management. LNGC, pp. 239–254. Springer, Heidelberg (2007). https://doi.org/10.1007/978-3-540-72108-6_16
11. Smart, P.D., Jones, C.B., Twaroch, F.A.: Multi-source toponym data integration and mediation for a meta-gazetteer service. In: Fabrikant, S.I., Reichenbacher, T., van Kreveld, M., Schlieder, C. (eds.) GIScience 2010. LNCS, vol. 6292, pp. 234–248. Springer, Heidelberg (2010). https://doi.org/10.1007/978-3-642-15300-6_17
12. Degrossi, L.C., Albuquerque, J., Fava, M.C., Mendiondo, E.M.: Flood citizen observatory: a crowdsourcing-based approach for flood risk management in Brazil. In: International Conference on Software Engineering and Knowledge Engineering (2014)
13. Longueville, B., Luraschi, G., Smits, P., Peedell, S., Groeve, T.: Citizens as sensors for natural hazards: a VGI integration workflow. Geomatica 64(1), 41–59 (2010)
14. Royston, J.P.: Some techiniques for assessing multivariate normality based on the Shapiro-Wilk W. J. Roy. Stat. Soc. 32(2), 121–133 (1983)
15. Olkin, I.: Contributions to Probability and Statistics: Essays in Honor of Harold Hotelling. Stanford University Press, Palo Alto (1960)
16. Wohlin, C., Runeson, P., Host, M., Ohlsson, M.C., Regnell, B., Wesslen, A.: Experimentation in Software Engineering: An Introduction. Kluwer Academic Publishers, Norwell (2000)

Multiresponse Optimization of Multistage Manufacturing Process Using a Patient Rule Induction Method

Dong-Hee Lee[(⊠)] and Jin-Kyung Yang

Division of Interdisciplinary Industrial Studies,
Hanyang University, Seoul, Republic of Korea
dh@hanyang.ac.kr

Abstract. Most of manufacturing industries produce products through a series of sequential processes. This is called multistage process. It is often difficult to optimize the multistage process due to the correlation between stages. Therefore, the relationships among the multiple processes should be considered in the multistage process optimization. Also, the processes often have multiple responses, thus, it is important to optimize multiple responses of multistage process. In these days, data mining techniques have been widely applied to process optimization. The proposed method attempts to optimize multiresponse of multistage process using a particular data mining method, called patient rule induction method. The proposed method obtains an optimal setting of input variables directly from the operational data in which multiple responses are optimized, simultaneously. The proposed approach is explained and illustrated by a step-by-step procedure with a case example.

Keywords: Data mining · Multiresponse optimization
Multistage manufacturing process · Patient rule induction method

1 Introduction

Most of manufacturing industries produce products through a series of sequential processes. This is called multistage manufacturing process. Figure 1 shows a typical multistage manufacturing process consisting of K stages. Here, Rectangles and circles represent the stages and inspection stations, respectively. The raw materials go through a total K sequential stages and becomes a product. The response of semi-finished product is gathered or measured at the inspection stations after each stage.

Multistage process has two properties which are often encountered in practice. First, result of preceding process affects to the afterward process. More specifically, the performance of Stage $k-1$ affects the performance of Stage k. Therefore, in order to optimize Stage k, it is necessary to consider responses of Stage $k-1$. Secondly, it is common to have multiple responses at each stage as shown in Fig. 1. Thus, it is important to simultaneously optimize the multiresponse of multistage process. x_k's and y_k's in Fig. 1 denote input variables and response variables at the kth stage, respectively. This work focuses on the multiresponse optimization (MRO) of multistage

© Springer International Publishing AG, part of Springer Nature 2018
O. Gervasi et al. (Eds.): ICCSA 2018, LNCS 10960, pp. 598–610, 2018.
https://doi.org/10.1007/978-3-319-95162-1_41

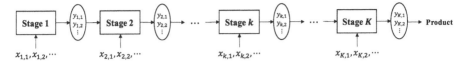

Fig. 1. Diagram of a multistage manufacturing process with multiresponse variables.

manufacturing process problem. The purpose of this optimization is maximizing the performance of multiresponse at each stage while considering the relationship between stages. To maximize the performance of multiresponse at Stage k, it is necessary to find the optimal control bounds of x_k's of Stage k while at the same time screening the multiresponse of Stage $k-1$.

Many manufacturing companies have a large volume and variety of operational data since diverse networked sensors and the internet of things are embedded in some smart factories (Wang and Zhang 2016). This trend is called era of big data, and big data analytics is being applied in various fields such as marketing, sales, and manufacturing (Lee et al. 2016). By applying big data analytics, improve existing analysis capabilities and provide new capabilities such as predictive analytics (Moyne and Iskandar, 2017).

A data mining approach is a good alternative for resolving the difficulties of existing MRO problem (Yang and Lee 2018). One of the attractive data mining approach is the patient rule induction method (PRIM) which is suggested by Friedman and Fisher (1999). PRIM searches a set of sub-regions of the search space within which the performance of the response is considerably better than that of the entire input domain (Chong et al. 2007).

Kwak et al. (2010) proposed a procedure for optimizing a multistage manufacturing process which is referred to as multistage PRIM. Multistage PRIM maximizes the performance of each stage considering the relationship between stages. The multistage PRIM assumes that there is only one response at each stage, however, considering several responses is common event in product and process development. Representative examples considering several response variables are machinery, chemical, semiconductor, steel, and food processing industry (Lee and Lee 2016).

Another recent study, Yang and Lee (2018) proposed a method for optimizing the mean and variance of multiple responses using PRIM. It is called EMR-PRIM. However, it considers only a single stage in the manufacturing process, thus, the correlation between stages cannot be considered in the optimization.

In this work, we propose a data mining-based approach to MRO of multistage manufacturing process which extends the multistage PRIM from single response to multiple response. The proposed method employs desirability functions and PRIM for the simultaneous optimization of multiresponse for multistage process.

The rest of the paper is organized as follows. Section 2 reviews the desirability function and PRIM. The proposed method is presented in Sect. 3 and illustrated with a case example in Sect. 4. Finally, discussion and concluding remarks are given in Sect. 5.

2 Literature Review

2.1 Desirability Function Approach

MRO attempts to find a set of input variables that simultaneously optimize the multiple response. It can be formally expressed as follows:

$$\text{Optimize}[\hat{y}_1(\mathbf{x}), \hat{y}_2(\mathbf{x}), \cdots, \hat{y}_J(\mathbf{x})]$$

$$\text{subject to } \mathbf{x} \in \Omega,$$

where $\mathbf{x}$ is a vector of input variables, and Ω is an experimental region of $\mathbf{x}$. $\hat{y}_j (j = 1, 2, \cdots, J)$ is the fitted response function of the jth response variable y_j, and J is the number of responses. The desirability function approach has been widely used for various MRO problems (Yang and Lee 2018). It converts each fitted response $\hat{y}_j$ as an individual desirability function d_j, ranging from 0 to 1. Then all of the individual desirability functions are aggregated into a single measure, called an overall desirability function. Geometric mean is often used as the aggregation as following Eq. (1). The desirability function is a good strategy that it reduces the multiple response models to one with a single aggregated measure and then solves as a single objective optimization problem. Thus, it is relatively simple in that an optimal solution can be obtained by maximizing the overall desirability function solely (Lee et al. 2018).

$$D = (d_1 \times d_2 \times \cdots \times d_J)^{\frac{1}{J}} \tag{1}$$

Derringer and Suich (1980) extended and modified Harrington (1965) by employing a different transformation scheme for estimating the response of multiresponse problems. When y_j is a LTB, NTB, and STB type response variable, individual d_j function is calculated as Eqs. (2), (3) and (4), respectively.

$$d_j(\hat{y}) = \begin{cases} 0, & \text{if } \hat{y}_j \leq y_j^{\min} \\ \left(\frac{\hat{y}_j - y_j^{\max}}{y_j^{\max} - y_j^{\min}} \right)^{s_j}, & \text{if } y_j^{\min} < \hat{y}_j < y_j^{\max} \\ 1, & \text{if } \hat{y}_j \geq y_j^{\max} \end{cases} \tag{2}$$

$$d_j(\hat{y}) = \begin{cases} 0, & \text{if } \hat{y}_j \leq y_j^{\min} \text{or } \hat{y}_j \geq y_j^{\max} \\ \left(\frac{\hat{y}_j - y_j^{\min}}{T_{y_j} - y_j^{\min}} \right)^{s_j}, & \text{if } y_j^{\min} < \hat{y}_j \leq T_{y_j} \\ \left(\frac{y_j^{\max} - \hat{y}_j}{y_j^{\max} - T_{y_j}} \right)^{t_j}, & \text{if } T_{y_j} \leq \hat{y}_j < y_j^{\max} \end{cases} \tag{3}$$

$$d_j(\hat{y}) = \begin{cases} 1, & \text{if } \hat{y}_j \leq y_j^{\min} \\ \left(\frac{y_j^{\max} - \hat{y}_j}{y_j^{\max} - y_j^{\min}} \right)^{t_j}, & \text{if } y_j^{\min} < \hat{y}_j < y_j^{\max} \\ 0, & \text{if } \hat{y}_j \geq y_j^{\max} \end{cases} \tag{4}$$

where $\hat{y}_j$ is the estimated jth response variable function. $y_j^{\min}$ and $y_j^{\max}$ is the minimum and maximum acceptable limits for the $\hat{y}_j$, respectively. T_{y_j} is the target value of $\hat{y}_j$ and parameters s_j and t_j determine the shape of the desirability function. For example, when $t_j = 1$, it represents linear, $0 < t_j < 1$ represents concave nonlinear, $t_j > 1$ represents convex. All of these parameters are determined according to the preferences of the process engineers. Thus, optimization process can be conducted in a flexible manner according to the preferences of the process engineers (Lee et al. 2017).

2.2 Patient Rule Induction Method

PRIM searches a set of sub regions of the input variable space within which the performance of the response is considerably better than that of the entire input domain (Chong et al. 2007). Here, a larger response is considered to be better. For the total I input variables, $x_1, x_2, \ldots, x_I$, a I-dimensional box B is defined as the intersection,

$$B = s_1 \times s_2 \times \cdots \times s_i \times \cdots \times s_I.$$

Here, s_i is a subrange of the ith input variable, x_i, denoted by $s_i = (l_i, u_i)$, where l_i and u_i are the lower and upper limits, respectively.

Suppose that we have total N observations denoted by $\{(y_n, \mathbf{x}_n), n = 1, 2, \ldots, N\}$, where y_n and $\mathbf{x}_n$ are values of the response and the input variables of the nth observation, respectively. $\mathbf{x}_n$ is a I-dimensional vector denoted by $\mathbf{x}_n = (x_{n1}, x_{n2}, \ldots, x_{ni})$. When $\mathbf{x}_n$ is located in box B (i.e., $l_1 \leq x_{n1} \leq u_1, l_2 \leq x_{n2} \leq u_2, \ldots, l_i \leq x_{ni} \leq u_i$), it is denoted by $\mathbf{x}_n \in B$.

Given a box B and observations $\{(y_n, \mathbf{x}_n), n = 1, 2, \ldots, N\}$, there are two statistics that describe the properties of box B. The first one is the support of box, β_B, which denotes the proportion of the observations located in box B.

$$\beta_B = \frac{n_B}{N},$$

where n_B denotes the number of observations that are located inside box B. The second useful statistic is the box objective Obj_B, which is the mean value of the response in box B.

$$Obj_B = \bar{y}_B = \frac{1}{n_B} \sum_{\mathbf{x}_n \in B} y_n.$$

The procedure of PRIM is presented below. Given observations $\{(y_n, \mathbf{x}_n), n = 1, 2, \ldots, N\}$, an initial box B_0 is formed by defining $l_i = \min_{n=1,2,\ldots,N} x_{ni}$ and $u_i = \max_{n=1,2,\ldots,N} x_{ni}$ for $i = 1, 2, \ldots, I$. From B_0, $2I$ candidate boxes, denoted by $\{C_{01-}, C_{01+}, C_{02-}, C_{02+}, \ldots, C_{0i-}, C_{0i+}, \ldots, C_{0I-}, C_{0I+}\}$, are created. The candidate boxes C_{0i-} and C_{0i+}, $i = 1, 2, \ldots, I$ are obtained by peeling $100\alpha\%$ of the observations in box B_0. The parameter α determines the peeling rate; its value is typically set between 0.05 and 0.1.

Once the $2I$ candidate boxes are obtained, PRIM chooses the one that has the largest box objective among the candidate boxes; this box becomes B_1. If the support of B_1 is greater than a stopping parameter, β_0, then PRIM continues to generate the next box B_2. Otherwise, the algorithm ends.

Among many data mining techniques, the patient rule induction method (PRIM) has been successfully applied for process optimization despite its recent emergence (Chong et al. 2007; Chong and Jun, 2008; Kwak et al. 2010; Lee and Kim 2008). This method directly seeks a set of sub-regions for input variables, in which higher quality values are observed from the historical data.

3 Proposed Method

In this section, the proposed method, which we refer to as multistage multiresponse PRIM (multistage MR-PRIM), is presented. Figure 2 shows the eight-step procedure of proposed method. Here, in dotted line, Steps 1–6 is PRIM procedure that iterate until the stopping criterion is satisfied. Details of each step are described below.

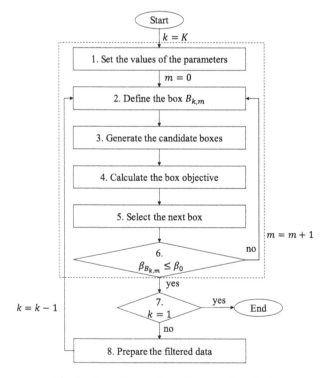

Fig. 2. Overall procedure of proposed method.

Step 1. Set the values of the parameters. The entire dataset with K stages process to be optimized is prepared. To avoid over-fitting problem, cross-validation is conducted.

The entire dataset is randomly split into learning and test sets. The size of the learning set is two times larger than the size of the test set in general. The stage iteration counter k is set as $k = K$ and starts to optimize with learning set only. The final stage (i.e., the Kth stage) is optimized first and then, going backward to the first stage sequentially.

The value of two initial parameters are set. The PRIM iteration counter m is set as $m = 0$, and the values of α and β_0 are determined. Typically, its value is set between 0.05 and 0.1.

Step 2. Define the box $B_{k,m}$. To reflect the relationship between Stage $k-1$ and Stage k, response variables of Stage $k-1$ is treated as the input variable of Stage k. Therefore, I_k-dimensional box is extended to $(I_k + J_{k-1})$-dimensional box, for the I input variables in that of the Stage k and J response variables of the Stage $k-1$. For a $(I_k + J_{k-1})$-dimensional box, $B_{k,m}$ in the mth PRIM iteration is defined by

$$B_{k,m} = \left(\prod_{j=1}^{J_{k-1}} s_{y_{k-1,j},m}\right) \times s_{x_{k,1},m} \times s_{x_{k,2},m} \times \cdots \times s_{x_{k,i},m} \times \cdots \times s_{x_{k,I_k},m},$$

where $s_{y_{k-1,j},m} = \left[LSL_{y_{k-1,j},m}, USL_{y_{k-1,j},m}\right]$ is an upper and lower specification limits of jth responses in the stage $k-1$ and mth PRIM iteration. $s_{x_{k,i},m} = \left[l_{x_{k,i},m}, u_{x_{k,i},m}\right]$ is a subrange of x_i in the Stage k and jth PRIM iteration where $i = 1, 2, \ldots, I_k$. When the PRIM iteration counter $m = 0$, the box $B_{k,0}$ contains all observations of the learning data $\{y_{k-1,j,0}(n), (y_{k,j,0}(n), \mathbf{x}_{k,0}(n)), n = 1, 2, \cdots, N\}$. Thus, the subranges are defined by $l_{0i} = \min_{n=1,2,\ldots,N} x_{ni}, u_{0i} = \max_{n=1,2,\ldots,N} x_{ni}$. As the PRIM iteration counter m increases by one, these subranges are updated.

Step 3. Generate the candidate boxes. For $x_{k,i}$ and $y_{k-1,j}$, two candidate boxes (denoted by $C_{x_{k,i}-m}, C_{x_{k,i}+m}$, and $C_{y_{k-1,j}-m}, C_{y_{k-1,j}+m}$, respectively.) are generated by peeling $100\alpha\%$ of the observations in box $B_{k,m}$. As a result, a total of $2(I_k + J_{k-1})$ candidate boxes are generated. For example, $C_{x_{k,i}-m}$ and $C_{x_{k,i}+m}$ for $x_{k,i}$ is shown as below.

$$C_{x_{k,i}-m} = s_{x_{k,1},m} \times s_{x_{k,2},m} \times \cdots \times s^{(-)}_{x_{k,i},m} \times \cdots \times s_{x_{k,I_k},m},$$

$$C_{x_{k,i}+m} = s_{x_{k,1},m} \times s_{x_{k,2},m} \times \cdots \times s^{(+)}_{x_{k,i},m} \times \cdots \times s_{x_{k,I_k},m},$$

where $s^{(-)}_{x_{k,i},m} = \left[x_{k,i(\alpha),m}, u_{x_{k,i},m}\right]$ and $s^{(+)}_{x_{k,i},m} = \left[l_{x_{k,i},m}, x_{k,i(1-\alpha)}\right]$. $x_{k,i(\alpha),m}$ is the α-percentile of $x_{k,i}$ in the box $B_{k,m}$ (i.e., $\Pr(x_{k,i} < x_{k,i(\alpha)} | x_k \in B_{k,m}) = \alpha$). Also, $y_{k-1,j}$'s candidate boxes can be generated in this way.

Step 4. Calculate the box objective. The box objective of each candidate box is calculated. We suggest using the desirability function as the box objective. When the optimizing Stage k, responses of the Stage $k-1$ are carefully screened as the interval of optimum conditions. Thus, it is a reasonable strategy to adopt desirability function for a multistage manufacturing process.

When constructing an overall desirability function (D) for the proposed method, geometric mean calculated by Eq. (5) is applied.

$$Obj_{B_{k,m}} = D_{k,m} = (d_{k,1} \times d_{k,2} \times \cdots \times d_{k,j} \times \cdots \times d_{k,J_k})^{1/J_k} \qquad (5)$$

where $Obj_{B_{k,m}}$ is the box objective of mth box at the Stage k. $d_{k,j}$ is an individual desirability for each mean of the jth response variables at the Stage k. An overall $D_{k,m}$ has the value ranging from 0 to 1. The individual $d_{k,j}$ function is calculated according to Eqs. (2), (3) and (4). In here, $\bar{y}_{k,j}$ is substituted for $\hat{y}_j$. Similarly, $y_{k,j}^{min}, y_{k,j}^{max}$, and $T_{y_{k,j}}$ which subscript k denotes for each Stage k is substituted for y_j^{min}, y_j^{max}, and T_{y_j}.

Step 5. Select the next box. In the desirability function, the candidate box with the largest box objective is selected as the next box. Once the next box is determined, iteration counter m is increased by one (i.e., $m = m + 1$).

Step 6. Check to see if the PRIM stopping criterion is satisfied. If the support of box $B_{k,m}, \beta_{B_{k,m}}$, is smaller than the predetermined threshold, β_0, the algorithm ends with box $B_{k,m}$. Otherwise, the algorithm returns to Step 2 to conduct another peeling process. Then, the next box is generated. This iterative procedure continues until the stopping criterion is satisfied.

Step 7. Check to see if the optimization stopping criterion is satisfied. If the Stage iteration counter $k = 1$, the optimization procedure ends with optimal box $B_{1,m}$, Otherwise, the algorithms goes to Step 8 to optimize the Stage $k-1$.

Step 8. Prepare the filtered data. In Step 8, prepare the filtered data and optimize the Stage $k-1$. The dataset of Stage $k-1$ to be optimized should meet the optimum conditions that was previously optimized in Stage k. In order to satisfy this restrictions, a filtered dataset $\left\{ y_{k-1,j}(n), (y_{k,j}(n), \mathbf{x}_k(n)) | y_{k-1,j}(n) \in y_{k-1,j}^*, n = 1, 2, \cdots, N_f \right\}$ should be used when the optimizing Stage $k-1$. $y_{k-1,j}^*$ is an optimum condition of jth response variable in Stage $k-1$ obtained from the previous optimization for Stage k. N_f is the number of filtered observations ($0 < N_f < N$) and the number of N_f changes each time in the optimizing process.

1:	Set the values of the initial parameters	Step 1
2:	Set the stage iteration counter $k = K$	
3:	**for** $k = K : 1$	
4:	**repeat**	
5:	Define the box	Step 2
6:	Generate candidate boxes to be peeled off	Step 3
7:	Calculate the box objective value using desirability function	Step 4
8:	Select the candidate box having the largest objective value as the next box	Step 5
9:	**until** *support* $< \beta_0$	Step 6
10:	Prepare the filtered data	Step 7
11:	Set the stage iteration counter $k = k-1$	Step 8
12:	**end**	

Fig. 3. Overall procedure of proposed method.

Stage iteration counter k is set as $k = k-1$ and repeat the Steps 2-6. This iterative process continues until the $k = 1$. At the end, for the optimal box, the box objective is recalculated with the test set.

To present the proposed method more clearly, we presented a pseudo-code of multistage MR-PRIM as shown in Fig. 3.

4 Case Study: Steel Manufacturing Process

In this section, the proposed method is illustrated by a particular example, steel manufacturing process problem. The steel manufacturing process consists of four stages to produce reinforcing bars. The scope of this case study, a dotted box in Fig. 4, is limited to the steel making and continuous casting stages (i.e., total 2-stage processes).

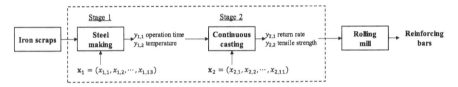

Fig. 4. Steel manufacturing process in the case study.

In the Stage 1, the iron scraps are melted to create molten iron. In the following Stage 2, the molten iron takes a solid shape called billets. The response variables of the Stage 1 are operating time ($y_{1,1}$, min) and molten iron temperature ($y_{1,2}$, °C). The operating time is a smaller-the-better (STB) type variable and molten iron temperature is a nominal-the-better (NTB) type variable. If the molten iron temperature is too high or too low, the equipment can be damaged or billets are solidified prematurely. Thus, it is important to meet the target of the temperature. Target value of $y_{1,2}$ is 1580 °C.

The response variables of the Stage 2 are return rate ($y_{2,1}$, %) and tensile strength ($y_{2,2}$, MPa). The return rate and tensile strength is a larger-the-better (LTB) type variable. The return rate, an important performance measure in the steel industry, means the ratio of the amount of iron scarps put into the steel making stage to the amount of billet produced in the continuous casting stage (Kwak et al. 2010). As we illustrated with Fig. 4, the number of input variables for each stage is 13 and 11, respectively. The purpose of this case study is to simultaneously optimize the mean of multiple responses for each stage, while optimally screening that of the preceding stages. The optimization is demonstrated by a step by step procedure as follows.

Step 1. Set the values of the parameters. The total number of observations, N is 5609. We randomly split the entire data into learning and test sets with ratio of 2:1. Since there are 2 stages in this example, the stage iteration counter k is set as $k = 2$. Then, optimization procedure for Stage 2 is performed with the learning set only. We set the initial parameter $\alpha = 0.05$ and $\beta_0 = 0.05$ which are typical values.

Table 1. Subranges of input variables for optimizing Stage 2.

	$y_{1,1}$	$y_{1,2}$	$x_{2,1}$	$x_{2,2}$	$x_{2,3}$	$x_{2,4}$	$x_{2,5}$	$x_{2,6}$	$x_{2,7}$	$x_{2,8}$	$x_{2,9}$	$x_{2,10}$	$x_{2,11}$
l_{01}	36	1447	1	13	1200	0	0	0	0	0	0	0	11
u_{01}	426	1666	264	121	12100	600	500	1425	25	270	120	89	163

Step 2. Define the box $B_{k,m}$. Because $m = 0$, the initial box $B_{2,0}$ is defined from the learning set: $B_{2,0} = s_{y_{1,1},0} \times s_{y_{1,2},0} \times s_{x_{2,1},0} \times s_{x_{2,2},0} \times \cdots \times s_{x_{2,11},0}$. $s_{y_{1,1},0}$ and $s_{y_{1,2},0}$ is the subranges of $y_{1,1}$ and $y_{1,2}$ in the Stage 1, respectively. The current subranges of each input variable for optimizing Stage 2 is given in Table 1.

Step 3. Generate the candidate boxes. For $x_{2,i}$, $y_{1,1}$ and $y_{1,2}$, two candidate boxes are generated by peeling $100\alpha\%$ of the observations in box $B_{2,0}$. As a result, a total of 26 (i.e., $2(11 + 2) = 26$) candidate boxes, $C_{y_{1,1}-0}, C_{y_{1,1}+0}, C_{y_{1,2}-0}, C_{y_{1,2}+0}, C_{x_{2,1}-0}, C_{x_{2,1}+0}, \cdots, C_{x_{2,11}-0}, C_{x_{2,11}+0}$ are generated.

Step 4. Calculate the box objective. The box objectives of the 26 candidate boxes are calculated by Eq. (5). The minimum and maximum acceptable limits for the $\bar{y}_{2,1}$ and $\bar{y}_{2,2}$ is [80, 100] and [200, 300], respectively. The minimum and maximum acceptable limits for the $\bar{y}_{1,1}$ and $\bar{y}_{1,2}$ is [30, 50] and [1530, 1620], respectively.

Step 5. Select the next box. The candidate box with the largest box objective is selected as the next box, $B_{2,1}$.

Step 6. Check to see if the stopping criterion is satisfied. Because $\beta_{B_{2,1}} > \beta_0$ (i.e., $0.95 > 0.05$), the algorithm goes back to Step 2. The iteration counter m is increased by one. Then, peeling and candidate box selection are conducted to generate the next box $B_{2,2}$. This iterative process continues until the support is less than 0.05. As a result, a total of 30 boxes (i.e., $B_{2,1}, B_{2,2}, \ldots, B_{2,30}$) were obtained.

Step 7. Check to see if the procedure stopping criterion is satisfied. Since the stage iteration counter k is $k = 2$, the algorithm goes to Step 8.

Step 8. Prepare the filtered data. The dataset for Stage $k-1$ to be optimized should meet the optimum conditions that was previously optimized in Stage k. Thus, the data where $y_{1,2}$ meets its optimal $y_{1,2}^* = ([1556, 1598])$ was filtered from the learning set. Here, $y_{1,1}$ does not peeled off. The number of filtered data, N_f, was 5033. Then, decrease the stage iteration counter $k = k-1$ and repeat the Steps 2–6. Since there are total 2-stages in this case study, optimization is completed only one repetition. Also, the preceding stage of Stage 1 does not exist, the performance of Stage 1 is maximized by optimizing the Stage 1 itself. Lastly, the box objective value of the optimal box is recalculated from the test set.

Table 2 summarizes the results of optimization for each stage. The optimum conditions obtained by Multistage MR-PRIM is expressed as an interval of input variables for each stage. Here, some of the optimum conditions for variables are not peeled off, which denoted by N/A. As can see in Table 2, the results indicate that the optimum conditions are significantly tight than the current level of subranges shown in Table 1.

The current level for the mean of $y_{2,1}$ and $y_{2,2}$ is 89.85 and 249.86, respectively. By contrast, the optimization results for the mean of $y_{2,1}$ and $y_{2,2}$ is improved to 92.06 and

Table 2. Results of the optimal box.

Variable	Continuous casting (stage 2)	Variable	Steel making (stage 1)
$x_{2,1}$	[N/A, N/A]	$x_{1,1}$	[8000, 10540]
$x_{2,2}$	[19, 31]	$x_{1,2}$	[4390, 6240]
$x_{2,3}$	[N/A, 3700]	$x_{1,3}$	[6530, 9750]
$x_{2,4}$	[195, 300]	$x_{1,4}$	[N/A, N/A]
$x_{2,5}$	[10, 120]	$x_{1,5}$	[N/A, N/A]
$x_{2,6}$	[N/A, 640]	$x_{1,6}$	[N/A, N/A]
$x_{2,7}$	[N/A, 10]	$x_{1,7}$	[N/A, N/A]
$x_{2,8}$	[15, 165]	$x_{1,8}$	[N/A, 400]
$x_{2,9}$	[4, 22]	$x_{1,9}$	[N/A, 1006]
$x_{2,10}$	[6, 34]	$x_{1,10}$	[N/A, N/A]
$x_{2,11}$	[39, 68]	$x_{1,11}$	[405, 826]
$y_{1,1}$	[N/A, N/A]	$x_{1,12}$	[86, 162]
$y_{1,2}$	[1556, 1598]	$x_{1,13}$	[1267, 2351]
$\bar{y}_{2,1}$	92.06	$\bar{y}_{1,1}$	42.25
$\bar{y}_{2,2}$	253.09	$\bar{y}_{1,2}$	1579.75
$s_{y_{2,1}}$	4.85	$s_{y_{1,1}}$	2.94
$s_{y_{2,2}}$	28.58	$s_{y_{1,2}}$	10.50

253.09, respectively. Also, the mean of $y_{1,1}$ and $y_{1,2}$ is improved from 46.40 and 1575.37 to 42.25 and 1579.75. Especially, $y_{1,2}$ is very close to the target of 1580(°C).

We plotted the peeling trajectories for each mean of the response variables in Fig. 5. The white dot represents the current level of the responses variables at box $B_{k,0}$. The two responses for Stage 2 is all LTB type variable, Fig. 5(a) and (b) shows that the mean of response increases with decreasing the value of support. In contrast, $y_{1,1}$ is a STB type variable, Fig. 5(c) clearly showed that the mean of $y_{1,1}$ was declining steadily. $y_{1,2}$ is a NTB type variable, As the support decreases, the mean of $y_{1,2}$ converges to the target value 1580 as shown in Fig. 5(d).

The cross-validation is conducted to determine whether the optimal box is over-fitted. In order that, the box objective of optimal box is recalculated by using the test set. The results obtained from the test set is compared with learning set in Table 3. The mean of responses from the learning set is 92.22 and 244.42 for the Stage 2. There was no significant difference in $y_{2,1}$, but not in $y_{2,2}$. The objective box was induced from the learning set only; thus, the recalculated box objective from the test set is worse than that of the learning set. In such a case, it is required to check whether outlier data exist in the dataset which can distort the box objective value (Hastie et al. 2009). Alternatively, new boxes can be obtained by changing the values of the initial parameters (α and β_0) or desirability function parameters. In the meanwhile, the recalculated mean of responses from the test set for Stage 1 is slightly larger than the learning set; however, the performances are sufficiently improved than that of the current level. Therefore, we can have concluded that the gap between the learning and test sets was not significant.

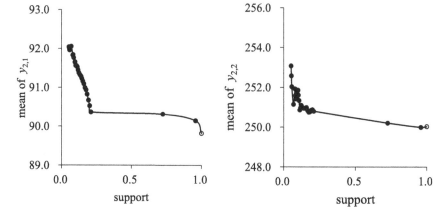

(a) Peeling trajectory for $\bar{y}_{2,1}$ and support.

(b) Peeling trajectory for $\bar{y}_{2,2}$ and support.

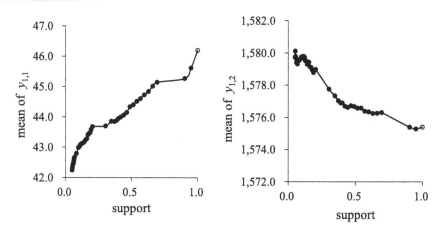

(c) Peeling trajectory for $\bar{y}_{1,1}$ and support.   (d) Peeling trajectory for $\bar{y}_{2,2}$ and support.

Fig. 5. Peeling trajectory for each of the responses and stages.

Table 3. Results of learning and test sets for optimal box.

	Continuous casting (stage 2)			Steel making (stage 1)	
	Learning set	Test set		Learning set	Test set
Box obj. (D)	0.57	0.52	Box obj. (D)	0.62	0.53
$\bar{y}_{2,1}$	92.06	92.22	$\bar{y}_{1,1}$	42.25	44.21
$\bar{y}_{2,2}$	253.09	244.42	$\bar{y}_{1,2}$	1579.75	1578.17

5   Concluding Remarks

Most of manufacturing industries produce products through a series of sequential processes. This is called multistage manufacturing process. We focused on the characteristics for the multistage manufacturing process as follows. First, the result of preceding process affects to the afterward process. Second, it is common to have multiple responses at each stage. Thus, it is important to simultaneously optimize the multiresponse of multistage process in practice.

In this paper, we proposed a multistage MR-PRIM which attempts to optimize the multiple responses of a multistage manufacturing process. The proposed method has advantageous to employing desirability function as the box objective for a multistage manufacturing process. We illustrated multistage MR-PRIM with a case example which it was shown that the multistage MR-PRIM works well for this case study. Also, it can find the optimum conditions directly from the historical data.

We suggest two future research topics. First of all, it is necessary to consider optimization of multistage process with more than two stages. In addition, we assumed that only Stage $k-1$ among various preceding stages affects the performance of Stage k, but the situations could occur in which two or more preceding stages affect to Stage k simultaneously. In case of that, it would be harder to directly find the optimal settings which meet some of the constraints. Secondly, not only the mean of responses, but also the standard deviation of the responses should be considered in determining the optimum conditions. It is often in conflict between the mean and variance of the response variables. By considering this trade-off, there is a chance that improve the stability of the MRO for a multistage manufacturing process.

References

Ames, A.E., Mattucci, N., Macdonald, S., Szonyi, G., Hawkins, D.M.: Quality loss function for optimization across multiple response surface. J. Qual. Technol. **29**, 339–346 (1997)

Derringer, G.: A balancing act: optimizing a product's properties. Qual. Prog **27**, 51–58 (1994)

Derringer, G., Suich, R.: Simultaneous optimization of several response variables. J. Qual. Technol. **12**, 214–219 (1980)

Friedman, J.H., Fisher, N.I.: Bump hunting in high dimensional data. Stat. Comput. Lond. **9**(2), 123–142 (1999)

Harrington, E.: The desirability function. Ind. Qual. Control **4**, 494–498 (1965)

Jeong, I., Kim, K.: An interactive desirability function method to multi-response optimization. Eur. J. Oper. Res. **195**, 412–426 (2009)

Kim, K., Lin, D.: Simultaneous optimization of multiple responses by maximizing exponential desirability functions. Appl. Stat. (J. Roy. Stat. Soc. Ser. C) **49**, 311–325 (2000)

Kim, K., Lin, D.: Optimization of multiple responses considering both location and dispersion effects. Eur. J. Oper. Res. **169**, 133–145 (2006)

Ko, Y., Kim, K., Jun, C.: A new loss function-based method for multi-response optimization. J. Qual. Technol. **37**, 50–59 (2005)

Kwak, D.S., Kim, K.J., Lee, M.S.: Multistage PRIM: patient rule induction method for optimisation of a multistage manufacturing process. Int. J. Prod. Res. **48**(12), 3461–3473 (2010)

Lee, D.H., Jeong, I.J., Kim, K.J.: A desirability function method for optimizing mean and variability of multiple responses using a posterior preference articulation approach. Qual. Reliab. Eng. Int. **34**(3), 1–17 (2018)

Lee, D.H., Yang, J.K., Kim, K.J.: Dual-response optimization using a patient rule induction method. Qual. Eng. 1–11 (2017)

Lee, M.S., Kim, K.J.: MR-PRIM: patient rule induction method for multiresponse optimization. Qual. Eng. **20**(2), 232–242 (2008)

Lee, H.J., Lee, D.H.: A solution selection approach to multiresponse surface optimization based on a clustering method. Qual. Eng. **28**(4), 388–401 (2016)

Lee, Y.H., Song, M.S., Ha, S.J., Baek, T.H., Son, S.Y.: Big data cloud service for manufacturing process analysis. Korean J. Bigdata **1**(1), 41–51 (2016)

Moyne, J., Iskandar, J.: Big data analytics for smart manufacturing: case studies in semiconductor manufacturing. Processes **5**(4), 39–58 (2017)

Pignatiello, J.: Strategies for robust multi-response quality engineering. IIE Trans. **25**, 5–15 (1993)

Vining, G.: A compromise approach to multi-response optimization. J. Qual. Technol. **30**, 309–313 (1998)

Wang, J., Zhang, J.: Big data analytics for forecasting cycle time in semiconductor wafer fabrication system. Int. J. Prod. Res. **54**(23), 7231–7244 (2016)

Yang, J.K., Lee, D.H.: Optimization of mean and standard deviation of multiple responses using patient rule induction method. Int. J. Data Warehouse.Min. **14**(1), 60–74 (2018)

Yoon, J., Shim, J.: Introduction to Ferrous Metallurgy. Daewoong Press, Seoul (2004)

A Scheduling Method for On-Demand Delivery of Selective Contents Considering Selection Time

Yusuke Gotoh$^{(\boxtimes)}$ and Ken Ohta

Okayama University, Okayama 7008530, Japan
gotoh@cs.okayama-u.ac.jp

Abstract. Due to the recent popularization of digital broadcasting services, on-demand delivery of selective contents on the Internet, i.e., watching contents selected by the users themselves, is attracting much attention. For example, in a quiz program, a user selects answer and watches the video content to learn the answer. When the waiting time for playing the data after the selection is lengthened, the continuity of playing them may be interrupted. In this paper, we propose a scheduling method to reduce the waiting time for the on-demand delivery of selective contents based on the selection time. In our proposed method, the server reduces the waiting time by delivering all the candidate contents during the selection time for watching subsequent content. Our evaluation confirmed that the average waiting time under our proposed method was reduced more than that under the conventional method.

Keywords: On-demand delivery · Scheduling · Selection time
Selective contents · Waiting time

1 Introduction

Due to the continued popularization of digital broadcasting services, on-demand delivery of selective contents is attracting much attention. For example, in news programs, after watching a summary of each story, the user selects one of interest and watches it. In quiz programs, the server delivers several potential answers from which the user selects answer. If the answer is correct, he watches the video content about the correct answer. Otherwise, he watches the content of the incorrect answer.

By having access to selective contents, clients can watch programs that meet their individual preferences. In such on-demand delivery systems as YouTube [1], the server delivers the contents based on the selections of clients. However, since some of the network bandwidth is wasted for each delivery, clients have to wait if insufficient bandwidth is provided. Here we assume that the server does not deliver contents if the available bandwidth is less than the data consumption rate. Therefore, users can watch the content without interruption after they start watching it.

© Springer International Publishing AG, part of Springer Nature 2018
O. Gervasi et al. (Eds.): ICCSA 2018, LNCS 10960, pp. 611–622, 2018.
https://doi.org/10.1007/978-3-319-95162-1_42

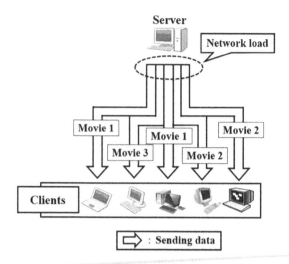

Fig. 1. VoD environment

In this paper, we propose a scheduling method for the on-demand delivery of selective contents to reduce the waiting times based on the selection times. Our proposed method reduces the waiting time by making a delivery schedule to distribute all the candidate contents while selecting subsequent content.

The remainder of our paper is organized as follows. We explain delivery systems for webcasts in Sect. 2 and introduce selective contents in Sect. 3. The waiting time for selective contents is explained in Sect. 4. Related works are introduced in Sect. 5. Our proposed method is explained in Sect. 6 and evaluated in Sect. 7. Finally, we conclude in Sect. 8.

2   Delivering System for Webcast

In webcasts, there are mainly two mainly types of delivery systems: Video on Demand (VoD) and broadcasting. First, we calculate the waiting times for VoD and broadcasting systems. Next, we explain waiting times for broadcasting data that are divided into several segments.

The situation that causes waiting time in VoD systems is shown in Fig. 1. In the VoD system, the server starts delivering data sequentially based on client requests. The waiting times under VoD systems are roughly equal to the receiving times.

On the other hand, the situation that causes waiting times in broadcasting systems is shown in Fig. 2. When the server repetitively broadcasts continuous media data, clients have to wait until the first portion of it is broadcast.

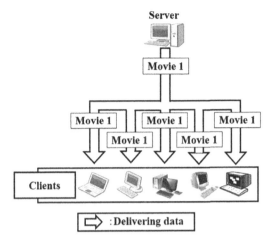

Fig. 2. Broadcasting environment

3 Selective Contents

3.1 Play-Sequence Graph

In this section, we explain a play-sequence graph [2], which is a state transition graph for describing the sequence of selective contents.

In a play-sequence graph, each node represents a state in which the client plays some content. When the client finishes playing it, the state transits to the next node. For example, a play-sequence graph for a quiz program is shown in Fig. 3. In Fig. 3–A, the user selects an answer from given answers X or Y. Node S_1 is a state where the client plays a video that presents the quiz. S_2 is a state where the client plays a video that explains answers X and Y. The user selects an answer from X or Y while playing the video. If she selects answer X, the state transits to S_3. If she selects answer Y, the state transits to S_4. In this way, the state transits to the next node based on her selections. When the user does not select an answer, the state transits to S_2 again or automatically transits to subsequent nodes S_3 or S_4. S_3 is the state where the user selects answer X, and a video for the correct answer is played. S_4 is the state where the user selects answer Y, and a video for the incorrect answer is played.

Play-sequence graphs can be simplified by applying the following three operations: abbreviate, merge, and split [3]. By applying them, we can simplify the play-sequence graph for a quiz program (Fig. 3–C).

3.2 Play-Sequence Graph Considering Selection Time

In this paper, we call the time for selecting one of the candidate contents after the user finishes watching the content the *selection time*. Based on Fig. 3–B, the play-sequence graph based on the selection time is shown in Fig. 4. S_i $(i = 1, 2, 3)$

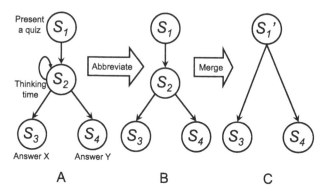

Fig. 3. Simplified play-sequence graph

is the video data, and T_i is the state of selecting the next content after watching S_i. In Fig. 4, clients start playing T_1 after 60 s of playing S_1. When clients select S_2 or S_3 during a maximum selection time (20 s), they play it within 60 s.

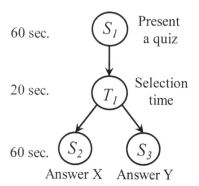

Fig. 4. Play-sequence graph considering selection time.

4   Mechanism for Waiting Time

In on-demand delivery of selective contents, the server needs to deliver contents effectively based on the client's selection. Many researchers have proposed scheduling methods to reduce waiting times considering the available bandwidth, the amount of contents, and the structure of play-sequence graphs.

In on-demand delivery, we explain the scheduling method to reduce waiting times. In the VoD system, when the server makes a delivery schedule called a VoD method, the server distributes contents to the client according to its own requirements. For example, the delivery schedule for selective contents is shown in Fig. 5. The server delivers a news program whose play-sequence graph is shown in Fig. 6. The playing time of $S_1, \cdots, S_7$ is 60 s, and that of T_1, T_2, and T_3 is 20 s. The consumption rate is 5.0 Mbps, and the available bandwidth is 8.0 Mbps.

In the VoD method, the server delivers contents selected by the clients. Therefore, the server does not deliver the data between finishing the delivery of S_t and starting to deliver the next content. In Fig. 5, when the client plays S_1, S_2, and S_4 sequentially and selects the next content within 10 s, the server does not use all of the bandwidth for delivering contents within 40 s.

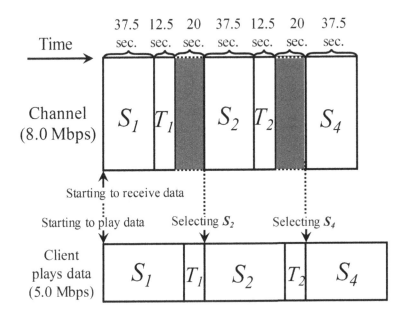

Fig. 5. Delivery schedule under VoD method

5   Related Works

Several methods have been proposed to reduce waiting times for broadcasting systems [4–10]. The Harmonic Broadcasting (HB) method [11] divides the data into several segments of equal sizes and broadcasts them to reduce the waiting time. By broadcasting divided data repetitively by each channel, the waiting time is reduced.

In the Optimized Periodic Broadcast (OPB) method [12], each segment of data is divided into two parts. After clients completely receive all of the preceding parts of the content, they start to receive the next part. Since clients can get the preceding parts in advance, the waiting time is reduced. However, the bandwidth increases as the number of segments increases.

In the Hierarchical Stream Merging (HSM) method [13], after clients have completely received all of the data, the server merges the channel that the client

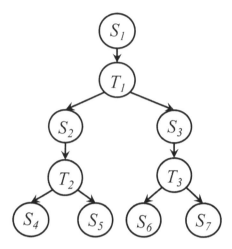

Fig. 6. Play-sequence graph for news program

is using. Since the method reduces the necessary bandwidth, the waiting time is reduced.

In the PolyHarmonic Broadcasting Protocol with Partial Preloading (PHP-PP) method [14], the data are divided into 20 segments. The number of segments is derived from the prefetching ratio and the bandwidths of the channels. The necessary bandwidth becomes 17.7 Mbps, which is less than the simple repetition method.

In Mayan Temple Broadcasting (MTB) [15], the data are divided into five segments. The necessary bandwidth becomes 21.3 Mbps. Although the necessary bandwidth is larger than that under the PHB-PP method, the number of channels needed to broadcast segments is fewer than under the PHB-PP method. Therefore, the implementation is easier than the PHB-PP method.

These schemes use a near-video-on-demand technique, i.e., reducing the waiting times by repetitively broadcasting the data. In this paper, we assume that the server does not repetitively broadcast the data. In addition, our assumed data are selective contents.

We previously proposed scheduling schemes to reduce the waiting times for selective contents broadcasting [2,16]. In these schemes, by acquiring channel bandwidth that is identical as the data consumption rate, the waiting time is effectively reduced. In this paper, we assume that the server creates a delivery schedule to distribute all the candidate contents while selecting the next content.

6   Proposed Method

6.1   Outline

We propose a scheduling scheme for on-demand delivery called the Contents Cumulated Broadcasting Considering Selection Time (CCB-ST) method, which reduces waiting times by making a delivery schedule for distributing all candidate contents while selecting the next content.

6.2   Assumed Environment

Our assumed system environment is listed below:

– The data are selective contents.
– The server provides an on-demand delivery system.
– The network is a guarantee type.
– The server only delivers content selected by the client.
– Clients have enough buffer to store the received data.

6.3   Scheduling Process

Let n be the number of states, and let b be the depth of play-sequence graph. S_i $(i = 1, \cdots, n)$ is the state of playing the content. T_i $(i = 1, \cdots, n)$ is the state of selecting the next content. The available bandwidth of the server is B, the amount of the stored contents on queue L is l, and the number of selections is e.

In the proposed method, in all the routes from the roots to the leaves, the server finds the longest route. The scheduling process continues as follows:

1. Insert the order of the early start time. If the start times of several contents are equivalent, they are inserted in a lower number of n.
2. The server removes the top content from L. We indicate the removed content by S_i.
3. Schedule S_i and T_i to C_j.
4. Schedule $S_{i+1}, \cdots, S_{i+e}$ to $C_1, \cdots, C_e$ during the selection time.
5. The client sends information about its selected content to the server.
6. From L, the server removes the other contents at the same depth and the contents on the routes that the client does not select.
7. If L is not empty, repeatedly go to process 2.

6.4   Practical Example

An example of a delivery schedule produced by the proposed method is shown in Fig. 7. We use the play-sequence graph shown in Fig. 6. Clients sequentially select S_1, S_2, and S_4. In our proposed scheduling method, when the available bandwidth is 8.0 Mbps and the consumption rate is 5.0 Mbps, the selection time is 10 s. As shown in Subsect. 6.3, while the client selects either S_2 or S_3 after it finishes playing S_1, the server delivers S_2 and S_3 by 4.0 Mbps, which takes 20 s. When the client selects S_2, the server delivers the rest of it by 8.0 Mbps, which takes 27.5 s. While the client selects either S_4 or S_5 after it finishes playing S_2, the server delivers S_4 and S_5 by 4.0 Mbps, which takes 30 s. When the client selects S_4, the server delivers the rest of it by 8.0 Mbps, which takes 22.5 s. Therefore, the CCB-ST method reduces the delivery time (162.5 s) more than the VoD method (177.5 s), and no waiting time occurred.

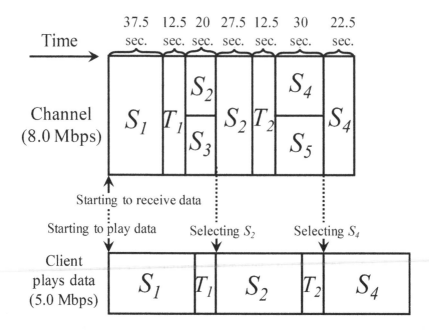

Fig. 7. Delivery schedule under proposed method

7   Evaluation

7.1   Evaluation Environment

According to delivery programs, play-sequence graphs have many patterns. However, evaluating the performance of our proposed method for all of these patterns is not realistic. Therefore, in this paper, we use the play-sequence graph shown in Fig. 8.

The number of potential answers e is 2, the playing time of S_i is 60 s, and that of T_i is 20 s. The consumption rate is 5.0 Mbps.

7.2   Effect of Arrival Interval

We evaluate the waiting time under several average arrival intervals. The result is shown in Fig. 9. The horizontal axis is the average arrival time that is set every 2 s in the 5 to 25 s range. The vertical axis is the average waiting time divided by the number of clients.

In this evaluation, we used the play-sequence graph shown in Fig. 8. The number of contents is 7 and the number of clients is 100. The available bandwidth is 100 Mbps, and the consumption rate is set every 0.1 Mbps in the 5.0 to 10 Mbps range. The selection time is 10 s after it finishes playing the content. In this paper, we assume that the arrival pattern of the user is independent of other users. Therefore, the simulation model used in the paper follows a Poisson distribution.

Depth

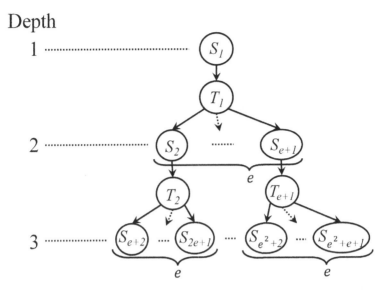

Fig. 8. Play-sequence graph for evaluating waiting times

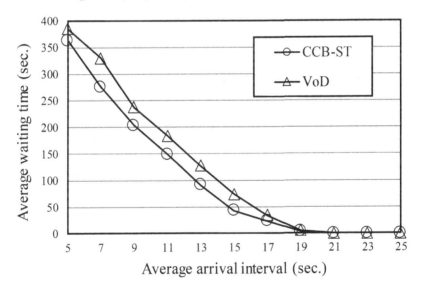

Fig. 9. Average arrival interval and waiting times

In Fig. 9, as the average arrival interval increases, the waiting times under the proposed and VoD methods are reduced further. When the arrival interval is lengthened, since the data size of the contents delivered by the server to the clients increases, the waiting time is reduced.

In addition, the waiting time in the CCB-ST method is shorter than the VoD method. In the CCB-ST method, since the delivery time of the program is reduced by distributing the candidate contents while selecting the next content, the waiting time can be reduced.

7.3   Effect of Selection Time

Next we evaluated the waiting time under several selection times. The result is shown in Fig. 10. The horizontal axis is a selection time that is set every sec. in the 0 to 20 s range. The vertical axis is the average waiting time divided by the number of clients. The number of contents is 7, and the number of clients is 100. The available bandwidth is 100 Mbps, and the consumption rate is set every 0.1 Mbps in the 5.0 to 10 Mbps range. The average arrival interval based on a Poisson distribution is 15 s.

In Fig. 10, as the average arrival interval increases, the waiting times under the proposed and VoD methods are lengthened. When the selection time is lengthened, the delivery time for each client is also lengthened. In the CCB-ST method, since the time that the server is unable to allocate bandwidth to the clients is reduced, the waiting time can be reduced.

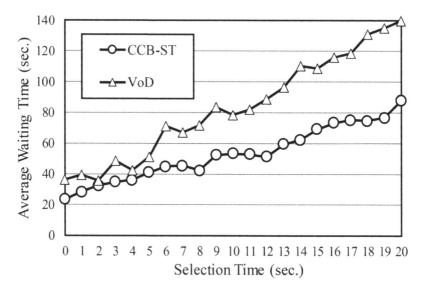

Fig. 10. Selection and waiting times

8   Conclusion

In this paper, we proposed and evaluated a scheduling method named the CCB-ST method for selective contents that considers selection time. The CCB-ST method reduces the waiting time by making a delivery schedule to distribute all the candidate contents while selecting the next content. In our evaluation, we confirmed that the waiting times are reduced more than the conventional VoD method.

A future direction of this study will make a scheduling method to consider the transition probability of play-sequence graphs.

Acknowledgement. This work was supported by JSPS KAKENHI Grant Number 18K11265 and 16K01065. In addition, this work was partially supported by the Telecommunications Advancement Foundation.

References

1. YouTube. http://www.youtube.com/
2. Gotoh, Y., Yoshihisa, T., Kanazawa, M.: A scheduling method considering available bandwidth in selective contents broadcasting. In: Proceedings of the IEEE Wireless Communications and Networking Conference, WCNC 2007, pp. 2597–2602 (2007)
3. Yoshihisa, T.: A scheduling method for bandwidth reduction on selective contents broadcasting. In: Proceedings of the IPSJ International Conference on Mobile Computing and Ubiquitous Networking, ICMU 2006, pp. 60–67 (2006)
4. Janakiraman, R., Waldvogel, M.: Fuzzycast: efficient video-on-demand over multicast. In: Proceedings of the IEEE INFOCOM, pp. 920–929 (2002)
5. Jinsuk, B., Jehan, F.P.: A tree-based reliable multicast scheme exploiting the temporal locality of transmission errors. In: Proceedings of the IEEE International Performance, Computing, and Communications Conference, IPCCC 2005, pp. 275–282 (2005)
6. Juhn, L.-S., Tseng, L.M.: Fast data broadcasting and receiving scheme for popular video service. IEEE Trans. Broadcast. **44**(1), 100–105 (1998)
7. Paris, J.-F.: An interactive broadcasting protocol for video-on-demand. In: Proceedings of the IEEE International Performance, Computing, and Communications Conference, IPCCC 2001, pp. 347–353 (2001)
8. Viswanathan, S., Imilelinski, T.: Pyramid broadcasting for video on demand service. In: Proceedings of the SPIE Multimedia Computing and Networking Conference, MMCN 1995, pp. 66–77 (1995)
9. Tantaoui, M., Hua, K., Do, T.: BroadCatch: a periodic broadcast technique for heterogeneous video-on-demand. IEEE Trans. Broadcast. **50**(3), 289–301 (2004)
10. Hua, K.A., Bagouet, O., Oger, D.: Periodic broadcast protocol for heterogeneous receivers. In: Proceedings of the MMCN, pp. 220–231 (2003)
11. Juhn, L.-S., Tseng, L.: Harmonic broadcasting for video-on-demand service. IEEE Trans. Broadcast. **43**(3), 268–271 (1997)
12. Carlsson, N., Mahanti, A., Li, Z., Eager, D.: Optimized periodic broadcast of nonlinear media. IEEE Trans. Multimed. **10**(5), 871–884 (2008)
13. Zhao, Y., Eager, D.L., Vernon, M.K.: Scalable on-demand streaming of non-linear media. In: Proceedings of the IEEE INFOCOM, vol. 3, pp. 1522–1533 (2004)
14. Mahanti, A., Eager, D.L., Vernon, M.K., Stukel, D.S.: Scalable on-demand media streaming with packet loss recovery. IEEE/ACM Trans. Netw. **11**(2), 195–209 (2003)

15. Paris, J.-F., Long, D.D.E., Mantey, P.E.: Zero-delay broadcasting protocols for video-on-demand. In: Proceedings of the ACM International Multimedia Conference, Multimedia 1999, pp. 189–197 (1999)
16. Gotoh, Y., Yoshihisa, T., Kanazawa, M., Takahashi, Y.: A broadcasting scheme for selective contents considering available bandwidth. IEEE Trans. Broadcast. **55**(2), 460–467 (2009)

Predicting Particulate Matter for Assessing Air Quality in Delhi Using Meteorological Features

Apeksha Aggarwal$^{(\boxtimes)}$ and Durga Toshniwal

Indian Institute of Technology, Roorkee, Roorkee, India
{aagar.dcs2016,durgafec}@iitr.ac.in

Abstract. Air pollution is one of the biggest threats to the environment. According to statistics of World Health Organization, more than 80% of people living in urban areas inhale poor air quality levels. Hence assessing air quality is important especially in urban areas where people suffer more health problems due to poor air quality. Data mining techniques can serve to be very useful for analyzing the air quality data. In the past, several research works were done for various developing countries of the world, except a few for developing countries, like India. Specifically for Delhi, where high concentrations of Oxides of Nitrogen, Oxides of Sulphur, Benzene, Toluene, Particulate Matter etc. are reported in its atmosphere. The presence of certain meteorological conditions in the atmosphere can be very helpful to identify the presence of such pollutants. Particulate matter with a diameter of 2.5 μm or less ($PM_{2.5}$) is focused upon in this work. Data mining techniques like multivariate linear regression model and regression trees etc. to identify the relationship between meteorological features and air quality are deployed. Further, the use of ensemble techniques such as random forests are also given in the present research work. Evaluation is done over root mean square error metrics and results are found to be promising.

Keywords: Data mining · Air quality · Air quality station
Meteorological feature · $PM_{2.5}$

1 Introduction

According to World Health Organization, Air pollution causes 1 million urban deaths per year [1]. However to abstain from inhaling poor levels of air quality, prior knowledge of air quality is obligatory. Air quality of any location is described by a list of several pollutants. Particularly for Delhi, Central Pollution Control Board (CPCB) [2], identified majorly following pollutants that define air quality namely, CO (Carbon mono oxide), NH_3 (Ammonia), $PM_{2.5}$ (Particulate Matter with a diameter of 2.5 μm or less), PM_{10} (Particulate Matter with a diameter of 10 μm or less), SO_2 (Sulphur Di Oxide), O_3 (Ozone), NO (Nitric Oxide), NO_2 (Nitrogen Di Oxide) and a few others. $PM_{2.5}$ is primarily focused

© Springer International Publishing AG, part of Springer Nature 2018
O. Gervasi et al. (Eds.): ICCSA 2018, LNCS 10960, pp. 623–638, 2018.
https://doi.org/10.1007/978-3-319-95162-1_43

upon in this work. Data mining can be useful for analyzing the air quality in terms of $PM_{2.5}$ concentration. To analyze the air quality, knowledge of domain experts is required. However, to apply statistical knowledge, a vast feature space is necessary to understand the data and address the data related issues such as noise, data dependencies. In the present work, we have tried to produce accurate prediction model, with less feature space as input.

In our research work main focus is on Delhi, which is the most polluted and 2nd most populated city in the world, witnessing alarming increase in pollution levels every year. Delhi government is taking major steps [3] to control air pollution, by reducing vehicle emissions and reducing emissions from factories. In addition to governments' step towards air pollution, this work is a helping hand to citizens as well as to government of Delhi by giving prior information about future air quality levels of the urban locality.

One of the major research challenge addressed in for our work is that huge amounts of meteorological data is generated these days so fitting a single model for large data might not give useful results. To handle this problem our proposed framework uses ensemble technique in which data is divided into number of trees with respect to features as well as data points and then model for each tree is fitted. Finally results are aggregated for each of these fits. Furthermore our method is applicable to any urban locality having air quality stations recording concentrations of pollutants as well as meteorological data.

Basic outline of paper is as follows. Section 2 discusses related work and comparison with previous approaches. Section 3 describes the proposed methodology used including various steps of data mining followed over Delhi data. Section 4 provides brief introduction to data mining classification and prediction models used in this research work. Results and discussions of the experiments are discussed in Sect. 5. Section 6 elaborates evaluation of results over RMSE error metrics. Section 7 includes conclusion and future scope.

2   Related Work

There are various methods of studying air pollution ranging from satellite sensing to handheld devices [4–6]. Nevertheless, most of these requires expensive hardware infrastructure to monitor air quality of any particular location in any city or area. Existing methods do not specifically analyze distribution of air pollution in developing countries except a few [7–9]. Zhang et al. [10] describes 3 categories of methods to collect data i.e simple empirical approaches, parametric or non-parametric statistical approaches and physically based more advanced approaches. Empirical approaches forecast next day's forecast using current day pollution values. These methods are simple and fast but have low accuracy and cannot handle sudden changes in weather. Parametric and non-parametric statistical models use statistical functions such as CART and regression methods, fuzzy logic, neural network etc. [11] to forecast pollutant concentration. These models have higher accuracy than deterministic models.

Multiple linear regression is used in Donnelly et al. [12] to forecast future concentrations of NO_2. Non-parametric kernel regression method is used as inputs to predict future concentrations of NO_2. Previous works have described that coefficients learned from linear regression explained the linear functionality between parameters and the prediction variable. While non parametric kernel regression methods describe it in a better way. In Feng et al. [13] various factors responsible for air pollution have been used to predict $PM_{2.5}$ concentration. The time series of $PM_{2.5}$ concentration is decomposed into few sub series by wavelet transform and multilayer perceptron model of ANN is applied to each of these sub series to sum up the results of prediction strategy. Prasad et al. [14] used ANFIS Adaptive-Network-based Fuzzy Inference System to model non-linear functions and predict a time series. Other very important research work includes air quality forecasting methods on big data using data mining [15–19].

One of the major research contribution is given by Zheng et al. [17], which explained relationship of spatial and temporal features with air quality. In the past, various researches have done on assessing air quality data from developed countries, but not for developing countries such as India. So, for better decision making and better planning, by policy makers and users, application of data mining techniques in such countries would be useful. Also, most of the existing research works on air quality data uses some specific classifier type for classification and prediction. But not much research works have used ensemble methods on air quality data for the purpose of air quality prediction. The main motive of our work is to identify the relationship between Delhi's meteorology with its air quality. Ensemble method gave good classifier accuracy for a limited studied area and limited feature space.

3   Proposed Methodology

As shown in Fig. 1 our framework consists of following major components namely, data preprocessing, feature selection, data mining and analysis of results.

Problem Statement: Given a collection of n number of features $F = (f_1, f_2, \ldots, f_n)$ where all f_i are meteorological features taken as input variable and Y is the output variable i.e. $PM_{2.5}$ concentration and $M = m_1, m_2, \ldots, m_t$ are the air quality monitoring stations at t locations. Aim is to provide a better fit for different models by identifying the dominating features of all f_is and predicting $PM_{2.5}$ concentration based on these features.

Problem solution is divided into following four steps.

1. Data preprocessing: Data collected from online source may contain missing values and other inconsistencies. Data Preprocessing is an important step so as to fetch the correct results from this data. Handling missing values and data normalization are the primary tasks that have been performed in this step.
2. Feature Selection: Feature selection includes selecting the best features and finding correlation among them.
3. Prediction: Multivariate linear regression, regression trees and ensemble methods have been applied in this research work for prediction of $PM_{2.5}$ concentration levels.

4. Analysis and knowledge discovery: Results over different models have been evaluated over RMSE metrics and further compared.

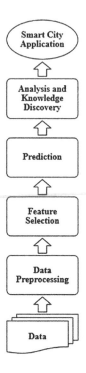

Fig. 1. Proposed methodology for analyzing air quality data.

4   Classification Techniques Used

This section gives a brief introduction about well known classification models that have been used in our research work to analyze the air quality data over four meteorological features for prediction of $PM_{2.5}$ concentration.

4.1   Multivariate Linear Regression

Technique for univariate linear regression [11] maps the predictors to a regression line so as to minimize the cost function of actual and observed values of dependent variables. Equation for linear regression is given in Eq. 1.

$$h_\theta = x_0 + \theta_1 x_1 + \theta_2 x_2 + \ldots + \theta_n x_n \tag{1}$$

where n is the number of features, $x^{(i)}$ is the input features of ith training example and $x_j^{(i)}$ is the value of feature j in the ith training example. Note that x_0 is an additional zero feature vector whose input value is chosen as 1.

Since our data shows a relationship between variables so in this research work Multivariate Linear Regression (MLR) technique is taken into account. From correlation maximum negative correlation of ambient temperature with $PM_{2.5}$ concentration is identified, represented in Table 3 along with other important features for classification i.e wind speed. Details are discussed in Sect. 5.

4.2   Regression Trees

Regression trees (RT) are a combination of decision trees and regression [20]. In case of categorical output, classification is performed, while in case of continuous data, a regression is performed on the decision tree. Root node consists of all the features, and recursive partitioning over each attribute is performed, until certain criteria's for split points are satisfied, such as minimum number of data points in the leaf nodes etc. Each of the non-terminal node specify some criteria or condition. Each of the leaf node represents a cell or a set of data points that is reached after traversing from root via other non-terminal nodes satisfying their set of conditions. For our data, features for splitting used are temperature, pressure, humidity and wind speed.

4.3   Ensemble Method

Ensemble methods take advantage of sampling by dividing data into subset of samples, fitting the model for each of the sampled data and finally aggregating the results. There are varied ensemble techniques, however we have used random forests in our work. Random forests (RF) are a class of ensemble methods which internally estimates the generalization error and generates a good classifier accuracy for dataset with large number of instances [21]. Algorithmic steps [21] to generate t trees for ensemble methods are shown further.

1. Repeat steps 2–4 for tree $b = 1$ to t.
2. Select bootstrap sample of size s from the training data, N.
3. Grow the random forest tree T_t to the bootstrapped data by recursively repeating the following steps for each terminal node of the tree, until the minimum node size, min is reached.
   (a) Select m variables at random from all 4 variables i.e. ambient temperature, barometric pressure, relative humidity and wind speed.
   (b) Pick the best variable to split among m.
   (c) Split the node into two daughter nodes.
4. Output the ensemble of trees $T_b{}_1^t$

To make a prediction at a new point x Eq. 2 is used:

$$\widehat{f} = \frac{1}{t} \sum_{i=1}^{t} T_i(x) \tag{2}$$

5   Experimental Study

In this section we discuss the experimental work done to analyze the air quality using meteorological features.

5.1   Data and Tools

Air quality data is taken from Central Pollution Control Board, Delhi [22] consisting of several attributes. For our work, we have considered four meteorological features namely, ambient temperature, barometric pressure, relative humidity and wind speed, at every 15 min interval, over a period of 1 year i.e. from 1'st Jan 2016 to 31'st Dec 2016, for five air quality stations of city of Delhi located at Punjabi Bagh, RK puram, Anand Vihar, Ihbas and Mandir Marg. These locations are shown in Fig. 2.

Fig. 2. Studied five locations of Delhi, marked on Google Maps.

Table 1 shows the number of records in the air quality data of five air quality stations at different locations in Delhi. Each record contains four meteorological features and $PM_{2.5}$ concentration as attributes. R is a well known language to perform statistical computing and data mining tasks. For experimental work, primarily 3 packages of R studios version 2.1 have been utilized i.e. **fit.models** [23] package of R for regression, package **rpart** [24] for regression tree and **randomForest** [25] package for random forest technique.

Table 1. Number of records in the data analyzed for 5 air quality stations of Delhi

Air quality station location	Number of records
Anand Vihar	25331
Punjabi Bagh	31014
Ihbas	20793
Mandir Marg	24181
RK puram	34854

5.2 Data Preprocessing

For removing missing values we have just ignored the tuple because number of missing values data is very less which is approximately 6% of total data. After removal of missing values, data is normalized with z-score transformation, so as to standardize the mean of the data. Table 2 shows the summary statistics of meteorological concentration for data of Delhi for the year 2016. Depending upon the minimum and maximum values, $PM_{2.5}$, pollutant concentration ranges from good (1–100), moderate (101–200), high (201–300), very high (301–400) and severe (401-above). Thus, the data normalization is done in order to make, 0 mean and 1 standard deviation of the given data without changing its distribution. We use z-score normalization with the given Eq. 3 where x' is the normalized value of x, $\hat{x}$ is the mean and s is the standard deviation.

$$x' = \frac{x - \hat{x}}{s} \tag{3}$$

Table 2. Summary statistics of data obtained for air quality monitoring station at Anand Vihar for the year 2016.

	Barometric pressure (mmHg)	Relative humidity (%)	Ambient temperature (°C)	Wind speed (m/s)	$PM_{2.5}$ ($\mu g/m^3$)
Minimum	739	3.67	5.27	0.3	−8
1st quantile	740	38	23.03	0.53	60
Median	740	53.33	29.17	1.33	101
Mean	739.93	51.95	27.90	1.58	163.02
3rd quantile	740	67	33.17	2.23	217
Maximum	740	86	47	8.5	985

5.3 Feature Selection

In this research work we identify 4 meteorological features viz. ambient temperature, barometric pressure, relative humidity and wind speed alongwith their relationships with concentration of $PM_{2.5}$ with respect to data availability of 2016 on hourly basis. To apply several data mining models, features should be independent of each other. However, meteorological features are sometimes dependent on each other. Note that this study aims at prediction analysis over a small set of meteorological features. So, other factors induced by global and local phenomenon are considered constant. Furthermore, prediction is performed from a limited data of 1 year only, hence it is justified to keep such factors constant. For example, increased wind speed might lead to somewhat decreased humidity at certain areas. Figure 3 shows the relationships of various meteorological features and $PM_{2.5}$ concentration for air quality station located at Punjabi Bagh.

To ensure independence between features, null hypothesis is rejected with a p-value less than 0.05 for analysis of variance. To identify the relationship between these features, three correlation methods [26] have been worked upon.

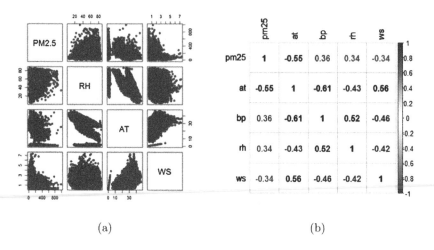

(a)   (b)

Fig. 3. Pearson correlation among features at air quality station of Punjabi Bagh for year 2016.

Pearson correlation coefficient [26] is given in Eq. 4, Kendall correlation coefficient [26] is given in Eq. 5 and Spearman correlation coefficient [26] is given in Eq. 6 respectively, where $x = x_1, x_2, \ldots, x_n$ and $y = y_1, y_2, \ldots, y_n$ are vectors with n values, n_c is the number of concordant [26], n_d is the number of discordant [26], d_i is the difference between the ranks of corresponding values x_i and y_i.

$$r = \frac{\sum_i^n (x_i - \widehat{x})(y_i - \widehat{y})}{\sqrt{\sum_i^n (x_i - \widehat{x})^2}\sqrt{\sum_i^n (y_i - \widehat{x})^2}} \tag{4}$$

$$\varsigma = \frac{n_c - n_d}{\frac{1}{2}n(n-1)} \tag{5}$$

$$\rho = 1 - \frac{6\sum_i^n d_i^2}{n(n^2-1)} \tag{6}$$

Pearson correlation coefficient depicts the linear relationship between two variables while Spearman correlation and Kendall correlation coefficients can identify non-linear relationship with the data. Spearman and Kendall are rank based correlation methods, thus instead of finding the linear change of one variable with respect to proportional change in other, they find the related change in these variables i.e. effect of amount of change in one variable to the amount of change in the other variable. Hence Spearman and Kendall perform better in our case. Data might contain error values, hence Kendall performs even better in such case.

However, results of all the three correlation coefficients are found to be almost similar for our data. For example, ambient temperature is negatively correlated with air quality i.e. locations with high temperature tends to have improved air quality as per values given by all these coefficients. Table 3 shows values of all these three correlation coefficients between different features with respect to $PM_{2.5}$ concentration in a sorted manner for air quality station of Punjabi Bagh. Similar relationships have been found for all other air quality stations. These results justifies the application of all combinations of these features to each of the three models during training.

Table 3. Correlation matrix of various features with $PM_{2.5}$ concentration.

Features	Pearson correlation coefficient	Kendall correlation coefficient	Spearman correlation coefficient
Ambient temperature (AT)	−0.57	−0.41	−0.61
Baromeric pressure (BP)	0.16	0.18	0.23
Relative humidity (RH)	0.14	0.01	0.003
Wind speed (WS)	−0.48	−0.43	−0.61

5.4   Model Training

We have divided the complete data available into training set and testing set. We have considered 75% data for training and 25% data as testing. For validation set training data is used as validation set. The sole purpose of this work is to analyze how well a model fits the data so that it can be applied on unseen data. For this, we have used three models for training purposes namely, MLR, RT and RF. Inputs to these three models are four meteorological features and all their combinations are used as inputs for modeling air quality in terms of $PM_{2.5}$ concentration. Figure 4 shows MLR fit for the data for different values of $PM_{2.5}$ for feature, ambient temperature. Figure 4 depicts estimated responses over residuals for Anand Vihar data over meteorological feature of ambient temperature. However, since all the data points scatter around the linear regression line, hence this relationship depicts heteroscedasticity among the response variable $PM_{2.5}$. So, we apply all the combinations of input features to train the model multivariate linear regression. Due to space constraints we restrict ourselves to plot a few graphs for a few air quality stations with a few features.

Regression trees are expected to prove a better fit because of fitting of regression line to a set of points which show similar characteristics by splitting over a certain set of attributes. For example Fig. 5 shows plots of regression trees of 2 air quality stations of Delhi i.e. Punjabi Bagh and Anand Vihar graphically, for features ambient temperature and relative humidity. However, regression trees might reduce variance in the data at each split but since we know single regression trees are prone to over-fitting, while combining trees formed by selecting a subset of features and subset of whole data, may provide a better generalization. Hence ensemble method is used to avoid over-fitting of data points. Specifically, random forests are used in the present work, because random selection of features allows reduction in correlation between trees in addition to reduced variance. Figure 6 shows the reduction in generalization error for random forests as number of trees keeps on increasing for two of the air quality stations. However this reduction in generalization reduces as number of trees goes on increasing because of increased repetition of sampled data points in newly generated trees. Note that to avoid overfitting and underfitting of the data, we have used 10-fold cross validation method for all the classification techniques.

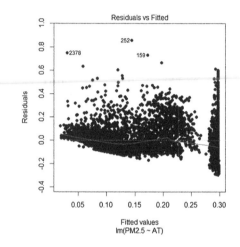

Fig. 4. Residual vs. fitted plot for linear regression model learned for Anand Vihar data over meteorological feature of ambient temperature against $PM_{2.5}$ concentration.

6   Evaluation

This section presents the results of different locations evaluated over different metrics.

6.1   Metrics

After model building evaluation over several metrics is done. The two most commonly used methods to measure the accuracy of a regression model are mean absolute error (MAE) and root mean square error (RMSE) given in Eq. 7.

$$RMSE = \sqrt{\frac{\sum_{k=1}^{n} o_k - a_k}{n}} \tag{7}$$

$$MAE = \frac{\sum_{k=1}^{n} |o_k - a_k|}{n} \tag{8}$$

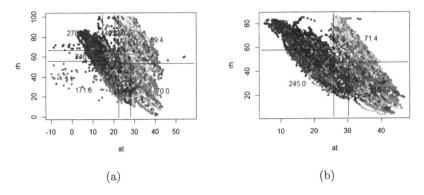

Fig. 5. Regression tree of two features ambient temperature and relative humidity for 2 air quality stations is shown with output variable is $PM_{2.5}$. (a) Air quality station of Punjabi Bagh. (b) Air quality station of Anand Vihar.

where o_k is the predicted values on test data, a_k are the actual values and n is the number of input data points. These metrics indicates absolute fit of the observed data points to the actual data points. However in this work we have used RMSE because our data does not shows more number of outliers in which case MAE would be a better metric to be used.

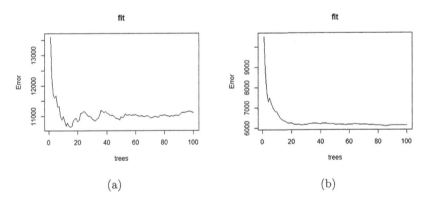

Fig. 6. Results showing generalization error for random forest algorithms for 2 air quality stations (a) Anand Vihar, (b) Punjabi Bagh.

6.2 Comparison

Tables 4 and 5 shows RMSE values for all the three prediction models for 2 air quality stations evaluated over test data. Table 4 i.e. Anand Vihar data shows the lowest RMSE values of 67.8 for AT+RH combination in random forests and lowest RMSE values of 117 and 108 for AT+RH+WS combination in MLR and regression trees. Similarly, data shows similar trends of lowest RMSEs for Mandir

Table 4. RMSE values for station Anand Vihar

Features	MLR	Regression trees	Random forests
AT	126.5336	-	-
RH	150.436	-	-
WS	135.6436	-	-
AT+BP	126.19	120	122
AT+WS	122.57	113	91.04
AT+RH	121.36	112	67.79
WS+RH	135.54	126	108
WS+BP	134.47	126	128.02
RH+BP	148.13	148.40	148.94
AT+RH+WS	117	108	68.39
AT+RH+WS+BP	117	108	102

Table 5. RMSE values for station Punjabi Bagh

Features	MLR	Regression trees	Random forests
AT	111.6844	-	-
RH	131.106	-	-
WS	122.7861	-	-
AT+BP	111.67	106.47	105.08
AT+WS	108.67	103.67	84.18
AT+RH	111.29	100.01	57.97
WS+RH	122.76	118.66	105.68
WS+BP	122.07	116.46	119.35
RH+BP	130.17	121.07	123.36
AT+RH+WS	107.81	97.19	60.64
AT+RH+WS+BP	107.76	97.19	87.25

Marg, RK Puram, Ihabas and Punjabi Bagh for the combination of AT+RH. This result is because of higher correlations of these two attributes with the $PM_{2.5}$ values. Note that due to space constraints we have not shown all the results of all five air quality stations.

Regression trees depicts a slight decrease for all combination of features on all the 5 stations with respect to MLR. However for Ihbas air quality station, results depicts a different trend at some points. Random Forests perform exceptionally well amongst all of these methods with a lower RMSE at all the air quality stations. Random forests perform best in AT+RH combination and AT+RH+WS combination with lowest RMSE of 60.19 and 55.03 in case of Mandir Marg, 67.8 and 68.3 in case of Anand Vihar, 58.8 and 61.6 in case of RK Puram and 57.9

and 60.6 in case of Pujabi Bagh. This result might be because of higher independence between these two features as identified in Sect. 5.3. Hence we could suggest AT and RH are the dominating features in most of the places, while WS also dominates along with these two at some places. BP has negligible effect over most of the places and with different models, this is because less variance in its data.

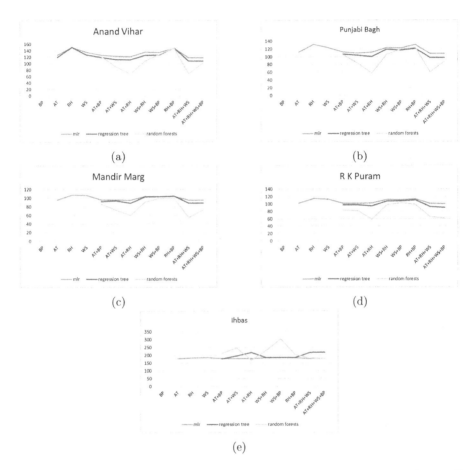

Fig. 7. Graph depicting RMSE metrics for MLR, regression tree and random forests. X axis shows the RMSE values and Y axis shows the feature combinations. (a) Air quality station of Anand Vihar. (b) Air quality station of Punjabi Bagh. (c) Air quality station of Mandir Marg. (d) Air quality station of RK Puram. (e) Air quality station of Ihbas.

Figure 7 represents RMSE of all of these stations graphically. From the results shown in Fig. 7 it is identified that random forest ensemble method shows much improved results as compared to other data mining models on four air quality stations of Anand Vihar, Mandir Marg, RK Puram, Punjabi Bagh. However, results of Ihbas shows the different trend. Reason for this might be more number of missing values in data of Ihbas station leading to imprecise training of the model over less amount of data. Since, random forests requires more data because more data means increasing probability of selecting varied random trees hence reduced generalization error. RMSE of MLE is more than regression trees because regression trees splits data into smaller chunks and then predict the output from that chunk itself. Thus causing reduction in generalization error of the data.

7   Conclusion and Future Scope

Air pollution is quite a major threat to environment as well as humans and there is urgency to tackle air pollution in efficient way. Knowledge of air pollution at any future instant can help decision making and planning. Primary aim of this work is to identify the correlations of meteorological features and to predict air quality using these features combinations. Further, dominant features are identified using data mining methods. Data of five air quality stations of Delhi is analyzed in this work. Data contains four meteorological features namely ambient temperature, barometric pressure, wind speed and relative humidity and $PM_{2.5}$ concentration as a response variable. $PM_{2.5}$ is a pollutant depicting air quality concentration.

Data preprocessing is done on this data of Delhi to make it suitable for analysis task. Preprocessing includes, handling of missing values, data normalization and feature selection as primary tasks in this research work. Correlation of these features with $PM_{2.5}$ concentration showed the highest negative correlation of temperature and highest positive correlation of humidity with $PM_{2.5}$ concentration. Correlation justified the use of these features for further analysis. We further applied renowned data mining methods of multivariate linear regression, regression trees and ensemble methods for model training.

Ensemble methods are advantage over other data mining models, as in addition to reduction in variance, they reduce the correlation among features by splitting, so as to give better generalization over data. Random forests ensemble method is used in this work. Data is divided into training and test set. Test data is evaluated for RMSE metrics. Evaluation over RMSE metrics showed the better results when only few of the dominating features were considered. In this case relative humidity and ambient temperature are most relevant features for model learning. Random forests did exceptionally well for our data. In future work, we tend to focus upon more features and other different data mining models for learning. Our method can be applied to various cities and urban establishments of the world striving for better air quality. There is a further a lot of scope for data sets of developing countries like India that can be worked upon for air quality.

References

1. UEP Agency: A guide to air quality and your health (2017). https://www3.epa.gov/airnow/aqibrochure0214.pdf. Accessed 30 July 2017
2. CPC Board: National air quality index (2017). http://cpcb.nic.in/FINAL-REPORTAQI.pdf. Accessed 30 July 2017
3. Express I: Delhi Govt. suggests centre to consider artificial rains (2016). http://indianexpress.com/article/india/india-news-india/delhi-air-pollution-smog-artificial-rain-ncr-region-3742222/. Accessed 13 Feb 2018
4. Völgyesi, P., Nádas, A., Koutsoukos, X., Lédeczi, Á.: Air quality monitoring with SensorMap. In: Proceedings of the 7th International Conference on Information Processing in Sensor Networks, pp. 529–530. IEEE Computer Society (2008)
5. Uyanik, I., Khatri, A., Tsiamyrtzis, P., Pavlidis, I.: Design and usage of an ozone mapping app. In: Proceedings of the Wireless Health 2014 on National Institutes of Health, pp. 1–7. ACM (2014)
6. Bales, E., Nikzad, N., Quick, N., Ziftci, C., Patrick, K., Griswold, W.: Citisense: mobile air quality sensing for individuals and communities design and deployment of the citisense mobile air-quality system. In: 2012 6th International Conference on Pervasive Computing Technologies for Healthcare (PervasiveHealth), pp. 155–158. IEEE (2012)
7. Tiwari, S., Pandithurai, G., Attri, S., Srivastava, A., Soni, V., Bisht, D., Kumar, V.A., Srivastava, M.K.: Aerosol optical properties and their relationship with meteorological parameters during wintertime in Delhi, India. Atmos. Res. **153**, 465–479 (2015)
8. Kumar, P., Jain, S., Gurjar, B., Sharma, P., Khare, M., Morawska, L., Britter, R.: New directions: can a blue sky return to indian megacities? Atmos. Environ. **71**, 198–201 (2013)
9. Nagendra, S.S., Khare, M.: Modelling urban air quality using artificial neural network. Clean Technol. Environ. Policy **7**(2), 116–126 (2005)
10. Zhang, Y., Bocquet, M., Mallet, V., Seigneur, C., Baklanov, A.: Real-time air quality forecasting, part I: History, techniques, and current status. Atmos. Environ. **60**, 632–655 (2012)
11. Han, J., Pei, J., Kamber, M.: Data Mining: Concepts and Techniques. Book (2011)
12. Donnelly, A., Misstear, B., Broderick, B.: Real time air quality forecasting using integrated parametric and non-parametric regression techniques. Atmos. Environ. **103**, 53–65 (2015)
13. Feng, X., Li, Q., Zhu, Y., Hou, J., Jin, L., Wang, J.: Artificial neural networks forecasting of $PM_{2.5}$ pollution using air mass trajectory based geographic model and wavelet transformation. Atmos. Environ. **107**, 118–128 (2015)
14. Prasad, K., Gorai, A.K., Goyal, P.: Development of anfis models for air quality forecasting and input optimization for reducing the computational cost and time. Atmos. Environ. **128**, 246–262 (2016)
15. Wang, K.M.: The relationship between carbon dioxide emissions and economic growth: Quantile panel-type analysis. Qual. Quant. **47**(3), 1337–1366 (2013)
16. Zheng, Y., Yi, X., Li, M., Li, R., Shan, Z., Chang, E., Li, T.: Forecasting fine-grained air quality based on big data. In: Proceedings of the 21th ACM SIGKDD International Conference on Knowledge Discovery and Data Mining, pp. 2267–2276. ACM (2015)
17. Zheng, Y., Liu, F., Hsieh, H.P.: U-air: when urban air quality inference meets big data. In: Proceedings of the 19th ACM SIGKDD International Conference on Knowledge Discovery and Data Mining, pp. 1436–1444. ACM (2013)

18. Engel-Cox, J.A., Holloman, C.H., Coutant, B.W., Hoff, R.M.: Qualitative and quantitative evaluation of modis satellite sensor data for regional and urban scale air quality. Atmos. Environ. **38**(16), 2495–2509 (2004)
19. Irfan, M., Shaw, K.: Modeling the effects of energy consumption and urbanization on environmental pollution in South Asian countries: a nonparametric panel approach. Qual. Quant. **51**(1), 65–78 (2017)
20. Tan, P.N., Steinbach, M., Kumar, V.: Introduction to Data Mining. Pearson Education Inc., London (2006)
21. Friedman, J., Hastie, T., Tibshirani, R.: The Elements of Statistical Learning. Springer Series in Statistics. Springer, New York (2001). https://doi.org/10.1007/978-0-387-21606-5
22. CPC Board: Air Quality Data (2017). Accessed 30 July 2017
23. Konis, K.: Package fit.models (2017). https://cran.r-project.org/web/packages/fit.models/fit.models.pdf. Accessed 13 Feb 2018
24. Therneau, T., Atkinson, B., Ripley, B.: Package rpart (2017). https://cran.r-project.org/web/packages/rpart/rpart.pdf. Accessed 13 Feb 2018
25. Liaw, A., Wiener, M.: Package randomforest (2018). https://cran.r-project.org/web/packages/randomForest/randomForest.pdf. Accessed 13 Feb 2018
26. Chok, N.S.: Pearson's versus Spearman's and Kendall's correlation coefficients for continuous data. University of Pittsburgh (2010)

Simulation Evaluation for Efficient Inventory Management Based on Demand Forecast

Jeong-A Kim and Jongpil Jeong[✉]

Department of Smart Factory Convergence, Sungkyunkwan University,
Suwon, Gyeonggi-do 16419, Republic of Korea
{jkop109,jpjeong}@skku.edu

Abstract. The AA manufacturing factory is a form of mass-producing and selling products in order to respond to customer's needs. This means an excessive amount of material supply and demand for companies to reduce losses associated with short inventory. This results in products that fail to respond to demand accumulating in managed warehouses, resulting in higher inventory maintenance costs. In this paper, as a measure to reduce costs and inventory shortage to complement these problems, we propose a plan that predicts future demand. In order to solve the problem, ARIMA model, which is a time series analysis technique, is used to predict demand in the temporal variability or seasonal factor, and to develop a demand-forecasting model based on the EOQ model. We also ran simulation to evaluate the effectiveness of the model, and in future research, we will apply it to small and medium enterprises, to demonstrate the effectiveness of the model.

Keywords: Inventory management · Demand forecasting
Economic order quantity
Autoregressive integrated moving average (ARIMA)

1 Introduce

In inventory control, it is possible to minimize the cost caused by important factors in corporate management and to grasp the effect of Business profit [1]. Companies are aware of the importance of inventory management, but practical practice in actual environments struggle to manage inefficient materials.

Practitioners incur costs due to the purchase of additional new materials in situations where there is no clear inventory location. In the current Industry market, in order to grasp the appropriate inventory quantity, inventory maintenance cost, and reorder point (ROP) by applying an economic order quantity model (EOQ) [2] with a new solution for efficient inventory management. Most companies apply EOQ to actual environments and manage inventory. Due to the development of the IoT environment, this has formulated various management strategies to meet the needs of customers [3]. EOQ has difficulty in grasping the

© Springer International Publishing AG, part of Springer Nature 2018
O. Gervasi et al. (Eds.): ICCSA 2018, LNCS 10960, pp. 639–650, 2018.
https://doi.org/10.1007/978-3-319-95162-1_44

customer's needs, determining the appropriate inventory quantity and forecasting future demand according to inventory items.

According to customer's needs increasingly diversified, the product life cycle of IT products is shorter [4]. This is a current situation where fluctuations in demand of products occur periodically and a new model for predicting inventory demand value according to time is proposed but it is difficult to apply because it is incompatible with trends. Suggested a solution in terms of inventory optimization, cost minimization, and inventory shortage problems due to demand forecasts. Customers have grasped the requirements and predicted many parameters, but systematic methods are necessary for effective improvement management [5]. Used research on deep learning to solve the problem of city taxi demand forecast [6]. We designed the Deep Neural Networks (DNN) [7] architecture by systematically comparing ST - ResNet and FLC - Net, but the case applied to small and medium - sized enterprises is short. The study developed an inventory management system for the supply chain distribution of products to suppliers from suppliers through central warehouses with minimal supply chain costs [8]. We calculated the minimization of supply chain costs according to customers' request, but it is necessary to present efficient inventory maintenance costs and storage costs. As a result, a new forecast model is required according to demand fluctuation, and demand forecasting must be made using accurate forecasting methods.

Fig. 1. Process for deriving demand forecasting model.

In this paper, in order to supplement the problems of the existing EOQ model, demand prediction is executed through the process as shown in Fig. 1. Forecast demand by using time series analyze autoregressive integrated moving average (ARIMA) [9] model. In this way, we use the improved economic order quantity modeling technique that can predict the demand, and grasp the optimum order quantity, the point of ordering and the cost of stock management. By doing this, it is considered that the effects are proved by selecting this small and medium-sized manufacturer in South Korea.

This paper is configured as follows; Sect. 2 explains the research on economic modeling, and demand forecasting method. Section 3 estimates the future demand value using the ARIMA model. Section 4 explains simulation for evaluating the EOQ model based on demand forecast and demonstrates the effectiveness. Finally, Sect. 5 concludes this study and the future research.

2   Related Work

Manufacturing company estimates the order of the customer roughly, purchases the material in bulk, and re-manufactures it according to the order. If the lead time of the material order are relatively long, it is difficult to meet to customer's needs. As a result, the EOQ can be used to grasp the accurate leadtime, and to understand the proper order quantity. Thus, it is possible to efficiently manage inventory by predicting various variables generated in the field.

2.1   Economic Order Quantity

Economic order quantity model for efficient inventory management optimum order quantity can derive appropriate lead time cycle, safety stock and order placement point.

Safety Inventory prevent risks associated with the occurrence of shortage Inventory events during leadtime periods [10]. It is also used to reduce inventory costs in order to calculate appropriate orders and reduce inventory maintenance costs, inventory quantity, etc. compared to demand.

2.2   Data Analysis with Data Mining Technology

Data mining can analyze past data to grasp special rules and patterns of data [11]. Based on the statistical methodology, a large amount of collected data is extracted using decision tree techniques, artificial neural network techniques, etc [12].

Recently it has been applied to the fields of finance, distribution, communication, and demand forecasting, using data mining techniques that are usefully used for large volume data collection methods.

2.3   Demand Forecasting with ARIMA

If demand values exist in past data, they can be used for Demand Forecast (DF) through time series analysis. Time series analyses recognize observed patterns according to weekly orders, and predict future demand based on trends and seasonal factors [13]. DF is essential to meet customer needs. The ARIMA model, which is a demand forecasting technique, is a mixed model that combines the Auto Regression (AR) model and the Moving Average (MA) model [14]. Therefore, utilize the ARIMA model, Forecasting future demand of reliable level based on actual demand value of SMEs, and satisfy the needs of customers timely, can be prevent inventory management shortage.

3   Customer's Demand Forecast Based on ARIMA Model

Company AA can use the EOQ model by grasp the proper order and the ordering time and present the effect of many economic improvement. However, this situation has a great impact on the company's sales due to frequent fluctuations, depending on the customer's needs for the raw materials. If company can't supply in a timely manner in response to customer demand, reliability is lowered and Economic losses rise.

Therefore, by using the ARIMA method, through the forecast of the demand quantity, reduce the inventory management cost and reduce the inventory shortage rate.

3.1   Future Demand Forecasting Through ARIMA Model

The monthly demand amount is predicted because it has demand during the lead time. It is possible to maintain and manage appropriate inventory quantity. The time series model predicts the demand pattern based on the past data by using a quantitative method in order to grasp the appropriate inventory quantity. As a result, demand patterns are searched from the past data according to the passage of time to predict the future demand quantity.

Figure 2 shows the time series data of AA company's demand for 10 years (2008–2017), judge the needs of customers using time series analysis technique.

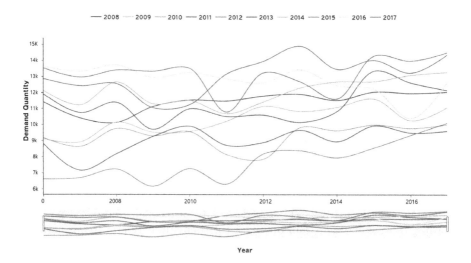

Fig. 2. Visualization of the year of demand value by company AA.

Figure 2 visualize and analyze the time series data of company AA noticed that the demand increased. As annual demand steadily increases, we can see that there are patterns like trends and seasonal factors. It was compared to other seasons.

The optimal $ARIMA(1,0,1)(0,0,2)_{12}$ model is calculated as the $MA(1) \times SMA(1)_{12}$ model.

$$Y_t = \beta_1 Y_{t-1} + \beta_1{}^* Y_{t-s} - \beta_1 \beta_1{}^* Y_{t-s-1} + \epsilon_t \tag{1}$$

The ARIMA model is calculated by Eq. (1) [14], where t is the weekly forecast, the coefficient of the model, the coefficient of the model, s is the period, t is the anticipated weekly, and the $epsilon_t$ is the error value.

The MA(1) value -0.8992 indicates β_1, which is the result of the derived ARIMA model of MA(1) means, the value of SMA(1) -0.3589 is β_1^* means. 0.5403 means $\beta_1 \times \beta_1^*$, and s is means 12.

$$Y_t = -0.8992_{t-1} - 0.3589 Y_{t-12} + 0.5403 Y_{t-12} + \epsilon_t \tag{2}$$

The analyzed model can be calculated according to Eq. (2). The backward operator represents seasonality and is denoted by B^s, and the period s is applied as a superscript.

$$
\begin{aligned}
Y_t &= \beta_1 Y_{t-1} + \beta_1{}^* Y_{t-s} - \beta_1 \beta_1{}^* Y_{t-s-1} + \epsilon_t \\
&\Leftrightarrow (1 + \beta_1 B + \beta_1^* B^s - \beta_1 \beta_1^* B^{s+1}) Y_t = \epsilon_t \\
&\Leftrightarrow (1 - \beta_1 B) + (1 - \beta_1^* B^s) Y_t = \epsilon_t \\
&\Leftrightarrow (1 - 0.8992 B)(1 - 0.3589 B^{12}) Y_t = \epsilon_t
\end{aligned}
\tag{3}
$$

According to Eq. (3), the demand in 2018–2020 of Fig. 3 can be measured. Figure 3 analyzes the data for 2008–2017, for 3 years using the ARIMA model.

This visualizes the forecasting demand based on the seasonal factors and trend patterns identified through the time series decomposition method.

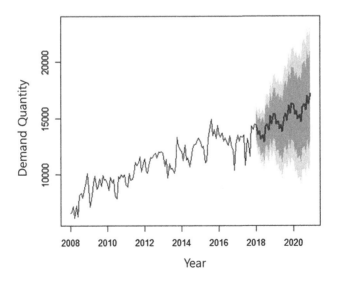

Fig. 3. The visualized demand forecast value of 3 years by ARIMA model.

Table 1 shows the values of the results obtained using $ARIMA(1,0,1)$ $(0,0,2)_{12}$ which is the model of company AA derived using the ARIMA model.

Table 1. Foretasted demand value of 2018-2020 forecast by ARIMA model.

Month	2018	2019	2020
1	15,837	17,232	18,600
2	15,746	17,324	18,710
3	15,934	17,446	18,820
4	16,044	17,566	18,929
5	16,176	17,685	19,037
6	15,649	17,803	19,144
7	16,385	17,920	19,251
8	16,301	18,036	19,357
9	16,167	18,150	19,463
10	16,957	18,264	19,568
11	17,074	18,377	19,673
12	17,174	18,489	19,777

Using the ARIMA model derived the result value of forecast demand for three years from 2018 to 2020. Data for 3 years was derived on average every month. The average demand value in 2018 was 16,287.12 the average demand value in 2019 was 17857.58 and the average demand value in 2020 was 19194.13.

The EOQ model is to overcome the shortcomings using of the forecasted demand value, and execute a simulation for accurate evaluation so that the company inventory shortage and inventory cost can be lowered. By doing this, we compare the results of applying the existing EOQ model of company AA and applying the EOQ model based on demand forecast, and grasp the effectiveness of the EOQ model based on the demand forecast, though simulation.

4   Verification of Demand Forecasting Efficiency Using Simulation

The ROP calculation uses the demand distribution value as the average value, from the point of ordering based on the value of the demand, until the week when the order arrived. Equation (4) shows the case where the leadtime is less than 53 weeks from the parking order ordered for the prediction of 53 weeks (1 year). where p is the demand value, $demand_i$ is the i th week of the weekly demand average (i = 1, 2, ..., 53), $leadtime$ is the leadtime, and $week$ is the weekly order.

$week + leadtime >= 53$

$$p = \sum_{i=week}^{53} demand_i \div leadtime \qquad (4)$$

In Eq. (4), ROP is the reorder point, $leadtime\_mean$ is the mean value of the leadtime, and $predict\_dstd$ is the standard deviation distribution according to the service level z .

$$ROP = p \times leadtime\_mean \\ + \sqrt{leadtime \times predict\_dstd^2 + p^2 \times leadtime^2} \qquad (5)$$

where, z is the level of service that can be determined by the inventory shortage risk. The higher the risk, the lower the service level, while the lower the risk, the higher the service level. $demand_i$ means the weekly demand average value. This demand generation that is higher than the demand average shortens the leadtime interval, which leads to a high probability of inventory shortage.

Therefore, it is necessary to derive the optimal order quantity.

$$order\_input = leadtime\_mean \times predict\_demand \qquad (6)$$

Equation (6) is an equation for calculating an order quantity.

In order to prevent the risk of inventory shortage in response to the customer's needs during the leadtime according to the demand value, it is possible to grasp the efficient order quantity according to the amount of safety inventory set in advance.

In order to judge the entry and exit of inventory, inventory is set as a variable, which means inventory quantity. When inventory was received, inventory = inventory + order_input, and when the demand is generated, the inventory amount is calculated by inventory = inventory - demand. The random value of the demand is calculated from the demand value (i = 1, 2, ..., 53) of the corresponding parking on the expected demand distribution data, and the standard deviation value (i = 1, 2, ..., 53). The distribution random value was calculated as. The demand for the corresponding weekly means D, and the calculation equation is Eq. (7):

$$D = Demand_i + Std_i \times rd \qquad (7)$$

In this way, the DF Model is satisfy customers meet and prevent inventory cost and shortage of inventory. Simulation is performed to demonstrate the effectiveness, and accurate assessment of DF model.

4.1   Simulation Implementation

This paper simulates the optimal reorder point and order quantity according to the demand forecast through the algorithm designed similar to the supply process of company AA.

In order to manage the inventory efficiently, simulation was performed assuming the situation that the management can consider. what was it analyzed as 1,000 times for simulation, 1 year simulation (53 weeks) per simulation, Demand/leadtime occurs randomly, Order can't requested during leadtime, Set service levels to 99%.

This is a simulation algorithm to evaluate the utility of the demand forecasting model developed as shown in Fig. 4.

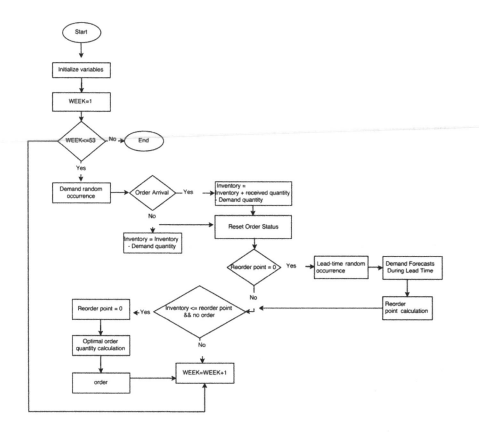

Fig. 4. The simulation algorithm for the demand forecasting based model.

The DF model performed through the algorithm for efficient inventory management uses the quantitative analysis method simulation to prevent inventory shortage risk.

When a customer's order is received, the amount requested is deducted from the inventory. The reorder point can't be set before the first order, the initial value is set to 0. Reorder point calculated as the average of the demand distribution during to generated leadtime with random.

An order is requested when the inventory level is below the reorder point, and is not yet in order. After an order request, the reorder point must be initialized to recalculate the reorder point according to the demand during the leadtime of the next order. Next, the optimal order quantity is calculated, and an order requested. After the set leadtime has passed, if the inventory was received, the decision variable is reset to 0, the existing will be added to inventory quantities, and the demand quantity is subtracted. If the WEEK variable exceeds 53 weeks, the simulation ends.

The demand forecast data value derived from AA company's actual collected raw material data through the ARIMA model is stored in the *demand_* distribution variable demand distribution as an average value. *demand_std* is a variable set so that the standard deviation of the demand average value and the random value of the normal distribution are generated.

As a result of analyzing the leadtime period of the original data, the average was determined to be 10 weeks, and the standard deviation was set to 2 weeks. In order to obtain future demand by demand forecasting through simulation, variables were set to derive the number of inventory shortages, inventory shortage period, and order quantity average for 53 weeks.

Evaluate when the service level of the EOQ model is 60% and the service level of the EOQ model based on the demand forecast is 90% by simulation. This proves the effect of the EOQ model based on the demand forecast when the service level is 90%.

4.2 Simulation Results with Service Level (60% and 90%)

It is 60% of the existing service level of company AA, the Inventory shortage rate is high, and it is difficult to Inventory management. In order to solve this, we confirm how the inventory shortage can be reduced by simulation of the EOQ model which raised the service level to 90% based on the demand forecast.

Table 2 shows the number of inventory shortage by simulation results when the service level is 60%, the period of shortage Inventory and the value of the result of calculating the order with the EOQ model.

Table 2. The simulation result value when the service level is 60% based on EOQ model.

An existing EOQ model with a service level of 60%					
Number of times	1	2	3	4	5
Inventory shortage count (time)	3.529	3.761	3.993	4.225	4.457
Inventory shortage period (week)	22.393	22.603	22.43	22.459	22.076
Count of orders (time)	4.438	4.445	4.454	4.444	4.471

Based on the results in Table 2, when the service level is 60% by the existing EOQ (Base) is about 4 of inventory shortage count, and the shortage of inventory period 22 weeks highly.

The manager raised the level of services that can accept the maintenance cost during the leadtime period. By choosing the service level to 90%, you can see how much you can lower the inventory shortage rate than when using the EOQ model (Base) with a service level of 60%.

Table 3 shows the number of inventory shortages by simulation results when the service level is 90%, the period of shortage inventory and the value of the result of calculating the order with the EOQ model base on Demand Forecasting.

Table 3. The simulation result value when the service level is 90% base on EOQ model.

Demand forecast based EOQ model with a service level of 90%					
Number of times	1	2	3	4	5
Inventory shortage count (time)	0.774	0.829	0.811	0.834	0.822
Inventory shortage period (week)	3.994	3.983	3.987	3.985	3.982
Count of orders (time)	3.994	3.983	3.987	3.985	3.982

Based on the results in Table 3, When the service level is 90%, the existing EOQ (Base) is about 4 of inventory shortage count, and the shortage of inventory period 22 weeks highly.

Figure 5 shows the results corresponding to the service levels in Table 2 (60%) and Table 3 (90%). This mean was showing the inventory shortage risk and the inventory management cost of the conventional model and the demand forecast model, and expressed this by visualization.

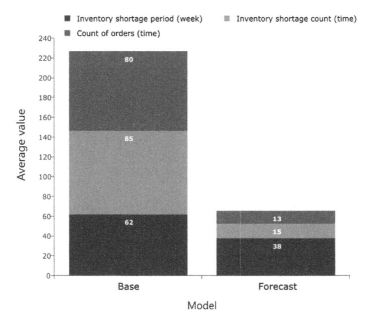

Fig. 5. Comparison of based on average value in simulation results with service levels of 60% and 90%.

As a result, we confirmed that the developed demand forecasting model was reduced by 53% from the existing economic investment model. SMEs in small quantity batch production system have set up a point of reference and a service level based on the relationship between various types of products. Difficulties in the order point and service level were overcome by prediction through simulations. We have overcome the shortcomings of the existing EOQ model for predicting demand through Arima forecasting method and have the effect of reducing inventory cost.

5 Conclusions

In this paper, manufacturing company AA researched how it could efficiently manage various inventories using EOQ models. In particular, time series forecasting techniques were used to predict customer needs and reduce the risk of shortage of inventory. The time series decomposition method identified demand patterns such as trends by disassembling the data of company AA for 10 years. ARIMA models also predicted demand over three years. The risk ratio of shortage of inventory with service levels of 60% and 90% was compared. 60% of service levels are those of current AA companies, with 76% of inventory risks. Raising service levels to more than 90% service levels and lowering the risk of shortage of inventory by 22% were identified. This resulted in a total 54% reduction in the demand forecast model compared to the existing economic order model. Service levels can be set at 60% and 90% to allow for consideration of enterprise management that may deteriorate due to shortage of inventory depending on the service level by comparing the risk rate of inventory shortage. The EOQ model was used not only in industrial plants but also in various fields to predict demand. This may lower the inventory shortage rate and increase cost savings. The economic order model was derived so that the demand prediction model reflected the actual situation of the inventory management system of small businesses.

This is expected to be applied to small businesses and provide results to meet their needs In the future, it will be applied to AA company's inventory supply process for accurate verification of development models.

Acknowledgment. This research was supported by Basic Science Research Program through the National Research Foundation of Korea (NRF) funded by the Ministry of Education (NRF-2016R1D1A1B03933828). Corresponding author: Prof. Jongpil Jeong.

References

1. Dhandayuthapani, S.P., Susmitha, G.: Inventory management at Arignar Anna Sugar mills, Kurungulam. IJSRD - Int. J. Sci. Res. Dev. 5(09), 1080–1082 (2017)
2. Harris, F.W.: How many parts to make at once. Int. J. Prod. Econ. 155, 8–11 (2014)

3. Wang, Y., Geng, X., Zhang, F., Ruan, J.: An immune genetic algorithm for multi-echelon inventory cost control of IOT based supply chains. IEEE Access **6**, 8547–8555 (2018)

4. Soliman, A.M., Zaki, A.M., El-Shafei, A.M., Mahgoub, O.A.: Application of grey jump model to forecast fluctuating inventory demand. In: 2008 IEEE International Conference on Service Operations and Logistics, and Informatics, vol. 1, pp. 1209–1214 (2008)

5. Okay Akyuz, A., Uysal, M., Atak Bulbul, B., Ozan Uysal, M.: Ensemble approach for time series analysis in demand forecasting. In: 2017 IEEE International Conference on INnovations in Intelligent SysTems and Applications (INISTA), pp. 7–12 (2017)

6. Liao, S., Zhou, L., Di, X., Yuan, B., Xiong, J.: Large-scale short-term urban taxi demand forecasting using deep learning. In: 2018 23rd Asia and South Pacific Design Automation Conference (ASP-DAC), pp. 428–433 (2018)

7. Dongardive, J., Abraham, S.: Reaching optimized parameter set: protein secondary structure prediction using neural network. Neural Comput. Appl. **28**(8), 1947–1974 (2016)

8. Efrilianda, D.A., Mustafid, R., Isnanto, R.: Inventory control systems with safety stock and reorder point approach. In: 2018 International Conference on Information and Communications Technology (ICOIACT), pp. 844–847 (2018)

9. Box, G.E.P., Jenkins, G.M., Reinsel, G.C., Ljung, G.M.: Time Series Analysis; Forecasting and Control, 8th edn. Wiley, Oxford (2008)

10. Persson, F., Axelsson, M., Edlund, F., Lanshed, C., Lindström, A., Persson, F.: Using simulation to determine the safety stock level for intermittent demand. In: 2017 Winter Simulation Conference (WSC), pp. 3768–3779 (2017)

11. Liu, G., Zong, X.: Research of second-hand real estate price forecasting based on data mining. In: IEEE 2nd Information Technology, Networking, Electronic and Automation Control Conference (ITNEC), Chengdu, pp. 1675–1679 (2017)

12. Yuniarti, T., Surjandari, I., Muslim, E., Laoh, E.: Data mining approach for short term load forecasting by combining wavelet transform and group method of data handling (WGMDH). In: 2017 3rd International Conference on Science in Information Technology (ICSITech), Bandung, pp. 53–58 (2017)

13. Alsudan, R.S.A., Liu, J.: The use of some of the information criterion in determining the best model for forecasting of Thalassemia cases depending on Iraqi patient data using ARIMA model. J. Appl. Math. Phys. **5**(3), 667–679 (2017)

14. Makridakis, S., Wheelwrigt, S.C., Hyndman, R.J.: Forecasting: Methods and Applications, 3rd edn. Wiley, New York (1998)

Territorial Statistical Analysis of National Student Mobility in Italian Universities

Massimo Iaquinta[1], Paola Perchinunno[2(✉)], and Francesco Rotondo[3]

[1] University Statistics Staff of the General Management, University of Bari,
Piazza Umberto, I - 70121 Bari, Italy
massimo.iaquinta@uniba.it
[2] DEMDI, University of Bari, Via C. Rosalba 53, 70100 Bari, Italy
paola.perchinunno@uniba.it
[3] DICAR, Politecnico di Bari, Via Orabona 4, 70125 Bari, Italy
francesco.rotondo@poliba.it

Abstract. The reforms in the university education system, motivated primarily by the need to bring universities closer to the professional needs of the economy and businesses, have changed the offer of Italian university education. The present work starts from a synthetic representation of national student mobility, both in terms of the allocation of university students in the various universities and the attractiveness of the various territorial areas. The comparison between the "potential" and "effective" catchment area and the structural availability, allows to define territories more attractive than others. By defining thematic maps, useful for summarizing national mobility, we will try to make a summary of the Italian situation trying to bring out the main causes of this phenomenon.

Keywords: Student mobility · Indicators · Territorial maps

1 Introduction

University autonomy and the growth of the student population have led to an expansion of the university system, especially in terms of the number of study courses offered and decentralized didactic sites. The dynamics of student flows linked to student mobility are increasingly becoming an important tool for boosting competitiveness among universities.

The meeting between university local supply and demand allows to identify territories starting from a general "law" that can be summarized as follows: "Everything is related to distant things" [1]. That is, the nearest universities can attract more than the distant ones. On the other hand, in the literature, the choice to study in a university far from home is mainly due to investment reasons (future possibilities of employment) and/or lifestyle (living in a city that guarantees a better quality of the life) [2, 3].

The contribution is the result of joint reflections by the authors, with the following contributions attributed to M. Iaquinta (chapters 1, 3 and paragraphs 2.1), to P. Perchinunno (paragraphs 2.2, 2.4, 2.5), and to F. Rotondo (chapters 4, 5 and paragraphs 2.3).

© Springer International Publishing AG, part of Springer Nature 2018
O. Gervasi et al. (Eds.): ICCSA 2018, LNCS 10960, pp. 651–664, 2018.
https://doi.org/10.1007/978-3-319-95162-1_45

It is therefore interesting to analyze the extent of these student flows and their directions, in order to understand the trend of movement, as well as the relationship between the profiles of the students and the location of movement [4, 5].

The analysis takes place through some indicators of the structure of the student population used to assess the attractiveness of the provinces where the university teaching facilities of different universities are located and the tendency of students residing outside the province, identifying relationships and possible motivations.

2   Student Mobility

2.1   Sources and Methods

For a correct understanding of the phenomena covered by this treatment it is useful to analyze data's sources and the methodology related to the calculation of the indices, as well as their effective representation for a correct understanding of the phenomena.

Data on the university student population were extracted from the web portal of the National Register of Students of MIUR-Cineca in April 2018.

In this paper, the representation of the values attributed to the individual geographic areas, corresponding to the provinces, occurs through cartograms, associated with "natural" interval classes, defined within the distribution. The determination of the intervals was obtained using an iterative optimization algorithm due to Jenks (1967), which identifies the fractures in the distribution of the variable using the statistical measure of "goodness of adaptation to variance", or Goodness of Variance Fit (GVF). This and other 'natural' methods produce classes with high internal homogeneity, which highlight the significant groupings of the phenomena, but which are difficult to compare with other maps [6].

The amounts of those enrolled in degree programs of all the universities present in the national territory, excluding foreign students, (state and non-state universities, including telematic universities) were surveyed on a provincial basis and for each university using segmentation variables, such as province of residence of the student and the province seat of the course, which allowed to define the appropriate subsets [7, 8].

2.2   Territorial Analysis of Student Mobility

Students, residing in Italy, enrolled in Italian universities in the A.A. 2016/17 are equal to 1,662,526; this value is almost unchanged, compared to that of A.A. 2006/07 in which they amounted to 1,625,484.

The percentage composition changes slightly, with an increase in the number of members in Campania (+11%) and Lombardy (+7%), while the number of Sardinian and Abruzzi members (with a decrease of 10%) is down, and of Molise (−8%). In the 2016/17 academic year more than half of the students enrolled at the university are concentrated in the following five Italian regions: Lombardy (13.3%), Campania (12.7%), Lazio (11.2%), Sicily (9.5%) and Puglia (7.7%) (Table 1).

The students who attend universities outside the region of residence in 2016/17 are 416,896 (equal to 25.1% of the total) while in 2006/07 they amounted to 322,794

Table 1. Students enrolled by region of residence (2006/07–2016/17)

Region	2006/07		2016/17	
	Enrolled	%	Enrolled	%
Abruzzo	50,203	3.1%	44,952	2.7%
Basilicata	21,707	1.3%	22,099	1.3%
Calabria	77,427	4.8%	74,361	4.5%
Campania	190,881	11.7%	211,517	12.7%
Emilia Romagna	93,293	5.7%	97,650	5.9%
Friuli Venezia Giulia	29,095	1.8%	27,990	1.7%
Lazio	184,561	11.4%	186,021	11.2%
Liguria	36,377	2.2%	37,576	2.3%
Lombardia	206,706	12.7%	220,536	13.3%
Marche	42,506	2.6%	43,518	2.6%
Molise	12,560	0.8%	11,549	0.7%
Piemonte	96,173	5.9%	97,977	5.9%
Autonomous Province of Bolzano	6,024	0.4%	5,449	0.3%
Autonomous Province of Trento	14,063	0.9%	13,279	0.8%
Puglia	127,850	7.9%	128,323	7.7%
Sardegna	53,155	3.3%	47,674	2.9%
Sicilia	153,677	9.5%	157,128	9.5%
Toscana	91,213	5.6%	93,406	5.6%
Umbria	23,820	1.5%	23,190	1.4%
Valle d'Aosta	3,118	0.2%	2,833	0.2%
Veneto	111,075	6.8%	115,498	6.9%
Total	**1,625,484**	**100.0%**	**1,662,526**	**100.0%**

Source: National Register of Students of MIUR-Cineca in April 2018.

(19.9%). Some of these students move a few kilometers going to neighboring provinces but belonging to different regions; in other cases, this shift is dictated by a targeted choice towards other universities that present different or higher quality educational offers. The territorial decentralization of university education has also widened the demand also in terms of greater possibilities of choice for the student and has fostered competition with distant universities (in the North and in the Center), historically attractive also for the best employment prospects [9–11].

We specifically look at the characteristics of these students by analyzing where they come from and where they are going, in terms of the region and the university.

2.3   Outgoing Mobility Index

First of all, let's analyze the *Outgoing mobility index*, given by the percentage ratio among students who choose to enroll in a university in a region other than that of residence on the total number of members resident in the region. It is the rate of "off-site" among resident students and therefore measures the tendency to emigrate.

In the 2016/17 academic year, the regions with percentages higher than 50% are Valle d'Aosta (75.6%), Basilicata (77.2%), Molise (67.5%) and the Autonomous Provinces of Bolzano (65.1%) and Trento (54.8%). Compared to the A.A. 2006/2007 it is noted that the regions that have undergone an increase in this index in 2016/17 are Sicily (from 16.2% to 32.9%), Abruzzo (from 27.3% to 38%), Umbria (from 24.6% to 35.3%) (Table 2).

It is also interesting to analyze the *Outgoing mobility index at the provincial level*, given by the percentage ratio among students who choose to enroll in a university in a region other than that of residence on the total number of members residing in the province.

Table 2. Outgoing mobility index at region level (ay 2006/07 – ay 2016/17)

Region	2006/07			2016/17		
	Enrolled outside the region	Enrolled resident in the region	Outgoing mobility index	Enrolled outside the region	Enrolled resident in the region	Outgoing mobility index
Abruzzo	13,693	50,203	27.3%	17,083	44,952	38.0%
Basilicata	16,121	21,707	74.3%	17,065	22,099	77.2%
Calabria	29,573	77,427	38.2%	32,590	74,361	43.8%
Campania	28,965	190,881	15.2%	36,321	211,517	17.2%
Emilia Romagna	12,123	93,293	13.0%	19,067	97,650	19.5%
Friuli Venezia Giulia	5,935	29,095	20.4%	7,792	27,990	27.8%
Lazio	19,551	184,561	10.6%	21,928	186,021	11.8%
Liguria	8,498	36,377	23.4%	11,541	37,576	30.7%
Lombardia	23,210	206,706	11.2%	29,102	220,536	13.2%
Marche	11,884	42,506	28.0%	14,321	43,518	32.9%
Molise	7,657	12,560	61.0%	7,797	11,549	67.5%
Piemonte	16,655	96,173	17.3%	19,460	97,977	19.9%
A. P. of Bolzano	4,411	6,024	73.2%	3,545	5,449	65.1%
A. P. of Trento	5,827	14,063	41.4%	7,279	13,279	54.8%
Puglia	40,724	127,850	31.9%	51,389	128,323	40.0%
Sardegna	8,216	53,155	15.5%	10,043	47,674	21.1%
Sicilia	24,918	153,677	16.2%	51,659	157,128	32.9%
Toscana	9,074	91,213	9.9%	14,079	93,406	15.1%
Umbria	5,849	23,820	24.6%	8,176	23,190	35.3%
Valle d'Aosta	2,254	3,118	72.3%	2,143	2,833	75.6%
Veneto	27,656	111,075	24.9%	34,516	115,498	29.9%
Total	**322,794**	**1,625,484**	**19.9%**	**416,896**	**1,662,526**	**25.1%**

Source: National Register of Students of MIUR-Cineca in April 2018.

From Fig. 1 emerges that the provinces with higher percentages are those that do not have a university in the same territory but in which there are perhaps universities in neighboring regions such as Matera (85%), Verbano Cusio Ossola (78%), Aosta (76%), Mantua (75%), La Spezia and Isernia (74%), Potenza (73%). Compared to 2006/07, Bolzano has a lower index, rising from 73% to 65% in 2016/17. Vice versa, in 2016/17 the provinces in which the percentage of students moving outside the region are very low, are Monza and Brianza (6%), Lecco (6%), Como and Bergamo, Pisa, Turin, Rome (8%) and Milan (9%).

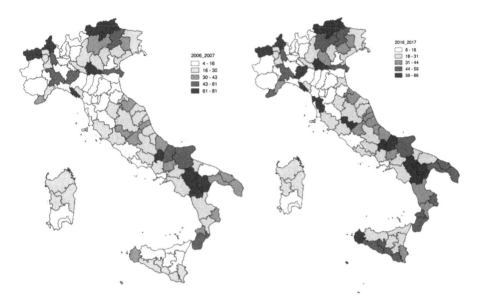

Fig. 1. Outgoing mobility index at provincial level (2006/07–2016/17)

2.4   Incoming Mobility Index

It is also interesting to analyze the *Incoming mobility index* in the regions (obtained as a percentage ratio among the students enrolled in a university in the region, but coming from other regions, out of the total enrollment in the region).

In this case it emerges as in the A.A. 2016/17 the regions with a high capacity to attract off-site students are the Autonomous Province of Trento with 62.6% of students coming from outside the region, Emilia Romagna with 43.5%; Molise with 46.6% and Abruzzo with 42.3% (Table 3).

Representing on the territory the total number of students enrolled who study outside the region (equal to 416,896 in 2016/17), it emerges that Lazio is the preferred destination, receiving 20% of the total number of students outside the region, Lombardy with 17.5% and Emilia Romagna with 14.5% (Fig. 2).

Let us now see, excluding the telematics universities, which universities are the most attractive for students residing outside the region (Table 4). First of all in the A.A. 2016/17 the University of Bologna (which attracts 8.2% of students outside the region), follows the Sapienza of Rome (5.2%), the University of Pisa (3.7%) and the

Table 3. Incoming mobility index in the region (ay 2006/07–ay 2016/17)

Region	2006/07			2016/17		
	Enrolled from different regions	Total enrolled in the region	Incoming mobility index	Enrolled from different regions	Total enrolled in the region	Incoming mobility index
Abruzzo	22,631	59,141	38.3%	20,431	48,300	42.3%
Basilicata	1,411	6,997	20.2%	1,498	6,532	22.9%
Calabria	1,664	49,518	3.4%	1,805	43,576	4.1%
Campania	8,971	170,887	5.2%	21,329	196,525	10.9%
Emilia Romagna	53,663	134,833	39.8%	60,510	139,093	43.5%
Friuli Venezia Giulia	8,381	31,541	26.6%	9,062	29,260	31.0%
Lazio	58,869	223,879	26.3%	83,354	247,447	33.7%
Liguria	4,720	32,599	14.5%	5,529	31,564	17.5%
Lombardia	47,433	230,929	20.5%	73,007	264,441	27.6%
Marche	15,200	45,822	33.2%	16,550	45,747	36.2%
Molise	3,043	7,946	38.3%	3,278	7,030	46.6%
Piemonte	11,818	91,336	12.9%	30,639	109,156	28.1%
A. P. of Bolzano	340	1,953	17.4%	1,090	2,994	36.4%
A. P. of Trento	6,073	14,309	42.4%	10,056	16,056	62.6%
Puglia	5,279	92,405	5.7%	5,037	81,971	6.1%
Sardegna	347	45,286	0.8%	647	38,278	1.7%
Sicilia	9,738	138,497	7.0%	6,158	111,627	5.5%
Toscana	31,955	114,094	28.0%	33,634	112,961	29.8%
Umbria	12,533	30,504	41.1%	8,268	23,282	35.5%
Valle d'Aosta	133	997	13.3%	362	1,052	34.4%
Veneto	18,592	102,011	18.2%	24,652	105,634	23.3%
Total	322,794	1,625,484	19.9%	416,896	1,662,526	25.1%

Source: National Register of Students of MIUR-Cineca in April 2018.

Polytechnic and the University of Turin (3.5% and 2.9% respectively), Catholic and Polytechnic of Milan (3.7% and 3.1% respectively).

2.5   Index of Attraction

The attraction index starts from the Migration Balance, that is calculated by the difference between the incoming flows, which measure the attractiveness of the didactic venues and the outgoing ones, which measure the propensity to emigrate of the resident students (Table 5).

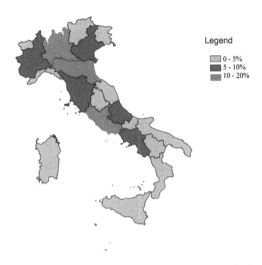

Fig. 2. Percentage location by region of destination of students enrolled at universities outside the region (A.A. 2016/17)

Table 4. Distribution of enrolled students not resident in the region on the basis of the destination university (ay 2006/07–ay 2016/17)

Universities	2006–07		2016/17	
	Number of students not resident in the region	%	Number of students not resident in the region	%
Bologna	31,366	9.7%	34,287	8.2%
Roma Sapienza	27,256	8.4%	21,646	5.2%
Pisa	11,601	3.6%	15,503	3.7%
Milano Cattolica	11,569	3.6%	15,470	3.7%
Torino Polytechnic	5,068	1.6%	14,626	3.5%
Milano Polytechnic	8,310	2.6%	13,126	3.1%
Torino	5,438	1.7%	12,209	2.9%
Chieti and Pescara	14,382	4.5%	11,409	2.7%
Parma	10,873	3.4%	11,359	2.7%
Padova	9,172	2.8%	10,819	2.6%
Milano	7,519	2.3%	10,234	2.5%
Trento	6,073	1.9%	10,056	2.4%
Firenze	9,818	3.0%	9,689	2.3%
Ferrara	7,826	2.4%	8,949	2.1%

Source: National Register of Students of MIUR-Cineca in April 2018.

Table 5. Index of attraction (2006/07–2016/17)

Region	2006/07			2016/17		
	Dynamic incoming	Dynamic output	Index of attraction	Dynamic incoming	Dynamic output	Index of attraction
Abruzzo	22,631	13,693	24.6%	20,431	17,083	8.9%
Basilicata	1,411	16,121	−83.9%	1,498	17,065	−83.9%
Calabria	1,664	29,573	−89.3%	1,805	32,590	−89.5%
Campania	8,971	28,965	−52.7%	21,329	36,321	−26.0%
Emilia Romagna	53,663	12,123	63.1%	60,510	19,067	52.1%
Friuli Venezia Giulia	8,381	5,935	17.1%	9,062	7,792	7.5%
Lazio	58,869	19,551	50.1%	83,354	21,928	58.3%
Liguria	4,720	8,498	−28.6%	5,529	11,541	−35.2%
Lombardia	47,433	23,210	34.3%	73,007	29,102	43.0%
Marche	15,200	11,884	12.2%	16,550	14,321	7.2%
Molise	3,043	7,657	−43.1%	3,278	7,797	−40.8%
Piemonte	11,818	16,655	−17.0%	30,639	19,460	22.3%
A. P. of Bolzano	340	4,411	−85.7%	1,090	3,545	−53.0%
A. P. of Trento	6,073	5,827	2.1%	10,056	7,279	16.0%
Puglia	5,279	40,724	−77.0%	5,037	51,389	−82.1%
Sardegna	347	8,216	−91.9%	647	10,043	−87.9%
Sicilia	9,738	24,918	−43.8%	6,158	51,659	−78.7%
Toscana	31,955	9,074	55.8%	33,634	14,079	41.0%
Umbria	12,533	5,849	36.4%	8,268	8,176	0.6%
Valle d'Aosta	133	2,254	−88.9%	362	2,143	−71.1%
Veneto	18,592	27,656	−19.6%	24,652	34,516	−16.7%

Negative or positive balances denote, respectively, the prevalence of the propensity to emigrate (of the residents) or the ability to attract students outside the province (of the universities). The attraction index is therefore obtained from the ratio between the balance of the incoming and outgoing flows and the total flows (incoming and outgoing) generated by the territorial domain in question.

Positive values are found in Lazio (58.3%) and Emilia Romagna (52.1%) while strongly negative values concern Calabria, Sardinia, Basilicata and Puglia (with a negative index of between 80% and 90%).

3 The Attractiveness of the Mega Italian Universities

A further aspect of considerable interest is the attractiveness for each University. In particular, we analyze in the following cartographies the origin of students enrolled in the main Italian Mega Universities (with more than 40,000 members), depending on their location in the South, Center and North of Italy.

Starting from the Mega universities located in the South of Italy (Fig. 3), we note that the areas of origin of the students who live outside the university are concentrated

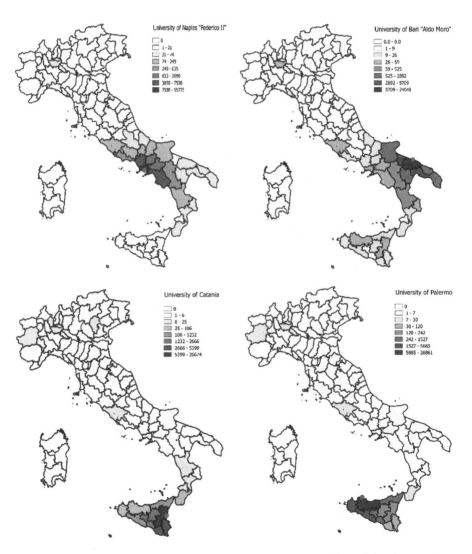

Fig. 3. Number of students enrolled in the main Mega Universities of Southern Italy by province of residence (A.A. 2016/17)

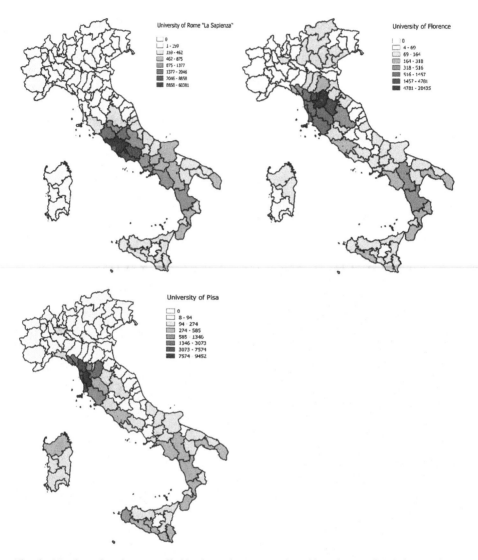

Fig. 4. Number of students enrolled in the main Mega Universities of Central Italy by province of residence (A.A. 2016/17)

in the regions and provinces bordering the location of the university. In fact, very concentrated areas, characterized by a little use in the area, are for Catania, Palermo, Bari and Naples. While the University of Naples gathers a diverse catchment area (76.934 enrolled students, excluding foreigners), which includes several regions of Southern Italy, the University of Catania (43.021 enrolled students) and Palermo (40.370 enrolled students), show an higher concentration with incoming flows coming almost completely from Sicily and Calabria. Interim situation occurs for the University of Bari (44,281 enrolled students) in which there is a substantial homogeneity of origin

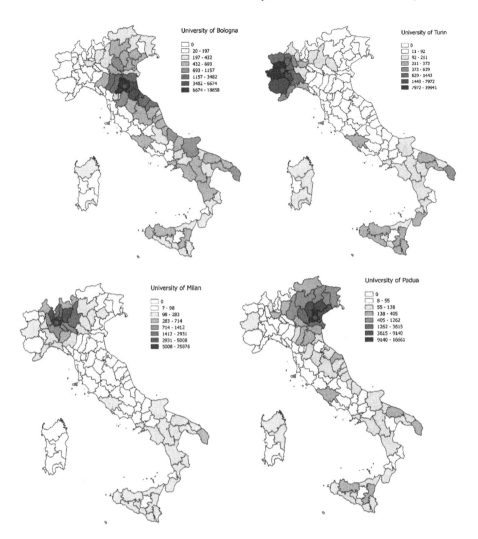

Fig. 5. Number of students enrolled in the main Mega Universities of Northern Italy by province of residence (A.A. 2016/17)

of incoming flows: students come mainly from Puglia but, to a consistent extent, also from Basilicata, Calabria, Molise and Sicily.

As for the universities of Central Italy (Rome, Florence and Pisa) while Florence (49,774 enrolled students) collects a widespread catchment area throughout the Italian territory, Rome (98,875 enrolled students) and Pisa (46,050 enrolled students) show a higher concentration with inflows coming in almost completely from central and southern Italy (Fig. 4).

The major areas of attraction are recorded for Bologna (76,892 enrolled students), Turin (67,008 enrolled students), Milan (60,329 enrolled students) and Padua (58,260 enrolled students). From Fig. 5 we understand the different collocation of the areas of origin of the students enrolled in these four universities. The University of Turin and the University of Milan present two areas of similar size. Bologna has a strong prevalence of the darkest areas in Emilia-Romagna and, with different intensities, along the Adriatic coast from the Veneto to Puglia. The markedly scientific training and the prestige enjoyed by these universities are attractive factors from all over Italy to these university institutions.

4 The Main Cause-Effect Relationships of Student Mobility

The mobility of university students is not a new phenomenon, even before the spread of university centers even in medium-sized cities, traditionally university courses have attracted students even from places very distant from those of residence.

Very often it is the capital city of a state where the most important university resides which attracts students from every area of the nation or, as more and more often happens in Europe after the introduction of the Erasmus program or habitually in the US universities and other nations [12].

In contemporary society, the importance of knowledge and higher education in the global economy is growing, as shown by the success stories of Facebook and Google, and universities play an often significant role for the development of a city and its urban region, as Wiewel and Perry [13] have shown, comparing the relationship between cities and universities all the way from Seoul to Helsinky via US universities.

As illustrated by Martinelli [14], the form of the relationship between city and university has evolved according to three main models:

- the university city like Oxford and Cambridge in England or Urbino in Italy, where the University is the driver of social and economic development determining its destiny;
- the city with the University, like most of the large cities in which the universities occupy a well - defined and attributed space, but still marginal with respect to the overall socio - economic dynamics;
- the University Campus, as in the case of Cincinnati in the United States, Sart-Tilman in Liege in Belgium or Arcavacata di Rende in Italy, which is physically separate and enclosed by the city, like a city in the city.

Often these three basic models have crossed and integrated into hybrid forms giving rise to mixed ways of relating with the city. The urban form and the relationship with the city are crucial for identifying the service offer and the urban quality that the city in which the university is located is able to offer students and which often helps to guide the choice of venue university together with the educational offer and opportunities to find work after the training period.

Analyzing the Italian case, as illustrated in this work on the basis of the ISTAT data, the most attractive university locations Bologna, Rome, Pisa, Milan and Turin represent the different models of the relationship between city and university and are able to provide a high level of social and cultural services that certainly constitute an element capable of influencing the choice of the student's home.

The quality of life assured by these cities is also confirmed by the position they occupy in the annual ranking of the Sole 24ore on the livability of the provinces and Italian cities where they are all among the first most livable provinces.

5 Final Remarks

The results reported in this work are undoubtedly encouraging. At the local level, the mobility analysis confirms the attractiveness of the provinces of central and northern Italy with respect to those of Southern Italy.

The comparison with other studies carried out on this topic have highlighted that between the causes that influence the incoming mobility it is necessary to distinguish endogenous and exogenous factors. Among the first we mention the quality of teaching provided and the quality of services to students. Among the exogenous factors are the accessibility of educational sites both in terms of transport costs (almost always as a function of distance) and quality of travel (comfort and duration), "the cultural atmosphere" and the quality of life of the city, in addition to the opportunities to find work after the training period.

Another fundamental element in the analysis of the Italian university system is that concerning the difference between the demand and supply of university education. The indexes calculated at the provincial level have highlighted the ability of some universities to contain not only the residents but also many students from other provinces: Milan, Bologna, Pisa, Rome and Turin are some of the universities that have this characteristic.

Interesting points of reflection emerge from the construction of the various indicators that highlight the particularities of the individual provinces and universities. Interesting findings that, although connected to a well-defined part of the youth population, must lead us to pay more attention to those who move. Basically, we need to know more about their characteristics, the motivations that drive them to go out of the region, their way of being "off-site", the quality of the services researched, etc.

References

1. Tobler, W.R.: A computer movie simulating urban growth in the Detroit region. Econ. Geogr. **46**, 234–240 (1970)
2. Sà, C., Florax, R.J.G.M., Rietveld, P.: Determinants of the regional demand for higher education in the Netherlands: a gravity model apporoach. Reg. Stud. **38**(4), 375–392 (2004)
3. Caleiro, A., Rego, C.: Universities and economically depressed regions: how 'attractive' is the University of Evora? In: ERSA Conference Papers. European Regional Science Association (2004)
4. Brait, F., Petrillo, R., Strozza, M.: Student and Graduate Mobility in Italy, Bulletin of Comparative Labour Relations, Volume 73 (2010)
5. Viesti, G.: Nuove migrazioni. Il trasferimento di forza lavoro giovane e qualificata dal Sud al Nord, Rivista Bimestrale di cultura e di politica, vol. 4, pp. 678–688, il Mulino (2005)

6. Demarinis, G., Iaquinta, M., Leogrande, D., Viola, D.: Analisi quantitativa della mobilità studentesca negli atenei italiani. Confronto territoriale fra domanda e offerta di formazione universitaria Valutazione e qualità degli atenei Modelli, metodi e indicatori, pp. 273–303. Università degli Studi di Bari, Bari (2011)
7. CNVSU: Analisi della mobilita regionale degli immatricolati (2001). www.cnvsu.it
8. CNVSU: Undicesimo Rapporto sullo Stato del Sistema Universitario (2011). www.cnvsu.it
9. Dal Bianco, A.: Determinants of Student Migration in Italy. XXVIII Conferenza Italiana di Scienze Regionali, Bolzano (2007)
10. Dal Bianco, A., Poggi, E., Spairani, A.: La mobilità degli studenti in Italia: un'analisi empirica. In: IRER Working Paper n. 12 (2009)
11. Miller, H.J.: Tobler's first law and spatial analysis. Ann. Assoc. Am. Geogr. **94**(2), 284–289 (2004)
12. Kelo, M., Teichler, U., Wächter, B. (eds.): EURODATA Student mobility in European higher education. Lemmens Verlags- & Mediengesellschaft, Bonn (2006)
13. Wiewel, W., Perry, D.C. (eds.): Global universities and cities development. Sharpe, New York (2008)
14. Martinelli, N.: Spazi della conoscenza. Università, città e territori, Adda Editore, Bari (2012)

Short Papers

Design and Implementation of a Dynamic GIS with Emphasis on Navigation Purpose in Urban Area

Alireza Vafaeinejad$^{(\boxtimes)}$

Faculty of Civil, Water and Environmental Engineering,
Shahid Beheshti University, Tehran, Iran
a_vafaei@sbu.ac.ir

Abstract. Dynamic GIS is a system that allows the changes in time for various features and objects be considered updating the system in real-time. An example of such a system is integration of Automatic Vehicle Location and Navigation System (AVLNS) with GIS. This paper describes design and implementation aspects of a Dynamic GIS with emphasis on analysis of optimum route finding. This system is able to monitor movements of vehicles in real-time at the control center. If a vehicle is located in traffic jam, an automatic message is sent to the user and then a buffer is established around the vehicle position on the digital map available in the computer at the control center. Based on analysis capabilities of dynamic GIS, the closest junction with respect to the vehicle position is found and from this junction the next shortest path to the final destination will be determined based on shortest time-distance functions. Then, a message containing new path for the vehicle is sent to the driver for changing his/her route. Using this system, it is possible to analyze Geo-referenced information based on real-time positioning data for various moving vehicles and make decisions for "optimum route finding in real-time" and "Defining exclusion and inclusion zones for vehicles and controlling their operational regions".

Keywords: Implementation · Dynamic GIS · Navigation · Urban area

1 Introduction

1.1 A Subsection Sample

Nowadays, GIS technology is acceptable to the high extent in the world and is improving [1–4]. However, most of the geographical phenomenon are dynamic, the traditional GIS has still remained static [5, 6]. Now, the users of GIS expect more from this system and for instance, adding the changes occurred with time on the data and entering these updated information to GIS is needed which makes it possible to create a dynamic GIS. Many of geographical phenomenon, studied in GIS, from geometrical and location point of view involve some changes with the time and considering these changes as they occur is necessary. These affairs and efforts lead us to the development of dynamic GIS that is one of the active research areas in GIS. The purpose of this research area is to provide users with a system that automatically transfers changes to the GIS model and update this model.

© Springer International Publishing AG, part of Springer Nature 2018
O. Gervasi et al. (Eds.): ICCSA 2018, LNCS 10960, pp. 667–675, 2018.
https://doi.org/10.1007/978-3-319-95162-1_46

Among the usages of dynamic geographical information systems, we can refer to the control of existing environment that depends on the analysis of the phenomenon that is continuously changing. For instance, the external factors like velocity and the direction of wind may possibly effect the distribution of pollution and most of the times, integrating such factors and dynamic phenomenon in the geographical database is necessary to provide the possibility for analysis and observing the changes.

Another example is integration of Automatic Vehicle Location and Navigation Systems (AVLNS) with GIS that a kind of dynamic GIS system is formed to the extent that the situations of vehicles in the geographical information system are updated. With such a system which is based on GIS and AVLNS, we can analyze Geo-referenced information on the existing data and make optimum decision for:

- Determining optimum route for the moving vehicles.
- Controlling of moving vehicles for the purpose of not entering to the banned region or not leaving from the described region (inclusion and exclusion zones).

This paper describes design and implementation of a dynamic geographical information system with emphasis on integration of GIS and AVLNS and modeling for analysis of optimum route finding.

2 Dynamic GIS Generated by Integration of GPS and GIS

In order to establish a dynamic GIS that is GPS-GIS integrated system, we need to have a real time tracking vehicle location system as an effective tool for monitoring moving vehicles [7].

This system consists of a control centre, mobile units, and communication link between control centre and mobile units. In addition to possibility of showing the position, velocity, and other information related to the vehicle at the control centre, the system has the ability of sending and receiving messages, guiding vehicle to desired destination; and limiting the vehicle activities on the basis of defined criterion, in banned or patrol regions.

2.1 Design and Implementation of a Dynamic GIS with Emphasis on Analysis of Optimum Route Finding

In this section, we describe design and implementation of a Dynamic Geographical Information System called DGIS. This system is able to monitor moving vehicles in real time.

The ability of cartography and editing, map matching, and analysis of route finding based on shortest time-distance functions using Dijkstra algorithm are some of the functionalities of the software. Time and position information of moving vehicles (i.e. bus, truck, …) is obtained using GPS component of AVLNS. Therefore, in the first step, software must be designed in such a way that it can receive output from AVLNS. In order to monitor the moving vehicles, latitude and longitude of vehicles are needed in real time. DGIS software should be able to receive these data from AVLNS and process them. To do this, DGIS uses an intermediate format to receive and store positional information from AVLNS. In this research, OZTRAK (Australian tracking system) was used as an AVLNS.

In order to monitor mobile units, maps of study area are required. We have used 1:2000 digital maps of Tehran covering vicinity of Vanak square with the extent of $2 \ km^2$.

DGIS software is also able to do some dynamic analyses that make it possible to consider changes occurred in time to the model and update the model in GIS. Based on updated model, various analyses can be done. The software was designed in such a way that other application development is also possible in future.

In the following sections, different steps for design and implementation of DGIS will be described.

2.1.1 Preparing Spatial and Attribute Information

Various analyses can be carried in GIS. These analyses should be based on accurate and up to date information. The primitive spatial information used in this research, was the 1:2000 digital maps of Tehran produced by Tehran municipality. The format of these maps was DWG readable in AutoCad environment. The reference ellipsoid of these maps were WGS84 and projection system was UTM. These maps were corrected and edited for some errors such as (overshoot, undershoot, sliver, …) to be ready for entering to GIS environment.

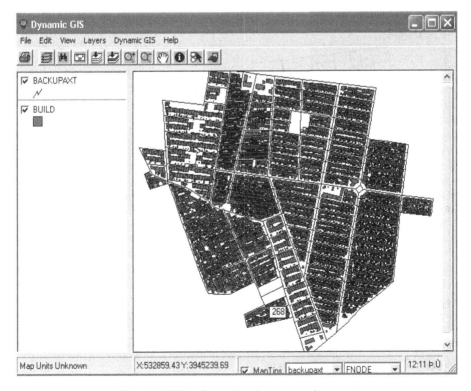

Fig. 1. DGIS software development environment

Attribute information such as name of streets, delay time and passing time for each route, etc. were also linked to the spatial information.

2.1.2 Integration of AVLNS and DGIS

The system was designed in such a way that according to the user needs, positional information of moving vehicles are stored in the Access database. Therefore, for the relation between AVLNS and DGIS software developed in this research, an additional program was written to communicate with Access database.

At first, the position of moving vehicle is determined via a GPS receiver and this positional data is sent to the control centre via VHF/UHF link. Then, the positional data will be received by the AVLNS software, and stored in Access database. In this case, DGIS software is connected to Access database via a program written in Visual Basic environment. The clock of this program starts with the period of 5 s and the first record of database is processed and information fields of latitude and longitude of moving

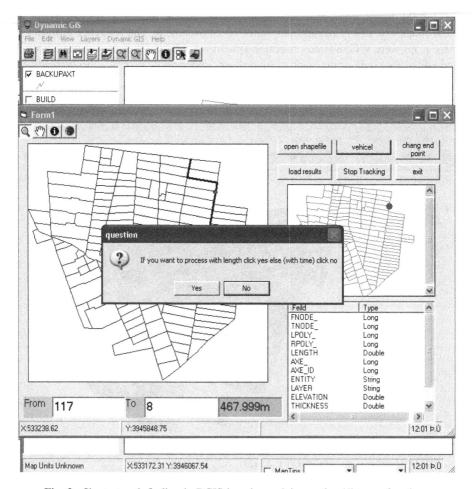

Fig. 2. Shortest path finding in DGIS based on minimum time/distance functions

vehicles are extracted. At the same time in DGIS environment, a point with the same coordinates will be shown as a graphical object in the monitor of a computer at control centre.

2.1.3   Map Matching Process

DGIS system can recognize the streets and roads from other features in the map and is able to apply map matching process. This means that it will correct for the positional errors introduced by GPS receiver. The vehicle usually moves on the street and, therefore, system will assign the receiving information from GPS receiver to the nearest street on the digital map.

At first, a buffer is established around the moving vehicle according to the accuracy of GPS position. Then, all routes having junctions with the buffer zone are determined and perpendicular distance from vehicle to all routes will be computed. Based on this calculation, the moving vehicle is placed on the nearest route.

2.1.4   Dynamic Modelling in DGIS Environment

After connection between the AVLNS and DGIS environment, it was decided to implement some dynamic modelling in DGIS with emphasis on analysis for optimum route finding. One of the important algorithms for route finding is Dijkstra algorithm that has low timing complexity (n^2) where n is the number of nodes.

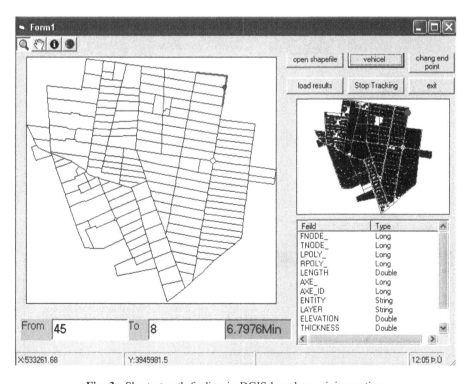

Fig. 3. Shortest path finding in DGIS based on minimum time

When a vehicle is moving, it is clear that it should not have causeless pause, but in traffic jam situations, the velocity of vehicle is reduced. Therefore, we have used this factor as a condition in the program in such a way that if the vehicle velocity is less than 15 km/h in 10 s, it is certain that the vehicle is in traffic jam. In this case, DGIS forms a buffer zone around the vehicle with a radius of 100 m and finds the nearest node in the zone with respect to the vehicle. Then, from this node, the new path to destination will be found based on minimum time or distance functions.

Now, a series of nodes of shortest paths in the form of text accompanied by distance or time required for driving each path between two nodes and total distance/time to final destination are presented.

These information provide valuable data for the user, for instance, if the driver is not familiar with the name of streets, we can guide him/her to his/her destination based on shortest time/distance modelling analyses.

Besides having the output of above analyses in the form of text, DGIS software can highlight the shortest path on the road network of digital map and based on this, driver is informed for the new path via a wireless communication link, and from the first node in his/her path, will drive on the new path towards his/her destination.

In order to find the shortest path in Dijkstra algorithm, sum of delay time and passing time are considered. Delay time is the time that each vehicle stops at traffic light and passing time is the time required to drive in a street based on information provided by traffic control centre.

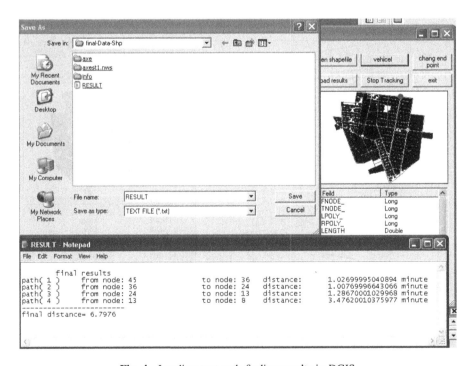

Fig. 4. Loading text path finding results in DGIS

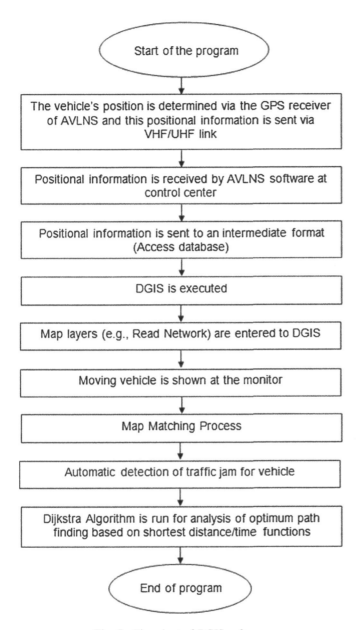

Fig. 5. Flowchart of DGIS software

Figures 1, 2, 3 and 4 show the software designed and the result of analysis for shortest path finding based on minimum time/distance functions.

In summary, Fig. 5 shows the flowchart of DGIS and various steps of running this system.

3 Discussion and Conclusion

Nowadays exploit of Geographical Information System (GIS) is used for power planning and better management, but most of them work in static environment, while we live in a dynamic world and everything around us changes at a different rates. So we must exert these changes to GIS that these operations guide us toward a dynamic GIS. In a dynamic GIS alterations just as happen must insert to the system and this alteration must be transferred automatically to relation model and model mentioned above must be controlled and then need analysis be accomplished.

With increase of GIS users and identification it's capabilities, usage and implementation of dynamic GIS will be increased. Concerning the wide use of these systems (dynamic GIS) and that till now there hasn't been so many researches, therefor this paper was a sample of research in this area.

Designing and implementation of dynamic GIS with emphasis on navigation purpose in urban area that earn from combination GPS data and GIS, was the main goal of this paper. In This system, GPS provides real-time positioning information of a moving vehicle which can be directly sent to the control center via a communication link and based on this information, GIS Database is updated. In this regard, after make ready spatial and non-spatial data that is required, out putting a vehicle navigation system received with using a Visual Basic Code, then a software called DGIS was designed and implemented successfully which has the main following abilities:

- Automatic recognition of location for vehicles in traffic jam situations.
- Map Matching process.
- Dynamic path finding based on minimum time/distance functions.
- Presentation of results of optimum route finding in the forms of text or graphic.

References

1. Vafaeinezhad, A.R., Alesheikh, A.A., Hamrah, M., Nourjou, R., Shad, R.: Using GIS to develop an efficient spatio-temporal task allocation algorithm to human groups in an entirely dynamic environment case study: earthquake rescue teams. In: Gervasi, O., Taniar, D., Murgante, B., Laganà, A., Mun, Y., Gavrilova, Marina L. (eds.) ICCSA 2009. LNCS, vol. 5592, pp. 66–78. Springer, Heidelberg (2009). https://doi.org/10.1007/978-3-642-02454-2_5
2. Vafaeinezhad, A.R., Alesheikh, A.A., Nouri, J.: Developing a spatio-temporal model of risk management for earthquake life detection rescue team. Int. J. Environ. Sci. Technol. 7(2), 243–250 (2010)
3. Bolouri, S., Vafaeinejad, A.R., Alesheikh, A.A., Aghamohammadi, H.: The ordered capacitated multi-objective location-allocation problem for fire stations using spatial optimization. ISPRS Int. J. Geo-Inf. 7(2), 44 (2018)
4. Vahidnia, M.H., Vafaeinejad, A.R., Shafiei, M.: Heuristic game-theoretic equilibrium establishment with application to task distribution among agents in spatial networks. J. Spat. Sci. https://doi.org/10.1080/14498596.2017.1395773
5. Vafaeinezhad, A.R., Alesheikh, A.A., Roshannejad, A.A., Shad, R.: A new approach for modeling spatio-temporal events in an earthquake rescue scenario. J. Appl. Sci. 9(3), 513–520 (2009)

6. Vafaeinejad, A.: Dynamic guidance of an autonomous vehicle with spatio-temporal GIS. In: Gervasi, O., et al. (eds.) ICCSA 2017. LNCS, vol. 10407, pp. 502–511. Springer, Cham (2017). https://doi.org/10.1007/978-3-319-62401-3_36
7. Zhao, Y.: Vehicle Location and Navigation System, 1st edn. Artech House, Inc., Norwood (1997)

A Girsanov Result Through Birkhoff Integral

Domenico Candeloro[ID] and Anna Rita Sambucini[(✉)][ID]

Department of Mathematics and Computer Science,
University of Perugia, Perugia, Italy
{domenico.candeloro,anna.sambucini}@unipg.it

Abstract. A vector-valued version of the Girsanov theorem is presented, for a scalar process with respect to a Banach-valued measure.
Previously, a short discussion about the Birkhoff-type integration is outlined, as for example integration by substitution, in order to fix the
measure-theoretic tools needed for the main result, Theorem 6, where
a martingale equivalent to the underlying vector probability has been
obtained in order to represent the modified process as a martingale with
the same marginals as the original one.

Keywords: Girsanov theorem · Martingale · Birkhoff integral

2010 AMS Classification: 28B05 · 60G44

1 Introduction

In probability theory, the so-called Girsanov Theorem is a well-known result,
whose interest lies both in its theoretical features and in its technical consequences, see for example [19]. The original formulation of this theorem is related
to the Wiener measure, i.e. the *distribution* of the standard Brownian Motion,
$(B_t)_{t \in [0,+\infty[}$, as a stochastic process on a probability space $(\Omega, \mathcal{A}, P)$.

The Girsanov Theorem is a fundamental tool for Stochastic Calculus and
Randow Walks; this last mathematical model has many uses as a simulation tool:
Brownian Motion of Molecules, stock prices and behavior of investors, modeling
of cascades of neuron firings in brain and it has important practical uses in
the internet: Twitter uses random walks to suggest who to follow, Google uses
random walks to order pages which match a search phrase.

In many concrete situations, particularly in stochastic calculus, the resultant
processes $(\widetilde{B}_t)_t$ are usually obtained as suitable *transformations* of $(B_t)_t$, and so
their distribution is different from the Wiener measure. A typical situation is the

Anna Rita Sambucini: The authors have been supported by Fondo Ricerca di Base
2015 University of Perugia - titles: "L^p Spaces in Banach Lattices with applications",
"The Choquet integral with respect to fuzzy measures and applications" and by
Grant Prot. N. U UFMBAZ2017/0000326 of GNAMPA – INDAM (Italy).

O. Gervasi et al. (Eds.): ICCSA 2018, LNCS 10960, pp. 676–683, 2018.
https://doi.org/10.1007/978-3-319-95162-1_47

following: assume that $a(t, \omega)$ is a stochastic process adapted to the Brownian Motion $(B_t)_t$, and define:

$$(\widetilde{B}_t)_t := \int_0^t a(t, \omega)dt + B(t).$$

Though the distribution of this process is different by the Wiener measure, the Girsanov theorem states that it is possible to endow the basic probability space with a new probability measure, Q (which turns out to be absolutely continuous w.r.t. P), in such a way that the distribution of $(\widetilde{B}_t)_t$ under the new probability Q is the Wiener measure, i.e. the same as $(B_t)_t$ under the original probability P. This clearly simplifies all calculations involving just the distribution of $(\widetilde{B}_t)_t$, since in the new probability space this process is the same as $(B_t)_t$.

In the example outlined above, the measure Q can be described by its derivative w.r.t. P :

$$\frac{dQ}{dP}(\omega) = \exp\left\{ -\int_0^T a(s, \omega)dB_s - \frac{1}{2}\int_0^T a^2(s, \omega)dt \right\}.$$

We also point out that, in this example, the process

$$\exp\left\{ -\int_0^t a(s, \omega)dB_s - \frac{1}{2}\int_0^t a^2(s, \omega)dt \right\}$$

is a martingale (Novikov condition).

Our research in this paper is motivated by the fact that, when the distributions involved are conditioned by some initial information (that can be represented as a particular sub-σ-algebra $\mathcal{F}$ of $\mathcal{A}$), then they should be evaluated with respect to $(P|\mathcal{F})$, which is a Banach space-valued measure.

So, in our setting here, continuing the study started in [8], changing a bit the notations, the basic space is $(T, \mathcal{A}, M)$ where $M : \mathcal{A} \to X$ is a Banach-valued σ-additive measure, and $(w_s)_{s \in [0,S]}$ is a scalar valued process, whose distribution admits a density $f_s : \mathbb{R} \to X$ w.r.t. M. (In this setting, we make use of a Birkhoff-type integral in order to integrate a scalar function with respect to M, as well as a *dual* type of integral in order to integrate a vector-valued function w.r.t. a scalar measure). In the paper, some conditions are assumed on the functions f_s in order to find an *equivalent* measure $\widetilde{M}$, under which some transform $\widetilde{w}_s$ of the process turns out to be a martingale, with the same marginal distributions as $(w_s)_s$ with respect to M.

2 Preliminaries

Let T be an abstract, non-empty set, $\mathcal{A}$ a σ-algebra of subsets of T, $\mathcal{B}$ the Borel σ-algebra in the real line and $\mu : \mathcal{A} \to \mathbb{R}_0^+$ a non-negative countably additive measure. Let $(X, \|\cdot\|)$ be a Banach space with the origin 0. We also will consider measures, taking values in X: in this case measures will be usually denoted with letters like m or M, while functions with capital letters, like F or W.

Definition 1. A *partition of* T is a finite or countable family of nonempty sets $P := \{A_n\}_{n \in \mathbb{N}} \subset \mathcal{A}$ such that $A_i \cap A_j = \emptyset, i \neq j$ and $\cup_{n \in \mathbb{N}} A_n = T$.
If P and P' are two partitions of T, then P' is said to be *finer than* P, denoted by $P' > P$, if every set of P' is included in some set of P. The *common refinement* of two partitions P and P' is the partition $P \vee P'$.

We shall make use of the Birkhoff integral, for two different cases. According with the results obtained in [4], and taking into account that we need measurable scalar functions f and strongly measurable vector functions F, we can adopt the following version:

Definition 2. Given two pairs (F, μ) and (f, m) with $F : T \to X$ and $f : T \to \mathbb{R}$, while μ and m denote two countably additive measures with values in $\mathbb{R}_0^+$ and X respectively, then

(α) a strongly measurable vector function F is B_1-*integrable* on T w.r.t μ
(β) a measurable scalar function f is B_2-*integrable* on T w.r.t m

if $\exists I \in X$ with the following property: $\forall \varepsilon > 0, \exists P_\varepsilon$ partition of T so that $\forall P = \{A_n\}_{n \in \mathbb{N}}$ of T, with $P \geq P_\varepsilon$ and $\forall t_n \in A_n, n \in \mathbb{N}$, one has (respectively)

$$\overline{\lim}_n \left\| \left(\sum_{i=1}^{n} F(t_i)\mu(A_i) - I \right) \right\| \leq \varepsilon; \qquad (1)$$

$$\overline{\lim}_n \left\| \left(\sum_{i=1}^{n} f(t_i)m(A_i) - I \right) \right\| \leq \varepsilon. \qquad (2)$$

The set I is called the B_1 (B_2) *integral of* F (f) *on* T *with respect to* μ (m) and is denoted by $\int_T F d\mu, (\int_T f dm)$; the corresponding spaces of B_i-integrable functions are denoted with $L_{B_1}(\mu, X)$ and $L_{B_2}(m, \mathbb{R}_0^+)$.

As proved in [4, Theorem 3.18], even if μ is σ-finite then this notion of integrability is equivalent to the classic Birkhoff integrability for Banach-valued strongly measurable mappings. Moreover in [7] B_1-integrability is named *strong Birkhoff integrability*. One can easily deduce, by means of a Cauchy criterion, that the B_1- or B_2-integrability on T implies the same in every subset $A \in \mathcal{A}$. For an extensive literature on the Birkhoff or non absolute integrals see for example [1–7,9–18,20–23].

3 Some Properties of the Birkhoff Integrals

We will deduce now some useful formulas for the notions of Birkhoff integral previously introduced. These formulas will also give a link between the B_1- and B_2-integral. First, let us mention a stronger result concerning the B_1-integrability.

Theorem 1. ([7, Theorem 3.14]) *Let* $F \in L_{B_1}(\mu, X)$, *then* $\forall \varepsilon > 0$ *there exists a countable partition* $P := \{A_n, n \in \mathbb{N}\} \subset \mathcal{A}$, *such that*

$$\sum_j \left\| F(t_j)\mu(E_j) - \int_{E_j} F d\mu \right\| \leq \varepsilon$$

holds true, for every partition $P' := \{E_j, j \in \mathbb{N}\} > P$ *and* $\forall t_j \in E_j$.

Remark 1. If f is measurable and F is B_1-integrable then the product $t \mapsto f(t)F(t)$ is strongly measurable. Moreover, thanks to the measurability of f, we can define a countable measurable partition of T, $(H_j)_j := (\{t \in T : j - 1 \leq |f(t)| < j\})_j$. Since F is B_1-integrable, according with Theorem 1, for every $\varepsilon > 0$ and for each integer j there exists a measurable countable partition $\{E_j^k, k \in \mathbb{N}\}$ of H_j such that

$$\sum_r \left\| F(t_j^r)\mu(E_j^r) - \int_{E_j^r} F d\mu \right\| \leq \frac{\varepsilon}{j2^j}$$

holds true, for every finer partition $\{E_j^r, r \in \mathbb{N}\}$ *and every choice of points* $t_j^r \in E_j^r$. Then, we have also

$$\sum_j \sum_r \| F(t_j^r) f(t_j^r)\mu(E_j^r) - f(t_j^r)M(E_j^r)\| \leq 2\varepsilon. \tag{3}$$

Theorem 2. (integration by substitution) *Given* $f : T \to \mathbb{R}$ *and* $F \in L_{B_1}(\mu, X)$, *the product* $t \mapsto f(t)F(t) \in L_{B_1}(\mu, X)$ *iff* $f \in L_{B_2}(M, \mathbb{R})$, *where* $M(A) := \int_A F d\mu$ *and*

$$\int_T f(t)F(t)d\mu = \int_T f(t)dM. \tag{4}$$

Another useful formula comes from probability theory. We just state it in a particular situation. Given a measurable $f : T \to \mathbb{R}$ and a countably additive measure $m : \mathcal{A} \to X$, we can set $m_f(B) = m(f^{-1}(B))$ for every Borel set $B \in \mathbb{R}$. Of course, m_f is a countably additive measure, called the *distribution* of f (with respect to m). We have the following result.

Theorem 3. *For any measurable function* $g : \mathbb{R} \to \mathbb{R}$, *one has*

$$\int_T g(f)dm = \int_{\mathbb{R}} g(t)dm_f$$

provided that both B_2-integrals exist.

We shall denote by σ_f the sub-σ-algebra of $\mathcal{A}$ induced by $f : T \to \mathbb{R}$, i.e. the family of all sets of the type $f^{-1}(B)$, $B \in \mathcal{B}$.

Definition 3. Let $F \in L_{B_1}(\mu, X)$. Given any sub-σ-algebra $\mathcal{E}$ of $\mathcal{A}$, the *conditional expectation* $\mathbb{E}(F|\mathcal{E})$ (if it exists) is a strongly $\mathcal{E}$-measurable mapping Z, in $L_{B_1}(\mu, X)$, such that

$$\int_E F d\mu = \int_E Z d\mu$$

for every $E \in \mathcal{E}$.

In case $\mathcal{E} = \sigma_f$, then we write $Z = \mathbb{E}(F|\mathcal{E}) = \mathbb{E}(F|f)$, and in this case Z turns out to be a measurable function of f, say $Z = h(f)$: then

$$\int_{f^{-1}(B)} F d\mu = \int_{f^{-1}(B)} h(f) d\mu$$

for every Borel set B.

The conditional expectation enjoys several properties, easy to deduce, among which linearity with respect to F, and the so-called *tower property*, i.e., whenever $\mathcal{E} \subset \mathcal{G} \subset \mathcal{A}$

$$\mathbb{E}(F|\mathcal{E}) = \mathbb{E}(\mathbb{E}(F|\mathcal{G})|\mathcal{E}),$$

provided that all the involved quantities exist.

The next theorem states another important property of the conditional expectation.

Theorem 4. *Let us assume that $\mathbb{E}(F|\mathcal{E})$ exists. Then, for every $\mathcal{E}$-measurable mapping $g : T \to \mathbb{R}$ it holds: $\mathbb{E}(F(t)g(t)|\mathcal{E}) = g(t)\mathbb{E}(F|\mathcal{E})$ provided that $F(t)g(t) \in L_{B_1}(\mu, X)$.*

4   Girsanov Theorem

We shall now state an analogous result as the well-known Girsanov Theorem. With this purpose, we shall assume that in the space $(T, \mathcal{A})$ a σ-additive measure $M : \mathcal{A} \to X$ is fixed.

Definition 4. A scalar process $(w_s)_s$ is said to be a *Martingale* in itself, if for every $s, v \in [0, S], s < v$, it holds $\mathbb{E}(w_v|\mathcal{E}_s) = w_s$, i.e.

$$\int_E w_v dM = \int_E w_s dM$$

holds true, $\forall v, s \in [0, S]$, $s < v$, and $\forall E \in \mathcal{E}_s$, where $\mathcal{E}_s$ is the least σ-algebra contained in $\mathcal{A}$ such that all w_r, $r \leq s$, are measurable.

Assumption 1. Let us assume that a scalar-valued process $(w_s)_{s \in [0,S]}$ is defined, in the space $(T, \mathcal{A}, M)$, with the property that

1.(a) $w_s \in L_{B_2}(M, \mathbb{R})$ for each s, with null integral, and that its distribution $M_s := M(w_s^{-1}(B))$, $\forall B \in \mathcal{B}$ has a density $f_s \in L_{B_1}(\lambda, X)$

1.(b) let $\widetilde{w}_s = w_s + sq$, with $q \in \mathbb{R}^+$; $\forall s$ there exists a measurable mapping $g_s : T \to \mathbb{R}$ such that $f_s(x) = g_s(x)f_s(x - qs)$, so that $\forall B \in \mathcal{B}$

$$M_s(B) = \int_B g_s(x)dM_{\widetilde{w}_s}; \tag{5}$$

(We observe that, since $g_s(x)f_s(x - qs) = f_s(x)$ is in $L_{B_1}(\lambda, X)$, from Theorem 2 it follows that g_s is B_2-integrable w.r.t. $M_{\widetilde{w}_s}$)

1.(c) $\{g_s(\widetilde{w}_s)\}_s$ is a Martingale.

As a consequence, we have

Theorem 5. *Set for every $A \in \mathcal{A}$, $Q(A) := \int_A g_S(\widetilde{w_S})dM$. Under Assumptions 1 it turns out that $Q_{\widetilde{w}_s} = M_{w_s}$, for every $s \in [0, S]$.*

The previous theorem shows that, under the new measure Q, every random variable $\widetilde{w}_s = w_s + sq$ has the same distribution as the corresponding w_s under M.

Our next step is to prove that the process $\{\widetilde{w_s}\}_s$ is a martingale, under Q. (This property is usually formulated by saying that Q is a *Martingale equivalent* measure). To this aim, we shall assume also the following:

Assumption 2. The scalar process $\{\tilde{w}_t \, g_t(\tilde{w}_t)\}_t$ is a martingale w.r.t. M.

Concerning the last assumption, we remark that, in case $\{w_t\}_t$ is the classical (scalar) Brownian Motion, then the process $\{\tilde{w}_t g_t(\tilde{w}_t)\}_t$ reduces to $\{w_t e^{-qw_t - \frac{1}{2}q^2 t} + qt e^{-qw_t - \frac{1}{2}q^2 t}\}_t$ which shows that the classic Brownian Motion satisfies the Assumption 2. So we have

Theorem 6. *Under Assumptions 1, 2 the process $(\widetilde{w_s})_s$ is a martingale with respect to Q.*

Proof. Fix arbitrarily s and v, with $s < v$, and fix $E \in \mathcal{E}_s$. We observe that

$$\int_E \tilde{w}_v dQ = \int_E w_v g_v(\tilde{w}_v)dM + qvQ(E).$$

Since $E \in \mathcal{E}_s$, it is clear that $Q(E) = \int_E g_s(\tilde{w}_s)dM$. Therefore,

$$\int_E \tilde{w}_v dQ = \int_E (w_v g_v(\tilde{w}_v) + qv g_v(\tilde{w}_v))dM = \int_E \tilde{w}_v g_v(\tilde{w}_v)dM.$$

By the Assumption 2 it follows then

$$\int_E \tilde{w}_v dQ = \int_E (w_s g_s(\tilde{w}_s)dM + qsQ(E).$$

But

$$\int_E w_s g_s(\tilde{w}_s)dM = \int_E w_s g_S(\tilde{w}_S)dM = \int_E w_s dQ$$

and in conclusion

$$\int_E \tilde{w}_v dQ = \int_E \tilde{w}_s dQ,$$

which shows the martingale property.

Conclusion

We have studied some theoretical aspects of the Birkhoff integral, both for scalar valued functions with respect to Banach-valued measures and for the dual situation of vector-valued functions with respect to scalar measures. These previous results are then used in order to state an abstract version of the Girsanov Theorem, where the underlying probability measure M is Banach-valued. The main results state that, under suitable conditions, a *Martingale Equivalent* to M is found, under which the transformed process is a martingale with the same marginals as the original one.

References

1. Boccuto, A., Candeloro, D., Sambucini, A.R.: Henstock multivalued integrability in Banach lattices with respect to pointwise non atomic measures. Atti Accad. Naz. Lincei Rend. Lincei Mat. Appl. **26**(4), 363–383 (2015). https://doi.org/10.4171/RLM/710
2. Boccuto, A., Minotti, A.M., Sambucini, A.R.: Set-valued Kurzweil-Henstock integral in Riesz space setting. PanAm. Math. J. **23**(1), 57–74 (2013)
3. Boccuto, A., Sambucini, A.R.: A note on comparison between Birkhoff and Mc Shane integrals for multifunctions. Real Anal. Exch. **37**(2), 3–15 (2012). https://doi.org/10.14321/realanalexch.37.2.0315
4. Candeloro, D., Croitoru, A., Gavriluţ, A., Sambucini, A.R.: An extension of the Birkhoff integrability for multifunctions. Mediterr. J. Math. **13**(5), 2551–2575 (2016). https://doi.org/10.1007/s00009-015-0639-7
5. Candeloro, D., Di Piazza, L., Musial, K., Sambucini, A.R.: Gauge integrals and selections of weakly compact valued multifunctions. J. Math. Anal. Appl. **441**(1), 293–308 (2016). https://doi.org/10.1016/j.jmaa.2016.04.009
6. Candeloro, D., Di Piazza, L., Musial, K., Sambucini, A.R.: Relations among gauge and Pettis integrals for multifunctions with weakly compact convex values. Annali di Matematica **197**(1), 171–183 (2018). https://doi.org/10.1007/s10231-017-0674-z
7. Candeloro, D., Di Piazza, L., Musial, K., Sambucini, A.R.: Some new results on integration for multifunction. Ricerche di Matematica (in press). https://doi.org/10.1007/s11587-018-0376-x
8. Candeloro, D., Labuschagne, C.C.A., Marraffa, V., Sambucini, A.R.: Set-valued Brownian motion. Ricerche di Matematica (in press). https://doi.org/10.1007/s11587-018-0372-1
9. Candeloro, D., Sambucini, A.R.: Order-type Henstock and Mc Shane integrals in Banach lattice setting. In: Proceedings of the SISY 2014 - IEEE 12th International Symposium on Intelligent Systems and Informatics, pp. 55–59 (2014). https://doi.org/10.1109/SISY.2014.6923557. ISBN 978-1-4799-5995-2
10. Candeloro, D., Sambucini, A.R.: Comparison between some norm and order gauge integrals in Banach lattices. PanAm. Math. J. **25**(3), 1–16 (2015)
11. Cascales, B., Rodríguez, J.: Birkhoff integral for multi-valued functions. J. Math. Anal. Appl. **297**, 540–560 (2004). https://doi.org/10.1016/j.jmaa.2004.03.026
12. Cascales, B., Rodríguez, J.: The Birkhoff integral and the property of Bourgain. Math. Ann. **331**(2), 259–279 (2005). https://doi.org/10.1007/s00208-004-0581-7

13. Cichoń, K., Cichoń, M.: Some applications of nonabsolute integrals in the theory of differential inclusions in Banach spaces. In: Curbera, G.P., Mockenhaupt, G., Ricker, W.J. (eds.) Vector Measures, Integration and Related Topics. Operator Theory: Advances and Applications, vol. 201, pp. 115–124. BirHauser-Verlag, Basel (2010). https://doi.org/10.1007/978-3-0346-0211-2_11. ISBN: 978-3-0346-0210-5
14. Croitoru, A., Gavriluţ, A.: Comparison between Birkhoff integral and Gould integral. Mediterr. J. Math. **12**, 329–347 (2015). https://doi.org/10.1007/50009-014-0410-5
15. Croitoru, A., Gavriluţ, A., Iosif, A.E.: Birkhoff weak integrability of multifunctions. Int. J. Pure Math. **2**, 47–54 (2015)
16. Croitoru, A., Iosif, A., Mastorakis, N., Gavriluţ, A.: Fuzzy multimeasures in Birkhoff weak set-valued integrability. In: 2016 Third International Conference on Mathematics and Computers in Sciences and in Industry (MCSI), Chania, pp. 128–135 (2016). https://doi.org/10.1109/MCSI.2016.034
17. Fremlin, D.H.: The Mc Shane and Birkhoff integrals of vector-valued functions, University of Essex Mathematics Department Research Report 92-10 (2004). http://www.essex.ac.uk/maths/staff/fremlin/preprints.htm
18. Marraffa, V.: A Birkhoff type integral and the Bourgain property in a locally convex space. Real Anal. Exch. **32**(2), 409–428 (2006–2007). https://doi.org/10.14321/realanalexch.32.2.0409
19. Mikosch, T.: Elementary Stochastic Calculus (with Finance in View). World Scientific Publ. Co., Singapore (1998)
20. Potyrala, M.M.: The Birkhoff and variational Mc Shane integrals of vector valued functions. Folia Mathematica, Acta Universitatis Lodziensis **13**, 31–40 (2006)
21. Potyrala, M.M.: Some remarks about Birkhoff and Riemann-Lebesgue integrability of vector valued functions. Tatra Mt. Math. Publ. **35**, 97–106 (2007)
22. Rodríguez, J.: On the existence of Pettis integrable functions which are not Birkhoff integrable. Proc. Amer. Math. Soc. **133**(4), 1157–1163 (2005). https://doi.org/10.1090/S0002-9939-04-07665-8
23. Rodríguez, J.: Some examples in vector integration. Bull. Aust. Math. Soc. **80**(3), 384–392 (2009). https://doi.org/10.1017/S0004972709000367

Design of a Facial Recognition Intelligent System for Non-authorized Person Detection Using High Definition Cameras

Alfredo Nuñez-Unda[✉], Jose Aguirre, Benita Canizalez, Viviana Pinos,
Silvia Medina, and Roberto Zurita

Universidad de Guayaquil, Guayaquil, Ecuador
alfredo.nunez.u@gmail.com,
{jose.aguirrea,benita.canizalezd,viviana.pinosm,silvia.medinaa,
roberto.zuritad}@ug.edu.ec

Abstract. Over the last decades video vigilance systems have experienced a considerable growth in public and private environments.This is true due to the increasing need of keeping areas safe in order to serve visitors. This work presents the design of an automated vigilance system using facial recognition. The system runs a real time comparison of data gathered through high definition cameras and stored information off authorized personnel for an specific area. The system generates different types of alerts depending on the event occurring at the time of comparison. The system was developed using Matlab simulations using Simulink. The simulations shows how the facial recognition works when detecting a non authorized person and the alerts triggered when this type of event occurs.

Keywords: Facial recognition · Detection · HD cameras · Matlab

1 Introduction

Non-authorized access to reserved areas or accessing areas by unknown personnel are just two common examples among the mentioned situations [3,6,12]. Given that context, many solutions have been implemented in order to solve this problem such as personnel manual registrar, credential control access, biometric control access, eye control access among others. Even though, the solutions have been under a continuous optimization process [3], those Unfortunately have not fully resolved the safety problem.

In spite all that, many companies have turned down their efforts to the aforementioned systems, instead, they have pointed their attention to a technology developed with just one goal which is enforcing security through and efficient and quick identification system: facial recognition [9]. Facial recognition system had their origins based on biometrics and they came to replacing systems using password protocols, PIN, tokens, smart cards, etc. Those systems have now been replaced by others that examine physical features of an individual [11]. They function in a very simple fashion: they extract information representing physical feature o features, analyze it, perform a comparison and make a decision.

Many of the systems that use access through passwords or codes, have their main disadvantage in that they depend on the memory of the individual. So if it is an extensive code or contains different types of characters so that it is a secure password it can be difficult to remember. Security, basic or smart cards can easily be duplicated, forgotten or lost, and the material they are composed of in which access information is found tends to become corrupted or become illegible. However, the verification of a person's identity based on physical characteristics such as eye color, fingerprints, facial features, height, weight, among others, are features that can hardly be duplicated, can not be forgotten or lose and much less can be replaced. This is one of the biggest advantages of this type of systems.

2   Related Work

One of the problems faced by facial recognition systems in the processing and recognition itself, is the selection of physiological characteristics that will be used for the representation of the face and the classification of these based on the representation of the chosen characteristics, the latter it is affected by variant factors in the images obtained, such as lighting, pose or expression [10]. In order to achieve this classification, the size of the data obtained must be reduced in such a way that a rapid and robust recognition is made, hence two methods of dimension reduction are obtained, one of which is characterized by the extraction of the main characteristics of the image. like the eyes, nose, etc. .; while the other takes the entire facial region as input, this method is known as a holistic method, this type of method is applied in systems such as Eigenfaces and Fisherfaces.

2.1   Holistic Methods

For the application and the correct understanding of this type of methods that will be described later, we start from the principles provided by statistical and algebra knowledge.

Main Component Analysis: PCA. According to the study carried out by Armengot [7], the analysis of main components is a typical method in the analysis of multivariate data since it has the objective of reducing the dimensionality of the same. According to Gámez [8] its function is to analyze if given c samples of a set of n values the information can be represented by a smaller number of variables, constructed as linear combinations of the originals.

PCA is a method that transforms a number of possibly correlated variables into a small number of incorrect variables called principal components, that is, it is a dimensional reduction algorithm that allows finding the vectors that best represent the distribution of a group of images. An image can be considered as a vector of pixels where the value of each component is a grayscale value, for example an image of 256×256 (NxN) will be a vector of dimension 65536 (N2), that is, the image will be in a space of dimension 65536. The images of faces are not randomly distributed in this space and can be described as a subspace of smaller dimension. The idea of principal component analysis is to find the vectors that best represent face images within the entire image space. These vectors define the subspace of face images (facespace). Each vector of length N2 is a linear combination of the original images. These vectors are the eigenvectors of the covariance matrix of the original space of face images and are called eigenfaces because they are similar to a face.

Independent Component Analysis: ICA. ICA is a generalization of the PCA method. This method tries to decompose an observed signal in a linear combination of independent sources. While PCA derelates the input signals using second order statistics, ICA minimizes higher dependency orders. We have a matrix of independent variables (sources): S = (S1 ......, Sn), and a matrix of observations X. In this observation matrix, each column is the result of a random experiment, and in each row we have the value of a test of that experiment. As it has been said the ICA method tries to decompose the signal observed in a combination of independent sources, the combination matrix (unknown) will be called A : X = A · S With the ICA algorithm, the separation matrix W is searched, which fulfills: U = W · X = W · A · S, where U is the maximum likelihood estimate (ML) of the independent components. There are two ways to implement the ICA method for face recognition: - You can put a different image in each row of the matrix X, so you will have that each image is a random variable and the pixels are tests. - Another option is to transpose the matrix X and have an image in each column, so that in this case, the pixels are random variables and each image a test.

Linear Discriminant Analysis: LDA. This method is a supervised learning technique for classifying data. The central idea of LDA is to obtain a projection of the data in a space of less (or even equal) dimension than the incoming data, in order that the separation of the classes is as large as possible. It is a supervised technique since in order to search for that projection the system must be trained with labeled patterns. The work scenario necessary to apply this method to face recognition is based on the fact that there is a set of training faces (xi) composed of a group of people with different facial expressions and different views. By definition all instances of faces of the same person are in a class (size Nc), and the faces of different people belong to different classes (there will be c classes), thus having the training space separated into groups. In addition, all instances in the training set must be labeled [5].

Methods Based in Kernels. These methods are a generalization of component analysis methods (PCA, ICA, LDA). In the component methods, a subspace is built that meets certain restrictions and then a base that generates it is chosen. Kernels methods take into account moments of higher order without having an excessively large computational cost. The classification problem is taken to a larger space where the classes are linearly separable. For this, the following is done [1]: 1. The training vectors are mapped through a non-linear function that takes the points to a larger space. 2. An equivalent problem is posed to the PCA, ICA or LDA problem in said space. 3. The equivalent problem is solved, using the trick kernel, which is a simplified way to solve the problem of PCA, ICA or LDA in the larger space. If you meet certain particular conditions, you can perform all the calculations of the resolution of the equivalent problem without the need to map the vectors in the largest space. For this there are different functions, called kernels, which make it possible.

Evolutionary Pursuit: EP. This method is a type of genetic algorithm that tries to find a base of faces through the rotation of defined axes in a suitable PCA white space. Evolution is driven by a fitness function that depends on the accuracy of the classification and the ability to generalize. The EP algorithm is used to search between the different rotations and base vectors to find an optimal subset of vectors (which have good classification accuracy and ability to generalize). The algorithm that is followed to find the EP-faces is [1] 1. Reduce the size of data through PCA. 2. Transform the previous space so that it is white. 3. Carry out the following loop until you reach a maximum number of iterations or find the solution you are looking for: (a) Perform several rotations between vector pairs of a space base and then select a set of them. Coding each rotation through a representation in bit words (in genetic algorithms the representation is done as a function of bits). (b) Calculate the fitness function to measure the accuracy and generalization. (c) Calculate the angles and vectors that maximize the function. They are saved as the best solution so far. (d) It iterates to a new subset of angles and therefore of rotated vectors. 4. With the optimal base found, the recognition of faces is made by some measure of similarity.

Support Vector Machine: SVM. SVM is a generic method to solve pattern recognition problems. Given a set of points in a given space belonging to two different classes, SVM finds the hyperplane that separates the most points of the same class from the same side. This is done by maximizing the distance of each class to the decision hyperplane, called OSH (Optimun Separating Hyperplane). The points closest to the hyperplane, of each set in question, are the so-called support vectors [1].

2.2   Methods Based on Local Characteristics

The representation of a face takes the form of tagged graphs. The graphs are formed by vectors and nodes; the vectors are labeled with geometric information (distances) and the nodes are labeled with a set of local characteristics called jets. The jets are based on Gabor transformations, which could be taken as a process of image preprocessing based on biological phenomena For an I image, the wavelet transform of one of its points, x, will be [13]:

$$\sigma_k = \frac{k^2}{\gamma^2} e^{-\frac{k^2}{2r^2}*x^2} \left(e^{jkx} - e^{\frac{\gamma^2}{2}} \right) \tag{1}$$

For that point the transform will be a flat wave where k is the wave vector and σ is a parameter that relates the wave vector to the size of the window in which the plane wave is defined. The second term in the parentheses eliminates the continuous component. A wave, centered on the x position of the image, is used to extract the Jk component of the I (x) image:

$$J_k(x) = \int I(x')\Psi(x - x')dx' = a_k e^{j\Phi_k} \tag{2}$$

where a_k is the amplitude and Φ_k the phase [4]. In a face recognition system using this method, the images of the faces must be subjected to a normalization process in which the values of the pixels are centered on the mean of the original image to obtain a zero mean signal. Geometric normalization is also performed, so that the coordinates of the eyes happen to have a predetermined value, and the values of the pixels are adjusted to have a signal of zero mean and standard deviation equal to one. In addition, the edges of the image are softened.

Local Binary Pattern: LBP. The operator LBP is an interesting tool as a texture's descriptor. This operator go through the image and label the pixels by a threshold of the difference between the central pixel and its neighbors, considering the result as a binary number. The labels concatenation of the neighbors can be used as a descriptor [2], as shown in Fig. 1 [15].

Fig. 1. Basic LBP operator

LBP is used for one face image description. It is built many local descriptors that are combined in a global descriptor.

Active Appearance Models: AAM. Active Appearance Model is a statistic model of the forms and appearance in the gray levels of the object of interest that can generalize to almost any valid example of the object mentioned [1].

The models are trained with faces images in a range of points of view. Per example to cover a 180° rotation is necessary just five models, to −90°, −45°, 0° (front view), 45° and 90° are the reflect of one each (assuming the symmetry of the faces), in reality it is enough with three models. Using the AAM algorithm, it can fit a new image in any model.

In the images of the training group, it is marked reference points. These points are represented in a vector and PCA is applied to them, so that the remaining model is: $x = x + P \bullet b$, where $x = (x_1, ..., x_n, y_1, ..., y_n)$, P is a matrix which columns are unitary vectors corresponding to the axis of maximum variation, and b is weight vector (eigenvalues).

3D Methods. In the methods based in local characteristics, the face recognition methods in two dimensions are sensitive to the illumination conditions, orientation, and facial expression, etc. These limitations come from the information limitation that exists in a two dimensions image. This has increased the faces data use in three dimensions, because it provides more orientation information and luminous conditions.

The general idea of the 3D methods is to look for a general model of a face that later has to adjust to a each particular face. The faces are tried as three dimensional surfaces, there are methods that are based in produce surface gradients and for those that is not necessary rebuild later the face surface. The classic methods to see the correspondence of two surfaces are based in find an Euclidean transformation that maximize a similarity criteria.

It has verified that the transformations of a facial surface can be modeled as isometric transformations. It is needed to find a representation for the isometric surfaces and for the faces recognition case it is often used MDS (Multi Dimensional Scaling) to obtain some forms called bending − invariant canonical [2]. One of the most important steps in the construction of the canonic form is the calculation of the surface distance, for which it is used the FMTD (Face Marching Method on Triangulates Domains) algorithm.

3 Architecture and Evaluation of the Proposed System

The proposed architecture was carried out using Matlab software applying the Principal Component Analysis technique. The purpose of this procedure is to analyze the main component by reducing the size of a set of samples. The main goal is to get the projection of data on a space within which, in theory, there is no covariance between the various variables of the observation vectors.

In Fig. 2 the program interface is shown. In Fig. 3 the camera turns on and captures the user's face. The program automatically enclose the user's face.

Once the data of the face has been captured, the program compares with the database of authorized users. Figure 4 shows an unauthorized user as an example.

As an additional security measure, the program sends an email to the security department with a picture of the unauthorized user, as shown in Fig. 5.

4 Conclusions and Future Work

A model for facial recognition was designed to detect unauthorized individuals in a monitored area, sending an alert through an email and thus validate the

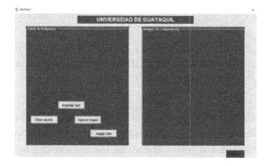

Fig. 2. Program interface.

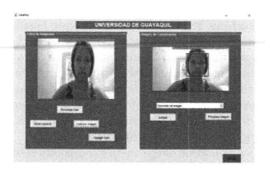

Fig. 3. User capture example.

Fig. 4. Unauthorized user example.

Fig. 5. Unauthorized user example.

presence of the individual. Using Matlab for the facial recognition algorithm demonstrating in real time how it performs the analysis of the images in the database and the detected one The results were evaluated obtaining through the simulation in which it was possible to detect in this way the individual arriving at the acceptable results in our project. It is recommended to use a rapid processing system that can handle database information, to make an effective comparison because the cameras have to detect several people at once. The cameras have to have specific characteristics such as the resolution of the image as far as quality is concerned for the detection of the individual. The information must be stored in a system with protection to provide greater security.

References

1. Aguerrebere Otegui, C., Capdehourat Longres, G., Delbracio Bentancor, M., Mateu Graside, M.: Proyecto aguará, Reconocimiento de caras (2006)
2. Bronstein, A.M., Bronstein, M.M., Kimmel, R., Spira, A.: 3D face recognition without facial surface reconstruction. Technical report, Computer Science Department, Technion (2003)
3. Cabello, E., Conde, C., Rodriguez, L.: Detección automática de conductas sospechosas, pp. 21–48 (2009)
4. Cabello Pardos, E.: Técnicas de reconocimiento facial mediante redes neuronales. Ph.D. thesis, Informatica (2004)
5. Etemad, K., Chellappa, R.: Discriminant analysis for recognition of human face images. JOSA A **14**(8), 1724–1733 (1997)
6. Gaggioli, D.N., Azpeitía, O., Di, P.: Debates sobre procedimientos de deteccion de conductas sospechosas en AVSEC, November 2014
7. Iborra, M.J.A.: Análisis comparativo de métodos basados en subespacios aplicados al reconocimiento de caras. Universidad. de Valencia (2006)
8. Jiménez, C.G., Virginia, C.: Diseño y desarrollo de un sistema de reconocimiento de caras. Universidad Carlos III de Madrid (2009)
9. Olguín, D.E.E., Guillen, P.I.J.: Reconocimiento facial (2015)
10. Ottado, G.: Reconocimiento de caras: Eigenfaces y fisherfaces (2010)
11. Parmar, D.N., Mehta, B.B.: Face recognition methods & applications. arXiv preprint arXiv:1403.0485 (2014)

12. Polo Herráez, R.: Etiquetado de elementos en entornos urbanos mediante visión estéreo y redes neuronales. Master's thesis (2013)
13. Wiskott, L., Krüger, N., Kuiger, N., Von Der Malsburg, C.: Face recognition by elastic bunch graph matching. IEEE Trans. Pattern Anal. Mach. Intell. **19**(7), 775–779 (1997)

Stochastic Epidemic Type Model for Analyzing Seismic Activity

Hasih Pratiwi[1]([✉]), Dody Chandra Priambodo[2], Respatiwulan[1],
and I. Wayan Mangku[3]

[1] Statistics Department, Universitas Sebelas Maret,
Jl. Ir. Sutami 36A, Surakarta, Indonesia
hpratiwi@mipa.uns.ac.id
[2] Mathematics Department, Universitas Sebelas Maret,
Jl. Ir. Sutami 36A, Surakarta, Indonesia
[3] Mathematics Department, Institut Pertanian Bogor,
Kampus Damaga, Bogor, Indonesia

Abstract. In statistical seismology, we can use stochastic process to explain random natural phenomena. One area of study in stochastic processes is point process. At a point process, earthquakes are viewed as a collection of random points in a space, where each point represents the time or/and location of an earthquake. In stochastic epidemic type model earthquake occurrence is assumed as an epidemic, i.e. a large earthquake triggers aftershocks at a certain time interval and the impact may extend to a region. By using point process approach, a stochastic model can be presented with its conditional intensity function, that is the probability of earthquake occurrence per time unit. It is expected that the analysis on the conditional intensity function of the epidemic type model provides information about the probability of earthquake occurrence based on its history. We apply the model to analyze seismic activity in Java Island, Indonesia.

Keywords: Point process · Earthquake · Epidemic type model
Conditional intensity function

1 Introduction

The geographical location of the Indonesian territory that lies between the three main tectonic plates causes Indonesia as one of the countries that have potential seismic activities high enough and prone to earthquake hazard (Katili [1]). Earthquakes are a natural event, that is a vibration on the earth's surface due to the sudden release of energy from the epicenter. Earthquake activity is still being studied both from seismology aspect and stochastic aspect. Part of the seismological statistics is a stochastic process. Stochastic process is one of the

Supported by the Ministry of Research, Technology, and Higher Education of the Republic of Indonesia through Grant of Pascadoctor No. 474/UN27.21/PP/2018.

© Springer International Publishing AG, part of Springer Nature 2018
O. Gervasi et al. (Eds.): ICCSA 2018, LNCS 10960, pp. 693–700, 2018.
https://doi.org/10.1007/978-3-319-95162-1_49

areas of study in mathematics that can be used to predict or to explain phenomena in everyday life. One of the stochastic processes that can explain earthquake phenomena is point process (Pratiwi et al. [4], Schoenberg [6]).

In stochastic process, earthquakes are viewed as points in a space where each point represents the time or/and location of an event. In a seismological research, one of the famous basic empirical laws is Omori law. This law was modified later by Utsu [4] into Omori-Utsu's law. The Omori-Utsu's law is not always appropriate to model the earthquake pattern for a long time.

According to Zhuang et al. [9], an appropriate model for explaining the sequence of aftershocks is the epidemic type aftershock sequence (ETAS) model. ETAS model shows the period between aftershocks and the next aftershocks. ETAS model is not optimal to explain the sequence of aftershocks because it has no location or spatial component (Veen and Schoenberg [8]). In this research we discuss spatial ETAS model. Ogata [2] explained that the conditional intensity function at a point process is defined as a derivative of the probability of earthquakes occurrence. The discussion of point process model, especially spatial ETAS model through the conditional intensity function, provides an information on the rate of earthquake occurrence based on its historical data.

2   Epidemic Type Model

In the epidemic type model, the number of individuals living at time t is controlled by immigration rate, birth rate, and mortality rate. In an earthquake, the immigration rate refers to the occurrence of the basic earthquake while the birth is associated with triggering aftershocks based on previous earthquake events. The birth and death processes are dependent on the age of every individual in the age x can survive at time t. For the interval $(t; t + dt)$ there are a probability of birth $g(x)\,dt$ and a probability of death $h(x)\,dt$ where they are mutually independent for each individual. The self-exciting process is the birth process that follows the immigration rate μ per unit time and the death process $h(x) = 0$. According to Ogata [2], the process has a conditional intensity function

$$\lambda(t) = \mu + \sum_{t_i < t} g(t - t_i) \tag{1}$$

where $N(t)$ is the number of events $\{t_i\}$ in time interval $(0, t]$.

Equation (1) is extended for point process that considering magnitude at time t_i. If m_i is magnitude associated with t_i then the conditional intensity function can be expressed by

$$\lambda(t) = \mu + \sum_{t_i < t} \kappa(m_i) g(t - t_i) \tag{2}$$

where t_i is the earthquake occurrence time of point process $N(t)$, m_i is the magnitude corresponding to t_i, and $\kappa(m_i)$ is a function of magnitude m_i.

One of epidemic model type in seismology is Omori's law. Omori's law stated that the number of occurrences of subsequent earthquakes decays pursuant to time. According to Utsu [7], Omori's law can be expressed as

$$n(t) = \frac{K}{(t+c)} \tag{3}$$

Equation (3) is modified by Utsu [7] with addition of the parameter p to obtain

$$n(t) = \frac{K}{(t+c)^p} \tag{4}$$

where K, c, p are parameters, t is a time since the beginning of the main earthquake, and $n(t)$ is the frequency of aftershocks. Equation (4) is known as the modified Omori law or Omori-Utsu law. Under Omori-Utsu's law (4) and epidemic type model (2) the following assumptions are given.

1. Basic seismic rate in a region is a constant expressed by μ.
2. All occurrences of earthquakes including aftershocks, trigger, secondary aftershocks. For each secondary aftershock also triggers the occurrence of subsequent secondary aftershocks independently. Probability the occurrence of aftershocks are expressed in form

$$\kappa(m) = A \; e^{\alpha(m-m_0)}$$

   where m_0 is the limit of magnitude, A and α are parameters.
3. Probability density function of the trigger earthquake time is

$$g(t) = \frac{p-1}{c} \left(1 + \frac{t}{c} \right)^{-p}$$

   where c and p are parameters and t_0 is the time when the main earthquake is happened.
4. Distribution of magnitudes independent from the rate of earthquake activity. The explicit form of the Guttenberg-Richter relationship is used as a probability density function of the magnitude

$$f(m) = \beta \; e^{\beta(m-m_0)}$$

Based on Eq. (2) and above assumptions, the conditional intensity function can be written as

$$\lambda(t|\mathcal{H}_t) = \mu + \sum_{t_i<t} \frac{A \; (p-1) \; c^{(p-1)} \; e^{\alpha(M_i-M_0)}}{(t-t_i+c)^p} \tag{5}$$

where A, α, c and p are parameters and $\mathcal{H}_t$ is historical data before time t. Equation (5) is called epidemic type aftershock sequence model (ETAS). Suppose that the incidence of $t_1, t_2, t_3, ..., t_N$ at the time interval $(0, t]$ and the conditional intensity function $\lambda(t|H_t)$ are given. According to Ogata and Zhuang [3], the log-likelihood function of ETAS model can be written as

$$\log L(\theta) = \sum_{i=1}^{N} \log(\lambda(t_i|H_t)) - \int_0^T \lambda(t|H_t)dt. \tag{6}$$

where $\theta = (\mu, A, \alpha, c, p)$.

ETAS model (5) is not optimal for explaining earthquake activity. This model has no spatial component. ETAS model can be developed by considering the components of time, magnitude, and location. According to Zhuang et al. [9], ETAS model was developed based on the following assumptions.

1. Main earthquake is assumed to be an immigrant in the earthquake branching process. The earthquake occurrence rate is assumed to be a function of location and magnitude expressed by $\mu(x, y)$.
2. Any aftershock is independent from another aftershock. The probability of aftershocks are expressed by $\kappa(m)$.
3. Probability distribution of the main earthquake time to the occurrence of aftershocks is assumed to be the lag time function of the main earthquake and it is expressed as $g(t|\tau) = g(t - \tau)$ with τ as the time between earthquake events.
4. Probability distribution of the locations (x, y) and the magnitude of the aftershock depend on the location (ξ, η) and magnitude of the main earthquake. The density probability function is

Based on that assumptions, a conditional intensity function can be obtained as

$$\lambda(t, x, y, m|\mathcal{H}_t) = j(m)\ \lambda(t, x, y|\mathcal{H}_t)$$

or

$$\lambda(t, x, y|\mathcal{H}_t) = \mu(x, y) + \sum_{\{i; t_i < t\}} \kappa(m_i)g(t - t_i)f(x - x_i, y - y_i|m_i) \tag{7}$$

where

1. $\mathcal{H}_t = (t_i, m_i); t_i < t$ is the occurrence of earthquake before time t,
2. $\mu(x, y) = \mu\ \rho(x, y)$ is base seismic rate with the location function (x, y),
3. $\kappa(m)$ is probability of aftershocks with the magnitude m can be expressed as

$$\kappa(m) = A\ e^{\alpha(m - m_0)};\ A, \alpha, m - m_0 > 0,$$

4. $g(t)$ is a probability density function of the time of the trigger earthquake as

$$g(t) = \frac{p - 1}{c}\left(1 + \frac{t}{c}\right)^{-p},$$

5. $f(x, y|m)$ is the location distribution of the trigger earthquake

$$f(x, y|m) = \frac{q - 1}{\pi D^2 e^{\gamma(M - M_0)}}\left(1 + \frac{x^2 + y^2}{D^2 e^{\gamma(M - M_0)}}\right)^{-q}.$$

Equation (7) is called a spatial epidemic type aftershock sequence (ETAS) model. According to Zhuang et al. [9], the maximum function of likelihood can be written as

$$\log\ L(\theta) = \prod_{i=1}^{N} \log\ \lambda(t_i, x_i, y_i) - \int_0^T \int_{y_0}^{y_1} \int_{x_0}^{x_1} \lambda(t, x, y)\ dx\ dy\ dt \qquad (8)$$

where i is the order of earthquakes that occur at location $(x_0, x_1) \times (y_0, y_1)$ and in time interval $(0, T]$. If the base seismic rate $\mu(x, y)$ is known then the model parameter $\theta = (\mu, A, c, \alpha, p, D, q, \gamma)$ can be estimated by the likelihood maximum method. The parameter estimation process also uses the Davidon Fletcher Powell method to maximize $\log L(\theta)$.

3   Application for Earthquake Data in Java Island

In this section we apply the spatial ETAS model to the earthquake data in Java Island. The earthquake data is a secondary data sourced from the United States Geological Survey (USGS). This earthquake data contains $\{t_i, x_i, y_i, m_i\}$ where t_i is the time of the i-th earthquake, (x_i, y_i) is the location of the i-th earthquake, and m_i is the magnitude of the i-th earthquake. The period of the earthquake occurred from January 1973 - December 2016 with a magnitude ≥ 5 and depth ≤ 70 km.

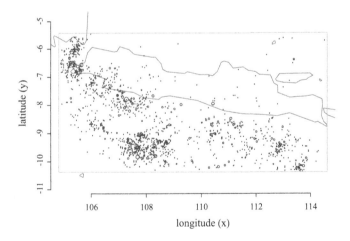

Fig. 1. Earthquake activity in Java Island

Java Island is located between $6° - 11°$ South Latitude and $105° - 114°$ East Longitude. The tectonic activities in Java Island are dominated by the movement of the Indo-Australian plate that moves to the north relatively and cause the collision with the Eurasian plate. The Indo-Australian plate subduction is about 100 to 200 km in the south of Java Island and 600 km in the north of Java

Island. The broken plates cause the movement of rock elements (Soehaimi [5]). This condition makes the area of Java Island to be an active tectonic area with a high seismic rate. The earthquake activity in the Java Island is presented in Fig. 1.

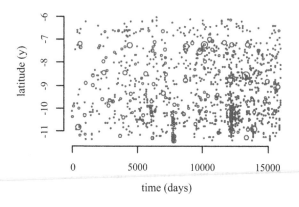

Fig. 2. Plot of location to time of the earthquake activity in Java Island

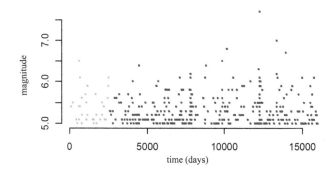

Fig. 3. Plot of magnitude to time of the earthquake activity in Java Island

Based on Fig. 1, it can be seen that earthquake activities in Java Island area tend to occur mostly along the southern sea of Java Island and around the Sunda Strait. Sunda Strait is located near the subduction line at the fault line between Sumatera Island and Java Island. It causes earthquakes with small magnitude often occur in that area. The relation of location to time and the relation of magnitude to time for earthquake activity in the Java Island are presented in Figs. 2 and 3. There are several earthquakes in Java Island that have large magnitude i.e. in Banyuwangi on June 2, 1994 with magnitude 7.2, in Yogyakarta on May 27, 2006 with magnitude 6.3, in Pangandaran offshore on July 17, 2006 with magnitude 7.7, in Tasikmalaya on September 2, 2009 with magnitude 7.0, and in Cilacap on April 4, 2011 with magnitude 6.7.

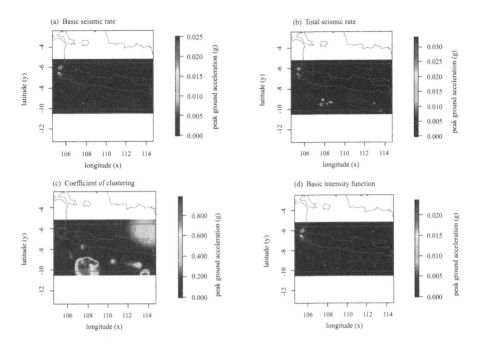

Fig. 4. The basic seismic rate, total seismic, coefficient of clustering, and intensity function of spatial ETAS model for earthquake activity in Java Island

All parameters of spatial ETAS model (7) on earthquake data in Java Island are estimated by the maximum likelihood estimation method and Davidon Fletcher Powell method. We have $\hat{\mu} = 0.916$, $\hat{A} = 0.143$, $\hat{c} = 0.015$, $\hat{\alpha} = 1.833$, $\hat{p} = 1.219$, $\hat{D} = 0.006$, $\hat{q} = 2.174$, $\hat{\gamma} = 1.279$, $log\ L = -2124.013$ and the spatial ETAS model for earthquake data in Java Island can be written as

$$\lambda(t, x, y | H_t) = 0.916\ \rho(x, y) + \sum_{t_i < t} 0.143\ e^{1.833(M_i - M_0)}$$

$$\left(\frac{0.219c^{0.219}}{(t - t_i + c)^{1.219}} \right) \left(\frac{1.174}{0.006^2 \pi e^{1.279(M_i - M_0)}} \right)$$

$$\left(\frac{\left(0.006^2 e^{1.279(M_i - M_0)} \right)^{2.174}}{((x - x_i)^2 + (y - y_i)^2 + 0.006^2 e^{1.279(M_i - M_0)})^{2.174}} \right). \quad (9)$$

The basic seismic rate, total seismic, clustering coefficient, and intensity function of spatial ETAS model are presented in Fig. 4. It is seen that the basic seismic rate in Java has been formed around the Sunda Strait and along the southern sea of Java Island. It can be seen also for the total seismic rate and the clustering coefficient that Java earthquake activities often occur on the southern coast of Java Island, especially in the southern sea of West Java and Central Java as well as a small part around the Sunda Strait, so it causes these areas prone to earthquake disaster.

4 Conclusion

Spatial epidemic type aftershock sequence (ETAS) model is an expansion of the ETAS model by considering time, location, and magnitude. The spatial ETAS model can be expressed through a conditional intensity function:

$$\lambda(t, x, y | H_t) = \mu(x, y) + K \sum_{t_i < t} \frac{e^{\alpha(m_i - m_0)}}{(t - t_i + c)^p} \times$$

$$\frac{(D^2 e^{\gamma(m_i - m_0)})^q}{e^{\gamma(m_i - m_0)} ((x - x_i)^2 + (y - y_i)^2 + D^2 e^{\gamma(m_i - m_0)})^q} \quad (10)$$

where $H_t = (t_i, m_i); t_i < t$ is historical data of earthquakes that occurs before time t, (x, y) is location of the earthquake, and m_0 is limit of magnitude.

Earthquake in Java Island often occurs in southern coast of Java Island, especially in the southern sea of West Java and Central Java as well as a small part around the Sunda Strait.

References

1. Katili, J.A.: Plate tectonics of indonesia with special reference to the Sundaland area. In: Proceedings Indonesian Petroleum Association (IPA) (1972)
2. Ogata, Y.: Statistical models for earthquake occurrences and residual analysis for point processes. J. Am. Stat. Assoc. **83**, 9–27 (1988)
3. Ogata, Y., Zhuang, J.: Space-time ETAS models and an improved extension. Tectonophysics **413**(1–2), 13–23 (2006)
4. Pratiwi, H., Slamet, I., Saputro, D.R.S.: Respatiwulan: self-exciting point process in modeling earthquake occurrences. J. Phys. Conf. Ser. **855**, 012033 (2017)
5. Soehaimi, A.: Seismotektonik dan Potensi Kegempaan Wilayah Jawa. Pusat Survei Geologi, Bandung 3 (2008)
6. Schoenberg, F.P., Brillinger, D.R., Guttorp, P.: Point processes, spatial-temporal. Encycl. Environ. **3**, 1573–1577 (2002)
7. Utsu, T.: Aftershock and earthquake statistics (I). J. Fac. Sci. Hokkaido Univ. **3**, 129–195 (1969)
8. Veen, A., Schoenberg, F.P.: Estimation of space-time branching process model in seismology using an EM-type algorithm. J. Am. Stat. Assoc. **103**(482), 614–624 (2008)
9. Zhuang, J., Ogata, Y., Vere-Jones, D.: Stochastic declustering of space-time earthquake occurences. J. Am. Stat. Assoc. **97**(458), 369–380 (2002)

Advance Multispectral Analysis
for Segmentation of Satellite Image

Paul E. Sterian[1,2(✉)] ⓘ, Florin Pop[3], and Dan Iordache[1,2]

[1] Faculty of Applied Sciences, Physics Department,
University "Politehnica" of Bucharest, 313 Splaiul Independentei,
060042 Bucharest, Romania
paulesterian@yahoo.com
[2] Academy of Romanian Scientists, Splaiul Independentei No. 54,
050094 Bucharest, Romania
[3] Faculty of Automatic Control and Computer Science,
University "Politehnica" of Bucharest, Bucharest, Romania

Abstract. This paper presents an application with record performance for electromagnetic spectrum analysis of multispectral satellite image. The analysis method is an application-specific pixels oriented to images segmentation. This kind of segmentation is used in remote sensing for land cover and land use classification and change detection. Regions of the image are clustered separately and then the results are combined, for this the processing method employs two types of clustering algorithms, each specialized to its task and steered towards obtaining a final meaningful segmentation. The results show good spatial coherency in segments and coherent borders between regions that were segmented separately.

Keywords: Multispectral images · Image segmentation · Remote sensing
Spectral characteristics · Spectral vector · Data clustering algorithm
Compatibility function · Fuzzy covariance matrix

1 Introduction

Satellite images are multispectral images formed by the instruments on board the earth orbiting satellites. Having a lot more spectral bands than the 3 usually associated with RGB images and higher than 8 bit resolution per spectral band satellite images require a lot of memory and processing time thus needing a distributed processing approach [1, 2, 7]. Multispectral image segmentation is used in various fields like medicine where it is employed in segmenting of magnetic resonance images (MRI) and detecting abnormalities, food quality assessment, separation of blood cells [3, 14], in detecting imperfect products, as well as satellite imagery. Satellite imagery is typically used to detect the distribution of vegetation, water bodies, snow, clouds, soil classes, roads, urban development and assessment of fire damage, floods and landslides. Detection of

© Springer International Publishing AG, part of Springer Nature 2018
O. Gervasi et al. (Eds.): ICCSA 2018, LNCS 10960, pp. 701–709, 2018.
https://doi.org/10.1007/978-3-319-95162-1_50

the various classes is called classification [4]. Some of them are supervised, meaning they are aided by humans, while the rest are unsupervised or hybrid.

2 Remote Sensing

Remote sensing is the acquisition of some types of information (spectral, spatial and temporal) of an array of target points within the sensed scene that correspond to objects, areas or phenomena, all this without coming into direct contact with them. Information transfer and processing in remote sensing is accomplished by use of electromagnetic radiation, force fields or acoustic energy, based on many more elaborated models of interaction at the classical or quantum models [4, 9–12]. The form of remote sensing used by satellites is by sensing reflected electromagnetic radiation. Satellites provide a unique view of our world and offer data on scales of time and space that otherwise would not be possible. Satellite sensors not only observe wavelengths of visible light but also wavelengths of radiant energy that our eyes cannot see, such as: infrared light, ultraviolet rays and microwaves.

By using the visible spectrum data combined with the data from the other lays software can classify objects found in those images by type and can quantify important climatic and environmental elements such as temperature, ozone concentrations, pollutants, cloud types, total cloud cover and many others [5].

3 Spectral Reflectance

Matter will emit or absorb electromagnetic radiation on a particular wavelength with respect to its inner state. This transfer of electromagnetic energy is unique with respect to the type of matter. The unique characteristics of matter are called spectral characteristics. Thus the proportions of energy reflected, absorbed and transmitted will vary for different earth features depending upon they material type and condition allowing us to distinguish them in an image.

These proportions depend also on the wavelength so that two features may be indistinguishable in one spectral range and are very different on another. Objects can be classified and differentiated by using what is called a spectral reflectance curve or spectral response, which shows how it reflects and absorbs differently at different wavelengths. In Fig. 1 the spectral responses of vegetation and different conditions of water and soil are shown. Six spectral bands are also highlighted which can be successfully used to distinguish between these kinds of land cover. Satellite sensors are primarily defined and compared by using four characteristics, their spatial, temporal, radiometric and spectral resolutions [6, 13]. Here are some important definitions that we use in data processing:

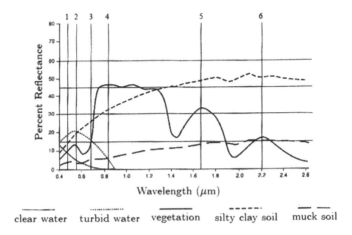

clear water   turbid water   vegetation   silty clay soil   muck soil

Fig. 1. Spectral response

Spatial Resolution is defined as the area on the ground represented by one pixel in the satellite image. The resolution is affected by the IFOV (Instantaneous Field Of View), the height of the sensor the optical characteristics of the sensor. For example, we specify some significant values:

- High spatial resolution: 0.6–4 m;
- Medium spatial resolution: 4–30 m;
- Low spatial resolution: >30 m.

Temporal Resolution specifies the revisiting frequency of a satellite sensor for a specific location and is characterised by values as:

1. High temporal resolution: <3 days;
2. Medium temporal resolution: 4–16 days;
3. Low temporal resolution: >16 days.

Spectral resolution defines the ability of a sensor to define fine wavelength intervals. The finer the spectral resolution, the narrower the wavelengths range for a particular channel or band. In can also be de.ned as the number of spectral bands in which the sensor can collect reflected radiance.

- Hyper spectral sensors: hundreds of bands;
- Moderate spectral resolution: tens of bands;
- Low spectral resolution: 3 bands.

Finally, we define the **Radiometric resolution** by the number of digital levels used to express the data collected by the sensor. It is expressed by the number of bits needed to store de maximum level. Usual values are 8 and 11 bits. High spatial resolution images are given by the IKONOS (1–4 m) and Quick-Bird (2:4 m) space programs. High spectral resolution instrument examples are MODIS and AIRS sensors flying on the Aqua and Terra satellites.

The MODIS sensor collects data in 36 spectral bands. It has a high radiometric sensitivity of 12 bits, acquiring values in the range from -100 to 16000. The first two bands have a spatial resolution of 250 m at nadir, the next five 500 m, while the remaining bands have 1 km spatial resolution. This means a pixel in the first and second band covers a 250 m by 250 m area on the surface of the Earth. The strengths of MODIS are the combination of global coverage and high spatial resolution, high radiometric accuracy and a spectral bands configuration which allows a wide range of studies of the land and ocean surfaces, and the atmosphere. With its sweeping 2330 km-wide viewing swath, MODIS sees every point on our world every one to two days. Terra's orbit around the Earth is timed so that it passes from north to south across the equator in the morning, while Aqua passes south to north over the equator in the afternoon. These data will improve our understanding of global dynamics and processes occurring on the land, in the oceans, and in the lower atmosphere. MODIS is playing a vital role in the development of validated, global, interactive Earth system models able to predict global change accurately enough to assist policy makers in making sound decisions concerning the protection of our environment.

MODIS provides imagery in 36 spectral bands from 0.4 to 14.5 μm, selected for their significance in monitoring the Earth [7, 8]:

- Bands 1–2 (620–876 nm) Land, cloud and aerosols boundaries;
- Bands 3–7 (459–2155 nm) Land, cloud and aerosols properties;
- Bands 8–16 (405–877 nm) Ocean color, phytoplankton and biogeochemistry;
- Bands 17–19 (890–965 nm) Atmospheric water vapor;
- Bands 20–23 (3660–4080 μm) Surface and cloud temperature;
- Bands 24–25 (4433–4549 μm) Atmospheric temperature;
- Bands 26–28 (1360–7475 μm) Cirrus clouds, water vapor;
- Band 29 (8400–8700 μm) Cloud properties;
- Band 30 (9580–9880 μm) Ozone;
- Bands 31–32 (10780–12270 μm) Surface and cloud temperature;
- Bands 33–36 (13285–14385 μm) Cloud top altitude.

The data that comes from the two satellites are transferred to ground stations in White Sands, New Mexico, via the Tracking and Data Relay Satellite System (TDRSS) and then to the EOS Data and Operations System (EDOS) at the Goddard Space Flight Center. In order to provide access to real-time MODIS imagery NASA has founded the Distributed Active Archive Center (DAAC) within the Goddard Earth Sciences Data and Information Services Center (GESDISC), providing an online data pool with the most recent two weeks of MODIS data.

The satellite images are stored in HDF-EOS files, which is an extension to the HDF file format used for storing scientific data. For example, Fig. 2 presents the possibility to classify the vegetation using wavelength. The data about wavelength is stored in HDF file [6].

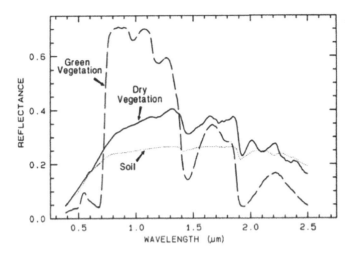

Fig. 2. Vegetation classification

4   Multispectral Analysis for Segmentation of Satellite Image

The segmentation of satellite images, also known as unsupervised classification, has the purpose of distinguishing the natural features in an image. A spectral vector is constructed for each point in the image. These vectors are grouped in classes according to their similarity. The difference between it and normal RGB image segmentation is that the results are clusters in the spectral domain as opposed to segments in 2D. Each cluster can be translated to multiple segments in 2D. Usual methods for doing the segmentation employ only the spectral vectors from each image location, discarding their spatial relationship in 2D. Other methods use the spatial neighborhood of a pixel to influence its classification, thus making it somewhat useful even in RGB image segmentation. The methods that work in the spatial domain as well as in the spectral are more robust and are more resistant to noise.

Fuzzy C-Means (FCM) [5, 6, 15] is a data clustering algorithm that uses a membership function that shows for each point and each cluster the degree to which the point belongs to the cluster. Thus the fractional degree of membership $u_{ij} \in [0, 1]$ shows the degree to which the point j is a member of the cluster i. It is an iterative method that tries to minimize an error function. At each step it recalculates the cluster centers and the cluster memberships of each point. The cluster centers are recomputed according to the formula:

$$c_j = \frac{\displaystyle\sum_{j=1}^{N} u_{ij}^m x_j}{\displaystyle\sum_{j=1}^{N} u_{ij}^m} \tag{1}$$

where x_j is the jth spectral vector and m is the fuzziness factor. A common value for m is 2. The new memberships are computed as:

$$u_{ij} = \sum_{k=1}^{c} \left(\frac{\|x_j - c_j\|}{\|x_j - c_k\|} \right)^{\frac{2}{1-m}} \tag{2}$$

where $\|V\|$ stands for the length of vector V [8].

The Gustafson-Kessel (GK) algorithm extends the FCM algorithm by using an adaptive distance norm, in order to detect clusters of different geometrical shapes in the d-dimensional space in which the patterns reside. To determine the shape of the cluster the algorithm computes for each cluster a norm-inducing matrix A_i. The norm inducing matrix is computed from the fuzzy covariance matrix of the cluster C_i. These matrices are computed as follows [8]:

$$C_i = \frac{\sum_{j=1}^{n} u_{ij}^m (x_j - c_i)(x_j - c_i)^T}{\sum_{j=1}^{n} u_{ij}^m} \tag{3}$$

$$A_i = \sqrt[n]{\det(C_i)} \cdot C_i^{-1}. \tag{4}$$

Now every cluster prototype is defined by the cluster center and covariance matrix. The cluster centers are computed the same way as in FCM but the distance function changes to include the covariance information:

$$d(c_i, x_j) = \sqrt{(x_j - c_i)^T A_i (x_j - c_i)}. \tag{5}$$

The Gustafson-Kessel algorithm detects ellipsoidal clusters in the d-dimensional feature space. By using the more complex distance function it has a higher execution time than FCM [5, 7].

The advantage is that the values are inherently normalized so that if two bands have different ranges of values, the band with the bigger values will not overwhelm the whole distance computation as it does with the Euclidian distance.

This characteristic is very important when there are multiple bands with different ranges of values as is the case with satellite images.

Patterns 2 and 3 (see Fig. 3) are compatible, while pattern 1 isn't compatible with any of them because in band 5 the amount of reflected energy decreases while in the other two patterns it increases.

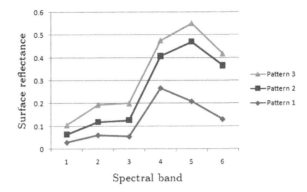

Fig. 3. Compatibility example

5   Experimental Results

The multispectral satellite image data comes from the MODIS instruments onboard the Terra and Aqua satellites. The data was downloaded in the form of HDF files. Six spectral bands were used in the segmentation, each band having a 2400 by 2400 resolution and 12 bit integer values. A point in the image represents an area of 500 by 500 m on the ground.

After the algorithm is run over the image the results are presented. The incompatibility borders are represented as borders over imposed on the true color composite in Fig. 4(a). The image show the borders found between distinct natural features.

(a) Incompatibility borders   (b) Using compatibility

Fig. 4. Satellite image segmentation borders

In Fig. 4(b) the borders found by the algorithm that uses the compatibility function are shown. The differences can be attributed to the influence of the incompatibility borders as can be seen from the images. The use of the compatibility function insures more spectrally correct clusters and more relevant borders. From both results it can be seen that the segments are spatially coherent, the image not being overly segmented. This is a result of the use of spatial information. The borders that intersect separately segmented regions are coherent, largely because of the overlapping region and the accurate hierarchical merging of clusters.

6   Conclusions

The inclusion of the compatibility function has shown to be a possibly valuable improvement to the normal fuzzy clustering with spatial information. Further improvements to the inclusion of the incompatibility in the formulae will be made to give even the incompatible clusters a little influence over the classification and make the algorithm more resistant to noise.

Stopping the hierarchical clustering at an optimum number of clusters will be investigated. Change classification between satellite images taken at different dates can be done with the same algorithm if a proper compatibility criterion is used.

The conflict of interest. The authors declare that there is no conflict of interest regarding the publication of this paper.

References

1. Duda, T., Canty, M., Klaus, D.: Unsupervised land-use classification of multispectral satellite images. A comparison of conventional and fuzzy-logic based clustering algorithms. In: Proceedings of IEEE 1999 International Geoscience and Remote Sensing Symposium, IGARSS 1999, vol. 2, pp. 1256–1258. IEEE (1999)
2. Muresan, O., Pop, F., Gorgan, D., Cristea, V.: Satellite image processing applications in MedioGRID. In: The Fifth International Symposium on Parallel and Distributed Computing, ISPDC 2006, pp. 253–262. IEEE, 6 July 2006
3. Iliescu, F.S., et al.: Continuous separation of white blood cell from blood in a microfluidic device. UPB Sci. Bull. Ser. A **71**(4), 21–30 (2009)
4. Walter V.: Automatic classification of remote sensing data for GIS database revision. Int. Arch. Photogramm. Remote Sens. **32**(4), 641–648 (1998)
5. Bezdek, J.C., Ehrlich, R., Full, W.: FCM: the fuzzy c-means clustering algorithm. Comput. Geosci. **10**(2–3), 191–203 (1984)
6. Cai, W., Chen, S., Zhang, D.: Fast and robust fuzzy c-means clustering algorithms incorporating local information for image segmentation. Pattern Recogn. **40**(3), 825–838 (2007)
7. Chuang, K.S., Tzeng, H.L., Chen, S., Wu, J., Chen, T.J.: Fuzzy c-means clustering with spatial information for image segmentation. Comput. Med. Imaging Graph. **30**(1), 9–15 (2006)
8. Jain, A.K., Murty, M.N., Flynn, P.J.: Data clustering: a review. ACM Comput. Surv. (CSUR). **31**(3), 264–323 (1999)
9. Sterian, A.R.: Computer Modeling of the Coherent Optical Amplifier and Laser Systems. In: Gervasi, O., Gavrilova, M.L. (eds.) ICCSA 2007. LNCS, vol. 4705, pp. 436–449. Springer, Heidelberg (2007). https://doi.org/10.1007/978-3-540-74472-6_35

10. Stefanescu, E., et al.: Study on the fermion systems coupled by electric dipol interaction with the free electromagnetic field. In: Proceedings of International Society for Optics and Photonics on Advanced Laser Technologies, vol. 5850, pp. 160–166, 7 June 2005

11. Sterian, A., Sterian, P.: Mathematical models of dissipative systems in quantum engineering. Math. Probl. Eng. (2012)

12. Dima M., et al.: The QUANTGRID project (RO)—quantum security in GRID computing applications. In: AIP Conference Proceedings, vol. 1203, no. 1, pp. 461–465. AIP, 21 January 2010

13. Ninulescu, V., Sterian, A.-R.: Dynamics of a Two-Level Medium Under the Action of Short Optical Pulses. In: Gervasi, O., Gavrilova, M.L., Kumar, V., Laganà, A., Lee, H.P., Mun, Y., Taniar, D., Tan, C.J.K. (eds.) ICCSA 2005. LNCS, vol. 3482, pp. 635–642. Springer, Heidelberg (2005). https://doi.org/10.1007/11424857_70

14. Iordache, D.A., et al.: Complex computer simulations, numerical artifacts, and numerical phenomena. Int. J. Comput. Commun. Control 5(5), 744–754 (2010)

15. Turčan, A., Ocelíková, E., Madarász, L.: Fuzzy C-means algorithms in remote sensing. In: Proceedings of the 1st Slovakian-Hungarian Joint Symposium on Applied Machine Intelligence (SAMI), Herlany, pp. 207–216, 12 February 2003

Characterisation of Intelligent Public Spaces and Technologies Applied for the Recreation of Ecuadorian Emigrants

Yovany Salazar Estrada[1(✉)], Marcelo León[2], Lídice Haz[3],
Rosa Iniguez-Apolo[2], Jimmy Sornoza Moreira[3],
and Christian Roberto Antón-Cedeño[3]

[1] Universidad Nacional de Loja, Loja, Ecuador
ysalazarec2002@yahoo.es
[2] Universidad Estatal Península de Santa Elena, La Libertad, Ecuador
marceloleonll@hotmail.com, rmia.rmia@gmail.com
[3] Universidad de Guayaquil, Guayaquil, Ecuador
victoria.haz@hotmail.com,
{jimmy.sornozam, christian.antonc}@ug.edu.ec

Abstract. This paper analyses and exemplifies the recreation in the use of preferred public spaces for social meeting, leisure and recreation of the original culture of Ecuadorian emigrants, while they remain outside of their country. The fundamental principles and the characterisation of public intelligent spaces are exposed, in which the use of information and communication technologies are combined with the Internet of Things. This combination of concepts signifies a very important resource that improves the recreation and communication of people who reside in large cities, creating a point of inflection that has a positive impact in the socio-technological development of these people.

Keywords: Ecuadorian emigration · Intelligent spaces
Socio-technological development · ICT · IoT · Value of cultural heritage

1 Introduction

The sociocultural development referred to the communication and coexistence between the people that inhabit a local community has been consolidated through the creation and management of public spaces that facilitate social recreation through artistic, sports and cultural expression. The places used for social recreation are usually parks, esplanades, streets or avenues, where the inhabitants of a city can develop activities of a social and cultural nature. Public spaces are ideal places for the development of leisure activities that are characterised to promote the development of life in society by facilitating the integration of leisure activities 24 h a day [1].

Recreation and recreation activities in the current society integrate the use of information and communication technologies that directly influence the conformation and expression of migrants, both individually and socially.

Developing recreational activities allows the individual to improve their emotional level with joy, reduce its stress levels and even create or produce something new. Recreation is defined as an activity that has a positive purpose in people. "Within leisure, recreation helps to renew the spirit and rejuvenate individuals. Specifically, in recreation there are activities such as games, art, crafts, outdoor recreation, etc." [2]. Recreation is also defined as an experience or leisure activity that man freely chooses, and from which he receives satisfaction, pleasure and creative enrichment, since through recreation he obtains values, both personal and social [3].

For the above reasons, emigrants would rather use public spaces to develop their recreational activities considering the amplitude and characteristics of the place, the use of technologies and the social groups that are concentrated there, which facilitates to perform different cultural activities and even economical activities. The public space represents a public domain that is used in a multifunctional and collective social manner. It is physically characterized by its accessibility, which makes it a centrality factor [4].

The purpose of using innovative technologies in these spaces is to approach the citizen to the concepts and application of the so-called Internet of things (IoT), through efficient management of technological resources in these public spaces that meets the needs of the city and its citizens. Likewise, another purpose of using innovative technologies is to relate the principles of development and technological innovation, and the cooperation between economic and social agents as fundamental axes for change.

2 Spaces for the Reencounter and the Recreation of the Original Culture

In virtue of the narrowness of the physical spaces for housing and rest in which Ecuadorian emigrants are forced to remain in the countries and cities of destination, Ecuadorian emigrants would rather use public spaces as places of meeting, recreation of the original culture, interaction with the compatriots and distraction during the days and hours that they have available and can enjoy in company [5]. From this perspective, emigrants who have chosen the United States as the destination country, when they arrive and get a job there, they try to enjoy the little free time they have left, with their countrymen and dedicate it to typical recreational activities of the country of origin, such as: listening national music, playing cards, drinking beer, playing sports, playing concerts, selling typical food and liquor [6].

For many Ecuadorian emigrants who are far from the native land, the best thing that can happen to them is to share the little free time they have among nationals, which is why they tend to meet with their compatriots and participate in associations that reinforce the links with the country of origin. On weekends, they usually enjoy being with their friends and families in the parks of the city, as a researcher shows about this sociological problem [7].

In public spaces, Ecuadorians try to reproduce their community spirit and Andean solidarity, which characterises them in the country of origin; for that reason they recognise as something typical of the collective "the need to meet the countrymen in the public space. They feel that this allows them to share their experiences, exchange their emotions, their pains, their shortcomings and the hopes they place in their migratory project" [8]. In view of the above, the occupation of public spaces, by emigrants, has some connotations among which we can mention: the need to overcome material difficulties such as the lack of information on the labour market or the administrative conditions of immigration; the precariousness or absolute lack of private spaces; or the impossibility of being able to access paid leisure and recreational facilities. In parallel, the act of meeting in a public space makes sense by itself, and responds to the will of being together the same kind of people or in similar conditions in a foreign state.

Emigration supposes the separation of an individual and its reference group, therefore, the communal gathering with the compatriots in a common space reverses that separation, and gives to an individual the possibility of rediscovering and reconstructing, although in a contingent and symbolic way, the gregarious spirit of origin; "This community gathering in the open spaces evokes the realization of collective identity in enjoyment, in laughter, celebration, well-being, but also activates pain, nostalgia and the construction of a collective identity charged with loss, abandonment, failures and frustrations" [8].

In this same city of Madrid, the meetings of Sundays in Casa de Campo have become a traditional act to which the Ecuadorians go individually, but also accompanied by their relatives: *"In this enclosure they play soccer championships, ecuavoley and other sports. Also, food, drink and various products are sold. In the routines of Sundays, wives and children join the sporting event and encourage their own fun meetings"* [9]. As shown in the previous citation and as can not be expected otherwise, these spaces of public and massive use serve to do several things at the same time, as an Ecuadorian emigrant recognizes [9].

In another places in Spain, public spaces are also preferred by Ecuadorian emigrants for communal gatherings and re-creation of their original culture. This is the case, for example, in the dry channel of the Turia River, in the city of Valencia, where people of a certain origin seek to be embodied as a collective, and perceive and recognize themselves as individuals and as a group (…). But in the public space, social interaction and family leisure are also staged" [10]. In this way, in an activity intended for leisure and fun, the individual can take psychologically refuge from an environment that is hostile. From the point of view of the Ecuadorian emigrants in Spain, the ecuavoley courts are there to remember the distant homeland, more than ten thousand kilometers away [11].

From this perspective, in the cities of emigrant destination of the Ecuadorians, the telephone boxes become the privileged spaces for transnational practices; because they *"become a meeting point where information circulates at all levels, facilitate the tasks of maternity practices and transnational paternity, operate as money and parcel delivery agencies; In addition, if the owners are Ecuadorian migrants, in some cases, it is articulated with others commercial activities such as the sale of consumer goods from the place of origin"* [12].

To the above expressed must be added that these telephone boxes not only serve to communicate at a distance but also offer other services such as purchase of prepaid cards, shipping of parcels, especially gifts that Ecuadorian emigrants want to send to their families; conversion of videos from the American system to European or vice versa or transfer to DVD, car or health insurance, food or sale of Latin American products; and, sometimes they are the places of gathering and reencounter between nationals [13]. Because of the multifunctionality of the telephone boxes, these may well be considered as a communicative, economic and symbolic space of high condensation and local reference in the global space.

The occupation and use of the public spaces described above have a varied range of representation and literary recreation in the Ecuadorian stories chosen as a narrative corpus of analysis, in which the leisure, recreation and entertainment spaces of the Ecuadorian emigrants and their respective families combine, at the same time, several options [14]. It is striking the importance of public parks in the city of Madry in several narrative papers analysed where these parks are the most crowded spaces for individuals that represent the Ecuadorian emigrants, in which they remember the distant land, they reflect about the emigration adventure, they share pains and joys between compatriots and try to find satisfactions, even if they are false, to the multiple problems that affect them. In this same metropolis, nightclubs are also a favorite place for the reunion, fun and leisure of Ecuadorian emigrants. Although, not all nigthclubs are safe, quiet and healthy places to relax, "where ordinary immigrants go, for killing time or the memory of a woman" [15].

3 Characterization of Intelligent Spaces

3.1 Information and Communication Technologies in Social Integration

Social and technological development is one of the most influential factors in modern society. The new information and communication technologies are the result of the inventions created by humanity in relation to the digitalization of data, products, services and processes, and their transfer through different channels, over long distances and in small time intervals, of reliable way, which cost-benefit is imperative for man [16].

According to what is exemplified in the section of spaces for migratory gathering, Ecuadorian emigrants seek various options for individual and family recreation and entertainment; as mentioned before, among them public spaces such as: parks, green spaces, sports courts, telephone boxes, discotheques and even movie theaters. These environments have something in common, which is the use of resources and technological tools that support migratory processes, and promote the indirect use of virtual spaces that foster collective social practices. Various studies have shown that ICTs (Information and Communication Technologies) play a significant role in shaping the social, cultural and, specifically, communicational universe of migrants by providing another expressive space for the conformation of identity and migratory sociotechnological development [17, 18].

The migratory groups appropriated various knowledge, such as those related to communication, to create newspapers and magazines of their communities that later have gone to cyberspace as web pages of newspapers or facebook accounts of associations. These virtual environments are disseminated as spaces for the conformation of social identities, they function as means of information and opinion, as bonds of community cohesion and as resources of visibility in the receiving society [19]. For migrants, sociocultural change, derived from the original geographical movement places them before a complex future, where cultural adaptation becomes a priority due to the longing for a distant homeland. In this sense, the omnipresence of ICTs in different social contexts contributes to the socio-technological and recreational integration of these people.

The frequent use of social communication networks and virtual spaces, become the preferred environments for young people and adults to interact with their friends and family, modifying the face-to-face environment by a virtual one [20]. Other studies have shown that there is a correlation between social interaction and the emotional psychological state of people according to the physical or virtual space where informal social communication is generated, associated with the various technological tools existing in the market [21, 22].

The foregoing is due to the presence of intelligent devices or objects that connect to the internet, joining collectively to an ecosystem that represents the current digital revolution, giving way to the so-called Internet of Things (IoT) [23]; which in turn integrates the so-called "intelligent public spaces". From this perspective, one of the defining features for this social group and in general of modern society, is the creation and exchange of constant information through the use of ICT, allowing the generation and transfer of new knowledge among different groups of people located at a distance. The logic of information systems integrated with an economic and social architecture is nourished by synchronous and asynchronous communication and exchange of information, facilitating the permanent interconnection of groups and individuals located at a distance with common interests [24].

3.2 Intelligent Spaces

Intelligent spaces or environments are described as an integration of various emerging technologies at the service of people. They are defined as a physical environment whose architectural design is integrated with technological resources of software and hardware, such as sensors, microcontrollers, actuators, screens and other electronic devices, these components work together and transparently in the everyday objects of the life of man. The most common intelligent environments are technified applications in closed spaces with relatively defined limits, such as home, office, motor vehicles, and also open spaces such as streets, bridges, parking lots, coliseums and smart cities [25].

An intelligent environment or space can be constituted as an ecosystem of technologies for the transmission of data, according to its level of integration with the technological resources that allow achieving the objective for which it has been designed. Studies on this field are presented and the following challenges are presented: defining new methods of modeling and collaboration, referencing the form of representation of the devices in the intelligent environment and the way in which new elements will be discovered in the system; another relevant issue is the way in which human interaction must be established with the devices, risks and security of the object for which they are designed, among other aspects [25].

Other studies analyse problematic situations such as: the need for a new semantic and ontological model for the integration of emerging technologies, the need for new protocols that allow a fluid dialogue between different technologies and in a transparent manner for the end user, hybrid topologies in accordance with the requirements of each technology, efficient energy management in the devices, development of complex Data Mining and Big Data systems that make it possible to take advantage of the information obtained, access to the cloud efficiently and in real time, among other parameters [26–28]. In this sense, the IoT represents a revolutionary concept at a technological level; presents the current reality and the future of information and communication technologies, supported by the integration and dynamic evolution of hardware and software resources and resources that together facilitate the invention of new tools that can be applied in different fields of studies, from medicine, education, transport, to social activity [29].

The IoT [30] is a network of networks that integrate into its ecosystem a diversity of things, objects, sensors and electronic devices that are interconnected through the information and connections infrastructure (ICI) that provides value-added services. The goal of the IoT is to learn more and better serve users. The IoT implies the widespread presence of a variety of things. Things are physical objects connected to the internet and between them, detecting and collecting data. These things or objects are interconnected with each other, and can interact with other objects close to the

Table 1. Fundamental principles for the technological design of intelligent spaces or environments.

Principles	Characteristics
Communication	Interoperability Transmission of data synchronously Reliability and security Device integration High availability Efficient implementation of IPv6 Data fusion for sending information
Functionality	Scalability Optimum performance (performance) Management of traffic level and performance (throughput) Quality of service (QoS) Efficient energy management
Analysis and data processing	Complex data processing systems Integrity and information privacy efficient integration of cloud and data mining technologies
Development and innovation	New semantic and ontological systems New technology integration infrastructure New validation and verification systems development of software that integrates technologies New framework for end user Include distributed computing Open architectures in the integration of technologies

ecosystem, allowing common objectives to be achieved [31]. Table 1 shows the fundamental principles that should be integrated into the technological design of intelligent spaces or environments in relation to what is proposed by the IoT [32].

The technological platform is the core of the organisational ecosystem, which is composed of an organisation of things. The core of an organisational ecosystem consists of the interconnections of the real world with the virtual world of the Internet, the hardware and software resources, the principles and design standards that allow the interconnection of objects [33]. To this end, it is necessary to know the socio-technological needs of migrants, in such a way that public spaces can provide adequate information and communication tools with specific technical criteria to achieve the design objective. Also, the organisational entities can structure a clear idea of what information is important for this group of people, and what type of information is required from the electronic devices, and what information is intended to analyse [34].

4 Conclusions

Migrants generate great effort to get used to the rhythm of life, social and technological development in countries of emigration destination. These social groups occupy a preferential place for the comunal and public gathering, the meeting, the socialisation and the recreation of the original culture, which takes place in public spaces, such as parks, squares, sports fields, telephone boxes, discotheques; places where the use of technology is a valuable resource that facilitates communication to manage migratory activities.

The socio-technological development of the world requires new proposals, which suggest a better use of the tools currently available and their integration. The proposal of an integrating architecture, which leads to the generation of a digital ecosystem through the creation of intelligent spaces or environments, fosters the development of various emerging technologies under clear principles for their design according to their objective and development environment.

An important and common element in the development of these technological platforms is the requirement for the transmission of data in real time that is prioritised in the communication process, which implies a challenge and important contribution in the integration of the objects through the IoT.

References

1. SEDESOL: Documento diagnóstico de rescate de espacios públicos (2010)
2. Aguilar Cortes, L.: La recreación como perfl proFesional: experiencia americana, enfunlibre
3. McLean, D.D., Hurd, A.R.: Kraus' Recreation and Leisure in Modern Society. Jones & Bartlett Publishers, Burlington (2011)
4. Borja, J.: Laberintos urbanos en América latina. Espacio Público y ciudadania. Abya-Yala, Quito (2000)

5. Salazar Estrada, Y.: La emigración internacional en la novelística ecuatoriana. Tesis de doctorado presentada al Departamento de Filosofía de la Universidad Complutense de Madrid (2014)
6. Carpio Benalcázar, P.: Entre pueblos y metrópolis: la migración internacional en comunidades austroandinas del Ecuador. Abya-Yala/Instituto Latinoamericano de Investigaciones Sociales, Quito (1992)
7. Marco, S.D.: Deporte e inmigración: el deporte como elemento de aculturación de los ecuatorianos en la ciudad de Madrid. Tesis de doctorado presentada a la Facultad de Ciencias de la Actividad Física y el Deporte de la Universidad Politécnica de Madrid (2009)
8. Thayer Correa, L.E.: La expropiación del tiempo y la apropiación del espacio: la incorporación de los inmigrantes latinoamericanos a la comunidad de Madrid. Tesis de Doctorado presentada al Departamento de Sociología III de la Universidad Complutense de Madrid (2009)
9. Retis, J.: Estudio exploratorio sobre el consumo cultural de los inmigrantes latinoamericanos en España: el contexto transnacional de las prácticas culturales (2011)
10. Herrera Mosquera, G., Carrillo Espinoza, M.C.: La migración ecuatoriana transnacionalismo, redes e identidades. FLACSO/Plan Comunicación, migración y desarrollo, Quito (2005)
11. Ampuero, M.F.: Vivir in between. "Me fui a volver": narrativa, autorías y lecturas teorizadas de las migraciones ecuatorianas, editado por Diego Falconí Trávez, pp. 29–41. Universidad Andina Simón Bolívar, Sede Ecuador Corporación Editora Nacional, Quito (2014)
12. Pedone, C.: Estrategias migratorias y poder: Tú siempre jalas a los tuyos. Abya-Yala, Quito (2006)
13. Ramírez Gallegos, F.: Con o sin pasaporte: análisis socioantroplógico sobre la migración ecuatoriana. Instituto de Altos Estudios Nacionales, Quito (2010)
14. Viteri Paredes, P.: Premoniciones del exilio. Puro cuento: antología, pp. 95–104. Casa de la Cultura Ecuatoriana "Benjamín Carrión", Quito (2004)
15. Carrión, C.: Ya no tengo que llorar. VIII Bienal del cuento ecuatoriano Pablo Palacio, pp. 15–34. CEDIC, Quito (2005)
16. Carrión, C.: La cachifa cojonuda. Hablo el rey y dijo muuu, pp. 117–129. El Conejo, Quito (2011)
17. Hevia, E.C.: El papel de las tecnologías de la información y las comunicaciones (TICs) en el proceso de enseñanza-aprendizaje a comienzos del siglo XXI
18. Melella, C.: Migración y Tecnologías de la Información y de la Comunicación (TIC). La presencia de los periódicos de migrantes en Internet y los desafíos del análisis de las redes sociales virtuales. Cuadernos de H Ideas, vol. 7, no. 7, pp. 1–18 (2013)
19. Peñaranda Cólera, M.C.: ¿Tecnologías que acercan distancias? Sobre los 'claroscuros' del estudios de la(s) tecnología(s) en los procesos migratorios transnacionales. In: Santamaría, E. (ed.) Retos epistemológicos de las migraciones transnacionales. Barcelona: Antrophos, pp. 135–167 (2008)
20. Melella, C.: Migración y TIC: Identidades andinas en Facebook. La Trama de la comunicación (2016)
21. Herrero, J., Meneses, J., Valiente, L., Rodríguez, F.: Participación social en contextos virtuales. Psicothema 16(3), 456–460 (2004)
22. Kraut, R., Fish, R., Root, R., Chalfonte, B.: Informal Comunication in Organizations: forma, function, and technology. In: Oskamp, S., Spacapan, S. (eds.) Human Reactions to Technology: The Claremont Symposium on Applies Social Psychology, pp. 145–149. Sage Publications, Beverly Hills (1990)
23. Wellman, B.: Physical place and cyberplace: changing portals and the rise of networked individualsim. Int. J. Urban Reg. Res. 25(2), 227–252 (2001)

24. Miorandi, D., Sicari, S., De Pellegrini, F., Chlamtac, I.: Internet of things: vision, applications and research challenges. Ad Hoc Netw. **10**(7), 1497–1516 (2012)
25. Castell, M.: La era de la información: Vol. I, II, III. Alianza, Madrid (1999)
26. Camarinha-Matos, L.M., Afsarmanesh, H.: Collaborative systems for smart environments: trends and challenges. In: Camarinha-Matos, L.M., Afsarmanesh, H. (eds.) PRO-VE 2014. IAICT, vol. 434, pp. 3–15. Springer, Heidelberg (2014). https://doi.org/10.1007/978-3-662-44745-1_1
27. Tsai, C.W., Lai, C.F., Chiang, M.C., Yang, L.T.: Data mining for internet of things: a survey. Commun. Surv. Tutor. IEEE **16**(1), 77–97 (2014)
28. Da Xu, L., He, W., Li, S.: Internet of things in industries: a survey. IEEE Trans. Ind. Inf. **10** (4), 2233–2243 (2014)
29. Botta, A., de Donato, W., Persico, V., Pescapé, A.: On the integration of cloud computing and internet of things. In: 2014 International Conference on Future Internet of Things and Cloud (FiCloud), pp. 23–30. IEEE (2014)
30. Madakam, S., Ramaswamy, R., Tripathi, S.: Internet of things (IoT): a literature review. J. Comput. Commun. **3**(05), 164–173 (2015)
31. Stankovic, J.: Research directions for the internet of things. Internet Things J. **1**, 3–9 (2014)
32. Chiti, F., Fantacci, R., Loreti, M., Pugliese, R., Chiti, F., Fantacci, R., Loreti, M., Pugliese, R.: Context-aware wireless mobile autonomic computing and communications: research trends and emerging applications. IEEE Wirel. Commun. **23**(2), 86–92 (2016)
33. Cabrera, A.A., Bastidas, S.E.C., Davinci-UNAD, G., Colciencias, C.: Ecosistemas digitales: redes de sensores inalámbricos, internet de las cosas y ambientes inteligentes
34. Muegge, S.: Platforms, communities, and business ecosystems: lessons learned about technology entrepreneurship in an interconnected world. Technol. Innov. Manage. Rev. **3**(2), 5–15 (2013)

Wireless Sensor Networks Based on Bio-Inspired Algorithms

Meonghun Lee[1] , Haengkon Kim[2] , and Hyun Yoe[3(✉)]

[1] Department of Agricultural Engineering, NAAS,
Jeonbuk 55365, Republic of Korea
leemh5544@gmail.com
[2] School of Information Technology Engineering,
Catholic University of Daegu, Gyeongbuk 38430, Republic of Korea
hangkon@cu.ac.kr
[3] Department of Information and Communication Engineering,
Sunchon National University, Jeonnam 57922, Republic of Korea
yhyun@sunchon.ac.kr

Abstract. The goal of bio-inspired is to resolve human problems by studying and mimicking the characteristics of organisms or design elements which can be found in nature. Wireless sensor networks are used in a variety of fields but have limited network lifespans, so various research is being performed on the subject. In particular, research is being performed on observing and modeling the behavioral principles of various organisms to use in bio-inspired algorithms for efficient routing techniques in large-scale networks. In this research, we studied the pheromones used in ant communication and designed the techniques for energy efficiency improvement and traffic distribution by applying them to the proposed network. We designed biomimicry technology called the Wireless Sensor Networks Based on Bio-inspired Algorithms, and by analyzing and applying the similarities between communication systems and biological systems, our system was able to show improved performance in terms of extended network lifespan, optimized path selection, etc. In simulation results, the proposed routing algorithm has a short information collection time and low energy consumption, and through this it is able to maximize network energy efficiency.

Keywords: Bio-inspired algorithm · ACO algorithm · WSN · Pheromone

1 Introduction

The small sensors that constitute wireless sensor networks have functions for detecting a variety of forms of information, such as light, sound, temperature, and pressure, processing the detected information as needed for a certain purpose, and transmitting it to a base node [1]. Due to the capabilities of these sensors, wireless sensor networks are used in a variety of scenarios in such fields as environmental surveillance, disaster prevention, and healthcare [2]. However, despite these features, cases often arise where the sensors cannot be recharged. Thus, path techniques for maximizing network lifespan have emerged an important area of research. The research has focused on

© Springer International Publishing AG, part of Springer Nature 2018
O. Gervasi et al. (Eds.): ICCSA 2018, LNCS 10960, pp. 719–725, 2018.
https://doi.org/10.1007/978-3-319-95162-1_52

efficient routing techniques for large-scale networks that apply biomimicry algorithms modeled on the behavioral principles of various organisms.

Unlike top-down centralized control methods, which control the behaviors of entities en masse, biomimicry algorithms are bottom-up distributed processing algorithms in which each entity independently performs simple movement to create a consistent overall form [3].

Pheromones are excretions used to communicate by animals of the same species. Pheromones are a substance similar to hormones, and act to strongly attract other entities of the same species. Ants can be seen as the typical example. Pheromones are also excreted by bees and other insects. It is clear that they play a significant role in communication and recognition among animals [4].

When ants find the shortest path to a destination, they exchange information in an indirect manner through pheromones. If an ant leaves a trail of pheromones along a path it has taken, when other ants travel along the path, they choose their route according to the strength or weakness of the pheromone that was left. If it is a path that has been traveled by several ants, the pheromones are strong, and the likelihood that the path is an optimal one is high. Once the path is determined, the ants all move along the optimal path along which the pheromones are concentrated.

If humans use these functions to create an algorithm based on natural principles and structures in organisms instead of mere trial and error, they can find answers to problems similar to ones faced by these organisms.

Biomimicry algorithms mainly have been applied to optimization algorithms, and of those, the ant colony optimization algorithm, which is modeled on the process of ants finding optimal paths based on the excreted pheromones, offers an efficient routing method for complex tasks using the average values of nearby information of entities in a large-scale network [5].

In this paper, we propose a technique for selecting optimal paths and improving energy efficiency in a wireless sensor network using the ant colony optimization algorithm, which is a biomimicry algorithm [6–8]. The basic design requirements of the proposed network are as follows:

a. Sensors have a limited amount of energy. Thus, the routing algorithm must be designed to find energy-efficient paths to extend the network's lifespan.
b. Aside from energy efficiency, the routing algorithm for the wireless sensor network must be designed so that it can operate many sensors for a long time by distributing data throughout the network.

In this paper, we qualitatively analyze the similarities between communications systems and biological systems to show that biomimicry algorithms can serve as a solution for the major problems in communication networks, i.e., path selection and energy efficiency. We design a set of algorithms called WiBiA (Wireless Sensor Networks Based on Bio-inspired Algorithms) using the ant colony optimization algorithm, which is the main biomimicry algorithm used in communication networks.

The remainder of this paper is organized as follows: Sect. 2 first describes the proposed network model to finding the optimal solution to the problem, and we analyze it using the experimental results. Section 3 contains the conclusions of this study and directions for future research.

2 Wireless Sensor Networks Based on Bio-Inspired Algorithms

The ACO algorithm is well known as a method suitable for selecting the optimal path in packet routing but it has the drawback of stagnation. It also leads to problems whereby it lowers the probability of selecting other paths, which causes congestion along the optimal path. The issue is that if congestion occurs along the optimal path, the path is no longer optimal, and the overall energy consumption of the network increases. In this paper, we propose the algorithm below with the intention of designing an efficient wireless sensor network and overcoming problems that occur when using biomimicry algorithms.

2.1 CFA: Congestion-Free Algorithm

As the path along which ants travel gets closer to the shortest path, a large amount of pheromones accumulate along it, and it is thus recognized as close to the shortest path and selected by ants. However, this kind of path setting leads to congestion in WSNs, and the energy of nodes along the optimal path is exhausted because sensor nodes have a limited amount of energy.

The goal of the CFA proposed in this paper is for nodes to resolve their own congestion and prevent excessive battery consumption in a WSN environment where network resources are limited.

The existing AODV protocol has a mechanism to set new paths and ones with the smallest delays whenever the network topology changes in an environment with high node mobility [9]. It can therefore be said to naturally achieve a balance in data traffic [10].

However, the typical environment where appropriate traffic distribution has not been achieved is one where node mobility is low and the density between nodes is high. Even if traffic congestion occurs, a mechanism for setting new paths is not available, because of which node congestion gradually worsens, and problems occur whereby the increase in end-to-end delays can degrade network performance. To resolve these problems, in the proposed CFA (congestion-free algorithm), once a node determines that excessive traffic is being sent to it, it can transmit a pheromone-PULL message to the source node to give notice of its intention to reject further data relays, so that nodes that receive this message can set new detours. Moreover, the node that transmits the pheromone-PULL message does not relay RREQ (Route Request) messages that arrive from nearby nodes, thus blocking the setting of a new path through the node [11] (Fig. 1).

Figure 2 shows a situation where congestion occurs because excessive traffic is concentrated on Node A and the actions of the congestion-free algorithm to resolve this. Node A is a relay node along the data paths of pairs $[S_1, D_1]$, $[S_2, D_2]$, and $[S_3, D_3]$. If the amount of traffic sent to Node A reaches a predefined threshold, Node A shifts to a pheromone-PULL state, and to do this, it transmits a pheromone-PULL message as it shifts states. The message goes to the source node that sent the last data packet to Node A (assumed to be S_2 in the figure) to request that a different detour be set. Node S_2 receives the pheromone-PULL message and broadcasts an RREQ to set a new path to Node D_2, and the mechanism of setting the new path is activated.

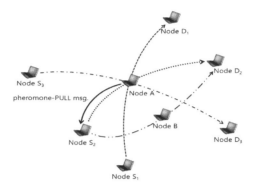

Fig. 1. The basic concept behind congestion-free algorithm.

Table 1. Operational process of CFA.

Algorithm 1: congestion-free algorithm

[When the node A receives a packet]

```
if RREQ message in a packet
if the node A is in pheromone-PULL state
ignore the packet
else
process the packet using the existing routing algorithm
else if pheromone-PULL state
if the pheromone-PULL state is destined to the node A
initiate the route discovery mechanism of the existing routing
algorithm
else
forward the packet with the alternative route
```

[At the end of a time interval]

```
if # of forwarding packets for the time interval ≥ threshold
change the state to pheromone-PULL
send a pheromone-PULL message to the src. of last received
packet
if # of forwarding packets for the time interval < threshold
change the state to normal
```

If node S_2 successfully completes the setting of a new detour and data transmission via the new path through a Node B begins, the path that maintains Node A is no longer used. The corresponding entry timer thus expires, and is naturally deleted from the routing table. Node A, which is in a pheromone-PULL state, does not provide packet relay service for RREQ messages sent by S_2 or any other node. The setting of new paths that pass through Node A is thus blocked. In this pheromone-PULL state, if Node A's congestion situation improves and the amount of traffic falls below a given threshold, the node shifts back into a normal state. Table 1 shows the operational process that has been described so far.

The congestion-free algorithm proposed in this paper takes into account the limitations of WSN and focuses on resolving node congestion by balancing traffic. It can resolve the problem of traffic concentration on a particular node, whether node mobility is high or low, and can support load-balancing features through the addition of a simple module to existing routing protocols.

2.2 Performance Evaluation

To execute a simulation using the proposed algorithm to test it, we distributed 500 nodes randomly in a square area with sides of 1000 m (W). Here, the node's communication radius was determined to be $2W/\sqrt{n}$. Considering a network topology where all nodes could connect to a multi-hub, it was assumed that the send/receive scheduling for data aggregation was perfect, and there were no collisions or transmission errors. All nodes periodically generated 100 kbits of sensing data. The channel bandwidth was assumed to be 100 kHz, and the power used to send and receive messages was assumed to be 100 mW. In the simulations, we compared the WiBiA protocol proposed in this paper and the LEACH (Low-energy Adaptive Clustering Hierarchy) protocol, which uses highly energy-efficient routing in WSNs [11].

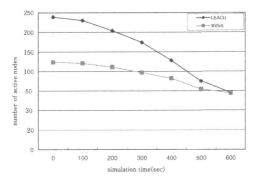

Fig. 2. The number of active nodes during the simulation in LEACH and the proposed WiBiA.

Figure 2 shows the number of active nodes during the simulation time in the existing LEACH and the proposed WiBiA. In the case of LEACH, energy consumption of all nodes was not balanced, and the time point at which energy was exhausted was not fixed so the number of active nodes rapidly decreased. On the other hand, in the case of WiBiA, we can see that all of the nodes consumed energy in a balanced way and maintained the network. WiBiA used alternative routes to re-form a direct path when path disconnection occurred, so the nodes' network delay and energy consumption activities were markedly reduced and the wireless sensor network was continuously maintained. We can see that in the WSN environment with limited network resources, the nodes resolved their own congestion situations and prevented excessive battery use.

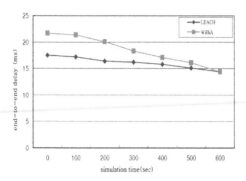

Fig. 3. The time taken to deliver a packet from the source node to the destination node during the simulation in LEACH and the proposed WiBiA.

Figure 3 shows the time taken to deliver a packet from the source node to the destination node. It can be seen that the proposed WiBiA's average delay time increased by 24% compared to LEACH's when the pause time was 0 s and increased by 12% when the pause time was 300 s. This is because when an alternative path is used, the distance of the path between the source node and the destination node becomes longer, and as the pause time grows longer the alternative path usage rate grows lower, so the difference between LEACH and WiBiA average delay times grew smaller. It can be seen that WiBiA shows excellent performance improvements in terms of packet distribution compared to the AODV or LEACH protocols, and therefore if we consider Figs. 2 and 3, we can ease the demand for battery sacrifices by the nodes where traffic is concentrated.

3   Conclusion

In this paper, we have described a biomimicry algorithm designed based on the similarity between biological systems and communication networks to resolve the problems of communication networks. Simulation results show that the proposed routing algorithm has short data collecting times and low energy consumption, and through this it can maximize network energy efficiency.

It can be seen that biomimicry algorithms like WiBiA reliably provide optimal solutions to given problems in complex environments by performing distributed operations according to simple behavioral rules. The rapid path setting and shortest path resetting between moving nodes in WiBiA can be considered the most important element for network lifespan.

Therefore, in order to provide efficient communications between each moving node, a routing method which can effectively and quickly restore disconnected paths is required. We expect that this kind of biomimicry algorithm can be effectively applied to the large-scale communications networks which will appear in the future.

Acknowledgements. This research was supported by the MSIP (Ministry of Science, ICT and Future Planning), Korea, under the ITRC (Information Technology Research Center) support program (IITP-2018-2013-1-00877) supervised by the IITP (Institute for Information & communications Technology Promotion).

References

1. Gubbi, J., Buyya, R., Marusic, S., Palaniswami, M.: Internet of Things (IoT): a vision, architectural elements, and future directions. Future Gener. Comput. Syst. **29**, 1645–1660 (2013)
2. Lee, M., Hwang, J., Yoe, H.: Agricultural production system based on IoT. In: 2013 IEEE 16th International Conference on Computational Science and Engineering (CSE), pp. 833–837. IEEE (2013)
3. Passino, K.M.: Biomimicry for Optimization, Control, and Automation. Springer, Heidelberg (2005). https://doi.org/10.1007/b138169
4. Dorigo, M., Birattari, M., Stutzle, T.: Ant colony optimization. IEEE Comput. Intell. Mag. **1**, 28–39 (2006)
5. Taneja, S., Kush, A.: A survey of routing protocols in mobile ad hoc networks. Int. J. Innov. Manag. Technol. **1**, 279 (2010)
6. Dorigo, M., Blum, C.: Ant colony optimization theory: a survey. Theor. Comput. Sci. **344**, 243–278 (2005)
7. Gunes, M., Sorges, U., Bouazizi, I.: ARA-the ant-colony based routing algorithm for MANETs. In: Proceedings. International Conference on Parallel Processing Workshops 2002, pp. 79–85. IEEE (2002)
8. Stützle, T.: Ant colony optimization. In: Ehrgott, M., Fonseca, C.M., Gandibleux, X., Hao, J.-K., Sevaux, M. (eds.) EMO 2009. LNCS, vol. 5467, p. 2. Springer, Heidelberg (2009). https://doi.org/10.1007/978-3-642-01020-0_2
9. Chakeres, I.D., Belding-Royer, E.M.: AODV routing protocol implementation design. In: Proceedings of the 24th International Conference on Distributed Computing Systems Workshops 2004, pp. 698–703. IEEE (2004)
10. Ganguli, A., Susca, S., Martínez, S., Bullo, F., Cortes, J.: On collective motion in sensor networks: sample problems and distributed algorithms. In: 44th IEEE Conference on Decision and Control, 2005 and 2005 European Control Conference CDC-ECC 2005, pp. 4239–4244. IEEE (2005)
11. Handy, M., Haase, M., Timmermann, D.: Low energy adaptive clustering hierarchy with deterministic cluster-head selection. In: 4th International Workshop on Mobile and Wireless Communications Network 2002, pp. 368–372. IEEE (2002)

Consideration of Host Nation Laws and Regulations by Japanese MNEs

Masayoshi Ike$^{(\boxtimes)}$, Jerome Donovan ⓘD, Cheree Topple,
and Eryadi K. Masli

Faculty of Business and Law, Swinburne University of Technology, Hawthorn,
VIC 3122, Australia
mike@swin.edu.au

Abstract. Multinational enterprises (MNEs) are key players in sustainable development. The ASEAN region represents an area of the planet of significant ecological value but hosting a large number of MNEs. Japanese MNEs are significant players in the region, with Vietnam, Thailand and Indonesia (VTI) representing the top three host nations. This study looks at how the Japanese MNEs work with sustainability related laws in VTI, and the challenges in meeting the requirements. It was found that in a majority of cases in this research, large Japanese MNEs operated at higher compliance levels than those required in the host nation. This implies that the host nation sustainability regulations could be tightened without threatening the economic benefits Japanese MNEs bring to them.

Keywords: Japanese · MNE · Sustainability · Regulation

1 Introduction

Multinational enterprises (MNEs) are key players in sustainable development in both a positive and negative sense [1, 2]. They are typically large-scale consumers of water and energy, as well as being the source of waste material, noise, water and airborne pollutants [3, 4]. Nevertheless, they are also the provider of economic and social development through employment, business development and products [2].

A region of the planet where there is significant MNE activity coinciding with a delicate biological environment is the ASEAN region [5]. Japan is a major participant of business activity in ASEAN, being the single largest contributor of foreign direct investment (FDI) into the region in 2016 [6]. The top three nations hosting the largest number of Japanese MNE subsidiaries in ASEAN is Vietnam, Thailand, Indonesia (VTI) [7]. The subsidiaries therefore have a substantial impact on the sustainable development of these nations.

The respective governments of VTI set laws and regulations to mitigate damage to the environment and negative effects to communities located in the vicinity of MNE subsidiary operations. The governments however would need to balance this with the economic benefits that the MNEs bring to the country. Sustainable development could be improved from a policy perspective by increasing demands for environmental and social contributions from MNEs through laws and regulation. The question remains as

© Springer International Publishing AG, part of Springer Nature 2018
O. Gervasi et al. (Eds.): ICCSA 2018, LNCS 10960, pp. 726–734, 2018.
https://doi.org/10.1007/978-3-319-95162-1_53

to how much they can be tightened, without affecting the investment by Japanese MNEs. As such, the research question for this paper is "can environmental and social contribution regulations be tightened in host countries without affecting inward FDI from the Japanese private sector?"

This paper will attempt to answer this research question by exploring the significance laws and regulations present to management, in the establishment and operation of MNE subsidiaries in VTI. The surveys conducted by the Japan External Trade Organization [7] provide some initial insight. Management of Japanese MNEs with ASEAN subsidiaries report top concerns in VTI as wage growth, difficulties in quality control, and quality of employees. Regulations pertaining to sustainability are not mentioned in this survey. In comparison, the equivalent survey in the United States of America shows environmental regulations as the seventh largest concern for management of Japanese MNEs [8].

If environmental and other sustainability related regulations are not presenting a current challenge to MNEs, it may be that the laws are not stringent enough. This paper will concentrate on manufacturing MNEs, as they pose a greater threat to the environment and human safety in operation than non-manufacturing industries.

2 Literature Review of Japanese MNEs Treatment of Sustainability Related Laws

There is significant extant literature related to Japanese manufacturing MNEs and environmental laws. Most center on Japanese environmental laws, instigated by major pollution disasters in the country in the 20th century [for example, see 9–13]. The industrial incidents not only resulted in significant ecological damage, but deaths and long-term illness of residents in the affected areas.

These papers were followed by various research on the laws implemented to prevent a recurrence, such as the study by Hara et al. [14] into the impact of government policies on the development of wastewater treatment technologies to reduce water pollution. In a similar vein, Kanada et al. [13] investigated the long-term effect of policies for air pollution in the Japanese city of Kawasaki. The results of these studies indicate Japanese MNEs will adhere to requirements and expectations placed upon it by governments of various jurisdictions, as some of the policies in these studies were specific to a prefecture or municipality.

A significant body of research exists for pollution haven theories and their impact on FDI [for example, see 15–17]. While debate continues regarding the existence of pollution havens, Elliott, Shimamoto [18] argues that in the case of Japanese MNEs in the ASEAN region, evidence for these are unable to be established. Nevertheless, no indications are made on the degree to which environmental regulations may be tightened before FDI from developed nations such as Japan may be driven away.

While the environment is often the focus of regulatory regimes, it is not the only aspect of sustainability which needs to be considered. For example, Indonesia has a mandatory corporate social responsibility (CSR) law [19]. CSR is understood to be the social benefits a company brings, as well as accountability through corporate governance, contributing to social sustainability [20, 21]. Very little research has been carried out on the impact of the Indonesian law on Japanese MNE activities, with the exception of Park et al. [22].

In this respect, there is a general paucity of literature pertaining to CSR as practiced by Japanese MNEs in VTI. Fukukawa, Teramoto [23] provide a global overview of some of the largest Japanese MNEs, while Murakami, Kimbara [24] investigate the correlation between the CSR assessment of Japanese MNEs and the transfer of their environmental management practices to their Vietnamese subsidiaries. Neither of these papers consider the impact of mandating CSR by law.

3 Framework and Methodology

A corporate sustainability assessment framework was used in order to captured sustainability related considerations in the data collection process. The framework used was developed by Donovan et al. [25], posing questions to the MNEs the sustainability considerations that had been taken into account when establishing the subsidiary operation, and its subsequent operation.

Data for this paper was collected using semi-structured interviews. The method was selected to allow for detailed exploration of topics of relevance in specific contexts and corporate situations [2, 26].

Japanese manufacturing MNEs with an investment greater than USD 20 million were approached. This amount of capital investment was assumed to create subsidiary operations with a noticeable impact on sustainability. Secondary data was collected from sustainability related information on their corporate websites for triangulation.

The MNEs approached were requested to provide up to 4 participants managing sustainability related activities within the company. Interviews were carried out at the subsidiary office, or by telephone where this was not possible. Interviews were obtained with 14 companies, with 37 individuals at the subsidiary level. Interviews were conducted between June 2013 and March 2017, varying in duration from 45 to 90 min.

The participating companies and interviewees are shown in Table 1.

Table 1. Participating companies and interviewees.

Subsidiary location	Company	Interviewees
Indonesia	A	Human Recourse/General Affairs manager Engineering Manager Finance Manager
	B	General Manager Human Resource & Planning Director of Marketing Corporate Planning Staff
Thailand	C	President Plant Manager Personnel and General Affairs Staff Deputy General Manager Business Administration Section Manager Business Relations

(continued)

Table 1. (*continued*)

Subsidiary location	Company	Interviewees
	D	General Manager – Legal
	E	Managing Director/Business Development Manager BOI Affairs Manager
	F	Senior Executive Vice President Finance Manager Public Relations Manager
	G	Vice President
	H	General Manager Director of Government Affairs Manager of Government Affairs and Corporate Planning
	I	Senior Vice President Corporate Strategy General Manager Government Regulations and External Affairs
	J	President Head of Marketing/Sales
Vietnam	K	President General Affairs Manager Senior Group Lead
	L	Chief Accountant
	M	Senior General Manager - Planning Assistant Manager to General Director
	N	General Director Director of Finance Director of Corporate Planning Assistant General Manager Legal and External Affairs Brand Promotion Team Member General Staff
14 Companies		37 Interviewees

Headquarter offices were also approached for interviews. The participants of Japanese headquarters are shown in Table 2.

Table 2. Headquarter interviewees

Subsidiary location	Company	Headquarter interviewees
Indonesia	A	Manager of Planning and Control
Thailand	D	General Manager Public Relations
	F	Chief Financial Officer
Vietnam	L	Manager – Products Staff - Products Staff - Public Relations/CSR/Environment

(*continued*)

Table 2. (*continued*)

Subsidiary location	Company	Headquarter interviewees
	N	Director of Planning, Environment and External Affairs (Regional Office) General Manager Environment and External Affairs (Regional Office) Staff - Environment and External Affairs (Regional Office) Director Of Corporate Planning (Vietnam) Assistant General Manager of Corporate Planning (Vietnam)
5 Companies		11 Interviewees

4 Results and Discussion

4.1 Japanese and Global Compliance

13 of the 14 companies interviewed indicated that they aimed for either compliance to Japanese regulations or corporate policies which were stricter than the respective host country regimes (Companies A, B, C, D, E, F, G, H, I, K, L, M, N). A certain degree of pride was noted in some of the responses regarding how much their company exceeded local regulations. For example, Company B indicated its corporate compliance levels were significantly above local regulations, that it allowed "the company to educate and give examples in form of cooperation to some of the related ministries" (Company B). A respondent at Company H stated:

"Whatever we do it beyond the regulations and any issues … We have our own handbook, which is higher standard. Even when we build a plant in a desert, it doesn't mean we can do anything we want or dump garbage to the area" (Company H).

Company F indicated internal standards set at the highest levels found around the world:

"… we have some internal regulation at headquarters … regulation based on research in Europe or US or China or South East Asia … so once a year [the company] send[s] some expert to the sites all over the world to comply." (Company F)

Company J did not indicate they followed any corporate guidance regarding environmental and CSR regulations, however they did state they acted above and beyond what was required by law.

While acknowledging the importance of aiming for higher standards in environmental and CSR requirements set by the government of the host nation, the interviewee from the head office of Company A noted challenges:

"…essentially we are a Japanese company, so we aim for Japanese compliance… As for the environment, the regulations and level of compliance varies depending on the country, so trying to replicate what we are aiming for in Japan to the countries we are extending to, is in my opinion very difficult." (Company A)

4.2   Meeting Changes in Regulation, the Environment and Sustainability

A challenge is posed to MNEs where governments make changes to laws and regulations. Company I illustrates how following global policies meant that it was able to meet changes subsequent to its establishment:

"When the company [was] established, there were still no environmental laws or social and communal regulations in Thailand, but in practice, the company has always [considered] the environment and local communities by involving in aiding and supporting the public and local community activities … The company has been able to comply with those new regulation [that came] after the establishment." (Company I)

A similar observation from Company K:

"[The subsidiary's establishment] was not influenced by the original investment approval given by the Government of Vietnam, as [the company] did all these development issues based on [global] vision and mission. As a matter of fact … issues like energy saving, waste water treatment much better or earlier than required by the Government of Vietnam" (Company K).

Concerns about the environmental future was identified by Company E. The respondent stated that the firm's main industry "impacts a lot on the environment, so the headquarters' policies have to focus on this" (Company E). The costs of meeting sustainability into the future was articulated as follows:

"We have to be more responsible on the nature. Even though the initial cost is increased, we have to do it because we do believe that we will have to face it in 10–20 years" (Company E).

4.3   Supply Chain Requirements

Companies D, H, K, L and N indicted supply chain requirements could set higher standards than the government regulatory framework for sustainability requirements. Company H stated that all suppliers were required to obtain ISO 14001 Environmental Management Certification. In a similar vein, Company D stated that it needed to obtain ISO 14001 as demanded by its customers. Company K stated that environmental management "was a must for the entire [Corporate] Group and was required by our customers".

4.4   Industrial Parks and Remote Locations

Three companies (A, C, and E) specifically mentioned operating in areas such as industrial parks or in areas far from urban developments to mitigate environmental and CSR risks. However, Company E noted challenges when urban growth resulted in local communities becoming established in the factory's vicinity which was once a remote area.

"Our method is that we focus specifically on the environment. We try to control whatever that might impact the local community like dust or bacteria so that there would be no complaint … We [were] here first, so we are responsible to the local area … We have to check the factors affecting the local [population] growth because the local community will expand until [they reach] us. We cannot pull out this factory to anywhere else. We better focus on environmental responsibility ... because this is the social responsibility" (Company E).

Company L was forced to relocate in a similar scenario when urban development caught up to its operational location. It is interesting to note in this case it was a lack of regulatory framework that made the relocation difficult:

"The company faces with difficulties in land acquisition during its moving to the new place. This process is lengthy. The land compensation cost to the affected people has to be based on negotiation, without regulations. This process takes time and increases the costs for compensation" (Company N).

4.5 Excessive, Complicated and Inconsistent Regulation

Three companies operating in Vietnam (L, M and N) reported difficulties in the complexities of the legal system in the country. These complexities were reported to cause challenges in getting clarification from government departments, as well as procedural overheads. For example:

"...some regulations and policies are complicated to follow, and overlapping and inclusive system particularly in customs, tax offices. Example: regulation to dispose waste is too troublesome, it takes 2 weeks" (Company N).

All three companies report various Vietnamese government departments having differing requirements. Company M claimed some laws in Vietnam to be inappropriate, as they were more stringent than those in Japan. Whether this view is justifiable or not, it does indicate a limit at which Japanese MNEs will reach a point where it deems local regulations to be too heavy a burden.

Both Companies M and N indicated approaching different government ministries allowed for better outcomes for their company, and that beyond this, MNEs could lobby for changes to the law.

If the company meets difficulties in operating in Vietnam, it will cooperate with other companies that face with the same problems and negotiate with Government of Vietnam when necessary. (Company M)

"...the government is not so stiff, foreign investors can negotiate with the government to find the way out" (Company N).

5   Conclusions and Limitations

This study has provided some evidence which suggest that large Japanese MNEs operating in VTI largely adhere to Japanese or global regulatory requirements related to environmental sustainability. These requirements are higher than those in VTI, with the exception of certain laws in Vietnam. This indicates the possibility that regulations in VTI can be tightened to match Japan, without significantly impacting the economic benefits these firms bring. There are limits however, where uncontrolled tightening of regulations can cause concern for Japanese MNEs as illustrated in Vietnam.

Furthermore, increasing environmental sustainability regulations may be beneficial to the natural ecology but local economies could suffer as a result of smaller local companies being unable to meet such requirements. Nevertheless, authors such as Kim et al. [27] suggest that in this situation, there may be beneficial spill-over effects.

In the aspect of social impact, the MNEs in the sample largely tended to deal with this aspect of sustainability by avoidance, setting up operations in remote regions or industrial parks.

Japanese MNEs are unique in their homogeneity of management personnel (being largely Japanese), and ultimately management styles across companies [28, 29]. It is argued that this may lead to greater transferability of findings from this paper to other Japanese MNEs. However, confirmation of this factor and the transferability of the findings to MNEs of other home nations, is not explored and is an area for further research. Similarly, the transferability of the findings to other host nations outside of VTI cannot be assumed.

References

1. Kolk, A., Kourula, A.E., Pisani, N.: Multinational enterprises and the sustainable development goals: what do we know and how to proceed? In: Zhan, J. (ed.) Transnational Corporations, vol. 24, no. 3, pp. 9–32. UNCTAD, New York (2017)
2. Myllyviita, T., Antikainen, R., Leskinen, P.: Sustainability assessment tools – their comprehensiveness and utilisation in company-level sustainability assessments in Finland. Int. J. Sustain. Dev. World Ecol. 24(3), 236–247 (2017). https://doi.org/10.1080/13504509.2016.1204636
3. Young, P., Byrne, G., Cotterell, M.: Manufacturing and the environment. Int. J. Adv. Manuf. Technol. 13(7), 488–493 (1997). https://doi.org/10.1007/BF01624609
4. Sarkis, J.: Manufacturing's role in corporate environmental sustainability - concerns for the new millennium. Int. J. Oper. Prod. Manag. 21(5/6), 666–686 (2001). https://doi.org/10.1108/01443570110390390
5. ASEAN Centre for Biodiversity: ASEAN Biodiversity Outlook. ASEAN Centre for Biodiversity (2010). http://environment.asean.org/asean-biodiversity-outlook/. Accessed 20 Sept 2015
6. ASEAN: ASEAN Investment Report 2017, Jakarta (2017)
7. Japan External Trade Organization: 2017 JETRO Survey on Business Conditions of Japanese Companies in Asia and Oceania (trans: Division ORDAaODCaNA). Survey of Japanese-Affiliated Firms in Asia and Oceania. Japan External Trade Organization (2017)
8. Japan External Trade Organization: FY2017 JETRO Survey on Business Conditions for Japanese Companies in the U.S. (36th Annual Survey) (trans: Americas Division ORD). Japan External Trade Organization (2018)
9. Wokutch, R.E.: Corporate social responsibility Japanese style. Executive 4(2), 56–74 (1990). https://doi.org/10.5465/AME.1990.4274797. ISSN 1938-9779
10. Harada, M.: Minamata disease: methylmercury poisoning in Japan caused by environmental pollution. Crit. Rev. Toxicol. 25(1), 1–24 (1995)
11. Kitagawa, T.: Cause analysis of the Yokkaichi asthma episode in Japan. J. Air Pollut. Control Assoc. 34(7), 743–746 (1984)
12. Avenell, S.: Japan's long environmental sixties and the birth of a green Leviathan. Jpn. Stud. 32(3), 423–444 (2012). https://doi.org/10.1080/10371397.2012.708402

13. Kanada, M., Fujita, T., Fujii, M., Ohnishi, S.: The long-term impacts of air pollution control policy: historical links between municipal actions and industrial energy efficiency in Kawasaki city, Japan. J. Clean. Prod. **58**, 92–101 (2013). https://doi.org/10.1016/j.jclepro.2013.04.015

14. Hara, K., Kuroda, M., Yabar, H., Kimura, M., Uwasu, M.: Historical development of wastewater and sewage sludge treatment technologies in Japan – an analysis of patent data from the past 50 years. Environ. Dev. **19**, 59–69 (2016). https://doi.org/10.1016/j.envdev.2016.05.001

15. Cai, X., Lu, Y., Wu, M., Yu, L.: Does environmental regulation drive away inbound foreign direct investment? Evidence from a quasi-natural experiment in China. J. Dev. Econ. **123**, 73–85 (2016)

16. Bakirtas, I., Cetin, M.A.: Revisiting the environmental Kuznets curve and pollution haven hypotheses: MIKTA sample. Environ. Sci. Pollut. Res. **24**(22), 18273–18283 (2017). https://doi.org/10.1007/s11356-017-9462-y

17. Candau, F., Dienesch, E.: Pollution haven and corruption paradise. J. Environ. Econ. Manag. **85**, 171–192 (2017)

18. Elliott, R.J.R., Shimamoto, K.: Are ASEAN countries havens for Japanese pollution-intensive industry? World Econ. **31**(2), 236–254 (2008). https://doi.org/10.1111/j.1467-9701.2007.01088.x

19. Waagstein, P.R.: The mandatory corporate social responsibility in Indonesia: problems and implications. J. Bus. Ethics **98**(3), 455–466 (2011)

20. Chapple, W., Moon, J.: Corporate social responsibility (CSR) in Asia a seven-country study of CSR web site reporting. Bus. Soc. **44**(4), 415–441 (2005)

21. Fukukawa, K., Moon, J.: A Japanese model of corporate social responsibility. J. Corp. Citizsh. **16**, 45–59 (2004). https://doi.org/10.9774/GLEAF.4700.2004.wi.00008

22. Park, Y.R., Song, S., Choe, S., Baik, Y.: Corporate social responsibility in international business: illustrations from Korean and Japanese electronics MNEs in Indonesia. J. Bus. Ethics **129**(3), 747–761 (2015). https://doi.org/10.1007/s10551-014-2212-x

23. Fukukawa, K., Teramoto, Y.: Understanding Japanese CSR: the reflections of managers in the field of global operations. J. Bus. Ethics **85**(1), 133–146 (2009). https://doi.org/10.1007/s10551-008-9933-7

24. Murakami, K., Kimbara, T.: Does CSR enhance the transfer of environmental practices to overseas subsidiaries? J. Bus. Adm. Res. **4**(2), 1 (2015)

25. Donovan, J.D., Topple, C., Masli, E.K., Vanichseni, T. (eds.): Corporate Sustainability Assessments: Sustainability Practices of Multinational Enterprises in Thailand. Routledge, Abingdon (2017)

26. Saunders, M.N., Thornhill, A., Lewis, P.: Research Methods for Business Students, 5th edn. Pearson Education, London (2009)

27. Kim, N., Moon, J.J., Yin, H.: Environmental pressure and the performance of foreign firms in an emerging economy. J. Bus. Ethics **137**(3), 475–490 (2016)

28. Wiersema, M.F., Bird, A.: Organizational demography in Japanese firms: group heterogeneity, individual dissimilarity, and top management team turnover. Acad. Manag. J. **36**(5), 996–1025 (1993). https://doi.org/10.2307/256643

29. Diefenbach, T.: Inclusiveness and exclusiveness of Japanese-style management abroad - some evidence from Southeast Asia. The South East Asian J. Manag. **9**(1), 52–69 (2015)

Real-Time Analytics and Visualization: Dengue Hemorrhagic Fever Epidemic Applying Mobile Augmented Reality

Siriwan Kajornkasirat$^{(\boxtimes)}$, Jirapond Muangprathub,
Naphatsawat Rachpibool, and Nitikorn Phomnui

Faculty of Science and Industrial Technology, Prince of Songkla University,
Surat Thani Campus, Surat Thani, Thailand
siriwan.wo@psu.ac.th

Abstract. This project aimed to develop a mobile application for visualization of the Dengue Hemorrhagic Fever (DHF) epidemic, by displaying the information and graph of the DHF epidemic in areas and to provide prediction of the DHF epidemic in Mueang District Surat Thani Province, Thailand. The weekly DHF cases were obtained from Surat Thani Provincial Public Health Office from January 2008 to April 2016. The application was developed by using Cordova platform, programming was completed with HTML5, JavaScripts, PHP, SQL, and JSON. The visualization of the DHF epidemic was completed with Augmented Reality (AR) technology. Google Map, Google Place, and Google Chart APIs were used for data representation of the DHF epidemic on Google Map™. *Mathematica* and Web*Mathematica* technology were used to develop a Time Series model for DHF prediction. The results showed that this application can be used via mobile devices on both iOS and Android operating system. The system allowed the users to visualize the DHF epidemic with AR. The DHF cases are shown as a bar chart on Google Map™. The different colors (gray, green, yellow, orange and red colors) of a marker in Google Map™ indicated the level of the DHF epidemic in the area. Moreover, the Time Series model was prepared a prediction of DHF cases in the area. This application could be used for monitoring the DHF epidemic and preparing for a health prevention campaign to protect against the DHF epidemic in the area. The information is useful to support the related organization for efficient planning regarding policies on DHF protection.

Keywords: Visualization · DHF · Augmented reality · Prediction
Time Series Model

1 Introduction

In recent years, mobile devices and services have become ever-present. For consumer electronics techniques, with the rise in popularity of mobile devices installed with integrated cameras, such as iPhones, Android phones, or tablet computers and augmented reality (AR) have been discussed for and implemented in interactive mobile services [1]. Augmented reality (AR) integrates computer-generated objects with the

© Springer International Publishing AG, part of Springer Nature 2018
O. Gervasi et al. (Eds.): ICCSA 2018, LNCS 10960, pp. 735–742, 2018.
https://doi.org/10.1007/978-3-319-95162-1_54

real environment and allows real-time interactions [2]. AR is rapidly gaining attention worldwide. Applications (apps) were first developed in the1990s, e.g. an aircraft wire bundle assembly guidance system supporting manufacturing and repairing for the Boeing Aircraft Company [3]. Mobile augmented reality (MAR) follows a different design paradigm. Instead of developing a virtual incarnation of the real world, MAR augments the real world with digital information. As such, the design canvas is expanded from the limited space of the mobile phone to also include the physical properties of the manufactured world. MAR is a relatively new technology that offers new advances for interaction. MAR has been used in tourism business [4], education [5], cultural [6], logistics [7] and health and safety [8].

From 1953–1964, Dengue Hemorrhagic Fever (DHF) occurred in several countries in Southeast Asia and the Asia Pacific including Philippines, Thailand, Vietnam, Singapore and India [9]. DHF was first reported in Thailand in 1949 and the first DHF epidemic occurred in 1958 in Bangkok [10], subsequently spreading to other areas outside Bangkok. Afterwards, DHF epidemics have been reported from almost all regions of the country. The Bureau of Epidemiology has reported that there have been several outbreaks reporting regularly in Thailand. The highest number of cases was reported in 1987 when the incidence rate was as high as 325 cases per 100,000 population based on the number of cases reported. The latest epidemic was in 1998 when the incidence rate was as high as 211 cases per 100,000 population. This was the second highest incidence rate in the 40-year history of DHF outbreaks [11].

Dengue Hemorrhagic Fever is transmitted mainly by *Aedes aegypti* and possible *Ae. albopictus* in the tropical and subtropical regions of the world [12]. These mosquitoes are well adapted to the dynamic environment; consequently, the effect of global warming, increased widespread transmission to other areas [13–15]. Moreover, the effect from environment, climatic including rainfall relative humidity effect change for mosquito-borne disease population and mosquito behavior [13, 16–18]. Movement of a population for business or other activities are supporting factors that continuously affect the increasing DHF epidemic. There are several supporting factors including age immunity and DHF infection in the area and other factors including mosquito larval abundance, population density and urban or rural area [19]. Social factors including knowledge, perception, and protection, public participation may affect the risk of DHF transmission. Well-designed and reliable strategies for a specific predictive model for the disease are needed. Since DHF transmission is highly dependent on local environmental factors, it may not be possible to predict incidence outside locations with extensive valid data [20, 21].

In this study, we developed real-time analytics and visualization of the DHF epidemic with Mobile Augmented Reality. This system supported visualization of the DHF epidemic with AR by providing the visualized patterns of the DHF epidemic with different colors (gray, green, yellow, orange and red colors) of a marker in Google Map™. The system also provided the prediction of DHF cases using Time series model. This application could be used for monitoring the DHF epidemic and preparing for the health education campaign to protect against the DHF epidemic in the area.

2 Materials and Method

The weekly DHF cases were obtained from the Surat Thani Provincial Public Health Office, Thailand from January 2008 to April 2016. The system was designed as a mobile application (i.e. iOS and Android). The application was developed by using Cordova platform, programming was completed with HTML5, JavaScripts, PHP, SQL, and JSON. The Real time visualization of the DHF epidemic on mobile devices was completed with Augmented Reality (AR) technology. Google Map, Google Place, and Google Chart APIs were used for data representation of the DHF epidemic on Google Map™. *Mathematica* and Web*Mathematica* program was used to develop a Time Series model for DHF prediction. The application has a complete data management system (Fig. 1).

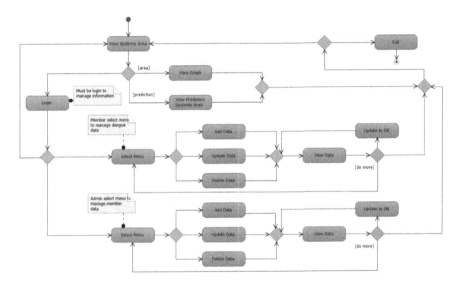

Fig. 1. State chart diagram.

The application displays the current location from the camera of the mobile device; also using GPS location and DHF area data from the database to display the results. The user can control the camera for surveillance in the area for the DHF epidemic prediction. The procedures are as follows (Fig. 1).

1. Retrieves and displays real-time images from mobile device cameras with Augmented Reality (AR) technology.
2. The GPS system retrieves the current location of the mobile device to find the nearby DHF epidemic area from the current area.
3. Retrieved the DHF epidemic area data from the database system.
4. Combined real-time image overlay from a mobile device and a current location of the DHF epidemic area data with Augmented Reality technology.
5. The system will display the DHF epidemic area.

6. Prediction of the DHF epidemic, the system retrieved data from the database system. Creating Time Series model with *Mathematica* and displayed the results with web*Mathematica* on the mobile application.

3 Results

The results show that this application can be used via mobile devices on both iOS and Android operating system. The system was designed for three groups of users: administrators, members, and general users. The users can access the system with or without login. For security reasons, an administrator and a member must use the login system with a username and password. The general user can access the system for AR visualization, DHF visualization on Google Map™ and prediction from the main menu. The member can choose two more functions: DHF management with data entry and data analysis (Fig. 2).

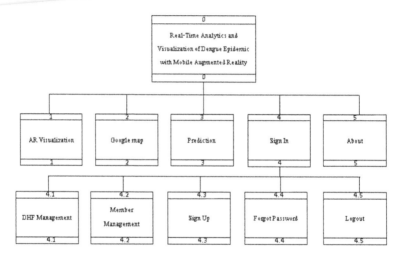

Fig. 2. Overview of the system functions.

The system allows the users to visualize the DHF epidemic with AR (Fig. 3). The number of DHF cases were represented as a bar chart on Google Map™. The different colors (gray, green, yellow, orange and red colors) of a marker in Google Map™ indicated the level of the DHF epidemic in the area (Fig. 4a–b).

Moreover, Time Series model was arranged for prediction of DHF cases in the area (Fig. 5). In addition, the system provided the data management including DHF management and member management. When users logged in to the system, the administrator and member can access the system to add more DHF cases, delete and edit the data via mobile application through the database (Fig. 6a–b). The system provided member management for the administrator. The administrator can add more members to the system, delete or update the information to the database system.

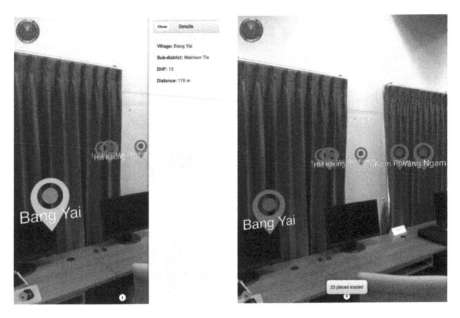

Fig. 3. Selected study with Augmented Reality (AR).

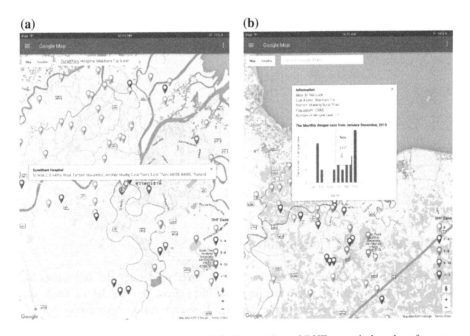

Fig. 4. (a) Marker at the selected area and (b) the number of DHF cases in bar chart format on Google Map™. (Color figure online)

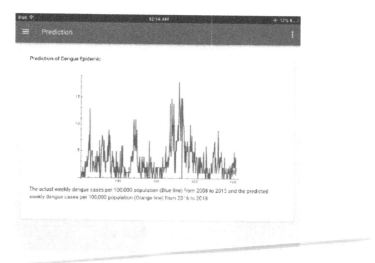

Fig. 5. Predicted DHF cases using Time Series Model.

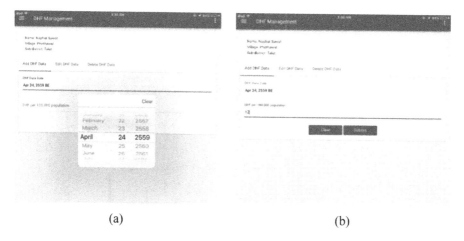

(a)   (b)

Fig. 6. DHF data management.

4 Discussion and Conclusion

This was an initial development to visualize the DHF epidemic with AR technology. Many studies in Thailand were completed with a predictive model of DHF using environmental, climatic or mosquito factors. However, using technology for DHF prediction via mobile phone appears interesting and easy to understand for people in the community. This study displayed the DHF cases as a bar chart on Google Map™. The different colors (gray, green, yellow, orange and red colors) of a marker in Google Map™ indicated the level of the DHF epidemic in the area. Moreover, the Time Series model was arranged for prediction of DHF cases in the area. This application could be used for monitoring the DHF epidemic and preparing for a health education campaign to guard against the DHF epidemic in the area. The information is useful to support the related organizations for efficient planning regarding policy implementation for DHF protection.

Acknowledgment. The researchers would like to thank Robert James Santos for comments on previous versions of this manuscript. This research was financially supported by Prince of Songkla University, Surat Thani Campus, 2015.

References

1. Lin, H.F., Chen, C.H.: Design and application of augmented reality query-answering system in mobile phone information navigation. Expert Syst. Appl. **42**, 810–820 (2015)
2. Azuma, R.: A survey of augmented reality. Presence: Teleoper. Virtual Environ. **6**(4), 355–385 (1997)
3. Caudell, T.P., Mizell, D.W.: Augmented reality: an application of heads-up display technology to manual manufacturing processes. Syst. Sci. **2**, 659–669 (1992)
4. Kourouthanassis, P., Boletsis, C., Bardaki, C., Chasanidou, D.: Tourists responses to mobile augmented reality travel guides: the role of emotions on adoption behavior. Pervasive. Mob. Comput. **18**(1), 71–87 (2015)
5. Coimbra, T., Cardoso, T., Mateus, A.: Augmented reality: an enhancer for higher education students in math's learning? Proc. Comput. Sci. **67**, 332–339 (2015)
6. Gutierrez, J.M., Molinero, M.A., Soto-Martín, O., Medina, C.R.: Augmented reality technology spreads information about historical graffiti in temple of Debod. Proc. Comput. Sci. **75**, 390–397 (2015)
7. Cirulis, A., Ginters, E.: Augmented reality in logistics. Proc. Comput. Sci. **14**, 14–20 (2013)
8. Kaklauskas, A., Zavadskas, E.K., Cerkauskas, J., Ubarte, I., Banaitis, A., Krutinis, M., Naimaviciene, J.: Housing health and safety decision support system with augmented reality. Proc. Eng. **122**, 143–150 (2015)
9. Gubler, D.J.: Epidemic dengue/dengue haemorrhagic fever: a global public health problem in the 21st century in the world health organization, the South East Asia and Western pacific Region. Dengue Bull. **21**, 1–13 (1997)
10. Hammon, W.M., Rudnik, A., Sather, G.E.: Viruses associated with epidemic hemorrhagic fever of the Philippines and Thailand. Science **131**, 1102–1103 (1960)
11. Bureau of Epidemiology. DHF situation in Thailand (2002)
12. Hay, S.I., Myers, M.F., Burke, D.S., Vaughn, D.W., Endy, T., Ananda, N., et al.: Etiology of interepidemic periods of mosquito-borne disease. Proc. Natl. Acad. Sci. U.S.A. **97**, 9335–9339 (2000)
13. Martens, W.J.M., Jetten, T.H., Focks, D.A.: Sensitivity of malaria, schistosomiasis, and dengue to global warming. Clim. Change **35**, 145–156 (1997)
14. Gubler, D.J., Reiter, P., Ebi, K.L., Yap, W., Nasci, R., Patz, J.A.: Climate variability and change in the United States: potential impacts on vector-and rodent-borne disease. Environ. Health Perspect. **109**, 223–233 (2001)
15. Hales, S., Wet, N., Maindonald, J., Woodward, A.: Potential effect of population and climate changes on global distribution of dengue fever: an empirical model. Lancet **360**, 830–834 (2002)

16. Suwonkerd, W., Mongkalngkoon, P., Parbaripai, A., Grieco, J., Achee, N., Roberts, D., Viriyaphap, T.: The effect of host type on movement patterns of Aedes aegypti (Diptera: Culicidae) into and out of experimental huts in Thailand. J. Vector Ecol. **31**(2), 311–318 (2006)
17. Shekhar, K.C., Huat, O.L.: Epidemiology of dengue/dengue hemorrhagic fever in Malaysia-a retrospective epidemiological study 1973–1987. Part I. dengue hemorrhagic fever. Asia Pacific. J. Public Health **6**, 15–25 (1992)
18. Wongkoon, S., Jaroensutasinee, M., Jaroensutasinee, K.: Distribution, seasonal variation and dengue transmission prediction at Sisaket. Thai. Indian J. Med. Res. **138**(3), 347–353 (2013)
19. Vanwambeke, S.O., Van Benthem, B.H.B., Khantikul, N., Burghoorn-Maas, C., Panart, K., Oskam, L., Lambin, E.F., Somboon, P.: Multi-level analyses of spatial and temporal determinants for dengue infection. Int. J. Health Geogr. **5**, 5 (2006)
20. Nagao, Y., Thavara, U., Chitnumsup, P., Tawatsin, A., Chansang, C., Campbell-Lendrum, D.: Climatic and social risk factors for Aedes infestation in rural Thailand. Trop. Med. Int. Health **8**, 650–659 (2003)
21. Wongkoon, S., Jaroensutasinee, M., Jaroensutasinee, K.: Climatic variability and dengue virus transmission in Chiang Rai. Thai. Biomed. **27**, 5–13 (2011)

Methodical Guide for Development on Mobile Applications Focused on M-learning

Garrido Fernando$^{(\boxtimes)}$ and Chiza Javier$^{(\boxtimes)}$

Department of Software Engineering and Artificial Intelligence,
Faculty of Engineering in Applied Sciences, Universidad Técnica del Norte,
Avenue 17 de Julio 5-21, Ibarra, Ecuador
{jfgarridos,fjchiza}@utn.edu.ec

Abstract. The vertiginous growth experienced in the use of mobile devices is evidenced in that 53% of the population in Latin America uses the internet through any technological equipment; at the same time, it has meant that e-learning in the field of teaching promotes the appearance of m-learning in turn with the availability of millions of applications for the end user. However, there is no Standardized Methodology under which such mobile applications are built. This research aims to propose a set of guidelines and techniques that facilitate the design and construction of web-based mobile applications for mobile devices. In order to achieve this objective, a methodology is proposed which consists of experimenting with source collections, designed for PC web pages, making an evaluation and carrying out a standardization, so that in the end valid guidelines are obtained for learning objects based on web for mobile devices. We cite theoretical references PMBOK, KANBAN, SCRUM. In conclusion, it was possible to propose a methodological guide that covers the necessary techniques and guidelines that allow the good design and construction of mobile applications of high quality oriented to m-learning, guaranteeing the success and acceptance of the end user.

Keywords: Software · Methodology · Research · Design · M-learning
Mobile applications

1 Introduction

Software engineering is defines as the technology discipline, worried about the systematic production and maintenance of software products which are developed and modified on time and within the defined budget. Software engineering: it is a discipline on an area of information technology or a computation science which offers technics and methods to develop and maintain good quality software to resolve any type [22].

Once the engineering universe has been conceived, we can say that software is considered, as a discipline, a technique, a tool or methodology in software development in order to get a model to follow in the development of software that is reliable and easy to modify. Now let's analyze that "A methodology is a collection of procedures, techniques, tools and auxiliary documents that help software developers in their efforts to implement new information systems. A methodology is formed by phases, each of

© Springer International Publishing AG, part of Springer Nature 2018
O. Gervasi et al. (Eds.): ICCSA 2018, LNCS 10960, pp. 743–752, 2018.
https://doi.org/10.1007/978-3-319-95162-1_55

which can be divided into sub-phases, which will guide system developers to choose the most appropriate techniques at each moment of the project and also to plan, manage, control and evaluate it" [15].

Achieving the construction of an efficient computer system that meets the requirements, is a really intense task and above all difficult to fulfill. Methodologies for software development impose a disciplined process on software development in order to make it more predictable and efficient. A software development methodology has as its main objective to increase the quality of the software that is produced in each and every one of its development phases. There is no universal software methodology, since every methodology must be adapted to the characteristics of each project (development team, resources), thus requiring that the process be configurable. Development methodologies can be divided into two groups according to their characteristics and the objectives they pursue: agile and robust. Then, today mobile technology has spread to the most remote corners of the planet, approximately 7,000 million inhabitants of the earth, almost the same amount today has access to a mobile device. And each user in turn makes use of dozens of applications of the m-learning type [3].

That is why the objective of this research is to propose an efficient Methodological Guide that allows, once it is turned off, the adequate development of efficient and above all quality applications that guarantee that the user fully meets their needs [9].

2 Methodological Foundation

This research is based on the qualitative-quantitative approach, which is directly related to the software development process, oriented to education through mobile devices, in order to verify the hypothesis and have logic in the development of the results to be obtained in said investigation [9].

Taking into account that information has been compiled and processed, allowing applying application performance processes in different environments to obtain results and observe the reality that is directly related to the problem posed. Software engineering is the area on which our research focuses on the methodologies that play a preponderant role in the development, portability, maintainability, functionality, adaptability and productivity of software. It is why we consider methodologies as processes for developing software specifically, assuming that we have them as traditional and agile. Then let's see that a methodology is a collection of procedures, techniques, tools and supporting documents which support software developers in their efforts to design, build and implement new information systems, oriented at all times to solve efficiently and effectively each of the needs of the users, that for the present investigation treats a universe of people who have access to Internet in search of mobile applications with academic aims that satisfy their needs in the field of the knowledge, At the same time, this is always oriented from the m-learning [13].

A methodology is structured in phases, each of which can be divided into sub-phases, which will guide the system developers to choose the most appropriate techniques in each moment of the project and also to plan, manage, control and evaluate it [8]. In our object of study and research are the agile methodologies. In general, they are classified according to their approach and essential characteristics; the most recent ones that were gestating at the end of the last century and that have begun to manifest since the beginning of the current one. They have been called "agile methodologies" and they emerge as an alternative to the traditional ones, and whose main objective is to reduce time of development, to be the most efficient and effective with the time resource.

Thus, the emergence of agile methodologies cannot be associated to a single cause, but to a whole set of events, although many relate them as a reaction to traditional methodologies and the factors commonly mentioned are heaviness, slowness of reaction and excess of documentation. Consequently, the lack of agility of formal development models. Another important point would be the explosion of the network, web applications and mobile applications, as well as the notorious growth of the open source movement and the vertiginous access to the internet in the world.

We can also add that the agile methodologies arise thanks to an important change, in terms of the demand of the software market, increasingly oriented to the web and mobile devices, with very volatile and constantly changing requirements, which require shorter development times, and, above all, they demand to compete with hundreds of models built under the same objective and they aim to capture the acceptance of millions of customers through electronic stores [13]. The agile methodologies analyzed in this research considered as more efficient in terms of their use and application, are the ones listed below:

2.1 Xtreme Programming XP

The methodology considered as Xtreme programming developed by Kent Beck focuses on the best practices, techniques and tools for software development, and it is comprised of twelve practices: the planning game, small emissions, metaphor, simple design, testing, refactoring, programming in pairs, collective ownership, continuous integration, on-site clients and coding standards. In the same way the XP2 version is composed of the following primary practices: meet as a team, consider an informative work space, energy effort, development of the programming in pairs, the stories, the cycle in weeks, the cycle in quarters, the Workflows, construction of time intervals that are very agile in time, with continuous integration, programming and delivery tests are generated [6].

2.2 Mobile D

It is appropriate for the development of mobile applications and its purpose is to achieve very fast development cycles in very small devices. The project cycle consists of five phases: exploration, initiation, production, stabilization and system testing. Each stage has a number of phases, tasks and associated practices. Full descriptions of the method are available in the first Stage, Explore, the development team must generate a plan and establish the characteristics of the project. This is done in three stages: establishment of actors, definition of the scope and establishment of functionalities of the product. The tasks in this phase enclose the entity of the client since they take an active part in the development process, the initial projection of the plan, the collection requirements, and the establishment of processes [10].

In the stabilization phase, the latest integration actions are carried out to ensure that the entire system works together. This will be the most important phase in multi-team projects with different subsystems developed by different teams. In this phase, the developers will perform tasks similar to those that had to be deployed in the "production" phase, although in this case all the effort is directed to the integration of the system. Additionally, documentation production can be considered in this phase. Finally, the last phase of testing and repair of the system has as its goal the availability of a stable and fully functional version of the system. The finished and integrated product is tested with the customer's requirements and all the defects found are eliminated, but new last-minute developments must never be carried out since the entire cycle would be broken [6].

2.3 Kanban

Kanban is an instrument supported by assessments of action and efforts, which expresses that the actors decide when and how much work they commit to do, within time. The actors take the job when they are ready. Just like a proofreader pulls on the next page only when it's ready to correct about it. Kanban deals with the optimization of continuous and empirical processes. It emphasizes the response to immediate change, by following a plan, Kanban is observed and exalted because it allows a faster response unlike other agile methodologies such as Scrum [10].

Kanban also participates in other methodologies such as FDD or Scrum the fact of creating a product Backlog, which has a series of items, user, stories, features, etc., as a priority. But the transcendentally is differentiated with other agile methodologies, since Kanban does not have iterations of the type timebox (time box), Kanban focuses on controlling the work in progress.

It is an excellent tool for visualizing the process, and the "Kanban Board" is one of the representative tools known as "information radiator in the jargon of agilism.

The proposed methodological guide for the development of mobile applications focused on m-learning is mainly based on the experience of previous research in mobile applications, the evaluation of the potential of success for third and fourth generation services, the engineering of educational software with oriented modeling by objects (ISE-OO), and especially in the values of progressive agile methodologies that are also considered as hybrid [9].

3 Presentation of the Proposal

In the research carried out regarding the Proposal of the Methodological Guide for the development of mobile applications focused on M-learning, it is considered the existence of three classes of applications that adapt to the nature of the requirements of the final user, and these are: native applications, mobile web applications and hybrid applications. In this methodology the hybrid application is considered since it combines the functionalities and advantages of the native ones and the webs. Therefore, the kindnesses and potentialities of each one in pleasure of those who use them in order to cover their needs. This methodological guide proposal integrates, therefore, the information sent and received through a web system that has as an essential requirement access to the Internet. The proposal seeks to facilitate the development of mobile applications focused on m-learning and provides functionality in an educational mobile learning environment through the proposed methodology in any educational context. This contribution is presented in two ways: first, a methodological guide for the development of mobile applications focused on learning. Secondly, it is proposed an application that can be implemented in education [10].

In the present methodology, it is recommended that, for each level or stage of the methodology, these correspond with well-structured design decisions, trying not to propose too many levels, since it would bring many concepts and would be very sensitive to the individual interpretation of each designer.

It is convenient to keep in mind the following considerations:

- Clearly explain the purpose of the proposed project or activity. The method derives directly from this purpose.
- Ask yourself, "what is trying to achieve participation in this particular project?". The answer to this question will make suggestions as to the methodology and the "most appropriate" techniques.
- Consider who will make up the team of multidisciplinary developers as well as which stakeholders will be considered in the project.

Other necessary aspects to consider, in the design process of the intermediate proposal of the methodology (see Fig. 1).

4   Generation of the Proposal of the Methodology –ADPE –

For the development of this Methodological Proposal some aspects have been considered described in what we call ADPE Methodology.

ADPE, whose name is the acronym of the 4 phases that allow an integral development of virtual education as support for the other modalities of education, and correspond to the following phases: D = Design, A = Scope, P = Tests, E = Delivery, likewise, characteristics of the proposed methodology for the achievement of success in the design and development of mobile applications oriented to m-learning have been added.

Fig. 1. Proposal of the methodology

5   Phases of the ADPE Methodology

5.1   Reach

This phase includes the activity that the user for the case the teacher will plan with respect to the academic scope of their mobile site, which covers in its entirety what the mobile application should and should not carry. This must be in accordance with the standards established for the assignment in relation to all educational activities within m-learning, ensuring that there is a close interrelation between the content of the virtual classroom and that of the mobile platform. It should be, at all times, and contemplated an emulation to the real physical activity that takes place in class.

It should analyze what activities can be created in the mobile environment to develop the skills and the abilities students should acquire. In general, the best resources of this platform are: documents, questionnaires, surveys, workshops that allow them to study for a qualified evaluation in the virtual classroom; study through flash animations and videos and audio files such as audio books or digital resources to support the learning process (see Fig. 2).

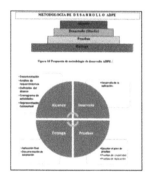

Fig. 2. Phases of the ADPE methodology

Likewise, in this phase, all the activities included in the educational activities must be contemplated in terms of evaluation and monitoring of units and content, which is why the scope phase covers the entire real environment and transfers it to the digital virtual environment of the application.

5.2   Development

The objective of this stage in the ADPE methodology is to capture the thinking of the solution through diagrams or schemes, considering the best alternative when integrating technical, functional, social and economic aspects. This phase is returned if you do not get what you want. In this stage, it is intended objectively to define the scenario, mobile applications can be designed to run in different scenarios, depending on the connection system and synchronization with the server or central application. The synchronization process is done to insert, modify or delete information [15].

We proceed to define times where the deadlines for each of the remaining activities are established, in order to finish the application in time for its release to the market. The computational design of the software performed in the previous task and the volatile and dynamic characteristics of the mobile services must be taken into account.

Allocation of resources. Resources are assigned here to carry out each activity and achieve the proposed objectives. Human, financial and technological resources must be considered. In addition, you must select the tools for the development of the mobile application. This phase is considered the most important within this methodology ADPE. It refers to the aspects and all the activities that have to do with the graphic design of the mobile learning environment, including the corporate image and visual impact that guarantees the comfort of the user and that should provide a welcoming environment that invites permanent customers to enter the application again. The corporate image should be similar in colors, graphics, modeling etc. to the one used in the virtual classroom, so that the user, whether is a teacher or a student, does not feel that they are different or strange environments from each other. The typography must be oriented to facilitate reading and navigation. For this, the typefaces must be simple and without overload of colors that facilitate their readability in any environment. Above all, they must present digital environments as exactly identical as possible [23].

5.3   Tests

The Mobile Learning allows to generate a great interaction between the users, for the case of the m-learning that we treat in our serious work it would be among the users of the academic environment. First, observing the distribution and the elements which arrange each section of the website so that the interaction is established from the content of the site itself. Secondly, the site can be designed complementing, not duplicating the virtual classroom. For example, the block or the communication section can be carried only on the mobile platform, since this allows the student to immediately know the innovations, the interactivity section can be potentiated with the use of chat. With Mobile Learning, students go from being simple passive receivers of content to being creative participants in permanent learning. It can be said that mobile learning is a new online and face-to-face trend that begins to take its first steps and opens a huge field of opportunities for teaching. For this phase, an adequate planning of the virtual resources available in Mobile Learning must be done to generate real learning opportunities for the students, programming collaborative activities such as chat and contributions in blogs so that knowledge is built. Here, mobile technology enhances learning as it allows you to experience it online, at the time and in the place the student requires. That is, it is the best time to learn.

5.4   Delivery

In this phase, the process demands the definitive delivery of the mobile applications attached to the proposed methodology where the parameters of development have been fully met in each of the previous phases, always with the consensus of criteria and especially compliance of the user's requirements.

6   Analysis of Results, Performance and Cadences

Once the prototype has been developed, it is necessary to analyze the performance of the modules built with the proposed ADPE methodology. Thereby, it is demonstrated that time resource efficiency is evident in the delivery of the different tasks of the prototype. In this way, the application of the ADPE methodology demonstrates that the sprints fully comply with the established times, even saving 10% less time compared to the methodology applied as an RUP adaptation (Figs. 3 and 4).

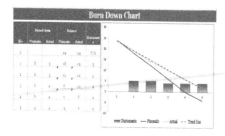

Fig. 3. Analysis of performance of the methodology

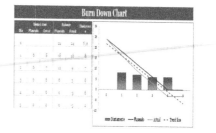

Fig. 4. ADPE methodology yields and cadence

7   Discussion

During the time of application of this methodological guide the effort has focused on demonstrating that its procedures, techniques and steps to follow achieved the optimization of the time of construction and development of a mobile application. Therefore, the prototype developer team, began these works with an alternation of methodologies. Finally, they opted for the ADPE methodological guide, based on time saving which was evident in the saving of resources, and therefore, in the effectiveness of the process. All this is demonstrated in the present research work. Through the metrics shown in the proposal where the time saving was 10% less.

8   Conclusions

The Methodological Guide proposed in this document groups and incorporates innovations to the best practices and artifacts of the most evaluated methodologies of the market, generating a considerably high level of productivity in conjunction with high levels of development and construction.

A significant improvement has been achieved regarding the occupation of time in the development of prototypes, since the Methodological Guide organizes the activities, artifacts and roles in such a way that the Scope, Development, Testing and Delivery are given in a prudent time, always maintaining control over the evolution of the product and the transparency of development towards the end user. Likewise, agile software development methodologies and this particular proposal guide allows small development groups to concentrate on the task of building software by fostering easy-to-adopt practices and an orderly environment that helps people to work better in what m-learning refers to and allows projects to be completed successfully in the shortest time possible without sacrificing the quality of the final product at any time.

References

1. Acosta Hoyos, L.E.: Guia practica para la investigacion y redaccion de informes. Ed. Piados, Buenos Aires (1978)
2. Americas, E.P.: Tendencias actuales en el uso de dispositivos móviles en educación. Educ. Digit. Mag. 21 (2012)
3. Arce, R.A.: Mobile learning: aprendizaje móvil como complemento de una estrategia de trabajo colaborativo con herramientas Web 2 y entorno virtual de aprendizaje WebUNLP en modalidad de blended learning. 10 (2013)
4. Arevalo, I.R.: Metodología para la implementación de Proyectos E-Learning, p. 12 (2005)
5. Boehm, B.W.: Software Engineering Economics. Prentice-Hall, New Jersey (1981)
6. Booth, T.: Index for Inclusion: Developing Learning and Participation in Schools (2002)
7. Brooks, F.P.: The Mythical Man-Month. Addison Wesley Publishing Company, Reading (1995)
8. Cancino, H.: tecno.americaeconomia.com. americaeconomia.com, 27 08 2015. http://tecno. americaeconomia.com/articulos/desafios-y-avances-del-desarrollo-movil-se-concentraran-en-latina
9. Castrillón, E.P.: Propuesta de metodología de desarrollo de software para objetos virtuales de aprendizaje -MESOVA. Revista Virtual Universidad Católica del Norte. No. 34, 25. concepto.de. (s.f.) (2011). http://concepto.de/pedagogia/.Homepage, http://concepto.de/pedagogia/
10. Curipallo, L., Paulina, E.: Creación de material M-Learning para el bachillerato de instituciones educativas de la provincia de tungurahua. Ambato, Tungurahua, Ecuador, 12 2010
11. ECURED. Metodologias de desarrollo de Software (2017). https://www.ecured.cu/Ingenier %C3%ADa_de_software
12. Fairley, R.: Ingeniería de Software. McGraw-Hill Interamericana, Mexico (2016)
13. de Fernández, C.: Guía Para la Elaboración de las Actividades de Aprendizaje. Editorial Octaedro, Barcelona (2010)
14. García, A.K.: angelicakarinaf.blogspot.com. ISEAS Coop., mobile learning, análisis prospectivo de las potencialidades asociadas al mobile learning. E-Isea, 58, 20 Feburary 2015
15. Jacobson, I.B.: El Proceso Unificado de Desarrollo de Software. España (2013)
16. Kruger-Corporation: 19 June 2013. http://krugercorporation.blogspot.com/2013/06/cuales-son-los-tres-beneficios-de.html
17. Labrador, R.M.: Tipos de Licencias de Software 3era Versión. España (2010)
18. Lemus, J.M.: Maestros del Web. http://www.maestrosdelweb.com/maquetacion-de-la-aplicacion-quinto-nivel5/
19. Ortíz, C.B.: Las Tecnologías De La Información y comunicación (T.I.C.). Unidad de Tecnología Educativa, Valencia (2014)

20. Requena, S.H., Guia Práctica para el Usuario: El modelo constructivista con las nuevas tecnologías: aplicado en el proceso de aprendizaje Stefany Hernández Requena. Revista de Universidad y Sociedad del Conocimiento, 10, (2010)
21. Rodríguez, T.: 11 September 2014. https://www.genbetadev.com/desarrollo-aplicaciones-moviles/metodos-aplicables-para-el-desarrollo-de-aplicaciones-moviles
22. Pressman, R.S.: Ingeniería del Software. Un Enfoque Práctico. Mcgraw-Hill Interamericana Editores S.A. de C.V., Mexico (2010)
23. Royce, W.: Managing the Development of Large. WESCON Western Electronic Show and Convention (1970)

Author Index

Printed in the United States
By Bookmasters